Health Care State Rankings 2010

Other titles in the State Fact Finder series

City Crime Rankings

Crime State Rankings

Education State Rankings

State Rankings

Health Care State Rankings 2010
Health Care Across America

Kathleen O'Leary Morgan

and

Scott Morgan

Editors

CQ PRESS

A Division of SAGE

Washington, D.C.

CQ Press
2300 N Street, NW, Suite 800
Washington, DC 20037

Phone: 202-729-1900; toll-free, 1-866-4CQ-PRESS (1-866-427-7737)

Web: www.cqpress.com

Cover design: Silverander Communications

♾ The paper used in this publication exceeds the requirements of the American
National Standard for Information Sciences--Permanence of Paper for Printed
Library Materials, ANSI Z39.48-1992.

Printed and bound in the United States of America

14   13   12   11   10   1   2   3   4   5

ISBN: 978-1-60426-617-7
ISSN: 1065-1403

Contents

Detailed Table of Contents

III. FACILITIES

IV. FINANCE

V. INCIDENCE OF DISEASE

VI. PROVIDERS

VII. PHYSICAL FITNESS

APPENDIX

Introduction and Methodology

Health Care State Rankings 2010 analyzes the latest health care data for each of the fifty states and the District of Columbia. The book provides state-by-state rankings of roughly 500 health care factors in the following seven categories: births and reproductive health, deaths, facilities, finance, incidence of disease, providers, and physical fitness.

Purpose of This Book

The purpose of *Health Care State Rankings 2010* is to serve as a resource for researchers, health policy professionals, and the community. The book provides the means by which individuals can compare the status of their state's health care to other states and the nation as a whole.

These data and rankings can be used in a variety of ways, by a variety of audiences, including the following examples:

- Health care policy makers can use them to help identify problems for further study.
- State governments can determine if their health care levels are on par with the rest of the nation.
- The federal government can use this type of analysis to allocate grant funding (Bauer, 2004).
- The media can rely on these results to report and compare health care rankings across states and years to the public.

In addition to the data and rankings, the volume offers numerous information-finding tools, including a thorough table of contents, table listings at the beginning of each chapter, and a detailed index. A directory of data sources the editors used is included, providing addresses, phone numbers, and Web sites. The Appendix consists of four charts: Population in 2009, Population in 2008, Male Population in 2008, and Female Population in 2008.

The Data and Their Limitations

The data featured in *Health Care State Rankings 2010* were chosen specifically by the editors from a variety of government and private-sector sources. Although the data provide more than a snapshot of the status of health care across the nation, they are not inclusive of all the possible health care data available.

Previous editions of the book have used the term "healthiest" when describing some states' place within the overall rankings. We no longer use this term because it is purely descriptive—at no time do we attempt to explain *why* a particular state is doing less well in health care than others or against the national average. Such as explanation—currently sought by health policy experts and other social science researchers—is beyond the scope of this book. Our selection of factors clearly affects the rankings; however, we believe the rankings provide a solid measurement of how the fifty states and Washington, D.C., are faring with regard to health care. Researchers, practitioners, and others can confidently use the data to understand health care issues and guide policy decisions.

Methodology

As noted previously, the health care rankings found on page xvi are based on seven overall categories (births and reproductive health, deaths, facilities, finance, incidence of disease, providers, and physical fitness), which are broken down into twenty-one factors that reflect access to health care providers, affordability of health care, and the general health of a population. These factors are then divided into two groups: those that are "negative," for which a high ranking would be considered troublesome for a state, and those that are "positive," for which a high ranking would be considered a good sign for a state:

Negative Factors

- Births of Low Birthweight as a Percent of All Births in 2007
- Teenage Birth Rate in 2006
- Percent of Women Receiving Late or No Prenatal Care in 2006
- Age-Adjusted Death Rate in 2007
- Infant Mortality Rate in 2006
- Age-Adjusted Death Rate by Malignant Neoplasms in 2006
- Age-Adjusted Death Rate by Suicide in 2006
- Average Annual Family Coverage Health Insurance Premium per Enrolled Employee in 2008
- Percent of Population Not Covered by Health Insurance in 2008

- Percent of Children Not Covered by Health Insurance in 2008
- Estimated Rate of New Cancer Cases in 2009
- AIDS Rate in 2007
- Sexually Transmitted Disease Rate in 2008
- Percent of Population Lacking Access to Primary Care in 2010
- Percent of Adults Who Are Binge Drinkers: 2008
- Percent of Adults Who Smoke: 2008
- Percent of Adults Obese: 2008
- Percent of Adults Who Do Not Exercise: 2008

Positive Factors

- Rate of Beds in Community Hospitals in 2008
- Percent of Children Aged 19 to 35 Months Fully Immunized in 2008
- Safety Belt Usage Rate in 2008

The twenty-one factors involve a rate or percent of frequency so that numbers are not biased toward population size, and the positive and negative nature of each factor is taken into account as part of the formula. Once we calculate the score for each individual factor, we add the scores to determine the overall ranking, with a positive score indicating a positive outlook for a state and a score that is above the national average.

"Comparison Score" Methodology

The methodology for determining the state health care rate rankings involves a multistep process in which rates for each of the twenty-one factors listed above is processed through a formula that measures how a state compares to the national average for a given category. The end result is that the farther below the national average a state's health ranking is, the lower it ranks overall. The farther above the national average a state's health ranking is, the higher it ranks overall. The methodology used for the most recent edition of the book has been used for the previous editions of *Health Care State Rankings*. The editors subjectively determine which factors are "negative" and which are "positive," as negative and positive factors are treated differently in the formula.

The methodology for *Health Care State Rankings* is described here in detail, using the following formula for these calculations:

$$\frac{\text{State Rate} - \text{National Rate}}{\text{National Rate}} \times 100$$

The following are steps for the "comparison score" calculation and examples that illustrate the calculations.

1. Let's use the following two factors for the state of Vermont as an example of both a positive and a negative factor: Positive Factor: Percent of Children Aged 19 to 35 Months Fully Immunized in 2008—64.5; Negative Factor: Births of Low Birthweight as a Percent of All Births in 2007—6.2.

2. The percent difference between the state rate and the national rate for all twenty-one factors is then computed. For the positive factor of percent of fully immunized children, Vermont's rate of 64.5 is divided by the national rate of 76.1 for a percent difference of 0.8476. For the negative factor of low birthweight, Vermont's rate of 6.2 is divided by the national rate of 8.2 for a percent difference of 0.7561.

3. The number "1" is then subtracted from the percent difference for each factor so that states with the national average would equal zero instead of one. The results are then multiplied by 100 for a more manageable number. For the positive factor, 1 is subtracted from 0.8476 to equal (0.1524), which is then multiplied by 100 to equal (15.24). For the negative factor, 1 is subtracted from 0.7561 to equal (0.2439), which is then multiplied by 100 to equal (24.39).

4. These numbers are then scaled to be one-twenty-first of the index by multiplying each score by 4.76% (since there are twenty-one equally weighted factors, each factor is multiplied by 4.76% or 1/21). For the positive factor, (15.24) times 0.0476 equals (0.725). For the negative factor, (24.39) times 0.0476 equals (1.1610).

5. The negative factors are then multiplied by negative one (–1). Positive factors are not multiplied by anything. Therefore, Vermont's score for Percent of Children Aged 19 to 35 Months Fully Immunized in 2008 is (0.725). Vermont's score for Births of Low Birthweight as a Percent of all Births in 2007 is 1.1610, or (1.1610) multiplied by –1 as this is a negative factor. Remember that a positive score illustrates that the state scored higher than the national average. Therefore, Vermont's score of (0.725) for the positive factor of Fully Immunized Children (a negative score of a positive factor) illustrates that Vermont has a lower than the national average score for children being fully immunized. Vermont's score of 1.1610 for the negative factor of Low Birthweight (a positive score of a negative number) illustrates that Vermont has a lower than the national average score for babies born with a low birthweight.

6. The final comparison score for each state is the sum of the individual scores for the equally weighted twenty-one factors ("SUM" on the 2010 Health Care State Rankings table on page xvi). This way, the states are assessed on how they stack up against the national average. In the case of Vermont, the SUM is 18.68 (note that we only illustrated the calculations of two of the twenty-one factors here). The interpretation of these scores is that the higher the state score, the farther above the national score; the lower the state score, the farther below the national score; and a score of zero is equal to the national score. With a SUM of 18.68, Vermont is significantly above the national average.

The scores are then sorted to produce the rankings. Note that the rankings do not indicate the actual difference between the scores, only their order, providing a means by which health care trends can be gauged in differing communities.

For the tables in the rest of *Health Care State Rankings 2010,* states are simply ranked from highest to lowest, with any ties among the states listed alphabetically for a given ranking. Negative numbers are reported in parentheses. Data reported as "NA" are not available or could not be calculated. In tables with national totals (as opposed to rates, per capita data, or the like), a separate column shows the percentage of the national total represented by each state. This "% of USA" column is particularly interesting when compared with a state's share of the nation's population for a particular year. Source information and other important notes are shown at the bottom of each page.

References

Bauer, L. 2004. *Local Law Enforcement Block Grant Program, 1996–2004.* Technical Report. Washington, D.C.: Bureau of Justice Studies.

The 2010 Health Care State Rankings

RANK	STATE	SUM	09 RANK	CHANGE
40	Alabama	(7.70)	42	2
42	Alaska	(9.35)	37	-5
43	Arizona	(9.73)	41	-2
38	Arkansas	(7.60)	38	0
16	California	5.84	17	1
27	Colorado	1.24	27	0
12	Connecticut	10.79	9	-3
37	Delaware	(6.32)	35	-2
45	Florida	(10.21)	45	0
39	Georgia	(7.64)	40	1
4	Hawaii	16.67	3	-1
19	Idaho	5.44	23	4
30	Illinois	(0.18)	28	-2
28	Indiana	1.03	25	-3
8	Iowa	14.27	4	-4
18	Kansas	5.71	16	-2
35	Kentucky	(4.73)	29	-6
49	Louisiana	(21.72)	49	0
7	Maine	15.68	8	1
29	Maryland	0.60	33	4
3	Massachusetts	17.38	2	-1
23	Michigan	4.51	20	-3
2	Minnesota	18.66	1	-1
50	Mississippi	(24.41)	50	0
34	Missouri	(4.03)	36	2
31	Montana	(1.23)	32	1
10	Nebraska	11.58	10	0
48	Nevada	(20.98)	47	-1
5	New Hampshire	16.51	5	0
14	New Jersey	8.04	14	0
47	New Mexico	(18.84)	48	1
26	New York	1.49	31	5
32	North Carolina	(1.32)	34	2
13	North Dakota	9.12	13	0
21	Ohio	5.13	26	5
44	Oklahoma	(10.02)	44	0
17	Oregon	5.72	19	2
24	Pennsylvania	4.39	21	-3
9	Rhode Island	12.28	11	2
46	South Carolina	(11.93)	46	0
25	South Dakota	1.95	22	-3
36	Tennessee	(5.63)	39	3
41	Texas	(8.87)	43	2
6	Utah	15.97	7	1
1	Vermont	18.68	6	5
20	Virginia	5.19	24	4
11	Washington	10.90	12	1
22	West Virginia	4.58	18	-4
15	Wisconsin	7.65	15	0
33	Wyoming	(1.87)	30	-3

RANK	STATE	SUM	09 RANK	CHANGE
1	Vermont	18.68	6	5
2	Minnesota	18.66	1	-1
3	Massachusetts	17.38	2	-1
4	Hawaii	16.67	3	-1
5	New Hampshire	16.51	5	0
6	Utah	15.97	7	1
7	Maine	15.68	8	1
8	Iowa	14.27	4	-4
9	Rhode Island	12.28	11	2
10	Nebraska	11.58	10	0
11	Washington	10.90	12	1
12	Connecticut	10.79	9	-3
13	North Dakota	9.12	13	0
14	New Jersey	8.04	14	0
15	Wisconsin	7.65	15	0
16	California	5.84	17	1
17	Oregon	5.72	19	2
18	Kansas	5.71	16	-2
19	Idaho	5.44	23	4
20	Virginia	5.19	24	4
21	Ohio	5.13	26	5
22	West Virginia	4.58	18	-4
23	Michigan	4.51	20	-3
24	Pennsylvania	4.39	21	-3
25	South Dakota	1.95	22	-3
26	New York	1.49	31	5
27	Colorado	1.24	27	0
28	Indiana	1.03	25	-3
29	Maryland	0.60	33	4
30	Illinois	(0.18)	28	-2
31	Montana	(1.23)	32	1
32	North Carolina	(1.32)	34	2
33	Wyoming	(1.87)	30	-3
34	Missouri	(4.03)	36	2
35	Kentucky	(4.73)	29	-6
36	Tennessee	(5.63)	39	3
37	Delaware	(6.32)	35	-2
38	Arkansas	(7.60)	38	0
39	Georgia	(7.64)	40	1
40	Alabama	(7.70)	42	2
41	Texas	(8.87)	43	2
42	Alaska	(9.35)	37	-5
43	Arizona	(9.73)	41	-2
44	Oklahoma	(10.02)	44	0
45	Florida	(10.21)	45	0
46	South Carolina	(11.93)	46	0
47	New Mexico	(18.84)	48	1
48	Nevada	(20.98)	47	-1
49	Louisiana	(21.72)	49	0
50	Mississippi	(24.41)	50	0

I. Births and Reproductive Health

Births in 2007

National Total = 4,317,119 Live Births*

ALPHA ORDER

RANK ORDER

RANK	STATE	BIRTHS	% of USA	RANK	STATE	BIRTHS	% of USA
24	Alabama	64,749	1.5%	1	California	566,352	13.1%
47	Alaska	11,101	0.3%	2	Texas	407,640	9.4%
13	Arizona	102,992	2.4%	3	New York	253,458	5.9%
33	Arkansas	41,377	1.0%	4	Florida	239,143	5.5%
1	California	566,352	13.1%	5	Illinois	180,856	4.2%
22	Colorado	70,805	1.6%	6	Georgia	152,021	3.5%
32	Connecticut	41,663	1.0%	7	Ohio	150,882	3.5%
46	Delaware	12,171	0.3%	8	Pennsylvania	150,731	3.5%
4	Florida	239,143	5.5%	9	North Carolina	131,016	3.0%
6	Georgia	152,021	3.5%	10	Michigan	125,394	2.9%
40	Hawaii	19,137	0.4%	11	New Jersey	116,060	2.7%
38	Idaho	25,019	0.6%	12	Virginia	108,874	2.5%
5	Illinois	180,856	4.2%	13	Arizona	102,992	2.4%
14	Indiana	89,847	2.1%	14	Indiana	89,847	2.1%
35	Iowa	40,885	0.9%	15	Washington	88,958	2.1%
31	Kansas	42,004	1.0%	16	Tennessee	86,707	2.0%
26	Kentucky	59,370	1.4%	17	Missouri	81,928	1.9%
23	Louisiana	66,260	1.5%	18	Maryland	78,096	1.8%
42	Maine	14,120	0.3%	19	Massachusetts	77,962	1.8%
18	Maryland	78,096	1.8%	20	Minnesota	73,745	1.7%
19	Massachusetts	77,962	1.8%	21	Wisconsin	72,796	1.7%
10	Michigan	125,394	2.9%	22	Colorado	70,805	1.6%
20	Minnesota	73,745	1.7%	23	Louisiana	66,260	1.5%
30	Mississippi	46,501	1.1%	24	Alabama	64,749	1.5%
17	Missouri	81,928	1.9%	25	South Carolina	62,891	1.5%
43	Montana	12,444	0.3%	26	Kentucky	59,370	1.4%
37	Nebraska	26,923	0.6%	27	Utah	55,131	1.3%
34	Nevada	41,202	1.0%	28	Oklahoma	55,078	1.3%
41	New Hampshire	14,169	0.3%	29	Oregon	49,372	1.1%
11	New Jersey	116,060	2.7%	30	Mississippi	46,501	1.1%
36	New Mexico	30,555	0.7%	31	Kansas	42,004	1.0%
3	New York	253,458	5.9%	32	Connecticut	41,663	1.0%
9	North Carolina	131,016	3.0%	33	Arkansas	41,377	1.0%
48	North Dakota	8,840	0.2%	34	Nevada	41,202	1.0%
7	Ohio	150,882	3.5%	35	Iowa	40,885	0.9%
28	Oklahoma	55,078	1.3%	36	New Mexico	30,555	0.7%
29	Oregon	49,372	1.1%	37	Nebraska	26,923	0.6%
8	Pennsylvania	150,731	3.5%	38	Idaho	25,019	0.6%
44	Rhode Island	12,375	0.3%	39	West Virginia	21,992	0.5%
25	South Carolina	62,891	1.5%	40	Hawaii	19,137	0.4%
45	South Dakota	12,259	0.3%	41	New Hampshire	14,169	0.3%
16	Tennessee	86,707	2.0%	42	Maine	14,120	0.3%
2	Texas	407,640	9.4%	43	Montana	12,444	0.3%
27	Utah	55,131	1.3%	44	Rhode Island	12,375	0.3%
50	Vermont	6,513	0.2%	45	South Dakota	12,259	0.3%
12	Virginia	108,874	2.5%	46	Delaware	12,171	0.3%
15	Washington	88,958	2.1%	47	Alaska	11,101	0.3%
39	West Virginia	21,992	0.5%	48	North Dakota	8,840	0.2%
21	Wisconsin	72,796	1.7%	49	Wyoming	7,893	0.2%
49	Wyoming	7,893	0.2%	50	Vermont	6,513	0.2%
					District of Columbia	8,862	0.2%

Source: U.S. Department of Health and Human Services, National Center for Health Statistics
"National Vital Statistics Reports" (Vol. 57, No. 12, March 18, 2009, http://www.cdc.gov/nchs/births.htm)
*Revised preliminary data by state of residence.

Birth Rate in 2007

National Rate = 14.3 Live Births per 1,000 Population*

ALPHA ORDER

RANK	STATE	RATE
28	Alabama	14.0
4	Alaska	16.2
4	Arizona	16.2
18	Arkansas	14.6
9	California	15.5
18	Colorado	14.6
46	Connecticut	11.9
24	Delaware	14.1
38	Florida	13.1
7	Georgia	15.9
17	Hawaii	14.9
3	Idaho	16.7
24	Illinois	14.1
22	Indiana	14.2
34	Iowa	13.7
15	Kansas	15.1
28	Kentucky	14.0
11	Louisiana	15.4
49	Maine	10.7
30	Maryland	13.9
43	Massachusetts	12.1
42	Michigan	12.4
22	Minnesota	14.2
7	Mississippi	15.9
30	Missouri	13.9
40	Montana	13.0
13	Nebraska	15.2
6	Nevada	16.1
48	New Hampshire	10.8
35	New Jersey	13.4
9	New Mexico	15.5
38	New York	13.1
20	North Carolina	14.5
32	North Dakota	13.8
36	Ohio	13.2
13	Oklahoma	15.2
36	Oregon	13.2
43	Pennsylvania	12.1
47	Rhode Island	11.7
21	South Carolina	14.3
11	South Dakota	15.4
24	Tennessee	14.1
2	Texas	17.1
1	Utah	20.8
50	Vermont	10.5
24	Virginia	14.1
32	Washington	13.8
43	West Virginia	12.1
40	Wisconsin	13.0
15	Wyoming	15.1

RANK ORDER

RANK	STATE	RATE
1	Utah	20.8
2	Texas	17.1
3	Idaho	16.7
4	Alaska	16.2
4	Arizona	16.2
6	Nevada	16.1
7	Georgia	15.9
7	Mississippi	15.9
9	California	15.5
9	New Mexico	15.5
11	Louisiana	15.4
11	South Dakota	15.4
13	Nebraska	15.2
13	Oklahoma	15.2
15	Kansas	15.1
15	Wyoming	15.1
17	Hawaii	14.9
18	Arkansas	14.6
18	Colorado	14.6
20	North Carolina	14.5
21	South Carolina	14.3
22	Indiana	14.2
22	Minnesota	14.2
24	Delaware	14.1
24	Illinois	14.1
24	Tennessee	14.1
24	Virginia	14.1
28	Alabama	14.0
28	Kentucky	14.0
30	Maryland	13.9
30	Missouri	13.9
32	North Dakota	13.8
32	Washington	13.8
34	Iowa	13.7
35	New Jersey	13.4
36	Ohio	13.2
36	Oregon	13.2
38	Florida	13.1
38	New York	13.1
40	Montana	13.0
40	Wisconsin	13.0
42	Michigan	12.4
43	Massachusetts	12.1
43	Pennsylvania	12.1
43	West Virginia	12.1
46	Connecticut	11.9
47	Rhode Island	11.7
48	New Hampshire	10.8
49	Maine	10.7
50	Vermont	10.5
	District of Columbia	15.1

Source: U.S. Department of Health and Human Services, National Center for Health Statistics
"National Vital Statistics Reports" (Vol. 57, No. 12, March 18, 2009, http://www.cdc.gov/nchs/births.htm)
*Revised preliminary data by state of residence.

Percent Change in Birth Rate: 1998 to 2007

National Percent Change = 0.0% Change*

ALPHA ORDER

RANK	STATE	PERCENT CHANGE
37	Alabama	(0.7)
29	Alaska	1.3
29	Arizona	1.3
13	Arkansas	4.3
39	California	(1.9)
31	Colorado	0.7
40	Connecticut	(8.5)
26	Delaware	1.4
14	Florida	4.0
24	Georgia	1.9
19	Hawaii	2.8
5	Idaho	7.7
46	Illinois	(5.4)
34	Indiana	0.0
7	Iowa	7.0
10	Kansas	4.9
17	Kentucky	2.9
22	Louisiana	2.0
38	Maine	(1.8)
31	Maryland	0.7
47	Massachusetts	(6.9)
49	Michigan	(8.8)
9	Minnesota	5.2
15	Mississippi	3.9
21	Missouri	2.2
6	Montana	7.4
4	Nebraska	9.4
15	Nevada	3.9
50	New Hampshire	(10.0)
42	New Jersey	(2.9)
22	New Mexico	2.0
45	New York	(5.1)
26	North Carolina	1.4
2	North Dakota	13.1
40	Ohio	(2.2)
11	Oklahoma	4.8
40	Oregon	(2.2)
25	Pennsylvania	1.7
43	Rhode Island	(4.1)
12	South Carolina	4.4
3	South Dakota	11.6
26	Tennessee	1.4
33	Texas	0.6
36	Utah	(0.5)
44	Vermont	(4.5)
17	Virginia	2.9
34	Washington	0.0
8	West Virginia	6.1
20	Wisconsin	2.4
1	Wyoming	18.9

RANK ORDER

RANK	STATE	PERCENT CHANGE
1	Wyoming	18.9
2	North Dakota	13.1
3	South Dakota	11.6
4	Nebraska	9.4
5	Idaho	7.7
6	Montana	7.4
7	Iowa	7.0
8	West Virginia	6.1
9	Minnesota	5.2
10	Kansas	4.9
11	Oklahoma	4.8
12	South Carolina	4.4
13	Arkansas	4.3
14	Florida	4.0
15	Mississippi	3.9
15	Nevada	3.9
17	Kentucky	2.9
17	Virginia	2.9
19	Hawaii	2.8
20	Wisconsin	2.4
21	Missouri	2.2
22	Louisiana	2.0
22	New Mexico	2.0
24	Georgia	1.9
25	Pennsylvania	1.7
26	Delaware	1.4
26	North Carolina	1.4
26	Tennessee	1.4
29	Alaska	1.3
29	Arizona	1.3
31	Colorado	0.7
31	Maryland	0.7
33	Texas	0.6
34	Indiana	0.0
34	Washington	0.0
36	Utah	(0.5)
37	Alabama	(0.7)
38	Maine	(1.8)
39	California	(1.9)
40	Ohio	(2.2)
40	Oregon	(2.2)
42	New Jersey	(2.9)
43	Rhode Island	(4.1)
44	Vermont	(4.5)
45	New York	(5.1)
46	Illinois	(5.4)
47	Massachusetts	(6.9)
48	Connecticut	(8.5)
49	Michigan	(8.8)
50	New Hampshire	(10.0)

District of Columbia	11.0

Source: CQ Press using data from U.S. Department of Health and Human Services, National Center for Health Statistics
"National Vital Statistics Reports" (Vol. 57, No. 12, March 18, 2009, http://www.cdc.gov/nchs/births.htm)
"VitalStats" (http://www.cdc.gov/nchs/datawh/vitalstats/VitalStats.htm)
*By state of residence.

Fertility Rate in 2007

National Rate = 69.5 Live Births per 1,000 Women 15 to 44 Years Old*

ALPHA ORDER

RANK	STATE	RATE
28	Alabama	68.7
8	Alaska	77.5
3	Arizona	81.1
17	Arkansas	73.1
18	California	72.5
21	Colorado	69.8
45	Connecticut	59.5
31	Delaware	68.4
31	Florida	68.4
15	Georgia	73.7
12	Hawaii	76.0
2	Idaho	83.4
33	Illinois	67.4
23	Indiana	69.7
19	Iowa	70.1
14	Kansas	75.6
29	Kentucky	68.6
16	Louisiana	73.3
48	Maine	55.6
38	Maryland	65.6
46	Massachusetts	57.4
44	Michigan	61.5
23	Minnesota	69.7
9	Mississippi	76.9
26	Missouri	68.8
29	Montana	68.6
11	Nebraska	76.2
6	Nevada	79.6
49	New Hampshire	53.8
36	New Jersey	66.1
10	New Mexico	76.4
42	New York	62.1
25	North Carolina	69.6
21	North Dakota	69.8
39	Ohio	65.5
12	Oklahoma	76.0
36	Oregon	66.1
43	Pennsylvania	61.9
47	Rhode Island	55.8
20	South Carolina	69.9
5	South Dakota	80.0
26	Tennessee	68.8
4	Texas	80.1
1	Utah	94.4
50	Vermont	53.2
34	Virginia	67.0
35	Washington	66.9
41	West Virginia	63.1
40	Wisconsin	65.0
7	Wyoming	77.7

RANK ORDER

RANK	STATE	RATE
1	Utah	94.4
2	Idaho	83.4
3	Arizona	81.1
4	Texas	80.1
5	South Dakota	80.0
6	Nevada	79.6
7	Wyoming	77.7
8	Alaska	77.5
9	Mississippi	76.9
10	New Mexico	76.4
11	Nebraska	76.2
12	Hawaii	76.0
12	Oklahoma	76.0
14	Kansas	75.6
15	Georgia	73.7
16	Louisiana	73.3
17	Arkansas	73.1
18	California	72.5
19	Iowa	70.1
20	South Carolina	69.9
21	Colorado	69.8
21	North Dakota	69.8
23	Indiana	69.7
23	Minnesota	69.7
25	North Carolina	69.6
26	Missouri	68.8
26	Tennessee	68.8
28	Alabama	68.7
29	Kentucky	68.6
29	Montana	68.6
31	Delaware	68.4
31	Florida	68.4
33	Illinois	67.4
34	Virginia	67.0
35	Washington	66.9
36	New Jersey	66.1
36	Oregon	66.1
38	Maryland	65.6
39	Ohio	65.5
40	Wisconsin	65.0
41	West Virginia	63.1
42	New York	62.1
43	Pennsylvania	61.9
44	Michigan	61.5
45	Connecticut	59.5
46	Massachusetts	57.4
47	Rhode Island	55.8
48	Maine	55.6
49	New Hampshire	53.8
50	Vermont	53.2

District of Columbia	60.0

Source: U.S. Department of Health and Human Services, National Center for Health Statistics
"National Vital Statistics Reports" (Vol. 57, No. 12, March 18, 2009, http://www.cdc.gov/nchs/births.htm)
*Preliminary data by state of residence.

Births to White Women in 2007

National Total = 2,312,473 Live Births to White Women*

ALPHA ORDER

RANK	STATE	BIRTHS	% of USA
24	Alabama	38,464	1.7%
47	Alaska	6,291	0.3%
22	Arizona	42,521	1.8%
32	Arkansas	27,720	1.2%
1	California	155,930	6.7%
23	Colorado	41,853	1.8%
33	Connecticut	24,897	1.1%
45	Delaware	6,494	0.3%
5	Florida	107,843	4.7%
10	Georgia	70,735	3.1%
50	Hawaii	4,557	0.2%
36	Idaho	20,190	0.9%
7	Illinois	95,508	4.1%
11	Indiana	68,907	3.0%
28	Iowa	34,521	1.5%
31	Kansas	30,512	1.3%
20	Kentucky	49,842	2.2%
25	Louisiana	36,172	1.6%
39	Maine	13,186	0.6%
26	Maryland	36,128	1.6%
19	Massachusetts	53,274	2.3%
8	Michigan	85,528	3.7%
18	Minnesota	53,856	2.3%
34	Mississippi	23,068	1.0%
12	Missouri	62,211	2.7%
41	Montana	9,623	0.4%
37	Nebraska	20,008	0.9%
38	Nevada	16,959	0.7%
40	New Hampshire	12,620	0.5%
16	New Jersey	56,139	2.4%
43	New Mexico	8,662	0.4%
3	New York	125,632	5.4%
9	North Carolina	72,416	3.1%
44	North Dakota	7,277	0.3%
4	Ohio	115,583	5.0%
27	Oklahoma	35,334	1.5%
30	Oregon	34,256	1.5%
6	Pennsylvania	107,818	4.7%
49	Rhode Island	5,999	0.3%
29	South Carolina	34,411	1.5%
42	South Dakota	9,351	0.4%
14	Tennessee	58,588	2.5%
2	Texas	140,272	6.1%
21	Utah	42,844	1.9%
48	Vermont	6,178	0.3%
13	Virginia	62,155	2.7%
15	Washington	56,299	2.4%
35	West Virginia	20,700	0.9%
17	Wisconsin	54,549	2.4%
46	Wyoming	6,361	0.3%

RANK ORDER

RANK	STATE	BIRTHS	% of USA
1	California	155,930	6.7%
2	Texas	140,272	6.1%
3	New York	125,632	5.4%
4	Ohio	115,583	5.0%
5	Florida	107,843	4.7%
6	Pennsylvania	107,818	4.7%
7	Illinois	95,508	4.1%
8	Michigan	85,528	3.7%
9	North Carolina	72,416	3.1%
10	Georgia	70,735	3.1%
11	Indiana	68,907	3.0%
12	Missouri	62,211	2.7%
13	Virginia	62,155	2.7%
14	Tennessee	58,588	2.5%
15	Washington	56,299	2.4%
16	New Jersey	56,139	2.4%
17	Wisconsin	54,549	2.4%
18	Minnesota	53,856	2.3%
19	Massachusetts	53,274	2.3%
20	Kentucky	49,842	2.2%
21	Utah	42,844	1.9%
22	Arizona	42,521	1.8%
23	Colorado	41,853	1.8%
24	Alabama	38,464	1.7%
25	Louisiana	36,172	1.6%
26	Maryland	36,128	1.6%
27	Oklahoma	35,334	1.5%
28	Iowa	34,521	1.5%
29	South Carolina	34,411	1.5%
30	Oregon	34,256	1.5%
31	Kansas	30,512	1.3%
32	Arkansas	27,720	1.2%
33	Connecticut	24,897	1.1%
34	Mississippi	23,068	1.0%
35	West Virginia	20,700	0.9%
36	Idaho	20,190	0.9%
37	Nebraska	20,008	0.9%
38	Nevada	16,959	0.7%
39	Maine	13,186	0.6%
40	New Hampshire	12,620	0.5%
41	Montana	9,623	0.4%
42	South Dakota	9,351	0.4%
43	New Mexico	8,662	0.4%
44	North Dakota	7,277	0.3%
45	Delaware	6,494	0.3%
46	Wyoming	6,361	0.3%
47	Alaska	6,291	0.3%
48	Vermont	6,178	0.3%
49	Rhode Island	5,999	0.3%
50	Hawaii	4,557	0.2%
	District of Columbia	2,227	0.1%

Source: U.S. Department of Health and Human Services, National Center for Health Statistics
  "National Vital Statistics Reports" (Vol. 57, No. 12, March 18, 2009, http://www.cdc.gov/nchs/births.htm)
*Preliminary data by state of residence. By race of mother. Does not include births to white Hispanic mothers.

White Births as a Percent of All Births in 2007

National Percent = 53.6% of Live Births*

ALPHA ORDER			RANK ORDER		
RANK	STATE	PERCENT	RANK	STATE	PERCENT
29	Alabama	59.4	1	Vermont	94.9
32	Alaska	56.7	2	West Virginia	94.1
45	Arizona	41.3	3	Maine	93.4
25	Arkansas	67.0	4	New Hampshire	89.1
49	California	27.5	5	Iowa	84.4
30	Colorado	59.1	6	Kentucky	84.0
28	Connecticut	59.8	7	North Dakota	82.3
36	Delaware	53.4	8	Idaho	80.7
44	Florida	45.1	9	Wyoming	80.6
42	Georgia	46.5	10	Utah	77.7
50	Hawaii	23.8	11	Montana	77.3
8	Idaho	80.7	12	Indiana	76.7
37	Illinois	52.8	13	Ohio	76.6
12	Indiana	76.7	14	South Dakota	76.3
5	Iowa	84.4	15	Missouri	75.9
19	Kansas	72.6	16	Wisconsin	74.9
6	Kentucky	84.0	17	Nebraska	74.3
35	Louisiana	54.6	18	Minnesota	73.0
3	Maine	93.4	19	Kansas	72.6
43	Maryland	46.3	20	Pennsylvania	71.5
22	Massachusetts	68.3	21	Oregon	69.4
23	Michigan	68.2	22	Massachusetts	68.3
18	Minnesota	73.0	23	Michigan	68.2
38	Mississippi	49.6	24	Tennessee	67.6
15	Missouri	75.9	25	Arkansas	67.0
11	Montana	77.3	26	Oklahoma	64.2
17	Nebraska	74.3	27	Washington	63.3
46	Nevada	41.2	28	Connecticut	59.8
4	New Hampshire	89.1	29	Alabama	59.4
41	New Jersey	48.4	30	Colorado	59.1
48	New Mexico	28.3	31	Virginia	57.1
38	New York	49.6	32	Alaska	56.7
33	North Carolina	55.3	33	North Carolina	55.3
7	North Dakota	82.3	34	South Carolina	54.7
13	Ohio	76.6	35	Louisiana	54.6
26	Oklahoma	64.2	36	Delaware	53.4
21	Oregon	69.4	37	Illinois	52.8
20	Pennsylvania	71.5	38	Mississippi	49.6
40	Rhode Island	48.5	38	New York	49.6
34	South Carolina	54.7	40	Rhode Island	48.5
14	South Dakota	76.3	41	New Jersey	48.4
24	Tennessee	67.6	42	Georgia	46.5
47	Texas	34.4	43	Maryland	46.3
10	Utah	77.7	44	Florida	45.1
1	Vermont	94.9	45	Arizona	41.3
31	Virginia	57.1	46	Nevada	41.2
27	Washington	63.3	47	Texas	34.4
2	West Virginia	94.1	48	New Mexico	28.3
16	Wisconsin	74.9	49	California	27.5
9.	Wyoming	80.6	50	Hawaii	23.8
			District of Columbia		25.1

Source: CQ Press using data from U.S. Department of Health and Human Services, National Center for Health Statistics
"National Vital Statistics Reports" (Vol. 57, No. 12, March 18, 2009, http://www.cdc.gov/nchs/births.htm)
*Preliminary data by state of residence. By race of mother. Does not include births to white Hispanic mothers.

Births to Black Women in 2007

National Total = 627,230 Live Births to Black Women*

<table>
<tr><td colspan="4">ALPHA ORDER</td><td colspan="4">RANK ORDER</td></tr>
<tr><th>RANK</th><th>STATE</th><th>BIRTHS</th><th>% of USA</th><th>RANK</th><th>STATE</th><th>BIRTHS</th><th>% of USA</th></tr>
<tr><td>16</td><td>Alabama</td><td>19,740</td><td>3.1%</td><td>1</td><td>Florida</td><td>51,835</td><td>8.3%</td></tr>
<tr><td>42</td><td>Alaska</td><td>409</td><td>0.1%</td><td>2</td><td>Georgia</td><td>49,278</td><td>7.9%</td></tr>
<tr><td>28</td><td>Arizona</td><td>3,914</td><td>0.6%</td><td>3</td><td>Texas</td><td>46,397</td><td>7.4%</td></tr>
<tr><td>21</td><td>Arkansas</td><td>8,080</td><td>1.3%</td><td>4</td><td>New York</td><td>42,738</td><td>6.8%</td></tr>
<tr><td>5</td><td>California</td><td>31,777</td><td>5.1%</td><td>5</td><td>California</td><td>31,777</td><td>5.1%</td></tr>
<tr><td>32</td><td>Colorado</td><td>3,122</td><td>0.5%</td><td>6</td><td>Illinois</td><td>31,655</td><td>5.0%</td></tr>
<tr><td>26</td><td>Connecticut</td><td>5,183</td><td>0.8%</td><td>7</td><td>North Carolina</td><td>30,635</td><td>4.9%</td></tr>
<tr><td>31</td><td>Delaware</td><td>3,215</td><td>0.5%</td><td>8</td><td>Maryland</td><td>26,198</td><td>4.2%</td></tr>
<tr><td>1</td><td>Florida</td><td>51,835</td><td>8.3%</td><td>9</td><td>Louisiana</td><td>25,343</td><td>4.0%</td></tr>
<tr><td>2</td><td>Georgia</td><td>49,278</td><td>7.9%</td><td>10</td><td>Ohio</td><td>24,222</td><td>3.9%</td></tr>
<tr><td>41</td><td>Hawaii</td><td>426</td><td>0.1%</td><td>11</td><td>Virginia</td><td>23,842</td><td>3.8%</td></tr>
<tr><td>46</td><td>Idaho</td><td>139</td><td>0.0%</td><td>12</td><td>Michigan</td><td>22,343</td><td>3.6%</td></tr>
<tr><td>6</td><td>Illinois</td><td>31,655</td><td>5.0%</td><td>13</td><td>Pennsylvania</td><td>21,281</td><td>3.4%</td></tr>
<tr><td>20</td><td>Indiana</td><td>10,229</td><td>1.6%</td><td>14</td><td>Mississippi</td><td>20,894</td><td>3.3%</td></tr>
<tr><td>34</td><td>Iowa</td><td>1,804</td><td>0.3%</td><td>15</td><td>South Carolina</td><td>20,489</td><td>3.3%</td></tr>
<tr><td>33</td><td>Kansas</td><td>3,059</td><td>0.5%</td><td>16</td><td>Alabama</td><td>19,740</td><td>3.1%</td></tr>
<tr><td>25</td><td>Kentucky</td><td>5,418</td><td>0.9%</td><td>17</td><td>New Jersey</td><td>17,863</td><td>2.8%</td></tr>
<tr><td>9</td><td>Louisiana</td><td>25,343</td><td>4.0%</td><td>18</td><td>Tennessee</td><td>17,768</td><td>2.8%</td></tr>
<tr><td>43</td><td>Maine</td><td>325</td><td>0.1%</td><td>19</td><td>Missouri</td><td>12,610</td><td>2.0%</td></tr>
<tr><td>8</td><td>Maryland</td><td>26,198</td><td>4.2%</td><td>20</td><td>Indiana</td><td>10,229</td><td>1.6%</td></tr>
<tr><td>22</td><td>Massachusetts</td><td>7,262</td><td>1.2%</td><td>21</td><td>Arkansas</td><td>8,080</td><td>1.3%</td></tr>
<tr><td>12</td><td>Michigan</td><td>22,343</td><td>3.6%</td><td>22</td><td>Massachusetts</td><td>7,262</td><td>1.2%</td></tr>
<tr><td>24</td><td>Minnesota</td><td>6,615</td><td>1.1%</td><td>23</td><td>Wisconsin</td><td>7,240</td><td>1.2%</td></tr>
<tr><td>14</td><td>Mississippi</td><td>20,894</td><td>3.3%</td><td>24</td><td>Minnesota</td><td>6,615</td><td>1.1%</td></tr>
<tr><td>19</td><td>Missouri</td><td>12,610</td><td>2.0%</td><td>25</td><td>Kentucky</td><td>5,418</td><td>0.9%</td></tr>
<tr><td>50</td><td>Montana</td><td>62</td><td>0.0%</td><td>26</td><td>Connecticut</td><td>5,183</td><td>0.8%</td></tr>
<tr><td>35</td><td>Nebraska</td><td>1,794</td><td>0.3%</td><td>27</td><td>Oklahoma</td><td>4,914</td><td>0.8%</td></tr>
<tr><td>30</td><td>Nevada</td><td>3,615</td><td>0.6%</td><td>28</td><td>Arizona</td><td>3,914</td><td>0.6%</td></tr>
<tr><td>45</td><td>New Hampshire</td><td>203</td><td>0.0%</td><td>29</td><td>Washington</td><td>3,812</td><td>0.6%</td></tr>
<tr><td>17</td><td>New Jersey</td><td>17,863</td><td>2.8%</td><td>30</td><td>Nevada</td><td>3,615</td><td>0.6%</td></tr>
<tr><td>40</td><td>New Mexico</td><td>522</td><td>0.1%</td><td>31</td><td>Delaware</td><td>3,215</td><td>0.5%</td></tr>
<tr><td>4</td><td>New York</td><td>42,738</td><td>6.8%</td><td>32</td><td>Colorado</td><td>3,122</td><td>0.5%</td></tr>
<tr><td>7</td><td>North Carolina</td><td>30,635</td><td>4.9%</td><td>33</td><td>Kansas</td><td>3,059</td><td>0.5%</td></tr>
<tr><td>47</td><td>North Dakota</td><td>129</td><td>0.0%</td><td>34</td><td>Iowa</td><td>1,804</td><td>0.3%</td></tr>
<tr><td>10</td><td>Ohio</td><td>24,222</td><td>3.9%</td><td>35</td><td>Nebraska</td><td>1,794</td><td>0.3%</td></tr>
<tr><td>27</td><td>Oklahoma</td><td>4,914</td><td>0.8%</td><td>36</td><td>Oregon</td><td>1,145</td><td>0.2%</td></tr>
<tr><td>36</td><td>Oregon</td><td>1,145</td><td>0.2%</td><td>37</td><td>Rhode Island</td><td>1,045</td><td>0.2%</td></tr>
<tr><td>13</td><td>Pennsylvania</td><td>21,281</td><td>3.4%</td><td>38</td><td>West Virginia</td><td>778</td><td>0.1%</td></tr>
<tr><td>37</td><td>Rhode Island</td><td>1,045</td><td>0.2%</td><td>39</td><td>Utah</td><td>539</td><td>0.1%</td></tr>
<tr><td>15</td><td>South Carolina</td><td>20,489</td><td>3.3%</td><td>40</td><td>New Mexico</td><td>522</td><td>0.1%</td></tr>
<tr><td>44</td><td>South Dakota</td><td>212</td><td>0.0%</td><td>41</td><td>Hawaii</td><td>426</td><td>0.1%</td></tr>
<tr><td>18</td><td>Tennessee</td><td>17,768</td><td>2.8%</td><td>42</td><td>Alaska</td><td>409</td><td>0.1%</td></tr>
<tr><td>3</td><td>Texas</td><td>46,397</td><td>7.4%</td><td>43</td><td>Maine</td><td>325</td><td>0.1%</td></tr>
<tr><td>39</td><td>Utah</td><td>539</td><td>0.1%</td><td>44</td><td>South Dakota</td><td>212</td><td>0.0%</td></tr>
<tr><td>48</td><td>Vermont</td><td>95</td><td>0.0%</td><td>45</td><td>New Hampshire</td><td>203</td><td>0.0%</td></tr>
<tr><td>11</td><td>Virginia</td><td>23,842</td><td>3.8%</td><td>46</td><td>Idaho</td><td>139</td><td>0.0%</td></tr>
<tr><td>29</td><td>Washington</td><td>3,812</td><td>0.6%</td><td>47</td><td>North Dakota</td><td>129</td><td>0.0%</td></tr>
<tr><td>38</td><td>West Virginia</td><td>778</td><td>0.1%</td><td>48</td><td>Vermont</td><td>95</td><td>0.0%</td></tr>
<tr><td>23</td><td>Wisconsin</td><td>7,240</td><td>1.2%</td><td>49</td><td>Wyoming</td><td>79</td><td>0.0%</td></tr>
<tr><td>49</td><td>Wyoming</td><td>79</td><td>0.0%</td><td>50</td><td>Montana</td><td>62</td><td>0.0%</td></tr>
<tr><td></td><td></td><td></td><td></td><td></td><td>District of Columbia</td><td>4,936</td><td>0.8%</td></tr>
</table>

Source: U.S. Department of Health and Human Services, National Center for Health Statistics
"National Vital Statistics Reports" (Vol. 57, No. 12, March 18, 2009, http://www.cdc.gov/nchs/births.htm)
*Preliminary data by state of residence. By race of mother. Does not include births to black Hispanic mothers.

Black Births as a Percent of All Births in 2007

National Percent = 14.5% of Live Births*

RANK	STATE	PERCENT		RANK	STATE	PERCENT
6	Alabama	30.5		1	Mississippi	44.9
37	Alaska	3.7		2	Louisiana	38.2
36	Arizona	3.8		3	Maryland	33.5
12	Arkansas	19.5		4	South Carolina	32.6
32	California	5.6		5	Georgia	32.4
33	Colorado	4.4		6	Alabama	30.5
20	Connecticut	12.4		7	Delaware	26.4
7	Delaware	26.4		8	North Carolina	23.4
10	Florida	21.7		9	Virginia	21.9
5	Georgia	32.4		10	Florida	21.7
41	Hawaii	2.2		11	Tennessee	20.5
49	Idaho	0.6		12	Arkansas	19.5
14	Illinois	17.5		13	Michigan	17.8
21	Indiana	11.4		14	Illinois	17.5
33	Iowa	4.4		15	New York	16.9
30	Kansas	7.3		16	Ohio	16.1
25	Kentucky	9.1		17	Missouri	15.4
2	Louisiana	38.2		17	New Jersey	15.4
39	Maine	2.3		19	Pennsylvania	14.1
3	Maryland	33.5		20	Connecticut	12.4
24	Massachusetts	9.3		21	Indiana	11.4
13	Michigan	17.8		21	Texas	11.4
26	Minnesota	9.0		23	Wisconsin	9.9
1	Mississippi	44.9		24	Massachusetts	9.3
17	Missouri	15.4		25	Kentucky	9.1
50	Montana	0.5		26	Minnesota	9.0
31	Nebraska	6.7		27	Oklahoma	8.9
28	Nevada	8.8		28	Nevada	8.8
46	New Hampshire	1.4		29	Rhode Island	8.4
17	New Jersey	15.4		30	Kansas	7.3
42	New Mexico	1.7		31	Nebraska	6.7
15	New York	16.9		32	California	5.6
8	North Carolina	23.4		33	Colorado	4.4
44	North Dakota	1.5		33	Iowa	4.4
16	Ohio	16.1		35	Washington	4.3
27	Oklahoma	8.9		36	Arizona	3.8
39	Oregon	2.3		37	Alaska	3.7
19	Pennsylvania	14.1		38	West Virginia	3.5
29	Rhode Island	8.4		39	Maine	2.3
4	South Carolina	32.6		39	Oregon	2.3
42	South Dakota	1.7		41	Hawaii	2.2
11	Tennessee	20.5		42	New Mexico	1.7
21	Texas	11.4		42	South Dakota	1.7
47	Utah	1.0		44	North Dakota	1.5
44	Vermont	1.5		44	Vermont	1.5
9	Virginia	21.9		46	New Hampshire	1.4
35	Washington	4.3		47	Utah	1.0
38	West Virginia	3.5		47	Wyoming	1.0
23	Wisconsin	9.9		49	Idaho	0.6
47	Wyoming	1.0		50	Montana	0.5

ALPHA ORDER — RANK ORDER

District of Columbia 55.7

Source: CQ Press using data from U.S. Department of Health and Human Services, National Center for Health Statistics
"National Vital Statistics Reports" (Vol. 57, No. 12, March 18, 2009, http://www.cdc.gov/nchs/births.htm)
*Preliminary data by state of residence. By race of mother. Does not include births to black Hispanic mothers.

Births to Hispanic Women in 2007

National Total = 1,061,970 Live Births to Hispanic Women*

ALPHA ORDER

RANK ORDER

RANK	STATE	BIRTHS	% of USA	RANK	STATE	BIRTHS	% of USA
30	Alabama	5,391	0.5%	1	California	296,942	28.0%
43	Alaska	825	0.1%	2	Texas	204,498	19.3%
5	Arizona	46,373	4.4%	3	Florida	70,833	6.7%
32	Arkansas	4,515	0.4%	4	New York	60,134	5.7%
1	California	296,942	28.0%	5	Arizona	46,373	4.4%
9	Colorado	22,221	2.1%	6	Illinois	44,151	4.2%
20	Connecticut	8,832	0.8%	7	New Jersey	30,027	2.8%
40	Delaware	1,912	0.2%	8	Georgia	24,319	2.3%
3	Florida	70,833	6.7%	9	Colorado	22,221	2.1%
8	Georgia	24,319	2.3%	10	North Carolina	22,113	2.1%
38	Hawaii	3,007	0.3%	11	New Mexico	17,007	1.6%
34	Idaho	3,870	0.4%	12	Washington	16,881	1.6%
6	Illinois	44,151	4.2%	13	Nevada	16,144	1.5%
21	Indiana	8,805	0.8%	14	Virginia	14,966	1.4%
35	Iowa	3,355	0.3%	15	Pennsylvania	13,793	1.3%
26	Kansas	6,689	0.6%	16	Massachusetts	10,900	1.0%
37	Kentucky	3,092	0.3%	17	Maryland	10,608	1.0%
36	Louisiana	3,188	0.3%	18	Oregon	10,133	1.0%
49	Maine	209	0.0%	19	Utah	9,042	0.9%
17	Maryland	10,608	1.0%	20	Connecticut	8,832	0.8%
16	Massachusetts	10,900	1.0%	21	Indiana	8,805	0.8%
22	Michigan	8,441	0.8%	22	Michigan	8,441	0.8%
29	Minnesota	5,939	0.6%	23	Tennessee	8,383	0.8%
41	Mississippi	1,708	0.2%	24	Oklahoma	7,173	0.7%
31	Missouri	4,667	0.4%	25	Wisconsin	6,934	0.7%
46	Montana	372	0.0%	26	Kansas	6,689	0.6%
33	Nebraska	4,068	0.4%	27	Ohio	6,611	0.6%
13	Nevada	16,144	1.5%	28	South Carolina	6,215	0.6%
44	New Hampshire	593	0.1%	29	Minnesota	5,939	0.6%
7	New Jersey	30,027	2.8%	30	Alabama	5,391	0.5%
11	New Mexico	17,007	1.6%	31	Missouri	4,667	0.4%
4	New York	60,134	5.7%	32	Arkansas	4,515	0.4%
10	North Carolina	22,113	2.1%	33	Nebraska	4,068	0.4%
47	North Dakota	278	0.0%	34	Idaho	3,870	0.4%
27	Ohio	6,611	0.6%	35	Iowa	3,355	0.3%
24	Oklahoma	7,173	0.7%	36	Louisiana	3,188	0.3%
18	Oregon	10,133	1.0%	37	Kentucky	3,092	0.3%
15	Pennsylvania	13,793	1.3%	38	Hawaii	3,007	0.3%
39	Rhode Island	2,588	0.2%	39	Rhode Island	2,588	0.2%
28	South Carolina	6,215	0.6%	40	Delaware	1,912	0.2%
45	South Dakota	471	0.0%	41	Mississippi	1,708	0.2%
23	Tennessee	8,383	0.8%	42	Wyoming	969	0.1%
2	Texas	204,498	19.3%	43	Alaska	825	0.1%
19	Utah	9,042	0.9%	44	New Hampshire	593	0.1%
50	Vermont	78	0.0%	45	South Dakota	471	0.0%
14	Virginia	14,966	1.4%	46	Montana	372	0.0%
12	Washington	16,881	1.6%	47	North Dakota	278	0.0%
48	West Virginia	253	0.0%	48	West Virginia	253	0.0%
25	Wisconsin	6,934	0.7%	49	Maine	209	0.0%
42	Wyoming	969	0.1%	50	Vermont	78	0.0%
					District of Columbia	1,450	0.1%

Source: U.S. Department of Health and Human Services, National Center for Health Statistics
  "National Vital Statistics Reports" (Vol. 57, No. 12, March 18, 2009, http://www.cdc.gov/nchs/births.htm)
*Preliminary data by state of residence. By race of mother. Persons of Hispanic origin may be of any race.

Hispanic Births as a Percent of All Births in 2007

National Percent = 24.6% of Live Births*

RANK	STATE	RATE
34	Alabama	8.3
37	Alaska	7.4
4	Arizona	45.0
28	Arkansas	10.9
2	California	52.4
6	Colorado	31.4
11	Connecticut	21.2
19	Delaware	15.7
7	Florida	29.6
17	Georgia	16.0
19	Hawaii	15.7
21	Idaho	15.5
9	Illinois	24.4
30	Indiana	9.8
35	Iowa	8.2
18	Kansas	15.9
40	Kentucky	5.2
41	Louisiana	4.8
48	Maine	1.5
25	Maryland	13.6
23	Massachusetts	14.0
38	Michigan	6.7
36	Minnesota	8.1
45	Mississippi	3.7
39	Missouri	5.7
47	Montana	3.0
22	Nebraska	15.1
5	Nevada	39.2
43	New Hampshire	4.2
8	New Jersey	25.9
1	New Mexico	55.7
10	New York	23.7
15	North Carolina	16.9
46	North Dakota	3.1
42	Ohio	4.4
26	Oklahoma	13.0
13	Oregon	20.5
33	Pennsylvania	9.2
12	Rhode Island	20.9
29	South Carolina	9.9
44	South Dakota	3.8
31	Tennessee	9.7
3	Texas	50.2
16	Utah	16.4
49	Vermont	1.2
24	Virginia	13.7
14	Washington	19.0
49	West Virginia	1.2
32	Wisconsin	9.5
27	Wyoming	12.3

RANK	STATE	RATE
1	New Mexico	55.7
2	California	52.4
3	Texas	50.2
4	Arizona	45.0
5	Nevada	39.2
6	Colorado	31.4
7	Florida	29.6
8	New Jersey	25.9
9	Illinois	24.4
10	New York	23.7
11	Connecticut	21.2
12	Rhode Island	20.9
13	Oregon	20.5
14	Washington	19.0
15	North Carolina	16.9
16	Utah	16.4
17	Georgia	16.0
18	Kansas	15.9
19	Delaware	15.7
19	Hawaii	15.7
21	Idaho	15.5
22	Nebraska	15.1
23	Massachusetts	14.0
24	Virginia	13.7
25	Maryland	13.6
26	Oklahoma	13.0
27	Wyoming	12.3
28	Arkansas	10.9
29	South Carolina	9.9
30	Indiana	9.8
31	Tennessee	9.7
32	Wisconsin	9.5
33	Pennsylvania	9.2
34	Alabama	8.3
35	Iowa	8.2
36	Minnesota	8.1
37	Alaska	7.4
38	Michigan	6.7
39	Missouri	5.7
40	Kentucky	5.2
41	Louisiana	4.8
42	Ohio	4.4
43	New Hampshire	4.2
44	South Dakota	3.8
45	Mississippi	3.7
46	North Dakota	3.1
47	Montana	3.0
48	Maine	1.5
49	Vermont	1.2
49	West Virginia	1.2
	District of Columbia	16.4

Source: CQ Press using data from U.S. Department of Health and Human Services, National Center for Health Statistics
"National Vital Statistics Reports" (Vol. 57, No. 12, March 18, 2009, http://www.cdc.gov/nchs/births.htm)
*Preliminary data by state of residence. By race of mother. Persons of Hispanic origin may be of any race.

Births of Low Birthweight in 2007

National Total = 354,004 Live Births*

ALPHA ORDER

RANK	STATE	BIRTHS	% of USA
18	Alabama	6,734	1.9%
48	Alaska	633	0.2%
15	Arizona	7,312	2.1%
29	Arkansas	3,765	1.1%
1	California	39,078	11.0%
20	Colorado	6,372	1.8%
32	Connecticut	3,375	1.0%
41	Delaware	1,132	0.3%
3	Florida	20,805	5.9%
6	Georgia	13,834	3.9%
40	Hawaii	1,531	0.4%
39	Idaho	1,626	0.5%
5	Illinois	15,373	4.3%
14	Indiana	7,637	2.2%
34	Iowa	2,780	0.8%
36	Kansas	2,520	0.7%
25	Kentucky	5,521	1.6%
16	Louisiana	7,289	2.1%
45	Maine	890	0.3%
17	Maryland	7,107	2.0%
22	Massachusetts	6,159	1.7%
10	Michigan	10,282	2.9%
27	Minnesota	4,941	1.4%
23	Mississippi	5,720	1.6%
19	Missouri	6,390	1.8%
43	Montana	896	0.3%
38	Nebraska	1,885	0.5%
31	Nevada	3,379	1.0%
44	New Hampshire	893	0.3%
11	New Jersey	9,865	2.8%
35	New Mexico	2,689	0.8%
4	New York	20,784	5.9%
9	North Carolina	12,053	3.4%
49	North Dakota	557	0.2%
7	Ohio	13,127	3.7%
28	Oklahoma	4,516	1.3%
33	Oregon	3,012	0.9%
8	Pennsylvania	12,661	3.6%
42	Rhode Island	990	0.3%
21	South Carolina	6,352	1.8%
46	South Dakota	858	0.2%
13	Tennessee	8,150	2.3%
2	Texas	34,242	9.7%
30	Utah	3,694	1.0%
50	Vermont	404	0.1%
12	Virginia	9,363	2.6%
24	Washington	5,604	1.6%
37	West Virginia	2,089	0.6%
26	Wisconsin	5,096	1.4%
47	Wyoming	718	0.2%

RANK ORDER

RANK	STATE	BIRTHS	% of USA
1	California	39,078	11.0%
2	Texas	34,242	9.7%
3	Florida	20,805	5.9%
4	New York	20,784	5.9%
5	Illinois	15,373	4.3%
6	Georgia	13,834	3.9%
7	Ohio	13,127	3.7%
8	Pennsylvania	12,661	3.6%
9	North Carolina	12,053	3.4%
10	Michigan	10,282	2.9%
11	New Jersey	9,865	2.8%
12	Virginia	9,363	2.6%
13	Tennessee	8,150	2.3%
14	Indiana	7,637	2.2%
15	Arizona	7,312	2.1%
16	Louisiana	7,289	2.1%
17	Maryland	7,107	2.0%
18	Alabama	6,734	1.9%
19	Missouri	6,390	1.8%
20	Colorado	6,372	1.8%
21	South Carolina	6,352	1.8%
22	Massachusetts	6,159	1.7%
23	Mississippi	5,720	1.6%
24	Washington	5,604	1.6%
25	Kentucky	5,521	1.6%
26	Wisconsin	5,096	1.4%
27	Minnesota	4,941	1.4%
28	Oklahoma	4,516	1.3%
29	Arkansas	3,765	1.1%
30	Utah	3,694	1.0%
31	Nevada	3,379	1.0%
32	Connecticut	3,375	1.0%
33	Oregon	3,012	0.9%
34	Iowa	2,780	0.8%
35	New Mexico	2,689	0.8%
36	Kansas	2,520	0.7%
37	West Virginia	2,089	0.6%
38	Nebraska	1,885	0.5%
39	Idaho	1,626	0.5%
40	Hawaii	1,531	0.4%
41	Delaware	1,132	0.3%
42	Rhode Island	990	0.3%
43	Montana	896	0.3%
44	New Hampshire	893	0.3%
45	Maine	890	0.3%
46	South Dakota	858	0.2%
47	Wyoming	718	0.2%
48	Alaska	633	0.2%
49	North Dakota	557	0.2%
50	Vermont	404	0.1%
	District of Columbia	984	0.3%

Source: CQ Press using data from U.S. Department of Health and Human Services, National Center for Health Statistics
"National Vital Statistics Reports" (Vol. 57, No. 12, March 18, 2009, http://www.cdc.gov/nchs/births.htm)
*Estimate based on preliminary data by state of residence. Births of less than 2,500 grams (5 pounds 8 ounces).

Births of Low Birthweight as a Percent of All Births in 2007

National Percent = 8.2% of Live Births*

ALPHA ORDER				RANK ORDER		
RANK	STATE	PERCENT		RANK	STATE	PERCENT
3	Alabama	10.4		1	Mississippi	12.3
50	Alaska	5.7		2	Louisiana	11.0
34	Arizona	7.1		3	Alabama	10.4
10	Arkansas	9.1		4	South Carolina	10.1
38	California	6.9		5	West Virginia	9.5
14	Colorado	9.0		6	Tennessee	9.4
28	Connecticut	8.1		7	Delaware	9.3
7	Delaware	9.3		7	Kentucky	9.3
16	Florida	8.7		9	North Carolina	9.2
10	Georgia	9.1		10	Arkansas	9.1
29	Hawaii	8.0		10	Georgia	9.1
42	Idaho	6.5		10	Maryland	9.1
19	Illinois	8.5		10	Wyoming	9.1
19	Indiana	8.5		14	Colorado	9.0
39	Iowa	6.8		15	New Mexico	8.8
49	Kansas	6.0		16	Florida	8.7
7	Kentucky	9.3		16	Ohio	8.7
2	Louisiana	11.0		18	Virginia	8.6
43	Maine	6.3		19	Illinois	8.5
10	Maryland	9.1		19	Indiana	8.5
31	Massachusetts	7.9		19	New Jersey	8.5
24	Michigan	8.2		22	Pennsylvania	8.4
40	Minnesota	6.7		22	Texas	8.4
1	Mississippi	12.3		24	Michigan	8.2
32	Missouri	7.8		24	Nevada	8.2
33	Montana	7.2		24	New York	8.2
35	Nebraska	7.0		24	Oklahoma	8.2
24	Nevada	8.2		28	Connecticut	8.1
43	New Hampshire	6.3		29	Hawaii	8.0
19	New Jersey	8.5		29	Rhode Island	8.0
15	New Mexico	8.8		31	Massachusetts	7.9
24	New York	8.2		32	Missouri	7.8
9	North Carolina	9.2		33	Montana	7.2
43	North Dakota	6.3		34	Arizona	7.1
16	Ohio	8.7		35	Nebraska	7.0
24	Oklahoma	8.2		35	South Dakota	7.0
48	Oregon	6.1		35	Wisconsin	7.0
22	Pennsylvania	8.4		38	California	6.9
29	Rhode Island	8.0		39	Iowa	6.8
4	South Carolina	10.1		40	Minnesota	6.7
35	South Dakota	7.0		40	Utah	6.7
6	Tennessee	9.4		42	Idaho	6.5
22	Texas	8.4		43	Maine	6.3
40	Utah	6.7		43	New Hampshire	6.3
47	Vermont	6.2		43	North Dakota	6.3
18	Virginia	8.6		43	Washington	6.3
43	Washington	6.3		47	Vermont	6.2
5	West Virginia	9.5		48	Oregon	6.1
35	Wisconsin	7.0		49	Kansas	6.0
10	Wyoming	9.1		50	Alaska	5.7
					District of Columbia	11.1

Source: U.S. Department of Health and Human Services, National Center for Health Statistics
    "National Vital Statistics Reports" (Vol. 57, No. 12, March 18, 2009, http://www.cdc.gov/nchs/births.htm)
*Preliminary data by state of residence. Births of less than 2,500 grams (5 pounds 8 ounces).

Births to Unmarried Women in 2007

National Total = 1,713,896 Births*

RANK	STATE	BIRTHS	% of USA
24	Alabama	24,864	1.5%
47	Alaska	4,130	0.2%
11	Arizona	46,552	2.7%
29	Arkansas	17,958	1.0%
1	California	220,311	12.9%
28	Colorado	17,984	1.0%
34	Connecticut	14,624	0.9%
41	Delaware	5,708	0.3%
3	Florida	110,245	6.4%
6	Georgia	65,825	3.8%
39	Hawaii	7,062	0.4%
40	Idaho	6,380	0.4%
5	Illinois	72,523	4.2%
14	Indiana	38,095	2.2%
35	Iowa	14,024	0.8%
33	Kansas	15,331	0.9%
26	Kentucky	23,332	1.4%
16	Louisiana	33,726	2.0%
42	Maine	5,521	0.3%
18	Maryland	31,941	1.9%
21	Massachusetts	26,039	1.5%
10	Michigan	49,405	2.9%
25	Minnesota	24,115	1.4%
23	Mississippi	24,971	1.5%
17	Missouri	33,181	1.9%
45	Montana	4,467	0.3%
37	Nebraska	8,992	0.5%
31	Nevada	17,305	1.0%
46	New Hampshire	4,449	0.3%
12	New Jersey	39,925	2.3%
32	New Mexico	15,827	0.9%
4	New York	103,157	6.0%
9	North Carolina	53,979	3.1%
48	North Dakota	2,882	0.2%
7	Ohio	63,672	3.7%
27	Oklahoma	22,747	1.3%
30	Oregon	17,330	1.0%
8	Pennsylvania	59,840	3.5%
43	Rhode Island	5,445	0.3%
20	South Carolina	29,307	1.7%
44	South Dakota	4,707	0.3%
15	Tennessee	37,111	2.2%
2	Texas	165,909	9.7%
36	Utah	10,806	0.6%
50	Vermont	2,384	0.1%
13	Virginia	38,324	2.2%
19	Washington	29,534	1.7%
38	West Virginia	8,863	0.5%
22	Wisconsin	25,770	1.5%
49	Wyoming	2,739	0.2%

RANK	STATE	BIRTHS	% of USA
1	California	220,311	12.9%
2	Texas	165,909	9.7%
3	Florida	110,245	6.4%
4	New York	103,157	6.0%
5	Illinois	72,523	4.2%
6	Georgia	65,825	3.8%
7	Ohio	63,672	3.7%
8	Pennsylvania	59,840	3.5%
9	North Carolina	53,979	3.1%
10	Michigan	49,405	2.9%
11	Arizona	46,552	2.7%
12	New Jersey	39,925	2.3%
13	Virginia	38,324	2.2%
14	Indiana	38,095	2.2%
15	Tennessee	37,111	2.2%
16	Louisiana	33,726	2.0%
17	Missouri	33,181	1.9%
18	Maryland	31,941	1.9%
19	Washington	29,534	1.7%
20	South Carolina	29,307	1.7%
21	Massachusetts	26,039	1.5%
22	Wisconsin	25,770	1.5%
23	Mississippi	24,971	1.5%
24	Alabama	24,864	1.5%
25	Minnesota	24,115	1.4%
26	Kentucky	23,332	1.4%
27	Oklahoma	22,747	1.3%
28	Colorado	17,984	1.0%
29	Arkansas	17,958	1.0%
30	Oregon	17,330	1.0%
31	Nevada	17,305	1.0%
32	New Mexico	15,827	0.9%
33	Kansas	15,331	0.9%
34	Connecticut	14,624	0.9%
35	Iowa	14,024	0.8%
36	Utah	10,806	0.6%
37	Nebraska	8,992	0.5%
38	West Virginia	8,863	0.5%
39	Hawaii	7,062	0.4%
40	Idaho	6,380	0.4%
41	Delaware	5,708	0.3%
42	Maine	5,521	0.3%
43	Rhode Island	5,445	0.3%
44	South Dakota	4,707	0.3%
45	Montana	4,467	0.3%
46	New Hampshire	4,449	0.3%
47	Alaska	4,130	0.2%
48	North Dakota	2,882	0.2%
49	Wyoming	2,739	0.2%
50	Vermont	2,384	0.1%
	District of Columbia	5,184	0.3%

Source: CQ Press using data from U.S. Department of Health and Human Services, National Center for Health Statistics
"National Vital Statistics Reports" (Vol. 57, No. 12, March 18, 2009, http://www.cdc.gov/nchs/births.htm)
*Estimate based on preliminary data by state of residence.

Births to Unmarried Women as a Percent of All Births in 2007

National Percent = 39.7% of Live Births*

<table>
<tr><td colspan="3">ALPHA ORDER</td><td colspan="3">RANK ORDER</td></tr>
<tr><td>RANK</td><td>STATE</td><td>PERCENT</td><td>RANK</td><td>STATE</td><td>PERCENT</td></tr>
<tr><td>28</td><td>Alabama</td><td>38.4</td><td>1</td><td>Mississippi</td><td>53.7</td></tr>
<tr><td>30</td><td>Alaska</td><td>37.2</td><td>2</td><td>New Mexico</td><td>51.8</td></tr>
<tr><td>7</td><td>Arizona</td><td>45.2</td><td>3</td><td>Louisiana</td><td>50.9</td></tr>
<tr><td>9</td><td>Arkansas</td><td>43.4</td><td>4</td><td>Delaware</td><td>46.9</td></tr>
<tr><td>27</td><td>California</td><td>38.9</td><td>5</td><td>South Carolina</td><td>46.6</td></tr>
<tr><td>49</td><td>Colorado</td><td>25.4</td><td>6</td><td>Florida</td><td>46.1</td></tr>
<tr><td>37</td><td>Connecticut</td><td>35.1</td><td>7</td><td>Arizona</td><td>45.2</td></tr>
<tr><td>4</td><td>Delaware</td><td>46.9</td><td>8</td><td>Rhode Island</td><td>44.0</td></tr>
<tr><td>6</td><td>Florida</td><td>46.1</td><td>9</td><td>Arkansas</td><td>43.4</td></tr>
<tr><td>10</td><td>Georgia</td><td>43.3</td><td>10</td><td>Georgia</td><td>43.3</td></tr>
<tr><td>31</td><td>Hawaii</td><td>36.9</td><td>11</td><td>Tennessee</td><td>42.8</td></tr>
<tr><td>48</td><td>Idaho</td><td>25.5</td><td>12</td><td>Indiana</td><td>42.4</td></tr>
<tr><td>22</td><td>Illinois</td><td>40.1</td><td>13</td><td>Ohio</td><td>42.2</td></tr>
<tr><td>12</td><td>Indiana</td><td>42.4</td><td>14</td><td>Nevada</td><td>42.0</td></tr>
<tr><td>41</td><td>Iowa</td><td>34.3</td><td>15</td><td>Oklahoma</td><td>41.3</td></tr>
<tr><td>33</td><td>Kansas</td><td>36.5</td><td>16</td><td>North Carolina</td><td>41.2</td></tr>
<tr><td>25</td><td>Kentucky</td><td>39.3</td><td>17</td><td>Maryland</td><td>40.9</td></tr>
<tr><td>3</td><td>Louisiana</td><td>50.9</td><td>18</td><td>New York</td><td>40.7</td></tr>
<tr><td>26</td><td>Maine</td><td>39.1</td><td>18</td><td>Texas</td><td>40.7</td></tr>
<tr><td>17</td><td>Maryland</td><td>40.9</td><td>20</td><td>Missouri</td><td>40.5</td></tr>
<tr><td>42</td><td>Massachusetts</td><td>33.4</td><td>21</td><td>West Virginia</td><td>40.3</td></tr>
<tr><td>24</td><td>Michigan</td><td>39.4</td><td>22</td><td>Illinois</td><td>40.1</td></tr>
<tr><td>45</td><td>Minnesota</td><td>32.7</td><td>23</td><td>Pennsylvania</td><td>39.7</td></tr>
<tr><td>1</td><td>Mississippi</td><td>53.7</td><td>24</td><td>Michigan</td><td>39.4</td></tr>
<tr><td>20</td><td>Missouri</td><td>40.5</td><td>25</td><td>Kentucky</td><td>39.3</td></tr>
<tr><td>34</td><td>Montana</td><td>35.9</td><td>26</td><td>Maine</td><td>39.1</td></tr>
<tr><td>42</td><td>Nebraska</td><td>33.4</td><td>27</td><td>California</td><td>38.9</td></tr>
<tr><td>14</td><td>Nevada</td><td>42.0</td><td>28</td><td>Alabama</td><td>38.4</td></tr>
<tr><td>47</td><td>New Hampshire</td><td>31.4</td><td>28</td><td>South Dakota</td><td>38.4</td></tr>
<tr><td>40</td><td>New Jersey</td><td>34.4</td><td>30</td><td>Alaska</td><td>37.2</td></tr>
<tr><td>2</td><td>New Mexico</td><td>51.8</td><td>31</td><td>Hawaii</td><td>36.9</td></tr>
<tr><td>18</td><td>New York</td><td>40.7</td><td>32</td><td>Vermont</td><td>36.6</td></tr>
<tr><td>16</td><td>North Carolina</td><td>41.2</td><td>33</td><td>Kansas</td><td>36.5</td></tr>
<tr><td>46</td><td>North Dakota</td><td>32.6</td><td>34</td><td>Montana</td><td>35.9</td></tr>
<tr><td>13</td><td>Ohio</td><td>42.2</td><td>35</td><td>Wisconsin</td><td>35.4</td></tr>
<tr><td>15</td><td>Oklahoma</td><td>41.3</td><td>36</td><td>Virginia</td><td>35.2</td></tr>
<tr><td>37</td><td>Oregon</td><td>35.1</td><td>37</td><td>Connecticut</td><td>35.1</td></tr>
<tr><td>23</td><td>Pennsylvania</td><td>39.7</td><td>37</td><td>Oregon</td><td>35.1</td></tr>
<tr><td>8</td><td>Rhode Island</td><td>44.0</td><td>39</td><td>Wyoming</td><td>34.7</td></tr>
<tr><td>5</td><td>South Carolina</td><td>46.6</td><td>40</td><td>New Jersey</td><td>34.4</td></tr>
<tr><td>28</td><td>South Dakota</td><td>38.4</td><td>41</td><td>Iowa</td><td>34.3</td></tr>
<tr><td>11</td><td>Tennessee</td><td>42.8</td><td>42</td><td>Massachusetts</td><td>33.4</td></tr>
<tr><td>18</td><td>Texas</td><td>40.7</td><td>42</td><td>Nebraska</td><td>33.4</td></tr>
<tr><td>50</td><td>Utah</td><td>19.6</td><td>44</td><td>Washington</td><td>33.2</td></tr>
<tr><td>32</td><td>Vermont</td><td>36.6</td><td>45</td><td>Minnesota</td><td>32.7</td></tr>
<tr><td>36</td><td>Virginia</td><td>35.2</td><td>46</td><td>North Dakota</td><td>32.6</td></tr>
<tr><td>44</td><td>Washington</td><td>33.2</td><td>47</td><td>New Hampshire</td><td>31.4</td></tr>
<tr><td>21</td><td>West Virginia</td><td>40.3</td><td>48</td><td>Idaho</td><td>25.5</td></tr>
<tr><td>35</td><td>Wisconsin</td><td>35.4</td><td>49</td><td>Colorado</td><td>25.4</td></tr>
<tr><td>39</td><td>Wyoming</td><td>34.7</td><td>50</td><td>Utah</td><td>19.6</td></tr>
<tr><td></td><td></td><td></td><td></td><td>District of Columbia</td><td>58.5</td></tr>
</table>

Source: U.S. Department of Health and Human Services, National Center for Health Statistics
"National Vital Statistics Reports" (Vol. 57, No. 12, March 18, 2009, http://www.cdc.gov/nchs/births.htm)
*Preliminary data by state of residence.

Births to Teenage Mothers in 2007

National Total = 453,297 Births*

ALPHA ORDER

RANK	STATE	BIRTHS	% of USA
17	Alabama	8,806	1.9%
46	Alaska	1,121	0.2%
10	Arizona	13,080	2.9%
27	Arkansas	6,041	1.3%
2	California	53,803	11.9%
25	Colorado	6,868	1.5%
36	Connecticut	2,875	0.6%
41	Delaware	1,266	0.3%
3	Florida	26,067	5.8%
4	Georgia	18,547	4.1%
40	Hawaii	1,627	0.4%
39	Idaho	2,277	0.5%
5	Illinois	18,266	4.0%
13	Indiana	10,063	2.2%
35	Iowa	3,557	0.8%
33	Kansas	4,326	1.0%
20	Kentucky	7,659	1.7%
16	Louisiana	9,078	2.0%
45	Maine	1,186	0.3%
24	Maryland	6,951	1.5%
29	Massachusetts	4,990	1.1%
11	Michigan	12,665	2.8%
28	Minnesota	5,236	1.2%
19	Mississippi	7,952	1.8%
15	Missouri	9,340	2.1%
42	Montana	1,207	0.3%
38	Nebraska	2,315	0.5%
31	Nevada	4,450	1.0%
47	New Hampshire	935	0.2%
23	New Jersey	7,428	1.6%
30	New Mexico	4,797	1.1%
6	New York	17,742	3.9%
8	North Carolina	15,329	3.4%
49	North Dakota	707	0.2%
7	Ohio	16,597	3.7%
21	Oklahoma	7,656	1.7%
32	Oregon	4,394	1.0%
9	Pennsylvania	14,018	3.1%
44	Rhode Island	1,200	0.3%
18	South Carolina	8,427	1.9%
43	South Dakota	1,201	0.3%
12	Tennessee	11,445	2.5%
1	Texas	55,031	12.1%
34	Utah	3,804	0.8%
50	Vermont	495	0.1%
14	Virginia	9,363	2.1%
22	Washington	7,472	1.6%
37	West Virginia	2,749	0.6%
26	Wisconsin	6,333	1.4%
48	Wyoming	931	0.2%

RANK ORDER

RANK	STATE	BIRTHS	% of USA
1	Texas	55,031	12.1%
2	California	53,803	11.9%
3	Florida	26,067	5.8%
4	Georgia	18,547	4.1%
5	Illinois	18,266	4.0%
6	New York	17,742	3.9%
7	Ohio	16,597	3.7%
8	North Carolina	15,329	3.4%
9	Pennsylvania	14,018	3.1%
10	Arizona	13,080	2.9%
11	Michigan	12,665	2.8%
12	Tennessee	11,445	2.5%
13	Indiana	10,063	2.2%
14	Virginia	9,363	2.1%
15	Missouri	9,340	2.1%
16	Louisiana	9,078	2.0%
17	Alabama	8,806	1.9%
18	South Carolina	8,427	1.9%
19	Mississippi	7,952	1.8%
20	Kentucky	7,659	1.7%
21	Oklahoma	7,656	1.7%
22	Washington	7,472	1.6%
23	New Jersey	7,428	1.6%
24	Maryland	6,951	1.5%
25	Colorado	6,868	1.5%
26	Wisconsin	6,333	1.4%
27	Arkansas	6,041	1.3%
28	Minnesota	5,236	1.2%
29	Massachusetts	4,990	1.1%
30	New Mexico	4,797	1.1%
31	Nevada	4,450	1.0%
32	Oregon	4,394	1.0%
33	Kansas	4,326	1.0%
34	Utah	3,804	0.8%
35	Iowa	3,557	0.8%
36	Connecticut	2,875	0.6%
37	West Virginia	2,749	0.6%
38	Nebraska	2,315	0.5%
39	Idaho	2,277	0.5%
40	Hawaii	1,627	0.4%
41	Delaware	1,266	0.3%
42	Montana	1,207	0.3%
43	South Dakota	1,201	0.3%
44	Rhode Island	1,200	0.3%
45	Maine	1,186	0.3%
46	Alaska	1,121	0.2%
47	New Hampshire	935	0.2%
48	Wyoming	931	0.2%
49	North Dakota	707	0.2%
50	Vermont	495	0.1%
	District of Columbia	1,072	0.2%

Source: CQ Press using data from U.S. Department of Health and Human Services, National Center for Health Statistics
"National Vital Statistics Reports" (Vol. 57, No. 12, March 18, 2009, http://www.cdc.gov/nchs/births.htm)
*Estimates based on preliminary data by state of residence.

Births to Teenage Mothers as a Percent of All Births in 2007

National Percent = 10.5% of Live Births*

ALPHA ORDER			RANK ORDER		
RANK	STATE	PERCENT	RANK	STATE	PERCENT
6	Alabama	13.6	1	Mississippi	17.1
23	Alaska	10.1	2	New Mexico	15.7
11	Arizona	12.7	3	Arkansas	14.6
3	Arkansas	14.6	4	Oklahoma	13.9
30	California	9.5	5	Louisiana	13.7
27	Colorado	9.7	6	Alabama	13.6
46	Connecticut	6.9	7	Texas	13.5
21	Delaware	10.4	8	South Carolina	13.4
19	Florida	10.9	9	Tennessee	13.2
13	Georgia	12.2	10	Kentucky	12.9
39	Hawaii	8.5	11	Arizona	12.7
32	Idaho	9.1	12	West Virginia	12.5
23	Illinois	10.1	13	Georgia	12.2
17	Indiana	11.2	14	Wyoming	11.8
35	Iowa	8.7	15	North Carolina	11.7
22	Kansas	10.3	16	Missouri	11.4
10	Kentucky	12.9	17	Indiana	11.2
5	Louisiana	13.7	18	Ohio	11.0
40	Maine	8.4	19	Florida	10.9
33	Maryland	8.9	20	Nevada	10.8
49	Massachusetts	6.4	21	Delaware	10.4
23	Michigan	10.1	22	Kansas	10.3
44	Minnesota	7.1	23	Alaska	10.1
1	Mississippi	17.1	23	Illinois	10.1
16	Missouri	11.4	23	Michigan	10.1
27	Montana	9.7	26	South Dakota	9.8
37	Nebraska	8.6	27	Colorado	9.7
20	Nevada	10.8	27	Montana	9.7
48	New Hampshire	6.6	27	Rhode Island	9.7
49	New Jersey	6.4	30	California	9.5
2	New Mexico	15.7	31	Pennsylvania	9.3
45	New York	7.0	32	Idaho	9.1
15	North Carolina	11.7	33	Maryland	8.9
42	North Dakota	8.0	33	Oregon	8.9
18	Ohio	11.0	35	Iowa	8.7
4	Oklahoma	13.9	35	Wisconsin	8.7
33	Oregon	8.9	37	Nebraska	8.6
31	Pennsylvania	9.3	37	Virginia	8.6
27	Rhode Island	9.7	39	Hawaii	8.5
8	South Carolina	13.4	40	Maine	8.4
26	South Dakota	9.8	40	Washington	8.4
9	Tennessee	13.2	42	North Dakota	8.0
7	Texas	13.5	43	Vermont	7.6
46	Utah	6.9	44	Minnesota	7.1
43	Vermont	7.6	45	New York	7.0
37	Virginia	8.6	46	Connecticut	6.9
40	Washington	8.4	46	Utah	6.9
12	West Virginia	12.5	48	New Hampshire	6.6
35	Wisconsin	8.7	49	Massachusetts	6.4
14	Wyoming	11.8	49	New Jersey	6.4
				District of Columbia	12.1

Source: U.S. Department of Health and Human Services, National Center for Health Statistics
  "National Vital Statistics Reports" (Vol. 57, No. 12, March 18, 2009, http://www.cdc.gov/nchs/births.htm)
*Preliminary data by state of residence.

Births in 2006

National Total = 4,265,555 Live Births*

ALPHA ORDER

RANK	STATE	BIRTHS	% of USA
24	Alabama	63,232	1.5%
47	Alaska	10,996	0.3%
13	Arizona	102,429	2.4%
33	Arkansas	40,961	1.0%
1	California	562,440	13.2%
22	Colorado	70,751	1.7%
31	Connecticut	41,820	1.0%
45	Delaware	11,989	0.3%
4	Florida	236,802	5.6%
8	Georgia	148,633	3.5%
40	Hawaii	18,982	0.4%
38	Idaho	24,184	0.6%
5	Illinois	180,572	4.2%
14	Indiana	88,631	2.1%
34	Iowa	40,607	1.0%
32	Kansas	40,968	1.0%
26	Kentucky	58,250	1.4%
23	Louisiana	63,376	1.5%
42	Maine	14,151	0.3%
19	Maryland	77,494	1.8%
18	Massachusetts	77,676	1.8%
10	Michigan	127,483	3.0%
20	Minnesota	73,525	1.7%
30	Mississippi	46,056	1.1%
17	Missouri	81,385	1.9%
43	Montana	12,508	0.3%
37	Nebraska	26,727	0.6%
35	Nevada	40,027	0.9%
41	New Hampshire	14,378	0.3%
11	New Jersey	115,020	2.7%
36	New Mexico	29,936	0.7%
3	New York	250,104	5.9%
9	North Carolina	127,859	3.0%
48	North Dakota	8,621	0.2%
6	Ohio	150,593	3.5%
27	Oklahoma	54,016	1.3%
29	Oregon	48,689	1.1%
7	Pennsylvania	149,090	3.5%
44	Rhode Island	12,372	0.3%
25	South Carolina	62,171	1.5%
46	South Dakota	11,919	0.3%
16	Tennessee	84,355	2.0%
2	Texas	399,603	9.4%
28	Utah	53,504	1.3%
50	Vermont	6,511	0.2%
12	Virginia	107,817	2.5%
15	Washington	86,876	2.0%
39	West Virginia	20,931	0.5%
21	Wisconsin	72,340	1.7%
49	Wyoming	7,672	0.2%

RANK ORDER

RANK	STATE	BIRTHS	% of USA
1	California	562,440	13.2%
2	Texas	399,603	9.4%
3	New York	250,104	5.9%
4	Florida	236,802	5.6%
5	Illinois	180,572	4.2%
6	Ohio	150,593	3.5%
7	Pennsylvania	149,090	3.5%
8	Georgia	148,633	3.5%
9	North Carolina	127,859	3.0%
10	Michigan	127,483	3.0%
11	New Jersey	115,020	2.7%
12	Virginia	107,817	2.5%
13	Arizona	102,429	2.4%
14	Indiana	88,631	2.1%
15	Washington	86,876	2.0%
16	Tennessee	84,355	2.0%
17	Missouri	81,385	1.9%
18	Massachusetts	77,676	1.8%
19	Maryland	77,494	1.8%
20	Minnesota	73,525	1.7%
21	Wisconsin	72,340	1.7%
22	Colorado	70,751	1.7%
23	Louisiana	63,376	1.5%
24	Alabama	63,232	1.5%
25	South Carolina	62,171	1.5%
26	Kentucky	58,250	1.4%
27	Oklahoma	54,016	1.3%
28	Utah	53,504	1.3%
29	Oregon	48,689	1.1%
30	Mississippi	46,056	1.1%
31	Connecticut	41,820	1.0%
32	Kansas	40,968	1.0%
33	Arkansas	40,961	1.0%
34	Iowa	40,607	1.0%
35	Nevada	40,027	0.9%
36	New Mexico	29,936	0.7%
37	Nebraska	26,727	0.6%
38	Idaho	24,184	0.6%
39	West Virginia	20,931	0.5%
40	Hawaii	18,982	0.4%
41	New Hampshire	14,378	0.3%
42	Maine	14,151	0.3%
43	Montana	12,508	0.3%
44	Rhode Island	12,372	0.3%
45	Delaware	11,989	0.3%
46	South Dakota	11,919	0.3%
47	Alaska	10,996	0.3%
48	North Dakota	8,621	0.2%
49	Wyoming	7,672	0.2%
50	Vermont	6,511	0.2%
	District of Columbia	8,523	0.2%

Source: U.S. Department of Health and Human Services, National Center for Health Statistics
"National Vital Statistics Reports" (Vol. 57, No. 7, January 7, 2009, http://www.cdc.gov/nchs/births.htm)
*Final data by state of residence.

Birth Rate in 2006

National Rate = 14.2 Live Births per 1,000 Population*

ALPHA ORDER				RANK ORDER		
RANK	**STATE**	**RATE**		**RANK**	**STATE**	**RATE**
31	Alabama	13.7		1	Utah	21.0
5	Alaska	16.4		2	Texas	17.0
3	Arizona	16.6		3	Arizona	16.6
19	Arkansas	14.6		4	Idaho	16.5
9	California	15.4		5	Alaska	16.4
14	Colorado	14.9		6	Nevada	16.0
45	Connecticut	11.9		7	Georgia	15.9
25	Delaware	14.0		8	Mississippi	15.8
38	Florida	13.1		9	California	15.4
7	Georgia	15.9		10	New Mexico	15.3
16	Hawaii	14.8		11	South Dakota	15.2
4	Idaho	16.5		12	Nebraska	15.1
23	Illinois	14.1		12	Oklahoma	15.1
25	Indiana	14.0		14	Colorado	14.9
32	Iowa	13.6		14	Wyoming	14.9
16	Kansas	14.8		16	Hawaii	14.8
29	Kentucky	13.8		16	Kansas	14.8
16	Louisiana	14.8		16	Louisiana	14.8
49	Maine	10.7		19	Arkansas	14.6
29	Maryland	13.8		20	North Carolina	14.4
43	Massachusetts	12.1		20	South Carolina	14.4
42	Michigan	12.6		22	Minnesota	14.2
22	Minnesota	14.2		23	Illinois	14.1
8	Mississippi	15.8		23	Virginia	14.1
28	Missouri	13.9		25	Delaware	14.0
35	Montana	13.2		25	Indiana	14.0
12	Nebraska	15.1		25	Tennessee	14.0
6	Nevada	16.0		28	Missouri	13.9
48	New Hampshire	10.9		29	Kentucky	13.8
35	New Jersey	13.2		29	Maryland	13.8
10	New Mexico	15.3		31	Alabama	13.7
40	New York	13.0		32	Iowa	13.6
20	North Carolina	14.4		32	North Dakota	13.6
32	North Dakota	13.6		32	Washington	13.6
38	Ohio	13.1		35	Montana	13.2
12	Oklahoma	15.1		35	New Jersey	13.2
35	Oregon	13.2		35	Oregon	13.2
44	Pennsylvania	12.0		38	Florida	13.1
46	Rhode Island	11.6		38	Ohio	13.1
20	South Carolina	14.4		40	New York	13.0
11	South Dakota	15.2		40	Wisconsin	13.0
25	Tennessee	14.0		42	Michigan	12.6
2	Texas	17.0		43	Massachusetts	12.1
1	Utah	21.0		44	Pennsylvania	12.0
50	Vermont	10.4		45	Connecticut	11.9
23	Virginia	14.1		46	Rhode Island	11.6
32	Washington	13.6		47	West Virginia	11.5
47	West Virginia	11.5		48	New Hampshire	10.9
40	Wisconsin	13.0		49	Maine	10.7
14	Wyoming	14.9		50	Vermont	10.4
					District of Columbia	14.7

Source: U.S. Department of Health and Human Services, National Center for Health Statistics
   "National Vital Statistics Reports" (Vol. 57, No. 7, January 7, 2009, http://www.cdc.gov/nchs/births.htm)
*Final data by state of residence.

Births of Low Birthweight in 2006

National Total = 351,974 Live Births*

ALPHA ORDER					RANK ORDER			
RANK	STATE		BIRTHS	% of USA	RANK	STATE	BIRTHS	% of USA
18	Alabama		6,624	1.9%	1	California	38,411	10.9%
48	Alaska		654	0.2%	2	Texas	33,727	9.6%
14	Arizona		7,289	2.1%	3	New York	20,790	5.9%
29	Arkansas		3,749	1.1%	4	Florida	20,614	5.9%
1	California		38,411	10.9%	5	Illinois	15,577	4.4%
20	Colorado		6,317	1.8%	6	Georgia	14,232	4.0%
31	Connecticut		3,395	1.0%	7	Ohio	13,180	3.7%
41	Delaware		1,108	0.3%	8	Pennsylvania	12,562	3.6%
4	Florida		20,614	5.9%	9	North Carolina	11,585	3.3%
6	Georgia		14,232	4.0%	10	Michigan	10,637	3.0%
40	Hawaii		1,531	0.4%	11	New Jersey	9,882	2.8%
39	Idaho		1,671	0.5%	12	Virginia	8,914	2.5%
5	Illinois		15,577	4.4%	13	Tennessee	8,108	2.3%
16	Indiana		7,268	2.1%	14	Arizona	7,289	2.1%
35	Iowa		2,809	0.8%	15	Maryland	7,269	2.1%
34	Kansas		2,933	0.8%	16	Indiana	7,268	2.1%
25	Kentucky		5,327	1.5%	17	Louisiana	7,231	2.1%
17	Louisiana		7,231	2.1%	18	Alabama	6,624	1.9%
44	Maine		967	0.3%	19	Missouri	6,555	1.9%
15	Maryland		7,269	2.1%	20	Colorado	6,317	1.8%
22	Massachusetts		6,138	1.7%	21	South Carolina	6,292	1.8%
10	Michigan		10,637	3.0%	22	Massachusetts	6,138	1.7%
27	Minnesota		4,807	1.4%	23	Mississippi	5,698	1.6%
23	Mississippi		5,698	1.6%	24	Washington	5,641	1.6%
19	Missouri		6,555	1.9%	25	Kentucky	5,327	1.5%
45	Montana		912	0.3%	26	Wisconsin	4,974	1.4%
38	Nebraska		1,900	0.5%	27	Minnesota	4,807	1.4%
32	Nevada		3,335	0.9%	28	Oklahoma	4,503	1.3%
42	New Hampshire		994	0.3%	29	Arkansas	3,749	1.1%
11	New Jersey		9,882	2.8%	30	Utah	3,700	1.1%
36	New Mexico		2,668	0.8%	31	Connecticut	3,395	1.0%
3	New York		20,790	5.9%	32	Nevada	3,335	0.9%
9	North Carolina		11,585	3.3%	33	Oregon	2,963	0.8%
49	North Dakota		576	0.2%	34	Kansas	2,933	0.8%
7	Ohio		13,180	3.7%	35	Iowa	2,809	0.8%
28	Oklahoma		4,503	1.3%	36	New Mexico	2,668	0.8%
33	Oregon		2,963	0.8%	37	West Virginia	2,024	0.6%
8	Pennsylvania		12,562	3.6%	38	Nebraska	1,900	0.5%
43	Rhode Island		988	0.3%	39	Idaho	1,671	0.5%
21	South Carolina		6,292	1.8%	40	Hawaii	1,531	0.4%
46	South Dakota		836	0.2%	41	Delaware	1,108	0.3%
13	Tennessee		8,108	2.3%	42	New Hampshire	994	0.3%
2	Texas		33,727	9.6%	43	Rhode Island	988	0.3%
30	Utah		3,700	1.1%	44	Maine	967	0.3%
50	Vermont		447	0.1%	45	Montana	912	0.3%
12	Virginia		8,914	2.5%	46	South Dakota	836	0.2%
24	Washington		5,641	1.6%	47	Wyoming	682	0.2%
37	West Virginia		2,024	0.6%	48	Alaska	654	0.2%
26	Wisconsin		4,974	1.4%	49	North Dakota	576	0.2%
47	Wyoming		682	0.2%	50	Vermont	447	0.1%
						District of Columbia	980	0.3%

Source: U.S. Department of Health and Human Services, National Center for Health Statistics
"National Vital Statistics Reports" (Vol. 57, No. 7, January 7, 2009, http://www.cdc.gov/nchs/births.htm)
*Final data by state of residence. Births of less than 2,500 grams (5 pounds 8 ounces).

Births of Low Birthweight as a Percent of All Births in 2006

National Percent = 8.3% of Live Births*

ALPHA ORDER			RANK ORDER		
RANK	STATE	PERCENT	RANK	STATE	PERCENT
3	Alabama	10.5	1	Mississippi	12.4
50	Alaska	0.0	2	Louisiana	11.4
35	Arizona	7.1	3	Alabama	10.5
10	Arkansas	9.2	4	South Carolina	10.1
44	California	6.8	5	West Virginia	9.7
13	Colorado	8.9	6	Georgia	9.6
28	Connecticut	8.1	6	Tennessee	9.6
9	Delaware	9.3	8	Maryland	9.4
17	Florida	8.7	9	Delaware	9.3
6	Georgia	9.6	10	Arkansas	9.2
28	Hawaii	8.1	11	Kentucky	9.1
38	Idaho	6.9	11	North Carolina	9.1
18	Illinois	8.6	13	Colorado	8.9
27	Indiana	8.2	13	New Mexico	8.9
38	Iowa	6.9	13	Wyoming	8.9
34	Kansas	7.2	16	Ohio	8.8
11	Kentucky	9.1	17	Florida	8.7
2	Louisiana	11.4	18	Illinois	8.6
44	Maine	6.8	18	New Jersey	8.6
8	Maryland	9.4	20	Pennsylvania	8.5
32	Massachusetts	7.9	21	Michigan	8.4
21	Michigan	8.4	21	Texas	8.4
47	Minnesota	6.5	23	Nevada	8.3
1	Mississippi	12.4	23	New York	8.3
28	Missouri	8.1	23	Oklahoma	8.3
33	Montana	7.3	23	Virginia	8.3
35	Nebraska	7.1	27	Indiana	8.2
23	Nevada	8.3	28	Connecticut	8.1
38	New Hampshire	6.9	28	Hawaii	8.1
18	New Jersey	8.6	28	Missouri	8.1
13	New Mexico	8.9	31	Rhode Island	8.0
23	New York	8.3	32	Massachusetts	7.9
11	North Carolina	9.1	33	Montana	7.3
46	North Dakota	6.7	34	Kansas	7.2
16	Ohio	8.8	35	Arizona	7.1
23	Oklahoma	8.3	35	Nebraska	7.1
49	Oregon	6.1	37	South Dakota	7.0
20	Pennsylvania	8.5	38	Idaho	6.9
31	Rhode Island	8.0	38	Iowa	6.9
4	South Carolina	10.1	38	New Hampshire	6.9
37	South Dakota	7.0	38	Utah	6.9
6	Tennessee	9.6	38	Vermont	6.9
21	Texas	8.4	38	Wisconsin	6.9
38	Utah	6.9	44	California	6.8
38	Vermont	6.9	44	Maine	6.8
23	Virginia	8.3	46	North Dakota	6.7
47	Washington	6.5	47	Minnesota	6.5
5	West Virginia	9.7	47	Washington	6.5
38	Wisconsin	6.9	49	Oregon	6.1
13	Wyoming	8.9	50	Alaska	0.0
				District of Columbia	11.5

Source: U.S. Department of Health and Human Services, National Center for Health Statistics
"National Vital Statistics Reports" (Vol. 57, No. 7, January 7, 2009, http://www.cdc.gov/nchs/births.htm)
*Final data by state of residence. Births of less than 2,500 grams (5 pounds 8 ounces).

Births of Low Birthweight to White Women
as a Percent of All Births to White Women in 2006
National Percent = 7.3% of Live Births to White Women*

ALPHA ORDER			RANK ORDER		
RANK	STATE	PERCENT	RANK	STATE	PERCENT
7	Alabama	8.5	1	West Virginia	9.5
46	Alaska	6.0	2	Wyoming	9.1
35	Arizona	6.8	3	Mississippi	8.9
11	Arkansas	7.9	4	Colorado	8.7
44	California	6.4	4	Kentucky	8.7
4	Colorado	8.7	4	New Mexico	8.7
33	Connecticut	6.9	7	Alabama	8.5
15	Delaware	7.7	7	Louisiana	8.5
18	Florida	7.6	9	Tennessee	8.4
22	Georgia	7.5	10	Nevada	8.3
50	Hawaii	5.9	11	Arkansas	7.9
32	Idaho	7.0	11	Oklahoma	7.9
23	Illinois	7.4	13	North Carolina	7.8
18	Indiana	7.6	13	South Carolina	7.8
35	Iowa	6.8	15	Delaware	7.7
33	Kansas	6.9	15	Ohio	7.7
4	Kentucky	8.7	15	Rhode Island	7.7
7	Louisiana	8.5	18	Florida	7.6
35	Maine	6.8	18	Indiana	7.6
18	Maryland	7.6	18	Maryland	7.6
27	Massachusetts	7.2	18	Texas	7.6
28	Michigan	7.1	22	Georgia	7.5
46	Minnesota	6.0	23	Illinois	7.4
3	Mississippi	8.9	23	New Jersey	7.4
28	Missouri	7.1	23	Pennsylvania	7.4
26	Montana	7.3	26	Montana	7.3
42	Nebraska	6.6	27	Massachusetts	7.2
10	Nevada	8.3	28	Michigan	7.1
35	New Hampshire	6.8	28	Missouri	7.1
23	New Jersey	7.4	28	New York	7.1
4	New Mexico	8.7	28	Virginia	7.1
28	New York	7.1	32	Idaho	7.0
13	North Carolina	7.8	33	Connecticut	6.9
39	North Dakota	6.7	33	Kansas	6.9
15	Ohio	7.7	35	Arizona	6.8
11	Oklahoma	7.9	35	Iowa	6.8
46	Oregon	6.0	35	Maine	6.8
23	Pennsylvania	7.4	35	New Hampshire	6.8
15	Rhode Island	7.7	39	North Dakota	6.7
13	South Carolina	7.8	39	South Dakota	6.7
39	South Dakota	6.7	39	Vermont	6.7
9	Tennessee	8.4	42	Nebraska	6.6
18	Texas	7.6	42	Utah	6.6
42	Utah	6.6	44	California	6.4
39	Vermont	6.7	45	Wisconsin	6.2
28	Virginia	7.1	46	Alaska	6.0
46	Washington	6.0	46	Minnesota	6.0
1	West Virginia	9.5	46	Oregon	6.0
45	Wisconsin	6.2	46	Washington	6.0
2	Wyoming	9.1	50	Hawaii	5.9
				District of Columbia	7.3

Source: U.S. Department of Health and Human Services, National Center for Health Statistics
"National Vital Statistics Reports" (Vol. 57, No. 7, January 7, 2009, http://www.cdc.gov/nchs/births.htm)
*Final data by state of residence. Births of less than 2,500 grams (5 pounds 8 ounces). Includes only non-Hispanic whites.

Births of Low Birthweight to Black Women
as a Percent of All Births to Black Women in 2006
National Percent = 14.0% of Live Births to Black Women*

ALPHA ORDER				RANK ORDER		
RANK	STATE	PERCENT		RANK	STATE	PERCENT
5	Alabama	15.5		1	Mississippi	16.7
44	Alaska	9.6		2	West Virginia	16.3
30	Arizona	12.8		3	Louisiana	16.2
8	Arkansas	15.0		4	Colorado	15.7
35	California	12.0		5	Alabama	15.5
4	Colorado	15.7		6	Oklahoma	15.4
32	Connecticut	12.5		7	South Carolina	15.2
11	Delaware	14.8		8	Arkansas	15.0
26	Florida	13.4		8	New Mexico	15.0
15	Georgia	14.4		8	Oregon	15.0
43	Hawaii	10.2		11	Delaware	14.8
NA	Idaho**	NA		11	Tennessee	14.8
16	Illinois	14.3		13	Kentucky	14.6
20	Indiana	14.1		14	Ohio	14.5
41	Iowa	10.6		15	Georgia	14.4
33	Kansas	12.4		16	Illinois	14.3
13	Kentucky	14.6		17	Michigan	14.2
3	Louisiana	16.2		17	North Carolina	14.2
45	Maine	7.5		17	Texas	14.2
26	Maryland	13.4		20	Indiana	14.1
34	Massachusetts	12.1		20	Nevada	14.1
17	Michigan	14.2		20	New Jersey	14.1
42	Minnesota	10.3		23	Nebraska	14.0
1	Mississippi	16.7		23	Pennsylvania	14.0
25	Missouri	13.6		25	Missouri	13.6
NA	Montana**	NA		26	Florida	13.4
23	Nebraska	14.0		26	Maryland	13.4
20	Nevada	14.1		26	Wisconsin	13.4
39	New Hampshire	10.8		29	Virginia	13.0
20	New Jersey	14.1		30	Arizona	12.8
8	New Mexico	15.0		31	New York	12.6
31	New York	12.6		32	Connecticut	12.5
17	North Carolina	14.2		33	Kansas	12.4
NA	North Dakota**	NA		34	Massachusetts	12.1
14	Ohio	14.5		35	California	12.0
6	Oklahoma	15.4		36	Rhode Island	11.6
8	Oregon	15.0		37	South Dakota	11.2
23	Pennsylvania	14.0		38	Utah	11.0
36	Rhode Island	11.6		39	New Hampshire	10.8
7	South Carolina	15.2		40	Washington	10.7
37	South Dakota	11.2		41	Iowa	10.6
11	Tennessee	14.8		42	Minnesota	10.3
17	Texas	14.2		43	Hawaii	10.2
38	Utah	11.0		44	Alaska	9.6
NA	Vermont**	NA		45	Maine	7.5
29	Virginia	13.0		NA	Idaho**	NA
40	Washington	10.7		NA	Montana**	NA
2	West Virginia	16.3		NA	North Dakota**	NA
26	Wisconsin	13.4		NA	Vermont**	NA
NA	Wyoming**	NA		NA	Wyoming**	NA
					District of Columbia	14.5

Source: U.S. Department of Health and Human Services, National Center for Health Statistics
"National Vital Statistics Reports" (Vol. 57, No. 7, January 7, 2009, http://www.cdc.gov/nchs/births.htm)
*Final data by state of residence. Births of less than 2,500 grams (5 pounds 8 ounces). Includes only non-Hispanic blacks.
**Not available. Fewer than 20 births of low birthweight to black women.

Births of Low Birthweight to Hispanic Women
as a Percent of All Births to Hispanic Women in 2006
National Percent = 7.0% of Live Births to Hispanic Women*

RANK	STATE	PERCENT
40	Alabama	6.1
48	Alaska	4.9
23	Arizona	6.9
23	Arkansas	6.9
35	California	6.3
7	Colorado	8.4
4	Connecticut	8.8
37	Delaware	6.2
21	Florida	7.0
40	Georgia	6.1
12	Hawaii	7.8
40	Idaho	6.1
16	Illinois	7.2
28	Indiana	6.7
33	Iowa	6.4
47	Kansas	5.6
16	Kentucky	7.2
16	Louisiana	7.2
1	Maine	9.6
25	Maryland	6.8
7	Massachusetts	8.4
21	Michigan	7.0
44	Minnesota	5.9
20	Mississippi	7.1
46	Missouri	5.8
25	Montana	6.8
28	Nebraska	6.7
30	Nevada	6.6
2	New Hampshire	9.3
14	New Jersey	7.5
3	New Mexico	9.1
10	New York	8.0
37	North Carolina	6.2
4	North Dakota	8.8
16	Ohio	7.2
30	Oklahoma	6.6
44	Oregon	5.9
6	Pennsylvania	8.7
10	Rhode Island	8.0
33	South Carolina	6.4
9	South Dakota	8.3
30	Tennessee	6.6
13	Texas	7.6
14	Utah	7.5
NA	Vermont**	NA
43	Virginia	6.0
35	Washington	6.3
NA	West Virginia**	NA
37	Wisconsin	6.2
25	Wyoming	6.8

RANK	STATE	PERCENT
1	Maine	9.6
2	New Hampshire	9.3
3	New Mexico	9.1
4	Connecticut	8.8
4	North Dakota	8.8
6	Pennsylvania	8.7
7	Colorado	8.4
7	Massachusetts	8.4
9	South Dakota	8.3
10	New York	8.0
10	Rhode Island	8.0
12	Hawaii	7.8
13	Texas	7.6
14	New Jersey	7.5
14	Utah	7.5
16	Illinois	7.2
16	Kentucky	7.2
16	Louisiana	7.2
16	Ohio	7.2
20	Mississippi	7.1
21	Florida	7.0
21	Michigan	7.0
23	Arizona	6.9
23	Arkansas	6.9
25	Maryland	6.8
25	Montana	6.8
25	Wyoming	6.8
28	Indiana	6.7
28	Nebraska	6.7
30	Nevada	6.6
30	Oklahoma	6.6
30	Tennessee	6.6
33	Iowa	6.4
33	South Carolina	6.4
35	California	6.3
35	Washington	6.3
37	Delaware	6.2
37	North Carolina	6.2
37	Wisconsin	6.2
40	Alabama	6.1
40	Georgia	6.1
40	Idaho	6.1
43	Virginia	6.0
44	Minnesota	5.9
44	Oregon	5.9
46	Missouri	5.8
47	Kansas	5.6
48	Alaska	4.9
NA	Vermont**	NA
NA	West Virginia**	NA
	District of Columbia	7.7

Source: U.S. Department of Health and Human Services, National Center for Health Statistics
"National Vital Statistics Reports" (Vol. 57, No. 7, January 7, 2009, http://www.cdc.gov/nchs/births.htm)
*Final data. Births of less than 2,500 grams (5 pounds 8 ounces). Hispanic can be of any race.
**Not available. Fewer than 20 births of low birthweight to Hispanic women.

Births to Unmarried Women in 2006

National Total = 1,641,946 Live Births*

ALPHA ORDER

RANK	STATE	BIRTHS	% of USA
25	Alabama	23,163	1.4%
47	Alaska	4,047	0.2%
11	Arizona	45,089	2.7%
29	Arkansas	17,114	1.0%
1	California	211,501	12.9%
28	Colorado	19,535	1.2%
34	Connecticut	14,209	0.9%
41	Delaware	5,456	0.3%
3	Florida	105,111	6.4%
6	Georgia	62,996	3.8%
39	Hawaii	6,832	0.4%
40	Idaho	5,878	0.4%
5	Illinois	69,961	4.3%
13	Indiana	36,703	2.2%
35	Iowa	13,720	0.8%
33	Kansas	14,430	0.9%
27	Kentucky	20,562	1.3%
17	Louisiana	31,543	1.9%
42	Maine	5,253	0.3%
18	Maryland	30,730	1.9%
21	Massachusetts	24,984	1.5%
10	Michigan	48,880	3.0%
24	Minnesota	23,341	1.4%
23	Mississippi	24,330	1.5%
16	Missouri	32,009	1.9%
44	Montana	4,500	0.3%
37	Nebraska	8,631	0.5%
31	Nevada	16,525	1.0%
46	New Hampshire	4,231	0.3%
12	New Jersey	37,900	2.3%
32	New Mexico	15,323	0.9%
4	New York	100,115	6.1%
9	North Carolina	51,271	3.1%
48	North Dakota	2,732	0.2%
7	Ohio	61,008	3.7%
26	Oklahoma	22,090	1.3%
30	Oregon	16,703	1.0%
8	Pennsylvania	57,065	3.5%
43	Rhode Island	5,013	0.3%
19	South Carolina	28,365	1.7%
45	South Dakota	4,422	0.3%
15	Tennessee	34,944	2.1%
2	Texas	157,302	9.6%
36	Utah	10,071	0.6%
50	Vermont	2,244	0.1%
14	Virginia	36,415	2.2%
20	Washington	27,690	1.7%
38	West Virginia	7,937	0.5%
22	Wisconsin	24,636	1.5%
49	Wyoming	2,530	0.2%

RANK ORDER

RANK	STATE	BIRTHS	% of USA
1	California	211,501	12.9%
2	Texas	157,302	9.6%
3	Florida	105,111	6.4%
4	New York	100,115	6.1%
5	Illinois	69,961	4.3%
6	Georgia	62,996	3.8%
7	Ohio	61,008	3.7%
8	Pennsylvania	57,065	3.5%
9	North Carolina	51,271	3.1%
10	Michigan	48,880	3.0%
11	Arizona	45,089	2.7%
12	New Jersey	37,900	2.3%
13	Indiana	36,703	2.2%
14	Virginia	36,415	2.2%
15	Tennessee	34,944	2.1%
16	Missouri	32,009	1.9%
17	Louisiana	31,543	1.9%
18	Maryland	30,730	1.9%
19	South Carolina	28,365	1.7%
20	Washington	27,690	1.7%
21	Massachusetts	24,984	1.5%
22	Wisconsin	24,636	1.5%
23	Mississippi	24,330	1.5%
24	Minnesota	23,341	1.4%
25	Alabama	23,163	1.4%
26	Oklahoma	22,090	1.3%
27	Kentucky	20,562	1.3%
28	Colorado	19,535	1.2%
29	Arkansas	17,114	1.0%
30	Oregon	16,703	1.0%
31	Nevada	16,525	1.0%
32	New Mexico	15,323	0.9%
33	Kansas	14,430	0.9%
34	Connecticut	14,209	0.9%
35	Iowa	13,720	0.8%
36	Utah	10,071	0.6%
37	Nebraska	8,631	0.5%
38	West Virginia	7,937	0.5%
39	Hawaii	6,832	0.4%
40	Idaho	5,878	0.4%
41	Delaware	5,456	0.3%
42	Maine	5,253	0.3%
43	Rhode Island	5,013	0.3%
44	Montana	4,500	0.3%
45	South Dakota	4,422	0.3%
46	New Hampshire	4,231	0.3%
47	Alaska	4,047	0.2%
48	North Dakota	2,732	0.2%
49	Wyoming	2,530	0.2%
50	Vermont	2,244	0.1%
	District of Columbia	4,906	0.3%

Source: U.S. Department of Health and Human Services, National Center for Health Statistics
   "National Vital Statistics Reports" (Vol. 57, No. 7, January 7, 2009, http://www.cdc.gov/nchs/births.htm)
*Final data by state of residence.

Births to Unmarried Women as a Percent of All Births in 2006

National Percent = 38.5% of Live Births*

<table>
<tr><td colspan="3">ALPHA ORDER</td><td colspan="3">RANK ORDER</td></tr>
<tr><th>RANK</th><th>STATE</th><th>PERCENT</th><th>RANK</th><th>STATE</th><th>PERCENT</th></tr>
<tr><td>29</td><td>Alabama</td><td>36.6</td><td>1</td><td>Mississippi</td><td>52.8</td></tr>
<tr><td>28</td><td>Alaska</td><td>36.8</td><td>2</td><td>New Mexico</td><td>51.2</td></tr>
<tr><td>7</td><td>Arizona</td><td>44.0</td><td>3</td><td>Louisiana</td><td>49.8</td></tr>
<tr><td>9</td><td>Arkansas</td><td>41.8</td><td>4</td><td>South Carolina</td><td>45.6</td></tr>
<tr><td>25</td><td>California</td><td>37.6</td><td>5</td><td>Delaware</td><td>45.5</td></tr>
<tr><td>48</td><td>Colorado</td><td>27.6</td><td>6</td><td>Florida</td><td>44.4</td></tr>
<tr><td>37</td><td>Connecticut</td><td>34.0</td><td>7</td><td>Arizona</td><td>44.0</td></tr>
<tr><td>5</td><td>Delaware</td><td>45.5</td><td>8</td><td>Georgia</td><td>42.4</td></tr>
<tr><td>6</td><td>Florida</td><td>44.4</td><td>9</td><td>Arkansas</td><td>41.8</td></tr>
<tr><td>8</td><td>Georgia</td><td>42.4</td><td>10</td><td>Indiana</td><td>41.4</td></tr>
<tr><td>30</td><td>Hawaii</td><td>36.0</td><td>10</td><td>Tennessee</td><td>41.4</td></tr>
<tr><td>49</td><td>Idaho</td><td>24.3</td><td>12</td><td>Nevada</td><td>41.3</td></tr>
<tr><td>21</td><td>Illinois</td><td>38.7</td><td>13</td><td>Oklahoma</td><td>40.9</td></tr>
<tr><td>10</td><td>Indiana</td><td>41.4</td><td>14</td><td>Ohio</td><td>40.5</td></tr>
<tr><td>38</td><td>Iowa</td><td>33.8</td><td>14</td><td>Rhode Island</td><td>40.5</td></tr>
<tr><td>33</td><td>Kansas</td><td>35.2</td><td>16</td><td>North Carolina</td><td>40.1</td></tr>
<tr><td>32</td><td>Kentucky</td><td>35.3</td><td>17</td><td>New York</td><td>40.0</td></tr>
<tr><td>3</td><td>Louisiana</td><td>49.8</td><td>18</td><td>Maryland</td><td>39.7</td></tr>
<tr><td>26</td><td>Maine</td><td>37.1</td><td>19</td><td>Texas</td><td>39.4</td></tr>
<tr><td>18</td><td>Maryland</td><td>39.7</td><td>20</td><td>Missouri</td><td>39.3</td></tr>
<tr><td>43</td><td>Massachusetts</td><td>32.2</td><td>21</td><td>Illinois</td><td>38.7</td></tr>
<tr><td>22</td><td>Michigan</td><td>38.3</td><td>22</td><td>Michigan</td><td>38.3</td></tr>
<tr><td>45</td><td>Minnesota</td><td>31.7</td><td>22</td><td>Pennsylvania</td><td>38.3</td></tr>
<tr><td>1</td><td>Mississippi</td><td>52.8</td><td>24</td><td>West Virginia</td><td>37.9</td></tr>
<tr><td>20</td><td>Missouri</td><td>39.3</td><td>25</td><td>California</td><td>37.6</td></tr>
<tr><td>30</td><td>Montana</td><td>36.0</td><td>26</td><td>Maine</td><td>37.1</td></tr>
<tr><td>42</td><td>Nebraska</td><td>32.3</td><td>26</td><td>South Dakota</td><td>37.1</td></tr>
<tr><td>12</td><td>Nevada</td><td>41.3</td><td>28</td><td>Alaska</td><td>36.8</td></tr>
<tr><td>47</td><td>New Hampshire</td><td>29.4</td><td>29</td><td>Alabama</td><td>36.6</td></tr>
<tr><td>40</td><td>New Jersey</td><td>33.0</td><td>30</td><td>Hawaii</td><td>36.0</td></tr>
<tr><td>2</td><td>New Mexico</td><td>51.2</td><td>30</td><td>Montana</td><td>36.0</td></tr>
<tr><td>17</td><td>New York</td><td>40.0</td><td>32</td><td>Kentucky</td><td>35.3</td></tr>
<tr><td>16</td><td>North Carolina</td><td>40.1</td><td>33</td><td>Kansas</td><td>35.2</td></tr>
<tr><td>45</td><td>North Dakota</td><td>31.7</td><td>34</td><td>Vermont</td><td>34.5</td></tr>
<tr><td>14</td><td>Ohio</td><td>40.5</td><td>35</td><td>Oregon</td><td>34.3</td></tr>
<tr><td>13</td><td>Oklahoma</td><td>40.9</td><td>36</td><td>Wisconsin</td><td>34.1</td></tr>
<tr><td>35</td><td>Oregon</td><td>34.3</td><td>37</td><td>Connecticut</td><td>34.0</td></tr>
<tr><td>22</td><td>Pennsylvania</td><td>38.3</td><td>38</td><td>Iowa</td><td>33.8</td></tr>
<tr><td>14</td><td>Rhode Island</td><td>40.5</td><td>38</td><td>Virginia</td><td>33.8</td></tr>
<tr><td>4</td><td>South Carolina</td><td>45.6</td><td>40</td><td>New Jersey</td><td>33.0</td></tr>
<tr><td>26</td><td>South Dakota</td><td>37.1</td><td>40</td><td>Wyoming</td><td>33.0</td></tr>
<tr><td>10</td><td>Tennessee</td><td>41.4</td><td>42</td><td>Nebraska</td><td>32.3</td></tr>
<tr><td>19</td><td>Texas</td><td>39.4</td><td>43</td><td>Massachusetts</td><td>32.2</td></tr>
<tr><td>50</td><td>Utah</td><td>18.8</td><td>44</td><td>Washington</td><td>31.9</td></tr>
<tr><td>34</td><td>Vermont</td><td>34.5</td><td>45</td><td>Minnesota</td><td>31.7</td></tr>
<tr><td>38</td><td>Virginia</td><td>33.8</td><td>45</td><td>North Dakota</td><td>31.7</td></tr>
<tr><td>44</td><td>Washington</td><td>31.9</td><td>47</td><td>New Hampshire</td><td>29.4</td></tr>
<tr><td>24</td><td>West Virginia</td><td>37.9</td><td>48</td><td>Colorado</td><td>27.6</td></tr>
<tr><td>36</td><td>Wisconsin</td><td>34.1</td><td>49</td><td>Idaho</td><td>24.3</td></tr>
<tr><td>40</td><td>Wyoming</td><td>33.0</td><td>50</td><td>Utah</td><td>18.8</td></tr>
<tr><td></td><td></td><td></td><td></td><td>District of Columbia</td><td>57.6</td></tr>
</table>

Source: U.S. Department of Health and Human Services, National Center for Health Statistics
"National Vital Statistics Reports" (Vol. 57, No. 7, January 7, 2009, http://www.cdc.gov/nchs/births.htm)
*Final data by state of residence.

Births to Unmarried White Women
as a Percent of All Births to White Women in 2006
National Percent = 26.6% of Live Births*

ALPHA ORDER

RANK	STATE	PERCENT
44	Alabama	22.2
37	Alaska	24.4
27	Arizona	27.9
11	Arkansas	31.2
43	California	22.4
48	Colorado	18.9
47	Connecticut	19.8
8	Delaware	31.8
6	Florida	32.6
34	Georgia	25.0
40	Hawaii	23.7
46	Idaho	20.6
39	Illinois	24.0
3	Indiana	34.8
13	Iowa	30.7
21	Kansas	28.8
12	Kentucky	30.9
9	Louisiana	31.6
1	Maine	37.2
37	Maryland	24.4
41	Massachusetts	23.5
22	Michigan	28.7
35	Minnesota	24.6
26	Mississippi	28.4
9	Missouri	31.6
19	Montana	29.4
32	Nebraska	25.4
18	Nevada	29.8
20	New Hampshire	29.2
49	New Jersey	15.5
15	New Mexico	30.4
42	New York	22.6
36	North Carolina	24.5
33	North Dakota	25.1
6	Ohio	32.6
5	Oklahoma	33.1
14	Oregon	30.5
23	Pennsylvania	28.6
17	Rhode Island	30.1
25	South Carolina	28.5
29	South Dakota	26.7
15	Tennessee	30.4
31	Texas	25.5
50	Utah	13.0
4	Vermont	34.6
45	Virginia	21.7
28	Washington	26.8
2	West Virginia	36.7
30	Wisconsin	25.7
23	Wyoming	28.6

RANK ORDER

RANK	STATE	PERCENT
1	Maine	37.2
2	West Virginia	36.7
3	Indiana	34.8
4	Vermont	34.6
5	Oklahoma	33.1
6	Florida	32.6
6	Ohio	32.6
8	Delaware	31.8
9	Louisiana	31.6
9	Missouri	31.6
11	Arkansas	31.2
12	Kentucky	30.9
13	Iowa	30.7
14	Oregon	30.5
15	New Mexico	30.4
15	Tennessee	30.4
17	Rhode Island	30.1
18	Nevada	29.8
19	Montana	29.4
20	New Hampshire	29.2
21	Kansas	28.8
22	Michigan	28.7
23	Pennsylvania	28.6
23	Wyoming	28.6
25	South Carolina	28.5
26	Mississippi	28.4
27	Arizona	27.9
28	Washington	26.8
29	South Dakota	26.7
30	Wisconsin	25.7
31	Texas	25.5
32	Nebraska	25.4
33	North Dakota	25.1
34	Georgia	25.0
35	Minnesota	24.6
36	North Carolina	24.5
37	Alaska	24.4
37	Maryland	24.4
39	Illinois	24.0
40	Hawaii	23.7
41	Massachusetts	23.5
42	New York	22.6
43	California	22.4
44	Alabama	22.2
45	Virginia	21.7
46	Idaho	20.6
47	Connecticut	19.8
48	Colorado	18.9
49	New Jersey	15.5
50	Utah	13.0

	District of Columbia	5.9

Source: U.S. Department of Health and Human Services, National Center for Health Statistics
    "National Vital Statistics Reports" (Vol. 57, No. 7, January 7, 2009, http://www.cdc.gov/nchs/births.htm)
*Final data by state of residence. By race of mother. Includes only non-Hispanic whites.

Births to Unmarried Black Women
as a Percent of All Births to Black Women in 2006
National Percent = 70.7% of Live Births*

ALPHA ORDER

RANK	STATE	PERCENT
20	Alabama	69.9
43	Alaska	44.3
33	Arizona	62.3
4	Arkansas	78.4
29	California	65.0
39	Colorado	53.4
25	Connecticut	68.0
18	Delaware	71.5
24	Florida	68.5
26	Georgia	67.8
49	Hawaii	25.1
45	Idaho	40.8
3	Illinois	78.7
5	Indiana	78.2
17	Iowa	72.4
15	Kansas	72.9
16	Kentucky	72.6
7	Louisiana	77.3
47	Maine	34.6
34	Maryland	62.0
35	Massachusetts	60.1
9	Michigan	76.9
35	Minnesota	60.1
2	Mississippi	79.1
6	Missouri	77.6
NA	Montana**	NA
22	Nebraska	69.4
21	Nevada	69.6
44	New Hampshire	41.8
27	New Jersey	67.1
38	New Mexico	56.0
23	New York	69.0
19	North Carolina	70.4
48	North Dakota	34.2
8	Ohio	77.2
11	Oklahoma	75.7
32	Oregon	62.8
9	Pennsylvania	76.9
31	Rhode Island	63.6
12	South Carolina	75.5
42	South Dakota	47.2
13	Tennessee	74.9
28	Texas	65.9
41	Utah	49.0
46	Vermont	35.1
30	Virginia	63.9
40	Washington	52.8
14	West Virginia	73.6
1	Wisconsin	83.4
37	Wyoming	60.0

RANK ORDER

RANK	STATE	PERCENT
1	Wisconsin	83.4
2	Mississippi	79.1
3	Illinois	78.7
4	Arkansas	78.4
5	Indiana	78.2
6	Missouri	77.6
7	Louisiana	77.3
8	Ohio	77.2
9	Michigan	76.9
9	Pennsylvania	76.9
11	Oklahoma	75.7
12	South Carolina	75.5
13	Tennessee	74.9
14	West Virginia	73.6
15	Kansas	72.9
16	Kentucky	72.6
17	Iowa	72.4
18	Delaware	71.5
19	North Carolina	70.4
20	Alabama	69.9
21	Nevada	69.6
22	Nebraska	69.4
23	New York	69.0
24	Florida	68.5
25	Connecticut	68.0
26	Georgia	67.8
27	New Jersey	67.1
28	Texas	65.9
29	California	65.0
30	Virginia	63.9
31	Rhode Island	63.6
32	Oregon	62.8
33	Arizona	62.3
34	Maryland	62.0
35	Massachusetts	60.1
35	Minnesota	60.1
37	Wyoming	60.0
38	New Mexico	56.0
39	Colorado	53.4
40	Washington	52.8
41	Utah	49.0
42	South Dakota	47.2
43	Alaska	44.3
44	New Hampshire	41.8
45	Idaho	40.8
46	Vermont	35.1
47	Maine	34.6
48	North Dakota	34.2
49	Hawaii	25.1
NA	Montana**	NA
	District of Columbia	79.3

Source: U.S. Department of Health and Human Services, National Center for Health Statistics
    "National Vital Statistics Reports" (Vol. 57, No. 7, January 7, 2009, http://www.cdc.gov/nchs/births.htm)
*Final data by state of residence. By race of mother. Includes only non-Hispanic blacks.
**Insufficient data.

Births to Unmarried Hispanic Women
as a Percent of All Births to Hispanic Women in 2006
National Percent = 49.9% of Live Births*

ALPHA ORDER

RANK ORDER

RANK	STATE	PERCENT	RANK	STATE	PERCENT
50	Alabama	21.4	1	Massachusetts	65.9
48	Alaska	36.8	2	New York	64.2
12	Arizona	55.5	3	Pennsylvania	63.3
38	Arkansas	46.5	4	Connecticut	63.1
31	California	48.2	5	Delaware	61.5
46	Colorado	41.4	5	Rhode Island	61.5
4	Connecticut	63.1	7	New Mexico	57.2
5	Delaware	61.5	8	New Jersey	57.1
33	Florida	47.8	9	Ohio	56.9
27	Georgia	48.6	10	Mississippi	56.1
34	Hawaii	47.4	11	Minnesota	55.9
47	Idaho	39.9	12	Arizona	55.5
25	Illinois	48.9	13	Indiana	55.0
13	Indiana	55.0	14	Maryland	53.9
24	Iowa	49.1	15	North Carolina	53.2
21	Kansas	49.6	16	Tennessee	52.3
29	Kentucky	48.4	17	Missouri	50.3
20	Louisiana	49.7	18	Virginia	50.2
45	Maine	42.7	18	Wisconsin	50.2
14	Maryland	53.9	20	Louisiana	49.7
1	Massachusetts	65.9	21	Kansas	49.6
31	Michigan	48.2	22	Nevada	49.3
11	Minnesota	55.9	22	Wyoming	49.3
10	Mississippi	56.1	24	Iowa	49.1
17	Missouri	50.3	25	Illinois	48.9
29	Montana	48.4	26	Nebraska	48.8
26	Nebraska	48.8	27	Georgia	48.6
22	Nevada	49.3	28	Oklahoma	48.5
41	New Hampshire	45.8	29	Kentucky	48.4
8	New Jersey	57.1	29	Montana	48.4
7	New Mexico	57.2	31	California	48.2
2	New York	64.2	31	Michigan	48.2
15	North Carolina	53.2	33	Florida	47.8
37	North Dakota	46.6	34	Hawaii	47.4
9	Ohio	56.9	34	South Dakota	47.4
28	Oklahoma	48.5	34	Washington	47.4
38	Oregon	46.5	37	North Dakota	46.6
3	Pennsylvania	63.3	38	Arkansas	46.5
5	Rhode Island	61.5	38	Oregon	46.5
40	South Carolina	45.9	40	South Carolina	45.9
34	South Dakota	47.4	41	New Hampshire	45.8
16	Tennessee	52.3	42	West Virginia	45.7
43	Texas	45.1	43	Texas	45.1
44	Utah	43.2	44	Utah	43.2
49	Vermont	36.5	45	Maine	42.7
18	Virginia	50.2	46	Colorado	41.4
34	Washington	47.4	47	Idaho	39.9
42	West Virginia	45.7	48	Alaska	36.8
18	Wisconsin	50.2	49	Vermont	36.5
22	Wyoming	49.3	50	Alabama	21.4
				District of Columbia	67.5

Source: U.S. Department of Health and Human Services, National Center for Health Statistics
"National Vital Statistics Reports" (Vol. 57, No. 7, January 7, 2009, http://www.cdc.gov/nchs/births.htm)
*Final data by state of residence. Hispanic can be of any race.

Pregnancy Rate in 2006

National Rate = 71.1 Births and Abortions per 1,000 Women 15 to 49 Years Old*

ALPHA ORDER

RANK	STATE	RATE
29	Alabama	66.9
11	Alaska	75.3
7	Arizona	77.6
22	Arkansas	69.0
NA	California**	NA
24	Colorado	68.8
32	Connecticut	65.8
4	Delaware	79.9
5	Florida	79.8
12	Georgia	75.0
9	Hawaii	76.9
14	Idaho	73.2
16	Illinois	71.4
35	Indiana	64.8
28	Iowa	67.9
6	Kansas	78.9
44	Kentucky	60.3
NA	Louisiana**	NA
47	Maine	53.6
42	Maryland	60.7
40	Massachusetts	62.4
41	Michigan	62.1
21	Minnesota	69.1
26	Mississippi	68.6
39	Missouri	62.5
30	Montana	66.7
18	Nebraska	70.7
2	Nevada	87.2
NA	New Hampshire**	NA
23	New Jersey	68.9
10	New Mexico	76.7
8	New York	77.4
13	North Carolina	74.5
33	North Dakota	65.7
31	Ohio	65.9
15	Oklahoma	71.7
24	Oregon	68.8
38	Pennsylvania	63.0
36	Rhode Island	64.5
34	South Carolina	65.4
20	South Dakota	69.4
27	Tennessee	68.5
3	Texas	82.2
1	Utah	87.6
46	Vermont	53.8
19	Virginia	70.1
17	Washington	71.2
45	West Virginia	54.6
43	Wisconsin	60.6
37	Wyoming	63.3

RANK ORDER

RANK	STATE	RATE
1	Utah	87.6
2	Nevada	87.2
3	Texas	82.2
4	Delaware	79.9
5	Florida	79.8
6	Kansas	78.9
7	Arizona	77.6
8	New York	77.4
9	Hawaii	76.9
10	New Mexico	76.7
11	Alaska	75.3
12	Georgia	75.0
13	North Carolina	74.5
14	Idaho	73.2
15	Oklahoma	71.7
16	Illinois	71.4
17	Washington	71.2
18	Nebraska	70.7
19	Virginia	70.1
20	South Dakota	69.4
21	Minnesota	69.1
22	Arkansas	69.0
23	New Jersey	68.9
24	Colorado	68.8
24	Oregon	68.8
26	Mississippi	68.6
27	Tennessee	68.5
28	Iowa	67.9
29	Alabama	66.9
30	Montana	66.7
31	Ohio	65.9
32	Connecticut	65.8
33	North Dakota	65.7
34	South Carolina	65.4
35	Indiana	64.8
36	Rhode Island	64.5
37	Wyoming	63.3
38	Pennsylvania	63.0
39	Missouri	62.5
40	Massachusetts	62.4
41	Michigan	62.1
42	Maryland	60.7
43	Wisconsin	60.6
44	Kentucky	60.3
45	West Virginia	54.6
46	Vermont	53.8
47	Maine	53.6
NA	California**	NA
NA	Louisiana**	NA
NA	New Hampshire**	NA

District of Columbia 67.3

Source: CQ Press using data from U.S. Department of Health and Human Services, Centers for Disease Control and Prevention "Abortion Surveillance-United States, 2006" (MMWR, Vol. 58, No. SS-8, 11/27/09, http://www.cdc.gov/mmwr/mmwr_ss.html)
*The sum of live births and legal induced abortions per 1,000 women 15 to 49 years old. Births by state of residence, abortions by state of occurrence. Miscarriages are not included in these rates. National rate includes only states reporting abortions and births.
**Not available.

Teenage Pregnancy Rate in 2006

National Rate = 57.7 Births and Abortions per 1,000 Women 15 to 19 Years Old*

ALPHA ORDER

RANK ORDER

RANK	STATE	RATE	RANK	STATE	RATE
11	Alabama	67.3	1	New Mexico	82.2
18	Alaska	58.5	2	Nevada	81.4
6	Arizona	72.2	3	Texas	76.6
5	Arkansas	72.3	4	Mississippi	73.0
NA	California**	NA	5	Arkansas	72.3
19	Colorado	57.0	6	Arizona	72.2
31	Connecticut	46.2	7	Georgia	69.3
12	Delaware	63.2	7	Tennessee	69.3
NA	Florida**	NA	9	Oklahoma	69.2
7	Georgia	69.3	10	North Carolina	68.4
13	Hawaii	62.6	11	Alabama	67.3
35	Idaho	44.5	12	Delaware	63.2
NA	Illinois**	NA	13	Hawaii	62.6
25	Indiana	51.7	14	Kansas	62.2
34	Iowa	44.7	15	South Carolina	61.7
14	Kansas	62.2	16	Kentucky	59.7
16	Kentucky	59.7	17	New York	59.6
NA	Louisiana**	NA	18	Alaska	58.5
42	Maine	37.0	19	Colorado	57.0
NA	Maryland**	NA	20	Ohio	55.1
41	Massachusetts	38.3	20	Washington	55.1
30	Michigan	46.9	22	Oregon	53.1
38	Minnesota	39.8	23	Missouri	52.1
4	Mississippi	73.0	23	Montana	52.1
23	Missouri	52.1	25	Indiana	51.7
23	Montana	52.1	26	West Virginia	51.4
37	Nebraska	40.9	27	Rhode Island	50.3
2	Nevada	81.4	28	Virginia	50.2
NA	New Hampshire**	NA	29	Wyoming	47.6
33	New Jersey	44.8	30	Michigan	46.9
1	New Mexico	82.2	31	Connecticut	46.2
17	New York	59.6	32	Pennsylvania	45.8
10	North Carolina	68.4	33	New Jersey	44.8
43	North Dakota	35.9	34	Iowa	44.7
20	Ohio	55.1	35	Idaho	44.5
9	Oklahoma	69.2	36	South Dakota	44.1
22	Oregon	53.1	37	Nebraska	40.9
32	Pennsylvania	45.8	38	Minnesota	39.8
27	Rhode Island	50.3	39	Utah	39.6
15	South Carolina	61.7	40	Wisconsin	39.4
36	South Dakota	44.1	41	Massachusetts	38.3
7	Tennessee	69.3	42	Maine	37.0
3	Texas	76.6	43	North Dakota	35.9
39	Utah	39.6	44	Vermont	34.0
44	Vermont	34.0	NA	California**	NA
28	Virginia	50.2	NA	Florida**	NA
20	Washington	55.1	NA	Illinois**	NA
26	West Virginia	51.4	NA	Louisiana**	NA
40	Wisconsin	39.4	NA	Maryland**	NA
29	Wyoming	47.6	NA	New Hampshire**	NA

District of Columbia 71.5

Source: CQ Press using data from U.S. Department of Health and Human Services, Centers for Disease Control and Prevention
"Abortion Surveillance-United States, 2006" (MMWR, Vol. 58, No. SS-8, 11/27/09, http://www.cdc.gov/mmwr/mmwr_ss.html)
*The sum of live births and legal induced abortions per 1,000 women 15 to 19 years old. Births by state of residence, abortions by state of occurrence. Miscarriages are not included in these rates. National rate includes only states reporting abortions and births.
**Not available.

Percent Change in Teenage Pregnancy Rate: 2002 to 2006

National Percent Change = 3.5% Decrease*

<table>
<tr><td colspan="3">ALPHA ORDER</td><td colspan="3">RANK ORDER</td></tr>
<tr><th>RANK</th><th>STATE</th><th>PERCENT CHANGE</th><th>RANK</th><th>STATE</th><th>PERCENT CHANGE</th></tr>
<tr><td>24</td><td>Alabama</td><td>(2.3)</td><td>1</td><td>Wyoming</td><td>18.4</td></tr>
<tr><td>NA</td><td>Alaska**</td><td>NA</td><td>2</td><td>Kentucky</td><td>18.0</td></tr>
<tr><td>17</td><td>Arizona</td><td>(0.7)</td><td>3</td><td>New Mexico</td><td>5.9</td></tr>
<tr><td>7</td><td>Arkansas</td><td>2.8</td><td>4</td><td>Hawaii</td><td>5.7</td></tr>
<tr><td>NA</td><td>California**</td><td>NA</td><td>5</td><td>Idaho</td><td>4.7</td></tr>
<tr><td>21</td><td>Colorado</td><td>(1.4)</td><td>6</td><td>Nevada</td><td>4.5</td></tr>
<tr><td>37</td><td>Connecticut</td><td>(8.7)</td><td>7</td><td>Arkansas</td><td>2.8</td></tr>
<tr><td>40</td><td>Delaware</td><td>(13.7)</td><td>7</td><td>Maine</td><td>2.8</td></tr>
<tr><td>NA</td><td>Florida**</td><td>NA</td><td>7</td><td>Mississippi</td><td>2.8</td></tr>
<tr><td>33</td><td>Georgia</td><td>(6.4)</td><td>10</td><td>Oklahoma</td><td>2.7</td></tr>
<tr><td>4</td><td>Hawaii</td><td>5.7</td><td>11</td><td>Missouri</td><td>2.2</td></tr>
<tr><td>5</td><td>Idaho</td><td>4.7</td><td>11</td><td>Montana</td><td>2.2</td></tr>
<tr><td>NA</td><td>Illinois**</td><td>NA</td><td>13</td><td>Iowa</td><td>1.6</td></tr>
<tr><td>27</td><td>Indiana</td><td>(3.2)</td><td>14</td><td>South Dakota</td><td>0.9</td></tr>
<tr><td>13</td><td>Iowa</td><td>1.6</td><td>15</td><td>South Carolina</td><td>0.2</td></tr>
<tr><td>31</td><td>Kansas</td><td>(5.9)</td><td>16</td><td>Minnesota</td><td>0.0</td></tr>
<tr><td>2</td><td>Kentucky</td><td>18.0</td><td>17</td><td>Arizona</td><td>(0.7)</td></tr>
<tr><td>NA</td><td>Louisiana**</td><td>NA</td><td>18</td><td>Tennessee</td><td>(0.9)</td></tr>
<tr><td>7</td><td>Maine</td><td>2.8</td><td>19</td><td>West Virginia</td><td>(1.0)</td></tr>
<tr><td>NA</td><td>Maryland**</td><td>NA</td><td>20</td><td>Ohio</td><td>(1.1)</td></tr>
<tr><td>38</td><td>Massachusetts</td><td>(10.1)</td><td>21</td><td>Colorado</td><td>(1.4)</td></tr>
<tr><td>28</td><td>Michigan</td><td>(4.7)</td><td>22</td><td>Pennsylvania</td><td>(1.9)</td></tr>
<tr><td>16</td><td>Minnesota</td><td>0.0</td><td>23</td><td>Washington</td><td>(2.0)</td></tr>
<tr><td>7</td><td>Mississippi</td><td>2.8</td><td>24</td><td>Alabama</td><td>(2.3)</td></tr>
<tr><td>11</td><td>Missouri</td><td>2.2</td><td>25</td><td>Texas</td><td>(2.7)</td></tr>
<tr><td>11</td><td>Montana</td><td>2.2</td><td>26</td><td>North Carolina</td><td>(3.0)</td></tr>
<tr><td>42</td><td>Nebraska</td><td>(14.8)</td><td>27</td><td>Indiana</td><td>(3.2)</td></tr>
<tr><td>6</td><td>Nevada</td><td>4.5</td><td>28</td><td>Michigan</td><td>(4.7)</td></tr>
<tr><td>NA</td><td>New Hampshire**</td><td>NA</td><td>29</td><td>Oregon</td><td>(5.3)</td></tr>
<tr><td>36</td><td>New Jersey</td><td>(7.1)</td><td>30</td><td>North Dakota</td><td>(5.8)</td></tr>
<tr><td>3</td><td>New Mexico</td><td>5.9</td><td>31</td><td>Kansas</td><td>(5.9)</td></tr>
<tr><td>39</td><td>New York</td><td>(10.2)</td><td>32</td><td>Wisconsin</td><td>(6.2)</td></tr>
<tr><td>26</td><td>North Carolina</td><td>(3.0)</td><td>33</td><td>Georgia</td><td>(6.4)</td></tr>
<tr><td>30</td><td>North Dakota</td><td>(5.8)</td><td>33</td><td>Utah</td><td>(6.4)</td></tr>
<tr><td>20</td><td>Ohio</td><td>(1.1)</td><td>35</td><td>Virginia</td><td>(6.7)</td></tr>
<tr><td>10</td><td>Oklahoma</td><td>2.7</td><td>36</td><td>New Jersey</td><td>(7.1)</td></tr>
<tr><td>29</td><td>Oregon</td><td>(5.3)</td><td>37</td><td>Connecticut</td><td>(8.7)</td></tr>
<tr><td>22</td><td>Pennsylvania</td><td>(1.9)</td><td>38</td><td>Massachusetts</td><td>(10.1)</td></tr>
<tr><td>43</td><td>Rhode Island</td><td>(21.9)</td><td>39</td><td>New York</td><td>(10.2)</td></tr>
<tr><td>15</td><td>South Carolina</td><td>0.2</td><td>40</td><td>Delaware</td><td>(13.7)</td></tr>
<tr><td>14</td><td>South Dakota</td><td>0.9</td><td>41</td><td>Vermont</td><td>(14.6)</td></tr>
<tr><td>18</td><td>Tennessee</td><td>(0.9)</td><td>42</td><td>Nebraska</td><td>(14.8)</td></tr>
<tr><td>25</td><td>Texas</td><td>(2.7)</td><td>43</td><td>Rhode Island</td><td>(21.9)</td></tr>
<tr><td>33</td><td>Utah</td><td>(6.4)</td><td>NA</td><td>Alaska**</td><td>NA</td></tr>
<tr><td>41</td><td>Vermont</td><td>(14.6)</td><td>NA</td><td>California**</td><td>NA</td></tr>
<tr><td>35</td><td>Virginia</td><td>(6.7)</td><td>NA</td><td>Florida**</td><td>NA</td></tr>
<tr><td>23</td><td>Washington</td><td>(2.0)</td><td>NA</td><td>Illinois**</td><td>NA</td></tr>
<tr><td>19</td><td>West Virginia</td><td>(1.0)</td><td>NA</td><td>Louisiana**</td><td>NA</td></tr>
<tr><td>32</td><td>Wisconsin</td><td>(6.2)</td><td>NA</td><td>Maryland**</td><td>NA</td></tr>
<tr><td>1</td><td>Wyoming</td><td>18.4</td><td>NA</td><td>New Hampshire**</td><td>NA</td></tr>
</table>

District of Columbia (53.5)

Source: CQ Press using data from U.S. Department of Health and Human Services, Centers for Disease Control and Prevention
"Abortion Surveillance-United States, 2006" (MMWR, Vol. 58, No. SS-8, 11/27/09, http://www.cdc.gov/mmwr/mmwr_ss.html)
*The sum of live births and legal induced abortions per 1,000 women 15 to 19 years old. Births by state of residence, abortions by state of occurrence. Miscarriages are not included in these rates. National rate includes only states reporting abortions and births.
**Not available.

Births to Teenage Mothers in 2006

National Total = 435,436 Births*

ALPHA ORDER				RANK ORDER			
RANK	STATE	BIRTHS	% of USA	RANK	STATE	BIRTHS	% of USA
17	Alabama	8,537	2.0%	1	Texas	53,093	12.2%
46	Alaska	1,101	0.3%	2	California	52,800	12.1%
10	Arizona	12,824	2.9%	3	Florida	25,384	5.8%
27	Arkansas	5,946	1.4%	4	Illinois	17,752	4.1%
2	California	52,800	12.1%	5	Georgia	17,693	4.1%
24	Colorado	6,719	1.5%	6	New York	17,442	4.0%
36	Connecticut	2,875	0.7%	7	Ohio	15,872	3.6%
42	Delaware	1,263	0.3%	8	North Carolina	14,701	3.4%
3	Florida	25,384	5.8%	9	Pennsylvania	13,599	3.1%
5	Georgia	17,693	4.1%	10	Arizona	12,824	2.9%
40	Hawaii	1,619	0.4%	11	Michigan	12,322	2.8%
38	Idaho	2,140	0.5%	12	Tennessee	10,784	2.5%
4	Illinois	17,752	4.1%	13	Indiana	9,549	2.2%
13	Indiana	9,549	2.2%	14	Missouri	9,183	2.1%
35	Iowa	3,495	0.8%	15	Virginia	9,105	2.1%
33	Kansas	4,109	0.9%	16	Louisiana	8,628	2.0%
19	Kentucky	7,412	1.7%	17	Alabama	8,537	2.0%
16	Louisiana	8,628	2.0%	18	South Carolina	8,175	1.9%
43	Maine	1,133	0.3%	19	Kentucky	7,412	1.7%
25	Maryland	6,705	1.5%	20	Mississippi	7,404	1.7%
29	Massachusetts	4,724	1.1%	21	Oklahoma	7,227	1.7%
11	Michigan	12,322	2.8%	22	New Jersey	7,159	1.6%
28	Minnesota	5,090	1.2%	23	Washington	7,110	1.6%
20	Mississippi	7,404	1.7%	24	Colorado	6,719	1.5%
14	Missouri	9,183	2.1%	25	Maryland	6,705	1.5%
41	Montana	1,283	0.3%	26	Wisconsin	6,015	1.4%
39	Nebraska	2,112	0.5%	27	Arkansas	5,946	1.4%
31	Nevada	4,287	1.0%	28	Minnesota	5,090	1.2%
47	New Hampshire	865	0.2%	29	Massachusetts	4,724	1.1%
22	New Jersey	7,159	1.6%	30	New Mexico	4,628	1.1%
30	New Mexico	4,628	1.1%	31	Nevada	4,287	1.0%
6	New York	17,442	4.0%	32	Oregon	4,285	1.0%
8	North Carolina	14,701	3.4%	33	Kansas	4,109	0.9%
49	North Dakota	633	0.1%	34	Utah	3,498	0.8%
7	Ohio	15,872	3.6%	35	Iowa	3,495	0.8%
21	Oklahoma	7,227	1.7%	36	Connecticut	2,875	0.7%
32	Oregon	4,285	1.0%	37	West Virginia	2,589	0.6%
9	Pennsylvania	13,599	3.1%	38	Idaho	2,140	0.5%
44	Rhode Island	1,127	0.3%	39	Nebraska	2,112	0.5%
18	South Carolina	8,175	1.9%	40	Hawaii	1,619	0.4%
45	South Dakota	1,123	0.3%	41	Montana	1,283	0.3%
12	Tennessee	10,784	2.5%	42	Delaware	1,263	0.3%
1	Texas	53,093	12.2%	43	Maine	1,133	0.3%
34	Utah	3,498	0.8%	44	Rhode Island	1,127	0.3%
50	Vermont	468	0.1%	45	South Dakota	1,123	0.3%
15	Virginia	9,105	2.1%	46	Alaska	1,101	0.3%
23	Washington	7,110	1.6%	47	New Hampshire	865	0.2%
37	West Virginia	2,589	0.6%	48	Wyoming	850	0.2%
26	Wisconsin	6,015	1.4%	49	North Dakota	633	0.1%
48	Wyoming	850	0.2%	50	Vermont	468	0.1%
					District of Columbia	999	0.2%

Source: U.S. Department of Health and Human Services, National Center for Health Statistics
"Vital Stats" (http://www.cdc.gov/nchs/VitalStats.htm)
*Final data. Live births to women 15 to 19 years old by state of residence of mother.

Births to Teenage Mothers as a Percent of All Births in 2006

National Percent = 10.2% of Live Births*

ALPHA ORDER

RANK	STATE	PERCENT	RANK	STATE	PERCENT
5	Alabama	13.5	1	Mississippi	16.1
23	Alaska	10.0	2	New Mexico	15.5
11	Arizona	12.5	3	Arkansas	14.5
3	Arkansas	14.5	4	Louisiana	13.6
28	California	9.4	5	Alabama	13.5
27	Colorado	9.5	6	Oklahoma	13.4
45	Connecticut	6.9	7	Texas	13.3
20	Delaware	10.5	8	South Carolina	13.1
18	Florida	10.7	9	Tennessee	12.8
13	Georgia	11.9	10	Kentucky	12.7
36	Hawaii	8.5	11	Arizona	12.5
32	Idaho	8.8	12	West Virginia	12.4
25	Illinois	9.8	13	Georgia	11.9
17	Indiana	10.8	14	North Carolina	11.5
35	Iowa	8.6	15	Missouri	11.3
23	Kansas	10.0	16	Wyoming	11.1
10	Kentucky	12.7	17	Indiana	10.8
4	Louisiana	13.6	18	Florida	10.7
40	Maine	8.0	18	Nevada	10.7
34	Maryland	8.7	20	Delaware	10.5
49	Massachusetts	6.1	20	Ohio	10.5
26	Michigan	9.7	22	Montana	10.3
45	Minnesota	6.9	23	Alaska	10.0
1	Mississippi	16.1	23	Kansas	10.0
15	Missouri	11.3	25	Illinois	9.8
22	Montana	10.3	26	Michigan	9.7
41	Nebraska	7.9	27	Colorado	9.5
18	Nevada	10.7	28	California	9.4
50	New Hampshire	6.0	28	South Dakota	9.4
48	New Jersey	6.2	30	Pennsylvania	9.1
2	New Mexico	15.5	30	Rhode Island	9.1
44	New York	7.0	32	Idaho	8.8
14	North Carolina	11.5	32	Oregon	8.8
42	North Dakota	7.3	34	Maryland	8.7
20	Ohio	10.5	35	Iowa	8.6
6	Oklahoma	13.4	36	Hawaii	8.5
32	Oregon	8.8	37	Virginia	8.4
30	Pennsylvania	9.1	38	Wisconsin	8.3
30	Rhode Island	9.1	39	Washington	8.2
8	South Carolina	13.1	40	Maine	8.0
28	South Dakota	9.4	41	Nebraska	7.9
9	Tennessee	12.8	42	North Dakota	7.3
7	Texas	13.3	43	Vermont	7.2
47	Utah	6.5	44	New York	7.0
43	Vermont	7.2	45	Connecticut	6.9
37	Virginia	8.4	45	Minnesota	6.9
39	Washington	8.2	47	Utah	6.5
12	West Virginia	12.4	48	New Jersey	6.2
38	Wisconsin	8.3	49	Massachusetts	6.1
16	Wyoming	11.1	50	New Hampshire	6.0

District of Columbia   11.7

Source: CQ Press using data from U.S. Department of Health and Human Services, National Center for Health Statistics
"National Vital Statistics Reports" (Vol. 57, No. 7, January 7, 2009, http://www.cdc.gov/nchs/births.htm) and
"Vital Stats" (http://www.cdc.gov/nchs/VitalStats.htm)
*Final data. Live births to women 15 to 19 years old by state of residence.

Teenage Birth Rate in 2006

National Rate = 41.9 Live Births per 1,000 Women 15 to 19 Years Old*

ALPHA ORDER

RANK	STATE	RATE
12	Alabama	53.5
19	Alaska	44.3
5	Arizona	62.0
4	Arkansas	62.3
27	California	39.9
20	Colorado	43.8
47	Connecticut	23.5
23	Delaware	41.9
17	Florida	45.2
10	Georgia	54.2
24	Hawaii	40.5
30	Idaho	39.2
29	Illinois	39.5
21	Indiana	43.5
38	Iowa	32.9
22	Kansas	42.0
9	Kentucky	54.6
11	Louisiana	53.9
44	Maine	25.8
35	Maryland	33.6
48	Massachusetts	21.3
34	Michigan	33.8
41	Minnesota	27.9
1	Mississippi	68.4
16	Missouri	45.7
28	Montana	39.6
36	Nebraska	33.4
7	Nevada	55.8
50	New Hampshire	18.7
46	New Jersey	24.9
2	New Mexico	64.1
45	New York	25.7
14	North Carolina	49.7
43	North Dakota	26.5
26	Ohio	40.0
6	Oklahoma	59.6
31	Oregon	35.7
39	Pennsylvania	31.0
42	Rhode Island	27.8
13	South Carolina	53.0
25	South Dakota	40.2
8	Tennessee	54.7
3	Texas	63.1
33	Utah	34.0
49	Vermont	20.8
32	Virginia	35.2
36	Washington	33.4
18	West Virginia	44.9
40	Wisconsin	30.9
15	Wyoming	47.3

RANK ORDER

RANK	STATE	RATE
1	Mississippi	68.4
2	New Mexico	64.1
3	Texas	63.1
4	Arkansas	62.3
5	Arizona	62.0
6	Oklahoma	59.6
7	Nevada	55.8
8	Tennessee	54.7
9	Kentucky	54.6
10	Georgia	54.2
11	Louisiana	53.9
12	Alabama	53.5
13	South Carolina	53.0
14	North Carolina	49.7
15	Wyoming	47.3
16	Missouri	45.7
17	Florida	45.2
18	West Virginia	44.9
19	Alaska	44.3
20	Colorado	43.8
21	Indiana	43.5
22	Kansas	42.0
23	Delaware	41.9
24	Hawaii	40.5
25	South Dakota	40.2
26	Ohio	40.0
27	California	39.9
28	Montana	39.6
29	Illinois	39.5
30	Idaho	39.2
31	Oregon	35.7
32	Virginia	35.2
33	Utah	34.0
34	Michigan	33.8
35	Maryland	33.6
36	Nebraska	33.4
36	Washington	33.4
38	Iowa	32.9
39	Pennsylvania	31.0
40	Wisconsin	30.9
41	Minnesota	27.9
42	Rhode Island	27.8
43	North Dakota	26.5
44	Maine	25.8
45	New York	25.7
46	New Jersey	24.9
47	Connecticut	23.5
48	Massachusetts	21.3
49	Vermont	20.8
50	New Hampshire	18.7
	District of Columbia	48.4

Source: U.S. Department of Health and Human Services, National Center for Health Statistics
"National Vital Statistics Reports" (Vol. 57, No. 7, January 7, 2009, http://www.cdc.gov/nchs/births.htm)
*Final data by state of residence.

Percent Change in Teenage Birth Rate: 2002 to 2006

National Percent Change = 2.6% Decrease*

ALPHA ORDER				RANK ORDER		
RANK	STATE	PERCENT CHANGE		RANK	STATE	PERCENT CHANGE
24	Alabama	(1.8)		1	Wyoming	18.5
2	Alaska	12.2		2	Alaska	12.2
16	Arizona	1.3		3	Montana	8.8
8	Arkansas	4.0		4	Kentucky	7.1
31	California	(2.9)		5	Hawaii	6.0
40	Colorado	(6.8)		6	South Dakota	5.8
45	Connecticut	(8.9)		7	Mississippi	5.7
46	Delaware	(9.5)		8	Arkansas	4.0
13	Florida	1.6		9	Missouri	3.6
30	Georgia	(2.7)		10	Nevada	3.5
5	Hawaii	6.0		11	Oklahoma	2.8
21	Idaho	0.3		12	New Mexico	2.7
37	Illinois	(6.4)		13	Florida	1.6
28	Indiana	(2.5)		13	Maine	1.6
18	Iowa	1.2		15	Minnesota	1.5
27	Kansas	(2.3)		16	Arizona	1.3
4	Kentucky	7.1		16	Ohio	1.3
42	Louisiana	(7.2)		18	Iowa	1.2
13	Maine	1.6		18	Washington	1.2
36	Maryland	(5.1)		20	Tennessee	0.7
44	Massachusetts	(8.6)		21	Idaho	0.3
31	Michigan	(2.9)		22	South Carolina	0.0
15	Minnesota	1.5		23	West Virginia	(1.3)
7	Mississippi	5.7		24	Alabama	(1.8)
9	Missouri	3.6		25	Pennsylvania	(1.9)
3	Montana	8.8		26	Texas	(2.0)
47	Nebraska	(9.7)		27	Kansas	(2.3)
10	Nevada	3.5		28	Indiana	(2.5)
39	New Hampshire	(6.5)		29	North Dakota	(2.6)
41	New Jersey	(7.1)		30	Georgia	(2.7)
12	New Mexico	2.7		31	California	(2.9)
48	New York	(12.9)		31	Michigan	(2.9)
35	North Carolina	(4.8)		33	Oregon	(3.0)
29	North Dakota	(2.6)		34	Wisconsin	(4.3)
16	Ohio	1.3		35	North Carolina	(4.8)
11	Oklahoma	2.8		36	Maryland	(5.1)
33	Oregon	(3.0)		37	Illinois	(6.4)
25	Pennsylvania	(1.9)		37	Virginia	(6.4)
50	Rhode Island	(21.9)		39	New Hampshire	(6.5)
22	South Carolina	0.0		40	Colorado	(6.8)
6	South Dakota	5.8		41	New Jersey	(7.1)
20	Tennessee	0.7		42	Louisiana	(7.2)
26	Texas	(2.0)		43	Utah	(7.6)
43	Utah	(7.6)		44	Massachusetts	(8.6)
49	Vermont	(14.0)		45	Connecticut	(8.9)
37	Virginia	(6.4)		46	Delaware	(9.5)
18	Washington	1.2		47	Nebraska	(9.7)
23	West Virginia	(1.3)		48	New York	(12.9)
34	Wisconsin	(4.3)		49	Vermont	(14.0)
1	Wyoming	18.5		50	Rhode Island	(21.9)
				District of Columbia		(30.0)

Source: CQ Press using data from U.S. Department of Health and Human Services, National Center for Health Statistics
"National Vital Statistics Reports" (Vol. 57, No. 7, January 7, 2009, http://www.cdc.gov/nchs/births.htm)
*Final data by state of residence. Births to women 15 to 19 years old.

Births to White Teenage Mothers in 2006

National Total = 308,344 Live Births*

ALPHA ORDER

RANK	STATE	BIRTHS	% of USA
20	Alabama	4,820	1.6%
47	Alaska	477	0.2%
5	Arizona	10,834	3.5%
22	Arkansas	4,182	1.4%
1	California	45,483	14.8%
16	Colorado	6,098	2.0%
37	Connecticut	2,051	0.7%
45	Delaware	731	0.2%
3	Florida	16,049	5.2%
8	Georgia	9,582	3.1%
50	Hawaii	347	0.1%
38	Idaho	2,032	0.7%
4	Illinois	11,039	3.6%
12	Indiana	7,512	2.4%
33	Iowa	3,133	1.0%
30	Kansas	3,389	1.1%
15	Kentucky	6,323	2.1%
27	Louisiana	3,772	1.2%
40	Maine	1,087	0.4%
35	Maryland	2,828	0.9%
28	Massachusetts	3,620	1.2%
11	Michigan	7,612	2.5%
31	Minnesota	3,346	1.1%
34	Mississippi	3,014	1.0%
14	Missouri	6,616	2.1%
41	Montana	916	0.3%
39	Nebraska	1,634	0.5%
29	Nevada	3,423	1.1%
43	New Hampshire	841	0.3%
21	New Jersey	4,252	1.4%
26	New Mexico	3,824	1.2%
7	New York	10,689	3.5%
9	North Carolina	8,947	2.9%
49	North Dakota	410	0.1%
6	Ohio	10,819	3.5%
19	Oklahoma	5,072	1.6%
25	Oregon	3,887	1.3%
10	Pennsylvania	8,461	2.7%
42	Rhode Island	891	0.3%
23	South Carolina	4,099	1.3%
46	South Dakota	658	0.2%
13	Tennessee	7,243	2.3%
2	Texas	44,177	14.3%
32	Utah	3,223	1.0%
48	Vermont	458	0.1%
18	Virginia	5,322	1.7%
17	Washington	5,802	1.9%
36	West Virginia	2,454	0.8%
24	Wisconsin	4,033	1.3%
44	Wyoming	765	0.2%

RANK ORDER

RANK	STATE	BIRTHS	% of USA
1	California	45,483	14.8%
2	Texas	44,177	14.3%
3	Florida	16,049	5.2%
4	Illinois	11,039	3.6%
5	Arizona	10,834	3.5%
6	Ohio	10,819	3.5%
7	New York	10,689	3.5%
8	Georgia	9,582	3.1%
9	North Carolina	8,947	2.9%
10	Pennsylvania	8,461	2.7%
11	Michigan	7,612	2.5%
12	Indiana	7,512	2.4%
13	Tennessee	7,243	2.3%
14	Missouri	6,616	2.1%
15	Kentucky	6,323	2.1%
16	Colorado	6,098	2.0%
17	Washington	5,802	1.9%
18	Virginia	5,322	1.7%
19	Oklahoma	5,072	1.6%
20	Alabama	4,820	1.6%
21	New Jersey	4,252	1.4%
22	Arkansas	4,182	1.4%
23	South Carolina	4,099	1.3%
24	Wisconsin	4,033	1.3%
25	Oregon	3,887	1.3%
26	New Mexico	3,824	1.2%
27	Louisiana	3,772	1.2%
28	Massachusetts	3,620	1.2%
29	Nevada	3,423	1.1%
30	Kansas	3,389	1.1%
31	Minnesota	3,346	1.1%
32	Utah	3,223	1.0%
33	Iowa	3,133	1.0%
34	Mississippi	3,014	1.0%
35	Maryland	2,828	0.9%
36	West Virginia	2,454	0.8%
37	Connecticut	2,051	0.7%
38	Idaho	2,032	0.7%
39	Nebraska	1,634	0.5%
40	Maine	1,087	0.4%
41	Montana	916	0.3%
42	Rhode Island	891	0.3%
43	New Hampshire	841	0.3%
44	Wyoming	765	0.2%
45	Delaware	731	0.2%
46	South Dakota	658	0.2%
47	Alaska	477	0.2%
48	Vermont	458	0.1%
49	North Dakota	410	0.1%
50	Hawaii	347	0.1%
	District of Columbia	67	0.0%

Source: U.S. Department of Health and Human Services, National Center for Health Statistics
"Vital Stats" (http://www.cdc.gov/nchs/VitalStats.htm)
*Final data. Live births to women 15 to 19 years old by state of residence.

White Teenage Birth Rate in 2006

National Rate = 38.2 Births per 1,000 White Teenage Women*

ALPHA ORDER

RANK	STATE	RATE
11	Alabama	46.8
34	Alaska	28.9
3	Arizona	62.0
4	Arkansas	57.3
14	California	44.5
16	Colorado	44.2
46	Connecticut	20.3
25	Delaware	34.3
23	Florida	38.5
9	Georgia	49.1
32	Hawaii	29.8
22	Idaho	38.8
29	Illinois	32.1
20	Indiana	39.4
31	Iowa	31.3
21	Kansas	39.1
8	Kentucky	52.4
18	Louisiana	40.1
38	Maine	25.6
41	Maryland	23.6
48	Massachusetts	19.2
37	Michigan	26.7
45	Minnesota	20.9
7	Mississippi	52.8
19	Missouri	39.8
30	Montana	32.0
35	Nebraska	28.5
6	Nevada	55.1
50	New Hampshire	18.8
47	New Jersey	19.8
1	New Mexico	65.3
43	New York	22.1
15	North Carolina	44.4
49	North Dakota	19.1
27	Ohio	32.9
5	Oklahoma	55.6
24	Oregon	35.8
42	Pennsylvania	23.2
39	Rhode Island	25.5
17	South Carolina	43.2
36	South Dakota	27.9
10	Tennessee	48.6
2	Texas	64.3
26	Utah	33.5
44	Vermont	21.0
33	Virginia	29.4
28	Washington	32.2
13	West Virginia	44.9
40	Wisconsin	23.7
12	Wyoming	45.2

RANK ORDER

RANK	STATE	RATE
1	New Mexico	65.3
2	Texas	64.3
3	Arizona	62.0
4	Arkansas	57.3
5	Oklahoma	55.6
6	Nevada	55.1
7	Mississippi	52.8
8	Kentucky	52.4
9	Georgia	49.1
10	Tennessee	48.6
11	Alabama	46.8
12	Wyoming	45.2
13	West Virginia	44.9
14	California	44.5
15	North Carolina	44.4
16	Colorado	44.2
17	South Carolina	43.2
18	Louisiana	40.1
19	Missouri	39.8
20	Indiana	39.4
21	Kansas	39.1
22	Idaho	38.8
23	Florida	38.5
24	Oregon	35.8
25	Delaware	34.3
26	Utah	33.5
27	Ohio	32.9
28	Washington	32.2
29	Illinois	32.1
30	Montana	32.0
31	Iowa	31.3
32	Hawaii	29.8
33	Virginia	29.4
34	Alaska	28.9
35	Nebraska	28.5
36	South Dakota	27.9
37	Michigan	26.7
38	Maine	25.6
39	Rhode Island	25.5
40	Wisconsin	23.7
41	Maryland	23.6
42	Pennsylvania	23.2
43	New York	22.1
44	Vermont	21.0
45	Minnesota	20.9
46	Connecticut	20.3
47	New Jersey	19.8
48	Massachusetts	19.2
49	North Dakota	19.1
50	New Hampshire	18.8

District of Columbia 9.6

Source: CQ Press using data from U.S. Department of Health and Human Services, National Center for Health Statistics
"Vital Stats" (http://www.cdc.gov/nchs/VitalStats.htm)
*Final data. Live births to women 15 to 19 years old by state of residence.

Births to White Teenage Mothers as a Percent of All White Births in 2006

National Percent = 9.3% of White Live Births*

ALPHA ORDER			RANK ORDER		
RANK	STATE	PERCENT	RANK	STATE	PERCENT
10	Alabama	11.3	1	New Mexico	15.4
37	Alaska	6.9	2	Texas	13.2
6	Arizona	12.2	3	Arkansas	13.0
3	Arkansas	13.0	4	Mississippi	12.5
16	California	10.0	5	West Virginia	12.3
20	Colorado	9.4	6	Arizona	12.2
46	Connecticut	6.1	6	Kentucky	12.2
25	Delaware	8.7	8	Oklahoma	12.1
20	Florida	9.4	9	Tennessee	11.4
14	Georgia	10.2	10	Alabama	11.3
43	Hawaii	6.3	11	Wyoming	10.7
25	Idaho	8.7	12	Nevada	10.5
32	Illinois	7.9	12	South Carolina	10.5
18	Indiana	9.8	14	Georgia	10.2
29	Iowa	8.3	15	Louisiana	10.1
20	Kansas	9.4	16	California	10.0
6	Kentucky	12.2	17	Missouri	9.9
15	Louisiana	10.1	18	Indiana	9.8
31	Maine	8.0	19	North Carolina	9.7
41	Maryland	6.4	20	Colorado	9.4
47	Massachusetts	5.8	20	Florida	9.4
33	Michigan	7.7	20	Kansas	9.4
48	Minnesota	5.7	23	Ohio	8.9
4	Mississippi	12.5	23	Oregon	8.9
17	Missouri	9.9	25	Delaware	8.7
27	Montana	8.6	25	Idaho	8.7
37	Nebraska	6.9	27	Montana	8.6
12	Nevada	10.5	28	Rhode Island	8.5
44	New Hampshire	6.2	29	Iowa	8.3
50	New Jersey	5.1	30	Washington	8.1
1	New Mexico	15.4	31	Maine	8.0
44	New York	6.2	32	Illinois	7.9
19	North Carolina	9.7	33	Michigan	7.7
49	North Dakota	5.6	34	Vermont	7.3
23	Ohio	8.9	35	Pennsylvania	7.2
8	Oklahoma	12.1	36	Virginia	7.0
23	Oregon	8.9	37	Alaska	6.9
35	Pennsylvania	7.2	37	Nebraska	6.9
28	Rhode Island	8.5	37	South Dakota	6.9
12	South Carolina	10.5	40	Wisconsin	6.6
37	South Dakota	6.9	41	Maryland	6.4
9	Tennessee	11.4	41	Utah	6.4
2	Texas	13.2	43	Hawaii	6.3
41	Utah	6.4	44	New Hampshire	6.2
34	Vermont	7.3	44	New York	6.2
36	Virginia	7.0	46	Connecticut	6.1
30	Washington	8.1	47	Massachusetts	5.8
5	West Virginia	12.3	48	Minnesota	5.7
40	Wisconsin	6.6	49	North Dakota	5.6
11	Wyoming	10.7	50	New Jersey	5.1
				District of Columbia	2.6

Source: CQ Press using data from U.S. Department of Health and Human Services, National Center for Health Statistics
"Vital Stats" (http://www.cdc.gov/nchs/VitalStats.htm)
*Final data. Live births to women 15 to 19 years old by state of residence.

Births to Black Teenage Mothers in 2006

National Total = 111,019 Live Births*

ALPHA ORDER

RANK	STATE	BIRTHS	% of USA
15	Alabama	3,666	3.3%
41	Alaska	61	0.1%
28	Arizona	629	0.6%
21	Arkansas	1,676	1.5%
9	California	4,843	4.4%
33	Colorado	444	0.4%
27	Connecticut	793	0.7%
32	Delaware	522	0.5%
1	Florida	8,951	8.1%
3	Georgia	7,977	7.2%
42	Hawaii	56	0.1%
47	Idaho	12	0.0%
4	Illinois	6,556	5.9%
20	Indiana	1,995	1.8%
35	Iowa	286	0.3%
29	Kansas	612	0.6%
23	Kentucky	1,038	0.9%
10	Louisiana	4,758	4.3%
43	Maine	23	0.0%
14	Maryland	3,741	3.4%
25	Massachusetts	925	0.8%
11	Michigan	4,479	4.0%
25	Minnesota	925	0.8%
12	Mississippi	4,314	3.9%
19	Missouri	2,443	2.2%
49	Montana	10	0.0%
34	Nebraska	338	0.3%
30	Nevada	603	0.5%
45	New Hampshire	13	0.0%
18	New Jersey	2,812	2.5%
39	New Mexico	105	0.1%
5	New York	6,361	5.7%
6	North Carolina	5,264	4.7%
45	North Dakota	13	0.0%
7	Ohio	4,937	4.4%
24	Oklahoma	968	0.9%
37	Oregon	154	0.1%
8	Pennsylvania	4,862	4.4%
36	Rhode Island	163	0.1%
13	South Carolina	3,971	3.6%
44	South Dakota	21	0.0%
17	Tennessee	3,407	3.1%
2	Texas	8,397	7.6%
40	Utah	71	0.1%
50	Vermont	8	0.0%
16	Virginia	3,643	3.3%
31	Washington	599	0.5%
38	West Virginia	129	0.1%
22	Wisconsin	1,515	1.4%
48	Wyoming	11	0.0%

RANK ORDER

RANK	STATE	BIRTHS	% of USA
1	Florida	8,951	8.1%
2	Texas	8,397	7.6%
3	Georgia	7,977	7.2%
4	Illinois	6,556	5.9%
5	New York	6,361	5.7%
6	North Carolina	5,264	4.7%
7	Ohio	4,937	4.4%
8	Pennsylvania	4,862	4.4%
9	California	4,843	4.4%
10	Louisiana	4,758	4.3%
11	Michigan	4,479	4.0%
12	Mississippi	4,314	3.9%
13	South Carolina	3,971	3.6%
14	Maryland	3,741	3.4%
15	Alabama	3,666	3.3%
16	Virginia	3,643	3.3%
17	Tennessee	3,407	3.1%
18	New Jersey	2,812	2.5%
19	Missouri	2,443	2.2%
20	Indiana	1,995	1.8%
21	Arkansas	1,676	1.5%
22	Wisconsin	1,515	1.4%
23	Kentucky	1,038	0.9%
24	Oklahoma	968	0.9%
25	Massachusetts	925	0.8%
25	Minnesota	925	0.8%
27	Connecticut	793	0.7%
28	Arizona	629	0.6%
29	Kansas	612	0.6%
30	Nevada	603	0.5%
31	Washington	599	0.5%
32	Delaware	522	0.5%
33	Colorado	444	0.4%
34	Nebraska	338	0.3%
35	Iowa	286	0.3%
36	Rhode Island	163	0.1%
37	Oregon	154	0.1%
38	West Virginia	129	0.1%
39	New Mexico	105	0.1%
40	Utah	71	0.1%
41	Alaska	61	0.1%
42	Hawaii	56	0.1%
43	Maine	23	0.0%
44	South Dakota	21	0.0%
45	New Hampshire	13	0.0%
45	North Dakota	13	0.0%
47	Idaho	12	0.0%
48	Wyoming	11	0.0%
49	Montana	10	0.0%
50	Vermont	8	0.0%
	District of Columbia	919	0.8%

Source: U.S. Department of Health and Human Services, National Center for Health Statistics
  "Vital Stats" (http://www.cdc.gov/nchs/VitalStats.htm)
*Final data. Live births to women 15 to 19 years old by state of residence.

Black Teenage Birth Rate in 2006

National Rate = 64.6 Births per 1,000 Black Teenage Women*

ALPHA ORDER

RANK	STATE	RATE
21	Alabama	67.8
35	Alaska	46.7
26	Arizona	59.6
4	Arkansas	82.6
43	California	41.7
33	Colorado	51.6
34	Connecticut	47.3
24	Delaware	64.7
18	Florida	69.8
23	Georgia	65.4
46	Hawaii	37.6
49	Idaho	21.5
14	Illinois	75.4
8	Indiana	78.4
15	Iowa	74.8
9	Kansas	78.2
11	Kentucky	76.5
13	Louisiana	76.2
47	Maine	36.6
28	Maryland	53.8
37	Massachusetts	44.2
22	Michigan	66.0
5	Minnesota	81.4
3	Mississippi	86.9
7	Missouri	79.0
45	Montana	37.7
2	Nebraska	87.5
17	Nevada	70.5
60	New Hampshire	18.7
30	New Jersey	52.7
37	New Mexico	44.2
40	New York	43.1
25	North Carolina	62.7
44	North Dakota	40.8
6	Ohio	80.0
16	Oklahoma	72.4
40	Oregon	43.1
10	Pennsylvania	77.9
36	Rhode Island	45.7
19	South Carolina	69.7
31	South Dakota	52.2
12	Tennessee	76.4
19	Texas	69.7
42	Utah	42.6
48	Vermont	28.3
27	Virginia	55.8
29	Washington	52.8
32	West Virginia	51.8
1	Wisconsin	90.8
39	Wyoming	43.7

RANK ORDER

RANK	STATE	RATE
1	Wisconsin	90.8
2	Nebraska	87.5
3	Mississippi	86.9
4	Arkansas	82.6
5	Minnesota	81.4
6	Ohio	80.0
7	Missouri	79.0
8	Indiana	78.4
9	Kansas	78.2
10	Pennsylvania	77.9
11	Kentucky	76.5
12	Tennessee	76.4
13	Louisiana	76.2
14	Illinois	75.4
15	Iowa	74.8
16	Oklahoma	72.4
17	Nevada	70.5
18	Florida	69.8
19	South Carolina	69.7
19	Texas	69.7
21	Alabama	67.8
22	Michigan	66.0
23	Georgia	65.4
24	Delaware	64.7
25	North Carolina	62.7
26	Arizona	59.6
27	Virginia	55.8
28	Maryland	53.8
29	Washington	52.8
30	New Jersey	52.7
31	South Dakota	52.2
32	West Virginia	51.8
33	Colorado	51.6
34	Connecticut	47.3
35	Alaska	46.7
36	Rhode Island	45.7
37	Massachusetts	44.2
37	New Mexico	44.2
39	Wyoming	43.7
40	New York	43.1
40	Oregon	43.1
42	Utah	42.6
43	California	41.7
44	North Dakota	40.8
45	Montana	37.7
46	Hawaii	37.6
47	Maine	36.6
48	Vermont	28.3
49	Idaho	21.5
50	New Hampshire	18.7

	District of Columbia	70.6

Source: CQ Press using data from U.S. Department of Health and Human Services, National Center for Health Statistics
"Vital Stats" (http://www.cdc.gov/nchs/VitalStats.htm)
*Final data. Live births to women 15 to 19 years old by state of residence.

Births to Black Teenage Mothers as a Percent of All Black Births in 2006

National Percent = 16.7% of Black Live Births*

ALPHA ORDER

RANK ORDER

RANK	STATE	PERCENT		RANK	STATE	PERCENT
14	Alabama	18.9		1	Wisconsin	21.3
34	Alaska	13.9		2	Arkansas	21.1
29	Arizona	15.4		3	Illinois	20.8
2	Arkansas	21.1		4	Mississippi	20.5
31	California	14.1		5	Missouri	19.6
31	Colorado	14.1		6	Louisiana	19.4
31	Connecticut	14.1		6	Michigan	19.4
23	Delaware	17.0		6	Ohio	19.4
28	Florida	15.7		6	Oklahoma	19.4
26	Georgia	16.1		6	Pennsylvania	19.4
47	Hawaii	9.2		11	Kansas	19.3
48	Idaho	8.2		12	Indiana	19.1
3	Illinois	20.8		13	Kentucky	19.0
12	Indiana	19.1		14	Alabama	18.9
19	Iowa	17.6		15	Tennessee	18.6
11	Kansas	19.3		16	South Carolina	18.5
13	Kentucky	19.0		17	West Virginia	18.4
6	Louisiana	19.4		18	Nebraska	17.9
49	Maine	7.7		19	Iowa	17.6
38	Maryland	13.3		19	North Carolina	17.6
44	Massachusetts	9.9		21	New Mexico	17.5
6	Michigan	19.4		22	Texas	17.1
41	Minnesota	12.2		23	Delaware	17.0
4	Mississippi	20.5		24	Nevada	16.9
5	Missouri	19.6		25	Wyoming	16.7
27	Montana	15.9		26	Georgia	16.1
18	Nebraska	17.9		27	Montana	15.9
24	Nevada	16.9		28	Florida	15.7
50	New Hampshire	4.9		29	Arizona	15.4
37	New Jersey	13.4		30	Virginia	14.9
21	New Mexico	17.5		31	California	14.1
42	New York	11.7		31	Colorado	14.1
19	North Carolina	17.6		31	Connecticut	14.1
45	North Dakota	9.8		34	Alaska	13.9
6	Ohio	19.4		35	Rhode Island	13.7
6	Oklahoma	19.4		35	Utah	13.7
38	Oregon	13.3		37	New Jersey	13.4
6	Pennsylvania	19.4		38	Maryland	13.3
35	Rhode Island	13.7		38	Oregon	13.3
16	South Carolina	18.5		40	Washington	12.6
46	South Dakota	9.6		41	Minnesota	12.2
15	Tennessee	18.6		42	New York	11.7
22	Texas	17.1		43	Vermont	10.0
35	Utah	13.7		44	Massachusetts	9.9
43	Vermont	10.0		45	North Dakota	9.8
30	Virginia	14.9		46	South Dakota	9.6
40	Washington	12.6		47	Hawaii	9.2
17	West Virginia	18.4		48	Idaho	8.2
1	Wisconsin	21.3		49	Maine	7.7
25	Wyoming	16.7		50	New Hampshire	4.9

District of Columbia   16.0

Source: CQ Press using data from U.S. Department of Health and Human Services, National Center for Health Statistics
   "Vital Stats" (http://www.cdc.gov/nchs/VitalStats.htm)
*Final data. Live births to women 15 to 19 years old by state of residence.

Births to Young Teenagers: 2004 to 2006

National Total = 19,899 Live Births*

ALPHA ORDER

RANK	STATE	BIRTHS	% of USA
15	Alabama	475	2.4%
44	Alaska	29	0.1%
11	Arizona	547	2.7%
23	Arkansas	305	1.5%
2	California	2,133	10.7%
22	Colorado	308	1.5%
35	Connecticut	102	0.5%
39	Delaware	61	0.3%
3	Florida	1,163	5.8%
4	Georgia	980	4.9%
42	Hawaii	48	0.2%
41	Idaho	51	0.3%
5	Illinois	890	4.5%
20	Indiana	339	1.7%
37	Iowa	86	0.4%
33	Kansas	151	0.8%
27	Kentucky	259	1.3%
11	Louisiana	547	2.7%
48	Maine	20	0.1%
18	Maryland	361	1.8%
31	Massachusetts	157	0.8%
10	Michigan	581	2.9%
30	Minnesota	186	0.9%
13	Mississippi	534	2.7%
19	Missouri	357	1.8%
45	Montana	28	0.1%
36	Nebraska	87	0.4%
29	Nevada	194	1.0%
49	New Hampshire	14	0.1%
24	New Jersey	287	1.4%
28	New Mexico	211	1.1%
7	New York	753	3.8%
6	North Carolina	796	4.0%
47	North Dakota	22	0.1%
8	Ohio	718	3.6%
21	Oklahoma	312	1.6%
32	Oregon	153	0.8%
9	Pennsylvania	639	3.2%
40	Rhode Island	55	0.3%
17	South Carolina	404	2.0%
43	South Dakota	32	0.2%
14	Tennessee	526	2.6%
1	Texas	2,786	14.0%
34	Utah	105	0.5%
50	Vermont	10	0.1%
16	Virginia	405	2.0%
26	Washington	261	1.3%
38	West Virginia	69	0.3%
25	Wisconsin	269	1.4%
46	Wyoming	24	0.1%

RANK ORDER

RANK	STATE	BIRTHS	% of USA
1	Texas	2,786	14.0%
2	California	2,133	10.7%
3	Florida	1,163	5.8%
4	Georgia	980	4.9%
5	Illinois	890	4.5%
6	North Carolina	796	4.0%
7	New York	753	3.8%
8	Ohio	718	3.6%
9	Pennsylvania	639	3.2%
10	Michigan	581	2.9%
11	Arizona	547	2.7%
11	Louisiana	547	2.7%
13	Mississippi	534	2.7%
14	Tennessee	526	2.6%
15	Alabama	475	2.4%
16	Virginia	405	2.0%
17	South Carolina	404	2.0%
18	Maryland	361	1.8%
19	Missouri	357	1.8%
20	Indiana	339	1.7%
21	Oklahoma	312	1.6%
22	Colorado	308	1.5%
23	Arkansas	305	1.5%
24	New Jersey	287	1.4%
25	Wisconsin	269	1.4%
26	Washington	261	1.3%
27	Kentucky	259	1.3%
28	New Mexico	211	1.1%
29	Nevada	194	1.0%
30	Minnesota	186	0.9%
31	Massachusetts	157	0.8%
32	Oregon	153	0.8%
33	Kansas	151	0.8%
34	Utah	105	0.5%
35	Connecticut	102	0.5%
36	Nebraska	87	0.4%
37	Iowa	86	0.4%
38	West Virginia	69	0.3%
39	Delaware	61	0.3%
40	Rhode Island	55	0.3%
41	Idaho	51	0.3%
42	Hawaii	48	0.2%
43	South Dakota	32	0.2%
44	Alaska	29	0.1%
45	Montana	28	0.1%
46	Wyoming	24	0.1%
47	North Dakota	22	0.1%
48	Maine	20	0.1%
49	New Hampshire	14	0.1%
50	Vermont	10	0.1%
	District of Columbia	69	0.3%

Source: CQ Press using data from U.S. Department of Health and Human Services, National Center for Health Statistics
"Vital Stats" (http://www.cdc.gov/nchs/VitalStats.htm)
*Final data. Births to 10- to 14-year-olds during the three years of 2004 to 2006 by state of residence.

Young Teen Birth Rate: 2004 to 2006

National Rate = 0.7 Live Births per 1,000 10- to 14-Year-Old Females*

ALPHA ORDER

RANK	STATE	RATE
5	Alabama	1.0
32	Alaska	0.4
8	Arizona	0.9
3	Arkansas	1.1
22	California	0.5
17	Colorado	0.6
42	Connecticut	0.3
14	Delaware	0.7
14	Florida	0.7
5	Georgia	1.0
32	Hawaii	0.4
42	Idaho	0.3
14	Illinois	0.7
22	Indiana	0.5
42	Iowa	0.3
22	Kansas	0.5
17	Kentucky	0.6
2	Louisiana	1.2
48	Maine	0.2
17	Maryland	0.6
42	Massachusetts	0.3
22	Michigan	0.5
32	Minnesota	0.4
1	Mississippi	1.7
17	Missouri	0.6
42	Montana	0.3
22	Nebraska	0.5
13	Nevada	0.8
NA	New Hampshire**	NA
42	New Jersey	0.3
5	New Mexico	1.0
32	New York	0.4
8	North Carolina	0.9
32	North Dakota	0.4
17	Ohio	0.6
8	Oklahoma	0.9
32	Oregon	0.4
22	Pennsylvania	0.5
22	Rhode Island	0.5
8	South Carolina	0.9
32	South Dakota	0.4
8	Tennessee	0.9
3	Texas	1.1
32	Utah	0.4
NA	Vermont**	NA
22	Virginia	0.5
32	Washington	0.4
32	West Virginia	0.4
22	Wisconsin	0.5
22	Wyoming	0.5

RANK ORDER

RANK	STATE	RATE
1	Mississippi	1.7
2	Louisiana	1.2
3	Arkansas	1.1
3	Texas	1.1
5	Alabama	1.0
5	Georgia	1.0
5	New Mexico	1.0
8	Arizona	0.9
8	North Carolina	0.9
8	Oklahoma	0.9
8	South Carolina	0.9
8	Tennessee	0.9
13	Nevada	0.8
14	Delaware	0.7
14	Florida	0.7
14	Illinois	0.7
17	Colorado	0.6
17	Kentucky	0.6
17	Maryland	0.6
17	Missouri	0.6
17	Ohio	0.6
22	California	0.5
22	Indiana	0.5
22	Kansas	0.5
22	Michigan	0.5
22	Nebraska	0.5
22	Pennsylvania	0.5
22	Rhode Island	0.5
22	Virginia	0.5
22	Wisconsin	0.5
22	Wyoming	0.5
32	Alaska	0.4
32	Hawaii	0.4
32	Minnesota	0.4
32	New York	0.4
32	North Dakota	0.4
32	Oregon	0.4
32	South Dakota	0.4
32	Utah	0.4
32	Washington	0.4
32	West Virginia	0.4
42	Connecticut	0.3
42	Idaho	0.3
42	Iowa	0.3
42	Massachusetts	0.3
42	Montana	0.3
42	New Jersey	0.3
48	Maine	0.2
NA	New Hampshire**	NA
NA	Vermont**	NA

	District of Columbia	1.5

Source: CQ Press using data from U.S. Department of Health and Human Services, National Center for Health Statistics
   "Vital Stats" (http://www.cdc.gov/nchs/VitalStats.htm)
*Final data. Births to 10- to 14-year-olds during the three years of 2004 to 2006 by state of residence.
**Insufficient data for a reliable rate.

Births to Women 35 to 54 Years Old in 2006

National Total = 611,129 Live Births*

RANK	STATE	BIRTHS	% of USA
26	Alabama	5,770	0.9%
45	Alaska	1,463	0.2%
16	Arizona	11,992	2.0%
38	Arkansas	3,114	0.5%
1	California	97,880	16.0%
18	Colorado	10,935	1.8%
20	Connecticut	9,433	1.5%
44	Delaware	1,653	0.3%
4	Florida	34,444	5.6%
8	Georgia	18,604	3.0%
35	Hawaii	3,284	0.5%
40	Idaho	2,315	0.4%
5	Illinois	28,033	4.6%
21	Indiana	9,219	1.5%
33	Iowa	4,440	0.7%
31	Kansas	4,563	0.7%
28	Kentucky	5,521	0.9%
27	Louisiana	5,570	0.9%
42	Maine	2,014	0.3%
14	Maryland	14,594	2.4%
10	Massachusetts	18,221	3.0%
12	Michigan	16,973	2.8%
17	Minnesota	11,260	1.8%
34	Mississippi	3,390	0.6%
23	Missouri	8,641	1.4%
46	Montana	1,439	0.2%
36	Nebraska	3,134	0.5%
29	Nevada	5,321	0.9%
39	New Hampshire	2,668	0.4%
6	New Jersey	25,296	4.1%
37	New Mexico	3,118	0.5%
2	New York	50,259	8.2%
13	North Carolina	16,069	2.6%
49	North Dakota	926	0.2%
9	Ohio	18,592	3.0%
32	Oklahoma	4,548	0.7%
24	Oregon	6,698	1.1%
7	Pennsylvania	23,705	3.9%
41	Rhode Island	2,269	0.4%
25	South Carolina	6,568	1.1%
47	South Dakota	1,212	0.2%
22	Tennessee	8,681	1.4%
3	Texas	45,476	7.4%
30	Utah	4,848	0.8%
48	Vermont	1,187	0.2%
11	Virginia	17,859	2.9%
15	Washington	13,713	2.2%
43	West Virginia	1,955	0.3%
19	Wisconsin	9,903	1.6%
50	Wyoming	676	0.1%

ALPHA ORDER

RANK ORDER

RANK	STATE	BIRTHS	% of USA
1	California	97,880	16.0%
2	New York	50,259	8.2%
3	Texas	45,476	7.4%
4	Florida	34,444	5.6%
5	Illinois	28,033	4.6%
6	New Jersey	25,296	4.1%
7	Pennsylvania	23,705	3.9%
8	Georgia	18,604	3.0%
9	Ohio	18,592	3.0%
10	Massachusetts	18,221	3.0%
11	Virginia	17,859	2.9%
12	Michigan	16,973	2.8%
13	North Carolina	16,069	2.6%
14	Maryland	14,594	2.4%
15	Washington	13,713	2.2%
16	Arizona	11,992	2.0%
17	Minnesota	11,260	1.8%
18	Colorado	10,935	1.8%
19	Wisconsin	9,903	1.6%
20	Connecticut	9,433	1.5%
21	Indiana	9,219	1.5%
22	Tennessee	8,681	1.4%
23	Missouri	8,641	1.4%
24	Oregon	6,698	1.1%
25	South Carolina	6,568	1.1%
26	Alabama	5,770	0.9%
27	Louisiana	5,570	0.9%
28	Kentucky	5,521	0.9%
29	Nevada	5,321	0.9%
30	Utah	4,848	0.8%
31	Kansas	4,563	0.7%
32	Oklahoma	4,548	0.7%
33	Iowa	4,440	0.7%
34	Mississippi	3,390	0.6%
35	Hawaii	3,284	0.5%
36	Nebraska	3,134	0.5%
37	New Mexico	3,118	0.5%
38	Arkansas	3,114	0.5%
39	New Hampshire	2,668	0.4%
40	Idaho	2,315	0.4%
41	Rhode Island	2,269	0.4%
42	Maine	2,014	0.3%
43	West Virginia	1,955	0.3%
44	Delaware	1,653	0.3%
45	Alaska	1,463	0.2%
46	Montana	1,439	0.2%
47	South Dakota	1,212	0.2%
48	Vermont	1,187	0.2%
49	North Dakota	926	0.2%
50	Wyoming	676	0.1%
	District of Columbia	1,683	0.3%

Source: CQ Press using data from U.S. Department of Health and Human Services, National Center for Health Statistics
"Vital Stats" (http://www.cdc.gov/nchs/VitalStats.htm)
*Final data by state of residence.

Births to Women 35 to 54 Years Old as a Percent of All Births in 2006

National Percent = 14.3% of Live Births*

ALPHA ORDER			RANK ORDER		
RANK	STATE	PERCENT	RANK	STATE	PERCENT
44	Alabama	9.1	1	Massachusetts	23.5
22	Alaska	13.3	2	Connecticut	22.6
28	Arizona	11.7	3	New Jersey	22.0
49	Arkansas	7.6	4	New York	20.1
9	California	17.4	5	Maryland	18.8
14	Colorado	15.5	6	New Hampshire	18.6
2	Connecticut	22.6	7	Rhode Island	18.3
19	Delaware	13.8	8	Vermont	18.2
17	Florida	14.5	9	California	17.4
26	Georgia	12.5	10	Hawaii	17.3
10	Hawaii	17.3	11	Virginia	16.6
41	Idaho	9.6	12	Pennsylvania	15.9
14	Illinois	15.5	13	Washington	15.8
37	Indiana	10.4	14	Colorado	15.5
33	Iowa	10.9	14	Illinois	15.5
32	Kansas	11.1	16	Minnesota	15.3
42	Kentucky	9.5	17	Florida	14.5
46	Louisiana	8.8	18	Maine	14.2
18	Maine	14.2	19	Delaware	13.8
5	Maryland	18.8	19	Oregon	13.8
1	Massachusetts	23.5	21	Wisconsin	13.7
22	Michigan	13.3	22	Alaska	13.3
16	Minnesota	15.3	22	Michigan	13.3
50	Mississippi	7.4	22	Nevada	13.3
35	Missouri	10.6	25	North Carolina	12.6
30	Montana	11.5	26	Georgia	12.5
28	Nebraska	11.7	27	Ohio	12.3
22	Nevada	13.3	28	Arizona	11.7
6	New Hampshire	18.6	28	Nebraska	11.7
3	New Jersey	22.0	30	Montana	11.5
37	New Mexico	10.4	31	Texas	11.4
4	New York	20.1	32	Kansas	11.1
25	North Carolina	12.6	33	Iowa	10.9
34	North Dakota	10.7	34	North Dakota	10.7
27	Ohio	12.3	35	Missouri	10.6
48	Oklahoma	8.4	35	South Carolina	10.6
19	Oregon	13.8	37	Indiana	10.4
12	Pennsylvania	15.9	37	New Mexico	10.4
7	Rhode Island	18.3	39	Tennessee	10.3
35	South Carolina	10.6	40	South Dakota	10.2
40	South Dakota	10.2	41	Idaho	9.6
39	Tennessee	10.3	42	Kentucky	9.5
31	Texas	11.4	43	West Virginia	9.3
44	Utah	9.1	44	Alabama	9.1
8	Vermont	18.2	44	Utah	9.1
11	Virginia	16.6	46	Louisiana	8.8
13	Washington	15.8	46	Wyoming	8.8
43	West Virginia	9.3	48	Oklahoma	8.4
21	Wisconsin	13.7	49	Arkansas	7.6
46	Wyoming	8.8	50	Mississippi	7.4
				District of Columbia	19.7

Source: CQ Press using data from U.S. Department of Health and Human Services, National Center for Health Statistics
"Vital Stats" (http://www.cdc.gov/nchs/VitalStats.htm)
*Final data by state of residence.

Average Age of Woman at First Birth in 2006

National Average = 25.0 Years Old

ALPHA ORDER			RANK ORDER		
RANK	STATE	AVERAGE AGE	RANK	STATE	AVERAGE AGE
45	Alabama	23.6	1	Massachusetts	27.7
31	Alaska	24.3	2	Connecticut	27.2
34	Arizona	24.0	2	New Jersey	27.2
48	Arkansas	23.0	4	New York	26.8
14	California	25.6	5	New Hampshire	26.7
12	Colorado	25.7	6	Vermont	26.5
2	Connecticut	27.2	7	Rhode Island	26.2
20	Delaware	25.0	8	Maryland	26.1
20	Florida	25.0	9	Washington	25.9
28	Georgia	24.5	10	Minnesota	25.8
12	Hawaii	25.7	10	Virginia	25.8
42	Idaho	23.8	12	Colorado	25.7
17	Illinois	25.4	12	Hawaii	25.7
34	Indiana	24.0	14	California	25.6
28	Iowa	24.5	14	Maine	25.6
32	Kansas	24.2	16	Pennsylvania	25.5
42	Kentucky	23.8	17	Illinois	25.4
46	Louisiana	23.3	17	Oregon	25.4
14	Maine	25.6	19	Wisconsin	25.3
8	Maryland	26.1	20	Delaware	25.0
1	Massachusetts	27.7	20	Florida	25.0
20	Michigan	25.0	20	Michigan	25.0
10	Minnesota	25.8	23	Nebraska	24.7
50	Mississippi	22.6	23	North Dakota	24.7
33	Missouri	24.1	23	Ohio	24.7
28	Montana	24.5	26	Nevada	24.6
23	Nebraska	24.7	26	North Carolina	24.6
26	Nevada	24.6	28	Georgia	24.5
5	New Hampshire	26.7	28	Iowa	24.5
2	New Jersey	27.2	28	Montana	24.5
48	New Mexico	23.0	31	Alaska	24.3
4	New York	26.8	32	Kansas	24.2
26	North Carolina	24.6	33	Missouri	24.1
23	North Dakota	24.7	34	Arizona	24.0
23	Ohio	24.7	34	Indiana	24.0
47	Oklahoma	23.1	34	South Carolina	24.0
17	Oregon	25.4	34	South Dakota	24.0
16	Pennsylvania	25.5	34	Tennessee	24.0
7	Rhode Island	26.2	39	Texas	23.9
34	South Carolina	24.0	39	Utah	23.9
34	South Dakota	24.0	39	West Virginia	23.9
34	Tennessee	24.0	42	Idaho	23.8
39	Texas	23.9	42	Kentucky	23.8
39	Utah	23.9	44	Wyoming	23.7
6	Vermont	26.5	45	Alabama	23.6
10	Virginia	25.8	46	Louisiana	23.3
9	Washington	25.9	47	Oklahoma	23.1
39	West Virginia	23.9	48	Arkansas	23.0
19	Wisconsin	25.3	48	New Mexico	23.0
44	Wyoming	23.7	50	Mississippi	22.6
				District of Columbia	26.5

Source: U.S. Department of Health and Human Services, National Center for Health Statistics
"Delayed Childbearing" (NCHS Data Brief, No. 21, August 2009, www.cdc.gov/nchs/data/databriefs/db21.pdf)

Births by Vaginal Delivery in 2007

National Total = 2,944,275 Live Births*

ALPHA ORDER

ALPHA ORDER / RANK ORDER

RANK	STATE	BIRTHS	% of USA	RANK	STATE	BIRTHS	% of USA
24	Alabama	42,864	1.5%	1	California	384,553	13.1%
45	Alaska	8,592	0.3%	2	Texas	270,265	9.2%
11	Arizona	76,008	2.6%	3	New York	168,043	5.7%
35	Arkansas	26,978	0.9%	4	Florida	150,182	5.1%
1	California	384,553	13.1%	5	Illinois	126,057	4.3%
20	Colorado	52,537	1.8%	6	Ohio	105,919	3.6%
34	Connecticut	27,248	0.9%	7	Pennsylvania	105,361	3.6%
47	Delaware	8,264	0.3%	8	Georgia	103,374	3.5%
4	Florida	150,182	5.1%	9	North Carolina	90,794	3.1%
8	Georgia	103,374	3.5%	10	Michigan	87,274	3.0%
40	Hawaii	14,085	0.5%	11	Arizona	76,008	2.6%
37	Idaho	19,014	0.6%	12	Virginia	72,401	2.5%
5	Illinois	126,057	4.3%	13	New Jersey	71,609	2.4%
14	Indiana	63,432	2.2%	14	Indiana	63,432	2.2%
32	Iowa	28,865	1.0%	15	Washington	63,160	2.1%
31	Kansas	29,487	1.0%	16	Tennessee	57,834	2.0%
27	Kentucky	38,828	1.3%	17	Missouri	57,104	1.9%
25	Louisiana	42,473	1.4%	18	Wisconsin	54,597	1.9%
41	Maine	9,884	0.3%	19	Minnesota	54,424	1.8%
21	Maryland	52,246	1.8%	20	Colorado	52,537	1.8%
22	Massachusetts	51,845	1.8%	21	Maryland	52,246	1.8%
10	Michigan	87,274	3.0%	22	Massachusetts	51,845	1.8%
19	Minnesota	54,424	1.8%	23	Utah	42,892	1.5%
30	Mississippi	29,668	1.0%	24	Alabama	42,864	1.5%
17	Missouri	57,104	1.9%	25	Louisiana	42,473	1.4%
44	Montana	8,785	0.3%	26	South Carolina	41,885	1.4%
38	Nebraska	18,604	0.6%	27	Kentucky	38,828	1.3%
33	Nevada	27,564	0.9%	28	Oklahoma	36,572	1.2%
42	New Hampshire	9,805	0.3%	29	Oregon	35,449	1.2%
13	New Jersey	71,609	2.4%	30	Mississippi	29,668	1.0%
36	New Mexico	23,436	0.8%	31	Kansas	29,487	1.0%
3	New York	168,043	5.7%	32	Iowa	28,865	1.0%
9	North Carolina	90,794	3.1%	33	Nevada	27,564	0.9%
48	North Dakota	6,329	0.2%	34	Connecticut	27,248	0.9%
6	Ohio	105,919	3.6%	35	Arkansas	26,978	0.9%
28	Oklahoma	36,572	1.2%	36	New Mexico	23,436	0.8%
29	Oregon	35,449	1.2%	37	Idaho	19,014	0.6%
7	Pennsylvania	105,361	3.6%	38	Nebraska	18,604	0.6%
46	Rhode Island	8,390	0.3%	39	West Virginia	14,251	0.5%
26	South Carolina	41,885	1.4%	40	Hawaii	14,085	0.5%
43	South Dakota	8,998	0.3%	41	Maine	9,884	0.3%
16	Tennessee	57,834	2.0%	42	New Hampshire	9,805	0.3%
2	Texas	270,265	9.2%	43	South Dakota	8,998	0.3%
23	Utah	42,892	1.5%	44	Montana	8,785	0.3%
50	Vermont	4,768	0.2%	45	Alaska	8,592	0.3%
12	Virginia	72,401	2.5%	46	Rhode Island	8,390	0.3%
15	Washington	63,160	2.1%	47	Delaware	8,264	0.3%
39	West Virginia	14,251	0.5%	48	North Dakota	6,329	0.2%
18	Wisconsin	54,597	1.9%	49	Wyoming	5,770	0.2%
49	Wyoming	5,770	0.2%	50	Vermont	4,768	0.2%
					District of Columbia	5,973	0.2%

Source: CQ Press using data from U.S. Department of Health and Human Services, National Center for Health Statistics
"National Vital Statistics Reports" (Vol. 57, No. 12, March 18, 2009, http://www.cdc.gov/nchs/births.htm)
*Estimates by state of residence.

Percent of Births by Vaginal Delivery in 2007

National Percent = 68.2% of Live Births*

<table>
<tr><td colspan="3">ALPHA ORDER</td><td colspan="3">RANK ORDER</td></tr>
<tr><td>RANK</td><td>STATE</td><td>PERCENT</td><td>RANK</td><td>STATE</td><td>PERCENT</td></tr>
<tr><td>42</td><td>Alabama</td><td>66.2</td><td>1</td><td>Utah</td><td>77.8</td></tr>
<tr><td>2</td><td>Alaska</td><td>77.4</td><td>2</td><td>Alaska</td><td>77.4</td></tr>
<tr><td>7</td><td>Arizona</td><td>73.8</td><td>3</td><td>New Mexico</td><td>76.7</td></tr>
<tr><td>45</td><td>Arkansas</td><td>65.2</td><td>4</td><td>Idaho</td><td>76.0</td></tr>
<tr><td>30</td><td>California</td><td>67.9</td><td>5</td><td>Wisconsin</td><td>75.0</td></tr>
<tr><td>6</td><td>Colorado</td><td>74.2</td><td>6</td><td>Colorado</td><td>74.2</td></tr>
<tr><td>43</td><td>Connecticut</td><td>65.4</td><td>7</td><td>Arizona</td><td>73.8</td></tr>
<tr><td>30</td><td>Delaware</td><td>67.9</td><td>7</td><td>Minnesota</td><td>73.8</td></tr>
<tr><td>49</td><td>Florida</td><td>62.8</td><td>9</td><td>Hawaii</td><td>73.6</td></tr>
<tr><td>29</td><td>Georgia</td><td>68.0</td><td>10</td><td>South Dakota</td><td>73.4</td></tr>
<tr><td>9</td><td>Hawaii</td><td>73.6</td><td>11</td><td>Vermont</td><td>73.2</td></tr>
<tr><td>4</td><td>Idaho</td><td>76.0</td><td>12</td><td>Wyoming</td><td>73.1</td></tr>
<tr><td>23</td><td>Illinois</td><td>69.7</td><td>13</td><td>Oregon</td><td>71.8</td></tr>
<tr><td>16</td><td>Indiana</td><td>70.6</td><td>14</td><td>North Dakota</td><td>71.6</td></tr>
<tr><td>16</td><td>Iowa</td><td>70.6</td><td>15</td><td>Washington</td><td>71.0</td></tr>
<tr><td>19</td><td>Kansas</td><td>70.2</td><td>16</td><td>Indiana</td><td>70.6</td></tr>
<tr><td>43</td><td>Kentucky</td><td>65.4</td><td>16</td><td>Iowa</td><td>70.6</td></tr>
<tr><td>47</td><td>Louisiana</td><td>64.1</td><td>16</td><td>Montana</td><td>70.6</td></tr>
<tr><td>21</td><td>Maine</td><td>70.0</td><td>19</td><td>Kansas</td><td>70.2</td></tr>
<tr><td>33</td><td>Maryland</td><td>66.9</td><td>19</td><td>Ohio</td><td>70.2</td></tr>
<tr><td>37</td><td>Massachusetts</td><td>66.5</td><td>21</td><td>Maine</td><td>70.0</td></tr>
<tr><td>25</td><td>Michigan</td><td>69.6</td><td>22</td><td>Pennsylvania</td><td>69.9</td></tr>
<tr><td>7</td><td>Minnesota</td><td>73.8</td><td>23</td><td>Illinois</td><td>69.7</td></tr>
<tr><td>48</td><td>Mississippi</td><td>63.8</td><td>23</td><td>Missouri</td><td>69.7</td></tr>
<tr><td>23</td><td>Missouri</td><td>69.7</td><td>25</td><td>Michigan</td><td>69.6</td></tr>
<tr><td>16</td><td>Montana</td><td>70.6</td><td>26</td><td>North Carolina</td><td>69.3</td></tr>
<tr><td>28</td><td>Nebraska</td><td>69.1</td><td>27</td><td>New Hampshire</td><td>69.2</td></tr>
<tr><td>33</td><td>Nevada</td><td>66.9</td><td>28</td><td>Nebraska</td><td>69.1</td></tr>
<tr><td>27</td><td>New Hampshire</td><td>69.2</td><td>29</td><td>Georgia</td><td>68.0</td></tr>
<tr><td>50</td><td>New Jersey</td><td>61.7</td><td>30</td><td>California</td><td>67.9</td></tr>
<tr><td>3</td><td>New Mexico</td><td>76.7</td><td>30</td><td>Delaware</td><td>67.9</td></tr>
<tr><td>40</td><td>New York</td><td>66.3</td><td>32</td><td>Rhode Island</td><td>67.8</td></tr>
<tr><td>26</td><td>North Carolina</td><td>69.3</td><td>33</td><td>Maryland</td><td>66.9</td></tr>
<tr><td>14</td><td>North Dakota</td><td>71.6</td><td>33</td><td>Nevada</td><td>66.9</td></tr>
<tr><td>19</td><td>Ohio</td><td>70.2</td><td>35</td><td>Tennessee</td><td>66.7</td></tr>
<tr><td>39</td><td>Oklahoma</td><td>66.4</td><td>36</td><td>South Carolina</td><td>66.6</td></tr>
<tr><td>13</td><td>Oregon</td><td>71.8</td><td>37</td><td>Massachusetts</td><td>66.5</td></tr>
<tr><td>22</td><td>Pennsylvania</td><td>69.9</td><td>37</td><td>Virginia</td><td>66.5</td></tr>
<tr><td>32</td><td>Rhode Island</td><td>67.8</td><td>39</td><td>Oklahoma</td><td>66.4</td></tr>
<tr><td>36</td><td>South Carolina</td><td>66.6</td><td>40</td><td>New York</td><td>66.3</td></tr>
<tr><td>10</td><td>South Dakota</td><td>73.4</td><td>40</td><td>Texas</td><td>66.3</td></tr>
<tr><td>35</td><td>Tennessee</td><td>66.7</td><td>42</td><td>Alabama</td><td>66.2</td></tr>
<tr><td>40</td><td>Texas</td><td>66.3</td><td>43</td><td>Connecticut</td><td>65.4</td></tr>
<tr><td>1</td><td>Utah</td><td>77.8</td><td>43</td><td>Kentucky</td><td>65.4</td></tr>
<tr><td>11</td><td>Vermont</td><td>73.2</td><td>45</td><td>Arkansas</td><td>65.2</td></tr>
<tr><td>37</td><td>Virginia</td><td>66.5</td><td>46</td><td>West Virginia</td><td>64.8</td></tr>
<tr><td>15</td><td>Washington</td><td>71.0</td><td>47</td><td>Louisiana</td><td>64.1</td></tr>
<tr><td>46</td><td>West Virginia</td><td>64.8</td><td>48</td><td>Mississippi</td><td>63.8</td></tr>
<tr><td>5</td><td>Wisconsin</td><td>75.0</td><td>49</td><td>Florida</td><td>62.8</td></tr>
<tr><td>12</td><td>Wyoming</td><td>73.1</td><td>50</td><td>New Jersey</td><td>61.7</td></tr>
<tr><td></td><td></td><td></td><td></td><td>District of Columbia</td><td>67.4</td></tr>
</table>

Source: CQ Press using data from U.S. Department of Health and Human Services, National Center for Health Statistics
"National Vital Statistics Reports" (Vol. 57, No. 12, March 18, 2009, http://www.cdc.gov/nchs/births.htm)
*Estimates by state of residence.

Births by Cesarean Delivery in 2007

National Total = 1,372,844 Live Cesarean Births*

<table>
<tr><td colspan="4">ALPHA ORDER</td><td colspan="4">RANK ORDER</td></tr>
<tr><th>RANK</th><th>STATE</th><th>BIRTHS</th><th>% of USA</th><th>RANK</th><th>STATE</th><th>BIRTHS</th><th>% of USA</th></tr>
<tr><td>21</td><td>Alabama</td><td>21,885</td><td>1.6%</td><td>1</td><td>California</td><td>181,799</td><td>13.2%</td></tr>
<tr><td>48</td><td>Alaska</td><td>2,509</td><td>0.2%</td><td>2</td><td>Texas</td><td>137,375</td><td>10.0%</td></tr>
<tr><td>14</td><td>Arizona</td><td>26,984</td><td>2.0%</td><td>3</td><td>Florida</td><td>88,961</td><td>6.5%</td></tr>
<tr><td>30</td><td>Arkansas</td><td>14,399</td><td>1.0%</td><td>4</td><td>New York</td><td>85,415</td><td>6.2%</td></tr>
<tr><td>1</td><td>California</td><td>181,799</td><td>13.2%</td><td>5</td><td>Illinois</td><td>54,799</td><td>4.0%</td></tr>
<tr><td>26</td><td>Colorado</td><td>18,268</td><td>1.3%</td><td>6</td><td>Georgia</td><td>48,647</td><td>3.5%</td></tr>
<tr><td>29</td><td>Connecticut</td><td>14,415</td><td>1.1%</td><td>7</td><td>Pennsylvania</td><td>45,370</td><td>3.3%</td></tr>
<tr><td>44</td><td>Delaware</td><td>3,907</td><td>0.3%</td><td>8</td><td>Ohio</td><td>44,963</td><td>3.3%</td></tr>
<tr><td>3</td><td>Florida</td><td>88,961</td><td>6.5%</td><td>9</td><td>New Jersey</td><td>44,451</td><td>3.2%</td></tr>
<tr><td>6</td><td>Georgia</td><td>48,647</td><td>3.5%</td><td>10</td><td>North Carolina</td><td>40,222</td><td>2.9%</td></tr>
<tr><td>40</td><td>Hawaii</td><td>5,052</td><td>0.4%</td><td>11</td><td>Michigan</td><td>38,120</td><td>2.8%</td></tr>
<tr><td>39</td><td>Idaho</td><td>6,005</td><td>0.4%</td><td>12</td><td>Virginia</td><td>36,473</td><td>2.7%</td></tr>
<tr><td>5</td><td>Illinois</td><td>54,799</td><td>4.0%</td><td>13</td><td>Tennessee</td><td>28,873</td><td>2.1%</td></tr>
<tr><td>15</td><td>Indiana</td><td>26,415</td><td>1.9%</td><td>14</td><td>Arizona</td><td>26,984</td><td>2.0%</td></tr>
<tr><td>35</td><td>Iowa</td><td>12,020</td><td>0.9%</td><td>15</td><td>Indiana</td><td>26,415</td><td>1.9%</td></tr>
<tr><td>33</td><td>Kansas</td><td>12,517</td><td>0.9%</td><td>16</td><td>Massachusetts</td><td>26,117</td><td>1.9%</td></tr>
<tr><td>23</td><td>Kentucky</td><td>20,542</td><td>1.5%</td><td>17</td><td>Maryland</td><td>25,850</td><td>1.9%</td></tr>
<tr><td>20</td><td>Louisiana</td><td>23,787</td><td>1.7%</td><td>18</td><td>Washington</td><td>25,798</td><td>1.9%</td></tr>
<tr><td>42</td><td>Maine</td><td>4,236</td><td>0.3%</td><td>19</td><td>Missouri</td><td>24,824</td><td>1.8%</td></tr>
<tr><td>17</td><td>Maryland</td><td>25,850</td><td>1.9%</td><td>20</td><td>Louisiana</td><td>23,787</td><td>1.7%</td></tr>
<tr><td>16</td><td>Massachusetts</td><td>26,117</td><td>1.9%</td><td>21</td><td>Alabama</td><td>21,885</td><td>1.6%</td></tr>
<tr><td>11</td><td>Michigan</td><td>38,120</td><td>2.8%</td><td>22</td><td>South Carolina</td><td>21,006</td><td>1.5%</td></tr>
<tr><td>24</td><td>Minnesota</td><td>19,321</td><td>1.4%</td><td>23</td><td>Kentucky</td><td>20,542</td><td>1.5%</td></tr>
<tr><td>28</td><td>Mississippi</td><td>16,833</td><td>1.2%</td><td>24</td><td>Minnesota</td><td>19,321</td><td>1.4%</td></tr>
<tr><td>19</td><td>Missouri</td><td>24,824</td><td>1.8%</td><td>25</td><td>Oklahoma</td><td>18,506</td><td>1.3%</td></tr>
<tr><td>45</td><td>Montana</td><td>3,659</td><td>0.3%</td><td>26</td><td>Colorado</td><td>18,268</td><td>1.3%</td></tr>
<tr><td>36</td><td>Nebraska</td><td>8,319</td><td>0.6%</td><td>27</td><td>Wisconsin</td><td>18,199</td><td>1.3%</td></tr>
<tr><td>32</td><td>Nevada</td><td>13,638</td><td>1.0%</td><td>28</td><td>Mississippi</td><td>16,833</td><td>1.2%</td></tr>
<tr><td>41</td><td>New Hampshire</td><td>4,364</td><td>0.3%</td><td>29</td><td>Connecticut</td><td>14,415</td><td>1.1%</td></tr>
<tr><td>9</td><td>New Jersey</td><td>44,451</td><td>3.2%</td><td>30</td><td>Arkansas</td><td>14,399</td><td>1.0%</td></tr>
<tr><td>38</td><td>New Mexico</td><td>7,119</td><td>0.5%</td><td>31</td><td>Oregon</td><td>13,923</td><td>1.0%</td></tr>
<tr><td>4</td><td>New York</td><td>85,415</td><td>6.2%</td><td>32</td><td>Nevada</td><td>13,638</td><td>1.0%</td></tr>
<tr><td>10</td><td>North Carolina</td><td>40,222</td><td>2.9%</td><td>33</td><td>Kansas</td><td>12,517</td><td>0.9%</td></tr>
<tr><td>47</td><td>North Dakota</td><td>2,511</td><td>0.2%</td><td>34</td><td>Utah</td><td>12,239</td><td>0.9%</td></tr>
<tr><td>8</td><td>Ohio</td><td>44,963</td><td>3.3%</td><td>35</td><td>Iowa</td><td>12,020</td><td>0.9%</td></tr>
<tr><td>25</td><td>Oklahoma</td><td>18,506</td><td>1.3%</td><td>36</td><td>Nebraska</td><td>8,319</td><td>0.6%</td></tr>
<tr><td>31</td><td>Oregon</td><td>13,923</td><td>1.0%</td><td>37</td><td>West Virginia</td><td>7,741</td><td>0.6%</td></tr>
<tr><td>7</td><td>Pennsylvania</td><td>45,370</td><td>3.3%</td><td>38</td><td>New Mexico</td><td>7,119</td><td>0.5%</td></tr>
<tr><td>43</td><td>Rhode Island</td><td>3,985</td><td>0.3%</td><td>39</td><td>Idaho</td><td>6,005</td><td>0.4%</td></tr>
<tr><td>22</td><td>South Carolina</td><td>21,006</td><td>1.5%</td><td>40</td><td>Hawaii</td><td>5,052</td><td>0.4%</td></tr>
<tr><td>46</td><td>South Dakota</td><td>3,261</td><td>0.2%</td><td>41</td><td>New Hampshire</td><td>4,364</td><td>0.3%</td></tr>
<tr><td>13</td><td>Tennessee</td><td>28,873</td><td>2.1%</td><td>42</td><td>Maine</td><td>4,236</td><td>0.3%</td></tr>
<tr><td>2</td><td>Texas</td><td>137,375</td><td>10.0%</td><td>43</td><td>Rhode Island</td><td>3,985</td><td>0.3%</td></tr>
<tr><td>34</td><td>Utah</td><td>12,239</td><td>0.9%</td><td>44</td><td>Delaware</td><td>3,907</td><td>0.3%</td></tr>
<tr><td>50</td><td>Vermont</td><td>1,745</td><td>0.1%</td><td>45</td><td>Montana</td><td>3,659</td><td>0.3%</td></tr>
<tr><td>12</td><td>Virginia</td><td>36,473</td><td>2.7%</td><td>46</td><td>South Dakota</td><td>3,261</td><td>0.2%</td></tr>
<tr><td>18</td><td>Washington</td><td>25,798</td><td>1.9%</td><td>47</td><td>North Dakota</td><td>2,511</td><td>0.2%</td></tr>
<tr><td>37</td><td>West Virginia</td><td>7,741</td><td>0.6%</td><td>48</td><td>Alaska</td><td>2,509</td><td>0.2%</td></tr>
<tr><td>27</td><td>Wisconsin</td><td>18,199</td><td>1.3%</td><td>49</td><td>Wyoming</td><td>2,123</td><td>0.2%</td></tr>
<tr><td>49</td><td>Wyoming</td><td>2,123</td><td>0.2%</td><td>50</td><td>Vermont</td><td>1,745</td><td>0.1%</td></tr>
<tr><td></td><td></td><td></td><td></td><td></td><td>District of Columbia</td><td>2,889</td><td>0.2%</td></tr>
</table>

Source: CQ Press using data from U.S. Department of Health and Human Services, National Center for Health Statistics
"National Vital Statistics Reports" (Vol. 57, No. 12, March 18, 2009, http://www.cdc.gov/nchs/births.htm)
*Estimates by state of residence.

Percent of Births by Cesarean Delivery in 2007

National Percent = 31.8% of Live Births*

ALPHA ORDER

RANK	STATE	PERCENT
9	Alabama	33.8
49	Alaska	22.6
43	Arizona	26.2
6	Arkansas	34.8
20	California	32.1
45	Colorado	25.8
7	Connecticut	34.6
20	Delaware	32.1
2	Florida	37.2
22	Georgia	32.0
42	Hawaii	26.4
47	Idaho	24.0
27	Illinois	30.3
33	Indiana	29.4
33	Iowa	29.4
31	Kansas	29.8
7	Kentucky	34.6
4	Louisiana	35.9
30	Maine	30.0
17	Maryland	33.1
13	Massachusetts	33.5
26	Michigan	30.4
43	Minnesota	26.2
3	Mississippi	36.2
27	Missouri	30.3
33	Montana	29.4
23	Nebraska	30.9
17	Nevada	33.1
24	New Hampshire	30.8
1	New Jersey	38.3
48	New Mexico	23.3
10	New York	33.7
25	North Carolina	30.7
37	North Dakota	28.4
31	Ohio	29.8
12	Oklahoma	33.6
38	Oregon	28.2
29	Pennsylvania	30.1
19	Rhode Island	32.2
15	South Carolina	33.4
41	South Dakota	26.6
16	Tennessee	33.3
10	Texas	33.7
50	Utah	22.2
40	Vermont	26.8
13	Virginia	33.5
36	Washington	29.0
5	West Virginia	35.2
46	Wisconsin	25.0
39	Wyoming	26.9

RANK ORDER

RANK	STATE	PERCENT
1	New Jersey	38.3
2	Florida	37.2
3	Mississippi	36.2
4	Louisiana	35.9
5	West Virginia	35.2
6	Arkansas	34.8
7	Connecticut	34.6
7	Kentucky	34.6
9	Alabama	33.8
10	New York	33.7
10	Texas	33.7
12	Oklahoma	33.6
13	Massachusetts	33.5
13	Virginia	33.5
15	South Carolina	33.4
16	Tennessee	33.3
17	Maryland	33.1
17	Nevada	33.1
19	Rhode Island	32.2
20	California	32.1
20	Delaware	32.1
22	Georgia	32.0
23	Nebraska	30.9
24	New Hampshire	30.8
25	North Carolina	30.7
26	Michigan	30.4
27	Illinois	30.3
27	Missouri	30.3
29	Pennsylvania	30.1
30	Maine	30.0
31	Kansas	29.8
31	Ohio	29.8
33	Indiana	29.4
33	Iowa	29.4
33	Montana	29.4
36	Washington	29.0
37	North Dakota	28.4
38	Oregon	28.2
39	Wyoming	26.9
40	Vermont	26.8
41	South Dakota	26.6
42	Hawaii	26.4
43	Arizona	26.2
43	Minnesota	26.2
45	Colorado	25.8
46	Wisconsin	25.0
47	Idaho	24.0
48	New Mexico	23.3
49	Alaska	22.6
50	Utah	22.2

	District of Columbia	32.6

Source: U.S. Department of Health and Human Services, National Center for Health Statistics
"National Vital Statistics Reports" (Vol. 57, No. 12, March 18, 2009, http://www.cdc.gov/nchs/births.htm)
*Preliminary data by state of residence.

Percent Change in Rate of Cesarean Births: 2003 to 2007

National Percent Change = 15.2% Increase*

ALPHA ORDER

RANK	STATE	PERCENT
29	Alabama	14.2
48	Alaska	6.1
10	Arizona	18.0
10	Arkansas	18.0
23	California	15.1
16	Colorado	16.2
1	Connecticut	27.2
46	Delaware	10.7
3	Florida	20.8
13	Georgia	17.2
4	Hawaii	20.0
34	Idaho	13.2
12	Illinois	17.9
25	Indiana	14.8
19	Iowa	15.7
37	Kansas	12.5
24	Kentucky	15.0
34	Louisiana	13.2
31	Maine	14.1
18	Maryland	16.1
27	Massachusetts	14.3
22	Michigan	15.2
39	Minnesota	12.4
40	Mississippi	12.1
45	Missouri	11.0
2	Montana	24.1
42	Nebraska	11.6
5	Nevada	19.9
16	New Hampshire	16.2
19	New Jersey	15.7
25	New Mexico	14.8
6	New York	18.7
41	North Carolina	12.0
14	North Dakota	16.9
6	Ohio	18.7
27	Oklahoma	14.3
33	Oregon	13.3
47	Pennsylvania	7.9
32	Rhode Island	13.8
37	South Carolina	12.5
50	South Dakota	4.7
15	Tennessee	16.4
42	Texas	11.6
21	Utah	15.6
8	Vermont	18.6
9	Virginia	18.4
49	Washington	5.8
44	West Virginia	11.4
29	Wisconsin	14.2
36	Wyoming	13.0

RANK ORDER

RANK	STATE	PERCENT
1	Connecticut	27.2
2	Montana	24.1
3	Florida	20.8
4	Hawaii	20.0
5	Nevada	19.9
6	New York	18.7
6	Ohio	18.7
8	Vermont	18.6
9	Virginia	18.4
10	Arizona	18.0
10	Arkansas	18.0
12	Illinois	17.9
13	Georgia	17.2
14	North Dakota	16.9
15	Tennessee	16.4
16	Colorado	16.2
16	New Hampshire	16.2
18	Maryland	16.1
19	Iowa	15.7
19	New Jersey	15.7
21	Utah	15.6
22	Michigan	15.2
23	California	15.1
24	Kentucky	15.0
25	Indiana	14.8
25	New Mexico	14.8
27	Massachusetts	14.3
27	Oklahoma	14.3
29	Alabama	14.2
29	Wisconsin	14.2
31	Maine	14.1
32	Rhode Island	13.8
33	Oregon	13.3
34	Idaho	13.2
34	Louisiana	13.2
36	Wyoming	13.0
37	Kansas	12.5
37	South Carolina	12.5
39	Minnesota	12.4
40	Mississippi	12.1
41	North Carolina	12.0
42	Nebraska	11.6
42	Texas	11.6
44	West Virginia	11.4
45	Missouri	11.0
46	Delaware	10.7
47	Pennsylvania	7.9
48	Alaska	6.1
49	Washington	5.8
50	South Dakota	4.7

District of Columbia	19.0

Source: CQ Press using data from U.S. Department of Health and Human Services, National Center for Health Statistics
    "National Vital Statistics Reports" (Vol. 57, No. 12, March 18, 2009, http://www.cdc.gov/nchs/births.htm)
*Estimates by state of residence.

Percent of Births That Are Pre-Term in 2007

National Percent = 12.7% of Births*

ALPHA ORDER			RANK ORDER		
RANK	STATE	PERCENT	RANK	STATE	PERCENT
2	Alabama	16.6	1	Mississippi	18.3
46	Alaska	10.4	2	Alabama	16.6
21	Arizona	12.7	3	Louisiana	16.5
9	Arkansas	13.9	4	South Carolina	15.5
40	California	10.9	5	Kentucky	15.2
28	Colorado	12.2	6	Delaware	14.3
44	Connecticut	10.5	6	Nevada	14.3
6	Delaware	14.3	8	Tennessee	14.2
11	Florida	13.8	9	Arkansas	13.9
12	Georgia	13.6	9	West Virginia	13.9
26	Hawaii	12.4	11	Florida	13.8
44	Idaho	10.5	12	Georgia	13.6
18	Illinois	13.1	12	Texas	13.6
19	Indiana	12.9	14	Oklahoma	13.5
35	Iowa	11.6	15	Maryland	13.4
37	Kansas	11.5	16	North Carolina	13.3
5	Kentucky	15.2	17	Ohio	13.2
3	Louisiana	16.5	18	Illinois	13.1
42	Maine	10.6	19	Indiana	12.9
15	Maryland	13.4	20	New Mexico	12.8
38	Massachusetts	11.2	21	Arizona	12.7
28	Michigan	12.2	21	New Jersey	12.7
46	Minnesota	10.4	21	Wyoming	12.7
1	Mississippi	18.3	24	South Dakota	12.6
25	Missouri	12.5	25	Missouri	12.5
32	Montana	11.9	26	Hawaii	12.4
32	Nebraska	11.9	27	New York	12.3
6	Nevada	14.3	28	Colorado	12.2
49	New Hampshire	9.4	28	Michigan	12.2
21	New Jersey	12.7	30	Virginia	12.1
20	New Mexico	12.8	31	Rhode Island	12.0
27	New York	12.3	32	Montana	11.9
16	North Carolina	13.3	32	Nebraska	11.9
35	North Dakota	11.6	34	Pennsylvania	11.8
17	Ohio	13.2	35	Iowa	11.6
14	Oklahoma	13.5	35	North Dakota	11.6
48	Oregon	10.3	37	Kansas	11.5
34	Pennsylvania	11.8	38	Massachusetts	11.2
31	Rhode Island	12.0	39	Wisconsin	11.1
4	South Carolina	15.5	40	California	10.9
24	South Dakota	12.6	40	Utah	10.9
8	Tennessee	14.2	42	Maine	10.6
12	Texas	13.6	42	Washington	10.6
40	Utah	10.9	44	Connecticut	10.5
50	Vermont	9.2	44	Idaho	10.5
30	Virginia	12.1	46	Alaska	10.4
42	Washington	10.6	46	Minnesota	10.4
9	West Virginia	13.9	48	Oregon	10.3
39	Wisconsin	11.1	49	New Hampshire	9.4
21	Wyoming	12.7	50	Vermont	9.2
				District of Columbia	15.6

Source: U.S. Department of Health and Human Services, National Center for Health Statistics
   "National Vital Statistics Reports" (Vol. 57, No. 12, March 18, 2009, http://www.cdc.gov/nchs/births.htm)
*Preliminary data by state of residence. Births before 37 weeks of gestation.

Assisted Reproductive Technology Procedures in 2006

National Total = 136,181 Procedures*

ALPHA ORDER

RANK	STATE	PROCEDURES	% of USA
30	Alabama	868	0.6%
47	Alaska	189	0.1%
17	Arizona	2,313	1.7%
40	Arkansas	415	0.3%
1	California	18,886	13.9%
21	Colorado	1,706	1.3%
12	Connecticut	3,341	2.5%
41	Delaware	301	0.2%
6	Florida	6,389	4.7%
14	Georgia	2,991	2.2%
37	Hawaii	570	0.4%
38	Idaho	506	0.4%
3	Illinois	9,594	7.0%
19	Indiana	1,844	1.4%
28	Iowa	899	0.7%
34	Kansas	704	0.5%
27	Kentucky	948	0.7%
29	Louisiana	891	0.7%
44	Maine	221	0.2%
8	Maryland	4,677	3.4%
5	Massachusetts	8,305	6.1%
13	Michigan	3,264	2.4%
18	Minnesota	2,008	1.5%
39	Mississippi	438	0.3%
20	Missouri	1,842	1.4%
49	Montana	176	0.1%
36	Nebraska	582	0.4%
23	Nevada	1,254	0.9%
32	New Hampshire	796	0.6%
4	New Jersey	9,237	6.8%
42	New Mexico	288	0.2%
2	New York	17,687	13.0%
15	North Carolina	2,608	1.9%
45	North Dakota	216	0.2%
11	Ohio	3,344	2.5%
35	Oklahoma	627	0.5%
24	Oregon	1,148	0.8%
9	Pennsylvania	4,611	3.4%
33	Rhode Island	760	0.6%
26	South Carolina	990	0.7%
46	South Dakota	197	0.1%
25	Tennessee	1,090	0.8%
7	Texas	6,181	4.5%
31	Utah	831	0.6%
48	Vermont	180	0.1%
10	Virginia	4,367	3.2%
16	Washington	2,382	1.7%
43	West Virginia	261	0.2%
22	Wisconsin	1,483	1.1%
50	Wyoming	63	0.0%

RANK ORDER

RANK	STATE	PROCEDURES	% of USA
1	California	18,886	13.9%
2	New York	17,687	13.0%
3	Illinois	9,594	7.0%
4	New Jersey	9,237	6.8%
5	Massachusetts	8,305	6.1%
6	Florida	6,389	4.7%
7	Texas	6,181	4.5%
8	Maryland	4,677	3.4%
9	Pennsylvania	4,611	3.4%
10	Virginia	4,367	3.2%
11	Ohio	3,344	2.5%
12	Connecticut	3,341	2.5%
13	Michigan	3,264	2.4%
14	Georgia	2,991	2.2%
15	North Carolina	2,608	1.9%
16	Washington	2,382	1.7%
17	Arizona	2,313	1.7%
18	Minnesota	2,008	1.5%
19	Indiana	1,844	1.4%
20	Missouri	1,842	1.4%
21	Colorado	1,706	1.3%
22	Wisconsin	1,483	1.1%
23	Nevada	1,254	0.9%
24	Oregon	1,148	0.8%
25	Tennessee	1,090	0.8%
26	South Carolina	990	0.7%
27	Kentucky	948	0.7%
28	Iowa	899	0.7%
29	Louisiana	891	0.7%
30	Alabama	868	0.6%
31	Utah	831	0.6%
32	New Hampshire	796	0.6%
33	Rhode Island	760	0.6%
34	Kansas	704	0.5%
35	Oklahoma	627	0.5%
36	Nebraska	582	0.4%
37	Hawaii	570	0.4%
38	Idaho	506	0.4%
39	Mississippi	438	0.3%
40	Arkansas	415	0.3%
41	Delaware	301	0.2%
42	New Mexico	288	0.2%
43	West Virginia	261	0.2%
44	Maine	221	0.2%
45	North Dakota	216	0.2%
46	South Dakota	197	0.1%
47	Alaska	189	0.1%
48	Vermont	180	0.1%
49	Montana	176	0.1%
50	Wyoming	63	0.0%
	District of Columbia	712	0.5%

Source: U.S. Department of Health and Human Services, Centers for Disease Control and Prevention
   "Assisted Reproductive Technology, 2006" (MMWR, Vol. 58, No. SS-5, 06/12/09, http://www.cdc.gov/mmwr/mmwr_ss.html)
*By patient's residence. Does not include 2,002 procedures for patients with residences outside the U.S. Assisted reproductive technology (ART) includes treatments in which both eggs and sperm are handled in the laboratory. In 2006, 72% of ART treatments were freshly fertilized embryos using the patient's eggs, 16% were thawed embryos using the patient's eggs, 8% were freshly fertilized embryos from donor eggs, and 4% were thawed embryos from donor eggs.

Infants Born from Assisted Reproductive Technology Procedures in 2006

National Total = 53,768 Live Births*

ALPHA ORDER					RANK ORDER			
RANK	STATE	BIRTHS	% of USA		RANK	STATE	BIRTHS	% of USA
30	Alabama	369	0.7%		1	California	7,288	13.6%
49	Alaska	73	0.1%		2	New York	5,802	10.8%
19	Arizona	890	1.7%		3	New Jersey	3,622	6.7%
38	Arkansas	203	0.4%		4	Illinois	3,297	6.1%
1	California	7,288	13.6%		5	Texas	2,996	5.6%
17	Colorado	1,025	1.9%		6	Massachusetts	2,965	5.5%
14	Connecticut	1,303	2.4%		7	Florida	2,505	4.7%
42	Delaware	138	0.3%		8	Maryland	1,798	3.3%
7	Florida	2,505	4.7%		9	Virginia	1,675	3.1%
13	Georgia	1,317	2.4%		10	Pennsylvania	1,643	3.1%
39	Hawaii	198	0.4%		11	Michigan	1,390	2.6%
37	Idaho	232	0.4%		12	Ohio	1,373	2.6%
4	Illinois	3,297	6.1%		13	Georgia	1,317	2.4%
21	Indiana	630	1.2%		14	Connecticut	1,303	2.4%
27	Iowa	437	0.8%		15	North Carolina	1,179	2.2%
34	Kansas	295	0.5%		16	Washington	1,082	2.0%
28	Kentucky	425	0.8%		17	Colorado	1,025	1.9%
31	Louisiana	343	0.6%		18	Minnesota	947	1.8%
43	Maine	128	0.2%		19	Arizona	890	1.7%
8	Maryland	1,798	3.3%		20	Missouri	795	1.5%
6	Massachusetts	2,965	5.5%		21	Indiana	630	1.2%
11	Michigan	1,390	2.6%		22	Nevada	563	1.0%
18	Minnesota	947	1.8%		23	Oregon	558	1.0%
40	Mississippi	178	0.3%		24	Wisconsin	557	1.0%
20	Missouri	795	1.5%		25	Tennessee	519	1.0%
44	Montana	109	0.2%		26	South Carolina	516	1.0%
36	Nebraska	243	0.5%		27	Iowa	437	0.8%
22	Nevada	563	1.0%		28	Kentucky	425	0.8%
33	New Hampshire	304	0.6%		29	Utah	416	0.8%
3	New Jersey	3,622	6.7%		30	Alabama	369	0.7%
41	New Mexico	163	0.3%		31	Louisiana	343	0.6%
2	New York	5,802	10.8%		32	Oklahoma	321	0.6%
15	North Carolina	1,179	2.2%		33	New Hampshire	304	0.6%
46	North Dakota	91	0.2%		34	Kansas	295	0.5%
12	Ohio	1,373	2.6%		35	Rhode Island	272	0.5%
32	Oklahoma	321	0.6%		36	Nebraska	243	0.5%
23	Oregon	558	1.0%		37	Idaho	232	0.4%
10	Pennsylvania	1,643	3.1%		38	Arkansas	203	0.4%
35	Rhode Island	272	0.5%		39	Hawaii	198	0.4%
26	South Carolina	516	1.0%		40	Mississippi	178	0.3%
47	South Dakota	85	0.2%		41	New Mexico	163	0.3%
25	Tennessee	519	1.0%		42	Delaware	138	0.3%
5	Texas	2,996	5.6%		43	Maine	128	0.2%
29	Utah	416	0.8%		44	Montana	109	0.2%
48	Vermont	76	0.1%		45	West Virginia	107	0.2%
9	Virginia	1,675	3.1%		46	North Dakota	91	0.2%
16	Washington	1,082	2.0%		47	South Dakota	85	0.2%
45	West Virginia	107	0.2%		48	Vermont	76	0.1%
24	Wisconsin	557	1.0%		49	Alaska	73	0.1%
50	Wyoming	39	0.1%		50	Wyoming	39	0.1%
						District of Columbia	288	0.5%

Source: U.S. Department of Health and Human Services, Centers for Disease Control and Prevention
"Assisted Reproductive Technology, 2006" (MMWR, Vol. 58, No. SS-5, 06/12/09, http://www.cdc.gov/mmwr/mmwr_ss.html)
*By patient's residence. Does not include 879 births for patients with residences outside the U.S. Assisted reproductive technology (ART) includes treatments in which both eggs and sperm are handled in the laboratory. In 2006, 72% of ART treatments were freshly fertilized embryos using the patient's eggs, 16% were thawed embryos using the patient's eggs, 8% were freshly fertilized embryos from donor eggs, and 4% were thawed embryos from donor eggs.

Percent of Assisted Reproductive Technology Procedures That Resulted in Live Births in 2006
National Percent = 29.9%*

ALPHA ORDER

RANK	STATE	PERCENT
24	Alabama	32.3
40	Alaska	29.1
38	Arizona	29.2
17	Arkansas	34.0
41	California	28.9
2	Colorado	44.3
32	Connecticut	30.6
13	Delaware	35.2
36	Florida	29.4
19	Georgia	33.1
49	Hawaii	25.4
15	Idaho	34.4
47	Illinois	26.3
48	Indiana	25.5
8	Iowa	38.0
21	Kansas	32.7
19	Kentucky	33.1
46	Louisiana	27.6
5	Maine	38.9
34	Maryland	29.7
43	Massachusetts	28.3
28	Michigan	31.5
10	Minnesota	36.4
29	Mississippi	31.1
26	Missouri	32.0
1	Montana	46.0
30	Nebraska	30.9
21	Nevada	32.7
35	New Hampshire	29.6
38	New Jersey	29.2
4	New Mexico	39.6
49	New York	25.4
16	North Carolina	34.1
33	North Dakota	30.1
31	Ohio	30.8
6	Oklahoma	38.8
14	Oregon	35.1
44	Pennsylvania	27.8
44	Rhode Island	27.8
7	South Carolina	38.4
23	South Dakota	32.5
12	Tennessee	35.4
11	Texas	35.5
9	Utah	37.2
25	Vermont	32.2
36	Virginia	29.4
17	Washington	34.0
27	West Virginia	31.8
41	Wisconsin	28.9
3	Wyoming	41.3

RANK ORDER

RANK	STATE	PERCENT
1	Montana	46.0
2	Colorado	44.3
3	Wyoming	41.3
4	New Mexico	39.6
5	Maine	38.9
6	Oklahoma	38.8
7	South Carolina	38.4
8	Iowa	38.0
9	Utah	37.2
10	Minnesota	36.4
11	Texas	35.5
12	Tennessee	35.4
13	Delaware	35.2
14	Oregon	35.1
15	Idaho	34.4
16	North Carolina	34.1
17	Arkansas	34.0
17	Washington	34.0
19	Georgia	33.1
19	Kentucky	33.1
21	Kansas	32.7
21	Nevada	32.7
23	South Dakota	32.5
24	Alabama	32.3
25	Vermont	32.2
26	Missouri	32.0
27	West Virginia	31.8
28	Michigan	31.5
29	Mississippi	31.1
30	Nebraska	30.9
31	Ohio	30.8
32	Connecticut	30.6
33	North Dakota	30.1
34	Maryland	29.7
35	New Hampshire	29.6
36	Florida	29.4
36	Virginia	29.4
38	Arizona	29.2
38	New Jersey	29.2
40	Alaska	29.1
41	California	28.9
41	Wisconsin	28.9
43	Massachusetts	28.3
44	Pennsylvania	27.8
44	Rhode Island	27.8
46	Louisiana	27.6
47	Illinois	26.3
48	Indiana	25.5
49	Hawaii	25.4
49	New York	25.4

District of Columbia	31.2

Source: CQ Press using data from U.S. Department of Health and Human Services, Centers for Disease Control and Prevention "Assisted Reproductive Technology, 2006" (MMWR, Vol. 58, No. SS-5, 06/12/09, http://www.cdc.gov/mmwr/mmwr_ss.html)
*By patient's residence. Assisted reproductive technology (ART) includes treatments in which both eggs and sperm are handled in the laboratory. In 2006, 72% of ART treatments were freshly fertilized embryos using the patient's eggs, 16% were thawed embryos using the patient's eggs, 8% were freshly fertilized embryos from donor eggs, and 4% were thawed embryos from donor eggs.

Percent of Total Live Births Resulting from
Assisted Reproductive Technology Procedures in 2006
National Percent = 1.3% of Live Births*

<table>
<tr><td colspan="3">ALPHA ORDER</td><td colspan="3">RANK ORDER</td></tr>
<tr><td>RANK</td><td>STATE</td><td>PERCENT</td><td>RANK</td><td>STATE</td><td>PERCENT</td></tr>
<tr><td>42</td><td>Alabama</td><td>0.6</td><td>1</td><td>Massachusetts</td><td>3.8</td></tr>
<tr><td>36</td><td>Alaska</td><td>0.7</td><td>2</td><td>Connecticut</td><td>3.1</td></tr>
<tr><td>26</td><td>Arizona</td><td>0.9</td><td>2</td><td>New Jersey</td><td>3.1</td></tr>
<tr><td>45</td><td>Arkansas</td><td>0.5</td><td>4</td><td>Maryland</td><td>2.3</td></tr>
<tr><td>12</td><td>California</td><td>1.3</td><td>4</td><td>New York</td><td>2.3</td></tr>
<tr><td>10</td><td>Colorado</td><td>1.4</td><td>6</td><td>Rhode Island</td><td>2.2</td></tr>
<tr><td>2</td><td>Connecticut</td><td>3.1</td><td>7</td><td>New Hampshire</td><td>2.1</td></tr>
<tr><td>14</td><td>Delaware</td><td>1.2</td><td>8</td><td>Illinois</td><td>1.8</td></tr>
<tr><td>17</td><td>Florida</td><td>1.1</td><td>9</td><td>Virginia</td><td>1.6</td></tr>
<tr><td>26</td><td>Georgia</td><td>0.9</td><td>10</td><td>Colorado</td><td>1.4</td></tr>
<tr><td>23</td><td>Hawaii</td><td>1.0</td><td>10</td><td>Nevada</td><td>1.4</td></tr>
<tr><td>23</td><td>Idaho</td><td>1.0</td><td>12</td><td>California</td><td>1.3</td></tr>
<tr><td>8</td><td>Illinois</td><td>1.8</td><td>12</td><td>Minnesota</td><td>1.3</td></tr>
<tr><td>36</td><td>Indiana</td><td>0.7</td><td>14</td><td>Delaware</td><td>1.2</td></tr>
<tr><td>17</td><td>Iowa</td><td>1.1</td><td>14</td><td>Vermont</td><td>1.2</td></tr>
<tr><td>36</td><td>Kansas</td><td>0.7</td><td>14</td><td>Washington</td><td>1.2</td></tr>
<tr><td>36</td><td>Kentucky</td><td>0.7</td><td>17</td><td>Florida</td><td>1.1</td></tr>
<tr><td>45</td><td>Louisiana</td><td>0.5</td><td>17</td><td>Iowa</td><td>1.1</td></tr>
<tr><td>26</td><td>Maine</td><td>0.9</td><td>17</td><td>Michigan</td><td>1.1</td></tr>
<tr><td>4</td><td>Maryland</td><td>2.3</td><td>17</td><td>North Dakota</td><td>1.1</td></tr>
<tr><td>1</td><td>Massachusetts</td><td>3.8</td><td>17</td><td>Oregon</td><td>1.1</td></tr>
<tr><td>17</td><td>Michigan</td><td>1.1</td><td>17</td><td>Pennsylvania</td><td>1.1</td></tr>
<tr><td>12</td><td>Minnesota</td><td>1.3</td><td>23</td><td>Hawaii</td><td>1.0</td></tr>
<tr><td>50</td><td>Mississippi</td><td>0.4</td><td>23</td><td>Idaho</td><td>1.0</td></tr>
<tr><td>23</td><td>Missouri</td><td>1.0</td><td>23</td><td>Missouri</td><td>1.0</td></tr>
<tr><td>26</td><td>Montana</td><td>0.9</td><td>26</td><td>Arizona</td><td>0.9</td></tr>
<tr><td>26</td><td>Nebraska</td><td>0.9</td><td>26</td><td>Georgia</td><td>0.9</td></tr>
<tr><td>10</td><td>Nevada</td><td>1.4</td><td>26</td><td>Maine</td><td>0.9</td></tr>
<tr><td>7</td><td>New Hampshire</td><td>2.1</td><td>26</td><td>Montana</td><td>0.9</td></tr>
<tr><td>2</td><td>New Jersey</td><td>3.1</td><td>26</td><td>Nebraska</td><td>0.9</td></tr>
<tr><td>45</td><td>New Mexico</td><td>0.5</td><td>26</td><td>North Carolina</td><td>0.9</td></tr>
<tr><td>4</td><td>New York</td><td>2.3</td><td>26</td><td>Ohio</td><td>0.9</td></tr>
<tr><td>26</td><td>North Carolina</td><td>0.9</td><td>33</td><td>South Carolina</td><td>0.8</td></tr>
<tr><td>17</td><td>North Dakota</td><td>1.1</td><td>33</td><td>Utah</td><td>0.8</td></tr>
<tr><td>26</td><td>Ohio</td><td>0.9</td><td>33</td><td>Wisconsin</td><td>0.8</td></tr>
<tr><td>42</td><td>Oklahoma</td><td>0.6</td><td>36</td><td>Alaska</td><td>0.7</td></tr>
<tr><td>17</td><td>Oregon</td><td>1.1</td><td>36</td><td>Indiana</td><td>0.7</td></tr>
<tr><td>17</td><td>Pennsylvania</td><td>1.1</td><td>36</td><td>Kansas</td><td>0.7</td></tr>
<tr><td>6</td><td>Rhode Island</td><td>2.2</td><td>36</td><td>Kentucky</td><td>0.7</td></tr>
<tr><td>33</td><td>South Carolina</td><td>0.8</td><td>36</td><td>South Dakota</td><td>0.7</td></tr>
<tr><td>36</td><td>South Dakota</td><td>0.7</td><td>36</td><td>Texas</td><td>0.7</td></tr>
<tr><td>42</td><td>Tennessee</td><td>0.6</td><td>42</td><td>Alabama</td><td>0.6</td></tr>
<tr><td>36</td><td>Texas</td><td>0.7</td><td>42</td><td>Oklahoma</td><td>0.6</td></tr>
<tr><td>33</td><td>Utah</td><td>0.8</td><td>42</td><td>Tennessee</td><td>0.6</td></tr>
<tr><td>14</td><td>Vermont</td><td>1.2</td><td>45</td><td>Arkansas</td><td>0.5</td></tr>
<tr><td>9</td><td>Virginia</td><td>1.6</td><td>45</td><td>Louisiana</td><td>0.5</td></tr>
<tr><td>14</td><td>Washington</td><td>1.2</td><td>45</td><td>New Mexico</td><td>0.5</td></tr>
<tr><td>45</td><td>West Virginia</td><td>0.5</td><td>45</td><td>West Virginia</td><td>0.5</td></tr>
<tr><td>33</td><td>Wisconsin</td><td>0.8</td><td>45</td><td>Wyoming</td><td>0.5</td></tr>
<tr><td>45</td><td>Wyoming</td><td>0.5</td><td>50</td><td>Mississippi</td><td>0.4</td></tr>
<tr><td></td><td></td><td></td><td></td><td>District of Columbia</td><td>3.4</td></tr>
</table>

Source: CQ Press using data from U.S. Department of Health and Human Services, Centers for Disease Control and Prevention
"Assisted Reproductive Technology, 2006" (MMWR, Vol. 58, No. SS-5, 06/12/09, http://www.cdc.gov/mmwr/mmwr_ss.html)
"National Vital Statistics Reports" (Vol. 57, No. 7, January 7, 2009, http://www.cdc.gov/nchs/births.htm)
*By patient's residence. Does not include births or procedures to patients with residences outside the U.S. Assisted reproductive technology (ART) includes treatments in which both eggs and sperm are handled in the laboratory (that is, in vitro fertilization and related procedures).

Percent of Assisted Reproductive Technology Procedure Infants Born in Multiple Birth Deliveries in 2006
National Percent = 47.5% of Assisted Reproductive Technology Births*

ALPHA ORDER

RANK	STATE	PERCENT
31	Alabama	47.2
27	Alaska	47.9
35	Arizona	46.2
3	Arkansas	59.1
23	California	48.8
13	Colorado	51.2
49	Connecticut	42.3
38	Delaware	45.7
22	Florida	48.9
24	Georgia	48.5
9	Hawaii	52.5
28	Idaho	47.8
39	Illinois	45.6
26	Indiana	48.1
47	Iowa	42.8
48	Kansas	42.7
14	Kentucky	50.6
7	Louisiana	53.4
2	Maine	61.7
42	Maryland	44.2
50	Massachusetts	40.9
17	Michigan	50.4
37	Minnesota	45.9
33	Mississippi	46.6
19	Missouri	49.7
16	Montana	50.5
14	Nebraska	50.6
8	Nevada	52.6
43	New Hampshire	44.1
18	New Jersey	50.0
4	New Mexico	57.1
41	New York	44.3
28	North Carolina	47.8
5	North Dakota	54.9
25	Ohio	48.3
30	Oklahoma	47.7
6	Oregon	54.5
46	Pennsylvania	43.5
45	Rhode Island	43.8
12	South Carolina	51.7
32	South Dakota	47.1
21	Tennessee	49.1
11	Texas	51.9
10	Utah	52.2
36	Vermont	46.1
34	Virginia	46.4
20	Washington	49.4
44	West Virginia	43.9
40	Wisconsin	45.4
1	Wyoming	64.1

RANK ORDER

RANK	STATE	PERCENT
1	Wyoming	64.1
2	Maine	61.7
3	Arkansas	59.1
4	New Mexico	57.1
5	North Dakota	54.9
6	Oregon	54.5
7	Louisiana	53.4
8	Nevada	52.6
9	Hawaii	52.5
10	Utah	52.2
11	Texas	51.9
12	South Carolina	51.7
13	Colorado	51.2
14	Kentucky	50.6
14	Nebraska	50.6
16	Montana	50.5
17	Michigan	50.4
18	New Jersey	50.0
19	Missouri	49.7
20	Washington	49.4
21	Tennessee	49.1
22	Florida	48.9
23	California	48.8
24	Georgia	48.5
25	Ohio	48.3
26	Indiana	48.1
27	Alaska	47.9
28	Idaho	47.8
28	North Carolina	47.8
30	Oklahoma	47.7
31	Alabama	47.2
32	South Dakota	47.1
33	Mississippi	46.6
34	Virginia	46.4
35	Arizona	46.2
36	Vermont	46.1
37	Minnesota	45.9
38	Delaware	45.7
39	Illinois	45.6
40	Wisconsin	45.4
41	New York	44.3
42	Maryland	44.2
43	New Hampshire	44.1
44	West Virginia	43.9
45	Rhode Island	43.8
46	Pennsylvania	43.5
47	Iowa	42.8
48	Kansas	42.7
49	Connecticut	42.3
50	Massachusetts	40.9

	District of Columbia	45.1

Source: U.S. Department of Health and Human Services, Centers for Disease Control and Prevention
   "Assisted Reproductive Technology, 2006" (MMWR, Vol. 58, No. SS-5, 06/12/09, http://www.cdc.gov/mmwr/mmwr_ss.html)
*By patient's residence. Includes births and procedures to patients with residences outside the U.S. Assisted reproductive technology (ART) includes treatments in which both eggs and sperm are handled in the laboratory (that is, in vitro fertilization and related procedures).

Percent of Women Beginning Prenatal Care in First Trimester in 2006

National Percent = 83.2% of Women*

ALPHA ORDER				RANK ORDER		
RANK	STATE	PERCENT		RANK	STATE	PERCENT
20	Alabama	81.7		1	Massachusetts	88.6
22	Alaska	81.1		2	Maine	87.7
29	Arizona	77.7		3	Missouri	87.2
26	Arkansas	79.5		4	Louisiana	87.0
8	California	85.9		5	Minnesota	86.5
25	Colorado	79.7		6	Iowa	86.4
9	Connecticut	85.8		7	Illinois	86.2
NA	Delaware**	NA		8	California	85.9
NA	Florida**	NA		9	Connecticut	85.8
15	Georgia	83.3		10	Michigan	85.4
19	Hawaii	81.8		11	Rhode Island	84.5
NA	Idaho**	NA		11	Wisconsin	84.5
7	Illinois	86.2		13	Virginia	84.2
28	Indiana	79.0		14	Montana	83.7
6	Iowa	86.4		15	Georgia	83.3
NA	Kansas**	NA		16	Mississippi	83.2
NA	Kentucky**	NA		17	West Virginia	82.8
4	Louisiana	87.0		18	North Carolina	82.6
2	Maine	87.7		19	Hawaii	81.8
20	Maryland	81.7		20	Alabama	81.7
1	Massachusetts	88.6		20	Maryland	81.7
10	Michigan	85.4		22	Alaska	81.1
5	Minnesota	86.5		23	Utah	80.2
16	Mississippi	83.2		24	New York*	79.9
3	Missouri	87.2		25	Colorado	79.7
14	Montana	83.7		26	Arkansas	79.5
NA	Nebraska**	NA		27	Oregon	79.2
33	Nevada	71.5		28	Indiana	79.0
NA	New Hampshire**	NA		29	Arizona	77.7
30	New Jersey	77.6		30	New Jersey	77.6
32	New Mexico	74.7		31	Oklahoma	75.6
24	New York*	79.9		32	New Mexico	74.7
18	North Carolina	82.6		33	Nevada	71.5
NA	North Dakota**	NA		NA	Delaware**	NA
NA	Ohio**	NA		NA	Florida**	NA
31	Oklahoma	75.6		NA	Idaho**	NA
27	Oregon	79.2		NA	Kansas**	NA
NA	Pennsylvania**	NA		NA	Kentucky**	NA
11	Rhode Island	84.5		NA	Nebraska**	NA
NA	South Carolina**	NA		NA	New Hampshire**	NA
NA	South Dakota**	NA		NA	North Dakota**	NA
NA	Tennessee**	NA		NA	Ohio**	NA
NA	Texas**	NA		NA	Pennsylvania**	NA
23	Utah	80.2		NA	South Carolina**	NA
NA	Vermont**	NA		NA	South Dakota**	NA
13	Virginia	84.2		NA	Tennessee**	NA
NA	Washington**	NA		NA	Texas**	NA
17	West Virginia	82.8		NA	Vermont**	NA
11	Wisconsin	84.5		NA	Washington**	NA
NA	Wyoming**	NA		NA	Wyoming**	NA
					District of Columbia	78.9

Source: U.S. Department of Health and Human Services, National Center for Health Statistics
  "National Vital Statistics Reports" (Vol. 57, No. 7, January 7, 2009, http://www.cdc.gov/nchs/births.htm)
*Final data by state of residence. New York's figure is for New York City only.
**Not available. These states have implemented the 2003 Revision of the U.S. Certificate of Live Birth and their prenatal care data are not comparable with those based on the 1989 revision.

Percent of White Women Beginning Prenatal Care in First Trimester in 2006

National Percent = 88.1% of White Women*

ALPHA ORDER

RANK	STATE	PERCENT
15	Alabama	88.5
25	Alaska	85.0
21	Arizona	86.8
28	Arkansas	83.0
7	California	89.8
23	Colorado	85.7
2	Connecticut	91.4
NA	Delaware**	NA
NA	Florida**	NA
13	Georgia	89.4
24	Hawaii	85.2
NA	Idaho**	NA
4	Illinois	90.7
29	Indiana	82.8
15	Iowa	88.5
NA	Kansas**	NA
NA	Kentucky**	NA
1	Louisiana	92.3
17	Maine	88.3
14	Maryland	89.2
2	Massachusetts	91.4
11	Michigan	89.5
5	Minnesota	90.4
10	Mississippi	89.6
11	Missouri	89.5
22	Montana	86.5
NA	Nebraska**	NA
32	Nevada	79.9
NA	New Hampshire**	NA
20	New Jersey	87.1
31	New Mexico	81.4
19	New York*	87.7
7	North Carolina	89.8
NA	North Dakota**	NA
NA	Ohio**	NA
33	Oklahoma	79.5
30	Oregon	82.4
NA	Pennsylvania**	NA
6	Rhode Island	90.0
NA	South Carolina**	NA
NA	South Dakota**	NA
NA	Tennessee**	NA
NA	Texas**	NA
26	Utah	84.1
NA	Vermont**	NA
9	Virginia	89.7
NA	Washington**	NA
27	West Virginia	83.5
18	Wisconsin	88.0
NA	Wyoming**	NA

RANK ORDER

RANK	STATE	PERCENT
1	Louisiana	92.3
2	Connecticut	91.4
2	Massachusetts	91.4
4	Illinois	90.7
5	Minnesota	90.4
6	Rhode Island	90.0
7	California	89.8
7	North Carolina	89.8
9	Virginia	89.7
10	Mississippi	89.6
11	Michigan	89.5
11	Missouri	89.5
13	Georgia	89.4
14	Maryland	89.2
15	Alabama	88.5
15	Iowa	88.5
17	Maine	88.3
18	Wisconsin	88.0
19	New York*	87.7
20	New Jersey	87.1
21	Arizona	86.8
22	Montana	86.5
23	Colorado	85.7
24	Hawaii	85.2
25	Alaska	85.0
26	Utah	84.1
27	West Virginia	83.5
28	Arkansas	83.0
29	Indiana	82.8
30	Oregon	82.4
31	New Mexico	81.4
32	Nevada	79.9
33	Oklahoma	79.5
NA	Delaware**	NA
NA	Florida**	NA
NA	Idaho**	NA
NA	Kansas**	NA
NA	Kentucky**	NA
NA	Nebraska**	NA
NA	New Hampshire**	NA
NA	North Dakota**	NA
NA	Ohio**	NA
NA	Pennsylvania**	NA
NA	South Carolina**	NA
NA	South Dakota**	NA
NA	Tennessee**	NA
NA	Texas**	NA
NA	Vermont**	NA
NA	Washington**	NA
NA	Wyoming**	NA
	District of Columbia	92.2

Source: U.S. Department of Health and Human Services, National Center for Health Statistics
   "National Vital Statistics Reports" (Vol. 57, No. 7, January 7, 2009, http://www.cdc.gov/nchs/births.htm)
*Final data by state of residence. New York's figure is for New York City only. Does not include whites of Hispanic origin.
**Not available. These states have implemented the 2003 Revision of the U.S. Certificate of Live Birth and their prenatal care data are not comparable with those based on the 1989 revision.

Percent of Black Women Beginning Prenatal Care in First Trimester in 2006

National Percent = 76.1% of Black Women*

ALPHA ORDER			RANK ORDER		
RANK	STATE	PERCENT	RANK	STATE	PERCENT
15	Alabama	76.0	1	Montana	86.7
3	Alaska	82.9	2	Hawaii	85.5
10	Arizona	77.9	3	Alaska	82.9
24	Arkansas	72.6	4	California	81.9
4	California	81.9	5	Massachusetts	80.4
22	Colorado	73.7	6	Louisiana	79.9
18	Connecticut	75.0	7	Virginia	79.4
NA	Delaware**	NA	8	Missouri	79.2
NA	Florida**	NA	9	Georgia	78.9
9	Georgia	78.9	10	Arizona	77.9
2	Hawaii	85.5	11	Mississippi	77.3
NA	Idaho**	NA	12	Illinois	76.7
12	Illinois	76.7	13	New Mexico	76.3
30	Indiana	66.5	14	Maryland	76.2
23	Iowa	73.0	15	Alabama	76.0
NA	Kansas**	NA	15	North Carolina	76.0
NA	Kentucky**	NA	17	Wisconsin	75.5
6	Louisiana	79.9	18	Connecticut	75.0
27	Maine	69.8	18	New York*	75.0
14	Maryland	76.2	20	Minnesota	74.5
5	Massachusetts	80.4	21	Rhode Island	74.2
26	Michigan	71.9	22	Colorado	73.7
20	Minnesota	74.5	23	Iowa	73.0
11	Mississippi	77.3	24	Arkansas	72.6
8	Missouri	79.2	25	Oregon	72.1
1	Montana	86.7	26	Michigan	71.9
NA	Nebraska**	NA	27	Maine	69.8
31	Nevada	66.3	28	Oklahoma	69.7
NA	New Hampshire**	NA	29	West Virginia	68.4
32	New Jersey	62.4	30	Indiana	66.5
13	New Mexico	76.3	31	Nevada	66.3
18	New York*	75.0	32	New Jersey	62.4
15	North Carolina	76.0	33	Utah	57.4
NA	North Dakota**	NA	NA	Delaware**	NA
NA	Ohio**	NA	NA	Florida**	NA
28	Oklahoma	69.7	NA	Idaho**	NA
25	Oregon	72.1	NA	Kansas**	NA
NA	Pennsylvania**	NA	NA	Kentucky**	NA
21	Rhode Island	74.2	NA	Nebraska**	NA
NA	South Carolina**	NA	NA	New Hampshire**	NA
NA	South Dakota**	NA	NA	North Dakota**	NA
NA	Tennessee**	NA	NA	Ohio**	NA
NA	Texas**	NA	NA	Pennsylvania**	NA
33	Utah	57.4	NA	South Carolina**	NA
NA	Vermont**	NA	NA	South Dakota**	NA
7	Virginia	79.4	NA	Tennessee**	NA
NA	Washington**	NA	NA	Texas**	NA
29	West Virginia	68.4	NA	Vermont**	NA
17	Wisconsin	75.5	NA	Washington**	NA
NA	Wyoming**	NA	NA	Wyoming**	NA
				District of Columbia	74.9

Source: U.S. Department of Health and Human Services, National Center for Health Statistics
    "National Vital Statistics Reports" (Vol. 57, No. 7, January 7, 2009, http://www.cdc.gov/nchs/births.htm)
*Final data by state of residence. New York's figure is for New York City only. Does not include blacks of Hispanic origin.
**Not available. These states have implemented the 2003 Revision of the U.S. Certificate of Live Birth and their prenatal care data are not comparable with those based on the 1989 revision.

Percent of Hispanic Women Beginning Prenatal Care in First Trimester in 2006

National Percent = 77.3% of Hispanic Women*

ALPHA ORDER

RANK	STATE	PERCENT
33	Alabama	50.6
4	Alaska	82.4
21	Arizona	70.2
23	Arkansas	69.7
1	California	83.8
24	Colorado	69.4
14	Connecticut	75.1
NA	Delaware**	NA
NA	Florida**	NA
16	Georgia	73.3
5	Hawaii	82.0
NA	Idaho**	NA
2	Illinois	82.5
31	Indiana	64.1
20	Iowa	71.7
NA	Kansas**	NA
NA	Kentucky**	NA
8	Louisiana	79.9
2	Maine	82.5
29	Maryland	65.0
6	Massachusetts	81.4
9	Michigan	78.6
19	Minnesota	72.1
18	Mississippi	73.1
11	Missouri	77.6
7	Montana	80.2
NA	Nebraska**	NA
32	Nevada	62.5
NA	New Hampshire**	NA
28	New Jersey	66.1
15	New Mexico	74.3
10	New York*	77.9
26	North Carolina	67.6
NA	North Dakota**	NA
NA	Ohio**	NA
30	Oklahoma	64.5
22	Oregon	70.1
NA	Pennsylvania**	NA
13	Rhode Island	75.7
NA	South Carolina**	NA
NA	South Dakota**	NA
NA	Tennessee**	NA
NA	Texas**	NA
27	Utah	66.4
NA	Vermont**	NA
25	Virginia	69.0
NA	Washington**	NA
12	West Virginia	76.1
17	Wisconsin	73.2
NA	Wyoming**	NA

RANK ORDER

RANK	STATE	PERCENT
1	California	83.8
2	Illinois	82.5
2	Maine	82.5
4	Alaska	82.4
5	Hawaii	82.0
6	Massachusetts	81.4
7	Montana	80.2
8	Louisiana	79.9
9	Michigan	78.6
10	New York*	77.9
11	Missouri	77.6
12	West Virginia	76.1
13	Rhode Island	75.7
14	Connecticut	75.1
15	New Mexico	74.3
16	Georgia	73.3
17	Wisconsin	73.2
18	Mississippi	73.1
19	Minnesota	72.1
20	Iowa	71.7
21	Arizona	70.2
22	Oregon	70.1
23	Arkansas	69.7
24	Colorado	69.4
25	Virginia	69.0
26	North Carolina	67.6
27	Utah	66.4
28	New Jersey	66.1
29	Maryland	65.0
30	Oklahoma	64.5
31	Indiana	64.1
32	Nevada	62.5
33	Alabama	50.6
NA	Delaware**	NA
NA	Florida**	NA
NA	Idaho**	NA
NA	Kansas**	NA
NA	Kentucky**	NA
NA	Nebraska**	NA
NA	New Hampshire**	NA
NA	North Dakota**	NA
NA	Ohio**	NA
NA	Pennsylvania**	NA
NA	South Carolina**	NA
NA	South Dakota**	NA
NA	Tennessee**	NA
NA	Texas**	NA
NA	Vermont**	NA
NA	Washington**	NA
NA	Wyoming**	NA

District of Columbia	67.0

Source: U.S. Department of Health and Human Services, National Center for Health Statistics
   "National Vital Statistics Reports" (Vol. 57, No. 7, January 7, 2009, http://www.cdc.gov/nchs/births.htm)
*Final data by state of residence. New York's figure is for New York City only. Persons of Hispanic origin may be of any race.
**Not available. These states have implemented the 2003 Revision of the U.S. Certificate of Live Birth and their prenatal care data are not comparable with those based on the 1989 revision.

Percent of Women Receiving Late or No Prenatal Care in 2006

National Percent = 3.6% of Women*

<table>
<tr><td colspan="3"><u>ALPHA ORDER</u></td><td colspan="3"><u>RANK ORDER</u></td></tr>
<tr><td>RANK</td><td>STATE</td><td>PERCENT</td><td>RANK</td><td>STATE</td><td>PERCENT</td></tr>
<tr><td>9</td><td>Alabama</td><td>4.5</td><td>1</td><td>Nevada</td><td>8.8</td></tr>
<tr><td>6</td><td>Alaska</td><td>4.9</td><td>2</td><td>New Mexico</td><td>6.7</td></tr>
<tr><td>3</td><td>Arizona</td><td>6.1</td><td>3</td><td>Arizona</td><td>6.1</td></tr>
<tr><td>8</td><td>Arkansas</td><td>4.7</td><td>3</td><td>Oklahoma</td><td>6.1</td></tr>
<tr><td>24</td><td>California</td><td>2.8</td><td>5</td><td>New Jersey</td><td>5.0</td></tr>
<tr><td>9</td><td>Colorado</td><td>4.5</td><td>6</td><td>Alaska</td><td>4.9</td></tr>
<tr><td>32</td><td>Connecticut</td><td>1.8</td><td>6</td><td>New York*</td><td>4.9</td></tr>
<tr><td>NA</td><td>Delaware**</td><td>NA</td><td>8</td><td>Arkansas</td><td>4.7</td></tr>
<tr><td>NA</td><td>Florida**</td><td>NA</td><td>9</td><td>Alabama</td><td>4.5</td></tr>
<tr><td>14</td><td>Georgia</td><td>4.1</td><td>9</td><td>Colorado</td><td>4.5</td></tr>
<tr><td>17</td><td>Hawaii</td><td>3.6</td><td>9</td><td>Indiana</td><td>4.5</td></tr>
<tr><td>NA</td><td>Idaho**</td><td>NA</td><td>12</td><td>Maryland</td><td>4.3</td></tr>
<tr><td>27</td><td>Illinois</td><td>2.4</td><td>12</td><td>Oregon</td><td>4.3</td></tr>
<tr><td>9</td><td>Indiana</td><td>4.5</td><td>14</td><td>Georgia</td><td>4.1</td></tr>
<tr><td>26</td><td>Iowa</td><td>2.5</td><td>14</td><td>Virginia</td><td>4.1</td></tr>
<tr><td>NA</td><td>Kansas**</td><td>NA</td><td>16</td><td>Utah</td><td>3.9</td></tr>
<tr><td>NA</td><td>Kentucky**</td><td>NA</td><td>17</td><td>Hawaii</td><td>3.6</td></tr>
<tr><td>25</td><td>Louisiana</td><td>2.6</td><td>18</td><td>Mississippi</td><td>3.2</td></tr>
<tr><td>32</td><td>Maine</td><td>1.8</td><td>18</td><td>West Virginia</td><td>3.2</td></tr>
<tr><td>12</td><td>Maryland</td><td>4.3</td><td>20</td><td>Michigan</td><td>3.1</td></tr>
<tr><td>28</td><td>Massachusetts</td><td>2.3</td><td>20</td><td>Montana</td><td>3.1</td></tr>
<tr><td>20</td><td>Michigan</td><td>3.1</td><td>20</td><td>North Carolina</td><td>3.1</td></tr>
<tr><td>30</td><td>Minnesota</td><td>2.1</td><td>20</td><td>Wisconsin</td><td>3.1</td></tr>
<tr><td>18</td><td>Mississippi</td><td>3.2</td><td>24</td><td>California</td><td>2.8</td></tr>
<tr><td>28</td><td>Missouri</td><td>2.3</td><td>25</td><td>Louisiana</td><td>2.6</td></tr>
<tr><td>20</td><td>Montana</td><td>3.1</td><td>26</td><td>Iowa</td><td>2.5</td></tr>
<tr><td>NA</td><td>Nebraska**</td><td>NA</td><td>27</td><td>Illinois</td><td>2.4</td></tr>
<tr><td>1</td><td>Nevada</td><td>8.8</td><td>28</td><td>Massachusetts</td><td>2.3</td></tr>
<tr><td>NA</td><td>New Hampshire**</td><td>NA</td><td>28</td><td>Missouri</td><td>2.3</td></tr>
<tr><td>5</td><td>New Jersey</td><td>5.0</td><td>30</td><td>Minnesota</td><td>2.1</td></tr>
<tr><td>2</td><td>New Mexico</td><td>6.7</td><td>31</td><td>Rhode Island</td><td>1.9</td></tr>
<tr><td>6</td><td>New York*</td><td>4.9</td><td>32</td><td>Connecticut</td><td>1.8</td></tr>
<tr><td>20</td><td>North Carolina</td><td>3.1</td><td>32</td><td>Maine</td><td>1.8</td></tr>
<tr><td>NA</td><td>North Dakota**</td><td>NA</td><td>NA</td><td>Delaware**</td><td>NA</td></tr>
<tr><td>NA</td><td>Ohio**</td><td>NA</td><td>NA</td><td>Florida**</td><td>NA</td></tr>
<tr><td>3</td><td>Oklahoma</td><td>6.1</td><td>NA</td><td>Idaho**</td><td>NA</td></tr>
<tr><td>12</td><td>Oregon</td><td>4.3</td><td>NA</td><td>Kansas**</td><td>NA</td></tr>
<tr><td>NA</td><td>Pennsylvania**</td><td>NA</td><td>NA</td><td>Kentucky**</td><td>NA</td></tr>
<tr><td>31</td><td>Rhode Island</td><td>1.9</td><td>NA</td><td>Nebraska**</td><td>NA</td></tr>
<tr><td>NA</td><td>South Carolina**</td><td>NA</td><td>NA</td><td>New Hampshire**</td><td>NA</td></tr>
<tr><td>NA</td><td>South Dakota**</td><td>NA</td><td>NA</td><td>North Dakota**</td><td>NA</td></tr>
<tr><td>NA</td><td>Tennessee**</td><td>NA</td><td>NA</td><td>Ohio**</td><td>NA</td></tr>
<tr><td>NA</td><td>Texas**</td><td>NA</td><td>NA</td><td>Pennsylvania**</td><td>NA</td></tr>
<tr><td>16</td><td>Utah</td><td>3.9</td><td>NA</td><td>South Carolina**</td><td>NA</td></tr>
<tr><td>NA</td><td>Vermont**</td><td>NA</td><td>NA</td><td>South Dakota**</td><td>NA</td></tr>
<tr><td>14</td><td>Virginia</td><td>4.1</td><td>NA</td><td>Tennessee**</td><td>NA</td></tr>
<tr><td>NA</td><td>Washington**</td><td>NA</td><td>NA</td><td>Texas**</td><td>NA</td></tr>
<tr><td>18</td><td>West Virginia</td><td>3.2</td><td>NA</td><td>Vermont**</td><td>NA</td></tr>
<tr><td>20</td><td>Wisconsin</td><td>3.1</td><td>NA</td><td>Washington**</td><td>NA</td></tr>
<tr><td>NA</td><td>Wyoming**</td><td>NA</td><td>NA</td><td>Wyoming**</td><td>NA</td></tr>
<tr><td></td><td></td><td></td><td></td><td>District of Columbia</td><td>5.5</td></tr>
</table>

Source: U.S. Department of Health and Human Services, National Center for Health Statistics
   "National Vital Statistics Reports" (Vol. 57, No. 7, January 7, 2009, http://www.cdc.gov/nchs/births.htm)
*Final data by state of residence. "Late" means care begun in third trimester. New York's figure is for New York City only.
**Not available. These states have implemented the 2003 Revision of the U.S. Certificate of Live Birth and their prenatal care data are not comparable with those based on the 1989 revision.

Percent of White Women Receiving Late or No Prenatal Care in 2006

National Percent = 2.3% of White Women*

<table>
<tr><td colspan="3"><u>ALPHA ORDER</u></td><td colspan="3"><u>RANK ORDER</u></td></tr>
<tr><th>RANK</th><th>STATE</th><th>PERCENT</th><th>RANK</th><th>STATE</th><th>PERCENT</th></tr>
<tr><td>17</td><td>Alabama</td><td>2.2</td><td>1</td><td>Nevada</td><td>6.4</td></tr>
<tr><td>4</td><td>Alaska</td><td>3.8</td><td>2</td><td>Oklahoma</td><td>5.4</td></tr>
<tr><td>8</td><td>Arizona</td><td>3.0</td><td>3</td><td>New Mexico</td><td>4.5</td></tr>
<tr><td>6</td><td>Arkansas</td><td>3.6</td><td>4</td><td>Alaska</td><td>3.8</td></tr>
<tr><td>22</td><td>California</td><td>2.1</td><td>5</td><td>Oregon</td><td>3.7</td></tr>
<tr><td>10</td><td>Colorado</td><td>2.8</td><td>6</td><td>Arkansas</td><td>3.6</td></tr>
<tr><td>32</td><td>Connecticut</td><td>1.1</td><td>7</td><td>Indiana</td><td>3.4</td></tr>
<tr><td>NA</td><td>Delaware**</td><td>NA</td><td>8</td><td>Arizona</td><td>3.0</td></tr>
<tr><td>NA</td><td>Florida**</td><td>NA</td><td>8</td><td>West Virginia</td><td>3.0</td></tr>
<tr><td>13</td><td>Georgia</td><td>2.3</td><td>10</td><td>Colorado</td><td>2.8</td></tr>
<tr><td>13</td><td>Hawaii</td><td>2.3</td><td>11</td><td>New Jersey</td><td>2.7</td></tr>
<tr><td>NA</td><td>Idaho**</td><td>NA</td><td>11</td><td>Utah</td><td>2.7</td></tr>
<tr><td>29</td><td>Illinois</td><td>1.5</td><td>13</td><td>Georgia</td><td>2.3</td></tr>
<tr><td>7</td><td>Indiana</td><td>3.4</td><td>13</td><td>Hawaii</td><td>2.3</td></tr>
<tr><td>23</td><td>Iowa</td><td>2.0</td><td>13</td><td>Virginia</td><td>2.3</td></tr>
<tr><td>NA</td><td>Kansas**</td><td>NA</td><td>13</td><td>Wisconsin</td><td>2.3</td></tr>
<tr><td>NA</td><td>Kentucky**</td><td>NA</td><td>17</td><td>Alabama</td><td>2.2</td></tr>
<tr><td>30</td><td>Louisiana</td><td>1.3</td><td>17</td><td>Maryland</td><td>2.2</td></tr>
<tr><td>25</td><td>Maine</td><td>1.7</td><td>17</td><td>Michigan</td><td>2.2</td></tr>
<tr><td>17</td><td>Maryland</td><td>2.2</td><td>17</td><td>Montana</td><td>2.2</td></tr>
<tr><td>28</td><td>Massachusetts</td><td>1.6</td><td>17</td><td>New York*</td><td>2.2</td></tr>
<tr><td>17</td><td>Michigan</td><td>2.2</td><td>22</td><td>California</td><td>2.1</td></tr>
<tr><td>30</td><td>Minnesota</td><td>1.3</td><td>23</td><td>Iowa</td><td>2.0</td></tr>
<tr><td>25</td><td>Mississippi</td><td>1.7</td><td>24</td><td>Missouri</td><td>1.8</td></tr>
<tr><td>24</td><td>Missouri</td><td>1.8</td><td>25</td><td>Maine</td><td>1.7</td></tr>
<tr><td>17</td><td>Montana</td><td>2.2</td><td>25</td><td>Mississippi</td><td>1.7</td></tr>
<tr><td>NA</td><td>Nebraska**</td><td>NA</td><td>25</td><td>North Carolina</td><td>1.7</td></tr>
<tr><td>1</td><td>Nevada</td><td>6.4</td><td>28</td><td>Massachusetts</td><td>1.6</td></tr>
<tr><td>NA</td><td>New Hampshire**</td><td>NA</td><td>29</td><td>Illinois</td><td>1.5</td></tr>
<tr><td>11</td><td>New Jersey</td><td>2.7</td><td>30</td><td>Louisiana</td><td>1.3</td></tr>
<tr><td>3</td><td>New Mexico</td><td>4.5</td><td>30</td><td>Minnesota</td><td>1.3</td></tr>
<tr><td>17</td><td>New York*</td><td>2.2</td><td>32</td><td>Connecticut</td><td>1.1</td></tr>
<tr><td>25</td><td>North Carolina</td><td>1.7</td><td>33</td><td>Rhode Island</td><td>1.0</td></tr>
<tr><td>NA</td><td>North Dakota**</td><td>NA</td><td>NA</td><td>Delaware**</td><td>NA</td></tr>
<tr><td>NA</td><td>Ohio**</td><td>NA</td><td>NA</td><td>Florida**</td><td>NA</td></tr>
<tr><td>2</td><td>Oklahoma</td><td>5.4</td><td>NA</td><td>Idaho**</td><td>NA</td></tr>
<tr><td>5</td><td>Oregon</td><td>3.7</td><td>NA</td><td>Kansas**</td><td>NA</td></tr>
<tr><td>NA</td><td>Pennsylvania**</td><td>NA</td><td>NA</td><td>Kentucky**</td><td>NA</td></tr>
<tr><td>33</td><td>Rhode Island</td><td>1.0</td><td>NA</td><td>Nebraska**</td><td>NA</td></tr>
<tr><td>NA</td><td>South Carolina**</td><td>NA</td><td>NA</td><td>New Hampshire**</td><td>NA</td></tr>
<tr><td>NA</td><td>South Dakota**</td><td>NA</td><td>NA</td><td>North Dakota**</td><td>NA</td></tr>
<tr><td>NA</td><td>Tennessee**</td><td>NA</td><td>NA</td><td>Ohio**</td><td>NA</td></tr>
<tr><td>NA</td><td>Texas**</td><td>NA</td><td>NA</td><td>Pennsylvania**</td><td>NA</td></tr>
<tr><td>11</td><td>Utah</td><td>2.7</td><td>NA</td><td>South Carolina**</td><td>NA</td></tr>
<tr><td>NA</td><td>Vermont**</td><td>NA</td><td>NA</td><td>South Dakota**</td><td>NA</td></tr>
<tr><td>13</td><td>Virginia</td><td>2.3</td><td>NA</td><td>Tennessee**</td><td>NA</td></tr>
<tr><td>NA</td><td>Washington**</td><td>NA</td><td>NA</td><td>Texas**</td><td>NA</td></tr>
<tr><td>8</td><td>West Virginia</td><td>3.0</td><td>NA</td><td>Vermont**</td><td>NA</td></tr>
<tr><td>13</td><td>Wisconsin</td><td>2.3</td><td>NA</td><td>Washington**</td><td>NA</td></tr>
<tr><td>NA</td><td>Wyoming**</td><td>NA</td><td>NA</td><td>Wyoming**</td><td>NA</td></tr>
</table>

District of Columbia   1.8

Source: U.S. Department of Health and Human Services, National Center for Health Statistics
"National Vital Statistics Reports" (Vol. 57, No. 7, January 7, 2009, http://www.cdc.gov/nchs/births.htm)
*Final data by state of residence. "Late" means care begun in third trimester. New York's figure is for New York City only.
Does not include whites of Hispanic origin.
**Not available. These states have implemented the 2003 Revision of the U.S. Certificate of Live Birth and their prenatal care
data are not comparable with those based on the 1989 revision.

Percent of Black Women Receiving Late or No Prenatal Care in 2006

National Percent = 5.7% of Black Women*

ALPHA ORDER				RANK ORDER		
RANK	STATE	PERCENT		RANK	STATE	PERCENT
21	Alabama	4.8		1	Utah	16.8
NA	Alaska**	NA		2	Nevada	11.6
21	Arizona	4.8		3	New Jersey	10.5
7	Arkansas	7.3		4	Indiana	8.5
29	California	3.8		5	Oklahoma	7.5
8	Colorado	7.0		6	New York*	7.4
28	Connecticut	3.9		7	Arkansas	7.3
NA	Delaware**	NA		8	Colorado	7.0
NA	Florida**	NA		9	West Virginia	6.8
20	Georgia	4.9		10	Michigan	6.6
NA	Hawaii**	NA		11	Iowa	6.2
NA	Idaho**	NA		11	Wisconsin	6.2
15	Illinois	5.4		13	Oregon	6.1
4	Indiana	8.5		14	Maryland	6.0
11	Iowa	6.2		15	Illinois	5.4
NA	Kansas**	NA		15	Minnesota	5.4
NA	Kentucky**	NA		17	New Mexico	5.3
26	Louisiana	4.2		18	Virginia	5.2
NA	Maine**	NA		19	Massachusetts	5.0
14	Maryland	6.0		20	Georgia	4.9
19	Massachusetts	5.0		21	Alabama	4.8
10	Michigan	6.6		21	Arizona	4.8
15	Minnesota	5.4		23	North Carolina	4.7
25	Mississippi	4.3		24	Missouri	4.5
24	Missouri	4.5		25	Mississippi	4.3
NA	Montana**	NA		26	Louisiana	4.2
NA	Nebraska**	NA		27	Rhode Island	4.0
2	Nevada	11.6		28	Connecticut	3.9
NA	New Hampshire**	NA		29	California	3.8
3	New Jersey	10.5		NA	Alaska**	NA
17	New Mexico	5.3		NA	Delaware**	NA
6	New York*	7.4		NA	Florida**	NA
23	North Carolina	4.7		NA	Hawaii**	NA
NA	North Dakota**	NA		NA	Idaho**	NA
NA	Ohio**	NA		NA	Kansas**	NA
5	Oklahoma	7.5		NA	Kentucky**	NA
13	Oregon	6.1		NA	Maine**	NA
NA	Pennsylvania**	NA		NA	Montana**	NA
27	Rhode Island	4.0		NA	Nebraska**	NA
NA	South Carolina**	NA		NA	New Hampshire**	NA
NA	South Dakota**	NA		NA	North Dakota**	NA
NA	Tennessee**	NA		NA	Ohio**	NA
NA	Texas**	NA		NA	Pennsylvania**	NA
1	Utah	16.8		NA	South Carolina**	NA
NA	Vermont**	NA		NA	South Dakota**	NA
18	Virginia	5.2		NA	Tennessee**	NA
NA	Washington**	NA		NA	Texas**	NA
9	West Virginia	6.8		NA	Vermont**	NA
11	Wisconsin	6.2		NA	Washington**	NA
NA	Wyoming**	NA		NA	Wyoming**	NA
					District of Columbia	7.4

Source: U.S. Department of Health and Human Services, National Center for Health Statistics
   "National Vital Statistics Reports" (Vol. 57, No. 7, January 7, 2009, http://www.cdc.gov/nchs/births.htm)
*Final data by state of residence. "Late" means care begun in third trimester. New York's figure is for New York City only.
Does not include blacks of Hispanic origin. **Not available. With the exception of Alaska, Hawaii, Maine, and Montana, these
states have implemented the 2003 Revision of the U.S. Certificate of Live Birth and their prenatal care data are not comparable
with those based on the 1989 revision.

Percent of Hispanic Women Receiving Late or No Prenatal Care in 2006

National Percent = 5.0% of Hispanic Women*

ALPHA ORDER			RANK ORDER		
RANK	**STATE**	**PERCENT**	**RANK**	**STATE**	**PERCENT**
1	Alabama	22.4	1	Alabama	22.4
22	Alaska	4.8	2	Nevada	11.1
5	Arizona	8.7	3	Mississippi	9.0
11	Arkansas	7.2	3	Virginia	9.0
28	California	3.2	5	Arizona	8.7
11	Colorado	7.2	6	Georgia	8.1
29	Connecticut	3.0	6	Maryland	8.1
NA	Delaware**	NA	8	Indiana	8.0
NA	Florida**	NA	9	Oklahoma	7.7
6	Georgia	8.1	10	Utah	7.5
26	Hawaii	3.4	11	Arkansas	7.2
NA	Idaho**	NA	11	Colorado	7.2
31	Illinois	2.4	13	New Jersey	6.8
8	Indiana	8.0	13	New Mexico	6.8
20	Iowa	4.9	15	North Carolina	5.7
NA	Kansas**	NA	16	Oregon	5.6
NA	Kentucky**	NA	17	Wisconsin	5.4
20	Louisiana	4.9	18	New York*	5.3
NA	Maine**	NA	19	Montana	5.1
6	Maryland	8.1	20	Iowa	4.9
26	Massachusetts	3.4	20	Louisiana	4.9
24	Michigan	4.0	22	Alaska	4.8
23	Minnesota	4.4	23	Minnesota	4.4
3	Mississippi	9.0	24	Michigan	4.0
25	Missouri	3.8	25	Missouri	3.8
19	Montana	5.1	26	Hawaii	3.4
NA	Nebraska**	NA	26	Massachusetts	3.4
2	Nevada	11.1	28	California	3.2
NA	New Hampshire**	NA	29	Connecticut	3.0
13	New Jersey	6.8	29	Rhode Island	3.0
13	New Mexico	6.8	31	Illinois	2.4
18	New York*	5.3	NA	Delaware**	NA
15	North Carolina	5.7	NA	Florida**	NA
NA	North Dakota**	NA	NA	Idaho**	NA
NA	Ohio**	NA	NA	Kansas**	NA
9	Oklahoma	7.7	NA	Kentucky**	NA
16	Oregon	5.6	NA	Maine**	NA
NA	Pennsylvania**	NA	NA	Nebraska**	NA
29	Rhode Island	3.0	NA	New Hampshire**	NA
NA	South Carolina**	NA	NA	North Dakota**	NA
NA	South Dakota**	NA	NA	Ohio**	NA
NA	Tennessee**	NA	NA	Pennsylvania**	NA
NA	Texas**	NA	NA	South Carolina**	NA
10	Utah	7.5	NA	South Dakota**	NA
NA	Vermont**	NA	NA	Tennessee**	NA
3	Virginia	9.0	NA	Texas**	NA
NA	Washington**	NA	NA	Vermont**	NA
NA	West Virginia**	NA	NA	Washington**	NA
17	Wisconsin	5.4	NA	West Virginia**	NA
NA	Wyoming**	NA	NA	Wyoming**	NA
				District of Columbia	6.3

Source: U.S. Department of Health and Human Services, National Center for Health Statistics
    "National Vital Statistics Reports" (Vol. 57, No. 7, January 7, 2009, http://www.cdc.gov/nchs/births.htm)
*Final data by state of residence. "Late" means care begun in third trimester. New York's figure is for New York City only.
Persons of Hispanic origin may be of any race. **Not available. With the exception of Maine and West Virginia, these states
have implemented the 2003 Revision of the U.S. Certificate of Live Birth and their prenatal care data are not comparable with
those based on the 1989 revision.

Reported Legal Abortions in 2006

Reporting States' Total = 846,181 Abortions*

ALPHA ORDER					RANK ORDER			
RANK	STATE	ABORTIONS	% of USA		RANK	STATE	ABORTIONS	% of USA
18	Alabama	11,654	1.4%		1	New York	127,437	15.1%
42	Alaska	1,923	0.2%		2	Florida	95,586	11.3%
22	Arizona	10,836	1.3%		3	Texas	81,883	9.7%
31	Arkansas	4,988	0.6%		4	Illinois	46,467	5.5%
NA	California**	NA	NA		5	Pennsylvania	36,731	4.3%
21	Colorado	11,048	1.3%		6	North Carolina	35,088	4.1%
15	Connecticut	14,112	1.7%		7	Ohio	32,936	3.9%
33	Delaware	4,804	0.6%		8	New Jersey	30,986	3.7%
2	Florida	95,586	11.3%		9	Georgia	30,550	3.6%
9	Georgia	30,550	3.6%		10	Virginia	27,349	3.2%
34	Hawaii	3,990	0.5%		11	Michigan	25,636	3.0%
45	Idaho	1,249	0.1%		12	Washington	24,627	2.9%
4	Illinois	46,467	5.5%		13	Massachusetts	24,246	2.9%
23	Indiana	10,614	1.3%		14	Tennessee	17,883	2.1%
29	Iowa	6,722	0.8%		15	Connecticut	14,112	1.7%
20	Kansas	11,173	1.3%		16	Minnesota	14,065	1.7%
35	Kentucky	3,912	0.5%		17	Oregon	11,732	1.4%
NA	Louisiana**	NA	NA		18	Alabama	11,654	1.4%
39	Maine	2,670	0.3%		19	Nevada	11,471	1.4%
25	Maryland	9,530	1.1%		20	Kansas	11,173	1.3%
13	Massachusetts	24,246	2.9%		21	Colorado	11,048	1.3%
11	Michigan	25,636	3.0%		22	Arizona	10,836	1.3%
16	Minnesota	14,065	1.7%		23	Indiana	10,614	1.3%
37	Mississippi	2,949	0.3%		24	Wisconsin	9,580	1.1%
26	Missouri	7,556	0.9%		25	Maryland	9,530	1.1%
40	Montana	2,119	0.3%		26	Missouri	7,556	0.9%
38	Nebraska	2,927	0.3%		27	Oklahoma	7,088	0.8%
19	Nevada	11,471	1.4%		28	South Carolina	7,005	0.8%
NA	New Hampshire**	NA	NA		29	Iowa	6,722	0.8%
8	New Jersey	30,986	3.7%		30	New Mexico	6,087	0.7%
30	New Mexico	6,087	0.7%		31	Arkansas	4,988	0.6%
1	New York	127,437	15.1%		32	Rhode Island	4,828	0.6%
6	North Carolina	35,088	4.1%		33	Delaware	4,804	0.6%
44	North Dakota	1,298	0.2%		34	Hawaii	3,990	0.5%
7	Ohio	32,936	3.9%		35	Kentucky	3,912	0.5%
27	Oklahoma	7,088	0.8%		36	Utah	3,753	0.4%
17	Oregon	11,732	1.4%		37	Mississippi	2,949	0.3%
5	Pennsylvania	36,731	4.3%		38	Nebraska	2,927	0.3%
32	Rhode Island	4,828	0.6%		39	Maine	2,670	0.3%
28	South Carolina	7,005	0.8%		40	Montana	2,119	0.3%
46	South Dakota	748	0.1%		41	West Virginia	2,036	0.2%
14	Tennessee	17,883	2.1%		42	Alaska	1,923	0.2%
3	Texas	81,883	9.7%		43	Vermont	1,610	0.2%
36	Utah	3,753	0.4%		44	North Dakota	1,298	0.2%
43	Vermont	1,610	0.2%		45	Idaho	1,249	0.1%
10	Virginia	27,349	3.2%		46	South Dakota	748	0.1%
12	Washington	24,627	2.9%		47	Wyoming	7	0.0%
41	West Virginia	2,036	0.2%		NA	California**	NA	NA
24	Wisconsin	9,580	1.1%		NA	Louisiana**	NA	NA
47	Wyoming	7	0.0%		NA	New Hampshire**	NA	NA
						District of Columbia	2,692	0.3%

Source: U.S. Department of Health and Human Services, Centers for Disease Control and Prevention
"Abortion Surveillance-United States, 2006" (MMWR, Vol. 58, No. SS-8, 11/27/09, http://www.cdc.gov/mmwr/mmwr_ss.html)
*By state of occurrence. Total is for reporting states only.
**Not reported.

Percent Change in Reported Legal Abortions: 2002 to 2006

National Percent Change = 0.1% Increase*

ALPHA ORDER

RANK	STATE	PERCENT CHANGE
30	Alabama	(4.9)
NA	Alaska**	NA
20	Arizona	1.5
34	Arkansas	(6.2)
NA	California**	NA
2	Colorado	42.4
16	Connecticut	4.8
12	Delaware	6.9
10	Florida	8.7
39	Georgia	(10.4)
19	Hawaii	1.8
1	Idaho	50.7
25	Illinois	(1.0)
28	Indiana	(3.0)
11	Iowa	7.7
31	Kansas	(5.0)
7	Kentucky	11.7
NA	Louisiana**	NA
5	Maine	15.3
45	Maryland	(29.9)
29	Massachusetts	(4.0)
41	Michigan	(12.3)
24	Minnesota	(0.9)
43	Mississippi	(18.2)
35	Missouri	(7.9)
32	Montana	(5.7)
44	Nebraska	(22.5)
6	Nevada	15.2
NA	New Hampshire**	NA
32	New Jersey	(5.7)
3	New Mexico	20.1
22	New York	(0.4)
4	North Carolina	20.0
13	North Dakota	6.5
36	Ohio	(8.1)
9	Oklahoma	9.0
40	Oregon	(10.9)
17	Pennsylvania	4.4
42	Rhode Island	(13.0)
15	South Carolina	5.2
38	South Dakota	(9.4)
21	Tennessee	0.4
18	Texas	2.4
13	Utah	6.5
26	Vermont	(1.5)
8	Virginia	9.4
27	Washington	(2.1)
23	West Virginia	(0.6)
37	Wisconsin	(8.7)
46	Wyoming	(30.0)

RANK ORDER

RANK	STATE	PERCENT CHANGE
1	Idaho	50.7
2	Colorado	42.4
3	New Mexico	20.1
4	North Carolina	20.0
5	Maine	15.3
6	Nevada	15.2
7	Kentucky	11.7
8	Virginia	9.4
9	Oklahoma	9.0
10	Florida	8.7
11	Iowa	7.7
12	Delaware	6.9
13	North Dakota	6.5
13	Utah	6.5
15	South Carolina	5.2
16	Connecticut	4.8
17	Pennsylvania	4.4
18	Texas	2.4
19	Hawaii	1.8
20	Arizona	1.5
21	Tennessee	0.4
22	New York	(0.4)
23	West Virginia	(0.6)
24	Minnesota	(0.9)
25	Illinois	(1.0)
26	Vermont	(1.5)
27	Washington	(2.1)
28	Indiana	(3.0)
29	Massachusetts	(4.0)
30	Alabama	(4.9)
31	Kansas	(5.0)
32	Montana	(5.7)
32	New Jersey	(5.7)
34	Arkansas	(6.2)
35	Missouri	(7.9)
36	Ohio	(8.1)
37	Wisconsin	(8.7)
38	South Dakota	(9.4)
39	Georgia	(10.4)
40	Oregon	(10.9)
41	Michigan	(12.3)
42	Rhode Island	(13.0)
43	Mississippi	(18.2)
44	Nebraska	(22.5)
45	Maryland	(29.9)
46	Wyoming	(30.0)
NA	Alaska**	NA
NA	California**	NA
NA	Louisiana**	NA
NA	New Hampshire**	NA

District of Columbia (51.2)

Source: CQ Press using data from U.S. Department of Health and Human Services, Centers for Disease Control and Prevention
"Abortion Surveillance-United States, 2006" (MMWR, Vol. 58, No. SS-8, 11/27/09, http://www.cdc.gov/mmwr/mmwr_ss.html)
"Abortion Surveillance-United States, 2002" (MMWR, Vol. 54, No. SS-7, 11/25/05)
*By state of occurrence. National percent change is only for states reporting in both years.
**Not reported.

Reported Legal Abortions per 1,000 Live Births in 2006

Reporting States' Ratio = 233 Abortions per 1,000 Live Births*

ALPHA ORDER			RANK ORDER		
RANK	STATE	RATIO	RANK	STATE	RATIO
26	Alabama	184	1	New York	510
27	Alaska	175	2	Florida	404
39	Arizona	106	3	Delaware	401
35	Arkansas	122	4	Rhode Island	390
NA	California**	NA	5	Connecticut	337
30	Colorado	156	6	Massachusetts	312
5	Connecticut	337	7	Nevada	287
3	Delaware	401	8	Washington	283
2	Florida	404	9	North Carolina	274
20	Georgia	206	10	Kansas	273
19	Hawaii	210	11	New Jersey	269
46	Idaho	52	12	Illinois	257
12	Illinois	257	13	Virginia	254
36	Indiana	120	14	Vermont	247
29	Iowa	166	15	Pennsylvania	246
10	Kansas	273	16	Oregon	241
43	Kentucky	67	17	Ohio	219
NA	Louisiana**	NA	18	Tennessee	212
25	Maine	189	19	Hawaii	210
34	Maryland	123	20	Georgia	206
6	Massachusetts	312	21	Texas	205
23	Michigan	201	22	New Mexico	203
24	Minnesota	191	23	Michigan	201
44	Mississippi	64	24	Minnesota	191
41	Missouri	93	25	Maine	189
28	Montana	169	26	Alabama	184
38	Nebraska	110	27	Alaska	175
7	Nevada	287	28	Montana	169
NA	New Hampshire**	NA	29	Iowa	166
11	New Jersey	269	30	Colorado	156
22	New Mexico	203	31	North Dakota	151
1	New York	510	32	Wisconsin	132
9	North Carolina	274	33	Oklahoma	131
31	North Dakota	151	34	Maryland	123
17	Ohio	219	35	Arkansas	122
33	Oklahoma	131	36	Indiana	120
16	Oregon	241	37	South Carolina	113
15	Pennsylvania	246	38	Nebraska	110
4	Rhode Island	390	39	Arizona	106
37	South Carolina	113	40	West Virginia	97
45	South Dakota	63	41	Missouri	93
18	Tennessee	212	42	Utah	70
21	Texas	205	43	Kentucky	67
42	Utah	70	44	Mississippi	64
14	Vermont	247	45	South Dakota	63
13	Virginia	254	46	Idaho	52
8	Washington	283	47	Wyoming	1
40	West Virginia	97	NA	California**	NA
32	Wisconsin	132	NA	Louisiana**	NA
47	Wyoming	1	NA	New Hampshire**	NA
				District of Columbia	316

Source: U.S. Department of Health and Human Services, Centers for Disease Control and Prevention
   "Abortion Surveillance-United States, 2006" (MMWR, Vol. 58, No. SS-8, 11/27/09, http://www.cdc.gov/mmwr/mmwr_ss.html)
*By state of occurrence. National figure is for reporting states only.
**Not reported.

Reported Legal Abortions per 1,000 Women 15 to 44 Years Old in 2006

Reporting States' Rate = 15.9 Abortions per 1,000 Women 15 to 44 Years Old*

ALPHA ORDER

RANK	STATE	RATE
25	Alabama	12.4
22	Alaska	13.4
34	Arizona	8.7
33	Arkansas	8.8
NA	California**	NA
29	Colorado	11.0
7	Connecticut	20.0
3	Delaware	27.1
2	Florida	27.3
18	Georgia	15.0
16	Hawaii	15.7
46	Idaho	4.2
12	Illinois	17.3
37	Indiana	8.2
28	Iowa	11.5
6	Kansas	20.1
45	Kentucky	4.5
NA	Louisiana**	NA
30	Maine	10.4
38	Maryland	7.9
10	Massachusetts	17.7
25	Michigan	12.4
23	Minnesota	13.2
43	Mississippi	4.9
41	Missouri	6.3
27	Montana	11.7
36	Nebraska	8.3
4	Nevada	22.7
NA	New Hampshire**	NA
11	New Jersey	17.5
17	New Mexico	15.3
1	New York	31.1
8	North Carolina	18.9
31	North Dakota	10.2
20	Ohio	14.2
32	Oklahoma	9.8
15	Oregon	15.9
18	Pennsylvania	15.0
5	Rhode Island	21.5
39	South Carolina	7.8
43	South Dakota	4.9
20	Tennessee	14.2
14	Texas	16.3
40	Utah	6.5
24	Vermont	13.0
13	Virginia	16.8
9	Washington	18.6
42	West Virginia	5.8
35	Wisconsin	8.5
47	Wyoming	0.1

RANK ORDER

RANK	STATE	RATE
1	New York	31.1
2	Florida	27.3
3	Delaware	27.1
4	Nevada	22.7
5	Rhode Island	21.5
6	Kansas	20.1
7	Connecticut	20.0
8	North Carolina	18.9
9	Washington	18.6
10	Massachusetts	17.7
11	New Jersey	17.5
12	Illinois	17.3
13	Virginia	16.8
14	Texas	16.3
15	Oregon	15.9
16	Hawaii	15.7
17	New Mexico	15.3
18	Georgia	15.0
18	Pennsylvania	15.0
20	Ohio	14.2
20	Tennessee	14.2
22	Alaska	13.4
23	Minnesota	13.2
24	Vermont	13.0
25	Alabama	12.4
25	Michigan	12.4
27	Montana	11.7
28	Iowa	11.5
29	Colorado	11.0
30	Maine	10.4
31	North Dakota	10.2
32	Oklahoma	9.8
33	Arkansas	8.8
34	Arizona	8.7
35	Wisconsin	8.5
36	Nebraska	8.3
37	Indiana	8.2
38	Maryland	7.9
39	South Carolina	7.8
40	Utah	6.5
41	Missouri	6.3
42	West Virginia	5.8
43	Mississippi	4.9
43	South Dakota	4.9
45	Kentucky	4.5
46	Idaho	4.2
47	Wyoming	0.1
NA	California**	NA
NA	Louisiana**	NA
NA	New Hampshire**	NA

District of Columbia   18.4

Source: U.S. Department of Health and Human Services, Centers for Disease Control and Prevention
"Abortion Surveillance-United States, 2006" (MMWR, Vol. 58, No. SS-8, 11/27/09, http://www.cdc.gov/mmwr/mmwr_ss.html)
*By state of occurrence. National figure is for reporting states only.
**Not reported.

Percent of Legal Abortions Obtained by Out-of-State Residents in 2006

Reporting States' Percent = 8.4% of Abortions*

ALPHA ORDER

RANK	STATE	PERCENT
6	Alabama	18.7
41	Alaska	0.6
34	Arizona	3.4
11	Arkansas	14.0
NA	California**	NA
42	Colorado	0.4
36	Connecticut	3.0
3	Delaware	28.2
NA	Florida**	NA
14	Georgia	10.7
43	Hawaii	0.3
38	Idaho	2.7
18	Illinois	8.7
31	Indiana	4.0
8	Iowa	16.7
1	Kansas	48.2
NA	Kentucky**	NA
NA	Louisiana**	NA
35	Maine	3.2
10	Maryland	14.3
30	Massachusetts	4.1
37	Michigan	2.8
20	Minnesota	7.9
39	Mississippi	2.5
21	Missouri	7.5
17	Montana	8.9
13	Nebraska	12.4
23	Nevada	5.7
NA	New Hampshire**	NA
26	New Jersey	5.2
24	New Mexico	5.3
NA	New York**	NA
7	North Carolina	17.4
2	North Dakota	40.1
22	Ohio	6.0
33	Oklahoma	3.5
12	Oregon	12.5
28	Pennsylvania	4.2
4	Rhode Island	23.6
28	South Carolina	4.2
9	South Dakota	15.4
5	Tennessee	22.2
32	Texas	3.6
19	Utah	8.2
16	Vermont	9.6
24	Virginia	5.3
27	Washington	4.8
15	West Virginia	10.3
40	Wisconsin	2.4
44	Wyoming	0.0

RANK ORDER

RANK	STATE	PERCENT
1	Kansas	48.2
2	North Dakota	40.1
3	Delaware	28.2
4	Rhode Island	23.6
5	Tennessee	22.2
6	Alabama	18.7
7	North Carolina	17.4
8	Iowa	16.7
9	South Dakota	15.4
10	Maryland	14.3
11	Arkansas	14.0
12	Oregon	12.5
13	Nebraska	12.4
14	Georgia	10.7
15	West Virginia	10.3
16	Vermont	9.6
17	Montana	8.9
18	Illinois	8.7
19	Utah	8.2
20	Minnesota	7.9
21	Missouri	7.5
22	Ohio	6.0
23	Nevada	5.7
24	New Mexico	5.3
24	Virginia	5.3
26	New Jersey	5.2
27	Washington	4.8
28	Pennsylvania	4.2
28	South Carolina	4.2
30	Massachusetts	4.1
31	Indiana	4.0
32	Texas	3.6
33	Oklahoma	3.5
34	Arizona	3.4
35	Maine	3.2
36	Connecticut	3.0
37	Michigan	2.8
38	Idaho	2.7
39	Mississippi	2.5
40	Wisconsin	2.4
41	Alaska	0.6
42	Colorado	0.4
43	Hawaii	0.3
44	Wyoming	0.0
NA	California**	NA
NA	Florida**	NA
NA	Kentucky**	NA
NA	Louisiana**	NA
NA	New Hampshire**	NA
NA	New York**	NA

District of Columbia   54.3

Source: U.S. Department of Health and Human Services, Centers for Disease Control and Prevention
"Abortion Surveillance-United States, 2006" (MMWR, Vol. 58, No. SS-8, 11/27/09, http://www.cdc.gov/mmwr/mmwr_ss.html)
*By state of occurrence. National figure is for reporting states only.
**Not reported.

Percent of Reported Legal Abortions That Were First-Time Abortions: 2006

Reporting States' Percent = 54.1% of Abortions*

ALPHA ORDER

RANK	STATE	PERCENT
7	Alabama	65.3
17	Alaska	59.6
15	Arizona	61.0
13	Arkansas	62.4
NA	California**	NA
9	Colorado	64.0
NA	Connecticut**	NA
20	Delaware	59.3
NA	Florida**	NA
16	Georgia	60.4
34	Hawaii	50.8
1	Idaho	78.1
NA	Illinois**	NA
26	Indiana	56.4
8	Iowa	65.0
14	Kansas	61.7
21	Kentucky	58.8
NA	Louisiana**	NA
6	Maine	65.8
40	Maryland	21.6
36	Massachusetts	48.1
32	Michigan	51.5
22	Minnesota	58.5
12	Mississippi	62.9
24	Missouri	57.8
39	Montana	32.2
10	Nebraska	63.9
35	Nevada	50.7
NA	New Hampshire**	NA
5	New Jersey	66.1
NA	New Mexico**	NA
38	New York	45.1
NA	North Carolina**	NA
3	North Dakota	68.8
36	Ohio	48.1
11	Oklahoma	63.4
28	Oregon	56.1
29	Pennsylvania	55.3
33	Rhode Island	51.3
25	South Carolina	57.0
2	South Dakota	70.5
31	Tennessee	52.2
23	Texas	58.0
4	Utah	66.4
18	Vermont	59.5
26	Virginia	56.4
30	Washington	53.3
18	West Virginia	59.5
NA	Wisconsin**	NA
NA	Wyoming**	NA

RANK ORDER

RANK	STATE	PERCENT
1	Idaho	78.1
2	South Dakota	70.5
3	North Dakota	68.8
4	Utah	66.4
5	New Jersey	66.1
6	Maine	65.8
7	Alabama	65.3
8	Iowa	65.0
9	Colorado	64.0
10	Nebraska	63.9
11	Oklahoma	63.4
12	Mississippi	62.9
13	Arkansas	62.4
14	Kansas	61.7
15	Arizona	61.0
16	Georgia	60.4
17	Alaska	59.6
18	Vermont	59.5
18	West Virginia	59.5
20	Delaware	59.3
21	Kentucky	58.8
22	Minnesota	58.5
23	Texas	58.0
24	Missouri	57.8
25	South Carolina	57.0
26	Indiana	56.4
26	Virginia	56.4
28	Oregon	56.1
29	Pennsylvania	55.3
30	Washington	53.3
31	Tennessee	52.2
32	Michigan	51.5
33	Rhode Island	51.3
34	Hawaii	50.8
35	Nevada	50.7
36	Massachusetts	48.1
36	Ohio	48.1
38	New York	45.1
39	Montana	32.2
40	Maryland	21.6
NA	California**	NA
NA	Connecticut**	NA
NA	Florida**	NA
NA	Illinois**	NA
NA	Louisiana**	NA
NA	New Hampshire**	NA
NA	New Mexico**	NA
NA	North Carolina**	NA
NA	Wisconsin**	NA
NA	Wyoming**	NA
	District of Columbia**	NA

Source: U.S. Department of Health and Human Services, Centers for Disease Control and Prevention

"Abortion Surveillance-United States, 2006" (MMWR, Vol. 58, No. SS-8, 11/27/09, http://www.cdc.gov/mmwr/mmwr_ss.html)

*By state of occurrence. National figure is for reporting states only. Percent of abortions to women who had no previous abortions.

**Not reported.

Percent of Reported Legal Abortions Obtained by White Women in 2006

Reporting States' Percent = 55.8% of Abortions*

ALPHA ORDER

RANK	STATE	PERCENT
31	Alabama	42.3
21	Alaska	57.8
NA	Arizona**	NA
19	Arkansas	61.7
NA	California**	NA
14	Colorado	67.2
NA	Connecticut**	NA
25	Delaware	53.8
NA	Florida**	NA
33	Georgia	37.9
35	Hawaii	24.1
2	Idaho	90.7
NA	Illinois**	NA
17	Indiana	64.1
9	Iowa	79.3
13	Kansas	68.2
15	Kentucky	66.6
NA	Louisiana**	NA
3	Maine	90.0
37	Maryland	20.5
27	Massachusetts	50.1
26	Michigan	53.5
18	Minnesota	62.9
36	Mississippi	22.6
24	Missouri	54.8
8	Montana	80.2
NA	Nebraska**	NA
NA	Nevada**	NA
NA	New Hampshire**	NA
34	New Jersey	31.8
NA	New Mexico**	NA
29	New York**	47.0
32	North Carolina	41.1
7	North Dakota	81.7
22	Ohio	56.8
10	Oklahoma	72.0
5	Oregon	84.2
23	Pennsylvania	55.9
16	Rhode Island	64.6
20	South Carolina	58.9
6	South Dakota	84.0
28	Tennessee	49.0
11	Texas	70.6
NA	Utah**	NA
1	Vermont	94.7
30	Virginia	44.5
NA	Washington**	NA
4	West Virginia	85.1
12	Wisconsin	69.1
NA	Wyoming**	NA

RANK ORDER

RANK	STATE	PERCENT
1	Vermont	94.7
2	Idaho	90.7
3	Maine	90.0
4	West Virginia	85.1
5	Oregon	84.2
6	South Dakota	84.0
7	North Dakota	81.7
8	Montana	80.2
9	Iowa	79.3
10	Oklahoma	72.0
11	Texas	70.6
12	Wisconsin	69.1
13	Kansas	68.2
14	Colorado	67.2
15	Kentucky	66.6
16	Rhode Island	64.6
17	Indiana	64.1
18	Minnesota	62.9
19	Arkansas	61.7
20	South Carolina	58.9
21	Alaska	57.8
22	Ohio	56.8
23	Pennsylvania	55.9
24	Missouri	54.8
25	Delaware	53.8
26	Michigan	53.5
27	Massachusetts	50.1
28	Tennessee	49.0
29	New York**	47.0
30	Virginia	44.5
31	Alabama	42.3
32	North Carolina	41.1
33	Georgia	37.9
34	New Jersey	31.8
35	Hawaii	24.1
36	Mississippi	22.6
37	Maryland	20.5
NA	Arizona**	NA
NA	California**	NA
NA	Connecticut**	NA
NA	Florida**	NA
NA	Illinois**	NA
NA	Louisiana**	NA
NA	Nebraska**	NA
NA	Nevada**	NA
NA	New Hampshire**	NA
NA	New Mexico**	NA
NA	Utah**	NA
NA	Washington**	NA
NA	Wyoming**	NA

District of Columbia	21.0

Source: U.S. Department of Health and Human Services, Centers for Disease Control and Prevention
"Abortion Surveillance-United States, 2006" (MMWR, Vol. 58, No. SS-8, 11/27/09, http://www.cdc.gov/mmwr/mmwr_ss.html)
*By state of occurrence. Includes those of Hispanic ethnicity. National percent is for reporting states only.
**Not reported. New York's number is for New York City only.

Percent of Reported Legal Abortions Obtained by Black Women in 2006

Reporting States' Percent = 36.4% of Abortions*

<table>
<tr><td colspan="3">ALPHA ORDER</td><td colspan="3">RANK ORDER</td></tr>
<tr><td>RANK</td><td>STATE</td><td>PERCENT</td><td>RANK</td><td>STATE</td><td>PERCENT</td></tr>
<tr><td>4</td><td>Alabama</td><td>56.0</td><td>1</td><td>Mississippi</td><td>76.3</td></tr>
<tr><td>28</td><td>Alaska</td><td>7.3</td><td>2</td><td>Maryland</td><td>67.4</td></tr>
<tr><td>NA</td><td>Arizona**</td><td>NA</td><td>3</td><td>Georgia</td><td>57.4</td></tr>
<tr><td>16</td><td>Arkansas</td><td>30.6</td><td>4</td><td>Alabama</td><td>56.0</td></tr>
<tr><td>NA</td><td>California**</td><td>NA</td><td>5</td><td>Tennessee</td><td>46.0</td></tr>
<tr><td>29</td><td>Colorado</td><td>6.2</td><td>6</td><td>North Carolina</td><td>45.4</td></tr>
<tr><td>NA</td><td>Connecticut**</td><td>NA</td><td>7</td><td>New Jersey</td><td>44.6</td></tr>
<tr><td>9</td><td>Delaware</td><td>41.5</td><td>8</td><td>Virginia</td><td>41.8</td></tr>
<tr><td>NA</td><td>Florida**</td><td>NA</td><td>9</td><td>Delaware</td><td>41.5</td></tr>
<tr><td>3</td><td>Georgia</td><td>57.4</td><td>10</td><td>New York**</td><td>40.9</td></tr>
<tr><td>32</td><td>Hawaii</td><td>3.6</td><td>11</td><td>Missouri</td><td>40.1</td></tr>
<tr><td>35</td><td>Idaho</td><td>1.1</td><td>12</td><td>Michigan</td><td>39.5</td></tr>
<tr><td>NA</td><td>Illinois**</td><td>NA</td><td>13</td><td>Pennsylvania</td><td>38.9</td></tr>
<tr><td>17</td><td>Indiana</td><td>28.7</td><td>14</td><td>South Carolina</td><td>38.5</td></tr>
<tr><td>27</td><td>Iowa</td><td>9.9</td><td>15</td><td>Ohio</td><td>35.5</td></tr>
<tr><td>22</td><td>Kansas</td><td>21.5</td><td>16</td><td>Arkansas</td><td>30.6</td></tr>
<tr><td>20</td><td>Kentucky</td><td>21.7</td><td>17</td><td>Indiana</td><td>28.7</td></tr>
<tr><td>NA</td><td>Louisiana**</td><td>NA</td><td>18</td><td>Wisconsin</td><td>24.3</td></tr>
<tr><td>34</td><td>Maine</td><td>1.9</td><td>19</td><td>Texas</td><td>23.2</td></tr>
<tr><td>2</td><td>Maryland</td><td>67.4</td><td>20</td><td>Kentucky</td><td>21.7</td></tr>
<tr><td>23</td><td>Massachusetts</td><td>19.2</td><td>20</td><td>Minnesota</td><td>21.7</td></tr>
<tr><td>12</td><td>Michigan</td><td>39.5</td><td>22</td><td>Kansas</td><td>21.5</td></tr>
<tr><td>20</td><td>Minnesota</td><td>21.7</td><td>23</td><td>Massachusetts</td><td>19.2</td></tr>
<tr><td>1</td><td>Mississippi</td><td>76.3</td><td>24</td><td>Oklahoma</td><td>18.8</td></tr>
<tr><td>11</td><td>Missouri</td><td>40.1</td><td>25</td><td>Rhode Island</td><td>15.2</td></tr>
<tr><td>36</td><td>Montana</td><td>0.7</td><td>26</td><td>West Virginia</td><td>11.2</td></tr>
<tr><td>NA</td><td>Nebraska**</td><td>NA</td><td>27</td><td>Iowa</td><td>9.9</td></tr>
<tr><td>NA</td><td>Nevada**</td><td>NA</td><td>28</td><td>Alaska</td><td>7.3</td></tr>
<tr><td>NA</td><td>New Hampshire**</td><td>NA</td><td>29</td><td>Colorado</td><td>6.2</td></tr>
<tr><td>7</td><td>New Jersey</td><td>44.6</td><td>30</td><td>Oregon</td><td>5.7</td></tr>
<tr><td>NA</td><td>New Mexico**</td><td>NA</td><td>31</td><td>North Dakota</td><td>3.7</td></tr>
<tr><td>10</td><td>New York**</td><td>40.9</td><td>32</td><td>Hawaii</td><td>3.6</td></tr>
<tr><td>6</td><td>North Carolina</td><td>45.4</td><td>33</td><td>Vermont</td><td>2.2</td></tr>
<tr><td>31</td><td>North Dakota</td><td>3.7</td><td>34</td><td>Maine</td><td>1.9</td></tr>
<tr><td>15</td><td>Ohio</td><td>35.5</td><td>35</td><td>Idaho</td><td>1.1</td></tr>
<tr><td>24</td><td>Oklahoma</td><td>18.8</td><td>36</td><td>Montana</td><td>0.7</td></tr>
<tr><td>30</td><td>Oregon</td><td>5.7</td><td>37</td><td>South Dakota</td><td>0.0</td></tr>
<tr><td>13</td><td>Pennsylvania</td><td>38.9</td><td>NA</td><td>Arizona**</td><td>NA</td></tr>
<tr><td>25</td><td>Rhode Island</td><td>15.2</td><td>NA</td><td>California**</td><td>NA</td></tr>
<tr><td>14</td><td>South Carolina</td><td>38.5</td><td>NA</td><td>Connecticut**</td><td>NA</td></tr>
<tr><td>37</td><td>South Dakota</td><td>0.0</td><td>NA</td><td>Florida**</td><td>NA</td></tr>
<tr><td>5</td><td>Tennessee</td><td>46.0</td><td>NA</td><td>Illinois**</td><td>NA</td></tr>
<tr><td>19</td><td>Texas</td><td>23.2</td><td>NA</td><td>Louisiana**</td><td>NA</td></tr>
<tr><td>NA</td><td>Utah**</td><td>NA</td><td>NA</td><td>Nebraska**</td><td>NA</td></tr>
<tr><td>33</td><td>Vermont</td><td>2.2</td><td>NA</td><td>Nevada**</td><td>NA</td></tr>
<tr><td>8</td><td>Virginia</td><td>41.8</td><td>NA</td><td>New Hampshire**</td><td>NA</td></tr>
<tr><td>NA</td><td>Washington**</td><td>NA</td><td>NA</td><td>New Mexico**</td><td>NA</td></tr>
<tr><td>26</td><td>West Virginia</td><td>11.2</td><td>NA</td><td>Utah**</td><td>NA</td></tr>
<tr><td>18</td><td>Wisconsin</td><td>24.3</td><td>NA</td><td>Washington**</td><td>NA</td></tr>
<tr><td>NA</td><td>Wyoming**</td><td>NA</td><td>NA</td><td>Wyoming**</td><td>NA</td></tr>
<tr><td></td><td></td><td></td><td></td><td>District of Columbia</td><td>52.5</td></tr>
</table>

Source: U.S. Department of Health and Human Services, Centers for Disease Control and Prevention
   "Abortion Surveillance-United States, 2006" (MMWR, Vol. 58, No. SS-8, 11/27/09, http://www.cdc.gov/mmwr/mmwr_ss.html)
*By state of occurrence. National percent is for reporting states only.
**Not reported. New York's number is for New York City only.

Percent of Reported Legal Abortions Obtained by Hispanic Women in 2006

Reporting States' Percent = 20.1%*

ALPHA ORDER			RANK ORDER		
RANK	STATE	PERCENT	RANK	STATE	PERCENT
NA	Alabama**	NA	1	New Mexico	50.9
NA	Alaska**	NA	2	Arizona	37.9
2	Arizona	37.9	3	Texas	36.7
19	Arkansas	5.0	4	New York	27.1
NA	California**	NA	5	New Jersey	26.9
7	Colorado	22.3	6	Utah	24.0
NA	Connecticut**	NA	7	Colorado	22.3
9	Delaware	11.2	8	Oregon	11.4
NA	Florida**	NA	9	Delaware	11.2
16	Georgia	5.7	10	Idaho	10.9
14	Hawaii	6.6	11	Kansas	10.5
10	Idaho	10.9	12	Wisconsin	9.1
NA	Illinois**	NA	13	Indiana	7.5
13	Indiana	7.5	14	Hawaii	6.6
NA	Iowa**	NA	15	Pennsylvania	6.0
11	Kansas	10.5	16	Georgia	5.7
NA	Kentucky**	NA	16	Minnesota	5.7
NA	Louisiana**	NA	18	South Dakota	5.2
23	Maine	2.3	19	Arkansas	5.0
NA	Maryland**	NA	20	Tennessee	4.3
NA	Massachusetts**	NA	21	Ohio	3.6
NA	Michigan**	NA	22	Missouri	3.1
16	Minnesota	5.7	23	Maine	2.3
25	Mississippi	1.2	24	Vermont	2.2
22	Missouri	3.1	25	Mississippi	1.2
NA	Montana**	NA	NA	Alabama**	NA
NA	Nebraska**	NA	NA	Alaska**	NA
NA	Nevada**	NA	NA	California**	NA
NA	New Hampshire**	NA	NA	Connecticut**	NA
5	New Jersey	26.9	NA	Florida**	NA
1	New Mexico	50.9	NA	Illinois**	NA
4	New York	27.1	NA	Iowa**	NA
NA	North Carolina**	NA	NA	Kentucky**	NA
NA	North Dakota**	NA	NA	Louisiana**	NA
21	Ohio	3.6	NA	Maryland**	NA
NA	Oklahoma**	NA	NA	Massachusetts**	NA
8	Oregon	11.4	NA	Michigan**	NA
15	Pennsylvania	6.0	NA	Montana**	NA
NA	Rhode Island**	NA	NA	Nebraska**	NA
NA	South Carolina**	NA	NA	Nevada**	NA
18	South Dakota	5.2	NA	New Hampshire**	NA
20	Tennessee	4.3	NA	North Carolina**	NA
3	Texas	36.7	NA	North Dakota**	NA
6	Utah	24.0	NA	Oklahoma**	NA
24	Vermont	2.2	NA	Rhode Island**	NA
NA	Virginia**	NA	NA	South Carolina**	NA
NA	Washington**	NA	NA	Virginia**	NA
NA	West Virginia**	NA	NA	Washington**	NA
12	Wisconsin	9.1	NA	West Virginia**	NA
NA	Wyoming**	NA	NA	Wyoming**	NA
				District of Columbia	13.7

Source: U.S. Department of Health and Human Services, Centers for Disease Control and Prevention
   "Abortion Surveillance-United States, 2006" (MMWR, Vol. 58, No. SS-8, 11/27/09, http://www.cdc.gov/mmwr/mmwr_ss.html)
*By state of occurrence. National percent is for reporting states only. Hispanic can be of any race.
**Not reported.

Percent of Reported Legal Abortions Obtained by Married Women in 2006

Reporting States' Percent = 16.5% of Abortions*

ALPHA ORDER				RANK ORDER		
RANK	STATE	PERCENT		RANK	STATE	PERCENT
38	Alabama	11.6		1	Utah	23.8
12	Alaska	17.6		2	Oklahoma	20.8
16	Arizona	16.9		3	Idaho	20.5
NA	Arkansas**	NA		4	North Carolina	20.3
NA	California**	NA		5	Nevada	19.6
11	Colorado	17.7		6	Oregon	19.4
NA	Connecticut**	NA		7	Texas	18.4
39	Delaware	11.4		8	Virginia	18.0
NA	Florida**	NA		9	Maryland	17.9
15	Georgia	17.0		10	Missouri	17.8
34	Hawaii	13.7		11	Colorado	17.7
3	Idaho	20.5		12	Alaska	17.6
23	Illinois	15.3		12	West Virginia	17.6
20	Indiana	16.1		14	Vermont	17.2
16	Iowa	16.9		15	Georgia	17.0
NA	Kansas**	NA		16	Arizona	16.9
25	Kentucky	15.1		16	Iowa	16.9
NA	Louisiana**	NA		16	Rhode Island	16.9
29	Maine	14.5		19	Minnesota	16.4
9	Maryland	17.9		20	Indiana	16.1
33	Massachusetts	13.8		20	South Carolina	16.1
37	Michigan	12.6		22	Tennessee	15.5
19	Minnesota	16.4		23	Illinois	15.3
NA	Mississippi**	NA		24	South Dakota	15.2
10	Missouri	17.8		25	Kentucky	15.1
27	Montana	14.8		26	Ohio	15.0
NA	Nebraska**	NA		27	Montana	14.8
5	Nevada	19.6		28	Pennsylvania	14.6
NA	New Hampshire**	NA		29	Maine	14.5
35	New Jersey	13.6		30	New Mexico	14.4
30	New Mexico	14.4		31	Wisconsin	14.3
32	New York**	14.1		32	New York**	14.1
4	North Carolina	20.3		33	Massachusetts	13.8
35	North Dakota	13.6		34	Hawaii	13.7
26	Ohio	15.0		35	New Jersey	13.6
2	Oklahoma	20.8		35	North Dakota	13.6
6	Oregon	19.4		37	Michigan	12.6
28	Pennsylvania	14.6		38	Alabama	11.6
16	Rhode Island	16.9		39	Delaware	11.4
20	South Carolina	16.1		NA	Arkansas**	NA
24	South Dakota	15.2		NA	California**	NA
22	Tennessee	15.5		NA	Connecticut**	NA
7	Texas	18.4		NA	Florida**	NA
1	Utah	23.8		NA	Kansas**	NA
14	Vermont	17.2		NA	Louisiana**	NA
8	Virginia	18.0		NA	Mississippi**	NA
NA	Washington**	NA		NA	Nebraska**	NA
12	West Virginia	17.6		NA	New Hampshire**	NA
31	Wisconsin	14.3		NA	Washington**	NA
NA	Wyoming**	NA		NA	Wyoming**	NA
					District of Columbia	10.0

Source: U.S. Department of Health and Human Services, Centers for Disease Control and Prevention
"Abortion Surveillance-United States, 2006" (MMWR, Vol. 58, No. SS-8, 11/27/09, http://www.cdc.gov/mmwr/mmwr_ss.html)
*By state of occurrence. National percent is for reporting states only.
**Not reported. New York's number is for New York City only.

Percent of Reported Legal Abortions Obtained by Unmarried Women in 2006

Reporting States' Percent = 83.5% of Abortions*

ALPHA ORDER			RANK ORDER		
RANK	STATE	PERCENT	RANK	STATE	PERCENT
2	Alabama	87.8	1	Mississippi	92.0
28	Alaska	79.7	2	Alabama	87.8
15	Arizona	83.1	3	Michigan	86.7
NA	Arkansas**	NA	4	Delaware	86.6
NA	California**	NA	5	New Jersey	86.4
32	Colorado	79.1	6	Hawaii	86.0
NA	Connecticut**	NA	6	North Dakota	86.0
4	Delaware	86.6	8	Wisconsin	85.5
NA	Florida**	NA	9	Pennsylvania	85.4
35	Georgia	77.4	10	Kentucky	84.9
6	Hawaii	86.0	11	South Dakota	84.8
29	Idaho	79.5	12	South Carolina	83.7
16	Illinois	82.8	13	New York**	83.6
21	Indiana	81.7	14	New Mexico	83.2
18	Iowa	82.7	15	Arizona	83.1
19	Kansas	82.6	16	Illinois	82.8
10	Kentucky	84.9	16	Minnesota	82.8
NA	Louisiana**	NA	18	Iowa	82.7
20	Maine	81.9	19	Kansas	82.6
32	Maryland	79.1	20	Maine	81.9
34	Massachusetts	77.7	21	Indiana	81.7
3	Michigan	86.7	22	Ohio	81.4
16	Minnesota	82.8	22	Tennessee	81.4
1	Mississippi	92.0	24	West Virginia	81.0
25	Missouri	80.7	25	Missouri	80.7
39	Montana	73.7	26	Texas	80.6
NA	Nebraska**	NA	26	Vermont	80.6
37	Nevada	74.5	28	Alaska	79.7
NA	New Hampshire**	NA	29	Idaho	79.5
5	New Jersey	86.4	29	Rhode Island	79.5
14	New Mexico	83.2	31	Oklahoma	79.2
13	New York**	83.6	32	Colorado	79.1
38	North Carolina	74.4	32	Maryland	79.1
6	North Dakota	86.0	34	Massachusetts	77.7
22	Ohio	81.4	35	Georgia	77.4
31	Oklahoma	79.2	36	Oregon	77.3
36	Oregon	77.3	37	Nevada	74.5
9	Pennsylvania	85.4	38	North Carolina	74.4
29	Rhode Island	79.5	39	Montana	73.7
12	South Carolina	83.7	40	Virginia	71.5
11	South Dakota	84.8	41	Utah	64.1
22	Tennessee	81.4	NA	Arkansas**	NA
26	Texas	80.6	NA	California**	NA
41	Utah	64.1	NA	Connecticut**	NA
26	Vermont	80.6	NA	Florida**	NA
40	Virginia	71.5	NA	Louisiana**	NA
NA	Washington**	NA	NA	Nebraska**	NA
24	West Virginia	81.0	NA	New Hampshire**	NA
8	Wisconsin	85.5	NA	Washington**	NA
NA	Wyoming**	NA	NA	Wyoming**	NA
				District of Columbia	89.6

Source: U.S. Department of Health and Human Services, Centers for Disease Control and Prevention
   "Abortion Surveillance-United States, 2006" (MMWR, Vol. 58, No. SS-8, 11/27/09, http://www.cdc.gov/mmwr/mmwr_ss.html)
*By state of occurrence. National percent is for reporting states only.
**Not reported. New York's number is for New York City only.

Reported Legal Abortions Obtained by Teenagers in 2006

Reporting States' Total = 116,613 Abortions Obtained by Teenagers*

ALPHA ORDER					RANK ORDER			
RANK	STATE	ABORTIONS	% of USA		RANK	STATE	ABORTIONS	% of USA
14	Alabama	2,180	1.9%		1	New York	23,286	20.0%
38	Alaska	369	0.3%		2	Texas	10,530	9.0%
18	Arizona	1,967	1.7%		3	Pennsylvania	6,415	5.5%
28	Arkansas	956	0.8%		4	Ohio	5,895	5.1%
NA	California**	NA	NA		5	New Jersey	5,592	4.8%
17	Colorado	1,994	1.7%		6	North Carolina	5,430	4.7%
13	Connecticut	2,733	2.3%		7	Michigan	4,694	4.0%
32	Delaware	632	0.5%		8	Georgia	4,520	3.9%
NA	Florida**	NA	NA		9	Washington	4,515	3.9%
8	Georgia	4,520	3.9%		10	Massachusetts	4,019	3.4%
30	Hawaii	824	0.7%		11	Virginia	3,981	3.4%
41	Idaho	265	0.2%		12	Tennessee	2,881	2.5%
NA	Illinois**	NA	NA		13	Connecticut	2,733	2.3%
21	Indiana	1,700	1.5%		14	Alabama	2,180	1.9%
25	Iowa	1,222	1.0%		15	Minnesota	2,141	1.8%
19	Kansas	1,950	1.7%		16	Oregon	2,053	1.8%
31	Kentucky	662	0.6%		17	Colorado	1,994	1.7%
NA	Louisiana**	NA	NA		18	Arizona	1,967	1.7%
34	Maine	483	0.4%		19	Kansas	1,950	1.7%
NA	Maryland**	NA	NA		20	Nevada	1,833	1.6%
10	Massachusetts	4,019	3.4%		21	Indiana	1,700	1.5%
7	Michigan	4,694	4.0%		22	Wisconsin	1,662	1.4%
15	Minnesota	2,141	1.8%		23	South Carolina	1,294	1.1%
35	Mississippi	467	0.4%		24	Missouri	1,278	1.1%
24	Missouri	1,278	1.1%		25	Iowa	1,222	1.0%
37	Montana	413	0.4%		26	New Mexico	1,208	1.0%
36	Nebraska	460	0.4%		27	Oklahoma	1,148	1.0%
20	Nevada	1,833	1.6%		28	Arkansas	956	0.8%
NA	New Hampshire**	NA	NA		29	Rhode Island	865	0.7%
5	New Jersey	5,592	4.8%		30	Hawaii	824	0.7%
26	New Mexico	1,208	1.0%		31	Kentucky	662	0.6%
1	New York	23,286	20.0%		32	Delaware	632	0.5%
6	North Carolina	5,430	4.7%		33	Utah	628	0.5%
42	North Dakota	229	0.2%		34	Maine	483	0.4%
4	Ohio	5,895	5.1%		35	Mississippi	467	0.4%
27	Oklahoma	1,148	1.0%		36	Nebraska	460	0.4%
16	Oregon	2,053	1.8%		37	Montana	413	0.4%
3	Pennsylvania	6,415	5.5%		38	Alaska	369	0.3%
29	Rhode Island	865	0.7%		39	West Virginia	320	0.3%
23	South Carolina	1,294	1.1%		40	Vermont	300	0.3%
43	South Dakota	124	0.1%		41	Idaho	265	0.2%
12	Tennessee	2,881	2.5%		42	North Dakota	229	0.2%
2	Texas	10,530	9.0%		43	South Dakota	124	0.1%
33	Utah	628	0.5%		44	Wyoming	1	0.0%
40	Vermont	300	0.3%		NA	California**	NA	NA
11	Virginia	3,981	3.4%		NA	Florida**	NA	NA
9	Washington	4,515	3.9%		NA	Illinois**	NA	NA
39	West Virginia	320	0.3%		NA	Louisiana**	NA	NA
22	Wisconsin	1,662	1.4%		NA	Maryland**	NA	NA
44	Wyoming	1	0.0%		NA	New Hampshire**	NA	NA
						District of Columbia	494	0.4%

Source: U.S. Department of Health and Human Services, Centers for Disease Control and Prevention
   "Abortion Surveillance-United States, 2006" (MMWR, Vol. 58, No. SS-8, 11/27/09, http://www.cdc.gov/mmwr/mmwr_ss.html)
*19 years old and younger by state of occurrence. National total is for reporting states only.
**Not reported.

Percent of Reported Legal Abortions Obtained by Teenagers in 2006

Reporting States' Percent = 16.8% of Abortions*

ALPHA ORDER				RANK ORDER		
RANK	STATE	PERCENT		RANK	STATE	PERCENT
8	Alabama	18.7		1	Idaho	21.2
6	Alaska	19.2		2	Hawaii	20.7
14	Arizona	18.2		3	New Mexico	19.8
6	Arkansas	19.2		4	Montana	19.5
NA	California**	NA		5	Connecticut	19.4
17	Colorado	18.0		6	Alaska	19.2
5	Connecticut	19.4		6	Arkansas	19.2
43	Delaware	13.2		8	Alabama	18.7
NA	Florida**	NA		9	Vermont	18.6
40	Georgia	14.8		10	South Carolina	18.5
2	Hawaii	20.7		11	Michigan	18.3
1	Idaho	21.2		11	New York	18.3
NA	Illinois**	NA		11	Washington	18.3
33	Indiana	16.0		14	Arizona	18.2
14	Iowa	18.2		14	Iowa	18.2
22	Kansas	17.5		16	Maine	18.1
26	Kentucky	16.9		17	Colorado	18.0
NA	Louisiana**	NA		17	New Jersey	18.0
16	Maine	18.1		19	Ohio	17.9
NA	Maryland**	NA		19	Rhode Island	17.9
29	Massachusetts	16.6		21	North Dakota	17.6
11	Michigan	18.3		22	Kansas	17.5
39	Minnesota	15.2		22	Oregon	17.5
35	Mississippi	15.8		22	Pennsylvania	17.5
26	Missouri	16.9		25	Wisconsin	17.3
4	Montana	19.5		26	Kentucky	16.9
36	Nebraska	15.7		26	Missouri	16.9
33	Nevada	16.0		28	Utah	16.7
NA	New Hampshire**	NA		29	Massachusetts	16.6
17	New Jersey	18.0		29	South Dakota	16.6
3	New Mexico	19.8		31	Oklahoma	16.2
11	New York	18.3		32	Tennessee	16.1
38	North Carolina	15.5		33	Indiana	16.0
21	North Dakota	17.6		33	Nevada	16.0
19	Ohio	17.9		35	Mississippi	15.8
31	Oklahoma	16.2		36	Nebraska	15.7
22	Oregon	17.5		36	West Virginia	15.7
22	Pennsylvania	17.5		38	North Carolina	15.5
19	Rhode Island	17.9		39	Minnesota	15.2
10	South Carolina	18.5		40	Georgia	14.8
29	South Dakota	16.6		41	Virginia	14.6
32	Tennessee	16.1		42	Wyoming	14.3
44	Texas	12.9		43	Delaware	13.2
28	Utah	16.7		44	Texas	12.9
9	Vermont	18.6		NA	California**	NA
41	Virginia	14.6		NA	Florida**	NA
11	Washington	18.3		NA	Illinois**	NA
36	West Virginia	15.7		NA	Louisiana**	NA
25	Wisconsin	17.3		NA	Maryland**	NA
42	Wyoming	14.3		NA	New Hampshire**	NA

District of Columbia 18.4

Source: CQ Press using data from U.S. Department of Health and Human Services, Centers for Disease Control and Prevention "Abortion Surveillance-United States, 2006" (MMWR, Vol. 58, No. SS-8, 11/27/09, http://www.cdc.gov/mmwr/mmwr_ss.html)
*19 years old and younger by state of occurrence. National percent is for reporting states only.
**Not reported.

Reported Legal Abortions Obtained by Teenagers 17 Years and Younger in 2006

Reporting States' Total = 44,322 Abortions*

RANK	STATE	ABORTIONS	% of USA
14	Alabama	842	1.9%
38	Alaska	128	0.3%
19	Arizona	705	1.6%
27	Arkansas	401	0.9%
NA	California**	NA	NA
20	Colorado	701	1.6%
12	Connecticut	1,147	2.6%
30	Delaware	264	0.6%
NA	Florida**	NA	NA
9	Georgia	1,687	3.8%
29	Hawaii	386	0.9%
39	Idaho	121	0.3%
NA	Illinois**	NA	NA
22	Indiana	595	1.3%
25	Iowa	463	1.0%
17	Kansas	758	1.7%
32	Kentucky	255	0.6%
NA	Louisiana**	NA	NA
34	Maine	189	0.4%
NA	Maryland**	NA	NA
10	Massachusetts	1,372	3.1%
7	Michigan	1,772	4.0%
16	Minnesota	793	1.8%
37	Mississippi	158	0.4%
26	Missouri	448	1.0%
36	Montana	161	0.4%
35	Nebraska	162	0.4%
18	Nevada	748	1.7%
NA	New Hampshire**	NA	NA
5	New Jersey	2,198	5.0%
24	New Mexico	502	1.1%
1	New York	9,953	22.5%
6	North Carolina	1,969	4.4%
42	North Dakota	64	0.1%
3	Ohio	2,380	5.4%
28	Oklahoma	400	0.9%
15	Oregon	829	1.9%
4	Pennsylvania	2,278	5.1%
31	Rhode Island	261	0.6%
23	South Carolina	549	1.2%
43	South Dakota	44	0.1%
13	Tennessee	1,002	2.3%
2	Texas	3,434	7.7%
33	Utah	197	0.4%
41	Vermont	103	0.2%
11	Virginia	1,249	2.8%
8	Washington	1,716	3.9%
40	West Virginia	108	0.2%
21	Wisconsin	596	1.3%
NA	Wyoming**	NA	NA

RANK	STATE	ABORTIONS	% of USA
1	New York	9,953	22.5%
2	Texas	3,434	7.7%
3	Ohio	2,380	5.4%
4	Pennsylvania	2,278	5.1%
5	New Jersey	2,198	5.0%
6	North Carolina	1,969	4.4%
7	Michigan	1,772	4.0%
8	Washington	1,716	3.9%
9	Georgia	1,687	3.8%
10	Massachusetts	1,372	3.1%
11	Virginia	1,249	2.8%
12	Connecticut	1,147	2.6%
13	Tennessee	1,002	2.3%
14	Alabama	842	1.9%
15	Oregon	829	1.9%
16	Minnesota	793	1.8%
17	Kansas	758	1.7%
18	Nevada	748	1.7%
19	Arizona	705	1.6%
20	Colorado	701	1.6%
21	Wisconsin	596	1.3%
22	Indiana	595	1.3%
23	South Carolina	549	1.2%
24	New Mexico	502	1.1%
25	Iowa	463	1.0%
26	Missouri	448	1.0%
27	Arkansas	401	0.9%
28	Oklahoma	400	0.9%
29	Hawaii	386	0.9%
30	Delaware	264	0.6%
31	Rhode Island	261	0.6%
32	Kentucky	255	0.6%
33	Utah	197	0.4%
34	Maine	189	0.4%
35	Nebraska	162	0.4%
36	Montana	161	0.4%
37	Mississippi	158	0.4%
38	Alaska	128	0.3%
39	Idaho	121	0.3%
40	West Virginia	108	0.2%
41	Vermont	103	0.2%
42	North Dakota	64	0.1%
43	South Dakota	44	0.1%
NA	California**	NA	NA
NA	Florida**	NA	NA
NA	Illinois**	NA	NA
NA	Louisiana**	NA	NA
NA	Maryland**	NA	NA
NA	New Hampshire**	NA	NA
NA	Wyoming**	NA	NA
	District of Columbia	241	0.5%

Source: U.S. Department of Health and Human Services, Centers for Disease Control and Prevention

"Abortion Surveillance-United States, 2006" (MMWR, Vol. 58, No. SS-8, 11/27/09, http://www.cdc.gov/mmwr/mmwr_ss.html)

*By state of occurrence. National total is for reporting states only.

**Not reported.

...f Teenage Abortions Obtained
...rs 17 Years and Younger in 2006
...Percent = 38.0% of Teenage Abortions*

RANK	STATE	PERCENT
1	Hawaii	46.8
2	Idaho	45.7
3	New York	42.7
4	South Carolina	42.4
5	Connecticut	42.0
6	Arkansas	41.9
7	Delaware	41.8
8	New Mexico	41.6
9	Nevada	40.8
10	Ohio	40.4
10	Oregon	40.4
12	New Jersey	39.3
13	Maine	39.1
14	Montana	39.0
15	Kansas	38.9
16	Alabama	38.6
17	Kentucky	38.5
18	Washington	38.0
19	Iowa	37.9
20	Michigan	37.8
21	Georgia	37.3
22	Minnesota	37.0
23	North Carolina	36.3
24	Wisconsin	35.9
25	Arizona	35.8
26	Pennsylvania	35.5
26	South Dakota	35.5
28	Colorado	35.2
28	Nebraska	35.2
30	Missouri	35.1
31	Indiana	35.0
32	Oklahoma	34.8
32	Tennessee	34.8
34	Alaska	34.7
35	Vermont	34.3
36	Massachusetts	34.1
37	Mississippi	33.8
37	West Virginia	33.8
39	Texas	32.6
40	Utah	31.4
40	Virginia	31.4
42	Rhode Island	30.2
43	North Dakota	27.9
NA	California**	NA
NA	Florida**	NA
NA	Illinois**	NA
NA	Louisiana**	NA
NA	Maryland**	NA
NA	New Hampshire**	NA
NA	Wyoming**	NA
	District of Columbia	48.8

...S. Department of Health and Human Services, Centers for Disease Control and Prevention

...tes, 2006" (MMWR, Vol. 58, No. SS-8, 11/27/09, http://www.cdc.gov/mmwr/mmwr_ss.html)

...cent is for reporting states only.

Reported Legal Abortions Performed at 12 Weeks or Fewer of Gestation in 2006

Reporting States' Total = 574,497 Abortions*

ALPHA ORDER

RANK	STATE	ABORTIONS	% of USA
15	Alabama	10,138	1.8%
35	Alaska	1,808	0.3%
16	Arizona	9,766	1.7%
27	Arkansas	4,264	0.7%
NA	California**	NA	NA
17	Colorado	9,751	1.7%
13	Connecticut	12,332	2.1%
32	Delaware	3,109	0.5%
NA	Florida**	NA	NA
6	Georgia	26,373	4.6%
29	Hawaii	3,429	0.6%
39	Idaho	1,197	0.2%
NA	Illinois**	NA	NA
20	Indiana	8,967	1.6%
25	Iowa	6,280	1.1%
18	Kansas	9,584	1.7%
30	Kentucky	3,248	0.6%
NA	Louisiana**	NA	NA
33	Maine	2,547	0.4%
NA	Maryland**	NA	NA
NA	Massachusetts**	NA	NA
9	Michigan	23,055	4.0%
12	Minnesota	12,462	2.2%
NA	Mississippi**	NA	NA
23	Missouri	6,838	1.2%
34	Montana	1,855	0.3%
NA	Nebraska**	NA	NA
19	Nevada	9,076	1.6%
NA	New Hampshire**	NA	NA
8	New Jersey	24,502	4.3%
26	New Mexico	5,162	0.9%
1	New York	105,653	18.4%
5	North Carolina	27,417	4.8%
38	North Dakota	1,215	0.2%
4	Ohio	27,817	4.8%
24	Oklahoma	6,357	1.1%
14	Oregon	10,202	1.8%
3	Pennsylvania	32,346	5.6%
28	Rhode Island	4,069	0.7%
22	South Carolina	6,906	1.2%
40	South Dakota	705	0.1%
11	Tennessee	16,904	2.9%
2	Texas	75,032	13.1%
31	Utah	3,219	0.6%
37	Vermont	1,511	0.3%
7	Virginia	26,077	4.5%
10	Washington	21,468	3.7%
36	West Virginia	1,793	0.3%
21	Wisconsin	7,821	1.4%
41	Wyoming	0	0.0%

RANK ORDER

RANK	STATE	ABORTIONS	% of USA
1	New York	105,653	18.4%
2	Texas	75,032	13.1%
3	Pennsylvania	32,346	5.6%
4	Ohio	27,817	4.8%
5	North Carolina	27,417	4.8%
6	Georgia	26,373	4.6%
7	Virginia	26,077	4.5%
8	New Jersey	24,502	4.3%
9	Michigan	23,055	4.0%
10	Washington	21,468	3.7%
11	Tennessee	16,904	2.9%
12	Minnesota	12,462	2.2%
13	Connecticut	12,332	2.1%
14	Oregon	10,202	1.8%
15	Alabama	10,138	1.8%
16	Arizona	9,766	1.7%
17	Colorado	9,751	1.7%
18	Kansas	9,584	1.7%
19	Nevada	9,076	1.6%
20	Indiana	8,967	1.6%
21	Wisconsin	7,821	1.4%
22	South Carolina	6,906	1.2%
23	Missouri	6,838	1.2%
24	Oklahoma	6,357	1.1%
25	Iowa	6,280	1.1%
26	New Mexico	5,162	0.9%
27	Arkansas	4,264	0.7%
28	Rhode Island	4,069	0.7%
29	Hawaii	3,429	0.6%
30	Kentucky	3,248	0.6%
31	Utah	3,219	0.6%
32	Delaware	3,109	0.5%
33	Maine	2,547	0.4%
34	Montana	1,855	0.3%
35	Alaska	1,808	0.3%
36	West Virginia	1,793	0.3%
37	Vermont	1,511	0.3%
38	North Dakota	1,215	0.2%
39	Idaho	1,197	0.2%
40	South Dakota	705	0.1%
41	Wyoming	0	0.0%
NA	California**	NA	NA
NA	Florida**	NA	NA
NA	Illinois**	NA	NA
NA	Louisiana**	NA	NA
NA	Maryland**	NA	NA
NA	Massachusetts**	NA	NA
NA	Mississippi**	NA	NA
NA	Nebraska**	NA	NA
NA	New Hampshire**	NA	NA
	District of Columbia	2,242	0.4%

Source: CQ Press using data from U.S. Department of Health and Human Services, Centers for Disease Control and Prevention "Abortion Surveillance-United States, 2006" (MMWR, Vol. 58, No. SS-8, 11/27/09, http://www.cdc.gov/mmwr/mmwr_ss.html)
*By state of occurrence. National total is for reporting states only.
**Not reported.

Reported Legal Abortions Obtained [by Moth]ers 17 Years and Younger in 2006

[Reporting S]tates' Percent = 6.4% of Abortions*

RANK ORDER

RANK	STATE	PERCENT
1	Hawaii	9.7
1	Idaho	9.7
3	New Mexico	8.2
4	Connecticut	8.1
5	Arkansas	8.0
6	New York	7.8
6	South Carolina	7.8
8	Montana	7.6
9	Alabama	7.2
9	Ohio	7.2
11	Maine	7.1
11	New Jersey	7.1
11	Oregon	7.1
14	Washington	7.0
15	Iowa	6.9
15	Michigan	6.9
17	Kansas	6.8
18	Alaska	6.7
19	Arizona	6.5
19	Kentucky	6.5
19	Nevada	6.5
22	Vermont	6.4
23	Colorado	6.3
24	Pennsylvania	6.2
24	Wisconsin	6.2
26	Missouri	5.9
26	South Dakota	5.9
28	Massachusetts	5.7
29	Indiana	5.6
29	Minnesota	5.6
29	North Carolina	5.6
29	Oklahoma	5.6
29	Tennessee	5.6
34	Delaware	5.5
34	Georgia	5.5
34	Nebraska	5.5
37	Mississippi	5.4
37	Rhode Island	5.4
39	West Virginia	5.3
40	Utah	5.2
41	North Dakota	4.9
42	Virginia	4.6
43	Texas	4.2
NA	California**	NA
NA	Florida**	NA
NA	Illinois**	NA
NA	Louisiana**	NA
NA	Maryland**	NA
NA	New Hampshire**	NA
NA	Wyoming**	NA
	District of Columbia	9.0

[U.]S. Department of Health and Human Services, Centers for Disease Control and Prevention
[...]tates, 2006" (MMWR, Vol. 58, No. SS-8, 11/27/09, http://www.cdc.gov/mmwr/mmwr_ss.html)
[...]rcent is for reporting states only.

Percent of Reported Legal Abortions Performed
at 12 Weeks or Fewer of Gestation in 2006
Reporting States' Percent = 86.5% of Abortions*

<table>
<tr><td colspan="3">ALPHA ORDER</td><td colspan="3">RANK ORDER</td></tr>
<tr><td>RANK</td><td>STATE</td><td>PERCENT</td><td>RANK</td><td>STATE</td><td>PERCENT</td></tr>
<tr><td>23</td><td>Alabama</td><td>87.0</td><td>1</td><td>South Carolina</td><td>98.6</td></tr>
<tr><td>7</td><td>Alaska</td><td>94.0</td><td>2</td><td>Idaho</td><td>95.8</td></tr>
<tr><td>13</td><td>Arizona</td><td>90.1</td><td>3</td><td>Maine</td><td>95.4</td></tr>
<tr><td>29</td><td>Arkansas</td><td>85.5</td><td>4</td><td>Virginia</td><td>95.3</td></tr>
<tr><td>NA</td><td>California**</td><td>NA</td><td>5</td><td>Tennessee</td><td>94.5</td></tr>
<tr><td>17</td><td>Colorado</td><td>88.3</td><td>6</td><td>South Dakota</td><td>94.3</td></tr>
<tr><td>21</td><td>Connecticut</td><td>87.4</td><td>7</td><td>Alaska</td><td>94.0</td></tr>
<tr><td>40</td><td>Delaware</td><td>64.7</td><td>8</td><td>Vermont</td><td>93.9</td></tr>
<tr><td>NA</td><td>Florida**</td><td>NA</td><td>9</td><td>North Dakota</td><td>93.6</td></tr>
<tr><td>25</td><td>Georgia</td><td>86.3</td><td>10</td><td>Iowa</td><td>93.4</td></tr>
<tr><td>26</td><td>Hawaii</td><td>85.9</td><td>11</td><td>Texas</td><td>91.6</td></tr>
<tr><td>2</td><td>Idaho</td><td>95.8</td><td>12</td><td>Missouri</td><td>90.5</td></tr>
<tr><td>NA</td><td>Illinois**</td><td>NA</td><td>13</td><td>Arizona</td><td>90.1</td></tr>
<tr><td>31</td><td>Indiana</td><td>84.5</td><td>14</td><td>Michigan</td><td>89.9</td></tr>
<tr><td>10</td><td>Iowa</td><td>93.4</td><td>15</td><td>Oklahoma</td><td>89.7</td></tr>
<tr><td>27</td><td>Kansas</td><td>85.8</td><td>16</td><td>Minnesota</td><td>88.6</td></tr>
<tr><td>34</td><td>Kentucky</td><td>83.0</td><td>17</td><td>Colorado</td><td>88.3</td></tr>
<tr><td>NA</td><td>Louisiana**</td><td>NA</td><td>18</td><td>Pennsylvania</td><td>88.1</td></tr>
<tr><td>3</td><td>Maine</td><td>95.4</td><td>18</td><td>West Virginia</td><td>88.1</td></tr>
<tr><td>NA</td><td>Maryland**</td><td>NA</td><td>20</td><td>Montana</td><td>87.5</td></tr>
<tr><td>NA</td><td>Massachusetts**</td><td>NA</td><td>21</td><td>Connecticut</td><td>87.4</td></tr>
<tr><td>14</td><td>Michigan</td><td>89.9</td><td>22</td><td>Washington</td><td>87.2</td></tr>
<tr><td>16</td><td>Minnesota</td><td>88.6</td><td>23</td><td>Alabama</td><td>87.0</td></tr>
<tr><td>NA</td><td>Mississippi**</td><td>NA</td><td>23</td><td>Oregon</td><td>87.0</td></tr>
<tr><td>12</td><td>Missouri</td><td>90.5</td><td>25</td><td>Georgia</td><td>86.3</td></tr>
<tr><td>20</td><td>Montana</td><td>87.5</td><td>26</td><td>Hawaii</td><td>85.9</td></tr>
<tr><td>NA</td><td>Nebraska**</td><td>NA</td><td>27</td><td>Kansas</td><td>85.8</td></tr>
<tr><td>37</td><td>Nevada</td><td>79.1</td><td>27</td><td>Utah</td><td>85.8</td></tr>
<tr><td>NA</td><td>New Hampshire**</td><td>NA</td><td>29</td><td>Arkansas</td><td>85.5</td></tr>
<tr><td>37</td><td>New Jersey</td><td>79.1</td><td>30</td><td>New Mexico</td><td>84.8</td></tr>
<tr><td>30</td><td>New Mexico</td><td>84.8</td><td>31</td><td>Indiana</td><td>84.5</td></tr>
<tr><td>35</td><td>New York</td><td>82.9</td><td>31</td><td>Ohio</td><td>84.5</td></tr>
<tr><td>39</td><td>North Carolina</td><td>78.1</td><td>33</td><td>Rhode Island</td><td>84.3</td></tr>
<tr><td>9</td><td>North Dakota</td><td>93.6</td><td>34</td><td>Kentucky</td><td>83.0</td></tr>
<tr><td>31</td><td>Ohio</td><td>84.5</td><td>35</td><td>New York</td><td>82.9</td></tr>
<tr><td>15</td><td>Oklahoma</td><td>89.7</td><td>36</td><td>Wisconsin</td><td>81.6</td></tr>
<tr><td>23</td><td>Oregon</td><td>87.0</td><td>37</td><td>Nevada</td><td>79.1</td></tr>
<tr><td>18</td><td>Pennsylvania</td><td>88.1</td><td>37</td><td>New Jersey</td><td>79.1</td></tr>
<tr><td>33</td><td>Rhode Island</td><td>84.3</td><td>39</td><td>North Carolina</td><td>78.1</td></tr>
<tr><td>1</td><td>South Carolina</td><td>98.6</td><td>40</td><td>Delaware</td><td>64.7</td></tr>
<tr><td>6</td><td>South Dakota</td><td>94.3</td><td>41</td><td>Wyoming</td><td>0.0</td></tr>
<tr><td>5</td><td>Tennessee</td><td>94.5</td><td>NA</td><td>California**</td><td>NA</td></tr>
<tr><td>11</td><td>Texas</td><td>91.6</td><td>NA</td><td>Florida**</td><td>NA</td></tr>
<tr><td>27</td><td>Utah</td><td>85.8</td><td>NA</td><td>Illinois**</td><td>NA</td></tr>
<tr><td>8</td><td>Vermont</td><td>93.9</td><td>NA</td><td>Louisiana**</td><td>NA</td></tr>
<tr><td>4</td><td>Virginia</td><td>95.3</td><td>NA</td><td>Maryland**</td><td>NA</td></tr>
<tr><td>22</td><td>Washington</td><td>87.2</td><td>NA</td><td>Massachusetts**</td><td>NA</td></tr>
<tr><td>18</td><td>West Virginia</td><td>88.1</td><td>NA</td><td>Mississippi**</td><td>NA</td></tr>
<tr><td>36</td><td>Wisconsin</td><td>81.6</td><td>NA</td><td>Nebraska**</td><td>NA</td></tr>
<tr><td>41</td><td>Wyoming</td><td>0.0</td><td>NA</td><td>New Hampshire**</td><td>NA</td></tr>
</table>

District of Columbia   83.3

Source: CQ Press using data from U.S. Department of Health and Human Services, Centers for Disease Control and Prevention
"Abortion Surveillance-United States, 2006" (MMWR, Vol. 58, No. SS-8, 11/27/09, http://www.cdc.gov/mmwr/mmwr_ss.html)
*By state of occurrence. National percent is for reporting states only.
**Not reported.

Reported Legal Abortions Performed at or after 21 Weeks of Gestation in 2006

Reporting States' Total = 8,360 Abortions*

ALPHA ORDER					RANK ORDER			
RANK	STATE	ABORTIONS	% of USA		RANK	STATE	ABORTIONS	% of USA
21	Alabama	26	0.3%		1	New York	2,974	35.6%
23	Alaska	15	0.2%		2	New Jersey	931	11.1%
13	Arizona	95	1.1%		3	Georgia	900	10.8%
33	Arkansas	0	0.0%		4	Texas	551	6.6%
NA	California**	NA	NA		5	Ohio	510	6.1%
8	Colorado	258	3.1%		6	Washington	431	5.2%
22	Connecticut	17	0.2%		7	Kansas	418	5.0%
23	Delaware	15	0.2%		8	Colorado	258	3.1%
NA	Florida**	NA	NA		9	Pennsylvania	247	3.0%
3	Georgia	900	10.8%		10	Oregon	230	2.8%
20	Hawaii	28	0.3%		11	Wisconsin	192	2.3%
33	Idaho	0	0.0%		12	New Mexico	114	1.4%
NA	Illinois**	NA	NA		13	Arizona	95	1.1%
33	Indiana	0	0.0%		14	Michigan	88	1.1%
28	Iowa	9	0.1%		15	Minnesota	53	0.6%
7	Kansas	418	5.0%		16	Kentucky	51	0.6%
16	Kentucky	51	0.6%		17	Nevada	48	0.6%
NA	Louisiana**	NA	NA		18	Missouri	46	0.6%
28	Maine	9	0.1%		19	Virginia	45	0.5%
NA	Maryland**	NA	NA		20	Hawaii	28	0.3%
NA	Massachusetts**	NA	NA		21	Alabama	26	0.3%
14	Michigan	88	1.1%		22	Connecticut	17	0.2%
15	Minnesota	53	0.6%		23	Alaska	15	0.2%
NA	Mississippi**	NA	NA		23	Delaware	15	0.2%
18	Missouri	46	0.6%		23	Tennessee	15	0.2%
33	Montana	0	0.0%		26	South Carolina	13	0.2%
NA	Nebraska**	NA	NA		26	Utah	13	0.2%
17	Nevada	48	0.6%		28	Iowa	9	0.1%
NA	New Hampshire**	NA	NA		28	Maine	9	0.1%
2	New Jersey	931	11.1%		30	South Dakota	7	0.1%
12	New Mexico	114	1.4%		31	West Virginia	6	0.1%
1	New York	2,974	35.6%		32	Vermont	5	0.1%
33	North Carolina	0	0.0%		33	Arkansas	0	0.0%
33	North Dakota	0	0.0%		33	Idaho	0	0.0%
5	Ohio	510	6.1%		33	Indiana	0	0.0%
33	Oklahoma	0	0.0%		33	Montana	0	0.0%
10	Oregon	230	2.8%		33	North Carolina	0	0.0%
9	Pennsylvania	247	3.0%		33	North Dakota	0	0.0%
33	Rhode Island	0	0.0%		33	Oklahoma	0	0.0%
26	South Carolina	13	0.2%		33	Rhode Island	0	0.0%
30	South Dakota	7	0.1%		33	Wyoming	0	0.0%
23	Tennessee	15	0.2%		NA	California**	NA	NA
4	Texas	551	6.6%		NA	Florida**	NA	NA
26	Utah	13	0.2%		NA	Illinois**	NA	NA
32	Vermont	5	0.1%		NA	Louisiana**	NA	NA
19	Virginia	45	0.5%		NA	Maryland**	NA	NA
6	Washington	431	5.2%		NA	Massachusetts**	NA	NA
31	West Virginia	6	0.1%		NA	Mississippi**	NA	NA
11	Wisconsin	192	2.3%		NA	Nebraska**	NA	NA
33	Wyoming	0	0.0%		NA	New Hampshire**	NA	NA
					District of Columbia		0	0.0%

Source: U.S. Department of Health and Human Services, Centers for Disease Control and Prevention
"Abortion Surveillance-United States, 2006" (MMWR, Vol. 58, No. SS-8, 11/27/09, http://www.cdc.gov/mmwr/mmwr_ss.html)
*By state of occurrence. National total is for reporting states only.
**Not reported.

Percent of Reported Legal Abortions Performed at or after
21 Weeks of Gestation in 2006
Reporting States' Percent = 1.3% of Abortions*

ALPHA ORDER

RANK	STATE	PERCENT
27	Alabama	0.2
14	Alaska	0.8
12	Arizona	0.9
33	Arkansas	0.0
NA	California**	NA
4	Colorado	2.3
30	Connecticut	0.1
19	Delaware	0.4
NA	Florida**	NA
3	Georgia	2.9
15	Hawaii	0.7
33	Idaho	0.0
NA	Illinois**	NA
33	Indiana	0.0
30	Iowa	0.1
1	Kansas	3.7
11	Kentucky	1.3
NA	Louisiana**	NA
22	Maine	0.3
NA	Maryland**	NA
NA	Massachusetts**	NA
22	Michigan	0.3
19	Minnesota	0.4
NA	Mississippi**	NA
18	Missouri	0.6
33	Montana	0.0
NA	Nebraska**	NA
19	Nevada	0.4
NA	New Hampshire**	NA
2	New Jersey	3.0
8	New Mexico	1.9
4	New York	2.3
33	North Carolina	0.0
33	North Dakota	0.0
10	Ohio	1.5
33	Oklahoma	0.0
7	Oregon	2.0
15	Pennsylvania	0.7
33	Rhode Island	0.0
27	South Carolina	0.2
12	South Dakota	0.9
30	Tennessee	0.1
15	Texas	0.7
22	Utah	0.3
22	Vermont	0.3
27	Virginia	0.2
9	Washington	1.8
22	West Virginia	0.3
6	Wisconsin	2.1
33	Wyoming	0.0

RANK ORDER

RANK	STATE	PERCENT
1	Kansas	3.7
2	New Jersey	3.0
3	Georgia	2.9
4	Colorado	2.3
4	New York	2.3
6	Wisconsin	2.1
7	Oregon	2.0
8	New Mexico	1.9
9	Washington	1.8
10	Ohio	1.5
11	Kentucky	1.3
12	Arizona	0.9
12	South Dakota	0.9
14	Alaska	0.8
15	Hawaii	0.7
15	Pennsylvania	0.7
15	Texas	0.7
18	Missouri	0.6
19	Delaware	0.4
19	Minnesota	0.4
19	Nevada	0.4
22	Maine	0.3
22	Michigan	0.3
22	Utah	0.3
22	Vermont	0.3
22	West Virginia	0.3
27	Alabama	0.2
27	South Carolina	0.2
27	Virginia	0.2
30	Connecticut	0.1
30	Iowa	0.1
30	Tennessee	0.1
33	Arkansas	0.0
33	Idaho	0.0
33	Indiana	0.0
33	Montana	0.0
33	North Carolina	0.0
33	North Dakota	0.0
33	Oklahoma	0.0
33	Rhode Island	0.0
33	Wyoming	0.0
NA	California**	NA
NA	Florida**	NA
NA	Illinois**	NA
NA	Louisiana**	NA
NA	Maryland**	NA
NA	Massachusetts**	NA
NA	Mississippi**	NA
NA	Nebraska**	NA
NA	New Hampshire**	NA
	District of Columbia	0.0

Source: U.S. Department of Health and Human Services, Centers for Disease Control and Prevention
   "Abortion Surveillance-United States, 2006" (MMWR, Vol. 58, No. SS-8, 11/27/09, http://www.cdc.gov/mmwr/mmwr_ss.html)
*By state of occurrence. National percent is for reporting states only.
**Not reported.

II. Deaths

Deaths in 2008

National Total = 2,452,590 Deaths*

ALPHA ORDER					RANK ORDER			
RANK	STATE	DEATHS	% of USA		RANK	STATE	DEATHS	% of USA
18	Alabama	47,821	1.9%		1	California	232,719	9.5%
50	Alaska	3,503	0.1%		2	Florida	170,535	7.0%
20	Arizona	45,493	1.9%		3	Texas	163,991	6.7%
29	Arkansas	29,330	1.2%		4	New York	149,634	6.1%
1	California	232,719	9.5%		5	Pennsylvania	125,754	5.1%
28	Colorado	31,402	1.3%		6	Ohio	109,831	4.5%
32	Connecticut	28,610	1.2%		7	Illinois	100,247	4.1%
45	Delaware	7,475	0.3%		8	Michigan	88,450	3.6%
2	Florida	170,535	7.0%		9	North Carolina	77,392	3.2%
11	Georgia	68,055	2.8%		10	New Jersey	68,506	2.8%
43	Hawaii	9,270	0.4%		11	Georgia	68,055	2.8%
40	Idaho	11,006	0.4%		12	Virginia	59,038	2.4%
7	Illinois	100,247	4.1%		13	Tennessee	58,676	2.4%
15	Indiana	54,612	2.2%		14	Missouri	56,919	2.3%
31	Iowa	28,731	1.2%		15	Indiana	54,612	2.2%
33	Kansas	24,643	1.0%		16	Massachusetts	52,892	2.2%
22	Kentucky	40,720	1.7%		17	Washington	48,347	2.0%
23	Louisiana	39,634	1.6%		18	Alabama	47,821	1.9%
39	Maine	12,433	0.5%		19	Wisconsin	46,813	1.9%
21	Maryland	43,786	1.8%		20	Arizona	45,493	1.9%
16	Massachusetts	52,892	2.2%		21	Maryland	43,786	1.8%
8	Michigan	88,450	3.6%		22	Kentucky	40,720	1.7%
24	Minnesota	38,529	1.6%		23	Louisiana	39,634	1.6%
30	Mississippi	28,910	1.2%		24	Minnesota	38,529	1.6%
14	Missouri	56,919	2.3%		25	South Carolina	38,354	1.6%
44	Montana	8,907	0.4%		26	Oklahoma	36,945	1.5%
37	Nebraska	15,492	0.6%		27	Oregon	31,767	1.3%
35	Nevada	18,942	0.8%		28	Colorado	31,402	1.3%
41	New Hampshire	10,272	0.4%		29	Arkansas	29,330	1.2%
10	New Jersey	68,506	2.8%		30	Mississippi	28,910	1.2%
36	New Mexico	15,586	0.6%		31	Iowa	28,731	1.2%
4	New York	149,634	6.1%		32	Connecticut	28,610	1.2%
9	North Carolina	77,392	3.2%		33	Kansas	24,643	1.0%
47	North Dakota	5,939	0.2%		34	West Virginia	21,486	0.9%
6	Ohio	109,831	4.5%		35	Nevada	18,942	0.8%
26	Oklahoma	36,945	1.5%		36	New Mexico	15,586	0.6%
27	Oregon	31,767	1.3%		37	Nebraska	15,492	0.6%
5	Pennsylvania	125,754	5.1%		38	Utah	14,064	0.6%
42	Rhode Island	9,774	0.4%		39	Maine	12,433	0.5%
25	South Carolina	38,354	1.6%		40	Idaho	11,006	0.4%
46	South Dakota	6,946	0.3%		41	New Hampshire	10,272	0.4%
13	Tennessee	58,676	2.4%		42	Rhode Island	9,774	0.4%
3	Texas	163,991	6.7%		43	Hawaii	9,270	0.4%
38	Utah	14,064	0.6%		44	Montana	8,907	0.4%
48	Vermont	5,119	0.2%		45	Delaware	7,475	0.3%
12	Virginia	59,038	2.4%		46	South Dakota	6,946	0.3%
17	Washington	48,347	2.0%		47	North Dakota	5,939	0.2%
34	West Virginia	21,486	0.9%		48	Vermont	5,119	0.2%
19	Wisconsin	46,813	1.9%		49	Wyoming	4,175	0.2%
49	Wyoming	4,175	0.2%		50	Alaska	3,503	0.1%
						District of Columbia	5,115	0.2%

Source: U.S. Department of Health and Human Services, National Center for Health Statistics
"National Vital Statistics Reports" (Vol. 57, No. 19, July 29, 2009, http://www.cdc.gov/nchs/deaths.htm)
*Provisional data for 12 months ending with December by state of residence.

Death Rate in 2008

National Rate = 805.8 Deaths per 100,000 Population*

ALPHA ORDER

RANK	STATE	RATE
3	Alabama	1,022.4
50	Alaska	509.1
45	Arizona	700.0
2	Arkansas	1,022.7
48	California	636.2
47	Colorado	636.3
29	Connecticut	816.7
23	Delaware	853.1
15	Florida	925.6
44	Georgia	701.8
43	Hawaii	720.0
42	Idaho	720.5
34	Illinois	780.6
22	Indiana	854.9
7	Iowa	959.6
19	Kansas	880.9
10	Kentucky	949.6
17	Louisiana	890.3
11	Maine	942.1
36	Maryland	773.8
30	Massachusetts	808.3
18	Michigan	884.3
39	Minnesota	736.6
6	Mississippi	983.3
8	Missouri	955.6
16	Montana	920.1
20	Nebraska	869.4
41	Nevada	724.1
35	New Hampshire	777.1
31	New Jersey	790.8
32	New Mexico	784.5
37	New York	768.6
26	North Carolina	836.9
14	North Dakota	925.9
9	Ohio	952.7
4	Oklahoma	1,013.9
25	Oregon	839.7
5	Pennsylvania	1,000.7
13	Rhode Island	927.8
24	South Carolina	851.7
21	South Dakota	863.4
12	Tennessee	940.3
46	Texas	674.7
49	Utah	515.7
28	Vermont	824.3
38	Virginia	757.3
40	Washington	736.3
1	West Virginia	1,183.9
27	Wisconsin	831.8
33	Wyoming	783.3

RANK ORDER

RANK	STATE	RATE
1	West Virginia	1,183.9
2	Arkansas	1,022.7
3	Alabama	1,022.4
4	Oklahoma	1,013.9
5	Pennsylvania	1,000.7
6	Mississippi	983.3
7	Iowa	959.6
8	Missouri	955.6
9	Ohio	952.7
10	Kentucky	949.6
11	Maine	942.1
12	Tennessee	940.3
13	Rhode Island	927.8
14	North Dakota	925.9
15	Florida	925.6
16	Montana	920.1
17	Louisiana	890.3
18	Michigan	884.3
19	Kansas	880.9
20	Nebraska	869.4
21	South Dakota	863.4
22	Indiana	854.9
23	Delaware	853.1
24	South Carolina	851.7
25	Oregon	839.7
26	North Carolina	836.9
27	Wisconsin	831.8
28	Vermont	824.3
29	Connecticut	816.7
30	Massachusetts	808.3
31	New Jersey	790.8
32	New Mexico	784.5
33	Wyoming	783.3
34	Illinois	780.6
35	New Hampshire	777.1
36	Maryland	773.8
37	New York	768.6
38	Virginia	757.3
39	Minnesota	736.6
40	Washington	736.3
41	Nevada	724.1
42	Idaho	720.5
43	Hawaii	720.0
44	Georgia	701.8
45	Arizona	700.0
46	Texas	674.7
47	Colorado	636.3
48	California	636.2
49	Utah	515.7
50	Alaska	509.1

District of Columbia   866.8

Source: CQ Press using data from U.S. Department of Health and Human Services, National Center for Health Statistics
   "National Vital Statistics Reports" (Vol. 57, No. 19, July 29, 2009, http://www.cdc.gov/nchs/deaths.htm)
*Provisional data for 12 months ending with December by state of residence. Not age-adjusted.

Deaths in 2007

National Total = 2,423,995 Deaths*

ALPHA ORDER

RANK	STATE	DEATHS	% of USA
15	Alabama	46,671	1.9%
47	Alaska	3,470	0.1%
17	Arizona	45,595	1.9%
28	Arkansas	28,164	1.2%
NA	California**	NA	NA
25	Colorado	29,993	1.2%
26	Connecticut	28,654	1.2%
42	Delaware	7,330	0.3%
1	Florida	168,043	6.9%
NA	Georgia**	NA	NA
40	Hawaii	9,499	0.4%
37	Idaho	10,829	0.4%
5	Illinois	100,318	4.1%
12	Indiana	54,172	2.2%
29	Iowa	27,247	1.1%
30	Kansas	24,477	1.0%
19	Kentucky	40,120	1.7%
20	Louisiana	39,765	1.6%
36	Maine	12,491	0.5%
18	Maryland	43,772	1.8%
13	Massachusetts	52,936	2.2%
6	Michigan	86,727	3.6%
22	Minnesota	37,176	1.5%
27	Mississippi	28,271	1.2%
11	Missouri	54,174	2.2%
41	Montana	8,629	0.4%
34	Nebraska	15,261	0.6%
32	Nevada	18,642	0.8%
38	New Hampshire	10,305	0.4%
8	New Jersey	69,648	2.9%
33	New Mexico	15,388	0.6%
2	New York	147,727	6.1%
7	North Carolina	76,033	3.1%
44	North Dakota	5,571	0.2%
4	Ohio	106,534	4.4%
23	Oklahoma	36,014	1.5%
24	Oregon	31,418	1.3%
3	Pennsylvania	125,200	5.2%
39	Rhode Island	9,721	0.4%
21	South Carolina	39,497	1.6%
43	South Dakota	6,824	0.3%
10	Tennessee	57,078	2.4%
NA	Texas**	NA	NA
35	Utah	14,143	0.6%
45	Vermont	5,186	0.2%
9	Virginia	58,220	2.4%
14	Washington	47,363	2.0%
31	West Virginia	21,087	0.9%
16	Wisconsin	46,271	1.9%
46	Wyoming	4,264	0.2%

RANK ORDER

RANK	STATE	DEATHS	% of USA
1	Florida	168,043	6.9%
2	New York	147,727	6.1%
3	Pennsylvania	125,200	5.2%
4	Ohio	106,534	4.4%
5	Illinois	100,318	4.1%
6	Michigan	86,727	3.6%
7	North Carolina	76,033	3.1%
8	New Jersey	69,648	2.9%
9	Virginia	58,220	2.4%
10	Tennessee	57,078	2.4%
11	Missouri	54,174	2.2%
12	Indiana	54,172	2.2%
13	Massachusetts	52,936	2.2%
14	Washington	47,363	2.0%
15	Alabama	46,671	1.9%
16	Wisconsin	46,271	1.9%
17	Arizona	45,595	1.9%
18	Maryland	43,772	1.8%
19	Kentucky	40,120	1.7%
20	Louisiana	39,765	1.6%
21	South Carolina	39,497	1.6%
22	Minnesota	37,176	1.5%
23	Oklahoma	36,014	1.5%
24	Oregon	31,418	1.3%
25	Colorado	29,993	1.2%
26	Connecticut	28,654	1.2%
27	Mississippi	28,271	1.2%
28	Arkansas	28,164	1.2%
29	Iowa	27,247	1.1%
30	Kansas	24,477	1.0%
31	West Virginia	21,087	0.9%
32	Nevada	18,642	0.8%
33	New Mexico	15,388	0.6%
34	Nebraska	15,261	0.6%
35	Utah	14,143	0.6%
36	Maine	12,491	0.5%
37	Idaho	10,829	0.4%
38	New Hampshire	10,305	0.4%
39	Rhode Island	9,721	0.4%
40	Hawaii	9,499	0.4%
41	Montana	8,629	0.4%
42	Delaware	7,330	0.3%
43	South Dakota	6,824	0.3%
44	North Dakota	5,571	0.2%
45	Vermont	5,186	0.2%
46	Wyoming	4,264	0.2%
47	Alaska	3,470	0.1%
NA	California**	NA	NA
NA	Georgia**	NA	NA
NA	Texas**	NA	NA
	District of Columbia	5,190	0.2%

Source: U.S. Department of Health and Human Services, National Center for Health Statistics
"National Vital Statistics Reports" (Vol. 58, No. 1, August 19, 2009, http://www.cdc.gov/nchs/deaths.htm)
*Preliminary data by state of residence.
**Not available. Data for these three states are not shown separately but are included in the U.S. total because their data did not meet the required criterion of completeness.

Death Rate in 2007

National Rate = 803.7 Deaths per 100,000 Population*

RANK	STATE	RATE
2	Alabama	1,008.5
47	Alaska	507.7
43	Arizona	719.3
5	Arkansas	993.5
NA	California**	NA
45	Colorado	616.9
30	Connecticut	818.1
24	Delaware	847.6
13	Florida	920.7
NA	Georgia**	NA
39	Hawaii	740.2
42	Idaho	722.2
35	Illinois	780.5
23	Indiana	853.7
15	Iowa	911.9
18	Kansas	881.7
8	Kentucky	945.9
11	Louisiana	926.2
7	Maine	948.3
36	Maryland	779.1
29	Massachusetts	820.7
20	Michigan	861.1
44	Minnesota	715.3
6	Mississippi	968.6
12	Missouri	921.6
16	Montana	900.9
21	Nebraska	860.0
41	Nevada	726.7
33	New Hampshire	783.2
32	New Jersey	801.8
34	New Mexico	781.2
37	New York	765.5
25	North Carolina	839.1
19	North Dakota	870.9
9	Ohio	929.1
4	Oklahoma	995.6
26	Oregon	838.4
3	Pennsylvania	1,007.0
14	Rhode Island	919.0
17	South Carolina	896.1
22	South Dakota	857.1
10	Tennessee	927.1
NA	Texas**	NA
46	Utah	534.6
27	Vermont	834.8
38	Virginia	754.9
40	Washington	732.2
1	West Virginia	1,163.7
28	Wisconsin	826.0
31	Wyoming	815.6

RANK	STATE	RATE
1	West Virginia	1,163.7
2	Alabama	1,008.5
3	Pennsylvania	1,007.0
4	Oklahoma	995.6
5	Arkansas	993.5
6	Mississippi	968.6
7	Maine	948.3
8	Kentucky	945.9
9	Ohio	929.1
10	Tennessee	927.1
11	Louisiana	926.2
12	Missouri	921.6
13	Florida	920.7
14	Rhode Island	919.0
15	Iowa	911.9
16	Montana	900.9
17	South Carolina	896.1
18	Kansas	881.7
19	North Dakota	870.9
20	Michigan	861.1
21	Nebraska	860.0
22	South Dakota	857.1
23	Indiana	853.7
24	Delaware	847.6
25	North Carolina	839.1
26	Oregon	838.4
27	Vermont	834.8
28	Wisconsin	826.0
29	Massachusetts	820.7
30	Connecticut	818.1
31	Wyoming	815.6
32	New Jersey	801.8
33	New Hampshire	783.2
34	New Mexico	781.2
35	Illinois	780.5
36	Maryland	779.1
37	New York	765.5
38	Virginia	754.9
39	Hawaii	740.2
40	Washington	732.2
41	Nevada	726.7
42	Idaho	722.2
43	Arizona	719.3
44	Minnesota	715.3
45	Colorado	616.9
46	Utah	534.6
47	Alaska	507.7
NA	California**	NA
NA	Georgia**	NA
NA	Texas**	NA
	District of Columbia	882.2

Source: U.S. Department of Health and Human Services, National Center for Health Statistics
   "National Vital Statistics Reports" (Vol. 58, No. 1, August 19, 2009, http://www.cdc.gov/nchs/deaths.htm)
*Preliminary data by state of residence. Not age-adjusted.
**Not available.

Age-Adjusted Death Rate in 2007

National Rate = 760.3 Deaths per 100,000 Population*

ALPHA ORDER

RANK	STATE	RATE
3	Alabama	930.3
25	Alaska	756.5
44	Arizona	682.5
8	Arkansas	881.8
NA	California**	NA
38	Colorado	700.8
40	Connecticut	694.1
20	Delaware	774.1
43	Florida	685.7
NA	Georgia**	NA
47	Hawaii	607.7
30	Idaho	734.9
24	Illinois	758.5
13	Indiana	812.5
36	Iowa	719.3
19	Kansas	782.5
6	Kentucky	897.6
4	Louisiana	921.8
21	Maine	773.5
18	Maryland	782.9
37	Massachusetts	707.7
14	Michigan	806.1
46	Minnesota	662.2
2	Mississippi	943.5
12	Missouri	826.8
22	Montana	772.9
29	Nebraska	743.5
15	Nevada	801.6
33	New Hampshire	727.2
34	New Jersey	724.0
27	New Mexico	751.0
42	New York	686.5
10	North Carolina	834.3
45	North Dakota	681.0
11	Ohio	830.8
5	Oklahoma	919.9
26	Oregon	753.9
17	Pennsylvania	790.7
28	Rhode Island	749.8
9	South Carolina	851.4
41	South Dakota	693.4
7	Tennessee	885.0
NA	Texas**	NA
39	Utah	694.2
32	Vermont	730.3
23	Virginia	770.6
35	Washington	722.8
1	West Virginia	951.7
31	Wisconsin	732.8
15	Wyoming	801.6

RANK ORDER

RANK	STATE	RATE
1	West Virginia	951.7
2	Mississippi	943.5
3	Alabama	930.3
4	Louisiana	921.8
5	Oklahoma	919.9
6	Kentucky	897.6
7	Tennessee	885.0
8	Arkansas	881.8
9	South Carolina	851.4
10	North Carolina	834.3
11	Ohio	830.8
12	Missouri	826.8
13	Indiana	812.5
14	Michigan	806.1
15	Nevada	801.6
15	Wyoming	801.6
17	Pennsylvania	790.7
18	Maryland	782.9
19	Kansas	782.5
20	Delaware	774.1
21	Maine	773.5
22	Montana	772.9
23	Virginia	770.6
24	Illinois	758.5
25	Alaska	756.5
26	Oregon	753.9
27	New Mexico	751.0
28	Rhode Island	749.8
29	Nebraska	743.5
30	Idaho	734.9
31	Wisconsin	732.8
32	Vermont	730.3
33	New Hampshire	727.2
34	New Jersey	724.0
35	Washington	722.8
36	Iowa	719.3
37	Massachusetts	707.7
38	Colorado	700.8
39	Utah	694.2
40	Connecticut	694.1
41	South Dakota	693.4
42	New York	686.5
43	Florida	685.7
44	Arizona	682.5
45	North Dakota	681.0
46	Minnesota	662.2
47	Hawaii	607.7
NA	California**	NA
NA	Georgia**	NA
NA	Texas**	NA

District of Columbia   866.9

Source: U.S. Department of Health and Human Services, National Center for Health Statistics
   "National Vital Statistics Reports" (Vol. 58, No. 1, August 19, 2009, http://www.cdc.gov/nchs/deaths.htm)
*Preliminary data by state of residence. Age-adjusted rates eliminate the distorting effects of the aging of the population. Rates based on the year 2000 standard population.
**Not available.

Percent Change in Death Rate: 1998 to 2007

National Percent Change = 7.1% Decrease*

ALPHA ORDER

RANK	STATE	PERCENT CHANGE	RANK	STATE	PERCENT CHANGE
7	Alabama	(0.1)	1	Alaska	21.3
1	Alaska	21.3	2	Hawaii	9.1
46	Arizona	(12.3)	3	New Mexico	5.1
37	Arkansas	(8.3)	4	Wyoming	1.8
NA	California**	NA	5	West Virginia	1.5
35	Colorado	(8.0)	6	Louisiana	0.3
42	Connecticut	(9.8)	7	Alabama	(0.1)
20	Delaware	(4.2)	8	Vermont	(0.3)
47	Florida	(13.2)	9	Montana	(0.6)
NA	Georgia**	NA	10	Michigan	(0.7)
2	Hawaii	9.1	11	South Carolina	(1.3)
18	Idaho	(3.1)	12	Kentucky	(1.6)
43	Illinois	(10.0)	13	Ohio	(1.7)
27	Indiana	(5.8)	14	Oklahoma	(1.8)
35	Iowa	(8.0)	15	New Hampshire	(2.2)
19	Kansas	(3.6)	16	Washington	(2.5)
12	Kentucky	(1.6)	17	Maine	(2.8)
6	Louisiana	0.3	18	Idaho	(3.1)
17	Maine	(2.8)	19	Kansas	(3.6)
23	Maryland	(4.9)	20	Delaware	(4.2)
38	Massachusetts	(8.7)	21	Mississippi	(4.3)
10	Michigan	(0.7)	22	Pennsylvania	(4.6)
40	Minnesota	(9.1)	23	Maryland	(4.9)
21	Mississippi	(4.3)	24	Utah	(5.1)
39	Missouri	(9.0)	25	Rhode Island	(5.4)
9	Montana	(0.6)	26	Tennessee	(5.7)
29	Nebraska	(5.9)	27	Indiana	(5.8)
45	Nevada	(12.2)	27	Virginia	(5.8)
15	New Hampshire	(2.2)	29	Nebraska	(5.9)
40	New Jersey	(9.1)	30	North Dakota	(6.1)
3	New Mexico	5.1	30	Wisconsin	(6.1)
44	New York	(11.2)	32	Oregon	(6.4)
33	North Carolina	(6.9)	33	North Carolina	(6.9)
30	North Dakota	(6.1)	34	South Dakota	(7.9)
13	Ohio	(1.7)	35	Colorado	(8.0)
14	Oklahoma	(1.8)	35	Iowa	(8.0)
32	Oregon	(6.4)	37	Arkansas	(8.3)
22	Pennsylvania	(4.6)	38	Massachusetts	(8.7)
25	Rhode Island	(5.4)	39	Missouri	(9.0)
11	South Carolina	(1.3)	40	Minnesota	(9.1)
34	South Dakota	(7.9)	40	New Jersey	(9.1)
26	Tennessee	(5.7)	42	Connecticut	(9.8)
NA	Texas**	NA	43	Illinois	(10.0)
24	Utah	(5.1)	44	New York	(11.2)
8	Vermont	(0.3)	45	Nevada	(12.2)
27	Virginia	(5.8)	46	Arizona	(12.3)
16	Washington	(2.5)	47	Florida	(13.2)
5	West Virginia	1.5	NA	California**	NA
30	Wisconsin	(6.1)	NA	Georgia**	NA
4	Wyoming	1.8	NA	Texas**	NA

District of Columbia   (23.8)

Source: CQ Press using data from U.S. Department of Health and Human Services, National Center for Health Statistics
"National Vital Statistics Reports" (Vol. 58, No. 1, August 19, 2009, http://www.cdc.gov/nchs/deaths.htm)
"National Vital Statistics Reports" (Vol. 48, No. 11, July 24, 2000, http://www.cdc.gov/nchs/data/nvsr/nvsr48/nvs48_11.pdf)
*By state of residence. Not age-adjusted.
**Not available.

Deaths in 2006

National Total = 2,426,264 Deaths*

ALPHA ORDER

RANK	STATE	DEATHS	% of USA
17	Alabama	46,977	1.9%
50	Alaska	3,354	0.1%
18	Arizona	46,365	1.9%
31	Arkansas	27,901	1.1%
1	California	237,126	9.8%
28	Colorado	29,521	1.2%
29	Connecticut	29,260	1.2%
45	Delaware	7,204	0.3%
2	Florida	170,066	7.0%
11	Georgia	67,808	2.8%
43	Hawaii	9,432	0.4%
40	Idaho	10,613	0.4%
7	Illinois	102,171	4.2%
14	Indiana	55,622	2.3%
32	Iowa	27,362	1.1%
33	Kansas	24,553	1.0%
22	Kentucky	40,102	1.7%
23	Louisiana	40,045	1.7%
39	Maine	12,294	0.5%
21	Maryland	43,582	1.8%
16	Massachusetts	53,450	2.2%
8	Michigan	86,042	3.5%
25	Minnesota	37,028	1.5%
30	Mississippi	28,564	1.2%
15	Missouri	54,681	2.3%
44	Montana	8,472	0.3%
37	Nebraska	14,899	0.6%
35	Nevada	18,872	0.8%
41	New Hampshire	10,060	0.4%
10	New Jersey	70,356	2.9%
36	New Mexico	15,296	0.6%
4	New York	148,806	6.1%
9	North Carolina	74,716	3.1%
47	North Dakota	5,868	0.2%
6	Ohio	106,825	4.4%
26	Oklahoma	35,427	1.5%
27	Oregon	31,380	1.3%
5	Pennsylvania	125,539	5.2%
42	Rhode Island	9,690	0.4%
24	South Carolina	38,761	1.6%
46	South Dakota	7,084	0.3%
13	Tennessee	56,838	2.3%
3	Texas	157,150	6.5%
38	Utah	13,764	0.6%
48	Vermont	5,048	0.2%
12	Virginia	57,690	2.4%
20	Washington	46,120	1.9%
34	West Virginia	20,672	0.9%
19	Wisconsin	46,153	1.9%
49	Wyoming	4,311	0.2%

RANK ORDER

RANK	STATE	DEATHS	% of USA
1	California	237,126	9.8%
2	Florida	170,066	7.0%
3	Texas	157,150	6.5%
4	New York	148,806	6.1%
5	Pennsylvania	125,539	5.2%
6	Ohio	106,825	4.4%
7	Illinois	102,171	4.2%
8	Michigan	86,042	3.5%
9	North Carolina	74,716	3.1%
10	New Jersey	70,356	2.9%
11	Georgia	67,808	2.8%
12	Virginia	57,690	2.4%
13	Tennessee	56,838	2.3%
14	Indiana	55,622	2.3%
15	Missouri	54,681	2.3%
16	Massachusetts	53,450	2.2%
17	Alabama	46,977	1.9%
18	Arizona	46,365	1.9%
19	Wisconsin	46,153	1.9%
20	Washington	46,120	1.9%
21	Maryland	43,582	1.8%
22	Kentucky	40,102	1.7%
23	Louisiana	40,045	1.7%
24	South Carolina	38,761	1.6%
25	Minnesota	37,028	1.5%
26	Oklahoma	35,427	1.5%
27	Oregon	31,380	1.3%
28	Colorado	29,521	1.2%
29	Connecticut	29,260	1.2%
30	Mississippi	28,564	1.2%
31	Arkansas	27,901	1.1%
32	Iowa	27,362	1.1%
33	Kansas	24,553	1.0%
34	West Virginia	20,672	0.9%
35	Nevada	18,872	0.8%
36	New Mexico	15,296	0.6%
37	Nebraska	14,899	0.6%
38	Utah	13,764	0.6%
39	Maine	12,294	0.5%
40	Idaho	10,613	0.4%
41	New Hampshire	10,060	0.4%
42	Rhode Island	9,690	0.4%
43	Hawaii	9,432	0.4%
44	Montana	8,472	0.3%
45	Delaware	7,204	0.3%
46	South Dakota	7,084	0.3%
47	North Dakota	5,868	0.2%
48	Vermont	5,048	0.2%
49	Wyoming	4,311	0.2%
50	Alaska	3,354	0.1%
	District of Columbia	5,344	0.2%

Source: U.S. Department of Health and Human Services, National Center for Health Statistics
"National Vital Statistics Reports" (Vol. 58, No. 1, August 19, 2009, http://www.cdc.gov/nchs/deaths.htm)
*Final data by state of residence.

Death Rate in 2006

National Rate = 810.4 Deaths per 100,000 Population*

<table>
<tr><td colspan="3">ALPHA ORDER</td><td colspan="3">RANK ORDER</td></tr>
<tr><td>RANK</td><td>STATE</td><td>RATE</td><td>RANK</td><td>STATE</td><td>RATE</td></tr>
<tr><td>2</td><td>Alabama</td><td>1,021.5</td><td>1</td><td>West Virginia</td><td>1,136.8</td></tr>
<tr><td>50</td><td>Alaska</td><td>500.6</td><td>2</td><td>Alabama</td><td>1,021.5</td></tr>
<tr><td>40</td><td>Arizona</td><td>751.9</td><td>3</td><td>Pennsylvania</td><td>1,009.1</td></tr>
<tr><td>4</td><td>Arkansas</td><td>992.6</td><td>4</td><td>Arkansas</td><td>992.6</td></tr>
<tr><td>47</td><td>California</td><td>650.4</td><td>5</td><td>Oklahoma</td><td>989.8</td></tr>
<tr><td>48</td><td>Colorado</td><td>621.1</td><td>6</td><td>Mississippi</td><td>981.4</td></tr>
<tr><td>28</td><td>Connecticut</td><td>834.9</td><td>7</td><td>Kentucky</td><td>953.4</td></tr>
<tr><td>24</td><td>Delaware</td><td>844.1</td><td>8</td><td>Tennessee</td><td>941.2</td></tr>
<tr><td>9</td><td>Florida</td><td>940.1</td><td>9</td><td>Florida</td><td>940.1</td></tr>
<tr><td>42</td><td>Georgia</td><td>724.1</td><td>10</td><td>Missouri</td><td>935.9</td></tr>
<tr><td>41</td><td>Hawaii</td><td>733.7</td><td>11</td><td>Louisiana</td><td>933.9</td></tr>
<tr><td>43</td><td>Idaho</td><td>723.7</td><td>12</td><td>Ohio</td><td>930.7</td></tr>
<tr><td>33</td><td>Illinois</td><td>796.2</td><td>13</td><td>Maine</td><td>930.3</td></tr>
<tr><td>21</td><td>Indiana</td><td>881.0</td><td>14</td><td>North Dakota</td><td>922.8</td></tr>
<tr><td>15</td><td>Iowa</td><td>917.5</td><td>15</td><td>Iowa</td><td>917.5</td></tr>
<tr><td>20</td><td>Kansas</td><td>888.3</td><td>16</td><td>Rhode Island</td><td>907.6</td></tr>
<tr><td>7</td><td>Kentucky</td><td>953.4</td><td>17</td><td>South Dakota</td><td>906.0</td></tr>
<tr><td>11</td><td>Louisiana</td><td>933.9</td><td>18</td><td>South Carolina</td><td>897.0</td></tr>
<tr><td>13</td><td>Maine</td><td>930.3</td><td>19</td><td>Montana</td><td>896.9</td></tr>
<tr><td>35</td><td>Maryland</td><td>776.1</td><td>20</td><td>Kansas</td><td>888.3</td></tr>
<tr><td>30</td><td>Massachusetts</td><td>830.3</td><td>21</td><td>Indiana</td><td>881.0</td></tr>
<tr><td>22</td><td>Michigan</td><td>852.3</td><td>22</td><td>Michigan</td><td>852.3</td></tr>
<tr><td>45</td><td>Minnesota</td><td>716.6</td><td>23</td><td>Oregon</td><td>847.9</td></tr>
<tr><td>6</td><td>Mississippi</td><td>981.4</td><td>24</td><td>Delaware</td><td>844.1</td></tr>
<tr><td>10</td><td>Missouri</td><td>935.9</td><td>25</td><td>North Carolina</td><td>843.6</td></tr>
<tr><td>19</td><td>Montana</td><td>896.9</td><td>26</td><td>Nebraska</td><td>842.5</td></tr>
<tr><td>26</td><td>Nebraska</td><td>842.5</td><td>27</td><td>Wyoming</td><td>837.1</td></tr>
<tr><td>38</td><td>Nevada</td><td>756.2</td><td>28</td><td>Connecticut</td><td>834.9</td></tr>
<tr><td>37</td><td>New Hampshire</td><td>765.1</td><td>29</td><td>Wisconsin</td><td>830.6</td></tr>
<tr><td>32</td><td>New Jersey</td><td>806.4</td><td>30</td><td>Massachusetts</td><td>830.3</td></tr>
<tr><td>34</td><td>New Mexico</td><td>782.6</td><td>31</td><td>Vermont</td><td>809.1</td></tr>
<tr><td>36</td><td>New York</td><td>770.8</td><td>32</td><td>New Jersey</td><td>806.4</td></tr>
<tr><td>25</td><td>North Carolina</td><td>843.6</td><td>33</td><td>Illinois</td><td>796.2</td></tr>
<tr><td>14</td><td>North Dakota</td><td>922.8</td><td>34</td><td>New Mexico</td><td>782.6</td></tr>
<tr><td>12</td><td>Ohio</td><td>930.7</td><td>35</td><td>Maryland</td><td>776.1</td></tr>
<tr><td>5</td><td>Oklahoma</td><td>989.8</td><td>36</td><td>New York</td><td>770.8</td></tr>
<tr><td>23</td><td>Oregon</td><td>847.9</td><td>37</td><td>New Hampshire</td><td>765.1</td></tr>
<tr><td>3</td><td>Pennsylvania</td><td>1,009.1</td><td>38</td><td>Nevada</td><td>756.2</td></tr>
<tr><td>16</td><td>Rhode Island</td><td>907.6</td><td>39</td><td>Virginia</td><td>754.8</td></tr>
<tr><td>18</td><td>South Carolina</td><td>897.0</td><td>40</td><td>Arizona</td><td>751.9</td></tr>
<tr><td>17</td><td>South Dakota</td><td>906.0</td><td>41</td><td>Hawaii</td><td>733.7</td></tr>
<tr><td>8</td><td>Tennessee</td><td>941.2</td><td>42</td><td>Georgia</td><td>724.1</td></tr>
<tr><td>46</td><td>Texas</td><td>668.5</td><td>43</td><td>Idaho</td><td>723.7</td></tr>
<tr><td>49</td><td>Utah</td><td>539.8</td><td>44</td><td>Washington</td><td>721.1</td></tr>
<tr><td>31</td><td>Vermont</td><td>809.1</td><td>45</td><td>Minnesota</td><td>716.6</td></tr>
<tr><td>39</td><td>Virginia</td><td>754.8</td><td>46</td><td>Texas</td><td>668.5</td></tr>
<tr><td>44</td><td>Washington</td><td>721.1</td><td>47</td><td>California</td><td>650.4</td></tr>
<tr><td>1</td><td>West Virginia</td><td>1,136.8</td><td>48</td><td>Colorado</td><td>621.1</td></tr>
<tr><td>29</td><td>Wisconsin</td><td>830.6</td><td>49</td><td>Utah</td><td>539.8</td></tr>
<tr><td>27</td><td>Wyoming</td><td>837.1</td><td>50</td><td>Alaska</td><td>500.6</td></tr>
<tr><td></td><td></td><td></td><td></td><td>District of Columbia</td><td>919.0</td></tr>
</table>

Source: U.S. Department of Health and Human Services, National Center for Health Statistics
"National Vital Statistics Reports" (Vol. 58, No. 1, August 19, 2009, http://www.cdc.gov/nchs/deaths.htm)
*Final data by state of residence. Not age-adjusted.

Age-Adjusted Death Rate in 2006

National Rate = 776.5 Deaths per 100,000 Population*

ALPHA ORDER

RANK	STATE	RATE
2	Alabama	952.4
26	Alaska	775.9
39	Arizona	724.1
8	Arkansas	888.9
48	California	700.2
43	Colorado	716.8
44	Connecticut	714.8
21	Delaware	784.0
45	Florida	711.3
10	Georgia	858.8
50	Hawaii	629.6
30	Idaho	747.4
24	Illinois	781.1
12	Indiana	847.6
36	Iowa	730.3
19	Kansas	794.7
6	Kentucky	915.2
4	Louisiana	930.1
28	Maine	775.0
20	Maryland	793.0
42	Massachusetts	719.7
17	Michigan	813.7
49	Minnesota	672.8
1	Mississippi	961.2
11	Missouri	848.3
23	Montana	781.4
35	Nebraska	735.3
13	Nevada	843.7
38	New Hampshire	724.9
34	New Jersey	736.6
27	New Mexico	775.5
47	New York	701.2
14	North Carolina	843.6
37	North Dakota	726.9
15	Ohio	840.8
5	Oklahoma	920.4
29	Oregon	770.5
18	Pennsylvania	800.8
30	Rhode Island	747.4
9	South Carolina	864.6
33	South Dakota	740.5
7	Tennessee	908.3
22	Texas	783.9
46	Utah	706.3
41	Vermont	721.7
25	Virginia	781.0
40	Washington	722.5
3	West Virginia	941.3
32	Wisconsin	746.6
16	Wyoming	822.8

RANK ORDER

RANK	STATE	RATE
1	Mississippi	961.2
2	Alabama	952.4
3	West Virginia	941.3
4	Louisiana	930.1
5	Oklahoma	920.4
6	Kentucky	915.2
7	Tennessee	908.3
8	Arkansas	888.9
9	South Carolina	864.6
10	Georgia	858.8
11	Missouri	848.3
12	Indiana	847.6
13	Nevada	843.7
14	North Carolina	843.6
15	Ohio	840.8
16	Wyoming	822.8
17	Michigan	813.7
18	Pennsylvania	800.8
19	Kansas	794.7
20	Maryland	793.0
21	Delaware	784.0
22	Texas	783.9
23	Montana	781.4
24	Illinois	781.1
25	Virginia	781.0
26	Alaska	775.9
27	New Mexico	775.5
28	Maine	775.0
29	Oregon	770.5
30	Idaho	747.4
30	Rhode Island	747.4
32	Wisconsin	746.6
33	South Dakota	740.5
34	New Jersey	736.6
35	Nebraska	735.3
36	Iowa	730.3
37	North Dakota	726.9
38	New Hampshire	724.9
39	Arizona	724.1
40	Washington	722.5
41	Vermont	721.7
42	Massachusetts	719.7
43	Colorado	716.8
44	Connecticut	714.8
45	Florida	711.3
46	Utah	706.3
47	New York	701.2
48	California	700.2
49	Minnesota	672.8
50	Hawaii	629.6

| | District of Columbia | 892.9 |

Source: U.S. Department of Health and Human Services, National Center for Health Statistics
"National Vital Statistics Reports" (Vol. 58, No. 1, August 19, 2009, http://www.cdc.gov/nchs/deaths.htm)
*Final data by state of residence. Age-adjusted rates eliminate the distorting effects of the aging of the population. Rates based on the year 2000 standard population.

Infant Deaths in 2006

National Total = 28,527 Infant Deaths*

ALPHA ORDER

RANK	STATE	DEATHS	% of USA
19	Alabama	571	2.0%
45	Alaska	76	0.3%
14	Arizona	651	2.3%
29	Arkansas	350	1.2%
1	California	2,835	9.9%
26	Colorado	404	1.4%
33	Connecticut	260	0.9%
41	Delaware	99	0.3%
3	Florida	1,717	6.0%
6	Georgia	1,206	4.2%
40	Hawaii	107	0.4%
37	Idaho	165	0.6%
5	Illinois	1,309	4.6%
13	Indiana	708	2.5%
35	Iowa	208	0.7%
30	Kansas	292	1.0%
23	Kentucky	438	1.5%
16	Louisiana	629	2.2%
42	Maine	89	0.3%
17	Maryland	616	2.2%
28	Massachusetts	370	1.3%
10	Michigan	940	3.3%
27	Minnesota	381	1.3%
21	Mississippi	488	1.7%
18	Missouri	603	2.1%
47	Montana	73	0.3%
39	Nebraska	149	0.5%
34	Nevada	257	0.9%
43	New Hampshire	87	0.3%
15	New Jersey	632	2.2%
36	New Mexico	173	0.6%
4	New York	1,407	4.9%
9	North Carolina	1,033	3.6%
49	North Dakota	50	0.2%
7	Ohio	1,170	4.1%
24	Oklahoma	432	1.5%
32	Oregon	267	0.9%
8	Pennsylvania	1,138	4.0%
45	Rhode Island	76	0.3%
20	South Carolina	522	1.8%
44	South Dakota	82	0.3%
12	Tennessee	733	2.6%
2	Texas	2,486	8.7%
31	Utah	273	1.0%
50	Vermont	36	0.1%
11	Virginia	765	2.7%
25	Washington	407	1.4%
38	West Virginia	155	0.5%
22	Wisconsin	462	1.6%
48	Wyoming	54	0.2%

RANK ORDER

RANK	STATE	DEATHS	% of USA
1	California	2,835	9.9%
2	Texas	2,486	8.7%
3	Florida	1,717	6.0%
4	New York	1,407	4.9%
5	Illinois	1,309	4.6%
6	Georgia	1,206	4.2%
7	Ohio	1,170	4.1%
8	Pennsylvania	1,138	4.0%
9	North Carolina	1,033	3.6%
10	Michigan	940	3.3%
11	Virginia	765	2.7%
12	Tennessee	733	2.6%
13	Indiana	708	2.5%
14	Arizona	651	2.3%
15	New Jersey	632	2.2%
16	Louisiana	629	2.2%
17	Maryland	616	2.2%
18	Missouri	603	2.1%
19	Alabama	571	2.0%
20	South Carolina	522	1.8%
21	Mississippi	488	1.7%
22	Wisconsin	462	1.6%
23	Kentucky	438	1.5%
24	Oklahoma	432	1.5%
25	Washington	407	1.4%
26	Colorado	404	1.4%
27	Minnesota	381	1.3%
28	Massachusetts	370	1.3%
29	Arkansas	350	1.2%
30	Kansas	292	1.0%
31	Utah	273	1.0%
32	Oregon	267	0.9%
33	Connecticut	260	0.9%
34	Nevada	257	0.9%
35	Iowa	208	0.7%
36	New Mexico	173	0.6%
37	Idaho	165	0.6%
38	West Virginia	155	0.5%
39	Nebraska	149	0.5%
40	Hawaii	107	0.4%
41	Delaware	99	0.3%
42	Maine	89	0.3%
43	New Hampshire	87	0.3%
44	South Dakota	82	0.3%
45	Alaska	76	0.3%
45	Rhode Island	76	0.3%
47	Montana	73	0.3%
48	Wyoming	54	0.2%
49	North Dakota	50	0.2%
50	Vermont	36	0.1%
	District of Columbia	96	0.3%

Source: U.S. Department of Health and Human Services, National Center for Health Statistics
"National Vital Statistics Reports" (Vol. 57, No. 14, April 17, 2009, http://www.cdc.gov/nchs/deaths.htm)
*Final data. Deaths of infants under 1 year old by state of residence.

Infant Mortality Rate in 2006

National Rate = 6.7 Infant Deaths per 1,000 Live Births*

ALPHA ORDER

RANK ORDER

RANK	STATE	RATE		RANK	STATE	RATE
3	Alabama	9.0		1	Mississippi	10.6
24	Alaska	6.9		2	Louisiana	9.9
27	Arizona	6.4		3	Alabama	9.0
5	Arkansas	8.5		4	Tennessee	8.7
48	California	5.0		5	Arkansas	8.5
38	Colorado	5.7		6	South Carolina	8.4
31	Connecticut	6.2		7	Delaware	8.3
7	Delaware	8.3		8	Georgia	8.1
19	Florida	7.3		8	North Carolina	8.1
8	Georgia	8.1		10	Indiana	8.0
39	Hawaii	5.6		10	Maryland	8.0
26	Idaho	6.8		10	Oklahoma	8.0
19	Illinois	7.3		13	Ohio	7.8
10	Indiana	8.0		14	Pennsylvania	7.6
46	Iowa	5.1		15	Kentucky	7.5
21	Kansas	7.1		16	Michigan	7.4
15	Kentucky	7.5		16	Missouri	7.4
2	Louisiana	9.9		16	West Virginia	7.4
30	Maine	6.3		19	Florida	7.3
10	Maryland	8.0		19	Illinois	7.3
49	Massachusetts	4.8		21	Kansas	7.1
16	Michigan	7.4		21	Virginia	7.1
45	Minnesota	5.2		23	Wyoming	7.0
1	Mississippi	10.6		24	Alaska	6.9
16	Missouri	7.4		24	South Dakota	6.9
35	Montana	5.8		26	Idaho	6.8
39	Nebraska	5.6		27	Arizona	6.4
27	Nevada	6.4		27	Nevada	6.4
33	New Hampshire	6.1		27	Wisconsin	6.4
42	New Jersey	5.5		30	Maine	6.3
35	New Mexico	5.8		31	Connecticut	6.2
39	New York	5.6		31	Texas	6.2
8	North Carolina	8.1		33	New Hampshire	6.1
35	North Dakota	5.8		33	Rhode Island	6.1
13	Ohio	7.8		35	Montana	5.8
10	Oklahoma	8.0		35	New Mexico	5.8
42	Oregon	5.5		35	North Dakota	5.8
14	Pennsylvania	7.6		38	Colorado	5.7
33	Rhode Island	6.1		39	Hawaii	5.6
6	South Carolina	8.4		39	Nebraska	5.6
24	South Dakota	6.9		39	New York	5.6
4	Tennessee	8.7		42	New Jersey	5.5
31	Texas	6.2		42	Oregon	5.5
46	Utah	5.1		42	Vermont	5.5
42	Vermont	5.5		45	Minnesota	5.2
21	Virginia	7.1		46	Iowa	5.1
50	Washington	4.7		46	Utah	5.1
16	West Virginia	7.4		48	California	5.0
27	Wisconsin	6.4		49	Massachusetts	4.8
23	Wyoming	7.0		50	Washington	4.7

District of Columbia   11.3

Source: U.S. Department of Health and Human Services, National Center for Health Statistics
"National Vital Statistics Reports" (Vol. 57, No. 14, April 17, 2009, http://www.cdc.gov/nchs/deaths.htm)
*Final data. Deaths of infants under 1 year old by state of residence.

White Infant Mortality Rate in 2006

National Rate = 5.6 White Infant Deaths per 1,000 White Live Births*

ALPHA ORDER

RANK	STATE	RATE
6	Alabama	6.7
47	Alaska	4.5
18	Arizona	6.0
2	Arkansas	6.9
44	California	4.8
31	Colorado	5.5
40	Connecticut	4.9
11	Delaware	6.2
22	Florida	5.9
23	Georgia	5.8
NA	Hawaii**	NA
6	Idaho	6.7
18	Illinois	6.0
6	Indiana	6.7
40	Iowa	4.9
15	Kansas	6.1
3	Kentucky	6.8
11	Louisiana	6.2
11	Maine	6.2
18	Maryland	6.0
46	Massachusetts	4.6
23	Michigan	5.8
45	Minnesota	4.7
1	Mississippi	7.1
15	Missouri	6.1
38	Montana	5.0
36	Nebraska	5.2
23	Nevada	5.8
26	New Hampshire	5.7
48	New Jersey	4.4
26	New Mexico	5.7
40	New York	4.9
18	North Carolina	6.0
40	North Dakota	4.9
15	Ohio	6.1
3	Oklahoma	6.8
34	Oregon	5.3
11	Pennsylvania	6.2
26	Rhode Island	5.7
26	South Carolina	5.7
34	South Dakota	5.3
3	Tennessee	6.8
31	Texas	5.5
37	Utah	5.1
30	Vermont	5.6
33	Virginia	5.4
48	Washington	4.4
6	West Virginia	6.7
38	Wisconsin	5.0
10	Wyoming	6.6

RANK ORDER

RANK	STATE	RATE
1	Mississippi	7.1
2	Arkansas	6.9
3	Kentucky	6.8
3	Oklahoma	6.8
3	Tennessee	6.8
6	Alabama	6.7
6	Idaho	6.7
6	Indiana	6.7
6	West Virginia	6.7
10	Wyoming	6.6
11	Delaware	6.2
11	Louisiana	6.2
11	Maine	6.2
11	Pennsylvania	6.2
15	Kansas	6.1
15	Missouri	6.1
15	Ohio	6.1
18	Arizona	6.0
18	Illinois	6.0
18	Maryland	6.0
18	North Carolina	6.0
22	Florida	5.9
23	Georgia	5.8
23	Michigan	5.8
23	Nevada	5.8
26	New Hampshire	5.7
26	New Mexico	5.7
26	Rhode Island	5.7
26	South Carolina	5.7
30	Vermont	5.6
31	Colorado	5.5
31	Texas	5.5
33	Virginia	5.4
34	Oregon	5.3
34	South Dakota	5.3
36	Nebraska	5.2
37	Utah	5.1
38	Montana	5.0
38	Wisconsin	5.0
40	Connecticut	4.9
40	Iowa	4.9
40	New York	4.9
40	North Dakota	4.9
44	California	4.8
45	Minnesota	4.7
46	Massachusetts	4.6
47	Alaska	4.5
48	New Jersey	4.4
48	Washington	4.4
NA	Hawaii**	NA
	District of Columbia**	NA

Source: U.S. Department of Health and Human Services, National Center for Health Statistics
"National Vital Statistics Reports" (Vol. 57, No. 14, April 17, 2009, http://www.cdc.gov/nchs/deaths.htm)
*Final data. Deaths of infants under 1 year old, exclusive of fetal deaths. Based on race of the mother.
**With fewer than 20 deaths, the rate would be considered statistically unreliable.

Black Infant Mortality Rate in 2006

National Rate = 13.3 Black Infant Deaths per 1,000 Black Live Births*

ALPHA ORDER

RANK	STATE	RATE
20	Alabama	14.2
NA	Alaska**	NA
5	Arizona	16.9
9	Arkansas	15.7
26	California	12.1
25	Colorado	12.4
17	Connecticut	14.8
19	Delaware	14.3
28	Florida	11.9
24	Georgia	12.9
NA	Hawaii**	NA
NA	Idaho**	NA
22	Illinois	13.7
3	Indiana	18.7
NA	Iowa**	NA
2	Kansas	19.3
14	Kentucky	15.0
8	Louisiana	15.8
NA	Maine**	NA
29	Maryland	11.8
34	Massachusetts	8.0
15	Michigan	14.9
33	Minnesota	8.3
18	Mississippi	14.6
15	Missouri	14.9
NA	Montana**	NA
31	Nebraska	10.6
9	Nevada	15.7
NA	New Hampshire**	NA
30	New Jersey	11.5
NA	New Mexico**	NA
32	New York	9.2
13	North Carolina	15.1
NA	North Dakota**	NA
5	Ohio	16.9
11	Oklahoma	15.4
NA	Oregon**	NA
12	Pennsylvania	15.2
NA	Rhode Island**	NA
21	South Carolina	13.8
NA	South Dakota**	NA
7	Tennessee	16.0
27	Texas	12.0
NA	Utah**	NA
NA	Vermont**	NA
23	Virginia	13.3
35	Washington	7.4
1	West Virginia	28.6
4	Wisconsin	18.3
NA	Wyoming**	NA

RANK ORDER

RANK	STATE	RATE
1	West Virginia	28.6
2	Kansas	19.3
3	Indiana	18.7
4	Wisconsin	18.3
5	Arizona	16.9
5	Ohio	16.9
7	Tennessee	16.0
8	Louisiana	15.8
9	Arkansas	15.7
9	Nevada	15.7
11	Oklahoma	15.4
12	Pennsylvania	15.2
13	North Carolina	15.1
14	Kentucky	15.0
15	Michigan	14.9
15	Missouri	14.9
17	Connecticut	14.8
18	Mississippi	14.6
19	Delaware	14.3
20	Alabama	14.2
21	South Carolina	13.8
22	Illinois	13.7
23	Virginia	13.3
24	Georgia	12.9
25	Colorado	12.4
26	California	12.1
27	Texas	12.0
28	Florida	11.9
29	Maryland	11.8
30	New Jersey	11.5
31	Nebraska	10.6
32	New York	9.2
33	Minnesota	8.3
34	Massachusetts	8.0
35	Washington	7.4
NA	Alaska**	NA
NA	Hawaii**	NA
NA	Idaho**	NA
NA	Iowa**	NA
NA	Maine**	NA
NA	Montana**	NA
NA	New Hampshire**	NA
NA	New Mexico**	NA
NA	North Dakota**	NA
NA	Oregon**	NA
NA	Rhode Island**	NA
NA	South Dakota**	NA
NA	Utah**	NA
NA	Vermont**	NA
NA	Wyoming**	NA

District of Columbia — 14.5

Source: U.S. Department of Health and Human Services, National Center for Health Statistics
"National Vital Statistics Reports" (Vol. 57, No. 14, April 17, 2009, http://www.cdc.gov/nchs/deaths.htm)
*Final data. Deaths of infants under 28 days old, exclusive of fetal deaths.
**With fewer than 20 deaths, the rate would be considered statistically unreliable.

Neonatal Deaths in 2006

National Total = 18,989 Deaths*

ALPHA ORDER

RANK	STATE	DEATHS	% of USA
19	Alabama	365	1.9%
46	Alaska	41	0.2%
15	Arizona	446	2.3%
29	Arkansas	202	1.1%
1	California	1,955	10.3%
22	Colorado	309	1.6%
30	Connecticut	199	1.0%
41	Delaware	72	0.4%
3	Florida	1,124	5.9%
7	Georgia	787	4.1%
39	Hawaii	84	0.4%
36	Idaho	112	0.6%
5	Illinois	885	4.7%
16	Indiana	438	2.3%
35	Iowa	132	0.7%
33	Kansas	175	0.9%
26	Kentucky	258	1.4%
18	Louisiana	388	2.0%
43	Maine	60	0.3%
14	Maryland	448	2.4%
24	Massachusetts	280	1.5%
10	Michigan	660	3.5%
27	Minnesota	241	1.3%
23	Mississippi	304	1.6%
17	Missouri	399	2.1%
48	Montana	33	0.2%
38	Nebraska	94	0.5%
34	Nevada	167	0.9%
44	New Hampshire	57	0.3%
13	New Jersey	450	2.4%
37	New Mexico	109	0.6%
4	New York	947	5.0%
9	North Carolina	711	3.7%
49	North Dakota	31	0.2%
8	Ohio	784	4.1%
28	Oklahoma	238	1.3%
32	Oregon	180	0.9%
6	Pennsylvania	815	4.3%
42	Rhode Island	62	0.3%
20	South Carolina	344	1.8%
45	South Dakota	43	0.2%
12	Tennessee	490	2.6%
2	Texas	1,586	8.4%
31	Utah	189	1.0%
50	Vermont	20	0.1%
11	Virginia	529	2.8%
25	Washington	260	1.4%
40	West Virginia	81	0.4%
21	Wisconsin	311	1.6%
47	Wyoming	34	0.2%

RANK ORDER

RANK	STATE	DEATHS	% of USA
1	California	1,955	10.3%
2	Texas	1,586	8.4%
3	Florida	1,124	5.9%
4	New York	947	5.0%
5	Illinois	885	4.7%
6	Pennsylvania	815	4.3%
7	Georgia	787	4.1%
8	Ohio	784	4.1%
9	North Carolina	711	3.7%
10	Michigan	660	3.5%
11	Virginia	529	2.8%
12	Tennessee	490	2.6%
13	New Jersey	450	2.4%
14	Maryland	448	2.4%
15	Arizona	446	2.3%
16	Indiana	438	2.3%
17	Missouri	399	2.1%
18	Louisiana	388	2.0%
19	Alabama	365	1.9%
20	South Carolina	344	1.8%
21	Wisconsin	311	1.6%
22	Colorado	309	1.6%
23	Mississippi	304	1.6%
24	Massachusetts	280	1.5%
25	Washington	260	1.4%
26	Kentucky	258	1.4%
27	Minnesota	241	1.3%
28	Oklahoma	238	1.3%
29	Arkansas	202	1.1%
30	Connecticut	199	1.0%
31	Utah	189	1.0%
32	Oregon	180	0.9%
33	Kansas	175	0.9%
34	Nevada	167	0.9%
35	Iowa	132	0.7%
36	Idaho	112	0.6%
37	New Mexico	109	0.6%
38	Nebraska	94	0.5%
39	Hawaii	84	0.4%
40	West Virginia	81	0.4%
41	Delaware	72	0.4%
42	Rhode Island	62	0.3%
43	Maine	60	0.3%
44	New Hampshire	57	0.3%
45	South Dakota	43	0.2%
46	Alaska	41	0.2%
47	Wyoming	34	0.2%
48	Montana	33	0.2%
49	North Dakota	31	0.2%
50	Vermont	20	0.1%
	District of Columbia	60	0.3%

Source: U.S. Department of Health and Human Services, National Center for Health Statistics
"National Vital Statistics Reports" (Vol. 57, No. 14, April 17, 2009, http://www.cdc.gov/nchs/deaths.htm)
*Final data. Deaths of infants under 28 days old, exclusive of fetal deaths.

Neonatal Death Rate in 2006

National Rate = 4.5 Deaths per 1,000 Live Births*

ALPHA ORDER

RANK	STATE	RATE
4	Alabama	5.8
37	Alaska	3.7
22	Arizona	4.4
14	Arkansas	4.9
43	California	3.5
22	Colorado	4.4
19	Connecticut	4.8
3	Delaware	6.0
19	Florida	4.8
10	Georgia	5.3
22	Hawaii	4.4
21	Idaho	4.6
14	Illinois	4.9
14	Indiana	4.9
46	Iowa	3.3
28	Kansas	4.3
22	Kentucky	4.4
2	Louisiana	6.1
30	Maine	4.2
4	Maryland	5.8
39	Massachusetts	3.6
11	Michigan	5.2
46	Minnesota	3.3
1	Mississippi	6.6
14	Missouri	4.9
50	Montana	2.6
43	Nebraska	3.5
30	Nevada	4.2
32	New Hampshire	4.0
34	New Jersey	3.9
39	New Mexico	3.6
36	New York	3.8
7	North Carolina	5.6
39	North Dakota	3.6
11	Ohio	5.2
22	Oklahoma	4.4
37	Oregon	3.7
8	Pennsylvania	5.5
13	Rhode Island	5.0
8	South Carolina	5.5
39	South Dakota	3.6
4	Tennessee	5.8
32	Texas	4.0
43	Utah	3.5
48	Vermont	3.1
14	Virginia	4.9
49	Washington	3.0
34	West Virginia	3.9
28	Wisconsin	4.3
22	Wyoming	4.4

RANK ORDER

RANK	STATE	RATE
1	Mississippi	6.6
2	Louisiana	6.1
3	Delaware	6.0
4	Alabama	5.8
4	Maryland	5.8
4	Tennessee	5.8
7	North Carolina	5.6
8	Pennsylvania	5.5
8	South Carolina	5.5
10	Georgia	5.3
11	Michigan	5.2
11	Ohio	5.2
13	Rhode Island	5.0
14	Arkansas	4.9
14	Illinois	4.9
14	Indiana	4.9
14	Missouri	4.9
14	Virginia	4.9
19	Connecticut	4.8
19	Florida	4.8
21	Idaho	4.6
22	Arizona	4.4
22	Colorado	4.4
22	Hawaii	4.4
22	Kentucky	4.4
22	Oklahoma	4.4
22	Wyoming	4.4
28	Kansas	4.3
28	Wisconsin	4.3
30	Maine	4.2
30	Nevada	4.2
32	New Hampshire	4.0
32	Texas	4.0
34	New Jersey	3.9
34	West Virginia	3.9
36	New York	3.8
37	Alaska	3.7
37	Oregon	3.7
39	Massachusetts	3.6
39	New Mexico	3.6
39	North Dakota	3.6
39	South Dakota	3.6
43	California	3.5
43	Nebraska	3.5
43	Utah	3.5
46	Iowa	3.3
46	Minnesota	3.3
48	Vermont	3.1
49	Washington	3.0
50	Montana	2.6
	District of Columbia	7.0

Source: U.S. Department of Health and Human Services, National Center for Health Statistics
    "National Vital Statistics Reports" (Vol. 57, No. 14, April 17, 2009, http://www.cdc.gov/nchs/deaths.htm)
*Final data. Deaths of infants under 28 days old, exclusive of fetal deaths.

White Neonatal Death Rate in 2006

National Rate = 3.7 White Neonatal Deaths per 1,000 White Live Births*

ALPHA ORDER

RANK	STATE	RATE
11	Alabama	4.1
NA	Alaska**	NA
5	Arizona	4.3
25	Arkansas	3.7
41	California	3.3
5	Colorado	4.3
25	Connecticut	3.7
5	Delaware	4.3
21	Florida	3.8
21	Georgia	3.8
NA	Hawaii**	NA
1	Idaho	4.7
3	Illinois	4.4
15	Indiana	4.0
43	Iowa	3.2
19	Kansas	3.9
11	Kentucky	4.1
31	Louisiana	3.5
11	Maine	4.1
3	Maryland	4.4
31	Massachusetts	3.5
15	Michigan	4.0
45	Minnesota	3.1
5	Mississippi	4.3
15	Missouri	4.0
47	Montana	2.2
41	Nebraska	3.3
21	Nevada	3.8
31	New Hampshire	3.5
36	New Jersey	3.4
31	New Mexico	3.5
36	New York	3.4
11	North Carolina	4.1
36	North Dakota	3.4
15	Ohio	4.0
21	Oklahoma	3.8
25	Oregon	3.7
5	Pennsylvania	4.3
2	Rhode Island	4.5
29	South Carolina	3.6
43	South Dakota	3.2
10	Tennessee	4.2
31	Texas	3.5
29	Utah	3.6
NA	Vermont**	NA
25	Virginia	3.7
46	Washington	2.8
36	West Virginia	3.4
36	Wisconsin	3.4
19	Wyoming	3.9

RANK ORDER

RANK	STATE	RATE
1	Idaho	4.7
2	Rhode Island	4.5
3	Illinois	4.4
3	Maryland	4.4
5	Arizona	4.3
5	Colorado	4.3
5	Delaware	4.3
5	Mississippi	4.3
5	Pennsylvania	4.3
10	Tennessee	4.2
11	Alabama	4.1
11	Kentucky	4.1
11	Maine	4.1
11	North Carolina	4.1
15	Indiana	4.0
15	Michigan	4.0
15	Missouri	4.0
15	Ohio	4.0
19	Kansas	3.9
19	Wyoming	3.9
21	Florida	3.8
21	Georgia	3.8
21	Nevada	3.8
21	Oklahoma	3.8
25	Arkansas	3.7
25	Connecticut	3.7
25	Oregon	3.7
25	Virginia	3.7
29	South Carolina	3.6
29	Utah	3.6
31	Louisiana	3.5
31	Massachusetts	3.5
31	New Hampshire	3.5
31	New Mexico	3.5
31	Texas	3.5
36	New Jersey	3.4
36	New York	3.4
36	North Dakota	3.4
36	West Virginia	3.4
36	Wisconsin	3.4
41	California	3.3
41	Nebraska	3.3
43	Iowa	3.2
43	South Dakota	3.2
45	Minnesota	3.1
46	Washington	2.8
47	Montana	2.2
NA	Alaska**	NA
NA	Hawaii**	NA
NA	Vermont**	NA
	District of Columbia**	NA

Source: U.S. Department of Health and Human Services, National Center for Health Statistics
   "National Vital Statistics Reports" (Vol. 57, No. 14, April 17, 2009, http://www.cdc.gov/nchs/deaths.htm)
*Final data. Deaths of infants under 28 days old, exclusive of fetal deaths. Based on race of the mother.
**With fewer than 20 deaths, the rate would be considered statistically unreliable.

Black Neonatal Death Rate in 2006

National Rate = 8.8 Black Neonatal Deaths per 1,000 Black Live Births*

ALPHA ORDER				RANK ORDER		
RANK	STATE	RATE		RANK	STATE	RATE
14	Alabama	9.6		1	Wisconsin	12.9
NA	Alaska**	NA		2	Indiana	12.6
14	Arizona	9.6		3	Connecticut	11.8
13	Arkansas	9.7		4	Tennessee	11.7
23	California	8.2		5	Ohio	11.5
25	Colorado	7.9		5	Pennsylvania	11.5
3	Connecticut	11.8		7	Delaware	10.7
7	Delaware	10.7		8	Michigan	10.5
24	Florida	8.0		9	North Carolina	10.3
22	Georgia	8.3		10	Louisiana	10.2
NA	Hawaii**	NA		11	Missouri	10.1
NA	Idaho**	NA		12	Kansas	9.8
27	Illinois	7.8		13	Arkansas	9.7
2	Indiana	12.6		14	Alabama	9.6
NA	Iowa**	NA		14	Arizona	9.6
12	Kansas	9.8		16	South Carolina	9.4
25	Kentucky	7.9		17	Mississippi	9.3
10	Louisiana	10.2		17	Virginia	9.3
NA	Maine**	NA		19	Nevada	9.0
20	Maryland	8.6		20	Maryland	8.6
30	Massachusetts	6.2		21	Oklahoma	8.4
8	Michigan	10.5		22	Georgia	8.3
33	Minnesota	4.9		23	California	8.2
17	Mississippi	9.3		24	Florida	8.0
11	Missouri	10.1		25	Colorado	7.9
NA	Montana**	NA		25	Kentucky	7.9
NA	Nebraska**	NA		27	Illinois	7.8
19	Nevada	9.0		28	New Jersey	7.4
NA	New Hampshire**	NA		29	Texas	7.3
28	New Jersey	7.4		30	Massachusetts	6.2
NA	New Mexico**	NA		31	New York	5.9
31	New York	5.9		32	Washington	5.1
9	North Carolina	10.3		33	Minnesota	4.9
NA	North Dakota**	NA		NA	Alaska**	NA
5	Ohio	11.5		NA	Hawaii**	NA
21	Oklahoma	8.4		NA	Idaho**	NA
NA	Oregon**	NA		NA	Iowa**	NA
5	Pennsylvania	11.5		NA	Maine**	NA
NA	Rhode Island**	NA		NA	Montana**	NA
16	South Carolina	9.4		NA	Nebraska**	NA
NA	South Dakota**	NA		NA	New Hampshire**	NA
4	Tennessee	11.7		NA	New Mexico**	NA
29	Texas	7.3		NA	North Dakota**	NA
NA	Utah**	NA		NA	Oregon**	NA
NA	Vermont**	NA		NA	Rhode Island**	NA
17	Virginia	9.3		NA	South Dakota**	NA
32	Washington	5.1		NA	Utah**	NA
NA	West Virginia**	NA		NA	Vermont**	NA
1	Wisconsin	12.9		NA	West Virginia**	NA
NA	Wyoming**	NA		NA	Wyoming**	NA
					District of Columbia	9.1

Source: U.S. Department of Health and Human Services, National Center for Health Statistics
"National Vital Statistics Reports" (Vol. 57, No. 14, April 17, 2009, http://www.cdc.gov/nchs/deaths.htm)
*Final data. Deaths of infants under 28 days old, exclusive of fetal deaths. Based on race of the mother.
**With fewer than 20 deaths, the rate would be considered statistically unreliable.

Estimated Deaths by Cancer in 2009

National Estimated Total = 562,340 Deaths

ALPHA ORDER

RANK	STATE	DEATHS	% of USA
21	Alabama	9,900	1.8%
50	Alaska	830	0.1%
20	Arizona	10,260	1.8%
31	Arkansas	6,230	1.1%
1	California	54,600	9.7%
29	Colorado	6,740	1.2%
28	Connecticut	6,990	1.2%
45	Delaware	1,860	0.3%
2	Florida	41,270	7.3%
11	Georgia	14,970	2.7%
42	Hawaii	2,270	0.4%
41	Idaho	2,450	0.4%
7	Illinois	23,220	4.1%
15	Indiana	12,820	2.3%
30	Iowa	6,360	1.1%
33	Kansas	5,290	0.9%
22	Kentucky	9,410	1.7%
25	Louisiana	8,810	1.6%
38	Maine	3,190	0.6%
19	Maryland	10,320	1.8%
14	Massachusetts	13,140	2.3%
8	Michigan	20,450	3.6%
24	Minnesota	9,020	1.6%
32	Mississippi	6,090	1.1%
16	Missouri	12,620	2.2%
44	Montana	1,980	0.4%
36	Nebraska	3,360	0.6%
34	Nevada	4,600	0.8%
40	New Hampshire	2,620	0.5%
10	New Jersey	16,480	2.9%
37	New Mexico	3,300	0.6%
4	New York	34,190	6.1%
9	North Carolina	18,550	3.3%
47	North Dakota	1,300	0.2%
6	Ohio	24,350	4.3%
26	Oklahoma	7,420	1.3%
27	Oregon	7,380	1.3%
5	Pennsylvania	28,690	5.1%
43	Rhode Island	2,220	0.4%
23	South Carolina	9,100	1.6%
46	South Dakota	1,640	0.3%
13	Tennessee	13,340	2.4%
3	Texas	36,030	6.4%
39	Utah	2,760	0.5%
48	Vermont	1,150	0.2%
12	Virginia	13,920	2.5%
17	Washington	11,210	2.0%
35	West Virginia	4,530	0.8%
18	Wisconsin	11,170	2.0%
49	Wyoming	990	0.2%

RANK ORDER

RANK	STATE	DEATHS	% of USA
1	California	54,600	9.7%
2	Florida	41,270	7.3%
3	Texas	36,030	6.4%
4	New York	34,190	6.1%
5	Pennsylvania	28,690	5.1%
6	Ohio	24,350	4.3%
7	Illinois	23,220	4.1%
8	Michigan	20,450	3.6%
9	North Carolina	18,550	3.3%
10	New Jersey	16,480	2.9%
11	Georgia	14,970	2.7%
12	Virginia	13,920	2.5%
13	Tennessee	13,340	2.4%
14	Massachusetts	13,140	2.3%
15	Indiana	12,820	2.3%
16	Missouri	12,620	2.2%
17	Washington	11,210	2.0%
18	Wisconsin	11,170	2.0%
19	Maryland	10,320	1.8%
20	Arizona	10,260	1.8%
21	Alabama	9,900	1.8%
22	Kentucky	9,410	1.7%
23	South Carolina	9,100	1.6%
24	Minnesota	9,020	1.6%
25	Louisiana	8,810	1.6%
26	Oklahoma	7,420	1.3%
27	Oregon	7,380	1.3%
28	Connecticut	6,990	1.2%
29	Colorado	6,740	1.2%
30	Iowa	6,360	1.1%
31	Arkansas	6,230	1.1%
32	Mississippi	6,090	1.1%
33	Kansas	5,290	0.9%
34	Nevada	4,600	0.8%
35	West Virginia	4,530	0.8%
36	Nebraska	3,360	0.6%
37	New Mexico	3,300	0.6%
38	Maine	3,190	0.6%
39	Utah	2,760	0.5%
40	New Hampshire	2,620	0.5%
41	Idaho	2,450	0.4%
42	Hawaii	2,270	0.4%
43	Rhode Island	2,220	0.4%
44	Montana	1,980	0.4%
45	Delaware	1,860	0.3%
46	South Dakota	1,640	0.3%
47	North Dakota	1,300	0.2%
48	Vermont	1,150	0.2%
49	Wyoming	990	0.2%
50	Alaska	830	0.1%
	District of Columbia	970	0.2%

Source: American Cancer Society
"Cancer Facts & Figures 2009" (Copyright 2009, American Cancer Society, http://www.cancer.org/docroot/stt/stt_0.asp)

Estimated Death Rate by Cancer in 2009

National Estimated Rate = 183.2 Deaths per 100,000 Population*

ALPHA ORDER

RANK	STATE	RATE
12	Alabama	210.2
49	Alaska	118.8
44	Arizona	155.6
6	Arkansas	215.6
46	California	147.7
48	Colorado	134.1
23	Connecticut	198.7
13	Delaware	210.1
4	Florida	222.6
45	Georgia	152.3
37	Hawaii	175.3
43	Idaho	158.5
35	Illinois	179.9
20	Indiana	199.6
8	Iowa	211.4
30	Kansas	187.7
5	Kentucky	218.1
27	Louisiana	196.1
2	Maine	242.0
34	Maryland	181.1
22	Massachusetts	199.3
15	Michigan	205.1
40	Minnesota	171.3
14	Mississippi	206.3
10	Missouri	210.8
16	Montana	203.1
31	Nebraska	187.0
39	Nevada	174.0
24	New Hampshire	197.8
29	New Jersey	189.3
42	New Mexico	164.2
38	New York	175.0
25	North Carolina	197.7
19	North Dakota	201.0
9	Ohio	211.0
18	Oklahoma	201.2
28	Oregon	192.9
3	Pennsylvania	227.6
10	Rhode Island	210.8
21	South Carolina	199.5
17	South Dakota	201.9
7	Tennessee	211.9
47	Texas	145.4
50	Utah	99.1
32	Vermont	185.0
36	Virginia	176.6
41	Washington	168.2
1	West Virginia	248.9
26	Wisconsin	197.5
33	Wyoming	181.9

RANK ORDER

RANK	STATE	RATE
1	West Virginia	248.9
2	Maine	242.0
3	Pennsylvania	227.6
4	Florida	222.6
5	Kentucky	218.1
6	Arkansas	215.6
7	Tennessee	211.9
8	Iowa	211.4
9	Ohio	211.0
10	Missouri	210.8
10	Rhode Island	210.8
12	Alabama	210.2
13	Delaware	210.1
14	Mississippi	206.3
15	Michigan	205.1
16	Montana	203.1
17	South Dakota	201.9
18	Oklahoma	201.2
19	North Dakota	201.0
20	Indiana	199.6
21	South Carolina	199.5
22	Massachusetts	199.3
23	Connecticut	198.7
24	New Hampshire	197.8
25	North Carolina	197.7
26	Wisconsin	197.5
27	Louisiana	196.1
28	Oregon	192.9
29	New Jersey	189.3
30	Kansas	187.7
31	Nebraska	187.0
32	Vermont	185.0
33	Wyoming	181.9
34	Maryland	181.1
35	Illinois	179.9
36	Virginia	176.6
37	Hawaii	175.3
38	New York	175.0
39	Nevada	174.0
40	Minnesota	171.3
41	Washington	168.2
42	New Mexico	164.2
43	Idaho	158.5
44	Arizona	155.6
45	Georgia	152.3
46	California	147.7
47	Texas	145.4
48	Colorado	134.1
49	Alaska	118.8
50	Utah	99.1

District of Columbia 161.8

Source: CQ Press using data from American Cancer Society
"Cancer Facts & Figures 2009" (Copyright 2009, American Cancer Society, http://www.cancer.org/docroot/stt/stt_0.asp)
*Rates calculated using 2009 Census resident population estimates. Not age-adjusted.

Age-Adjusted Death Rate by Cancer for Males in 2005

National Rate = 234.4 Deaths per 100,000 Male Population*

ALPHA ORDER

RANK	STATE	RATE
5	Alabama	271.7
33	Alaska	226.7
47	Arizona	201.3
6	Arkansas	266.8
45	California	206.4
48	Colorado	199.3
35	Connecticut	225.1
12	Delaware	252.8
39	Florida	219.9
16	Georgia	250.9
49	Hawaii	189.4
44	Idaho	208.4
18	Illinois	245.6
9	Indiana	257.7
28	Iowa	231.3
27	Kansas	231.9
1	Kentucky	286.9
2	Louisiana	285.9
10	Maine	256.0
21	Maryland	241.4
23	Massachusetts	237.8
22	Michigan	240.2
40	Minnesota	219.2
3	Mississippi	282.6
14	Missouri	252.1
37	Montana	222.0
38	Nebraska	220.6
30	Nevada	229.4
24	New Hampshire	237.6
25	New Jersey	232.4
46	New Mexico	203.4
41	New York	217.1
15	North Carolina	251.8
42	North Dakota	216.3
11	Ohio	254.9
13	Oklahoma	252.2
31	Oregon	228.2
17	Pennsylvania	246.4
20	Rhode Island	243.3
8	South Carolina	263.7
31	South Dakota	228.2
4	Tennessee	272.4
26	Texas	232.3
50	Utah	172.5
34	Vermont	226.2
19	Virginia	244.8
36	Washington	222.8
7	West Virginia	265.6
29	Wisconsin	230.8
43	Wyoming	211.2

RANK ORDER

RANK	STATE	RATE
1	Kentucky	286.9
2	Louisiana	285.9
3	Mississippi	282.6
4	Tennessee	272.4
5	Alabama	271.7
6	Arkansas	266.8
7	West Virginia	265.6
8	South Carolina	263.7
9	Indiana	257.7
10	Maine	256.0
11	Ohio	254.9
12	Delaware	252.8
13	Oklahoma	252.2
14	Missouri	252.1
15	North Carolina	251.8
16	Georgia	250.9
17	Pennsylvania	246.4
18	Illinois	245.6
19	Virginia	244.8
20	Rhode Island	243.3
21	Maryland	241.4
22	Michigan	240.2
23	Massachusetts	237.8
24	New Hampshire	237.6
25	New Jersey	232.4
26	Texas	232.3
27	Kansas	231.9
28	Iowa	231.3
29	Wisconsin	230.8
30	Nevada	229.4
31	Oregon	228.2
31	South Dakota	228.2
33	Alaska	226.7
34	Vermont	226.2
35	Connecticut	225.1
36	Washington	222.8
37	Montana	222.0
38	Nebraska	220.6
39	Florida	219.9
40	Minnesota	219.2
41	New York	217.1
42	North Dakota	216.3
43	Wyoming	211.2
44	Idaho	208.4
45	California	206.4
46	New Mexico	203.4
47	Arizona	201.3
48	Colorado	199.3
49	Hawaii	189.4
50	Utah	172.5

District of Columbia		275.5

Source: American Cancer Society
    "Cancer Facts & Figures 2009" (Copyright 2009, American Cancer Society, http://www.cancer.org/docroot/stt/stt_0.asp)
*For 2001 to 2005. Age-adjusted to the 2000 U.S. standard population.

Age-Adjusted Death Rate by Cancer for Females in 2005

National Rate = 159.9 Deaths per 100,000 Female Population*

ALPHA ORDER

RANK	STATE	RATE
23	Alabama	163.6
37	Alaska	155.9
47	Arizona	142.0
16	Arkansas	166.2
42	California	150.5
46	Colorado	145.4
29	Connecticut	158.6
8	Delaware	171.0
43	Florida	149.9
30	Georgia	158.3
49	Hawaii	123.0
45	Idaho	147.6
14	Illinois	167.3
7	Indiana	171.1
36	Iowa	156.1
33	Kansas	157.3
1	Kentucky	180.5
3	Louisiana	178.0
4	Maine	173.8
13	Maryland	167.6
16	Massachusetts	166.2
19	Michigan	165.7
38	Minnesota	153.0
18	Mississippi	165.8
11	Missouri	168.6
26	Montana	162.0
40	Nebraska	152.4
5	Nevada	171.6
22	New Hampshire	164.2
10	New Jersey	169.2
48	New Mexico	140.9
34	New York	156.8
27	North Carolina	160.1
44	North Dakota	149.6
6	Ohio	171.2
20	Oklahoma	164.5
15	Oregon	166.9
12	Pennsylvania	168.0
21	Rhode Island	164.4
28	South Carolina	159.0
41	South Dakota	150.8
9	Tennessee	170.9
39	Texas	152.6
50	Utah	117.9
35	Vermont	156.2
25	Virginia	162.5
24	Washington	162.7
2	West Virginia	178.2
31	Wisconsin	157.6
32	Wyoming	157.4

RANK ORDER

RANK	STATE	RATE
1	Kentucky	180.5
2	West Virginia	178.2
3	Louisiana	178.0
4	Maine	173.8
5	Nevada	171.6
6	Ohio	171.2
7	Indiana	171.1
8	Delaware	171.0
9	Tennessee	170.9
10	New Jersey	169.2
11	Missouri	168.6
12	Pennsylvania	168.0
13	Maryland	167.6
14	Illinois	167.3
15	Oregon	166.9
16	Arkansas	166.2
16	Massachusetts	166.2
18	Mississippi	165.8
19	Michigan	165.7
20	Oklahoma	164.5
21	Rhode Island	164.4
22	New Hampshire	164.2
23	Alabama	163.6
24	Washington	162.7
25	Virginia	162.5
26	Montana	162.0
27	North Carolina	160.1
28	South Carolina	159.0
29	Connecticut	158.6
30	Georgia	158.3
31	Wisconsin	157.6
32	Wyoming	157.4
33	Kansas	157.3
34	New York	156.8
35	Vermont	156.2
36	Iowa	156.1
37	Alaska	155.9
38	Minnesota	153.0
39	Texas	152.6
40	Nebraska	152.4
41	South Dakota	150.8
42	California	150.5
43	Florida	149.9
44	North Dakota	149.6
45	Idaho	147.6
46	Colorado	145.4
47	Arizona	142.0
48	New Mexico	140.9
49	Hawaii	123.0
50	Utah	117.9

| | District of Columbia | 169.4 |

Source: American Cancer Society
   "Cancer Facts & Figures 2009" (Copyright 2009, American Cancer Society, http://www.cancer.org/docroot/stt/stt_0.asp)
*For 2001 to 2005. Age-adjusted to the 2000 U.S. standard population.

Estimated Deaths by Brain Cancer in 2009

National Estimated Total = 12,920 Deaths

ALPHA ORDER

RANK	STATE	DEATHS	% of USA
23	Alabama	200	1.5%
NA	Alaska*	NA	NA
16	Arizona	280	2.2%
33	Arkansas	130	1.0%
1	California	1,460	11.3%
23	Colorado	200	1.5%
30	Connecticut	150	1.2%
42	Delaware	50	0.4%
3	Florida	810	6.3%
12	Georgia	320	2.5%
NA	Hawaii*	NA	NA
36	Idaho	90	0.7%
8	Illinois	470	3.6%
14	Indiana	290	2.2%
28	Iowa	160	1.2%
30	Kansas	150	1.2%
30	Kentucky	150	1.2%
21	Louisiana	210	1.6%
38	Maine	80	0.6%
23	Maryland	200	1.5%
17	Massachusetts	270	2.1%
7	Michigan	490	3.8%
20	Minnesota	230	1.8%
28	Mississippi	160	1.2%
17	Missouri	270	2.1%
42	Montana	50	0.4%
38	Nebraska	80	0.6%
34	Nevada	120	0.9%
41	New Hampshire	70	0.5%
12	New Jersey	320	2.5%
38	New Mexico	80	0.6%
4	New York	790	6.1%
11	North Carolina	330	2.6%
NA	North Dakota*	NA	NA
5	Ohio	550	4.3%
27	Oklahoma	170	1.3%
21	Oregon	210	1.6%
5	Pennsylvania	550	4.3%
42	Rhode Island	50	0.4%
26	South Carolina	190	1.5%
NA	South Dakota*	NA	NA
10	Tennessee	350	2.7%
2	Texas	850	6.6%
35	Utah	100	0.8%
NA	Vermont*	NA	NA
14	Virginia	290	2.2%
9	Washington	380	2.9%
36	West Virginia	90	0.7%
19	Wisconsin	260	2.0%
NA	Wyoming*	NA	NA

RANK ORDER

RANK	STATE	DEATHS	% of USA
1	California	1,460	11.3%
2	Texas	850	6.6%
3	Florida	810	6.3%
4	New York	790	6.1%
5	Ohio	550	4.3%
5	Pennsylvania	550	4.3%
7	Michigan	490	3.8%
8	Illinois	470	3.6%
9	Washington	380	2.9%
10	Tennessee	350	2.7%
11	North Carolina	330	2.6%
12	Georgia	320	2.5%
12	New Jersey	320	2.5%
14	Indiana	290	2.2%
14	Virginia	290	2.2%
16	Arizona	280	2.2%
17	Massachusetts	270	2.1%
17	Missouri	270	2.1%
19	Wisconsin	260	2.0%
20	Minnesota	230	1.8%
21	Louisiana	210	1.6%
21	Oregon	210	1.6%
23	Alabama	200	1.5%
23	Colorado	200	1.5%
23	Maryland	200	1.5%
26	South Carolina	190	1.5%
27	Oklahoma	170	1.3%
28	Iowa	160	1.2%
28	Mississippi	160	1.2%
30	Connecticut	150	1.2%
30	Kansas	150	1.2%
30	Kentucky	150	1.2%
33	Arkansas	130	1.0%
34	Nevada	120	0.9%
35	Utah	100	0.8%
36	Idaho	90	0.7%
36	West Virginia	90	0.7%
38	Maine	80	0.6%
38	Nebraska	80	0.6%
38	New Mexico	80	0.6%
41	New Hampshire	70	0.5%
42	Delaware	50	0.4%
42	Montana	50	0.4%
42	Rhode Island	50	0.4%
NA	Alaska*	NA	NA
NA	Hawaii*	NA	NA
NA	North Dakota*	NA	NA
NA	South Dakota*	NA	NA
NA	Vermont*	NA	NA
NA	Wyoming*	NA	NA
	District of Columbia*	NA	NA

Source: American Cancer Society
"Cancer Facts & Figures 2009" (Copyright 2009, American Cancer Society, http://www.cancer.org/docroot/stt/stt_0.asp)
*Fewer than 50 deaths.

Estimated Death Rate by Brain Cancer in 2009

National Estimated Rate = 4.2 Deaths per 100,000 Population*

ALPHA ORDER			RANK ORDER		
RANK	STATE	RATE	RANK	STATE	RATE
28	Alabama	4.2	1	Maine	6.1
NA	Alaska**	NA	2	Idaho	5.8
28	Arizona	4.2	3	Washington	5.7
19	Arkansas	4.5	4	Delaware	5.6
32	California	4.0	4	Tennessee	5.6
32	Colorado	4.0	6	Oregon	5.5
27	Connecticut	4.3	7	Mississippi	5.4
4	Delaware	5.6	8	Iowa	5.3
24	Florida	4.4	8	Kansas	5.3
44	Georgia	3.3	8	New Hampshire	5.3
NA	Hawaii**	NA	11	Montana	5.1
2	Idaho	5.8	12	Michigan	4.9
38	Illinois	3.6	12	West Virginia	4.9
19	Indiana	4.5	14	Ohio	4.8
8	Iowa	5.3	15	Louisiana	4.7
8	Kansas	5.3	15	Rhode Island	4.7
40	Kentucky	3.5	17	Oklahoma	4.6
15	Louisiana	4.7	17	Wisconsin	4.6
1	Maine	6.1	19	Arkansas	4.5
40	Maryland	3.5	19	Indiana	4.5
31	Massachusetts	4.1	19	Missouri	4.5
12	Michigan	4.9	19	Nebraska	4.5
24	Minnesota	4.4	19	Nevada	4.5
7	Mississippi	5.4	24	Florida	4.4
19	Missouri	4.5	24	Minnesota	4.4
11	Montana	5.1	24	Pennsylvania	4.4
19	Nebraska	4.5	27	Connecticut	4.3
19	Nevada	4.5	28	Alabama	4.2
8	New Hampshire	5.3	28	Arizona	4.2
36	New Jersey	3.7	28	South Carolina	4.2
32	New Mexico	4.0	31	Massachusetts	4.1
32	New York	4.0	32	California	4.0
40	North Carolina	3.5	32	Colorado	4.0
NA	North Dakota**	NA	32	New Mexico	4.0
14	Ohio	4.8	32	New York	4.0
17	Oklahoma	4.6	36	New Jersey	3.7
6	Oregon	5.5	36	Virginia	3.7
24	Pennsylvania	4.4	38	Illinois	3.6
15	Rhode Island	4.7	38	Utah	3.6
28	South Carolina	4.2	40	Kentucky	3.5
NA	South Dakota**	NA	40	Maryland	3.5
4	Tennessee	5.6	40	North Carolina	3.5
43	Texas	3.4	43	Texas	3.4
38	Utah	3.6	44	Georgia	3.3
NA	Vermont**	NA	NA	Alaska**	NA
36	Virginia	3.7	NA	Hawaii**	NA
3	Washington	5.7	NA	North Dakota**	NA
12	West Virginia	4.9	NA	South Dakota**	NA
17	Wisconsin	4.6	NA	Vermont**	NA
NA	Wyoming**	NA	NA	Wyoming**	NA
				District of Columbia**	NA

Source: CQ Press using data from American Cancer Society
     "Cancer Facts & Figures 2009" (Copyright 2009, American Cancer Society, http://www.cancer.org/docroot/stt/stt_0.asp)
*Rates calculated using 2009 Census resident population estimates. Not age-adjusted.
**Fewer than 50 deaths.

Estimated Deaths by Female Breast Cancer in 2009

National Estimated Total = 40,170 Deaths

ALPHA ORDER				RANK ORDER			
RANK	STATE	DEATHS	% of USA	RANK	STATE	DEATHS	% of USA
21	Alabama	700	1.7%	1	California	4,030	10.0%
49	Alaska	60	0.1%	2	Florida	2,730	6.8%
20	Arizona	740	1.8%	3	Texas	2,570	6.4%
31	Arkansas	410	1.0%	4	New York	2,550	6.3%
1	California	4,030	10.0%	5	Pennsylvania	2,070	5.2%
26	Colorado	520	1.3%	6	Ohio	1,790	4.5%
29	Connecticut	480	1.2%	7	Illinois	1,770	4.4%
45	Delaware	110	0.3%	8	New Jersey	1,470	3.7%
2	Florida	2,730	6.8%	9	Michigan	1,350	3.4%
12	Georgia	1,130	2.8%	10	North Carolina	1,310	3.3%
42	Hawaii	140	0.3%	11	Virginia	1,140	2.8%
41	Idaho	160	0.4%	12	Georgia	1,130	2.8%
7	Illinois	1,770	4.4%	13	Tennessee	910	2.3%
16	Indiana	860	2.1%	14	Missouri	890	2.2%
32	Iowa	400	1.0%	15	Massachusetts	870	2.2%
33	Kansas	370	0.9%	16	Indiana	860	2.1%
25	Kentucky	590	1.5%	17	Maryland	810	2.0%
22	Louisiana	690	1.7%	18	Washington	790	2.0%
39	Maine	180	0.4%	19	Wisconsin	750	1.9%
17	Maryland	810	2.0%	20	Arizona	740	1.8%
15	Massachusetts	870	2.2%	21	Alabama	700	1.7%
9	Michigan	1,350	3.4%	22	Louisiana	690	1.7%
24	Minnesota	600	1.5%	23	South Carolina	640	1.6%
30	Mississippi	430	1.1%	24	Minnesota	600	1.5%
14	Missouri	890	2.2%	25	Kentucky	590	1.5%
44	Montana	120	0.3%	26	Colorado	520	1.3%
38	Nebraska	210	0.5%	26	Oklahoma	520	1.3%
34	Nevada	330	0.8%	28	Oregon	500	1.2%
40	New Hampshire	170	0.4%	29	Connecticut	480	1.2%
8	New Jersey	1,470	3.7%	30	Mississippi	430	1.1%
37	New Mexico	240	0.6%	31	Arkansas	410	1.0%
4	New York	2,550	6.3%	32	Iowa	400	1.0%
10	North Carolina	1,310	3.3%	33	Kansas	370	0.9%
47	North Dakota	80	0.2%	34	Nevada	330	0.8%
6	Ohio	1,790	4.5%	35	West Virginia	280	0.7%
26	Oklahoma	520	1.3%	36	Utah	260	0.6%
28	Oregon	500	1.2%	37	New Mexico	240	0.6%
5	Pennsylvania	2,070	5.2%	38	Nebraska	210	0.5%
43	Rhode Island	130	0.3%	39	Maine	180	0.4%
23	South Carolina	640	1.6%	40	New Hampshire	170	0.4%
46	South Dakota	100	0.2%	41	Idaho	160	0.4%
13	Tennessee	910	2.3%	42	Hawaii	140	0.3%
3	Texas	2,570	6.4%	43	Rhode Island	130	0.3%
36	Utah	260	0.6%	44	Montana	120	0.3%
47	Vermont	80	0.2%	45	Delaware	110	0.3%
11	Virginia	1,140	2.8%	46	South Dakota	100	0.2%
18	Washington	790	2.0%	47	North Dakota	80	0.2%
35	West Virginia	280	0.7%	47	Vermont	80	0.2%
19	Wisconsin	750	1.9%	49	Alaska	60	0.1%
49	Wyoming	60	0.1%	49	Wyoming	60	0.1%
					District of Columbia	70	0.2%

Source: American Cancer Society
"Cancer Facts & Figures 2009" (Copyright 2009, American Cancer Society, http://www.cancer.org/docroot/stt/stt_0.asp)

Age-Adjusted Death Rate by Female Breast Cancer in 2005

National Rate = 25.0 Deaths per 100,000 Female Population*

ALPHA ORDER				RANK ORDER		
RANK	STATE	RATE		RANK	STATE	RATE
11	Alabama	26.0		1	Louisiana	29.7
49	Alaska	20.5		2	New Jersey	27.8
46	Arizona	22.2		3	Ohio	27.6
26	Arkansas	24.4		4	Maryland	27.4
35	California	23.7		5	Pennsylvania	27.0
44	Colorado	22.6		6	Mississippi	26.9
19	Connecticut	25.1		7	Missouri	26.6
19	Delaware	25.1		8	Virginia	26.5
41	Florida	23.0		9	Illinois	26.2
24	Georgia	24.7		9	Tennessee	26.2
50	Hawaii	18.0		11	Alabama	26.0
47	Idaho	22.1		12	Kentucky	25.6
9	Illinois	26.2		12	New York	25.6
22	Indiana	25.0		14	North Carolina	25.4
39	Iowa	23.1		14	Oklahoma	25.4
27	Kansas	24.3		16	Michigan	25.3
12	Kentucky	25.6		16	Nevada	25.3
1	Louisiana	29.7		16	South Carolina	25.3
37	Maine	23.5		19	Connecticut	25.1
4	Maryland	27.4		19	Delaware	25.1
23	Massachusetts	24.8		19	West Virginia	25.1
16	Michigan	25.3		22	Indiana	25.0
41	Minnesota	23.0		23	Massachusetts	24.8
6	Mississippi	26.9		24	Georgia	24.7
7	Missouri	26.6		25	Oregon	24.5
33	Montana	23.8		26	Arkansas	24.4
30	Nebraska	24.0		27	Kansas	24.3
16	Nevada	25.3		27	New Hampshire	24.3
27	New Hampshire	24.3		29	Vermont	24.2
2	New Jersey	27.8		30	Nebraska	24.0
47	New Mexico	22.1		30	North Dakota	24.0
12	New York	25.6		30	Wisconsin	24.0
14	North Carolina	25.4		33	Montana	23.8
30	North Dakota	24.0		33	Texas	23.8
3	Ohio	27.6		35	California	23.7
14	Oklahoma	25.4		36	Washington	23.6
25	Oregon	24.5		37	Maine	23.5
5	Pennsylvania	27.0		37	Rhode Island	23.5
37	Rhode Island	23.5		39	Iowa	23.1
16	South Carolina	25.3		39	Utah	23.1
43	South Dakota	22.9		41	Florida	23.0
9	Tennessee	26.2		41	Minnesota	23.0
33	Texas	23.8		43	South Dakota	22.9
39	Utah	23.1		44	Colorado	22.6
29	Vermont	24.2		44	Wyoming	22.6
8	Virginia	26.5		46	Arizona	22.2
36	Washington	23.6		47	Idaho	22.1
19	West Virginia	25.1		47	New Mexico	22.1
30	Wisconsin	24.0		49	Alaska	20.5
44	Wyoming	22.6		50	Hawaii	18.0
				District of Columbia		31.0

Source: American Cancer Society
"Cancer Facts & Figures 2009" (Copyright 2009, American Cancer Society, http://www.cancer.org/docroot/stt/stt_0.asp)
*For 2001 to 2005. Age-adjusted to the 2000 U.S. standard population.

Estimated Deaths by Colon and Rectum Cancer in 2008

National Estimated Total = 49,920 Deaths

ALPHA ORDER

RANK	STATE	CASES	% of USA
18	Alabama	940	1.9%
50	Alaska	70	0.1%
17	Arizona	970	1.9%
31	Arkansas	580	1.2%
1	California	4,830	9.7%
26	Colorado	670	1.3%
32	Connecticut	550	1.1%
45	Delaware	150	0.3%
2	Florida	3,460	6.9%
11	Georgia	1,370	2.7%
41	Hawaii	210	0.4%
42	Idaho	200	0.4%
6	Illinois	2,260	4.5%
14	Indiana	1,130	2.3%
28	Iowa	600	1.2%
33	Kansas	510	1.0%
23	Kentucky	840	1.7%
21	Louisiana	910	1.8%
38	Maine	260	0.5%
18	Maryland	940	1.9%
16	Massachusetts	1,070	2.1%
8	Michigan	1,720	3.4%
25	Minnesota	760	1.5%
28	Mississippi	600	1.2%
15	Missouri	1,100	2.2%
43	Montana	170	0.3%
36	Nebraska	350	0.7%
34	Nevada	500	1.0%
40	New Hampshire	220	0.4%
9	New Jersey	1,580	3.2%
37	New Mexico	320	0.6%
4	New York	3,110	6.2%
10	North Carolina	1,410	2.8%
47	North Dakota	120	0.2%
7	Ohio	2,210	4.4%
28	Oklahoma	600	1.2%
27	Oregon	610	1.2%
5	Pennsylvania	2,550	5.1%
44	Rhode Island	160	0.3%
24	South Carolina	780	1.6%
45	South Dakota	150	0.3%
13	Tennessee	1,140	2.3%
3	Texas	3,140	6.3%
39	Utah	240	0.5%
47	Vermont	120	0.2%
12	Virginia	1,270	2.5%
18	Washington	940	1.9%
35	West Virginia	430	0.9%
22	Wisconsin	900	1.8%
49	Wyoming	100	0.2%

RANK ORDER

RANK	STATE	CASES	% of USA
1	California	4,830	9.7%
2	Florida	3,460	6.9%
3	Texas	3,140	6.3%
4	New York	3,110	6.2%
5	Pennsylvania	2,550	5.1%
6	Illinois	2,260	4.5%
7	Ohio	2,210	4.4%
8	Michigan	1,720	3.4%
9	New Jersey	1,580	3.2%
10	North Carolina	1,410	2.8%
11	Georgia	1,370	2.7%
12	Virginia	1,270	2.5%
13	Tennessee	1,140	2.3%
14	Indiana	1,130	2.3%
15	Missouri	1,100	2.2%
16	Massachusetts	1,070	2.1%
17	Arizona	970	1.9%
18	Alabama	940	1.9%
18	Maryland	940	1.9%
18	Washington	940	1.9%
21	Louisiana	910	1.8%
22	Wisconsin	900	1.8%
23	Kentucky	840	1.7%
24	South Carolina	780	1.6%
25	Minnesota	760	1.5%
26	Colorado	670	1.3%
27	Oregon	610	1.2%
28	Iowa	600	1.2%
28	Mississippi	600	1.2%
28	Oklahoma	600	1.2%
31	Arkansas	580	1.2%
32	Connecticut	550	1.1%
33	Kansas	510	1.0%
34	Nevada	500	1.0%
35	West Virginia	430	0.9%
36	Nebraska	350	0.7%
37	New Mexico	320	0.6%
38	Maine	260	0.5%
39	Utah	240	0.5%
40	New Hampshire	220	0.4%
41	Hawaii	210	0.4%
42	Idaho	200	0.4%
43	Montana	170	0.3%
44	Rhode Island	160	0.3%
45	Delaware	150	0.3%
45	South Dakota	150	0.3%
47	North Dakota	120	0.2%
47	Vermont	120	0.2%
49	Wyoming	100	0.2%
50	Alaska	70	0.1%
	District of Columbia	100	0.2%

Source: American Cancer Society
"Cancer Facts & Figures 2009" (Copyright 2009, American Cancer Society, http://www.cancer.org/docroot/stt/stt_0.asp)

Estimated Death Rate by Colon and Rectum Cancer in 2009

National Estimated Rate = 16.3 Deaths per 100,000 Population*

ALPHA ORDER			RANK ORDER		
RANK	STATE	RATE	RANK	STATE	RATE
6	Alabama	20.0	1	West Virginia	23.6
49	Alaska	10.0	2	Louisiana	20.3
41	Arizona	14.7	2	Mississippi	20.3
5	Arkansas	20.1	4	Pennsylvania	20.2
46	California	13.1	5	Arkansas	20.1
45	Colorado	13.3	6	Alabama	20.0
38	Connecticut	15.6	7	Iowa	19.9
27	Delaware	16.9	8	Maine	19.7
14	Florida	18.7	9	Kentucky	19.5
44	Georgia	13.9	9	Nebraska	19.5
31	Hawaii	16.2	11	Vermont	19.3
47	Idaho	12.9	12	Ohio	19.1
23	Illinois	17.5	13	Nevada	18.9
22	Indiana	17.6	14	Florida	18.7
7	Iowa	19.9	15	North Dakota	18.6
19	Kansas	18.1	16	South Dakota	18.5
9	Kentucky	19.5	17	Missouri	18.4
2	Louisiana	20.3	17	Wyoming	18.4
8	Maine	19.7	19	Kansas	18.1
29	Maryland	16.5	19	New Jersey	18.1
31	Massachusetts	16.2	19	Tennessee	18.1
25	Michigan	17.3	22	Indiana	17.6
42	Minnesota	14.4	23	Illinois	17.5
2	Mississippi	20.3	24	Montana	17.4
17	Missouri	18.4	25	Michigan	17.3
24	Montana	17.4	26	South Carolina	17.1
9	Nebraska	19.5	27	Delaware	16.9
13	Nevada	18.9	28	New Hampshire	16.6
28	New Hampshire	16.6	29	Maryland	16.5
19	New Jersey	18.1	30	Oklahoma	16.3
34	New Mexico	15.9	31	Hawaii	16.2
34	New York	15.9	31	Massachusetts	16.2
40	North Carolina	15.0	33	Virginia	16.1
15	North Dakota	18.6	34	New Mexico	15.9
12	Ohio	19.1	34	New York	15.9
30	Oklahoma	16.3	34	Oregon	15.9
34	Oregon	15.9	34	Wisconsin	15.9
4	Pennsylvania	20.2	38	Connecticut	15.6
39	Rhode Island	15.2	39	Rhode Island	15.2
26	South Carolina	17.1	40	North Carolina	15.0
16	South Dakota	18.5	41	Arizona	14.7
19	Tennessee	18.1	42	Minnesota	14.4
48	Texas	12.7	43	Washington	14.1
50	Utah	8.6	44	Georgia	13.9
11	Vermont	19.3	45	Colorado	13.3
33	Virginia	16.1	46	California	13.1
43	Washington	14.1	47	Idaho	12.9
1	West Virginia	23.6	48	Texas	12.7
34	Wisconsin	15.9	49	Alaska	10.0
17	Wyoming	18.4	50	Utah	8.6
				District of Columbia	16.7

Source: CQ Press using data from American Cancer Society
"Cancer Facts & Figures 2009" (Copyright 2009, American Cancer Society, http://www.cancer.org/docroot/stt/stt_0.asp)
*Rates calculated using 2009 Census resident population estimates. Not age-adjusted.

Estimated Deaths by Leukemia in 2009

National Estimated Total = 21,870 Deaths

ALPHA ORDER

RANK	STATE	DEATHS	% of USA
22	Alabama	340	1.6%
NA	Alaska*	NA	NA
19	Arizona	410	1.9%
31	Arkansas	250	1.1%
1	California	2,200	10.1%
26	Colorado	300	1.4%
30	Connecticut	270	1.2%
45	Delaware	70	0.3%
2	Florida	1,650	7.5%
11	Georgia	550	2.5%
44	Hawaii	80	0.4%
38	Idaho	120	0.5%
6	Illinois	950	4.3%
13	Indiana	520	2.4%
26	Iowa	300	1.4%
33	Kansas	200	0.9%
24	Kentucky	320	1.5%
25	Louisiana	310	1.4%
40	Maine	110	0.5%
20	Maryland	390	1.8%
16	Massachusetts	490	2.2%
8	Michigan	820	3.7%
21	Minnesota	370	1.7%
32	Mississippi	220	1.0%
12	Missouri	530	2.4%
42	Montana	90	0.4%
34	Nebraska	150	0.7%
35	Nevada	140	0.6%
41	New Hampshire	100	0.5%
10	New Jersey	610	2.8%
38	New Mexico	120	0.5%
4	New York	1,380	6.3%
9	North Carolina	640	2.9%
48	North Dakota	50	0.2%
7	Ohio	890	4.1%
28	Oklahoma	290	1.3%
28	Oregon	290	1.3%
5	Pennsylvania	1,080	4.9%
42	Rhode Island	90	0.4%
23	South Carolina	330	1.5%
46	South Dakota	60	0.3%
17	Tennessee	480	2.2%
3	Texas	1,430	6.5%
37	Utah	130	0.6%
46	Vermont	60	0.3%
14	Virginia	500	2.3%
18	Washington	450	2.1%
35	West Virginia	140	0.6%
14	Wisconsin	500	2.3%
NA	Wyoming*	NA	NA

RANK ORDER

RANK	STATE	DEATHS	% of USA
1	California	2,200	10.1%
2	Florida	1,650	7.5%
3	Texas	1,430	6.5%
4	New York	1,380	6.3%
5	Pennsylvania	1,080	4.9%
6	Illinois	950	4.3%
7	Ohio	890	4.1%
8	Michigan	820	3.7%
9	North Carolina	640	2.9%
10	New Jersey	610	2.8%
11	Georgia	550	2.5%
12	Missouri	530	2.4%
13	Indiana	520	2.4%
14	Virginia	500	2.3%
14	Wisconsin	500	2.3%
16	Massachusetts	490	2.2%
17	Tennessee	480	2.2%
18	Washington	450	2.1%
19	Arizona	410	1.9%
20	Maryland	390	1.8%
21	Minnesota	370	1.7%
22	Alabama	340	1.6%
23	South Carolina	330	1.5%
24	Kentucky	320	1.5%
25	Louisiana	310	1.4%
26	Colorado	300	1.4%
26	Iowa	300	1.4%
28	Oklahoma	290	1.3%
28	Oregon	290	1.3%
30	Connecticut	270	1.2%
31	Arkansas	250	1.1%
32	Mississippi	220	1.0%
33	Kansas	200	0.9%
34	Nebraska	150	0.7%
35	Nevada	140	0.6%
35	West Virginia	140	0.6%
37	Utah	130	0.6%
38	Idaho	120	0.5%
38	New Mexico	120	0.5%
40	Maine	110	0.5%
41	New Hampshire	100	0.5%
42	Montana	90	0.4%
42	Rhode Island	90	0.4%
44	Hawaii	80	0.4%
45	Delaware	70	0.3%
46	South Dakota	60	0.3%
46	Vermont	60	0.3%
48	North Dakota	50	0.2%
NA	Alaska*	NA	NA
NA	Wyoming*	NA	NA
	District of Columbia	50	0.2%

Source: American Cancer Society
"Cancer Facts & Figures 2009" (Copyright 2009, American Cancer Society, http://www.cancer.org/docroot/stt/stt_0.asp)
*Fewer than 50 deaths.

Estimated Death Rate by Leukemia in 2009

National Estimated Rate = 7.1 Deaths per 100,000 Population*

ALPHA ORDER				RANK ORDER		
RANK	STATE	RATE		RANK	STATE	RATE
29	Alabama	7.2		1	Iowa	10.0
NA	Alaska**	NA		2	Vermont	9.7
40	Arizona	6.2		3	Montana	9.2
7	Arkansas	8.7		4	Florida	8.9
42	California	6.0		4	Missouri	8.9
42	Colorado	6.0		6	Wisconsin	8.8
17	Connecticut	7.7		7	Arkansas	8.7
14	Delaware	7.9		8	Pennsylvania	8.6
4	Florida	8.9		9	Rhode Island	8.5
46	Georgia	5.6		10	Maine	8.3
40	Hawaii	6.2		10	Nebraska	8.3
16	Idaho	7.8		12	Michigan	8.2
25	Illinois	7.4		13	Indiana	8.1
13	Indiana	8.1		14	Delaware	7.9
1	Iowa	10.0		14	Oklahoma	7.9
31	Kansas	7.1		16	Idaho	7.8
25	Kentucky	7.4		17	Connecticut	7.7
35	Louisiana	6.9		17	North Dakota	7.7
10	Maine	8.3		17	Ohio	7.7
36	Maryland	6.8		17	West Virginia	7.7
25	Massachusetts	7.4		21	Oregon	7.6
12	Michigan	8.2		21	Tennessee	7.6
33	Minnesota	7.0		23	Mississippi	7.5
23	Mississippi	7.5		23	New Hampshire	7.5
4	Missouri	8.9		25	Illinois	7.4
3	Montana	9.2		25	Kentucky	7.4
10	Nebraska	8.3		25	Massachusetts	7.4
47	Nevada	5.3		25	South Dakota	7.4
23	New Hampshire	7.5		29	Alabama	7.2
33	New Jersey	7.0		29	South Carolina	7.2
42	New Mexico	6.0		31	Kansas	7.1
31	New York	7.1		31	New York	7.1
36	North Carolina	6.8		33	Minnesota	7.0
17	North Dakota	7.7		33	New Jersey	7.0
17	Ohio	7.7		35	Louisiana	6.9
14	Oklahoma	7.9		36	Maryland	6.8
21	Oregon	7.6		36	North Carolina	6.8
8	Pennsylvania	8.6		36	Washington	6.8
9	Rhode Island	8.5		39	Virginia	6.3
29	South Carolina	7.2		40	Arizona	6.2
25	South Dakota	7.4		40	Hawaii	6.2
21	Tennessee	7.6		42	California	6.0
45	Texas	5.8		42	Colorado	6.0
48	Utah	4.7		42	New Mexico	6.0
2	Vermont	9.7		45	Texas	5.8
39	Virginia	6.3		46	Georgia	5.6
36	Washington	6.8		47	Nevada	5.3
17	West Virginia	7.7		48	Utah	4.7
6	Wisconsin	8.8		NA	Alaska**	NA
NA	Wyoming**	NA		NA	Wyoming**	NA
				District of Columbia		8.3

Source: CQ Press using data from American Cancer Society
   "Cancer Facts & Figures 2009" (Copyright 2009, American Cancer Society, http://www.cancer.org/docroot/stt/stt_0.asp)
*Rates calculated using 2009 Census resident population estimates. Not age-adjusted.
**Fewer than 50 deaths.

Estimated Deaths by Liver Cancer in 2009

National Estimated Total = 18,160 Deaths

ALPHA ORDER

RANK	STATE	DEATHS	% of USA
22	Alabama	280	1.5%
NA	Alaska*	NA	NA
15	Arizona	360	2.0%
30	Arkansas	190	1.0%
1	California	2,450	13.5%
26	Colorado	210	1.2%
26	Connecticut	210	1.2%
44	Delaware	50	0.3%
3	Florida	1,300	7.2%
13	Georgia	400	2.2%
36	Hawaii	120	0.7%
38	Idaho	80	0.4%
6	Illinois	700	3.9%
17	Indiana	350	1.9%
33	Iowa	150	0.8%
35	Kansas	140	0.8%
25	Kentucky	240	1.3%
19	Louisiana	330	1.8%
38	Maine	80	0.4%
20	Maryland	320	1.8%
11	Massachusetts	420	2.3%
8	Michigan	610	3.4%
23	Minnesota	260	1.4%
30	Mississippi	190	1.0%
15	Missouri	360	2.0%
44	Montana	50	0.3%
38	Nebraska	80	0.4%
32	Nevada	160	0.9%
41	New Hampshire	70	0.4%
9	New Jersey	540	3.0%
33	New Mexico	150	0.8%
4	New York	1,210	6.7%
10	North Carolina	470	2.6%
NA	North Dakota*	NA	NA
7	Ohio	640	3.5%
29	Oklahoma	200	1.1%
26	Oregon	210	1.2%
5	Pennsylvania	790	4.4%
41	Rhode Island	70	0.4%
24	South Carolina	250	1.4%
NA	South Dakota*	NA	NA
17	Tennessee	350	1.9%
2	Texas	1,650	9.1%
41	Utah	70	0.4%
NA	Vermont*	NA	NA
14	Virginia	390	2.1%
12	Washington	410	2.3%
37	West Virginia	110	0.6%
20	Wisconsin	320	1.8%
NA	Wyoming*	NA	NA

RANK ORDER

RANK	STATE	DEATHS	% of USA
1	California	2,450	13.5%
2	Texas	1,650	9.1%
3	Florida	1,300	7.2%
4	New York	1,210	6.7%
5	Pennsylvania	790	4.4%
6	Illinois	700	3.9%
7	Ohio	640	3.5%
8	Michigan	610	3.4%
9	New Jersey	540	3.0%
10	North Carolina	470	2.6%
11	Massachusetts	420	2.3%
12	Washington	410	2.3%
13	Georgia	400	2.2%
14	Virginia	390	2.1%
15	Arizona	360	2.0%
15	Missouri	360	2.0%
17	Indiana	350	1.9%
17	Tennessee	350	1.9%
19	Louisiana	330	1.8%
20	Maryland	320	1.8%
20	Wisconsin	320	1.8%
22	Alabama	280	1.5%
23	Minnesota	260	1.4%
24	South Carolina	250	1.4%
25	Kentucky	240	1.3%
26	Colorado	210	1.2%
26	Connecticut	210	1.2%
26	Oregon	210	1.2%
29	Oklahoma	200	1.1%
30	Arkansas	190	1.0%
30	Mississippi	190	1.0%
32	Nevada	160	0.9%
33	Iowa	150	0.8%
33	New Mexico	150	0.8%
35	Kansas	140	0.8%
36	Hawaii	120	0.7%
37	West Virginia	110	0.6%
38	Idaho	80	0.4%
38	Maine	80	0.4%
38	Nebraska	80	0.4%
41	New Hampshire	70	0.4%
41	Rhode Island	70	0.4%
41	Utah	70	0.4%
44	Delaware	50	0.3%
44	Montana	50	0.3%
NA	Alaska*	NA	NA
NA	North Dakota*	NA	NA
NA	South Dakota*	NA	NA
NA	Vermont*	NA	NA
NA	Wyoming*	NA	NA
	District of Columbia*	NA	NA

Source: American Cancer Society
  "Cancer Facts & Figures 2009" (Copyright 2009, American Cancer Society, http://www.cancer.org/docroot/stt/stt_0.asp)
*Fewer than 50 deaths.

Estimated Death Rate by Liver Cancer in 2009

National Estimated Rate = 5.9 Deaths per 100,000 Population*

ALPHA ORDER				RANK ORDER		
RANK	STATE	RATE		RANK	STATE	RATE
21	Alabama	5.9		1	Hawaii	9.3
NA	Alaska**	NA		2	New Mexico	7.5
27	Arizona	5.5		3	Louisiana	7.3
6	Arkansas	6.6		4	Florida	7.0
6	California	6.6		5	Texas	6.7
43	Colorado	4.2		6	Arkansas	6.6
18	Connecticut	6.0		6	California	6.6
23	Delaware	5.6		6	Rhode Island	6.6
4	Florida	7.0		9	Massachusetts	6.4
44	Georgia	4.1		9	Mississippi	6.4
1	Hawaii	9.3		11	Pennsylvania	6.3
35	Idaho	5.2		12	New Jersey	6.2
31	Illinois	5.4		12	New York	6.2
31	Indiana	5.4		12	Washington	6.2
37	Iowa	5.0		15	Maine	6.1
37	Kansas	5.0		15	Michigan	6.1
23	Kentucky	5.6		15	Nevada	6.1
3	Louisiana	7.3		18	Connecticut	6.0
15	Maine	6.1		18	Missouri	6.0
23	Maryland	5.6		18	West Virginia	6.0
9	Massachusetts	6.4		21	Alabama	5.9
15	Michigan	6.1		22	Wisconsin	5.7
40	Minnesota	4.9		23	Delaware	5.6
9	Mississippi	6.4		23	Kentucky	5.6
18	Missouri	6.0		23	Maryland	5.6
36	Montana	5.1		23	Tennessee	5.6
42	Nebraska	4.5		27	Arizona	5.5
15	Nevada	6.1		27	Ohio	5.5
34	New Hampshire	5.3		27	Oregon	5.5
12	New Jersey	6.2		27	South Carolina	5.5
2	New Mexico	7.5		31	Illinois	5.4
12	New York	6.2		31	Indiana	5.4
37	North Carolina	5.0		31	Oklahoma	5.4
NA	North Dakota**	NA		34	New Hampshire	5.3
27	Ohio	5.5		35	Idaho	5.2
31	Oklahoma	5.4		36	Montana	5.1
27	Oregon	5.5		37	Iowa	5.0
11	Pennsylvania	6.3		37	Kansas	5.0
6	Rhode Island	6.6		37	North Carolina	5.0
27	South Carolina	5.5		40	Minnesota	4.9
NA	South Dakota**	NA		40	Virginia	4.9
23	Tennessee	5.6		42	Nebraska	4.5
5	Texas	6.7		43	Colorado	4.2
45	Utah	2.5		44	Georgia	4.1
NA	Vermont**	NA		45	Utah	2.5
40	Virginia	4.9		NA	Alaska**	NA
12	Washington	6.2		NA	North Dakota**	NA
18	West Virginia	6.0		NA	South Dakota**	NA
22	Wisconsin	5.7		NA	Vermont**	NA
NA	Wyoming**	NA		NA	Wyoming**	NA
				District of Columbia**		NA

Source: CQ Press using data from American Cancer Society
"Cancer Facts & Figures 2009" (Copyright 2009, American Cancer Society, http://www.cancer.org/docroot/stt/stt_0.asp)
*Rates calculated using 2009 Census resident population estimates. Not age-adjusted.
**Fewer than 50 deaths.

Estimated Deaths by Lung Cancer in 2009

National Estimated Total = 159,390 Deaths

ALPHA ORDER

RANK	STATE	DEATHS	% of USA
18	Alabama	3,140	2.0%
50	Alaska	220	0.1%
23	Arizona	2,820	1.8%
27	Arkansas	2,160	1.4%
1	California	12,750	8.0%
32	Colorado	1,670	1.0%
30	Connecticut	1,810	1.1%
41	Delaware	590	0.4%
2	Florida	12,210	7.7%
10	Georgia	4,660	2.9%
42	Hawaii	570	0.4%
40	Idaho	630	0.4%
7	Illinois	6,460	4.1%
15	Indiana	4,000	2.5%
31	Iowa	1,760	1.1%
33	Kansas	1,620	1.0%
17	Kentucky	3,430	2.2%
24	Louisiana	2,700	1.7%
36	Maine	980	0.6%
21	Maryland	2,880	1.8%
16	Massachusetts	3,610	2.3%
8	Michigan	5,840	3.7%
26	Minnesota	2,380	1.5%
29	Mississippi	2,030	1.3%
14	Missouri	4,100	2.6%
44	Montana	550	0.3%
37	Nebraska	890	0.6%
35	Nevada	1,340	0.8%
38	New Hampshire	750	0.5%
13	New Jersey	4,190	2.6%
39	New Mexico	710	0.4%
4	New York	8,780	5.5%
9	North Carolina	5,630	3.5%
47	North Dakota	370	0.2%
6	Ohio	7,300	4.6%
25	Oklahoma	2,390	1.5%
28	Oregon	2,140	1.3%
5	Pennsylvania	8,090	5.1%
43	Rhode Island	560	0.4%
21	South Carolina	2,880	1.8%
46	South Dakota	450	0.3%
11	Tennessee	4,520	2.8%
3	Texas	9,780	6.1%
45	Utah	480	0.3%
48	Vermont	350	0.2%
12	Virginia	4,250	2.7%
19	Washington	3,090	1.9%
34	West Virginia	1,500	0.9%
20	Wisconsin	2,910	1.8%
49	Wyoming	260	0.2%

RANK ORDER

RANK	STATE	DEATHS	% of USA
1	California	12,750	8.0%
2	Florida	12,210	7.7%
3	Texas	9,780	6.1%
4	New York	8,780	5.5%
5	Pennsylvania	8,090	5.1%
6	Ohio	7,300	4.6%
7	Illinois	6,460	4.1%
8	Michigan	5,840	3.7%
9	North Carolina	5,630	3.5%
10	Georgia	4,660	2.9%
11	Tennessee	4,520	2.8%
12	Virginia	4,250	2.7%
13	New Jersey	4,190	2.6%
14	Missouri	4,100	2.6%
15	Indiana	4,000	2.5%
16	Massachusetts	3,610	2.3%
17	Kentucky	3,430	2.2%
18	Alabama	3,140	2.0%
19	Washington	3,090	1.9%
20	Wisconsin	2,910	1.8%
21	Maryland	2,880	1.8%
21	South Carolina	2,880	1.8%
23	Arizona	2,820	1.8%
24	Louisiana	2,700	1.7%
25	Oklahoma	2,390	1.5%
26	Minnesota	2,380	1.5%
27	Arkansas	2,160	1.4%
28	Oregon	2,140	1.3%
29	Mississippi	2,030	1.3%
30	Connecticut	1,810	1.1%
31	Iowa	1,760	1.1%
32	Colorado	1,670	1.0%
33	Kansas	1,620	1.0%
34	West Virginia	1,500	0.9%
35	Nevada	1,340	0.8%
36	Maine	980	0.6%
37	Nebraska	890	0.6%
38	New Hampshire	750	0.5%
39	New Mexico	710	0.4%
40	Idaho	630	0.4%
41	Delaware	590	0.4%
42	Hawaii	570	0.4%
43	Rhode Island	560	0.4%
44	Montana	550	0.3%
45	Utah	480	0.3%
46	South Dakota	450	0.3%
47	North Dakota	370	0.2%
48	Vermont	350	0.2%
49	Wyoming	260	0.2%
50	Alaska	220	0.1%
	District of Columbia	240	0.2%

Source: American Cancer Society
"Cancer Facts & Figures 2009" (Copyright 2009, American Cancer Society, http://www.cancer.org/docroot/stt/stt_0.asp)

Estimated Death Rate by Lung Cancer in 2009

National Estimated Rate = 51.9 Deaths per 100,000 Population*

ALPHA ORDER

RANK	STATE	RATE
8	Alabama	66.7
49	Alaska	31.5
43	Arizona	42.8
3	Arkansas	74.8
47	California	34.5
48	Colorado	33.2
31	Connecticut	51.4
8	Delaware	66.7
10	Florida	65.9
38	Georgia	47.4
42	Hawaii	44.0
44	Idaho	40.8
34	Illinois	50.0
15	Indiana	62.3
19	Iowa	58.5
20	Kansas	57.5
2	Kentucky	79.5
16	Louisiana	60.1
4	Maine	74.3
33	Maryland	50.5
27	Massachusetts	54.8
18	Michigan	58.6
40	Minnesota	45.2
6	Mississippi	68.8
7	Missouri	68.5
23	Montana	56.4
35	Nebraska	49.5
32	Nevada	50.7
22	New Hampshire	56.6
36	New Jersey	48.1
46	New Mexico	35.3
41	New York	44.9
17	North Carolina	60.0
21	North Dakota	57.2
13	Ohio	63.2
11	Oklahoma	64.8
25	Oregon	55.9
12	Pennsylvania	64.2
29	Rhode Island	53.2
14	South Carolina	63.1
26	South Dakota	55.4
5	Tennessee	71.8
45	Texas	39.5
50	Utah	17.2
24	Vermont	56.3
28	Virginia	53.9
39	Washington	46.4
1	West Virginia	82.4
30	Wisconsin	51.5
37	Wyoming	47.8

RANK ORDER

RANK	STATE	RATE
1	West Virginia	82.4
2	Kentucky	79.5
3	Arkansas	74.8
4	Maine	74.3
5	Tennessee	71.8
6	Mississippi	68.8
7	Missouri	68.5
8	Alabama	66.7
8	Delaware	66.7
10	Florida	65.9
11	Oklahoma	64.8
12	Pennsylvania	64.2
13	Ohio	63.2
14	South Carolina	63.1
15	Indiana	62.3
16	Louisiana	60.1
17	North Carolina	60.0
18	Michigan	58.6
19	Iowa	58.5
20	Kansas	57.5
21	North Dakota	57.2
22	New Hampshire	56.6
23	Montana	56.4
24	Vermont	56.3
25	Oregon	55.9
26	South Dakota	55.4
27	Massachusetts	54.8
28	Virginia	53.9
29	Rhode Island	53.2
30	Wisconsin	51.5
31	Connecticut	51.4
32	Nevada	50.7
33	Maryland	50.5
34	Illinois	50.0
35	Nebraska	49.5
36	New Jersey	48.1
37	Wyoming	47.8
38	Georgia	47.4
39	Washington	46.4
40	Minnesota	45.2
41	New York	44.9
42	Hawaii	44.0
43	Arizona	42.8
44	Idaho	40.8
45	Texas	39.5
46	New Mexico	35.3
47	California	34.5
48	Colorado	33.2
49	Alaska	31.5
50	Utah	17.2

District of Columbia 40.0

Source: CQ Press using data from American Cancer Society
    "Cancer Facts & Figures 2009" (Copyright 2009, American Cancer Society, http://www.cancer.org/docroot/stt/stt_0.asp)
*Rates calculated using 2009 Census resident population estimates. Not age-adjusted.

Estimated Deaths by Non-Hodgkin's Lymphoma in 2009

National Estimated Total = 19,500 Deaths

ALPHA ORDER

RANK	STATE	DEATHS	% of USA
26	Alabama	290	1.5%
NA	Alaska*	NA	NA
19	Arizona	350	1.8%
31	Arkansas	200	1.0%
1	California	1,900	9.7%
29	Colorado	230	1.2%
30	Connecticut	220	1.1%
46	Delaware	50	0.3%
2	Florida	1,560	8.0%
11	Georgia	460	2.4%
40	Hawaii	80	0.4%
40	Idaho	80	0.4%
6	Illinois	770	3.9%
15	Indiana	420	2.2%
27	Iowa	280	1.4%
32	Kansas	180	0.9%
24	Kentucky	300	1.5%
22	Louisiana	310	1.6%
39	Maine	90	0.5%
24	Maryland	300	1.5%
13	Massachusetts	430	2.2%
8	Michigan	710	3.6%
21	Minnesota	320	1.6%
32	Mississippi	180	0.9%
13	Missouri	430	2.2%
42	Montana	70	0.4%
35	Nebraska	130	0.7%
35	Nevada	130	0.7%
45	New Hampshire	60	0.3%
9	New Jersey	610	3.1%
38	New Mexico	110	0.6%
3	New York	1,430	7.3%
10	North Carolina	530	2.7%
NA	North Dakota*	NA	NA
7	Ohio	740	3.8%
28	Oklahoma	240	1.2%
20	Oregon	330	1.7%
5	Pennsylvania	1,090	5.6%
42	Rhode Island	70	0.4%
22	South Carolina	310	1.6%
42	South Dakota	70	0.4%
12	Tennessee	440	2.3%
4	Texas	1,300	6.7%
35	Utah	130	0.7%
NA	Vermont*	NA	NA
16	Virginia	410	2.1%
16	Washington	410	2.1%
32	West Virginia	180	0.9%
18	Wisconsin	400	2.1%
NA	Wyoming*	NA	NA

RANK ORDER

RANK	STATE	DEATHS	% of USA
1	California	1,900	9.7%
2	Florida	1,560	8.0%
3	New York	1,430	7.3%
4	Texas	1,300	6.7%
5	Pennsylvania	1,090	5.6%
6	Illinois	770	3.9%
7	Ohio	740	3.8%
8	Michigan	710	3.6%
9	New Jersey	610	3.1%
10	North Carolina	530	2.7%
11	Georgia	460	2.4%
12	Tennessee	440	2.3%
13	Massachusetts	430	2.2%
13	Missouri	430	2.2%
15	Indiana	420	2.2%
16	Virginia	410	2.1%
16	Washington	410	2.1%
18	Wisconsin	400	2.1%
19	Arizona	350	1.8%
20	Oregon	330	1.7%
21	Minnesota	320	1.6%
22	Louisiana	310	1.6%
22	South Carolina	310	1.6%
24	Kentucky	300	1.5%
24	Maryland	300	1.5%
26	Alabama	290	1.5%
27	Iowa	280	1.4%
28	Oklahoma	240	1.2%
29	Colorado	230	1.2%
30	Connecticut	220	1.1%
31	Arkansas	200	1.0%
32	Kansas	180	0.9%
32	Mississippi	180	0.9%
32	West Virginia	180	0.9%
35	Nebraska	130	0.7%
35	Nevada	130	0.7%
35	Utah	130	0.7%
38	New Mexico	110	0.6%
39	Maine	90	0.5%
40	Hawaii	80	0.4%
40	Idaho	80	0.4%
42	Montana	70	0.4%
42	Rhode Island	70	0.4%
42	South Dakota	70	0.4%
45	New Hampshire	60	0.3%
46	Delaware	50	0.3%
NA	Alaska*	NA	NA
NA	North Dakota*	NA	NA
NA	Vermont*	NA	NA
NA	Wyoming*	NA	NA
	District of Columbia*	NA	NA

Source: American Cancer Society
"Cancer Facts & Figures 2009" (Copyright 2009, American Cancer Society, http://www.cancer.org/docroot/stt/stt_0.asp)
*Fewer than 50 deaths.

Estimated Death Rate by Non-Hodgkin's Lymphoma in 2009

National Estimated Rate = 6.4 Deaths per 100,000 Population*

ALPHA ORDER				RANK ORDER		
RANK	STATE	RATE		RANK	STATE	RATE
27	Alabama	6.2		1	West Virginia	9.9
NA	Alaska**	NA		2	Iowa	9.3
36	Arizona	5.3		3	Oregon	8.6
16	Arkansas	6.9		3	Pennsylvania	8.6
41	California	5.1		3	South Dakota	8.6
45	Colorado	4.6		6	Florida	8.4
26	Connecticut	6.3		7	New York	7.3
33	Delaware	5.6		8	Missouri	7.2
6	Florida	8.4		8	Montana	7.2
43	Georgia	4.7		8	Nebraska	7.2
27	Hawaii	6.2		11	Michigan	7.1
38	Idaho	5.2		11	Wisconsin	7.1
32	Illinois	6.0		13	Kentucky	7.0
21	Indiana	6.5		13	New Jersey	7.0
2	Iowa	9.3		13	Tennessee	7.0
24	Kansas	6.4		16	Arkansas	6.9
13	Kentucky	7.0		16	Louisiana	6.9
16	Louisiana	6.9		18	Maine	6.8
18	Maine	6.8		18	South Carolina	6.8
36	Maryland	5.3		20	Rhode Island	6.6
21	Massachusetts	6.5		21	Indiana	6.5
11	Michigan	7.1		21	Massachusetts	6.5
30	Minnesota	6.1		21	Oklahoma	6.5
30	Mississippi	6.1		24	Kansas	6.4
8	Missouri	7.2		24	Ohio	6.4
8	Montana	7.2		26	Connecticut	6.3
8	Nebraska	7.2		27	Alabama	6.2
42	Nevada	4.9		27	Hawaii	6.2
46	New Hampshire	4.5		27	Washington	6.2
13	New Jersey	7.0		30	Minnesota	6.1
35	New Mexico	5.5		30	Mississippi	6.1
7	New York	7.3		32	Illinois	6.0
33	North Carolina	5.6		33	Delaware	5.6
NA	North Dakota**	NA		33	North Carolina	5.6
24	Ohio	6.4		35	New Mexico	5.5
21	Oklahoma	6.5		36	Arizona	5.3
3	Oregon	8.6		36	Maryland	5.3
3	Pennsylvania	8.6		38	Idaho	5.2
20	Rhode Island	6.6		38	Texas	5.2
18	South Carolina	6.8		38	Virginia	5.2
3	South Dakota	8.6		41	California	5.1
13	Tennessee	7.0		42	Nevada	4.9
38	Texas	5.2		43	Georgia	4.7
43	Utah	4.7		43	Utah	4.7
NA	Vermont**	NA		45	Colorado	4.6
38	Virginia	5.2		46	New Hampshire	4.5
27	Washington	6.2		NA	Alaska**	NA
1	West Virginia	9.9		NA	North Dakota**	NA
11	Wisconsin	7.1		NA	Vermont**	NA
NA	Wyoming**	NA		NA	Wyoming**	NA
					District of Columbia**	NA

Source: CQ Press using data from American Cancer Society
    "Cancer Facts & Figures 2009" (Copyright 2009, American Cancer Society, http://www.cancer.org/docroot/stt/stt_0.asp)
*Rates calculated using 2009 Census resident population estimates. Not age-adjusted.
**Fewer than 50 deaths.

Estimated Deaths by Ovarian Cancer in 2009

National Estimated Total = 14,600 Deaths

ALPHA ORDER

RANK	STATE	DEATHS	% of USA
20	Alabama	270	1.8%
NA	Alaska*	NA	NA
18	Arizona	290	2.0%
33	Arkansas	130	0.9%
1	California	1,580	10.8%
24	Colorado	210	1.4%
28	Connecticut	180	1.2%
NA	Delaware*	NA	NA
2	Florida	970	6.6%
11	Georgia	400	2.7%
42	Hawaii	50	0.3%
42	Idaho	50	0.3%
6	Illinois	600	4.1%
14	Indiana	340	2.3%
29	Iowa	170	1.2%
31	Kansas	150	1.0%
24	Kentucky	210	1.4%
24	Louisiana	210	1.4%
39	Maine	70	0.5%
21	Maryland	260	1.8%
13	Massachusetts	350	2.4%
8	Michigan	520	3.6%
22	Minnesota	240	1.6%
32	Mississippi	140	1.0%
18	Missouri	290	2.0%
42	Montana	50	0.3%
36	Nebraska	90	0.6%
34	Nevada	120	0.8%
40	New Hampshire	60	0.4%
9	New Jersey	450	3.1%
36	New Mexico	90	0.6%
2	New York	970	6.6%
10	North Carolina	430	2.9%
NA	North Dakota*	NA	NA
7	Ohio	580	4.0%
29	Oklahoma	170	1.2%
23	Oregon	220	1.5%
5	Pennsylvania	760	5.2%
40	Rhode Island	60	0.4%
24	South Carolina	210	1.4%
42	South Dakota	50	0.3%
16	Tennessee	310	2.1%
4	Texas	890	6.1%
36	Utah	90	0.6%
NA	Vermont*	NA	NA
12	Virginia	380	2.6%
14	Washington	340	2.3%
34	West Virginia	120	0.8%
17	Wisconsin	300	2.1%
NA	Wyoming*	NA	NA

RANK ORDER

RANK	STATE	DEATHS	% of USA
1	California	1,580	10.8%
2	Florida	970	6.6%
2	New York	970	6.6%
4	Texas	890	6.1%
5	Pennsylvania	760	5.2%
6	Illinois	600	4.1%
7	Ohio	580	4.0%
8	Michigan	520	3.6%
9	New Jersey	450	3.1%
10	North Carolina	430	2.9%
11	Georgia	400	2.7%
12	Virginia	380	2.6%
13	Massachusetts	350	2.4%
14	Indiana	340	2.3%
14	Washington	340	2.3%
16	Tennessee	310	2.1%
17	Wisconsin	300	2.1%
18	Arizona	290	2.0%
18	Missouri	290	2.0%
20	Alabama	270	1.8%
21	Maryland	260	1.8%
22	Minnesota	240	1.6%
23	Oregon	220	1.5%
24	Colorado	210	1.4%
24	Kentucky	210	1.4%
24	Louisiana	210	1.4%
24	South Carolina	210	1.4%
28	Connecticut	180	1.2%
29	Iowa	170	1.2%
29	Oklahoma	170	1.2%
31	Kansas	150	1.0%
32	Mississippi	140	1.0%
33	Arkansas	130	0.9%
34	Nevada	120	0.8%
34	West Virginia	120	0.8%
36	Nebraska	90	0.6%
36	New Mexico	90	0.6%
36	Utah	90	0.6%
39	Maine	70	0.5%
40	New Hampshire	60	0.4%
40	Rhode Island	60	0.4%
42	Hawaii	50	0.3%
42	Idaho	50	0.3%
42	Montana	50	0.3%
42	South Dakota	50	0.3%
NA	Alaska*	NA	NA
NA	Delaware*	NA	NA
NA	North Dakota*	NA	NA
NA	Vermont*	NA	NA
NA	Wyoming*	NA	NA
	District of Columbia*	NA	NA

Source: American Cancer Society
"Cancer Facts & Figures 2009" (Copyright 2009, American Cancer Society, http://www.cancer.org/docroot/stt/stt_0.asp)
*Fewer than 50 deaths.

Estimated Death Rate by Ovarian Cancer in 2009

National Estimated Rate = 9.5 Deaths per 100,000 Female Population*

ALPHA ORDER				RANK ORDER		
RANK	STATE	RATE		RANK	STATE	RATE
5	Alabama	11.2		1	West Virginia	13.0
NA	Alaska**	NA		2	South Dakota	12.4
35	Arizona	8.9		3	Pennsylvania	11.9
35	Arkansas	8.9		4	Oregon	11.5
39	California	8.6		5	Alabama	11.2
39	Colorado	8.6		5	Iowa	11.2
18	Connecticut	10.0		7	Rhode Island	11.1
NA	Delaware**	NA		8	Kansas	10.6
12	Florida	10.4		8	Wisconsin	10.6
41	Georgia	8.1		10	Indiana	10.5
42	Hawaii	7.8		10	Massachusetts	10.5
44	Idaho	6.6		12	Florida	10.4
28	Illinois	9.2		12	Maine	10.4
10	Indiana	10.5		12	Montana	10.4
5	Iowa	11.2		12	Washington	10.4
8	Kansas	10.6		16	Michigan	10.2
23	Kentucky	9.6		16	New Jersey	10.2
27	Louisiana	9.3		18	Connecticut	10.0
12	Maine	10.4		18	Nebraska	10.0
35	Maryland	8.9		20	Ohio	9.9
10	Massachusetts	10.5		21	New York	9.7
16	Michigan	10.2		21	Tennessee	9.7
28	Minnesota	9.2		23	Kentucky	9.6
28	Mississippi	9.2		23	Missouri	9.6
23	Missouri	9.6		23	Virginia	9.6
12	Montana	10.4		26	Nevada	9.4
18	Nebraska	10.0		27	Louisiana	9.3
26	Nevada	9.4		28	Illinois	9.2
34	New Hampshire	9.0		28	Minnesota	9.2
16	New Jersey	10.2		28	Mississippi	9.2
35	New Mexico	8.9		28	Oklahoma	9.2
21	New York	9.7		32	North Carolina	9.1
32	North Carolina	9.1		32	South Carolina	9.1
NA	North Dakota**	NA		34	New Hampshire	9.0
20	Ohio	9.9		35	Arizona	8.9
28	Oklahoma	9.2		35	Arkansas	8.9
4	Oregon	11.5		35	Maryland	8.9
3	Pennsylvania	11.9		35	New Mexico	8.9
7	Rhode Island	11.1		39	California	8.6
32	South Carolina	9.1		39	Colorado	8.6
2	South Dakota	12.4		41	Georgia	8.1
21	Tennessee	9.7		42	Hawaii	7.8
43	Texas	7.3		43	Texas	7.3
44	Utah	6.6		44	Idaho	6.6
NA	Vermont**	NA		44	Utah	6.6
23	Virginia	9.6		NA	Alaska**	NA
12	Washington	10.4		NA	Delaware**	NA
1	West Virginia	13.0		NA	North Dakota**	NA
8	Wisconsin	10.6		NA	Vermont**	NA
NA	Wyoming**	NA		NA	Wyoming**	NA
					District of Columbia**	NA

Source: CQ Press using data from American Cancer Society
   "Cancer Facts & Figures 2009" (Copyright 2009, American Cancer Society, http://www.cancer.org/docroot/stt/stt_0.asp)
*Rates calculated using 2008 Census female population estimates. Not age-adjusted.
**Fewer than 50 deaths.

Estimated Deaths by Pancreatic Cancer in 2009

National Estimated Total = 35,240 Deaths

ALPHA ORDER

RANK	STATE	DEATHS	% of USA
22	Alabama	550	1.6%
50	Alaska	50	0.1%
20	Arizona	630	1.8%
29	Arkansas	400	1.1%
1	California	3,740	10.6%
28	Colorado	430	1.2%
23	Connecticut	540	1.5%
45	Delaware	110	0.3%
2	Florida	2,470	7.0%
13	Georgia	870	2.5%
41	Hawaii	170	0.5%
37	Idaho	200	0.6%
6	Illinois	1,560	4.4%
14	Indiana	770	2.2%
30	Iowa	380	1.1%
33	Kansas	330	0.9%
26	Kentucky	500	1.4%
24	Louisiana	530	1.5%
37	Maine	200	0.6%
19	Maryland	690	2.0%
11	Massachusetts	880	2.5%
8	Michigan	1,250	3.5%
21	Minnesota	580	1.6%
32	Mississippi	350	1.0%
15	Missouri	750	2.1%
43	Montana	120	0.3%
39	Nebraska	190	0.5%
34	Nevada	280	0.8%
41	New Hampshire	170	0.5%
10	New Jersey	1,080	3.1%
35	New Mexico	220	0.6%
3	New York	2,360	6.7%
9	North Carolina	1,090	3.1%
47	North Dakota	90	0.3%
7	Ohio	1,430	4.1%
30	Oklahoma	380	1.1%
27	Oregon	470	1.3%
5	Pennsylvania	1,920	5.4%
43	Rhode Island	120	0.3%
24	South Carolina	530	1.5%
46	South Dakota	100	0.3%
16	Tennessee	730	2.1%
4	Texas	2,120	6.0%
39	Utah	190	0.5%
48	Vermont	70	0.2%
11	Virginia	880	2.5%
17	Washington	710	2.0%
36	West Virginia	210	0.6%
17	Wisconsin	710	2.0%
49	Wyoming	60	0.2%

RANK ORDER

RANK	STATE	DEATHS	% of USA
1	California	3,740	10.6%
2	Florida	2,470	7.0%
3	New York	2,360	6.7%
4	Texas	2,120	6.0%
5	Pennsylvania	1,920	5.4%
6	Illinois	1,560	4.4%
7	Ohio	1,430	4.1%
8	Michigan	1,250	3.5%
9	North Carolina	1,090	3.1%
10	New Jersey	1,080	3.1%
11	Massachusetts	880	2.5%
11	Virginia	880	2.5%
13	Georgia	870	2.5%
14	Indiana	770	2.2%
15	Missouri	750	2.1%
16	Tennessee	730	2.1%
17	Washington	710	2.0%
17	Wisconsin	710	2.0%
19	Maryland	690	2.0%
20	Arizona	630	1.8%
21	Minnesota	580	1.6%
22	Alabama	550	1.6%
23	Connecticut	540	1.5%
24	Louisiana	530	1.5%
24	South Carolina	530	1.5%
26	Kentucky	500	1.4%
27	Oregon	470	1.3%
28	Colorado	430	1.2%
29	Arkansas	400	1.1%
30	Iowa	380	1.1%
30	Oklahoma	380	1.1%
32	Mississippi	350	1.0%
33	Kansas	330	0.9%
34	Nevada	280	0.8%
35	New Mexico	220	0.6%
36	West Virginia	210	0.6%
37	Idaho	200	0.6%
37	Maine	200	0.6%
39	Nebraska	190	0.5%
39	Utah	190	0.5%
41	Hawaii	170	0.5%
41	New Hampshire	170	0.5%
43	Montana	120	0.3%
43	Rhode Island	120	0.3%
45	Delaware	110	0.3%
46	South Dakota	100	0.3%
47	North Dakota	90	0.3%
48	Vermont	70	0.2%
49	Wyoming	60	0.2%
50	Alaska	50	0.1%
	District of Columbia	60	0.2%

Source: American Cancer Society
"Cancer Facts & Figures 2009" (Copyright 2009, American Cancer Society, http://www.cancer.org/docroot/stt/stt_0.asp)

Estimated Death Rate by Pancreatic Cancer in 2009

National Estimated Rate = 11.5 Deaths per 100,000 Population*

ALPHA ORDER

RANK	STATE	RATE
27	Alabama	11.7
49	Alaska	7.2
45	Arizona	9.6
5	Arkansas	13.8
44	California	10.1
47	Colorado	8.6
1	Connecticut	15.3
15	Delaware	12.4
6	Florida	13.3
46	Georgia	8.9
8	Hawaii	13.1
9	Idaho	12.9
21	Illinois	12.1
24	Indiana	12.0
11	Iowa	12.6
27	Kansas	11.7
29	Kentucky	11.6
26	Louisiana	11.8
2	Maine	15.2
21	Maryland	12.1
6	Massachusetts	13.3
13	Michigan	12.5
37	Minnesota	11.0
25	Mississippi	11.9
13	Missouri	12.5
18	Montana	12.3
41	Nebraska	10.6
41	Nevada	10.6
10	New Hampshire	12.8
15	New Jersey	12.4
39	New Mexico	10.9
21	New York	12.1
29	North Carolina	11.6
4	North Dakota	13.9
15	Ohio	12.4
43	Oklahoma	10.3
18	Oregon	12.3
2	Pennsylvania	15.2
34	Rhode Island	11.4
29	South Carolina	11.6
18	South Dakota	12.3
29	Tennessee	11.6
47	Texas	8.6
50	Utah	6.8
35	Vermont	11.3
36	Virginia	11.2
40	Washington	10.7
33	West Virginia	11.5
11	Wisconsin	12.6
37	Wyoming	11.0

RANK ORDER

RANK	STATE	RATE
1	Connecticut	15.3
2	Maine	15.2
2	Pennsylvania	15.2
4	North Dakota	13.9
5	Arkansas	13.8
6	Florida	13.3
6	Massachusetts	13.3
8	Hawaii	13.1
9	Idaho	12.9
10	New Hampshire	12.8
11	Iowa	12.6
11	Wisconsin	12.6
13	Michigan	12.5
13	Missouri	12.5
15	Delaware	12.4
15	New Jersey	12.4
15	Ohio	12.4
18	Montana	12.3
18	Oregon	12.3
18	South Dakota	12.3
21	Illinois	12.1
21	Maryland	12.1
21	New York	12.1
24	Indiana	12.0
25	Mississippi	11.9
26	Louisiana	11.8
27	Alabama	11.7
27	Kansas	11.7
29	Kentucky	11.6
29	North Carolina	11.6
29	South Carolina	11.6
29	Tennessee	11.6
33	West Virginia	11.5
34	Rhode Island	11.4
35	Vermont	11.3
36	Virginia	11.2
37	Minnesota	11.0
37	Wyoming	11.0
39	New Mexico	10.9
40	Washington	10.7
41	Nebraska	10.6
41	Nevada	10.6
43	Oklahoma	10.3
44	California	10.1
45	Arizona	9.6
46	Georgia	8.9
47	Colorado	8.6
47	Texas	8.6
49	Alaska	7.2
50	Utah	6.8

District of Columbia   10.0

Source: CQ Press using data from American Cancer Society
   "Cancer Facts & Figures 2009" (Copyright 2009, American Cancer Society, http://www.cancer.org/docroot/stt/stt_0.asp)
*Rates calculated using 2009 Census resident population estimates. Not age-adjusted.

Estimated Deaths by Prostate Cancer in 2009

National Estimated Total = 27,360 Deaths

ALPHA ORDER

RANK	STATE	DEATHS	% of USA
20	Alabama	510	1.9%
NA	Alaska*	NA	NA
15	Arizona	580	2.1%
29	Arkansas	340	1.2%
1	California	2,780	10.2%
28	Colorado	350	1.3%
25	Connecticut	390	1.4%
47	Delaware	90	0.3%
2	Florida	2,280	8.3%
10	Georgia	800	2.9%
43	Hawaii	100	0.4%
38	Idaho	160	0.6%
7	Illinois	1,150	4.2%
19	Indiana	520	1.9%
30	Iowa	330	1.2%
34	Kansas	210	0.8%
25	Kentucky	390	1.4%
22	Louisiana	450	1.6%
38	Maine	160	0.6%
17	Maryland	550	2.0%
18	Massachusetts	540	2.0%
9	Michigan	820	3.0%
24	Minnesota	410	1.5%
31	Mississippi	300	1.1%
12	Missouri	660	2.4%
42	Montana	120	0.4%
36	Nebraska	200	0.7%
33	Nevada	230	0.8%
41	New Hampshire	130	0.5%
12	New Jersey	660	2.4%
34	New Mexico	210	0.8%
4	New York	1,470	5.4%
8	North Carolina	860	3.1%
43	North Dakota	100	0.4%
6	Ohio	1,200	4.4%
32	Oklahoma	280	1.0%
25	Oregon	390	1.4%
5	Pennsylvania	1,440	5.3%
43	Rhode Island	100	0.4%
23	South Carolina	420	1.5%
43	South Dakota	100	0.4%
16	Tennessee	570	2.1%
3	Texas	1,700	6.2%
37	Utah	170	0.6%
48	Vermont	60	0.2%
14	Virginia	620	2.3%
11	Washington	680	2.5%
40	West Virginia	140	0.5%
21	Wisconsin	500	1.8%
NA	Wyoming*	NA	NA

RANK ORDER

RANK	STATE	DEATHS	% of USA
1	California	2,780	10.2%
2	Florida	2,280	8.3%
3	Texas	1,700	6.2%
4	New York	1,470	5.4%
5	Pennsylvania	1,440	5.3%
6	Ohio	1,200	4.4%
7	Illinois	1,150	4.2%
8	North Carolina	860	3.1%
9	Michigan	820	3.0%
10	Georgia	800	2.9%
11	Washington	680	2.5%
12	Missouri	660	2.4%
12	New Jersey	660	2.4%
14	Virginia	620	2.3%
15	Arizona	580	2.1%
16	Tennessee	570	2.1%
17	Maryland	550	2.0%
18	Massachusetts	540	2.0%
19	Indiana	520	1.9%
20	Alabama	510	1.9%
21	Wisconsin	500	1.8%
22	Louisiana	450	1.6%
23	South Carolina	420	1.5%
24	Minnesota	410	1.5%
25	Connecticut	390	1.4%
25	Kentucky	390	1.4%
25	Oregon	390	1.4%
28	Colorado	350	1.3%
29	Arkansas	340	1.2%
30	Iowa	330	1.2%
31	Mississippi	300	1.1%
32	Oklahoma	280	1.0%
33	Nevada	230	0.8%
34	Kansas	210	0.8%
34	New Mexico	210	0.8%
36	Nebraska	200	0.7%
37	Utah	170	0.6%
38	Idaho	160	0.6%
38	Maine	160	0.6%
40	West Virginia	140	0.5%
41	New Hampshire	130	0.5%
42	Montana	120	0.4%
43	Hawaii	100	0.4%
43	North Dakota	100	0.4%
43	Rhode Island	100	0.4%
43	South Dakota	100	0.4%
47	Delaware	90	0.3%
48	Vermont	60	0.2%
NA	Alaska*	NA	NA
NA	Wyoming*	NA	NA
	District of Columbia	60	0.2%

Source: American Cancer Society
"Cancer Facts & Figures 2009" (Copyright 2009, American Cancer Society, http://www.cancer.org/docroot/stt/stt_0.asp)
*Fewer than 50 deaths.

Age-Adjusted Death Rate by Prostate Cancer in 2005

National Rate = 26.7 Deaths per 100,000 Male Population*

ALPHA ORDER

RANK	STATE	RATE
2	Alabama	33.0
38	Alaska	26.1
48	Arizona	23.2
13	Arkansas	28.9
43	California	25.0
33	Colorado	26.5
26	Connecticut	27.0
8	Delaware	29.4
49	Florida	22.3
5	Georgia	30.6
50	Hawaii	18.8
12	Idaho	29.0
19	Illinois	28.1
23	Indiana	27.8
25	Iowa	27.5
43	Kansas	25.0
28	Kentucky	26.9
4	Louisiana	32.2
19	Maine	28.1
9	Maryland	29.3
36	Massachusetts	26.4
33	Michigan	26.5
16	Minnesota	28.6
1	Mississippi	36.2
47	Missouri	24.3
11	Montana	29.2
42	Nebraska	25.1
32	Nevada	26.6
17	New Hampshire	28.3
37	New Jersey	26.2
28	New Mexico	26.9
39	New York	26.0
7	North Carolina	29.9
19	North Dakota	28.1
22	Ohio	27.9
46	Oklahoma	24.9
24	Oregon	27.7
28	Pennsylvania	26.9
26	Rhode Island	27.0
3	South Carolina	32.4
14	South Dakota	28.8
9	Tennessee	29.3
41	Texas	25.5
33	Utah	26.5
17	Vermont	28.3
6	Virginia	30.1
31	Washington	26.8
43	West Virginia	25.0
14	Wisconsin	28.8
40	Wyoming	25.8

RANK ORDER

RANK	STATE	RATE
1	Mississippi	36.2
2	Alabama	33.0
3	South Carolina	32.4
4	Louisiana	32.2
5	Georgia	30.6
6	Virginia	30.1
7	North Carolina	29.9
8	Delaware	29.4
9	Maryland	29.3
9	Tennessee	29.3
11	Montana	29.2
12	Idaho	29.0
13	Arkansas	28.9
14	South Dakota	28.8
14	Wisconsin	28.8
16	Minnesota	28.6
17	New Hampshire	28.3
17	Vermont	28.3
19	Illinois	28.1
19	Maine	28.1
19	North Dakota	28.1
22	Ohio	27.9
23	Indiana	27.8
24	Oregon	27.7
25	Iowa	27.5
26	Connecticut	27.0
26	Rhode Island	27.0
28	Kentucky	26.9
28	New Mexico	26.9
28	Pennsylvania	26.9
31	Washington	26.8
32	Nevada	26.6
33	Colorado	26.5
33	Michigan	26.5
33	Utah	26.5
36	Massachusetts	26.4
37	New Jersey	26.2
38	Alaska	26.1
39	New York	26.0
40	Wyoming	25.8
41	Texas	25.5
42	Nebraska	25.1
43	California	25.0
43	Kansas	25.0
43	West Virginia	25.0
46	Oklahoma	24.9
47	Missouri	24.3
48	Arizona	23.2
49	Florida	22.3
50	Hawaii	18.8
	District of Columbia	43.8

Source: American Cancer Society
"Cancer Facts & Figures 2009" (Copyright 2009, American Cancer Society, http://www.cancer.org/docroot/stt/stt_0.asp)
*For 2001 to 2005. Age-adjusted to the 2000 U.S. standard population.

Deaths by AIDS in 2006

National Total = 12,113 Deaths*

ALPHA ORDER

ALPHA ORDER

RANK	STATE	DEATHS	% of USA
16	Alabama	189	1.6%
44	Alaska	10	0.1%
21	Arizona	138	1.1%
28	Arkansas	74	0.6%
3	California	1,176	9.7%
26	Colorado	83	0.7%
22	Connecticut	127	1.0%
30	Delaware	54	0.4%
1	Florida	1,753	14.5%
5	Georgia	684	5.6%
40	Hawaii	18	0.1%
45	Idaho	8	0.1%
9	Illinois	382	3.2%
20	Indiana	141	1.2%
41	Iowa	16	0.1%
35	Kansas	28	0.2%
27	Kentucky	81	0.7%
11	Louisiana	338	2.8%
42	Maine	12	0.1%
7	Maryland	483	4.0%
19	Massachusetts	182	1.5%
18	Michigan	184	1.5%
31	Minnesota	53	0.4%
17	Mississippi	187	1.5%
23	Missouri	120	1.0%
47	Montana	6	0.0%
38	Nebraska	24	0.2%
28	Nevada	74	0.6%
42	New Hampshire	12	0.1%
6	New Jersey	539	4.4%
34	New Mexico	39	0.3%
2	New York	1,471	12.1%
8	North Carolina	427	3.5%
50	North Dakota	2	0.0%
15	Ohio	232	1.9%
25	Oklahoma	89	0.7%
33	Oregon	50	0.4%
10	Pennsylvania	367	3.0%
37	Rhode Island	27	0.2%
12	South Carolina	256	2.1%
45	South Dakota	8	0.1%
12	Tennessee	256	2.1%
4	Texas	1,034	8.5%
35	Utah	28	0.2%
47	Vermont	6	0.0%
14	Virginia	251	2.1%
24	Washington	100	0.8%
39	West Virginia	22	0.2%
32	Wisconsin	52	0.4%
49	Wyoming	3	0.0%

RANK ORDER

RANK	STATE	DEATHS	% of USA
1	Florida	1,753	14.5%
2	New York	1,471	12.1%
3	California	1,176	9.7%
4	Texas	1,034	8.5%
5	Georgia	684	5.6%
6	New Jersey	539	4.4%
7	Maryland	483	4.0%
8	North Carolina	427	3.5%
9	Illinois	382	3.2%
10	Pennsylvania	367	3.0%
11	Louisiana	338	2.8%
12	South Carolina	256	2.1%
12	Tennessee	256	2.1%
14	Virginia	251	2.1%
15	Ohio	232	1.9%
16	Alabama	189	1.6%
17	Mississippi	187	1.5%
18	Michigan	184	1.5%
19	Massachusetts	182	1.5%
20	Indiana	141	1.2%
21	Arizona	138	1.1%
22	Connecticut	127	1.0%
23	Missouri	120	1.0%
24	Washington	100	0.8%
25	Oklahoma	89	0.7%
26	Colorado	83	0.7%
27	Kentucky	81	0.7%
28	Arkansas	74	0.6%
28	Nevada	74	0.6%
30	Delaware	54	0.4%
31	Minnesota	53	0.4%
32	Wisconsin	52	0.4%
33	Oregon	50	0.4%
34	New Mexico	39	0.3%
35	Kansas	28	0.2%
35	Utah	28	0.2%
37	Rhode Island	27	0.2%
38	Nebraska	24	0.2%
39	West Virginia	22	0.2%
40	Hawaii	18	0.1%
41	Iowa	16	0.1%
42	Maine	12	0.1%
42	New Hampshire	12	0.1%
44	Alaska	10	0.1%
45	Idaho	8	0.1%
45	South Dakota	8	0.1%
47	Montana	6	0.0%
47	Vermont	6	0.0%
49	Wyoming	3	0.0%
50	North Dakota	2	0.0%
	District of Columbia	217	1.8%

Source: U.S. Department of Health and Human Services, National Center for Health Statistics
   "National Vital Statistics Reports" (Vol. 57, No. 14, April 17, 2009, http://www.cdc.gov/nchs/deaths.htm)
*Final data by state of residence. AIDS is Acquired Immunodeficiency Syndrome. It is a specific group of diseases or
conditions which are indicative of severe immunosuppression related to infection with the Human Immunodeficiency Virus (HIV).

Death Rate by AIDS in 2006

National Rate = 4.0 Deaths per 100,000 Population*

ALPHA ORDER

RANK	STATE	RATE
13	Alabama	4.1
NA	Alaska**	NA
24	Arizona	2.2
21	Arkansas	2.6
16	California	3.2
31	Colorado	1.7
14	Connecticut	3.6
7	Delaware	6.3
1	Florida	9.7
5	Georgia	7.3
NA	Hawaii**	NA
NA	Idaho**	NA
17	Illinois	3.0
24	Indiana	2.2
NA	Iowa**	NA
37	Kansas	1.0
29	Kentucky	1.9
3	Louisiana	7.9
NA	Maine**	NA
2	Maryland	8.6
20	Massachusetts	2.8
30	Michigan	1.8
37	Minnesota	1.0
6	Mississippi	6.4
26	Missouri	2.1
NA	Montana**	NA
33	Nebraska	1.4
17	Nevada	3.0
NA	New Hampshire**	NA
8	New Jersey	6.2
27	New Mexico	2.0
4	New York	7.6
10	North Carolina	4.8
NA	North Dakota**	NA
27	Ohio	2.0
22	Oklahoma	2.5
33	Oregon	1.4
17	Pennsylvania	3.0
22	Rhode Island	2.5
9	South Carolina	5.9
NA	South Dakota**	NA
12	Tennessee	4.2
11	Texas	4.4
36	Utah	1.1
NA	Vermont**	NA
15	Virginia	3.3
32	Washington	1.6
35	West Virginia	1.2
39	Wisconsin	0.9
NA	Wyoming**	NA

RANK ORDER

RANK	STATE	RATE
1	Florida	9.7
2	Maryland	8.6
3	Louisiana	7.9
4	New York	7.6
5	Georgia	7.3
6	Mississippi	6.4
7	Delaware	6.3
8	New Jersey	6.2
9	South Carolina	5.9
10	North Carolina	4.8
11	Texas	4.4
12	Tennessee	4.2
13	Alabama	4.1
14	Connecticut	3.6
15	Virginia	3.3
16	California	3.2
17	Illinois	3.0
17	Nevada	3.0
17	Pennsylvania	3.0
20	Massachusetts	2.8
21	Arkansas	2.6
22	Oklahoma	2.5
22	Rhode Island	2.5
24	Arizona	2.2
24	Indiana	2.2
26	Missouri	2.1
27	New Mexico	2.0
27	Ohio	2.0
29	Kentucky	1.9
30	Michigan	1.8
31	Colorado	1.7
32	Washington	1.6
33	Nebraska	1.4
33	Oregon	1.4
35	West Virginia	1.2
36	Utah	1.1
37	Kansas	1.0
37	Minnesota	1.0
39	Wisconsin	0.9
NA	Alaska**	NA
NA	Hawaii**	NA
NA	Idaho**	NA
NA	Iowa**	NA
NA	Maine**	NA
NA	Montana**	NA
NA	New Hampshire**	NA
NA	North Dakota**	NA
NA	South Dakota**	NA
NA	Vermont**	NA
NA	Wyoming**	NA

District of Columbia — 37.3

Source: U.S. Department of Health and Human Services, National Center for Health Statistics
    "National Vital Statistics Reports" (Vol. 57, No. 14, April 17, 2009, http://www.cdc.gov/nchs/deaths.htm)
*Final data by state of residence. AIDS is Acquired Immunodeficiency Syndrome. It is a specific group of diseases or conditions which are indicative of severe immunosuppression related to infection with the Human Immunodeficiency Virus (HIV). Not age-adjusted.
**Insufficient data to determine a reliable rate.

Age-Adjusted Death Rate by AIDS in 2006

National Rate = 4.0 Deaths per 100,000 Population*

RANK	STATE	RATE
12	Alabama	4.2
NA	Alaska**	NA
23	Arizona	2.4
20	Arkansas	2.8
15	California	3.3
31	Colorado	1.7
14	Connecticut	3.4
7	Delaware	6.1
1	Florida	9.7
5	Georgia	7.2
NA	Hawaii**	NA
NA	Idaho**	NA
17	Illinois	3.0
25	Indiana	2.2
NA	Iowa**	NA
37	Kansas	1.1
29	Kentucky	1.9
2	Louisiana	8.1
NA	Maine**	NA
2	Maryland	8.1
21	Massachusetts	2.7
30	Michigan	1.8
38	Minnesota	1.0
6	Mississippi	6.7
27	Missouri	2.1
NA	Montana**	NA
32	Nebraska	1.4
18	Nevada	2.9
NA	New Hampshire**	NA
9	New Jersey	5.8
25	New Mexico	2.2
4	New York	7.3
10	North Carolina	4.7
NA	North Dakota**	NA
28	Ohio	2.0
22	Oklahoma	2.6
32	Oregon	1.4
18	Pennsylvania	2.9
23	Rhode Island	2.4
8	South Carolina	5.9
NA	South Dakota**	NA
12	Tennessee	4.2
11	Texas	4.5
35	Utah	1.3
NA	Vermont**	NA
16	Virginia	3.1
32	Washington	1.4
36	West Virginia	1.2
39	Wisconsin	0.9
NA	Wyoming**	NA

RANK	STATE	RATE
1	Florida	9.7
2	Louisiana	8.1
2	Maryland	8.1
4	New York	7.3
5	Georgia	7.2
6	Mississippi	6.7
7	Delaware	6.1
8	South Carolina	5.9
9	New Jersey	5.8
10	North Carolina	4.7
11	Texas	4.5
12	Alabama	4.2
12	Tennessee	4.2
14	Connecticut	3.4
15	California	3.3
16	Virginia	3.1
17	Illinois	3.0
18	Nevada	2.9
18	Pennsylvania	2.9
20	Arkansas	2.8
21	Massachusetts	2.7
22	Oklahoma	2.6
23	Arizona	2.4
23	Rhode Island	2.4
25	Indiana	2.2
25	New Mexico	2.2
27	Missouri	2.1
28	Ohio	2.0
29	Kentucky	1.9
30	Michigan	1.8
31	Colorado	1.7
32	Nebraska	1.4
32	Oregon	1.4
32	Washington	1.4
35	Utah	1.3
36	West Virginia	1.2
37	Kansas	1.1
38	Minnesota	1.0
39	Wisconsin	0.9
NA	Alaska**	NA
NA	Hawaii**	NA
NA	Idaho**	NA
NA	Iowa**	NA
NA	Maine**	NA
NA	Montana**	NA
NA	New Hampshire**	NA
NA	North Dakota**	NA
NA	South Dakota**	NA
NA	Vermont**	NA
NA	Wyoming**	NA

District of Columbia   37.3

Source: U.S. Department of Health and Human Services, National Center for Health Statistics
"National Vital Statistics Reports" (Vol. 57, No. 14, April 17, 2009, http://www.cdc.gov/nchs/deaths.htm)
*Final data by state of residence. AIDS is Acquired Immunodeficiency Syndrome. It is a specific group of diseases or conditions which are indicative of severe immunosuppression related to infection with the Human Immunodeficiency Virus (HIV). Age-adjusted rates based on the year 2000 standard population.
**Insufficient data to determine a reliable rate.

Deaths by Alzheimer's Disease in 2006

National Total = 72,432 Deaths*

ALPHA ORDER

RANK	STATE	DEATHS	% of USA
20	Alabama	1,497	2.1%
50	Alaska	73	0.1%
11	Arizona	2,066	2.9%
31	Arkansas	783	1.1%
1	California	8,146	11.2%
27	Colorado	1,058	1.5%
33	Connecticut	728	1.0%
47	Delaware	189	0.3%
3	Florida	4,689	6.5%
13	Georgia	1,820	2.5%
46	Hawaii	201	0.3%
37	Idaho	400	0.6%
6	Illinois	2,794	3.9%
14	Indiana	1,696	2.3%
26	Iowa	1,121	1.5%
30	Kansas	830	1.1%
25	Kentucky	1,153	1.6%
23	Louisiana	1,282	1.8%
36	Maine	477	0.7%
29	Maryland	915	1.3%
19	Massachusetts	1,560	2.2%
8	Michigan	2,331	3.2%
22	Minnesota	1,299	1.8%
32	Mississippi	744	1.0%
16	Missouri	1,632	2.3%
45	Montana	226	0.3%
34	Nebraska	500	0.7%
44	Nevada	281	0.4%
39	New Hampshire	372	0.5%
15	New Jersey	1,649	2.3%
40	New Mexico	348	0.5%
12	New York	2,021	2.8%
9	North Carolina	2,265	3.1%
42	North Dakota	318	0.4%
4	Ohio	3,565	4.9%
28	Oklahoma	928	1.3%
24	Oregon	1,231	1.7%
5	Pennsylvania	3,311	4.6%
43	Rhode Island	297	0.4%
21	South Carolina	1,364	1.9%
41	South Dakota	329	0.5%
10	Tennessee	2,115	2.9%
2	Texas	4,887	6.7%
38	Utah	390	0.5%
48	Vermont	186	0.3%
18	Virginia	1,574	2.2%
7	Washington	2,470	3.4%
35	West Virginia	496	0.7%
17	Wisconsin	1,596	2.2%
49	Wyoming	112	0.2%

RANK ORDER

RANK	STATE	DEATHS	% of USA
1	California	8,146	11.2%
2	Texas	4,887	6.7%
3	Florida	4,689	6.5%
4	Ohio	3,565	4.9%
5	Pennsylvania	3,311	4.6%
6	Illinois	2,794	3.9%
7	Washington	2,470	3.4%
8	Michigan	2,331	3.2%
9	North Carolina	2,265	3.1%
10	Tennessee	2,115	2.9%
11	Arizona	2,066	2.9%
12	New York	2,021	2.8%
13	Georgia	1,820	2.5%
14	Indiana	1,696	2.3%
15	New Jersey	1,649	2.3%
16	Missouri	1,632	2.3%
17	Wisconsin	1,596	2.2%
18	Virginia	1,574	2.2%
19	Massachusetts	1,560	2.2%
20	Alabama	1,497	2.1%
21	South Carolina	1,364	1.9%
22	Minnesota	1,299	1.8%
23	Louisiana	1,282	1.8%
24	Oregon	1,231	1.7%
25	Kentucky	1,153	1.6%
26	Iowa	1,121	1.5%
27	Colorado	1,058	1.5%
28	Oklahoma	928	1.3%
29	Maryland	915	1.3%
30	Kansas	830	1.1%
31	Arkansas	783	1.1%
32	Mississippi	744	1.0%
33	Connecticut	728	1.0%
34	Nebraska	500	0.7%
35	West Virginia	496	0.7%
36	Maine	477	0.7%
37	Idaho	400	0.6%
38	Utah	390	0.5%
39	New Hampshire	372	0.5%
40	New Mexico	348	0.5%
41	South Dakota	329	0.5%
42	North Dakota	318	0.4%
43	Rhode Island	297	0.4%
44	Nevada	281	0.4%
45	Montana	226	0.3%
46	Hawaii	201	0.3%
47	Delaware	189	0.3%
48	Vermont	186	0.3%
49	Wyoming	112	0.2%
50	Alaska	73	0.1%
	District of Columbia	117	0.2%

Source: U.S. Department of Health and Human Services, National Center for Health Statistics
"National Vital Statistics Reports" (Vol. 57, No. 14, April 17, 2009, http://www.cdc.gov/nchs/deaths.htm)
*Final data by state of residence. A degenerative disease of the brain cells producing loss of memory and general intellectual impairment. It usually affects people over age 65. As the disease progresses, a variety of symptoms may become apparent, including confusion, irritability, and restlessness, as well as disorientation and impaired judgment and concentration.

Death Rate by Alzheimer's Disease in 2006

National Rate = 24.2 Deaths per 100,000 Population*

ALPHA ORDER

ALPHA ORDER

RANK	STATE	RATE
9	Alabama	32.6
49	Alaska	10.9
7	Arizona	33.5
18	Arkansas	27.9
34	California	22.3
34	Colorado	22.3
39	Connecticut	20.8
36	Delaware	22.1
26	Florida	25.9
42	Georgia	19.4
46	Hawaii	15.6
22	Idaho	27.3
37	Illinois	21.8
24	Indiana	26.9
4	Iowa	37.6
12	Kansas	30.0
21	Kentucky	27.4
13	Louisiana	29.9
5	Maine	36.1
45	Maryland	16.3
31	Massachusetts	24.2
33	Michigan	23.1
30	Minnesota	25.1
28	Mississippi	25.6
18	Missouri	27.9
32	Montana	23.9
16	Nebraska	28.3
48	Nevada	11.3
16	New Hampshire	28.3
43	New Jersey	18.9
44	New Mexico	17.8
50	New York	10.5
28	North Carolina	25.6
1	North Dakota	50.0
11	Ohio	31.1
26	Oklahoma	25.9
8	Oregon	33.3
25	Pennsylvania	26.6
20	Rhode Island	27.8
10	South Carolina	31.6
2	South Dakota	42.1
6	Tennessee	35.0
39	Texas	20.8
47	Utah	15.3
14	Vermont	29.8
41	Virginia	20.6
3	Washington	38.6
22	West Virginia	27.3
15	Wisconsin	28.7
38	Wyoming	21.7

RANK ORDER

RANK	STATE	RATE
1	North Dakota	50.0
2	South Dakota	42.1
3	Washington	38.6
4	Iowa	37.6
5	Maine	36.1
6	Tennessee	35.0
7	Arizona	33.5
8	Oregon	33.3
9	Alabama	32.6
10	South Carolina	31.6
11	Ohio	31.1
12	Kansas	30.0
13	Louisiana	29.9
14	Vermont	29.8
15	Wisconsin	28.7
16	Nebraska	28.3
16	New Hampshire	28.3
18	Arkansas	27.9
18	Missouri	27.9
20	Rhode Island	27.8
21	Kentucky	27.4
22	Idaho	27.3
22	West Virginia	27.3
24	Indiana	26.9
25	Pennsylvania	26.6
26	Florida	25.9
26	Oklahoma	25.9
28	Mississippi	25.6
28	North Carolina	25.6
30	Minnesota	25.1
31	Massachusetts	24.2
32	Montana	23.9
33	Michigan	23.1
34	California	22.3
34	Colorado	22.3
36	Delaware	22.1
37	Illinois	21.8
38	Wyoming	21.7
39	Connecticut	20.8
39	Texas	20.8
41	Virginia	20.6
42	Georgia	19.4
43	New Jersey	18.9
44	New Mexico	17.8
45	Maryland	16.3
46	Hawaii	15.6
47	Utah	15.3
48	Nevada	11.3
49	Alaska	10.9
50	New York	10.5
	District of Columbia	20.1

Source: U.S. Department of Health and Human Services, National Center for Health Statistics
"National Vital Statistics Reports" (Vol. 57, No. 14, April 17, 2009, http://www.cdc.gov/nchs/deaths.htm)

*Final data by state of residence. A degenerative disease of the brain cells producing loss of memory and general intellectual impairment. It usually affects people over age 65. As the disease progresses, a variety of symptoms may become apparent, including confusion, irritability, and restlessness, as well as disorientation and impaired judgment and concentration. Not age-adjusted.

Age-Adjusted Death Rate by Alzheimer's Disease in 2006

National Rate = 22.6 Deaths per 100,000 Population*

ALPHA ORDER

RANK	STATE	RATE
7	Alabama	30.3
23	Alaska	24.7
5	Arizona	31.4
28	Arkansas	23.9
26	California	24.1
12	Colorado	27.7
47	Connecticut	16.2
38	Delaware	20.4
45	Florida	17.0
20	Georgia	25.7
49	Hawaii	12.2
11	Idaho	28.1
37	Illinois	20.6
21	Indiana	25.2
17	Iowa	26.3
24	Kansas	24.3
14	Kentucky	26.7
6	Louisiana	30.5
9	Maine	29.0
44	Maryland	17.1
41	Massachusetts	19.4
35	Michigan	21.7
32	Minnesota	22.2
22	Mississippi	25.0
26	Missouri	24.1
40	Montana	19.6
30	Nebraska	22.6
48	Nevada	14.7
15	New Hampshire	26.5
46	New Jersey	16.5
43	New Mexico	17.7
50	New York	9.1
16	North Carolina	26.4
3	North Dakota	33.6
13	Ohio	27.0
29	Oklahoma	23.5
9	Oregon	29.0
42	Pennsylvania	18.9
39	Rhode Island	20.3
4	South Carolina	31.5
8	South Dakota	29.8
2	Tennessee	34.6
19	Texas	25.9
36	Utah	21.4
18	Vermont	26.2
31	Virginia	22.3
1	Washington	38.3
33	West Virginia	21.8
25	Wisconsin	24.2
33	Wyoming	21.8

RANK ORDER

RANK	STATE	RATE
1	Washington	38.3
2	Tennessee	34.6
3	North Dakota	33.6
4	South Carolina	31.5
5	Arizona	31.4
6	Louisiana	30.5
7	Alabama	30.3
8	South Dakota	29.8
9	Maine	29.0
9	Oregon	29.0
11	Idaho	28.1
12	Colorado	27.7
13	Ohio	27.0
14	Kentucky	26.7
15	New Hampshire	26.5
16	North Carolina	26.4
17	Iowa	26.3
18	Vermont	26.2
19	Texas	25.9
20	Georgia	25.7
21	Indiana	25.2
22	Mississippi	25.0
23	Alaska	24.7
24	Kansas	24.3
25	Wisconsin	24.2
26	California	24.1
26	Missouri	24.1
28	Arkansas	23.9
29	Oklahoma	23.5
30	Nebraska	22.6
31	Virginia	22.3
32	Minnesota	22.2
33	West Virginia	21.8
33	Wyoming	21.8
35	Michigan	21.7
36	Utah	21.4
37	Illinois	20.6
38	Delaware	20.4
39	Rhode Island	20.3
40	Montana	19.6
41	Massachusetts	19.4
42	Pennsylvania	18.9
43	New Mexico	17.7
44	Maryland	17.1
45	Florida	17.0
46	New Jersey	16.5
47	Connecticut	16.2
48	Nevada	14.7
49	Hawaii	12.2
50	New York	9.1

District of Columbia	18.3

Source: U.S. Department of Health and Human Services, National Center for Health Statistics
   "National Vital Statistics Reports" (Vol. 57, No. 14, April 17, 2009, http://www.cdc.gov/nchs/deaths.htm)
*Final data by state of residence. A degenerative disease of the brain cells producing loss of memory and general intellectual impairment. It usually affects people over age 65. As the disease progresses, a variety of symptoms may become apparent, including confusion, irritability, and restlessness, as well as disorientation and impaired judgment and concentration. Age-adjusted rates based on the year 2000 standard population.

Deaths by Cerebrovascular Diseases in 2006

National Total = 137,119 Deaths*

ALPHA ORDER

RANK	STATE	DEATHS	% of USA
18	Alabama	2,740	2.0%
50	Alaska	177	0.1%
22	Arizona	2,226	1.6%
28	Arkansas	1,884	1.4%
1	California	15,039	11.0%
32	Colorado	1,532	1.1%
31	Connecticut	1,547	1.1%
47	Delaware	384	0.3%
3	Florida	8,925	6.5%
10	Georgia	3,889	2.8%
41	Hawaii	665	0.5%
38	Idaho	725	0.5%
6	Illinois	5,989	4.4%
15	Indiana	3,238	2.4%
29	Iowa	1,718	1.3%
33	Kansas	1,489	1.1%
24	Kentucky	2,197	1.6%
25	Louisiana	2,195	1.6%
40	Maine	670	0.5%
20	Maryland	2,365	1.7%
16	Massachusetts	2,880	2.1%
8	Michigan	4,752	3.5%
23	Minnesota	2,219	1.6%
30	Mississippi	1,585	1.2%
14	Missouri	3,247	2.4%
43	Montana	461	0.3%
35	Nebraska	922	0.7%
36	Nevada	847	0.6%
42	New Hampshire	494	0.4%
12	New Jersey	3,468	2.5%
37	New Mexico	739	0.5%
5	New York	6,398	4.7%
9	North Carolina	4,572	3.3%
45	North Dakota	428	0.3%
7	Ohio	5,828	4.3%
26	Oklahoma	2,085	1.5%
27	Oregon	1,978	1.4%
4	Pennsylvania	7,151	5.2%
46	Rhode Island	421	0.3%
21	South Carolina	2,291	1.7%
44	South Dakota	442	0.3%
13	Tennessee	3,407	2.5%
2	Texas	9,366	6.8%
39	Utah	674	0.5%
48	Vermont	264	0.2%
11	Virginia	3,523	2.6%
19	Washington	2,725	2.0%
34	West Virginia	1,072	0.8%
17	Wisconsin	2,829	2.1%
49	Wyoming	236	0.2%

RANK ORDER

RANK	STATE	DEATHS	% of USA
1	California	15,039	11.0%
2	Texas	9,366	6.8%
3	Florida	8,925	6.5%
4	Pennsylvania	7,151	5.2%
5	New York	6,398	4.7%
6	Illinois	5,989	4.4%
7	Ohio	5,828	4.3%
8	Michigan	4,752	3.5%
9	North Carolina	4,572	3.3%
10	Georgia	3,889	2.8%
11	Virginia	3,523	2.6%
12	New Jersey	3,468	2.5%
13	Tennessee	3,407	2.5%
14	Missouri	3,247	2.4%
15	Indiana	3,238	2.4%
16	Massachusetts	2,880	2.1%
17	Wisconsin	2,829	2.1%
18	Alabama	2,740	2.0%
19	Washington	2,725	2.0%
20	Maryland	2,365	1.7%
21	South Carolina	2,291	1.7%
22	Arizona	2,226	1.6%
23	Minnesota	2,219	1.6%
24	Kentucky	2,197	1.6%
25	Louisiana	2,195	1.6%
26	Oklahoma	2,085	1.5%
27	Oregon	1,978	1.4%
28	Arkansas	1,884	1.4%
29	Iowa	1,718	1.3%
30	Mississippi	1,585	1.2%
31	Connecticut	1,547	1.1%
32	Colorado	1,532	1.1%
33	Kansas	1,489	1.1%
34	West Virginia	1,072	0.8%
35	Nebraska	922	0.7%
36	Nevada	847	0.6%
37	New Mexico	739	0.5%
38	Idaho	725	0.5%
39	Utah	674	0.5%
40	Maine	670	0.5%
41	Hawaii	665	0.5%
42	New Hampshire	494	0.4%
43	Montana	461	0.3%
44	South Dakota	442	0.3%
45	North Dakota	428	0.3%
46	Rhode Island	421	0.3%
47	Delaware	384	0.3%
48	Vermont	264	0.2%
49	Wyoming	236	0.2%
50	Alaska	177	0.1%
	District of Columbia	221	0.2%

Source: U.S. Department of Health and Human Services, National Center for Health Statistics
   "National Vital Statistics Reports" (Vol. 57, No. 14, April 17, 2009, http://www.cdc.gov/nchs/deaths.htm)
*Final data by state of residence. Cerebrovascular diseases include stroke and other disorders of the blood vessels of the brain.

Death Rate by Cerebrovascular Diseases in 2006

National Rate = 45.8 Deaths per 100,000 Population*

ALPHA ORDER

RANK	STATE	RATE
3	Alabama	59.6
49	Alaska	26.4
45	Arizona	36.1
2	Arkansas	67.0
39	California	41.3
48	Colorado	32.2
33	Connecticut	44.1
31	Delaware	45.0
25	Florida	49.3
38	Georgia	41.5
17	Hawaii	51.7
24	Idaho	49.4
28	Illinois	46.7
19	Indiana	51.3
6	Iowa	57.6
12	Kansas	53.9
15	Kentucky	52.2
20	Louisiana	51.2
23	Maine	50.7
37	Maryland	42.1
32	Massachusetts	44.7
27	Michigan	47.1
34	Minnesota	42.9
11	Mississippi	54.5
10	Missouri	55.6
26	Montana	48.8
16	Nebraska	52.1
46	Nevada	33.9
44	New Hampshire	37.6
41	New Jersey	39.7
43	New Mexico	37.8
47	New York	33.1
18	North Carolina	51.6
1	North Dakota	67.3
22	Ohio	50.8
5	Oklahoma	58.3
13	Oregon	53.4
7	Pennsylvania	57.5
42	Rhode Island	39.4
14	South Carolina	53.0
8	South Dakota	56.5
9	Tennessee	56.4
40	Texas	39.8
49	Utah	26.4
36	Vermont	42.3
29	Virginia	46.1
35	Washington	42.6
4	West Virginia	59.0
21	Wisconsin	50.9
30	Wyoming	45.8

RANK ORDER

RANK	STATE	RATE
1	North Dakota	67.3
2	Arkansas	67.0
3	Alabama	59.6
4	West Virginia	59.0
5	Oklahoma	58.3
6	Iowa	57.6
7	Pennsylvania	57.5
8	South Dakota	56.5
9	Tennessee	56.4
10	Missouri	55.6
11	Mississippi	54.5
12	Kansas	53.9
13	Oregon	53.4
14	South Carolina	53.0
15	Kentucky	52.2
16	Nebraska	52.1
17	Hawaii	51.7
18	North Carolina	51.6
19	Indiana	51.3
20	Louisiana	51.2
21	Wisconsin	50.9
22	Ohio	50.8
23	Maine	50.7
24	Idaho	49.4
25	Florida	49.3
26	Montana	48.8
27	Michigan	47.1
28	Illinois	46.7
29	Virginia	46.1
30	Wyoming	45.8
31	Delaware	45.0
32	Massachusetts	44.7
33	Connecticut	44.1
34	Minnesota	42.9
35	Washington	42.6
36	Vermont	42.3
37	Maryland	42.1
38	Georgia	41.5
39	California	41.3
40	Texas	39.8
41	New Jersey	39.7
42	Rhode Island	39.4
43	New Mexico	37.8
44	New Hampshire	37.6
45	Arizona	36.1
46	Nevada	33.9
47	New York	33.1
48	Colorado	32.2
49	Alaska	26.4
49	Utah	26.4
	District of Columbia	38.0

Source: U.S. Department of Health and Human Services, National Center for Health Statistics
   "National Vital Statistics Reports" (Vol. 57, No. 14, April 17, 2009, http://www.cdc.gov/nchs/deaths.htm)
*Final data by state of residence. Cerebrovascular diseases include stroke and other disorders of the blood vessels of the brain.
Not age-adjusted.

Age-Adjusted Death Rate by Cerebrovascular Diseases in 2006

National Rate = 43.6 Deaths per 100,000 Population*

ALPHA ORDER

RANK	STATE	RATE
2	Alabama	55.3
19	Alaska	47.2
48	Arizona	34.5
1	Arkansas	58.8
24	California	44.9
39	Colorado	38.9
44	Connecticut	36.3
34	Delaware	41.7
47	Florida	35.3
10	Georgia	51.3
30	Hawaii	43.2
7	Idaho	51.8
21	Illinois	45.3
14	Indiana	49.0
31	Iowa	42.9
20	Kansas	46.5
11	Kentucky	50.3
9	Louisiana	51.5
35	Maine	41.3
28	Maryland	43.6
41	Massachusetts	37.6
25	Michigan	44.7
38	Minnesota	39.4
4	Mississippi	53.4
12	Missouri	49.5
35	Montana	41.3
27	Nebraska	43.8
37	Nevada	39.6
46	New Hampshire	35.5
45	New Jersey	35.8
41	New Mexico	37.6
50	New York	29.8
6	North Carolina	52.4
13	North Dakota	49.3
23	Ohio	45.1
4	Oklahoma	53.4
17	Oregon	47.9
29	Pennsylvania	43.4
49	Rhode Island	31.2
8	South Carolina	51.6
31	South Dakota	42.9
3	Tennessee	54.9
16	Texas	48.3
43	Utah	36.4
40	Vermont	37.8
15	Virginia	48.8
31	Washington	42.9
18	West Virginia	47.6
26	Wisconsin	44.6
21	Wyoming	45.3

RANK ORDER

RANK	STATE	RATE
1	Arkansas	58.8
2	Alabama	55.3
3	Tennessee	54.9
4	Mississippi	53.4
4	Oklahoma	53.4
6	North Carolina	52.4
7	Idaho	51.8
8	South Carolina	51.6
9	Louisiana	51.5
10	Georgia	51.3
11	Kentucky	50.3
12	Missouri	49.5
13	North Dakota	49.3
14	Indiana	49.0
15	Virginia	48.8
16	Texas	48.3
17	Oregon	47.9
18	West Virginia	47.6
19	Alaska	47.2
20	Kansas	46.5
21	Illinois	45.3
21	Wyoming	45.3
23	Ohio	45.1
24	California	44.9
25	Michigan	44.7
26	Wisconsin	44.6
27	Nebraska	43.8
28	Maryland	43.6
29	Pennsylvania	43.4
30	Hawaii	43.2
31	Iowa	42.9
31	South Dakota	42.9
31	Washington	42.9
34	Delaware	41.7
35	Maine	41.3
35	Montana	41.3
37	Nevada	39.6
38	Minnesota	39.4
39	Colorado	38.9
40	Vermont	37.8
41	Massachusetts	37.6
41	New Mexico	37.6
43	Utah	36.4
44	Connecticut	36.3
45	New Jersey	35.8
46	New Hampshire	35.5
47	Florida	35.3
48	Arizona	34.5
49	Rhode Island	31.2
50	New York	29.8

District of Columbia	36.9

Source: U.S. Department of Health and Human Services, National Center for Health Statistics
   "National Vital Statistics Reports" (Vol. 57, No. 14, April 17, 2009, http://www.cdc.gov/nchs/deaths.htm)
*Final data by state of residence. Cerebrovascular diseases include stroke and other disorders of the blood vessels of the brain.
Age-adjusted rates based on the year 2000 standard population.

Deaths by Chronic Liver Disease and Cirrhosis in 2006

National Total = 27,555 Deaths*

<table>
<tr><td colspan="4">ALPHA ORDER</td><td colspan="4">RANK ORDER</td></tr>
<tr><td>RANK</td><td>STATE</td><td>DEATHS</td><td>% of USA</td><td>RANK</td><td>STATE</td><td>DEATHS</td><td>% of USA</td></tr>
<tr><td>18</td><td>Alabama</td><td>489</td><td>1.8%</td><td>1</td><td>California</td><td>3,840</td><td>13.9%</td></tr>
<tr><td>50</td><td>Alaska</td><td>46</td><td>0.2%</td><td>2</td><td>Texas</td><td>2,385</td><td>8.7%</td></tr>
<tr><td>10</td><td>Arizona</td><td>716</td><td>2.6%</td><td>3</td><td>Florida</td><td>2,185</td><td>7.9%</td></tr>
<tr><td>33</td><td>Arkansas</td><td>259</td><td>0.9%</td><td>4</td><td>New York</td><td>1,223</td><td>4.4%</td></tr>
<tr><td>1</td><td>California</td><td>3,840</td><td>13.9%</td><td>5</td><td>Ohio</td><td>1,096</td><td>4.0%</td></tr>
<tr><td>20</td><td>Colorado</td><td>463</td><td>1.7%</td><td>6</td><td>Illinois</td><td>1,071</td><td>3.9%</td></tr>
<tr><td>31</td><td>Connecticut</td><td>273</td><td>1.0%</td><td>7</td><td>Pennsylvania</td><td>1,057</td><td>3.8%</td></tr>
<tr><td>46</td><td>Delaware</td><td>74</td><td>0.3%</td><td>8</td><td>Michigan</td><td>981</td><td>3.6%</td></tr>
<tr><td>3</td><td>Florida</td><td>2,185</td><td>7.9%</td><td>9</td><td>North Carolina</td><td>804</td><td>2.9%</td></tr>
<tr><td>12</td><td>Georgia</td><td>664</td><td>2.4%</td><td>10</td><td>Arizona</td><td>716</td><td>2.6%</td></tr>
<tr><td>44</td><td>Hawaii</td><td>91</td><td>0.3%</td><td>11</td><td>New Jersey</td><td>674</td><td>2.4%</td></tr>
<tr><td>39</td><td>Idaho</td><td>124</td><td>0.5%</td><td>12</td><td>Georgia</td><td>664</td><td>2.4%</td></tr>
<tr><td>6</td><td>Illinois</td><td>1,071</td><td>3.9%</td><td>13</td><td>Tennessee</td><td>636</td><td>2.3%</td></tr>
<tr><td>16</td><td>Indiana</td><td>510</td><td>1.9%</td><td>14</td><td>Washington</td><td>601</td><td>2.2%</td></tr>
<tr><td>36</td><td>Iowa</td><td>167</td><td>0.6%</td><td>15</td><td>Virginia</td><td>567</td><td>2.1%</td></tr>
<tr><td>35</td><td>Kansas</td><td>224</td><td>0.8%</td><td>16</td><td>Indiana</td><td>510</td><td>1.9%</td></tr>
<tr><td>26</td><td>Kentucky</td><td>359</td><td>1.3%</td><td>17</td><td>Massachusetts</td><td>508</td><td>1.8%</td></tr>
<tr><td>27</td><td>Louisiana</td><td>342</td><td>1.2%</td><td>18</td><td>Alabama</td><td>489</td><td>1.8%</td></tr>
<tr><td>37</td><td>Maine</td><td>147</td><td>0.5%</td><td>19</td><td>South Carolina</td><td>479</td><td>1.7%</td></tr>
<tr><td>25</td><td>Maryland</td><td>408</td><td>1.5%</td><td>20</td><td>Colorado</td><td>463</td><td>1.7%</td></tr>
<tr><td>17</td><td>Massachusetts</td><td>508</td><td>1.8%</td><td>21</td><td>Missouri</td><td>458</td><td>1.7%</td></tr>
<tr><td>8</td><td>Michigan</td><td>981</td><td>3.6%</td><td>22</td><td>Wisconsin</td><td>452</td><td>1.6%</td></tr>
<tr><td>28</td><td>Minnesota</td><td>325</td><td>1.2%</td><td>23</td><td>Oklahoma</td><td>445</td><td>1.6%</td></tr>
<tr><td>32</td><td>Mississippi</td><td>267</td><td>1.0%</td><td>24</td><td>Oregon</td><td>422</td><td>1.5%</td></tr>
<tr><td>21</td><td>Missouri</td><td>458</td><td>1.7%</td><td>25</td><td>Maryland</td><td>408</td><td>1.5%</td></tr>
<tr><td>41</td><td>Montana</td><td>113</td><td>0.4%</td><td>26</td><td>Kentucky</td><td>359</td><td>1.3%</td></tr>
<tr><td>40</td><td>Nebraska</td><td>123</td><td>0.4%</td><td>27</td><td>Louisiana</td><td>342</td><td>1.2%</td></tr>
<tr><td>30</td><td>Nevada</td><td>291</td><td>1.1%</td><td>28</td><td>Minnesota</td><td>325</td><td>1.2%</td></tr>
<tr><td>43</td><td>New Hampshire</td><td>100</td><td>0.4%</td><td>29</td><td>New Mexico</td><td>308</td><td>1.1%</td></tr>
<tr><td>11</td><td>New Jersey</td><td>674</td><td>2.4%</td><td>30</td><td>Nevada</td><td>291</td><td>1.1%</td></tr>
<tr><td>29</td><td>New Mexico</td><td>308</td><td>1.1%</td><td>31</td><td>Connecticut</td><td>273</td><td>1.0%</td></tr>
<tr><td>4</td><td>New York</td><td>1,223</td><td>4.4%</td><td>32</td><td>Mississippi</td><td>267</td><td>1.0%</td></tr>
<tr><td>9</td><td>North Carolina</td><td>804</td><td>2.9%</td><td>33</td><td>Arkansas</td><td>259</td><td>0.9%</td></tr>
<tr><td>49</td><td>North Dakota</td><td>51</td><td>0.2%</td><td>34</td><td>West Virginia</td><td>237</td><td>0.9%</td></tr>
<tr><td>5</td><td>Ohio</td><td>1,096</td><td>4.0%</td><td>35</td><td>Kansas</td><td>224</td><td>0.8%</td></tr>
<tr><td>23</td><td>Oklahoma</td><td>445</td><td>1.6%</td><td>36</td><td>Iowa</td><td>167</td><td>0.6%</td></tr>
<tr><td>24</td><td>Oregon</td><td>422</td><td>1.5%</td><td>37</td><td>Maine</td><td>147</td><td>0.5%</td></tr>
<tr><td>7</td><td>Pennsylvania</td><td>1,057</td><td>3.8%</td><td>38</td><td>Utah</td><td>134</td><td>0.5%</td></tr>
<tr><td>42</td><td>Rhode Island</td><td>106</td><td>0.4%</td><td>39</td><td>Idaho</td><td>124</td><td>0.5%</td></tr>
<tr><td>19</td><td>South Carolina</td><td>479</td><td>1.7%</td><td>40</td><td>Nebraska</td><td>123</td><td>0.4%</td></tr>
<tr><td>45</td><td>South Dakota</td><td>82</td><td>0.3%</td><td>41</td><td>Montana</td><td>113</td><td>0.4%</td></tr>
<tr><td>13</td><td>Tennessee</td><td>636</td><td>2.3%</td><td>42</td><td>Rhode Island</td><td>106</td><td>0.4%</td></tr>
<tr><td>2</td><td>Texas</td><td>2,385</td><td>8.7%</td><td>43</td><td>New Hampshire</td><td>100</td><td>0.4%</td></tr>
<tr><td>38</td><td>Utah</td><td>134</td><td>0.5%</td><td>44</td><td>Hawaii</td><td>91</td><td>0.3%</td></tr>
<tr><td>48</td><td>Vermont</td><td>55</td><td>0.2%</td><td>45</td><td>South Dakota</td><td>82</td><td>0.3%</td></tr>
<tr><td>15</td><td>Virginia</td><td>567</td><td>2.1%</td><td>46</td><td>Delaware</td><td>74</td><td>0.3%</td></tr>
<tr><td>14</td><td>Washington</td><td>601</td><td>2.2%</td><td>47</td><td>Wyoming</td><td>69</td><td>0.3%</td></tr>
<tr><td>34</td><td>West Virginia</td><td>237</td><td>0.9%</td><td>48</td><td>Vermont</td><td>55</td><td>0.2%</td></tr>
<tr><td>22</td><td>Wisconsin</td><td>452</td><td>1.6%</td><td>49</td><td>North Dakota</td><td>51</td><td>0.2%</td></tr>
<tr><td>47</td><td>Wyoming</td><td>69</td><td>0.3%</td><td>50</td><td>Alaska</td><td>46</td><td>0.2%</td></tr>
<tr><td></td><td></td><td></td><td></td><td></td><td>District of Columbia</td><td>54</td><td>0.2%</td></tr>
</table>

Source: U.S. Department of Health and Human Services, National Center for Health Statistics
"National Vital Statistics Reports" (Vol. 57, No. 14, April 17, 2009, http://www.cdc.gov/nchs/deaths.htm)
*Final data by state of residence. Cirrhosis of the liver is characterized by the replacement of normal tissue with fibrous tissue and the loss of functional liver cells. It can result from alcohol abuse, nutritional deprivation, or infection especially by the hepatitis virus.

Death Rate by Chronic Liver Disease and Cirrhosis in 2006

National Rate = 9.2 Deaths per 100,000 Population*

<table>
<tr><td colspan="3">ALPHA ORDER</td><td colspan="3">RANK ORDER</td></tr>
<tr><td>RANK</td><td>STATE</td><td>RATE</td><td>RANK</td><td>STATE</td><td>RATE</td></tr>
<tr><td>12</td><td>Alabama</td><td>10.6</td><td>1</td><td>New Mexico</td><td>15.8</td></tr>
<tr><td>46</td><td>Alaska</td><td>6.9</td><td>2</td><td>Wyoming</td><td>13.4</td></tr>
<tr><td>8</td><td>Arizona</td><td>11.6</td><td>3</td><td>West Virginia</td><td>13.0</td></tr>
<tr><td>22</td><td>Arkansas</td><td>9.2</td><td>4</td><td>Oklahoma</td><td>12.4</td></tr>
<tr><td>13</td><td>California</td><td>10.5</td><td>5</td><td>Florida</td><td>12.1</td></tr>
<tr><td>18</td><td>Colorado</td><td>9.7</td><td>6</td><td>Montana</td><td>12.0</td></tr>
<tr><td>37</td><td>Connecticut</td><td>7.8</td><td>7</td><td>Nevada</td><td>11.7</td></tr>
<tr><td>26</td><td>Delaware</td><td>8.7</td><td>8</td><td>Arizona</td><td>11.6</td></tr>
<tr><td>5</td><td>Florida</td><td>12.1</td><td>9</td><td>Oregon</td><td>11.4</td></tr>
<tr><td>43</td><td>Georgia</td><td>7.1</td><td>10</td><td>Maine</td><td>11.1</td></tr>
<tr><td>43</td><td>Hawaii</td><td>7.1</td><td>10</td><td>South Carolina</td><td>11.1</td></tr>
<tr><td>27</td><td>Idaho</td><td>8.5</td><td>12</td><td>Alabama</td><td>10.6</td></tr>
<tr><td>30</td><td>Illinois</td><td>8.3</td><td>13</td><td>California</td><td>10.5</td></tr>
<tr><td>31</td><td>Indiana</td><td>8.1</td><td>13</td><td>South Dakota</td><td>10.5</td></tr>
<tr><td>49</td><td>Iowa</td><td>5.6</td><td>13</td><td>Tennessee</td><td>10.5</td></tr>
<tr><td>31</td><td>Kansas</td><td>8.1</td><td>16</td><td>Texas</td><td>10.1</td></tr>
<tr><td>27</td><td>Kentucky</td><td>8.5</td><td>17</td><td>Rhode Island</td><td>9.9</td></tr>
<tr><td>34</td><td>Louisiana</td><td>8.0</td><td>18</td><td>Colorado</td><td>9.7</td></tr>
<tr><td>10</td><td>Maine</td><td>11.1</td><td>18</td><td>Michigan</td><td>9.7</td></tr>
<tr><td>42</td><td>Maryland</td><td>7.3</td><td>20</td><td>Ohio</td><td>9.5</td></tr>
<tr><td>36</td><td>Massachusetts</td><td>7.9</td><td>21</td><td>Washington</td><td>9.4</td></tr>
<tr><td>18</td><td>Michigan</td><td>9.7</td><td>22</td><td>Arkansas</td><td>9.2</td></tr>
<tr><td>47</td><td>Minnesota</td><td>6.3</td><td>22</td><td>Mississippi</td><td>9.2</td></tr>
<tr><td>22</td><td>Mississippi</td><td>9.2</td><td>24</td><td>North Carolina</td><td>9.1</td></tr>
<tr><td>37</td><td>Missouri</td><td>7.8</td><td>25</td><td>Vermont</td><td>8.8</td></tr>
<tr><td>6</td><td>Montana</td><td>12.0</td><td>26</td><td>Delaware</td><td>8.7</td></tr>
<tr><td>45</td><td>Nebraska</td><td>7.0</td><td>27</td><td>Idaho</td><td>8.5</td></tr>
<tr><td>7</td><td>Nevada</td><td>11.7</td><td>27</td><td>Kentucky</td><td>8.5</td></tr>
<tr><td>40</td><td>New Hampshire</td><td>7.6</td><td>27</td><td>Pennsylvania</td><td>8.5</td></tr>
<tr><td>39</td><td>New Jersey</td><td>7.7</td><td>30</td><td>Illinois</td><td>8.3</td></tr>
<tr><td>1</td><td>New Mexico</td><td>15.8</td><td>31</td><td>Indiana</td><td>8.1</td></tr>
<tr><td>47</td><td>New York</td><td>6.3</td><td>31</td><td>Kansas</td><td>8.1</td></tr>
<tr><td>24</td><td>North Carolina</td><td>9.1</td><td>31</td><td>Wisconsin</td><td>8.1</td></tr>
<tr><td>34</td><td>North Dakota</td><td>8.0</td><td>34</td><td>Louisiana</td><td>8.0</td></tr>
<tr><td>20</td><td>Ohio</td><td>9.5</td><td>34</td><td>North Dakota</td><td>8.0</td></tr>
<tr><td>4</td><td>Oklahoma</td><td>12.4</td><td>36</td><td>Massachusetts</td><td>7.9</td></tr>
<tr><td>9</td><td>Oregon</td><td>11.4</td><td>37</td><td>Connecticut</td><td>7.8</td></tr>
<tr><td>27</td><td>Pennsylvania</td><td>8.5</td><td>37</td><td>Missouri</td><td>7.8</td></tr>
<tr><td>17</td><td>Rhode Island</td><td>9.9</td><td>39</td><td>New Jersey</td><td>7.7</td></tr>
<tr><td>10</td><td>South Carolina</td><td>11.1</td><td>40</td><td>New Hampshire</td><td>7.6</td></tr>
<tr><td>13</td><td>South Dakota</td><td>10.5</td><td>41</td><td>Virginia</td><td>7.4</td></tr>
<tr><td>13</td><td>Tennessee</td><td>10.5</td><td>42</td><td>Maryland</td><td>7.3</td></tr>
<tr><td>16</td><td>Texas</td><td>10.1</td><td>43</td><td>Georgia</td><td>7.1</td></tr>
<tr><td>50</td><td>Utah</td><td>5.3</td><td>43</td><td>Hawaii</td><td>7.1</td></tr>
<tr><td>25</td><td>Vermont</td><td>8.8</td><td>45</td><td>Nebraska</td><td>7.0</td></tr>
<tr><td>41</td><td>Virginia</td><td>7.4</td><td>46</td><td>Alaska</td><td>6.9</td></tr>
<tr><td>21</td><td>Washington</td><td>9.4</td><td>47</td><td>Minnesota</td><td>6.3</td></tr>
<tr><td>3</td><td>West Virginia</td><td>13.0</td><td>47</td><td>New York</td><td>6.3</td></tr>
<tr><td>31</td><td>Wisconsin</td><td>8.1</td><td>49</td><td>Iowa</td><td>5.6</td></tr>
<tr><td>2</td><td>Wyoming</td><td>13.4</td><td>50</td><td>Utah</td><td>5.3</td></tr>
<tr><td></td><td></td><td></td><td></td><td>District of Columbia</td><td>9.3</td></tr>
</table>

Source: U.S. Department of Health and Human Services, National Center for Health Statistics
   "National Vital Statistics Reports" (Vol. 57, No. 14, April 17, 2009, http://www.cdc.gov/nchs/deaths.htm)
*Final data by state of residence. Cirrhosis of the liver is characterized by the replacement of normal tissue with fibrous tissue and the loss of functional liver cells. It can result from alcohol abuse, nutritional deprivation, or infection especially by the hepatitis virus. Not age-adjusted.

Age-Adjusted Death Rate by Chronic Liver Disease and Cirrhosis in 2006

National Rate = 8.8 Deaths per 100,000 Population*

ALPHA ORDER

RANK	STATE	RATE
16	Alabama	9.6
36	Alaska	7.3
4	Arizona	11.6
25	Arkansas	8.5
8	California	10.9
14	Colorado	9.9
42	Connecticut	7.0
27	Delaware	8.1
11	Florida	10.3
35	Georgia	7.5
47	Hawaii	6.5
23	Idaho	8.6
26	Illinois	8.2
29	Indiana	7.8
50	Iowa	5.0
32	Kansas	7.7
28	Kentucky	7.9
29	Louisiana	7.8
17	Maine	9.3
43	Maryland	6.9
39	Massachusetts	7.1
18	Michigan	9.1
48	Minnesota	6.0
19	Mississippi	9.0
36	Missouri	7.3
9	Montana	10.8
45	Nebraska	6.7
5	Nevada	11.4
43	New Hampshire	6.9
39	New Jersey	7.1
1	New Mexico	15.2
49	New York	5.9
23	North Carolina	8.6
33	North Dakota	7.6
22	Ohio	8.7
3	Oklahoma	11.9
10	Oregon	10.4
36	Pennsylvania	7.3
20	Rhode Island	8.9
12	South Carolina	10.2
13	South Dakota	10.1
15	Tennessee	9.7
6	Texas	11.0
45	Utah	6.7
29	Vermont	7.8
39	Virginia	7.1
20	Washington	8.9
6	West Virginia	11.0
33	Wisconsin	7.6
2	Wyoming	12.4

RANK ORDER

RANK	STATE	RATE
1	New Mexico	15.2
2	Wyoming	12.4
3	Oklahoma	11.9
4	Arizona	11.6
5	Nevada	11.4
6	Texas	11.0
6	West Virginia	11.0
8	California	10.9
9	Montana	10.8
10	Oregon	10.4
11	Florida	10.3
12	South Carolina	10.2
13	South Dakota	10.1
14	Colorado	9.9
15	Tennessee	9.7
16	Alabama	9.6
17	Maine	9.3
18	Michigan	9.1
19	Mississippi	9.0
20	Rhode Island	8.9
20	Washington	8.9
22	Ohio	8.7
23	Idaho	8.6
23	North Carolina	8.6
25	Arkansas	8.5
26	Illinois	8.2
27	Delaware	8.1
28	Kentucky	7.9
29	Indiana	7.8
29	Louisiana	7.8
29	Vermont	7.8
32	Kansas	7.7
33	North Dakota	7.6
33	Wisconsin	7.6
35	Georgia	7.5
36	Alaska	7.3
36	Missouri	7.3
36	Pennsylvania	7.3
39	Massachusetts	7.1
39	New Jersey	7.1
39	Virginia	7.1
42	Connecticut	7.0
43	Maryland	6.9
43	New Hampshire	6.9
45	Nebraska	6.7
45	Utah	6.7
47	Hawaii	6.5
48	Minnesota	6.0
49	New York	5.9
50	Iowa	5.0

	District of Columbia	9.3

Source: U.S. Department of Health and Human Services, National Center for Health Statistics
 "National Vital Statistics Reports" (Vol. 57, No. 14, April 17, 2009, http://www.cdc.gov/nchs/deaths.htm)
*Final data by state of residence. Cirrhosis of the liver is characterized by the replacement of normal tissue with fibrous tissue
and the loss of functional liver cells. It can result from alcohol abuse, nutritional deprivation, or infection especially by the
hepatitis virus. Age-adjusted rates based on the year 2000 standard population.

Deaths by Chronic Lower Respiratory Diseases in 2006

National Total = 124,583 Deaths*

RANK	STATE	DEATHS	% of USA
21	Alabama	2,309	1.9%
50	Alaska	140	0.1%
15	Arizona	2,799	2.2%
31	Arkansas	1,498	1.2%
1	California	12,829	10.3%
24	Colorado	1,932	1.6%
32	Connecticut	1,458	1.2%
46	Delaware	344	0.3%
2	Florida	8,912	7.2%
10	Georgia	3,387	2.7%
48	Hawaii	293	0.2%
39	Idaho	644	0.5%
7	Illinois	4,731	3.8%
11	Indiana	3,291	2.6%
29	Iowa	1,655	1.3%
30	Kansas	1,501	1.2%
19	Kentucky	2,407	1.9%
28	Louisiana	1,687	1.4%
38	Maine	783	0.6%
25	Maryland	1,832	1.5%
18	Massachusetts	2,535	2.0%
8	Michigan	4,474	3.6%
27	Minnesota	1,770	1.4%
33	Mississippi	1,378	1.1%
12	Missouri	3,017	2.4%
42	Montana	579	0.5%
37	Nebraska	878	0.7%
35	Nevada	1,066	0.9%
40	New Hampshire	603	0.5%
14	New Jersey	2,862	2.3%
36	New Mexico	888	0.7%
4	New York	6,329	5.1%
9	North Carolina	4,017	3.2%
49	North Dakota	283	0.2%
5	Ohio	6,054	4.9%
22	Oklahoma	2,192	1.8%
26	Oregon	1,828	1.5%
6	Pennsylvania	5,621	4.5%
43	Rhode Island	485	0.4%
23	South Carolina	1,935	1.6%
44	South Dakota	376	0.3%
13	Tennessee	2,980	2.4%
3	Texas	7,639	6.1%
41	Utah	591	0.5%
47	Vermont	320	0.3%
16	Virginia	2,697	2.2%
17	Washington	2,662	2.1%
34	West Virginia	1,267	1.0%
20	Wisconsin	2,354	1.9%
45	Wyoming	345	0.3%

RANK	STATE	DEATHS	% of USA
1	California	12,829	10.3%
2	Florida	8,912	7.2%
3	Texas	7,639	6.1%
4	New York	6,329	5.1%
5	Ohio	6,054	4.9%
6	Pennsylvania	5,621	4.5%
7	Illinois	4,731	3.8%
8	Michigan	4,474	3.6%
9	North Carolina	4,017	3.2%
10	Georgia	3,387	2.7%
11	Indiana	3,291	2.6%
12	Missouri	3,017	2.4%
13	Tennessee	2,980	2.4%
14	New Jersey	2,862	2.3%
15	Arizona	2,799	2.2%
16	Virginia	2,697	2.2%
17	Washington	2,662	2.1%
18	Massachusetts	2,535	2.0%
19	Kentucky	2,407	1.9%
20	Wisconsin	2,354	1.9%
21	Alabama	2,309	1.9%
22	Oklahoma	2,192	1.8%
23	South Carolina	1,935	1.6%
24	Colorado	1,932	1.6%
25	Maryland	1,832	1.5%
26	Oregon	1,828	1.5%
27	Minnesota	1,770	1.4%
28	Louisiana	1,687	1.4%
29	Iowa	1,655	1.3%
30	Kansas	1,501	1.2%
31	Arkansas	1,498	1.2%
32	Connecticut	1,458	1.2%
33	Mississippi	1,378	1.1%
34	West Virginia	1,267	1.0%
35	Nevada	1,066	0.9%
36	New Mexico	888	0.7%
37	Nebraska	878	0.7%
38	Maine	783	0.6%
39	Idaho	644	0.5%
40	New Hampshire	603	0.5%
41	Utah	591	0.5%
42	Montana	579	0.5%
43	Rhode Island	485	0.4%
44	South Dakota	376	0.3%
45	Wyoming	345	0.3%
46	Delaware	344	0.3%
47	Vermont	320	0.3%
48	Hawaii	293	0.2%
49	North Dakota	283	0.2%
50	Alaska	140	0.1%
	District of Columbia	126	0.1%

Source: U.S. Department of Health and Human Services, National Center for Health Statistics
"National Vital Statistics Reports" (Vol. 57, No. 14, April 17, 2009, http://www.cdc.gov/nchs/deaths.htm)
*Final data by state of residence. Chronic lower respiratory diseases are diseases of the lungs including bronchitis, emphysema, and asthma. Includes allied conditions.

Death Rate by Chronic Lower Respiratory Diseases in 2006

National Rate = 41.6 Deaths per 100,000 Population*

RANK	STATE	RATE		RANK	STATE	RATE
14	Alabama	50.2		1	West Virginia	69.7
50	Alaska	20.9		2	Wyoming	67.0
22	Arizona	45.4		3	Montana	61.3
9	Arkansas	53.3		4	Oklahoma	61.2
42	California	35.2		5	Maine	59.2
35	Colorado	40.6		6	Kentucky	57.2
33	Connecticut	41.6		7	Iowa	55.5
36	Delaware	40.3		8	Kansas	54.3
17	Florida	49.3		9	Arkansas	53.3
40	Georgia	36.2		10	Ohio	52.7
49	Hawaii	22.8		11	Indiana	52.1
30	Idaho	43.9		12	Missouri	51.6
39	Illinois	36.9		13	Vermont	51.3
11	Indiana	52.1		14	Alabama	50.2
7	Iowa	55.5		15	Nebraska	49.7
8	Kansas	54.3		16	Oregon	49.4
6	Kentucky	57.2		17	Florida	49.3
38	Louisiana	39.3		17	Tennessee	49.3
5	Maine	59.2		19	South Dakota	48.1
46	Maryland	32.6		20	Mississippi	47.3
37	Massachusetts	39.4		21	New Hampshire	45.9
29	Michigan	44.3		22	Arizona	45.4
43	Minnesota	34.3		22	New Mexico	45.4
20	Mississippi	47.3		22	North Carolina	45.4
12	Missouri	51.6		22	Rhode Island	45.4
3	Montana	61.3		26	Pennsylvania	45.2
15	Nebraska	49.7		27	South Carolina	44.8
31	Nevada	42.7		28	North Dakota	44.5
21	New Hampshire	45.9		29	Michigan	44.3
44	New Jersey	32.8		30	Idaho	43.9
22	New Mexico	45.4		31	Nevada	42.7
44	New York	32.8		32	Wisconsin	42.4
22	North Carolina	45.4		33	Connecticut	41.6
28	North Dakota	44.5		33	Washington	41.6
10	Ohio	52.7		35	Colorado	40.6
4	Oklahoma	61.2		36	Delaware	40.3
16	Oregon	49.4		37	Massachusetts	39.4
26	Pennsylvania	45.2		38	Louisiana	39.3
22	Rhode Island	45.4		39	Illinois	36.9
27	South Carolina	44.8		40	Georgia	36.2
19	South Dakota	48.1		41	Virginia	35.3
17	Tennessee	49.3		42	California	35.2
47	Texas	32.5		43	Minnesota	34.3
48	Utah	23.2		44	New Jersey	32.8
13	Vermont	51.3		44	New York	32.8
41	Virginia	35.3		46	Maryland	32.6
33	Washington	41.6		47	Texas	32.5
1	West Virginia	69.7		48	Utah	23.2
32	Wisconsin	42.4		49	Hawaii	22.8
2	Wyoming	67.0		50	Alaska	20.9
					District of Columbia	21.7

ALPHA ORDER

RANK ORDER

Source: U.S. Department of Health and Human Services, National Center for Health Statistics
   "National Vital Statistics Reports" (Vol. 57, No. 14, April 17, 2009, http://www.cdc.gov/nchs/deaths.htm)
*Final data by state of residence. Chronic lower respiratory diseases are diseases of the lungs including bronchitis, emphysema, and asthma. Includes allied conditions. Not age-adjusted.

Age-Adjusted Death Rate by Chronic Lower Respiratory Diseases in 2006

National Rate = 40.5 Deaths per 100,000 Population*

ALPHA ORDER

RANK	STATE	RATE
15	Alabama	46.7
38	Alaska	37.2
26	Arizona	43.7
13	Arkansas	47.4
33	California	39.1
8	Colorado	49.3
41	Connecticut	35.5
36	Delaware	37.5
40	Florida	35.9
23	Georgia	45.1
50	Hawaii	19.4
17	Idaho	46.6
39	Illinois	36.9
6	Indiana	50.8
22	Iowa	45.3
7	Kansas	49.9
4	Kentucky	55.0
32	Louisiana	39.6
8	Maine	49.3
45	Maryland	34.3
43	Massachusetts	34.5
29	Michigan	42.9
46	Minnesota	33.3
15	Mississippi	46.7
14	Missouri	47.3
5	Montana	53.6
25	Nebraska	44.2
10	Nevada	49.0
24	New Hampshire	44.4
48	New Jersey	30.3
21	New Mexico	45.5
49	New York	30.1
19	North Carolina	45.9
43	North Dakota	34.5
11	Ohio	47.9
2	Oklahoma	57.1
20	Oregon	45.7
42	Pennsylvania	35.4
35	Rhode Island	38.2
27	South Carolina	43.2
31	South Dakota	39.7
12	Tennessee	47.8
30	Texas	39.9
47	Utah	31.9
18	Vermont	46.3
37	Virginia	37.4
28	Washington	43.1
3	West Virginia	56.6
34	Wisconsin	38.8
1	Wyoming	67.0

RANK ORDER

RANK	STATE	RATE
1	Wyoming	67.0
2	Oklahoma	57.1
3	West Virginia˙	56.6
4	Kentucky	55.0
5	Montana	53.6
6	Indiana	50.8
7	Kansas	49.9
8	Colorado	49.3
8	Maine	49.3
10	Nevada	49.0
11	Ohio	47.9
12	Tennessee	47.8
13	Arkansas	47.4
14	Missouri	47.3
15	Alabama	46.7
15	Mississippi	46.7
17	Idaho	46.6
18	Vermont	46.3
19	North Carolina	45.9
20	Oregon	45.7
21	New Mexico	45.5
22	Iowa	45.3
23	Georgia	45.1
24	New Hampshire	44.4
25	Nebraska	44.2
26	Arizona	43.7
27	South Carolina	43.2
28	Washington	43.1
29	Michigan	42.9
30	Texas	39.9
31	South Dakota	39.7
32	Louisiana	39.6
33	California	39.1
34	Wisconsin	38.8
35	Rhode Island	38.2
36	Delaware	37.5
37	Virginia	37.4
38	Alaska	37.2
39	Illinois	36.9
40	Florida	35.9
41	Connecticut	35.5
42	Pennsylvania	35.4
43	Massachusetts	34.5
43	North Dakota	34.5
45	Maryland	34.3
46	Minnesota	33.3
47	Utah	31.9
48	New Jersey	30.3
49	New York	30.1
50	Hawaii	19.4

	District of Columbia	21.5

Source: U.S. Department of Health and Human Services, National Center for Health Statistics
    "National Vital Statistics Reports" (Vol. 57, No. 14, April 17, 2009, http://www.cdc.gov/nchs/deaths.htm)
*Final data by state of residence. Chronic lower respiratory diseases are diseases of the lungs including bronchitis, emphysema,
and asthma. Includes allied conditions. Age-adjusted rates based on the year 2000 standard population.

Deaths by Diabetes Mellitus in 2006

National Total = 72,449 Deaths*

ALPHA ORDER

RANK ORDER

RANK	STATE	DEATHS	% of USA
18	Alabama	1,453	2.0%
50	Alaska	109	0.2%
21	Arizona	1,206	1.7%
28	Arkansas	839	1.2%
1	California	7,376	10.2%
34	Colorado	677	0.9%
30	Connecticut	782	1.1%
47	Delaware	191	0.3%
3	Florida	5,172	7.1%
13	Georgia	1,657	2.3%
42	Hawaii	271	0.4%
39	Idaho	320	0.4%
8	Illinois	2,795	3.9%
12	Indiana	1,682	2.3%
29	Iowa	804	1.1%
31	Kansas	749	1.0%
24	Kentucky	1,141	1.6%
16	Louisiana	1,536	2.1%
38	Maine	343	0.5%
19	Maryland	1,237	1.7%
27	Massachusetts	1,132	1.6%
7	Michigan	2,830	3.9%
23	Minnesota	1,158	1.6%
33	Mississippi	707	1.0%
17	Missouri	1,493	2.1%
44	Montana	249	0.3%
37	Nebraska	437	0.6%
41	Nevada	294	0.4%
40	New Hampshire	296	0.4%
9	New Jersey	2,454	3.4%
35	New Mexico	606	0.8%
4	New York	3,848	5.3%
10	North Carolina	2,234	3.1%
45	North Dakota	208	0.3%
5	Ohio	3,761	5.2%
22	Oklahoma	1,166	1.6%
25	Oregon	1,139	1.6%
6	Pennsylvania	3,466	4.8%
46	Rhode Island	206	0.3%
26	South Carolina	1,136	1.6%
43	South Dakota	262	0.4%
11	Tennessee	1,715	2.4%
2	Texas	5,201	7.2%
36	Utah	496	0.7%
48	Vermont	175	0.2%
14	Virginia	1,632	2.3%
15	Washington	1,543	2.1%
32	West Virginia	743	1.0%
20	Wisconsin	1,212	1.7%
49	Wyoming	126	0.2%

RANK	STATE	DEATHS	% of USA
1	California	7,376	10.2%
2	Texas	5,201	7.2%
3	Florida	5,172	7.1%
4	New York	3,848	5.3%
5	Ohio	3,761	5.2%
6	Pennsylvania	3,466	4.8%
7	Michigan	2,830	3.9%
8	Illinois	2,795	3.9%
9	New Jersey	2,454	3.4%
10	North Carolina	2,234	3.1%
11	Tennessee	1,715	2.4%
12	Indiana	1,682	2.3%
13	Georgia	1,657	2.3%
14	Virginia	1,632	2.3%
15	Washington	1,543	2.1%
16	Louisiana	1,536	2.1%
17	Missouri	1,493	2.1%
18	Alabama	1,453	2.0%
19	Maryland	1,237	1.7%
20	Wisconsin	1,212	1.7%
21	Arizona	1,206	1.7%
22	Oklahoma	1,166	1.6%
23	Minnesota	1,158	1.6%
24	Kentucky	1,141	1.6%
25	Oregon	1,139	1.6%
26	South Carolina	1,136	1.6%
27	Massachusetts	1,132	1.6%
28	Arkansas	839	1.2%
29	Iowa	804	1.1%
30	Connecticut	782	1.1%
31	Kansas	749	1.0%
32	West Virginia	743	1.0%
33	Mississippi	707	1.0%
34	Colorado	677	0.9%
35	New Mexico	606	0.8%
36	Utah	496	0.7%
37	Nebraska	437	0.6%
38	Maine	343	0.5%
39	Idaho	320	0.4%
40	New Hampshire	296	0.4%
41	Nevada	294	0.4%
42	Hawaii	271	0.4%
43	South Dakota	262	0.4%
44	Montana	249	0.3%
45	North Dakota	208	0.3%
46	Rhode Island	206	0.3%
47	Delaware	191	0.3%
48	Vermont	175	0.2%
49	Wyoming	126	0.2%
50	Alaska	109	0.2%
	District of Columbia	184	0.3%

Source: U.S. Department of Health and Human Services, National Center for Health Statistics
"National Vital Statistics Reports" (Vol. 57, No. 14, April 17, 2009, http://www.cdc.gov/nchs/deaths.htm)
*Final data by state of residence. A severe, chronic form of diabetes caused by insufficient production of insulin and resulting in abnormal metabolism of carbohydrates, fats, and proteins. The disease, which typically appears in childhood or adolescence, is characterized by increased sugar levels in the blood and urine, excessive thirst, and frequent urination.

Death Rate by Diabetes Mellitus in 2006

National Rate = 24.2 Deaths per 100,000 Population*

ALPHA ORDER				RANK ORDER		
RANK	STATE	RATE		RANK	STATE	RATE
7	Alabama	31.6		1	West Virginia	40.9
48	Alaska	16.3		2	Louisiana	35.8
43	Arizona	19.6		3	South Dakota	33.5
10	Arkansas	29.8		4	Ohio	32.8
41	California	20.2		5	North Dakota	32.7
49	Colorado	14.2		6	Oklahoma	32.6
33	Connecticut	22.3		7	Alabama	31.6
31	Delaware	22.4		8	New Mexico	31.0
11	Florida	28.6		9	Oregon	30.8
46	Georgia	17.7		10	Arkansas	29.8
40	Hawaii	21.1		11	Florida	28.6
36	Idaho	21.8		12	Tennessee	28.4
36	Illinois	21.8		13	New Jersey	28.1
20	Indiana	26.6		14	Michigan	28.0
19	Iowa	27.0		14	Vermont	28.0
17	Kansas	27.1		16	Pennsylvania	27.9
17	Kentucky	27.1		17	Kansas	27.1
2	Louisiana	35.8		17	Kentucky	27.1
23	Maine	26.0		19	Iowa	27.0
35	Maryland	22.0		20	Indiana	26.6
47	Massachusetts	17.6		21	Montana	26.4
14	Michigan	28.0		22	South Carolina	26.3
31	Minnesota	22.4		23	Maine	26.0
28	Mississippi	24.3		24	Missouri	25.6
24	Missouri	25.6		25	North Carolina	25.2
21	Montana	26.4		26	Nebraska	24.7
26	Nebraska	24.7		27	Wyoming	24.5
50	Nevada	11.8		28	Mississippi	24.3
30	New Hampshire	22.5		29	Washington	24.1
13	New Jersey	28.1		30	New Hampshire	22.5
8	New Mexico	31.0		31	Delaware	22.4
42	New York	19.9		31	Minnesota	22.4
25	North Carolina	25.2		33	Connecticut	22.3
5	North Dakota	32.7		34	Texas	22.1
4	Ohio	32.8		35	Maryland	22.0
6	Oklahoma	32.6		36	Idaho	21.8
9	Oregon	30.8		36	Illinois	21.8
16	Pennsylvania	27.9		36	Wisconsin	21.8
45	Rhode Island	19.3		39	Virginia	21.4
22	South Carolina	26.3		40	Hawaii	21.1
3	South Dakota	33.5		41	California	20.2
12	Tennessee	28.4		42	New York	19.9
34	Texas	22.1		43	Arizona	19.6
44	Utah	19.5		44	Utah	19.5
14	Vermont	28.0		45	Rhode Island	19.3
39	Virginia	21.4		46	Georgia	17.7
29	Washington	24.1		47	Massachusetts	17.6
1	West Virginia	40.9		48	Alaska	16.3
36	Wisconsin	21.8		49	Colorado	14.2
27	Wyoming	24.5		50	Nevada	11.8

District of Columbia   31.6

Source: U.S. Department of Health and Human Services, National Center for Health Statistics
"National Vital Statistics Reports" (Vol. 57, No. 14, April 17, 2009, http://www.cdc.gov/nchs/deaths.htm)
*Final data by state of residence. A severe, chronic form of diabetes caused by insufficient production of insulin and resulting in abnormal metabolism of carbohydrates, fats, and proteins. The disease, which typically appears in childhood or adolescence, is characterized by increased sugar levels in the blood and urine, excessive thirst, and frequent urination. Not age-adjusted.

Age-Adjusted Death Rate by Diabetes Mellitus in 2006

National Rate = 23.3 Deaths per 100,000 Population*

ALPHA ORDER

RANK	STATE	RATE
6	Alabama	29.3
18	Alaska	25.6
44	Arizona	19.0
10	Arkansas	26.9
31	California	22.1
47	Colorado	16.6
43	Connecticut	19.2
41	Delaware	20.5
35	Florida	21.7
40	Georgia	20.6
46	Hawaii	18.1
27	Idaho	23.0
36	Illinois	21.6
17	Indiana	25.8
33	Iowa	21.9
22	Kansas	24.7
15	Kentucky	25.9
1	Louisiana	35.5
37	Maine	21.4
29	Maryland	22.4
49	Massachusetts	15.4
11	Michigan	26.8
37	Minnesota	21.4
24	Mississippi	23.8
26	Missouri	23.4
27	Montana	23.0
31	Nebraska	22.1
50	Nevada	12.8
39	New Hampshire	21.2
15	New Jersey	25.9
3	New Mexico	30.5
45	New York	18.3
20	North Carolina	24.9
12	North Dakota	26.3
5	Ohio	29.6
4	Oklahoma	30.3
7	Oregon	28.2
30	Pennsylvania	22.2
48	Rhode Island	16.2
19	South Carolina	25.0
8	South Dakota	27.1
8	Tennessee	27.1
13	Texas	26.1
13	Utah	26.1
20	Vermont	24.9
34	Virginia	21.8
23	Washington	24.4
2	West Virginia	33.1
42	Wisconsin	19.7
25	Wyoming	23.7

RANK ORDER

RANK	STATE	RATE
1	Louisiana	35.5
2	West Virginia	33.1
3	New Mexico	30.5
4	Oklahoma	30.3
5	Ohio	29.6
6	Alabama	29.3
7	Oregon	28.2
8	South Dakota	27.1
8	Tennessee	27.1
10	Arkansas	26.9
11	Michigan	26.8
12	North Dakota	26.3
13	Texas	26.1
13	Utah	26.1
15	Kentucky	25.9
15	New Jersey	25.9
17	Indiana	25.8
18	Alaska	25.6
19	South Carolina	25.0
20	North Carolina	24.9
20	Vermont	24.9
22	Kansas	24.7
23	Washington	24.4
24	Mississippi	23.8
25	Wyoming	23.7
26	Missouri	23.4
27	Idaho	23.0
27	Montana	23.0
29	Maryland	22.4
30	Pennsylvania	22.2
31	California	22.1
31	Nebraska	22.1
33	Iowa	21.9
34	Virginia	21.8
35	Florida	21.7
36	Illinois	21.6
37	Maine	21.4
37	Minnesota	21.4
39	New Hampshire	21.2
40	Georgia	20.6
41	Delaware	20.5
42	Wisconsin	19.7
43	Connecticut	19.2
44	Arizona	19.0
45	New York	18.3
46	Hawaii	18.1
47	Colorado	16.6
48	Rhode Island	16.2
49	Massachusetts	15.4
50	Nevada	12.8
	District of Columbia	30.6

Source: U.S. Department of Health and Human Services, National Center for Health Statistics
   "National Vital Statistics Reports" (Vol. 57, No. 14, April 17, 2009, http://www.cdc.gov/nchs/deaths.htm)
*Final data by state of residence. A severe, chronic form of diabetes caused by insufficient production of insulin and resulting in abnormal metabolism of carbohydrates, fats, and proteins. The disease, which typically appears in childhood or adolescence, is characterized by increased sugar levels in the blood and urine, excessive thirst, and frequent urination. Age-adjusted rates based on the year 2000 standard population.

Deaths by Diseases of the Heart in 2006

National Total = 631,636 Deaths*

ALPHA ORDER

ALPHA ORDER | RANK ORDER

RANK	STATE	DEATHS	% of USA	RANK	STATE	DEATHS	% of USA
17	Alabama	12,583	2.0%	1	California	64,871	10.3%
50	Alaska	645	0.1%	2	New York	50,470	8.0%
20	Arizona	10,607	1.7%	3	Florida	44,305	7.0%
29	Arkansas	7,431	1.2%	4	Texas	38,782	6.1%
1	California	64,871	10.3%	5	Pennsylvania	33,744	5.3%
32	Colorado	6,124	1.0%	6	Ohio	27,886	4.4%
28	Connecticut	7,490	1.2%	7	Illinois	27,007	4.3%
45	Delaware	1,866	0.3%	8	Michigan	24,255	3.8%
3	Florida	44,305	7.0%	9	New Jersey	19,548	3.1%
11	Georgia	16,478	2.6%	10	North Carolina	17,271	2.7%
43	Hawaii	2,244	0.4%	11	Georgia	16,478	2.6%
42	Idaho	2,399	0.4%	12	Missouri	14,749	2.3%
7	Illinois	27,007	4.3%	13	Tennessee	14,642	2.3%
14	Indiana	14,375	2.3%	14	Indiana	14,375	2.3%
30	Iowa	7,172	1.1%	15	Virginia	14,021	2.2%
33	Kansas	5,849	0.9%	16	Massachusetts	12,947	2.0%
22	Kentucky	10,353	1.6%	17	Alabama	12,583	2.0%
23	Louisiana	10,026	1.6%	18	Wisconsin	11,451	1.8%
39	Maine	2,815	0.4%	19	Maryland	11,268	1.8%
19	Maryland	11,268	1.8%	20	Arizona	10,607	1.7%
16	Massachusetts	12,947	2.0%	21	Washington	10,604	1.7%
8	Michigan	24,255	3.8%	22	Kentucky	10,353	1.6%
27	Minnesota	7,525	1.2%	23	Louisiana	10,026	1.6%
26	Mississippi	8,097	1.3%	24	Oklahoma	9,798	1.6%
12	Missouri	14,749	2.3%	25	South Carolina	9,030	1.4%
44	Montana	1,869	0.3%	26	Mississippi	8,097	1.3%
36	Nebraska	3,445	0.5%	27	Minnesota	7,525	1.2%
35	Nevada	5,013	0.8%	28	Connecticut	7,490	1.2%
41	New Hampshire	2,501	0.4%	29	Arkansas	7,431	1.2%
9	New Jersey	19,548	3.1%	30	Iowa	7,172	1.1%
37	New Mexico	3,411	0.5%	31	Oregon	6,620	1.0%
2	New York	50,470	8.0%	32	Colorado	6,124	1.0%
10	North Carolina	17,271	2.7%	33	Kansas	5,849	0.9%
47	North Dakota	1,527	0.2%	34	West Virginia	5,311	0.8%
6	Ohio	27,886	4.4%	35	Nevada	5,013	0.8%
24	Oklahoma	9,798	1.6%	36	Nebraska	3,445	0.5%
31	Oregon	6,620	1.0%	37	New Mexico	3,411	0.5%
5	Pennsylvania	33,744	5.3%	38	Utah	2,932	0.5%
40	Rhode Island	2,718	0.4%	39	Maine	2,815	0.4%
25	South Carolina	9,030	1.4%	40	Rhode Island	2,718	0.4%
46	South Dakota	1,757	0.3%	41	New Hampshire	2,501	0.4%
13	Tennessee	14,642	2.3%	42	Idaho	2,399	0.4%
4	Texas	38,782	6.1%	43	Hawaii	2,244	0.4%
38	Utah	2,932	0.5%	44	Montana	1,869	0.3%
48	Vermont	1,244	0.2%	45	Delaware	1,866	0.3%
15	Virginia	14,021	2.2%	46	South Dakota	1,757	0.3%
21	Washington	10,604	1.7%	47	North Dakota	1,527	0.2%
34	West Virginia	5,311	0.8%	48	Vermont	1,244	0.2%
18	Wisconsin	11,451	1.8%	49	Wyoming	994	0.2%
49	Wyoming	994	0.2%	50	Alaska	645	0.1%
					District of Columbia	1,566	0.2%

Source: U.S. Department of Health and Human Services, National Center for Health Statistics
"National Vital Statistics Reports" (Vol. 57, No. 14, April 17, 2009, http://www.cdc.gov/nchs/deaths.htm)
*Final data by state of residence.

Death Rate by Diseases of the Heart in 2006

National Rate = 211.0 Deaths per 100,000 Population*

ALPHA ORDER

RANK	STATE	RATE
4	Alabama	273.6
50	Alaska	96.3
43	Arizona	172.0
6	Arkansas	264.4
39	California	177.9
48	Colorado	128.8
22	Connecticut	213.7
21	Delaware	218.6
11	Florida	244.9
40	Georgia	176.0
41	Hawaii	174.6
46	Idaho	163.6
25	Illinois	210.5
18	Indiana	227.7
14	Iowa	240.5
24	Kansas	211.6
10	Kentucky	246.1
17	Louisiana	233.8
23	Maine	213.0
30	Maryland	200.7
28	Massachusetts	201.1
15	Michigan	240.3
47	Minnesota	145.6
2	Mississippi	278.2
9	Missouri	252.4
32	Montana	197.9
34	Nebraska	194.8
29	Nevada	200.9
36	New Hampshire	190.2
20	New Jersey	224.1
42	New Mexico	174.5
7	New York	261.4
33	North Carolina	195.0
16	North Dakota	240.1
12	Ohio	243.0
3	Oklahoma	273.7
38	Oregon	178.9
5	Pennsylvania	271.2
8	Rhode Island	254.6
26	South Carolina	209.0
19	South Dakota	224.7
13	Tennessee	242.5
45	Texas	165.0
49	Utah	115.0
31	Vermont	199.4
37	Virginia	183.5
44	Washington	165.8
1	West Virginia	292.1
27	Wisconsin	206.1
35	Wyoming	193.0

RANK ORDER

RANK	STATE	RATE
1	West Virginia	292.1
2	Mississippi	278.2
3	Oklahoma	273.7
4	Alabama	273.6
5	Pennsylvania	271.2
6	Arkansas	264.4
7	New York	261.4
8	Rhode Island	254.6
9	Missouri	252.4
10	Kentucky	246.1
11	Florida	244.9
12	Ohio	243.0
13	Tennessee	242.5
14	Iowa	240.5
15	Michigan	240.3
16	North Dakota	240.1
17	Louisiana	233.8
18	Indiana	227.7
19	South Dakota	224.7
20	New Jersey	224.1
21	Delaware	218.6
22	Connecticut	213.7
23	Maine	213.0
24	Kansas	211.6
25	Illinois	210.5
26	South Carolina	209.0
27	Wisconsin	206.1
28	Massachusetts	201.1
29	Nevada	200.9
30	Maryland	200.7
31	Vermont	199.4
32	Montana	197.9
33	North Carolina	195.0
34	Nebraska	194.8
35	Wyoming	193.0
36	New Hampshire	190.2
37	Virginia	183.5
38	Oregon	178.9
39	California	177.9
40	Georgia	176.0
41	Hawaii	174.6
42	New Mexico	174.5
43	Arizona	172.0
44	Washington	165.8
45	Texas	165.0
46	Idaho	163.6
47	Minnesota	145.6
48	Colorado	128.8
49	Utah	115.0
50	Alaska	96.3

District of Columbia	269.3

Source: U.S. Department of Health and Human Services, National Center for Health Statistics
"National Vital Statistics Reports" (Vol. 57, No. 14, April 17, 2009, http://www.cdc.gov/nchs/deaths.htm)
*Final data by state of residence. Not age-adjusted.

Age-Adjusted Death Rate by Diseases of the Heart in 2006

National Rate = 200.2 Deaths per 100,000 Population*

ALPHA ORDER

RANK	STATE	RATE
2	Alabama	253.3
42	Alaska	167.2
45	Arizona	164.2
8	Arkansas	233.0
25	California	192.5
48	Colorado	151.6
33	Connecticut	177.3
19	Delaware	201.2
36	Florida	175.1
15	Georgia	213.2
49	Hawaii	147.2
40	Idaho	168.5
18	Illinois	204.4
13	Indiana	217.2
28	Iowa	184.7
29	Kansas	183.6
5	Kentucky	235.5
9	Louisiana	232.3
37	Maine	174.0
17	Maryland	205.6
39	Massachusetts	169.5
10	Michigan	227.0
50	Minnesota	133.9
1	Mississippi	270.9
12	Missouri	224.4
41	Montana	168.4
44	Nebraska	165.0
11	Nevada	226.7
32	New Hampshire	178.3
20	New Jersey	200.9
38	New Mexico	172.6
7	New York	233.1
24	North Carolina	195.3
30	North Dakota	181.5
14	Ohio	216.1
3	Oklahoma	251.1
46	Oregon	160.0
16	Pennsylvania	207.1
21	Rhode Island	200.8
22	South Carolina	200.2
34	South Dakota	177.0
6	Tennessee	233.3
23	Texas	197.4
47	Utah	156.3
35	Vermont	175.5
26	Virginia	190.8
43	Washington	165.8
4	West Virginia	236.9
31	Wisconsin	181.1
27	Wyoming	189.4

RANK ORDER

RANK	STATE	RATE
1	Mississippi	270.9
2	Alabama	253.3
3	Oklahoma	251.1
4	West Virginia	236.9
5	Kentucky	235.5
6	Tennessee	233.3
7	New York	233.1
8	Arkansas	233.0
9	Louisiana	232.3
10	Michigan	227.0
11	Nevada	226.7
12	Missouri	224.4
13	Indiana	217.2
14	Ohio	216.1
15	Georgia	213.2
16	Pennsylvania	207.1
17	Maryland	205.6
18	Illinois	204.4
19	Delaware	201.2
20	New Jersey	200.9
21	Rhode Island	200.8
22	South Carolina	200.2
23	Texas	197.4
24	North Carolina	195.3
25	California	192.5
26	Virginia	190.8
27	Wyoming	189.4
28	Iowa	184.7
29	Kansas	183.6
30	North Dakota	181.5
31	Wisconsin	181.1
32	New Hampshire	178.3
33	Connecticut	177.3
34	South Dakota	177.0
35	Vermont	175.5
36	Florida	175.1
37	Maine	174.0
38	New Mexico	172.6
39	Massachusetts	169.5
40	Idaho	168.5
41	Montana	168.4
42	Alaska	167.2
43	Washington	165.8
44	Nebraska	165.0
45	Arizona	164.2
46	Oregon	160.0
47	Utah	156.3
48	Colorado	151.6
49	Hawaii	147.2
50	Minnesota	133.9
	District of Columbia	260.0

Source: U.S. Department of Health and Human Services, National Center for Health Statistics
"National Vital Statistics Reports" (Vol. 57, No. 14, April 17, 2009, http://www.cdc.gov/nchs/deaths.htm)
*Final data by state of residence. Age-adjusted rates based on the year 2000 standard population.

Deaths by Malignant Neoplasms in 2006

National Total = 559,888 Deaths*

ALPHA ORDER

ALPHA ORDER

RANK	STATE	DEATHS	% of USA
21	Alabama	9,899	1.8%
50	Alaska	790	0.1%
20	Arizona	9,919	1.8%
32	Arkansas	6,177	1.1%
1	California	54,140	9.7%
29	Colorado	6,550	1.2%
28	Connecticut	7,044	1.3%
45	Delaware	1,780	0.3%
2	Florida	40,415	7.2%
11	Georgia	14,474	2.6%
43	Hawaii	2,171	0.4%
41	Idaho	2,306	0.4%
7	Illinois	24,084	4.3%
15	Indiana	12,903	2.3%
30	Iowa	6,359	1.1%
33	Kansas	5,343	1.0%
22	Kentucky	9,394	1.7%
24	Louisiana	8,853	1.6%
38	Maine	3,089	0.6%
19	Maryland	10,350	1.8%
13	Massachusetts	13,407	2.4%
8	Michigan	20,192	3.6%
23	Minnesota	9,079	1.6%
31	Mississippi	6,236	1.1%
16	Missouri	12,519	2.2%
44	Montana	1,943	0.3%
36	Nebraska	3,430	0.6%
35	Nevada	4,226	0.8%
40	New Hampshire	2,534	0.5%
10	New Jersey	17,180	3.1%
37	New Mexico	3,147	0.6%
3	New York	35,284	6.3%
9	North Carolina	17,318	3.1%
47	North Dakota	1,387	0.2%
6	Ohio	24,975	4.5%
26	Oklahoma	7,491	1.3%
27	Oregon	7,309	1.3%
5	Pennsylvania	29,172	5.2%
42	Rhode Island	2,250	0.4%
24	South Carolina	8,853	1.6%
46	South Dakota	1,570	0.3%
14	Tennessee	13,051	2.3%
4	Texas	34,939	6.2%
39	Utah	2,615	0.5%
48	Vermont	1,214	0.2%
12	Virginia	13,829	2.5%
17	Washington	11,055	2.0%
34	West Virginia	4,613	0.8%
18	Wisconsin	10,925	2.0%
49	Wyoming	927	0.2%

RANK ORDER

RANK	STATE	DEATHS	% of USA
1	California	54,140	9.7%
2	Florida	40,415	7.2%
3	New York	35,284	6.3%
4	Texas	34,939	6.2%
5	Pennsylvania	29,172	5.2%
6	Ohio	24,975	4.5%
7	Illinois	24,084	4.3%
8	Michigan	20,192	3.6%
9	North Carolina	17,318	3.1%
10	New Jersey	17,180	3.1%
11	Georgia	14,474	2.6%
12	Virginia	13,829	2.5%
13	Massachusetts	13,407	2.4%
14	Tennessee	13,051	2.3%
15	Indiana	12,903	2.3%
16	Missouri	12,519	2.2%
17	Washington	11,055	2.0%
18	Wisconsin	10,925	2.0%
19	Maryland	10,350	1.8%
20	Arizona	9,919	1.8%
21	Alabama	9,899	1.8%
22	Kentucky	9,394	1.7%
23	Minnesota	9,079	1.6%
24	Louisiana	8,853	1.6%
24	South Carolina	8,853	1.6%
26	Oklahoma	7,491	1.3%
27	Oregon	7,309	1.3%
28	Connecticut	7,044	1.3%
29	Colorado	6,550	1.2%
30	Iowa	6,359	1.1%
31	Mississippi	6,236	1.1%
32	Arkansas	6,177	1.1%
33	Kansas	5,343	1.0%
34	West Virginia	4,613	0.8%
35	Nevada	4,226	0.8%
36	Nebraska	3,430	0.6%
37	New Mexico	3,147	0.6%
38	Maine	3,089	0.6%
39	Utah	2,615	0.5%
40	New Hampshire	2,534	0.5%
41	Idaho	2,306	0.4%
42	Rhode Island	2,250	0.4%
43	Hawaii	2,171	0.4%
44	Montana	1,943	0.3%
45	Delaware	1,780	0.3%
46	South Dakota	1,570	0.3%
47	North Dakota	1,387	0.2%
48	Vermont	1,214	0.2%
49	Wyoming	927	0.2%
50	Alaska	790	0.1%
	District of Columbia	1,178	0.2%

Source: U.S. Department of Health and Human Services, National Center for Health Statistics
  "National Vital Statistics Reports" (Vol. 57, No. 14, April 17, 2009, http://www.cdc.gov/nchs/deaths.htm)
*Final data by state of residence. Neoplasms are abnormal tissue, tumors. Includes many cancers.

Death Rate by Malignant Neoplasms in 2006

National Rate = 187.0 Deaths per 100,000 Population*

<table>
<tr><td colspan="3">ALPHA ORDER</td><td colspan="3">RANK ORDER</td></tr>
<tr><td>RANK</td><td>STATE</td><td>RATE</td><td>RANK</td><td>STATE</td><td>RATE</td></tr>
<tr><td>10</td><td>Alabama</td><td>215.2</td><td>1</td><td>West Virginia</td><td>253.7</td></tr>
<tr><td>49</td><td>Alaska</td><td>117.9</td><td>2</td><td>Pennsylvania</td><td>234.5</td></tr>
<tr><td>43</td><td>Arizona</td><td>160.9</td><td>3</td><td>Maine</td><td>233.7</td></tr>
<tr><td>6</td><td>Arkansas</td><td>219.8</td><td>4</td><td>Florida</td><td>223.4</td></tr>
<tr><td>47</td><td>California</td><td>148.5</td><td>5</td><td>Kentucky</td><td>223.3</td></tr>
<tr><td>48</td><td>Colorado</td><td>137.8</td><td>6</td><td>Arkansas</td><td>219.8</td></tr>
<tr><td>22</td><td>Connecticut</td><td>201.0</td><td>7</td><td>North Dakota</td><td>218.1</td></tr>
<tr><td>16</td><td>Delaware</td><td>208.6</td><td>8</td><td>Ohio</td><td>217.6</td></tr>
<tr><td>4</td><td>Florida</td><td>223.4</td><td>9</td><td>Tennessee</td><td>216.1</td></tr>
<tr><td>45</td><td>Georgia</td><td>154.6</td><td>10</td><td>Alabama</td><td>215.2</td></tr>
<tr><td>41</td><td>Hawaii</td><td>168.9</td><td>11</td><td>Mississippi</td><td>214.3</td></tr>
<tr><td>44</td><td>Idaho</td><td>157.2</td><td>11</td><td>Missouri</td><td>214.3</td></tr>
<tr><td>33</td><td>Illinois</td><td>187.7</td><td>13</td><td>Iowa</td><td>213.2</td></tr>
<tr><td>21</td><td>Indiana</td><td>204.4</td><td>14</td><td>Rhode Island</td><td>210.8</td></tr>
<tr><td>13</td><td>Iowa</td><td>213.2</td><td>15</td><td>Oklahoma</td><td>209.3</td></tr>
<tr><td>31</td><td>Kansas</td><td>193.3</td><td>16</td><td>Delaware</td><td>208.6</td></tr>
<tr><td>5</td><td>Kentucky</td><td>223.3</td><td>17</td><td>Massachusetts</td><td>208.3</td></tr>
<tr><td>18</td><td>Louisiana</td><td>206.5</td><td>18</td><td>Louisiana</td><td>206.5</td></tr>
<tr><td>3</td><td>Maine</td><td>233.7</td><td>19</td><td>Montana</td><td>205.7</td></tr>
<tr><td>34</td><td>Maryland</td><td>184.3</td><td>20</td><td>South Carolina</td><td>204.9</td></tr>
<tr><td>17</td><td>Massachusetts</td><td>208.3</td><td>21</td><td>Indiana</td><td>204.4</td></tr>
<tr><td>24</td><td>Michigan</td><td>200.0</td><td>22</td><td>Connecticut</td><td>201.0</td></tr>
<tr><td>38</td><td>Minnesota</td><td>175.7</td><td>23</td><td>South Dakota</td><td>200.8</td></tr>
<tr><td>11</td><td>Mississippi</td><td>214.3</td><td>24</td><td>Michigan</td><td>200.0</td></tr>
<tr><td>11</td><td>Missouri</td><td>214.3</td><td>25</td><td>Oregon</td><td>197.5</td></tr>
<tr><td>19</td><td>Montana</td><td>205.7</td><td>26</td><td>New Jersey</td><td>196.9</td></tr>
<tr><td>30</td><td>Nebraska</td><td>194.0</td><td>27</td><td>Wisconsin</td><td>196.6</td></tr>
<tr><td>40</td><td>Nevada</td><td>169.3</td><td>28</td><td>North Carolina</td><td>195.5</td></tr>
<tr><td>32</td><td>New Hampshire</td><td>192.7</td><td>29</td><td>Vermont</td><td>194.6</td></tr>
<tr><td>26</td><td>New Jersey</td><td>196.9</td><td>30</td><td>Nebraska</td><td>194.0</td></tr>
<tr><td>42</td><td>New Mexico</td><td>161.0</td><td>31</td><td>Kansas</td><td>193.3</td></tr>
<tr><td>35</td><td>New York</td><td>182.8</td><td>32</td><td>New Hampshire</td><td>192.7</td></tr>
<tr><td>28</td><td>North Carolina</td><td>195.5</td><td>33</td><td>Illinois</td><td>187.7</td></tr>
<tr><td>7</td><td>North Dakota</td><td>218.1</td><td>34</td><td>Maryland</td><td>184.3</td></tr>
<tr><td>8</td><td>Ohio</td><td>217.6</td><td>35</td><td>New York</td><td>182.8</td></tr>
<tr><td>15</td><td>Oklahoma</td><td>209.3</td><td>36</td><td>Virginia</td><td>180.9</td></tr>
<tr><td>25</td><td>Oregon</td><td>197.5</td><td>37</td><td>Wyoming</td><td>180.0</td></tr>
<tr><td>2</td><td>Pennsylvania</td><td>234.5</td><td>38</td><td>Minnesota</td><td>175.7</td></tr>
<tr><td>14</td><td>Rhode Island</td><td>210.8</td><td>39</td><td>Washington</td><td>172.8</td></tr>
<tr><td>20</td><td>South Carolina</td><td>204.9</td><td>40</td><td>Nevada</td><td>169.3</td></tr>
<tr><td>23</td><td>South Dakota</td><td>200.8</td><td>41</td><td>Hawaii</td><td>168.9</td></tr>
<tr><td>9</td><td>Tennessee</td><td>216.1</td><td>42</td><td>New Mexico</td><td>161.0</td></tr>
<tr><td>46</td><td>Texas</td><td>148.6</td><td>43</td><td>Arizona</td><td>160.9</td></tr>
<tr><td>50</td><td>Utah</td><td>102.5</td><td>44</td><td>Idaho</td><td>157.2</td></tr>
<tr><td>29</td><td>Vermont</td><td>194.6</td><td>45</td><td>Georgia</td><td>154.6</td></tr>
<tr><td>36</td><td>Virginia</td><td>180.9</td><td>46</td><td>Texas</td><td>148.6</td></tr>
<tr><td>39</td><td>Washington</td><td>172.8</td><td>47</td><td>California</td><td>148.5</td></tr>
<tr><td>1</td><td>West Virginia</td><td>253.7</td><td>48</td><td>Colorado</td><td>137.8</td></tr>
<tr><td>27</td><td>Wisconsin</td><td>196.6</td><td>49</td><td>Alaska</td><td>117.9</td></tr>
<tr><td>37</td><td>Wyoming</td><td>180.0</td><td>50</td><td>Utah</td><td>102.5</td></tr>
</table>

District of Columbia   202.6

Source: U.S. Department of Health and Human Services, National Center for Health Statistics
   "National Vital Statistics Reports" (Vol. 57, No. 14, April 17, 2009, http://www.cdc.gov/nchs/deaths.htm)
*Final data by state of residence. Neoplasms are abnormal tissue, tumors. Includes many cancers. Not age-adjusted.

Age-Adjusted Death Rate by Malignant Neoplasms in 2006

National Rate = 180.7 Deaths per 100,000 Population*

ALPHA ORDER

RANK	STATE	RATE
7	Alabama	197.7
34	Alaska	177.4
48	Arizona	155.7
10	Arkansas	196.0
45	California	162.3
47	Colorado	157.7
33	Connecticut	177.8
15	Delaware	191.4
39	Florida	172.0
30	Georgia	180.4
49	Hawaii	147.6
44	Idaho	163.2
18	Illinois	187.2
7	Indiana	197.7
31	Iowa	179.6
29	Kansas	180.5
1	Kentucky	211.2
5	Louisiana	203.5
12	Maine	193.8
19	Maryland	186.8
20	Massachusetts	186.7
16	Michigan	191.0
42	Minnesota	171.2
2	Mississippi	209.2
9	Missouri	196.2
31	Montana	179.6
35	Nebraska	176.9
22	Nevada	183.2
24	New Hampshire	182.6
25	New Jersey	182.3
46	New Mexico	158.3
43	New York	169.0
14	North Carolina	192.8
22	North Dakota	183.2
6	Ohio	198.0
11	Oklahoma	194.8
27	Oregon	181.3
17	Pennsylvania	190.8
26	Rhode Island	181.7
13	South Carolina	193.2
40	South Dakota	171.9
4	Tennessee	204.7
37	Texas	174.5
50	Utah	136.4
41	Vermont	171.8
21	Virginia	183.9
38	Washington	174.2
3	West Virginia	205.9
28	Wisconsin	181.2
36	Wyoming	175.4

RANK ORDER

RANK	STATE	RATE
1	Kentucky	211.2
2	Mississippi	209.2
3	West Virginia	205.9
4	Tennessee	204.7
5	Louisiana	203.5
6	Ohio	198.0
7	Alabama	197.7
7	Indiana	197.7
9	Missouri	196.2
10	Arkansas	196.0
11	Oklahoma	194.8
12	Maine	193.8
13	South Carolina	193.2
14	North Carolina	192.8
15	Delaware	191.4
16	Michigan	191.0
17	Pennsylvania	190.8
18	Illinois	187.2
19	Maryland	186.8
20	Massachusetts	186.7
21	Virginia	183.9
22	Nevada	183.2
22	North Dakota	183.2
24	New Hampshire	182.6
25	New Jersey	182.3
26	Rhode Island	181.7
27	Oregon	181.3
28	Wisconsin	181.2
29	Kansas	180.5
30	Georgia	180.4
31	Iowa	179.6
31	Montana	179.6
33	Connecticut	177.8
34	Alaska	177.4
35	Nebraska	176.9
36	Wyoming	175.4
37	Texas	174.5
38	Washington	174.2
39	Florida	172.0
40	South Dakota	171.9
41	Vermont	171.8
42	Minnesota	171.2
43	New York	169.0
44	Idaho	163.2
45	California	162.3
46	New Mexico	158.3
47	Colorado	157.7
48	Arizona	155.7
49	Hawaii	147.6
50	Utah	136.4

	District of Columbia	198.7

Source: U.S. Department of Health and Human Services, National Center for Health Statistics
   "National Vital Statistics Reports" (Vol. 56, No. 10, April 24, 2008, http://www.cdc.gov/nchs/deaths.htm)
*Final data by state of residence. Neoplasms are abnormal tissue, tumors. Includes many cancers. Age-adjusted rates based on the year 2000 standard population.

Deaths by Nephritis and Other Kidney Diseases in 2006

National Total = 45,344 Deaths*

ALPHA ORDER

RANK	STATE	DEATHS	% of USA
16	Alabama	1,104	2.4%
50	Alaska	44	0.1%
29	Arizona	565	1.2%
25	Arkansas	616	1.4%
3	California	2,676	5.9%
31	Colorado	472	1.0%
28	Connecticut	567	1.3%
43	Delaware	152	0.3%
4	Florida	2,620	5.8%
9	Georgia	1,668	3.7%
40	Hawaii	179	0.4%
45	Idaho	130	0.3%
5	Illinois	2,502	5.5%
14	Indiana	1,372	3.0%
38	Iowa	225	0.5%
26	Kansas	594	1.3%
19	Kentucky	922	2.0%
17	Louisiana	1,074	2.4%
36	Maine	252	0.6%
22	Maryland	767	1.7%
12	Massachusetts	1,406	3.1%
8	Michigan	1,673	3.7%
23	Minnesota	711	1.6%
24	Mississippi	673	1.5%
15	Missouri	1,118	2.5%
44	Montana	132	0.3%
37	Nebraska	249	0.5%
30	Nevada	475	1.0%
42	New Hampshire	160	0.4%
11	New Jersey	1,645	3.6%
35	New Mexico	262	0.6%
6	New York	2,351	5.2%
10	North Carolina	1,661	3.7%
47	North Dakota	59	0.1%
7	Ohio	1,758	3.9%
26	Oklahoma	594	1.3%
34	Oregon	353	0.8%
1	Pennsylvania	3,084	6.8%
41	Rhode Island	167	0.4%
20	South Carolina	846	1.9%
46	South Dakota	62	0.1%
21	Tennessee	768	1.7%
2	Texas	2,995	6.6%
39	Utah	210	0.5%
49	Vermont	52	0.1%
13	Virginia	1,400	3.1%
33	Washington	423	0.9%
32	West Virginia	468	1.0%
18	Wisconsin	962	2.1%
48	Wyoming	58	0.1%

RANK ORDER

RANK	STATE	DEATHS	% of USA
1	Pennsylvania	3,084	6.8%
2	Texas	2,995	6.6%
3	California	2,676	5.9%
4	Florida	2,620	5.8%
5	Illinois	2,502	5.5%
6	New York	2,351	5.2%
7	Ohio	1,758	3.9%
8	Michigan	1,673	3.7%
9	Georgia	1,668	3.7%
10	North Carolina	1,661	3.7%
11	New Jersey	1,645	3.6%
12	Massachusetts	1,406	3.1%
13	Virginia	1,400	3.1%
14	Indiana	1,372	3.0%
15	Missouri	1,118	2.5%
16	Alabama	1,104	2.4%
17	Louisiana	1,074	2.4%
18	Wisconsin	962	2.1%
19	Kentucky	922	2.0%
20	South Carolina	846	1.9%
21	Tennessee	768	1.7%
22	Maryland	767	1.7%
23	Minnesota	711	1.6%
24	Mississippi	673	1.5%
25	Arkansas	616	1.4%
26	Kansas	594	1.3%
26	Oklahoma	594	1.3%
28	Connecticut	567	1.3%
29	Arizona	565	1.2%
30	Nevada	475	1.0%
31	Colorado	472	1.0%
32	West Virginia	468	1.0%
33	Washington	423	0.9%
34	Oregon	353	0.8%
35	New Mexico	262	0.6%
36	Maine	252	0.6%
37	Nebraska	249	0.5%
38	Iowa	225	0.5%
39	Utah	210	0.5%
40	Hawaii	179	0.4%
41	Rhode Island	167	0.4%
42	New Hampshire	160	0.4%
43	Delaware	152	0.3%
44	Montana	132	0.3%
45	Idaho	130	0.3%
46	South Dakota	62	0.1%
47	North Dakota	59	0.1%
48	Wyoming	58	0.1%
49	Vermont	52	0.1%
50	Alaska	44	0.1%
	District of Columbia	68	0.1%

Source: U.S. Department of Health and Human Services, National Center for Health Statistics
"National Vital Statistics Reports" (Vol. 57, No. 14, April 17, 2009, http://www.cdc.gov/nchs/deaths.htm)
*Final data by state of residence. Includes nephrotic syndrome and nephrosis.

Death Rate by Nephritis and Other Kidney Diseases in 2006

National Rate = 15.1 Deaths per 100,000 Population*

ALPHA ORDER

RANK	STATE	RATE
4	Alabama	24.0
49	Alaska	6.6
42	Arizona	9.2
6	Arkansas	21.9
48	California	7.3
39	Colorado	9.9
24	Connecticut	16.2
19	Delaware	17.8
27	Florida	14.5
19	Georgia	17.8
30	Hawaii	13.9
43	Idaho	8.9
12	Illinois	19.5
9	Indiana	21.7
47	Iowa	7.5
10	Kansas	21.5
6	Kentucky	21.9
2	Louisiana	25.0
13	Maine	19.1
32	Maryland	13.7
8	Massachusetts	21.8
22	Michigan	16.6
31	Minnesota	13.8
5	Mississippi	23.1
13	Missouri	19.1
29	Montana	14.0
28	Nebraska	14.1
15	Nevada	19.0
36	New Hampshire	12.2
16	New Jersey	18.9
33	New Mexico	13.4
36	New York	12.2
17	North Carolina	18.8
41	North Dakota	9.3
26	Ohio	15.3
22	Oklahoma	16.6
40	Oregon	9.5
3	Pennsylvania	24.8
25	Rhode Island	15.6
11	South Carolina	19.6
46	South Dakota	7.9
34	Tennessee	12.7
34	Texas	12.7
45	Utah	8.2
44	Vermont	8.3
18	Virginia	18.3
49	Washington	6.6
1	West Virginia	25.7
21	Wisconsin	17.3
38	Wyoming	11.3

RANK ORDER

RANK	STATE	RATE
1	West Virginia	25.7
2	Louisiana	25.0
3	Pennsylvania	24.8
4	Alabama	24.0
5	Mississippi	23.1
6	Arkansas	21.9
6	Kentucky	21.9
8	Massachusetts	21.8
9	Indiana	21.7
10	Kansas	21.5
11	South Carolina	19.6
12	Illinois	19.5
13	Maine	19.1
13	Missouri	19.1
15	Nevada	19.0
16	New Jersey	18.9
17	North Carolina	18.8
18	Virginia	18.3
19	Delaware	17.8
19	Georgia	17.8
21	Wisconsin	17.3
22	Michigan	16.6
22	Oklahoma	16.6
24	Connecticut	16.2
25	Rhode Island	15.6
26	Ohio	15.3
27	Florida	14.5
28	Nebraska	14.1
29	Montana	14.0
30	Hawaii	13.9
31	Minnesota	13.8
32	Maryland	13.7
33	New Mexico	13.4
34	Tennessee	12.7
34	Texas	12.7
36	New Hampshire	12.2
36	New York	12.2
38	Wyoming	11.3
39	Colorado	9.9
40	Oregon	9.5
41	North Dakota	9.3
42	Arizona	9.2
43	Idaho	8.9
44	Vermont	8.3
45	Utah	8.2
46	South Dakota	7.9
47	Iowa	7.5
48	California	7.3
49	Alaska	6.6
49	Washington	6.6
	District of Columbia	11.7

Source: U.S. Department of Health and Human Services, National Center for Health Statistics
   "National Vital Statistics Reports" (Vol. 57, No. 14, April 17, 2009, http://www.cdc.gov/nchs/deaths.htm)
*Final data by state of residence. Includes nephrotic syndrome and nephrosis. Not age-adjusted.

Age-Adjusted Death Rate by Nephritis and Other Kidney Diseases in 2006

National Rate = 14.5 Deaths per 100,000 Population*

ALPHA ORDER

RANK	STATE	RATE
3	Alabama	22.2
31	Alaska	12.6
43	Arizona	8.8
9	Arkansas	19.3
45	California	8.0
34	Colorado	12.1
27	Connecticut	13.7
19	Delaware	16.5
41	Florida	10.5
5	Georgia	21.7
36	Hawaii	11.8
42	Idaho	9.2
10	Illinois	19.2
7	Indiana	20.8
50	Iowa	5.7
15	Kansas	18.8
6	Kentucky	21.0
1	Louisiana	25.2
21	Maine	15.7
25	Maryland	14.1
16	Massachusetts	18.5
20	Michigan	15.8
30	Minnesota	12.8
2	Mississippi	22.5
17	Missouri	17.1
35	Montana	11.9
33	Nebraska	12.2
4	Nevada	22.0
37	New Hampshire	11.6
17	New Jersey	17.1
28	New Mexico	13.2
40	New York	11.0
13	North Carolina	18.9
48	North Dakota	6.5
26	Ohio	13.8
22	Oklahoma	15.4
44	Oregon	8.7
12	Pennsylvania	19.0
29	Rhode Island	12.9
13	South Carolina	18.9
49	South Dakota	6.2
32	Tennessee	12.4
24	Texas	15.3
39	Utah	11.1
46	Vermont	7.4
10	Virginia	19.2
47	Washington	6.6
7	West Virginia	20.8
22	Wisconsin	15.4
38	Wyoming	11.2

RANK ORDER

RANK	STATE	RATE
1	Louisiana	25.2
2	Mississippi	22.5
3	Alabama	22.2
4	Nevada	22.0
5	Georgia	21.7
6	Kentucky	21.0
7	Indiana	20.8
7	West Virginia	20.8
9	Arkansas	19.3
10	Illinois	19.2
10	Virginia	19.2
12	Pennsylvania	19.0
13	North Carolina	18.9
13	South Carolina	18.9
15	Kansas	18.8
16	Massachusetts	18.5
17	Missouri	17.1
17	New Jersey	17.1
19	Delaware	16.5
20	Michigan	15.8
21	Maine	15.7
22	Oklahoma	15.4
22	Wisconsin	15.4
24	Texas	15.3
25	Maryland	14.1
26	Ohio	13.8
27	Connecticut	13.7
28	New Mexico	13.2
29	Rhode Island	12.9
30	Minnesota	12.8
31	Alaska	12.6
32	Tennessee	12.4
33	Nebraska	12.2
34	Colorado	12.1
35	Montana	11.9
36	Hawaii	11.8
37	New Hampshire	11.6
38	Wyoming	11.2
39	Utah	11.1
40	New York	11.0
41	Florida	10.5
42	Idaho	9.2
43	Arizona	8.8
44	Oregon	8.7
45	California	8.0
46	Vermont	7.4
47	Washington	6.6
48	North Dakota	6.5
49	South Dakota	6.2
50	Iowa	5.7

District of Columbia	11.1

Source: U.S. Department of Health and Human Services, National Center for Health Statistics
"National Vital Statistics Reports" (Vol. 57, No. 14, April 17, 2009, http://www.cdc.gov/nchs/deaths.htm)
*Final data by state of residence. Includes nephrotic syndrome and nephrosis. Age-adjusted rates based on the year 2000 standard population.

Deaths by Influenza and Pneumonia in 2006

National Total = 56,326 Deaths*

RANK	STATE	DEATHS	% of USA
21	Alabama	918	1.6%
50	Alaska	49	0.1%
16	Arizona	1,166	2.1%
26	Arkansas	772	1.4%
1	California	7,338	13.0%
32	Colorado	614	1.1%
25	Connecticut	800	1.4%
46	Delaware	138	0.2%
6	Florida	2,454	4.4%
12	Georgia	1,463	2.6%
41	Hawaii	257	0.5%
42	Idaho	225	0.4%
5	Illinois	2,668	4.7%
17	Indiana	1,129	2.0%
27	Iowa	770	1.4%
29	Kansas	647	1.1%
20	Kentucky	927	1.6%
23	Louisiana	833	1.5%
39	Maine	269	0.5%
18	Maryland	1,082	1.9%
8	Massachusetts	1,750	3.1%
10	Michigan	1,679	3.0%
30	Minnesota	630	1.1%
31	Mississippi	621	1.1%
14	Missouri	1,285	2.3%
45	Montana	169	0.3%
37	Nebraska	345	0.6%
35	Nevada	426	0.8%
43	New Hampshire	212	0.4%
13	New Jersey	1,315	2.3%
36	New Mexico	353	0.6%
2	New York	4,892	8.7%
9	North Carolina	1,705	3.0%
46	North Dakota	138	0.2%
7	Ohio	1,947	3.5%
22	Oklahoma	879	1.6%
33	Oregon	522	0.9%
4	Pennsylvania	2,716	4.8%
40	Rhode Island	268	0.5%
28	South Carolina	724	1.3%
44	South Dakota	173	0.3%
11	Tennessee	1,535	2.7%
3	Texas	3,342	5.9%
38	Utah	343	0.6%
49	Vermont	77	0.1%
15	Virginia	1,281	2.3%
24	Washington	814	1.4%
34	West Virginia	459	0.8%
19	Wisconsin	1,014	1.8%
48	Wyoming	117	0.2%

RANK	STATE	DEATHS	% of USA
1	California	7,338	13.0%
2	New York	4,892	8.7%
3	Texas	3,342	5.9%
4	Pennsylvania	2,716	4.8%
5	Illinois	2,668	4.7%
6	Florida	2,454	4.4%
7	Ohio	1,947	3.5%
8	Massachusetts	1,750	3.1%
9	North Carolina	1,705	3.0%
10	Michigan	1,679	3.0%
11	Tennessee	1,535	2.7%
12	Georgia	1,463	2.6%
13	New Jersey	1,315	2.3%
14	Missouri	1,285	2.3%
15	Virginia	1,281	2.3%
16	Arizona	1,166	2.1%
17	Indiana	1,129	2.0%
18	Maryland	1,082	1.9%
19	Wisconsin	1,014	1.8%
20	Kentucky	927	1.6%
21	Alabama	918	1.6%
22	Oklahoma	879	1.6%
23	Louisiana	833	1.5%
24	Washington	814	1.4%
25	Connecticut	800	1.4%
26	Arkansas	772	1.4%
27	Iowa	770	1.4%
28	South Carolina	724	1.3%
29	Kansas	647	1.1%
30	Minnesota	630	1.1%
31	Mississippi	621	1.1%
32	Colorado	614	1.1%
33	Oregon	522	0.9%
34	West Virginia	459	0.8%
35	Nevada	426	0.8%
36	New Mexico	353	0.6%
37	Nebraska	345	0.6%
38	Utah	343	0.6%
39	Maine	269	0.5%
40	Rhode Island	268	0.5%
41	Hawaii	257	0.5%
42	Idaho	225	0.4%
43	New Hampshire	212	0.4%
44	South Dakota	173	0.3%
45	Montana	169	0.3%
46	Delaware	138	0.2%
46	North Dakota	138	0.2%
48	Wyoming	117	0.2%
49	Vermont	77	0.1%
50	Alaska	49	0.1%
	District of Columbia	76	0.1%

Source: U.S. Department of Health and Human Services, National Center for Health Statistics
   "National Vital Statistics Reports" (Vol. 57, No. 14, April 17, 2009, http://www.cdc.gov/nchs/deaths.htm)
*Final data by state of residence.

Death Rate by Influenza and Pneumonia in 2006

National Rate = 18.8 Deaths per 100,000 Population*

<table>
<tr><td colspan="3">ALPHA ORDER</td><td colspan="3">RANK ORDER</td></tr>
<tr><td>RANK</td><td>STATE</td><td>RATE</td><td>RANK</td><td>STATE</td><td>RATE</td></tr>
<tr><td>21</td><td>Alabama</td><td>20.0</td><td>1</td><td>Arkansas</td><td>27.5</td></tr>
<tr><td>50</td><td>Alaska</td><td>7.3</td><td>2</td><td>Massachusetts</td><td>27.2</td></tr>
<tr><td>27</td><td>Arizona</td><td>18.9</td><td>3</td><td>Iowa</td><td>25.8</td></tr>
<tr><td>1</td><td>Arkansas</td><td>27.5</td><td>4</td><td>Tennessee</td><td>25.4</td></tr>
<tr><td>20</td><td>California</td><td>20.1</td><td>5</td><td>New York</td><td>25.3</td></tr>
<tr><td>46</td><td>Colorado</td><td>12.9</td><td>6</td><td>West Virginia</td><td>25.2</td></tr>
<tr><td>10</td><td>Connecticut</td><td>22.8</td><td>7</td><td>Rhode Island</td><td>25.1</td></tr>
<tr><td>37</td><td>Delaware</td><td>16.2</td><td>8</td><td>Oklahoma</td><td>24.6</td></tr>
<tr><td>44</td><td>Florida</td><td>13.6</td><td>9</td><td>Kansas</td><td>23.4</td></tr>
<tr><td>39</td><td>Georgia</td><td>15.6</td><td>10</td><td>Connecticut</td><td>22.8</td></tr>
<tr><td>21</td><td>Hawaii</td><td>20.0</td><td>11</td><td>Wyoming</td><td>22.7</td></tr>
<tr><td>40</td><td>Idaho</td><td>15.3</td><td>12</td><td>South Dakota</td><td>22.1</td></tr>
<tr><td>18</td><td>Illinois</td><td>20.8</td><td>13</td><td>Kentucky</td><td>22.0</td></tr>
<tr><td>30</td><td>Indiana</td><td>17.9</td><td>13</td><td>Missouri</td><td>22.0</td></tr>
<tr><td>3</td><td>Iowa</td><td>25.8</td><td>15</td><td>Pennsylvania</td><td>21.8</td></tr>
<tr><td>9</td><td>Kansas</td><td>23.4</td><td>16</td><td>North Dakota</td><td>21.7</td></tr>
<tr><td>13</td><td>Kentucky</td><td>22.0</td><td>17</td><td>Mississippi</td><td>21.3</td></tr>
<tr><td>24</td><td>Louisiana</td><td>19.4</td><td>18</td><td>Illinois</td><td>20.8</td></tr>
<tr><td>19</td><td>Maine</td><td>20.4</td><td>19</td><td>Maine</td><td>20.4</td></tr>
<tr><td>25</td><td>Maryland</td><td>19.3</td><td>20</td><td>California</td><td>20.1</td></tr>
<tr><td>2</td><td>Massachusetts</td><td>27.2</td><td>21</td><td>Alabama</td><td>20.0</td></tr>
<tr><td>36</td><td>Michigan</td><td>16.6</td><td>21</td><td>Hawaii</td><td>20.0</td></tr>
<tr><td>49</td><td>Minnesota</td><td>12.2</td><td>23</td><td>Nebraska</td><td>19.5</td></tr>
<tr><td>17</td><td>Mississippi</td><td>21.3</td><td>24</td><td>Louisiana</td><td>19.4</td></tr>
<tr><td>13</td><td>Missouri</td><td>22.0</td><td>25</td><td>Maryland</td><td>19.3</td></tr>
<tr><td>30</td><td>Montana</td><td>17.9</td><td>25</td><td>North Carolina</td><td>19.3</td></tr>
<tr><td>23</td><td>Nebraska</td><td>19.5</td><td>27</td><td>Arizona</td><td>18.9</td></tr>
<tr><td>32</td><td>Nevada</td><td>17.1</td><td>28</td><td>Wisconsin</td><td>18.2</td></tr>
<tr><td>38</td><td>New Hampshire</td><td>16.1</td><td>29</td><td>New Mexico</td><td>18.1</td></tr>
<tr><td>41</td><td>New Jersey</td><td>15.1</td><td>30</td><td>Indiana</td><td>17.9</td></tr>
<tr><td>29</td><td>New Mexico</td><td>18.1</td><td>30</td><td>Montana</td><td>17.9</td></tr>
<tr><td>5</td><td>New York</td><td>25.3</td><td>32</td><td>Nevada</td><td>17.1</td></tr>
<tr><td>25</td><td>North Carolina</td><td>19.3</td><td>33</td><td>Ohio</td><td>17.0</td></tr>
<tr><td>16</td><td>North Dakota</td><td>21.7</td><td>34</td><td>South Carolina</td><td>16.8</td></tr>
<tr><td>33</td><td>Ohio</td><td>17.0</td><td>34</td><td>Virginia</td><td>16.8</td></tr>
<tr><td>8</td><td>Oklahoma</td><td>24.6</td><td>36</td><td>Michigan</td><td>16.6</td></tr>
<tr><td>43</td><td>Oregon</td><td>14.1</td><td>37</td><td>Delaware</td><td>16.2</td></tr>
<tr><td>15</td><td>Pennsylvania</td><td>21.8</td><td>38</td><td>New Hampshire</td><td>16.1</td></tr>
<tr><td>7</td><td>Rhode Island</td><td>25.1</td><td>39</td><td>Georgia</td><td>15.6</td></tr>
<tr><td>34</td><td>South Carolina</td><td>16.8</td><td>40</td><td>Idaho</td><td>15.3</td></tr>
<tr><td>12</td><td>South Dakota</td><td>22.1</td><td>41</td><td>New Jersey</td><td>15.1</td></tr>
<tr><td>4</td><td>Tennessee</td><td>25.4</td><td>42</td><td>Texas</td><td>14.2</td></tr>
<tr><td>42</td><td>Texas</td><td>14.2</td><td>43</td><td>Oregon</td><td>14.1</td></tr>
<tr><td>45</td><td>Utah</td><td>13.5</td><td>44</td><td>Florida</td><td>13.6</td></tr>
<tr><td>48</td><td>Vermont</td><td>12.3</td><td>45</td><td>Utah</td><td>13.5</td></tr>
<tr><td>34</td><td>Virginia</td><td>16.8</td><td>46</td><td>Colorado</td><td>12.9</td></tr>
<tr><td>47</td><td>Washington</td><td>12.7</td><td>47</td><td>Washington</td><td>12.7</td></tr>
<tr><td>6</td><td>West Virginia</td><td>25.2</td><td>48</td><td>Vermont</td><td>12.3</td></tr>
<tr><td>28</td><td>Wisconsin</td><td>18.2</td><td>49</td><td>Minnesota</td><td>12.2</td></tr>
<tr><td>11</td><td>Wyoming</td><td>22.7</td><td>50</td><td>Alaska</td><td>7.3</td></tr>
<tr><td></td><td></td><td></td><td></td><td>District of Columbia</td><td>13.1</td></tr>
</table>

Source: U.S. Department of Health and Human Services, National Center for Health Statistics
   "National Vital Statistics Reports" (Vol. 57, No. 14, April 17, 2009, http://www.cdc.gov/nchs/deaths.htm)
*Final data by state of residence. Not age-adjusted.

Age-Adjusted Death Rate by Influenza and Pneumonia in 2006

National Rate = 17.8 Deaths per 100,000 Population*

ALPHA ORDER

RANK	STATE	RATE
21	Alabama	18.6
44	Alaska	13.5
24	Arizona	18.1
2	Arkansas	23.9
7	California	21.8
38	Colorado	15.4
22	Connecticut	18.5
39	Delaware	15.1
50	Florida	9.7
14	Georgia	19.7
32	Hawaii	16.2
34	Idaho	15.8
11	Illinois	20.1
28	Indiana	17.0
20	Iowa	18.8
18	Kansas	19.4
8	Kentucky	21.3
15	Louisiana	19.6
29	Maine	16.6
12	Maryland	19.9
5	Massachusetts	22.5
34	Michigan	15.8
48	Minnesota	10.8
9	Mississippi	20.8
19	Missouri	19.3
42	Montana	15.0
34	Nebraska	15.8
13	Nevada	19.8
39	New Hampshire	15.1
44	New Jersey	13.5
25	New Mexico	18.0
5	New York	22.5
15	North Carolina	19.6
39	North Dakota	15.1
42	Ohio	15.0
3	Oklahoma	22.7
47	Oregon	12.5
33	Pennsylvania	16.1
17	Rhode Island	19.5
31	South Carolina	16.4
30	South Dakota	16.5
1	Tennessee	24.9
27	Texas	17.3
23	Utah	18.2
48	Vermont	10.8
26	Virginia	17.9
46	Washington	12.7
10	West Virginia	20.6
37	Wisconsin	15.7
4	Wyoming	22.6

RANK ORDER

RANK	STATE	RATE
1	Tennessee	24.9
2	Arkansas	23.9
3	Oklahoma	22.7
4	Wyoming	22.6
5	Massachusetts	22.5
5	New York	22.5
7	California	21.8
8	Kentucky	21.3
9	Mississippi	20.8
10	West Virginia	20.6
11	Illinois	20.1
12	Maryland	19.9
13	Nevada	19.8
14	Georgia	19.7
15	Louisiana	19.6
15	North Carolina	19.6
17	Rhode Island	19.5
18	Kansas	19.4
19	Missouri	19.3
20	Iowa	18.8
21	Alabama	18.6
22	Connecticut	18.5
23	Utah	18.2
24	Arizona	18.1
25	New Mexico	18.0
26	Virginia	17.9
27	Texas	17.3
28	Indiana	17.0
29	Maine	16.6
30	South Dakota	16.5
31	South Carolina	16.4
32	Hawaii	16.2
33	Pennsylvania	16.1
34	Idaho	15.8
34	Michigan	15.8
34	Nebraska	15.8
37	Wisconsin	15.7
38	Colorado	15.4
39	Delaware	15.1
39	New Hampshire	15.1
39	North Dakota	15.1
42	Montana	15.0
42	Ohio	15.0
44	Alaska	13.5
44	New Jersey	13.5
46	Washington	12.7
47	Oregon	12.5
48	Minnesota	10.8
48	Vermont	10.8
50	Florida	9.7
	District of Columbia	12.6

Source: U.S. Department of Health and Human Services, National Center for Health Statistics
"National Vital Statistics Reports" (Vol. 57, No. 14, April 17, 2009, http://www.cdc.gov/nchs/deaths.htm)
*Final data by state of residence. Age-adjusted rates based on the year 2000 standard population.

Deaths by Injury in 2006

National Total = 179,065 Deaths*

ALPHA ORDER

ALPHA ORDER

RANK	STATE	DEATHS	% of USA
18	Alabama	3,626	2.0%
46	Alaska	506	0.3%
11	Arizona	5,023	2.8%
30	Arkansas	2,174	1.2%
1	California	17,758	9.9%
24	Colorado	2,975	1.7%
33	Connecticut	1,751	1.0%
47	Delaware	491	0.3%
3	Florida	12,739	7.1%
10	Georgia	5,597	3.1%
42	Hawaii	666	0.4%
39	Idaho	974	0.5%
7	Illinois	6,403	3.6%
15	Indiana	3,909	2.2%
35	Iowa	1,632	0.9%
34	Kansas	1,742	1.0%
21	Kentucky	3,351	1.9%
19	Louisiana	3,580	2.0%
41	Maine	763	0.4%
23	Maryland	3,264	1.8%
25	Massachusetts	2,931	1.6%
9	Michigan	5,712	3.2%
27	Minnesota	2,668	1.5%
28	Mississippi	2,574	1.4%
13	Missouri	4,310	2.4%
40	Montana	810	0.5%
38	Nebraska	975	0.5%
31	Nevada	1,849	1.0%
43	New Hampshire	646	0.4%
17	New Jersey	3,698	2.1%
32	New Mexico	1,836	1.0%
4	New York	7,800	4.4%
8	North Carolina	5,946	3.3%
50	North Dakota	386	0.2%
6	Ohio	6,927	3.9%
26	Oklahoma	2,864	1.6%
29	Oregon	2,393	1.3%
5	Pennsylvania	7,634	4.3%
45	Rhode Island	603	0.3%
22	South Carolina	3,270	1.8%
44	South Dakota	606	0.3%
12	Tennessee	4,856	2.7%
2	Texas	13,197	7.4%
37	Utah	1,466	0.8%
49	Vermont	401	0.2%
14	Virginia	4,058	2.3%
16	Washington	3,811	2.1%
36	West Virginia	1,601	0.9%
20	Wisconsin	3,454	1.9%
48	Wyoming	435	0.2%

RANK ORDER

RANK	STATE	DEATHS	% of USA
1	California	17,758	9.9%
2	Texas	13,197	7.4%
3	Florida	12,739	7.1%
4	New York	7,800	4.4%
5	Pennsylvania	7,634	4.3%
6	Ohio	6,927	3.9%
7	Illinois	6,403	3.6%
8	North Carolina	5,946	3.3%
9	Michigan	5,712	3.2%
10	Georgia	5,597	3.1%
11	Arizona	5,023	2.8%
12	Tennessee	4,856	2.7%
13	Missouri	4,310	2.4%
14	Virginia	4,058	2.3%
15	Indiana	3,909	2.2%
16	Washington	3,811	2.1%
17	New Jersey	3,698	2.1%
18	Alabama	3,626	2.0%
19	Louisiana	3,580	2.0%
20	Wisconsin	3,454	1.9%
21	Kentucky	3,351	1.9%
22	South Carolina	3,270	1.8%
23	Maryland	3,264	1.8%
24	Colorado	2,975	1.7%
25	Massachusetts	2,931	1.6%
26	Oklahoma	2,864	1.6%
27	Minnesota	2,668	1.5%
28	Mississippi	2,574	1.4%
29	Oregon	2,393	1.3%
30	Arkansas	2,174	1.2%
31	Nevada	1,849	1.0%
32	New Mexico	1,836	1.0%
33	Connecticut	1,751	1.0%
34	Kansas	1,742	1.0%
35	Iowa	1,632	0.9%
36	West Virginia	1,601	0.9%
37	Utah	1,466	0.8%
38	Nebraska	975	0.5%
39	Idaho	974	0.5%
40	Montana	810	0.5%
41	Maine	763	0.4%
42	Hawaii	666	0.4%
43	New Hampshire	646	0.4%
44	South Dakota	606	0.3%
45	Rhode Island	603	0.3%
46	Alaska	506	0.3%
47	Delaware	491	0.3%
48	Wyoming	435	0.2%
49	Vermont	401	0.2%
50	North Dakota	386	0.2%
	District of Columbia	424	0.2%

Source: U.S. Department of Health and Human Services, National Center for Health Statistics
(http://wonder.cdc.gov)
*By state of residence. Injury as used here includes accidents (including motor vehicle), suicides, homicides, and "other" undetermined.

Death Rate by Injury in 2006

National Rate = 59.9 Deaths per 100,000 Population*

ALPHA ORDER				RANK ORDER		
RANK	STATE	RATE		RANK	STATE	RATE
11	Alabama	79.0		1	New Mexico	94.5
15	Alaska	74.7		2	Mississippi	88.8
7	Arizona	81.5		3	West Virginia	88.5
12	Arkansas	77.4		4	Montana	85.6
47	California	49.0		5	Wyoming	84.8
24	Colorado	62.4		6	Louisiana	84.4
44	Connecticut	50.1		7	Arizona	81.5
34	Delaware	57.6		8	Oklahoma	80.1
18	Florida	70.5		9	Tennessee	79.9
30	Georgia	59.9		10	Kentucky	79.7
42	Hawaii	52.1		11	Alabama	79.0
20	Idaho	66.5		12	Arkansas	77.4
44	Illinois	50.1		13	South Dakota	76.9
25	Indiana	62.0		14	South Carolina	75.5
40	Iowa	54.9		15	Alaska	74.7
23	Kansas	63.2		16	Nevada	74.2
10	Kentucky	79.7		17	Missouri	73.8
6	Louisiana	84.4		18	Florida	70.5
33	Maine	58.0		19	North Carolina	67.0
32	Maryland	58.3		20	Idaho	66.5
48	Massachusetts	45.6		21	Oregon	64.8
37	Michigan	56.5		22	Vermont	64.6
43	Minnesota	51.8		23	Kansas	63.2
2	Mississippi	88.8		24	Colorado	62.4
17	Missouri	73.8		25	Indiana	62.0
4	Montana	85.6		25	Wisconsin	62.0
39	Nebraska	55.3		27	Pennsylvania	61.6
16	Nevada	74.2		28	North Dakota	60.6
46	New Hampshire	49.2		29	Ohio	60.4
49	New Jersey	42.7		30	Georgia	59.9
1	New Mexico	94.5		31	Washington	59.8
50	New York	40.5		32	Maryland	58.3
19	North Carolina	67.0		33	Maine	58.0
28	North Dakota	60.6		34	Delaware	57.6
29	Ohio	60.4		35	Rhode Island	56.8
8	Oklahoma	80.1		35	Utah	56.8
21	Oregon	64.8		37	Michigan	56.5
27	Pennsylvania	61.6		38	Texas	56.4
35	Rhode Island	56.8		39	Nebraska	55.3
14	South Carolina	75.5		40	Iowa	54.9
13	South Dakota	76.9		41	Virginia	53.1
9	Tennessee	79.9		42	Hawaii	52.1
38	Texas	56.4		43	Minnesota	51.8
35	Utah	56.8		44	Connecticut	50.1
22	Vermont	64.6		44	Illinois	50.1
41	Virginia	53.1		46	New Hampshire	49.2
31	Washington	59.8		47	California	49.0
3	West Virginia	88.5		48	Massachusetts	45.6
25	Wisconsin	62.0		49	New Jersey	42.7
5	Wyoming	84.8		50	New York	40.5
					District of Columbia	72.4

Source: U.S. Department of Health and Human Services, National Center for Health Statistics
(http://wonder.cdc.gov)
*By state of residence. Injury as used here includes accidents (including motor vehicle), suicides, homicides, and "other" undetermined. Not age-adjusted.

Age-Adjusted Death Rate by Injury in 2006

National Rate = 58.9 Deaths per 100,000 Population*

ALPHA ORDER

RANK ORDER

RANK	STATE	RATE		RANK	STATE	RATE
12	Alabama	78.3		1	New Mexico	94.9
9	Alaska	79.2		2	Mississippi	89.5
7	Arizona	81.1		3	West Virginia	85.3
13	Arkansas	76.6		4	Louisiana	84.3
44	California	49.1		5	Wyoming	83.9
21	Colorado	63.8		6	Montana	82.1
47	Connecticut	47.5		7	Arizona	81.1
34	Delaware	57.1		8	Oklahoma	79.4
20	Florida	66.7		9	Alaska	79.2
22	Georgia	62.4		9	Tennessee	79.2
45	Hawaii	48.5		11	Kentucky	79.0
18	Idaho	67.8		12	Alabama	78.3
42	Illinois	49.6		13	Arkansas	76.6
26	Indiana	61.4		14	Nevada	75.4
41	Iowa	50.4		15	South Carolina	75.0
25	Kansas	61.5		16	South Dakota	72.4
11	Kentucky	79.0		17	Missouri	72.0
4	Louisiana	84.3		18	Idaho	67.8
37	Maine	54.5		19	North Carolina	66.9
33	Maryland	58.0		20	Florida	66.7
48	Massachusetts	42.8		21	Colorado	63.8
36	Michigan	55.7		22	Georgia	62.4
42	Minnesota	49.6		23	Utah	62.1
2	Mississippi	89.5		24	Oregon	61.9
17	Missouri	72.0		25	Kansas	61.5
6	Montana	82.1		26	Indiana	61.4
39	Nebraska	52.3		27	Vermont	60.5
14	Nevada	75.4		28	Wisconsin	59.1
46	New Hampshire	47.6		29	Texas	58.7
49	New Jersey	41.6		30	Ohio	58.5
1	New Mexico	94.9		30	Washington	58.5
50	New York	38.9		32	Pennsylvania	58.2
19	North Carolina	66.9		33	Maryland	58.0
35	North Dakota	56.2		34	Delaware	57.1
30	Ohio	58.5		35	North Dakota	56.2
8	Oklahoma	79.4		36	Michigan	55.7
24	Oregon	61.9		37	Maine	54.5
32	Pennsylvania	58.2		38	Virginia	53.1
40	Rhode Island	52.1		39	Nebraska	52.3
15	South Carolina	75.0		40	Rhode Island	52.1
16	South Dakota	72.4		41	Iowa	50.4
9	Tennessee	79.2		42	Illinois	49.6
29	Texas	58.7		42	Minnesota	49.6
23	Utah	62.1		44	California	49.1
27	Vermont	60.5		45	Hawaii	48.5
38	Virginia	53.1		46	New Hampshire	47.6
30	Washington	58.5		47	Connecticut	47.5
3	West Virginia	85.3		48	Massachusetts	42.8
28	Wisconsin	59.1		49	New Jersey	41.6
5	Wyoming	83.9		50	New York	38.9

District of Columbia 69.5

Source: U.S. Department of Health and Human Services, National Center for Health Statistics
(http://wonder.cdc.gov)

*By state of residence. Injury as used here includes accidents (including motor vehicle), suicides, homicides, and "other" undetermined. Age-adjusted rates based on the year 2000 standard population.

Deaths by Accidents in 2006

National Total = 121,599 Deaths*

ALPHA ORDER				RANK ORDER			
RANK	STATE	DEATHS	% of USA	RANK	STATE	DEATHS	% of USA
18	Alabama	2,506	2.1%	1	California	11,375	9.4%
47	Alaska	316	0.3%	2	Texas	9,140	7.5%
11	Arizona	3,352	2.8%	3	Florida	8,917	7.3%
30	Arkansas	1,415	1.2%	4	Pennsylvania	5,299	4.4%
1	California	11,375	9.4%	5	New York	5,235	4.3%
26	Colorado	1,917	1.6%	6	Ohio	4,821	4.0%
31	Connecticut	1,302	1.1%	7	Illinois	4,451	3.7%
46	Delaware	329	0.3%	8	North Carolina	4,156	3.4%
3	Florida	8,917	7.3%	9	Georgia	3,879	3.2%
9	Georgia	3,879	3.2%	10	Michigan	3,590	3.0%
44	Hawaii	441	0.4%	11	Arizona	3,352	2.8%
39	Idaho	682	0.6%	12	Tennessee	3,307	2.7%
7	Illinois	4,451	3.7%	13	Missouri	3,009	2.5%
19	Indiana	2,480	2.0%	14	Virginia	2,703	2.2%
34	Iowa	1,188	1.0%	15	Washington	2,679	2.2%
33	Kansas	1,198	1.0%	16	New Jersey	2,590	2.1%
20	Kentucky	2,446	2.0%	17	Wisconsin	2,524	2.1%
21	Louisiana	2,422	2.0%	18	Alabama	2,506	2.1%
40	Maine	572	0.5%	19	Indiana	2,480	2.0%
29	Maryland	1,456	1.2%	20	Kentucky	2,446	2.0%
23	Massachusetts	2,214	1.8%	21	Louisiana	2,422	2.0%
10	Michigan	3,590	3.0%	22	South Carolina	2,315	1.9%
25	Minnesota	1,919	1.6%	23	Massachusetts	2,214	1.8%
27	Mississippi	1,856	1.5%	24	Oklahoma	2,039	1.7%
13	Missouri	3,009	2.5%	25	Minnesota	1,919	1.6%
41	Montana	558	0.5%	26	Colorado	1,917	1.6%
38	Nebraska	683	0.6%	27	Mississippi	1,856	1.5%
36	Nevada	1,091	0.9%	28	Oregon	1,586	1.3%
42	New Hampshire	460	0.4%	29	Maryland	1,456	1.2%
16	New Jersey	2,590	2.1%	30	Arkansas	1,415	1.2%
32	New Mexico	1,297	1.1%	31	Connecticut	1,302	1.1%
5	New York	5,235	4.3%	32	New Mexico	1,297	1.1%
8	North Carolina	4,156	3.4%	33	Kansas	1,198	1.0%
50	North Dakota	275	0.2%	34	Iowa	1,188	1.0%
6	Ohio	4,821	4.0%	35	West Virginia	1,177	1.0%
24	Oklahoma	2,039	1.7%	36	Nevada	1,091	0.9%
28	Oregon	1,586	1.3%	37	Utah	715	0.6%
4	Pennsylvania	5,299	4.4%	38	Nebraska	683	0.6%
45	Rhode Island	434	0.4%	39	Idaho	682	0.6%
22	South Carolina	2,315	1.9%	40	Maine	572	0.5%
43	South Dakota	452	0.4%	41	Montana	558	0.5%
12	Tennessee	3,307	2.7%	42	New Hampshire	460	0.4%
2	Texas	9,140	7.5%	43	South Dakota	452	0.4%
37	Utah	715	0.6%	44	Hawaii	441	0.4%
49	Vermont	301	0.2%	45	Rhode Island	434	0.4%
14	Virginia	2,703	2.2%	46	Delaware	329	0.3%
15	Washington	2,679	2.2%	47	Alaska	316	0.3%
35	West Virginia	1,177	1.0%	48	Wyoming	306	0.3%
17	Wisconsin	2,524	2.1%	49	Vermont	301	0.2%
48	Wyoming	306	0.3%	50	North Dakota	275	0.2%
					District of Columbia	224	0.2%

Source: U.S. Department of Health and Human Services, National Center for Health Statistics
   "National Vital Statistics Reports" (Vol. 57, No. 14, April 17, 2009, http://www.cdc.gov/nchs/deaths.htm)
*Final data by state of residence. Includes motor vehicle deaths, poisoning, falls, drowning, and other accidents.

Death Rate by Accidents in 2006

National Rate = 40.6 Deaths per 100,000 Population*

ALPHA ORDER

RANK	STATE	RATE
11	Alabama	54.5
18	Alaska	47.2
12	Arizona	54.4
15	Arkansas	50.3
46	California	31.2
32	Colorado	40.3
38	Connecticut	37.1
37	Delaware	38.5
16	Florida	49.3
30	Georgia	41.4
45	Hawaii	34.3
20	Idaho	46.5
43	Illinois	34.7
34	Indiana	39.3
33	Iowa	39.8
23	Kansas	43.3
6	Kentucky	58.2
9	Louisiana	56.5
23	Maine	43.3
50	Maryland	25.9
44	Massachusetts	34.4
40	Michigan	35.6
38	Minnesota	37.1
3	Mississippi	63.8
14	Missouri	51.5
5	Montana	59.1
36	Nebraska	38.6
22	Nevada	43.7
42	New Hampshire	35.0
47	New Jersey	29.7
1	New Mexico	66.4
49	New York	27.1
19	North Carolina	46.9
25	North Dakota	43.2
28	Ohio	42.0
8	Oklahoma	57.0
26	Oregon	42.9
27	Pennsylvania	42.6
31	Rhode Island	40.7
13	South Carolina	53.6
7	South Dakota	57.8
10	Tennessee	54.8
35	Texas	38.9
48	Utah	28.0
17	Vermont	48.2
41	Virginia	35.4
29	Washington	41.9
2	West Virginia	64.7
21	Wisconsin	45.4
4	Wyoming	59.4

RANK ORDER

RANK	STATE	RATE
1	New Mexico	66.4
2	West Virginia	64.7
3	Mississippi	63.8
4	Wyoming	59.4
5	Montana	59.1
6	Kentucky	58.2
7	South Dakota	57.8
8	Oklahoma	57.0
9	Louisiana	56.5
10	Tennessee	54.8
11	Alabama	54.5
12	Arizona	54.4
13	South Carolina	53.6
14	Missouri	51.5
15	Arkansas	50.3
16	Florida	49.3
17	Vermont	48.2
18	Alaska	47.2
19	North Carolina	46.9
20	Idaho	46.5
21	Wisconsin	45.4
22	Nevada	43.7
23	Kansas	43.3
23	Maine	43.3
25	North Dakota	43.2
26	Oregon	42.9
27	Pennsylvania	42.6
28	Ohio	42.0
29	Washington	41.9
30	Georgia	41.4
31	Rhode Island	40.7
32	Colorado	40.3
33	Iowa	39.8
34	Indiana	39.3
35	Texas	38.9
36	Nebraska	38.6
37	Delaware	38.5
38	Connecticut	37.1
38	Minnesota	37.1
40	Michigan	35.6
41	Virginia	35.4
42	New Hampshire	35.0
43	Illinois	34.7
44	Massachusetts	34.4
45	Hawaii	34.3
46	California	31.2
47	New Jersey	29.7
48	Utah	28.0
49	New York	27.1
50	Maryland	25.9
	District of Columbia	38.5

Source: U.S. Department of Health and Human Services, National Center for Health Statistics
"National Vital Statistics Reports" (Vol. 57, No. 14, April 17, 2009, http://www.cdc.gov/nchs/deaths.htm)
*Final data by state of residence. Includes motor vehicle deaths, poisoning, falls, drowning, and other accidents. Not age-adjusted.

Age-Adjusted Death Rate by Accidents in 2006

National Rate = 39.8 Deaths per 100,000 Population*

ALPHA ORDER

RANK	STATE	RATE
10	Alabama	53.8
14	Alaska	51.9
10	Arizona	53.8
16	Arkansas	49.1
46	California	31.6
24	Colorado	42.1
41	Connecticut	34.6
34	Delaware	37.9
19	Florida	46.0
22	Georgia	43.8
45	Hawaii	31.7
17	Idaho	47.0
42	Illinois	34.3
33	Indiana	38.7
38	Iowa	35.4
25	Kansas	41.5
5	Kentucky	57.5
6	Louisiana	56.6
28	Maine	40.6
49	Maryland	26.1
44	Massachusetts	32.0
40	Michigan	34.9
39	Minnesota	35.2
2	Mississippi	63.8
15	Missouri	49.7
8	Montana	55.8
36	Nebraska	35.9
21	Nevada	44.5
43	New Hampshire	33.7
48	New Jersey	28.7
1	New Mexico	67.1
50	New York	25.9
17	North Carolina	47.0
31	North Dakota	39.5
30	Ohio	40.2
7	Oklahoma	56.3
29	Oregon	40.5
32	Pennsylvania	39.4
35	Rhode Island	36.4
12	South Carolina	53.2
13	South Dakota	53.0
9	Tennessee	54.2
27	Texas	41.0
47	Utah	30.9
20	Vermont	45.2
37	Virginia	35.7
26	Washington	41.1
3	West Virginia	62.2
23	Wisconsin	42.7
4	Wyoming	58.9

RANK ORDER

RANK	STATE	RATE
1	New Mexico	67.1
2	Mississippi	63.8
3	West Virginia	62.2
4	Wyoming	58.9
5	Kentucky	57.5
6	Louisiana	56.6
7	Oklahoma	56.3
8	Montana	55.8
9	Tennessee	54.2
10	Alabama	53.8
10	Arizona	53.8
12	South Carolina	53.2
13	South Dakota	53.0
14	Alaska	51.9
15	Missouri	49.7
16	Arkansas	49.1
17	Idaho	47.0
17	North Carolina	47.0
19	Florida	46.0
20	Vermont	45.2
21	Nevada	44.5
22	Georgia	43.8
23	Wisconsin	42.7
24	Colorado	42.1
25	Kansas	41.5
26	Washington	41.1
27	Texas	41.0
28	Maine	40.6
29	Oregon	40.5
30	Ohio	40.2
31	North Dakota	39.5
32	Pennsylvania	39.4
33	Indiana	38.7
34	Delaware	37.9
35	Rhode Island	36.4
36	Nebraska	35.9
37	Virginia	35.7
38	Iowa	35.4
39	Minnesota	35.2
40	Michigan	34.9
41	Connecticut	34.6
42	Illinois	34.3
43	New Hampshire	33.7
44	Massachusetts	32.0
45	Hawaii	31.7
46	California	31.6
47	Utah	30.9
48	New Jersey	28.7
49	Maryland	26.1
50	New York	25.9

	District of Columbia	38.1

Source: U.S. Department of Health and Human Services, National Center for Health Statistics
"National Vital Statistics Reports" (Vol. 57, No. 14, April 17, 2009, http://www.cdc.gov/nchs/deaths.htm)
*Final data by state of residence. Includes motor vehicle deaths, poisoning, falls, drowning, and other accidents. Age-adjusted rates based on the year 2000 standard population.

Deaths by Motor Vehicle Accidents in 2006

National Total = 45,316 Deaths*

ALPHA ORDER

RANK	STATE	DEATHS	% of USA
12	Alabama	1,224	2.7%
50	Alaska	85	0.2%
11	Arizona	1,323	2.9%
25	Arkansas	729	1.6%
1	California	4,464	9.9%
28	Colorado	591	1.3%
36	Connecticut	363	0.8%
45	Delaware	140	0.3%
3	Florida	3,466	7.6%
4	Georgia	1,751	3.9%
43	Hawaii	157	0.3%
38	Idaho	298	0.7%
8	Illinois	1,416	3.1%
19	Indiana	954	2.1%
33	Iowa	457	1.0%
30	Kansas	491	1.1%
20	Kentucky	932	2.1%
16	Louisiana	1,017	2.2%
41	Maine	193	0.4%
26	Maryland	727	1.6%
31	Massachusetts	487	1.1%
13	Michigan	1,176	2.6%
27	Minnesota	610	1.3%
17	Mississippi	968	2.1%
14	Missouri	1,111	2.5%
40	Montana	264	0.6%
39	Nebraska	270	0.6%
34	Nevada	442	1.0%
46	New Hampshire	129	0.3%
22	New Jersey	774	1.7%
32	New Mexico	469	1.0%
7	New York	1,599	3.5%
5	North Carolina	1,704	3.8%
47	North Dakota	114	0.3%
10	Ohio	1,367	3.0%
21	Oklahoma	787	1.7%
29	Oregon	510	1.1%
6	Pennsylvania	1,625	3.6%
49	Rhode Island	89	0.2%
15	South Carolina	1,044	2.3%
41	South Dakota	193	0.4%
9	Tennessee	1,379	3.0%
2	Texas	3,907	8.6%
37	Utah	342	0.8%
48	Vermont	91	0.2%
18	Virginia	962	2.1%
24	Washington	743	1.6%
35	West Virginia	420	0.9%
23	Wisconsin	769	1.7%
44	Wyoming	153	0.3%

RANK ORDER

RANK	STATE	DEATHS	% of USA
1	California	4,464	9.9%
2	Texas	3,907	8.6%
3	Florida	3,466	7.6%
4	Georgia	1,751	3.9%
5	North Carolina	1,704	3.8%
6	Pennsylvania	1,625	3.6%
7	New York	1,599	3.5%
8	Illinois	1,416	3.1%
9	Tennessee	1,379	3.0%
10	Ohio	1,367	3.0%
11	Arizona	1,323	2.9%
12	Alabama	1,224	2.7%
13	Michigan	1,176	2.6%
14	Missouri	1,111	2.5%
15	South Carolina	1,044	2.3%
16	Louisiana	1,017	2.2%
17	Mississippi	968	2.1%
18	Virginia	962	2.1%
19	Indiana	954	2.1%
20	Kentucky	932	2.1%
21	Oklahoma	787	1.7%
22	New Jersey	774	1.7%
23	Wisconsin	769	1.7%
24	Washington	743	1.6%
25	Arkansas	729	1.6%
26	Maryland	727	1.6%
27	Minnesota	610	1.3%
28	Colorado	591	1.3%
29	Oregon	510	1.1%
30	Kansas	491	1.1%
31	Massachusetts	487	1.1%
32	New Mexico	469	1.0%
33	Iowa	457	1.0%
34	Nevada	442	1.0%
35	West Virginia	420	0.9%
36	Connecticut	363	0.8%
37	Utah	342	0.8%
38	Idaho	298	0.7%
39	Nebraska	270	0.6%
40	Montana	264	0.6%
41	Maine	193	0.4%
41	South Dakota	193	0.4%
43	Hawaii	157	0.3%
44	Wyoming	153	0.3%
45	Delaware	140	0.3%
46	New Hampshire	129	0.3%
47	North Dakota	114	0.3%
48	Vermont	91	0.2%
49	Rhode Island	89	0.2%
50	Alaska	85	0.2%
	District of Columbia	40	0.1%

Source: U.S. Department of Health and Human Services, National Center for Health Statistics
"National Vital Statistics Reports" (Vol. 57, No. 14, April 17, 2009, http://www.cdc.gov/nchs/deaths.htm)
*Final data by state of residence. These numbers are compiled from death certificates by the Centers for Disease Control and Prevention. They may differ from motor vehicle deaths collected by the U.S. Department of Transportation from other sources.

Death Rate by Motor Vehicle Accidents in 2006

National Rate = 15.1 Deaths per 100,000 Population*

RANK	STATE	RATE
4	Alabama	26.6
35	Alaska	12.7
14	Arizona	21.5
5	Arkansas	25.9
38	California	12.2
37	Colorado	12.4
45	Connecticut	10.4
24	Delaware	16.4
16	Florida	19.2
19	Georgia	18.7
38	Hawaii	12.2
15	Idaho	20.3
44	Illinois	11.0
27	Indiana	15.1
25	Iowa	15.3
21	Kansas	17.8
12	Kentucky	22.2
9	Louisiana	23.7
28	Maine	14.6
34	Maryland	12.9
50	Massachusetts	7.6
42	Michigan	11.6
41	Minnesota	11.8
1	Mississippi	33.3
18	Missouri	19.0
3	Montana	27.9
25	Nebraska	15.3
22	Nevada	17.7
46	New Hampshire	9.8
47	New Jersey	8.9
8	New Mexico	24.0
48	New York	8.3
16	North Carolina	19.2
20	North Dakota	17.9
40	Ohio	11.9
13	Oklahoma	22.0
30	Oregon	13.8
33	Pennsylvania	13.1
48	Rhode Island	8.3
7	South Carolina	24.2
6	South Dakota	24.7
11	Tennessee	22.8
23	Texas	16.6
32	Utah	13.4
28	Vermont	14.6
36	Virginia	12.6
42	Washington	11.6
10	West Virginia	23.1
30	Wisconsin	13.8
2	Wyoming	29.7

RANK	STATE	RATE
1	Mississippi	33.3
2	Wyoming	29.7
3	Montana	27.9
4	Alabama	26.6
5	Arkansas	25.9
6	South Dakota	24.7
7	South Carolina	24.2
8	New Mexico	24.0
9	Louisiana	23.7
10	West Virginia	23.1
11	Tennessee	22.8
12	Kentucky	22.2
13	Oklahoma	22.0
14	Arizona	21.5
15	Idaho	20.3
16	Florida	19.2
16	North Carolina	19.2
18	Missouri	19.0
19	Georgia	18.7
20	North Dakota	17.9
21	Kansas	17.8
22	Nevada	17.7
23	Texas	16.6
24	Delaware	16.4
25	Iowa	15.3
25	Nebraska	15.3
27	Indiana	15.1
28	Maine	14.6
28	Vermont	14.6
30	Oregon	13.8
30	Wisconsin	13.8
32	Utah	13.4
33	Pennsylvania	13.1
34	Maryland	12.9
35	Alaska	12.7
36	Virginia	12.6
37	Colorado	12.4
38	California	12.2
38	Hawaii	12.2
40	Ohio	11.9
41	Minnesota	11.8
42	Michigan	11.6
42	Washington	11.6
44	Illinois	11.0
45	Connecticut	10.4
46	New Hampshire	9.8
47	New Jersey	8.9
48	New York	8.3
48	Rhode Island	8.3
50	Massachusetts	7.6

District of Columbia	6.9

Source: U.S. Department of Health and Human Services, National Center for Health Statistics
   "National Vital Statistics Reports" (Vol. 57, No. 14, April 17, 2009, http://www.cdc.gov/nchs/deaths.htm)
*Final data by state of residence. These numbers are compiled from death certificates by the Centers for Disease Control and Prevention. They may differ from motor vehicle deaths collected by the U.S. Department of Transportation from other sources. Not age-adjusted.

Age-Adjusted Death Rate by Motor Vehicle Accidents in 2006

National Rate = 15.0 Deaths per 100,000 Population*

<table>
<tr><td colspan="3">ALPHA ORDER</td><td colspan="3">RANK ORDER</td></tr>
<tr><th>RANK</th><th>STATE</th><th>RATE</th><th>RANK</th><th>STATE</th><th>RATE</th></tr>
<tr><td>4</td><td>Alabama</td><td>26.6</td><td>1</td><td>Mississippi</td><td>33.3</td></tr>
<tr><td>33</td><td>Alaska</td><td>13.1</td><td>2</td><td>Wyoming</td><td>29.7</td></tr>
<tr><td>14</td><td>Arizona</td><td>21.4</td><td>3</td><td>Montana</td><td>27.3</td></tr>
<tr><td>5</td><td>Arkansas</td><td>25.9</td><td>4</td><td>Alabama</td><td>26.6</td></tr>
<tr><td>38</td><td>California</td><td>12.2</td><td>5</td><td>Arkansas</td><td>25.9</td></tr>
<tr><td>37</td><td>Colorado</td><td>12.3</td><td>6</td><td>South Dakota</td><td>24.2</td></tr>
<tr><td>45</td><td>Connecticut</td><td>10.1</td><td>7</td><td>New Mexico</td><td>24.1</td></tr>
<tr><td>24</td><td>Delaware</td><td>16.4</td><td>7</td><td>South Carolina</td><td>24.1</td></tr>
<tr><td>17</td><td>Florida</td><td>18.9</td><td>9</td><td>Louisiana</td><td>23.7</td></tr>
<tr><td>17</td><td>Georgia</td><td>18.9</td><td>10</td><td>West Virginia</td><td>23.1</td></tr>
<tr><td>39</td><td>Hawaii</td><td>11.9</td><td>11</td><td>Tennessee</td><td>22.8</td></tr>
<tr><td>15</td><td>Idaho</td><td>20.4</td><td>12</td><td>Kentucky</td><td>22.0</td></tr>
<tr><td>44</td><td>Illinois</td><td>10.9</td><td>13</td><td>Oklahoma</td><td>21.8</td></tr>
<tr><td>25</td><td>Indiana</td><td>15.0</td><td>14</td><td>Arizona</td><td>21.4</td></tr>
<tr><td>27</td><td>Iowa</td><td>14.6</td><td>15</td><td>Idaho</td><td>20.4</td></tr>
<tr><td>22</td><td>Kansas</td><td>17.4</td><td>16</td><td>North Carolina</td><td>19.2</td></tr>
<tr><td>12</td><td>Kentucky</td><td>22.0</td><td>17</td><td>Florida</td><td>18.9</td></tr>
<tr><td>9</td><td>Louisiana</td><td>23.7</td><td>17</td><td>Georgia</td><td>18.9</td></tr>
<tr><td>28</td><td>Maine</td><td>14.3</td><td>19</td><td>Missouri</td><td>18.8</td></tr>
<tr><td>34</td><td>Maryland</td><td>12.9</td><td>20</td><td>Nevada</td><td>17.9</td></tr>
<tr><td>50</td><td>Massachusetts</td><td>7.3</td><td>20</td><td>North Dakota</td><td>17.9</td></tr>
<tr><td>42</td><td>Michigan</td><td>11.5</td><td>22</td><td>Kansas</td><td>17.4</td></tr>
<tr><td>41</td><td>Minnesota</td><td>11.6</td><td>23</td><td>Texas</td><td>16.8</td></tr>
<tr><td>1</td><td>Mississippi</td><td>33.3</td><td>24</td><td>Delaware</td><td>16.4</td></tr>
<tr><td>19</td><td>Missouri</td><td>18.8</td><td>25</td><td>Indiana</td><td>15.0</td></tr>
<tr><td>3</td><td>Montana</td><td>27.3</td><td>26</td><td>Nebraska</td><td>14.8</td></tr>
<tr><td>26</td><td>Nebraska</td><td>14.8</td><td>27</td><td>Iowa</td><td>14.6</td></tr>
<tr><td>20</td><td>Nevada</td><td>17.9</td><td>28</td><td>Maine</td><td>14.3</td></tr>
<tr><td>46</td><td>New Hampshire</td><td>9.5</td><td>29</td><td>Vermont</td><td>14.1</td></tr>
<tr><td>47</td><td>New Jersey</td><td>8.8</td><td>30</td><td>Utah</td><td>13.9</td></tr>
<tr><td>7</td><td>New Mexico</td><td>24.1</td><td>31</td><td>Oregon</td><td>13.5</td></tr>
<tr><td>48</td><td>New York</td><td>8.1</td><td>31</td><td>Wisconsin</td><td>13.5</td></tr>
<tr><td>16</td><td>North Carolina</td><td>19.2</td><td>33</td><td>Alaska</td><td>13.1</td></tr>
<tr><td>20</td><td>North Dakota</td><td>17.9</td><td>34</td><td>Maryland</td><td>12.9</td></tr>
<tr><td>40</td><td>Ohio</td><td>11.7</td><td>35</td><td>Pennsylvania</td><td>12.8</td></tr>
<tr><td>13</td><td>Oklahoma</td><td>21.8</td><td>36</td><td>Virginia</td><td>12.5</td></tr>
<tr><td>31</td><td>Oregon</td><td>13.5</td><td>37</td><td>Colorado</td><td>12.3</td></tr>
<tr><td>35</td><td>Pennsylvania</td><td>12.8</td><td>38</td><td>California</td><td>12.2</td></tr>
<tr><td>49</td><td>Rhode Island</td><td>7.8</td><td>39</td><td>Hawaii</td><td>11.9</td></tr>
<tr><td>7</td><td>South Carolina</td><td>24.1</td><td>40</td><td>Ohio</td><td>11.7</td></tr>
<tr><td>6</td><td>South Dakota</td><td>24.2</td><td>41</td><td>Minnesota</td><td>11.6</td></tr>
<tr><td>11</td><td>Tennessee</td><td>22.8</td><td>42</td><td>Michigan</td><td>11.5</td></tr>
<tr><td>23</td><td>Texas</td><td>16.8</td><td>43</td><td>Washington</td><td>11.4</td></tr>
<tr><td>30</td><td>Utah</td><td>13.9</td><td>44</td><td>Illinois</td><td>10.9</td></tr>
<tr><td>29</td><td>Vermont</td><td>14.1</td><td>45</td><td>Connecticut</td><td>10.1</td></tr>
<tr><td>36</td><td>Virginia</td><td>12.5</td><td>46</td><td>New Hampshire</td><td>9.5</td></tr>
<tr><td>43</td><td>Washington</td><td>11.4</td><td>47</td><td>New Jersey</td><td>8.8</td></tr>
<tr><td>10</td><td>West Virginia</td><td>23.1</td><td>48</td><td>New York</td><td>8.1</td></tr>
<tr><td>31</td><td>Wisconsin</td><td>13.5</td><td>49</td><td>Rhode Island</td><td>7.8</td></tr>
<tr><td>2</td><td>Wyoming</td><td>29.7</td><td>50</td><td>Massachusetts</td><td>7.3</td></tr>
<tr><td></td><td></td><td></td><td></td><td>District of Columbia</td><td>6.8</td></tr>
</table>

Source: U.S. Department of Health and Human Services, National Center for Health Statistics
"National Vital Statistics Reports" (Vol. 57, No. 14, April 17, 2009, http://www.cdc.gov/nchs/deaths.htm)
*Final data by state of residence. These numbers are compiled from death certificates by the Centers for Disease Control and Prevention. They may differ from motor vehicle deaths collected by the U.S. Department of Transportation from other sources. Age-adjusted rates based on the year 2000 standard population.

Deaths by Firearm Injury in 2006

National Total = 30,896 Deaths*

ALPHA ORDER

RANK	STATE	DEATHS	% of USA
15	Alabama	780	2.5%
41	Alaska	111	0.4%
11	Arizona	982	3.2%
26	Arkansas	426	1.4%
1	California	3,363	10.9%
22	Colorado	497	1.6%
38	Connecticut	173	0.6%
45	Delaware	79	0.3%
3	Florida	2,083	6.7%
6	Georgia	1,144	3.7%
50	Hawaii	33	0.1%
37	Idaho	180	0.6%
9	Illinois	1,036	3.4%
17	Indiana	742	2.4%
36	Iowa	193	0.6%
31	Kansas	299	1.0%
21	Kentucky	531	1.7%
13	Louisiana	831	2.7%
42	Maine	105	0.3%
18	Maryland	678	2.2%
35	Massachusetts	211	0.7%
5	Michigan	1,157	3.7%
30	Minnesota	329	1.1%
25	Mississippi	475	1.5%
16	Missouri	767	2.5%
40	Montana	120	0.4%
39	Nebraska	141	0.5%
28	Nevada	405	1.3%
43	New Hampshire	82	0.3%
23	New Jersey	492	1.6%
32	New Mexico	283	0.9%
10	New York	1,002	3.2%
7	North Carolina	1,133	3.7%
49	North Dakota	46	0.1%
8	Ohio	1,114	3.6%
24	Oklahoma	482	1.6%
29	Oregon	384	1.2%
4	Pennsylvania	1,371	4.4%
48	Rhode Island	47	0.2%
19	South Carolina	616	2.0%
46	South Dakota	77	0.2%
12	Tennessee	943	3.1%
2	Texas	2,422	7.8%
34	Utah	224	0.7%
47	Vermont	54	0.2%
14	Virginia	816	2.6%
20	Washington	546	1.8%
33	West Virginia	253	0.8%
27	Wisconsin	424	1.4%
44	Wyoming	80	0.3%

RANK ORDER

RANK	STATE	DEATHS	% of USA
1	California	3,363	10.9%
2	Texas	2,422	7.8%
3	Florida	2,083	6.7%
4	Pennsylvania	1,371	4.4%
5	Michigan	1,157	3.7%
6	Georgia	1,144	3.7%
7	North Carolina	1,133	3.7%
8	Ohio	1,114	3.6%
9	Illinois	1,036	3.4%
10	New York	1,002	3.2%
11	Arizona	982	3.2%
12	Tennessee	943	3.1%
13	Louisiana	831	2.7%
14	Virginia	816	2.6%
15	Alabama	780	2.5%
16	Missouri	767	2.5%
17	Indiana	742	2.4%
18	Maryland	678	2.2%
19	South Carolina	616	2.0%
20	Washington	546	1.8%
21	Kentucky	531	1.7%
22	Colorado	497	1.6%
23	New Jersey	492	1.6%
24	Oklahoma	482	1.6%
25	Mississippi	475	1.5%
26	Arkansas	426	1.4%
27	Wisconsin	424	1.4%
28	Nevada	405	1.3%
29	Oregon	384	1.2%
30	Minnesota	329	1.1%
31	Kansas	299	1.0%
32	New Mexico	283	0.9%
33	West Virginia	253	0.8%
34	Utah	224	0.7%
35	Massachusetts	211	0.7%
36	Iowa	193	0.6%
37	Idaho	180	0.6%
38	Connecticut	173	0.6%
39	Nebraska	141	0.5%
40	Montana	120	0.4%
41	Alaska	111	0.4%
42	Maine	105	0.3%
43	New Hampshire	82	0.3%
44	Wyoming	80	0.3%
45	Delaware	79	0.3%
46	South Dakota	77	0.2%
47	Vermont	54	0.2%
48	Rhode Island	47	0.2%
49	North Dakota	46	0.1%
50	Hawaii	33	0.1%
	District of Columbia	134	0.4%

Source: U.S. Department of Health and Human Services, National Center for Health Statistics
"National Vital Statistics Reports" (Vol. 57, No. 14, April 17, 2009, http://www.cdc.gov/nchs/deaths.htm)
*Final data by state of residence.

Death Rate by Firearm Injury in 2006

National Rate = 10.3 Deaths per 100,000 Population*

ALPHA ORDER			RANK ORDER		
RANK	STATE	RATE	RANK	STATE	RATE
2	Alabama	17.0	1	Louisiana	19.4
3	Alaska	16.6	2	Alabama	17.0
6	Arizona	15.9	3	Alaska	16.6
9	Arkansas	15.2	4	Mississippi	16.3
33	California	9.2	5	Nevada	16.2
27	Colorado	10.5	6	Arizona	15.9
47	Connecticut	4.9	7	Tennessee	15.6
32	Delaware	9.3	8	Wyoming	15.5
22	Florida	11.5	9	Arkansas	15.2
19	Georgia	12.2	10	New Mexico	14.5
50	Hawaii	2.6	11	South Carolina	14.3
18	Idaho	12.3	12	West Virginia	13.9
37	Illinois	8.1	13	Oklahoma	13.5
21	Indiana	11.8	14	Missouri	13.1
42	Iowa	6.5	15	North Carolina	12.8
25	Kansas	10.8	16	Montana	12.7
17	Kentucky	12.6	17	Kentucky	12.6
1	Louisiana	19.4	18	Idaho	12.3
39	Maine	7.9	19	Georgia	12.2
20	Maryland	12.1	20	Maryland	12.1
49	Massachusetts	3.3	21	Indiana	11.8
22	Michigan	11.5	22	Florida	11.5
43	Minnesota	6.4	22	Michigan	11.5
4	Mississippi	16.3	24	Pennsylvania	11.0
14	Missouri	13.1	25	Kansas	10.8
16	Montana	12.7	26	Virginia	10.7
38	Nebraska	8.0	27	Colorado	10.5
5	Nevada	16.2	28	Oregon	10.4
44	New Hampshire	6.2	29	Texas	10.3
45	New Jersey	5.6	30	South Dakota	9.8
10	New Mexico	14.5	31	Ohio	9.7
46	New York	5.2	32	Delaware	9.3
15	North Carolina	12.8	33	California	9.2
41	North Dakota	7.2	34	Utah	8.8
31	Ohio	9.7	35	Vermont	8.7
13	Oklahoma	13.5	36	Washington	8.5
28	Oregon	10.4	37	Illinois	8.1
24	Pennsylvania	11.0	38	Nebraska	8.0
48	Rhode Island	4.4	39	Maine	7.9
11	South Carolina	14.3	40	Wisconsin	7.6
30	South Dakota	9.8	41	North Dakota	7.2
7	Tennessee	15.6	42	Iowa	6.5
29	Texas	10.3	43	Minnesota	6.4
34	Utah	8.8	44	New Hampshire	6.2
35	Vermont	8.7	45	New Jersey	5.6
26	Virginia	10.7	46	New York	5.2
36	Washington	8.5	47	Connecticut	4.9
12	West Virginia	13.9	48	Rhode Island	4.4
40	Wisconsin	7.6	49	Massachusetts	3.3
8	Wyoming	15.5	50	Hawaii	2.6
				District of Columbia	23.0

Source: U.S. Department of Health and Human Services, National Center for Health Statistics
   "National Vital Statistics Reports" (Vol. 57, No. 14, April 17, 2009, http://www.cdc.gov/nchs/deaths.htm)
*Final data by state of residence. Not age-adjusted.

Age-Adjusted Death Rate by Firearm Injury in 2006

National Rate = 10.2 Deaths per 100,000 Population*

ALPHA ORDER

RANK	STATE	RATE
3	Alabama	16.8
2	Alaska	17.1
6	Arizona	15.9
8	Arkansas	15.1
34	California	9.1
27	Colorado	10.4
47	Connecticut	5.0
33	Delaware	9.2
23	Florida	11.1
19	Georgia	12.2
50	Hawaii	2.5
16	Idaho	12.6
36	Illinois	8.0
21	Indiana	11.6
42	Iowa	6.3
24	Kansas	10.9
17	Kentucky	12.5
1	Louisiana	19.3
40	Maine	7.3
20	Maryland	12.1
49	Massachusetts	3.2
22	Michigan	11.4
42	Minnesota	6.3
4	Mississippi	16.6
14	Missouri	13.0
18	Montana	12.4
38	Nebraska	7.7
5	Nevada	16.5
44	New Hampshire	6.1
45	New Jersey	5.7
10	New Mexico	14.5
46	New York	5.1
15	North Carolina	12.7
41	North Dakota	6.7
32	Ohio	9.6
12	Oklahoma	13.4
29	Oregon	10.0
24	Pennsylvania	10.9
48	Rhode Island	4.2
11	South Carolina	14.0
30	South Dakota	9.7
7	Tennessee	15.4
27	Texas	10.4
30	Utah	9.7
36	Vermont	8.0
26	Virginia	10.5
35	Washington	8.4
13	West Virginia	13.2
39	Wisconsin	7.5
9	Wyoming	15.0

RANK ORDER

RANK	STATE	RATE
1	Louisiana	19.3
2	Alaska	17.1
3	Alabama	16.8
4	Mississippi	16.6
5	Nevada	16.5
6	Arizona	15.9
7	Tennessee	15.4
8	Arkansas	15.1
9	Wyoming	15.0
10	New Mexico	14.5
11	South Carolina	14.0
12	Oklahoma	13.4
13	West Virginia	13.2
14	Missouri	13.0
15	North Carolina	12.7
16	Idaho	12.6
17	Kentucky	12.5
18	Montana	12.4
19	Georgia	12.2
20	Maryland	12.1
21	Indiana	11.6
22	Michigan	11.4
23	Florida	11.1
24	Kansas	10.9
24	Pennsylvania	10.9
26	Virginia	10.5
27	Colorado	10.4
27	Texas	10.4
29	Oregon	10.0
30	South Dakota	9.7
30	Utah	9.7
32	Ohio	9.6
33	Delaware	9.2
34	California	9.1
35	Washington	8.4
36	Illinois	8.0
36	Vermont	8.0
38	Nebraska	7.7
39	Wisconsin	7.5
40	Maine	7.3
41	North Dakota	6.7
42	Iowa	6.3
42	Minnesota	6.3
44	New Hampshire	6.1
45	New Jersey	5.7
46	New York	5.1
47	Connecticut	5.0
48	Rhode Island	4.2
49	Massachusetts	3.2
50	Hawaii	2.5

District of Columbia	20.6

Source: U.S. Department of Health and Human Services, National Center for Health Statistics
"National Vital Statistics Reports" (Vol. 57, No. 14, April 17, 2009, http://www.cdc.gov/nchs/deaths.htm)
*Final data by state of residence. Age-adjusted rates based on the year 2000 standard population.

Deaths by Homicide in 2006

National Total = 18,573 Homicides*

ALPHA ORDER

RANK	STATE	DEATHS	% of USA
16	Alabama	445	2.4%
40	Alaska	43	0.2%
13	Arizona	549	3.0%
22	Arkansas	234	1.3%
1	California	2,616	14.1%
29	Colorado	181	1.0%
31	Connecticut	132	0.7%
39	Delaware	50	0.3%
3	Florida	1,214	6.5%
8	Georgia	687	3.7%
44	Hawaii	28	0.2%
42	Idaho	38	0.2%
5	Illinois	865	4.7%
20	Indiana	375	2.0%
36	Iowa	73	0.4%
33	Kansas	114	0.6%
27	Kentucky	192	1.0%
12	Louisiana	554	3.0%
46	Maine	20	0.1%
11	Maryland	568	3.1%
28	Massachusetts	183	1.0%
7	Michigan	722	3.9%
32	Minnesota	128	0.7%
21	Mississippi	318	1.7%
17	Missouri	412	2.2%
43	Montana	35	0.2%
37	Nebraska	55	0.3%
25	Nevada	219	1.2%
46	New Hampshire	20	0.1%
15	New Jersey	449	2.4%
30	New Mexico	135	0.7%
4	New York	962	5.2%
10	North Carolina	622	3.3%
49	North Dakota	11	0.1%
9	Ohio	666	3.6%
23	Oklahoma	226	1.2%
34	Oregon	113	0.6%
6	Pennsylvania	769	4.1%
41	Rhode Island	39	0.2%
19	South Carolina	391	2.1%
45	South Dakota	21	0.1%
14	Tennessee	486	2.6%
2	Texas	1,467	7.9%
38	Utah	52	0.3%
48	Vermont	13	0.1%
18	Virginia	410	2.2%
24	Washington	221	1.2%
35	West Virginia	97	0.5%
26	Wisconsin	194	1.0%
50	Wyoming	9	0.0%

RANK ORDER

RANK	STATE	DEATHS	% of USA
1	California	2,616	14.1%
2	Texas	1,467	7.9%
3	Florida	1,214	6.5%
4	New York	962	5.2%
5	Illinois	865	4.7%
6	Pennsylvania	769	4.1%
7	Michigan	722	3.9%
8	Georgia	687	3.7%
9	Ohio	666	3.6%
10	North Carolina	622	3.3%
11	Maryland	568	3.1%
12	Louisiana	554	3.0%
13	Arizona	549	3.0%
14	Tennessee	486	2.6%
15	New Jersey	449	2.4%
16	Alabama	445	2.4%
17	Missouri	412	2.2%
18	Virginia	410	2.2%
19	South Carolina	391	2.1%
20	Indiana	375	2.0%
21	Mississippi	318	1.7%
22	Arkansas	234	1.3%
23	Oklahoma	226	1.2%
24	Washington	221	1.2%
25	Nevada	219	1.2%
26	Wisconsin	194	1.0%
27	Kentucky	192	1.0%
28	Massachusetts	183	1.0%
29	Colorado	181	1.0%
30	New Mexico	135	0.7%
31	Connecticut	132	0.7%
32	Minnesota	128	0.7%
33	Kansas	114	0.6%
34	Oregon	113	0.6%
35	West Virginia	97	0.5%
36	Iowa	73	0.4%
37	Nebraska	55	0.3%
38	Utah	52	0.3%
39	Delaware	50	0.3%
40	Alaska	43	0.2%
41	Rhode Island	39	0.2%
42	Idaho	38	0.2%
43	Montana	35	0.2%
44	Hawaii	28	0.2%
45	South Dakota	21	0.1%
46	Maine	20	0.1%
46	New Hampshire	20	0.1%
48	Vermont	13	0.1%
49	North Dakota	11	0.1%
50	Wyoming	9	0.0%
	District of Columbia	150	0.8%

Source: U.S. Department of Health and Human Services, National Center for Health Statistics
   "National Vital Statistics Reports" (Vol. 57, No. 14, April 17, 2009, http://www.cdc.gov/nchs/deaths.htm)
*Final data by state of residence. Includes legal intervention. Homicide data shown here are collected by the Centers for Disease Control and Prevention based on death certificates and differ from murder data collected by the F.B.I. from other sources.

Death Rate by Homicide in 2006

National Rate = 6.2 Deaths per 100,000 Population*

ALPHA ORDER

RANK	STATE	RATE
4	Alabama	9.7
18	Alaska	6.4
6	Arizona	8.9
8	Arkansas	8.3
11	California	7.2
31	Colorado	3.8
31	Connecticut	3.8
22	Delaware	5.9
16	Florida	6.7
10	Georgia	7.3
44	Hawaii	2.2
41	Idaho	2.6
16	Illinois	6.7
22	Indiana	5.9
43	Iowa	2.4
30	Kansas	4.1
29	Kentucky	4.6
1	Louisiana	12.9
46	Maine	1.5
3	Maryland	10.1
39	Massachusetts	2.8
11	Michigan	7.2
42	Minnesota	2.5
2	Mississippi	10.9
13	Missouri	7.1
33	Montana	3.7
37	Nebraska	3.1
7	Nevada	8.8
46	New Hampshire	1.5
27	New Jersey	5.1
15	New Mexico	6.9
28	New York	5.0
14	North Carolina	7.0
NA	North Dakota**	NA
24	Ohio	5.8
19	Oklahoma	6.3
37	Oregon	3.1
20	Pennsylvania	6.2
33	Rhode Island	3.7
5	South Carolina	9.0
40	South Dakota	2.7
9	Tennessee	8.0
20	Texas	6.2
45	Utah	2.0
NA	Vermont**	NA
25	Virginia	5.4
35	Washington	3.5
26	West Virginia	5.3
35	Wisconsin	3.5
NA	Wyoming**	NA

RANK ORDER

RANK	STATE	RATE
1	Louisiana	12.9
2	Mississippi	10.9
3	Maryland	10.1
4	Alabama	9.7
5	South Carolina	9.0
6	Arizona	8.9
7	Nevada	8.8
8	Arkansas	8.3
9	Tennessee	8.0
10	Georgia	7.3
11	California	7.2
11	Michigan	7.2
13	Missouri	7.1
14	North Carolina	7.0
15	New Mexico	6.9
16	Florida	6.7
16	Illinois	6.7
18	Alaska	6.4
19	Oklahoma	6.3
20	Pennsylvania	6.2
20	Texas	6.2
22	Delaware	5.9
22	Indiana	5.9
24	Ohio	5.8
25	Virginia	5.4
26	West Virginia	5.3
27	New Jersey	5.1
28	New York	5.0
29	Kentucky	4.6
30	Kansas	4.1
31	Colorado	3.8
31	Connecticut	3.8
33	Montana	3.7
33	Rhode Island	3.7
35	Washington	3.5
35	Wisconsin	3.5
37	Nebraska	3.1
37	Oregon	3.1
39	Massachusetts	2.8
40	South Dakota	2.7
41	Idaho	2.6
42	Minnesota	2.5
43	Iowa	2.4
44	Hawaii	2.2
45	Utah	2.0
46	Maine	1.5
46	New Hampshire	1.5
NA	North Dakota**	NA
NA	Vermont**	NA
NA	Wyoming**	NA

District of Columbia   25.8

Source: U.S. Department of Health and Human Services, National Center for Health Statistics
"National Vital Statistics Reports" (Vol. 57, No. 14, April 17, 2009, http://www.cdc.gov/nchs/deaths.htm)
*Final data by state of residence. Includes legal intervention. Homicide data shown here are collected by the Centers for Disease Control and Prevention based on death certificates and differ from murder data collected by the F.B.I. from other sources. Not age-adjusted.
**Insufficient data to determine a reliable rate.

Age-Adjusted Death Rate by Homicide in 2006

National Rate = 6.2 Deaths per 100,000 Population*

ALPHA ORDER

RANK	STATE	RATE		RANK	STATE	RATE
4	Alabama	9.8		1	Louisiana	12.8
20	Alaska	6.1		2	Mississippi	11.0
6	Arizona	8.9		3	Maryland	10.2
8	Arkansas	8.5		4	Alabama	9.8
16	California	6.9		5	South Carolina	9.1
33	Colorado	3.7		6	Arizona	8.9
31	Connecticut	3.9		6	Nevada	8.9
20	Delaware	6.1		8	Arkansas	8.5
13	Florida	7.0		9	Tennessee	8.0
11	Georgia	7.1		10	Michigan	7.2
44	Hawaii	2.1		11	Georgia	7.1
41	Idaho	2.6		11	Missouri	7.1
17	Illinois	6.7		13	Florida	7.0
23	Indiana	5.9		13	New Mexico	7.0
42	Iowa	2.5		13	North Carolina	7.0
30	Kansas	4.1		16	California	6.9
29	Kentucky	4.6		17	Illinois	6.7
1	Louisiana	12.8		18	Oklahoma	6.4
47	Maine	1.5		18	Pennsylvania	6.4
3	Maryland	10.2		20	Alaska	6.1
39	Massachusetts	2.9		20	Delaware	6.1
10	Michigan	7.2		20	Texas	6.1
42	Minnesota	2.5		23	Indiana	5.9
2	Mississippi	11.0		23	Ohio	5.9
11	Missouri	7.1		25	West Virginia	5.4
32	Montana	3.8		26	New Jersey	5.3
37	Nebraska	3.1		26	Virginia	5.3
6	Nevada	8.9		28	New York	5.0
46	New Hampshire	1.6		29	Kentucky	4.6
26	New Jersey	5.3		30	Kansas	4.1
13	New Mexico	7.0		31	Connecticut	3.9
28	New York	5.0		32	Montana	3.8
13	North Carolina	7.0		33	Colorado	3.7
NA	North Dakota**	NA		34	Rhode Island	3.6
23	Ohio	5.9		35	Wisconsin	3.5
18	Oklahoma	6.4		36	Washington	3.4
37	Oregon	3.1		37	Nebraska	3.1
18	Pennsylvania	6.4		37	Oregon	3.1
34	Rhode Island	3.6		39	Massachusetts	2.9
5	South Carolina	9.1		39	South Dakota	2.9
39	South Dakota	2.9		41	Idaho	2.6
9	Tennessee	8.0		42	Iowa	2.5
20	Texas	6.1		42	Minnesota	2.5
45	Utah	2.0		44	Hawaii	2.1
NA	Vermont**	NA		45	Utah	2.0
26	Virginia	5.3		46	New Hampshire	1.6
36	Washington	3.4		47	Maine	1.5
25	West Virginia	5.4		NA	North Dakota**	NA
35	Wisconsin	3.5		NA	Vermont**	NA
NA	Wyoming**	NA		NA	Wyoming**	NA

RANK ORDER

District of Columbia 23.3

Source: U.S. Department of Health and Human Services, National Center for Health Statistics
"National Vital Statistics Reports" (Vol. 57, No. 14, April 17, 2009, http://www.cdc.gov/nchs/deaths.htm)
*Final data by state of residence. Includes legal intervention. Homicide data shown here are collected by the Centers for Disease Control and Prevention based on death certificates and differ from murder data collected by the F.B.I. from other sources. Age-adjusted rates based on the year 2000 standard population.
**Insufficient data to determine a reliable rate.

Deaths by Suicide in 2006

National Total = 33,300 Suicides*

ALPHA ORDER

RANK	STATE	DEATHS	% of USA
21	Alabama	580	1.7%
43	Alaska	135	0.4%
10	Arizona	979	2.9%
31	Arkansas	376	1.1%
1	California	3,334	10.0%
17	Colorado	730	2.2%
36	Connecticut	292	0.9%
47	Delaware	91	0.3%
2	Florida	2,440	7.3%
11	Georgia	923	2.8%
45	Hawaii	120	0.4%
38	Idaho	222	0.7%
9	Illinois	1,010	3.0%
14	Indiana	824	2.5%
34	Iowa	334	1.0%
30	Kansas	379	1.1%
19	Kentucky	622	1.9%
27	Louisiana	492	1.5%
41	Maine	158	0.5%
26	Maryland	495	1.5%
29	Massachusetts	450	1.4%
7	Michigan	1,139	3.4%
23	Minnesota	554	1.7%
35	Mississippi	325	1.0%
16	Missouri	799	2.4%
40	Montana	189	0.6%
39	Nebraska	202	0.6%
28	Nevada	486	1.5%
42	New Hampshire	151	0.5%
20	New Jersey	585	1.8%
33	New Mexico	352	1.1%
5	New York	1,326	4.0%
8	North Carolina	1,106	3.3%
48	North Dakota	90	0.3%
6	Ohio	1,325	4.0%
24	Oklahoma	537	1.6%
22	Oregon	579	1.7%
4	Pennsylvania	1,396	4.2%
48	Rhode Island	90	0.3%
25	South Carolina	524	1.6%
44	South Dakota	125	0.4%
13	Tennessee	874	2.6%
3	Texas	2,347	7.0%
32	Utah	362	1.1%
50	Vermont	81	0.2%
12	Virginia	876	2.6%
15	Washington	809	2.4%
37	West Virginia	269	0.8%
18	Wisconsin	670	2.0%
46	Wyoming	116	0.3%

RANK ORDER

RANK	STATE	DEATHS	% of USA
1	California	3,334	10.0%
2	Florida	2,440	7.3%
3	Texas	2,347	7.0%
4	Pennsylvania	1,396	4.2%
5	New York	1,326	4.0%
6	Ohio	1,325	4.0%
7	Michigan	1,139	3.4%
8	North Carolina	1,106	3.3%
9	Illinois	1,010	3.0%
10	Arizona	979	2.9%
11	Georgia	923	2.8%
12	Virginia	876	2.6%
13	Tennessee	874	2.6%
14	Indiana	824	2.5%
15	Washington	809	2.4%
16	Missouri	799	2.4%
17	Colorado	730	2.2%
18	Wisconsin	670	2.0%
19	Kentucky	622	1.9%
20	New Jersey	585	1.8%
21	Alabama	580	1.7%
22	Oregon	579	1.7%
23	Minnesota	554	1.7%
24	Oklahoma	537	1.6%
25	South Carolina	524	1.6%
26	Maryland	495	1.5%
27	Louisiana	492	1.5%
28	Nevada	486	1.5%
29	Massachusetts	450	1.4%
30	Kansas	379	1.1%
31	Arkansas	376	1.1%
32	Utah	362	1.1%
33	New Mexico	352	1.1%
34	Iowa	334	1.0%
35	Mississippi	325	1.0%
36	Connecticut	292	0.9%
37	West Virginia	269	0.8%
38	Idaho	222	0.7%
39	Nebraska	202	0.6%
40	Montana	189	0.6%
41	Maine	158	0.5%
42	New Hampshire	151	0.5%
43	Alaska	135	0.4%
44	South Dakota	125	0.4%
45	Hawaii	120	0.4%
46	Wyoming	116	0.3%
47	Delaware	91	0.3%
48	North Dakota	90	0.3%
48	Rhode Island	90	0.3%
50	Vermont	81	0.2%
	District of Columbia	30	0.1%

Source: U.S. Department of Health and Human Services, National Center for Health Statistics
"National Vital Statistics Reports" (Vol. 57, No. 14, April 17, 2009, http://www.cdc.gov/nchs/deaths.htm)
*Final data by state of residence.

Death Rate by Suicide in 2006

National Rate = 11.1 Deaths per 100,000 Population*

ALPHA ORDER

RANK	STATE	RATE
23	Alabama	12.6
2	Alaska	20.1
7	Arizona	15.9
20	Arkansas	13.4
43	California	9.1
9	Colorado	15.4
46	Connecticut	8.3
38	Delaware	10.7
19	Florida	13.5
41	Georgia	9.9
42	Hawaii	9.3
10	Idaho	15.1
47	Illinois	7.9
21	Indiana	13.1
35	Iowa	11.2
17	Kansas	13.7
12	Kentucky	14.8
29	Louisiana	11.5
28	Maine	12.0
44	Maryland	8.8
48	Massachusetts	7.0
34	Michigan	11.3
38	Minnesota	10.7
35	Mississippi	11.2
17	Missouri	13.7
3	Montana	20.0
33	Nebraska	11.4
4	Nevada	19.5
29	New Hampshire	11.5
50	New Jersey	6.7
5	New Mexico	18.0
49	New York	6.9
25	North Carolina	12.5
15	North Dakota	14.2
29	Ohio	11.5
11	Oklahoma	15.0
8	Oregon	15.6
35	Pennsylvania	11.2
45	Rhode Island	8.4
26	South Carolina	12.1
6	South Dakota	16.0
14	Tennessee	14.5
40	Texas	10.0
15	Utah	14.2
22	Vermont	13.0
29	Virginia	11.5
23	Washington	12.6
12	West Virginia	14.8
26	Wisconsin	12.1
1	Wyoming	22.5

RANK ORDER

RANK	STATE	RATE
1	Wyoming	22.5
2	Alaska	20.1
3	Montana	20.0
4	Nevada	19.5
5	New Mexico	18.0
6	South Dakota	16.0
7	Arizona	15.9
8	Oregon	15.6
9	Colorado	15.4
10	Idaho	15.1
11	Oklahoma	15.0
12	Kentucky	14.8
12	West Virginia	14.8
14	Tennessee	14.5
15	North Dakota	14.2
15	Utah	14.2
17	Kansas	13.7
17	Missouri	13.7
19	Florida	13.5
20	Arkansas	13.4
21	Indiana	13.1
22	Vermont	13.0
23	Alabama	12.6
23	Washington	12.6
25	North Carolina	12.5
26	South Carolina	12.1
26	Wisconsin	12.1
28	Maine	12.0
29	Louisiana	11.5
29	New Hampshire	11.5
29	Ohio	11.5
29	Virginia	11.5
33	Nebraska	11.4
34	Michigan	11.3
35	Iowa	11.2
35	Mississippi	11.2
35	Pennsylvania	11.2
38	Delaware	10.7
38	Minnesota	10.7
40	Texas	10.0
41	Georgia	9.9
42	Hawaii	9.3
43	California	9.1
44	Maryland	8.8
45	Rhode Island	8.4
46	Connecticut	8.3
47	Illinois	7.9
48	Massachusetts	7.0
49	New York	6.9
50	New Jersey	6.7
	District of Columbia	5.2

Source: U.S. Department of Health and Human Services, National Center for Health Statistics
    "National Vital Statistics Reports" (Vol. 57, No. 14, April 17, 2009, http://www.cdc.gov/nchs/deaths.htm)
*Final data by state of residence. Not age-adjusted.

Age-Adjusted Death Rate by Suicide in 2006

National Rate = 10.9 Deaths per 100,000 Population*

ALPHA ORDER				RANK ORDER		
RANK	STATE	RATE		RANK	STATE	RATE
22	Alabama	12.4		1	Wyoming	21.7
2	Alaska	20.0		2	Alaska	20.0
6	Arizona	16.0		3	Montana	19.7
19	Arkansas	13.3		4	Nevada	19.5
42	California	9.2		5	New Mexico	18.0
10	Colorado	15.2		6	Arizona	16.0
46	Connecticut	8.0		6	South Dakota	16.0
39	Delaware	10.4		8	Utah	15.8
21	Florida	12.6		9	Idaho	15.6
41	Georgia	10.0		10	Colorado	15.2
42	Hawaii	9.2		10	Oregon	15.2
9	Idaho	15.6		12	Oklahoma	15.0
47	Illinois	7.8		13	Kentucky	14.6
20	Indiana	13.0		14	Tennessee	14.2
32	Iowa	11.1		15	West Virginia	14.1
16	Kansas	13.8		16	Kansas	13.8
13	Kentucky	14.6		17	North Dakota	13.6
28	Louisiana	11.6		18	Missouri	13.5
35	Maine	11.0		19	Arkansas	13.3
44	Maryland	8.6		20	Indiana	13.0
48	Massachusetts	6.7		21	Florida	12.6
32	Michigan	11.1		22	Alabama	12.4
38	Minnesota	10.6		23	Washington	12.3
29	Mississippi	11.4		24	North Carolina	12.2
18	Missouri	13.5		25	Vermont	12.0
3	Montana	19.7		26	South Carolina	11.9
30	Nebraska	11.2		26	Wisconsin	11.9
4	Nevada	19.5		28	Louisiana	11.6
35	New Hampshire	11.0		29	Mississippi	11.4
50	New Jersey	6.5		30	Nebraska	11.2
5	New Mexico	18.0		30	Ohio	11.2
49	New York	6.6		32	Iowa	11.1
24	North Carolina	12.2		32	Michigan	11.1
17	North Dakota	13.6		32	Virginia	11.1
30	Ohio	11.2		35	Maine	11.0
12	Oklahoma	15.0		35	New Hampshire	11.0
10	Oregon	15.2		37	Pennsylvania	10.8
37	Pennsylvania	10.8		38	Minnesota	10.6
45	Rhode Island	8.1		39	Delaware	10.4
26	South Carolina	11.9		40	Texas	10.3
6	South Dakota	16.0		41	Georgia	10.0
14	Tennessee	14.2		42	California	9.2
40	Texas	10.3		42	Hawaii	9.2
8	Utah	15.8		44	Maryland	8.6
25	Vermont	12.0		45	Rhode Island	8.1
32	Virginia	11.1		46	Connecticut	8.0
23	Washington	12.3		47	Illinois	7.8
15	West Virginia	14.1		48	Massachusetts	6.7
26	Wisconsin	11.9		49	New York	6.6
1	Wyoming	21.7		50	New Jersey	6.5
					District of Columbia	5.1

Source: U.S. Department of Health and Human Services, National Center for Health Statistics
"National Vital Statistics Reports" (Vol. 57, No. 14, April 17, 2009, http://www.cdc.gov/nchs/deaths.htm)
*Final data by state of residence. Age-adjusted rates based on the year 2000 standard population.

Alcohol-Induced Deaths in 2006

National Total = 22,073 Deaths*

ALPHA ORDER					RANK ORDER			
RANK	**STATE**	**DEATHS**	**% of USA**		**RANK**	**STATE**	**DEATHS**	**% of USA**
27	Alabama	249	1.1%		1	California	3,932	17.8%
38	Alaska	143	0.6%		2	Florida	1,746	7.9%
7	Arizona	664	3.0%		3	Texas	1,371	6.2%
34	Arkansas	171	0.8%		4	New York	1,101	5.0%
1	California	3,932	17.8%		5	Ohio	708	3.2%
11	Colorado	526	2.4%		6	Michigan	695	3.1%
31	Connecticut	186	0.8%		7	Arizona	664	3.0%
50	Delaware	58	0.3%		8	Washington	663	3.0%
2	Florida	1,746	7.9%		9	Illinois	610	2.8%
13	Georgia	500	2.3%		9	North Carolina	610	2.8%
47	Hawaii	65	0.3%		11	Colorado	526	2.4%
40	Idaho	129	0.6%		12	Pennsylvania	503	2.3%
9	Illinois	610	2.8%		13	Georgia	500	2.3%
25	Indiana	332	1.5%		14	Tennessee	485	2.2%
32	Iowa	185	0.8%		15	Oregon	475	2.2%
33	Kansas	184	0.8%		16	New Jersey	466	2.1%
28	Kentucky	232	1.1%		17	Wisconsin	424	1.9%
29	Louisiana	221	1.0%		18	Missouri	385	1.7%
41	Maine	114	0.5%		19	Massachusetts	371	1.7%
26	Maryland	294	1.3%		19	Minnesota	371	1.7%
19	Massachusetts	371	1.7%		21	Oklahoma	353	1.6%
6	Michigan	695	3.1%		22	New Mexico	351	1.6%
19	Minnesota	371	1.7%		22	South Carolina	351	1.6%
35	Mississippi	159	0.7%		24	Virginia	348	1.6%
18	Missouri	385	1.7%		25	Indiana	332	1.5%
36	Montana	149	0.7%		26	Maryland	294	1.3%
42	Nebraska	105	0.5%		27	Alabama	249	1.1%
30	Nevada	217	1.0%		28	Kentucky	232	1.1%
43	New Hampshire	100	0.5%		29	Louisiana	221	1.0%
16	New Jersey	466	2.1%		30	Nevada	217	1.0%
22	New Mexico	351	1.6%		31	Connecticut	186	0.8%
4	New York	1,101	5.0%		32	Iowa	185	0.8%
9	North Carolina	610	2.8%		33	Kansas	184	0.8%
48	North Dakota	64	0.3%		34	Arkansas	171	0.8%
5	Ohio	708	3.2%		35	Mississippi	159	0.7%
21	Oklahoma	353	1.6%		36	Montana	149	0.7%
15	Oregon	475	2.2%		37	Utah	144	0.7%
12	Pennsylvania	503	2.3%		38	Alaska	143	0.6%
45	Rhode Island	95	0.4%		39	West Virginia	137	0.6%
22	South Carolina	351	1.6%		40	Idaho	129	0.6%
44	South Dakota	98	0.4%		41	Maine	114	0.5%
14	Tennessee	485	2.2%		42	Nebraska	105	0.5%
3	Texas	1,371	6.2%		43	New Hampshire	100	0.5%
37	Utah	144	0.7%		44	South Dakota	98	0.4%
49	Vermont	63	0.3%		45	Rhode Island	95	0.4%
24	Virginia	348	1.6%		46	Wyoming	88	0.4%
8	Washington	663	3.0%		47	Hawaii	65	0.3%
39	West Virginia	137	0.6%		48	North Dakota	64	0.3%
17	Wisconsin	424	1.9%		49	Vermont	63	0.3%
46	Wyoming	88	0.4%		50	Delaware	58	0.3%
						District of Columbia	82	0.4%

Source: U.S. Department of Health and Human Services, National Center for Health Statistics
   "National Vital Statistics Reports" (Vol. 57, No. 14, April 17, 2009, http://www.cdc.gov/nchs/deaths.htm)
*Final data by state of residence. Includes excessive blood level of alcohol, accidental poisoning by alcohol and the following
alcohol-related causes: psychoses, dependence syndrome, polyneuropathy, cardiomyopathy, gastritis, chronic liver disease, and
cirrhosis. Excludes accidents, homicides, and other causes indirectly related to alcohol use.

Death Rate by Alcohol-Induced Deaths in 2006

National Rate = 7.4 Deaths per 100,000 Population*

ALPHA ORDER			RANK ORDER		
RANK	STATE	RATE	RANK	STATE	RATE
40	Alabama	5.4	1	Alaska	21.3
1	Alaska	21.3	2	New Mexico	18.0
8	Arizona	10.8	3	Wyoming	17.1
32	Arkansas	6.1	4	Montana	15.8
8	California	10.8	5	Oregon	12.8
7	Colorado	11.1	6	South Dakota	12.5
41	Connecticut	5.3	7	Colorado	11.1
27	Delaware	6.8	8	Arizona	10.8
14	Florida	9.7	8	California	10.8
41	Georgia	5.3	10	Washington	10.4
47	Hawaii	5.1	11	North Dakota	10.1
16	Idaho	8.8	11	Vermont	10.1
48	Illinois	4.8	13	Oklahoma	9.9
41	Indiana	5.3	14	Florida	9.7
30	Iowa	6.2	15	Rhode Island	8.9
28	Kansas	6.7	16	Idaho	8.8
38	Kentucky	5.5	17	Nevada	8.7
45	Louisiana	5.2	18	Maine	8.6
18	Maine	8.6	19	South Carolina	8.1
45	Maryland	5.2	20	Tennessee	8.0
34	Massachusetts	5.8	21	New Hampshire	7.6
25	Michigan	6.9	21	Wisconsin	7.6
24	Minnesota	7.2	23	West Virginia	7.5
38	Mississippi	5.5	24	Minnesota	7.2
29	Missouri	6.6	25	Michigan	6.9
4	Montana	15.8	25	North Carolina	6.9
33	Nebraska	5.9	27	Delaware	6.8
17	Nevada	8.7	28	Kansas	6.7
21	New Hampshire	7.6	29	Missouri	6.6
41	New Jersey	5.3	30	Iowa	6.2
2	New Mexico	18.0	30	Ohio	6.2
36	New York	5.7	32	Arkansas	6.1
25	North Carolina	6.9	33	Nebraska	5.9
11	North Dakota	10.1	34	Massachusetts	5.8
30	Ohio	6.2	34	Texas	5.8
13	Oklahoma	9.9	36	New York	5.7
5	Oregon	12.8	37	Utah	5.6
50	Pennsylvania	4.0	38	Kentucky	5.5
15	Rhode Island	8.9	38	Mississippi	5.5
19	South Carolina	8.1	40	Alabama	5.4
6	South Dakota	12.5	41	Connecticut	5.3
20	Tennessee	8.0	41	Georgia	5.3
34	Texas	5.8	41	Indiana	5.3
37	Utah	5.6	41	New Jersey	5.3
11	Vermont	10.1	45	Louisiana	5.2
49	Virginia	4.6	45	Maryland	5.2
10	Washington	10.4	47	Hawaii	5.1
23	West Virginia	7.5	48	Illinois	4.8
21	Wisconsin	7.6	49	Virginia	4.6
3	Wyoming	17.1	50	Pennsylvania	4.0

	District of Columbia	14.1

Source: U.S. Department of Health and Human Services, National Center for Health Statistics
"National Vital Statistics Reports" (Vol. 57, No. 14, April 17, 2009, http://www.cdc.gov/nchs/deaths.htm)
*Final data by state of residence. Includes excessive blood level of alcohol, accidental poisoning by alcohol and the following alcohol-related causes: psychoses, dependence syndrome, polyneuropathy, cardiomyopathy, gastritis, chronic liver disease, and cirrhosis. Excludes accidents, homicides, and other causes indirectly related to alcohol use. Not age-adjusted.

Age-Adjusted Death Rate by Alcohol-Induced Deaths in 2006

National Rate = 7.0 Deaths per 100,000 Population*

ALPHA ORDER				RANK ORDER		
RANK	STATE	RATE		RANK	STATE	RATE
40	Alabama	5.0		1	Alaska	21.6
1	Alaska	21.6		2	New Mexico	17.7
8	Arizona	10.8		3	Wyoming	15.9
32	Arkansas	5.8		4	Montana	14.3
7	California	11.0		5	South Dakota	12.1
9	Colorado	10.6		6	Oregon	11.6
47	Connecticut	4.7		7	California	11.0
29	Delaware	6.3		8	Arizona	10.8
13	Florida	8.7		9	Colorado	10.6
36	Georgia	5.4		10	North Dakota	9.8
46	Hawaii	4.8		10	Washington	9.8
13	Idaho	8.7		12	Oklahoma	9.5
48	Illinois	4.6		13	Florida	8.7
40	Indiana	5.0		13	Idaho	8.7
34	Iowa	5.7		15	Vermont	8.6
27	Kansas	6.4		16	Nevada	8.3
40	Kentucky	5.0		17	Rhode Island	8.1
40	Louisiana	5.0		18	Maine	7.4
18	Maine	7.4		18	South Carolina	7.4
44	Maryland	4.9		18	Tennessee	7.4
39	Massachusetts	5.2		21	Wisconsin	7.1
27	Michigan	6.4		22	Utah	6.9
23	Minnesota	6.8		23	Minnesota	6.8
36	Mississippi	5.4		24	West Virginia	6.7
30	Missouri	6.2		25	New Hampshire	6.6
4	Montana	14.3		26	North Carolina	6.5
32	Nebraska	5.8		27	Kansas	6.4
16	Nevada	8.3		27	Michigan	6.4
25	New Hampshire	6.6		29	Delaware	6.3
44	New Jersey	4.9		30	Missouri	6.2
2	New Mexico	17.7		31	Texas	6.1
38	New York	5.3		32	Arkansas	5.8
26	North Carolina	6.5		32	Nebraska	5.8
10	North Dakota	9.8		34	Iowa	5.7
35	Ohio	5.6		35	Ohio	5.6
12	Oklahoma	9.5		36	Georgia	5.4
6	Oregon	11.6		36	Mississippi	5.4
50	Pennsylvania	3.6		38	New York	5.3
17	Rhode Island	8.1		39	Massachusetts	5.2
18	South Carolina	7.4		40	Alabama	5.0
5	South Dakota	12.1		40	Indiana	5.0
18	Tennessee	7.4		40	Kentucky	5.0
31	Texas	6.1		40	Louisiana	5.0
22	Utah	6.9		44	Maryland	4.9
15	Vermont	8.6		44	New Jersey	4.9
49	Virginia	4.3		46	Hawaii	4.8
10	Washington	9.8		47	Connecticut	4.7
24	West Virginia	6.7		48	Illinois	4.6
21	Wisconsin	7.1		49	Virginia	4.3
3	Wyoming	15.9		50	Pennsylvania	3.6
					District of Columbia	13.9

Source: U.S. Department of Health and Human Services, National Center for Health Statistics
"National Vital Statistics Reports" (Vol. 57, No. 14, April 17, 2009, http://www.cdc.gov/nchs/deaths.htm)
*Final data by state of residence. Includes excessive blood level of alcohol, accidental poisoning by alcohol and the following alcohol-related causes: psychoses, dependence syndrome, polyneuropathy, cardiomyopathy, gastritis, chronic liver disease, and cirrhosis. Excludes accidents, homicides, and other causes indirectly related to alcohol use. Age-adjusted rates based on the year 2000 standard population.

Drug-Induced Deaths in 2006

National Total = 38,396 Deaths*

ALPHA ORDER

RANK	STATE	DEATHS	% of USA
29	Alabama	466	1.2%
45	Alaska	85	0.2%
14	Arizona	959	2.5%
35	Arkansas	307	0.8%
1	California	4,026	10.5%
22	Colorado	660	1.7%
30	Connecticut	458	1.2%
46	Delaware	83	0.2%
2	Florida	2,928	7.6%
15	Georgia	912	2.4%
42	Hawaii	131	0.3%
41	Idaho	147	0.4%
8	Illinois	1,423	3.7%
18	Indiana	773	2.0%
37	Iowa	199	0.5%
36	Kansas	292	0.8%
19	Kentucky	766	2.0%
17	Louisiana	800	2.1%
39	Maine	166	0.4%
16	Maryland	805	2.1%
11	Massachusetts	1,021	2.7%
6	Michigan	1,661	4.3%
32	Minnesota	378	1.0%
34	Mississippi	368	1.0%
20	Missouri	765	2.0%
44	Montana	121	0.3%
42	Nebraska	131	0.3%
28	Nevada	471	1.2%
40	New Hampshire	160	0.4%
12	New Jersey	1,009	2.6%
31	New Mexico	435	1.1%
4	New York	1,949	5.1%
9	North Carolina	1,120	2.9%
50	North Dakota	16	0.0%
7	Ohio	1,606	4.2%
25	Oklahoma	619	1.6%
26	Oregon	584	1.5%
5	Pennsylvania	1,834	4.8%
38	Rhode Island	179	0.5%
24	South Carolina	641	1.7%
49	South Dakota	43	0.1%
10	Tennessee	1,030	2.7%
3	Texas	2,452	6.4%
27	Utah	481	1.3%
46	Vermont	83	0.2%
21	Virginia	670	1.7%
13	Washington	970	2.5%
32	West Virginia	378	1.0%
23	Wisconsin	642	1.7%
48	Wyoming	64	0.2%

RANK ORDER

RANK	STATE	DEATHS	% of USA
1	California	4,026	10.5%
2	Florida	2,928	7.6%
3	Texas	2,452	6.4%
4	New York	1,949	5.1%
5	Pennsylvania	1,834	4.8%
6	Michigan	1,661	4.3%
7	Ohio	1,606	4.2%
8	Illinois	1,423	3.7%
9	North Carolina	1,120	2.9%
10	Tennessee	1,030	2.7%
11	Massachusetts	1,021	2.7%
12	New Jersey	1,009	2.6%
13	Washington	970	2.5%
14	Arizona	959	2.5%
15	Georgia	912	2.4%
16	Maryland	805	2.1%
17	Louisiana	800	2.1%
18	Indiana	773	2.0%
19	Kentucky	766	2.0%
20	Missouri	765	2.0%
21	Virginia	670	1.7%
22	Colorado	660	1.7%
23	Wisconsin	642	1.7%
24	South Carolina	641	1.7%
25	Oklahoma	619	1.6%
26	Oregon	584	1.5%
27	Utah	481	1.3%
28	Nevada	471	1.2%
29	Alabama	466	1.2%
30	Connecticut	458	1.2%
31	New Mexico	435	1.1%
32	Minnesota	378	1.0%
32	West Virginia	378	1.0%
34	Mississippi	368	1.0%
35	Arkansas	307	0.8%
36	Kansas	292	0.8%
37	Iowa	199	0.5%
38	Rhode Island	179	0.5%
39	Maine	166	0.4%
40	New Hampshire	160	0.4%
41	Idaho	147	0.4%
42	Hawaii	131	0.3%
42	Nebraska	131	0.3%
44	Montana	121	0.3%
45	Alaska	85	0.2%
46	Delaware	83	0.2%
46	Vermont	83	0.2%
48	Wyoming	64	0.2%
49	South Dakota	43	0.1%
50	North Dakota	16	0.0%
	District of Columbia	129	0.3%

Source: U.S. Department of Health and Human Services, National Center for Health Statistics
   "National Vital Statistics Reports" (Vol. 57, No. 14, April 17, 2009, http://www.cdc.gov/nchs/deaths.htm)
*Final data by state of residence. Includes drug psychoses, drug dependence, nondependent use excluding alcohol and tobacco, accidental poisoning or suicide by drugs, medicaments, and biologicals. Excludes accidents, homicides, and other causes indirectly related to drug use.

Death Rate by Drug-Induced Deaths in 2006

National Rate = 12.8 Deaths per 100,000 Population*

ALPHA ORDER				RANK ORDER		
RANK	STATE	RATE		RANK	STATE	RATE
40	Alabama	10.1		1	New Mexico	22.3
25	Alaska	12.7		2	West Virginia	20.8
14	Arizona	15.6		3	Nevada	18.9
36	Arkansas	10.9		3	Utah	18.9
35	California	11.0		5	Louisiana	18.7
20	Colorado	13.9		6	Kentucky	18.2
22	Connecticut	13.1		7	Oklahoma	17.3
43	Delaware	9.7		8	Tennessee	17.1
11	Florida	16.2		9	Rhode Island	16.8
43	Georgia	9.7		10	Michigan	16.5
39	Hawaii	10.2		11	Florida	16.2
42	Idaho	10.0		12	Massachusetts	15.9
34	Illinois	11.1		13	Oregon	15.8
30	Indiana	12.2		14	Arizona	15.6
48	Iowa	6.7		15	Washington	15.2
37	Kansas	10.6		16	South Carolina	14.8
6	Kentucky	18.2		17	Pennsylvania	14.7
5	Louisiana	18.7		18	Maryland	14.3
26	Maine	12.6		19	Ohio	14.0
18	Maryland	14.3		20	Colorado	13.9
12	Massachusetts	15.9		21	Vermont	13.3
10	Michigan	16.5		22	Connecticut	13.1
47	Minnesota	7.3		22	Missouri	13.1
26	Mississippi	12.6		24	Montana	12.8
22	Missouri	13.1		25	Alaska	12.7
24	Montana	12.8		26	Maine	12.6
46	Nebraska	7.4		26	Mississippi	12.6
3	Nevada	18.9		26	North Carolina	12.6
30	New Hampshire	12.2		29	Wyoming	12.4
32	New Jersey	11.6		30	Indiana	12.2
1	New Mexico	22.3		30	New Hampshire	12.2
40	New York	10.1		32	New Jersey	11.6
26	North Carolina	12.6		32	Wisconsin	11.6
NA	North Dakota**	NA		34	Illinois	11.1
19	Ohio	14.0		35	California	11.0
7	Oklahoma	17.3		36	Arkansas	10.9
13	Oregon	15.8		37	Kansas	10.6
17	Pennsylvania	14.7		38	Texas	10.4
9	Rhode Island	16.8		39	Hawaii	10.2
16	South Carolina	14.8		40	Alabama	10.1
49	South Dakota	5.5		40	New York	10.1
8	Tennessee	17.1		42	Idaho	10.0
38	Texas	10.4		43	Delaware	9.7
3	Utah	18.9		43	Georgia	9.7
21	Vermont	13.3		45	Virginia	8.8
45	Virginia	8.8		46	Nebraska	7.4
15	Washington	15.2		47	Minnesota	7.3
2	West Virginia	20.8		48	Iowa	6.7
32	Wisconsin	11.6		49	South Dakota	5.5
29	Wyoming	12.4		NA	North Dakota**	NA
					District of Columbia	22.2

Source: U.S. Department of Health and Human Services, National Center for Health Statistics
"National Vital Statistics Reports" (Vol. 57, No. 14, April 17, 2009, http://www.cdc.gov/nchs/deaths.htm)
*Final data by state of residence. Includes drug psychoses, drug dependence, nondependent use excluding alcohol and tobacco, accidental poisoning or suicide by drugs, medicaments, and biologicals. Excludes accidents, homicides, and other causes indirectly related to drug use. Not age-adjusted.

Age-Adjusted Death Rate by Drug-Induced Deaths in 2006

National Rate = 12.7 Deaths per 100,000 Population*

ALPHA ORDER

RANK	STATE	RATE
40	Alabama	10.3
25	Alaska	12.6
12	Arizona	16.0
33	Arkansas	11.3
36	California	11.0
20	Colorado	13.3
24	Connecticut	12.8
42	Delaware	9.9
11	Florida	16.2
44	Georgia	9.6
41	Hawaii	10.0
39	Idaho	10.4
35	Illinois	11.1
29	Indiana	12.2
48	Iowa	6.9
37	Kansas	10.7
6	Kentucky	18.1
4	Louisiana	19.0
28	Maine	12.3
18	Maryland	13.9
13	Massachusetts	15.3
10	Michigan	16.3
47	Minnesota	7.1
23	Mississippi	13.1
22	Missouri	13.2
26	Montana	12.5
46	Nebraska	7.4
5	Nevada	18.7
31	New Hampshire	11.8
33	New Jersey	11.3
1	New Mexico	22.8
43	New York	9.8
26	North Carolina	12.5
NA	North Dakota**	NA
18	Ohio	13.9
7	Oklahoma	17.8
14	Oregon	15.2
15	Pennsylvania	14.9
9	Rhode Island	16.6
16	South Carolina	14.7
49	South Dakota	5.7
8	Tennessee	16.9
38	Texas	10.6
3	Utah	20.7
20	Vermont	13.3
45	Virginia	8.6
17	Washington	14.6
2	West Virginia	21.2
32	Wisconsin	11.4
29	Wyoming	12.2

RANK ORDER

RANK	STATE	RATE
1	New Mexico	22.8
2	West Virginia	21.2
3	Utah	20.7
4	Louisiana	19.0
5	Nevada	18.7
6	Kentucky	18.1
7	Oklahoma	17.8
8	Tennessee	16.9
9	Rhode Island	16.6
10	Michigan	16.3
11	Florida	16.2
12	Arizona	16.0
13	Massachusetts	15.3
14	Oregon	15.2
15	Pennsylvania	14.9
16	South Carolina	14.7
17	Washington	14.6
18	Maryland	13.9
18	Ohio	13.9
20	Colorado	13.3
20	Vermont	13.3
22	Missouri	13.2
23	Mississippi	13.1
24	Connecticut	12.8
25	Alaska	12.6
26	Montana	12.5
26	North Carolina	12.5
28	Maine	12.3
29	Indiana	12.2
29	Wyoming	12.2
31	New Hampshire	11.8
32	Wisconsin	11.4
33	Arkansas	11.3
33	New Jersey	11.3
35	Illinois	11.1
36	California	11.0
37	Kansas	10.7
38	Texas	10.6
39	Idaho	10.4
40	Alabama	10.3
41	Hawaii	10.0
42	Delaware	9.9
43	New York	9.8
44	Georgia	9.6
45	Virginia	8.6
46	Nebraska	7.4
47	Minnesota	7.1
48	Iowa	6.9
49	South Dakota	5.7
NA	North Dakota**	NA

District of Columbia	22.4

Source: U.S. Department of Health and Human Services, National Center for Health Statistics
"National Vital Statistics Reports" (Vol. 57, No. 14, April 17, 2009, http://www.cdc.gov/nchs/deaths.htm)
*Final data by state of residence. Includes drug psychoses, drug dependence, nondependent use excluding alcohol and tobacco, accidental poisoning or suicide by drugs, medicaments, and biologicals. Excludes accidents, homicides, and other causes indirectly related to drug use. Age-adjusted rates based on the year 2000 standard population.

Occupational Fatalities in 2008

National Total = 5,071 Deaths*

ALPHA ORDER

RANK	STATE	DEATHS	% of USA
19	Alabama	97	1.9%
39	Alaska	33	0.7%
22	Arizona	86	1.7%
23	Arkansas	85	1.7%
2	California	404	8.0%
17	Colorado	102	2.0%
43	Connecticut	28	0.6%
47	Delaware	11	0.2%
3	Florida	290	5.7%
7	Georgia	171	3.4%
46	Hawaii	18	0.4%
38	Idaho	36	0.7%
6	Illinois	193	3.8%
14	Indiana	132	2.6%
20	Iowa	93	1.8%
28	Kansas	73	1.4%
16	Kentucky	105	2.1%
12	Louisiana	134	2.6%
45	Maine	24	0.5%
32	Maryland	59	1.2%
31	Massachusetts	61	1.2%
15	Michigan	123	2.4%
29	Minnesota	65	1.3%
26	Mississippi	80	1.6%
11	Missouri	147	2.9%
37	Montana	39	0.8%
34	Nebraska	53	1.0%
36	Nevada	40	0.8%
49	New Hampshire	7	0.1%
21	New Jersey	91	1.8%
41	New Mexico	31	0.6%
5	New York	212	4.2%
9	North Carolina	160	3.2%
44	North Dakota	27	0.5%
8	Ohio	167	3.3%
17	Oklahoma	102	2.0%
33	Oregon	54	1.1%
4	Pennsylvania	240	4.7%
50	Rhode Island	6	0.1%
23	South Carolina	85	1.7%
42	South Dakota	30	0.6%
12	Tennessee	134	2.6%
1	Texas	457	9.0%
29	Utah	65	1.3%
48	Vermont	10	0.2%
10	Virginia	154	3.0%
25	Washington	83	1.6%
34	West Virginia	53	1.0%
27	Wisconsin	77	1.5%
39	Wyoming	33	0.7%

RANK ORDER

RANK	STATE	DEATHS	% of USA
1	Texas	457	9.0%
2	California	404	8.0%
3	Florida	290	5.7%
4	Pennsylvania	240	4.7%
5	New York	212	4.2%
6	Illinois	193	3.8%
7	Georgia	171	3.4%
8	Ohio	167	3.3%
9	North Carolina	160	3.2%
10	Virginia	154	3.0%
11	Missouri	147	2.9%
12	Louisiana	134	2.6%
12	Tennessee	134	2.6%
14	Indiana	132	2.6%
15	Michigan	123	2.4%
16	Kentucky	105	2.1%
17	Colorado	102	2.0%
17	Oklahoma	102	2.0%
19	Alabama	97	1.9%
20	Iowa	93	1.8%
21	New Jersey	91	1.8%
22	Arizona	86	1.7%
23	Arkansas	85	1.7%
23	South Carolina	85	1.7%
25	Washington	83	1.6%
26	Mississippi	80	1.6%
27	Wisconsin	77	1.5%
28	Kansas	73	1.4%
29	Minnesota	65	1.3%
29	Utah	65	1.3%
31	Massachusetts	61	1.2%
32	Maryland	59	1.2%
33	Oregon	54	1.1%
34	Nebraska	53	1.0%
34	West Virginia	53	1.0%
36	Nevada	40	0.8%
37	Montana	39	0.8%
38	Idaho	36	0.7%
39	Alaska	33	0.7%
39	Wyoming	33	0.7%
41	New Mexico	31	0.6%
42	South Dakota	30	0.6%
43	Connecticut	28	0.6%
44	North Dakota	27	0.5%
45	Maine	24	0.5%
46	Hawaii	18	0.4%
47	Delaware	11	0.2%
48	Vermont	10	0.2%
49	New Hampshire	7	0.1%
50	Rhode Island	6	0.1%
	District of Columbia	9	0.2%

Source: U.S. Department of Labor, Bureau of Labor Statistics
"National Census of Fatal Occupational Injuries in 2008" (press release, August 20, 2009, http://www.bls.gov/iif/home.htm)
*Preliminary data. Includes two fatalities that occurred within the territorial boundaries of the United States but for which a state of incident could not be determined.

Occupational Fatality Rate in 2008

National Rate = 3.5 Deaths per 100,000 Workers*

ALPHA ORDER

RANK	STATE	RATE
18	Alabama	4.8
2	Alaska	9.9
36	Arizona	2.9
8	Arkansas	6.6
42	California	2.4
24	Colorado	3.9
48	Connecticut	1.6
40	Delaware	2.6
29	Florida	3.4
26	Georgia	3.8
36	Hawaii	2.9
15	Idaho	5.1
31	Illinois	3.1
20	Indiana	4.5
11	Iowa	5.8
15	Kansas	5.1
12	Kentucky	5.6
7	Louisiana	6.9
28	Maine	3.6
46	Maryland	2.1
47	Massachusetts	1.9
38	Michigan	2.8
42	Minnesota	2.4
8	Mississippi	6.6
14	Missouri	5.3
3	Montana	8.2
13	Nebraska	5.5
31	Nevada	3.1
50	New Hampshire	1.0
45	New Jersey	2.2
29	New Mexico	3.4
42	New York	2.4
26	North Carolina	3.8
4	North Dakota	7.5
33	Ohio	3.0
10	Oklahoma	6.1
33	Oregon	3.0
23	Pennsylvania	4.0
49	Rhode Island	1.2
21	South Carolina	4.3
5	South Dakota	7.0
18	Tennessee	4.8
22	Texas	4.1
17	Utah	4.9
33	Vermont	3.0
24	Virginia	3.9
41	Washington	2.5
5	West Virginia	7.0
39	Wisconsin	2.7
1	Wyoming	11.6

RANK ORDER

RANK	STATE	RATE
1	Wyoming	11.6
2	Alaska	9.9
3	Montana	8.2
4	North Dakota	7.5
5	South Dakota	7.0
5	West Virginia	7.0
7	Louisiana	6.9
8	Arkansas	6.6
8	Mississippi	6.6
10	Oklahoma	6.1
11	Iowa	5.8
12	Kentucky	5.6
13	Nebraska	5.5
14	Missouri	5.3
15	Idaho	5.1
15	Kansas	5.1
17	Utah	4.9
18	Alabama	4.8
18	Tennessee	4.8
20	Indiana	4.5
21	South Carolina	4.3
22	Texas	4.1
23	Pennsylvania	4.0
24	Colorado	3.9
24	Virginia	3.9
26	Georgia	3.8
26	North Carolina	3.8
28	Maine	3.6
29	Florida	3.4
29	New Mexico	3.4
31	Illinois	3.1
31	Nevada	3.1
33	Ohio	3.0
33	Oregon	3.0
33	Vermont	3.0
36	Arizona	2.9
36	Hawaii	2.9
38	Michigan	2.8
39	Wisconsin	2.7
40	Delaware	2.6
41	Washington	2.5
42	California	2.4
42	Minnesota	2.4
42	New York	2.4
45	New Jersey	2.2
46	Maryland	2.1
47	Massachusetts	1.9
48	Connecticut	1.6
49	Rhode Island	1.2
50	New Hampshire	1.0

| | District of Columbia | 3.0 |

Source: CQ Press using data from U.S. Department of Labor, Bureau of Labor Statistics
"National Census of Fatal Occupational Injuries in 2008" (press release, August 20, 2009, http://www.bls.gov/iif/home.htm)
*Preliminary data. Rates based on employed civilian labor force.

III. Facilities

Community Hospitals in 2008

National Total = 5,010 Hospitals*

RANK	STATE	HOSPITALS	% of USA
20	Alabama	109	2.2%
47	Alaska	22	0.4%
30	Arizona	71	1.4%
24	Arkansas	86	1.7%
2	California	352	7.0%
27	Colorado	78	1.6%
42	Connecticut	35	0.7%
50	Delaware	7	0.1%
3	Florida	211	4.2%
8	Georgia	153	3.1%
45	Hawaii	25	0.5%
39	Idaho	39	0.8%
6	Illinois	191	3.8%
15	Indiana	123	2.5%
17	Iowa	118	2.4%
11	Kansas	132	2.6%
21	Kentucky	105	2.1%
12	Louisiana	130	2.6%
40	Maine	37	0.7%
35	Maryland	50	1.0%
28	Massachusetts	75	1.5%
8	Michigan	153	3.1%
12	Minnesota	130	2.6%
22	Mississippi	98	2.0%
15	Missouri	123	2.5%
36	Montana	48	1.0%
24	Nebraska	86	1.7%
42	Nevada	35	0.7%
44	New Hampshire	28	0.6%
29	New Jersey	73	1.5%
41	New Mexico	36	0.7%
5	New York	194	3.9%
18	North Carolina	116	2.3%
38	North Dakota	41	0.8%
7	Ohio	181	3.6%
19	Oklahoma	115	2.3%
32	Oregon	58	1.2%
4	Pennsylvania	201	4.0%
49	Rhode Island	11	0.2%
31	South Carolina	69	1.4%
34	South Dakota	53	1.1%
10	Tennessee	137	2.7%
1	Texas	426	8.5%
37	Utah	43	0.9%
48	Vermont	14	0.3%
23	Virginia	90	1.8%
24	Washington	86	1.7%
33	West Virginia	56	1.1%
14	Wisconsin	126	2.5%
46	Wyoming	24	0.5%

RANK	STATE	HOSPITALS	% of USA
1	Texas	426	8.5%
2	California	352	7.0%
3	Florida	211	4.2%
4	Pennsylvania	201	4.0%
5	New York	194	3.9%
6	Illinois	191	3.8%
7	Ohio	181	3.6%
8	Georgia	153	3.1%
8	Michigan	153	3.1%
10	Tennessee	137	2.7%
11	Kansas	132	2.6%
12	Louisiana	130	2.6%
12	Minnesota	130	2.6%
14	Wisconsin	126	2.5%
15	Indiana	123	2.5%
15	Missouri	123	2.5%
17	Iowa	118	2.4%
18	North Carolina	116	2.3%
19	Oklahoma	115	2.3%
20	Alabama	109	2.2%
21	Kentucky	105	2.1%
22	Mississippi	98	2.0%
23	Virginia	90	1.8%
24	Arkansas	86	1.7%
24	Nebraska	86	1.7%
24	Washington	86	1.7%
27	Colorado	78	1.6%
28	Massachusetts	75	1.5%
29	New Jersey	73	1.5%
30	Arizona	71	1.4%
31	South Carolina	69	1.4%
32	Oregon	58	1.2%
33	West Virginia	56	1.1%
34	South Dakota	53	1.1%
35	Maryland	50	1.0%
36	Montana	48	1.0%
37	Utah	43	0.9%
38	North Dakota	41	0.8%
39	Idaho	39	0.8%
40	Maine	37	0.7%
41	New Mexico	36	0.7%
42	Connecticut	35	0.7%
42	Nevada	35	0.7%
44	New Hampshire	28	0.6%
45	Hawaii	25	0.5%
46	Wyoming	24	0.5%
47	Alaska	22	0.4%
48	Vermont	14	0.3%
49	Rhode Island	11	0.2%
50	Delaware	7	0.1%
	District of Columbia	10	0.2%

Source: American Hospital Association (Chicago, IL)
"Hospital Statistics" (2010 edition)

*Community hospitals are all nonfederal, short-term general, and special hospitals whose facilities and services are available to the public.

Rate of Community Hospitals in 2008

National Rate = 1.6 Community Hospitals per 100,000 Population*

ALPHA ORDER

RANK	STATE	RATE
18	Alabama	2.3
9	Alaska	3.2
41	Arizona	1.1
12	Arkansas	3.0
44	California	1.0
28	Colorado	1.6
44	Connecticut	1.0
49	Delaware	0.8
41	Florida	1.1
28	Georgia	1.6
24	Hawaii	1.9
15	Idaho	2.6
33	Illinois	1.5
24	Indiana	1.9
7	Iowa	3.9
5	Kansas	4.7
17	Kentucky	2.4
13	Louisiana	2.9
14	Maine	2.8
48	Maryland	0.9
41	Massachusetts	1.1
33	Michigan	1.5
16	Minnesota	2.5
8	Mississippi	3.3
22	Missouri	2.1
3	Montana	5.0
4	Nebraska	4.8
37	Nevada	1.3
22	New Hampshire	2.1
49	New Jersey	0.8
26	New Mexico	1.8
44	New York	1.0
37	North Carolina	1.3
2	North Dakota	6.4
28	Ohio	1.6
9	Oklahoma	3.2
33	Oregon	1.5
28	Pennsylvania	1.6
44	Rhode Island	1.0
33	South Carolina	1.5
1	South Dakota	6.6
20	Tennessee	2.2
26	Texas	1.8
28	Utah	1.6
18	Vermont	2.3
40	Virginia	1.2
37	Washington	1.3
11	West Virginia	3.1
20	Wisconsin	2.2
6	Wyoming	4.5

RANK ORDER

RANK	STATE	RATE
1	South Dakota	6.6
2	North Dakota	6.4
3	Montana	5.0
4	Nebraska	4.8
5	Kansas	4.7
6	Wyoming	4.5
7	Iowa	3.9
8	Mississippi	3.3
9	Alaska	3.2
9	Oklahoma	3.2
11	West Virginia	3.1
12	Arkansas	3.0
13	Louisiana	2.9
14	Maine	2.8
15	Idaho	2.6
16	Minnesota	2.5
17	Kentucky	2.4
18	Alabama	2.3
18	Vermont	2.3
20	Tennessee	2.2
20	Wisconsin	2.2
22	Missouri	2.1
22	New Hampshire	2.1
24	Hawaii	1.9
24	Indiana	1.9
26	New Mexico	1.8
26	Texas	1.8
28	Colorado	1.6
28	Georgia	1.6
28	Ohio	1.6
28	Pennsylvania	1.6
28	Utah	1.6
33	Illinois	1.5
33	Michigan	1.5
33	Oregon	1.5
33	South Carolina	1.5
37	Nevada	1.3
37	North Carolina	1.3
37	Washington	1.3
40	Virginia	1.2
41	Arizona	1.1
41	Florida	1.1
41	Massachusetts	1.1
44	California	1.0
44	Connecticut	1.0
44	New York	1.0
44	Rhode Island	1.0
48	Maryland	0.9
49	Delaware	0.8
49	New Jersey	0.8

District of Columbia 1.7

Source: CQ Press using data from American Hospital Association (Chicago, IL)
"Hospital Statistics" (2010 edition)
*Community hospitals are all nonfederal, short-term general, and special hospitals whose facilities and services are available to the public.

Community Hospitals per 1,000 Square Miles in 2008

National Rate = 1.3 Community Hospitals*

ALPHA ORDER

RANK	STATE	RATE
23	Alabama	2.1
50	Alaska**	0.0
41	Arizona	0.6
29	Arkansas	1.6
20	California	2.2
39	Colorado	0.7
4	Connecticut	6.3
14	Delaware	2.8
12	Florida	3.2
15	Georgia	2.6
18	Hawaii	2.3
44	Idaho	0.5
10	Illinois	3.3
9	Indiana	3.4
23	Iowa	2.1
29	Kansas	1.6
15	Kentucky	2.6
17	Louisiana	2.5
38	Maine	1.0
6	Maryland	4.0
2	Massachusetts	7.1
29	Michigan	1.6
34	Minnesota	1.5
26	Mississippi	2.0
28	Missouri	1.8
46	Montana	0.3
37	Nebraska	1.1
46	Nevada	0.3
13	New Hampshire	3.0
1	New Jersey	8.4
46	New Mexico	0.3
8	New York	3.6
20	North Carolina	2.2
41	North Dakota	0.6
6	Ohio	4.0
29	Oklahoma	1.6
41	Oregon	0.6
5	Pennsylvania	4.4
2	Rhode Island	7.1
20	South Carolina	2.2
39	South Dakota	0.7
10	Tennessee	3.3
29	Texas	1.6
44	Utah	0.5
34	Vermont	1.5
23	Virginia	2.1
36	Washington	1.2
18	West Virginia	2.3
27	Wisconsin	1.9
49	Wyoming	0.2

RANK ORDER

RANK	STATE	RATE
1	New Jersey	8.4
2	Massachusetts	7.1
2	Rhode Island	7.1
4	Connecticut	6.3
5	Pennsylvania	4.4
6	Maryland	4.0
6	Ohio	4.0
8	New York	3.6
9	Indiana	3.4
10	Illinois	3.3
10	Tennessee	3.3
12	Florida	3.2
13	New Hampshire	3.0
14	Delaware	2.8
15	Georgia	2.6
15	Kentucky	2.6
17	Louisiana	2.5
18	Hawaii	2.3
18	West Virginia	2.3
20	California	2.2
20	North Carolina	2.2
20	South Carolina	2.2
23	Alabama	2.1
23	Iowa	2.1
23	Virginia	2.1
26	Mississippi	2.0
27	Wisconsin	1.9
28	Missouri	1.8
29	Arkansas	1.6
29	Kansas	1.6
29	Michigan	1.6
29	Oklahoma	1.6
29	Texas	1.6
34	Minnesota	1.5
34	Vermont	1.5
36	Washington	1.2
37	Nebraska	1.1
38	Maine	1.0
39	Colorado	0.7
39	South Dakota	0.7
41	Arizona	0.6
41	North Dakota	0.6
41	Oregon	0.6
44	Idaho	0.5
44	Utah	0.5
46	Montana	0.3
46	Nevada	0.3
46	New Mexico	0.3
49	Wyoming	0.2
50	Alaska**	0.0

District of Columbia***   NA

Source: CQ Press using data from American Hospital Association (Chicago, IL)
    "Hospital Statistics" (2010 edition)
*Based on land and water area figures. Community hospitals are nonfederal, short-term general, and other special hospitals whose facilities and services are available to the public.
**Alaska has 22 community hospitals for its 663,267 square miles.
***The District of Columbia has 10 community hospitals for its 68 square miles.

Community Hospitals in Urban Areas in 2008

National Total = 3,012 Hospitals*

ALPHA ORDER					RANK ORDER			
RANK	STATE		HOSPITALS	% of USA	RANK	STATE	HOSPITALS	% of USA
17	Alabama		60	2.0%	1	California	321	10.7%
46	Alaska		5	0.2%	2	Texas	275	9.1%
20	Arizona		57	1.9%	3	Florida	181	6.0%
28	Arkansas		37	1.2%	4	New York	154	5.1%
1	California		321	10.7%	5	Pennsylvania	152	5.0%
26	Colorado		41	1.4%	6	Illinois	127	4.2%
31	Connecticut		30	1.0%	7	Ohio	126	4.2%
46	Delaware		5	0.2%	8	Michigan	94	3.1%
3	Florida		181	6.0%	9	Georgia	87	2.9%
9	Georgia		87	2.9%	10	Indiana	83	2.8%
39	Hawaii		14	0.5%	11	Tennessee	81	2.7%
39	Idaho		14	0.5%	12	Louisiana	80	2.7%
6	Illinois		127	4.2%	13	Massachusetts	73	2.4%
10	Indiana		83	2.8%	13	New Jersey	73	2.4%
29	Iowa		34	1.1%	15	Missouri	70	2.3%
30	Kansas		33	1.1%	16	Wisconsin	69	2.3%
26	Kentucky		41	1.4%	17	Alabama	60	2.0%
12	Louisiana		80	2.7%	17	Virginia	60	2.0%
38	Maine		15	0.5%	19	North Carolina	58	1.9%
24	Maryland		44	1.5%	20	Arizona	57	1.9%
13	Massachusetts		73	2.4%	21	Washington	51	1.7%
8	Michigan		94	3.1%	22	Oklahoma	50	1.7%
23	Minnesota		49	1.6%	23	Minnesota	49	1.6%
32	Mississippi		29	1.0%	24	Maryland	44	1.5%
15	Missouri		70	2.3%	24	South Carolina	44	1.5%
46	Montana		5	0.2%	26	Colorado	41	1.4%
37	Nebraska		16	0.5%	26	Kentucky	41	1.4%
36	Nevada		24	0.8%	28	Arkansas	37	1.2%
42	New Hampshire		11	0.4%	29	Iowa	34	1.1%
13	New Jersey		73	2.4%	30	Kansas	33	1.1%
39	New Mexico		14	0.5%	31	Connecticut	30	1.0%
4	New York		154	5.1%	32	Mississippi	29	1.0%
19	North Carolina		58	1.9%	32	Oregon	29	1.0%
45	North Dakota		7	0.2%	34	West Virginia	27	0.9%
7	Ohio		126	4.2%	35	Utah	26	0.9%
22	Oklahoma		50	1.7%	36	Nevada	24	0.8%
32	Oregon		29	1.0%	37	Nebraska	16	0.5%
5	Pennsylvania		152	5.0%	38	Maine	15	0.5%
42	Rhode Island		11	0.4%	39	Hawaii	14	0.5%
24	South Carolina		44	1.5%	39	Idaho	14	0.5%
42	South Dakota		11	0.4%	39	New Mexico	14	0.5%
11	Tennessee		81	2.7%	42	New Hampshire	11	0.4%
2	Texas		275	9.1%	42	Rhode Island	11	0.4%
35	Utah		26	0.9%	42	South Dakota	11	0.4%
49	Vermont		2	0.1%	45	North Dakota	7	0.2%
17	Virginia		60	2.0%	46	Alaska	5	0.2%
21	Washington		51	1.7%	46	Delaware	5	0.2%
34	West Virginia		27	0.9%	46	Montana	5	0.2%
16	Wisconsin		69	2.3%	49	Vermont	2	0.1%
49	Wyoming		2	0.1%	49	Wyoming	2	0.1%
						District of Columbia	10	0.3%

Source: American Hospital Association (Chicago, IL)
"Hospital Statistics" (2010 edition)

*Community hospitals are all nonfederal, short-term general, and special hospitals whose facilities and services are available to the public. Urban is defined as any area inside a metropolitan statistical area as defined by the U.S. Office of Management and Budget.

Percent of Community Hospitals in Urban Areas in 2008

National Percent = 60.1% of Community Hospitals*

ALPHA ORDER

RANK	STATE	PERCENT
27	Alabama	55.0
44	Alaska	22.7
8	Arizona	80.3
34	Arkansas	43.0
4	California	91.2
29	Colorado	52.6
7	Connecticut	85.7
11	Delaware	71.4
6	Florida	85.8
24	Georgia	56.9
26	Hawaii	56.0
40	Idaho	35.9
16	Illinois	66.5
14	Indiana	67.5
42	Iowa	28.8
43	Kansas	25.0
37	Kentucky	39.0
19	Louisiana	61.5
35	Maine	40.5
5	Maryland	88.0
3	Massachusetts	97.3
20	Michigan	61.4
39	Minnesota	37.7
41	Mississippi	29.6
24	Missouri	56.9
49	Montana	10.4
46	Nebraska	18.6
13	Nevada	68.6
36	New Hampshire	39.3
1	New Jersey	100.0
38	New Mexico	38.9
9	New York	79.4
30	North Carolina	50.0
47	North Dakota	17.1
12	Ohio	69.6
33	Oklahoma	43.5
30	Oregon	50.0
10	Pennsylvania	75.6
1	Rhode Island	100.0
18	South Carolina	63.8
45	South Dakota	20.8
23	Tennessee	59.1
17	Texas	64.6
21	Utah	60.5
48	Vermont	14.3
15	Virginia	66.7
22	Washington	59.3
32	West Virginia	48.2
28	Wisconsin	54.8
50	Wyoming	8.3

RANK ORDER

RANK	STATE	PERCENT
1	New Jersey	100.0
1	Rhode Island	100.0
3	Massachusetts	97.3
4	California	91.2
5	Maryland	88.0
6	Florida	85.8
7	Connecticut	85.7
8	Arizona	80.3
9	New York	79.4
10	Pennsylvania	75.6
11	Delaware	71.4
12	Ohio	69.6
13	Nevada	68.6
14	Indiana	67.5
15	Virginia	66.7
16	Illinois	66.5
17	Texas	64.6
18	South Carolina	63.8
19	Louisiana	61.5
20	Michigan	61.4
21	Utah	60.5
22	Washington	59.3
23	Tennessee	59.1
24	Georgia	56.9
24	Missouri	56.9
26	Hawaii	56.0
27	Alabama	55.0
28	Wisconsin	54.8
29	Colorado	52.6
30	North Carolina	50.0
30	Oregon	50.0
32	West Virginia	48.2
33	Oklahoma	43.5
34	Arkansas	43.0
35	Maine	40.5
36	New Hampshire	39.3
37	Kentucky	39.0
38	New Mexico	38.9
39	Minnesota	37.7
40	Idaho	35.9
41	Mississippi	29.6
42	Iowa	28.8
43	Kansas	25.0
44	Alaska	22.7
45	South Dakota	20.8
46	Nebraska	18.6
47	North Dakota	17.1
48	Vermont	14.3
49	Montana	10.4
50	Wyoming	8.3

District of Columbia		100.0

Source: CQ Press using data from American Hospital Association (Chicago, IL)
    "Hospital Statistics" (2010 edition)
*Community hospitals are all nonfederal, short-term general, and special hospitals whose facilities and services are available to the public. Urban is defined as any area inside a metropolitan statistical area as defined by the U.S. Office of Management and Budget.

Community Hospitals in Rural Areas in 2008

National Total = 1,998 Hospitals*

ALPHA ORDER					RANK ORDER			

RANK	STATE	HOSPITALS	% of USA		RANK	STATE	HOSPITALS	% of USA
18	Alabama	49	2.5%		1	Texas	151	7.6%
38	Alaska	17	0.9%		2	Kansas	99	5.0%
41	Arizona	14	0.7%		3	Iowa	84	4.2%
18	Arkansas	49	2.5%		4	Minnesota	81	4.1%
28	California	31	1.6%		5	Nebraska	70	3.5%
25	Colorado	37	1.9%		6	Mississippi	69	3.5%
46	Connecticut	5	0.3%		7	Georgia	66	3.3%
47	Delaware	2	0.1%		8	Oklahoma	65	3.3%
29	Florida	30	1.5%		9	Illinois	64	3.2%
7	Georgia	66	3.3%		9	Kentucky	64	3.2%
43	Hawaii	11	0.6%		11	Michigan	59	3.0%
33	Idaho	25	1.3%		12	North Carolina	58	2.9%
9	Illinois	64	3.2%		13	Wisconsin	57	2.9%
23	Indiana	40	2.0%		14	Tennessee	56	2.8%
3	Iowa	84	4.2%		15	Ohio	55	2.8%
2	Kansas	99	5.0%		16	Missouri	53	2.7%
9	Kentucky	64	3.2%		17	Louisiana	50	2.5%
17	Louisiana	50	2.5%		18	Alabama	49	2.5%
35	Maine	22	1.1%		18	Arkansas	49	2.5%
45	Maryland	6	0.3%		18	Pennsylvania	49	2.5%
47	Massachusetts	2	0.1%		21	Montana	43	2.2%
11	Michigan	59	3.0%		22	South Dakota	42	2.1%
4	Minnesota	81	4.1%		23	Indiana	40	2.0%
6	Mississippi	69	3.5%		23	New York	40	2.0%
16	Missouri	53	2.7%		25	Colorado	37	1.9%
21	Montana	43	2.2%		26	Washington	35	1.8%
5	Nebraska	70	3.5%		27	North Dakota	34	1.7%
43	Nevada	11	0.6%		28	California	31	1.6%
38	New Hampshire	17	0.9%		29	Florida	30	1.5%
49	New Jersey	0	0.0%		29	Virginia	30	1.5%
35	New Mexico	22	1.1%		31	Oregon	29	1.5%
23	New York	40	2.0%		31	West Virginia	29	1.5%
12	North Carolina	58	2.9%		33	Idaho	25	1.3%
27	North Dakota	34	1.7%		33	South Carolina	25	1.3%
15	Ohio	55	2.8%		35	Maine	22	1.1%
8	Oklahoma	65	3.3%		35	New Mexico	22	1.1%
31	Oregon	29	1.5%		35	Wyoming	22	1.1%
18	Pennsylvania	49	2.5%		38	Alaska	17	0.9%
49	Rhode Island	0	0.0%		38	New Hampshire	17	0.9%
33	South Carolina	25	1.3%		38	Utah	17	0.9%
22	South Dakota	42	2.1%		41	Arizona	14	0.7%
14	Tennessee	56	2.8%		42	Vermont	12	0.6%
1	Texas	151	7.6%		43	Hawaii	11	0.6%
38	Utah	17	0.9%		43	Nevada	11	0.6%
42	Vermont	12	0.6%		45	Maryland	6	0.3%
29	Virginia	30	1.5%		46	Connecticut	5	0.3%
26	Washington	35	1.8%		47	Delaware	2	0.1%
31	West Virginia	29	1.5%		47	Massachusetts	2	0.1%
13	Wisconsin	57	2.9%		49	New Jersey	0	0.0%
35	Wyoming	22	1.1%		49	Rhode Island	0	0.0%
					District of Columbia		0	0.0%

Source: American Hospital Association (Chicago, IL)
"Hospital Statistics" (2010 edition)

*Community hospitals are all nonfederal, short-term general, and special hospitals whose facilities and services are available to the public. Rural is defined as any area outside a metropolitan statistical area as defined by the U.S. Office of Management and Budget.

Percent of Community Hospitals in Rural Areas in 2008

National Percent = 39.9% of Community Hospitals*

<table>
<tr><td colspan="3">ALPHA ORDER</td><td colspan="3">RANK ORDER</td></tr>
<tr><td>RANK</td><td>STATE</td><td>PERCENT</td><td>RANK</td><td>STATE</td><td>PERCENT</td></tr>
<tr><td>24</td><td>Alabama</td><td>45.0</td><td>1</td><td>Wyoming</td><td>91.7</td></tr>
<tr><td>7</td><td>Alaska</td><td>77.3</td><td>2</td><td>Montana</td><td>89.6</td></tr>
<tr><td>43</td><td>Arizona</td><td>19.7</td><td>3</td><td>Vermont</td><td>85.7</td></tr>
<tr><td>17</td><td>Arkansas</td><td>57.0</td><td>4</td><td>North Dakota</td><td>82.9</td></tr>
<tr><td>47</td><td>California</td><td>8.8</td><td>5</td><td>Nebraska</td><td>81.4</td></tr>
<tr><td>22</td><td>Colorado</td><td>47.4</td><td>6</td><td>South Dakota</td><td>79.2</td></tr>
<tr><td>44</td><td>Connecticut</td><td>14.3</td><td>7</td><td>Alaska</td><td>77.3</td></tr>
<tr><td>40</td><td>Delaware</td><td>28.6</td><td>8</td><td>Kansas</td><td>75.0</td></tr>
<tr><td>45</td><td>Florida</td><td>14.2</td><td>9</td><td>Iowa</td><td>71.2</td></tr>
<tr><td>26</td><td>Georgia</td><td>43.1</td><td>10</td><td>Mississippi</td><td>70.4</td></tr>
<tr><td>25</td><td>Hawaii</td><td>44.0</td><td>11</td><td>Idaho</td><td>64.1</td></tr>
<tr><td>11</td><td>Idaho</td><td>64.1</td><td>12</td><td>Minnesota</td><td>62.3</td></tr>
<tr><td>35</td><td>Illinois</td><td>33.5</td><td>13</td><td>New Mexico</td><td>61.1</td></tr>
<tr><td>37</td><td>Indiana</td><td>32.5</td><td>14</td><td>Kentucky</td><td>61.0</td></tr>
<tr><td>9</td><td>Iowa</td><td>71.2</td><td>15</td><td>New Hampshire</td><td>60.7</td></tr>
<tr><td>8</td><td>Kansas</td><td>75.0</td><td>16</td><td>Maine</td><td>59.5</td></tr>
<tr><td>14</td><td>Kentucky</td><td>61.0</td><td>17</td><td>Arkansas</td><td>57.0</td></tr>
<tr><td>32</td><td>Louisiana</td><td>38.5</td><td>18</td><td>Oklahoma</td><td>56.5</td></tr>
<tr><td>16</td><td>Maine</td><td>59.5</td><td>19</td><td>West Virginia</td><td>51.8</td></tr>
<tr><td>46</td><td>Maryland</td><td>12.0</td><td>20</td><td>North Carolina</td><td>50.0</td></tr>
<tr><td>48</td><td>Massachusetts</td><td>2.7</td><td>20</td><td>Oregon</td><td>50.0</td></tr>
<tr><td>31</td><td>Michigan</td><td>38.6</td><td>22</td><td>Colorado</td><td>47.4</td></tr>
<tr><td>12</td><td>Minnesota</td><td>62.3</td><td>23</td><td>Wisconsin</td><td>45.2</td></tr>
<tr><td>10</td><td>Mississippi</td><td>70.4</td><td>24</td><td>Alabama</td><td>45.0</td></tr>
<tr><td>26</td><td>Missouri</td><td>43.1</td><td>25</td><td>Hawaii</td><td>44.0</td></tr>
<tr><td>2</td><td>Montana</td><td>89.6</td><td>26</td><td>Georgia</td><td>43.1</td></tr>
<tr><td>5</td><td>Nebraska</td><td>81.4</td><td>26</td><td>Missouri</td><td>43.1</td></tr>
<tr><td>38</td><td>Nevada</td><td>31.4</td><td>28</td><td>Tennessee</td><td>40.9</td></tr>
<tr><td>15</td><td>New Hampshire</td><td>60.7</td><td>29</td><td>Washington</td><td>40.7</td></tr>
<tr><td>49</td><td>New Jersey</td><td>0.0</td><td>30</td><td>Utah</td><td>39.5</td></tr>
<tr><td>13</td><td>New Mexico</td><td>61.1</td><td>31</td><td>Michigan</td><td>38.6</td></tr>
<tr><td>42</td><td>New York</td><td>20.6</td><td>32</td><td>Louisiana</td><td>38.5</td></tr>
<tr><td>20</td><td>North Carolina</td><td>50.0</td><td>33</td><td>South Carolina</td><td>36.2</td></tr>
<tr><td>4</td><td>North Dakota</td><td>82.9</td><td>34</td><td>Texas</td><td>35.4</td></tr>
<tr><td>39</td><td>Ohio</td><td>30.4</td><td>35</td><td>Illinois</td><td>33.5</td></tr>
<tr><td>18</td><td>Oklahoma</td><td>56.5</td><td>36</td><td>Virginia</td><td>33.3</td></tr>
<tr><td>20</td><td>Oregon</td><td>50.0</td><td>37</td><td>Indiana</td><td>32.5</td></tr>
<tr><td>41</td><td>Pennsylvania</td><td>24.4</td><td>38</td><td>Nevada</td><td>31.4</td></tr>
<tr><td>49</td><td>Rhode Island</td><td>0.0</td><td>39</td><td>Ohio</td><td>30.4</td></tr>
<tr><td>33</td><td>South Carolina</td><td>36.2</td><td>40</td><td>Delaware</td><td>28.6</td></tr>
<tr><td>6</td><td>South Dakota</td><td>79.2</td><td>41</td><td>Pennsylvania</td><td>24.4</td></tr>
<tr><td>28</td><td>Tennessee</td><td>40.9</td><td>42</td><td>New York</td><td>20.6</td></tr>
<tr><td>34</td><td>Texas</td><td>35.4</td><td>43</td><td>Arizona</td><td>19.7</td></tr>
<tr><td>30</td><td>Utah</td><td>39.5</td><td>44</td><td>Connecticut</td><td>14.3</td></tr>
<tr><td>3</td><td>Vermont</td><td>85.7</td><td>45</td><td>Florida</td><td>14.2</td></tr>
<tr><td>36</td><td>Virginia</td><td>33.3</td><td>46</td><td>Maryland</td><td>12.0</td></tr>
<tr><td>29</td><td>Washington</td><td>40.7</td><td>47</td><td>California</td><td>8.8</td></tr>
<tr><td>19</td><td>West Virginia</td><td>51.8</td><td>48</td><td>Massachusetts</td><td>2.7</td></tr>
<tr><td>23</td><td>Wisconsin</td><td>45.2</td><td>49</td><td>New Jersey</td><td>0.0</td></tr>
<tr><td>1</td><td>Wyoming</td><td>91.7</td><td>49</td><td>Rhode Island</td><td>0.0</td></tr>
<tr><td></td><td></td><td></td><td></td><td>District of Columbia</td><td>0.0</td></tr>
</table>

Source: CQ Press using data from American Hospital Association (Chicago, IL)
   "Hospital Statistics" (2010 edition)
*Community hospitals are all nonfederal, short-term general, and special hospitals whose facilities and services are available to the public. Rural is defined as any area outside a metropolitan statistical area as defined by the U.S. Office of Management and Budget.

Nongovernment, Not-for-Profit Hospitals in 2008

National Total = 2,923 Hospitals*

ALPHA ORDER

RANK	STATE	HOSPITALS	% of USA
38	Alabama	27	0.9%
46	Alaska	13	0.4%
25	Arizona	44	1.5%
23	Arkansas	46	1.6%
1	California	202	6.9%
32	Colorado	37	1.3%
35	Connecticut	32	1.1%
49	Delaware	6	0.2%
10	Florida	86	2.9%
15	Georgia	63	2.2%
42	Hawaii	17	0.6%
43	Idaho	14	0.5%
5	Illinois	149	5.1%
19	Indiana	59	2.0%
20	Iowa	58	2.0%
21	Kansas	53	1.8%
12	Kentucky	71	2.4%
31	Louisiana	38	1.3%
34	Maine	34	1.2%
22	Maryland	48	1.6%
13	Massachusetts	65	2.2%
7	Michigan	123	4.2%
9	Minnesota	93	3.2%
37	Mississippi	30	1.0%
16	Missouri	62	2.1%
29	Montana	39	1.3%
23	Nebraska	46	1.6%
46	Nevada	13	0.4%
40	New Hampshire	24	0.8%
17	New Jersey	61	2.1%
43	New Mexico	14	0.5%
2	New York	167	5.7%
11	North Carolina	74	2.5%
29	North Dakota	39	1.3%
6	Ohio	139	4.8%
32	Oklahoma	37	1.3%
27	Oregon	43	1.5%
3	Pennsylvania	160	5.5%
48	Rhode Island	11	0.4%
39	South Carolina	25	0.9%
25	South Dakota	44	1.5%
18	Tennessee	60	2.1%
4	Texas	152	5.2%
41	Utah	23	0.8%
43	Vermont	14	0.5%
13	Virginia	65	2.2%
28	Washington	40	1.4%
35	West Virginia	32	1.1%
8	Wisconsin	119	4.1%
50	Wyoming	5	0.2%

RANK ORDER

RANK	STATE	HOSPITALS	% of USA
1	California	202	6.9%
2	New York	167	5.7%
3	Pennsylvania	160	5.5%
4	Texas	152	5.2%
5	Illinois	149	5.1%
6	Ohio	139	4.8%
7	Michigan	123	4.2%
8	Wisconsin	119	4.1%
9	Minnesota	93	3.2%
10	Florida	86	2.9%
11	North Carolina	74	2.5%
12	Kentucky	71	2.4%
13	Massachusetts	65	2.2%
13	Virginia	65	2.2%
15	Georgia	63	2.2%
16	Missouri	62	2.1%
17	New Jersey	61	2.1%
18	Tennessee	60	2.1%
19	Indiana	59	2.0%
20	Iowa	58	2.0%
21	Kansas	53	1.8%
22	Maryland	48	1.6%
23	Arkansas	46	1.6%
23	Nebraska	46	1.6%
25	Arizona	44	1.5%
25	South Dakota	44	1.5%
27	Oregon	43	1.5%
28	Washington	40	1.4%
29	Montana	39	1.3%
29	North Dakota	39	1.3%
31	Louisiana	38	1.3%
32	Colorado	37	1.3%
32	Oklahoma	37	1.3%
34	Maine	34	1.2%
35	Connecticut	32	1.1%
35	West Virginia	32	1.1%
37	Mississippi	30	1.0%
38	Alabama	27	0.9%
39	South Carolina	25	0.9%
40	New Hampshire	24	0.8%
41	Utah	23	0.8%
42	Hawaii	17	0.6%
43	Idaho	14	0.5%
43	New Mexico	14	0.5%
43	Vermont	14	0.5%
46	Alaska	13	0.4%
46	Nevada	13	0.4%
48	Rhode Island	11	0.4%
49	Delaware	6	0.2%
50	Wyoming	5	0.2%
	District of Columbia	7	0.2%

Source: American Hospital Association (Chicago, IL)
   "Hospital Statistics" (2010 edition)
*Nongovernment, not-for-profit hospitals are a subset of community hospitals. Community hospitals are all nonfederal,
short-term general, and other special hospitals whose facilities and services are available to the public.

Investor-Owned, For-Profit Hospitals in 2008

National Total = 982 Hospitals*

<table>
<tr><td colspan="4">ALPHA ORDER</td><td colspan="4">RANK ORDER</td></tr>
<tr><td>RANK</td><td>STATE</td><td>HOSPITALS</td><td>% of USA</td><td>RANK</td><td>STATE</td><td>HOSPITALS</td><td>% of USA</td></tr>
<tr><td>6</td><td>Alabama</td><td>40</td><td>4.1%</td><td>1</td><td>Texas</td><td>157</td><td>16.0%</td></tr>
<tr><td>36</td><td>Alaska</td><td>2</td><td>0.2%</td><td>2</td><td>Florida</td><td>100</td><td>10.2%</td></tr>
<tr><td>15</td><td>Arizona</td><td>23</td><td>2.3%</td><td>3</td><td>California</td><td>79</td><td>8.0%</td></tr>
<tr><td>10</td><td>Arkansas</td><td>27</td><td>2.7%</td><td>4</td><td>Tennessee</td><td>55</td><td>5.6%</td></tr>
<tr><td>3</td><td>California</td><td>79</td><td>8.0%</td><td>5</td><td>Louisiana</td><td>42</td><td>4.3%</td></tr>
<tr><td>26</td><td>Colorado</td><td>13</td><td>1.3%</td><td>6</td><td>Alabama</td><td>40</td><td>4.1%</td></tr>
<tr><td>36</td><td>Connecticut</td><td>2</td><td>0.2%</td><td>7</td><td>Pennsylvania</td><td>38</td><td>3.9%</td></tr>
<tr><td>42</td><td>Delaware</td><td>1</td><td>0.1%</td><td>8</td><td>Georgia</td><td>34</td><td>3.5%</td></tr>
<tr><td>2</td><td>Florida</td><td>100</td><td>10.2%</td><td>9</td><td>Oklahoma</td><td>33</td><td>3.4%</td></tr>
<tr><td>8</td><td>Georgia</td><td>34</td><td>3.5%</td><td>10</td><td>Arkansas</td><td>27</td><td>2.7%</td></tr>
<tr><td>47</td><td>Hawaii</td><td>0</td><td>0.0%</td><td>10</td><td>Mississippi</td><td>27</td><td>2.7%</td></tr>
<tr><td>34</td><td>Idaho</td><td>3</td><td>0.3%</td><td>12</td><td>Missouri</td><td>26</td><td>2.6%</td></tr>
<tr><td>20</td><td>Illinois</td><td>16</td><td>1.6%</td><td>13</td><td>Indiana</td><td>25</td><td>2.5%</td></tr>
<tr><td>13</td><td>Indiana</td><td>25</td><td>2.5%</td><td>14</td><td>South Carolina</td><td>24</td><td>2.4%</td></tr>
<tr><td>42</td><td>Iowa</td><td>1</td><td>0.1%</td><td>15</td><td>Arizona</td><td>23</td><td>2.3%</td></tr>
<tr><td>19</td><td>Kansas</td><td>17</td><td>1.7%</td><td>16</td><td>Ohio</td><td>21</td><td>2.1%</td></tr>
<tr><td>18</td><td>Kentucky</td><td>20</td><td>2.0%</td><td>16</td><td>Virginia</td><td>21</td><td>2.1%</td></tr>
<tr><td>5</td><td>Louisiana</td><td>42</td><td>4.3%</td><td>18</td><td>Kentucky</td><td>20</td><td>2.0%</td></tr>
<tr><td>42</td><td>Maine</td><td>1</td><td>0.1%</td><td>19</td><td>Kansas</td><td>17</td><td>1.7%</td></tr>
<tr><td>36</td><td>Maryland</td><td>2</td><td>0.2%</td><td>20</td><td>Illinois</td><td>16</td><td>1.6%</td></tr>
<tr><td>28</td><td>Massachusetts</td><td>8</td><td>0.8%</td><td>20</td><td>Nevada</td><td>16</td><td>1.6%</td></tr>
<tr><td>22</td><td>Michigan</td><td>15</td><td>1.5%</td><td>22</td><td>Michigan</td><td>15</td><td>1.5%</td></tr>
<tr><td>47</td><td>Minnesota</td><td>0</td><td>0.0%</td><td>22</td><td>New Mexico</td><td>15</td><td>1.5%</td></tr>
<tr><td>10</td><td>Mississippi</td><td>27</td><td>2.7%</td><td>22</td><td>Utah</td><td>15</td><td>1.5%</td></tr>
<tr><td>12</td><td>Missouri</td><td>26</td><td>2.6%</td><td>25</td><td>West Virginia</td><td>14</td><td>1.4%</td></tr>
<tr><td>42</td><td>Montana</td><td>1</td><td>0.1%</td><td>26</td><td>Colorado</td><td>13</td><td>1.3%</td></tr>
<tr><td>36</td><td>Nebraska</td><td>2</td><td>0.2%</td><td>27</td><td>North Carolina</td><td>10</td><td>1.0%</td></tr>
<tr><td>20</td><td>Nevada</td><td>16</td><td>1.6%</td><td>28</td><td>Massachusetts</td><td>8</td><td>0.8%</td></tr>
<tr><td>31</td><td>New Hampshire</td><td>4</td><td>0.4%</td><td>28</td><td>New Jersey</td><td>8</td><td>0.8%</td></tr>
<tr><td>28</td><td>New Jersey</td><td>8</td><td>0.8%</td><td>30</td><td>Wisconsin</td><td>5</td><td>0.5%</td></tr>
<tr><td>22</td><td>New Mexico</td><td>15</td><td>1.5%</td><td>31</td><td>New Hampshire</td><td>4</td><td>0.4%</td></tr>
<tr><td>42</td><td>New York</td><td>1</td><td>0.1%</td><td>31</td><td>South Dakota</td><td>4</td><td>0.4%</td></tr>
<tr><td>27</td><td>North Carolina</td><td>10</td><td>1.0%</td><td>31</td><td>Washington</td><td>4</td><td>0.4%</td></tr>
<tr><td>36</td><td>North Dakota</td><td>2</td><td>0.2%</td><td>34</td><td>Idaho</td><td>3</td><td>0.3%</td></tr>
<tr><td>16</td><td>Ohio</td><td>21</td><td>2.1%</td><td>34</td><td>Wyoming</td><td>3</td><td>0.3%</td></tr>
<tr><td>9</td><td>Oklahoma</td><td>33</td><td>3.4%</td><td>36</td><td>Alaska</td><td>2</td><td>0.2%</td></tr>
<tr><td>36</td><td>Oregon</td><td>2</td><td>0.2%</td><td>36</td><td>Connecticut</td><td>2</td><td>0.2%</td></tr>
<tr><td>7</td><td>Pennsylvania</td><td>38</td><td>3.9%</td><td>36</td><td>Maryland</td><td>2</td><td>0.2%</td></tr>
<tr><td>47</td><td>Rhode Island</td><td>0</td><td>0.0%</td><td>36</td><td>Nebraska</td><td>2</td><td>0.2%</td></tr>
<tr><td>14</td><td>South Carolina</td><td>24</td><td>2.4%</td><td>36</td><td>North Dakota</td><td>2</td><td>0.2%</td></tr>
<tr><td>31</td><td>South Dakota</td><td>4</td><td>0.4%</td><td>36</td><td>Oregon</td><td>2</td><td>0.2%</td></tr>
<tr><td>4</td><td>Tennessee</td><td>55</td><td>5.6%</td><td>42</td><td>Delaware</td><td>1</td><td>0.1%</td></tr>
<tr><td>1</td><td>Texas</td><td>157</td><td>16.0%</td><td>42</td><td>Iowa</td><td>1</td><td>0.1%</td></tr>
<tr><td>22</td><td>Utah</td><td>15</td><td>1.5%</td><td>42</td><td>Maine</td><td>1</td><td>0.1%</td></tr>
<tr><td>47</td><td>Vermont</td><td>0</td><td>0.0%</td><td>42</td><td>Montana</td><td>1</td><td>0.1%</td></tr>
<tr><td>16</td><td>Virginia</td><td>21</td><td>2.1%</td><td>42</td><td>New York</td><td>1</td><td>0.1%</td></tr>
<tr><td>31</td><td>Washington</td><td>4</td><td>0.4%</td><td>47</td><td>Hawaii</td><td>0</td><td>0.0%</td></tr>
<tr><td>25</td><td>West Virginia</td><td>14</td><td>1.4%</td><td>47</td><td>Minnesota</td><td>0</td><td>0.0%</td></tr>
<tr><td>30</td><td>Wisconsin</td><td>5</td><td>0.5%</td><td>47</td><td>Rhode Island</td><td>0</td><td>0.0%</td></tr>
<tr><td>34</td><td>Wyoming</td><td>3</td><td>0.3%</td><td>47</td><td>Vermont</td><td>0</td><td>0.0%</td></tr>
<tr><td></td><td></td><td></td><td></td><td colspan="2">District of Columbia</td><td>3</td><td>0.3%</td></tr>
</table>

Source: American Hospital Association (Chicago, IL)
"Hospital Statistics" (2010 edition)
*Investor-owned, for-profit hospitals are a subset of community hospitals. Community hospitals are all nonfederal, short-term general, and other special hospitals whose facilities and services are available to the public.

State and Local Government-Owned Hospitals in 2008

National Total = 1,105 Hospitals*

ALPHA ORDER

RANK	STATE	HOSPITALS	% of USA
8	Alabama	42	3.8%
32	Alaska	7	0.6%
37	Arizona	4	0.4%
27	Arkansas	13	1.2%
2	California	71	6.4%
16	Colorado	28	2.5%
44	Connecticut	1	0.1%
45	Delaware	0	0.0%
19	Florida	25	2.3%
5	Georgia	56	5.1%
30	Hawaii	8	0.7%
20	Idaho	22	2.0%
17	Illinois	26	2.4%
11	Indiana	39	3.5%
4	Iowa	59	5.3%
3	Kansas	62	5.6%
26	Kentucky	14	1.3%
6	Louisiana	50	4.5%
41	Maine	2	0.2%
45	Maryland	0	0.0%
41	Massachusetts	2	0.2%
25	Michigan	15	1.4%
13	Minnesota	37	3.3%
10	Mississippi	41	3.7%
14	Missouri	35	3.2%
30	Montana	8	0.7%
12	Nebraska	38	3.4%
34	Nevada	6	0.5%
45	New Hampshire	0	0.0%
37	New Jersey	4	0.4%
32	New Mexico	7	0.6%
17	New York	26	2.4%
15	North Carolina	32	2.9%
45	North Dakota	0	0.0%
22	Ohio	21	1.9%
7	Oklahoma	45	4.1%
27	Oregon	13	1.2%
40	Pennsylvania	3	0.3%
45	Rhode Island	0	0.0%
23	South Carolina	20	1.8%
35	South Dakota	5	0.5%
20	Tennessee	22	2.0%
1	Texas	117	10.6%
35	Utah	5	0.5%
45	Vermont	0	0.0%
37	Virginia	4	0.4%
8	Washington	42	3.8%
29	West Virginia	10	0.9%
41	Wisconsin	2	0.2%
24	Wyoming	16	1.4%

RANK ORDER

RANK	STATE	HOSPITALS	% of USA
1	Texas	117	10.6%
2	California	71	6.4%
3	Kansas	62	5.6%
4	Iowa	59	5.3%
5	Georgia	56	5.1%
6	Louisiana	50	4.5%
7	Oklahoma	45	4.1%
8	Alabama	42	3.8%
8	Washington	42	3.8%
10	Mississippi	41	3.7%
11	Indiana	39	3.5%
12	Nebraska	38	3.4%
13	Minnesota	37	3.3%
14	Missouri	35	3.2%
15	North Carolina	32	2.9%
16	Colorado	28	2.5%
17	Illinois	26	2.4%
17	New York	26	2.4%
19	Florida	25	2.3%
20	Idaho	22	2.0%
20	Tennessee	22	2.0%
22	Ohio	21	1.9%
23	South Carolina	20	1.8%
24	Wyoming	16	1.4%
25	Michigan	15	1.4%
26	Kentucky	14	1.3%
27	Arkansas	13	1.2%
27	Oregon	13	1.2%
29	West Virginia	10	0.9%
30	Hawaii	8	0.7%
30	Montana	8	0.7%
32	Alaska	7	0.6%
32	New Mexico	7	0.6%
34	Nevada	6	0.5%
35	South Dakota	5	0.5%
35	Utah	5	0.5%
37	Arizona	4	0.4%
37	New Jersey	4	0.4%
37	Virginia	4	0.4%
40	Pennsylvania	3	0.3%
41	Maine	2	0.2%
41	Massachusetts	2	0.2%
41	Wisconsin	2	0.2%
44	Connecticut	1	0.1%
45	Delaware	0	0.0%
45	Maryland	0	0.0%
45	New Hampshire	0	0.0%
45	North Dakota	0	0.0%
45	Rhode Island	0	0.0%
45	Vermont	0	0.0%
	District of Columbia	0	0.0%

Source: American Hospital Association (Chicago, IL)
   "Hospital Statistics" (2010 edition)
*State and local government-owned hospitals are a subset of community hospitals. Community hospitals are all nonfederal,
short-term general, and other special hospitals whose facilities and services are available to the public.

Beds in Community Hospitals in 2008

National Total = 808,069 Beds*

ALPHA ORDER

ALPHA ORDER

RANK	STATE	BEDS	% of USA
19	Alabama	15,250	1.9%
49	Alaska	1,553	0.2%
22	Arizona	13,138	1.6%
31	Arkansas	9,686	1.2%
1	California	69,587	8.6%
30	Colorado	10,053	1.2%
32	Connecticut	7,906	1.0%
48	Delaware	2,071	0.3%
4	Florida	52,836	6.5%
8	Georgia	25,583	3.2%
44	Hawaii	3,087	0.4%
43	Idaho	3,311	0.4%
6	Illinois	34,506	4.3%
15	Indiana	17,612	2.2%
28	Iowa	10,531	1.3%
29	Kansas	10,269	1.3%
20	Kentucky	14,180	1.8%
16	Louisiana	16,007	2.0%
41	Maine	3,504	0.4%
25	Maryland	12,018	1.5%
17	Massachusetts	15,710	1.9%
9	Michigan	25,272	3.1%
18	Minnesota	15,621	1.9%
23	Mississippi	13,094	1.6%
13	Missouri	18,968	2.3%
40	Montana	3,765	0.5%
34	Nebraska	7,264	0.9%
36	Nevada	5,144	0.6%
45	New Hampshire	2,858	0.4%
12	New Jersey	20,867	2.6%
39	New Mexico	3,935	0.5%
2	New York	61,237	7.6%
10	North Carolina	23,140	2.9%
42	North Dakota	3,442	0.4%
7	Ohio	33,860	4.2%
27	Oklahoma	10,988	1.4%
35	Oregon	6,814	0.8%
5	Pennsylvania	40,407	5.0%
46	Rhode Island	2,463	0.3%
24	South Carolina	12,498	1.5%
38	South Dakota	4,113	0.5%
11	Tennessee	21,102	2.6%
3	Texas	61,039	7.6%
37	Utah	4,874	0.6%
50	Vermont	1,302	0.2%
14	Virginia	17,648	2.2%
26	Washington	11,348	1.4%
33	West Virginia	7,470	0.9%
21	Wisconsin	13,707	1.7%
47	Wyoming	2,073	0.3%

RANK ORDER

RANK	STATE	BEDS	% of USA
1	California	69,587	8.6%
2	New York	61,237	7.6%
3	Texas	61,039	7.6%
4	Florida	52,836	6.5%
5	Pennsylvania	40,407	5.0%
6	Illinois	34,506	4.3%
7	Ohio	33,860	4.2%
8	Georgia	25,583	3.2%
9	Michigan	25,272	3.1%
10	North Carolina	23,140	2.9%
11	Tennessee	21,102	2.6%
12	New Jersey	20,867	2.6%
13	Missouri	18,968	2.3%
14	Virginia	17,648	2.2%
15	Indiana	17,612	2.2%
16	Louisiana	16,007	2.0%
17	Massachusetts	15,710	1.9%
18	Minnesota	15,621	1.9%
19	Alabama	15,250	1.9%
20	Kentucky	14,180	1.8%
21	Wisconsin	13,707	1.7%
22	Arizona	13,138	1.6%
23	Mississippi	13,094	1.6%
24	South Carolina	12,498	1.5%
25	Maryland	12,018	1.5%
26	Washington	11,348	1.4%
27	Oklahoma	10,988	1.4%
28	Iowa	10,531	1.3%
29	Kansas	10,269	1.3%
30	Colorado	10,053	1.2%
31	Arkansas	9,686	1.2%
32	Connecticut	7,906	1.0%
33	West Virginia	7,470	0.9%
34	Nebraska	7,264	0.9%
35	Oregon	6,814	0.8%
36	Nevada	5,144	0.6%
37	Utah	4,874	0.6%
38	South Dakota	4,113	0.5%
39	New Mexico	3,935	0.5%
40	Montana	3,765	0.5%
41	Maine	3,504	0.4%
42	North Dakota	3,442	0.4%
43	Idaho	3,311	0.4%
44	Hawaii	3,087	0.4%
45	New Hampshire	2,858	0.4%
46	Rhode Island	2,463	0.3%
47	Wyoming	2,073	0.3%
48	Delaware	2,071	0.3%
49	Alaska	1,553	0.2%
50	Vermont	1,302	0.2%
	District of Columbia	3,358	0.4%

Source: American Hospital Association (Chicago, IL)
   "Hospital Statistics" (2010 edition)

*All nonfederal, short-term general, and other special hospitals whose facilities and services are available to the public. Includes beds in hospital and nursing home units.

Rate of Beds in Community Hospitals in 2008

National Rate = 265 Beds per 100,000 Population*

ALPHA ORDER

RANK	STATE	RATE
14	Alabama	326
36	Alaska	226
44	Arizona	202
11	Arkansas	338
47	California	190
43	Colorado	204
36	Connecticut	226
34	Delaware	236
21	Florida	287
26	Georgia	264
32	Hawaii	240
39	Idaho	217
24	Illinois	269
23	Indiana	276
10	Iowa	352
8	Kansas	367
13	Kentucky	331
9	Louisiana	360
25	Maine	266
41	Maryland	212
32	Massachusetts	240
27	Michigan	253
19	Minnesota	299
3	Mississippi	445
16	Missouri	318
6	Montana	389
5	Nebraska	408
46	Nevada	197
40	New Hampshire	216
31	New Jersey	241
45	New Mexico	198
17	New York	315
29	North Carolina	250
1	North Dakota	537
20	Ohio	294
18	Oklahoma	302
48	Oregon	180
15	Pennsylvania	322
35	Rhode Island	234
22	South Carolina	278
2	South Dakota	511
11	Tennessee	338
28	Texas	251
49	Utah	179
42	Vermont	210
36	Virginia	226
50	Washington	173
4	West Virginia	412
30	Wisconsin	244
6	Wyoming	389

RANK ORDER

RANK	STATE	RATE
1	North Dakota	537
2	South Dakota	511
3	Mississippi	445
4	West Virginia	412
5	Nebraska	408
6	Montana	389
6	Wyoming	389
8	Kansas	367
9	Louisiana	360
10	Iowa	352
11	Arkansas	338
11	Tennessee	338
13	Kentucky	331
14	Alabama	326
15	Pennsylvania	322
16	Missouri	318
17	New York	315
18	Oklahoma	302
19	Minnesota	299
20	Ohio	294
21	Florida	287
22	South Carolina	278
23	Indiana	276
24	Illinois	269
25	Maine	266
26	Georgia	264
27	Michigan	253
28	Texas	251
29	North Carolina	250
30	Wisconsin	244
31	New Jersey	241
32	Hawaii	240
32	Massachusetts	240
34	Delaware	236
35	Rhode Island	234
36	Alaska	226
36	Connecticut	226
36	Virginia	226
39	Idaho	217
40	New Hampshire	216
41	Maryland	212
42	Vermont	210
43	Colorado	204
44	Arizona	202
45	New Mexico	198
46	Nevada	197
47	California	190
48	Oregon	180
49	Utah	179
50	Washington	173

| | District of Columbia | 569 |

Source: CQ Press using data from American Hospital Association (Chicago, IL)
   "Hospital Statistics" (2010 edition)
*All nonfederal, short-term general, and other special hospitals whose facilities and services are available to the public. Includes beds in hospital and nursing home units.

Average Number of Beds per Community Hospital in 2008

National Average = 161 Beds per Community Hospital*

ALPHA ORDER

RANK	STATE	RATE
24	Alabama	140
50	Alaska	71
14	Arizona	185
34	Arkansas	113
11	California	198
29	Colorado	129
6	Connecticut	226
2	Delaware	296
4	Florida	250
17	Georgia	167
30	Hawaii	123
44	Idaho	85
15	Illinois	181
22	Indiana	143
42	Iowa	89
47	Kansas	78
25	Kentucky	135
30	Louisiana	123
40	Maine	95
5	Maryland	240
8	Massachusetts	209
18	Michigan	165
32	Minnesota	120
26	Mississippi	134
19	Missouri	154
47	Montana	78
45	Nebraska	84
21	Nevada	147
38	New Hampshire	102
3	New Jersey	286
36	New Mexico	109
1	New York	316
10	North Carolina	199
45	North Dakota	84
13	Ohio	187
39	Oklahoma	96
33	Oregon	117
9	Pennsylvania	201
7	Rhode Island	224
15	South Carolina	181
47	South Dakota	78
19	Tennessee	154
22	Texas	143
34	Utah	113
41	Vermont	93
12	Virginia	196
28	Washington	132
27	West Virginia	133
36	Wisconsin	109
43	Wyoming	86

RANK ORDER

RANK	STATE	RATE
1	New York	316
2	Delaware	296
3	New Jersey	286
4	Florida	250
5	Maryland	240
6	Connecticut	226
7	Rhode Island	224
8	Massachusetts	209
9	Pennsylvania	201
10	North Carolina	199
11	California	198
12	Virginia	196
13	Ohio	187
14	Arizona	185
15	Illinois	181
15	South Carolina	181
17	Georgia	167
18	Michigan	165
19	Missouri	154
19	Tennessee	154
21	Nevada	147
22	Indiana	143
22	Texas	143
24	Alabama	140
25	Kentucky	135
26	Mississippi	134
27	West Virginia	133
28	Washington	132
29	Colorado	129
30	Hawaii	123
30	Louisiana	123
32	Minnesota	120
33	Oregon	117
34	Arkansas	113
34	Utah	113
36	New Mexico	109
36	Wisconsin	109
38	New Hampshire	102
39	Oklahoma	96
40	Maine	95
41	Vermont	93
42	Iowa	89
43	Wyoming	86
44	Idaho	85
45	Nebraska	84
45	North Dakota	84
47	Kansas	78
47	Montana	78
47	South Dakota	78
50	Alaska	71

District of Columbia   336

Source: CQ Press using data from American Hospital Association (Chicago, IL)
 "Hospital Statistics" (2010 edition)

*All nonfederal, short-term general, and other special hospitals whose facilities and services are available to the public. Includes beds in hospital and nursing home units.

Admissions to Community Hospitals in 2008

National Total = 35,760,750 Admissions*

ALPHA ORDER

RANK	STATE	ADMISSIONS	% of USA
19	Alabama	687,446	1.9%
48	Alaska	58,204	0.2%
17	Arizona	716,136	2.0%
30	Arkansas	376,158	1.1%
1	California	3,460,688	9.7%
27	Colorado	442,161	1.2%
29	Connecticut	400,632	1.1%
45	Delaware	103,726	0.3%
4	Florida	2,396,691	6.7%
11	Georgia	959,375	2.7%
43	Hawaii	111,310	0.3%
40	Idaho	135,697	0.4%
6	Illinois	1,610,844	4.5%
16	Indiana	732,627	2.0%
31	Iowa	373,330	1.0%
33	Kansas	328,279	0.9%
23	Kentucky	610,449	1.7%
21	Louisiana	636,767	1.8%
39	Maine	148,635	0.4%
18	Maryland	711,267	2.0%
14	Massachusetts	808,489	2.3%
8	Michigan	1,221,970	3.4%
20	Minnesota	640,976	1.8%
28	Mississippi	430,680	1.2%
13	Missouri	841,118	2.4%
44	Montana	103,840	0.3%
37	Nebraska	214,808	0.6%
35	Nevada	247,232	0.7%
42	New Hampshire	124,184	0.3%
9	New Jersey	1,086,445	3.0%
38	New Mexico	174,169	0.5%
3	New York	2,528,191	7.1%
10	North Carolina	1,041,918	2.9%
47	North Dakota	89,225	0.2%
7	Ohio	1,547,720	4.3%
26	Oklahoma	462,954	1.3%
32	Oregon	348,600	1.0%
5	Pennsylvania	1,901,417	5.3%
41	Rhode Island	127,413	0.4%
25	South Carolina	528,872	1.5%
46	South Dakota	102,116	0.3%
12	Tennessee	859,344	2.4%
2	Texas	2,585,680	7.2%
36	Utah	226,376	0.6%
50	Vermont	51,301	0.1%
15	Virginia	795,578	2.2%
24	Washington	578,856	1.6%
34	West Virginia	283,673	0.8%
22	Wisconsin	617,295	1.7%
49	Wyoming	52,628	0.1%

RANK ORDER

RANK	STATE	ADMISSIONS	% of USA
1	California	3,460,688	9.7%
2	Texas	2,585,680	7.2%
3	New York	2,528,191	7.1%
4	Florida	2,396,691	6.7%
5	Pennsylvania	1,901,417	5.3%
6	Illinois	1,610,844	4.5%
7	Ohio	1,547,720	4.3%
8	Michigan	1,221,970	3.4%
9	New Jersey	1,086,445	3.0%
10	North Carolina	1,041,918	2.9%
11	Georgia	959,375	2.7%
12	Tennessee	859,344	2.4%
13	Missouri	841,118	2.4%
14	Massachusetts	808,489	2.3%
15	Virginia	795,578	2.2%
16	Indiana	732,627	2.0%
17	Arizona	716,136	2.0%
18	Maryland	711,267	2.0%
19	Alabama	687,446	1.9%
20	Minnesota	640,976	1.8%
21	Louisiana	636,767	1.8%
22	Wisconsin	617,295	1.7%
23	Kentucky	610,449	1.7%
24	Washington	578,856	1.6%
25	South Carolina	528,872	1.5%
26	Oklahoma	462,954	1.3%
27	Colorado	442,161	1.2%
28	Mississippi	430,680	1.2%
29	Connecticut	400,632	1.1%
30	Arkansas	376,158	1.1%
31	Iowa	373,330	1.0%
32	Oregon	348,600	1.0%
33	Kansas	328,279	0.9%
34	West Virginia	283,673	0.8%
35	Nevada	247,232	0.7%
36	Utah	226,376	0.6%
37	Nebraska	214,808	0.6%
38	New Mexico	174,169	0.5%
39	Maine	148,635	0.4%
40	Idaho	135,697	0.4%
41	Rhode Island	127,413	0.4%
42	New Hampshire	124,184	0.3%
43	Hawaii	111,310	0.3%
44	Montana	103,840	0.3%
45	Delaware	103,726	0.3%
46	South Dakota	102,116	0.3%
47	North Dakota	89,225	0.2%
48	Alaska	58,204	0.2%
49	Wyoming	52,628	0.1%
50	Vermont	51,301	0.1%
	District of Columbia	137,260	0.4%

Source: American Hospital Association (Chicago, IL)
    "Hospital Statistics" (2010 edition)
*Admissions to all nonfederal, short-term general, and other special hospitals whose facilities and services are available to the public. Includes admissions to hospital and nursing home units.

Inpatient Days in Community Hospitals in 2008

National Total = 196,078,468 Inpatient Days*

ALPHA ORDER

RANK	STATE	DAYS	% of USA		RANK	STATE	DAYS	% of USA
18	Alabama	3,524,687	1.8%		1	California	18,044,888	9.2%
49	Alaska	346,837	0.2%		2	New York	17,973,047	9.2%
21	Arizona	3,235,063	1.6%		3	Texas	13,430,355	6.8%
32	Arkansas	1,989,969	1.0%		4	Florida	12,192,327	6.2%
1	California	18,044,888	9.2%		5	Pennsylvania	10,353,793	5.3%
30	Colorado	2,210,340	1.1%		6	Illinois	8,069,859	4.1%
28	Connecticut	2,296,558	1.2%		7	Ohio	7,814,849	4.0%
47	Delaware	613,049	0.3%		8	Michigan	6,350,025	3.2%
4	Florida	12,192,327	6.2%		9	Georgia	6,172,510	3.1%
9	Georgia	6,172,510	3.1%		10	North Carolina	6,019,401	3.1%
40	Hawaii	846,756	0.4%		11	New Jersey	5,595,966	2.9%
46	Idaho	643,039	0.3%		12	Tennessee	4,911,215	2.5%
6	Illinois	8,069,859	4.1%		13	Virginia	4,452,740	2.3%
17	Indiana	3,829,835	2.0%		14	Missouri	4,396,779	2.2%
29	Iowa	2,248,874	1.1%		15	Massachusetts	4,190,441	2.1%
31	Kansas	2,079,667	1.1%		16	Minnesota	3,873,690	2.0%
22	Kentucky	3,216,149	1.6%		17	Indiana	3,829,835	2.0%
19	Louisiana	3,378,368	1.7%		18	Alabama	3,524,687	1.8%
41	Maine	845,428	0.4%		19	Louisiana	3,378,368	1.7%
20	Maryland	3,298,930	1.7%		20	Maryland	3,298,930	1.7%
15	Massachusetts	4,190,441	2.1%		21	Arizona	3,235,063	1.6%
8	Michigan	6,350,025	3.2%		22	Kentucky	3,216,149	1.6%
16	Minnesota	3,873,690	2.0%		23	Wisconsin	3,172,566	1.6%
25	Mississippi	2,807,964	1.4%		24	South Carolina	2,962,830	1.5%
14	Missouri	4,396,779	2.2%		25	Mississippi	2,807,964	1.4%
39	Montana	903,981	0.5%		26	Washington	2,663,704	1.4%
34	Nebraska	1,562,960	0.8%		27	Oklahoma	2,436,253	1.2%
36	Nevada	1,300,514	0.7%		28	Connecticut	2,296,558	1.2%
45	New Hampshire	664,659	0.3%		29	Iowa	2,248,874	1.1%
11	New Jersey	5,595,966	2.9%		30	Colorado	2,210,340	1.1%
42	New Mexico	809,916	0.4%		31	Kansas	2,079,667	1.1%
2	New York	17,973,047	9.2%		32	Arkansas	1,989,969	1.0%
10	North Carolina	6,019,401	3.1%		33	West Virginia	1,665,076	0.8%
43	North Dakota	744,876	0.4%		34	Nebraska	1,562,960	0.8%
7	Ohio	7,814,849	4.0%		35	Oregon	1,551,894	0.8%
27	Oklahoma	2,436,253	1.2%		36	Nevada	1,300,514	0.7%
35	Oregon	1,551,894	0.8%		37	Utah	1,015,945	0.5%
5	Pennsylvania	10,353,793	5.3%		38	South Dakota	1,005,766	0.5%
44	Rhode Island	666,745	0.3%		39	Montana	903,981	0.5%
24	South Carolina	2,962,830	1.5%		40	Hawaii	846,756	0.4%
38	South Dakota	1,005,766	0.5%		41	Maine	845,428	0.4%
12	Tennessee	4,911,215	2.5%		42	New Mexico	809,916	0.4%
3	Texas	13,430,355	6.8%		43	North Dakota	744,876	0.4%
37	Utah	1,015,945	0.5%		44	Rhode Island	666,745	0.3%
50	Vermont	328,506	0.2%		45	New Hampshire	664,659	0.3%
13	Virginia	4,452,740	2.3%		46	Idaho	643,039	0.3%
26	Washington	2,663,704	1.4%		47	Delaware	613,049	0.3%
33	West Virginia	1,665,076	0.8%		48	Wyoming	414,463	0.2%
23	Wisconsin	3,172,566	1.6%		49	Alaska	346,837	0.2%
48	Wyoming	414,463	0.2%		50	Vermont	328,506	0.2%
						District of Columbia	954,416	0.5%

Source: American Hospital Association (Chicago, IL)
   "Hospital Statistics" (2010 edition)
*Inpatient days in all nonfederal, short-term general, and other special hospitals whose facilities and services are available to the public. Includes days in hospital and nursing home units.

Average Daily Census in Community Hospitals in 2008

National Average = 537,201 Inpatients*

RANK	STATE	INPATIENTS	% of USA		RANK	STATE	INPATIENTS	% of USA
18	Alabama	9,657	1.8%		1	California	49,438	9.2%
49	Alaska	950	0.2%		2	New York	49,241	9.2%
21	Arizona	8,863	1.6%		3	Texas	36,795	6.8%
32	Arkansas	5,452	1.0%		4	Florida	33,404	6.2%
1	California	49,438	9.2%		5	Pennsylvania	28,367	5.3%
30	Colorado	6,056	1.1%		6	Illinois	22,109	4.1%
28	Connecticut	6,292	1.2%		7	Ohio	21,411	4.0%
47	Delaware	1,680	0.3%		8	Michigan	17,397	3.2%
4	Florida	33,404	6.2%		9	Georgia	16,911	3.1%
9	Georgia	16,911	3.1%		10	North Carolina	16,492	3.1%
40	Hawaii	2,320	0.4%		11	New Jersey	15,331	2.9%
46	Idaho	1,762	0.3%		12	Tennessee	13,455	2.5%
6	Illinois	22,109	4.1%		13	Virginia	12,199	2.3%
17	Indiana	10,493	2.0%		14	Missouri	12,046	2.2%
29	Iowa	6,161	1.1%		15	Massachusetts	11,481	2.1%
31	Kansas	5,698	1.1%		16	Minnesota	10,613	2.0%
22	Kentucky	8,811	1.6%		17	Indiana	10,493	2.0%
19	Louisiana	9,256	1.7%		18	Alabama	9,657	1.8%
41	Maine	2,316	0.4%		19	Louisiana	9,256	1.7%
20	Maryland	9,038	1.7%		20	Maryland	9,038	1.7%
15	Massachusetts	11,481	2.1%		21	Arizona	8,863	1.6%
8	Michigan	17,397	3.2%		22	Kentucky	8,811	1.6%
16	Minnesota	10,613	2.0%		23	Wisconsin	8,692	1.6%
25	Mississippi	7,693	1.4%		24	South Carolina	8,117	1.5%
14	Missouri	12,046	2.2%		25	Mississippi	7,693	1.4%
39	Montana	2,477	0.5%		26	Washington	7,298	1.4%
34	Nebraska	4,282	0.8%		27	Oklahoma	6,675	1.2%
36	Nevada	3,563	0.7%		28	Connecticut	6,292	1.2%
45	New Hampshire	1,821	0.3%		29	Iowa	6,161	1.1%
11	New Jersey	15,331	2.9%		30	Colorado	6,056	1.1%
42	New Mexico	2,219	0.4%		31	Kansas	5,698	1.1%
2	New York	49,241	9.2%		32	Arkansas	5,452	1.0%
10	North Carolina	16,492	3.1%		33	West Virginia	4,562	0.8%
43	North Dakota	2,041	0.4%		34	Nebraska	4,282	0.8%
7	Ohio	21,411	4.0%		35	Oregon	4,252	0.8%
27	Oklahoma	6,675	1.2%		36	Nevada	3,563	0.7%
35	Oregon	4,252	0.8%		37	Utah	2,783	0.5%
5	Pennsylvania	28,367	5.3%		38	South Dakota	2,756	0.5%
44	Rhode Island	1,827	0.3%		39	Montana	2,477	0.5%
24	South Carolina	8,117	1.5%		40	Hawaii	2,320	0.4%
38	South Dakota	2,756	0.5%		41	Maine	2,316	0.4%
12	Tennessee	13,455	2.5%		42	New Mexico	2,219	0.4%
3	Texas	36,795	6.8%		43	North Dakota	2,041	0.4%
37	Utah	2,783	0.5%		44	Rhode Island	1,827	0.3%
50	Vermont	900	0.2%		45	New Hampshire	1,821	0.3%
13	Virginia	12,199	2.3%		46	Idaho	1,762	0.3%
26	Washington	7,298	1.4%		47	Delaware	1,680	0.3%
33	West Virginia	4,562	0.8%		48	Wyoming	1,136	0.2%
23	Wisconsin	8,692	1.6%		49	Alaska	950	0.2%
48	Wyoming	1,136	0.2%		50	Vermont	900	0.2%
						District of Columbia	2,615	0.5%

ALPHA ORDER

RANK ORDER

Source: CQ Press using data from American Hospital Association (Chicago, IL)
"Hospital Statistics" (2010 edition)
*Average total of inpatients receiving care in all nonfederal, short-term general, and other special hospitals whose facilities and services are available to the public. Excludes newborns.

Average Stay in Community Hospitals in 2008

National Average = 5.5 Days*

ALPHA ORDER

RANK	STATE	DAYS
38	Alabama	5.1
12	Alaska	6.0
48	Arizona	4.5
25	Arkansas	5.3
30	California	5.2
41	Colorado	5.0
18	Connecticut	5.7
15	Delaware	5.9
38	Florida	5.1
9	Georgia	6.4
5	Hawaii	7.6
44	Idaho	4.7
41	Illinois	5.0
30	Indiana	5.2
12	Iowa	6.0
11	Kansas	6.3
25	Kentucky	5.3
25	Louisiana	5.3
18	Maine	5.7
46	Maryland	4.6
30	Massachusetts	5.2
30	Michigan	5.2
12	Minnesota	6.0
8	Mississippi	6.5
30	Missouri	5.2
2	Montana	8.7
6	Nebraska	7.3
25	Nevada	5.3
23	New Hampshire	5.4
30	New Jersey	5.2
44	New Mexico	4.7
7	New York	7.1
17	North Carolina	5.8
3	North Dakota	8.3
41	Ohio	5.0
25	Oklahoma	5.3
48	Oregon	4.5
23	Pennsylvania	5.4
30	Rhode Island	5.2
21	South Carolina	5.6
1	South Dakota	9.8
18	Tennessee	5.7
30	Texas	5.2
48	Utah	4.5
9	Vermont	6.4
21	Virginia	5.6
46	Washington	4.6
15	West Virginia	5.9
38	Wisconsin	5.1
4	Wyoming	7.9

RANK ORDER

RANK	STATE	DAYS
1	South Dakota	9.8
2	Montana	8.7
3	North Dakota	8.3
4	Wyoming	7.9
5	Hawaii	7.6
6	Nebraska	7.3
7	New York	7.1
8	Mississippi	6.5
9	Georgia	6.4
9	Vermont	6.4
11	Kansas	6.3
12	Alaska	6.0
12	Iowa	6.0
12	Minnesota	6.0
15	Delaware	5.9
15	West Virginia	5.9
17	North Carolina	5.8
18	Connecticut	5.7
18	Maine	5.7
18	Tennessee	5.7
21	South Carolina	5.6
21	Virginia	5.6
23	New Hampshire	5.4
23	Pennsylvania	5.4
25	Arkansas	5.3
25	Kentucky	5.3
25	Louisiana	5.3
25	Nevada	5.3
25	Oklahoma	5.3
30	California	5.2
30	Indiana	5.2
30	Massachusetts	5.2
30	Michigan	5.2
30	Missouri	5.2
30	New Jersey	5.2
30	Rhode Island	5.2
30	Texas	5.2
38	Alabama	5.1
38	Florida	5.1
38	Wisconsin	5.1
41	Colorado	5.0
41	Illinois	5.0
41	Ohio	5.0
44	Idaho	4.7
44	New Mexico	4.7
46	Maryland	4.6
46	Washington	4.6
48	Arizona	4.5
48	Oregon	4.5
48	Utah	4.5
	District of Columbia	7.0

Source: American Hospital Association (Chicago, IL)
 "Hospital Statistics" (2010 edition)
*All nonfederal, short-term general, and other special hospitals whose facilities and services are available to the public.

Occupancy Rate in Community Hospitals in 2008

National Rate = 66.5% of Community Hospital Beds Occupied*

ALPHA ORDER

RANK	STATE	RATE
29	Alabama	63.3
34	Alaska	61.2
17	Arizona	67.5
47	Arkansas	56.3
10	California	71.0
38	Colorado	60.2
3	Connecticut	79.6
1	Delaware	81.1
30	Florida	63.2
19	Georgia	66.1
4	Hawaii	75.2
50	Idaho	53.2
24	Illinois	64.1
39	Indiana	59.6
43	Iowa	58.5
48	Kansas	55.5
33	Kentucky	62.1
44	Louisiana	57.8
19	Maine	66.1
4	Maryland	75.2
8	Massachusetts	73.1
15	Michigan	68.8
16	Minnesota	67.9
42	Mississippi	58.8
27	Missouri	63.5
21	Montana	65.8
41	Nebraska	58.9
12	Nevada	69.3
26	New Hampshire	63.7
7	New Jersey	73.5
46	New Mexico	56.4
2	New York	80.4
9	North Carolina	71.3
40	North Dakota	59.3
30	Ohio	63.2
36	Oklahoma	60.7
32	Oregon	62.4
11	Pennsylvania	70.2
6	Rhode Island	74.2
22	South Carolina	64.9
18	South Dakota	67.0
25	Tennessee	63.8
37	Texas	60.3
45	Utah	57.1
13	Vermont	69.1
13	Virginia	69.1
23	Washington	64.3
35	West Virginia	61.1
28	Wisconsin	63.4
49	Wyoming	54.8

RANK ORDER

RANK	STATE	RATE
1	Delaware	81.1
2	New York	80.4
3	Connecticut	79.6
4	Hawaii	75.2
4	Maryland	75.2
6	Rhode Island	74.2
7	New Jersey	73.5
8	Massachusetts	73.1
9	North Carolina	71.3
10	California	71.0
11	Pennsylvania	70.2
12	Nevada	69.3
13	Vermont	69.1
13	Virginia	69.1
15	Michigan	68.8
16	Minnesota	67.9
17	Arizona	67.5
18	South Dakota	67.0
19	Georgia	66.1
19	Maine	66.1
21	Montana	65.8
22	South Carolina	64.9
23	Washington	64.3
24	Illinois	64.1
25	Tennessee	63.8
26	New Hampshire	63.7
27	Missouri	63.5
28	Wisconsin	63.4
29	Alabama	63.3
30	Florida	63.2
30	Ohio	63.2
32	Oregon	62.4
33	Kentucky	62.1
34	Alaska	61.2
35	West Virginia	61.1
36	Oklahoma	60.7
37	Texas	60.3
38	Colorado	60.2
39	Indiana	59.6
40	North Dakota	59.3
41	Nebraska	58.9
42	Mississippi	58.8
43	Iowa	58.5
44	Louisiana	57.8
45	Utah	57.1
46	New Mexico	56.4
47	Arkansas	56.3
48	Kansas	55.5
49	Wyoming	54.8
50	Idaho	53.2

District of Columbia   77.9

Source: CQ Press using data from American Hospital Association (Chicago, IL)
"Hospital Statistics" (2010 edition)

*Average daily census compared to number of community hospital beds. Community hospitals are all nonfederal, short-term general, and other special hospitals whose facilities and services are available to the public.

Outpatient Visits to Community Hospitals in 2008

National Total = 624,098,296 Visits*

<table>
<tr><td colspan="4">ALPHA ORDER</td><td colspan="4">RANK ORDER</td></tr>
<tr><td>RANK</td><td>STATE</td><td>VISITS</td><td>% of USA</td><td>RANK</td><td>STATE</td><td>VISITS</td><td>% of USA</td></tr>
<tr><td>23</td><td>Alabama</td><td>9,018,521</td><td>1.4%</td><td>1</td><td>New York</td><td>52,569,640</td><td>8.4%</td></tr>
<tr><td>48</td><td>Alaska</td><td>1,693,342</td><td>0.3%</td><td>2</td><td>California</td><td>48,877,149</td><td>7.8%</td></tr>
<tr><td>28</td><td>Arizona</td><td>7,714,351</td><td>1.2%</td><td>3</td><td>Pennsylvania</td><td>38,456,395</td><td>6.2%</td></tr>
<tr><td>36</td><td>Arkansas</td><td>4,972,752</td><td>0.8%</td><td>4</td><td>Texas</td><td>34,819,068</td><td>5.6%</td></tr>
<tr><td>2</td><td>California</td><td>48,877,149</td><td>7.8%</td><td>5</td><td>Ohio</td><td>32,891,862</td><td>5.3%</td></tr>
<tr><td>25</td><td>Colorado</td><td>8,407,972</td><td>1.3%</td><td>6</td><td>Illinois</td><td>30,986,757</td><td>5.0%</td></tr>
<tr><td>27</td><td>Connecticut</td><td>8,074,634</td><td>1.3%</td><td>7</td><td>Michigan</td><td>27,998,296</td><td>4.5%</td></tr>
<tr><td>49</td><td>Delaware</td><td>1,681,076</td><td>0.3%</td><td>8</td><td>Florida</td><td>24,429,940</td><td>3.9%</td></tr>
<tr><td>8</td><td>Florida</td><td>24,429,940</td><td>3.9%</td><td>9</td><td>Massachusetts</td><td>20,459,758</td><td>3.3%</td></tr>
<tr><td>15</td><td>Georgia</td><td>14,184,092</td><td>2.3%</td><td>10</td><td>Missouri</td><td>18,828,585</td><td>3.0%</td></tr>
<tr><td>45</td><td>Hawaii</td><td>2,019,132</td><td>0.3%</td><td>11</td><td>New Jersey</td><td>18,139,915</td><td>2.9%</td></tr>
<tr><td>42</td><td>Idaho</td><td>2,940,411</td><td>0.5%</td><td>12</td><td>North Carolina</td><td>17,733,068</td><td>2.8%</td></tr>
<tr><td>6</td><td>Illinois</td><td>30,986,757</td><td>5.0%</td><td>13</td><td>Indiana</td><td>17,022,314</td><td>2.7%</td></tr>
<tr><td>13</td><td>Indiana</td><td>17,022,314</td><td>2.7%</td><td>14</td><td>Wisconsin</td><td>14,203,427</td><td>2.3%</td></tr>
<tr><td>20</td><td>Iowa</td><td>10,380,628</td><td>1.7%</td><td>15</td><td>Georgia</td><td>14,184,092</td><td>2.3%</td></tr>
<tr><td>30</td><td>Kansas</td><td>6,526,203</td><td>1.0%</td><td>16</td><td>Virginia</td><td>13,314,419</td><td>2.1%</td></tr>
<tr><td>22</td><td>Kentucky</td><td>9,658,798</td><td>1.5%</td><td>17</td><td>Washington</td><td>11,378,054</td><td>1.8%</td></tr>
<tr><td>19</td><td>Louisiana</td><td>11,161,368</td><td>1.8%</td><td>18</td><td>Tennessee</td><td>11,246,995</td><td>1.8%</td></tr>
<tr><td>34</td><td>Maine</td><td>5,093,378</td><td>0.8%</td><td>19</td><td>Louisiana</td><td>11,161,368</td><td>1.8%</td></tr>
<tr><td>26</td><td>Maryland</td><td>8,083,115</td><td>1.3%</td><td>20</td><td>Iowa</td><td>10,380,628</td><td>1.7%</td></tr>
<tr><td>9</td><td>Massachusetts</td><td>20,459,758</td><td>3.3%</td><td>21</td><td>Minnesota</td><td>10,006,069</td><td>1.6%</td></tr>
<tr><td>7</td><td>Michigan</td><td>27,998,296</td><td>4.5%</td><td>22</td><td>Kentucky</td><td>9,658,798</td><td>1.5%</td></tr>
<tr><td>21</td><td>Minnesota</td><td>10,006,069</td><td>1.6%</td><td>23</td><td>Alabama</td><td>9,018,521</td><td>1.4%</td></tr>
<tr><td>35</td><td>Mississippi</td><td>5,015,607</td><td>0.8%</td><td>24</td><td>Oregon</td><td>8,558,164</td><td>1.4%</td></tr>
<tr><td>10</td><td>Missouri</td><td>18,828,585</td><td>3.0%</td><td>25</td><td>Colorado</td><td>8,407,972</td><td>1.3%</td></tr>
<tr><td>41</td><td>Montana</td><td>3,154,274</td><td>0.5%</td><td>26</td><td>Maryland</td><td>8,083,115</td><td>1.3%</td></tr>
<tr><td>37</td><td>Nebraska</td><td>4,627,089</td><td>0.7%</td><td>27</td><td>Connecticut</td><td>8,074,634</td><td>1.3%</td></tr>
<tr><td>43</td><td>Nevada</td><td>2,916,309</td><td>0.5%</td><td>28</td><td>Arizona</td><td>7,714,351</td><td>1.2%</td></tr>
<tr><td>38</td><td>New Hampshire</td><td>4,468,523</td><td>0.7%</td><td>29</td><td>West Virginia</td><td>6,615,109</td><td>1.1%</td></tr>
<tr><td>11</td><td>New Jersey</td><td>18,139,915</td><td>2.9%</td><td>30</td><td>Kansas</td><td>6,526,203</td><td>1.0%</td></tr>
<tr><td>39</td><td>New Mexico</td><td>4,251,559</td><td>0.7%</td><td>31</td><td>South Carolina</td><td>5,924,215</td><td>0.9%</td></tr>
<tr><td>1</td><td>New York</td><td>52,569,640</td><td>8.4%</td><td>32</td><td>Oklahoma</td><td>5,431,621</td><td>0.9%</td></tr>
<tr><td>12</td><td>North Carolina</td><td>17,733,068</td><td>2.8%</td><td>33</td><td>Utah</td><td>5,305,448</td><td>0.9%</td></tr>
<tr><td>47</td><td>North Dakota</td><td>1,695,560</td><td>0.3%</td><td>34</td><td>Maine</td><td>5,093,378</td><td>0.8%</td></tr>
<tr><td>5</td><td>Ohio</td><td>32,891,862</td><td>5.3%</td><td>35</td><td>Mississippi</td><td>5,015,607</td><td>0.8%</td></tr>
<tr><td>32</td><td>Oklahoma</td><td>5,431,621</td><td>0.9%</td><td>36</td><td>Arkansas</td><td>4,972,752</td><td>0.8%</td></tr>
<tr><td>24</td><td>Oregon</td><td>8,558,164</td><td>1.4%</td><td>37</td><td>Nebraska</td><td>4,627,089</td><td>0.7%</td></tr>
<tr><td>3</td><td>Pennsylvania</td><td>38,456,395</td><td>6.2%</td><td>38</td><td>New Hampshire</td><td>4,468,523</td><td>0.7%</td></tr>
<tr><td>44</td><td>Rhode Island</td><td>2,634,226</td><td>0.4%</td><td>39</td><td>New Mexico</td><td>4,251,559</td><td>0.7%</td></tr>
<tr><td>31</td><td>South Carolina</td><td>5,924,215</td><td>0.9%</td><td>40</td><td>Vermont</td><td>3,306,095</td><td>0.5%</td></tr>
<tr><td>46</td><td>South Dakota</td><td>1,857,956</td><td>0.3%</td><td>41</td><td>Montana</td><td>3,154,274</td><td>0.5%</td></tr>
<tr><td>18</td><td>Tennessee</td><td>11,246,995</td><td>1.8%</td><td>42</td><td>Idaho</td><td>2,940,411</td><td>0.5%</td></tr>
<tr><td>4</td><td>Texas</td><td>34,819,068</td><td>5.6%</td><td>43</td><td>Nevada</td><td>2,916,309</td><td>0.5%</td></tr>
<tr><td>33</td><td>Utah</td><td>5,305,448</td><td>0.9%</td><td>44</td><td>Rhode Island</td><td>2,634,226</td><td>0.4%</td></tr>
<tr><td>40</td><td>Vermont</td><td>3,306,095</td><td>0.5%</td><td>45</td><td>Hawaii</td><td>2,019,132</td><td>0.3%</td></tr>
<tr><td>16</td><td>Virginia</td><td>13,314,419</td><td>2.1%</td><td>46</td><td>South Dakota</td><td>1,857,956</td><td>0.3%</td></tr>
<tr><td>17</td><td>Washington</td><td>11,378,054</td><td>1.8%</td><td>47</td><td>North Dakota</td><td>1,695,560</td><td>0.3%</td></tr>
<tr><td>29</td><td>West Virginia</td><td>6,615,109</td><td>1.1%</td><td>48</td><td>Alaska</td><td>1,693,342</td><td>0.3%</td></tr>
<tr><td>14</td><td>Wisconsin</td><td>14,203,427</td><td>2.3%</td><td>49</td><td>Delaware</td><td>1,681,076</td><td>0.3%</td></tr>
<tr><td>50</td><td>Wyoming</td><td>1,008,994</td><td>0.2%</td><td>50</td><td>Wyoming</td><td>1,008,994</td><td>0.2%</td></tr>
<tr><td></td><td></td><td></td><td></td><td></td><td>District of Columbia</td><td>2,356,063</td><td>0.4%</td></tr>
</table>

Source: American Hospital Association (Chicago, IL)
"Hospital Statistics" (2010 edition)
*All nonfederal, short-term general, and other special hospitals whose facilities and services are available to the public. Includes emergency and other visits.

Emergency Outpatient Visits to Community Hospitals in 2008

National Total = 123,024,024 Visits*

RANK	STATE	VISITS	% of USA		RANK	STATE	VISITS	% of USA
21	Alabama	2,271,755	1.8%		1	California	10,068,613	8.2%
46	Alaska	328,164	0.3%		2	Texas	8,819,272	7.2%
22	Arizona	2,172,149	1.8%		3	New York	8,114,078	6.6%
31	Arkansas	1,301,330	1.1%		4	Florida	7,161,108	5.8%
1	California	10,068,613	8.2%		5	Ohio	6,023,705	4.9%
28	Colorado	1,621,056	1.3%		6	Pennsylvania	6,006,841	4.9%
29	Connecticut	1,524,545	1.2%		7	Illinois	5,123,091	4.2%
43	Delaware	363,979	0.3%		8	Michigan	4,428,070	3.6%
4	Florida	7,161,108	5.8%		9	North Carolina	4,166,718	3.4%
10	Georgia	3,843,244	3.1%		10	Georgia	3,843,244	3.1%
44	Hawaii	361,068	0.3%		11	New Jersey	3,350,786	2.7%
41	Idaho	520,941	0.4%		12	Tennessee	3,251,592	2.6%
7	Illinois	5,123,091	4.2%		13	Massachusetts	3,119,580	2.5%
15	Indiana	3,041,160	2.5%		14	Virginia	3,091,131	2.5%
32	Iowa	1,226,568	1.0%		15	Indiana	3,041,160	2.5%
34	Kansas	1,028,706	0.8%		16	Missouri	2,860,410	2.3%
19	Kentucky	2,339,390	1.9%		17	Washington	2,385,734	1.9%
18	Louisiana	2,381,889	1.9%		18	Louisiana	2,381,889	1.9%
36	Maine	780,874	0.6%		19	Kentucky	2,339,390	1.9%
20	Maryland	2,282,417	1.9%		20	Maryland	2,282,417	1.9%
13	Massachusetts	3,119,580	2.5%		21	Alabama	2,271,755	1.8%
8	Michigan	4,428,070	3.6%		22	Arizona	2,172,149	1.8%
25	Minnesota	1,772,982	1.4%		23	Wisconsin	2,066,654	1.7%
26	Mississippi	1,694,645	1.4%		24	South Carolina	1,954,264	1.6%
16	Missouri	2,860,410	2.3%		25	Minnesota	1,772,982	1.4%
45	Montana	346,670	0.3%		26	Mississippi	1,694,645	1.4%
39	Nebraska	639,756	0.5%		27	Oklahoma	1,645,625	1.3%
37	Nevada	780,500	0.6%		28	Colorado	1,621,056	1.3%
40	New Hampshire	623,814	0.5%		29	Connecticut	1,524,545	1.2%
11	New Jersey	3,350,786	2.7%		30	Oregon	1,330,142	1.1%
38	New Mexico	770,475	0.6%		31	Arkansas	1,301,330	1.1%
3	New York	8,114,078	6.6%		32	Iowa	1,226,568	1.0%
9	North Carolina	4,166,718	3.4%		33	West Virginia	1,183,158	1.0%
48	North Dakota	289,070	0.2%		34	Kansas	1,028,706	0.8%
5	Ohio	6,023,705	4.9%		35	Utah	856,277	0.7%
27	Oklahoma	1,645,625	1.3%		36	Maine	780,874	0.6%
30	Oregon	1,330,142	1.1%		37	Nevada	780,500	0.6%
6	Pennsylvania	6,006,841	4.9%		38	New Mexico	770,475	0.6%
42	Rhode Island	494,817	0.4%		39	Nebraska	639,756	0.5%
24	South Carolina	1,954,264	1.6%		40	New Hampshire	623,814	0.5%
49	South Dakota	239,192	0.2%		41	Idaho	520,941	0.4%
12	Tennessee	3,251,592	2.6%		42	Rhode Island	494,817	0.4%
2	Texas	8,819,272	7.2%		43	Delaware	363,979	0.3%
35	Utah	856,277	0.7%		44	Hawaii	361,068	0.3%
47	Vermont	304,717	0.2%		45	Montana	346,670	0.3%
14	Virginia	3,091,131	2.5%		46	Alaska	328,164	0.3%
17	Washington	2,385,734	1.9%		47	Vermont	304,717	0.2%
33	West Virginia	1,183,158	1.0%		48	North Dakota	289,070	0.2%
23	Wisconsin	2,066,654	1.7%		49	South Dakota	239,192	0.2%
50	Wyoming	234,384	0.2%		50	Wyoming	234,384	0.2%
						District of Columbia	436,918	0.4%

ALPHA ORDER / RANK ORDER

Source: American Hospital Association (Chicago, IL)
   "Hospital Statistics" (2010 edition)
*All nonfederal, short-term general, and other special hospitals whose facilities and services are available to the public.

Medicare and Medicaid Certified Facilities in 2010

National Total = 280,728 Facilities*

ALPHA ORDER

RANK	STATE	FACILITIES	% of USA
19	Alabama	4,798	1.7%
48	Alaska	675	0.2%
17	Arizona	5,074	1.8%
32	Arkansas	2,998	1.1%
2	California	25,869	9.2%
28	Colorado	3,735	1.3%
30	Connecticut	3,362	1.2%
46	Delaware	952	0.3%
3	Florida	20,330	7.2%
9	Georgia	8,811	3.1%
44	Hawaii	991	0.4%
39	Idaho	1,420	0.5%
6	Illinois	12,090	4.3%
11	Indiana	7,087	2.5%
27	Iowa	4,150	1.5%
29	Kansas	3,542	1.3%
21	Kentucky	4,595	1.6%
16	Louisiana	5,809	2.1%
40	Maine	1,419	0.5%
22	Maryland	4,567	1.6%
18	Massachusetts	4,839	1.7%
8	Michigan	9,320	3.3%
20	Minnesota	4,596	1.6%
31	Mississippi	3,333	1.2%
13	Missouri	6,727	2.4%
43	Montana	1,035	0.4%
34	Nebraska	2,476	0.9%
37	Nevada	1,823	0.6%
42	New Hampshire	1,205	0.4%
12	New Jersey	6,744	2.4%
38	New Mexico	1,781	0.6%
4	New York	12,896	4.6%
10	North Carolina	8,489	3.0%
47	North Dakota	915	0.3%
5	Ohio	12,747	4.5%
25	Oklahoma	4,413	1.6%
33	Oregon	2,963	1.1%
7	Pennsylvania	10,667	3.8%
45	Rhode Island	962	0.3%
23	South Carolina	4,532	1.6%
41	South Dakota	1,216	0.4%
14	Tennessee	6,433	2.3%
1	Texas	27,196	9.7%
36	Utah	1,920	0.7%
49	Vermont	624	0.2%
15	Virginia	6,168	2.2%
26	Washington	4,353	1.6%
35	West Virginia	2,397	0.9%
24	Wisconsin	4,446	1.6%
50	Wyoming	578	0.2%

RANK ORDER

RANK	STATE	FACILITIES	% of USA
1	Texas	27,196	9.7%
2	California	25,869	9.2%
3	Florida	20,330	7.2%
4	New York	12,896	4.6%
5	Ohio	12,747	4.5%
6	Illinois	12,090	4.3%
7	Pennsylvania	10,667	3.8%
8	Michigan	9,320	3.3%
9	Georgia	8,811	3.1%
10	North Carolina	8,489	3.0%
11	Indiana	7,087	2.5%
12	New Jersey	6,744	2.4%
13	Missouri	6,727	2.4%
14	Tennessee	6,433	2.3%
15	Virginia	6,168	2.2%
16	Louisiana	5,809	2.1%
17	Arizona	5,074	1.8%
18	Massachusetts	4,839	1.7%
19	Alabama	4,798	1.7%
20	Minnesota	4,596	1.6%
21	Kentucky	4,595	1.6%
22	Maryland	4,567	1.6%
23	South Carolina	4,532	1.6%
24	Wisconsin	4,446	1.6%
25	Oklahoma	4,413	1.6%
26	Washington	4,353	1.6%
27	Iowa	4,150	1.5%
28	Colorado	3,735	1.3%
29	Kansas	3,542	1.3%
30	Connecticut	3,362	1.2%
31	Mississippi	3,333	1.2%
32	Arkansas	2,998	1.1%
33	Oregon	2,963	1.1%
34	Nebraska	2,476	0.9%
35	West Virginia	2,397	0.9%
36	Utah	1,920	0.7%
37	Nevada	1,823	0.6%
38	New Mexico	1,781	0.6%
39	Idaho	1,420	0.5%
40	Maine	1,419	0.5%
41	South Dakota	1,216	0.4%
42	New Hampshire	1,205	0.4%
43	Montana	1,035	0.4%
44	Hawaii	991	0.4%
45	Rhode Island	962	0.3%
46	Delaware	952	0.3%
47	North Dakota	915	0.3%
48	Alaska	675	0.2%
49	Vermont	624	0.2%
50	Wyoming	578	0.2%
	District of Columbia	660	0.2%

Source: U.S. Department of Health and Human Services, Centers for Medicare and Medicaid Services
    OSCAR Report 10 (January 08, 2010)
*Certified by CMS to participate in the Medicare/Medicaid programs. All provider groups including hospitals, home health agencies, rural health centers, community mental health centers, nursing facilities, outpatient physical therapy facilities, hospices, and laboratories. National total does not include 1,544 certified facilities in U.S. territories.

Medicare and Medicaid Certified Hospitals in 2010

National Total = 6,235 Hospitals*

ALPHA ORDER

RANK	STATE	HOSPITALS	% of USA
19	Alabama	129	2.1%
47	Alaska	25	0.4%
25	Arizona	107	1.7%
26	Arkansas	104	1.7%
2	California	423	6.8%
29	Colorado	97	1.6%
42	Connecticut	46	0.7%
50	Delaware	12	0.2%
3	Florida	247	4.0%
10	Georgia	178	2.9%
46	Hawaii	27	0.4%
38	Idaho	51	0.8%
8	Illinois	214	3.4%
11	Indiana	169	2.7%
20	Iowa	125	2.0%
12	Kansas	159	2.6%
21	Kentucky	120	1.9%
7	Louisiana	228	3.7%
43	Maine	43	0.7%
32	Maryland	65	1.0%
22	Massachusetts	118	1.9%
9	Michigan	180	2.9%
16	Minnesota	149	2.4%
24	Mississippi	112	1.8%
14	Missouri	154	2.5%
34	Montana	64	1.0%
30	Nebraska	95	1.5%
38	Nevada	51	0.8%
44	New Hampshire	31	0.5%
28	New Jersey	101	1.6%
37	New Mexico	53	0.9%
5	New York	239	3.8%
18	North Carolina	138	2.2%
41	North Dakota	49	0.8%
6	Ohio	230	3.7%
13	Oklahoma	157	2.5%
36	Oregon	63	1.0%
4	Pennsylvania	244	3.9%
48	Rhode Island	16	0.3%
31	South Carolina	81	1.3%
32	South Dakota	65	1.0%
14	Tennessee	154	2.5%
1	Texas	580	9.3%
40	Utah	50	0.8%
48	Vermont	16	0.3%
23	Virginia	117	1.9%
27	Washington	102	1.6%
34	West Virginia	64	1.0%
17	Wisconsin	148	2.4%
45	Wyoming	30	0.5%

RANK ORDER

RANK	STATE	HOSPITALS	% of USA
1	Texas	580	9.3%
2	California	423	6.8%
3	Florida	247	4.0%
4	Pennsylvania	244	3.9%
5	New York	239	3.8%
6	Ohio	230	3.7%
7	Louisiana	228	3.7%
8	Illinois	214	3.4%
9	Michigan	180	2.9%
10	Georgia	178	2.9%
11	Indiana	169	2.7%
12	Kansas	159	2.6%
13	Oklahoma	157	2.5%
14	Missouri	154	2.5%
14	Tennessee	154	2.5%
16	Minnesota	149	2.4%
17	Wisconsin	148	2.4%
18	North Carolina	138	2.2%
19	Alabama	129	2.1%
20	Iowa	125	2.0%
21	Kentucky	120	1.9%
22	Massachusetts	118	1.9%
23	Virginia	117	1.9%
24	Mississippi	112	1.8%
25	Arizona	107	1.7%
26	Arkansas	104	1.7%
27	Washington	102	1.6%
28	New Jersey	101	1.6%
29	Colorado	97	1.6%
30	Nebraska	95	1.5%
31	South Carolina	81	1.3%
32	Maryland	65	1.0%
32	South Dakota	65	1.0%
34	Montana	64	1.0%
34	West Virginia	64	1.0%
36	Oregon	63	1.0%
37	New Mexico	53	0.9%
38	Idaho	51	0.8%
38	Nevada	51	0.8%
40	Utah	50	0.8%
41	North Dakota	49	0.8%
42	Connecticut	46	0.7%
43	Maine	43	0.7%
44	New Hampshire	31	0.5%
45	Wyoming	30	0.5%
46	Hawaii	27	0.4%
47	Alaska	25	0.4%
48	Rhode Island	16	0.3%
48	Vermont	16	0.3%
50	Delaware	12	0.2%
	District of Columbia	15	0.2%

Source: U.S. Department of Health and Human Services, Centers for Medicare and Medicaid Services
OSCAR Report 10 (January 08, 2010)
*Certified by CMS to participate in the Medicare/Medicaid programs. Excludes licensed facilities that do not accept federal funding and facilities managed by the Department of Veterans Affairs. National total does not include 64 certified hospitals in U.S. territories.

Beds in Medicare and Medicaid Certified Hospitals in 2010

National Total = 915,327 Beds*

ALPHA ORDER

RANK	STATE	BEDS	% of USA
17	Alabama	19,295	2.1%
49	Alaska	1,607	0.2%
21	Arizona	16,165	1.8%
31	Arkansas	10,445	1.1%
1	California	78,637	8.6%
28	Colorado	12,488	1.4%
32	Connecticut	10,177	1.1%
47	Delaware	2,520	0.3%
4	Florida	59,497	6.5%
11	Georgia	24,610	2.7%
46	Hawaii	2,735	0.3%
42	Idaho	3,403	0.4%
6	Illinois	40,753	4.5%
18	Indiana	18,989	2.1%
30	Iowa	10,450	1.1%
29	Kansas	11,532	1.3%
20	Kentucky	17,462	1.9%
14	Louisiana	20,647	2.3%
39	Maine	4,081	0.4%
22	Maryland	15,470	1.7%
15	Massachusetts	20,114	2.2%
8	Michigan	28,187	3.1%
23	Minnesota	15,464	1.7%
27	Mississippi	13,024	1.4%
13	Missouri	23,804	2.6%
44	Montana	3,143	0.3%
35	Nebraska	6,563	0.7%
36	Nevada	6,476	0.7%
41	New Hampshire	3,529	0.4%
10	New Jersey	26,619	2.9%
38	New Mexico	4,919	0.5%
3	New York	64,513	7.0%
9	North Carolina	26,656	2.9%
45	North Dakota	3,103	0.3%
5	Ohio	43,853	4.8%
24	Oklahoma	14,594	1.6%
34	Oregon	8,034	0.9%
7	Pennsylvania	35,103	3.8%
40	Rhode Island	3,657	0.4%
25	South Carolina	13,649	1.5%
43	South Dakota	3,382	0.4%
12	Tennessee	24,519	2.7%
2	Texas	67,981	7.4%
37	Utah	5,256	0.6%
48	Vermont	1,788	0.2%
16	Virginia	19,881	2.2%
26	Washington	13,426	1.5%
33	West Virginia	8,952	1.0%
19	Wisconsin	18,481	2.0%
50	Wyoming	1,541	0.2%

RANK ORDER

RANK	STATE	BEDS	% of USA
1	California	78,637	8.6%
2	Texas	67,981	7.4%
3	New York	64,513	7.0%
4	Florida	59,497	6.5%
5	Ohio	43,853	4.8%
6	Illinois	40,753	4.5%
7	Pennsylvania	35,103	3.8%
8	Michigan	28,187	3.1%
9	North Carolina	26,656	2.9%
10	New Jersey	26,619	2.9%
11	Georgia	24,610	2.7%
12	Tennessee	24,519	2.7%
13	Missouri	23,804	2.6%
14	Louisiana	20,647	2.3%
15	Massachusetts	20,114	2.2%
16	Virginia	19,881	2.2%
17	Alabama	19,295	2.1%
18	Indiana	18,989	2.1%
19	Wisconsin	18,481	2.0%
20	Kentucky	17,462	1.9%
21	Arizona	16,165	1.8%
22	Maryland	15,470	1.7%
23	Minnesota	15,464	1.7%
24	Oklahoma	14,594	1.6%
25	South Carolina	13,649	1.5%
26	Washington	13,426	1.5%
27	Mississippi	13,024	1.4%
28	Colorado	12,488	1.4%
29	Kansas	11,532	1.3%
30	Iowa	10,450	1.1%
31	Arkansas	10,445	1.1%
32	Connecticut	10,177	1.1%
33	West Virginia	8,952	1.0%
34	Oregon	8,034	0.9%
35	Nebraska	6,563	0.7%
36	Nevada	6,476	0.7%
37	Utah	5,256	0.6%
38	New Mexico	4,919	0.5%
39	Maine	4,081	0.4%
40	Rhode Island	3,657	0.4%
41	New Hampshire	3,529	0.4%
42	Idaho	3,403	0.4%
43	South Dakota	3,382	0.4%
44	Montana	3,143	0.3%
45	North Dakota	3,103	0.3%
46	Hawaii	2,735	0.3%
47	Delaware	2,520	0.3%
48	Vermont	1,788	0.2%
49	Alaska	1,607	0.2%
50	Wyoming	1,541	0.2%
	District of Columbia	4,153	0.5%

Source: U.S. Department of Health and Human Services, Centers for Medicare and Medicaid Services
 OSCAR Database (January 08, 2010)

*Beds in hospitals certified by CMS to participate in the Medicare/Medicaid programs. Excludes licensed facilities that do not accept federal funding and facilities managed by the Department of Veterans Affairs. National total does not include 11,705 beds in U.S. territories.

Medicare and Medicaid Certified Children's Hospitals in 2010

National Total = 77 Hospitals*

ALPHA ORDER				RANK ORDER			
RANK	STATE	HOSPITALS	% of USA	RANK	STATE	HOSPITALS	% of USA
9	Alabama	2	2.6%	1	California	10	13.0%
32	Alaska	0	0.0%	2	Texas	8	10.4%
9	Arizona	2	2.6%	3	Ohio	6	7.8%
21	Arkansas	1	1.3%	4	Pennsylvania	5	6.5%
1	California	10	13.0%	5	Minnesota	3	3.9%
21	Colorado	1	1.3%	5	Missouri	3	3.9%
21	Connecticut	1	1.3%	5	Virginia	3	3.9%
21	Delaware	1	1.3%	5	Wisconsin	3	3.9%
9	Florida	2	2.6%	9	Alabama	2	2.6%
9	Georgia	2	2.6%	9	Arizona	2	2.6%
21	Hawaii	1	1.3%	9	Florida	2	2.6%
32	Idaho	0	0.0%	9	Georgia	2	2.6%
9	Illinois	2	2.6%	9	Illinois	2	2.6%
32	Indiana	0	0.0%	9	Maryland	2	2.6%
32	Iowa	0	0.0%	9	Massachusetts	2	2.6%
21	Kansas	1	1.3%	9	Nebraska	2	2.6%
32	Kentucky	0	0.0%	9	New Jersey	2	2.6%
21	Louisiana	1	1.3%	9	Oklahoma	2	2.6%
32	Maine	0	0.0%	9	Tennessee	2	2.6%
9	Maryland	2	2.6%	9	Washington	2	2.6%
9	Massachusetts	2	2.6%	21	Arkansas	1	1.3%
21	Michigan	1	1.3%	21	Colorado	1	1.3%
5	Minnesota	3	3.9%	21	Connecticut	1	1.3%
32	Mississippi	0	0.0%	21	Delaware	1	1.3%
5	Missouri	3	3.9%	21	Hawaii	1	1.3%
32	Montana	0	0.0%	21	Kansas	1	1.3%
9	Nebraska	2	2.6%	21	Louisiana	1	1.3%
32	Nevada	0	0.0%	21	Michigan	1	1.3%
32	New Hampshire	0	0.0%	21	New York	1	1.3%
9	New Jersey	2	2.6%	21	South Dakota	1	1.3%
32	New Mexico	0	0.0%	21	Utah	1	1.3%
21	New York	1	1.3%	32	Alaska	0	0.0%
32	North Carolina	0	0.0%	32	Idaho	0	0.0%
32	North Dakota	0	0.0%	32	Indiana	0	0.0%
3	Ohio	6	7.8%	32	Iowa	0	0.0%
9	Oklahoma	2	2.6%	32	Kentucky	0	0.0%
32	Oregon	0	0.0%	32	Maine	0	0.0%
4	Pennsylvania	5	6.5%	32	Mississippi	0	0.0%
32	Rhode Island	0	0.0%	32	Montana	0	0.0%
32	South Carolina	0	0.0%	32	Nevada	0	0.0%
21	South Dakota	1	1.3%	32	New Hampshire	0	0.0%
9	Tennessee	2	2.6%	32	New Mexico	0	0.0%
2	Texas	8	10.4%	32	North Carolina	0	0.0%
21	Utah	1	1.3%	32	North Dakota	0	0.0%
32	Vermont	0	0.0%	32	Oregon	0	0.0%
5	Virginia	3	3.9%	32	Rhode Island	0	0.0%
9	Washington	2	2.6%	32	South Carolina	0	0.0%
32	West Virginia	0	0.0%	32	Vermont	0	0.0%
5	Wisconsin	3	3.9%	32	West Virginia	0	0.0%
32	Wyoming	0	0.0%	32	Wyoming	0	0.0%
					District of Columbia	1	1.3%

Source: U.S. Department of Health and Human Services, Centers for Medicare and Medicaid Services
OSCAR Report 10 (January 08, 2010)
*Certified by CMS to participate in the Medicare/Medicaid programs. National total does not include one facility in U.S. territories.
Excludes licensed facilities that do not accept federal funding and facilities managed by the Department of Veterans Affairs.

Beds in Medicare and Medicaid Certified Children's Hospitals in 2010

National Total = 12,266 Beds*

ALPHA ORDER

RANK ORDER

RANK	STATE	BEDS	% of USA
6	Alabama	434	3.5%
32	Alaska	0	0.0%
17	Arizona	250	2.0%
14	Arkansas	280	2.3%
1	California	1,722	14.0%
16	Colorado	253	2.1%
27	Connecticut	129	1.1%
24	Delaware	180	1.5%
8	Florida	424	3.5%
5	Georgia	483	3.9%
20	Hawaii	207	1.7%
32	Idaho	0	0.0%
11	Illinois	339	2.8%
32	Indiana	0	0.0%
32	Iowa	0	0.0%
31	Kansas	34	0.3%
32	Kentucky	0	0.0%
21	Louisiana	201	1.6%
32	Maine	0	0.0%
26	Maryland	150	1.2%
9	Massachusetts	421	3.4%
19	Michigan	228	1.9%
11	Minnesota	339	2.8%
32	Mississippi	0	0.0%
7	Missouri	432	3.5%
32	Montana	0	0.0%
22	Nebraska	200	1.6%
32	Nevada	0	0.0%
32	New Hampshire	0	0.0%
29	New Jersey	100	0.8%
32	New Mexico	0	0.0%
30	New York	92	0.8%
32	North Carolina	0	0.0%
32	North Dakota	0	0.0%
3	Ohio	1,356	11.1%
25	Oklahoma	160	1.3%
32	Oregon	0	0.0%
4	Pennsylvania	759	6.2%
32	Rhode Island	0	0.0%
32	South Carolina	0	0.0%
28	South Dakota	114	0.9%
23	Tennessee	197	1.6%
2	Texas	1,385	11.3%
18	Utah	232	1.9%
32	Vermont	0	0.0%
13	Virginia	296	2.4%
15	Washington	276	2.3%
32	West Virginia	0	0.0%
10	Wisconsin	350	2.9%
32	Wyoming	0	0.0%

RANK	STATE	BEDS	% of USA
1	California	1,722	14.0%
2	Texas	1,385	11.3%
3	Ohio	1,356	11.1%
4	Pennsylvania	759	6.2%
5	Georgia	483	3.9%
6	Alabama	434	3.5%
7	Missouri	432	3.5%
8	Florida	424	3.5%
9	Massachusetts	421	3.4%
10	Wisconsin	350	2.9%
11	Illinois	339	2.8%
11	Minnesota	339	2.8%
13	Virginia	296	2.4%
14	Arkansas	280	2.3%
15	Washington	276	2.3%
16	Colorado	253	2.1%
17	Arizona	250	2.0%
18	Utah	232	1.9%
19	Michigan	228	1.9%
20	Hawaii	207	1.7%
21	Louisiana	201	1.6%
22	Nebraska	200	1.6%
23	Tennessee	197	1.6%
24	Delaware	180	1.5%
25	Oklahoma	160	1.3%
26	Maryland	150	1.2%
27	Connecticut	129	1.1%
28	South Dakota	114	0.9%
29	New Jersey	100	0.8%
30	New York	92	0.8%
31	Kansas	34	0.3%
32	Alaska	0	0.0%
32	Idaho	0	0.0%
32	Indiana	0	0.0%
32	Iowa	0	0.0%
32	Kentucky	0	0.0%
32	Maine	0	0.0%
32	Mississippi	0	0.0%
32	Montana	0	0.0%
32	Nevada	0	0.0%
32	New Hampshire	0	0.0%
32	New Mexico	0	0.0%
32	North Carolina	0	0.0%
32	North Dakota	0	0.0%
32	Oregon	0	0.0%
32	Rhode Island	0	0.0%
32	South Carolina	0	0.0%
32	Vermont	0	0.0%
32	West Virginia	0	0.0%
32	Wyoming	0	0.0%
	District of Columbia	243	2.0%

Source: U.S. Department of Health and Human Services, Centers for Medicare and Medicaid Services
OSCAR Database (January 08, 2010)

*Certified by CMS to participate in the Medicare/Medicaid programs. National total does not include 215 beds in one facility in U.S. territories. Excludes licensed facilities that do not accept federal funding and facilities managed by the Department of Veterans Affairs.

Medicare and Medicaid Certified Rehabilitation Hospitals in 2010

National Total = 225 Hospitals*

ALPHA ORDER

RANK	STATE	HOSPITALS	% of USA
8	Alabama	7	3.1%
41	Alaska	0	0.0%
8	Arizona	7	3.1%
5	Arkansas	8	3.6%
14	California	5	2.2%
22	Colorado	3	1.3%
31	Connecticut	1	0.4%
41	Delaware	0	0.0%
4	Florida	13	5.8%
22	Georgia	3	1.3%
31	Hawaii	1	0.4%
31	Idaho	1	0.4%
18	Illinois	4	1.8%
11	Indiana	6	2.7%
41	Iowa	0	0.0%
18	Kansas	4	1.8%
14	Kentucky	5	2.2%
2	Louisiana	21	9.3%
31	Maine	1	0.4%
26	Maryland	2	0.9%
5	Massachusetts	8	3.6%
18	Michigan	4	1.8%
31	Minnesota	1	0.4%
41	Mississippi	0	0.0%
18	Missouri	4	1.8%
41	Montana	0	0.0%
31	Nebraska	1	0.4%
22	Nevada	3	1.3%
26	New Hampshire	2	0.9%
5	New Jersey	8	3.6%
14	New Mexico	5	2.2%
41	New York	0	0.0%
26	North Carolina	2	0.9%
41	North Dakota	0	0.0%
22	Ohio	3	1.3%
26	Oklahoma	2	0.9%
41	Oregon	0	0.0%
3	Pennsylvania	17	7.6%
31	Rhode Island	1	0.4%
11	South Carolina	6	2.7%
41	South Dakota	0	0.0%
11	Tennessee	6	2.7%
1	Texas	42	18.7%
31	Utah	1	0.4%
41	Vermont	0	0.0%
8	Virginia	7	3.1%
31	Washington	1	0.4%
14	West Virginia	5	2.2%
26	Wisconsin	2	0.9%
31	Wyoming	1	0.4%

RANK ORDER

RANK	STATE	HOSPITALS	% of USA
1	Texas	42	18.7%
2	Louisiana	21	9.3%
3	Pennsylvania	17	7.6%
4	Florida	13	5.8%
5	Arkansas	8	3.6%
5	Massachusetts	8	3.6%
5	New Jersey	8	3.6%
8	Alabama	7	3.1%
8	Arizona	7	3.1%
8	Virginia	7	3.1%
11	Indiana	6	2.7%
11	South Carolina	6	2.7%
11	Tennessee	6	2.7%
14	California	5	2.2%
14	Kentucky	5	2.2%
14	New Mexico	5	2.2%
14	West Virginia	5	2.2%
18	Illinois	4	1.8%
18	Kansas	4	1.8%
18	Michigan	4	1.8%
18	Missouri	4	1.8%
22	Colorado	3	1.3%
22	Georgia	3	1.3%
22	Nevada	3	1.3%
22	Ohio	3	1.3%
26	Maryland	2	0.9%
26	New Hampshire	2	0.9%
26	North Carolina	2	0.9%
26	Oklahoma	2	0.9%
26	Wisconsin	2	0.9%
31	Connecticut	1	0.4%
31	Hawaii	1	0.4%
31	Idaho	1	0.4%
31	Maine	1	0.4%
31	Minnesota	1	0.4%
31	Nebraska	1	0.4%
31	Rhode Island	1	0.4%
31	Utah	1	0.4%
31	Washington	1	0.4%
31	Wyoming	1	0.4%
41	Alaska	0	0.0%
41	Delaware	0	0.0%
41	Iowa	0	0.0%
41	Mississippi	0	0.0%
41	Montana	0	0.0%
41	New York	0	0.0%
41	North Dakota	0	0.0%
41	Oregon	0	0.0%
41	South Dakota	0	0.0%
41	Vermont	0	0.0%
	District of Columbia	1	0.4%

Source: U.S. Department of Health and Human Services, Centers for Medicare and Medicaid Services
OSCAR Report 10 (January 08, 2010)
*Certified by CMS to participate in the Medicare/Medicaid programs. Excludes licensed facilities that do not accept federal funding and facilities managed by the Department of Veterans Affairs. National total does not include two certified hospitals in U.S. territories.

Beds in Medicare and Medicaid Certified Rehabilitation Hospitals in 2010

National Total = 14,397 Beds*

RANK	STATE	BEDS	% of USA
9	Alabama	392	2.7%
41	Alaska	0	0.0%
10	Arizona	371	2.6%
7	Arkansas	463	3.2%
12	California	367	2.5%
21	Colorado	226	1.6%
37	Connecticut	60	0.4%
41	Delaware	0	0.0%
4	Florida	1,022	7.1%
26	Georgia	168	1.2%
32	Hawaii	100	0.7%
38	Idaho	46	0.3%
8	Illinois	448	3.1%
14	Indiana	290	2.0%
41	Iowa	0	0.0%
18	Kansas	257	1.8%
15	Kentucky	288	2.0%
6	Louisiana	577	4.0%
32	Maine	100	0.7%
28	Maryland	131	0.9%
3	Massachusetts	1,040	7.2%
19	Michigan	240	1.7%
40	Minnesota	16	0.1%
41	Mississippi	0	0.0%
20	Missouri	237	1.6%
41	Montana	0	0.0%
36	Nebraska	72	0.5%
25	Nevada	181	1.3%
27	New Hampshire	152	1.1%
5	New Jersey	774	5.4%
23	New Mexico	212	1.5%
41	New York	0	0.0%
22	North Carolina	213	1.5%
41	North Dakota	0	0.0%
24	Ohio	199	1.4%
30	Oklahoma	107	0.7%
41	Oregon	0	0.0%
2	Pennsylvania	1,365	9.5%
35	Rhode Island	82	0.6%
13	South Carolina	344	2.4%
41	South Dakota	0	0.0%
11	Tennessee	370	2.6%
1	Texas	2,421	16.8%
34	Utah	84	0.6%
41	Vermont	0	0.0%
15	Virginia	288	2.0%
31	Washington	102	0.7%
17	West Virginia	270	1.9%
29	Wisconsin	121	0.8%
39	Wyoming	41	0.3%

RANK	STATE	BEDS	% of USA
1	Texas	2,421	16.8%
2	Pennsylvania	1,365	9.5%
3	Massachusetts	1,040	7.2%
4	Florida	1,022	7.1%
5	New Jersey	774	5.4%
6	Louisiana	577	4.0%
7	Arkansas	463	3.2%
8	Illinois	448	3.1%
9	Alabama	392	2.7%
10	Arizona	371	2.6%
11	Tennessee	370	2.6%
12	California	367	2.5%
13	South Carolina	344	2.4%
14	Indiana	290	2.0%
15	Kentucky	288	2.0%
15	Virginia	288	2.0%
17	West Virginia	270	1.9%
18	Kansas	257	1.8%
19	Michigan	240	1.7%
20	Missouri	237	1.6%
21	Colorado	226	1.6%
22	North Carolina	213	1.5%
23	New Mexico	212	1.5%
24	Ohio	199	1.4%
25	Nevada	181	1.3%
26	Georgia	168	1.2%
27	New Hampshire	152	1.1%
28	Maryland	131	0.9%
29	Wisconsin	121	0.8%
30	Oklahoma	107	0.7%
31	Washington	102	0.7%
32	Hawaii	100	0.7%
32	Maine	100	0.7%
34	Utah	84	0.6%
35	Rhode Island	82	0.6%
36	Nebraska	72	0.5%
37	Connecticut	60	0.4%
38	Idaho	46	0.3%
39	Wyoming	41	0.3%
40	Minnesota	16	0.1%
41	Alaska	0	0.0%
41	Delaware	0	0.0%
41	Iowa	0	0.0%
41	Mississippi	0	0.0%
41	Montana	0	0.0%
41	New York	0	0.0%
41	North Dakota	0	0.0%
41	Oregon	0	0.0%
41	South Dakota	0	0.0%
41	Vermont	0	0.0%
	District of Columbia	160	1.1%

Source: U.S. Department of Health and Human Services, Centers for Medicare and Medicaid Services
OSCAR Database (January 08, 2010)

*Beds in hospitals certified by CMS to participate in the Medicare/Medicaid programs. Excludes licensed facilities that do not accept federal funding and facilities managed by the Department of Veterans Affairs. National total does not include 72 beds in U.S. territories.

Medicare and Medicaid Certified Psychiatric Hospitals in 2010

National Total = 503 Psychiatric Hospitals*

ALPHA ORDER

RANK	STATE	HOSPITALS	% of USA
14	Alabama	11	2.2%
42	Alaska	2	0.4%
26	Arizona	7	1.4%
24	Arkansas	8	1.6%
3	California	33	6.6%
21	Colorado	9	1.8%
28	Connecticut	6	1.2%
33	Delaware	4	0.8%
5	Florida	24	4.8%
9	Georgia	15	3.0%
48	Hawaii	1	0.2%
30	Idaho	5	1.0%
12	Illinois	14	2.8%
7	Indiana	22	4.4%
33	Iowa	4	0.8%
33	Kansas	4	0.8%
14	Kentucky	11	2.2%
1	Louisiana	37	7.4%
33	Maine	4	0.8%
21	Maryland	9	1.8%
9	Massachusetts	15	3.0%
18	Michigan	10	2.0%
26	Minnesota	7	1.4%
30	Mississippi	5	1.0%
12	Missouri	14	2.8%
42	Montana	2	0.4%
38	Nebraska	3	0.6%
28	Nevada	6	1.2%
42	New Hampshire	2	0.4%
8	New Jersey	17	3.4%
42	New Mexico	2	0.4%
4	New York	28	5.6%
18	North Carolina	10	2.0%
38	North Dakota	3	0.6%
9	Ohio	15	3.0%
18	Oklahoma	10	2.0%
38	Oregon	3	0.6%
5	Pennsylvania	24	4.8%
42	Rhode Island	2	0.4%
24	South Carolina	8	1.6%
48	South Dakota	1	0.2%
14	Tennessee	11	2.2%
1	Texas	37	7.4%
38	Utah	3	0.6%
48	Vermont	1	0.2%
21	Virginia	9	1.8%
30	Washington	5	1.0%
33	West Virginia	4	0.8%
14	Wisconsin	11	2.2%
42	Wyoming	2	0.4%

RANK ORDER

RANK	STATE	HOSPITALS	% of USA
1	Louisiana	37	7.4%
1	Texas	37	7.4%
3	California	33	6.6%
4	New York	28	5.6%
5	Florida	24	4.8%
5	Pennsylvania	24	4.8%
7	Indiana	22	4.4%
8	New Jersey	17	3.4%
9	Georgia	15	3.0%
9	Massachusetts	15	3.0%
9	Ohio	15	3.0%
12	Illinois	14	2.8%
12	Missouri	14	2.8%
14	Alabama	11	2.2%
14	Kentucky	11	2.2%
14	Tennessee	11	2.2%
14	Wisconsin	11	2.2%
18	Michigan	10	2.0%
18	North Carolina	10	2.0%
18	Oklahoma	10	2.0%
21	Colorado	9	1.8%
21	Maryland	9	1.8%
21	Virginia	9	1.8%
24	Arkansas	8	1.6%
24	South Carolina	8	1.6%
26	Arizona	7	1.4%
26	Minnesota	7	1.4%
28	Connecticut	6	1.2%
28	Nevada	6	1.2%
30	Idaho	5	1.0%
30	Mississippi	5	1.0%
30	Washington	5	1.0%
33	Delaware	4	0.8%
33	Iowa	4	0.8%
33	Kansas	4	0.8%
33	Maine	4	0.8%
33	West Virginia	4	0.8%
38	Nebraska	3	0.6%
38	North Dakota	3	0.6%
38	Oregon	3	0.6%
38	Utah	3	0.6%
42	Alaska	2	0.4%
42	Montana	2	0.4%
42	New Hampshire	2	0.4%
42	New Mexico	2	0.4%
42	Rhode Island	2	0.4%
42	Wyoming	2	0.4%
48	Hawaii	1	0.2%
48	South Dakota	1	0.2%
48	Vermont	1	0.2%
	District of Columbia	3	0.6%

Source: U.S. Department of Health and Human Services, Centers for Medicare and Medicaid Services
OSCAR Report 10 (January 08, 2010)
*Certified by CMS to participate in the Medicare/Medicaid programs. Excludes licensed facilities that do not accept federal funding and facilities managed by the Department of Veterans Affairs. National total does not include four certified psychiatric hospitals in U.S. territories.

Beds in Medicare and Medicaid Certified Psychiatric Hospitals in 2010

National Total = 55,112 Beds*

ALPHA ORDER

RANK	STATE	BEDS	% of USA
27	Alabama	758	1.4%
42	Alaska	205	0.4%
23	Arizona	941	1.7%
25	Arkansas	787	1.4%
7	California	2,444	4.4%
24	Colorado	889	1.6%
20	Connecticut	1,012	1.8%
38	Delaware	307	0.6%
6	Florida	2,545	4.6%
11	Georgia	1,514	2.7%
49	Hawaii	88	0.2%
41	Idaho	263	0.5%
13	Illinois	1,461	2.7%
21	Indiana	1,002	1.8%
40	Iowa	287	0.5%
30	Kansas	561	1.0%
14	Kentucky	1,392	2.5%
8	Louisiana	1,749	3.2%
35	Maine	386	0.7%
9	Maryland	1,731	3.1%
10	Massachusetts	1,541	2.8%
16	Michigan	1,221	2.2%
33	Minnesota	442	0.8%
29	Mississippi	585	1.1%
22	Missouri	958	1.7%
44	Montana	153	0.3%
36	Nebraska	369	0.7%
28	Nevada	589	1.1%
37	New Hampshire	341	0.6%
5	New Jersey	2,877	5.2%
48	New Mexico	124	0.2%
1	New York	6,373	11.6%
3	North Carolina	3,390	6.2%
39	North Dakota	303	0.5%
19	Ohio	1,019	1.8%
31	Oklahoma	536	1.0%
47	Oregon	127	0.2%
2	Pennsylvania	3,454	6.3%
43	Rhode Island	177	0.3%
17	South Carolina	1,093	2.0%
46	South Dakota	133	0.2%
18	Tennessee	1,034	1.9%
4	Texas	3,051	5.5%
34	Utah	391	0.7%
45	Vermont	149	0.3%
26	Virginia	767	1.4%
15	Washington	1,241	2.3%
32	West Virginia	485	0.9%
12	Wisconsin	1,491	2.7%
50	Wyoming	84	0.2%

RANK ORDER

RANK	STATE	BEDS	% of USA
1	New York	6,373	11.6%
2	Pennsylvania	3,454	6.3%
3	North Carolina	3,390	6.2%
4	Texas	3,051	5.5%
5	New Jersey	2,877	5.2%
6	Florida	2,545	4.6%
7	California	2,444	4.4%
8	Louisiana	1,749	3.2%
9	Maryland	1,731	3.1%
10	Massachusetts	1,541	2.8%
11	Georgia	1,514	2.7%
12	Wisconsin	1,491	2.7%
13	Illinois	1,461	2.7%
14	Kentucky	1,392	2.5%
15	Washington	1,241	2.3%
16	Michigan	1,221	2.2%
17	South Carolina	1,093	2.0%
18	Tennessee	1,034	1.9%
19	Ohio	1,019	1.8%
20	Connecticut	1,012	1.8%
21	Indiana	1,002	1.8%
22	Missouri	958	1.7%
23	Arizona	941	1.7%
24	Colorado	889	1.6%
25	Arkansas	787	1.4%
26	Virginia	767	1.4%
27	Alabama	758	1.4%
28	Nevada	589	1.1%
29	Mississippi	585	1.1%
30	Kansas	561	1.0%
31	Oklahoma	536	1.0%
32	West Virginia	485	0.9%
33	Minnesota	442	0.8%
34	Utah	391	0.7%
35	Maine	386	0.7%
36	Nebraska	369	0.7%
37	New Hampshire	341	0.6%
38	Delaware	307	0.6%
39	North Dakota	303	0.5%
40	Iowa	287	0.5%
41	Idaho	263	0.5%
42	Alaska	205	0.4%
43	Rhode Island	177	0.3%
44	Montana	153	0.3%
45	Vermont	149	0.3%
46	South Dakota	133	0.2%
47	Oregon	127	0.2%
48	New Mexico	124	0.2%
49	Hawaii	88	0.2%
50	Wyoming	84	0.2%
	District of Columbia	292	0.5%

Source: U.S. Department of Health and Human Services, Centers for Medicare and Medicaid Services
        OSCAR Database (January 08, 2010)

*Beds in hospitals certified by CMS to participate in the Medicare/Medicaid programs. Excludes licensed facilities that do not accept federal funding and facilities managed by the Department of Veterans Affairs. National total does not include 492 beds in U.S. territories.

Medicare and Medicaid Certified Outpatient Surgery Centers in 2010

National Total = 5,232 Centers*

ALPHA ORDER					RANK ORDER			
RANK	STATE		CENTERS	% of USA	RANK	STATE	CENTERS	% of USA
35	Alabama		38	0.7%	1	California	725	13.9%
49	Alaska		9	0.2%	2	Florida	398	7.6%
10	Arizona		150	2.9%	3	Maryland	359	6.9%
23	Arkansas		62	1.2%	3	Texas	359	6.9%
1	California		725	13.9%	5	Georgia	266	5.1%
15	Colorado		102	1.9%	6	Pennsylvania	230	4.4%
34	Connecticut		43	0.8%	7	Washington	224	4.3%
38	Delaware		24	0.5%	8	New Jersey	221	4.2%
2	Florida		398	7.6%	9	Ohio	204	3.9%
5	Georgia		266	5.1%	10	Arizona	150	2.9%
46	Hawaii		12	0.2%	11	Tennessee	148	2.8%
27	Idaho		58	1.1%	12	Illinois	121	2.3%
12	Illinois		121	2.3%	13	Indiana	118	2.3%
13	Indiana		118	2.3%	14	Missouri	103	2.0%
37	Iowa		26	0.5%	15	Colorado	102	1.9%
26	Kansas		61	1.2%	16	New York	92	1.8%
36	Kentucky		36	0.7%	17	Michigan	88	1.7%
20	Louisiana		77	1.5%	18	North Carolina	82	1.6%
42	Maine		17	0.3%	19	Oregon	79	1.5%
3	Maryland		359	6.9%	20	Louisiana	77	1.5%
23	Massachusetts		62	1.2%	21	South Carolina	71	1.4%
17	Michigan		88	1.7%	22	Mississippi	64	1.2%
28	Minnesota		53	1.0%	23	Arkansas	62	1.2%
22	Mississippi		64	1.2%	23	Massachusetts	62	1.2%
14	Missouri		103	2.0%	23	Wisconsin	62	1.2%
44	Montana		15	0.3%	26	Kansas	61	1.2%
32	Nebraska		48	0.9%	27	Idaho	58	1.1%
31	Nevada		52	1.0%	28	Minnesota	53	1.0%
39	New Hampshire		22	0.4%	28	Oklahoma	53	1.0%
8	New Jersey		221	4.2%	28	Virginia	53	1.0%
40	New Mexico		20	0.4%	31	Nevada	52	1.0%
16	New York		92	1.8%	32	Nebraska	48	0.9%
18	North Carolina		82	1.6%	33	Utah	46	0.9%
43	North Dakota		16	0.3%	34	Connecticut	43	0.8%
9	Ohio		204	3.9%	35	Alabama	38	0.7%
28	Oklahoma		53	1.0%	36	Kentucky	36	0.7%
19	Oregon		79	1.5%	37	Iowa	26	0.5%
6	Pennsylvania		230	4.4%	38	Delaware	24	0.5%
46	Rhode Island		12	0.2%	39	New Hampshire	22	0.4%
21	South Carolina		71	1.4%	40	New Mexico	20	0.4%
44	South Dakota		15	0.3%	40	Wyoming	20	0.4%
11	Tennessee		148	2.8%	42	Maine	17	0.3%
3	Texas		359	6.9%	43	North Dakota	16	0.3%
33	Utah		46	0.9%	44	Montana	15	0.3%
50	Vermont		1	0.0%	44	South Dakota	15	0.3%
28	Virginia		53	1.0%	46	Hawaii	12	0.2%
7	Washington		224	4.3%	46	Rhode Island	12	0.2%
48	West Virginia		11	0.2%	48	West Virginia	11	0.2%
23	Wisconsin		62	1.2%	49	Alaska	9	0.2%
40	Wyoming		20	0.4%	50	Vermont	1	0.0%
						District of Columbia	4	0.1%

Source: U.S. Department of Health and Human Services, Centers for Medicare and Medicaid Services
OSCAR Report 10 (January 08, 2010)
*Certified by CMS to participate in the Medicare/Medicaid programs. Excludes licensed facilities that do not accept federal funding and facilities managed by the Department of Veterans Affairs. National total does not include 29 certified outpatient surgery centers in U.S. territories. Also known as Ambulatory Surgical Centers.

Medicare and Medicaid Certified Community Mental Health Centers in 2010

National Total = 639 Centers*

ALPHA ORDER

RANK ORDER

RANK	STATE	CENTERS	% of USA		RANK	STATE	CENTERS	% of USA
2	Alabama	61	9.5%		1	Florida	143	22.4%
40	Alaska	0	0.0%		2	Alabama	61	9.5%
30	Arizona	3	0.5%		3	Louisiana	53	8.3%
15	Arkansas	13	2.0%		4	Texas	44	6.9%
7	California	20	3.1%		5	New Jersey	28	4.4%
11	Colorado	14	2.2%		6	Washington	25	3.9%
27	Connecticut	5	0.8%		7	California	20	3.1%
40	Delaware	0	0.0%		7	North Carolina	20	3.1%
1	Florida	143	22.4%		9	Tennessee	18	2.8%
20	Georgia	10	1.6%		10	Pennsylvania	16	2.5%
40	Hawaii	0	0.0%		11	Colorado	14	2.2%
40	Idaho	0	0.0%		11	Massachusetts	14	2.2%
18	Illinois	11	1.7%		11	Minnesota	14	2.2%
25	Indiana	7	1.1%		11	New Mexico	14	2.2%
27	Iowa	5	0.8%		15	Arkansas	13	2.0%
22	Kansas	9	1.4%		15	Ohio	13	2.0%
20	Kentucky	10	1.6%		17	Oregon	12	1.9%
3	Louisiana	53	8.3%		18	Illinois	11	1.7%
40	Maine	0	0.0%		18	Missouri	11	1.7%
33	Maryland	2	0.3%		20	Georgia	10	1.6%
11	Massachusetts	14	2.2%		20	Kentucky	10	1.6%
25	Michigan	7	1.1%		22	Kansas	9	1.4%
11	Minnesota	14	2.2%		22	Mississippi	9	1.4%
22	Mississippi	9	1.4%		24	Oklahoma	8	1.3%
18	Missouri	11	1.7%		25	Indiana	7	1.1%
40	Montana	0	0.0%		25	Michigan	7	1.1%
38	Nebraska	1	0.2%		27	Connecticut	5	0.8%
33	Nevada	2	0.3%		27	Iowa	5	0.8%
40	New Hampshire	0	0.0%		29	New York	4	0.6%
5	New Jersey	28	4.4%		30	Arizona	3	0.5%
11	New Mexico	14	2.2%		30	South Carolina	3	0.5%
29	New York	4	0.6%		30	Wyoming	3	0.5%
7	North Carolina	20	3.1%		33	Maryland	2	0.3%
40	North Dakota	0	0.0%		33	Nevada	2	0.3%
15	Ohio	13	2.0%		33	Utah	2	0.3%
24	Oklahoma	8	1.3%		33	Virginia	2	0.3%
17	Oregon	12	1.9%		33	West Virginia	2	0.3%
10	Pennsylvania	16	2.5%		38	Nebraska	1	0.2%
40	Rhode Island	0	0.0%		38	South Dakota	1	0.2%
30	South Carolina	3	0.5%		40	Alaska	0	0.0%
38	South Dakota	1	0.2%		40	Delaware	0	0.0%
9	Tennessee	18	2.8%		40	Hawaii	0	0.0%
4	Texas	44	6.9%		40	Idaho	0	0.0%
33	Utah	2	0.3%		40	Maine	0	0.0%
40	Vermont	0	0.0%		40	Montana	0	0.0%
33	Virginia	2	0.3%		40	New Hampshire	0	0.0%
6	Washington	25	3.9%		40	North Dakota	0	0.0%
33	West Virginia	2	0.3%		40	Rhode Island	0	0.0%
40	Wisconsin	0	0.0%		40	Vermont	0	0.0%
30	Wyoming	3	0.5%		40	Wisconsin	0	0.0%
						District of Columbia	0	0.0%

Source: U.S. Department of Health and Human Services, Centers for Medicare and Medicaid Services
OSCAR Report 10 (January 08, 2010)
*Certified by CMS to participate in the Medicare/Medicaid programs. Excludes licensed facilities that do not accept federal funding and facilities managed by the Department of Veterans Affairs. National total does not include 13 certified mental health centers in U.S. territories.

Medicare and Medicaid Certified Outpatient Physical Therapy Facilities in 2010

National Total = 2,638 Facilities*

<table>
<tr><td colspan="4">ALPHA ORDER</td><td colspan="4">RANK ORDER</td></tr>
<tr><td>RANK</td><td>STATE</td><td>FACILITIES</td><td>% of USA</td><td>RANK</td><td>STATE</td><td>FACILITIES</td><td>% of USA</td></tr>
<tr><td>25</td><td>Alabama</td><td>32</td><td>1.2%</td><td>1</td><td>Florida</td><td>343</td><td>13.0%</td></tr>
<tr><td>36</td><td>Alaska</td><td>13</td><td>0.5%</td><td>2</td><td>Texas</td><td>234</td><td>8.9%</td></tr>
<tr><td>29</td><td>Arizona</td><td>23</td><td>0.9%</td><td>3</td><td>Michigan</td><td>219</td><td>8.3%</td></tr>
<tr><td>29</td><td>Arkansas</td><td>23</td><td>0.9%</td><td>4</td><td>California</td><td>160</td><td>6.1%</td></tr>
<tr><td>4</td><td>California</td><td>160</td><td>6.1%</td><td>5</td><td>Ohio</td><td>125</td><td>4.7%</td></tr>
<tr><td>16</td><td>Colorado</td><td>56</td><td>2.1%</td><td>6</td><td>Virginia</td><td>120</td><td>4.5%</td></tr>
<tr><td>23</td><td>Connecticut</td><td>36</td><td>1.4%</td><td>7</td><td>Pennsylvania</td><td>99</td><td>3.8%</td></tr>
<tr><td>38</td><td>Delaware</td><td>10</td><td>0.4%</td><td>8</td><td>Kentucky</td><td>95</td><td>3.6%</td></tr>
<tr><td>1</td><td>Florida</td><td>343</td><td>13.0%</td><td>9</td><td>Maryland</td><td>86</td><td>3.3%</td></tr>
<tr><td>12</td><td>Georgia</td><td>75</td><td>2.8%</td><td>10</td><td>Illinois</td><td>84</td><td>3.2%</td></tr>
<tr><td>44</td><td>Hawaii</td><td>5</td><td>0.2%</td><td>11</td><td>Tennessee</td><td>76</td><td>2.9%</td></tr>
<tr><td>40</td><td>Idaho</td><td>9</td><td>0.3%</td><td>12</td><td>Georgia</td><td>75</td><td>2.8%</td></tr>
<tr><td>10</td><td>Illinois</td><td>84</td><td>3.2%</td><td>13</td><td>New Jersey</td><td>59</td><td>2.2%</td></tr>
<tr><td>17</td><td>Indiana</td><td>55</td><td>2.1%</td><td>14</td><td>Missouri</td><td>58</td><td>2.2%</td></tr>
<tr><td>24</td><td>Iowa</td><td>35</td><td>1.3%</td><td>15</td><td>North Carolina</td><td>57</td><td>2.2%</td></tr>
<tr><td>28</td><td>Kansas</td><td>24</td><td>0.9%</td><td>16</td><td>Colorado</td><td>56</td><td>2.1%</td></tr>
<tr><td>8</td><td>Kentucky</td><td>95</td><td>3.6%</td><td>17</td><td>Indiana</td><td>55</td><td>2.1%</td></tr>
<tr><td>18</td><td>Louisiana</td><td>49</td><td>1.9%</td><td>18</td><td>Louisiana</td><td>49</td><td>1.9%</td></tr>
<tr><td>35</td><td>Maine</td><td>16</td><td>0.6%</td><td>19</td><td>Oklahoma</td><td>48</td><td>1.8%</td></tr>
<tr><td>9</td><td>Maryland</td><td>86</td><td>3.3%</td><td>20</td><td>South Carolina</td><td>47</td><td>1.8%</td></tr>
<tr><td>33</td><td>Massachusetts</td><td>17</td><td>0.6%</td><td>21</td><td>Minnesota</td><td>42</td><td>1.6%</td></tr>
<tr><td>3</td><td>Michigan</td><td>219</td><td>8.3%</td><td>22</td><td>Wisconsin</td><td>38</td><td>1.4%</td></tr>
<tr><td>21</td><td>Minnesota</td><td>42</td><td>1.6%</td><td>23</td><td>Connecticut</td><td>36</td><td>1.4%</td></tr>
<tr><td>25</td><td>Mississippi</td><td>32</td><td>1.2%</td><td>24</td><td>Iowa</td><td>35</td><td>1.3%</td></tr>
<tr><td>14</td><td>Missouri</td><td>58</td><td>2.2%</td><td>25</td><td>Alabama</td><td>32</td><td>1.2%</td></tr>
<tr><td>47</td><td>Montana</td><td>1</td><td>0.0%</td><td>25</td><td>Mississippi</td><td>32</td><td>1.2%</td></tr>
<tr><td>42</td><td>Nebraska</td><td>8</td><td>0.3%</td><td>27</td><td>New Mexico</td><td>25</td><td>0.9%</td></tr>
<tr><td>32</td><td>Nevada</td><td>19</td><td>0.7%</td><td>28</td><td>Kansas</td><td>24</td><td>0.9%</td></tr>
<tr><td>37</td><td>New Hampshire</td><td>11</td><td>0.4%</td><td>29</td><td>Arizona</td><td>23</td><td>0.9%</td></tr>
<tr><td>13</td><td>New Jersey</td><td>59</td><td>2.2%</td><td>29</td><td>Arkansas</td><td>23</td><td>0.9%</td></tr>
<tr><td>27</td><td>New Mexico</td><td>25</td><td>0.9%</td><td>31</td><td>Washington</td><td>21</td><td>0.8%</td></tr>
<tr><td>33</td><td>New York</td><td>17</td><td>0.6%</td><td>32</td><td>Nevada</td><td>19</td><td>0.7%</td></tr>
<tr><td>15</td><td>North Carolina</td><td>57</td><td>2.2%</td><td>33</td><td>Massachusetts</td><td>17</td><td>0.6%</td></tr>
<tr><td>47</td><td>North Dakota</td><td>1</td><td>0.0%</td><td>33</td><td>New York</td><td>17</td><td>0.6%</td></tr>
<tr><td>5</td><td>Ohio</td><td>125</td><td>4.7%</td><td>35</td><td>Maine</td><td>16</td><td>0.6%</td></tr>
<tr><td>19</td><td>Oklahoma</td><td>48</td><td>1.8%</td><td>36</td><td>Alaska</td><td>13</td><td>0.5%</td></tr>
<tr><td>38</td><td>Oregon</td><td>10</td><td>0.4%</td><td>37</td><td>New Hampshire</td><td>11</td><td>0.4%</td></tr>
<tr><td>7</td><td>Pennsylvania</td><td>99</td><td>3.8%</td><td>38</td><td>Delaware</td><td>10</td><td>0.4%</td></tr>
<tr><td>45</td><td>Rhode Island</td><td>3</td><td>0.1%</td><td>38</td><td>Oregon</td><td>10</td><td>0.4%</td></tr>
<tr><td>20</td><td>South Carolina</td><td>47</td><td>1.8%</td><td>40</td><td>Idaho</td><td>9</td><td>0.3%</td></tr>
<tr><td>46</td><td>South Dakota</td><td>2</td><td>0.1%</td><td>40</td><td>West Virginia</td><td>9</td><td>0.3%</td></tr>
<tr><td>11</td><td>Tennessee</td><td>76</td><td>2.9%</td><td>42</td><td>Nebraska</td><td>8</td><td>0.3%</td></tr>
<tr><td>2</td><td>Texas</td><td>234</td><td>8.9%</td><td>43</td><td>Utah</td><td>6</td><td>0.2%</td></tr>
<tr><td>43</td><td>Utah</td><td>6</td><td>0.2%</td><td>44</td><td>Hawaii</td><td>5</td><td>0.2%</td></tr>
<tr><td>47</td><td>Vermont</td><td>1</td><td>0.0%</td><td>45</td><td>Rhode Island</td><td>3</td><td>0.1%</td></tr>
<tr><td>6</td><td>Virginia</td><td>120</td><td>4.5%</td><td>46</td><td>South Dakota</td><td>2</td><td>0.1%</td></tr>
<tr><td>31</td><td>Washington</td><td>21</td><td>0.8%</td><td>47</td><td>Montana</td><td>1</td><td>0.0%</td></tr>
<tr><td>40</td><td>West Virginia</td><td>9</td><td>0.3%</td><td>47</td><td>North Dakota</td><td>1</td><td>0.0%</td></tr>
<tr><td>22</td><td>Wisconsin</td><td>38</td><td>1.4%</td><td>47</td><td>Vermont</td><td>1</td><td>0.0%</td></tr>
<tr><td>47</td><td>Wyoming</td><td>1</td><td>0.0%</td><td>47</td><td>Wyoming</td><td>1</td><td>0.0%</td></tr>
<tr><td></td><td></td><td></td><td></td><td></td><td>District of Columbia</td><td>3</td><td>0.1%</td></tr>
</table>

Source: U.S. Department of Health and Human Services, Centers for Medicare and Medicaid Services
OSCAR Report 10 (January 08, 2010)

*Certified by CMS to participate in the Medicare/Medicaid programs. Excludes licensed facilities that do not accept federal funding and facilities managed by the Department of Veterans Affairs. National total does not include two certified outpatient physical therapy facilities in U.S. territories.

Medicare and Medicaid Certified Rural Health Clinics in 2010

National Total = 3,752 Rural Health Clinics*

ALPHA ORDER

RANK	STATE	CLINICS	% of USA
19	Alabama	70	1.9%
43	Alaska	2	0.1%
35	Arizona	17	0.5%
18	Arkansas	71	1.9%
3	California	264	7.0%
28	Colorado	47	1.3%
46	Connecticut	0	0.0%
46	Delaware	0	0.0%
10	Florida	137	3.7%
16	Georgia	84	2.2%
43	Hawaii	2	0.1%
30	Idaho	46	1.2%
4	Illinois	210	5.6%
20	Indiana	61	1.6%
9	Iowa	139	3.7%
5	Kansas	175	4.7%
8	Kentucky	142	3.8%
14	Louisiana	107	2.9%
33	Maine	39	1.0%
46	Maryland	0	0.0%
45	Massachusetts	1	0.0%
7	Michigan	156	4.2%
17	Minnesota	76	2.0%
6	Mississippi	157	4.2%
1	Missouri	341	9.1%
30	Montana	46	1.2%
12	Nebraska	125	3.3%
42	Nevada	6	0.2%
38	New Hampshire	12	0.3%
46	New Jersey	0	0.0%
38	New Mexico	12	0.3%
41	New York	8	0.2%
15	North Carolina	86	2.3%
22	North Dakota	59	1.6%
40	Ohio	10	0.3%
32	Oklahoma	40	1.1%
23	Oregon	58	1.5%
23	Pennsylvania	58	1.5%
46	Rhode Island	0	0.0%
13	South Carolina	118	3.1%
20	South Dakota	61	1.6%
25	Tennessee	57	1.5%
2	Texas	314	8.4%
34	Utah	18	0.5%
35	Vermont	17	0.5%
26	Virginia	54	1.4%
11	Washington	132	3.5%
27	West Virginia	53	1.4%
28	Wisconsin	47	1.3%
35	Wyoming	17	0.5%

RANK ORDER

RANK	STATE	CLINICS	% of USA
1	Missouri	341	9.1%
2	Texas	314	8.4%
3	California	264	7.0%
4	Illinois	210	5.6%
5	Kansas	175	4.7%
6	Mississippi	157	4.2%
7	Michigan	156	4.2%
8	Kentucky	142	3.8%
9	Iowa	139	3.7%
10	Florida	137	3.7%
11	Washington	132	3.5%
12	Nebraska	125	3.3%
13	South Carolina	118	3.1%
14	Louisiana	107	2.9%
15	North Carolina	86	2.3%
16	Georgia	84	2.2%
17	Minnesota	76	2.0%
18	Arkansas	71	1.9%
19	Alabama	70	1.9%
20	Indiana	61	1.6%
20	South Dakota	61	1.6%
22	North Dakota	59	1.6%
23	Oregon	58	1.5%
23	Pennsylvania	58	1.5%
25	Tennessee	57	1.5%
26	Virginia	54	1.4%
27	West Virginia	53	1.4%
28	Colorado	47	1.3%
28	Wisconsin	47	1.3%
30	Idaho	46	1.2%
30	Montana	46	1.2%
32	Oklahoma	40	1.1%
33	Maine	39	1.0%
34	Utah	18	0.5%
35	Arizona	17	0.5%
35	Vermont	17	0.5%
35	Wyoming	17	0.5%
38	New Hampshire	12	0.3%
38	New Mexico	12	0.3%
40	Ohio	10	0.3%
41	New York	8	0.2%
42	Nevada	6	0.2%
43	Alaska	2	0.1%
43	Hawaii	2	0.1%
45	Massachusetts	1	0.0%
46	Connecticut	0	0.0%
46	Delaware	0	0.0%
46	Maryland	0	0.0%
46	New Jersey	0	0.0%
46	Rhode Island	0	0.0%
	District of Columbia	0	0.0%

Source: U.S. Department of Health and Human Services, Centers for Medicare and Medicaid Services
OSCAR Report 10 (January 08, 2010)
*Certified by CMS to participate in the Medicare/Medicaid programs. Excludes licensed facilities that do not accept federal funding and facilities managed by the Department of Veterans Affairs. There are no certified rural health centers in U.S. territories.

Medicare and Medicaid Certified Home Health Agencies in 2010

National Total = 10,525 Home Health Agencies*

ALPHA ORDER				RANK ORDER			
RANK	STATE	AGENCIES	% of USA	RANK	STATE	AGENCIES	% of USA
18	Alabama	150	1.4%	1	Texas	2,190	20.8%
48	Alaska	15	0.1%	2	Florida	1,236	11.7%
26	Arizona	102	1.0%	3	California	848	8.1%
16	Arkansas	170	1.6%	4	Illinois	597	5.7%
3	California	848	8.1%	5	Michigan	523	5.0%
19	Colorado	145	1.4%	5	Ohio	523	5.0%
28	Connecticut	85	0.8%	7	Pennsylvania	353	3.4%
47	Delaware	20	0.2%	8	Oklahoma	236	2.2%
2	Florida	1,236	11.7%	9	Indiana	231	2.2%
24	Georgia	103	1.0%	10	Louisiana	219	2.1%
49	Hawaii	14	0.1%	11	Minnesota	207	2.0%
39	Idaho	45	0.4%	12	Virginia	196	1.9%
4	Illinois	597	5.7%	13	New York	195	1.9%
9	Indiana	231	2.2%	14	Missouri	177	1.7%
15	Iowa	173	1.6%	15	Iowa	173	1.6%
22	Kansas	132	1.3%	16	Arkansas	170	1.6%
24	Kentucky	103	1.0%	17	North Carolina	169	1.6%
10	Louisiana	219	2.1%	18	Alabama	150	1.4%
43	Maine	30	0.3%	19	Colorado	145	1.4%
37	Maryland	51	0.5%	20	Tennessee	142	1.3%
21	Massachusetts	134	1.3%	21	Massachusetts	134	1.3%
5	Michigan	523	5.0%	22	Kansas	132	1.3%
11	Minnesota	207	2.0%	23	Wisconsin	125	1.2%
36	Mississippi	55	0.5%	24	Georgia	103	1.0%
14	Missouri	177	1.7%	24	Kentucky	103	1.0%
41	Montana	36	0.3%	26	Arizona	102	1.0%
30	Nebraska	74	0.7%	27	Nevada	91	0.9%
27	Nevada	91	0.9%	28	Connecticut	85	0.8%
42	New Hampshire	35	0.3%	29	Utah	83	0.8%
37	New Jersey	51	0.5%	30	Nebraska	74	0.7%
31	New Mexico	72	0.7%	31	New Mexico	72	0.7%
13	New York	195	1.9%	32	South Carolina	68	0.6%
17	North Carolina	169	1.6%	33	Washington	59	0.6%
46	North Dakota	21	0.2%	34	West Virginia	57	0.5%
5	Ohio	523	5.0%	35	Oregon	56	0.5%
8	Oklahoma	236	2.2%	36	Mississippi	55	0.5%
35	Oregon	56	0.5%	37	Maryland	51	0.5%
7	Pennsylvania	353	3.4%	37	New Jersey	51	0.5%
45	Rhode Island	23	0.2%	39	Idaho	45	0.4%
32	South Carolina	68	0.6%	40	South Dakota	39	0.4%
40	South Dakota	39	0.4%	41	Montana	36	0.3%
20	Tennessee	142	1.3%	42	New Hampshire	35	0.3%
1	Texas	2,190	20.8%	43	Maine	30	0.3%
29	Utah	83	0.8%	44	Wyoming	27	0.3%
50	Vermont	12	0.1%	45	Rhode Island	23	0.2%
12	Virginia	196	1.9%	46	North Dakota	21	0.2%
33	Washington	59	0.6%	47	Delaware	20	0.2%
34	West Virginia	57	0.5%	48	Alaska	15	0.1%
23	Wisconsin	125	1.2%	49	Hawaii	14	0.1%
44	Wyoming	27	0.3%	50	Vermont	12	0.1%
					District of Columbia	27	0.3%

Source: U.S. Department of Health and Human Services, Centers for Medicare and Medicaid Services
   OSCAR Report 10 (January 08, 2010)
*Certified by CMS to participate in the Medicare/Medicaid programs. Excludes agencies that do not accept federal funding. National total does not include 56 certified home health agencies in U.S. territories. A home health agency provides health services to individuals in their homes for the purpose of promoting, maintaining, or restoring health or maximizing the level of independence, while minimizing the effects of disability and illness.

Medicare and Medicaid Certified Hospices in 2010

National Total = 3,366 Hospices*

<table>
<tr><td colspan="4">ALPHA ORDER</td><td colspan="4">RANK ORDER</td></tr>
<tr><th>RANK</th><th>STATE</th><th>HOSPICES</th><th>% of USA</th><th>RANK</th><th>STATE</th><th>HOSPICES</th><th>% of USA</th></tr>
<tr><td>7</td><td>Alabama</td><td>124</td><td>3.7%</td><td>1</td><td>Texas</td><td>325</td><td>9.7%</td></tr>
<tr><td>50</td><td>Alaska</td><td>4</td><td>0.1%</td><td>2</td><td>California</td><td>243</td><td>7.2%</td></tr>
<tr><td>22</td><td>Arizona</td><td>63</td><td>1.9%</td><td>3</td><td>Pennsylvania</td><td>171</td><td>5.1%</td></tr>
<tr><td>26</td><td>Arkansas</td><td>51</td><td>1.5%</td><td>4</td><td>Georgia</td><td>142</td><td>4.2%</td></tr>
<tr><td>2</td><td>California</td><td>243</td><td>7.2%</td><td>5</td><td>Oklahoma</td><td>140</td><td>4.2%</td></tr>
<tr><td>27</td><td>Colorado</td><td>49</td><td>1.5%</td><td>6</td><td>Louisiana</td><td>126</td><td>3.7%</td></tr>
<tr><td>35</td><td>Connecticut</td><td>31</td><td>0.9%</td><td>7</td><td>Alabama</td><td>124</td><td>3.7%</td></tr>
<tr><td>47</td><td>Delaware</td><td>9</td><td>0.3%</td><td>8</td><td>Mississippi</td><td>118</td><td>3.5%</td></tr>
<tr><td>30</td><td>Florida</td><td>41</td><td>1.2%</td><td>9</td><td>Ohio</td><td>112</td><td>3.3%</td></tr>
<tr><td>4</td><td>Georgia</td><td>142</td><td>4.2%</td><td>10</td><td>Illinois</td><td>102</td><td>3.0%</td></tr>
<tr><td>48</td><td>Hawaii</td><td>8</td><td>0.2%</td><td>10</td><td>Missouri</td><td>102</td><td>3.0%</td></tr>
<tr><td>32</td><td>Idaho</td><td>38</td><td>1.1%</td><td>12</td><td>Michigan</td><td>98</td><td>2.9%</td></tr>
<tr><td>10</td><td>Illinois</td><td>102</td><td>3.0%</td><td>13</td><td>Indiana</td><td>84</td><td>2.5%</td></tr>
<tr><td>13</td><td>Indiana</td><td>84</td><td>2.5%</td><td>14</td><td>South Carolina</td><td>82</td><td>2.4%</td></tr>
<tr><td>16</td><td>Iowa</td><td>78</td><td>2.3%</td><td>15</td><td>North Carolina</td><td>81</td><td>2.4%</td></tr>
<tr><td>24</td><td>Kansas</td><td>56</td><td>1.7%</td><td>16</td><td>Iowa</td><td>78</td><td>2.3%</td></tr>
<tr><td>37</td><td>Kentucky</td><td>27</td><td>0.8%</td><td>17</td><td>Virginia</td><td>75</td><td>2.2%</td></tr>
<tr><td>6</td><td>Louisiana</td><td>126</td><td>3.7%</td><td>18</td><td>Massachusetts</td><td>71</td><td>2.1%</td></tr>
<tr><td>40</td><td>Maine</td><td>20</td><td>0.6%</td><td>19</td><td>Utah</td><td>67</td><td>2.0%</td></tr>
<tr><td>37</td><td>Maryland</td><td>27</td><td>0.8%</td><td>20</td><td>Minnesota</td><td>65</td><td>1.9%</td></tr>
<tr><td>18</td><td>Massachusetts</td><td>71</td><td>2.1%</td><td>20</td><td>Wisconsin</td><td>65</td><td>1.9%</td></tr>
<tr><td>12</td><td>Michigan</td><td>98</td><td>2.9%</td><td>22</td><td>Arizona</td><td>63</td><td>1.9%</td></tr>
<tr><td>20</td><td>Minnesota</td><td>65</td><td>1.9%</td><td>23</td><td>New Jersey</td><td>57</td><td>1.7%</td></tr>
<tr><td>8</td><td>Mississippi</td><td>118</td><td>3.5%</td><td>24</td><td>Kansas</td><td>56</td><td>1.7%</td></tr>
<tr><td>10</td><td>Missouri</td><td>102</td><td>3.0%</td><td>25</td><td>Tennessee</td><td>55</td><td>1.6%</td></tr>
<tr><td>36</td><td>Montana</td><td>29</td><td>0.9%</td><td>26</td><td>Arkansas</td><td>51</td><td>1.5%</td></tr>
<tr><td>33</td><td>Nebraska</td><td>33</td><td>1.0%</td><td>27</td><td>Colorado</td><td>49</td><td>1.5%</td></tr>
<tr><td>42</td><td>Nevada</td><td>19</td><td>0.6%</td><td>27</td><td>New York</td><td>49</td><td>1.5%</td></tr>
<tr><td>39</td><td>New Hampshire</td><td>22</td><td>0.7%</td><td>29</td><td>Oregon</td><td>47</td><td>1.4%</td></tr>
<tr><td>23</td><td>New Jersey</td><td>57</td><td>1.7%</td><td>30</td><td>Florida</td><td>41</td><td>1.2%</td></tr>
<tr><td>31</td><td>New Mexico</td><td>40</td><td>1.2%</td><td>31</td><td>New Mexico</td><td>40</td><td>1.2%</td></tr>
<tr><td>27</td><td>New York</td><td>49</td><td>1.5%</td><td>32</td><td>Idaho</td><td>38</td><td>1.1%</td></tr>
<tr><td>15</td><td>North Carolina</td><td>81</td><td>2.4%</td><td>33</td><td>Nebraska</td><td>33</td><td>1.0%</td></tr>
<tr><td>45</td><td>North Dakota</td><td>14</td><td>0.4%</td><td>34</td><td>Washington</td><td>32</td><td>1.0%</td></tr>
<tr><td>9</td><td>Ohio</td><td>112</td><td>3.3%</td><td>35</td><td>Connecticut</td><td>31</td><td>0.9%</td></tr>
<tr><td>5</td><td>Oklahoma</td><td>140</td><td>4.2%</td><td>36</td><td>Montana</td><td>29</td><td>0.9%</td></tr>
<tr><td>29</td><td>Oregon</td><td>47</td><td>1.4%</td><td>37</td><td>Kentucky</td><td>27</td><td>0.8%</td></tr>
<tr><td>3</td><td>Pennsylvania</td><td>171</td><td>5.1%</td><td>37</td><td>Maryland</td><td>27</td><td>0.8%</td></tr>
<tr><td>48</td><td>Rhode Island</td><td>8</td><td>0.2%</td><td>39</td><td>New Hampshire</td><td>22</td><td>0.7%</td></tr>
<tr><td>14</td><td>South Carolina</td><td>82</td><td>2.4%</td><td>40</td><td>Maine</td><td>20</td><td>0.6%</td></tr>
<tr><td>44</td><td>South Dakota</td><td>16</td><td>0.5%</td><td>40</td><td>West Virginia</td><td>20</td><td>0.6%</td></tr>
<tr><td>25</td><td>Tennessee</td><td>55</td><td>1.6%</td><td>42</td><td>Nevada</td><td>19</td><td>0.6%</td></tr>
<tr><td>1</td><td>Texas</td><td>325</td><td>9.7%</td><td>43</td><td>Wyoming</td><td>17</td><td>0.5%</td></tr>
<tr><td>19</td><td>Utah</td><td>67</td><td>2.0%</td><td>44</td><td>South Dakota</td><td>16</td><td>0.5%</td></tr>
<tr><td>46</td><td>Vermont</td><td>10</td><td>0.3%</td><td>45</td><td>North Dakota</td><td>14</td><td>0.4%</td></tr>
<tr><td>17</td><td>Virginia</td><td>75</td><td>2.2%</td><td>46</td><td>Vermont</td><td>10</td><td>0.3%</td></tr>
<tr><td>34</td><td>Washington</td><td>32</td><td>1.0%</td><td>47</td><td>Delaware</td><td>9</td><td>0.3%</td></tr>
<tr><td>40</td><td>West Virginia</td><td>20</td><td>0.6%</td><td>48</td><td>Hawaii</td><td>8</td><td>0.2%</td></tr>
<tr><td>20</td><td>Wisconsin</td><td>65</td><td>1.9%</td><td>48</td><td>Rhode Island</td><td>8</td><td>0.2%</td></tr>
<tr><td>43</td><td>Wyoming</td><td>17</td><td>0.5%</td><td>50</td><td>Alaska</td><td>4</td><td>0.1%</td></tr>
<tr><td></td><td></td><td></td><td></td><td></td><td>District of Columbia</td><td>3</td><td>0.1%</td></tr>
</table>

Source: U.S. Department of Health and Human Services, Centers for Medicare and Medicaid Services
    OSCAR Report 10 (January 08, 2010)
*Certified by CMS to participate in the Medicare/Medicaid programs. Excludes licensed facilities that do not accept federal funding and facilities managed by the Department of Veterans Affairs. National total does not include 41 certified hospices in U.S. territories. A hospice provides specialized services for terminally ill people and their families.

Hospice Patients in Residential Facilities in 2010

National Total = 81,654 Patients*

ALPHA ORDER

RANK	STATE	PATIENTS	% of USA
22	Alabama	1,238	1.5%
50	Alaska	9	0.0%
12	Arizona	2,335	2.9%
37	Arkansas	439	0.5%
6	California	3,315	4.1%
28	Colorado	1,068	1.3%
20	Connecticut	1,339	1.6%
40	Delaware	383	0.5%
1	Florida	9,111	11.2%
11	Georgia	2,359	2.9%
48	Hawaii	56	0.1%
44	Idaho	151	0.2%
5	Illinois	3,909	4.8%
13	Indiana	1,842	2.3%
27	Iowa	1,086	1.3%
30	Kansas	822	1.0%
32	Kentucky	601	0.7%
31	Louisiana	633	0.8%
17	Maine	1,633	2.0%
41	Maryland	358	0.4%
8	Massachusetts	2,831	3.5%
9	Michigan	2,657	3.3%
25	Minnesota	1,180	1.4%
34	Mississippi	514	0.6%
10	Missouri	2,585	3.2%
29	Montana	962	1.2%
37	Nebraska	439	0.5%
44	Nevada	151	0.2%
36	New Hampshire	441	0.5%
21	New Jersey	1,299	1.6%
35	New Mexico	466	0.6%
18	New York	1,371	1.7%
7	North Carolina	2,857	3.5%
46	North Dakota	80	0.1%
4	Ohio	4,464	5.5%
14	Oklahoma	1,805	2.2%
15	Oregon	1,780	2.2%
2	Pennsylvania	8,211	10.1%
26	Rhode Island	1,143	1.4%
33	South Carolina	582	0.7%
42	South Dakota	357	0.4%
23	Tennessee	1,218	1.5%
3	Texas	6,446	7.9%
39	Utah	391	0.5%
47	Vermont	59	0.1%
24	Virginia	1,202	1.5%
19	Washington	1,367	1.7%
43	West Virginia	203	0.2%
16	Wisconsin	1,767	2.2%
49	Wyoming	33	0.0%

RANK ORDER

RANK	STATE	PATIENTS	% of USA
1	Florida	9,111	11.2%
2	Pennsylvania	8,211	10.1%
3	Texas	6,446	7.9%
4	Ohio	4,464	5.5%
5	Illinois	3,909	4.8%
6	California	3,315	4.1%
7	North Carolina	2,857	3.5%
8	Massachusetts	2,831	3.5%
9	Michigan	2,657	3.3%
10	Missouri	2,585	3.2%
11	Georgia	2,359	2.9%
12	Arizona	2,335	2.9%
13	Indiana	1,842	2.3%
14	Oklahoma	1,805	2.2%
15	Oregon	1,780	2.2%
16	Wisconsin	1,767	2.2%
17	Maine	1,633	2.0%
18	New York	1,371	1.7%
19	Washington	1,367	1.7%
20	Connecticut	1,339	1.6%
21	New Jersey	1,299	1.6%
22	Alabama	1,238	1.5%
23	Tennessee	1,218	1.5%
24	Virginia	1,202	1.5%
25	Minnesota	1,180	1.4%
26	Rhode Island	1,143	1.4%
27	Iowa	1,086	1.3%
28	Colorado	1,068	1.3%
29	Montana	962	1.2%
30	Kansas	822	1.0%
31	Louisiana	633	0.8%
32	Kentucky	601	0.7%
33	South Carolina	582	0.7%
34	Mississippi	514	0.6%
35	New Mexico	466	0.6%
36	New Hampshire	441	0.5%
37	Arkansas	439	0.5%
37	Nebraska	439	0.5%
39	Utah	391	0.5%
40	Delaware	383	0.5%
41	Maryland	358	0.4%
42	South Dakota	357	0.4%
43	West Virginia	203	0.2%
44	Idaho	151	0.2%
44	Nevada	151	0.2%
46	North Dakota	80	0.1%
47	Vermont	59	0.1%
48	Hawaii	56	0.1%
49	Wyoming	33	0.0%
50	Alaska	9	0.0%
	District of Columbia	106	0.1%

Source: U.S. Department of Health and Human Services, Centers for Medicare and Medicaid Services
   OSCAR Database (January 08, 2010)
*Patients in facilities certified by CMS to participate in the Medicare/Medicaid programs. Excludes licensed facilities that do not accept federal funding and facilities managed by the Department of Veterans Affairs. National total does not include 28 patients in U.S. territories. A hospice provides specialized services for terminally ill people and their families.

Medicare and Medicaid Certified Nursing Care Facilities in 2010

National Total = 15,711 Nursing Care Facilities*

ALPHA ORDER

RANK	STATE	FACILITIES	% of USA
26	Alabama	231	1.5%
50	Alaska	15	0.1%
34	Arizona	135	0.9%
26	Arkansas	231	1.5%
1	California	1,252	8.0%
30	Colorado	211	1.3%
24	Connecticut	239	1.5%
46	Delaware	47	0.3%
6	Florida	676	4.3%
16	Georgia	360	2.3%
46	Hawaii	47	0.3%
43	Idaho	79	0.5%
4	Illinois	794	5.1%
9	Indiana	503	3.2%
10	Iowa	447	2.8%
18	Kansas	341	2.2%
21	Kentucky	287	1.8%
22	Louisiana	283	1.8%
36	Maine	109	0.7%
26	Maryland	231	1.5%
11	Massachusetts	429	2.7%
11	Michigan	429	2.7%
15	Minnesota	385	2.5%
31	Mississippi	202	1.3%
8	Missouri	513	3.3%
39	Montana	90	0.6%
29	Nebraska	225	1.4%
45	Nevada	49	0.3%
42	New Hampshire	80	0.5%
17	New Jersey	359	2.3%
44	New Mexico	71	0.5%
7	New York	640	4.1%
13	North Carolina	424	2.7%
41	North Dakota	83	0.5%
3	Ohio	962	6.1%
20	Oklahoma	317	2.0%
33	Oregon	137	0.9%
5	Pennsylvania	713	4.5%
40	Rhode Island	86	0.5%
32	South Carolina	178	1.1%
36	South Dakota	109	0.7%
19	Tennessee	320	2.0%
2	Texas	1,167	7.4%
38	Utah	96	0.6%
48	Vermont	40	0.3%
23	Virginia	281	1.8%
25	Washington	232	1.5%
35	West Virginia	128	0.8%
14	Wisconsin	391	2.5%
49	Wyoming	38	0.2%

RANK ORDER

RANK	STATE	FACILITIES	% of USA
1	California	1,252	8.0%
2	Texas	1,167	7.4%
3	Ohio	962	6.1%
4	Illinois	794	5.1%
5	Pennsylvania	713	4.5%
6	Florida	676	4.3%
7	New York	640	4.1%
8	Missouri	513	3.3%
9	Indiana	503	3.2%
10	Iowa	447	2.8%
11	Massachusetts	429	2.7%
11	Michigan	429	2.7%
13	North Carolina	424	2.7%
14	Wisconsin	391	2.5%
15	Minnesota	385	2.5%
16	Georgia	360	2.3%
17	New Jersey	359	2.3%
18	Kansas	341	2.2%
19	Tennessee	320	2.0%
20	Oklahoma	317	2.0%
21	Kentucky	287	1.8%
22	Louisiana	283	1.8%
23	Virginia	281	1.8%
24	Connecticut	239	1.5%
25	Washington	232	1.5%
26	Alabama	231	1.5%
26	Arkansas	231	1.5%
26	Maryland	231	1.5%
29	Nebraska	225	1.4%
30	Colorado	211	1.3%
31	Mississippi	202	1.3%
32	South Carolina	178	1.1%
33	Oregon	137	0.9%
34	Arizona	135	0.9%
35	West Virginia	128	0.8%
36	Maine	109	0.7%
36	South Dakota	109	0.7%
38	Utah	96	0.6%
39	Montana	90	0.6%
40	Rhode Island	86	0.5%
41	North Dakota	83	0.5%
42	New Hampshire	80	0.5%
43	Idaho	79	0.5%
44	New Mexico	71	0.5%
45	Nevada	49	0.3%
46	Delaware	47	0.3%
46	Hawaii	47	0.3%
48	Vermont	40	0.3%
49	Wyoming	38	0.2%
50	Alaska	15	0.1%
	District of Columbia	19	0.1%

Source: U.S. Department of Health and Human Services, Centers for Medicare and Medicaid Services
OSCAR Report 10 (January 08, 2010)
*Certified by CMS to participate in the Medicare/Medicaid programs. Excludes licensed facilities that do not accept federal funding and facilities managed by the Department of Veterans Affairs. National total does not include nine certified nursing facilities in U.S. territories.

Beds in Medicare and Medicaid Certified Nursing Care Facilities in 2010

National Total = 1,670,469 Beds*

ALPHA ORDER

RANK	STATE	BEDS	% of USA
24	Alabama	26,790	1.6%
50	Alaska	716	0.0%
33	Arizona	15,387	0.9%
26	Arkansas	24,466	1.5%
2	California	121,447	7.3%
29	Colorado	19,906	1.2%
22	Connecticut	28,848	1.7%
46	Delaware	5,004	0.3%
7	Florida	81,598	4.9%
14	Georgia	39,993	2.4%
47	Hawaii	4,135	0.2%
44	Idaho	6,159	0.4%
4	Illinois	96,097	5.8%
10	Indiana	48,782	2.9%
19	Iowa	32,057	1.9%
27	Kansas	22,817	1.4%
25	Kentucky	25,848	1.5%
17	Louisiana	34,916	2.1%
39	Maine	7,084	0.4%
23	Maryland	28,715	1.7%
11	Massachusetts	48,429	2.9%
12	Michigan	46,988	2.8%
18	Minnesota	32,698	2.0%
31	Mississippi	18,472	1.1%
8	Missouri	51,995	3.1%
40	Montana	7,038	0.4%
32	Nebraska	15,923	1.0%
45	Nevada	5,679	0.3%
38	New Hampshire	7,742	0.5%
9	New Jersey	50,965	3.1%
41	New Mexico	6,827	0.4%
3	New York	118,911	7.1%
13	North Carolina	43,491	2.6%
43	North Dakota	6,305	0.4%
5	Ohio	93,203	5.6%
21	Oklahoma	28,981	1.7%
34	Oregon	12,313	0.7%
6	Pennsylvania	88,895	5.3%
36	Rhode Island	8,795	0.5%
30	South Carolina	18,642	1.1%
42	South Dakota	6,469	0.4%
15	Tennessee	37,116	2.2%
1	Texas	126,034	7.5%
37	Utah	7,990	0.5%
48	Vermont	3,285	0.2%
20	Virginia	31,685	1.9%
28	Washington	21,921	1.3%
35	West Virginia	10,805	0.6%
16	Wisconsin	36,428	2.2%
49	Wyoming	2,974	0.2%

RANK ORDER

RANK	STATE	BEDS	% of USA
1	Texas	126,034	7.5%
2	California	121,447	7.3%
3	New York	118,911	7.1%
4	Illinois	96,097	5.8%
5	Ohio	93,203	5.6%
6	Pennsylvania	88,895	5.3%
7	Florida	81,598	4.9%
8	Missouri	51,995	3.1%
9	New Jersey	50,965	3.1%
10	Indiana	48,782	2.9%
11	Massachusetts	48,429	2.9%
12	Michigan	46,988	2.8%
13	North Carolina	43,491	2.6%
14	Georgia	39,993	2.4%
15	Tennessee	37,116	2.2%
16	Wisconsin	36,428	2.2%
17	Louisiana	34,916	2.1%
18	Minnesota	32,698	2.0%
19	Iowa	32,057	1.9%
20	Virginia	31,685	1.9%
21	Oklahoma	28,981	1.7%
22	Connecticut	28,848	1.7%
23	Maryland	28,715	1.7%
24	Alabama	26,790	1.6%
25	Kentucky	25,848	1.5%
26	Arkansas	24,466	1.5%
27	Kansas	22,817	1.4%
28	Washington	21,921	1.3%
29	Colorado	19,906	1.2%
30	South Carolina	18,642	1.1%
31	Mississippi	18,472	1.1%
32	Nebraska	15,923	1.0%
33	Arizona	15,387	0.9%
34	Oregon	12,313	0.7%
35	West Virginia	10,805	0.6%
36	Rhode Island	8,795	0.5%
37	Utah	7,990	0.5%
38	New Hampshire	7,742	0.5%
39	Maine	7,084	0.4%
40	Montana	7,038	0.4%
41	New Mexico	6,827	0.4%
42	South Dakota	6,469	0.4%
43	North Dakota	6,305	0.4%
44	Idaho	6,159	0.4%
45	Nevada	5,679	0.3%
46	Delaware	5,004	0.3%
47	Hawaii	4,135	0.2%
48	Vermont	3,285	0.2%
49	Wyoming	2,974	0.2%
50	Alaska	716	0.0%
	District of Columbia	2,705	0.2%

Source: U.S. Department of Health and Human Services, Centers for Medicare and Medicaid Services
OSCAR Database (January 08, 2010)
*Beds in nursing care facilities certified by CMS to participate in the Medicare/Medicaid programs. National total does not include 353 beds in U.S. territories.

Rate of Beds in Medicare and Medicaid Certified Nursing Care Facilities in 2010

National Rate = 292 Beds per 1,000 Population 85 Years and Older*

ALPHA ORDER

RANK	STATE	RATE
23	Alabama	315
48	Alaska	148
50	Arizona	125
3	Arkansas	417
42	California	198
30	Colorado	296
12	Connecticut	365
27	Delaware	310
47	Florida	157
21	Georgia	327
49	Hawaii	131
41	Idaho	242
8	Illinois	402
5	Indiana	411
7	Iowa	407
11	Kansas	366
17	Kentucky	346
1	Louisiana	483
38	Maine	247
24	Maryland	313
18	Massachusetts	338
37	Michigan	252
28	Minnesota	306
14	Mississippi	354
2	Missouri	427
16	Montana	348
9	Nebraska	388
45	Nevada	178
22	New Hampshire	316
32	New Jersey	291
44	New Mexico	190
29	New York	299
31	North Carolina	294
13	North Dakota	355
6	Ohio	408
4	Oklahoma	415
46	Oregon	162
33	Pennsylvania	287
18	Rhode Island	338
39	South Carolina	243
24	South Dakota	313
15	Tennessee	350
10	Texas	379
39	Utah	243
35	Vermont	266
36	Virginia	260
43	Washington	191
34	West Virginia	281
26	Wisconsin	311
20	Wyoming	331

RANK ORDER

RANK	STATE	RATE
1	Louisiana	483
2	Missouri	427
3	Arkansas	417
4	Oklahoma	415
5	Indiana	411
6	Ohio	408
7	Iowa	407
8	Illinois	402
9	Nebraska	388
10	Texas	379
11	Kansas	366
12	Connecticut	365
13	North Dakota	355
14	Mississippi	354
15	Tennessee	350
16	Montana	348
17	Kentucky	346
18	Massachusetts	338
18	Rhode Island	338
20	Wyoming	331
21	Georgia	327
22	New Hampshire	316
23	Alabama	315
24	Maryland	313
24	South Dakota	313
26	Wisconsin	311
27	Delaware	310
28	Minnesota	306
29	New York	299
30	Colorado	296
31	North Carolina	294
32	New Jersey	291
33	Pennsylvania	287
34	West Virginia	281
35	Vermont	266
36	Virginia	260
37	Michigan	252
38	Maine	247
39	South Carolina	243
39	Utah	243
41	Idaho	242
42	California	198
43	Washington	191
44	New Mexico	190
45	Nevada	178
46	Oregon	162
47	Florida	157
48	Alaska	148
49	Hawaii	131
50	Arizona	125

District of Columbia	243

Source: CQ Press using data from U.S. Department of Health and Human Services, Centers for Medicare and Medicaid Services OSCAR Database (January 08, 2010)
*Beds in nursing care facilities certified by CMS to participate in the Medicare/Medicaid programs. National rate does not include beds or population in U.S. territories. Calculated using 2008 Census population estimates.

Nursing Home Occupancy Rate in 2007

National Rate = 83.2% of Beds in Nursing Homes Occupied

ALPHA ORDER

RANK	STATE	RATE
20	Alabama	87.8
27	Alaska	86.6
38	Arizona	76.6
43	Arkansas	72.7
31	California	83.9
32	Colorado	83.7
10	Connecticut	90.8
33	Delaware	83.4
21	Florida	87.7
19	Georgia	88.8
2	Hawaii	92.5
41	Idaho	74.6
40	Illinois	74.9
48	Indiana	69.2
37	Iowa	77.6
39	Kansas	75.5
13	Kentucky	89.7
42	Louisiana	73.2
11	Maine	90.6
24	Maryland	87.3
18	Massachusetts	89.2
30	Michigan	86.1
7	Minnesota	91.2
13	Mississippi	89.7
47	Missouri	69.3
44	Montana	72.4
35	Nebraska	80.9
34	Nevada	83.2
13	New Hampshire	89.7
17	New Jersey	89.3
28	New Mexico	86.5
4	New York	92.2
26	North Carolina	86.9
5	North Dakota	92.1
25	Ohio	87.1
49	Oklahoma	65.8
50	Oregon	65.2
8	Pennsylvania	91.1
3	Rhode Island	92.4
9	South Carolina	91.0
1	South Dakota	100.0
23	Tennessee	87.4
45	Texas	71.7
46	Utah	69.4
6	Vermont	91.3
16	Virginia	89.4
29	Washington	86.2
12	West Virginia	89.8
22	Wisconsin	87.6
36	Wyoming	80.1

RANK ORDER

RANK	STATE	RATE
1	South Dakota	100.0
2	Hawaii	92.5
3	Rhode Island	92.4
4	New York	92.2
5	North Dakota	92.1
6	Vermont	91.3
7	Minnesota	91.2
8	Pennsylvania	91.1
9	South Carolina	91.0
10	Connecticut	90.8
11	Maine	90.6
12	West Virginia	89.8
13	Kentucky	89.7
13	Mississippi	89.7
13	New Hampshire	89.7
16	Virginia	89.4
17	New Jersey	89.3
18	Massachusetts	89.2
19	Georgia	88.8
20	Alabama	87.8
21	Florida	87.7
22	Wisconsin	87.6
23	Tennessee	87.4
24	Maryland	87.3
25	Ohio	87.1
26	North Carolina	86.9
27	Alaska	86.6
28	New Mexico	86.5
29	Washington	86.2
30	Michigan	86.1
31	California	83.9
32	Colorado	83.7
33	Delaware	83.4
34	Nevada	83.2
35	Nebraska	80.9
36	Wyoming	80.1
37	Iowa	77.6
38	Arizona	76.6
39	Kansas	75.5
40	Illinois	74.9
41	Idaho	74.6
42	Louisiana	73.2
43	Arkansas	72.7
44	Montana	72.4
45	Texas	71.7
46	Utah	69.4
47	Missouri	69.3
48	Indiana	69.2
49	Oklahoma	65.8
50	Oregon	65.2

District of Columbia	94.0

Source: U.S. Department of Health and Human Services, Centers for Medicare and Medicaid Services
"Health, United States, 2008" (www.cdc.gov/nchs/data/hus/hus08.pdf)

Nursing Home Resident Rate in 2007

National Rate = 258.5 Residents per 1,000 Population Age 85 and Older*

ALPHA ORDER				RANK ORDER		
RANK	STATE	RATE		RANK	STATE	RATE
24	Alabama	285.2		1	Louisiana	387.0
47	Alaska	138.2		2	Ohio	365.8
50	Arizona	110.4		3	Connecticut	350.5
17	Arkansas	314.6		4	Indiana	348.7
41	California	179.0		5	Iowa	342.5
34	Colorado	256.5		6	North Dakota	339.6
3	Connecticut	350.5		7	Illinois	329.6
33	Delaware	261.1		8	Nebraska	328.8
46	Florida	146.5		9	South Dakota	326.2
19	Georgia	302.3		10	Kentucky	326.1
48	Hawaii	130.3		11	Mississippi	325.6
40	Idaho	182.9		12	Kansas	324.5
7	Illinois	329.6		13	Massachusetts	320.2
4	Indiana	348.7		13	Missouri	320.2
5	Iowa	342.5		15	Rhode Island	319.9
12	Kansas	324.5		16	Tennessee	319.1
10	Kentucky	326.1		17	Arkansas	314.6
1	Louisiana	387.0		18	Minnesota	304.3
37	Maine	236.3		19	Georgia	302.3
26	Maryland	284.9		20	New Hampshire	291.4
13	Massachusetts	320.2		21	New York	289.9
39	Michigan	223.5		22	Oklahoma	289.6
18	Minnesota	304.3		23	Wisconsin	288.1
11	Mississippi	325.6		24	Alabama	285.2
13	Missouri	320.2		24	Wyoming	285.2
32	Montana	262.3		26	Maryland	284.9
8	Nebraska	328.8		27	Texas	282.6
45	Nevada	158.2		28	New Jersey	269.2
20	New Hampshire	291.4		29	North Carolina	267.7
28	New Jersey	269.2		30	Pennsylvania	265.5
43	New Mexico	176.5		31	West Virginia	262.6
21	New York	289.9		32	Montana	262.3
29	North Carolina	267.7		33	Delaware	261.1
6	North Dakota	339.6		34	Colorado	256.5
2	Ohio	365.8		35	Vermont	252.8
22	Oklahoma	289.6		36	Virginia	241.7
49	Oregon	111.1		37	Maine	236.3
30	Pennsylvania	265.5		38	South Carolina	232.1
15	Rhode Island	319.9		39	Michigan	223.5
38	South Carolina	232.1		40	Idaho	182.9
9	South Dakota	326.2		41	California	179.0
16	Tennessee	319.1		42	Utah	176.8
27	Texas	282.6		43	New Mexico	176.5
42	Utah	176.8		44	Washington	172.5
35	Vermont	252.8		45	Nevada	158.2
36	Virginia	241.7		46	Florida	146.5
44	Washington	172.5		47	Alaska	138.2
31	West Virginia	262.6		48	Hawaii	130.3
23	Wisconsin	288.1		49	Oregon	111.1
24	Wyoming	285.2		50	Arizona	110.4
					District of Columbia	262.6

Source: U.S. Department of Health and Human Services, Centers for Medicare and Medicaid Services
"Health, United States, 2008" (www.cdc.gov/nchs/data/hus/hus08.pdf)
*Number of nursing home residents (all ages) per 1,000 resident population 85 years of age and over.

Nursing Home Population in 2007

National Total = 1,442,824

ALPHA ORDER

RANK	STATE	POPULATION	% of USA
24	Alabama	23,392	1.6%
50	Alaska	628	0.0%
33	Arizona	12,447	0.9%
28	Arkansas	17,857	1.3%
2	California	104,610	7.3%
30	Colorado	16,608	1.2%
19	Connecticut	27,257	1.9%
46	Delaware	4,004	0.3%
7	Florida	72,326	5.1%
14	Georgia	35,682	2.5%
47	Hawaii	3,830	0.3%
45	Idaho	4,513	0.3%
6	Illinois	76,974	5.4%
11	Indiana	39,986	2.8%
21	Iowa	26,505	1.9%
26	Kansas	19,701	1.4%
23	Kentucky	23,393	1.6%
20	Louisiana	26,556	1.9%
38	Maine	6,598	0.5%
22	Maryland	25,456	1.8%
9	Massachusetts	44,746	3.1%
10	Michigan	40,626	2.9%
17	Minnesota	31,909	2.2%
31	Mississippi	16,498	1.2%
13	Missouri	37,794	2.7%
43	Montana	5,204	0.4%
32	Nebraska	13,176	0.9%
44	Nevada	4,724	0.3%
37	New Hampshire	6,978	0.5%
8	New Jersey	45,551	3.2%
40	New Mexico	5,981	0.4%
1	New York	111,510	7.8%
12	North Carolina	38,176	2.7%
41	North Dakota	5,926	0.4%
4	Ohio	81,146	5.7%
25	Oklahoma	19,769	1.4%
35	Oregon	8,134	0.6%
5	Pennsylvania	80,266	5.6%
36	Rhode Island	8,112	0.6%
29	South Carolina	16,827	1.2%
39	South Dakota	6,553	0.5%
16	Tennessee	32,633	2.3%
3	Texas	89,967	6.3%
42	Utah	5,486	0.4%
48	Vermont	3,051	0.2%
18	Virginia	28,321	2.0%
27	Washington	19,223	1.3%
34	West Virginia	9,826	0.7%
15	Wisconsin	33,139	2.3%
49	Wyoming	2,445	0.2%

RANK ORDER

RANK	STATE	POPULATION	% of USA
1	New York	111,510	7.8%
2	California	104,610	7.3%
3	Texas	89,967	6.3%
4	Ohio	81,146	5.7%
5	Pennsylvania	80,266	5.6%
6	Illinois	76,974	5.4%
7	Florida	72,326	5.1%
8	New Jersey	45,551	3.2%
9	Massachusetts	44,746	3.1%
10	Michigan	40,626	2.9%
11	Indiana	39,986	2.8%
12	North Carolina	38,176	2.7%
13	Missouri	37,794	2.7%
14	Georgia	35,682	2.5%
15	Wisconsin	33,139	2.3%
16	Tennessee	32,633	2.3%
17	Minnesota	31,909	2.2%
18	Virginia	28,321	2.0%
19	Connecticut	27,257	1.9%
20	Louisiana	26,556	1.9%
21	Iowa	26,505	1.9%
22	Maryland	25,456	1.8%
23	Kentucky	23,393	1.6%
24	Alabama	23,392	1.6%
25	Oklahoma	19,769	1.4%
26	Kansas	19,701	1.4%
27	Washington	19,223	1.3%
28	Arkansas	17,857	1.3%
29	South Carolina	16,827	1.2%
30	Colorado	16,608	1.2%
31	Mississippi	16,498	1.2%
32	Nebraska	13,176	0.9%
33	Arizona	12,447	0.9%
34	West Virginia	9,826	0.7%
35	Oregon	8,134	0.6%
36	Rhode Island	8,112	0.6%
37	New Hampshire	6,978	0.5%
38	Maine	6,598	0.5%
39	South Dakota	6,553	0.5%
40	New Mexico	5,981	0.4%
41	North Dakota	5,926	0.4%
42	Utah	5,486	0.4%
43	Montana	5,204	0.4%
44	Nevada	4,724	0.3%
45	Idaho	4,513	0.3%
46	Delaware	4,004	0.3%
47	Hawaii	3,830	0.3%
48	Vermont	3,051	0.2%
49	Wyoming	2,445	0.2%
50	Alaska	628	0.0%
	District of Columbia	2,804	0.2%

Source: U.S. Department of Health and Human Services, Centers for Medicare and Medicaid Services
"Health, United States, 2008" (www.cdc.gov/nchs/data/hus/hus08.pdf)

Health Care Establishments in 2007

National Total = 630,141 Establishments*

ALPHA ORDER

RANK	STATE	ESTABLISH'S	% of USA
27	Alabama	8,171	1.3%
47	Alaska	1,642	0.3%
15	Arizona	13,315	2.1%
32	Arkansas	5,546	0.9%
1	California	80,757	12.8%
20	Colorado	11,152	1.8%
28	Connecticut	7,917	1.3%
45	Delaware	1,839	0.3%
3	Florida	44,163	7.0%
10	Georgia	16,689	2.6%
41	Hawaii	2,868	0.5%
39	Idaho	3,493	0.6%
6	Illinois	25,277	4.0%
18	Indiana	11,776	1.9%
30	Iowa	5,935	0.9%
31	Kansas	5,867	0.9%
25	Kentucky	8,366	1.3%
23	Louisiana	9,148	1.5%
40	Maine	3,463	0.5%
16	Maryland	12,496	2.0%
14	Massachusetts	13,655	2.2%
9	Michigan	21,355	3.4%
22	Minnesota	10,398	1.7%
35	Mississippi	4,506	0.7%
17	Missouri	11,816	1.9%
44	Montana	2,392	0.4%
38	Nebraska	3,652	0.6%
34	Nevada	5,070	0.8%
43	New Hampshire	2,543	0.4%
8	New Jersey	21,518	3.4%
37	New Mexico	3,687	0.6%
4	New York	43,463	6.9%
11	North Carolina	16,669	2.6%
49	North Dakota	1,269	0.2%
7	Ohio	22,675	3.6%
26	Oklahoma	8,187	1.3%
24	Oregon	9,110	1.4%
5	Pennsylvania	27,830	4.4%
42	Rhode Island	2,628	0.4%
29	South Carolina	7,351	1.2%
46	South Dakota	1,644	0.3%
19	Tennessee	11,484	1.8%
2	Texas	45,552	7.2%
33	Utah	5,308	0.8%
48	Vermont	1,521	0.2%
13	Virginia	13,911	2.2%
12	Washington	14,079	2.2%
36	West Virginia	3,831	0.6%
21	Wisconsin	10,496	1.7%
50	Wyoming	1,268	0.2%

RANK ORDER

RANK	STATE	ESTABLISH'S	% of USA
1	California	80,757	12.8%
2	Texas	45,552	7.2%
3	Florida	44,163	7.0%
4	New York	43,463	6.9%
5	Pennsylvania	27,830	4.4%
6	Illinois	25,277	4.0%
7	Ohio	22,675	3.6%
8	New Jersey	21,518	3.4%
9	Michigan	21,355	3.4%
10	Georgia	16,689	2.6%
11	North Carolina	16,669	2.6%
12	Washington	14,079	2.2%
13	Virginia	13,911	2.2%
14	Massachusetts	13,655	2.2%
15	Arizona	13,315	2.1%
16	Maryland	12,496	2.0%
17	Missouri	11,816	1.9%
18	Indiana	11,776	1.9%
19	Tennessee	11,484	1.8%
20	Colorado	11,152	1.8%
21	Wisconsin	10,496	1.7%
22	Minnesota	10,398	1.7%
23	Louisiana	9,148	1.5%
24	Oregon	9,110	1.4%
25	Kentucky	8,366	1.3%
26	Oklahoma	8,187	1.3%
27	Alabama	8,171	1.3%
28	Connecticut	7,917	1.3%
29	South Carolina	7,351	1.2%
30	Iowa	5,935	0.9%
31	Kansas	5,867	0.9%
32	Arkansas	5,546	0.9%
33	Utah	5,308	0.8%
34	Nevada	5,070	0.8%
35	Mississippi	4,506	0.7%
36	West Virginia	3,831	0.6%
37	New Mexico	3,687	0.6%
38	Nebraska	3,652	0.6%
39	Idaho	3,493	0.6%
40	Maine	3,463	0.5%
41	Hawaii	2,868	0.5%
42	Rhode Island	2,628	0.4%
43	New Hampshire	2,543	0.4%
44	Montana	2,392	0.4%
45	Delaware	1,839	0.3%
46	South Dakota	1,644	0.3%
47	Alaska	1,642	0.3%
48	Vermont	1,521	0.2%
49	North Dakota	1,269	0.2%
50	Wyoming	1,268	0.2%
	District of Columbia	1,393	0.2%

Source: U.S. Bureau of the Census
     "County Business Patterns 2007 (NAICS)" (http://censtats.census.gov/cbpnaic/cbpnaic.shtml)
*Includes establishments exempt from as well as subject to the federal income tax. Includes those establishments within the
North American Industry Classification System (NAICS) classifications 621 (ambulatory health care services), 622 (hospitals),
and 623 (nursing and residential care facilities). Does not include classification 624 (social assistance facilities).

IV. Finance

Average Medical Malpractice Payment in 2006

National Average = $311,965*

ALPHA ORDER

RANK	STATE	AVERAGE PAYMENT
7	Alabama	$453,665
39	Alaska	240,511
30	Arizona	286,898
37	Arkansas	246,959
41	California	223,039
24	Colorado	312,138
4	Connecticut	500,289
3	Delaware	521,177
40	Florida**	240,363
29	Georgia	292,902
14	Hawaii	342,316
31	Idaho	281,751
1	Illinois	619,205
20	Indiana**	322,822
34	Iowa	274,281
48	Kansas**	155,285
32	Kentucky	280,599
43	Louisiana**	207,878
21	Maine	322,325
13	Maryland	347,477
6	Massachusetts	465,236
49	Michigan	138,433
5	Minnesota	480,822
35	Mississippi	258,806
18	Missouri	330,115
22	Montana	320,849
42	Nebraska**	213,081
15	Nevada	340,211
16	New Hampshire	336,032
11	New Jersey	401,144
45	New Mexico**	199,917
10	New York	405,558
12	North Carolina	366,966
27	North Dakota	301,422
25	Ohio	310,573
38	Oklahoma	245,127
26	Oregon	305,725
17	Pennsylvania**	332,376
19	Rhode Island	326,542
47	South Carolina**	174,454
8	South Dakota	422,033
23	Tennessee	317,305
46	Texas	175,644
36	Utah	247,349
50	Vermont	125,795
28	Virginia	295,840
33	Washington	277,493
44	West Virginia	204,794
2	Wisconsin**	524,041
9	Wyoming	413,553

RANK ORDER

RANK	STATE	AVERAGE PAYMENT
1	Illinois	$619,205
2	Wisconsin**	524,041
3	Delaware	521,177
4	Connecticut	500,289
5	Minnesota	480,822
6	Massachusetts	465,236
7	Alabama	453,665
8	South Dakota	422,033
9	Wyoming	413,553
10	New York	405,558
11	New Jersey	401,144
12	North Carolina	366,966
13	Maryland	347,477
14	Hawaii	342,316
15	Nevada	340,211
16	New Hampshire	336,032
17	Pennsylvania**	332,376
18	Missouri	330,115
19	Rhode Island	326,542
20	Indiana**	322,822
21	Maine	322,325
22	Montana	320,849
23	Tennessee	317,305
24	Colorado	312,138
25	Ohio	310,573
26	Oregon	305,725
27	North Dakota	301,422
28	Virginia	295,840
29	Georgia	292,902
30	Arizona	286,898
31	Idaho	281,751
32	Kentucky	280,599
33	Washington	277,493
34	Iowa	274,281
35	Mississippi	258,806
36	Utah	247,349
37	Arkansas	246,959
38	Oklahoma	245,127
39	Alaska	240,511
40	Florida**	240,363
41	California	223,039
42	Nebraska**	213,081
43	Louisiana**	207,878
44	West Virginia	204,794
45	New Mexico**	199,917
46	Texas	175,644
47	South Carolina**	174,454
48	Kansas**	155,285
49	Michigan	138,433
50	Vermont	125,795
	District of Columbia	331,628

Source: U.S. Department of Health and Human Services, Bureau of Health Professions
"National Practitioner Data Bank, 2006 Annual Report" (http://www.npdb-hipdb.com/annualrpt.html)
*National figure includes U.S. territories and U.S. Armed Forces locations overseas.
**The figures for these states have not been adjusted for payments by state compensation funds and other similar funds.
Average payments for these states understate the actual average amounts received by claimants.

Percent of Private-Sector Establishments That Offer Health Insurance: 2008

National Percent = 56.4%

<u>ALPHA ORDER</u>

RANK	STATE	PERCENT
7	Alabama	62.9
45	Alaska	46.0
32	Arizona	53.4
45	Arkansas	46.0
16	California	57.6
38	Colorado	52.1
5	Connecticut	63.6
10	Delaware	61.4
26	Florida	55.1
32	Georgia	53.4
1	Hawaii	88.5
49	Idaho	43.9
23	Illinois	55.6
29	Indiana	53.8
25	Iowa	55.2
24	Kansas	55.3
20	Kentucky	56.6
34	Louisiana	52.8
17	Maine	57.1
15	Maryland	58.2
2	Massachusetts	68.7
18	Michigan	56.9
31	Minnesota	53.5
43	Mississippi	47.7
18	Missouri	56.9
50	Montana	40.2
48	Nebraska	44.8
8	Nevada	62.8
4	New Hampshire	64.8
3	New Jersey	67.5
39	New Mexico	51.1
13	New York	58.7
28	North Carolina	54.4
36	North Dakota	52.2
9	Ohio	61.6
41	Oklahoma	50.8
35	Oregon	52.6
11	Pennsylvania	61.3
6	Rhode Island	63.0
27	South Carolina	54.8
44	South Dakota	47.3
21	Tennessee	56.3
42	Texas	48.8
39	Utah	51.1
22	Vermont	56.0
12	Virginia	59.1
14	Washington	58.6
30	West Virginia	53.7
36	Wisconsin	52.2
45	Wyoming	46.0

<u>RANK ORDER</u>

RANK	STATE	PERCENT
1	Hawaii	88.5
2	Massachusetts	68.7
3	New Jersey	67.5
4	New Hampshire	64.8
5	Connecticut	63.6
6	Rhode Island	63.0
7	Alabama	62.9
8	Nevada	62.8
9	Ohio	61.6
10	Delaware	61.4
11	Pennsylvania	61.3
12	Virginia	59.1
13	New York	58.7
14	Washington	58.6
15	Maryland	58.2
16	California	57.6
17	Maine	57.1
18	Michigan	56.9
18	Missouri	56.9
20	Kentucky	56.6
21	Tennessee	56.3
22	Vermont	56.0
23	Illinois	55.6
24	Kansas	55.3
25	Iowa	55.2
26	Florida	55.1
27	South Carolina	54.8
28	North Carolina	54.4
29	Indiana	53.8
30	West Virginia	53.7
31	Minnesota	53.5
32	Arizona	53.4
32	Georgia	53.4
34	Louisiana	52.8
35	Oregon	52.6
36	North Dakota	52.2
36	Wisconsin	52.2
38	Colorado	52.1
39	New Mexico	51.1
39	Utah	51.1
41	Oklahoma	50.8
42	Texas	48.8
43	Mississippi	47.7
44	South Dakota	47.3
45	Alaska	46.0
45	Arkansas	46.0
45	Wyoming	46.0
48	Nebraska	44.8
49	Idaho	43.9
50	Montana	40.2
	District of Columbia	72.5

Source: U.S. Department of Health and Human Services, Agency for Healthcare Research and Quality
"Private-Sector Data by Firm Size and State" (Table II Series, Medical Expenditures Panel Survey)
(http://www.meps.ahrq.gov/mepsweb/survey_comp/Insurance.jsp)

Percent of Private-Sector Establishments with Fewer Than 50 Employees That Offer Health Insurance: 2008
National Percent = 43.2%

<table>
<tr><td colspan="3">ALPHA ORDER</td><td colspan="3">RANK ORDER</td></tr>
<tr><td>RANK</td><td>STATE</td><td>PERCENT</td><td>RANK</td><td>STATE</td><td>PERCENT</td></tr>
<tr><td>10</td><td>Alabama</td><td>48.1</td><td>1</td><td>Hawaii</td><td>84.8</td></tr>
<tr><td>46</td><td>Alaska</td><td>31.6</td><td>2</td><td>New Jersey</td><td>59.6</td></tr>
<tr><td>41</td><td>Arizona</td><td>35.2</td><td>3</td><td>Massachusetts</td><td>58.9</td></tr>
<tr><td>50</td><td>Arkansas</td><td>27.1</td><td>4</td><td>New Hampshire</td><td>53.9</td></tr>
<tr><td>13</td><td>California</td><td>46.5</td><td>5</td><td>Rhode Island</td><td>53.3</td></tr>
<tr><td>32</td><td>Colorado</td><td>38.1</td><td>6</td><td>Connecticut</td><td>53.1</td></tr>
<tr><td>6</td><td>Connecticut</td><td>53.1</td><td>7</td><td>Nevada</td><td>49.3</td></tr>
<tr><td>11</td><td>Delaware</td><td>47.7</td><td>7</td><td>New York</td><td>49.3</td></tr>
<tr><td>21</td><td>Florida</td><td>42.0</td><td>9</td><td>Pennsylvania</td><td>48.7</td></tr>
<tr><td>35</td><td>Georgia</td><td>37.8</td><td>10</td><td>Alabama</td><td>48.1</td></tr>
<tr><td>1</td><td>Hawaii</td><td>84.8</td><td>11</td><td>Delaware</td><td>47.7</td></tr>
<tr><td>44</td><td>Idaho</td><td>32.8</td><td>12</td><td>Washington</td><td>47.5</td></tr>
<tr><td>23</td><td>Illinois</td><td>41.4</td><td>13</td><td>California</td><td>46.5</td></tr>
<tr><td>32</td><td>Indiana</td><td>38.1</td><td>14</td><td>Vermont</td><td>45.8</td></tr>
<tr><td>22</td><td>Iowa</td><td>41.9</td><td>15</td><td>Maine</td><td>45.6</td></tr>
<tr><td>24</td><td>Kansas</td><td>41.3</td><td>16</td><td>Ohio</td><td>45.5</td></tr>
<tr><td>25</td><td>Kentucky</td><td>41.2</td><td>17</td><td>Virginia</td><td>44.4</td></tr>
<tr><td>37</td><td>Louisiana</td><td>37.4</td><td>18</td><td>Maryland</td><td>44.0</td></tr>
<tr><td>15</td><td>Maine</td><td>45.6</td><td>19</td><td>Michigan</td><td>43.6</td></tr>
<tr><td>18</td><td>Maryland</td><td>44.0</td><td>20</td><td>Missouri</td><td>42.8</td></tr>
<tr><td>3</td><td>Massachusetts</td><td>58.9</td><td>21</td><td>Florida</td><td>42.0</td></tr>
<tr><td>19</td><td>Michigan</td><td>43.6</td><td>22</td><td>Iowa</td><td>41.9</td></tr>
<tr><td>28</td><td>Minnesota</td><td>40.0</td><td>23</td><td>Illinois</td><td>41.4</td></tr>
<tr><td>47</td><td>Mississippi</td><td>30.2</td><td>24</td><td>Kansas</td><td>41.3</td></tr>
<tr><td>20</td><td>Missouri</td><td>42.8</td><td>25</td><td>Kentucky</td><td>41.2</td></tr>
<tr><td>48</td><td>Montana</td><td>29.4</td><td>26</td><td>North Dakota</td><td>40.9</td></tr>
<tr><td>48</td><td>Nebraska</td><td>29.4</td><td>27</td><td>Oregon</td><td>40.3</td></tr>
<tr><td>7</td><td>Nevada</td><td>49.3</td><td>28</td><td>Minnesota</td><td>40.0</td></tr>
<tr><td>4</td><td>New Hampshire</td><td>53.9</td><td>29</td><td>Tennessee</td><td>38.7</td></tr>
<tr><td>2</td><td>New Jersey</td><td>59.6</td><td>30</td><td>South Carolina</td><td>38.5</td></tr>
<tr><td>40</td><td>New Mexico</td><td>35.9</td><td>31</td><td>North Carolina</td><td>38.2</td></tr>
<tr><td>7</td><td>New York</td><td>49.3</td><td>32</td><td>Colorado</td><td>38.1</td></tr>
<tr><td>31</td><td>North Carolina</td><td>38.2</td><td>32</td><td>Indiana</td><td>38.1</td></tr>
<tr><td>26</td><td>North Dakota</td><td>40.9</td><td>32</td><td>Utah</td><td>38.1</td></tr>
<tr><td>16</td><td>Ohio</td><td>45.5</td><td>35</td><td>Georgia</td><td>37.8</td></tr>
<tr><td>39</td><td>Oklahoma</td><td>36.3</td><td>36</td><td>Wisconsin</td><td>37.6</td></tr>
<tr><td>27</td><td>Oregon</td><td>40.3</td><td>37</td><td>Louisiana</td><td>37.4</td></tr>
<tr><td>9</td><td>Pennsylvania</td><td>48.7</td><td>38</td><td>West Virginia</td><td>37.2</td></tr>
<tr><td>5</td><td>Rhode Island</td><td>53.3</td><td>39</td><td>Oklahoma</td><td>36.3</td></tr>
<tr><td>30</td><td>South Carolina</td><td>38.5</td><td>40</td><td>New Mexico</td><td>35.9</td></tr>
<tr><td>42</td><td>South Dakota</td><td>35.0</td><td>41</td><td>Arizona</td><td>35.2</td></tr>
<tr><td>29</td><td>Tennessee</td><td>38.7</td><td>42</td><td>South Dakota</td><td>35.0</td></tr>
<tr><td>45</td><td>Texas</td><td>32.5</td><td>43</td><td>Wyoming</td><td>33.8</td></tr>
<tr><td>32</td><td>Utah</td><td>38.1</td><td>44</td><td>Idaho</td><td>32.8</td></tr>
<tr><td>14</td><td>Vermont</td><td>45.8</td><td>45</td><td>Texas</td><td>32.5</td></tr>
<tr><td>17</td><td>Virginia</td><td>44.4</td><td>46</td><td>Alaska</td><td>31.6</td></tr>
<tr><td>12</td><td>Washington</td><td>47.5</td><td>47</td><td>Mississippi</td><td>30.2</td></tr>
<tr><td>38</td><td>West Virginia</td><td>37.2</td><td>48</td><td>Montana</td><td>29.4</td></tr>
<tr><td>36</td><td>Wisconsin</td><td>37.6</td><td>48</td><td>Nebraska</td><td>29.4</td></tr>
<tr><td>43</td><td>Wyoming</td><td>33.8</td><td>50</td><td>Arkansas</td><td>27.1</td></tr>
<tr><td></td><td></td><td></td><td colspan="2">District of Columbia</td><td>60.1</td></tr>
</table>

Source: U.S. Department of Health and Human Services, Agency for Healthcare Research and Quality
   "Private-Sector Data by Firm Size and State" (Table II Series, Medical Expenditures Panel Survey)
   (http://www.meps.ahrq.gov/mepsweb/survey_comp/Insurance.jsp)

Percent of Private-Sector Establishments with More Than 50 Employees That Offer Health Insurance: 2008
National Percent = 96.5%

ALPHA ORDER

RANK	STATE	PERCENT
14	Alabama	97.8
10	Alaska	98.5
26	Arizona	96.7
31	Arkansas	96.4
40	California	95.4
11	Colorado	98.4
18	Connecticut	97.4
49	Delaware	92.3
31	Florida	96.4
22	Georgia	97.0
7	Hawaii	98.8
47	Idaho	92.9
20	Illinois	97.2
24	Indiana	96.8
16	Iowa	97.5
24	Kansas	96.8
29	Kentucky	96.5
27	Louisiana	96.6
3	Maine	99.6
7	Maryland	98.8
1	Massachusetts	99.8
33	Michigan	96.3
41	Minnesota	95.3
36	Mississippi	96.1
37	Missouri	95.9
35	Montana	96.2
22	Nebraska	97.0
44	Nevada	93.9
1	New Hampshire	99.8
4	New Jersey	99.4
46	New Mexico	93.5
16	New York	97.5
12	North Carolina	98.1
33	North Dakota	96.3
18	Ohio	97.4
42	Oklahoma	94.2
38	Oregon	95.6
27	Pennsylvania	96.6
12	Rhode Island	98.1
15	South Carolina	97.6
45	South Dakota	93.7
29	Tennessee	96.5
50	Texas	91.6
47	Utah	92.9
5	Vermont	99.3
6	Virginia	99.0
21	Washington	97.1
38	West Virginia	95.6
9	Wisconsin	98.6
43	Wyoming	94.0

RANK ORDER

RANK	STATE	PERCENT
1	Massachusetts	99.8
1	New Hampshire	99.8
3	Maine	99.6
4	New Jersey	99.4
5	Vermont	99.3
6	Virginia	99.0
7	Hawaii	98.8
7	Maryland	98.8
9	Wisconsin	98.6
10	Alaska	98.5
11	Colorado	98.4
12	North Carolina	98.1
12	Rhode Island	98.1
14	Alabama	97.8
15	South Carolina	97.6
16	Iowa	97.5
16	New York	97.5
18	Connecticut	97.4
18	Ohio	97.4
20	Illinois	97.2
21	Washington	97.1
22	Georgia	97.0
22	Nebraska	97.0
24	Indiana	96.8
24	Kansas	96.8
26	Arizona	96.7
27	Louisiana	96.6
27	Pennsylvania	96.6
29	Kentucky	96.5
29	Tennessee	96.5
31	Arkansas	96.4
31	Florida	96.4
33	Michigan	96.3
33	North Dakota	96.3
35	Montana	96.2
36	Mississippi	96.1
37	Missouri	95.9
38	Oregon	95.6
38	West Virginia	95.6
40	California	95.4
41	Minnesota	95.3
42	Oklahoma	94.2
43	Wyoming	94.0
44	Nevada	93.9
45	South Dakota	93.7
46	New Mexico	93.5
47	Idaho	92.9
47	Utah	92.9
49	Delaware	92.3
50	Texas	91.6

	District of Columbia	96.4

Source: U.S. Department of Health and Human Services, Agency for Healthcare Research and Quality
"Private-Sector Data by Firm Size and State" (Table II Series, Medical Expenditures Panel Survey)
(http://www.meps.ahrq.gov/mepsweb/survey_comp/Insurance.jsp)

Average Annual Single Coverage Health Insurance Premium per Enrolled Employee in 2008
National Average = $4,386*

ALPHA ORDER

RANK	STATE	PREMIUM
38	Alabama	$4,139
1	Alaska	5,293
31	Arizona	4,214
48	Arkansas	3,923
28	California	4,280
27	Colorado	4,303
10	Connecticut	4,740
11	Delaware	4,733
15	Florida	4,517
36	Georgia	4,160
49	Hawaii	3,831
41	Idaho	4,104
12	Illinois	4,643
17	Indiana	4,495
37	Iowa	4,146
34	Kansas	4,197
46	Kentucky	4,009
45	Louisiana	4,055
4	Maine	4,910
25	Maryland	4,360
7	Massachusetts	4,836
23	Michigan	4,388
20	Minnesota	4,432
39	Mississippi	4,124
39	Missouri	4,124
26	Montana	4,355
22	Nebraska	4,392
47	Nevada	3,927
2	New Hampshire	5,247
8	New Jersey	4,798
43	New Mexico	4,074
13	New York	4,638
19	North Carolina	4,460
50	North Dakota	3,830
42	Ohio	4,089
44	Oklahoma	4,072
24	Oregon	4,384
16	Pennsylvania	4,499
3	Rhode Island	4,930
18	South Carolina	4,477
30	South Dakota	4,233
29	Tennessee	4,276
32	Texas	4,205
34	Utah	4,197
5	Vermont	4,900
33	Virginia	4,202
21	Washington	4,404
6	West Virginia	4,892
9	Wisconsin	4,777
14	Wyoming	4,622

RANK ORDER

RANK	STATE	PREMIUM
1	Alaska	$5,293
2	New Hampshire	5,247
3	Rhode Island	4,930
4	Maine	4,910
5	Vermont	4,900
6	West Virginia	4,892
7	Massachusetts	4,836
8	New Jersey	4,798
9	Wisconsin	4,777
10	Connecticut	4,740
11	Delaware	4,733
12	Illinois	4,643
13	New York	4,638
14	Wyoming	4,622
15	Florida	4,517
16	Pennsylvania	4,499
17	Indiana	4,495
18	South Carolina	4,477
19	North Carolina	4,460
20	Minnesota	4,432
21	Washington	4,404
22	Nebraska	4,392
23	Michigan	4,388
24	Oregon	4,384
25	Maryland	4,360
26	Montana	4,355
27	Colorado	4,303
28	California	4,280
29	Tennessee	4,276
30	South Dakota	4,233
31	Arizona	4,214
32	Texas	4,205
33	Virginia	4,202
34	Kansas	4,197
34	Utah	4,197
36	Georgia	4,160
37	Iowa	4,146
38	Alabama	4,139
39	Mississippi	4,124
39	Missouri	4,124
41	Idaho	4,104
42	Ohio	4,089
43	New Mexico	4,074
44	Oklahoma	4,072
45	Louisiana	4,055
46	Kentucky	4,009
47	Nevada	3,927
48	Arkansas	3,923
49	Hawaii	3,831
50	North Dakota	3,830
	District of Columbia	4,890

Source: U.S. Department of Health and Human Services, Agency for Healthcare Research and Quality
"Private-Sector Data by Firm Size and State" (Table II Series, Medical Expenditures Panel Survey)
(http://www.meps.ahrq.gov/mepsweb/survey_comp/Insurance.jsp)
*Enrolled employees at private-sector establishments that offer health insurance coverage.

Average Annual Employee Contribution for
Single Coverage Health Insurance in 2008
National Average = $882*

ALPHA ORDER

RANK	STATE	CONTRIBUTION
16	Alabama	$959
33	Alaska	814
34	Arizona	811
38	Arkansas	781
43	California	741
10	Colorado	998
11	Connecticut	992
25	Delaware	885
4	Florida	1,065
14	Georgia	972
50	Hawaii	451
49	Idaho	476
18	Illinois	954
19	Indiana	950
39	Iowa	756
35	Kansas	807
36	Kentucky	806
27	Louisiana	868
5	Maine	1,054
15	Maryland	964
2	Massachusetts	1,110
44	Michigan	735
23	Minnesota	891
42	Mississippi	749
17	Missouri	956
47	Montana	583
9	Nebraska	1,010
28	Nevada	863
1	New Hampshire	1,264
8	New Jersey	1,033
19	New Mexico	950
21	New York	947
32	North Carolina	827
40	North Dakota	754
25	Ohio	885
37	Oklahoma	787
46	Oregon	612
29	Pennsylvania	852
6	Rhode Island	1,050
30	South Carolina	849
24	South Dakota	887
22	Tennessee	914
31	Texas	844
41	Utah	752
13	Vermont	986
12	Virginia	988
48	Washington	569
7	West Virginia	1,049
3	Wisconsin	1,069
45	Wyoming	717

RANK ORDER

RANK	STATE	CONTRIBUTION
1	New Hampshire	$1,264
2	Massachusetts	1,110
3	Wisconsin	1,069
4	Florida	1,065
5	Maine	1,054
6	Rhode Island	1,050
7	West Virginia	1,049
8	New Jersey	1,033
9	Nebraska	1,010
10	Colorado	998
11	Connecticut	992
12	Virginia	988
13	Vermont	986
14	Georgia	972
15	Maryland	964
16	Alabama	959
17	Missouri	956
18	Illinois	954
19	Indiana	950
19	New Mexico	950
21	New York	947
22	Tennessee	914
23	Minnesota	891
24	South Dakota	887
25	Delaware	885
25	Ohio	885
27	Louisiana	868
28	Nevada	863
29	Pennsylvania	852
30	South Carolina	849
31	Texas	844
32	North Carolina	827
33	Alaska	814
34	Arizona	811
35	Kansas	807
36	Kentucky	806
37	Oklahoma	787
38	Arkansas	781
39	Iowa	756
40	North Dakota	754
41	Utah	752
42	Mississippi	749
43	California	741
44	Michigan	735
45	Wyoming	717
46	Oregon	612
47	Montana	583
48	Washington	569
49	Idaho	476
50	Hawaii	451
	District of Columbia	991

Source: U.S. Department of Health and Human Services, Agency for Healthcare Research and Quality
"Private-Sector Data by Firm Size and State" (Table II Series, Medical Expenditures Panel Survey)
(http://www.meps.ahrq.gov/mepsweb/survey_comp/Insurance.jsp)
*Enrolled employees at private-sector establishments that offer health insurance coverage.

Percent of Total Premiums for Single Coverage
Health Insurance Paid by Employees in 2008
National Average = 20.1%*

ALPHA ORDER

RANK	STATE	PERCENT
6	Alabama	23.2
45	Alaska	15.4
33	Arizona	19.2
30	Arkansas	19.9
42	California	17.3
6	Colorado	23.2
23	Connecticut	20.9
37	Delaware	18.7
2	Florida	23.6
4	Georgia	23.4
49	Hawaii	11.8
50	Idaho	11.6
24	Illinois	20.5
21	Indiana	21.1
39	Iowa	18.2
33	Kansas	19.2
26	Kentucky	20.1
17	Louisiana	21.4
15	Maine	21.5
12	Maryland	22.1
9	Massachusetts	23.0
43	Michigan	16.8
26	Minnesota	20.1
39	Mississippi	18.2
6	Missouri	23.2
47	Montana	13.4
9	Nebraska	23.0
13	Nevada	22.0
1	New Hampshire	24.1
15	New Jersey	21.5
5	New Mexico	23.3
25	New York	20.4
38	North Carolina	18.5
31	North Dakota	19.7
14	Ohio	21.6
32	Oklahoma	19.3
46	Oregon	14.0
36	Pennsylvania	18.9
20	Rhode Island	21.3
35	South Carolina	19.0
22	South Dakota	21.0
17	Tennessee	21.4
26	Texas	20.1
41	Utah	17.9
26	Vermont	20.1
3	Virginia	23.5
48	Washington	12.9
17	West Virginia	21.4
11	Wisconsin	22.4
44	Wyoming	15.5

RANK ORDER

RANK	STATE	PERCENT
1	New Hampshire	24.1
2	Florida	23.6
3	Virginia	23.5
4	Georgia	23.4
5	New Mexico	23.3
6	Alabama	23.2
6	Colorado	23.2
6	Missouri	23.2
9	Massachusetts	23.0
9	Nebraska	23.0
11	Wisconsin	22.4
12	Maryland	22.1
13	Nevada	22.0
14	Ohio	21.6
15	Maine	21.5
15	New Jersey	21.5
17	Louisiana	21.4
17	Tennessee	21.4
17	West Virginia	21.4
20	Rhode Island	21.3
21	Indiana	21.1
22	South Dakota	21.0
23	Connecticut	20.9
24	Illinois	20.5
25	New York	20.4
26	Kentucky	20.1
26	Minnesota	20.1
26	Texas	20.1
26	Vermont	20.1
30	Arkansas	19.9
31	North Dakota	19.7
32	Oklahoma	19.3
33	Arizona	19.2
33	Kansas	19.2
35	South Carolina	19.0
36	Pennsylvania	18.9
37	Delaware	18.7
38	North Carolina	18.5
39	Iowa	18.2
39	Mississippi	18.2
41	Utah	17.9
42	California	17.3
43	Michigan	16.8
44	Wyoming	15.5
45	Alaska	15.4
46	Oregon	14.0
47	Montana	13.4
48	Washington	12.9
49	Hawaii	11.8
50	Idaho	11.6

	District of Columbia	20.3

Source: U.S. Department of Health and Human Services, Agency for Healthcare Research and Quality
"Private-Sector Data by Firm Size and State" (Table II Series, Medical Expenditures Panel Survey)
(http://www.meps.ahrq.gov/mepsweb/survey_comp/Insurance.jsp)
*Enrolled employees at private-sector establishments that offer health insurance coverage.

Average Annual Family Coverage Health Insurance Premium per Enrolled Employee in 2008
National Average = $12,298*

<table>
<tr><th colspan="3">ALPHA ORDER</th><th colspan="3">RANK ORDER</th></tr>
<tr><th>RANK</th><th>STATE</th><th>PREMIUM</th><th>RANK</th><th>STATE</th><th>PREMIUM</th></tr>
<tr><td>46</td><td>Alabama</td><td>$11,119</td><td>1</td><td>Massachusetts</td><td>$13,788</td></tr>
<tr><td>7</td><td>Alaska</td><td>13,383</td><td>2</td><td>Minnesota</td><td>13,639</td></tr>
<tr><td>24</td><td>Arizona</td><td>12,292</td><td>3</td><td>New Hampshire</td><td>13,592</td></tr>
<tr><td>43</td><td>Arkansas</td><td>11,220</td><td>4</td><td>Indiana</td><td>13,504</td></tr>
<tr><td>25</td><td>California</td><td>12,254</td><td>5</td><td>Connecticut</td><td>13,436</td></tr>
<tr><td>29</td><td>Colorado</td><td>11,952</td><td>6</td><td>Delaware</td><td>13,386</td></tr>
<tr><td>5</td><td>Connecticut</td><td>13,436</td><td>7</td><td>Alaska</td><td>13,383</td></tr>
<tr><td>6</td><td>Delaware</td><td>13,386</td><td>8</td><td>Rhode Island</td><td>13,363</td></tr>
<tr><td>17</td><td>Florida</td><td>12,697</td><td>9</td><td>Maine</td><td>13,102</td></tr>
<tr><td>33</td><td>Georgia</td><td>11,659</td><td>10</td><td>Vermont</td><td>13,091</td></tr>
<tr><td>48</td><td>Hawaii</td><td>11,044</td><td>11</td><td>Washington</td><td>13,036</td></tr>
<tr><td>50</td><td>Idaho</td><td>10,837</td><td>12</td><td>Wisconsin</td><td>12,956</td></tr>
<tr><td>18</td><td>Illinois</td><td>12,603</td><td>13</td><td>West Virginia</td><td>12,887</td></tr>
<tr><td>4</td><td>Indiana</td><td>13,504</td><td>14</td><td>New York</td><td>12,824</td></tr>
<tr><td>49</td><td>Iowa</td><td>10,947</td><td>15</td><td>New Jersey</td><td>12,789</td></tr>
<tr><td>32</td><td>Kansas</td><td>11,662</td><td>16</td><td>Wyoming</td><td>12,734</td></tr>
<tr><td>36</td><td>Kentucky</td><td>11,506</td><td>17</td><td>Florida</td><td>12,697</td></tr>
<tr><td>44</td><td>Louisiana</td><td>11,207</td><td>18</td><td>Illinois</td><td>12,603</td></tr>
<tr><td>9</td><td>Maine</td><td>13,102</td><td>19</td><td>Oregon</td><td>12,585</td></tr>
<tr><td>20</td><td>Maryland</td><td>12,541</td><td>20</td><td>Maryland</td><td>12,541</td></tr>
<tr><td>1</td><td>Massachusetts</td><td>13,788</td><td>21</td><td>Pennsylvania</td><td>12,339</td></tr>
<tr><td>42</td><td>Michigan</td><td>11,321</td><td>22</td><td>North Carolina</td><td>12,308</td></tr>
<tr><td>2</td><td>Minnesota</td><td>13,639</td><td>23</td><td>Tennessee</td><td>12,302</td></tr>
<tr><td>41</td><td>Mississippi</td><td>11,363</td><td>24</td><td>Arizona</td><td>12,292</td></tr>
<tr><td>35</td><td>Missouri</td><td>11,557</td><td>25</td><td>California</td><td>12,254</td></tr>
<tr><td>38</td><td>Montana</td><td>11,438</td><td>26</td><td>New Mexico</td><td>12,071</td></tr>
<tr><td>34</td><td>Nebraska</td><td>11,648</td><td>27</td><td>South Carolina</td><td>12,068</td></tr>
<tr><td>37</td><td>Nevada</td><td>11,487</td><td>28</td><td>Texas</td><td>11,967</td></tr>
<tr><td>3</td><td>New Hampshire</td><td>13,592</td><td>29</td><td>Colorado</td><td>11,952</td></tr>
<tr><td>15</td><td>New Jersey</td><td>12,789</td><td>30</td><td>Virginia</td><td>11,935</td></tr>
<tr><td>26</td><td>New Mexico</td><td>12,071</td><td>31</td><td>Utah</td><td>11,783</td></tr>
<tr><td>14</td><td>New York</td><td>12,824</td><td>32</td><td>Kansas</td><td>11,662</td></tr>
<tr><td>22</td><td>North Carolina</td><td>12,308</td><td>33</td><td>Georgia</td><td>11,659</td></tr>
<tr><td>45</td><td>North Dakota</td><td>11,178</td><td>34</td><td>Nebraska</td><td>11,648</td></tr>
<tr><td>39</td><td>Ohio</td><td>11,425</td><td>35</td><td>Missouri</td><td>11,557</td></tr>
<tr><td>47</td><td>Oklahoma</td><td>11,053</td><td>36</td><td>Kentucky</td><td>11,506</td></tr>
<tr><td>19</td><td>Oregon</td><td>12,585</td><td>37</td><td>Nevada</td><td>11,487</td></tr>
<tr><td>21</td><td>Pennsylvania</td><td>12,339</td><td>38</td><td>Montana</td><td>11,438</td></tr>
<tr><td>8</td><td>Rhode Island</td><td>13,363</td><td>39</td><td>Ohio</td><td>11,425</td></tr>
<tr><td>27</td><td>South Carolina</td><td>12,068</td><td>40</td><td>South Dakota</td><td>11,382</td></tr>
<tr><td>40</td><td>South Dakota</td><td>11,382</td><td>41</td><td>Mississippi</td><td>11,363</td></tr>
<tr><td>23</td><td>Tennessee</td><td>12,302</td><td>42</td><td>Michigan</td><td>11,321</td></tr>
<tr><td>28</td><td>Texas</td><td>11,967</td><td>43</td><td>Arkansas</td><td>11,220</td></tr>
<tr><td>31</td><td>Utah</td><td>11,783</td><td>44</td><td>Louisiana</td><td>11,207</td></tr>
<tr><td>10</td><td>Vermont</td><td>13,091</td><td>45</td><td>North Dakota</td><td>11,178</td></tr>
<tr><td>30</td><td>Virginia</td><td>11,935</td><td>46</td><td>Alabama</td><td>11,119</td></tr>
<tr><td>11</td><td>Washington</td><td>13,036</td><td>47</td><td>Oklahoma</td><td>11,053</td></tr>
<tr><td>13</td><td>West Virginia</td><td>12,887</td><td>48</td><td>Hawaii</td><td>11,044</td></tr>
<tr><td>12</td><td>Wisconsin</td><td>12,956</td><td>49</td><td>Iowa</td><td>10,947</td></tr>
<tr><td>16</td><td>Wyoming</td><td>12,734</td><td>50</td><td>Idaho</td><td>10,837</td></tr>
<tr><td></td><td></td><td></td><td></td><td>District of Columbia</td><td>13,427</td></tr>
</table>

Source: U.S. Department of Health and Human Services, Agency for Healthcare Research and Quality
   "Private-Sector Data by Firm Size and State" (Table II Series, Medical Expenditures Panel Survey)
      (http://www.meps.ahrq.gov/mepsweb/survey_comp/Insurance.jsp)
*Enrolled employees at private-sector establishments that offer health insurance coverage.

Average Annual Employee Contribution for
Family Coverage Health Insurance in 2008
National Average = $3,394*

ALPHA ORDER

RANK	STATE	CONTRIBUTION
31	Alabama	$3,265
33	Alaska	3,248
3	Arizona	4,136
35	Arkansas	3,085
19	California	3,398
2	Colorado	4,151
36	Connecticut	3,075
23	Delaware	3,373
1	Florida	4,412
12	Georgia	3,814
46	Hawaii	2,597
47	Idaho	2,562
24	Illinois	3,366
50	Indiana	2,472
48	Iowa	2,524
42	Kansas	2,954
43	Kentucky	2,918
14	Louisiana	3,607
6	Maine	4,017
8	Maryland	3,920
26	Massachusetts	3,363
49	Michigan	2,522
30	Minnesota	3,279
17	Mississippi	3,458
39	Missouri	2,994
11	Montana	3,823
34	Nebraska	3,173
15	Nevada	3,575
7	New Hampshire	3,922
29	New Jersey	3,286
5	New Mexico	4,021
22	New York	3,376
4	North Carolina	4,115
20	North Dakota	3,388
45	Ohio	2,642
13	Oklahoma	3,619
28	Oregon	3,297
40	Pennsylvania	2,971
41	Rhode Island	2,960
21	South Carolina	3,377
16	South Dakota	3,503
24	Tennessee	3,366
9	Texas	3,872
44	Utah	2,760
18	Vermont	3,435
10	Virginia	3,854
32	Washington	3,258
37	West Virginia	3,056
27	Wisconsin	3,301
38	Wyoming	3,052

RANK ORDER

RANK	STATE	CONTRIBUTION
1	Florida	$4,412
2	Colorado	4,151
3	Arizona	4,136
4	North Carolina	4,115
5	New Mexico	4,021
6	Maine	4,017
7	New Hampshire	3,922
8	Maryland	3,920
9	Texas	3,872
10	Virginia	3,854
11	Montana	3,823
12	Georgia	3,814
13	Oklahoma	3,619
14	Louisiana	3,607
15	Nevada	3,575
16	South Dakota	3,503
17	Mississippi	3,458
18	Vermont	3,435
19	California	3,398
20	North Dakota	3,388
21	South Carolina	3,377
22	New York	3,376
23	Delaware	3,373
24	Illinois	3,366
24	Tennessee	3,366
26	Massachusetts	3,363
27	Wisconsin	3,301
28	Oregon	3,297
29	New Jersey	3,286
30	Minnesota	3,279
31	Alabama	3,265
32	Washington	3,258
33	Alaska	3,248
34	Nebraska	3,173
35	Arkansas	3,085
36	Connecticut	3,075
37	West Virginia	3,056
38	Wyoming	3,052
39	Missouri	2,994
40	Pennsylvania	2,971
41	Rhode Island	2,960
42	Kansas	2,954
43	Kentucky	2,918
44	Utah	2,760
45	Ohio	2,642
46	Hawaii	2,597
47	Idaho	2,562
48	Iowa	2,524
49	Michigan	2,522
50	Indiana	2,472

District of Columbia	3,834

Source: U.S. Department of Health and Human Services, Agency for Healthcare Research and Quality
"Private-Sector Data by Firm Size and State" (Table II Series, Medical Expenditures Panel Survey)
(http://www.meps.ahrq.gov/mepsweb/survey_comp/Insurance.jsp)
*Enrolled employees at private-sector establishments that offer health insurance coverage.

Percent of Total Premiums for Family Coverage
Health Insurance Paid by Employees in 2008
National Average = 27.6%*

ALPHA ORDER

RANK	STATE	PERCENT
18	Alabama	29.4
37	Alaska	24.3
3	Arizona	33.6
22	Arkansas	27.5
21	California	27.7
2	Colorado	34.7
47	Connecticut	22.9
34	Delaware	25.2
1	Florida	34.8
7	Georgia	32.7
43	Hawaii	23.5
42	Idaho	23.6
25	Illinois	26.7
50	Indiana	18.3
45	Iowa	23.1
33	Kansas	25.3
32	Kentucky	25.4
11	Louisiana	32.2
15	Maine	30.7
12	Maryland	31.3
36	Massachusetts	24.4
48	Michigan	22.3
39	Minnesota	24.0
16	Mississippi	30.4
29	Missouri	25.9
4	Montana	33.4
24	Nebraska	27.2
13	Nevada	31.1
19	New Hampshire	28.9
30	New Jersey	25.7
6	New Mexico	33.3
26	New York	26.3
4	North Carolina	33.4
17	North Dakota	30.3
45	Ohio	23.1
7	Oklahoma	32.7
27	Oregon	26.2
38	Pennsylvania	24.1
49	Rhode Island	22.1
20	South Carolina	28.0
14	South Dakota	30.8
23	Tennessee	27.4
9	Texas	32.4
44	Utah	23.4
27	Vermont	26.2
10	Virginia	32.3
35	Washington	25.0
41	West Virginia	23.7
31	Wisconsin	25.5
39	Wyoming	24.0

RANK ORDER

RANK	STATE	PERCENT
1	Florida	34.8
2	Colorado	34.7
3	Arizona	33.6
4	Montana	33.4
4	North Carolina	33.4
6	New Mexico	33.3
7	Georgia	32.7
7	Oklahoma	32.7
9	Texas	32.4
10	Virginia	32.3
11	Louisiana	32.2
12	Maryland	31.3
13	Nevada	31.1
14	South Dakota	30.8
15	Maine	30.7
16	Mississippi	30.4
17	North Dakota	30.3
18	Alabama	29.4
19	New Hampshire	28.9
20	South Carolina	28.0
21	California	27.7
22	Arkansas	27.5
23	Tennessee	27.4
24	Nebraska	27.2
25	Illinois	26.7
26	New York	26.3
27	Oregon	26.2
27	Vermont	26.2
29	Missouri	25.9
30	New Jersey	25.7
31	Wisconsin	25.5
32	Kentucky	25.4
33	Kansas	25.3
34	Delaware	25.2
35	Washington	25.0
36	Massachusetts	24.4
37	Alaska	24.3
38	Pennsylvania	24.1
39	Minnesota	24.0
39	Wyoming	24.0
41	West Virginia	23.7
42	Idaho	23.6
43	Hawaii	23.5
44	Utah	23.4
45	Iowa	23.1
45	Ohio	23.1
47	Connecticut	22.9
48	Michigan	22.3
49	Rhode Island	22.1
50	Indiana	18.3

| | District of Columbia | 28.6 |

Source: U.S. Department of Health and Human Services, Agency for Healthcare Research and Quality
"Private-Sector Data by Firm Size and State" (Table II Series, Medical Expenditures Panel Survey)
(http://www.meps.ahrq.gov/mepsweb/survey_comp/Insurance.jsp)
*Enrolled employees at private-sector establishments that offer health insurance coverage.

Persons Not Covered by Health Insurance in 2008

National Total = 46,340,000 Uninsured

ALPHA ORDER

RANK	STATE	UNINSURED	% of USA
24	Alabama	561,000	1.2%
42	Alaska	133,000	0.3%
9	Arizona	1,273,000	2.7%
27	Arkansas	505,000	1.1%
1	California	6,822,000	14.7%
17	Colorado	780,000	1.7%
34	Connecticut	343,000	0.7%
47	Delaware	94,000	0.2%
3	Florida	3,619,000	7.8%
5	Georgia	1,703,000	3.7%
46	Hawaii	98,000	0.2%
38	Idaho	236,000	0.5%
6	Illinois	1,638,000	3.5%
18	Indiana	772,000	1.7%
36	Iowa	283,000	0.6%
35	Kansas	330,000	0.7%
21	Kentucky	682,000	1.5%
15	Louisiana	869,000	1.9%
41	Maine	137,000	0.3%
22	Maryland	669,000	1.4%
33	Massachusetts	352,000	0.8%
12	Michigan	1,151,000	2.5%
31	Minnesota	444,000	1.0%
26	Mississippi	519,000	1.1%
19	Missouri	739,000	1.6%
40	Montana	158,000	0.3%
39	Nebraska	211,000	0.5%
29	Nevada	487,000	1.1%
42	New Hampshire	133,000	0.3%
11	New Jersey	1,201,000	2.6%
30	New Mexico	468,000	1.0%
4	New York	2,720,000	5.9%
7	North Carolina	1,421,000	3.1%
48	North Dakota	74,000	0.2%
8	Ohio	1,309,000	2.8%
28	Oklahoma	498,000	1.1%
23	Oregon	621,000	1.3%
10	Pennsylvania	1,211,000	2.6%
44	Rhode Island	123,000	0.3%
20	South Carolina	707,000	1.5%
45	South Dakota	100,000	0.2%
14	Tennessee	931,000	2.0%
2	Texas	6,084,000	13.1%
32	Utah	364,000	0.8%
50	Vermont	57,000	0.1%
13	Virginia	962,000	2.1%
16	Washington	808,000	1.7%
37	West Virginia	271,000	0.6%
25	Wisconsin	535,000	1.2%
49	Wyoming	72,000	0.2%

RANK ORDER

RANK	STATE	UNINSURED	% of USA
1	California	6,822,000	14.7%
2	Texas	6,084,000	13.1%
3	Florida	3,619,000	7.8%
4	New York	2,720,000	5.9%
5	Georgia	1,703,000	3.7%
6	Illinois	1,638,000	3.5%
7	North Carolina	1,421,000	3.1%
8	Ohio	1,309,000	2.8%
9	Arizona	1,273,000	2.7%
10	Pennsylvania	1,211,000	2.6%
11	New Jersey	1,201,000	2.6%
12	Michigan	1,151,000	2.5%
13	Virginia	962,000	2.1%
14	Tennessee	931,000	2.0%
15	Louisiana	869,000	1.9%
16	Washington	808,000	1.7%
17	Colorado	780,000	1.7%
18	Indiana	772,000	1.7%
19	Missouri	739,000	1.6%
20	South Carolina	707,000	1.5%
21	Kentucky	682,000	1.5%
22	Maryland	669,000	1.4%
23	Oregon	621,000	1.3%
24	Alabama	561,000	1.2%
25	Wisconsin	535,000	1.2%
26	Mississippi	519,000	1.1%
27	Arkansas	505,000	1.1%
28	Oklahoma	498,000	1.1%
29	Nevada	487,000	1.1%
30	New Mexico	468,000	1.0%
31	Minnesota	444,000	1.0%
32	Utah	364,000	0.8%
33	Massachusetts	352,000	0.8%
34	Connecticut	343,000	0.7%
35	Kansas	330,000	0.7%
36	Iowa	283,000	0.6%
37	West Virginia	271,000	0.6%
38	Idaho	236,000	0.5%
39	Nebraska	211,000	0.5%
40	Montana	158,000	0.3%
41	Maine	137,000	0.3%
42	Alaska	133,000	0.3%
42	New Hampshire	133,000	0.3%
44	Rhode Island	123,000	0.3%
45	South Dakota	100,000	0.2%
46	Hawaii	98,000	0.2%
47	Delaware	94,000	0.2%
48	North Dakota	74,000	0.2%
49	Wyoming	72,000	0.2%
50	Vermont	57,000	0.1%
	District of Columbia	59,000	0.1%

Source: U.S. Bureau of the Census
"Health Insurance Coverage Status by State for All People: 2008" (http://www.census.gov/hhes/www/hlthins/hlthin08.html)

Percent of Population Not Covered by Health Insurance in 2008

National Percent = 15.5% of Population*

ALPHA ORDER

RANK	STATE	PERCENT
29	Alabama	13.0
9	Alaska	18.2
5	Arizona	19.6
11	Arkansas	17.6
7	California	18.5
15	Colorado	16.5
45	Connecticut	9.6
36	Delaware	11.4
3	Florida	20.5
10	Georgia	17.7
49	Hawaii	8.1
19	Idaho	15.0
27	Illinois	13.4
33	Indiana	11.8
43	Iowa	9.8
32	Kansas	12.4
19	Kentucky	15.0
4	Louisiana	20.1
46	Maine	9.5
28	Maryland	13.2
50	Massachusetts	7.1
38	Michigan	11.3
48	Minnesota	8.7
6	Mississippi	19.1
30	Missouri	12.8
16	Montana	16.3
31	Nebraska	12.5
7	Nevada	18.5
40	New Hampshire	10.7
18	New Jersey	15.1
2	New Mexico	23.0
25	New York	13.8
14	North Carolina	16.6
36	North Dakota	11.4
39	Ohio	11.1
13	Oklahoma	16.9
12	Oregon	17.0
43	Pennsylvania	9.8
41	Rhode Island	10.4
17	South Carolina	16.1
35	South Dakota	11.5
22	Tennessee	14.4
1	Texas	24.9
21	Utah	14.5
42	Vermont	10.2
26	Virginia	13.5
33	Washington	11.8
23	West Virginia	14.2
47	Wisconsin	8.9
24	Wyoming	13.9

RANK ORDER

RANK	STATE	PERCENT
1	Texas	24.9
2	New Mexico	23.0
3	Florida	20.5
4	Louisiana	20.1
5	Arizona	19.6
6	Mississippi	19.1
7	California	18.5
7	Nevada	18.5
9	Alaska	18.2
10	Georgia	17.7
11	Arkansas	17.6
12	Oregon	17.0
13	Oklahoma	16.9
14	North Carolina	16.6
15	Colorado	16.5
16	Montana	16.3
17	South Carolina	16.1
18	New Jersey	15.1
19	Idaho	15.0
19	Kentucky	15.0
21	Utah	14.5
22	Tennessee	14.4
23	West Virginia	14.2
24	Wyoming	13.9
25	New York	13.8
26	Virginia	13.5
27	Illinois	13.4
28	Maryland	13.2
29	Alabama	13.0
30	Missouri	12.8
31	Nebraska	12.5
32	Kansas	12.4
33	Indiana	11.8
33	Washington	11.8
35	South Dakota	11.5
36	Delaware	11.4
36	North Dakota	11.4
38	Michigan	11.3
39	Ohio	11.1
40	New Hampshire	10.7
41	Rhode Island	10.4
42	Vermont	10.2
43	Iowa	9.8
43	Pennsylvania	9.8
45	Connecticut	9.6
46	Maine	9.5
47	Wisconsin	8.9
48	Minnesota	8.7
49	Hawaii	8.1
50	Massachusetts	7.1
	District of Columbia	10.4

Source: U.S. Bureau of the Census
"Health Insurance Coverage Status by State for All People: 2008" (http://www.census.gov/hhes/www/hlthins/hlthin08.html)
*Three-year average for 2006 through 2008.

Numerical Change in Persons Uninsured: 2004 to 2008

National Change = 2,842,000 Increase

ALPHA ORDER

RANK	STATE	GAIN/LOSS
36	Alabama	(1,000)
26	Alaska	26,000
4	Arizona	312,000
15	Arkansas	64,000
2	California	381,000
16	Colorado	61,000
45	Connecticut	(38,000)
41	Delaware	(16,000)
5	Florida	237,000
6	Georgia	234,000
38	Hawaii	(6,000)
24	Idaho	36,000
37	Illinois	(2,000)
47	Indiana	(75,000)
28	Iowa	17,000
20	Kansas	44,000
10	Kentucky	126,000
9	Louisiana	162,000
27	Maine	22,000
46	Maryland	(73,000)
50	Massachusetts	(368,000)
21	Michigan	42,000
32	Minnesota	10,000
22	Mississippi	41,000
14	Missouri	69,000
39	Montana	(8,000)
25	Nebraska	31,000
18	Nevada	47,000
34	New Hampshire	2,000
35	New Jersey	0
13	New Mexico	91,000
3	New York	318,000
7	North Carolina	169,000
31	North Dakota	11,000
11	Ohio	116,000
49	Oklahoma	(163,000)
23	Oregon	38,000
48	Pennsylvania	(120,000)
30	Rhode Island	14,000
12	South Carolina	99,000
29	South Dakota	16,000
8	Tennessee	165,000
1	Texas	679,000
19	Utah	46,000
39	Vermont	(8,000)
44	Virginia	(24,000)
17	Washington	49,000
43	West Virginia	(18,000)
41	Wisconsin	(16,000)
33	Wyoming	8,000

RANK ORDER

RANK	STATE	GAIN/LOSS
1	Texas	679,000
2	California	381,000
3	New York	318,000
4	Arizona	312,000
5	Florida	237,000
6	Georgia	234,000
7	North Carolina	169,000
8	Tennessee	165,000
9	Louisiana	162,000
10	Kentucky	126,000
11	Ohio	116,000
12	South Carolina	99,000
13	New Mexico	91,000
14	Missouri	69,000
15	Arkansas	64,000
16	Colorado	61,000
17	Washington	49,000
18	Nevada	47,000
19	Utah	46,000
20	Kansas	44,000
21	Michigan	42,000
22	Mississippi	41,000
23	Oregon	38,000
24	Idaho	36,000
25	Nebraska	31,000
26	Alaska	26,000
27	Maine	22,000
28	Iowa	17,000
29	South Dakota	16,000
30	Rhode Island	14,000
31	North Dakota	11,000
32	Minnesota	10,000
33	Wyoming	8,000
34	New Hampshire	2,000
35	New Jersey	0
36	Alabama	(1,000)
37	Illinois	(2,000)
38	Hawaii	(6,000)
39	Montana	(8,000)
39	Vermont	(8,000)
41	Delaware	(16,000)
41	Wisconsin	(16,000)
43	West Virginia	(18,000)
44	Virginia	(24,000)
45	Connecticut	(38,000)
46	Maryland	(73,000)
47	Indiana	(75,000)
48	Pennsylvania	(120,000)
49	Oklahoma	(163,000)
50	Massachusetts	(368,000)

District of Columbia   (8,000)

Source: CQ Press using data from U.S. Bureau of the Census
  "Health Insurance Coverage Status by State for All People: 2008" (http://www.census.gov/hhes/www/hlthins/hlthin08.html)
  "Health Insurance Coverage Status by State for All People: 2004"

Percent Change in Persons Uninsured: 2004 to 2008

National Percent Change = 6.5% Increase

ALPHA ORDER				RANK ORDER		
RANK	STATE	PERCENT CHANGE		RANK	STATE	PERCENT CHANGE
37	Alabama	(0.2)		1	Arizona	32.5
2	Alaska	24.3		2	Alaska	24.3
1	Arizona	32.5		3	New Mexico	24.1
15	Arkansas	14.5		4	Louisiana	22.9
31	California	5.9		5	Kentucky	22.7
26	Colorado	8.5		6	Tennessee	21.5
46	Connecticut	(10.0)		7	Maine	19.1
48	Delaware	(14.5)		8	South Dakota	19.0
27	Florida	7.0		9	Idaho	18.0
13	Georgia	15.9		10	North Dakota	17.5
41	Hawaii	(5.8)		11	Nebraska	17.2
9	Idaho	18.0		12	South Carolina	16.3
36	Illinois	(0.1)		13	Georgia	15.9
43	Indiana	(8.9)		14	Kansas	15.4
30	Iowa	6.4		15	Arkansas	14.5
14	Kansas	15.4		15	Utah	14.5
5	Kentucky	22.7		17	North Carolina	13.5
4	Louisiana	22.9		18	New York	13.2
7	Maine	19.1		19	Rhode Island	12.8
45	Maryland	(9.8)		20	Texas	12.6
50	Massachusetts	(51.1)		21	Wyoming	12.5
32	Michigan	3.8		22	Nevada	10.7
33	Minnesota	2.3		23	Missouri	10.3
25	Mississippi	8.6		24	Ohio	9.7
23	Missouri	10.3		25	Mississippi	8.6
40	Montana	(4.8)		26	Colorado	8.5
11	Nebraska	17.2		27	Florida	7.0
22	Nevada	10.7		28	Oregon	6.5
34	New Hampshire	1.5		28	Washington	6.5
35	New Jersey	0.0		30	Iowa	6.4
3	New Mexico	24.1		31	California	5.9
18	New York	13.2		32	Michigan	3.8
17	North Carolina	13.5		33	Minnesota	2.3
10	North Dakota	17.5		34	New Hampshire	1.5
24	Ohio	9.7		35	New Jersey	0.0
49	Oklahoma	(24.7)		36	Illinois	(0.1)
28	Oregon	6.5		37	Alabama	(0.2)
44	Pennsylvania	(9.0)		38	Virginia	(2.4)
19	Rhode Island	12.8		39	Wisconsin	(2.9)
12	South Carolina	16.3		40	Montana	(4.8)
8	South Dakota	19.0		41	Hawaii	(5.8)
6	Tennessee	21.5		42	West Virginia	(6.2)
20	Texas	12.6		43	Indiana	(8.9)
15	Utah	14.5		44	Pennsylvania	(9.0)
47	Vermont	(12.3)		45	Maryland	(9.8)
38	Virginia	(2.4)		46	Connecticut	(10.0)
28	Washington	6.5		47	Vermont	(12.3)
42	West Virginia	(6.2)		48	Delaware	(14.5)
39	Wisconsin	(2.9)		49	Oklahoma	(24.7)
21	Wyoming	12.5		50	Massachusetts	(51.1)
					District of Columbia	(11.9)

Source: CQ Press using data from U.S. Bureau of the Census
"Health Insurance Coverage Status by State for All People: 2008" (http://www.census.gov/hhes/www/hlthins/hlthin08.html)
"Health Insurance Coverage Status by State for All People: 2004"

Change in Percent of Population Uninsured: 2004 to 2008

National Percent Change = 0.0% Change*

<table>
<tr><td colspan="3">ALPHA ORDER</td><td colspan="3">RANK ORDER</td></tr>
<tr><th>RANK</th><th>STATE</th><th>PERCENT CHANGE</th><th>RANK</th><th>STATE</th><th>PERCENT CHANGE</th></tr>
<tr><td>33</td><td>Alabama</td><td>(3.7)</td><td>1</td><td>South Carolina</td><td>16.7</td></tr>
<tr><td>21</td><td>Alaska</td><td>0.0</td><td>2</td><td>Arizona</td><td>15.3</td></tr>
<tr><td>2</td><td>Arizona</td><td>15.3</td><td>3</td><td>Kansas</td><td>14.8</td></tr>
<tr><td>15</td><td>Arkansas</td><td>5.4</td><td>4</td><td>Nebraska</td><td>13.6</td></tr>
<tr><td>20</td><td>California</td><td>0.5</td><td>5</td><td>Tennessee</td><td>13.4</td></tr>
<tr><td>27</td><td>Colorado</td><td>(1.8)</td><td>6</td><td>Mississippi</td><td>11.0</td></tr>
<tr><td>41</td><td>Connecticut</td><td>(11.9)</td><td>7</td><td>Florida</td><td>10.8</td></tr>
<tr><td>31</td><td>Delaware</td><td>(3.4)</td><td>8</td><td>Missouri</td><td>9.4</td></tr>
<tr><td>7</td><td>Florida</td><td>10.8</td><td>9</td><td>Utah</td><td>8.2</td></tr>
<tr><td>13</td><td>Georgia</td><td>6.6</td><td>10</td><td>Kentucky</td><td>7.9</td></tr>
<tr><td>49</td><td>Hawaii</td><td>(18.2)</td><td>11</td><td>New Mexico</td><td>7.5</td></tr>
<tr><td>44</td><td>Idaho</td><td>(13.3)</td><td>12</td><td>Louisiana</td><td>6.9</td></tr>
<tr><td>34</td><td>Illinois</td><td>(5.6)</td><td>13</td><td>Georgia</td><td>6.6</td></tr>
<tr><td>45</td><td>Indiana</td><td>(13.9)</td><td>14</td><td>Oregon</td><td>5.6</td></tr>
<tr><td>29</td><td>Iowa</td><td>(3.0)</td><td>15</td><td>Arkansas</td><td>5.4</td></tr>
<tr><td>3</td><td>Kansas</td><td>14.8</td><td>16</td><td>New Jersey</td><td>4.9</td></tr>
<tr><td>10</td><td>Kentucky</td><td>7.9</td><td>17</td><td>North Dakota</td><td>3.6</td></tr>
<tr><td>12</td><td>Louisiana</td><td>6.9</td><td>18</td><td>Minnesota</td><td>2.4</td></tr>
<tr><td>39</td><td>Maine</td><td>(10.4)</td><td>19</td><td>New Hampshire</td><td>0.9</td></tr>
<tr><td>35</td><td>Maryland</td><td>(5.7)</td><td>20</td><td>California</td><td>0.5</td></tr>
<tr><td>50</td><td>Massachusetts</td><td>(34.3)</td><td>21</td><td>Alaska</td><td>0.0</td></tr>
<tr><td>25</td><td>Michigan</td><td>(0.9)</td><td>21</td><td>North Carolina</td><td>0.0</td></tr>
<tr><td>18</td><td>Minnesota</td><td>2.4</td><td>23</td><td>Virginia</td><td>(0.7)</td></tr>
<tr><td>6</td><td>Mississippi</td><td>11.0</td><td>24</td><td>Texas</td><td>(0.8)</td></tr>
<tr><td>8</td><td>Missouri</td><td>9.4</td><td>25</td><td>Michigan</td><td>(0.9)</td></tr>
<tr><td>38</td><td>Montana</td><td>(8.9)</td><td>26</td><td>Rhode Island</td><td>(1.0)</td></tr>
<tr><td>4</td><td>Nebraska</td><td>13.6</td><td>27</td><td>Colorado</td><td>(1.8)</td></tr>
<tr><td>30</td><td>Nevada</td><td>(3.1)</td><td>28</td><td>Vermont</td><td>(2.9)</td></tr>
<tr><td>19</td><td>New Hampshire</td><td>0.9</td><td>29</td><td>Iowa</td><td>(3.0)</td></tr>
<tr><td>16</td><td>New Jersey</td><td>4.9</td><td>30</td><td>Nevada</td><td>(3.1)</td></tr>
<tr><td>11</td><td>New Mexico</td><td>7.5</td><td>31</td><td>Delaware</td><td>(3.4)</td></tr>
<tr><td>37</td><td>New York</td><td>(8.0)</td><td>31</td><td>South Dakota</td><td>(3.4)</td></tr>
<tr><td>21</td><td>North Carolina</td><td>0.0</td><td>33</td><td>Alabama</td><td>(3.7)</td></tr>
<tr><td>17</td><td>North Dakota</td><td>3.6</td><td>34</td><td>Illinois</td><td>(5.6)</td></tr>
<tr><td>36</td><td>Ohio</td><td>(5.9)</td><td>35</td><td>Maryland</td><td>(5.7)</td></tr>
<tr><td>42</td><td>Oklahoma</td><td>(12.0)</td><td>36</td><td>Ohio</td><td>(5.9)</td></tr>
<tr><td>14</td><td>Oregon</td><td>5.6</td><td>37</td><td>New York</td><td>(8.0)</td></tr>
<tr><td>47</td><td>Pennsylvania</td><td>(14.8)</td><td>38</td><td>Montana</td><td>(8.9)</td></tr>
<tr><td>26</td><td>Rhode Island</td><td>(1.0)</td><td>39</td><td>Maine</td><td>(10.4)</td></tr>
<tr><td>1</td><td>South Carolina</td><td>16.7</td><td>40</td><td>West Virginia</td><td>(10.7)</td></tr>
<tr><td>31</td><td>South Dakota</td><td>(3.4)</td><td>41</td><td>Connecticut</td><td>(11.9)</td></tr>
<tr><td>5</td><td>Tennessee</td><td>13.4</td><td>42</td><td>Oklahoma</td><td>(12.0)</td></tr>
<tr><td>24</td><td>Texas</td><td>(0.8)</td><td>43</td><td>Wyoming</td><td>(12.6)</td></tr>
<tr><td>9</td><td>Utah</td><td>8.2</td><td>44</td><td>Idaho</td><td>(13.3)</td></tr>
<tr><td>28</td><td>Vermont</td><td>(2.9)</td><td>45</td><td>Indiana</td><td>(13.9)</td></tr>
<tr><td>23</td><td>Virginia</td><td>(0.7)</td><td>46</td><td>Wisconsin</td><td>(14.4)</td></tr>
<tr><td>48</td><td>Washington</td><td>(16.9)</td><td>47</td><td>Pennsylvania</td><td>(14.8)</td></tr>
<tr><td>40</td><td>West Virginia</td><td>(10.7)</td><td>48</td><td>Washington</td><td>(16.9)</td></tr>
<tr><td>46</td><td>Wisconsin</td><td>(14.4)</td><td>49</td><td>Hawaii</td><td>(18.2)</td></tr>
<tr><td>43</td><td>Wyoming</td><td>(12.6)</td><td>50</td><td>Massachusetts</td><td>(34.3)</td></tr>
<tr><td></td><td></td><td></td><td></td><td>District of Columbia</td><td>(23.0)</td></tr>
</table>

Source: CQ Press using data from U.S. Bureau of the Census
"Health Insurance Coverage Status by State for All People: 2008" (http://www.census.gov/hhes/www/hlthins/hlthin08.html)
"Health Insurance Coverage Status by State for All People: 2004"
*Based on three-year averages for 2006 through 2008 and 2002 through 2004.

Percent of Children Not Covered by Health Insurance in 2008

National Percent = 9.9% of Children*

ALPHA ORDER				RANK ORDER		
RANK	STATE	PERCENT		RANK	STATE	PERCENT
48	Alabama	3.6		1	Nevada	19.1
6	Alaska	14.5		2	Texas	17.9
5	Arizona	16.0		3	Florida	16.7
23	Arkansas	9.2		4	New Mexico	16.1
14	California	10.5		5	Arizona	16.0
9	Colorado	12.3		6	Alaska	14.5
43	Connecticut	5.4		7	Mississippi	13.4
24	Delaware	9.1		8	South Carolina	12.8
3	Florida	16.7		9	Colorado	12.3
14	Georgia	10.5		10	Oregon	11.6
43	Hawaii	5.4		11	Louisiana	11.3
25	Idaho	8.9		11	New Jersey	11.3
36	Illinois	6.4		13	Kansas	11.0
38	Indiana	6.0		14	California	10.5
45	Iowa	5.3		14	Georgia	10.5
13	Kansas	11.0		14	Montana	10.5
18	Kentucky	10.0		17	Nebraska	10.1
11	Louisiana	11.3		18	Kentucky	10.0
42	Maine	5.7		19	South Dakota	9.9
38	Maryland	6.0		20	Utah	9.5
50	Massachusetts	3.4		21	Tennessee	9.4
46	Michigan	4.7		22	North Carolina	9.3
35	Minnesota	6.6		23	Arkansas	9.2
7	Mississippi	13.4		24	Delaware	9.1
32	Missouri	6.8		25	Idaho	8.9
14	Montana	10.5		26	Wyoming	8.8
17	Nebraska	10.1		27	North Dakota	7.9
1	Nevada	19.1		27	Rhode Island	7.9
48	New Hampshire	3.6		29	Oklahoma	7.2
11	New Jersey	11.3		30	New York	7.1
4	New Mexico	16.1		31	Virginia	6.9
30	New York	7.1		32	Missouri	6.8
22	North Carolina	9.3		32	Washington	6.8
27	North Dakota	7.9		34	Pennsylvania	6.7
40	Ohio	5.8		35	Minnesota	6.6
29	Oklahoma	7.2		36	Illinois	6.4
10	Oregon	11.6		37	West Virginia	6.3
34	Pennsylvania	6.7		38	Indiana	6.0
27	Rhode Island	7.9		38	Maryland	6.0
8	South Carolina	12.8		40	Ohio	5.8
19	South Dakota	9.9		40	Wisconsin	5.8
21	Tennessee	9.4		42	Maine	5.7
2	Texas	17.9		43	Connecticut	5.4
20	Utah	9.5		43	Hawaii	5.4
47	Vermont	3.8		45	Iowa	5.3
31	Virginia	6.9		46	Michigan	4.7
32	Washington	6.8		47	Vermont	3.8
37	West Virginia	6.3		48	Alabama	3.6
40	Wisconsin	5.8		48	New Hampshire	3.6
26	Wyoming	8.8		50	Massachusetts	3.4
					District of Columbia	6.3

Source: U.S. Bureau of the Census
  "Health Insurance Coverage Status by State for All People: 2008" (http://www.census.gov/hhes/www/hlthins/hlthin08.html)
*Children under 18 years old.

Persons Covered by Health Insurance in 2008

National Total = 255,143,000 Insured

<table>
<tr><td colspan="4">ALPHA ORDER</td><td colspan="4">RANK ORDER</td></tr>
<tr><td>RANK</td><td>STATE</td><td>INSURED</td><td>% of USA</td><td>RANK</td><td>STATE</td><td>INSURED</td><td>% of USA</td></tr>
<tr><td>22</td><td>Alabama</td><td>4,159,000</td><td>1.6%</td><td>1</td><td>California</td><td>29,868,000</td><td>11.7%</td></tr>
<tr><td>49</td><td>Alaska</td><td>539,000</td><td>0.2%</td><td>2</td><td>Texas</td><td>18,110,000</td><td>7.1%</td></tr>
<tr><td>16</td><td>Arizona</td><td>5,264,000</td><td>2.1%</td><td>3</td><td>New York</td><td>16,617,000</td><td>6.5%</td></tr>
<tr><td>34</td><td>Arkansas</td><td>2,322,000</td><td>0.9%</td><td>4</td><td>Florida</td><td>14,430,000</td><td>5.7%</td></tr>
<tr><td>1</td><td>California</td><td>29,868,000</td><td>11.7%</td><td>5</td><td>Illinois</td><td>11,065,000</td><td>4.3%</td></tr>
<tr><td>23</td><td>Colorado</td><td>4,136,000</td><td>1.6%</td><td>6</td><td>Pennsylvania</td><td>10,984,000</td><td>4.3%</td></tr>
<tr><td>28</td><td>Connecticut</td><td>3,094,000</td><td>1.2%</td><td>7</td><td>Ohio</td><td>10,088,000</td><td>4.0%</td></tr>
<tr><td>45</td><td>Delaware</td><td>769,000</td><td>0.3%</td><td>8</td><td>Michigan</td><td>8,665,000</td><td>3.4%</td></tr>
<tr><td>4</td><td>Florida</td><td>14,430,000</td><td>5.7%</td><td>9</td><td>Georgia</td><td>7,850,000</td><td>3.1%</td></tr>
<tr><td>9</td><td>Georgia</td><td>7,850,000</td><td>3.1%</td><td>10</td><td>North Carolina</td><td>7,832,000</td><td>3.1%</td></tr>
<tr><td>42</td><td>Hawaii</td><td>1,159,000</td><td>0.5%</td><td>11</td><td>New Jersey</td><td>7,323,000</td><td>2.9%</td></tr>
<tr><td>39</td><td>Idaho</td><td>1,282,000</td><td>0.5%</td><td>12</td><td>Virginia</td><td>6,786,000</td><td>2.7%</td></tr>
<tr><td>5</td><td>Illinois</td><td>11,065,000</td><td>4.3%</td><td>13</td><td>Massachusetts</td><td>6,069,000</td><td>2.4%</td></tr>
<tr><td>15</td><td>Indiana</td><td>5,522,000</td><td>2.2%</td><td>14</td><td>Washington</td><td>5,732,000</td><td>2.2%</td></tr>
<tr><td>30</td><td>Iowa</td><td>2,707,000</td><td>1.1%</td><td>15</td><td>Indiana</td><td>5,522,000</td><td>2.2%</td></tr>
<tr><td>32</td><td>Kansas</td><td>2,394,000</td><td>0.9%</td><td>16</td><td>Arizona</td><td>5,264,000</td><td>2.1%</td></tr>
<tr><td>25</td><td>Kentucky</td><td>3,574,000</td><td>1.4%</td><td>17</td><td>Tennessee</td><td>5,252,000</td><td>2.1%</td></tr>
<tr><td>26</td><td>Louisiana</td><td>3,465,000</td><td>1.4%</td><td>18</td><td>Missouri</td><td>5,132,000</td><td>2.0%</td></tr>
<tr><td>40</td><td>Maine</td><td>1,182,000</td><td>0.5%</td><td>19</td><td>Wisconsin</td><td>5,020,000</td><td>2.0%</td></tr>
<tr><td>20</td><td>Maryland</td><td>4,870,000</td><td>1.9%</td><td>20</td><td>Maryland</td><td>4,870,000</td><td>1.9%</td></tr>
<tr><td>13</td><td>Massachusetts</td><td>6,069,000</td><td>2.4%</td><td>21</td><td>Minnesota</td><td>4,676,000</td><td>1.8%</td></tr>
<tr><td>8</td><td>Michigan</td><td>8,665,000</td><td>3.4%</td><td>22</td><td>Alabama</td><td>4,159,000</td><td>1.6%</td></tr>
<tr><td>21</td><td>Minnesota</td><td>4,676,000</td><td>1.8%</td><td>23</td><td>Colorado</td><td>4,136,000</td><td>1.6%</td></tr>
<tr><td>33</td><td>Mississippi</td><td>2,388,000</td><td>0.9%</td><td>24</td><td>South Carolina</td><td>3,762,000</td><td>1.5%</td></tr>
<tr><td>18</td><td>Missouri</td><td>5,132,000</td><td>2.0%</td><td>25</td><td>Kentucky</td><td>3,574,000</td><td>1.4%</td></tr>
<tr><td>44</td><td>Montana</td><td>819,000</td><td>0.3%</td><td>26</td><td>Louisiana</td><td>3,465,000</td><td>1.4%</td></tr>
<tr><td>36</td><td>Nebraska</td><td>1,565,000</td><td>0.6%</td><td>27</td><td>Oregon</td><td>3,194,000</td><td>1.3%</td></tr>
<tr><td>35</td><td>Nevada</td><td>2,097,000</td><td>0.8%</td><td>28</td><td>Connecticut</td><td>3,094,000</td><td>1.2%</td></tr>
<tr><td>41</td><td>New Hampshire</td><td>1,168,000</td><td>0.5%</td><td>29</td><td>Oklahoma</td><td>3,060,000</td><td>1.2%</td></tr>
<tr><td>11</td><td>New Jersey</td><td>7,323,000</td><td>2.9%</td><td>30</td><td>Iowa</td><td>2,707,000</td><td>1.1%</td></tr>
<tr><td>38</td><td>New Mexico</td><td>1,510,000</td><td>0.6%</td><td>31</td><td>Utah</td><td>2,396,000</td><td>0.9%</td></tr>
<tr><td>3</td><td>New York</td><td>16,617,000</td><td>6.5%</td><td>32</td><td>Kansas</td><td>2,394,000</td><td>0.9%</td></tr>
<tr><td>10</td><td>North Carolina</td><td>7,832,000</td><td>3.1%</td><td>33</td><td>Mississippi</td><td>2,388,000</td><td>0.9%</td></tr>
<tr><td>48</td><td>North Dakota</td><td>552,000</td><td>0.2%</td><td>34</td><td>Arkansas</td><td>2,322,000</td><td>0.9%</td></tr>
<tr><td>7</td><td>Ohio</td><td>10,088,000</td><td>4.0%</td><td>35</td><td>Nevada</td><td>2,097,000</td><td>0.8%</td></tr>
<tr><td>29</td><td>Oklahoma</td><td>3,060,000</td><td>1.2%</td><td>36</td><td>Nebraska</td><td>1,565,000</td><td>0.6%</td></tr>
<tr><td>27</td><td>Oregon</td><td>3,194,000</td><td>1.3%</td><td>37</td><td>West Virginia</td><td>1,528,000</td><td>0.6%</td></tr>
<tr><td>6</td><td>Pennsylvania</td><td>10,984,000</td><td>4.3%</td><td>38</td><td>New Mexico</td><td>1,510,000</td><td>0.6%</td></tr>
<tr><td>43</td><td>Rhode Island</td><td>921,000</td><td>0.4%</td><td>39</td><td>Idaho</td><td>1,282,000</td><td>0.5%</td></tr>
<tr><td>24</td><td>South Carolina</td><td>3,762,000</td><td>1.5%</td><td>40</td><td>Maine</td><td>1,182,000</td><td>0.5%</td></tr>
<tr><td>46</td><td>South Dakota</td><td>698,000</td><td>0.3%</td><td>41</td><td>New Hampshire</td><td>1,168,000</td><td>0.5%</td></tr>
<tr><td>17</td><td>Tennessee</td><td>5,252,000</td><td>2.1%</td><td>42</td><td>Hawaii</td><td>1,159,000</td><td>0.5%</td></tr>
<tr><td>2</td><td>Texas</td><td>18,110,000</td><td>7.1%</td><td>43</td><td>Rhode Island</td><td>921,000</td><td>0.4%</td></tr>
<tr><td>31</td><td>Utah</td><td>2,396,000</td><td>0.9%</td><td>44</td><td>Montana</td><td>819,000</td><td>0.3%</td></tr>
<tr><td>47</td><td>Vermont</td><td>555,000</td><td>0.2%</td><td>45</td><td>Delaware</td><td>769,000</td><td>0.3%</td></tr>
<tr><td>12</td><td>Virginia</td><td>6,786,000</td><td>2.7%</td><td>46</td><td>South Dakota</td><td>698,000</td><td>0.3%</td></tr>
<tr><td>14</td><td>Washington</td><td>5,732,000</td><td>2.2%</td><td>47</td><td>Vermont</td><td>555,000</td><td>0.2%</td></tr>
<tr><td>37</td><td>West Virginia</td><td>1,528,000</td><td>0.6%</td><td>48</td><td>North Dakota</td><td>552,000</td><td>0.2%</td></tr>
<tr><td>19</td><td>Wisconsin</td><td>5,020,000</td><td>2.0%</td><td>49</td><td>Alaska</td><td>539,000</td><td>0.2%</td></tr>
<tr><td>50</td><td>Wyoming</td><td>458,000</td><td>0.2%</td><td>50</td><td>Wyoming</td><td>458,000</td><td>0.2%</td></tr>
<tr><td></td><td></td><td></td><td></td><td colspan="2">District of Columbia</td><td>533,000</td><td>0.2%</td></tr>
</table>

Source: U.S. Bureau of the Census
"Health Insurance Coverage Status by State for All People: 2008" (http://www.census.gov/hhes/www/hlthins/hlthin08.html)

Percent of Population Covered by Health Insurance in 2008

National Percent = 84.6% of Population

ALPHA ORDER

RANK	STATE	PERCENT
16	Alabama	88.1
46	Alaska	80.2
45	Arizona	80.5
40	Arkansas	82.2
43	California	81.4
36	Colorado	84.1
8	Connecticut	90.0
11	Delaware	89.2
47	Florida	80.0
40	Georgia	82.2
2	Hawaii	92.2
34	Idaho	84.4
25	Illinois	87.1
20	Indiana	87.7
5	Iowa	90.5
18	Kansas	87.9
37	Kentucky	84.0
48	Louisiana	79.9
10	Maine	89.6
18	Maryland	87.9
1	Massachusetts	94.5
13	Michigan	88.3
3	Minnesota	91.3
42	Mississippi	82.1
24	Missouri	87.4
38	Montana	83.9
16	Nebraska	88.1
44	Nevada	81.2
9	New Hampshire	89.8
29	New Jersey	85.9
49	New Mexico	76.3
29	New York	85.9
33	North Carolina	84.6
14	North Dakota	88.2
12	Ohio	88.5
28	Oklahoma	86.0
39	Oregon	83.7
7	Pennsylvania	90.1
14	Rhode Island	88.2
35	South Carolina	84.2
23	South Dakota	87.5
32	Tennessee	84.9
50	Texas	74.9
26	Utah	86.8
4	Vermont	90.8
21	Virginia	87.6
21	Washington	87.6
31	West Virginia	85.0
6	Wisconsin	90.4
27	Wyoming	86.4

RANK ORDER

RANK	STATE	PERCENT
1	Massachusetts	94.5
2	Hawaii	92.2
3	Minnesota	91.3
4	Vermont	90.8
5	Iowa	90.5
6	Wisconsin	90.4
7	Pennsylvania	90.1
8	Connecticut	90.0
9	New Hampshire	89.8
10	Maine	89.6
11	Delaware	89.2
12	Ohio	88.5
13	Michigan	88.3
14	North Dakota	88.2
14	Rhode Island	88.2
16	Alabama	88.1
16	Nebraska	88.1
18	Kansas	87.9
18	Maryland	87.9
20	Indiana	87.7
21	Virginia	87.6
21	Washington	87.6
23	South Dakota	87.5
24	Missouri	87.4
25	Illinois	87.1
26	Utah	86.8
27	Wyoming	86.4
28	Oklahoma	86.0
29	New Jersey	85.9
29	New York	85.9
31	West Virginia	85.0
32	Tennessee	84.9
33	North Carolina	84.6
34	Idaho	84.4
35	South Carolina	84.2
36	Colorado	84.1
37	Kentucky	84.0
38	Montana	83.9
39	Oregon	83.7
40	Arkansas	82.2
40	Georgia	82.2
42	Mississippi	82.1
43	California	81.4
44	Nevada	81.2
45	Arizona	80.5
46	Alaska	80.2
47	Florida	80.0
48	Louisiana	79.9
49	New Mexico	76.3
50	Texas	74.9

District of Columbia	90.0

Source: U.S. Bureau of the Census
"Health Insurance Coverage Status by State for All People: 2008" (http://www.census.gov/hhes/www/hlthins/hlthin08.html)

Percent of Population Covered by Private Health Insurance in 2008

National Percent = 66.7% of Population*

ALPHA ORDER

RANK	STATE	PERCENT		RANK	STATE	PERCENT
31	Alabama	67.8		1	Utah	78.1
42	Alaska	62.2		2	Iowa	78.0
45	Arizona	59.5		3	New Hampshire	77.5
47	Arkansas	57.9		4	Minnesota	76.8
41	California	62.3		4	North Dakota	76.8
27	Colorado	69.6		6	Massachusetts	76.3
8	Connecticut	74.9		7	Maryland	75.3
14	Delaware	72.6		8	Connecticut	74.9
43	Florida	61.7		9	Nebraska	74.7
38	Georgia	64.5		10	Wisconsin	74.4
18	Hawaii	71.5		11	Pennsylvania	74.1
21	Idaho	71.1		12	Kansas	72.7
17	Illinois	71.7		12	New Jersey	72.7
25	Indiana	70.6		14	Delaware	72.6
2	Iowa	78.0		14	Michigan	72.6
12	Kansas	72.7		16	South Dakota	72.4
40	Kentucky	63.5		17	Illinois	71.7
46	Louisiana	58.6		18	Hawaii	71.5
30	Maine	67.9		19	Virginia	71.3
7	Maryland	75.3		20	Ohio	71.2
6	Massachusetts	76.3		21	Idaho	71.1
14	Michigan	72.6		22	Vermont	71.0
4	Minnesota	76.8		23	Wyoming	70.8
48	Mississippi	56.6		24	Rhode Island	70.7
29	Missouri	68.5		25	Indiana	70.6
32	Montana	66.4		26	Oregon	69.7
9	Nebraska	74.7		27	Colorado	69.6
34	Nevada	66.3		28	Washington	69.1
3	New Hampshire	77.5		29	Missouri	68.5
12	New Jersey	72.7		30	Maine	67.9
50	New Mexico	53.5		31	Alabama	67.8
36	New York	65.0		32	Montana	66.4
37	North Carolina	64.6		32	Oklahoma	66.4
4	North Dakota	76.8		34	Nevada	66.3
20	Ohio	71.2		34	West Virginia	66.3
32	Oklahoma	66.4		36	New York	65.0
26	Oregon	69.7		37	North Carolina	64.6
11	Pennsylvania	74.1		38	Georgia	64.5
24	Rhode Island	70.7		38	South Carolina	64.5
38	South Carolina	64.5		40	Kentucky	63.5
16	South Dakota	72.4		41	California	62.3
44	Tennessee	60.9		42	Alaska	62.2
49	Texas	55.6		43	Florida	61.7
1	Utah	78.1		44	Tennessee	60.9
22	Vermont	71.0		45	Arizona	59.5
19	Virginia	71.3		46	Louisiana	58.6
28	Washington	69.1		47	Arkansas	57.9
34	West Virginia	66.3		48	Mississippi	56.6
10	Wisconsin	74.4		49	Texas	55.6
23	Wyoming	70.8		50	New Mexico	53.5
					District of Columbia	68.2

Source: U.S. Bureau of the Census

"Health Insurance Coverage Status by State for All People: 2008" (http://www.census.gov/hhes/www/hlthins/hlthin08.html)

*Private health insurance is coverage by a health plan provided through an employer or union or purchased by an individual from a private health insurance company.

Percent of Population Covered by
Employment-Based Health Insurance in 2008
National Percent = 58.5% of Population*

ALPHA ORDER

RANK	STATE	PERCENT
21	Alabama	60.9
38	Alaska	56.2
44	Arizona	52.1
47	Arkansas	49.9
41	California	53.8
26	Colorado	60.3
7	Connecticut	65.7
6	Delaware	66.1
45	Florida	51.8
31	Georgia	58.9
5	Hawaii	66.3
32	Idaho	58.8
15	Illinois	63.6
16	Indiana	63.2
11	Iowa	64.2
27	Kansas	60.1
38	Kentucky	56.2
46	Louisiana	50.9
34	Maine	57.9
4	Maryland	68.0
2	Massachusetts	70.1
9	Michigan	64.9
11	Minnesota	64.2
49	Mississippi	48.8
30	Missouri	59.1
42	Montana	52.9
16	Nebraska	63.2
20	Nevada	61.3
1	New Hampshire	70.3
8	New Jersey	65.5
50	New Mexico	46.6
33	New York	58.7
40	North Carolina	55.5
21	North Dakota	60.9
13	Ohio	63.9
37	Oklahoma	56.9
29	Oregon	59.4
16	Pennsylvania	63.2
23	Rhode Island	60.6
36	South Carolina	57.4
35	South Dakota	57.7
43	Tennessee	52.8
48	Texas	49.5
3	Utah	69.1
19	Vermont	63.1
10	Virginia	64.4
24	Washington	60.5
28	West Virginia	59.8
14	Wisconsin	63.8
25	Wyoming	60.4

RANK ORDER

RANK	STATE	PERCENT
1	New Hampshire	70.3
2	Massachusetts	70.1
3	Utah	69.1
4	Maryland	68.0
5	Hawaii	66.3
6	Delaware	66.1
7	Connecticut	65.7
8	New Jersey	65.5
9	Michigan	64.9
10	Virginia	64.4
11	Iowa	64.2
11	Minnesota	64.2
13	Ohio	63.9
14	Wisconsin	63.8
15	Illinois	63.6
16	Indiana	63.2
16	Nebraska	63.2
16	Pennsylvania	63.2
19	Vermont	63.1
20	Nevada	61.3
21	Alabama	60.9
21	North Dakota	60.9
23	Rhode Island	60.6
24	Washington	60.5
25	Wyoming	60.4
26	Colorado	60.3
27	Kansas	60.1
28	West Virginia	59.8
29	Oregon	59.4
30	Missouri	59.1
31	Georgia	58.9
32	Idaho	58.8
33	New York	58.7
34	Maine	57.9
35	South Dakota	57.7
36	South Carolina	57.4
37	Oklahoma	56.9
38	Alaska	56.2
38	Kentucky	56.2
40	North Carolina	55.5
41	California	53.8
42	Montana	52.9
43	Tennessee	52.8
44	Arizona	52.1
45	Florida	51.8
46	Louisiana	50.9
47	Arkansas	49.9
48	Texas	49.5
49	Mississippi	48.8
50	New Mexico	46.6

District of Columbia   61.0

Source: U.S. Bureau of the Census
    "Health Insurance Coverage Status by State for All People: 2008" (http://www.census.gov/hhes/www/hlthins/hlthin08.html)
*Employment-based health insurance is private insurance coverage offered through one's own employment or a relative's. It may be offered by an employer or by a union.

Percent of Population Covered by Direct-Purchase Health Insurance in 2008

National Percent = 8.9% of Population*

ALPHA ORDER

RANK	STATE	PERCENT
48	Alabama	6.0
42	Alaska	7.1
35	Arizona	7.9
22	Arkansas	9.4
24	California	9.2
20	Colorado	9.8
22	Connecticut	9.4
45	Delaware	6.5
12	Florida	11.3
49	Georgia	5.9
47	Hawaii	6.2
3	Idaho	15.0
25	Illinois	8.8
25	Indiana	8.8
5	Iowa	14.5
8	Kansas	12.8
29	Kentucky	8.1
28	Louisiana	8.5
13	Maine	11.2
36	Maryland	7.8
44	Massachusetts	6.6
41	Michigan	7.4
6	Minnesota	13.6
29	Mississippi	8.1
14	Missouri	10.8
4	Montana	14.9
6	Nebraska	13.6
50	Nevada	5.5
29	New Hampshire	8.1
36	New Jersey	7.8
39	New Mexico	7.5
45	New York	6.5
20	North Carolina	9.8
2	North Dakota	15.7
27	Ohio	8.7
10	Oklahoma	11.7
9	Oregon	12.5
14	Pennsylvania	10.8
17	Rhode Island	10.0
29	South Carolina	8.1
1	South Dakota	16.6
34	Tennessee	8.0
43	Texas	6.8
16	Utah	10.5
29	Vermont	8.1
39	Virginia	7.5
19	Washington	9.9
38	West Virginia	7.7
11	Wisconsin	11.4
17	Wyoming	10.0

RANK ORDER

RANK	STATE	PERCENT
1	South Dakota	16.6
2	North Dakota	15.7
3	Idaho	15.0
4	Montana	14.9
5	Iowa	14.5
6	Minnesota	13.6
6	Nebraska	13.6
8	Kansas	12.8
9	Oregon	12.5
10	Oklahoma	11.7
11	Wisconsin	11.4
12	Florida	11.3
13	Maine	11.2
14	Missouri	10.8
14	Pennsylvania	10.8
16	Utah	10.5
17	Rhode Island	10.0
17	Wyoming	10.0
19	Washington	9.9
20	Colorado	9.8
20	North Carolina	9.8
22	Arkansas	9.4
22	Connecticut	9.4
24	California	9.2
25	Illinois	8.8
25	Indiana	8.8
27	Ohio	8.7
28	Louisiana	8.5
29	Kentucky	8.1
29	Mississippi	8.1
29	New Hampshire	8.1
29	South Carolina	8.1
29	Vermont	8.1
34	Tennessee	8.0
35	Arizona	7.9
36	Maryland	7.8
36	New Jersey	7.8
38	West Virginia	7.7
39	New Mexico	7.5
39	Virginia	7.5
41	Michigan	7.4
42	Alaska	7.1
43	Texas	6.8
44	Massachusetts	6.6
45	Delaware	6.5
45	New York	6.5
47	Hawaii	6.2
48	Alabama	6.0
49	Georgia	5.9
50	Nevada	5.5

	District of Columbia	8.0

Source: U.S. Bureau of the Census
   "Health Insurance Coverage Status by State for All People: 2008" (http://www.census.gov/hhes/www/hlthins/hlthin08.html)
*Direct-purchase health insurance is private insurance coverage through a plan purchased by an individual from a private company.

Percent of Population Covered by Government Health Insurance in 2008

National Percent = 33.2% of Population*

ALPHA ORDER				RANK ORDER		
RANK	STATE	PERCENT		RANK	STATE	PERCENT
10	Alabama	32.6		1	Maine	37.9
22	Alaska	30.2		2	Hawaii	36.7
14	Arizona	31.2		3	Mississippi	36.6
7	Arkansas	34.5		4	West Virginia	36.1
33	California	28.0		5	Vermont	35.6
47	Colorado	23.4		6	Tennessee	35.1
37	Connecticut	27.0		7	Arkansas	34.5
25	Delaware	29.5		8	Oklahoma	33.7
19	Florida	30.6		9	New Mexico	33.0
39	Georgia	26.5		10	Alabama	32.6
2	Hawaii	36.7		11	North Carolina	32.4
43	Idaho	25.8		12	Kentucky	32.3
42	Illinois	26.1		13	New York	32.0
31	Indiana	28.4		14	Arizona	31.2
38	Iowa	26.6		14	Montana	31.2
40	Kansas	26.4		16	Massachusetts	31.1
12	Kentucky	32.3		16	South Carolina	31.1
24	Louisiana	29.7		18	South Dakota	30.9
1	Maine	37.9		19	Florida	30.6
44	Maryland	24.4		20	Missouri	30.5
16	Massachusetts	31.1		21	Washington	30.4
28	Michigan	29.0		22	Alaska	30.2
36	Minnesota	27.1		22	Rhode Island	30.2
3	Mississippi	36.6		24	Louisiana	29.7
20	Missouri	30.5		25	Delaware	29.5
14	Montana	31.2		25	Pennsylvania	29.5
34	Nebraska	27.3		27	Wisconsin	29.3
49	Nevada	21.9		28	Michigan	29.0
48	New Hampshire	22.5		29	Virginia	28.8
46	New Jersey	23.6		30	Ohio	28.5
9	New Mexico	33.0		31	Indiana	28.4
13	New York	32.0		31	Wyoming	28.4
11	North Carolina	32.4		33	California	28.0
45	North Dakota	24.3		34	Nebraska	27.3
30	Ohio	28.5		34	Texas	27.3
8	Oklahoma	33.7		36	Minnesota	27.1
40	Oregon	26.4		37	Connecticut	27.0
25	Pennsylvania	29.5		38	Iowa	26.6
22	Rhode Island	30.2		39	Georgia	26.5
16	South Carolina	31.1		40	Kansas	26.4
18	South Dakota	30.9		40	Oregon	26.4
6	Tennessee	35.1		42	Illinois	26.1
34	Texas	27.3		43	Idaho	25.8
50	Utah	17.0		44	Maryland	24.4
5	Vermont	35.6		45	North Dakota	24.3
29	Virginia	28.8		46	New Jersey	23.6
21	Washington	30.4		47	Colorado	23.4
4	West Virginia	36.1		48	New Hampshire	22.5
27	Wisconsin	29.3		49	Nevada	21.9
31	Wyoming	28.4		50	Utah	17.0
				District of Columbia		30.8

Source: U.S. Bureau of the Census

"Health Insurance Coverage Status by State for All People: 2008" (http://www.census.gov/hhes/www/hlthins/hlthin08.html)

*Includes Medicaid, Medicare, State Children's Health Insurance Program (SCHIP), and military health care.

Percent of Population Covered by Military Health Care in 2008

National Percent = 3.8% of Population*

ALPHA ORDER

RANK	STATE	PERCENT
30	Alabama	3.7
1	Alaska	12.1
23	Arizona	4.4
15	Arkansas	5.6
40	California	2.4
14	Colorado	5.7
44	Connecticut	2.1
36	Delaware	2.8
16	Florida	5.3
8	Georgia	6.3
2	Hawaii	11.1
33	Idaho	3.4
46	Illinois	1.9
49	Indiana	1.5
34	Iowa	3.3
18	Kansas	5.1
28	Kentucky	3.9
43	Louisiana	2.3
10	Maine	6.0
29	Maryland	3.8
38	Massachusetts	2.6
46	Michigan	1.9
40	Minnesota	2.4
20	Mississippi	4.8
19	Missouri	4.9
7	Montana	7.0
16	Nebraska	5.3
26	Nevada	4.2
32	New Hampshire	3.5
48	New Jersey	1.6
8	New Mexico	6.3
50	New York	1.4
10	North Carolina	6.0
27	North Dakota	4.1
44	Ohio	2.1
12	Oklahoma	5.9
35	Oregon	3.2
40	Pennsylvania	2.4
30	Rhode Island	3.7
20	South Carolina	4.8
6	South Dakota	7.3
13	Tennessee	5.8
22	Texas	4.7
38	Utah	2.6
25	Vermont	4.3
3	Virginia	10.2
4	Washington	8.0
23	West Virginia	4.4
36	Wisconsin	2.8
5	Wyoming	7.4

RANK ORDER

RANK	STATE	PERCENT
1	Alaska	12.1
2	Hawaii	11.1
3	Virginia	10.2
4	Washington	8.0
5	Wyoming	7.4
6	South Dakota	7.3
7	Montana	7.0
8	Georgia	6.3
8	New Mexico	6.3
10	Maine	6.0
10	North Carolina	6.0
12	Oklahoma	5.9
13	Tennessee	5.8
14	Colorado	5.7
15	Arkansas	5.6
16	Florida	5.3
16	Nebraska	5.3
18	Kansas	5.1
19	Missouri	4.9
20	Mississippi	4.8
20	South Carolina	4.8
22	Texas	4.7
23	Arizona	4.4
23	West Virginia	4.4
25	Vermont	4.3
26	Nevada	4.2
27	North Dakota	4.1
28	Kentucky	3.9
29	Maryland	3.8
30	Alabama	3.7
30	Rhode Island	3.7
32	New Hampshire	3.5
33	Idaho	3.4
34	Iowa	3.3
35	Oregon	3.2
36	Delaware	2.8
36	Wisconsin	2.8
38	Massachusetts	2.6
38	Utah	2.6
40	California	2.4
40	Minnesota	2.4
40	Pennsylvania	2.4
43	Louisiana	2.3
44	Connecticut	2.1
44	Ohio	2.1
46	Illinois	1.9
46	Michigan	1.9
48	New Jersey	1.6
49	Indiana	1.5
50	New York	1.4

District of Columbia 1.6

Source: U.S. Bureau of the Census
"Health Insurance Coverage Status by State for All People: 2008" (http://www.census.gov/hhes/www/hlthins/hlthin08.html)
*Includes CHAMPUS (Comprehensive Health and Medical Plan for Uniformed Services)/Tricare, Veterans, and military health care.

Percent of Children Covered by Health Insurance in 2008

National Percent = 90.1% of Children*

ALPHA ORDER				RANK ORDER		
RANK	STATE	PERCENT		RANK	STATE	PERCENT
2	Alabama	96.4		1	Massachusetts	96.6
45	Alaska	85.5		2	Alabama	96.4
46	Arizona	84.0		2	New Hampshire	96.4
28	Arkansas	90.8		4	Vermont	96.2
35	California	89.5		5	Michigan	95.3
42	Colorado	87.7		6	Iowa	94.7
7	Connecticut	94.6		7	Connecticut	94.6
27	Delaware	90.9		7	Hawaii	94.6
48	Florida	83.3		9	Maine	94.3
35	Georgia	89.5		10	Ohio	94.2
7	Hawaii	94.6		10	Wisconsin	94.2
26	Idaho	91.1		12	Indiana	94.0
15	Illinois	93.6		12	Maryland	94.0
12	Indiana	94.0		14	West Virginia	93.7
6	Iowa	94.7		15	Illinois	93.6
38	Kansas	89.0		16	Minnesota	93.4
33	Kentucky	90.0		17	Pennsylvania	93.3
39	Louisiana	88.7		18	Missouri	93.2
9	Maine	94.3		18	Washington	93.2
12	Maryland	94.0		20	Virginia	93.1
1	Massachusetts	96.6		21	New York	92.9
5	Michigan	95.3		22	Oklahoma	92.8
16	Minnesota	93.4		23	North Dakota	92.1
44	Mississippi	86.6		23	Rhode Island	92.1
18	Missouri	93.2		25	Wyoming	91.2
35	Montana	89.5		26	Idaho	91.1
34	Nebraska	89.9		27	Delaware	90.9
50	Nevada	80.9		28	Arkansas	90.8
2	New Hampshire	96.4		29	North Carolina	90.7
39	New Jersey	88.7		30	Tennessee	90.6
47	New Mexico	83.9		31	Utah	90.5
21	New York	92.9		32	South Dakota	90.1
29	North Carolina	90.7		33	Kentucky	90.0
23	North Dakota	92.1		34	Nebraska	89.9
10	Ohio	94.2		35	California	89.5
22	Oklahoma	92.8		35	Georgia	89.5
41	Oregon	88.4		35	Montana	89.5
17	Pennsylvania	93.3		38	Kansas	89.0
23	Rhode Island	92.1		39	Louisiana	88.7
43	South Carolina	87.2		39	New Jersey	88.7
32	South Dakota	90.1		41	Oregon	88.4
30	Tennessee	90.6		42	Colorado	87.7
49	Texas	82.1		43	South Carolina	87.2
31	Utah	90.5		44	Mississippi	86.6
4	Vermont	96.2		45	Alaska	85.5
20	Virginia	93.1		46	Arizona	84.0
18	Washington	93.2		47	New Mexico	83.9
14	West Virginia	93.7		48	Florida	83.3
10	Wisconsin	94.2		49	Texas	82.1
25	Wyoming	91.2		50	Nevada	80.9
				District of Columbia		93.7

Source: U.S. Bureau of the Census

"Health Insurance Coverage Status by State for All People: 2008" (http://www.census.gov/hhes/www/hlthins/hlthin08.html)

*Children under 18 covered by either private or government health insurance.

Percent of Children Covered by Private Health Insurance in 2008

National Percent = 63.5% of Children*

ALPHA ORDER

RANK	STATE	PERCENT
32	Alabama	63.7
40	Alaska	60.1
46	Arizona	52.3
50	Arkansas	49.1
44	California	58.7
20	Colorado	68.4
5	Connecticut	74.8
12	Delaware	70.6
39	Florida	60.5
37	Georgia	61.0
29	Hawaii	64.1
18	Idaho	69.6
21	Illinois	67.8
27	Indiana	64.7
4	Iowa	75.1
33	Kansas	63.4
42	Kentucky	59.2
43	Louisiana	58.9
24	Maine	66.4
7	Maryland	74.1
3	Massachusetts	75.5
11	Michigan	71.3
8	Minnesota	73.5
48	Mississippi	49.5
15	Missouri	69.9
30	Montana	64.0
22	Nebraska	67.3
26	Nevada	65.3
2	New Hampshire	79.5
16	New Jersey	69.8
49	New Mexico	49.2
34	New York	63.3
38	North Carolina	60.9
9	North Dakota	73.3
17	Ohio	69.7
41	Oklahoma	59.8
25	Oregon	66.2
14	Pennsylvania	70.0
23	Rhode Island	67.0
36	South Carolina	61.3
30	South Dakota	64.0
45	Tennessee	56.1
47	Texas	50.7
1	Utah	83.2
19	Vermont	69.2
9	Virginia	73.3
28	Washington	64.3
35	West Virginia	61.9
6	Wisconsin	74.7
12	Wyoming	70.6

RANK ORDER

RANK	STATE	PERCENT
1	Utah	83.2
2	New Hampshire	79.5
3	Massachusetts	75.5
4	Iowa	75.1
5	Connecticut	74.8
6	Wisconsin	74.7
7	Maryland	74.1
8	Minnesota	73.5
9	North Dakota	73.3
9	Virginia	73.3
11	Michigan	71.3
12	Delaware	70.6
12	Wyoming	70.6
14	Pennsylvania	70.0
15	Missouri	69.9
16	New Jersey	69.8
17	Ohio	69.7
18	Idaho	69.6
19	Vermont	69.2
20	Colorado	68.4
21	Illinois	67.8
22	Nebraska	67.3
23	Rhode Island	67.0
24	Maine	66.4
25	Oregon	66.2
26	Nevada	65.3
27	Indiana	64.7
28	Washington	64.3
29	Hawaii	64.1
30	Montana	64.0
30	South Dakota	64.0
32	Alabama	63.7
33	Kansas	63.4
34	New York	63.3
35	West Virginia	61.9
36	South Carolina	61.3
37	Georgia	61.0
38	North Carolina	60.9
39	Florida	60.5
40	Alaska	60.1
41	Oklahoma	59.8
42	Kentucky	59.2
43	Louisiana	58.9
44	California	58.7
45	Tennessee	56.1
46	Arizona	52.3
47	Texas	50.7
48	Mississippi	49.5
49	New Mexico	49.2
50	Arkansas	49.1
	District of Columbia	57.5

Source: U.S. Bureau of the Census
  "Health Insurance Coverage Status by State for All People: 2008" (http://www.census.gov/hhes/www/hlthins/hlthin08.html)
*Children under 18. Private health insurance is coverage by a health plan provided through an employer or union or purchased by an individual from a private health insurance company.

Percent of Children Covered by Employment-Based Health Insurance in 2008

National Percent = 58.9% of Children*

ALPHA ORDER

RANK	STATE	PERCENT
29	Alabama	59.6
43	Alaska	53.5
46	Arizona	47.9
49	Arkansas	45.0
42	California	53.7
26	Colorado	61.1
6	Connecticut	69.1
12	Delaware	66.6
40	Florida	54.2
35	Georgia	57.8
29	Hawaii	59.6
20	Idaho	63.5
18	Illinois	64.3
25	Indiana	61.4
8	Iowa	68.6
36	Kansas	57.7
41	Kentucky	54.1
44	Louisiana	53.1
24	Maine	61.7
7	Maryland	69.0
3	Massachusetts	73.5
11	Michigan	67.4
10	Minnesota	67.5
48	Mississippi	46.0
19	Missouri	64.0
32	Montana	59.3
22	Nebraska	62.2
23	Nevada	62.1
1	New Hampshire	75.8
13	New Jersey	65.9
50	New Mexico	44.4
31	New York	59.5
39	North Carolina	54.8
9	North Dakota	67.8
15	Ohio	65.7
38	Oklahoma	55.5
27	Oregon	60.8
13	Pennsylvania	65.9
21	Rhode Island	62.5
34	South Carolina	58.3
37	South Dakota	56.9
45	Tennessee	52.6
47	Texas	46.5
1	Utah	75.8
16	Vermont	65.6
5	Virginia	69.2
28	Washington	59.8
33	West Virginia	59.1
4	Wisconsin	69.9
17	Wyoming	65.3

RANK ORDER

RANK	STATE	PERCENT
1	New Hampshire	75.8
1	Utah	75.8
3	Massachusetts	73.5
4	Wisconsin	69.9
5	Virginia	69.2
6	Connecticut	69.1
7	Maryland	69.0
8	Iowa	68.6
9	North Dakota	67.8
10	Minnesota	67.5
11	Michigan	67.4
12	Delaware	66.6
13	New Jersey	65.9
13	Pennsylvania	65.9
15	Ohio	65.7
16	Vermont	65.6
17	Wyoming	65.3
18	Illinois	64.3
19	Missouri	64.0
20	Idaho	63.5
21	Rhode Island	62.5
22	Nebraska	62.2
23	Nevada	62.1
24	Maine	61.7
25	Indiana	61.4
26	Colorado	61.1
27	Oregon	60.8
28	Washington	59.8
29	Alabama	59.6
29	Hawaii	59.6
31	New York	59.5
32	Montana	59.3
33	West Virginia	59.1
34	South Carolina	58.3
35	Georgia	57.8
36	Kansas	57.7
37	South Dakota	56.9
38	Oklahoma	55.5
39	North Carolina	54.8
40	Florida	54.2
41	Kentucky	54.1
42	California	53.7
43	Alaska	53.5
44	Louisiana	53.1
45	Tennessee	52.6
46	Arizona	47.9
47	Texas	46.5
48	Mississippi	46.0
49	Arkansas	45.0
50	New Mexico	44.4

District of Columbia 53.7

Source: U.S. Bureau of the Census
    "Health Insurance Coverage Status by State for All People: 2008" (http://www.census.gov/hhes/www/hlthins/hlthin08.html)
*Children under 18. Employment-based health insurance is private insurance coverage offered through one's own employment or a relative's. It may be offered by an employer or by a union.

Percent of Children Covered by Direct-Purchase Health Insurance in 2008

National Percent = 5.1% of Children*

ALPHA ORDER

RANK	STATE	PERCENT
49	Alabama	2.6
15	Alaska	6.2
33	Arizona	4.2
22	Arkansas	5.1
18	California	5.8
7	Colorado	7.5
24	Connecticut	4.9
41	Delaware	3.4
8	Florida	7.3
41	Georgia	3.4
30	Hawaii	4.5
2	Idaho	8.9
36	Illinois	3.9
44	Indiana	2.9
11	Iowa	6.7
18	Kansas	5.8
27	Kentucky	4.7
8	Louisiana	7.3
40	Maine	3.6
20	Maryland	5.7
47	Massachusetts	2.7
44	Michigan	2.9
10	Minnesota	6.9
49	Mississippi	2.6
6	Missouri	7.8
14	Montana	6.3
5	Nebraska	8.4
37	Nevada	3.8
37	New Hampshire	3.8
32	New Jersey	4.4
16	New Mexico	6.1
29	New York	4.6
16	North Carolina	6.1
13	North Dakota	6.4
22	Ohio	5.1
12	Oklahoma	6.5
1	Oregon	9.4
33	Pennsylvania	4.2
30	Rhode Island	4.5
43	South Carolina	3.3
3	South Dakota	8.7
39	Tennessee	3.7
26	Texas	4.8
4	Utah	8.5
47	Vermont	2.7
27	Virginia	4.7
21	Washington	5.4
46	West Virginia	2.8
24	Wisconsin	4.9
33	Wyoming	4.2

RANK ORDER

RANK	STATE	PERCENT
1	Oregon	9.4
2	Idaho	8.9
3	South Dakota	8.7
4	Utah	8.5
5	Nebraska	8.4
6	Missouri	7.8
7	Colorado	7.5
8	Florida	7.3
8	Louisiana	7.3
10	Minnesota	6.9
11	Iowa	6.7
12	Oklahoma	6.5
13	North Dakota	6.4
14	Montana	6.3
15	Alaska	6.2
16	New Mexico	6.1
16	North Carolina	6.1
18	California	5.8
18	Kansas	5.8
20	Maryland	5.7
21	Washington	5.4
22	Arkansas	5.1
22	Ohio	5.1
24	Connecticut	4.9
24	Wisconsin	4.9
26	Texas	4.8
27	Kentucky	4.7
27	Virginia	4.7
29	New York	4.6
30	Hawaii	4.5
30	Rhode Island	4.5
32	New Jersey	4.4
33	Arizona	4.2
33	Pennsylvania	4.2
33	Wyoming	4.2
36	Illinois	3.9
37	Nevada	3.8
37	New Hampshire	3.8
39	Tennessee	3.7
40	Maine	3.6
41	Delaware	3.4
41	Georgia	3.4
43	South Carolina	3.3
44	Indiana	2.9
44	Michigan	2.9
46	West Virginia	2.8
47	Massachusetts	2.7
47	Vermont	2.7
49	Alabama	2.6
49	Mississippi	2.6
	District of Columbia	3.9

Source: U.S. Bureau of the Census

"Health Insurance Coverage Status by State for All People: 2008" (http://www.census.gov/hhes/www/hlthins/hlthin08.html)

*Children under 18. Direct-purchase health insurance is private insurance coverage through a plan purchased by an individual from a private company.

Percent of Children Covered by Government Health Insurance in 2008

National Percent = 33.2% of Children*

RANK	STATE	PERCENT
11	Alabama	37.2
18	Alaska	36.5
9	Arizona	38.1
1	Arkansas	47.2
16	California	36.6
47	Colorado	22.6
43	Connecticut	26.9
41	Delaware	27.2
38	Florida	28.2
20	Georgia	35.3
4	Hawaii	42.8
36	Idaho	28.9
24	Illinois	32.6
21	Indiana	34.7
39	Iowa	28.1
30	Kansas	30.2
13	Kentucky	37.1
19	Louisiana	35.6
16	Maine	36.6
40	Maryland	27.6
42	Massachusetts	27.1
25	Michigan	31.8
44	Minnesota	24.7
2	Mississippi	43.8
27	Missouri	31.2
26	Montana	31.5
33	Nebraska	29.6
49	Nevada	19.2
46	New Hampshire	23.5
48	New Jersey	22.3
8	New Mexico	39.7
11	New York	37.2
14	North Carolina	36.8
45	North Dakota	24.1
28	Ohio	31.1
3	Oklahoma	43.2
34	Oregon	29.4
31	Pennsylvania	29.9
22	Rhode Island	33.5
29	South Carolina	30.8
23	South Dakota	33.2
5	Tennessee	42.7
10	Texas	37.5
50	Utah	13.4
6	Vermont	42.0
35	Virginia	29.1
15	Washington	36.7
7	West Virginia	41.5
37	Wisconsin	28.8
32	Wyoming	29.7

RANK	STATE	PERCENT
1	Arkansas	47.2
2	Mississippi	43.8
3	Oklahoma	43.2
4	Hawaii	42.8
5	Tennessee	42.7
6	Vermont	42.0
7	West Virginia	41.5
8	New Mexico	39.7
9	Arizona	38.1
10	Texas	37.5
11	Alabama	37.2
11	New York	37.2
13	Kentucky	37.1
14	North Carolina	36.8
15	Washington	36.7
16	California	36.6
16	Maine	36.6
18	Alaska	36.5
19	Louisiana	35.6
20	Georgia	35.3
21	Indiana	34.7
22	Rhode Island	33.5
23	South Dakota	33.2
24	Illinois	32.6
25	Michigan	31.8
26	Montana	31.5
27	Missouri	31.2
28	Ohio	31.1
29	South Carolina	30.8
30	Kansas	30.2
31	Pennsylvania	29.9
32	Wyoming	29.7
33	Nebraska	29.6
34	Oregon	29.4
35	Virginia	29.1
36	Idaho	28.9
37	Wisconsin	28.8
38	Florida	28.2
39	Iowa	28.1
40	Maryland	27.6
41	Delaware	27.2
42	Massachusetts	27.1
43	Connecticut	26.9
44	Minnesota	24.7
45	North Dakota	24.1
46	New Hampshire	23.5
47	Colorado	22.6
48	New Jersey	22.3
49	Nevada	19.2
50	Utah	13.4
	District of Columbia	44.9

Source: U.S. Bureau of the Census
    "Health Insurance Coverage Status by State for All People: 2008" (http://www.census.gov/hhes/www/hlthins/hlthin08.html)
*Children under 18. Includes Medicaid, Medicare, State Children's Health Insurance Program (SCHIP), and military health care.

Percent of Children Covered by Military Health Care in 2008

National Percent = 3.0% of Children*

ALPHA ORDER				RANK ORDER		
RANK	STATE	PERCENT		RANK	STATE	PERCENT
28	Alabama	2.6		1	Alaska	16.9
1	Alaska	16.9		2	Hawaii	13.3
30	Arizona	2.5		3	Virginia	9.5
25	Arkansas	3.0		4	Washington	8.7
39	California	1.6		5	Wyoming	7.1
12	Colorado	4.5		6	North Carolina	6.7
35	Connecticut	1.9		7	Tennessee	6.1
35	Delaware	1.9		8	Georgia	5.8
14	Florida	4.2		9	Montana	5.3
8	Georgia	5.8		10	Oklahoma	4.7
2	Hawaii	13.3		11	Nebraska	4.6
28	Idaho	2.6		12	Colorado	4.5
39	Illinois	1.6		13	Kansas	4.4
50	Indiana	0.3		14	Florida	4.2
34	Iowa	2.0		15	New Mexico	3.9
13	Kansas	4.4		15	South Dakota	3.9
31	Kentucky	2.3		15	West Virginia	3.9
46	Louisiana	1.2		18	Missouri	3.8
19	Maine	3.7		19	Maine	3.7
24	Maryland	3.2		19	Mississippi	3.7
48	Massachusetts	1.1		21	Texas	3.6
46	Michigan	1.2		22	North Dakota	3.4
44	Minnesota	1.3		23	Vermont	3.3
19	Mississippi	3.7		24	Maryland	3.2
18	Missouri	3.8		25	Arkansas	3.0
9	Montana	5.3		26	New Hampshire	2.7
11	Nebraska	4.6		26	South Carolina	2.7
32	Nevada	2.2		28	Alabama	2.6
26	New Hampshire	2.7		28	Idaho	2.6
39	New Jersey	1.6		30	Arizona	2.5
15	New Mexico	3.9		31	Kentucky	2.3
49	New York	0.7		32	Nevada	2.2
6	North Carolina	6.7		32	Rhode Island	2.2
22	North Dakota	3.4		34	Iowa	2.0
38	Ohio	1.7		35	Connecticut	1.9
10	Oklahoma	4.7		35	Delaware	1.9
42	Oregon	1.5		35	Wisconsin	1.9
44	Pennsylvania	1.3		38	Ohio	1.7
32	Rhode Island	2.2		39	California	1.6
26	South Carolina	2.7		39	Illinois	1.6
15	South Dakota	3.9		39	New Jersey	1.6
7	Tennessee	6.1		42	Oregon	1.5
21	Texas	3.6		43	Utah	1.4
43	Utah	1.4		44	Minnesota	1.3
23	Vermont	3.3		44	Pennsylvania	1.3
3	Virginia	9.5		46	Louisiana	1.2
4	Washington	8.7		46	Michigan	1.2
15	West Virginia	3.9		48	Massachusetts	1.1
35	Wisconsin	1.9		49	New York	0.7
5	Wyoming	7.1		50	Indiana	0.3
					District of Columbia	1.3

Source: U.S. Bureau of the Census
"Health Insurance Coverage Status by State for All People: 2008" (http://www.census.gov/hhes/www/hlthins/hlthin08.html)
*Children under 18. Includes CHAMPUS (Comprehensive Health and Medical Plan for Uniformed Services)/Tricare, Veterans, and military health care.

Percent of Children Covered by Medicaid in 2008

National Percent = 30.3% of Children*

ALPHA ORDER

RANK	STATE	PERCENT
12	Alabama	34.4
45	Alaska	19.9
8	Arizona	35.9
1	Arkansas	44.1
10	California	34.9
48	Colorado	18.1
38	Connecticut	24.9
37	Delaware	25.4
39	Florida	24.4
21	Georgia	30.0
21	Hawaii	30.0
33	Idaho	26.4
18	Illinois	31.0
13	Indiana	34.3
30	Iowa	26.6
33	Kansas	26.4
9	Kentucky	35.4
11	Louisiana	34.5
14	Maine	33.9
39	Maryland	24.4
35	Massachusetts	26.0
19	Michigan	30.7
41	Minnesota	23.5
2	Mississippi	40.3
27	Missouri	28.1
30	Montana	26.6
36	Nebraska	25.7
49	Nevada	17.0
44	New Hampshire	20.7
46	New Jersey	19.7
14	New Mexico	33.9
7	New York	36.2
20	North Carolina	30.5
43	North Dakota	20.9
24	Ohio	29.1
4	Oklahoma	38.1
28	Oregon	28.0
25	Pennsylvania	28.6
17	Rhode Island	31.2
28	South Carolina	28.0
26	South Dakota	28.3
6	Tennessee	37.0
14	Texas	33.9
50	Utah	11.9
3	Vermont	39.3
46	Virginia	19.7
23	Washington	29.3
5	West Virginia	37.7
30	Wisconsin	26.6
42	Wyoming	23.3

RANK ORDER

RANK	STATE	PERCENT
1	Arkansas	44.1
2	Mississippi	40.3
3	Vermont	39.3
4	Oklahoma	38.1
5	West Virginia	37.7
6	Tennessee	37.0
7	New York	36.2
8	Arizona	35.9
9	Kentucky	35.4
10	California	34.9
11	Louisiana	34.5
12	Alabama	34.4
13	Indiana	34.3
14	Maine	33.9
14	New Mexico	33.9
14	Texas	33.9
17	Rhode Island	31.2
18	Illinois	31.0
19	Michigan	30.7
20	North Carolina	30.5
21	Georgia	30.0
21	Hawaii	30.0
23	Washington	29.3
24	Ohio	29.1
25	Pennsylvania	28.6
26	South Dakota	28.3
27	Missouri	28.1
28	Oregon	28.0
28	South Carolina	28.0
30	Iowa	26.6
30	Montana	26.6
30	Wisconsin	26.6
33	Idaho	26.4
33	Kansas	26.4
35	Massachusetts	26.0
36	Nebraska	25.7
37	Delaware	25.4
38	Connecticut	24.9
39	Florida	24.4
39	Maryland	24.4
41	Minnesota	23.5
42	Wyoming	23.3
43	North Dakota	20.9
44	New Hampshire	20.7
45	Alaska	19.9
46	New Jersey	19.7
46	Virginia	19.7
48	Colorado	18.1
49	Nevada	17.0
50	Utah	11.9
	District of Columbia	43.6

Source: U.S. Bureau of the Census

"Health Insurance Coverage Status by State for All People: 2008" (http://www.census.gov/hhes/www/hlthins/hlthin08.html)

*Children under 18. Medicaid is a form of government insurance.

State Children's Health Insurance Program (SCHIP) Enrollment in 2008

National Total = 7,368,479 Children*

ALPHA ORDER

RANK	STATE	ENROLLMENT	% of USA
19	Alabama	110,821	1.5%
41	Alaska	18,707	0.3%
18	Arizona	112,072	1.5%
21	Arkansas	93,446	1.3%
1	California	1,692,087	23.0%
20	Colorado	99,555	1.4%
40	Connecticut	22,270	0.3%
46	Delaware	11,192	0.2%
5	Florida	354,385	4.8%
6	Georgia	311,234	4.2%
37	Hawaii	28,803	0.4%
33	Idaho	43,526	0.6%
4	Illinois	356,460	4.8%
16	Indiana	124,954	1.7%
31	Iowa	50,390	0.7%
29	Kansas	51,162	0.7%
26	Kentucky	67,717	0.9%
13	Louisiana	147,863	2.0%
36	Maine	30,947	0.4%
15	Maryland	132,864	1.8%
10	Massachusetts	200,950	2.7%
25	Michigan	67,763	0.9%
50	Minnesota	5,621	0.1%
22	Mississippi	84,370	1.1%
14	Missouri	136,135	1.8%
39	Montana	22,679	0.3%
32	Nebraska	48,827	0.7%
34	Nevada	38,592	0.5%
45	New Hampshire	12,236	0.2%
12	New Jersey	151,805	2.1%
44	New Mexico	14,944	0.2%
3	New York	517,256	7.0%
8	North Carolina	251,653	3.4%
48	North Dakota	7,617	0.1%
9	Ohio	251,278	3.4%
17	Oklahoma	117,507	1.6%
23	Oregon	73,686	1.0%
7	Pennsylvania	256,627	3.5%
38	Rhode Island	26,031	0.4%
24	South Carolina	73,620	1.0%
43	South Dakota	15,277	0.2%
27	Tennessee	63,619	0.9%
2	Texas	731,916	9.9%
30	Utah	51,092	0.7%
49	Vermont	6,496	0.1%
11	Virginia	155,289	2.1%
42	Washington	16,831	0.2%
35	West Virginia	37,645	0.5%
28	Wisconsin	52,940	0.7%
47	Wyoming	8,976	0.1%

RANK ORDER

RANK	STATE	ENROLLMENT	% of USA
1	California	1,692,087	23.0%
2	Texas	731,916	9.9%
3	New York	517,256	7.0%
4	Illinois	356,460	4.8%
5	Florida	354,385	4.8%
6	Georgia	311,234	4.2%
7	Pennsylvania	256,627	3.5%
8	North Carolina	251,653	3.4%
9	Ohio	251,278	3.4%
10	Massachusetts	200,950	2.7%
11	Virginia	155,289	2.1%
12	New Jersey	151,805	2.1%
13	Louisiana	147,863	2.0%
14	Missouri	136,135	1.8%
15	Maryland	132,864	1.8%
16	Indiana	124,954	1.7%
17	Oklahoma	117,507	1.6%
18	Arizona	112,072	1.5%
19	Alabama	110,821	1.5%
20	Colorado	99,555	1.4%
21	Arkansas	93,446	1.3%
22	Mississippi	84,370	1.1%
23	Oregon	73,686	1.0%
24	South Carolina	73,620	1.0%
25	Michigan	67,763	0.9%
26	Kentucky	67,717	0.9%
27	Tennessee	63,619	0.9%
28	Wisconsin	52,940	0.7%
29	Kansas	51,162	0.7%
30	Utah	51,092	0.7%
31	Iowa	50,390	0.7%
32	Nebraska	48,827	0.7%
33	Idaho	43,526	0.6%
34	Nevada	38,592	0.5%
35	West Virginia	37,645	0.5%
36	Maine	30,947	0.4%
37	Hawaii	28,803	0.4%
38	Rhode Island	26,031	0.4%
39	Montana	22,679	0.3%
40	Connecticut	22,270	0.3%
41	Alaska	18,707	0.3%
42	Washington	16,831	0.2%
43	South Dakota	15,277	0.2%
44	New Mexico	14,944	0.2%
45	New Hampshire	12,236	0.2%
46	Delaware	11,192	0.2%
47	Wyoming	8,976	0.1%
48	North Dakota	7,617	0.1%
49	Vermont	6,496	0.1%
50	Minnesota	5,621	0.1%
	District of Columbia	8,746	0.1%

Source: U.S. Department of Health and Human Services, Centers for Medicare and Medicaid Services
"Children's Health Insurance Program Annual Enrollment Report" (http://www.cms.hhs.gov/NationalSCHIPPolicy/)
*Figures for fiscal year 2008. The State Children's Health Insurance Program (SCHIP) was created in 1997 to help states expand health insurance to children whose families earn too much to qualify for Medicaid, yet not enough to afford private health insurance.

Percent Change in State Children's Health Insurance Program (SCHIP) Enrollment: 2007 to 2008
National Percent Change = 3.8% Increase*

RANK	STATE	PERCENT CHANGE
26	Alabama	3.9
19	Alaska	6.5
18	Arizona	7.5
25	Arkansas	4.2
13	California	10.0
7	Colorado	17.6
45	Connecticut	(5.8)
35	Delaware	0.4
14	Florida	9.5
48	Georgia	(12.6)
6	Hawaii	20.2
4	Idaho	31.7
30	Illinois	3.1
43	Indiana	(4.2)
37	Iowa	0.3
29	Kansas	3.3
42	Kentucky	(3.5)
43	Louisiana	(4.2)
40	Maine	(0.3)
38	Maryland	0.0
15	Massachusetts	8.9
24	Michigan	4.6
26	Minnesota	3.9
28	Mississippi	3.4
1	Missouri	66.5
12	Montana	12.7
21	Nebraska	5.7
46	Nevada	(7.8)
33	New Hampshire	1.2
34	New Jersey	1.0
47	New Mexico	(9.6)
50	New York	(20.6)
22	North Carolina	4.8
3	North Dakota	39.3
16	Ohio	8.5
35	Oklahoma	0.4
8	Oregon	16.8
11	Pennsylvania	12.9
39	Rhode Island	(0.1)
5	South Carolina	22.9
32	South Dakota	2.0
2	Tennessee	53.8
31	Texas	3.0
10	Utah	14.1
20	Vermont	5.9
17	Virginia	7.7
9	Washington	14.2
41	West Virginia	(2.4)
49	Wisconsin	(15.3)
23	Wyoming	4.7

RANK	STATE	PERCENT CHANGE
1	Missouri	66.5
2	Tennessee	53.8
3	North Dakota	39.3
4	Idaho	31.7
5	South Carolina	22.9
6	Hawaii	20.2
7	Colorado	17.6
8	Oregon	16.8
9	Washington	14.2
10	Utah	14.1
11	Pennsylvania	12.9
12	Montana	12.7
13	California	10.0
14	Florida	9.5
15	Massachusetts	8.9
16	Ohio	8.5
17	Virginia	7.7
18	Arizona	7.5
19	Alaska	6.5
20	Vermont	5.9
21	Nebraska	5.7
22	North Carolina	4.8
23	Wyoming	4.7
24	Michigan	4.6
25	Arkansas	4.2
26	Alabama	3.9
26	Minnesota	3.9
28	Mississippi	3.4
29	Kansas	3.3
30	Illinois	3.1
31	Texas	3.0
32	South Dakota	2.0
33	New Hampshire	1.2
34	New Jersey	1.0
35	Delaware	0.4
35	Oklahoma	0.4
37	Iowa	0.3
38	Maryland	0.0
39	Rhode Island	(0.1)
40	Maine	(0.3)
41	West Virginia	(2.4)
42	Kentucky	(3.5)
43	Indiana	(4.2)
43	Louisiana	(4.2)
45	Connecticut	(5.8)
46	Nevada	(7.8)
47	New Mexico	(9.6)
48	Georgia	(12.6)
49	Wisconsin	(15.3)
50	New York	(20.6)
	District of Columbia	33.2

Source: CQ Press using data from U.S. Department of Health and Human Services, Centers for Medicare and Medicaid Services "Children's Health Insurance Program Annual Enrollment Report" (http://www.cms.hhs.gov/NationalSCHIPPolicy/)

*Figures for fiscal years. The State Children's Health Insurance Program (SCHIP) was created in 1997 to help states expand health insurance to children whose families earn too much to qualify for Medicaid, yet not enough to afford private health insurance.

Percent of Children Enrolled in State Children's Health Insurance Program (SCHIP) in 2008
National Percent = 10.0% of Children 17 Years and Younger*

ALPHA ORDER

RANK	STATE	PERCENT
19	Alabama	9.9
16	Alaska	10.4
37	Arizona	6.6
3	Arkansas	13.3
1	California	18.1
28	Colorado	8.2
48	Connecticut	2.7
40	Delaware	5.4
25	Florida	8.9
6	Georgia	12.2
18	Hawaii	10.1
15	Idaho	10.5
10	Illinois	11.2
29	Indiana	7.9
33	Iowa	7.1
32	Kansas	7.3
36	Kentucky	6.7
3	Louisiana	13.3
9	Maine	11.3
19	Maryland	9.9
2	Massachusetts	14.1
47	Michigan	2.8
50	Minnesota	0.4
12	Mississippi	11.0
22	Missouri	9.6
17	Montana	10.3
13	Nebraska	10.9
39	Nevada	5.8
44	New Hampshire	4.2
31	New Jersey	7.4
46	New Mexico	3.0
7	New York	11.7
10	North Carolina	11.2
41	North Dakota	5.3
24	Ohio	9.2
5	Oklahoma	13.0
26	Oregon	8.5
23	Pennsylvania	9.3
8	Rhode Island	11.4
35	South Carolina	6.9
30	South Dakota	7.7
43	Tennessee	4.3
13	Texas	10.9
38	Utah	6.0
42	Vermont	5.0
26	Virginia	8.5
49	Washington	1.1
21	West Virginia	9.7
45	Wisconsin	4.0
34	Wyoming	7.0

RANK ORDER

RANK	STATE	PERCENT
1	California	18.1
2	Massachusetts	14.1
3	Arkansas	13.3
3	Louisiana	13.3
5	Oklahoma	13.0
6	Georgia	12.2
7	New York	11.7
8	Rhode Island	11.4
9	Maine	11.3
10	Illinois	11.2
10	North Carolina	11.2
12	Mississippi	11.0
13	Nebraska	10.9
13	Texas	10.9
15	Idaho	10.5
16	Alaska	10.4
17	Montana	10.3
18	Hawaii	10.1
19	Alabama	9.9
19	Maryland	9.9
21	West Virginia	9.7
22	Missouri	9.6
23	Pennsylvania	9.3
24	Ohio	9.2
25	Florida	8.9
26	Oregon	8.5
26	Virginia	8.5
28	Colorado	8.2
29	Indiana	7.9
30	South Dakota	7.7
31	New Jersey	7.4
32	Kansas	7.3
33	Iowa	7.1
34	Wyoming	7.0
35	South Carolina	6.9
36	Kentucky	6.7
37	Arizona	6.6
38	Utah	6.0
39	Nevada	5.8
40	Delaware	5.4
41	North Dakota	5.3
42	Vermont	5.0
43	Tennessee	4.3
44	New Hampshire	4.2
45	Wisconsin	4.0
46	New Mexico	3.0
47	Michigan	2.8
48	Connecticut	2.7
49	Washington	1.1
50	Minnesota	0.4

| | District of Columbia | 7.8 |

Source: CQ Press using data from U.S. Department of Health and Human Services, Centers for Medicare and Medicaid Services "Children's Health Insurance Program Annual Enrollment Report" (http://www.cms.hhs.gov/NationalSCHIPPolicy/)
*Figures for fiscal year 2008. The State Children's Health Insurance Program (SCHIP) was created in 1997 to help states expand health insurance to children whose families earn too much to qualify for Medicaid, yet not enough to afford private health insurance. Calculated using 2008 Census estimates for 17 and younger.

Expenditures for State Children's Health Insurance Program (SCHIP) in 2008

National Total = $6,896,600,000*

ALPHA ORDER

RANK	STATE	EXPENDITURES	% of USA
20	Alabama	$108,800,000	1.6%
45	Alaska	14,400,000	0.2%
18	Arizona	119,400,000	1.7%
19	Arkansas	113,200,000	1.6%
1	California	1,259,300,000	18.3%
24	Colorado	82,500,000	1.2%
41	Connecticut	26,300,000	0.4%
48	Delaware	9,700,000	0.1%
6	Florida	272,300,000	3.9%
9	Georgia	225,000,000	3.3%
43	Hawaii	17,600,000	0.3%
38	Idaho	35,400,000	0.5%
5	Illinois	292,900,000	4.2%
21	Indiana	102,400,000	1.5%
32	Iowa	55,300,000	0.8%
34	Kansas	47,900,000	0.7%
23	Kentucky	90,300,000	1.3%
13	Louisiana	159,200,000	2.3%
39	Maine	33,400,000	0.5%
14	Maryland	156,200,000	2.3%
7	Massachusetts	259,300,000	3.8%
12	Michigan	172,900,000	2.5%
28	Minnesota	71,400,000	1.0%
15	Mississippi	142,900,000	2.1%
25	Missouri	79,600,000	1.2%
42	Montana	24,900,000	0.4%
37	Nebraska	35,600,000	0.5%
40	Nevada	28,800,000	0.4%
47	New Hampshire	11,200,000	0.2%
4	New Jersey	323,100,000	4.7%
17	New Mexico	124,300,000	1.8%
3	New York	326,900,000	4.7%
11	North Carolina	193,700,000	2.8%
46	North Dakota	13,500,000	0.2%
8	Ohio	227,500,000	3.3%
22	Oklahoma	99,400,000	1.4%
29	Oregon	66,300,000	1.0%
10	Pennsylvania	204,500,000	3.0%
30	Rhode Island	59,100,000	0.9%
31	South Carolina	57,800,000	0.8%
44	South Dakota	15,600,000	0.2%
26	Tennessee	77,500,000	1.1%
2	Texas	698,000,000	10.1%
33	Utah	50,300,000	0.7%
50	Vermont	5,700,000	0.1%
16	Virginia	131,300,000	1.9%
35	Washington	43,400,000	0.6%
36	West Virginia	36,800,000	0.5%
27	Wisconsin	75,300,000	1.1%
49	Wyoming	8,700,000	0.1%

RANK ORDER

RANK	STATE	EXPENDITURES	% of USA
1	California	$1,259,300,000	18.3%
2	Texas	698,000,000	10.1%
3	New York	326,900,000	4.7%
4	New Jersey	323,100,000	4.7%
5	Illinois	292,900,000	4.2%
6	Florida	272,300,000	3.9%
7	Massachusetts	259,300,000	3.8%
8	Ohio	227,500,000	3.3%
9	Georgia	225,000,000	3.3%
10	Pennsylvania	204,500,000	3.0%
11	North Carolina	193,700,000	2.8%
12	Michigan	172,900,000	2.5%
13	Louisiana	159,200,000	2.3%
14	Maryland	156,200,000	2.3%
15	Mississippi	142,900,000	2.1%
16	Virginia	131,300,000	1.9%
17	New Mexico	124,300,000	1.8%
18	Arizona	119,400,000	1.7%
19	Arkansas	113,200,000	1.6%
20	Alabama	108,800,000	1.6%
21	Indiana	102,400,000	1.5%
22	Oklahoma	99,400,000	1.4%
23	Kentucky	90,300,000	1.3%
24	Colorado	82,500,000	1.2%
25	Missouri	79,600,000	1.2%
26	Tennessee	77,500,000	1.1%
27	Wisconsin	75,300,000	1.1%
28	Minnesota	71,400,000	1.0%
29	Oregon	66,300,000	1.0%
30	Rhode Island	59,100,000	0.9%
31	South Carolina	57,800,000	0.8%
32	Iowa	55,300,000	0.8%
33	Utah	50,300,000	0.7%
34	Kansas	47,900,000	0.7%
35	Washington	43,400,000	0.6%
36	West Virginia	36,800,000	0.5%
37	Nebraska	35,600,000	0.5%
38	Idaho	35,400,000	0.5%
39	Maine	33,400,000	0.5%
40	Nevada	28,800,000	0.4%
41	Connecticut	26,300,000	0.4%
42	Montana	24,900,000	0.4%
43	Hawaii	17,600,000	0.3%
44	South Dakota	15,600,000	0.2%
45	Alaska	14,400,000	0.2%
46	North Dakota	13,500,000	0.2%
47	New Hampshire	11,200,000	0.2%
48	Delaware	9,700,000	0.1%
49	Wyoming	8,700,000	0.1%
50	Vermont	5,700,000	0.1%
	District of Columbia	10,100,000	0.1%

Source: U.S. Department of Health and Human Services, Centers for Medicare and Medicaid Services
"Statement of Expenditures for the SCHIP Program" (CMS-21 Report, http://www.cms.hhs.gov)
*Federal and state expenditures for fiscal year 2008. National total does not include funds spent in U.S. territories. The State Children's Health Insurance Program (SCHIP) was created in 1997 to help states expand health insurance to children whose families earn too much to qualify for Medicaid, yet not enough to afford private health insurance.

Per Capita Expenditures for State Children's Health Insurance Program (SCHIP) in 2008
National Per Capita = $22.66*

ALPHA ORDER

RANK	STATE	PER CAPITA
14	Alabama	$23.26
21	Alaska	20.93
28	Arizona	18.37
5	Arkansas	39.47
8	California	34.43
34	Colorado	16.72
49	Connecticut	7.51
45	Delaware	11.07
38	Florida	14.78
15	Georgia	23.20
39	Hawaii	13.67
16	Idaho	23.18
17	Illinois	22.81
37	Indiana	16.03
26	Iowa	18.47
31	Kansas	17.12
18	Kentucky	21.06
7	Louisiana	35.76
13	Maine	25.31
10	Maryland	27.60
4	Massachusetts	39.63
30	Michigan	17.29
40	Minnesota	13.65
3	Mississippi	48.60
42	Missouri	13.36
12	Montana	25.72
23	Nebraska	19.98
46	Nevada	11.01
48	New Hampshire	8.47
6	New Jersey	37.29
1	New Mexico	62.56
33	New York	16.79
20	North Carolina	20.95
19	North Dakota	21.05
24	Ohio	19.73
11	Oklahoma	27.28
29	Oregon	17.53
36	Pennsylvania	16.27
2	Rhode Island	56.10
43	South Carolina	12.84
25	South Dakota	19.39
44	Tennessee	12.42
9	Texas	28.72
27	Utah	18.44
47	Vermont	9.18
32	Virginia	16.84
50	Washington	6.61
22	West Virginia	20.28
41	Wisconsin	13.38
35	Wyoming	16.32

RANK ORDER

RANK	STATE	PER CAPITA
1	New Mexico	$62.56
2	Rhode Island	56.10
3	Mississippi	48.60
4	Massachusetts	39.63
5	Arkansas	39.47
6	New Jersey	37.29
7	Louisiana	35.76
8	California	34.43
9	Texas	28.72
10	Maryland	27.60
11	Oklahoma	27.28
12	Montana	25.72
13	Maine	25.31
14	Alabama	23.26
15	Georgia	23.20
16	Idaho	23.18
17	Illinois	22.81
18	Kentucky	21.06
19	North Dakota	21.05
20	North Carolina	20.95
21	Alaska	20.93
22	West Virginia	20.28
23	Nebraska	19.98
24	Ohio	19.73
25	South Dakota	19.39
26	Iowa	18.47
27	Utah	18.44
28	Arizona	18.37
29	Oregon	17.53
30	Michigan	17.29
31	Kansas	17.12
32	Virginia	16.84
33	New York	16.79
34	Colorado	16.72
35	Wyoming	16.32
36	Pennsylvania	16.27
37	Indiana	16.03
38	Florida	14.78
39	Hawaii	13.67
40	Minnesota	13.65
41	Wisconsin	13.38
42	Missouri	13.36
43	South Carolina	12.84
44	Tennessee	12.42
45	Delaware	11.07
46	Nevada	11.01
47	Vermont	9.18
48	New Hampshire	8.47
49	Connecticut	7.51
50	Washington	6.61
	District of Columbia	17.12

Source: CQ Press using data from U.S. Department of Health and Human Services, Centers for Medicare and Medicaid Services "Statement of Expenditures for the SCHIP Program" (CMS-21 Report, http://www.cms.hhs.gov)

*Federal and state expenditures for fiscal year 2008. National figure does not include funds spent in U.S. territories. The State Children's Health Insurance Program (SCHIP) was created in 1997 to help states expand health insurance to children whose families earn too much to qualify for Medicaid, yet not enough to afford private health insurance.

Expenditures per State Children's Health Insurance Program (SCHIP) Participant in 2008
National Per Participant = $936*

ALPHA ORDER

RANK	STATE	PER PARTICIPANT
23	Alabama	$982
41	Alaska	770
20	Arizona	1,065
13	Arkansas	1,211
45	California	744
35	Colorado	829
14	Connecticut	1,181
32	Delaware	867
43	Florida	768
47	Georgia	723
49	Hawaii	611
38	Idaho	813
36	Illinois	822
37	Indiana	820
17	Iowa	1,097
27	Kansas	936
10	Kentucky	1,333
19	Louisiana	1,077
18	Maine	1,079
15	Maryland	1,176
11	Massachusetts	1,290
4	Michigan	2,552
1	Minnesota	12,702
8	Mississippi	1,694
50	Missouri	585
16	Montana	1,098
46	Nebraska	729
44	Nevada	746
28	New Hampshire	915
6	New Jersey	2,128
2	New Mexico	8,318
48	New York	632
41	North Carolina	770
7	North Dakota	1,772
29	Ohio	905
33	Oklahoma	846
30	Oregon	900
39	Pennsylvania	797
5	Rhode Island	2,270
40	South Carolina	785
21	South Dakota	1,021
12	Tennessee	1,218
26	Texas	954
22	Utah	984
31	Vermont	877
33	Virginia	846
3	Washington	2,579
24	West Virginia	978
9	Wisconsin	1,422
25	Wyoming	969

RANK ORDER

RANK	STATE	PER PARTICIPANT
1	Minnesota	$12,702
2	New Mexico	8,318
3	Washington	2,579
4	Michigan	2,552
5	Rhode Island	2,270
6	New Jersey	2,128
7	North Dakota	1,772
8	Mississippi	1,694
9	Wisconsin	1,422
10	Kentucky	1,333
11	Massachusetts	1,290
12	Tennessee	1,218
13	Arkansas	1,211
14	Connecticut	1,181
15	Maryland	1,176
16	Montana	1,098
17	Iowa	1,097
18	Maine	1,079
19	Louisiana	1,077
20	Arizona	1,065
21	South Dakota	1,021
22	Utah	984
23	Alabama	982
24	West Virginia	978
25	Wyoming	969
26	Texas	954
27	Kansas	936
28	New Hampshire	915
29	Ohio	905
30	Oregon	900
31	Vermont	877
32	Delaware	867
33	Oklahoma	846
33	Virginia	846
35	Colorado	829
36	Illinois	822
37	Indiana	820
38	Idaho	813
39	Pennsylvania	797
40	South Carolina	785
41	Alaska	770
41	North Carolina	770
43	Florida	768
44	Nevada	746
45	California	744
46	Nebraska	729
47	Georgia	723
48	New York	632
49	Hawaii	611
50	Missouri	585

District of Columbia 1,155

Source: CQ Press using data from U.S. Department of Health and Human Services, Centers for Medicare and Medicaid Services "Statement of Expenditures for the SCHIP Program" (CMS-21 Report, http://www.cms.hhs.gov)

*Federal and state expenditures for fiscal year 2008. National figure does not include funds spent in U.S. territories. The State Children's Health Insurance Program (SCHIP) was created in 1997 to help states expand health insurance to children whose families earn too much to qualify for Medicaid, yet not enough to afford private health insurance.

Health Maintenance Organizations (HMOs) in 2009

National Total = 462 HMOs*

RANK	STATE	HMOs	% of USA
31	Alabama	43	9.3%
50	Alaska	20	4.3%
6	Arizona	72	15.6%
25	Arkansas	51	11.0%
1	California	102	22.1%
20	Colorado	55	11.9%
28	Connecticut	46	10.0%
35	Delaware	41	8.9%
2	Florida	98	21.2%
9	Georgia	62	13.4%
40	Hawaii	35	7.6%
40	Idaho	35	7.6%
7	Illinois	65	14.1%
17	Indiana	57	12.3%
37	Iowa	38	8.2%
31	Kansas	43	9.3%
27	Kentucky	47	10.2%
28	Louisiana	46	10.0%
40	Maine	35	7.6%
24	Maryland	52	11.3%
16	Massachusetts	58	12.6%
14	Michigan	60	13.0%
30	Minnesota	45	9.7%
38	Mississippi	37	8.0%
15	Missouri	59	12.8%
47	Montana	26	5.6%
44	Nebraska	30	6.5%
20	Nevada	55	11.9%
43	New Hampshire	33	7.1%
19	New Jersey	56	12.1%
35	New Mexico	41	8.9%
3	New York	88	19.0%
20	North Carolina	55	11.9%
45	North Dakota	27	5.8%
8	Ohio	64	13.9%
31	Oklahoma	43	9.3%
23	Oregon	53	11.5%
5	Pennsylvania	73	15.8%
47	Rhode Island	26	5.6%
10	South Carolina	61	13.2%
38	South Dakota	37	8.0%
10	Tennessee	61	13.2%
4	Texas	83	18.0%
26	Utah	48	10.4%
49	Vermont	25	5.4%
10	Virginia	61	13.2%
17	Washington	57	12.3%
34	West Virginia	42	9.1%
10	Wisconsin	61	13.2%
45	Wyoming	27	5.8%

RANK	STATE	HMOs	% of USA
1	California	102	22.1%
2	Florida	98	21.2%
3	New York	88	19.0%
4	Texas	83	18.0%
5	Pennsylvania	73	15.8%
6	Arizona	72	15.6%
7	Illinois	65	14.1%
8	Ohio	64	13.9%
9	Georgia	62	13.4%
10	South Carolina	61	13.2%
10	Tennessee	61	13.2%
10	Virginia	61	13.2%
10	Wisconsin	61	13.2%
14	Michigan	60	13.0%
15	Missouri	59	12.8%
16	Massachusetts	58	12.6%
17	Indiana	57	12.3%
17	Washington	57	12.3%
19	New Jersey	56	12.1%
20	Colorado	55	11.9%
20	Nevada	55	11.9%
20	North Carolina	55	11.9%
23	Oregon	53	11.5%
24	Maryland	52	11.3%
25	Arkansas	51	11.0%
26	Utah	48	10.4%
27	Kentucky	47	10.2%
28	Connecticut	46	10.0%
28	Louisiana	46	10.0%
30	Minnesota	45	9.7%
31	Alabama	43	9.3%
31	Kansas	43	9.3%
31	Oklahoma	43	9.3%
34	West Virginia	42	9.1%
35	Delaware	41	8.9%
35	New Mexico	41	8.9%
37	Iowa	38	8.2%
38	Mississippi	37	8.0%
38	South Dakota	37	8.0%
40	Hawaii	35	7.6%
40	Idaho	35	7.6%
40	Maine	35	7.6%
43	New Hampshire	33	7.1%
44	Nebraska	30	6.5%
45	North Dakota	27	5.8%
45	Wyoming	27	5.8%
47	Montana	26	5.6%
47	Rhode Island	26	5.6%
49	Vermont	25	5.4%
50	Alaska	20	4.3%
	District of Columbia	38	8.2%

Source: Lance Wolkenbrod, Data Analyst
HealthLeaders - InterStudy (Nashville, TN, http://home.healthleaders-interstudy.com)
*As of January 2009. National total reflects the total HMOs nationwide and does not count HMOs in more than one state as multiple HMOs. The total for all HMO programs by state is 2,573.

Enrollees in Health Maintenance Organizations (HMOs) in 2009

National Total = 74,494,844 Enrollees*

ALPHA ORDER

RANK	STATE	ENROLLEES	% of USA
37	Alabama	257,584	0.3%
50	Alaska	8,825	0.0%
11	Arizona	1,836,849	2.5%
44	Arkansas	104,516	0.1%
1	California	16,489,216	22.1%
22	Colorado	916,295	1.2%
23	Connecticut	915,376	1.2%
36	Delaware	262,859	0.4%
3	Florida	4,123,318	5.5%
9	Georgia	2,346,939	3.2%
25	Hawaii	665,435	0.9%
43	Idaho	112,507	0.2%
16	Illinois	1,604,723	2.2%
18	Indiana	1,109,757	1.5%
33	Iowa	330,092	0.4%
32	Kansas	369,312	0.5%
30	Kentucky	443,904	0.6%
31	Louisiana	382,110	0.5%
41	Maine	143,367	0.2%
12	Maryland	1,781,237	2.4%
6	Massachusetts	2,991,311	4.0%
7	Michigan	2,848,966	3.8%
20	Minnesota	993,494	1.3%
45	Mississippi	60,868	0.1%
21	Missouri	928,378	1.2%
46	Montana	56,322	0.1%
40	Nebraska	150,259	0.2%
28	Nevada	510,864	0.7%
35	New Hampshire	271,608	0.4%
10	New Jersey	2,001,474	2.7%
26	New Mexico	611,926	0.8%
2	New York	6,195,912	8.3%
27	North Carolina	545,636	0.7%
48	North Dakota	21,556	0.0%
8	Ohio	2,477,375	3.3%
38	Oklahoma	256,128	0.3%
19	Oregon	1,099,721	1.5%
4	Pennsylvania	3,780,412	5.1%
39	Rhode Island	198,618	0.3%
29	South Carolina	503,594	0.7%
42	South Dakota	140,247	0.2%
15	Tennessee	1,607,946	2.2%
5	Texas	3,732,750	5.0%
24	Utah	836,248	1.1%
47	Vermont	48,531	0.1%
13	Virginia	1,694,815	2.3%
17	Washington	1,302,266	1.7%
34	West Virginia	285,232	0.4%
14	Wisconsin	1,672,688	2.2%
49	Wyoming	11,348	0.0%

RANK ORDER

RANK	STATE	ENROLLEES	% of USA
1	California	16,489,216	22.1%
2	New York	6,195,912	8.3%
3	Florida	4,123,318	5.5%
4	Pennsylvania	3,780,412	5.1%
5	Texas	3,732,750	5.0%
6	Massachusetts	2,991,311	4.0%
7	Michigan	2,848,966	3.8%
8	Ohio	2,477,375	3.3%
9	Georgia	2,346,939	3.2%
10	New Jersey	2,001,474	2.7%
11	Arizona	1,836,849	2.5%
12	Maryland	1,781,237	2.4%
13	Virginia	1,694,815	2.3%
14	Wisconsin	1,672,688	2.2%
15	Tennessee	1,607,946	2.2%
16	Illinois	1,604,723	2.2%
17	Washington	1,302,266	1.7%
18	Indiana	1,109,757	1.5%
19	Oregon	1,099,721	1.5%
20	Minnesota	993,494	1.3%
21	Missouri	928,378	1.2%
22	Colorado	916,295	1.2%
23	Connecticut	915,376	1.2%
24	Utah	836,248	1.1%
25	Hawaii	665,435	0.9%
26	New Mexico	611,926	0.8%
27	North Carolina	545,636	0.7%
28	Nevada	510,864	0.7%
29	South Carolina	503,594	0.7%
30	Kentucky	443,904	0.6%
31	Louisiana	382,110	0.5%
32	Kansas	369,312	0.5%
33	Iowa	330,092	0.4%
34	West Virginia	285,232	0.4%
35	New Hampshire	271,608	0.4%
36	Delaware	262,859	0.4%
37	Alabama	257,584	0.3%
38	Oklahoma	256,128	0.3%
39	Rhode Island	198,618	0.3%
40	Nebraska	150,259	0.2%
41	Maine	143,367	0.2%
42	South Dakota	140,247	0.2%
43	Idaho	112,507	0.2%
44	Arkansas	104,516	0.1%
45	Mississippi	60,868	0.1%
46	Montana	56,322	0.1%
47	Vermont	48,531	0.1%
48	North Dakota	21,556	0.0%
49	Wyoming	11,348	0.0%
50	Alaska	8,825	0.0%
	District of Columbia	274,160	0.4%

Source: Lance Wolkenbrod, Data Analyst
  HealthLeaders - InterStudy (Nashville, TN, http://home.healthleaders-interstudy.com)
*As of January 2009.

Percent Change in Enrollees in Health Maintenance Organizations (HMOs): 2008 to 2009
National Percent Change = 1.2% Decrease*

ALPHA ORDER

RANK	STATE	PERCENT CHANGE
7	Alabama	9.5
16	Alaska	2.2
33	Arizona	(6.6)
10	Arkansas	5.6
20	California	0.2
43	Colorado	(13.5)
27	Connecticut	(2.0)
2	Delaware	35.1
37	Florida	(9.6)
11	Georgia	5.3
8	Hawaii	8.5
5	Idaho	11.0
41	Illinois	(12.9)
30	Indiana	(4.7)
3	Iowa	24.8
46	Kansas	(19.7)
14	Kentucky	3.5
25	Louisiana	(1.6)
45	Maine	(18.0)
15	Maryland	2.6
13	Massachusetts	4.7
22	Michigan	(0.2)
39	Minnesota	(11.4)
35	Mississippi	(7.6)
38	Missouri	(9.7)
24	Montana	(1.3)
1	Nebraska	64.4
34	Nevada	(7.0)
42	New Hampshire	(13.2)
36	New Jersey	(9.3)
18	New Mexico	0.5
9	New York	6.6
48	North Carolina	(35.8)
4	North Dakota	16.4
12	Ohio	4.8
28	Oklahoma	(2.5)
17	Oregon	1.8
32	Pennsylvania	(5.9)
47	Rhode Island	(22.1)
26	South Carolina	(1.7)
31	South Dakota	(5.2)
44	Tennessee	(15.0)
29	Texas	(3.1)
40	Utah	(11.8)
49	Vermont	(43.5)
20	Virginia	0.2
19	Washington	0.3
23	West Virginia	(1.1)
6	Wisconsin	9.8
50	Wyoming	(53.6)

RANK ORDER

RANK	STATE	PERCENT CHANGE
1	Nebraska	64.4
2	Delaware	35.1
3	Iowa	24.8
4	North Dakota	16.4
5	Idaho	11.0
6	Wisconsin	9.8
7	Alabama	9.5
8	Hawaii	8.5
9	New York	6.6
10	Arkansas	5.6
11	Georgia	5.3
12	Ohio	4.8
13	Massachusetts	4.7
14	Kentucky	3.5
15	Maryland	2.6
16	Alaska	2.2
17	Oregon	1.8
18	New Mexico	0.5
19	Washington	0.3
20	California	0.2
20	Virginia	0.2
22	Michigan	(0.2)
23	West Virginia	(1.1)
24	Montana	(1.3)
25	Louisiana	(1.6)
26	South Carolina	(1.7)
27	Connecticut	(2.0)
28	Oklahoma	(2.5)
29	Texas	(3.1)
30	Indiana	(4.7)
31	South Dakota	(5.2)
32	Pennsylvania	(5.9)
33	Arizona	(6.6)
34	Nevada	(7.0)
35	Mississippi	(7.6)
36	New Jersey	(9.3)
37	Florida	(9.6)
38	Missouri	(9.7)
39	Minnesota	(11.4)
40	Utah	(11.8)
41	Illinois	(12.9)
42	New Hampshire	(13.2)
43	Colorado	(13.5)
44	Tennessee	(15.0)
45	Maine	(18.0)
46	Kansas	(19.7)
47	Rhode Island	(22.1)
48	North Carolina	(35.8)
49	Vermont	(43.5)
50	Wyoming	(53.6)

District of Columbia (12.5)

Source: CQ Press using data from Lance Wolkenbrod, Data Analyst
HealthLeaders - InterStudy (Nashville, TN, http://home.healthleaders-interstudy.com)
*As of January 2009. National figure does not include enrollees in U.S. territories.

Percent of Population Enrolled in Health Maintenance Organizations (HMOs) in 2009
National Percent = 24.2% Enrolled in HMOs*

ALPHA ORDER

RANK	STATE	PERCENT
45	Alabama	5.5
50	Alaska	1.3
13	Arizona	28.3
46	Arkansas	3.7
3	California	44.9
26	Colorado	18.6
14	Connecticut	26.1
9	Delaware	30.1
18	Florida	22.5
16	Georgia	24.2
1	Hawaii	51.7
41	Idaho	7.4
33	Illinois	12.4
27	Indiana	17.4
35	Iowa	11.0
32	Kansas	13.2
37	Kentucky	10.4
38	Louisiana	8.7
36	Maine	10.9
5	Maryland	31.6
2	Massachusetts	46.0
12	Michigan	28.5
24	Minnesota	19.0
48	Mississippi	2.1
29	Missouri	15.7
44	Montana	5.8
39	Nebraska	8.4
23	Nevada	19.6
21	New Hampshire	20.6
17	New Jersey	23.1
6	New Mexico	30.8
4	New York	31.8
43	North Carolina	5.9
47	North Dakota	3.4
20	Ohio	21.6
42	Oklahoma	7.0
11	Oregon	29.0
8	Pennsylvania	30.4
25	Rhode Island	18.9
34	South Carolina	11.2
27	South Dakota	17.4
15	Tennessee	25.9
31	Texas	15.3
7	Utah	30.6
40	Vermont	7.8
19	Virginia	21.8
22	Washington	19.9
29	West Virginia	15.7
10	Wisconsin	29.7
48	Wyoming	2.1

RANK ORDER

RANK	STATE	PERCENT
1	Hawaii	51.7
2	Massachusetts	46.0
3	California	44.9
4	New York	31.8
5	Maryland	31.6
6	New Mexico	30.8
7	Utah	30.6
8	Pennsylvania	30.4
9	Delaware	30.1
10	Wisconsin	29.7
11	Oregon	29.0
12	Michigan	28.5
13	Arizona	28.3
14	Connecticut	26.1
15	Tennessee	25.9
16	Georgia	24.2
17	New Jersey	23.1
18	Florida	22.5
19	Virginia	21.8
20	Ohio	21.6
21	New Hampshire	20.6
22	Washington	19.9
23	Nevada	19.6
24	Minnesota	19.0
25	Rhode Island	18.9
26	Colorado	18.6
27	Indiana	17.4
27	South Dakota	17.4
29	Missouri	15.7
29	West Virginia	15.7
31	Texas	15.3
32	Kansas	13.2
33	Illinois	12.4
34	South Carolina	11.2
35	Iowa	11.0
36	Maine	10.9
37	Kentucky	10.4
38	Louisiana	8.7
39	Nebraska	8.4
40	Vermont	7.8
41	Idaho	7.4
42	Oklahoma	7.0
43	North Carolina	5.9
44	Montana	5.8
45	Alabama	5.5
46	Arkansas	3.7
47	North Dakota	3.4
48	Mississippi	2.1
48	Wyoming	2.1
50	Alaska	1.3
	District of Columbia	46.3

Source: Lance Wolkenbrod, Data Analyst
  HealthLeaders - InterStudy (Nashville, TN, http://home.healthleaders-interstudy.com)
*As of January 2009.

Percent of Insured Population Enrolled in
Health Maintenance Organizations (HMOs) in 2009
National Percent = 29.2% of Insured Are Enrolled in HMOs*

ALPHA ORDER

RANK	STATE	PERCENT
45	Alabama	6.2
50	Alaska	1.6
7	Arizona	34.9
46	Arkansas	4.5
2	California	55.2
24	Colorado	22.2
16	Connecticut	29.6
11	Delaware	34.2
17	Florida	28.6
15	Georgia	29.9
1	Hawaii	57.4
40	Idaho	8.8
33	Illinois	14.5
28	Indiana	20.1
36	Iowa	12.2
32	Kansas	15.4
35	Kentucky	12.4
38	Louisiana	11.0
37	Maine	12.1
6	Maryland	36.6
3	Massachusetts	49.3
13	Michigan	32.9
26	Minnesota	21.2
48	Mississippi	2.5
31	Missouri	18.1
44	Montana	6.9
39	Nebraska	9.6
21	Nevada	24.4
22	New Hampshire	23.3
18	New Jersey	27.3
4	New Mexico	40.5
5	New York	37.3
43	North Carolina	7.0
47	North Dakota	3.9
20	Ohio	24.6
42	Oklahoma	8.4
9	Oregon	34.4
9	Pennsylvania	34.4
25	Rhode Island	21.6
34	South Carolina	13.4
28	South Dakota	20.1
14	Tennessee	30.6
27	Texas	20.6
7	Utah	34.9
41	Vermont	8.7
19	Virginia	25.0
23	Washington	22.7
30	West Virginia	18.7
12	Wisconsin	33.3
48	Wyoming	2.5

RANK ORDER

RANK	STATE	PERCENT
1	Hawaii	57.4
2	California	55.2
3	Massachusetts	49.3
4	New Mexico	40.5
5	New York	37.3
6	Maryland	36.6
7	Arizona	34.9
7	Utah	34.9
9	Oregon	34.4
9	Pennsylvania	34.4
11	Delaware	34.2
12	Wisconsin	33.3
13	Michigan	32.9
14	Tennessee	30.6
15	Georgia	29.9
16	Connecticut	29.6
17	Florida	28.6
18	New Jersey	27.3
19	Virginia	25.0
20	Ohio	24.6
21	Nevada	24.4
22	New Hampshire	23.3
23	Washington	22.7
24	Colorado	22.2
25	Rhode Island	21.6
26	Minnesota	21.2
27	Texas	20.6
28	Indiana	20.1
28	South Dakota	20.1
30	West Virginia	18.7
31	Missouri	18.1
32	Kansas	15.4
33	Illinois	14.5
34	South Carolina	13.4
35	Kentucky	12.4
36	Iowa	12.2
37	Maine	12.1
38	Louisiana	11.0
39	Nebraska	9.6
40	Idaho	8.8
41	Vermont	8.7
42	Oklahoma	8.4
43	North Carolina	7.0
44	Montana	6.9
45	Alabama	6.2
46	Arkansas	4.5
47	North Dakota	3.9
48	Mississippi	2.5
48	Wyoming	2.5
50	Alaska	1.6

District of Columbia   51.4

Source: CQ Press using data from Lance Wolkenbrod, Data Analyst
HealthLeaders - InterStudy (Nashville, TN, http://home.healthleaders-interstudy.com)
*As of January 2009. Calculated using estimated number of insured as of 2008 from the U.S. Census Bureau.

Medicare Enrollees in 2008

National Total = 45,411,883 Enrollees*

RANK	STATE	ENROLLEES	% of USA
20	Alabama	809,193	1.8%
50	Alaska	59,781	0.1%
19	Arizona	869,591	1.9%
30	Arkansas	508,767	1.1%
1	California	4,491,586	9.9%
27	Colorado	579,322	1.3%
29	Connecticut	548,703	1.2%
45	Delaware	141,080	0.3%
2	Florida	3,211,813	7.1%
11	Georgia	1,152,522	2.5%
42	Hawaii	194,183	0.4%
40	Idaho	214,247	0.5%
7	Illinois	1,774,555	3.9%
16	Indiana	964,240	2.1%
31	Iowa	506,152	1.1%
33	Kansas	417,996	0.9%
23	Kentucky	728,218	1.6%
25	Louisiana	656,392	1.4%
39	Maine	253,188	0.6%
22	Maryland	744,564	1.6%
13	Massachusetts	1,018,689	2.2%
8	Michigan	1,579,631	3.5%
21	Minnesota	749,065	1.6%
32	Mississippi	479,231	1.1%
15	Missouri	966,061	2.1%
44	Montana	160,441	0.4%
37	Nebraska	271,368	0.6%
35	Nevada	330,003	0.7%
41	New Hampshire	211,657	0.5%
10	New Jersey	1,282,636	2.8%
36	New Mexico	294,269	0.6%
3	New York	2,891,085	6.4%
9	North Carolina	1,404,787	3.1%
47	North Dakota	106,666	0.2%
6	Ohio	1,840,714	4.1%
28	Oklahoma	578,488	1.3%
26	Oregon	584,222	1.3%
5	Pennsylvania	2,221,376	4.9%
43	Rhode Island	177,874	0.4%
24	South Carolina	723,726	1.6%
46	South Dakota	132,046	0.3%
14	Tennessee	1,004,176	2.2%
4	Texas	2,801,840	6.2%
38	Utah	264,086	0.6%
48	Vermont	104,917	0.2%
12	Virginia	1,078,534	2.4%
17	Washington	903,249	2.0%
34	West Virginia	372,995	0.8%
18	Wisconsin	873,782	1.9%
49	Wyoming	76,122	0.2%

RANK	STATE	ENROLLEES	% of USA
1	California	4,491,586	9.9%
2	Florida	3,211,813	7.1%
3	New York	2,891,085	6.4%
4	Texas	2,801,840	6.2%
5	Pennsylvania	2,221,376	4.9%
6	Ohio	1,840,714	4.1%
7	Illinois	1,774,555	3.9%
8	Michigan	1,579,631	3.5%
9	North Carolina	1,404,787	3.1%
10	New Jersey	1,282,636	2.8%
11	Georgia	1,152,522	2.5%
12	Virginia	1,078,534	2.4%
13	Massachusetts	1,018,689	2.2%
14	Tennessee	1,004,176	2.2%
15	Missouri	966,061	2.1%
16	Indiana	964,240	2.1%
17	Washington	903,249	2.0%
18	Wisconsin	873,782	1.9%
19	Arizona	869,591	1.9%
20	Alabama	809,193	1.8%
21	Minnesota	749,065	1.6%
22	Maryland	744,564	1.6%
23	Kentucky	728,218	1.6%
24	South Carolina	723,726	1.6%
25	Louisiana	656,392	1.4%
26	Oregon	584,222	1.3%
27	Colorado	579,322	1.3%
28	Oklahoma	578,488	1.3%
29	Connecticut	548,703	1.2%
30	Arkansas	508,767	1.1%
31	Iowa	506,152	1.1%
32	Mississippi	479,231	1.1%
33	Kansas	417,996	0.9%
34	West Virginia	372,995	0.8%
35	Nevada	330,003	0.7%
36	New Mexico	294,269	0.6%
37	Nebraska	271,368	0.6%
38	Utah	264,086	0.6%
39	Maine	253,188	0.6%
40	Idaho	214,247	0.5%
41	New Hampshire	211,657	0.5%
42	Hawaii	194,183	0.4%
43	Rhode Island	177,874	0.4%
44	Montana	160,441	0.4%
45	Delaware	141,080	0.3%
46	South Dakota	132,046	0.3%
47	North Dakota	106,666	0.2%
48	Vermont	104,917	0.2%
49	Wyoming	76,122	0.2%
50	Alaska	59,781	0.1%
	District of Columbia	75,125	0.2%

Source: U.S. Department of Health and Human Services, Centers for Medicare and Medicaid Services
"2009 Data Compendium" (http://www.cms.hhs.gov/DataCompendium/)
*Includes aged and disabled enrollees. Total includes 636,922 enrollees in Puerto Rico and other outlying areas, foreign countries, or whose address is unknown.

Percent Change in Medicare Enrollees: 2007 to 2008

National Percent Change = 2.6% Increase*

RANK	STATE	PERCENT CHANGE
26	Alabama	2.5
1	Alaska	5.2
10	Arizona	3.5
26	Arkansas	2.5
21	California	2.8
4	Colorado	3.8
35	Connecticut	2.2
8	Delaware	3.6
26	Florida	2.5
4	Georgia	3.8
26	Hawaii	2.5
7	Idaho	3.7
42	Illinois	1.9
26	Indiana	2.5
50	Iowa	1.2
46	Kansas	1.5
32	Kentucky	2.4
25	Louisiana	2.6
22	Maine	2.7
20	Maryland	2.9
35	Massachusetts	2.2
26	Michigan	2.5
22	Minnesota	2.7
37	Mississippi	2.1
37	Missouri	2.1
17	Montana	3.0
48	Nebraska	1.4
2	Nevada	3.9
8	New Hampshire	3.6
40	New Jersey	2.0
14	New Mexico	3.3
43	New York	1.8
12	North Carolina	3.4
49	North Dakota	1.3
40	Ohio	2.0
32	Oklahoma	2.4
17	Oregon	3.0
44	Pennsylvania	1.7
45	Rhode Island	1.6
4	South Carolina	3.8
37	South Dakota	2.1
17	Tennessee	3.0
10	Texas	3.5
2	Utah	3.9
14	Vermont	3.3
16	Virginia	3.2
12	Washington	3.4
46	West Virginia	1.5
34	Wisconsin	2.3
22	Wyoming	2.7

RANK	STATE	PERCENT CHANGE
1	Alaska	5.2
2	Nevada	3.9
2	Utah	3.9
4	Colorado	3.8
4	Georgia	3.8
4	South Carolina	3.8
7	Idaho	3.7
8	Delaware	3.6
8	New Hampshire	3.6
10	Arizona	3.5
10	Texas	3.5
12	North Carolina	3.4
12	Washington	3.4
14	New Mexico	3.3
14	Vermont	3.3
16	Virginia	3.2
17	Montana	3.0
17	Oregon	3.0
17	Tennessee	3.0
20	Maryland	2.9
21	California	2.8
22	Maine	2.7
22	Minnesota	2.7
22	Wyoming	2.7
25	Louisiana	2.6
26	Alabama	2.5
26	Arkansas	2.5
26	Florida	2.5
26	Hawaii	2.5
26	Indiana	2.5
26	Michigan	2.5
32	Kentucky	2.4
32	Oklahoma	2.4
34	Wisconsin	2.3
35	Connecticut	2.2
35	Massachusetts	2.2
37	Mississippi	2.1
37	Missouri	2.1
37	South Dakota	2.1
40	New Jersey	2.0
40	Ohio	2.0
42	Illinois	1.9
43	New York	1.8
44	Pennsylvania	1.7
45	Rhode Island	1.6
46	Kansas	1.5
46	West Virginia	1.5
48	Nebraska	1.4
49	North Dakota	1.3
50	Iowa	1.2

	District of Columbia	1.4

Source: CQ Press using data from U.S. Department of Health and Human Services, Centers for Medicare and Medicaid Services
"2009 Data Compendium" (http://www.cms.hhs.gov/DataCompendium/)
*Includes aged and disabled enrollees. National rate includes enrollees in Puerto Rico and other outlying areas, foreign countries, or whose address is unknown.

Percent of Population Enrolled in Medicare in 2008

National Percent = 14.6% of Population*

ALPHA ORDER			RANK ORDER		
RANK	STATE	PERCENT	RANK	STATE	PERCENT
6	Alabama	17.4	1	West Virginia	20.6
50	Alaska	8.7	2	Maine	19.2
42	Arizona	13.4	3	Arkansas	17.8
3	Arkansas	17.8	3	Pennsylvania	17.8
45	California	12.2	5	Florida	17.5
47	Colorado	11.7	6	Alabama	17.4
23	Connecticut	15.7	7	Kentucky	17.1
16	Delaware	16.2	8	Iowa	16.9
5	Florida	17.5	8	Rhode Island	16.9
46	Georgia	11.9	8	Vermont	16.9
29	Hawaii	15.1	11	Montana	16.6
38	Idaho	14.1	11	North Dakota	16.6
40	Illinois	13.8	13	South Dakota	16.4
29	Indiana	15.1	14	Mississippi	16.3
8	Iowa	16.9	14	Missouri	16.3
31	Kansas	14.9	16	Delaware	16.2
7	Kentucky	17.1	16	South Carolina	16.2
31	Louisiana	14.9	16	Tennessee	16.2
2	Maine	19.2	19	New Hampshire	16.1
43	Maryland	13.2	20	Ohio	16.0
23	Massachusetts	15.7	21	Oklahoma	15.9
22	Michigan	15.8	22	Michigan	15.8
36	Minnesota	14.3	23	Connecticut	15.7
14	Mississippi	16.3	23	Massachusetts	15.7
14	Missouri	16.3	25	Wisconsin	15.5
11	Montana	16.6	26	Oregon	15.4
27	Nebraska	15.2	27	Nebraska	15.2
44	Nevada	12.7	27	North Carolina	15.2
19	New Hampshire	16.1	29	Hawaii	15.1
33	New Jersey	14.8	29	Indiana	15.1
33	New Mexico	14.8	31	Kansas	14.9
33	New York	14.8	31	Louisiana	14.9
27	North Carolina	15.2	33	New Jersey	14.8
11	North Dakota	16.6	33	New Mexico	14.8
20	Ohio	16.0	33	New York	14.8
21	Oklahoma	15.9	36	Minnesota	14.3
26	Oregon	15.4	36	Wyoming	14.3
3	Pennsylvania	17.8	38	Idaho	14.1
8	Rhode Island	16.9	39	Virginia	13.9
16	South Carolina	16.2	40	Illinois	13.8
13	South Dakota	16.4	40	Washington	13.8
16	Tennessee	16.2	42	Arizona	13.4
48	Texas	11.5	43	Maryland	13.2
49	Utah	9.7	44	Nevada	12.7
8	Vermont	16.9	45	California	12.2
39	Virginia	13.9	46	Georgia	11.9
40	Washington	13.8	47	Colorado	11.7
1	West Virginia	20.6	48	Texas	11.5
25	Wisconsin	15.5	49	Utah	9.7
36	Wyoming	14.3	50	Alaska	8.7
				District of Columbia	12.7

Source: U.S. Department of Health and Human Services, Centers for Medicare and Medicaid Services
   "2009 Data Compendium" (http://www.cms.hhs.gov/DataCompendium/)
*Includes aged and disabled enrollees. National rate includes only residents of the 50 states and the District of Columbia.

Percent of Medicare Enrollees in Managed Care Programs in 2008

National Percent = 22.2% of Medicare Enrollees*

<table>
<tr><td colspan="3">ALPHA ORDER</td><td colspan="3">RANK ORDER</td></tr>
<tr><td>RANK</td><td>STATE</td><td>PERCENT</td><td>RANK</td><td>STATE</td><td>PERCENT</td></tr>
<tr><td>22</td><td>Alabama</td><td>19.4</td><td>1</td><td>Oregon</td><td>40.6</td></tr>
<tr><td>50</td><td>Alaska</td><td>0.7</td><td>2</td><td>Hawaii</td><td>37.5</td></tr>
<tr><td>4</td><td>Arizona</td><td>36.4</td><td>3</td><td>Pennsylvania</td><td>37.1</td></tr>
<tr><td>35</td><td>Arkansas</td><td>12.4</td><td>4</td><td>Arizona</td><td>36.4</td></tr>
<tr><td>7</td><td>California</td><td>34.3</td><td>5</td><td>Rhode Island</td><td>36.1</td></tr>
<tr><td>8</td><td>Colorado</td><td>32.3</td><td>6</td><td>Minnesota</td><td>34.8</td></tr>
<tr><td>28</td><td>Connecticut</td><td>14.8</td><td>7</td><td>California</td><td>34.3</td></tr>
<tr><td>48</td><td>Delaware</td><td>4.2</td><td>8</td><td>Colorado</td><td>32.3</td></tr>
<tr><td>12</td><td>Florida</td><td>27.5</td><td>9</td><td>Nevada</td><td>30.2</td></tr>
<tr><td>32</td><td>Georgia</td><td>13.2</td><td>10</td><td>Utah</td><td>28.0</td></tr>
<tr><td>2</td><td>Hawaii</td><td>37.5</td><td>11</td><td>New York</td><td>27.8</td></tr>
<tr><td>14</td><td>Idaho</td><td>25.2</td><td>12</td><td>Florida</td><td>27.5</td></tr>
<tr><td>40</td><td>Illinois</td><td>9.4</td><td>13</td><td>Ohio</td><td>25.6</td></tr>
<tr><td>33</td><td>Indiana</td><td>13.0</td><td>14</td><td>Idaho</td><td>25.2</td></tr>
<tr><td>37</td><td>Iowa</td><td>10.6</td><td>15</td><td>Wisconsin</td><td>25.1</td></tr>
<tr><td>42</td><td>Kansas</td><td>8.4</td><td>16</td><td>New Mexico</td><td>23.1</td></tr>
<tr><td>29</td><td>Kentucky</td><td>13.8</td><td>17</td><td>Washington</td><td>22.4</td></tr>
<tr><td>21</td><td>Louisiana</td><td>20.7</td><td>17</td><td>West Virginia</td><td>22.4</td></tr>
<tr><td>45</td><td>Maine</td><td>5.9</td><td>19</td><td>Michigan</td><td>22.3</td></tr>
<tr><td>44</td><td>Maryland</td><td>7.3</td><td>20</td><td>Tennessee</td><td>20.8</td></tr>
<tr><td>23</td><td>Massachusetts</td><td>18.7</td><td>21</td><td>Louisiana</td><td>20.7</td></tr>
<tr><td>19</td><td>Michigan</td><td>22.3</td><td>22</td><td>Alabama</td><td>19.4</td></tr>
<tr><td>6</td><td>Minnesota</td><td>34.8</td><td>23</td><td>Massachusetts</td><td>18.7</td></tr>
<tr><td>41</td><td>Mississippi</td><td>8.6</td><td>24</td><td>Missouri</td><td>18.6</td></tr>
<tr><td>24</td><td>Missouri</td><td>18.6</td><td>25</td><td>Texas</td><td>17.2</td></tr>
<tr><td>27</td><td>Montana</td><td>15.3</td><td>26</td><td>North Carolina</td><td>16.4</td></tr>
<tr><td>36</td><td>Nebraska</td><td>11.3</td><td>27</td><td>Montana</td><td>15.3</td></tr>
<tr><td>9</td><td>Nevada</td><td>30.2</td><td>28</td><td>Connecticut</td><td>14.8</td></tr>
<tr><td>47</td><td>New Hampshire</td><td>4.8</td><td>29</td><td>Kentucky</td><td>13.8</td></tr>
<tr><td>37</td><td>New Jersey</td><td>10.6</td><td>30</td><td>South Carolina</td><td>13.6</td></tr>
<tr><td>16</td><td>New Mexico</td><td>23.1</td><td>31</td><td>Oklahoma</td><td>13.5</td></tr>
<tr><td>11</td><td>New York</td><td>27.8</td><td>32</td><td>Georgia</td><td>13.2</td></tr>
<tr><td>26</td><td>North Carolina</td><td>16.4</td><td>33</td><td>Indiana</td><td>13.0</td></tr>
<tr><td>43</td><td>North Dakota</td><td>7.5</td><td>34</td><td>Virginia</td><td>12.5</td></tr>
<tr><td>13</td><td>Ohio</td><td>25.6</td><td>35</td><td>Arkansas</td><td>12.4</td></tr>
<tr><td>31</td><td>Oklahoma</td><td>13.5</td><td>36</td><td>Nebraska</td><td>11.3</td></tr>
<tr><td>1</td><td>Oregon</td><td>40.6</td><td>37</td><td>Iowa</td><td>10.6</td></tr>
<tr><td>3</td><td>Pennsylvania</td><td>37.1</td><td>37</td><td>New Jersey</td><td>10.6</td></tr>
<tr><td>5</td><td>Rhode Island</td><td>36.1</td><td>39</td><td>South Dakota</td><td>9.7</td></tr>
<tr><td>30</td><td>South Carolina</td><td>13.6</td><td>40</td><td>Illinois</td><td>9.4</td></tr>
<tr><td>39</td><td>South Dakota</td><td>9.7</td><td>41</td><td>Mississippi</td><td>8.6</td></tr>
<tr><td>20</td><td>Tennessee</td><td>20.8</td><td>42</td><td>Kansas</td><td>8.4</td></tr>
<tr><td>25</td><td>Texas</td><td>17.2</td><td>43</td><td>North Dakota</td><td>7.5</td></tr>
<tr><td>10</td><td>Utah</td><td>28.0</td><td>44</td><td>Maryland</td><td>7.3</td></tr>
<tr><td>49</td><td>Vermont</td><td>3.4</td><td>45</td><td>Maine</td><td>5.9</td></tr>
<tr><td>34</td><td>Virginia</td><td>12.5</td><td>46</td><td>Wyoming</td><td>5.3</td></tr>
<tr><td>17</td><td>Washington</td><td>22.4</td><td>47</td><td>New Hampshire</td><td>4.8</td></tr>
<tr><td>17</td><td>West Virginia</td><td>22.4</td><td>48</td><td>Delaware</td><td>4.2</td></tr>
<tr><td>15</td><td>Wisconsin</td><td>25.1</td><td>49</td><td>Vermont</td><td>3.4</td></tr>
<tr><td>46</td><td>Wyoming</td><td>5.3</td><td>50</td><td>Alaska</td><td>0.7</td></tr>
<tr><td></td><td></td><td></td><td></td><td>District of Columbia</td><td>10.4</td></tr>
</table>

Source: U.S. Department of Health and Human Services, Centers for Medicare and Medicaid Services
"Health Care Financing Review, 2009 Statistical Supplement" (http://cms.hhs.gov/MedicareMedicaidStatSupp)
*As of December 2008. National rate is a weighted average calculated by the editors. Includes Medicare Advantage and Employer Direct Plans. Regional Preferred Provider Organizations, Special Needs Plans, and employer only plans are also included.

Percent of Physicians Participating in Medicare in 2009

National Percent = 95.3% of Physicians Participate in Medicare*

ALPHA ORDER				RANK ORDER		
RANK	STATE	PERCENT		RANK	STATE	PERCENT
9	Alabama	97.7		1	Massachusetts	99.1
49	Alaska	91.0		2	Maine	98.7
44	Arizona	93.7		2	Rhode Island	98.7
10	Arkansas	97.6		4	Delaware	98.3
48	California	91.2		4	Michigan	98.3
43	Colorado	93.8		6	Pennsylvania	98.0
34	Connecticut	95.9		7	New Hampshire	97.9
4	Delaware	98.3		7	Utah	97.9
32	Florida	96.1		9	Alabama	97.7
39	Georgia	94.6		10	Arkansas	97.6
29	Hawaii	96.4		10	Kansas	97.6
47	Idaho	91.5		10	Vermont	97.6
31	Illinois	96.2		10	West Virginia	97.6
30	Indiana	96.3		14	North Dakota	97.5
28	Iowa	96.5		14	Ohio	97.5
10	Kansas	97.6		16	Maryland	97.3
23	Kentucky	96.8		16	Nebraska	97.3
33	Louisiana	96.0		18	Nevada	97.1
2	Maine	98.7		19	South Carolina	96.9
16	Maryland	97.3		19	Tennessee	96.9
1	Massachusetts	99.1		19	Virginia	96.9
4	Michigan	98.3		19	Washington	96.9
50	Minnesota	81.6		23	Kentucky	96.8
35	Mississippi	95.6		23	North Carolina	96.8
36	Missouri	95.4		23	Oklahoma	96.8
38	Montana	95.1		23	Wisconsin	96.8
16	Nebraska	97.3		27	New Mexico	96.7
18	Nevada	97.1		28	Iowa	96.5
7	New Hampshire	97.9		29	Hawaii	96.4
46	New Jersey	93.0		30	Indiana	96.3
27	New Mexico	96.7		31	Illinois	96.2
40	New York	94.5		32	Florida	96.1
23	North Carolina	96.8		33	Louisiana	96.0
14	North Dakota	97.5		34	Connecticut	95.9
14	Ohio	97.5		35	Mississippi	95.6
23	Oklahoma	96.8		36	Missouri	95.4
36	Oregon	95.4		36	Oregon	95.4
6	Pennsylvania	98.0		38	Montana	95.1
2	Rhode Island	98.7		39	Georgia	94.6
19	South Carolina	96.9		40	New York	94.5
42	South Dakota	93.9		40	Texas	94.5
19	Tennessee	96.9		42	South Dakota	93.9
40	Texas	94.5		43	Colorado	93.8
7	Utah	97.9		44	Arizona	93.7
10	Vermont	97.6		45	Wyoming	93.6
19	Virginia	96.9		46	New Jersey	93.0
19	Washington	96.9		47	Idaho	91.5
10	West Virginia	97.6		48	California	91.2
23	Wisconsin	96.8		49	Alaska	91.0
45	Wyoming	93.6		50	Minnesota	81.6
					District of Columbia	94.8

Source: U.S. Department of Health and Human Services, Centers for Medicare and Medicaid Services
   "2009 Data Compendium" (http://www.cms.hhs.gov/DataCompendium/)
*As of January 2009. Refers to Medicare Part B. Physicians include MDs, DOs, limited license practitioners, and non-physician practitioners. National average is a weighted average based on state population.

Enrollees in Medicare Prescription Drug Program in 2009

National Total = 27,197,965 Enrollees*

RANK	STATE	ENROLLEES	% of USA
20	Alabama	483,246	1.8%
50	Alaska	24,412	0.1%
16	Arizona	547,402	2.0%
31	Arkansas	312,621	1.1%
1	California	3,188,179	11.7%
26	Colorado	351,312	1.3%
32	Connecticut	304,040	1.1%
47	Delaware	72,067	0.3%
2	Florida	1,954,907	7.2%
10	Georgia	707,098	2.6%
40	Hawaii	131,815	0.5%
41	Idaho	126,873	0.5%
6	Illinois	994,552	3.7%
17	Indiana	541,935	2.0%
28	Iowa	338,925	1.2%
33	Kansas	259,887	1.0%
22	Kentucky	416,152	1.5%
23	Louisiana	413,319	1.5%
38	Maine	158,986	0.6%
29	Maryland	332,185	1.2%
14	Massachusetts	599,759	2.2%
8	Michigan	860,845	3.2%
18	Minnesota	522,004	1.9%
30	Mississippi	313,416	1.2%
13	Missouri	609,886	2.2%
44	Montana	93,587	0.3%
37	Nebraska	176,513	0.6%
35	Nevada	189,226	0.7%
43	New Hampshire	98,410	0.4%
11	New Jersey	679,498	2.5%
36	New Mexico	186,806	0.7%
3	New York	1,715,823	6.3%
9	North Carolina	851,850	3.1%
46	North Dakota	74,630	0.3%
7	Ohio	993,897	3.7%
27	Oklahoma	350,468	1.3%
25	Oregon	385,465	1.4%
5	Pennsylvania	1,415,090	5.2%
42	Rhode Island	120,755	0.4%
24	South Carolina	401,449	1.5%
45	South Dakota	87,537	0.3%
12	Tennessee	655,436	2.4%
4	Texas	1,633,369	6.0%
39	Utah	151,304	0.6%
48	Vermont	59,811	0.2%
15	Virginia	574,055	2.1%
19	Washington	492,147	1.8%
34	West Virginia	228,240	0.8%
21	Wisconsin	475,078	1.7%
49	Wyoming	41,976	0.2%

RANK	STATE	ENROLLEES	% of USA
1	California	3,188,179	11.7%
2	Florida	1,954,907	7.2%
3	New York	1,715,823	6.3%
4	Texas	1,633,369	6.0%
5	Pennsylvania	1,415,090	5.2%
6	Illinois	994,552	3.7%
7	Ohio	993,897	3.7%
8	Michigan	860,845	3.2%
9	North Carolina	851,850	3.1%
10	Georgia	707,098	2.6%
11	New Jersey	679,498	2.5%
12	Tennessee	655,436	2.4%
13	Missouri	609,886	2.2%
14	Massachusetts	599,759	2.2%
15	Virginia	574,055	2.1%
16	Arizona	547,402	2.0%
17	Indiana	541,935	2.0%
18	Minnesota	522,004	1.9%
19	Washington	492,147	1.8%
20	Alabama	483,246	1.8%
21	Wisconsin	475,078	1.7%
22	Kentucky	416,152	1.5%
23	Louisiana	413,319	1.5%
24	South Carolina	401,449	1.5%
25	Oregon	385,465	1.4%
26	Colorado	351,312	1.3%
27	Oklahoma	350,468	1.3%
28	Iowa	338,925	1.2%
29	Maryland	332,185	1.2%
30	Mississippi	313,416	1.2%
31	Arkansas	312,621	1.1%
32	Connecticut	304,040	1.1%
33	Kansas	259,887	1.0%
34	West Virginia	228,240	0.8%
35	Nevada	189,226	0.7%
36	New Mexico	186,806	0.7%
37	Nebraska	176,513	0.6%
38	Maine	158,986	0.6%
39	Utah	151,304	0.6%
40	Hawaii	131,815	0.5%
41	Idaho	126,873	0.5%
42	Rhode Island	120,755	0.4%
43	New Hampshire	98,410	0.4%
44	Montana	93,587	0.3%
45	South Dakota	87,537	0.3%
46	North Dakota	74,630	0.3%
47	Delaware	72,067	0.3%
48	Vermont	59,811	0.2%
49	Wyoming	41,976	0.2%
50	Alaska	24,412	0.1%
	District of Columbia	36,049	0.1%

Source: U.S. Department of Health and Human Services, Centers for Medicare and Medicaid Services
   "2009 Data Compendium" (http://www.cms.hhs.gov/DataCompendium/)
*Total includes 447,309 enrollees in U.S. territories.

Percent of Medicare Enrollees Participating in the
Medicare Prescription Drug Program: 2009
National Percent = 58.3%*

ALPHA ORDER

RANK	STATE	PERCENT
25	Alabama	58.3
50	Alaska	38.6
17	Arizona	60.9
20	Arkansas	59.8
2	California	68.8
26	Colorado	58.2
38	Connecticut	54.4
47	Delaware	49.7
21	Florida	59.5
23	Georgia	58.8
6	Hawaii	65.6
29	Idaho	57.0
36	Illinois	54.9
36	Indiana	54.9
5	Iowa	66.1
17	Kansas	60.9
32	Kentucky	55.8
14	Louisiana	61.3
16	Maine	61.2
49	Maryland	43.3
28	Massachusetts	57.5
41	Michigan	53.1
3	Minnesota	67.7
8	Mississippi	64.1
13	Missouri	61.7
30	Montana	56.6
9	Nebraska	63.9
33	Nevada	55.1
48	New Hampshire	46.4
45	New Jersey	51.9
14	New Mexico	61.3
26	New York	58.2
24	North Carolina	58.7
1	North Dakota	69.3
42	Ohio	53.0
22	Oklahoma	59.0
9	Oregon	63.9
12	Pennsylvania	62.7
4	Rhode Island	66.8
39	South Carolina	53.6
7	South Dakota	64.9
11	Tennessee	63.5
31	Texas	56.1
33	Utah	55.1
33	Vermont	55.1
46	Virginia	51.5
44	Washington	52.3
19	West Virginia	60.4
42	Wisconsin	53.0
39	Wyoming	53.6

RANK ORDER

RANK	STATE	PERCENT
1	North Dakota	69.3
2	California	68.8
3	Minnesota	67.7
4	Rhode Island	66.8
5	Iowa	66.1
6	Hawaii	65.6
7	South Dakota	64.9
8	Mississippi	64.1
9	Nebraska	63.9
9	Oregon	63.9
11	Tennessee	63.5
12	Pennsylvania	62.7
13	Missouri	61.7
14	Louisiana	61.3
14	New Mexico	61.3
16	Maine	61.2
17	Arizona	60.9
17	Kansas	60.9
19	West Virginia	60.4
20	Arkansas	59.8
21	Florida	59.5
22	Oklahoma	59.0
23	Georgia	58.8
24	North Carolina	58.7
25	Alabama	58.3
26	Colorado	58.2
26	New York	58.2
28	Massachusetts	57.5
29	Idaho	57.0
30	Montana	56.6
31	Texas	56.1
32	Kentucky	55.8
33	Nevada	55.1
33	Utah	55.1
33	Vermont	55.1
36	Illinois	54.9
36	Indiana	54.9
38	Connecticut	54.4
39	South Carolina	53.6
39	Wyoming	53.6
41	Michigan	53.1
42	Ohio	53.0
42	Wisconsin	53.0
44	Washington	52.3
45	New Jersey	51.9
46	Virginia	51.5
47	Delaware	49.7
48	New Hampshire	46.4
49	Maryland	43.3
50	Alaska	38.6
	District of Columbia	46.9

Source: U.S. Department of Health and Human Services, Centers for Medicare and Medicaid Services
   "2009 Data Compendium" (http://www.cms.hhs.gov/DataCompendium/)
*National figure includes enrollees in U.S. territories.

Medicare Program Payments in 2008

National Total = $300,045,000,000*

ALPHA ORDER				RANK ORDER			
RANK	STATE	PAYMENTS	% of USA	RANK	STATE	PAYMENTS	% of USA
18	Alabama	$5,429,000,000	1.8%	1	California	$26,290,000,000	8.8%
50	Alaska	413,000,000	0.1%	2	Florida	24,025,000,000	8.0%
25	Arizona	4,381,000,000	1.5%	3	Texas	22,693,000,000	7.6%
29	Arkansas	3,278,000,000	1.1%	4	New York	20,158,000,000	6.7%
1	California	26,290,000,000	8.8%	5	Illinois	14,387,000,000	4.8%
32	Colorado	2,956,000,000	1.0%	6	Pennsylvania	12,271,000,000	4.1%
24	Connecticut	4,436,000,000	1.5%	7	Ohio	12,146,000,000	4.0%
41	Delaware	1,232,000,000	0.4%	8	Michigan	11,680,000,000	3.9%
2	Florida	24,025,000,000	8.0%	9	New Jersey	11,555,000,000	3.9%
11	Georgia	7,932,000,000	2.6%	10	North Carolina	9,229,000,000	3.1%
48	Hawaii	680,000,000	0.2%	11	Georgia	7,932,000,000	2.6%
42	Idaho	1,051,000,000	0.4%	12	Massachusetts	7,597,000,000	2.5%
5	Illinois	14,387,000,000	4.8%	13	Maryland	7,002,000,000	2.3%
15	Indiana	6,881,000,000	2.3%	14	Virginia	6,959,000,000	2.3%
30	Iowa	3,034,000,000	1.0%	15	Indiana	6,881,000,000	2.3%
31	Kansas	2,965,000,000	1.0%	16	Tennessee	6,491,000,000	2.2%
20	Kentucky	5,077,000,000	1.7%	17	Missouri	6,395,000,000	2.1%
19	Louisiana	5,169,000,000	1.7%	18	Alabama	5,429,000,000	1.8%
37	Maine	1,657,000,000	0.6%	19	Louisiana	5,169,000,000	1.7%
13	Maryland	7,002,000,000	2.3%	20	Kentucky	5,077,000,000	1.7%
12	Massachusetts	7,597,000,000	2.5%	21	South Carolina	4,952,000,000	1.7%
8	Michigan	11,680,000,000	3.9%	22	Wisconsin	4,926,000,000	1.6%
28	Minnesota	3,880,000,000	1.3%	23	Washington	4,896,000,000	1.6%
27	Mississippi	3,973,000,000	1.3%	24	Connecticut	4,436,000,000	1.5%
17	Missouri	6,395,000,000	2.1%	25	Arizona	4,381,000,000	1.5%
44	Montana	883,000,000	0.3%	26	Oklahoma	4,247,000,000	1.4%
36	Nebraska	1,825,000,000	0.6%	27	Mississippi	3,973,000,000	1.3%
35	Nevada	1,931,000,000	0.6%	28	Minnesota	3,880,000,000	1.3%
39	New Hampshire	1,484,000,000	0.5%	29	Arkansas	3,278,000,000	1.1%
9	New Jersey	11,555,000,000	3.9%	30	Iowa	3,034,000,000	1.0%
38	New Mexico	1,527,000,000	0.5%	31	Kansas	2,965,000,000	1.0%
4	New York	20,158,000,000	6.7%	32	Colorado	2,956,000,000	1.0%
10	North Carolina	9,229,000,000	3.1%	33	West Virginia	2,248,000,000	0.7%
47	North Dakota	723,000,000	0.2%	34	Oregon	2,171,000,000	0.7%
7	Ohio	12,146,000,000	4.0%	35	Nevada	1,931,000,000	0.6%
26	Oklahoma	4,247,000,000	1.4%	36	Nebraska	1,825,000,000	0.6%
34	Oregon	2,171,000,000	0.7%	37	Maine	1,657,000,000	0.6%
6	Pennsylvania	12,271,000,000	4.1%	38	New Mexico	1,527,000,000	0.5%
43	Rhode Island	917,000,000	0.3%	39	New Hampshire	1,484,000,000	0.5%
21	South Carolina	4,952,000,000	1.7%	40	Utah	1,349,000,000	0.4%
45	South Dakota	752,000,000	0.3%	41	Delaware	1,232,000,000	0.4%
16	Tennessee	6,491,000,000	2.2%	42	Idaho	1,051,000,000	0.4%
3	Texas	22,693,000,000	7.6%	43	Rhode Island	917,000,000	0.3%
40	Utah	1,349,000,000	0.4%	44	Montana	883,000,000	0.3%
46	Vermont	740,000,000	0.2%	45	South Dakota	752,000,000	0.3%
14	Virginia	6,959,000,000	2.3%	46	Vermont	740,000,000	0.2%
23	Washington	4,896,000,000	1.6%	47	North Dakota	723,000,000	0.2%
33	West Virginia	2,248,000,000	0.7%	48	Hawaii	680,000,000	0.2%
22	Wisconsin	4,926,000,000	1.6%	49	Wyoming	471,000,000	0.2%
49	Wyoming	471,000,000	0.2%	50	Alaska	413,000,000	0.1%
					District of Columbia	703,000,000	0.2%

Source: U.S. Department of Health and Human Services, Centers for Medicare and Medicaid Services
"Health Care Financing Review, 2009 Statistical Supplement" (http://cms.hhs.gov/MedicareMedicaidStatSupp)
*Figures for calendar year 2008. Includes payments to aged and disabled enrollees. Total does not include payments to beneficiaries in Puerto Rico and other outlying areas.

Per Capita Medicare Program Payments in 2008

National Per Capita = $986*

ALPHA ORDER			RANK ORDER		
RANK	STATE	PER CAPITA	RANK	STATE	PER CAPITA
13	Alabama	$1,161	1	Delaware	$1,406
46	Alaska	600	2	Mississippi	1,351
45	Arizona	674	3	New Jersey	1,334
16	Arkansas	1,143	4	Florida	1,304
43	California	719	5	Connecticut	1,266
47	Colorado	599	6	Maine	1,256
5	Connecticut	1,266	7	West Virginia	1,239
1	Delaware	1,406	8	Maryland	1,237
4	Florida	1,304	9	Vermont	1,192
38	Georgia	818	10	Kentucky	1,184
49	Hawaii	528	11	Michigan	1,168
44	Idaho	688	12	Oklahoma	1,165
19	Illinois	1,120	13	Alabama	1,161
21	Indiana	1,077	13	Louisiana	1,161
28	Iowa	1,013	13	Massachusetts	1,161
23	Kansas	1,060	16	Arkansas	1,143
10	Kentucky	1,184	17	North Dakota	1,127
13	Louisiana	1,161	18	New Hampshire	1,123
6	Maine	1,256	19	Illinois	1,120
8	Maryland	1,237	20	South Carolina	1,100
13	Massachusetts	1,161	21	Indiana	1,077
11	Michigan	1,168	22	Missouri	1,074
41	Minnesota	742	23	Kansas	1,060
2	Mississippi	1,351	24	Ohio	1,054
22	Missouri	1,074	25	Tennessee	1,040
33	Montana	912	26	New York	1,035
27	Nebraska	1,024	27	Nebraska	1,024
42	Nevada	738	28	Iowa	1,013
18	New Hampshire	1,123	29	North Carolina	998
3	New Jersey	1,334	30	Pennsylvania	976
39	New Mexico	769	31	South Dakota	935
26	New York	1,035	32	Texas	934
29	North Carolina	998	33	Montana	912
17	North Dakota	1,127	34	Virginia	893
24	Ohio	1,054	35	Wyoming	884
12	Oklahoma	1,165	36	Wisconsin	875
48	Oregon	574	37	Rhode Island	870
30	Pennsylvania	976	38	Georgia	818
37	Rhode Island	870	39	New Mexico	769
20	South Carolina	1,100	40	Washington	746
31	South Dakota	935	41	Minnesota	742
25	Tennessee	1,040	42	Nevada	738
32	Texas	934	43	California	719
50	Utah	495	44	Idaho	688
9	Vermont	1,192	45	Arizona	674
34	Virginia	893	46	Alaska	600
40	Washington	746	47	Colorado	599
7	West Virginia	1,239	48	Oregon	574
36	Wisconsin	875	49	Hawaii	528
35	Wyoming	884	50	Utah	495

District of Columbia   1,191

Source: CQ Press using data from U.S. Department of Health and Human Services, Centers for Medicare and Medicaid Services "Health Care Financing Review, 2009 Statistical Supplement" (http://cms.hhs.gov/MedicareMedicaidStatSupp)

*Figures for calendar year 2008. Includes payments to aged and disabled enrollees. National rate does not include payments or enrollees in Puerto Rico and other outlying areas.

Medicare Program Payments per Enrollee in 2008

National Rate = $8,649*

RANK	STATE	PER ENROLLEE		RANK	STATE	PER ENROLLEE
	ALPHA ORDER				**RANK ORDER**	
17	Alabama	$8,306		1	Florida	$10,317
40	Alaska	7,043		2	Maryland	10,092
25	Arizona	7,945		3	New Jersey	9,974
32	Arkansas	7,528		4	Louisiana	9,894
13	California	8,862		5	Texas	9,769
34	Colorado	7,496		6	New York	9,545
8	Connecticut	9,419		7	Michigan	9,448
11	Delaware	8,959		8	Connecticut	9,419
1	Florida	10,317		9	Massachusetts	9,115
28	Georgia	7,857		10	Mississippi	9,089
50	Hawaii	5,531		11	Delaware	8,959
45	Idaho	6,494		12	Illinois	8,893
12	Illinois	8,893		13	California	8,862
19	Indiana	8,202		14	Ohio	8,780
43	Iowa	6,842		15	Pennsylvania	8,711
27	Kansas	7,864		16	Oklahoma	8,498
23	Kentucky	8,044		17	Alabama	8,306
4	Louisiana	9,894		18	Nevada	8,249
42	Maine	6,937		19	Indiana	8,202
2	Maryland	10,092		20	Tennessee	8,103
9	Massachusetts	9,115		21	Rhode Island	8,086
7	Michigan	9,448		22	Missouri	8,052
26	Minnesota	7,895		23	Kentucky	8,044
10	Mississippi	9,089		24	South Carolina	7,972
22	Missouri	8,052		25	Arizona	7,945
46	Montana	6,414		26	Minnesota	7,895
33	Nebraska	7,509		27	Kansas	7,864
18	Nevada	8,249		28	Georgia	7,857
35	New Hampshire	7,469		29	North Carolina	7,853
3	New Jersey	9,974		30	West Virginia	7,659
44	New Mexico	6,782		31	Wisconsin	7,532
6	New York	9,545		32	Arkansas	7,528
29	North Carolina	7,853		33	Nebraska	7,509
37	North Dakota	7,152		34	Colorado	7,496
14	Ohio	8,780		35	New Hampshire	7,469
16	Oklahoma	8,498		36	Virginia	7,320
49	Oregon	6,176		37	North Dakota	7,152
15	Pennsylvania	8,711		38	Vermont	7,114
21	Rhode Island	8,086		39	Utah	7,059
24	South Carolina	7,972		40	Alaska	7,043
48	South Dakota	6,307		41	Washington	6,958
20	Tennessee	8,103		42	Maine	6,937
5	Texas	9,769		43	Iowa	6,842
39	Utah	7,059		44	New Mexico	6,782
38	Vermont	7,114		45	Idaho	6,494
36	Virginia	7,320		46	Montana	6,414
41	Washington	6,958		47	Wyoming	6,397
30	West Virginia	7,659		48	South Dakota	6,307
31	Wisconsin	7,532		49	Oregon	6,176
47	Wyoming	6,397		50	Hawaii	5,531
					District of Columbia	10,215

Source: U.S. Department of Health and Human Services, Centers for Medicare and Medicaid Services
   "Health Care Financing Review, 2009 Statistical Supplement" (http://cms.hhs.gov/MedicareMedicaidStatSupp)
*Figures for calendar year 2008. Includes payments to aged and disabled enrollees. National figure does not include enrollees in managed care plans in the denominator used to calculate average payments. National rate also does not include payments or enrollees in Puerto Rico and other outlying areas.

Medicaid Enrollment in 2008

National Total = 47,142,791 Enrollees*

ALPHA ORDER

RANK	STATE	ENROLLEES	% of USA
20	Alabama	764,914	1.6%
47	Alaska	96,807	0.2%
13	Arizona	1,048,635	2.2%
26	Arkansas	622,491	1.3%
1	California	6,606,893	14.0%
31	Colorado	429,895	0.9%
30	Connecticut	435,419	0.9%
43	Delaware	152,899	0.3%
4	Florida	2,276,014	4.8%
10	Georgia	1,271,355	2.7%
37	Hawaii	211,105	0.4%
41	Idaho	187,394	0.4%
5	Illinois	2,106,700	4.5%
18	Indiana	881,888	1.9%
33	Iowa	362,807	0.8%
35	Kansas	278,705	0.6%
22	Kentucky	731,911	1.6%
14	Louisiana	1,006,842	2.1%
36	Maine	258,751	0.5%
23	Maryland	710,790	1.5%
12	Massachusetts	1,155,134	2.5%
8	Michigan	1,547,246	3.3%
27	Minnesota	617,397	1.3%
25	Mississippi	669,690	1.4%
19	Missouri	833,112	1.8%
48	Montana	82,852	0.2%
39	Nebraska	202,297	0.4%
40	Nevada	188,831	0.4%
45	New Hampshire	113,496	0.2%
16	New Jersey	914,503	1.9%
29	New Mexico	472,629	1.0%
2	New York	4,147,101	8.8%
9	North Carolina	1,353,760	2.9%
50	North Dakota	53,556	0.1%
7	Ohio	1,783,993	3.8%
28	Oklahoma	583,057	1.2%
32	Oregon	417,946	0.9%
6	Pennsylvania	1,833,489	3.9%
42	Rhode Island	178,119	0.4%
24	South Carolina	689,338	1.5%
46	South Dakota	102,444	0.2%
11	Tennessee	1,207,136	2.6%
3	Texas	3,041,201	6.5%
38	Utah	208,009	0.4%
44	Vermont	141,260	0.3%
21	Virginia	753,714	1.6%
15	Washington	960,881	2.0%
34	West Virginia	311,064	0.7%
17	Wisconsin	907,455	1.9%
49	Wyoming	61,083	0.1%

RANK ORDER

RANK	STATE	ENROLLEES	% of USA
1	California	6,606,893	14.0%
2	New York	4,147,101	8.8%
3	Texas	3,041,201	6.5%
4	Florida	2,276,014	4.8%
5	Illinois	2,106,700	4.5%
6	Pennsylvania	1,833,489	3.9%
7	Ohio	1,783,993	3.8%
8	Michigan	1,547,246	3.3%
9	North Carolina	1,353,760	2.9%
10	Georgia	1,271,355	2.7%
11	Tennessee	1,207,136	2.6%
12	Massachusetts	1,155,134	2.5%
13	Arizona	1,048,635	2.2%
14	Louisiana	1,006,842	2.1%
15	Washington	960,881	2.0%
16	New Jersey	914,503	1.9%
17	Wisconsin	907,455	1.9%
18	Indiana	881,888	1.9%
19	Missouri	833,112	1.8%
20	Alabama	764,914	1.6%
21	Virginia	753,714	1.6%
22	Kentucky	731,911	1.6%
23	Maryland	710,790	1.5%
24	South Carolina	689,338	1.5%
25	Mississippi	669,690	1.4%
26	Arkansas	622,491	1.3%
27	Minnesota	617,397	1.3%
28	Oklahoma	583,057	1.2%
29	New Mexico	472,629	1.0%
30	Connecticut	435,419	0.9%
31	Colorado	429,895	0.9%
32	Oregon	417,946	0.9%
33	Iowa	362,807	0.8%
34	West Virginia	311,064	0.7%
35	Kansas	278,705	0.6%
36	Maine	258,751	0.5%
37	Hawaii	211,105	0.4%
38	Utah	208,009	0.4%
39	Nebraska	202,297	0.4%
40	Nevada	188,831	0.4%
41	Idaho	187,394	0.4%
42	Rhode Island	178,119	0.4%
43	Delaware	152,899	0.3%
44	Vermont	141,260	0.3%
45	New Hampshire	113,496	0.2%
46	South Dakota	102,444	0.2%
47	Alaska	96,807	0.2%
48	Montana	82,852	0.2%
49	Wyoming	61,083	0.1%
50	North Dakota	53,556	0.1%
	District of Columbia	146,072	0.3%

Source: U.S. Department of Health and Human Services, Centers for Medicare and Medicaid Services
   "2008 Medicaid Managed Care Enrollment Report" (http://www.cms.hhs.gov/MedicaidDataSourcesGenInfo/)
*Unduplicated enrollment as of June 30, 2008. National total includes 1,022,711 Medicaid enrollees in Puerto Rico and the Virgin Islands.

Percent of Population Enrolled in Medicaid in 2008

National Percent = 15.2% of Population*

RANK	STATE	PERCENT
15	Alabama	16.4
27	Alaska	14.1
18	Arizona	16.1
5	Arkansas	21.7
9	California	18.1
45	Colorado	8.7
34	Connecticut	12.4
11	Delaware	17.5
34	Florida	12.4
30	Georgia	13.1
15	Hawaii	16.4
36	Idaho	12.3
15	Illinois	16.4
29	Indiana	13.8
37	Iowa	12.1
43	Kansas	10.0
12	Kentucky	17.1
4	Louisiana	22.6
7	Maine	19.6
32	Maryland	12.6
10	Massachusetts	17.7
21	Michigan	15.5
38	Minnesota	11.8
2	Mississippi	22.8
28	Missouri	14.0
46	Montana	8.6
40	Nebraska	11.4
50	Nevada	7.2
46	New Hampshire	8.6
42	New Jersey	10.6
1	New Mexico	23.8
6	New York	21.3
24	North Carolina	14.6
48	North Dakota	8.3
21	Ohio	15.5
20	Oklahoma	16.0
41	Oregon	11.0
24	Pennsylvania	14.6
14	Rhode Island	16.9
23	South Carolina	15.3
31	South Dakota	12.7
8	Tennessee	19.3
33	Texas	12.5
49	Utah	7.6
3	Vermont	22.7
44	Virginia	9.7
24	Washington	14.6
12	West Virginia	17.1
18	Wisconsin	16.1
39	Wyoming	11.5

RANK	STATE	PERCENT
1	New Mexico	23.8
2	Mississippi	22.8
3	Vermont	22.7
4	Louisiana	22.6
5	Arkansas	21.7
6	New York	21.3
7	Maine	19.6
8	Tennessee	19.3
9	California	18.1
10	Massachusetts	17.7
11	Delaware	17.5
12	Kentucky	17.1
12	West Virginia	17.1
14	Rhode Island	16.9
15	Alabama	16.4
15	Hawaii	16.4
15	Illinois	16.4
18	Arizona	16.1
18	Wisconsin	16.1
20	Oklahoma	16.0
21	Michigan	15.5
21	Ohio	15.5
23	South Carolina	15.3
24	North Carolina	14.6
24	Pennsylvania	14.6
24	Washington	14.6
27	Alaska	14.1
28	Missouri	14.0
29	Indiana	13.8
30	Georgia	13.1
31	South Dakota	12.7
32	Maryland	12.6
33	Texas	12.5
34	Connecticut	12.4
34	Florida	12.4
36	Idaho	12.3
37	Iowa	12.1
38	Minnesota	11.8
39	Wyoming	11.5
40	Nebraska	11.4
41	Oregon	11.0
42	New Jersey	10.6
43	Kansas	10.0
44	Virginia	9.7
45	Colorado	8.7
46	Montana	8.6
46	New Hampshire	8.6
48	North Dakota	8.3
49	Utah	7.6
50	Nevada	7.2

| | District of Columbia | 24.8 |

Source: CQ Press using data from U.S. Department of Health and Human Services, Centers for Medicare and Medicaid Services
"2008 Medicaid Managed Care Enrollment Report" (http://www.cms.hhs.gov/MedicaidDataSourcesGenInfo/)
*Unduplicated enrollment as of June 30, 2008. National percent does not include recipients or population in U.S. territories.

Medicaid Managed Care Enrollment in 2008

National Total = 33,427,582 Enrollees*

ALPHA ORDER

RANK	STATE	ENROLLEES	% of USA
23	Alabama	504,466	1.5%
49	Alaska	0	0.0%
11	Arizona	949,404	2.8%
24	Arkansas	500,214	1.5%
1	California	3,408,909	10.2%
28	Colorado	414,245	1.2%
33	Connecticut	284,465	0.9%
43	Delaware	115,236	0.3%
5	Florida	1,441,624	4.3%
9	Georgia	1,167,887	3.5%
37	Hawaii	166,948	0.5%
40	Idaho	156,268	0.5%
10	Illinois	1,167,500	3.5%
20	Indiana	629,710	1.9%
31	Iowa	295,887	0.9%
34	Kansas	233,505	0.7%
17	Kentucky	664,790	2.0%
16	Louisiana	692,099	2.1%
38	Maine	163,285	0.5%
21	Maryland	516,454	1.5%
15	Massachusetts	696,801	2.1%
6	Michigan	1,363,482	4.1%
29	Minnesota	385,025	1.2%
25	Mississippi	485,143	1.5%
14	Missouri	810,828	2.4%
48	Montana	29,831	0.1%
36	Nebraska	171,623	0.5%
39	Nevada	156,539	0.5%
46	New Hampshire	88,026	0.3%
18	New Jersey	659,586	2.0%
32	New Mexico	293,066	0.9%
2	New York	2,713,731	8.1%
12	North Carolina	905,327	2.7%
47	North Dakota	31,216	0.1%
7	Ohio	1,275,466	3.8%
22	Oklahoma	510,768	1.5%
30	Oregon	381,101	1.1%
4	Pennsylvania	1,487,082	4.4%
44	Rhode Island	110,196	0.3%
19	South Carolina	646,741	1.9%
45	South Dakota	101,259	0.3%
8	Tennessee	1,207,136	3.6%
3	Texas	2,116,493	6.3%
35	Utah	178,345	0.5%
42	Vermont	128,608	0.4%
27	Virginia	472,401	1.4%
13	Washington	858,331	2.6%
41	West Virginia	138,699	0.4%
26	Wisconsin	474,168	1.4%
49	Wyoming	0	0.0%

RANK ORDER

RANK	STATE	ENROLLEES	% of USA
1	California	3,408,909	10.2%
2	New York	2,713,731	8.1%
3	Texas	2,116,493	6.3%
4	Pennsylvania	1,487,082	4.4%
5	Florida	1,441,624	4.3%
6	Michigan	1,363,482	4.1%
7	Ohio	1,275,466	3.8%
8	Tennessee	1,207,136	3.6%
9	Georgia	1,167,887	3.5%
10	Illinois	1,167,500	3.5%
11	Arizona	949,404	2.8%
12	North Carolina	905,327	2.7%
13	Washington	858,331	2.6%
14	Missouri	810,828	2.4%
15	Massachusetts	696,801	2.1%
16	Louisiana	692,099	2.1%
17	Kentucky	664,790	2.0%
18	New Jersey	659,586	2.0%
19	South Carolina	646,741	1.9%
20	Indiana	629,710	1.9%
21	Maryland	516,454	1.5%
22	Oklahoma	510,768	1.5%
23	Alabama	504,466	1.5%
24	Arkansas	500,214	1.5%
25	Mississippi	485,143	1.5%
26	Wisconsin	474,168	1.4%
27	Virginia	472,401	1.4%
28	Colorado	414,245	1.2%
29	Minnesota	385,025	1.2%
30	Oregon	381,101	1.1%
31	Iowa	295,887	0.9%
32	New Mexico	293,066	0.9%
33	Connecticut	284,465	0.9%
34	Kansas	233,505	0.7%
35	Utah	178,345	0.5%
36	Nebraska	171,623	0.5%
37	Hawaii	166,948	0.5%
38	Maine	163,285	0.5%
39	Nevada	156,539	0.5%
40	Idaho	156,268	0.5%
41	West Virginia	138,699	0.4%
42	Vermont	128,608	0.4%
43	Delaware	115,236	0.3%
44	Rhode Island	110,196	0.3%
45	South Dakota	101,259	0.3%
46	New Hampshire	88,026	0.3%
47	North Dakota	31,216	0.1%
48	Montana	29,831	0.1%
49	Alaska	0	0.0%
49	Wyoming	0	0.0%
	District of Columbia	92,985	0.3%

Source: U.S. Department of Health and Human Services, Centers for Medicare and Medicaid Services
"2008 Medicaid Managed Care Enrollment Report" (http://www.cms.hhs.gov/MedicaidDataSourcesGenInfo/)
*Unduplicated enrollment as of June 30, 2008. Enrollment in state health care reform programs that expand eligibility beyond traditional Medicaid standards. National total includes 984,683 Medicaid managed care enrollees in Puerto Rico.

Percent of Medicaid Enrollees in Managed Care in 2008

National Percent = 70.9% of Medicaid Enrollees*

ALPHA ORDER

RANK	STATE	PERCENT
33	Alabama	66.0
49	Alaska	0.0
10	Arizona	90.5
21	Arkansas	80.4
46	California	51.6
4	Colorado	96.4
35	Connecticut	65.3
24	Delaware	75.4
36	Florida	63.3
6	Georgia	91.9
22	Hawaii	79.1
17	Idaho	83.4
44	Illinois	55.4
29	Indiana	71.4
19	Iowa	81.6
16	Kansas	83.8
9	Kentucky	90.8
31	Louisiana	68.7
37	Maine	63.1
25	Maryland	72.7
42	Massachusetts	60.3
12	Michigan	88.1
39	Minnesota	62.4
26	Mississippi	72.4
3	Missouri	97.3
48	Montana	36.0
15	Nebraska	84.8
18	Nevada	82.9
23	New Hampshire	77.6
27	New Jersey	72.1
40	New Mexico	62.0
34	New York	65.4
32	North Carolina	66.9
43	North Dakota	58.3
28	Ohio	71.5
13	Oklahoma	87.6
7	Oregon	91.2
20	Pennsylvania	81.1
41	Rhode Island	61.9
5	South Carolina	93.8
2	South Dakota	98.8
1	Tennessee	100.0
30	Texas	69.6
14	Utah	85.7
8	Vermont	91.0
38	Virginia	62.7
11	Washington	89.3
47	West Virginia	44.6
45	Wisconsin	52.3
49	Wyoming	0.0

RANK ORDER

RANK	STATE	PERCENT
1	Tennessee	100.0
2	South Dakota	98.8
3	Missouri	97.3
4	Colorado	96.4
5	South Carolina	93.8
6	Georgia	91.9
7	Oregon	91.2
8	Vermont	91.0
9	Kentucky	90.8
10	Arizona	90.5
11	Washington	89.3
12	Michigan	88.1
13	Oklahoma	87.6
14	Utah	85.7
15	Nebraska	84.8
16	Kansas	83.8
17	Idaho	83.4
18	Nevada	82.9
19	Iowa	81.6
20	Pennsylvania	81.1
21	Arkansas	80.4
22	Hawaii	79.1
23	New Hampshire	77.6
24	Delaware	75.4
25	Maryland	72.7
26	Mississippi	72.4
27	New Jersey	72.1
28	Ohio	71.5
29	Indiana	71.4
30	Texas	69.6
31	Louisiana	68.7
32	North Carolina	66.9
33	Alabama	66.0
34	New York	65.4
35	Connecticut	65.3
36	Florida	63.3
37	Maine	63.1
38	Virginia	62.7
39	Minnesota	62.4
40	New Mexico	62.0
41	Rhode Island	61.9
42	Massachusetts	60.3
43	North Dakota	58.3
44	Illinois	55.4
45	Wisconsin	52.3
46	California	51.6
47	West Virginia	44.6
48	Montana	36.0
49	Alaska	0.0
49	Wyoming	0.0

	District of Columbia	63.7

Source: U.S. Department of Health and Human Services, Centers for Medicare and Medicaid Services
"2008 Medicaid Managed Care Enrollment Report" (http://www.cms.hhs.gov/MedicaidDataSourcesGenInfo/)
*Unduplicated enrollment as of June 30, 2008. Enrollment in state health care reform programs that expand eligibility beyond traditional Medicaid standards. National percent includes Medicaid enrollees in Puerto Rico and the Virgin Islands.

Estimated Medicaid Expenditures in 2009

National Total = $335,177,000,000*

RANK	STATE	EXPENDITURES	% of USA
24	Alabama	$4,871,000,000	1.5%
44	Alaska	1,201,000,000	0.4%
13	Arizona	7,972,000,000	2.4%
29	Arkansas	3,766,000,000	1.1%
1	California	39,903,000,000	11.9%
32	Colorado	3,114,000,000	0.9%
25	Connecticut	4,671,000,000	1.4%
46	Delaware	1,077,000,000	0.3%
4	Florida	16,119,000,000	4.8%
14	Georgia	7,615,000,000	2.3%
42	Hawaii	1,331,000,000	0.4%
40	Idaho	1,437,000,000	0.4%
5	Illinois	14,488,000,000	4.3%
22	Indiana	5,595,000,000	1.7%
33	Iowa	3,110,000,000	0.9%
34	Kansas	2,593,000,000	0.8%
23	Kentucky	5,509,000,000	1.6%
18	Louisiana	6,588,000,000	2.0%
36	Maine	2,462,000,000	0.7%
19	Maryland	6,353,000,000	1.9%
11	Massachusetts	8,688,000,000	2.6%
9	Michigan	10,551,000,000	3.1%
17	Minnesota	6,658,000,000	2.0%
27	Mississippi	4,203,000,000	1.3%
12	Missouri	8,619,000,000	2.6%
47	Montana	841,000,000	0.3%
39	Nebraska	1,629,000,000	0.5%
41	Nevada	1,332,000,000	0.4%
43	New Hampshire	1,316,000,000	0.4%
10	New Jersey	9,851,000,000	2.9%
31	New Mexico	3,401,000,000	1.0%
2	New York	32,428,000,000	9.7%
8	North Carolina	10,721,000,000	3.2%
50	North Dakota	549,000,000	0.2%
7	Ohio	14,051,000,000	4.2%
28	Oklahoma	3,968,000,000	1.2%
30	Oregon	3,532,000,000	1.1%
3	Pennsylvania	18,750,000,000	5.6%
37	Rhode Island	1,766,000,000	0.5%
26	South Carolina	4,562,000,000	1.4%
48	South Dakota	776,000,000	0.2%
15	Tennessee	7,389,000,000	2.2%
6	Texas	14,471,000,000	4.3%
38	Utah	1,720,000,000	0.5%
45	Vermont	1,088,000,000	0.3%
21	Virginia	6,079,000,000	1.8%
16	Washington	7,223,000,000	2.2%
35	West Virginia	2,467,000,000	0.7%
20	Wisconsin	6,198,000,000	1.8%
49	Wyoming	575,000,000	0.2%

RANK ORDER

RANK	STATE	EXPENDITURES	% of USA
1	California	$39,903,000,000	11.9%
2	New York	32,428,000,000	9.7%
3	Pennsylvania	18,750,000,000	5.6%
4	Florida	16,119,000,000	4.8%
5	Illinois	14,488,000,000	4.3%
6	Texas	14,471,000,000	4.3%
7	Ohio	14,051,000,000	4.2%
8	North Carolina	10,721,000,000	3.2%
9	Michigan	10,551,000,000	3.1%
10	New Jersey	9,851,000,000	2.9%
11	Massachusetts	8,688,000,000	2.6%
12	Missouri	8,619,000,000	2.6%
13	Arizona	7,972,000,000	2.4%
14	Georgia	7,615,000,000	2.3%
15	Tennessee	7,389,000,000	2.2%
16	Washington	7,223,000,000	2.2%
17	Minnesota	6,658,000,000	2.0%
18	Louisiana	6,588,000,000	2.0%
19	Maryland	6,353,000,000	1.9%
20	Wisconsin	6,198,000,000	1.8%
21	Virginia	6,079,000,000	1.8%
22	Indiana	5,595,000,000	1.7%
23	Kentucky	5,509,000,000	1.6%
24	Alabama	4,871,000,000	1.5%
25	Connecticut	4,671,000,000	1.4%
26	South Carolina	4,562,000,000	1.4%
27	Mississippi	4,203,000,000	1.3%
28	Oklahoma	3,968,000,000	1.2%
29	Arkansas	3,766,000,000	1.1%
30	Oregon	3,532,000,000	1.1%
31	New Mexico	3,401,000,000	1.0%
32	Colorado	3,114,000,000	0.9%
33	Iowa	3,110,000,000	0.9%
34	Kansas	2,593,000,000	0.8%
35	West Virginia	2,467,000,000	0.7%
36	Maine	2,462,000,000	0.7%
37	Rhode Island	1,766,000,000	0.5%
38	Utah	1,720,000,000	0.5%
39	Nebraska	1,629,000,000	0.5%
40	Idaho	1,437,000,000	0.4%
41	Nevada	1,332,000,000	0.4%
42	Hawaii	1,331,000,000	0.4%
43	New Hampshire	1,316,000,000	0.4%
44	Alaska	1,201,000,000	0.4%
45	Vermont	1,088,000,000	0.3%
46	Delaware	1,077,000,000	0.3%
47	Montana	841,000,000	0.3%
48	South Dakota	776,000,000	0.2%
49	Wyoming	575,000,000	0.2%
50	North Dakota	549,000,000	0.2%
	District of Columbia**	NA	NA

Source: National Association of State Budget Officers
"2008 State Expenditure Report" (http://www.nasbo.org)
*Estimates for fiscal year 2009.
**Not available.

Estimated Per Capita Medicaid Expenditures in 2009

National Per Capita = $1,092*

ALPHA ORDER

RANK	STATE	PER CAPITA
31	Alabama	$1,034
3	Alaska	1,719
19	Arizona	1,209
14	Arkansas	1,303
27	California	1,080
47	Colorado	620
12	Connecticut	1,328
17	Delaware	1,217
42	Florida	870
45	Georgia	775
33	Hawaii	1,028
37	Idaho	930
23	Illinois	1,122
41	Indiana	871
31	Iowa	1,034
39	Kansas	920
15	Kentucky	1,277
8	Louisiana	1,467
1	Maine	1,868
24	Maryland	1,115
13	Massachusetts	1,318
29	Michigan	1,058
16	Minnesota	1,264
10	Mississippi	1,424
9	Missouri	1,439
43	Montana	863
40	Nebraska	907
50	Nevada	504
35	New Hampshire	994
22	New Jersey	1,131
4	New Mexico	1,692
6	New York	1,659
21	North Carolina	1,143
44	North Dakota	849
17	Ohio	1,217
28	Oklahoma	1,076
38	Oregon	923
7	Pennsylvania	1,488
5	Rhode Island	1,677
34	South Carolina	1,000
36	South Dakota	955
20	Tennessee	1,174
49	Texas	584
48	Utah	618
2	Vermont	1,750
46	Virginia	771
26	Washington	1,084
11	West Virginia	1,356
25	Wisconsin	1,096
30	Wyoming	1,056

RANK ORDER

RANK	STATE	PER CAPITA
1	Maine	$1,868
2	Vermont	1,750
3	Alaska	1,719
4	New Mexico	1,692
5	Rhode Island	1,677
6	New York	1,659
7	Pennsylvania	1,488
8	Louisiana	1,467
9	Missouri	1,439
10	Mississippi	1,424
11	West Virginia	1,356
12	Connecticut	1,328
13	Massachusetts	1,318
14	Arkansas	1,303
15	Kentucky	1,277
16	Minnesota	1,264
17	Delaware	1,217
17	Ohio	1,217
19	Arizona	1,209
20	Tennessee	1,174
21	North Carolina	1,143
22	New Jersey	1,131
23	Illinois	1,122
24	Maryland	1,115
25	Wisconsin	1,096
26	Washington	1,084
27	California	1,080
28	Oklahoma	1,076
29	Michigan	1,058
30	Wyoming	1,056
31	Alabama	1,034
31	Iowa	1,034
33	Hawaii	1,028
34	South Carolina	1,000
35	New Hampshire	994
36	South Dakota	955
37	Idaho	930
38	Oregon	923
39	Kansas	920
40	Nebraska	907
41	Indiana	871
42	Florida	870
43	Montana	863
44	North Dakota	849
45	Georgia	775
46	Virginia	771
47	Colorado	620
48	Utah	618
49	Texas	584
50	Nevada	504

District of Columbia**   NA

Source: CQ Press using data from National Association of State Budget Officers
    "2008 State Expenditure Report" (http://www.nasbo.org)
*Estimates for fiscal year 2009.
**Not available.

Estimated Medicaid Expenditures as a Percent of Total Expenditures in 2009

National Percent = 21.0%*

ALPHA ORDER

RANK	STATE	PERCENT
48	Alabama	10.5
49	Alaska	8.4
5	Arizona	29.4
24	Arkansas	20.5
31	California	19.1
46	Colorado	11.6
33	Connecticut	18.7
44	Delaware	12.3
10	Florida	24.6
22	Georgia	21.0
47	Hawaii	11.3
21	Idaho	21.2
3	Illinois	29.9
18	Indiana	21.8
35	Iowa	17.6
29	Kansas	19.4
13	Kentucky	22.9
26	Louisiana	20.1
2	Maine	30.4
26	Maryland	20.1
31	Massachusetts	19.1
18	Michigan	21.8
22	Minnesota	21.0
20	Mississippi	21.7
1	Missouri	38.4
34	Montana	18.6
40	Nebraska	15.0
39	Nevada	16.0
6	New Hampshire	27.0
28	New Jersey	20.0
16	New Mexico	22.0
7	New York	26.7
8	North Carolina	26.6
43	North Dakota	13.6
11	Ohio	24.3
29	Oklahoma	19.4
42	Oregon	14.4
4	Pennsylvania	29.8
12	Rhode Island	23.3
14	South Carolina	22.2
14	South Dakota	22.2
9	Tennessee	25.9
37	Texas	16.1
41	Utah	14.8
25	Vermont	20.4
36	Virginia	16.4
16	Washington	22.0
45	West Virginia	12.1
37	Wisconsin	16.1
50	Wyoming	8.1

RANK ORDER

RANK	STATE	PERCENT
1	Missouri	38.4
2	Maine	30.4
3	Illinois	29.9
4	Pennsylvania	29.8
5	Arizona	29.4
6	New Hampshire	27.0
7	New York	26.7
8	North Carolina	26.6
9	Tennessee	25.9
10	Florida	24.6
11	Ohio	24.3
12	Rhode Island	23.3
13	Kentucky	22.9
14	South Carolina	22.2
14	South Dakota	22.2
16	New Mexico	22.0
16	Washington	22.0
18	Indiana	21.8
18	Michigan	21.8
20	Mississippi	21.7
21	Idaho	21.2
22	Georgia	21.0
22	Minnesota	21.0
24	Arkansas	20.5
25	Vermont	20.4
26	Louisiana	20.1
26	Maryland	20.1
28	New Jersey	20.0
29	Kansas	19.4
29	Oklahoma	19.4
31	California	19.1
31	Massachusetts	19.1
33	Connecticut	18.7
34	Montana	18.6
35	Iowa	17.6
36	Virginia	16.4
37	Texas	16.1
37	Wisconsin	16.1
39	Nevada	16.0
40	Nebraska	15.0
41	Utah	14.8
42	Oregon	14.4
43	North Dakota	13.6
44	Delaware	12.3
45	West Virginia	12.1
46	Colorado	11.6
47	Hawaii	11.3
48	Alabama	10.5
49	Alaska	8.4
50	Wyoming	8.1

District of Columbia**	NA

Source: National Association of State Budget Officers
    "2008 State Expenditure Report" (http://www.nasbo.org)
*Estimates for fiscal year 2009.
**Not available.

Percent Change in Medicaid Expenditures: 2008 to 2009

National Percent Change = 7.8% Increase*

ALPHA ORDER				RANK ORDER		
RANK	STATE	PERCENT CHANGE		RANK	STATE	PERCENT CHANGE
18	Alabama	10.7		1	Arizona	41.2
7	Alaska	16.5		2	Wisconsin	27.1
1	Arizona	41.2		3	Mississippi	20.3
21	Arkansas	9.8		4	Missouri	17.9
42	California	4.2		5	Maine	17.7
15	Colorado	11.8		6	Nevada	16.9
22	Connecticut	9.5		7	Alaska	16.5
25	Delaware	8.7		8	Washington	16.1
28	Florida	8.0		9	Wyoming	14.1
35	Georgia	5.6		10	Louisiana	14.0
31	Hawaii	6.9		10	Oregon	14.0
20	Idaho	10.5		12	Virginia	13.8
40	Illinois	4.8		13	Maryland	13.1
34	Indiana	6.5		14	Kentucky	12.3
29	Iowa	7.5		15	Colorado	11.8
23	Kansas	9.3		16	Montana	11.7
14	Kentucky	12.3		17	New Mexico	10.8
10	Louisiana	14.0		18	Alabama	10.7
5	Maine	17.7		18	South Dakota	10.7
13	Maryland	13.1		20	Idaho	10.5
38	Massachusetts	5.3		21	Arkansas	9.8
27	Michigan	8.2		22	Connecticut	9.5
45	Minnesota	3.4		23	Kansas	9.3
3	Mississippi	20.3		24	West Virginia	9.1
4	Missouri	17.9		25	Delaware	8.7
16	Montana	11.7		26	Vermont	8.5
36	Nebraska	5.5		27	Michigan	8.2
6	Nevada	16.9		28	Florida	8.0
38	New Hampshire	5.3		29	Iowa	7.5
44	New Jersey	3.6		29	Texas	7.5
17	New Mexico	10.8		31	Hawaii	6.9
41	New York	4.5		32	Ohio	6.7
49	North Carolina	(2.5)		32	Oklahoma	6.7
47	North Dakota	1.1		34	Indiana	6.5
32	Ohio	6.7		35	Georgia	5.6
32	Oklahoma	6.7		36	Nebraska	5.5
10	Oregon	14.0		37	Pennsylvania	5.4
37	Pennsylvania	5.4		38	Massachusetts	5.3
50	Rhode Island	(3.9)		38	New Hampshire	5.3
43	South Carolina	4.1		40	Illinois	4.8
18	South Dakota	10.7		41	New York	4.5
48	Tennessee	(1.4)		42	California	4.2
29	Texas	7.5		43	South Carolina	4.1
46	Utah	1.5		44	New Jersey	3.6
26	Vermont	8.5		45	Minnesota	3.4
12	Virginia	13.8		46	Utah	1.5
8	Washington	16.1		47	North Dakota	1.1
24	West Virginia	9.1		48	Tennessee	(1.4)
2	Wisconsin	27.1		49	North Carolina	(2.5)
9	Wyoming	14.1		50	Rhode Island	(3.9)
				District of Columbia**		NA

Source: National Association of State Budget Officers
   "2008 State Expenditure Report" (http://www.nasbo.org)
*Estimates for fiscal year 2009.
**Not available.

Medicaid Expenditures in 2007

National Total = $315,771,772,844*

ALPHA ORDER

RANK	STATE	EXPENDITURES	% of USA
25	Alabama	$4,099,163,829	1.3%
46	Alaska	947,339,783	0.3%
14	Arizona	6,609,346,183	2.1%
29	Arkansas	3,060,407,830	1.0%
2	California	34,884,518,837	11.0%
30	Colorado	2,911,647,539	0.9%
24	Connecticut	4,229,689,762	1.3%
45	Delaware	990,683,309	0.3%
5	Florida	13,450,490,934	4.3%
13	Georgia	6,844,102,301	2.2%
42	Hawaii	1,089,577,939	0.3%
43	Idaho	1,078,074,833	0.3%
7	Illinois	12,508,958,330	4.0%
20	Indiana	5,080,277,554	1.6%
33	Iowa	2,465,590,698	0.8%
35	Kansas	2,121,598,065	0.7%
23	Kentucky	4,513,988,817	1.4%
19	Louisiana	5,207,246,125	1.6%
36	Maine	1,977,693,124	0.6%
18	Maryland	5,383,477,265	1.7%
8	Massachusetts	10,166,110,000	3.2%
10	Michigan	9,213,679,007	2.9%
16	Minnesota	6,327,281,799	2.0%
28	Mississippi	3,256,111,556	1.0%
15	Missouri	6,515,259,281	2.1%
47	Montana	724,679,158	0.2%
38	Nebraska	1,495,709,937	0.5%
40	Nevada	1,241,248,471	0.4%
41	New Hampshire	1,153,993,168	0.4%
11	New Jersey	8,855,366,275	2.8%
32	New Mexico	2,626,097,407	0.8%
1	New York	43,564,119,806	13.8%
9	North Carolina	9,397,798,245	3.0%
49	North Dakota	503,564,400	0.2%
6	Ohio	12,821,041,986	4.1%
27	Oklahoma	3,263,204,924	1.0%
31	Oregon	2,851,153,656	0.9%
4	Pennsylvania	15,825,480,891	5.0%
37	Rhode Island	1,687,169,653	0.5%
26	South Carolina	4,039,243,153	1.3%
48	South Dakota	616,113,377	0.2%
12	Tennessee	7,070,169,782	2.2%
3	Texas	20,278,820,695	6.4%
39	Utah	1,365,289,240	0.4%
44	Vermont	1,056,251,605	0.3%
21	Virginia	4,882,347,418	1.5%
17	Washington	5,722,427,414	1.8%
34	West Virginia	2,158,876,640	0.7%
22	Wisconsin	4,875,516,535	1.5%
50	Wyoming	424,952,159	0.1%

RANK ORDER

RANK	STATE	EXPENDITURES	% of USA
1	New York	$43,564,119,806	13.8%
2	California	34,884,518,837	11.0%
3	Texas	20,278,820,695	6.4%
4	Pennsylvania	15,825,480,891	5.0%
5	Florida	13,450,490,934	4.3%
6	Ohio	12,821,041,986	4.1%
7	Illinois	12,508,958,330	4.0%
8	Massachusetts	10,166,110,000	3.2%
9	North Carolina	9,397,798,245	3.0%
10	Michigan	9,213,679,007	2.9%
11	New Jersey	8,855,366,275	2.8%
12	Tennessee	7,070,169,782	2.2%
13	Georgia	6,844,102,301	2.2%
14	Arizona	6,609,346,183	2.1%
15	Missouri	6,515,259,281	2.1%
16	Minnesota	6,327,281,799	2.0%
17	Washington	5,722,427,414	1.8%
18	Maryland	5,383,477,265	1.7%
19	Louisiana	5,207,246,125	1.6%
20	Indiana	5,080,277,554	1.6%
21	Virginia	4,882,347,418	1.5%
22	Wisconsin	4,875,516,535	1.5%
23	Kentucky	4,513,988,817	1.4%
24	Connecticut	4,229,689,762	1.3%
25	Alabama	4,099,163,829	1.3%
26	South Carolina	4,039,243,153	1.3%
27	Oklahoma	3,263,204,924	1.0%
28	Mississippi	3,256,111,556	1.0%
29	Arkansas	3,060,407,830	1.0%
30	Colorado	2,911,647,539	0.9%
31	Oregon	2,851,153,656	0.9%
32	New Mexico	2,626,097,407	0.8%
33	Iowa	2,465,590,698	0.8%
34	West Virginia	2,158,876,640	0.7%
35	Kansas	2,121,598,065	0.7%
36	Maine	1,977,693,124	0.6%
37	Rhode Island	1,687,169,653	0.5%
38	Nebraska	1,495,709,937	0.5%
39	Utah	1,365,289,240	0.4%
40	Nevada	1,241,248,471	0.4%
41	New Hampshire	1,153,993,168	0.4%
42	Hawaii	1,089,577,939	0.3%
43	Idaho	1,078,074,833	0.3%
44	Vermont	1,056,251,605	0.3%
45	Delaware	990,683,309	0.3%
46	Alaska	947,339,783	0.3%
47	Montana	724,679,158	0.2%
48	South Dakota	616,113,377	0.2%
49	North Dakota	503,564,400	0.2%
50	Wyoming	424,952,159	0.1%
	District of Columbia	1,378,323,404	0.4%

Source: U.S. Department of Health and Human Services, Centers for Medicare and Medicaid Services
   "2008 Data Compendium" (http://www.cms.hhs.gov/DataCompendium/)
*For fiscal year 2007. National total includes $960,498,745 in expenditures in U.S. territories. Net expenditures reported from Form CMS-64. Excludes ADM, Medicaid SCHIP expansions, and CMS adjustments.

Per Capita Medicaid Expenditures in 2007

National Per Capita = $1,045*

ALPHA ORDER

RANK	STATE	PER CAPITA
30	Alabama	$886
6	Alaska	1,391
20	Arizona	1,040
18	Arkansas	1,081
24	California	959
48	Colorado	601
10	Connecticut	1,212
14	Delaware	1,149
44	Florida	739
46	Georgia	719
33	Hawaii	853
45	Idaho	721
23	Illinois	975
38	Indiana	802
36	Iowa	826
41	Kansas	764
19	Kentucky	1,066
12	Louisiana	1,191
5	Maine	1,503
25	Maryland	958
4	Massachusetts	1,572
26	Michigan	917
9	Minnesota	1,221
16	Mississippi	1,115
17	Missouri	1,108
43	Montana	758
35	Nebraska	845
50	Nevada	486
31	New Hampshire	879
22	New Jersey	1,023
7	New Mexico	1,337
1	New York	2,242
21	North Carolina	1,039
39	North Dakota	789
15	Ohio	1,117
28	Oklahoma	904
42	Oregon	763
8	Pennsylvania	1,274
3	Rhode Island	1,602
26	South Carolina	917
40	South Dakota	774
13	Tennessee	1,150
34	Texas	850
49	Utah	512
2	Vermont	1,702
47	Virginia	634
29	Washington	887
11	West Virginia	1,193
32	Wisconsin	871
37	Wyoming	812

RANK ORDER

RANK	STATE	PER CAPITA
1	New York	$2,242
2	Vermont	1,702
3	Rhode Island	1,602
4	Massachusetts	1,572
5	Maine	1,503
6	Alaska	1,391
7	New Mexico	1,337
8	Pennsylvania	1,274
9	Minnesota	1,221
10	Connecticut	1,212
11	West Virginia	1,193
12	Louisiana	1,191
13	Tennessee	1,150
14	Delaware	1,149
15	Ohio	1,117
16	Mississippi	1,115
17	Missouri	1,108
18	Arkansas	1,081
19	Kentucky	1,066
20	Arizona	1,040
21	North Carolina	1,039
22	New Jersey	1,023
23	Illinois	975
24	California	959
25	Maryland	958
26	Michigan	917
26	South Carolina	917
28	Oklahoma	904
29	Washington	887
30	Alabama	886
31	New Hampshire	879
32	Wisconsin	871
33	Hawaii	853
34	Texas	850
35	Nebraska	845
36	Iowa	826
37	Wyoming	812
38	Indiana	802
39	North Dakota	789
40	South Dakota	774
41	Kansas	764
42	Oregon	763
43	Montana	758
44	Florida	739
45	Idaho	721
46	Georgia	719
47	Virginia	634
48	Colorado	601
49	Utah	512
50	Nevada	486

District of Columbia   2,345

Source: CQ Press using data from U.S. Department of Health and Human Services, Centers for Medicare and Medicaid Services "2008 Data Compendium" (http://www.cms.hhs.gov/DataCompendium/)
*Figures for fiscal year 2007. National figure does not include expenditures or population in U.S. territories. Net expenditures reported from Form CMS-64. Excludes ADM, Medicaid SCHIP expansions, and CMS adjustments.

Medicaid Expenditures per Beneficiary in 2007

National Rate = $7,014 per Beneficiary*

ALPHA ORDER

RANK	STATE	PER BENEFICIARY	RANK	STATE	PER BENEFICIARY
44	Alabama	$5,662	1	Minnesota	$10,652
6	Alaska	9,868	2	New Hampshire	10,587
30	Arizona	6,676	3	New York	10,574
49	Arkansas	4,889	4	Connecticut	10,444
47	California	5,396	5	New Jersey	10,086
16	Colorado	7,642	6	Alaska	9,868
4	Connecticut	10,444	7	North Dakota	9,684
26	Delaware	6,880	8	Massachusetts	9,396
36	Florida	6,128	9	Rhode Island	9,321
50	Georgia	4,557	10	Montana	9,058
48	Hawaii	5,394	11	Pennsylvania	8,926
39	Idaho	5,989	12	Missouri	7,916
33	Illinois	6,245	13	Kansas	7,800
35	Indiana	6,150	14	Maine	7,786
29	Iowa	6,737	15	Maryland	7,768
13	Kansas	7,800	16	Colorado	7,642
32	Kentucky	6,322	17	Ohio	7,458
45	Louisiana	5,569	18	Nevada	7,301
14	Maine	7,786	19	Vermont	7,235
15	Maryland	7,768	20	Oregon	7,200
8	Massachusetts	9,396	21	North Carolina	7,136
38	Michigan	6,062	22	Nebraska	7,122
1	Minnesota	10,652	23	West Virginia	7,102
41	Mississippi	5,942	24	Virginia	7,025
12	Missouri	7,916	25	Wyoming	6,966
10	Montana	9,058	26	Delaware	6,880
22	Nebraska	7,122	27	Utah	6,792
18	Nevada	7,301	28	Texas	6,755
2	New Hampshire	10,587	29	Iowa	6,737
5	New Jersey	10,086	30	Arizona	6,676
31	New Mexico	6,343	31	New Mexico	6,343
3	New York	10,574	32	Kentucky	6,322
21	North Carolina	7,136	33	Illinois	6,245
7	North Dakota	9,684	34	South Carolina	6,167
17	Ohio	7,458	35	Indiana	6,150
46	Oklahoma	5,512	36	Florida	6,128
20	Oregon	7,200	37	South Dakota	6,100
11	Pennsylvania	8,926	38	Michigan	6,062
9	Rhode Island	9,321	39	Idaho	5,989
34	South Carolina	6,167	40	Tennessee	5,982
37	South Dakota	6,100	41	Mississippi	5,942
40	Tennessee	5,982	42	Washington	5,763
28	Texas	6,755	43	Wisconsin	5,722
27	Utah	6,792	44	Alabama	5,662
19	Vermont	7,235	45	Louisiana	5,569
24	Virginia	7,025	46	Oklahoma	5,512
42	Washington	5,763	47	California	5,396
23	West Virginia	7,102	48	Hawaii	5,394
43	Wisconsin	5,722	49	Arkansas	4,889
25	Wyoming	6,966	50	Georgia	4,557

District of Columbia   9,707

Source: CQ Press using data from U.S. Department of Health and Human Services, Centers for Medicare and Medicaid Services
"2008 Data Compendium" (http://www.cms.hhs.gov/DataCompendium/)

*Figures for fiscal year 2007. National figure does not include expenditures or enrollees in U.S. territories. Net expenditures reported from Form CMS-64. Excludes ADM, Medicaid SCHIP expansions, and CMS adjustments.

Federal Medicaid Matching Fund Rate for 2010

National Average = 71.92% of States' Funds Matched by Federal Government*

ALPHA ORDER

RANK	STATE	PERCENT
9	Alabama	77.98
38	Alaska	65.00
12	Arizona	76.10
4	Arkansas	79.96
38	California	65.00
38	Colorado	65.00
38	Connecticut	65.00
33	Delaware	67.21
32	Florida	68.82
15	Georgia	75.73
35	Hawaii	66.25
8	Idaho	78.20
37	Illinois	65.14
11	Indiana	76.56
23	Iowa	73.84
28	Kansas	71.34
3	Kentucky	80.04
20	Louisiana	74.53
18	Maine	74.66
38	Maryland	65.00
38	Massachusetts	65.00
14	Michigan	76.05
38	Minnesota	65.00
1	Mississippi	82.31
21	Missouri	74.30
10	Montana	76.77
30	Nebraska	70.91
36	Nevada	66.13
38	New Hampshire	65.00
38	New Jersey	65.00
7	New Mexico	78.85
38	New York	65.00
17	North Carolina	75.30
26	North Dakota	72.25
19	Ohio	74.58
16	Oklahoma	75.46
22	Oregon	74.00
31	Pennsylvania	68.95
34	Rhode Island	67.08
6	South Carolina	79.03
24	South Dakota	72.88
12	Tennessee	76.10
25	Texas	72.39
5	Utah	79.79
29	Vermont	71.10
38	Virginia	65.00
38	Washington	65.00
2	West Virginia	81.27
27	Wisconsin	72.11
38	Wyoming	65.00

RANK ORDER

RANK	STATE	PERCENT
1	Mississippi	82.31
2	West Virginia	81.27
3	Kentucky	80.04
4	Arkansas	79.96
5	Utah	79.79
6	South Carolina	79.03
7	New Mexico	78.85
8	Idaho	78.20
9	Alabama	77.98
10	Montana	76.77
11	Indiana	76.56
12	Arizona	76.10
12	Tennessee	76.10
14	Michigan	76.05
15	Georgia	75.73
16	Oklahoma	75.46
17	North Carolina	75.30
18	Maine	74.66
19	Ohio	74.58
20	Louisiana	74.53
21	Missouri	74.30
22	Oregon	74.00
23	Iowa	73.84
24	South Dakota	72.88
25	Texas	72.39
26	North Dakota	72.25
27	Wisconsin	72.11
28	Kansas	71.34
29	Vermont	71.10
30	Nebraska	70.91
31	Pennsylvania	68.95
32	Florida	68.82
33	Delaware	67.21
34	Rhode Island	67.08
35	Hawaii	66.25
36	Nevada	66.13
37	Illinois	65.14
38	Alaska	65.00
38	California	65.00
38	Colorado	65.00
38	Connecticut	65.00
38	Maryland	65.00
38	Massachusetts	65.00
38	Minnesota	65.00
38	New Hampshire	65.00
38	New Jersey	65.00
38	New York	65.00
38	Virginia	65.00
38	Washington	65.00
38	Wyoming	65.00
	District of Columbia	79.00

Source: U.S. Department of Health and Human Services, Centers for Medicare and Medicaid Services
    "Enhanced Federal Medical Assistance Percentages" (Federal Register, Vol. 74, No. 227, Nov. 27, 2009, pages 62316-62317)
        (http://www.gpoaccess.gov/fr/index.html)
*For fiscal year 2011. These are "enhanced" matching rates established by the Children's Health Insurance Program, signed into law in August 1997. Sixty-five percent is the minimum. National average is a simple average of the 51 individual rates and is not weighted for population or funds.

State and Local Government Expenditures for Hospitals in 2007

National Total = $118,512,132,000*

ALPHA ORDER					RANK ORDER			
RANK	STATE	EXPENDITURES	% of USA		RANK	STATE	EXPENDITURES	% of USA
8	Alabama	$3,651,431,000	3.1%		1	California	$17,221,969,000	14.5%
42	Alaska	228,573,000	0.2%		2	New York	11,552,549,000	9.7%
29	Arizona	1,146,562,000	1.0%		3	Texas	9,489,407,000	8.0%
32	Arkansas	926,642,000	0.8%		4	Florida	6,586,759,000	5.6%
1	California	17,221,969,000	14.5%		5	North Carolina	4,936,390,000	4.2%
22	Colorado	1,787,411,000	1.5%		6	Georgia	4,773,750,000	4.0%
26	Connecticut	1,284,057,000	1.1%		7	South Carolina	3,913,938,000	3.3%
47	Delaware	63,217,000	0.1%		8	Alabama	3,651,431,000	3.1%
4	Florida	6,586,759,000	5.6%		9	Washington	3,507,557,000	3.0%
6	Georgia	4,773,750,000	4.0%		10	Ohio	3,333,282,000	2.8%
40	Hawaii	454,936,000	0.4%		11	Michigan	3,080,794,000	2.6%
37	Idaho	725,897,000	0.6%		12	Indiana	2,989,683,000	2.5%
17	Illinois	2,414,080,000	2.0%		13	Tennessee	2,851,280,000	2.4%
12	Indiana	2,989,683,000	2.5%		14	Louisiana	2,851,114,000	2.4%
21	Iowa	2,157,861,000	1.8%		15	Virginia	2,768,138,000	2.3%
31	Kansas	938,145,000	0.8%		16	Mississippi	2,623,494,000	2.2%
24	Kentucky	1,434,448,000	1.2%		17	Illinois	2,414,080,000	2.0%
14	Louisiana	2,851,114,000	2.4%		18	Missouri	2,410,546,000	2.0%
43	Maine	125,359,000	0.1%		19	Pennsylvania	2,182,545,000	1.8%
39	Maryland	480,529,000	0.4%		20	New Jersey	2,176,114,000	1.8%
25	Massachusetts	1,375,276,000	1.2%		21	Iowa	2,157,861,000	1.8%
11	Michigan	3,080,794,000	2.6%		22	Colorado	1,787,411,000	1.5%
23	Minnesota	1,703,855,000	1.4%		23	Minnesota	1,703,855,000	1.4%
16	Mississippi	2,623,494,000	2.2%		24	Kentucky	1,434,448,000	1.2%
18	Missouri	2,410,546,000	2.0%		25	Massachusetts	1,375,276,000	1.2%
44	Montana	99,630,000	0.1%		26	Connecticut	1,284,057,000	1.1%
36	Nebraska	809,544,000	0.7%		27	Oregon	1,274,428,000	1.1%
33	Nevada	898,625,000	0.8%		28	Wisconsin	1,187,295,000	1.0%
48	New Hampshire	56,244,000	0.0%		29	Arizona	1,146,562,000	1.0%
20	New Jersey	2,176,114,000	1.8%		30	Oklahoma	1,024,085,000	0.9%
34	New Mexico	851,855,000	0.7%		31	Kansas	938,145,000	0.8%
2	New York	11,552,549,000	9.7%		32	Arkansas	926,642,000	0.8%
5	North Carolina	4,936,390,000	4.2%		33	Nevada	898,625,000	0.8%
50	North Dakota	17,752,000	0.0%		34	New Mexico	851,855,000	0.7%
10	Ohio	3,333,282,000	2.8%		35	Utah	817,997,000	0.7%
30	Oklahoma	1,024,085,000	0.9%		36	Nebraska	809,544,000	0.7%
27	Oregon	1,274,428,000	1.1%		37	Idaho	725,897,000	0.6%
19	Pennsylvania	2,182,545,000	1.8%		38	Wyoming	649,059,000	0.5%
46	Rhode Island	93,996,000	0.1%		39	Maryland	480,529,000	0.4%
7	South Carolina	3,913,938,000	3.3%		40	Hawaii	454,936,000	0.4%
45	South Dakota	95,974,000	0.1%		41	West Virginia	324,979,000	0.3%
13	Tennessee	2,851,280,000	2.4%		42	Alaska	228,573,000	0.2%
3	Texas	9,489,407,000	8.0%		43	Maine	125,359,000	0.1%
35	Utah	817,997,000	0.7%		44	Montana	99,630,000	0.1%
49	Vermont	18,166,000	0.0%		45	South Dakota	95,974,000	0.1%
15	Virginia	2,768,138,000	2.3%		46	Rhode Island	93,996,000	0.1%
9	Washington	3,507,557,000	3.0%		47	Delaware	63,217,000	0.1%
41	West Virginia	324,979,000	0.3%		48	New Hampshire	56,244,000	0.0%
28	Wisconsin	1,187,295,000	1.0%		49	Vermont	18,166,000	0.0%
38	Wyoming	649,059,000	0.5%		50	North Dakota	17,752,000	0.0%
						District of Columbia	144,915,000	0.1%

Source: U.S. Bureau of the Census, Governments Division
   "State and Local Government Finances 2006-2007" (http://www.census.gov/govs/estimate/index.html)
*Financing, construction, acquisition, maintenance or operation of hospital facilities, provision of hospital care, and support of public or private hospitals.

Per Capita State and Local Government Expenditures for Hospitals in 2007

National Per Capita = $393*

ALPHA ORDER

RANK	STATE	PER CAPITA
4	Alabama	$789
28	Alaska	336
39	Arizona	180
30	Arkansas	327
12	California	473
19	Colorado	369
20	Connecticut	368
47	Delaware	73
21	Florida	362
10	Georgia	501
23	Hawaii	356
11	Idaho	485
38	Illinois	188
13	Indiana	472
5	Iowa	723
27	Kansas	338
26	Kentucky	339
6	Louisiana	652
44	Maine	95
46	Maryland	86
36	Massachusetts	213
31	Michigan	307
29	Minnesota	329
2	Mississippi	898
17	Missouri	410
43	Montana	104
15	Nebraska	458
24	Nevada	352
48	New Hampshire	43
35	New Jersey	251
16	New Mexico	434
7	New York	595
8	North Carolina	546
50	North Dakota	28
33	Ohio	290
34	Oklahoma	284
25	Oregon	341
41	Pennsylvania	176
45	Rhode Island	89
3	South Carolina	889
42	South Dakota	121
14	Tennessee	464
18	Texas	398
32	Utah	306
49	Vermont	29
22	Virginia	360
9	Washington	544
39	West Virginia	180
37	Wisconsin	212
1	Wyoming	1,240

RANK ORDER

RANK	STATE	PER CAPITA
1	Wyoming	$1,240
2	Mississippi	898
3	South Carolina	889
4	Alabama	789
5	Iowa	723
6	Louisiana	652
7	New York	595
8	North Carolina	546
9	Washington	544
10	Georgia	501
11	Idaho	485
12	California	473
13	Indiana	472
14	Tennessee	464
15	Nebraska	458
16	New Mexico	434
17	Missouri	410
18	Texas	398
19	Colorado	369
20	Connecticut	368
21	Florida	362
22	Virginia	360
23	Hawaii	356
24	Nevada	352
25	Oregon	341
26	Kentucky	339
27	Kansas	338
28	Alaska	336
29	Minnesota	329
30	Arkansas	327
31	Michigan	307
32	Utah	306
33	Ohio	290
34	Oklahoma	284
35	New Jersey	251
36	Massachusetts	213
37	Wisconsin	212
38	Illinois	188
39	Arizona	180
39	West Virginia	180
41	Pennsylvania	176
42	South Dakota	121
43	Montana	104
44	Maine	95
45	Rhode Island	89
46	Maryland	86
47	Delaware	73
48	New Hampshire	43
49	Vermont	29
50	North Dakota	28

District of Columbia — 247

Source: CQ Press using data from U.S. Bureau of the Census, Governments Division
   "State and Local Government Finances 2006-2007" (http://www.census.gov/govs/estimate/index.html)
*Financing, construction, acquisition, maintenance or operation of hospital facilities, provision of hospital care, and support of public or private hospitals.

Percent of State and Local Government Expenditures
Used for Hospitals in 2007
National Percent = 5.2%*

ALPHA ORDER

RANK	STATE	PERCENT
2	Alabama	11.9
41	Alaska	2.2
34	Arizona	2.9
18	Arkansas	5.4
17	California	5.5
19	Colorado	5.3
29	Connecticut	4.4
47	Delaware	0.8
24	Florida	5.0
10	Georgia	7.5
31	Hawaii	4.2
8	Idaho	8.1
37	Illinois	2.7
11	Indiana	7.1
5	Iowa	10.0
24	Kansas	5.0
19	Kentucky	5.3
7	Louisiana	8.2
44	Maine	1.2
45	Maryland	1.1
39	Massachusetts	2.5
29	Michigan	4.4
31	Minnesota	4.2
3	Mississippi	11.8
13	Missouri	6.6
43	Montana	1.5
14	Nebraska	6.5
22	Nevada	5.2
48	New Hampshire	0.7
34	New Jersey	2.9
19	New Mexico	5.3
16	New York	5.7
6	North Carolina	8.3
49	North Dakota	0.4
33	Ohio	3.9
28	Oklahoma	4.5
27	Oregon	4.8
40	Pennsylvania	2.3
45	Rhode Island	1.1
1	South Carolina	12.6
42	South Dakota	1.9
9	Tennessee	7.9
15	Texas	6.4
26	Utah	4.9
50	Vermont	0.3
22	Virginia	5.2
12	Washington	7.0
37	West Virginia	2.7
34	Wisconsin	2.9
4	Wyoming	10.7

RANK ORDER

RANK	STATE	PERCENT
1	South Carolina	12.6
2	Alabama	11.9
3	Mississippi	11.8
4	Wyoming	10.7
5	Iowa	10.0
6	North Carolina	8.3
7	Louisiana	8.2
8	Idaho	8.1
9	Tennessee	7.9
10	Georgia	7.5
11	Indiana	7.1
12	Washington	7.0
13	Missouri	6.6
14	Nebraska	6.5
15	Texas	6.4
16	New York	5.7
17	California	5.5
18	Arkansas	5.4
19	Colorado	5.3
19	Kentucky	5.3
19	New Mexico	5.3
22	Nevada	5.2
22	Virginia	5.2
24	Florida	5.0
24	Kansas	5.0
26	Utah	4.9
27	Oregon	4.8
28	Oklahoma	4.5
29	Connecticut	4.4
29	Michigan	4.4
31	Hawaii	4.2
31	Minnesota	4.2
33	Ohio	3.9
34	Arizona	2.9
34	New Jersey	2.9
34	Wisconsin	2.9
37	Illinois	2.7
37	West Virginia	2.7
39	Massachusetts	2.5
40	Pennsylvania	2.3
41	Alaska	2.2
42	South Dakota	1.9
43	Montana	1.5
44	Maine	1.2
45	Maryland	1.1
45	Rhode Island	1.1
47	Delaware	0.8
48	New Hampshire	0.7
49	North Dakota	0.4
50	Vermont	0.3

District of Columbia 1.7

Source: CQ Press using data from U.S. Bureau of the Census, Governments Division
"State and Local Government Finances 2006-2007" (http://www.census.gov/govs/estimate/index.html)
*As a percent of direct general expenditures. Financing, construction, acquisition, maintenance or operation of hospital facilities, provision of hospital care, and support of public or private hospitals.

State and Local Government Expenditures for Health Programs in 2007

National Total = $74,515,211,000*

ALPHA ORDER				RANK ORDER			
RANK	STATE	EXPENDITURES	% of USA	RANK	STATE	EXPENDITURES	% of USA
24	Alabama	$885,772,000	1.2%	1	California	$12,473,853,000	16.7%
45	Alaska	184,028,000	0.2%	2	New York	5,651,066,000	7.6%
13	Arizona	1,620,254,000	2.2%	3	Florida	4,167,605,000	5.6%
43	Arkansas	270,646,000	0.4%	4	Ohio	3,929,189,000	5.3%
1	California	12,473,853,000	16.7%	5	Pennsylvania	3,776,406,000	5.1%
20	Colorado	1,061,808,000	1.4%	6	Texas	3,558,926,000	4.8%
27	Connecticut	684,872,000	0.9%	7	Michigan	3,313,621,000	4.4%
37	Delaware	388,644,000	0.5%	8	Illinois	2,770,895,000	3.7%
3	Florida	4,167,605,000	5.6%	9	North Carolina	2,755,975,000	3.7%
11	Georgia	1,968,466,000	2.6%	10	Washington	2,393,440,000	3.2%
30	Hawaii	631,985,000	0.8%	11	Georgia	1,968,466,000	2.6%
44	Idaho	202,977,000	0.3%	12	New Jersey	1,650,635,000	2.2%
8	Illinois	2,770,895,000	3.7%	13	Arizona	1,620,254,000	2.2%
25	Indiana	758,295,000	1.0%	14	Maryland	1,593,001,000	2.1%
34	Iowa	476,293,000	0.6%	15	Virginia	1,551,381,000	2.1%
38	Kansas	375,964,000	0.5%	16	Tennessee	1,535,395,000	2.1%
29	Kentucky	646,778,000	0.9%	17	Wisconsin	1,510,404,000	2.0%
26	Louisiana	744,725,000	1.0%	18	Missouri	1,427,862,000	1.9%
32	Maine	503,789,000	0.7%	19	South Carolina	1,105,427,000	1.5%
14	Maryland	1,593,001,000	2.1%	20	Colorado	1,061,808,000	1.4%
21	Massachusetts	1,055,748,000	1.4%	21	Massachusetts	1,055,748,000	1.4%
7	Michigan	3,313,621,000	4.4%	22	Minnesota	1,004,802,000	1.3%
22	Minnesota	1,004,802,000	1.3%	23	Oregon	948,389,000	1.3%
36	Mississippi	402,242,000	0.5%	24	Alabama	885,772,000	1.2%
18	Missouri	1,427,862,000	1.9%	25	Indiana	758,295,000	1.0%
40	Montana	366,083,000	0.5%	26	Louisiana	744,725,000	1.0%
35	Nebraska	416,213,000	0.6%	27	Connecticut	684,872,000	0.9%
39	Nevada	368,863,000	0.5%	28	Oklahoma	674,260,000	0.9%
49	New Hampshire	139,849,000	0.2%	29	Kentucky	646,778,000	0.9%
12	New Jersey	1,650,635,000	2.2%	30	Hawaii	631,985,000	0.8%
33	New Mexico	496,211,000	0.7%	31	Utah	515,461,000	0.7%
2	New York	5,651,066,000	7.6%	32	Maine	503,789,000	0.7%
9	North Carolina	2,755,975,000	3.7%	33	New Mexico	496,211,000	0.7%
50	North Dakota	89,799,000	0.1%	34	Iowa	476,293,000	0.6%
4	Ohio	3,929,189,000	5.3%	35	Nebraska	416,213,000	0.6%
28	Oklahoma	674,260,000	0.9%	36	Mississippi	402,242,000	0.5%
23	Oregon	948,389,000	1.3%	37	Delaware	388,644,000	0.5%
5	Pennsylvania	3,776,406,000	5.1%	38	Kansas	375,964,000	0.5%
46	Rhode Island	170,867,000	0.2%	39	Nevada	368,863,000	0.5%
19	South Carolina	1,105,427,000	1.5%	40	Montana	366,083,000	0.5%
48	South Dakota	144,344,000	0.2%	41	West Virginia	314,550,000	0.4%
16	Tennessee	1,535,395,000	2.1%	42	Wyoming	293,882,000	0.4%
6	Texas	3,558,926,000	4.8%	43	Arkansas	270,646,000	0.4%
31	Utah	515,461,000	0.7%	44	Idaho	202,977,000	0.3%
47	Vermont	156,561,000	0.2%	45	Alaska	184,028,000	0.2%
15	Virginia	1,551,381,000	2.1%	46	Rhode Island	170,867,000	0.2%
10	Washington	2,393,440,000	3.2%	47	Vermont	156,561,000	0.2%
41	West Virginia	314,550,000	0.4%	48	South Dakota	144,344,000	0.2%
17	Wisconsin	1,510,404,000	2.0%	49	New Hampshire	139,849,000	0.2%
42	Wyoming	293,882,000	0.4%	50	North Dakota	89,799,000	0.1%
					District of Columbia	386,710,000	0.5%

Source: U.S. Bureau of the Census, Governments Division
"State and Local Government Finances 2006-2007" (http://www.census.gov/govs/estimate/index.html)
*Includes outpatient health services other than hospital care, research and education, categorical health programs, treatment and immunization clinics, nursing, and environmental health activities. Includes capital expenditures.

Per Capita State and Local Government Expenditures for
Health Programs in 2007
National Per Capita = $247*

ALPHA ORDER

RANK	STATE	PER CAPITA
32	Alabama	$191
14	Alaska	270
16	Arizona	255
50	Arkansas	96
7	California	343
25	Colorado	219
29	Connecticut	196
3	Delaware	451
24	Florida	229
27	Georgia	207
2	Hawaii	495
46	Idaho	136
26	Illinois	216
48	Indiana	120
40	Iowa	160
47	Kansas	135
41	Kentucky	153
37	Louisiana	170
4	Maine	383
13	Maryland	284
38	Massachusetts	163
9	Michigan	330
30	Minnesota	194
45	Mississippi	138
22	Missouri	243
4	Montana	383
23	Nebraska	235
43	Nevada	144
49	New Hampshire	107
32	New Jersey	191
18	New Mexico	253
12	New York	291
10	North Carolina	305
44	North Dakota	141
8	Ohio	342
34	Oklahoma	187
17	Oregon	254
11	Pennsylvania	304
39	Rhode Island	162
20	South Carolina	251
35	South Dakota	181
21	Tennessee	250
42	Texas	149
31	Utah	193
19	Vermont	252
28	Virginia	202
6	Washington	371
36	West Virginia	174
14	Wisconsin	270
1	Wyoming	562

RANK ORDER

RANK	STATE	PER CAPITA
1	Wyoming	$562
2	Hawaii	495
3	Delaware	451
4	Maine	383
4	Montana	383
6	Washington	371
7	California	343
8	Ohio	342
9	Michigan	330
10	North Carolina	305
11	Pennsylvania	304
12	New York	291
13	Maryland	284
14	Alaska	270
14	Wisconsin	270
16	Arizona	255
17	Oregon	254
18	New Mexico	253
19	Vermont	252
20	South Carolina	251
21	Tennessee	250
22	Missouri	243
23	Nebraska	235
24	Florida	229
25	Colorado	219
26	Illinois	216
27	Georgia	207
28	Virginia	202
29	Connecticut	196
30	Minnesota	194
31	Utah	193
32	Alabama	191
32	New Jersey	191
34	Oklahoma	187
35	South Dakota	181
36	West Virginia	174
37	Louisiana	170
38	Massachusetts	163
39	Rhode Island	162
40	Iowa	160
41	Kentucky	153
42	Texas	149
43	Nevada	144
44	North Dakota	141
45	Mississippi	138
46	Idaho	136
47	Kansas	135
48	Indiana	120
49	New Hampshire	107
50	Arkansas	96

District of Columbia   658

Source: CQ Press using data from U.S. Bureau of the Census, Governments Division
   "State and Local Government Finances 2006-2007" (http://www.census.gov/govs/estimate/index.html)
*Includes outpatient health services other than hospital care, research and education, categorical health programs, treatment and immunization clinics, nursing, and environmental health activities. Includes capital expenditures.

Percent of State and Local Government Expenditures
Used for Health Programs in 2007
National Percent = 3.3%*

ALPHA ORDER

RANK	STATE	PERCENT
28	Alabama	2.9
46	Alaska	1.8
11	Arizona	4.1
50	Arkansas	1.6
13	California	3.9
20	Colorado	3.2
34	Connecticut	2.4
3	Delaware	5.0
20	Florida	3.2
22	Georgia	3.1
1	Hawaii	5.8
37	Idaho	2.3
22	Illinois	3.1
46	Indiana	1.8
38	Iowa	2.2
42	Kansas	2.0
34	Kentucky	2.4
38	Louisiana	2.2
3	Maine	5.0
15	Maryland	3.7
42	Massachusetts	2.0
7	Michigan	4.7
33	Minnesota	2.5
46	Mississippi	1.8
13	Missouri	3.9
2	Montana	5.5
19	Nebraska	3.3
41	Nevada	2.1
49	New Hampshire	1.7
38	New Jersey	2.2
22	New Mexico	3.1
31	New York	2.8
8	North Carolina	4.6
45	North Dakota	1.9
8	Ohio	4.6
26	Oklahoma	3.0
17	Oregon	3.6
12	Pennsylvania	4.0
42	Rhode Island	2.0
18	South Carolina	3.5
28	South Dakota	2.9
10	Tennessee	4.3
34	Texas	2.4
22	Utah	3.1
26	Vermont	3.0
28	Virginia	2.9
6	Washington	4.8
32	West Virginia	2.7
15	Wisconsin	3.7
5	Wyoming	4.9

RANK ORDER

RANK	STATE	PERCENT
1	Hawaii	5.8
2	Montana	5.5
3	Delaware	5.0
3	Maine	5.0
5	Wyoming	4.9
6	Washington	4.8
7	Michigan	4.7
8	North Carolina	4.6
8	Ohio	4.6
10	Tennessee	4.3
11	Arizona	4.1
12	Pennsylvania	4.0
13	California	3.9
13	Missouri	3.9
15	Maryland	3.7
15	Wisconsin	3.7
17	Oregon	3.6
18	South Carolina	3.5
19	Nebraska	3.3
20	Colorado	3.2
20	Florida	3.2
22	Georgia	3.1
22	Illinois	3.1
22	New Mexico	3.1
22	Utah	3.1
26	Oklahoma	3.0
26	Vermont	3.0
28	Alabama	2.9
28	South Dakota	2.9
28	Virginia	2.9
31	New York	2.8
32	West Virginia	2.7
33	Minnesota	2.5
34	Connecticut	2.4
34	Kentucky	2.4
34	Texas	2.4
37	Idaho	2.3
38	Iowa	2.2
38	Louisiana	2.2
38	New Jersey	2.2
41	Nevada	2.1
42	Kansas	2.0
42	Massachusetts	2.0
42	Rhode Island	2.0
45	North Dakota	1.9
46	Alaska	1.8
46	Indiana	1.8
46	Mississippi	1.8
49	New Hampshire	1.7
50	Arkansas	1.6
	District of Columbia	4.6

Source: CQ Press using data from U.S. Bureau of the Census, Governments Division
   "State and Local Government Finances 2006-2007" (http://www.census.gov/govs/estimate/index.html)
*As a percent of direct general expenditures. Includes outpatient health services other than hospital care, research and education, categorical health programs, treatment and immunization clinics, nursing, and environmental health activities. Includes capital expenditures.

Estimated Tobacco Settlement Revenues in Fiscal Year 2010

National Total = $8,100,000,000*

ALPHA ORDER

RANK	STATE	REVENUES	% of USA
26	Alabama	$107,000,000	1.3%
46	Alaska	34,300,000	0.4%
24	Arizona	115,400,000	1.4%
35	Arkansas	57,600,000	0.7%
2	California	838,700,000	10.4%
27	Colorado	103,700,000	1.3%
21	Connecticut	141,300,000	1.7%
47	Delaware	30,500,000	0.4%
5	Florida	369,300,000	4.6%
15	Georgia	160,800,000	2.0%
36	Hawaii	55,600,000	0.7%
48	Idaho	28,500,000	0.4%
7	Illinois	312,100,000	3.9%
20	Indiana	147,800,000	1.8%
31	Iowa	75,000,000	0.9%
33	Kansas	66,200,000	0.8%
23	Kentucky	116,000,000	1.4%
14	Louisiana	161,100,000	2.0%
34	Maine	58,200,000	0.7%
13	Maryland	166,500,000	2.1%
9	Massachusetts	289,400,000	3.6%
8	Michigan	292,100,000	3.6%
12	Minnesota	168,600,000	2.1%
25	Mississippi	114,100,000	1.4%
18	Missouri	154,200,000	1.9%
45	Montana	34,500,000	0.4%
41	Nebraska	43,000,000	0.5%
39	Nevada	46,000,000	0.6%
38	New Hampshire	48,500,000	0.6%
10	New Jersey	263,800,000	3.3%
40	New Mexico	44,900,000	0.6%
1	New York	841,000,000	10.4%
15	North Carolina	160,800,000	2.0%
44	North Dakota	36,100,000	0.4%
6	Ohio	336,600,000	4.2%
29	Oklahoma	88,500,000	1.1%
28	Oregon	90,100,000	1.1%
4	Pennsylvania	384,600,000	4.7%
37	Rhode Island	53,300,000	0.7%
30	South Carolina	83,800,000	1.0%
49	South Dakota	27,600,000	0.3%
17	Tennessee	158,600,000	2.0%
3	Texas	472,600,000	5.8%
42	Utah	41,700,000	0.5%
43	Vermont	39,500,000	0.5%
22	Virginia	133,800,000	1.7%
11	Washington	172,200,000	2.1%
32	West Virginia	72,700,000	0.9%
19	Wisconsin	149,600,000	1.8%
50	Wyoming	21,300,000	0.3%

RANK ORDER

RANK	STATE	REVENUES	% of USA
1	New York	$841,000,000	10.4%
2	California	838,700,000	10.4%
3	Texas	472,600,000	5.8%
4	Pennsylvania	384,600,000	4.7%
5	Florida	369,300,000	4.6%
6	Ohio	336,600,000	4.2%
7	Illinois	312,100,000	3.9%
8	Michigan	292,100,000	3.6%
9	Massachusetts	289,400,000	3.6%
10	New Jersey	263,800,000	3.3%
11	Washington	172,200,000	2.1%
12	Minnesota	168,600,000	2.1%
13	Maryland	166,500,000	2.1%
14	Louisiana	161,100,000	2.0%
15	Georgia	160,800,000	2.0%
15	North Carolina	160,800,000	2.0%
17	Tennessee	158,600,000	2.0%
18	Missouri	154,200,000	1.9%
19	Wisconsin	149,600,000	1.8%
20	Indiana	147,800,000	1.8%
21	Connecticut	141,300,000	1.7%
22	Virginia	133,800,000	1.7%
23	Kentucky	116,000,000	1.4%
24	Arizona	115,400,000	1.4%
25	Mississippi	114,100,000	1.4%
26	Alabama	107,000,000	1.3%
27	Colorado	103,700,000	1.3%
28	Oregon	90,100,000	1.1%
29	Oklahoma	88,500,000	1.1%
30	South Carolina	83,800,000	1.0%
31	Iowa	75,000,000	0.9%
32	West Virginia	72,700,000	0.9%
33	Kansas	66,200,000	0.8%
34	Maine	58,200,000	0.7%
35	Arkansas	57,600,000	0.7%
36	Hawaii	55,600,000	0.7%
37	Rhode Island	53,300,000	0.7%
38	New Hampshire	48,500,000	0.6%
39	Nevada	46,000,000	0.6%
40	New Mexico	44,900,000	0.6%
41	Nebraska	43,000,000	0.5%
42	Utah	41,700,000	0.5%
43	Vermont	39,500,000	0.5%
44	North Dakota	36,100,000	0.4%
45	Montana	34,500,000	0.4%
46	Alaska	34,300,000	0.4%
47	Delaware	30,500,000	0.4%
48	Idaho	28,500,000	0.4%
49	South Dakota	27,600,000	0.3%
50	Wyoming	21,300,000	0.3%
	District of Columbia	43,700,000	0.5%

Source: Campaign for Tobacco-Free Kids
  "A Broken Promise to Our Children" (http://tobaccofreekids.org/reports/settlements/)
*For fiscal year 2010. Settlement originally reached in November 1998 and called for an estimated 25 years of payments.

Annual Smoking-Related Health Costs in 2009

National Estimate = $95,900,000,000*

ALPHA ORDER

RANK	STATE	COSTS	% of USA
23	Alabama	$1,490,000,000	1.6%
49	Alaska	169,000,000	0.2%
26	Arizona	1,300,000,000	1.4%
32	Arkansas	812,000,000	0.8%
1	California	9,140,000,000	9.5%
25	Colorado	1,310,000,000	1.4%
21	Connecticut	1,630,000,000	1.7%
44	Delaware	284,000,000	0.3%
3	Florida	6,320,000,000	6.6%
12	Georgia	2,250,000,000	2.3%
42	Hawaii	336,000,000	0.4%
43	Idaho	319,000,000	0.3%
7	Illinois	4,100,000,000	4.3%
15	Indiana	2,080,000,000	2.2%
30	Iowa	1,010,000,000	1.1%
31	Kansas	927,000,000	1.0%
22	Kentucky	1,500,000,000	1.6%
24	Louisiana	1,470,000,000	1.5%
35	Maine	602,000,000	0.6%
19	Maryland	1,960,000,000	2.0%
8	Massachusetts	3,540,000,000	3.7%
9	Michigan	3,400,000,000	3.5%
17	Minnesota	2,060,000,000	2.1%
33	Mississippi	719,000,000	0.7%
14	Missouri	2,130,000,000	2.2%
45	Montana	277,000,000	0.3%
38	Nebraska	537,000,000	0.6%
36	Nevada	565,000,000	0.6%
37	New Hampshire	564,000,000	0.6%
10	New Jersey	3,170,000,000	3.3%
40	New Mexico	461,000,000	0.5%
2	New York	8,170,000,000	8.5%
11	North Carolina	2,460,000,000	2.6%
47	North Dakota	247,000,000	0.3%
6	Ohio	4,370,000,000	4.6%
27	Oklahoma	1,160,000,000	1.2%
28	Oregon	1,110,000,000	1.2%
5	Pennsylvania	5,190,000,000	5.4%
39	Rhode Island	506,000,000	0.5%
29	South Carolina	1,090,000,000	1.1%
46	South Dakota	274,000,000	0.3%
13	Tennessee	2,160,000,000	2.3%
4	Texas	5,830,000,000	6.1%
41	Utah	345,000,000	0.4%
48	Vermont	233,000,000	0.2%
15	Virginia	2,080,000,000	2.2%
20	Washington	1,950,000,000	2.0%
34	West Virginia	690,000,000	0.7%
18	Wisconsin	2,020,000,000	2.1%
50	Wyoming	136,000,000	0.1%

RANK ORDER

RANK	STATE	COSTS	% of USA
1	California	$9,140,000,000	9.5%
2	New York	8,170,000,000	8.5%
3	Florida	6,320,000,000	6.6%
4	Texas	5,830,000,000	6.1%
5	Pennsylvania	5,190,000,000	5.4%
6	Ohio	4,370,000,000	4.6%
7	Illinois	4,100,000,000	4.3%
8	Massachusetts	3,540,000,000	3.7%
9	Michigan	3,400,000,000	3.5%
10	New Jersey	3,170,000,000	3.3%
11	North Carolina	2,460,000,000	2.6%
12	Georgia	2,250,000,000	2.3%
13	Tennessee	2,160,000,000	2.3%
14	Missouri	2,130,000,000	2.2%
15	Indiana	2,080,000,000	2.2%
15	Virginia	2,080,000,000	2.2%
17	Minnesota	2,060,000,000	2.1%
18	Wisconsin	2,020,000,000	2.1%
19	Maryland	1,960,000,000	2.0%
20	Washington	1,950,000,000	2.0%
21	Connecticut	1,630,000,000	1.7%
22	Kentucky	1,500,000,000	1.6%
23	Alabama	1,490,000,000	1.6%
24	Louisiana	1,470,000,000	1.5%
25	Colorado	1,310,000,000	1.4%
26	Arizona	1,300,000,000	1.4%
27	Oklahoma	1,160,000,000	1.2%
28	Oregon	1,110,000,000	1.2%
29	South Carolina	1,090,000,000	1.1%
30	Iowa	1,010,000,000	1.1%
31	Kansas	927,000,000	1.0%
32	Arkansas	812,000,000	0.8%
33	Mississippi	719,000,000	0.7%
34	West Virginia	690,000,000	0.7%
35	Maine	602,000,000	0.6%
36	Nevada	565,000,000	0.6%
37	New Hampshire	564,000,000	0.6%
38	Nebraska	537,000,000	0.6%
39	Rhode Island	506,000,000	0.5%
40	New Mexico	461,000,000	0.5%
41	Utah	345,000,000	0.4%
42	Hawaii	336,000,000	0.4%
43	Idaho	319,000,000	0.3%
44	Delaware	284,000,000	0.3%
45	Montana	277,000,000	0.3%
46	South Dakota	274,000,000	0.3%
47	North Dakota	247,000,000	0.3%
48	Vermont	233,000,000	0.2%
49	Alaska	169,000,000	0.2%
50	Wyoming	136,000,000	0.1%
	District of Columbia	243,000,000	0.3%

Source: Campaign for Tobacco-Free Kids
"A Decade of Broken Promises" (http://tobaccofreekids.org/reports/settlements/)
*Estimate based on figures from Centers for Disease Control and Prevention.

Personal Health Care Expenditures in 2004

National Total = $1,551,255,000,000*

ALPHA ORDER

RANK ORDER

RANK	STATE	EXPENDITURES	% of USA
22	Alabama	$23,199,000,000	1.5%
46	Alaska	4,237,000,000	0.3%
21	Arizona	23,576,000,000	1.5%
33	Arkansas	13,357,000,000	0.9%
1	California	166,236,000,000	10.7%
26	Colorado	21,691,000,000	1.4%
25	Connecticut	22,167,000,000	1.4%
44	Delaware	5,226,000,000	0.3%
4	Florida	95,223,000,000	6.1%
12	Georgia	41,097,000,000	2.6%
42	Hawaii	6,222,000,000	0.4%
43	Idaho	6,197,000,000	0.4%
6	Illinois	67,292,000,000	4.3%
14	Indiana	32,951,000,000	2.1%
30	Iowa	15,892,000,000	1.0%
31	Kansas	14,736,000,000	0.9%
23	Kentucky	22,662,000,000	1.5%
24	Louisiana	22,658,000,000	1.5%
38	Maine	8,593,000,000	0.6%
19	Maryland	31,044,000,000	2.0%
11	Massachusetts	43,009,000,000	2.8%
8	Michigan	51,048,000,000	3.3%
20	Minnesota	29,524,000,000	1.9%
32	Mississippi	14,634,000,000	0.9%
17	Missouri	31,317,000,000	2.0%
45	Montana	4,706,000,000	0.3%
36	Nebraska	9,782,000,000	0.6%
35	Nevada	10,656,000,000	0.7%
40	New Hampshire	7,050,000,000	0.5%
9	New Jersey	50,384,000,000	3.2%
39	New Mexico	8,498,000,000	0.5%
2	New York	126,076,000,000	8.1%
10	North Carolina	44,281,000,000	2.9%
49	North Dakota	3,693,000,000	0.2%
7	Ohio	65,622,000,000	4.2%
29	Oklahoma	17,323,000,000	1.1%
28	Oregon	17,516,000,000	1.1%
5	Pennsylvania	73,441,000,000	4.7%
41	Rhode Island	6,682,000,000	0.4%
27	South Carolina	21,450,000,000	1.4%
47	South Dakota	4,103,000,000	0.3%
15	Tennessee	32,161,000,000	2.1%
3	Texas	103,600,000,000	6.7%
37	Utah	9,618,000,000	0.6%
48	Vermont	3,768,000,000	0.2%
13	Virginia	36,032,000,000	2.3%
16	Washington	31,600,000,000	2.0%
34	West Virginia	10,783,000,000	0.7%
18	Wisconsin	31,177,000,000	2.0%
50	Wyoming	2,662,000,000	0.2%

RANK	STATE	EXPENDITURES	% of USA
1	California	$166,236,000,000	10.7%
2	New York	126,076,000,000	8.1%
3	Texas	103,600,000,000	6.7%
4	Florida	95,223,000,000	6.1%
5	Pennsylvania	73,441,000,000	4.7%
6	Illinois	67,292,000,000	4.3%
7	Ohio	65,622,000,000	4.2%
8	Michigan	51,048,000,000	3.3%
9	New Jersey	50,384,000,000	3.2%
10	North Carolina	44,281,000,000	2.9%
11	Massachusetts	43,009,000,000	2.8%
12	Georgia	41,097,000,000	2.6%
13	Virginia	36,032,000,000	2.3%
14	Indiana	32,951,000,000	2.1%
15	Tennessee	32,161,000,000	2.1%
16	Washington	31,600,000,000	2.0%
17	Missouri	31,317,000,000	2.0%
18	Wisconsin	31,177,000,000	2.0%
19	Maryland	31,044,000,000	2.0%
20	Minnesota	29,524,000,000	1.9%
21	Arizona	23,576,000,000	1.5%
22	Alabama	23,199,000,000	1.5%
23	Kentucky	22,662,000,000	1.5%
24	Louisiana	22,658,000,000	1.5%
25	Connecticut	22,167,000,000	1.4%
26	Colorado	21,691,000,000	1.4%
27	South Carolina	21,450,000,000	1.4%
28	Oregon	17,516,000,000	1.1%
29	Oklahoma	17,323,000,000	1.1%
30	Iowa	15,892,000,000	1.0%
31	Kansas	14,736,000,000	0.9%
32	Mississippi	14,634,000,000	0.9%
33	Arkansas	13,357,000,000	0.9%
34	West Virginia	10,783,000,000	0.7%
35	Nevada	10,656,000,000	0.7%
36	Nebraska	9,782,000,000	0.6%
37	Utah	9,618,000,000	0.6%
38	Maine	8,593,000,000	0.6%
39	New Mexico	8,498,000,000	0.5%
40	New Hampshire	7,050,000,000	0.5%
41	Rhode Island	6,682,000,000	0.4%
42	Hawaii	6,222,000,000	0.4%
43	Idaho	6,197,000,000	0.4%
44	Delaware	5,226,000,000	0.3%
45	Montana	4,706,000,000	0.3%
46	Alaska	4,237,000,000	0.3%
47	South Dakota	4,103,000,000	0.3%
48	Vermont	3,768,000,000	0.2%
49	North Dakota	3,693,000,000	0.2%
50	Wyoming	2,662,000,000	0.2%

| | District of Columbia | 4,809,000,000 | 0.3% |

Source: U.S. Department of Health and Human Services, Centers for Medicare and Medicaid Services
"State Health Care Expenditures" (http://www.cms.hhs.gov/NationalHealthExpendData/)
*By state of residence. Includes hospital care, physician services, dental services, home health care, drugs, vision products, nursing home care, and other personal health care services and products.

Health Care Expenditures as a Percent of Gross State Product in 2004

National Percent = 13.3% of Total Gross State Product*

ALPHA ORDER

RANK	STATE	PERCENT
7	Alabama	16.2
44	Alaska	11.6
36	Arizona	12.5
16	Arkansas	15.4
46	California	11.0
45	Colorado	11.1
40	Connecticut	12.1
49	Delaware	9.7
13	Florida	15.6
38	Georgia	12.2
36	Hawaii	12.5
32	Idaho	13.0
38	Illinois	12.2
20	Indiana	14.4
27	Iowa	13.7
20	Kansas	14.4
5	Kentucky	16.9
23	Louisiana	14.2
2	Maine	19.4
31	Maryland	13.3
24	Massachusetts	14.1
29	Michigan	13.5
27	Minnesota	13.7
3	Mississippi	18.1
11	Missouri	15.7
6	Montana	16.7
19	Nebraska	14.5
46	Nevada	11.0
29	New Hampshire	13.5
42	New Jersey	11.8
34	New Mexico	12.6
25	New York	13.9
26	North Carolina	13.8
4	North Dakota	17.6
15	Ohio	15.5
17	Oklahoma	14.8
32	Oregon	13.0
10	Pennsylvania	16.1
7	Rhode Island	16.2
11	South Carolina	15.7
20	South Dakota	14.4
13	Tennessee	15.6
43	Texas	11.7
40	Utah	12.1
7	Vermont	16.2
48	Virginia	10.9
34	Washington	12.6
1	West Virginia	20.3
17	Wisconsin	14.8
50	Wyoming	9.4

RANK ORDER

RANK	STATE	PERCENT
1	West Virginia	20.3
2	Maine	19.4
3	Mississippi	18.1
4	North Dakota	17.6
5	Kentucky	16.9
6	Montana	16.7
7	Alabama	16.2
7	Rhode Island	16.2
7	Vermont	16.2
10	Pennsylvania	16.1
11	Missouri	15.7
11	South Carolina	15.7
13	Florida	15.6
13	Tennessee	15.6
15	Ohio	15.5
16	Arkansas	15.4
17	Oklahoma	14.8
17	Wisconsin	14.8
19	Nebraska	14.5
20	Indiana	14.4
20	Kansas	14.4
20	South Dakota	14.4
23	Louisiana	14.2
24	Massachusetts	14.1
25	New York	13.9
26	North Carolina	13.8
27	Iowa	13.7
27	Minnesota	13.7
29	Michigan	13.5
29	New Hampshire	13.5
31	Maryland	13.3
32	Idaho	13.0
32	Oregon	13.0
34	New Mexico	12.6
34	Washington	12.6
36	Arizona	12.5
36	Hawaii	12.5
38	Georgia	12.2
38	Illinois	12.2
40	Connecticut	12.1
40	Utah	12.1
42	New Jersey	11.8
43	Texas	11.7
44	Alaska	11.6
45	Colorado	11.1
46	California	11.0
46	Nevada	11.0
48	Virginia	10.9
49	Delaware	9.7
50	Wyoming	9.4
	District of Columbia	8.1

Source: U.S. Department of Health and Human Services, Centers for Medicare and Medicaid Services
"State Health Care Expenditures" (http://www.cms.hhs.gov/NationalHealthExpendData/)
*By state of provider. Includes hospital care, physician services, dental services, home health care, drugs, vision products, nursing home care, and other personal health care services and products.

Per Capita Personal Health Care Expenditures in 2004

National Per Capita = $5,283*

ALPHA ORDER

RANK	STATE	PER CAPITA
30	Alabama	$5,135
4	Alaska	6,450
49	Arizona	4,103
40	Arkansas	4,863
43	California	4,638
42	Colorado	4,717
5	Connecticut	6,344
6	Delaware	6,306
18	Florida	5,483
45	Georgia	4,600
37	Hawaii	4,941
48	Idaho	4,444
27	Illinois	5,293
26	Indiana	5,295
24	Iowa	5,380
23	Kansas	5,382
19	Kentucky	5,473
36	Louisiana	5,040
2	Maine	6,540
17	Maryland	5,590
1	Massachusetts	6,683
35	Michigan	5,058
13	Minnesota	5,795
34	Mississippi	5,059
21	Missouri	5,444
33	Montana	5,080
16	Nebraska	5,599
46	Nevada	4,569
22	New Hampshire	5,432
12	New Jersey	5,807
47	New Mexico	4,471
3	New York	6,535
29	North Carolina	5,191
11	North Dakota	5,808
14	Ohio	5,725
38	Oklahoma	4,917
39	Oregon	4,880
10	Pennsylvania	5,933
7	Rhode Island	6,193
31	South Carolina	5,114
25	South Dakota	5,327
20	Tennessee	5,464
44	Texas	4,601
50	Utah	3,972
8	Vermont	6,069
41	Virginia	4,822
32	Washington	5,092
9	West Virginia	5,954
15	Wisconsin	5,670
28	Wyoming	5,265

RANK ORDER

RANK	STATE	PER CAPITA
1	Massachusetts	$6,683
2	Maine	6,540
3	New York	6,535
4	Alaska	6,450
5	Connecticut	6,344
6	Delaware	6,306
7	Rhode Island	6,193
8	Vermont	6,069
9	West Virginia	5,954
10	Pennsylvania	5,933
11	North Dakota	5,808
12	New Jersey	5,807
13	Minnesota	5,795
14	Ohio	5,725
15	Wisconsin	5,670
16	Nebraska	5,599
17	Maryland	5,590
18	Florida	5,483
19	Kentucky	5,473
20	Tennessee	5,464
21	Missouri	5,444
22	New Hampshire	5,432
23	Kansas	5,382
24	Iowa	5,380
25	South Dakota	5,327
26	Indiana	5,295
27	Illinois	5,293
28	Wyoming	5,265
29	North Carolina	5,191
30	Alabama	5,135
31	South Carolina	5,114
32	Washington	5,092
33	Montana	5,080
34	Mississippi	5,059
35	Michigan	5,058
36	Louisiana	5,040
37	Hawaii	4,941
38	Oklahoma	4,917
39	Oregon	4,880
40	Arkansas	4,863
41	Virginia	4,822
42	Colorado	4,717
43	California	4,638
44	Texas	4,601
45	Georgia	4,600
46	Nevada	4,569
47	New Mexico	4,471
48	Idaho	4,444
49	Arizona	4,103
50	Utah	3,972
	District of Columbia	8,295

Source: U.S. Department of Health and Human Services, Centers for Medicare and Medicaid Services
"State Health Care Expenditures" (http://www.cms.hhs.gov/NationalHealthExpendData/)
*By state of provider. Includes hospital care, physician services, dental services, home health care, drugs, vision products, nursing home care, and other personal health care services and products.

Average Annual Growth in Personal Health Care Expenditures: 1991 to 2004

National Average = 6.7% Annual Growth*

ALPHA ORDER

RANK ORDER

RANK	STATE	ANNUAL GROWTH	RANK	STATE	ANNUAL GROWTH
37	Alabama	6.4	1	Nevada	10.0
3	Alaska	8.4	2	North Carolina	8.6
10	Arizona	7.7	3	Alaska	8.4
30	Arkansas	6.9	3	Idaho	8.4
48	California	5.7	3	Vermont	8.4
10	Colorado	7.7	6	Maine	8.3
48	Connecticut	5.7	6	Utah	8.3
8	Delaware	8.0	8	Delaware	8.0
26	Florida	7.1	9	South Carolina	7.8
23	Georgia	7.2	10	Arizona	7.7
45	Hawaii	5.9	10	Colorado	7.7
3	Idaho	8.4	10	Oregon	7.7
44	Illinois	6.1	10	Wyoming	7.7
31	Indiana	6.8	14	Minnesota	7.6
37	Iowa	6.4	14	Mississippi	7.6
34	Kansas	6.6	14	Nebraska	7.6
18	Kentucky	7.5	14	New Hampshire	7.6
48	Louisiana	5.7	18	Kentucky	7.5
6	Maine	8.3	19	Tennessee	7.4
34	Maryland	6.6	19	Texas	7.4
40	Massachusetts	6.3	21	Montana	7.3
46	Michigan	5.8	21	Washington	7.3
14	Minnesota	7.6	23	Georgia	7.2
14	Mississippi	7.6	23	New Mexico	7.2
27	Missouri	7.0	23	Wisconsin	7.2
21	Montana	7.3	26	Florida	7.1
14	Nebraska	7.6	27	Missouri	7.0
1	Nevada	10.0	27	South Dakota	7.0
14	New Hampshire	7.6	27	Virginia	7.0
40	New Jersey	6.3	30	Arkansas	6.9
23	New Mexico	7.2	31	Indiana	6.8
40	New York	6.3	31	West Virginia	6.8
2	North Carolina	8.6	33	Oklahoma	6.7
40	North Dakota	6.3	34	Kansas	6.6
37	Ohio	6.4	34	Maryland	6.6
33	Oklahoma	6.7	34	Rhode Island	6.6
10	Oregon	7.7	37	Alabama	6.4
46	Pennsylvania	5.8	37	Iowa	6.4
34	Rhode Island	6.6	37	Ohio	6.4
9	South Carolina	7.8	40	Massachusetts	6.3
27	South Dakota	7.0	40	New Jersey	6.3
19	Tennessee	7.4	40	New York	6.3
19	Texas	7.4	40	North Dakota	6.3
6	Utah	8.3	44	Illinois	6.1
3	Vermont	8.4	45	Hawaii	5.9
27	Virginia	7.0	46	Michigan	5.8
21	Washington	7.3	46	Pennsylvania	5.8
31	West Virginia	6.8	48	California	5.7
23	Wisconsin	7.2	48	Connecticut	5.7
10	Wyoming	7.7	48	Louisiana	5.7
				District of Columbia	4.1

Source: U.S. Department of Health and Human Services, Centers for Medicare and Medicaid Services
"State Health Care Expenditures" (http://www.cms.hhs.gov/NationalHealthExpendData/)
*By state of residence. Includes hospital care, physician services, dental services, home health care, drugs, vision products, nursing home care, and other personal health care services and products.

Expenditures for Hospital Care in 2004

National Total = $566,886,000,000*

<table>
<tr><td colspan="4">ALPHA ORDER</td><td colspan="4">RANK ORDER</td></tr>
<tr><td>RANK</td><td>STATE</td><td>EXPENDITURES</td><td>% of USA</td><td>RANK</td><td>STATE</td><td>EXPENDITURES</td><td>% of USA</td></tr>
<tr><td>25</td><td>Alabama</td><td>$7,938,000,000</td><td>1.4%</td><td>1</td><td>California</td><td>$57,805,000,000</td><td>10.2%</td></tr>
<tr><td>47</td><td>Alaska</td><td>1,704,000,000</td><td>0.3%</td><td>2</td><td>New York</td><td>45,569,000,000</td><td>8.0%</td></tr>
<tr><td>22</td><td>Arizona</td><td>8,499,000,000</td><td>1.5%</td><td>3</td><td>Texas</td><td>38,910,000,000</td><td>6.9%</td></tr>
<tr><td>33</td><td>Arkansas</td><td>5,092,000,000</td><td>0.9%</td><td>4</td><td>Florida</td><td>31,494,000,000</td><td>5.6%</td></tr>
<tr><td>1</td><td>California</td><td>57,805,000,000</td><td>10.2%</td><td>5</td><td>Pennsylvania</td><td>26,715,000,000</td><td>4.7%</td></tr>
<tr><td>26</td><td>Colorado</td><td>7,624,000,000</td><td>1.3%</td><td>6</td><td>Illinois</td><td>25,801,000,000</td><td>4.6%</td></tr>
<tr><td>27</td><td>Connecticut</td><td>7,029,000,000</td><td>1.2%</td><td>7</td><td>Ohio</td><td>24,822,000,000</td><td>4.4%</td></tr>
<tr><td>45</td><td>Delaware</td><td>1,917,000,000</td><td>0.3%</td><td>8</td><td>Michigan</td><td>20,206,000,000</td><td>3.6%</td></tr>
<tr><td>4</td><td>Florida</td><td>31,494,000,000</td><td>5.6%</td><td>9</td><td>New Jersey</td><td>17,024,000,000</td><td>3.0%</td></tr>
<tr><td>12</td><td>Georgia</td><td>14,613,000,000</td><td>2.6%</td><td>10</td><td>Massachusetts</td><td>16,865,000,000</td><td>3.0%</td></tr>
<tr><td>42</td><td>Hawaii</td><td>2,310,000,000</td><td>0.4%</td><td>11</td><td>North Carolina</td><td>16,294,000,000</td><td>2.9%</td></tr>
<tr><td>43</td><td>Idaho</td><td>2,298,000,000</td><td>0.4%</td><td>12</td><td>Georgia</td><td>14,613,000,000</td><td>2.6%</td></tr>
<tr><td>6</td><td>Illinois</td><td>25,801,000,000</td><td>4.6%</td><td>13</td><td>Virginia</td><td>13,361,000,000</td><td>2.4%</td></tr>
<tr><td>15</td><td>Indiana</td><td>12,761,000,000</td><td>2.3%</td><td>14</td><td>Missouri</td><td>12,993,000,000</td><td>2.3%</td></tr>
<tr><td>29</td><td>Iowa</td><td>6,179,000,000</td><td>1.1%</td><td>15</td><td>Indiana</td><td>12,761,000,000</td><td>2.3%</td></tr>
<tr><td>32</td><td>Kansas</td><td>5,157,000,000</td><td>0.9%</td><td>16</td><td>Wisconsin</td><td>11,625,000,000</td><td>2.1%</td></tr>
<tr><td>24</td><td>Kentucky</td><td>8,283,000,000</td><td>1.5%</td><td>17</td><td>Maryland</td><td>11,559,000,000</td><td>2.0%</td></tr>
<tr><td>21</td><td>Louisiana</td><td>9,145,000,000</td><td>1.6%</td><td>18</td><td>Tennessee</td><td>10,744,000,000</td><td>1.9%</td></tr>
<tr><td>39</td><td>Maine</td><td>3,035,000,000</td><td>0.5%</td><td>19</td><td>Washington</td><td>10,702,000,000</td><td>1.9%</td></tr>
<tr><td>17</td><td>Maryland</td><td>11,559,000,000</td><td>2.0%</td><td>20</td><td>Minnesota</td><td>10,009,000,000</td><td>1.8%</td></tr>
<tr><td>10</td><td>Massachusetts</td><td>16,865,000,000</td><td>3.0%</td><td>21</td><td>Louisiana</td><td>9,145,000,000</td><td>1.6%</td></tr>
<tr><td>8</td><td>Michigan</td><td>20,206,000,000</td><td>3.6%</td><td>22</td><td>Arizona</td><td>8,499,000,000</td><td>1.5%</td></tr>
<tr><td>20</td><td>Minnesota</td><td>10,009,000,000</td><td>1.8%</td><td>23</td><td>South Carolina</td><td>8,316,000,000</td><td>1.5%</td></tr>
<tr><td>30</td><td>Mississippi</td><td>6,129,000,000</td><td>1.1%</td><td>24</td><td>Kentucky</td><td>8,283,000,000</td><td>1.5%</td></tr>
<tr><td>14</td><td>Missouri</td><td>12,993,000,000</td><td>2.3%</td><td>25</td><td>Alabama</td><td>7,938,000,000</td><td>1.4%</td></tr>
<tr><td>44</td><td>Montana</td><td>1,944,000,000</td><td>0.3%</td><td>26</td><td>Colorado</td><td>7,624,000,000</td><td>1.3%</td></tr>
<tr><td>35</td><td>Nebraska</td><td>3,938,000,000</td><td>0.7%</td><td>27</td><td>Connecticut</td><td>7,029,000,000</td><td>1.2%</td></tr>
<tr><td>37</td><td>Nevada</td><td>3,459,000,000</td><td>0.6%</td><td>28</td><td>Oklahoma</td><td>6,659,000,000</td><td>1.2%</td></tr>
<tr><td>40</td><td>New Hampshire</td><td>2,519,000,000</td><td>0.4%</td><td>29</td><td>Iowa</td><td>6,179,000,000</td><td>1.1%</td></tr>
<tr><td>9</td><td>New Jersey</td><td>17,024,000,000</td><td>3.0%</td><td>30</td><td>Mississippi</td><td>6,129,000,000</td><td>1.1%</td></tr>
<tr><td>38</td><td>New Mexico</td><td>3,315,000,000</td><td>0.6%</td><td>31</td><td>Oregon</td><td>5,998,000,000</td><td>1.1%</td></tr>
<tr><td>2</td><td>New York</td><td>45,569,000,000</td><td>8.0%</td><td>32</td><td>Kansas</td><td>5,157,000,000</td><td>0.9%</td></tr>
<tr><td>11</td><td>North Carolina</td><td>16,294,000,000</td><td>2.9%</td><td>33</td><td>Arkansas</td><td>5,092,000,000</td><td>0.9%</td></tr>
<tr><td>48</td><td>North Dakota</td><td>1,533,000,000</td><td>0.3%</td><td>34</td><td>West Virginia</td><td>4,432,000,000</td><td>0.8%</td></tr>
<tr><td>7</td><td>Ohio</td><td>24,822,000,000</td><td>4.4%</td><td>35</td><td>Nebraska</td><td>3,938,000,000</td><td>0.7%</td></tr>
<tr><td>28</td><td>Oklahoma</td><td>6,659,000,000</td><td>1.2%</td><td>36</td><td>Utah</td><td>3,468,000,000</td><td>0.6%</td></tr>
<tr><td>31</td><td>Oregon</td><td>5,998,000,000</td><td>1.1%</td><td>37</td><td>Nevada</td><td>3,459,000,000</td><td>0.6%</td></tr>
<tr><td>5</td><td>Pennsylvania</td><td>26,715,000,000</td><td>4.7%</td><td>38</td><td>New Mexico</td><td>3,315,000,000</td><td>0.6%</td></tr>
<tr><td>41</td><td>Rhode Island</td><td>2,437,000,000</td><td>0.4%</td><td>39</td><td>Maine</td><td>3,035,000,000</td><td>0.5%</td></tr>
<tr><td>23</td><td>South Carolina</td><td>8,316,000,000</td><td>1.5%</td><td>40</td><td>New Hampshire</td><td>2,519,000,000</td><td>0.4%</td></tr>
<tr><td>46</td><td>South Dakota</td><td>1,753,000,000</td><td>0.3%</td><td>41</td><td>Rhode Island</td><td>2,437,000,000</td><td>0.4%</td></tr>
<tr><td>18</td><td>Tennessee</td><td>10,744,000,000</td><td>1.9%</td><td>42</td><td>Hawaii</td><td>2,310,000,000</td><td>0.4%</td></tr>
<tr><td>3</td><td>Texas</td><td>38,910,000,000</td><td>6.9%</td><td>43</td><td>Idaho</td><td>2,298,000,000</td><td>0.4%</td></tr>
<tr><td>36</td><td>Utah</td><td>3,468,000,000</td><td>0.6%</td><td>44</td><td>Montana</td><td>1,944,000,000</td><td>0.3%</td></tr>
<tr><td>49</td><td>Vermont</td><td>1,446,000,000</td><td>0.3%</td><td>45</td><td>Delaware</td><td>1,917,000,000</td><td>0.3%</td></tr>
<tr><td>13</td><td>Virginia</td><td>13,361,000,000</td><td>2.4%</td><td>46</td><td>South Dakota</td><td>1,753,000,000</td><td>0.3%</td></tr>
<tr><td>19</td><td>Washington</td><td>10,702,000,000</td><td>1.9%</td><td>47</td><td>Alaska</td><td>1,704,000,000</td><td>0.3%</td></tr>
<tr><td>34</td><td>West Virginia</td><td>4,432,000,000</td><td>0.8%</td><td>48</td><td>North Dakota</td><td>1,533,000,000</td><td>0.3%</td></tr>
<tr><td>16</td><td>Wisconsin</td><td>11,625,000,000</td><td>2.1%</td><td>49</td><td>Vermont</td><td>1,446,000,000</td><td>0.3%</td></tr>
<tr><td>50</td><td>Wyoming</td><td>1,095,000,000</td><td>0.2%</td><td>50</td><td>Wyoming</td><td>1,095,000,000</td><td>0.2%</td></tr>
<tr><td></td><td></td><td></td><td></td><td></td><td>District of Columbia</td><td>2,366,000,000</td><td>0.4%</td></tr>
</table>

Source: U.S. Department of Health and Human Services, Centers for Medicare and Medicaid Services
   "State Health Care Expenditures" (http://www.cms.hhs.gov/NationalHealthExpendData/)
*By state of residence.

Percent of Total Personal Health Care Expenditures
Spent on Hospital Care in 2004
National Percent = 36.5%*

RANK	STATE	PERCENT
42	Alabama	34.2
10	Alaska	40.2
35	Arizona	36.0
20	Arkansas	38.1
41	California	34.8
39	Colorado	35.1
50	Connecticut	31.7
29	Delaware	36.7
48	Florida	33.1
37	Georgia	35.6
25	Hawaii	37.1
25	Idaho	37.1
19	Illinois	38.3
16	Indiana	38.7
14	Iowa	38.9
40	Kansas	35.0
30	Kentucky	36.6
8	Louisiana	40.4
38	Maine	35.3
24	Maryland	37.2
12	Massachusetts	39.2
11	Michigan	39.6
44	Minnesota	33.9
2	Mississippi	41.9
3	Missouri	41.5
5	Montana	41.3
9	Nebraska	40.3
49	Nevada	32.5
36	New Hampshire	35.7
46	New Jersey	33.8
13	New Mexico	39.0
33	New York	36.1
28	North Carolina	36.8
3	North Dakota	41.5
21	Ohio	37.8
17	Oklahoma	38.4
42	Oregon	34.2
32	Pennsylvania	36.4
31	Rhode Island	36.5
15	South Carolina	38.8
1	South Dakota	42.7
47	Tennessee	33.4
22	Texas	37.6
33	Utah	36.1
17	Vermont	38.4
25	Virginia	37.1
44	Washington	33.9
6	West Virginia	41.1
23	Wisconsin	37.3
6	Wyoming	41.1

RANK	STATE	PERCENT
1	South Dakota	42.7
2	Mississippi	41.9
3	Missouri	41.5
3	North Dakota	41.5
5	Montana	41.3
6	West Virginia	41.1
6	Wyoming	41.1
8	Louisiana	40.4
9	Nebraska	40.3
10	Alaska	40.2
11	Michigan	39.6
12	Massachusetts	39.2
13	New Mexico	39.0
14	Iowa	38.9
15	South Carolina	38.8
16	Indiana	38.7
17	Oklahoma	38.4
17	Vermont	38.4
19	Illinois	38.3
20	Arkansas	38.1
21	Ohio	37.8
22	Texas	37.6
23	Wisconsin	37.3
24	Maryland	37.2
25	Hawaii	37.1
25	Idaho	37.1
25	Virginia	37.1
28	North Carolina	36.8
29	Delaware	36.7
30	Kentucky	36.6
31	Rhode Island	36.5
32	Pennsylvania	36.4
33	New York	36.1
33	Utah	36.1
35	Arizona	36.0
36	New Hampshire	35.7
37	Georgia	35.6
38	Maine	35.3
39	Colorado	35.1
40	Kansas	35.0
41	California	34.8
42	Alabama	34.2
42	Oregon	34.2
44	Minnesota	33.9
44	Washington	33.9
46	New Jersey	33.8
47	Tennessee	33.4
48	Florida	33.1
49	Nevada	32.5
50	Connecticut	31.7

| | District of Columbia | 49.2 |

Source: CQ Press using data from U.S. Department of Health and Human Services, Centers for Medicare and Medicaid Services
"State Health Care Expenditures" (http://www.cms.hhs.gov/NationalHealthExpendData/)
*By state of residence.

Per Capita Expenditures for Hospital Care in 2004

National Per Capita = $1,931*

ALPHA ORDER

RANK	STATE	PER CAPITA
39	Alabama	$1,757
2	Alaska	2,594
49	Arizona	1,479
34	Arkansas	1,854
47	California	1,613
44	Colorado	1,658
24	Connecticut	2,012
7	Delaware	2,313
37	Florida	1,813
46	Georgia	1,635
35	Hawaii	1,834
45	Idaho	1,648
23	Illinois	2,029
21	Indiana	2,051
19	Iowa	2,092
33	Kansas	1,883
26	Kentucky	2,001
22	Louisiana	2,034
8	Maine	2,310
20	Maryland	2,081
1	Massachusetts	2,620
25	Michigan	2,002
28	Minnesota	1,965
16	Mississippi	2,119
10	Missouri	2,259
18	Montana	2,099
12	Nebraska	2,254
48	Nevada	1,483
30	New Hampshire	1,941
29	New Jersey	1,962
40	New Mexico	1,744
5	New York	2,362
31	North Carolina	1,910
4	North Dakota	2,411
13	Ohio	2,166
32	Oklahoma	1,890
43	Oregon	1,671
15	Pennsylvania	2,158
10	Rhode Island	2,259
27	South Carolina	1,982
9	South Dakota	2,276
36	Tennessee	1,826
41	Texas	1,728
50	Utah	1,432
6	Vermont	2,329
38	Virginia	1,788
42	Washington	1,725
3	West Virginia	2,447
17	Wisconsin	2,114
14	Wyoming	2,165

RANK ORDER

RANK	STATE	PER CAPITA
1	Massachusetts	$2,620
2	Alaska	2,594
3	West Virginia	2,447
4	North Dakota	2,411
5	New York	2,362
6	Vermont	2,329
7	Delaware	2,313
8	Maine	2,310
9	South Dakota	2,276
10	Missouri	2,259
10	Rhode Island	2,259
12	Nebraska	2,254
13	Ohio	2,166
14	Wyoming	2,165
15	Pennsylvania	2,158
16	Mississippi	2,119
17	Wisconsin	2,114
18	Montana	2,099
19	Iowa	2,092
20	Maryland	2,081
21	Indiana	2,051
22	Louisiana	2,034
23	Illinois	2,029
24	Connecticut	2,012
25	Michigan	2,002
26	Kentucky	2,001
27	South Carolina	1,982
28	Minnesota	1,965
29	New Jersey	1,962
30	New Hampshire	1,941
31	North Carolina	1,910
32	Oklahoma	1,890
33	Kansas	1,883
34	Arkansas	1,854
35	Hawaii	1,834
36	Tennessee	1,826
37	Florida	1,813
38	Virginia	1,788
39	Alabama	1,757
40	New Mexico	1,744
41	Texas	1,728
42	Washington	1,725
43	Oregon	1,671
44	Colorado	1,658
45	Idaho	1,648
46	Georgia	1,635
47	California	1,613
48	Nevada	1,483
49	Arizona	1,479
50	Utah	1,432

District of Columbia	4,081

Source: U.S. Department of Health and Human Services, Centers for Medicare and Medicaid Services
   "State Health Care Expenditures" (http://www.cms.hhs.gov/NationalHealthExpendData/)
*By state of residence.

Expenditures for Physician and Clinical Services in 2004

National Total = $393,713,000,000*

ALPHA ORDER

RANK	STATE	EXPENDITURES	% of USA
23	Alabama	$6,200,000,000	1.6%
45	Alaska	1,220,000,000	0.3%
21	Arizona	6,855,000,000	1.7%
33	Arkansas	3,316,000,000	0.8%
1	California	49,417,000,000	12.6%
22	Colorado	6,375,000,000	1.6%
27	Connecticut	5,155,000,000	1.3%
44	Delaware	1,228,000,000	0.3%
3	Florida	26,439,000,000	6.7%
10	Georgia	11,227,000,000	2.9%
41	Hawaii	1,587,000,000	0.4%
42	Idaho	1,466,000,000	0.4%
5	Illinois	16,984,000,000	4.3%
18	Indiana	7,869,000,000	2.0%
31	Iowa	3,719,000,000	0.9%
30	Kansas	4,144,000,000	1.1%
24	Kentucky	5,748,000,000	1.5%
26	Louisiana	5,271,000,000	1.3%
38	Maine	2,075,000,000	0.5%
17	Maryland	7,891,000,000	2.0%
13	Massachusetts	9,116,000,000	2.3%
9	Michigan	11,757,000,000	3.0%
19	Minnesota	7,757,000,000	2.0%
34	Mississippi	3,219,000,000	0.8%
20	Missouri	6,891,000,000	1.8%
46	Montana	1,157,000,000	0.3%
37	Nebraska	2,287,000,000	0.6%
32	Nevada	3,386,000,000	0.9%
40	New Hampshire	1,757,000,000	0.4%
8	New Jersey	12,265,000,000	3.1%
39	New Mexico	1,925,000,000	0.5%
4	New York	25,643,000,000	6.5%
11	North Carolina	10,248,000,000	2.6%
49	North Dakota	763,000,000	0.2%
7	Ohio	15,322,000,000	3.9%
29	Oklahoma	4,305,000,000	1.1%
28	Oregon	5,142,000,000	1.3%
6	Pennsylvania	16,942,000,000	4.3%
43	Rhode Island	1,325,000,000	0.3%
25	South Carolina	5,491,000,000	1.4%
47	South Dakota	920,000,000	0.2%
14	Tennessee	9,069,000,000	2.3%
2	Texas	28,769,000,000	7.3%
36	Utah	2,393,000,000	0.6%
48	Vermont	874,000,000	0.2%
12	Virginia	9,220,000,000	2.3%
15	Washington	9,004,000,000	2.3%
35	West Virginia	2,444,000,000	0.6%
16	Wisconsin	8,441,000,000	2.1%
50	Wyoming	670,000,000	0.2%

RANK ORDER

RANK	STATE	EXPENDITURES	% of USA
1	California	$49,417,000,000	12.6%
2	Texas	28,769,000,000	7.3%
3	Florida	26,439,000,000	6.7%
4	New York	25,643,000,000	6.5%
5	Illinois	16,984,000,000	4.3%
6	Pennsylvania	16,942,000,000	4.3%
7	Ohio	15,322,000,000	3.9%
8	New Jersey	12,265,000,000	3.1%
9	Michigan	11,757,000,000	3.0%
10	Georgia	11,227,000,000	2.9%
11	North Carolina	10,248,000,000	2.6%
12	Virginia	9,220,000,000	2.3%
13	Massachusetts	9,116,000,000	2.3%
14	Tennessee	9,069,000,000	2.3%
15	Washington	9,004,000,000	2.3%
16	Wisconsin	8,441,000,000	2.1%
17	Maryland	7,891,000,000	2.0%
18	Indiana	7,869,000,000	2.0%
19	Minnesota	7,757,000,000	2.0%
20	Missouri	6,891,000,000	1.8%
21	Arizona	6,855,000,000	1.7%
22	Colorado	6,375,000,000	1.6%
23	Alabama	6,200,000,000	1.6%
24	Kentucky	5,748,000,000	1.5%
25	South Carolina	5,491,000,000	1.4%
26	Louisiana	5,271,000,000	1.3%
27	Connecticut	5,155,000,000	1.3%
28	Oregon	5,142,000,000	1.3%
29	Oklahoma	4,305,000,000	1.1%
30	Kansas	4,144,000,000	1.1%
31	Iowa	3,719,000,000	0.9%
32	Nevada	3,386,000,000	0.9%
33	Arkansas	3,316,000,000	0.8%
34	Mississippi	3,219,000,000	0.8%
35	West Virginia	2,444,000,000	0.6%
36	Utah	2,393,000,000	0.6%
37	Nebraska	2,287,000,000	0.6%
38	Maine	2,075,000,000	0.5%
39	New Mexico	1,925,000,000	0.5%
40	New Hampshire	1,757,000,000	0.4%
41	Hawaii	1,587,000,000	0.4%
42	Idaho	1,466,000,000	0.4%
43	Rhode Island	1,325,000,000	0.3%
44	Delaware	1,228,000,000	0.3%
45	Alaska	1,220,000,000	0.3%
46	Montana	1,157,000,000	0.3%
47	South Dakota	920,000,000	0.2%
48	Vermont	874,000,000	0.2%
49	North Dakota	763,000,000	0.2%
50	Wyoming	670,000,000	0.2%
	District of Columbia	1,024,000,000	0.3%

Source: U.S. Department of Health and Human Services, Centers for Medicare and Medicaid Services
"State Health Care Expenditures" (http://www.cms.hhs.gov/NationalHealthExpendData/)
*By state of residence. Includes private physician offices and clinics, independently billing laboratories, and clinics run by U.S. Department of Veteran Affairs and the U.S. Indian Health Service.

Percent of Total Personal Health Care Expenditures
Spent on Physician and Clinical Services in 2004
National Percent = 25.4%*

ALPHA ORDER

RANK	STATE	PERCENT
14	Alabama	26.7
6	Alaska	28.8
5	Arizona	29.1
26	Arkansas	24.8
2	California	29.7
3	Colorado	29.4
35	Connecticut	23.3
32	Delaware	23.5
10	Florida	27.8
12	Georgia	27.3
18	Hawaii	25.5
31	Idaho	23.7
21	Illinois	25.2
30	Indiana	23.9
33	Iowa	23.4
9	Kansas	28.1
19	Kentucky	25.4
35	Louisiana	23.3
29	Maine	24.1
19	Maryland	25.4
47	Massachusetts	21.2
41	Michigan	23.0
15	Minnesota	26.3
45	Mississippi	22.0
45	Missouri	22.0
27	Montana	24.6
33	Nebraska	23.4
1	Nevada	31.8
23	New Hampshire	24.9
28	New Jersey	24.3
42	New Mexico	22.7
49	New York	20.3
39	North Carolina	23.1
48	North Dakota	20.7
35	Ohio	23.3
23	Oklahoma	24.9
3	Oregon	29.4
39	Pennsylvania	23.1
50	Rhode Island	19.8
16	South Carolina	25.6
44	South Dakota	22.4
8	Tennessee	28.2
10	Texas	27.8
23	Utah	24.9
38	Vermont	23.2
16	Virginia	25.6
7	Washington	28.5
42	West Virginia	22.7
13	Wisconsin	27.1
21	Wyoming	25.2

RANK ORDER

RANK	STATE	PERCENT
1	Nevada	31.8
2	California	29.7
3	Colorado	29.4
3	Oregon	29.4
5	Arizona	29.1
6	Alaska	28.8
7	Washington	28.5
8	Tennessee	28.2
9	Kansas	28.1
10	Florida	27.8
10	Texas	27.8
12	Georgia	27.3
13	Wisconsin	27.1
14	Alabama	26.7
15	Minnesota	26.3
16	South Carolina	25.6
16	Virginia	25.6
18	Hawaii	25.5
19	Kentucky	25.4
19	Maryland	25.4
21	Illinois	25.2
21	Wyoming	25.2
23	New Hampshire	24.9
23	Oklahoma	24.9
23	Utah	24.9
26	Arkansas	24.8
27	Montana	24.6
28	New Jersey	24.3
29	Maine	24.1
30	Indiana	23.9
31	Idaho	23.7
32	Delaware	23.5
33	Iowa	23.4
33	Nebraska	23.4
35	Connecticut	23.3
35	Louisiana	23.3
35	Ohio	23.3
38	Vermont	23.2
39	North Carolina	23.1
39	Pennsylvania	23.1
41	Michigan	23.0
42	New Mexico	22.7
42	West Virginia	22.7
44	South Dakota	22.4
45	Mississippi	22.0
45	Missouri	22.0
47	Massachusetts	21.2
48	North Dakota	20.7
49	New York	20.3
50	Rhode Island	19.8

District of Columbia 21.3

Source: CQ Press using data from U.S. Department of Health and Human Services, Centers for Medicare and Medicaid Services "State Health Care Expenditures" (http://www.cms.hhs.gov/NationalHealthExpendData/)
*By state of residence. Includes private physician offices and clinics, independently billing laboratories, and clinics run by U.S. Department of Veteran Affairs and the U.S. Indian Health Service.

Finance 313

Per Capita Expenditures for Physician and Clinical Services in 2004

National Per Capita = $1,341*

ALPHA ORDER

RANK	STATE	PER CAPITA
20	Alabama	$1,372
1	Alaska	1,858
44	Arizona	1,193
39	Arkansas	1,207
19	California	1,379
18	Colorado	1,386
9	Connecticut	1,475
8	Delaware	1,482
6	Florida	1,522
34	Georgia	1,257
32	Hawaii	1,260
48	Idaho	1,051
25	Illinois	1,336
31	Indiana	1,264
33	Iowa	1,259
7	Kansas	1,513
17	Kentucky	1,388
45	Louisiana	1,173
2	Maine	1,579
13	Maryland	1,421
14	Massachusetts	1,416
46	Michigan	1,165
5	Minnesota	1,523
47	Mississippi	1,113
42	Missouri	1,198
35	Montana	1,249
28	Nebraska	1,309
10	Nevada	1,451
22	New Hampshire	1,354
15	New Jersey	1,414
49	New Mexico	1,013
26	New York	1,329
40	North Carolina	1,201
41	North Dakota	1,200
24	Ohio	1,337
38	Oklahoma	1,222
12	Oregon	1,433
21	Pennsylvania	1,369
37	Rhode Island	1,228
28	South Carolina	1,309
43	South Dakota	1,195
3	Tennessee	1,541
30	Texas	1,278
50	Utah	988
16	Vermont	1,408
36	Virginia	1,234
10	Washington	1,451
23	West Virginia	1,350
4	Wisconsin	1,535
27	Wyoming	1,326

RANK ORDER

RANK	STATE	PER CAPITA
1	Alaska	$1,858
2	Maine	1,579
3	Tennessee	1,541
4	Wisconsin	1,535
5	Minnesota	1,523
6	Florida	1,522
7	Kansas	1,513
8	Delaware	1,482
9	Connecticut	1,475
10	Nevada	1,451
10	Washington	1,451
12	Oregon	1,433
13	Maryland	1,421
14	Massachusetts	1,416
15	New Jersey	1,414
16	Vermont	1,408
17	Kentucky	1,388
18	Colorado	1,386
19	California	1,379
20	Alabama	1,372
21	Pennsylvania	1,369
22	New Hampshire	1,354
23	West Virginia	1,350
24	Ohio	1,337
25	Illinois	1,336
26	New York	1,329
27	Wyoming	1,326
28	Nebraska	1,309
28	South Carolina	1,309
30	Texas	1,278
31	Indiana	1,264
32	Hawaii	1,260
33	Iowa	1,259
34	Georgia	1,257
35	Montana	1,249
36	Virginia	1,234
37	Rhode Island	1,228
38	Oklahoma	1,222
39	Arkansas	1,207
40	North Carolina	1,201
41	North Dakota	1,200
42	Missouri	1,198
43	South Dakota	1,195
44	Arizona	1,193
45	Louisiana	1,173
46	Michigan	1,165
47	Mississippi	1,113
48	Idaho	1,051
49	New Mexico	1,013
50	Utah	988

| | District of Columbia | 1,767 |

Source: U.S. Department of Health and Human Services, Centers for Medicare and Medicaid Services
   "State Health Care Expenditures" (http://www.cms.hhs.gov/NationalHealthExpendData/)
*By state of residence. Includes private physician offices and clinics, independently billing laboratories, and clinics run by U.S. Department of Veteran Affairs and the U.S. Indian Health Service.

Expenditures for Dental Services in 2004

National Total = $81,476,000,000*

<table>
<tr><td colspan="4">ALPHA ORDER</td><td colspan="4">RANK ORDER</td></tr>
<tr><th>RANK</th><th>STATE</th><th>EXPENDITURES</th><th>% of USA</th><th>RANK</th><th>STATE</th><th>EXPENDITURES</th><th>% of USA</th></tr>
<tr><td>26</td><td>Alabama</td><td>$977,000,000</td><td>1.2%</td><td>1</td><td>California</td><td>$11,625,000,000</td><td>14.3%</td></tr>
<tr><td>46</td><td>Alaska</td><td>241,000,000</td><td>0.3%</td><td>2</td><td>New York</td><td>5,445,000,000</td><td>6.7%</td></tr>
<tr><td>20</td><td>Arizona</td><td>1,457,000,000</td><td>1.8%</td><td>3</td><td>Texas</td><td>4,749,000,000</td><td>5.8%</td></tr>
<tr><td>34</td><td>Arkansas</td><td>601,000,000</td><td>0.7%</td><td>4</td><td>Florida</td><td>4,494,000,000</td><td>5.5%</td></tr>
<tr><td>1</td><td>California</td><td>11,625,000,000</td><td>14.3%</td><td>5</td><td>Illinois</td><td>3,488,000,000</td><td>4.3%</td></tr>
<tr><td>19</td><td>Colorado</td><td>1,537,000,000</td><td>1.9%</td><td>6</td><td>Pennsylvania</td><td>3,189,000,000</td><td>3.9%</td></tr>
<tr><td>22</td><td>Connecticut</td><td>1,336,000,000</td><td>1.6%</td><td>7</td><td>Michigan</td><td>3,147,000,000</td><td>3.9%</td></tr>
<tr><td>44</td><td>Delaware</td><td>279,000,000</td><td>0.3%</td><td>8</td><td>New Jersey</td><td>2,903,000,000</td><td>3.6%</td></tr>
<tr><td>4</td><td>Florida</td><td>4,494,000,000</td><td>5.5%</td><td>9</td><td>Ohio</td><td>2,901,000,000</td><td>3.6%</td></tr>
<tr><td>12</td><td>Georgia</td><td>2,257,000,000</td><td>2.8%</td><td>10</td><td>Washington</td><td>2,505,000,000</td><td>3.1%</td></tr>
<tr><td>41</td><td>Hawaii</td><td>382,000,000</td><td>0.5%</td><td>11</td><td>Massachusetts</td><td>2,276,000,000</td><td>2.8%</td></tr>
<tr><td>37</td><td>Idaho</td><td>468,000,000</td><td>0.6%</td><td>12</td><td>Georgia</td><td>2,257,000,000</td><td>2.8%</td></tr>
<tr><td>5</td><td>Illinois</td><td>3,488,000,000</td><td>4.3%</td><td>13</td><td>North Carolina</td><td>2,253,000,000</td><td>2.8%</td></tr>
<tr><td>17</td><td>Indiana</td><td>1,606,000,000</td><td>2.0%</td><td>14</td><td>Virginia</td><td>2,043,000,000</td><td>2.5%</td></tr>
<tr><td>30</td><td>Iowa</td><td>735,000,000</td><td>0.9%</td><td>15</td><td>Wisconsin</td><td>1,694,000,000</td><td>2.1%</td></tr>
<tr><td>31</td><td>Kansas</td><td>723,000,000</td><td>0.9%</td><td>16</td><td>Minnesota</td><td>1,678,000,000</td><td>2.1%</td></tr>
<tr><td>27</td><td>Kentucky</td><td>876,000,000</td><td>1.1%</td><td>17</td><td>Indiana</td><td>1,606,000,000</td><td>2.0%</td></tr>
<tr><td>29</td><td>Louisiana</td><td>781,000,000</td><td>1.0%</td><td>18</td><td>Maryland</td><td>1,553,000,000</td><td>1.9%</td></tr>
<tr><td>42</td><td>Maine</td><td>363,000,000</td><td>0.4%</td><td>19</td><td>Colorado</td><td>1,537,000,000</td><td>1.9%</td></tr>
<tr><td>18</td><td>Maryland</td><td>1,553,000,000</td><td>1.9%</td><td>20</td><td>Arizona</td><td>1,457,000,000</td><td>1.8%</td></tr>
<tr><td>11</td><td>Massachusetts</td><td>2,276,000,000</td><td>2.8%</td><td>21</td><td>Tennessee</td><td>1,428,000,000</td><td>1.8%</td></tr>
<tr><td>7</td><td>Michigan</td><td>3,147,000,000</td><td>3.9%</td><td>22</td><td>Connecticut</td><td>1,336,000,000</td><td>1.6%</td></tr>
<tr><td>16</td><td>Minnesota</td><td>1,678,000,000</td><td>2.1%</td><td>22</td><td>Missouri</td><td>1,336,000,000</td><td>1.6%</td></tr>
<tr><td>35</td><td>Mississippi</td><td>507,000,000</td><td>0.6%</td><td>24</td><td>Oregon</td><td>1,269,000,000</td><td>1.6%</td></tr>
<tr><td>22</td><td>Missouri</td><td>1,336,000,000</td><td>1.6%</td><td>25</td><td>South Carolina</td><td>1,003,000,000</td><td>1.2%</td></tr>
<tr><td>45</td><td>Montana</td><td>249,000,000</td><td>0.3%</td><td>26</td><td>Alabama</td><td>977,000,000</td><td>1.2%</td></tr>
<tr><td>39</td><td>Nebraska</td><td>423,000,000</td><td>0.5%</td><td>27</td><td>Kentucky</td><td>876,000,000</td><td>1.1%</td></tr>
<tr><td>33</td><td>Nevada</td><td>679,000,000</td><td>0.8%</td><td>28</td><td>Oklahoma</td><td>842,000,000</td><td>1.0%</td></tr>
<tr><td>36</td><td>New Hampshire</td><td>471,000,000</td><td>0.6%</td><td>29</td><td>Louisiana</td><td>781,000,000</td><td>1.0%</td></tr>
<tr><td>8</td><td>New Jersey</td><td>2,903,000,000</td><td>3.6%</td><td>30</td><td>Iowa</td><td>735,000,000</td><td>0.9%</td></tr>
<tr><td>38</td><td>New Mexico</td><td>425,000,000</td><td>0.5%</td><td>31</td><td>Kansas</td><td>723,000,000</td><td>0.9%</td></tr>
<tr><td>2</td><td>New York</td><td>5,445,000,000</td><td>6.7%</td><td>32</td><td>Utah</td><td>718,000,000</td><td>0.9%</td></tr>
<tr><td>13</td><td>North Carolina</td><td>2,253,000,000</td><td>2.8%</td><td>33</td><td>Nevada</td><td>679,000,000</td><td>0.8%</td></tr>
<tr><td>49</td><td>North Dakota</td><td>174,000,000</td><td>0.2%</td><td>34</td><td>Arkansas</td><td>601,000,000</td><td>0.7%</td></tr>
<tr><td>9</td><td>Ohio</td><td>2,901,000,000</td><td>3.6%</td><td>35</td><td>Mississippi</td><td>507,000,000</td><td>0.6%</td></tr>
<tr><td>28</td><td>Oklahoma</td><td>842,000,000</td><td>1.0%</td><td>36</td><td>New Hampshire</td><td>471,000,000</td><td>0.6%</td></tr>
<tr><td>24</td><td>Oregon</td><td>1,269,000,000</td><td>1.6%</td><td>37</td><td>Idaho</td><td>468,000,000</td><td>0.6%</td></tr>
<tr><td>6</td><td>Pennsylvania</td><td>3,189,000,000</td><td>3.9%</td><td>38</td><td>New Mexico</td><td>425,000,000</td><td>0.5%</td></tr>
<tr><td>43</td><td>Rhode Island</td><td>294,000,000</td><td>0.4%</td><td>39</td><td>Nebraska</td><td>423,000,000</td><td>0.5%</td></tr>
<tr><td>25</td><td>South Carolina</td><td>1,003,000,000</td><td>1.2%</td><td>40</td><td>West Virginia</td><td>384,000,000</td><td>0.5%</td></tr>
<tr><td>48</td><td>South Dakota</td><td>195,000,000</td><td>0.2%</td><td>41</td><td>Hawaii</td><td>382,000,000</td><td>0.5%</td></tr>
<tr><td>21</td><td>Tennessee</td><td>1,428,000,000</td><td>1.8%</td><td>42</td><td>Maine</td><td>363,000,000</td><td>0.4%</td></tr>
<tr><td>3</td><td>Texas</td><td>4,749,000,000</td><td>5.8%</td><td>43</td><td>Rhode Island</td><td>294,000,000</td><td>0.4%</td></tr>
<tr><td>32</td><td>Utah</td><td>718,000,000</td><td>0.9%</td><td>44</td><td>Delaware</td><td>279,000,000</td><td>0.3%</td></tr>
<tr><td>47</td><td>Vermont</td><td>198,000,000</td><td>0.2%</td><td>45</td><td>Montana</td><td>249,000,000</td><td>0.3%</td></tr>
<tr><td>14</td><td>Virginia</td><td>2,043,000,000</td><td>2.5%</td><td>46</td><td>Alaska</td><td>241,000,000</td><td>0.3%</td></tr>
<tr><td>10</td><td>Washington</td><td>2,505,000,000</td><td>3.1%</td><td>47</td><td>Vermont</td><td>198,000,000</td><td>0.2%</td></tr>
<tr><td>40</td><td>West Virginia</td><td>384,000,000</td><td>0.5%</td><td>48</td><td>South Dakota</td><td>195,000,000</td><td>0.2%</td></tr>
<tr><td>15</td><td>Wisconsin</td><td>1,694,000,000</td><td>2.1%</td><td>49</td><td>North Dakota</td><td>174,000,000</td><td>0.2%</td></tr>
<tr><td>50</td><td>Wyoming</td><td>134,000,000</td><td>0.2%</td><td>50</td><td>Wyoming</td><td>134,000,000</td><td>0.2%</td></tr>
<tr><td></td><td></td><td></td><td></td><td></td><td>District of Columbia</td><td>183,000,000</td><td>0.2%</td></tr>
</table>

Source: U.S. Department of Health and Human Services, Centers for Medicare and Medicaid Services
   "State Health Care Expenditures" (http://www.cms.hhs.gov/NationalHealthExpendData/)
*By state of residence.

Percent of Total Personal Health Care Expenditures
Spent on Dental Services in 2004
National Percent = 5.3%*

ALPHA ORDER

RANK ORDER

RANK	STATE	PERCENT		RANK	STATE	PERCENT
45	Alabama	4.2		1	Washington	7.9
14	Alaska	5.7		2	Idaho	7.6
9	Arizona	6.2		3	Utah	7.5
37	Arkansas	4.5		4	Oregon	7.2
6	California	7.0		5	Colorado	7.1
5	Colorado	7.1		6	California	7.0
12	Connecticut	6.0		7	New Hampshire	6.7
19	Delaware	5.3		8	Nevada	6.4
32	Florida	4.7		9	Arizona	6.2
17	Georgia	5.5		9	Michigan	6.2
11	Hawaii	6.1		11	Hawaii	6.1
2	Idaho	7.6		12	Connecticut	6.0
23	Illinois	5.2		13	New Jersey	5.8
28	Indiana	4.9		14	Alaska	5.7
35	Iowa	4.6		14	Minnesota	5.7
28	Kansas	4.9		14	Virginia	5.7
47	Kentucky	3.9		17	Georgia	5.5
50	Louisiana	3.4		18	Wisconsin	5.4
45	Maine	4.2		19	Delaware	5.3
25	Maryland	5.0		19	Massachusetts	5.3
19	Massachusetts	5.3		19	Montana	5.3
9	Michigan	6.2		19	Vermont	5.3
14	Minnesota	5.7		23	Illinois	5.2
49	Mississippi	3.5		24	North Carolina	5.1
41	Missouri	4.3		25	Maryland	5.0
19	Montana	5.3		25	New Mexico	5.0
41	Nebraska	4.3		25	Wyoming	5.0
8	Nevada	6.4		28	Indiana	4.9
7	New Hampshire	6.7		28	Kansas	4.9
13	New Jersey	5.8		28	Oklahoma	4.9
25	New Mexico	5.0		31	South Dakota	4.8
41	New York	4.3		32	Florida	4.7
24	North Carolina	5.1		32	North Dakota	4.7
32	North Dakota	4.7		32	South Carolina	4.7
38	Ohio	4.4		35	Iowa	4.6
28	Oklahoma	4.9		35	Texas	4.6
4	Oregon	7.2		37	Arkansas	4.5
41	Pennsylvania	4.3		38	Ohio	4.4
38	Rhode Island	4.4		38	Rhode Island	4.4
32	South Carolina	4.7		38	Tennessee	4.4
31	South Dakota	4.8		41	Missouri	4.3
38	Tennessee	4.4		41	Nebraska	4.3
35	Texas	4.6		41	New York	4.3
3	Utah	7.5		41	Pennsylvania	4.3
19	Vermont	5.3		45	Alabama	4.2
14	Virginia	5.7		45	Maine	4.2
1	Washington	7.9		47	Kentucky	3.9
48	West Virginia	3.6		48	West Virginia	3.6
18	Wisconsin	5.4		49	Mississippi	3.5
25	Wyoming	5.0		50	Louisiana	3.4

District of Columbia 3.8

Source: CQ Press using data from U.S. Department of Health and Human Services, Centers for Medicare and Medicaid Services
"State Health Care Expenditures" (http://www.cms.hhs.gov/NationalHealthExpendData/)
*By state of residence.

Per Capita Expenditures for Dental Care in 2004

National Per Capita = $277*

ALPHA ORDER

RANK	STATE	PER CAPITA
45	Alabama	$216
3	Alaska	366
33	Arizona	254
44	Arkansas	219
12	California	324
10	Colorado	334
2	Connecticut	382
7	Delaware	337
30	Florida	259
34	Georgia	253
16	Hawaii	303
8	Idaho	336
22	Illinois	274
31	Indiana	258
37	Iowa	249
28	Kansas	264
46	Kentucky	212
50	Louisiana	174
21	Maine	276
20	Maryland	280
5	Massachusetts	354
14	Michigan	312
11	Minnesota	329
49	Mississippi	175
42	Missouri	232
26	Montana	269
39	Nebraska	242
18	Nevada	291
4	New Hampshire	363
9	New Jersey	335
43	New Mexico	224
19	New York	282
28	North Carolina	264
22	North Dakota	274
34	Ohio	253
40	Oklahoma	239
5	Oregon	354
31	Pennsylvania	258
25	Rhode Island	272
40	South Carolina	239
34	South Dakota	253
38	Tennessee	243
48	Texas	211
17	Utah	297
13	Vermont	319
24	Virginia	273
1	Washington	404
46	West Virginia	212
15	Wisconsin	308
27	Wyoming	265

RANK ORDER

RANK	STATE	PER CAPITA
1	Washington	$404
2	Connecticut	382
3	Alaska	366
4	New Hampshire	363
5	Massachusetts	354
5	Oregon	354
7	Delaware	337
8	Idaho	336
9	New Jersey	335
10	Colorado	334
11	Minnesota	329
12	California	324
13	Vermont	319
14	Michigan	312
15	Wisconsin	308
16	Hawaii	303
17	Utah	297
18	Nevada	291
19	New York	282
20	Maryland	280
21	Maine	276
22	Illinois	274
22	North Dakota	274
24	Virginia	273
25	Rhode Island	272
26	Montana	269
27	Wyoming	265
28	Kansas	264
28	North Carolina	264
30	Florida	259
31	Indiana	258
31	Pennsylvania	258
33	Arizona	254
34	Georgia	253
34	Ohio	253
34	South Dakota	253
37	Iowa	249
38	Tennessee	243
39	Nebraska	242
40	Oklahoma	239
40	South Carolina	239
42	Missouri	232
43	New Mexico	224
44	Arkansas	219
45	Alabama	216
46	Kentucky	212
46	West Virginia	212
48	Texas	211
49	Mississippi	175
50	Louisiana	174
	District of Columbia	315

Source: U.S. Department of Health and Human Services, Centers for Medicare and Medicaid Services
"State Health Care Expenditures" (http://www.cms.hhs.gov/NationalHealthExpendData/)
*By state of residence.

Expenditures for Other Professional Health Care Services in 2004

National Total = $52,636,000,000*

ALPHA ORDER

RANK	STATE	EXPENDITURES	% of USA
27	Alabama	$681,000,000	1.3%
46	Alaska	164,000,000	0.3%
22	Arizona	932,000,000	1.8%
32	Arkansas	463,000,000	0.9%
1	California	6,178,000,000	11.7%
21	Colorado	939,000,000	1.8%
23	Connecticut	855,000,000	1.6%
43	Delaware	210,000,000	0.4%
3	Florida	3,529,000,000	6.7%
13	Georgia	1,252,000,000	2.4%
42	Hawaii	224,000,000	0.4%
40	Idaho	303,000,000	0.6%
6	Illinois	2,365,000,000	4.5%
19	Indiana	1,002,000,000	1.9%
29	Iowa	557,000,000	1.1%
31	Kansas	499,000,000	0.9%
24	Kentucky	796,000,000	1.5%
26	Louisiana	705,000,000	1.3%
38	Maine	305,000,000	0.6%
16	Maryland	1,034,000,000	2.0%
12	Massachusetts	1,289,000,000	2.4%
9	Michigan	1,896,000,000	3.6%
18	Minnesota	1,005,000,000	1.9%
35	Mississippi	351,000,000	0.7%
20	Missouri	958,000,000	1.8%
45	Montana	172,000,000	0.3%
39	Nebraska	304,000,000	0.6%
33	Nevada	370,000,000	0.7%
41	New Hampshire	229,000,000	0.4%
8	New Jersey	1,919,000,000	3.6%
37	New Mexico	321,000,000	0.6%
2	New York	3,587,000,000	6.8%
11	North Carolina	1,336,000,000	2.5%
50	North Dakota	103,000,000	0.2%
7	Ohio	2,285,000,000	4.3%
28	Oklahoma	561,000,000	1.1%
25	Oregon	715,000,000	1.4%
5	Pennsylvania	2,613,000,000	5.0%
44	Rhode Island	193,000,000	0.4%
30	South Carolina	534,000,000	1.0%
47	South Dakota	135,000,000	0.3%
15	Tennessee	1,035,000,000	2.0%
4	Texas	3,177,000,000	6.0%
36	Utah	332,000,000	0.6%
48	Vermont	132,000,000	0.3%
14	Virginia	1,123,000,000	2.1%
10	Washington	1,363,000,000	2.6%
34	West Virginia	361,000,000	0.7%
17	Wisconsin	1,031,000,000	2.0%
49	Wyoming	117,000,000	0.2%

RANK ORDER

RANK	STATE	EXPENDITURES	% of USA
1	California	$6,178,000,000	11.7%
2	New York	3,587,000,000	6.8%
3	Florida	3,529,000,000	6.7%
4	Texas	3,177,000,000	6.0%
5	Pennsylvania	2,613,000,000	5.0%
6	Illinois	2,365,000,000	4.5%
7	Ohio	2,285,000,000	4.3%
8	New Jersey	1,919,000,000	3.6%
9	Michigan	1,896,000,000	3.6%
10	Washington	1,363,000,000	2.6%
11	North Carolina	1,336,000,000	2.5%
12	Massachusetts	1,289,000,000	2.4%
13	Georgia	1,252,000,000	2.4%
14	Virginia	1,123,000,000	2.1%
15	Tennessee	1,035,000,000	2.0%
16	Maryland	1,034,000,000	2.0%
17	Wisconsin	1,031,000,000	2.0%
18	Minnesota	1,005,000,000	1.9%
19	Indiana	1,002,000,000	1.9%
20	Missouri	958,000,000	1.8%
21	Colorado	939,000,000	1.8%
22	Arizona	932,000,000	1.8%
23	Connecticut	855,000,000	1.6%
24	Kentucky	796,000,000	1.5%
25	Oregon	715,000,000	1.4%
26	Louisiana	705,000,000	1.3%
27	Alabama	681,000,000	1.3%
28	Oklahoma	561,000,000	1.1%
29	Iowa	557,000,000	1.1%
30	South Carolina	534,000,000	1.0%
31	Kansas	499,000,000	0.9%
32	Arkansas	463,000,000	0.9%
33	Nevada	370,000,000	0.7%
34	West Virginia	361,000,000	0.7%
35	Mississippi	351,000,000	0.7%
36	Utah	332,000,000	0.6%
37	New Mexico	321,000,000	0.6%
38	Maine	305,000,000	0.6%
39	Nebraska	304,000,000	0.6%
40	Idaho	303,000,000	0.6%
41	New Hampshire	229,000,000	0.4%
42	Hawaii	224,000,000	0.4%
43	Delaware	210,000,000	0.4%
44	Rhode Island	193,000,000	0.4%
45	Montana	172,000,000	0.3%
46	Alaska	164,000,000	0.3%
47	South Dakota	135,000,000	0.3%
48	Vermont	132,000,000	0.3%
49	Wyoming	117,000,000	0.2%
50	North Dakota	103,000,000	0.2%
	District of Columbia	98,000,000	0.2%

Source: U.S. Department of Health and Human Services, Centers for Medicare and Medicaid Services
"State Health Care Expenditures" (http://www.cms.hhs.gov/NationalHealthExpendData/)
*By state of residence. Includes services of licensed professionals such as chiropractors, optometrists, podiatrists, and independently practicing nurses. Also includes Medicare ambulance services.

Percent of Total Personal Health Care Expenditures Spent on Other Professional Health Care Services in 2004
National Percent = 3.4%*

ALPHA ORDER

RANK	STATE	PERCENT
45	Alabama	2.9
8	Alaska	3.9
6	Arizona	4.0
18	Arkansas	3.5
12	California	3.7
3	Colorado	4.3
8	Connecticut	3.9
6	Delaware	4.0
12	Florida	3.7
41	Georgia	3.0
16	Hawaii	3.6
1	Idaho	4.9
18	Illinois	3.5
41	Indiana	3.0
18	Iowa	3.5
27	Kansas	3.4
18	Kentucky	3.5
36	Louisiana	3.1
18	Maine	3.5
29	Maryland	3.3
41	Massachusetts	3.0
12	Michigan	3.7
27	Minnesota	3.4
50	Mississippi	2.4
36	Missouri	3.1
12	Montana	3.7
36	Nebraska	3.1
18	Nevada	3.5
33	New Hampshire	3.2
10	New Jersey	3.8
10	New Mexico	3.8
47	New York	2.8
41	North Carolina	3.0
47	North Dakota	2.8
18	Ohio	3.5
33	Oklahoma	3.2
5	Oregon	4.1
16	Pennsylvania	3.6
45	Rhode Island	2.9
49	South Carolina	2.5
29	South Dakota	3.3
33	Tennessee	3.2
36	Texas	3.1
18	Utah	3.5
18	Vermont	3.5
36	Virginia	3.1
3	Washington	4.3
29	West Virginia	3.3
29	Wisconsin	3.3
2	Wyoming	4.4

RANK ORDER

RANK	STATE	PERCENT
1	Idaho	4.9
2	Wyoming	4.4
3	Colorado	4.3
3	Washington	4.3
5	Oregon	4.1
6	Arizona	4.0
6	Delaware	4.0
8	Alaska	3.9
8	Connecticut	3.9
10	New Jersey	3.8
10	New Mexico	3.8
12	California	3.7
12	Florida	3.7
12	Michigan	3.7
12	Montana	3.7
16	Hawaii	3.6
16	Pennsylvania	3.6
18	Arkansas	3.5
18	Illinois	3.5
18	Iowa	3.5
18	Kentucky	3.5
18	Maine	3.5
18	Nevada	3.5
18	Ohio	3.5
18	Utah	3.5
18	Vermont	3.5
27	Kansas	3.4
27	Minnesota	3.4
29	Maryland	3.3
29	South Dakota	3.3
29	West Virginia	3.3
29	Wisconsin	3.3
33	New Hampshire	3.2
33	Oklahoma	3.2
33	Tennessee	3.2
36	Louisiana	3.1
36	Missouri	3.1
36	Nebraska	3.1
36	Texas	3.1
36	Virginia	3.1
41	Georgia	3.0
41	Indiana	3.0
41	Massachusetts	3.0
41	North Carolina	3.0
45	Alabama	2.9
45	Rhode Island	2.9
47	New York	2.8
47	North Dakota	2.8
49	South Carolina	2.5
50	Mississippi	2.4

District of Columbia — 2.0

Source: CQ Press using data from U.S. Department of Health and Human Services, Centers for Medicare and Medicaid Services "State Health Care Expenditures" (http://www.cms.hhs.gov/NationalHealthExpendData/)

*By state of residence. Includes services of licensed professionals such as chiropractors, optometrists, podiatrists, and independently practicing nurses. Also includes Medicare ambulance services.

Per Capita Expenditures for Other Professional Health Care Services in 2004

National Per Capita = $179*

ALPHA ORDER				RANK ORDER		
RANK	STATE	PER CAPITA		RANK	STATE	PER CAPITA
44	Alabama	$151		1	Delaware	$253
2	Alaska	249		2	Alaska	249
37	Arizona	162		3	Connecticut	245
35	Arkansas	168		4	Maine	232
33	California	172		5	Wyoming	231
11	Colorado	204		6	New Jersey	221
3	Connecticut	245		7	Washington	220
1	Delaware	253		8	Idaho	217
12	Florida	203		9	Vermont	212
47	Georgia	140		10	Pennsylvania	211
27	Hawaii	178		11	Colorado	204
8	Idaho	217		12	Florida	203
22	Illinois	186		13	Massachusetts	200
39	Indiana	161		14	Ohio	199
19	Iowa	188		14	Oregon	199
26	Kansas	182		14	West Virginia	199
18	Kentucky	192		17	Minnesota	197
42	Louisiana	157		18	Kentucky	192
4	Maine	232		19	Iowa	188
22	Maryland	186		19	Michigan	188
13	Massachusetts	200		21	Wisconsin	187
19	Michigan	188		22	Illinois	186
17	Minnesota	197		22	Maryland	186
50	Mississippi	121		22	Montana	186
36	Missouri	167		22	New York	186
22	Montana	186		26	Kansas	182
32	Nebraska	174		27	Hawaii	178
40	Nevada	159		27	Rhode Island	178
29	New Hampshire	176		29	New Hampshire	176
6	New Jersey	221		29	South Dakota	176
34	New Mexico	169		29	Tennessee	176
22	New York	186		32	Nebraska	174
42	North Carolina	157		33	California	172
37	North Dakota	162		34	New Mexico	169
14	Ohio	199		35	Arkansas	168
40	Oklahoma	159		36	Missouri	167
14	Oregon	199		37	Arizona	162
10	Pennsylvania	211		37	North Dakota	162
27	Rhode Island	178		39	Indiana	161
49	South Carolina	127		40	Nevada	159
29	South Dakota	176		40	Oklahoma	159
29	Tennessee	176		42	Louisiana	157
46	Texas	141		42	North Carolina	157
48	Utah	137		44	Alabama	151
9	Vermont	212		45	Virginia	150
45	Virginia	150		46	Texas	141
7	Washington	220		47	Georgia	140
14	West Virginia	199		48	Utah	137
21	Wisconsin	187		49	South Carolina	127
5	Wyoming	231		50	Mississippi	121
					District of Columbia	170

Source: U.S. Department of Health and Human Services, Centers for Medicare and Medicaid Services
"State Health Care Expenditures" (http://www.cms.hhs.gov/NationalHealthExpendData/)
*By state of residence. Includes services of licensed professionals such as chiropractors, optometrists, podiatrists, and independently practicing nurses. Also includes Medicare ambulance services.

Expenditures for Nursing Home Care in 2004

National Total = $115,015,000,000*

ALPHA ORDER

RANK	STATE	EXPENDITURES	% of USA
25	Alabama	$1,475,000,000	1.3%
50	Alaska	80,000,000	0.1%
32	Arizona	1,023,000,000	0.9%
31	Arkansas	1,040,000,000	0.9%
2	California	8,424,000,000	7.3%
27	Colorado	1,178,000,000	1.0%
13	Connecticut	2,711,000,000	2.4%
40	Delaware	409,000,000	0.4%
5	Florida	6,503,000,000	5.7%
19	Georgia	2,272,000,000	2.0%
47	Hawaii	293,000,000	0.3%
44	Idaho	361,000,000	0.3%
7	Illinois	5,173,000,000	4.5%
12	Indiana	2,871,000,000	2.5%
22	Iowa	1,623,000,000	1.4%
29	Kansas	1,110,000,000	1.0%
24	Kentucky	1,526,000,000	1.3%
23	Louisiana	1,617,000,000	1.4%
36	Maine	630,000,000	0.5%
16	Maryland	2,419,000,000	2.1%
9	Massachusetts	4,124,000,000	3.6%
11	Michigan	3,193,000,000	2.8%
18	Minnesota	2,367,000,000	2.1%
30	Mississippi	1,094,000,000	1.0%
14	Missouri	2,479,000,000	2.2%
46	Montana	322,000,000	0.3%
34	Nebraska	860,000,000	0.7%
45	Nevada	341,000,000	0.3%
38	New Hampshire	548,000,000	0.5%
8	New Jersey	4,261,000,000	3.7%
43	New Mexico	372,000,000	0.3%
1	New York	13,364,000,000	11.6%
10	North Carolina	3,354,000,000	2.9%
42	North Dakota	387,000,000	0.3%
4	Ohio	6,834,000,000	5.9%
28	Oklahoma	1,157,000,000	1.0%
33	Oregon	897,000,000	0.8%
3	Pennsylvania	7,562,000,000	6.6%
37	Rhode Island	616,000,000	0.5%
26	South Carolina	1,236,000,000	1.1%
41	South Dakota	406,000,000	0.4%
20	Tennessee	2,211,000,000	1.9%
6	Texas	5,600,000,000	4.9%
39	Utah	428,000,000	0.4%
48	Vermont	235,000,000	0.2%
15	Virginia	2,448,000,000	2.1%
21	Washington	1,860,000,000	1.6%
35	West Virginia	716,000,000	0.6%
17	Wisconsin	2,405,000,000	2.1%
49	Wyoming	150,000,000	0.1%

RANK ORDER

RANK	STATE	EXPENDITURES	% of USA
1	New York	$13,364,000,000	11.6%
2	California	8,424,000,000	7.3%
3	Pennsylvania	7,562,000,000	6.6%
4	Ohio	6,834,000,000	5.9%
5	Florida	6,503,000,000	5.7%
6	Texas	5,600,000,000	4.9%
7	Illinois	5,173,000,000	4.5%
8	New Jersey	4,261,000,000	3.7%
9	Massachusetts	4,124,000,000	3.6%
10	North Carolina	3,354,000,000	2.9%
11	Michigan	3,193,000,000	2.8%
12	Indiana	2,871,000,000	2.5%
13	Connecticut	2,711,000,000	2.4%
14	Missouri	2,479,000,000	2.2%
15	Virginia	2,448,000,000	2.1%
16	Maryland	2,419,000,000	2.1%
17	Wisconsin	2,405,000,000	2.1%
18	Minnesota	2,367,000,000	2.1%
19	Georgia	2,272,000,000	2.0%
20	Tennessee	2,211,000,000	1.9%
21	Washington	1,860,000,000	1.6%
22	Iowa	1,623,000,000	1.4%
23	Louisiana	1,617,000,000	1.4%
24	Kentucky	1,526,000,000	1.3%
25	Alabama	1,475,000,000	1.3%
26	South Carolina	1,236,000,000	1.1%
27	Colorado	1,178,000,000	1.0%
28	Oklahoma	1,157,000,000	1.0%
29	Kansas	1,110,000,000	1.0%
30	Mississippi	1,094,000,000	1.0%
31	Arkansas	1,040,000,000	0.9%
32	Arizona	1,023,000,000	0.9%
33	Oregon	897,000,000	0.8%
34	Nebraska	860,000,000	0.7%
35	West Virginia	716,000,000	0.6%
36	Maine	630,000,000	0.5%
37	Rhode Island	616,000,000	0.5%
38	New Hampshire	548,000,000	0.5%
39	Utah	428,000,000	0.4%
40	Delaware	409,000,000	0.4%
41	South Dakota	406,000,000	0.4%
42	North Dakota	387,000,000	0.3%
43	New Mexico	372,000,000	0.3%
44	Idaho	361,000,000	0.3%
45	Nevada	341,000,000	0.3%
46	Montana	322,000,000	0.3%
47	Hawaii	293,000,000	0.3%
48	Vermont	235,000,000	0.2%
49	Wyoming	150,000,000	0.1%
50	Alaska	80,000,000	0.1%
	District of Columbia	452,000,000	0.4%

Source: U.S. Department of Health and Human Services, Centers for Medicare and Medicaid Services
   "State Health Care Expenditures" (http://www.cms.hhs.gov/NationalHealthExpendData/)
*By state of residence. Includes all freestanding nursing homes. Does not include nursing home services provided in long-term care units of hospitals.

Percent of Total Personal Health Care Expenditures
Spent on Nursing Home Care in 2004
National Percent = 7.4%*

ALPHA ORDER

RANK	STATE	PERCENT
33	Alabama	6.4
50	Alaska	1.9
48	Arizona	4.3
15	Arkansas	7.8
43	California	5.1
41	Colorado	5.4
1	Connecticut	12.2
15	Delaware	7.8
27	Florida	6.8
40	Georgia	5.5
45	Hawaii	4.7
37	Idaho	5.8
19	Illinois	7.7
11	Indiana	8.7
6	Iowa	10.2
22	Kansas	7.5
30	Kentucky	6.7
25	Louisiana	7.1
24	Maine	7.3
15	Maryland	7.8
8	Massachusetts	9.6
34	Michigan	6.3
13	Minnesota	8.0
22	Mississippi	7.5
14	Missouri	7.9
27	Montana	6.8
10	Nebraska	8.8
49	Nevada	3.2
15	New Hampshire	7.8
12	New Jersey	8.5
46	New Mexico	4.4
2	New York	10.6
21	North Carolina	7.6
3	North Dakota	10.5
4	Ohio	10.4
30	Oklahoma	6.7
43	Oregon	5.1
5	Pennsylvania	10.3
9	Rhode Island	9.2
37	South Carolina	5.8
7	South Dakota	9.9
26	Tennessee	6.9
41	Texas	5.4
46	Utah	4.4
35	Vermont	6.2
27	Virginia	6.8
36	Washington	5.9
32	West Virginia	6.6
19	Wisconsin	7.7
39	Wyoming	5.6

RANK ORDER

RANK	STATE	PERCENT
1	Connecticut	12.2
2	New York	10.6
3	North Dakota	10.5
4	Ohio	10.4
5	Pennsylvania	10.3
6	Iowa	10.2
7	South Dakota	9.9
8	Massachusetts	9.6
9	Rhode Island	9.2
10	Nebraska	8.8
11	Indiana	8.7
12	New Jersey	8.5
13	Minnesota	8.0
14	Missouri	7.9
15	Arkansas	7.8
15	Delaware	7.8
15	Maryland	7.8
15	New Hampshire	7.8
19	Illinois	7.7
19	Wisconsin	7.7
21	North Carolina	7.6
22	Kansas	7.5
22	Mississippi	7.5
24	Maine	7.3
25	Louisiana	7.1
26	Tennessee	6.9
27	Florida	6.8
27	Montana	6.8
27	Virginia	6.8
30	Kentucky	6.7
30	Oklahoma	6.7
32	West Virginia	6.6
33	Alabama	6.4
34	Michigan	6.3
35	Vermont	6.2
36	Washington	5.9
37	Idaho	5.8
37	South Carolina	5.8
39	Wyoming	5.6
40	Georgia	5.5
41	Colorado	5.4
41	Texas	5.4
43	California	5.1
43	Oregon	5.1
45	Hawaii	4.7
46	New Mexico	4.4
46	Utah	4.4
48	Arizona	4.3
49	Nevada	3.2
50	Alaska	1.9

District of Columbia   9.4

Source: CQ Press using data from U.S. Department of Health and Human Services, Centers for Medicare and Medicaid Services "State Health Care Expenditures" (http://www.cms.hhs.gov/NationalHealthExpendData/)
*By state of residence. Includes all freestanding nursing homes. Does not include nursing home services provided in long-term care units of hospitals.

Per Capita Expenditures for Nursing Home Care in 2004

National Per Capita = $392*

ALPHA ORDER

RANK	STATE	PER CAPITA
34	Alabama	$326
50	Alaska	122
47	Arizona	178
24	Arkansas	378
44	California	235
40	Colorado	256
1	Connecticut	776
10	Delaware	493
28	Florida	374
41	Georgia	254
45	Hawaii	233
39	Idaho	259
20	Illinois	407
15	Indiana	461
8	Iowa	549
21	Kansas	406
29	Kentucky	369
30	Louisiana	360
13	Maine	480
17	Maryland	436
3	Massachusetts	641
35	Michigan	316
14	Minnesota	465
24	Mississippi	378
18	Missouri	431
31	Montana	348
11	Nebraska	492
49	Nevada	146
19	New Hampshire	422
12	New Jersey	491
46	New Mexico	196
2	New York	693
23	North Carolina	393
5	North Dakota	608
6	Ohio	596
32	Oklahoma	329
42	Oregon	250
4	Pennsylvania	611
7	Rhode Island	570
38	South Carolina	295
9	South Dakota	527
27	Tennessee	376
43	Texas	249
48	Utah	177
24	Vermont	378
33	Virginia	328
36	Washington	300
22	West Virginia	395
16	Wisconsin	437
37	Wyoming	297

RANK ORDER

RANK	STATE	PER CAPITA
1	Connecticut	$776
2	New York	693
3	Massachusetts	641
4	Pennsylvania	611
5	North Dakota	608
6	Ohio	596
7	Rhode Island	570
8	Iowa	549
9	South Dakota	527
10	Delaware	493
11	Nebraska	492
12	New Jersey	491
13	Maine	480
14	Minnesota	465
15	Indiana	461
16	Wisconsin	437
17	Maryland	436
18	Missouri	431
19	New Hampshire	422
20	Illinois	407
21	Kansas	406
22	West Virginia	395
23	North Carolina	393
24	Arkansas	378
24	Mississippi	378
24	Vermont	378
27	Tennessee	376
28	Florida	374
29	Kentucky	369
30	Louisiana	360
31	Montana	348
32	Oklahoma	329
33	Virginia	328
34	Alabama	326
35	Michigan	316
36	Washington	300
37	Wyoming	297
38	South Carolina	295
39	Idaho	259
40	Colorado	256
41	Georgia	254
42	Oregon	250
43	Texas	249
44	California	235
45	Hawaii	233
46	New Mexico	196
47	Arizona	178
48	Utah	177
49	Nevada	146
50	Alaska	122
	District of Columbia	780

Source: U.S. Department of Health and Human Services, Centers for Medicare and Medicaid Services
   "State Health Care Expenditures" (http://www.cms.hhs.gov/NationalHealthExpendData/)
*By state of residence. Includes all freestanding nursing homes. Does not include nursing home services provided in long-term care units of hospitals.

Expenditures for Home Health Care in 2004

National Total = $42,710,000,000*

ALPHA ORDER

RANK	STATE	EXPENDITURES	% of USA
18	Alabama	$661,000,000	1.5%
47	Alaska	64,000,000	0.1%
19	Arizona	656,000,000	1.5%
31	Arkansas	325,000,000	0.8%
2	California	5,537,000,000	13.0%
30	Colorado	367,000,000	0.9%
15	Connecticut	708,000,000	1.7%
43	Delaware	94,000,000	0.2%
4	Florida	2,876,000,000	6.7%
12	Georgia	876,000,000	2.1%
42	Hawaii	105,000,000	0.2%
41	Idaho	115,000,000	0.3%
11	Illinois	1,269,000,000	3.0%
25	Indiana	509,000,000	1.2%
32	Iowa	310,000,000	0.7%
34	Kansas	241,000,000	0.6%
23	Kentucky	531,000,000	1.2%
21	Louisiana	624,000,000	1.5%
38	Maine	173,000,000	0.4%
24	Maryland	511,000,000	1.2%
5	Massachusetts	1,743,000,000	4.1%
10	Michigan	1,326,000,000	3.1%
17	Minnesota	679,000,000	1.6%
26	Mississippi	484,000,000	1.1%
15	Missouri	708,000,000	1.7%
45	Montana	89,000,000	0.2%
46	Nebraska	79,000,000	0.2%
35	Nevada	231,000,000	0.5%
39	New Hampshire	168,000,000	0.4%
8	New Jersey	1,427,000,000	3.3%
28	New Mexico	451,000,000	1.1%
1	New York	6,021,000,000	14.1%
9	North Carolina	1,413,000,000	3.3%
50	North Dakota	18,000,000	0.0%
7	Ohio	1,519,000,000	3.6%
27	Oklahoma	464,000,000	1.1%
36	Oregon	201,000,000	0.5%
6	Pennsylvania	1,527,000,000	3.6%
40	Rhode Island	116,000,000	0.3%
29	South Carolina	422,000,000	1.0%
49	South Dakota	20,000,000	0.0%
14	Tennessee	738,000,000	1.7%
3	Texas	3,604,000,000	8.4%
33	Utah	245,000,000	0.6%
43	Vermont	94,000,000	0.2%
22	Virginia	605,000,000	1.4%
13	Washington	823,000,000	1.9%
37	West Virginia	197,000,000	0.5%
20	Wisconsin	642,000,000	1.5%
48	Wyoming	28,000,000	0.1%

RANK ORDER

RANK	STATE	EXPENDITURES	% of USA
1	New York	$6,021,000,000	14.1%
2	California	5,537,000,000	13.0%
3	Texas	3,604,000,000	8.4%
4	Florida	2,876,000,000	6.7%
5	Massachusetts	1,743,000,000	4.1%
6	Pennsylvania	1,527,000,000	3.6%
7	Ohio	1,519,000,000	3.6%
8	New Jersey	1,427,000,000	3.3%
9	North Carolina	1,413,000,000	3.3%
10	Michigan	1,326,000,000	3.1%
11	Illinois	1,269,000,000	3.0%
12	Georgia	876,000,000	2.1%
13	Washington	823,000,000	1.9%
14	Tennessee	738,000,000	1.7%
15	Connecticut	708,000,000	1.7%
15	Missouri	708,000,000	1.7%
17	Minnesota	679,000,000	1.6%
18	Alabama	661,000,000	1.5%
19	Arizona	656,000,000	1.5%
20	Wisconsin	642,000,000	1.5%
21	Louisiana	624,000,000	1.5%
22	Virginia	605,000,000	1.4%
23	Kentucky	531,000,000	1.2%
24	Maryland	511,000,000	1.2%
25	Indiana	509,000,000	1.2%
26	Mississippi	484,000,000	1.1%
27	Oklahoma	464,000,000	1.1%
28	New Mexico	451,000,000	1.1%
29	South Carolina	422,000,000	1.0%
30	Colorado	367,000,000	0.9%
31	Arkansas	325,000,000	0.8%
32	Iowa	310,000,000	0.7%
33	Utah	245,000,000	0.6%
34	Kansas	241,000,000	0.6%
35	Nevada	231,000,000	0.5%
36	Oregon	201,000,000	0.5%
37	West Virginia	197,000,000	0.5%
38	Maine	173,000,000	0.4%
39	New Hampshire	168,000,000	0.4%
40	Rhode Island	116,000,000	0.3%
41	Idaho	115,000,000	0.3%
42	Hawaii	105,000,000	0.2%
43	Delaware	94,000,000	0.2%
43	Vermont	94,000,000	0.2%
45	Montana	89,000,000	0.2%
46	Nebraska	79,000,000	0.2%
47	Alaska	64,000,000	0.1%
48	Wyoming	28,000,000	0.1%
49	South Dakota	20,000,000	0.0%
50	North Dakota	18,000,000	0.0%
	District of Columbia	78,000,000	0.2%

Source: U.S. Department of Health and Human Services, Centers for Medicare and Medicaid Services
   "State Health Care Expenditures" (http://www.cms.hhs.gov/NationalHealthExpendData/)
*By state of residence. Includes spending for services and products by public and private freestanding home health agencies.
Excludes home health care services provided by hospital-based agencies which are included in hospital expenditures.

Percent of Total Personal Health Care Expenditures
Spent on Home Health Care in 2004
National Percent = 2.8%*

<table>
<tr><td colspan="3">ALPHA ORDER</td><td colspan="3">RANK ORDER</td></tr>
<tr><td>RANK</td><td>STATE</td><td>PERCENT</td><td>RANK</td><td>STATE</td><td>PERCENT</td></tr>
<tr><td>10</td><td>Alabama</td><td>2.8</td><td>1</td><td>New Mexico</td><td>5.3</td></tr>
<tr><td>44</td><td>Alaska</td><td>1.5</td><td>2</td><td>New York</td><td>4.8</td></tr>
<tr><td>10</td><td>Arizona</td><td>2.8</td><td>3</td><td>Massachusetts</td><td>4.1</td></tr>
<tr><td>19</td><td>Arkansas</td><td>2.4</td><td>4</td><td>Texas</td><td>3.5</td></tr>
<tr><td>5</td><td>California</td><td>3.3</td><td>5</td><td>California</td><td>3.3</td></tr>
<tr><td>38</td><td>Colorado</td><td>1.7</td><td>5</td><td>Mississippi</td><td>3.3</td></tr>
<tr><td>7</td><td>Connecticut</td><td>3.2</td><td>7</td><td>Connecticut</td><td>3.2</td></tr>
<tr><td>36</td><td>Delaware</td><td>1.8</td><td>7</td><td>North Carolina</td><td>3.2</td></tr>
<tr><td>9</td><td>Florida</td><td>3.0</td><td>9</td><td>Florida</td><td>3.0</td></tr>
<tr><td>27</td><td>Georgia</td><td>2.1</td><td>10</td><td>Alabama</td><td>2.8</td></tr>
<tr><td>38</td><td>Hawaii</td><td>1.7</td><td>10</td><td>Arizona</td><td>2.8</td></tr>
<tr><td>33</td><td>Idaho</td><td>1.9</td><td>10</td><td>Louisiana</td><td>2.8</td></tr>
<tr><td>33</td><td>Illinois</td><td>1.9</td><td>10</td><td>New Jersey</td><td>2.8</td></tr>
<tr><td>44</td><td>Indiana</td><td>1.5</td><td>14</td><td>Oklahoma</td><td>2.7</td></tr>
<tr><td>30</td><td>Iowa</td><td>2.0</td><td>15</td><td>Michigan</td><td>2.6</td></tr>
<tr><td>42</td><td>Kansas</td><td>1.6</td><td>15</td><td>Washington</td><td>2.6</td></tr>
<tr><td>21</td><td>Kentucky</td><td>2.3</td><td>17</td><td>Utah</td><td>2.5</td></tr>
<tr><td>10</td><td>Louisiana</td><td>2.8</td><td>17</td><td>Vermont</td><td>2.5</td></tr>
<tr><td>30</td><td>Maine</td><td>2.0</td><td>19</td><td>Arkansas</td><td>2.4</td></tr>
<tr><td>42</td><td>Maryland</td><td>1.6</td><td>19</td><td>New Hampshire</td><td>2.4</td></tr>
<tr><td>3</td><td>Massachusetts</td><td>4.1</td><td>21</td><td>Kentucky</td><td>2.3</td></tr>
<tr><td>15</td><td>Michigan</td><td>2.6</td><td>21</td><td>Minnesota</td><td>2.3</td></tr>
<tr><td>21</td><td>Minnesota</td><td>2.3</td><td>21</td><td>Missouri</td><td>2.3</td></tr>
<tr><td>5</td><td>Mississippi</td><td>3.3</td><td>21</td><td>Ohio</td><td>2.3</td></tr>
<tr><td>21</td><td>Missouri</td><td>2.3</td><td>21</td><td>Tennessee</td><td>2.3</td></tr>
<tr><td>33</td><td>Montana</td><td>1.9</td><td>26</td><td>Nevada</td><td>2.2</td></tr>
<tr><td>48</td><td>Nebraska</td><td>0.8</td><td>27</td><td>Georgia</td><td>2.1</td></tr>
<tr><td>26</td><td>Nevada</td><td>2.2</td><td>27</td><td>Pennsylvania</td><td>2.1</td></tr>
<tr><td>19</td><td>New Hampshire</td><td>2.4</td><td>27</td><td>Wisconsin</td><td>2.1</td></tr>
<tr><td>10</td><td>New Jersey</td><td>2.8</td><td>30</td><td>Iowa</td><td>2.0</td></tr>
<tr><td>1</td><td>New Mexico</td><td>5.3</td><td>30</td><td>Maine</td><td>2.0</td></tr>
<tr><td>2</td><td>New York</td><td>4.8</td><td>30</td><td>South Carolina</td><td>2.0</td></tr>
<tr><td>7</td><td>North Carolina</td><td>3.2</td><td>33</td><td>Idaho</td><td>1.9</td></tr>
<tr><td>49</td><td>North Dakota</td><td>0.5</td><td>33</td><td>Illinois</td><td>1.9</td></tr>
<tr><td>21</td><td>Ohio</td><td>2.3</td><td>33</td><td>Montana</td><td>1.9</td></tr>
<tr><td>14</td><td>Oklahoma</td><td>2.7</td><td>36</td><td>Delaware</td><td>1.8</td></tr>
<tr><td>46</td><td>Oregon</td><td>1.1</td><td>36</td><td>West Virginia</td><td>1.8</td></tr>
<tr><td>27</td><td>Pennsylvania</td><td>2.1</td><td>38</td><td>Colorado</td><td>1.7</td></tr>
<tr><td>38</td><td>Rhode Island</td><td>1.7</td><td>38</td><td>Hawaii</td><td>1.7</td></tr>
<tr><td>30</td><td>South Carolina</td><td>2.0</td><td>38</td><td>Rhode Island</td><td>1.7</td></tr>
<tr><td>49</td><td>South Dakota</td><td>0.5</td><td>38</td><td>Virginia</td><td>1.7</td></tr>
<tr><td>21</td><td>Tennessee</td><td>2.3</td><td>42</td><td>Kansas</td><td>1.6</td></tr>
<tr><td>4</td><td>Texas</td><td>3.5</td><td>42</td><td>Maryland</td><td>1.6</td></tr>
<tr><td>17</td><td>Utah</td><td>2.5</td><td>44</td><td>Alaska</td><td>1.5</td></tr>
<tr><td>17</td><td>Vermont</td><td>2.5</td><td>44</td><td>Indiana</td><td>1.5</td></tr>
<tr><td>38</td><td>Virginia</td><td>1.7</td><td>46</td><td>Oregon</td><td>1.1</td></tr>
<tr><td>15</td><td>Washington</td><td>2.6</td><td>46</td><td>Wyoming</td><td>1.1</td></tr>
<tr><td>36</td><td>West Virginia</td><td>1.8</td><td>48</td><td>Nebraska</td><td>0.8</td></tr>
<tr><td>27</td><td>Wisconsin</td><td>2.1</td><td>49</td><td>North Dakota</td><td>0.5</td></tr>
<tr><td>46</td><td>Wyoming</td><td>1.1</td><td>49</td><td>South Dakota</td><td>0.5</td></tr>
<tr><td></td><td></td><td></td><td></td><td>District of Columbia</td><td>1.6</td></tr>
</table>

Source: CQ Press using data from U.S. Department of Health and Human Services, Centers for Medicare and Medicaid Services
"State Health Care Expenditures" (http://www.cms.hhs.gov/NationalHealthExpendData/)

*By state of residence. Includes spending for services and products by public and private freestanding home health agencies.
Excludes home health care services provided by hospital-based agencies which are included in hospital expenditures.

Per Capita Expenditures for Home Health Care in 2004

National Per Capita = $145*

ALPHA ORDER				RANK ORDER		
RANK	STATE	PER CAPITA		RANK	STATE	PER CAPITA
12	Alabama	$146		1	New York	$312
36	Alaska	98		2	Massachusetts	271
27	Arizona	114		3	New Mexico	237
25	Arkansas	118		4	Connecticut	203
10	California	154		5	Mississippi	167
45	Colorado	80		6	Florida	166
4	Connecticut	203		6	North Carolina	166
28	Delaware	113		8	New Jersey	164
6	Florida	166		9	Texas	160
36	Georgia	98		10	California	154
41	Hawaii	84		11	Vermont	152
42	Idaho	82		12	Alabama	146
34	Illinois	100		13	Louisiana	139
42	Indiana	82		14	Minnesota	133
31	Iowa	105		14	Ohio	133
40	Kansas	88		14	Washington	133
21	Kentucky	128		17	Maine	132
13	Louisiana	139		17	Oklahoma	132
17	Maine	132		19	Michigan	131
39	Maryland	92		20	New Hampshire	130
2	Massachusetts	271		21	Kentucky	128
19	Michigan	131		22	Tennessee	125
14	Minnesota	133		23	Missouri	123
5	Mississippi	167		23	Pennsylvania	123
23	Missouri	123		25	Arkansas	118
38	Montana	96		26	Wisconsin	117
48	Nebraska	45		27	Arizona	114
35	Nevada	99		28	Delaware	113
20	New Hampshire	130		29	West Virginia	109
8	New Jersey	164		30	Rhode Island	107
3	New Mexico	237		31	Iowa	105
1	New York	312		32	South Carolina	101
6	North Carolina	166		32	Utah	101
49	North Dakota	28		34	Illinois	100
14	Ohio	133		35	Nevada	99
17	Oklahoma	132		36	Alaska	98
46	Oregon	56		36	Georgia	98
23	Pennsylvania	123		38	Montana	96
30	Rhode Island	107		39	Maryland	92
32	South Carolina	101		40	Kansas	88
50	South Dakota	26		41	Hawaii	84
22	Tennessee	125		42	Idaho	82
9	Texas	160		42	Indiana	82
32	Utah	101		44	Virginia	81
11	Vermont	152		45	Colorado	80
44	Virginia	81		46	Oregon	56
14	Washington	133		47	Wyoming	55
29	West Virginia	109		48	Nebraska	45
26	Wisconsin	117		49	North Dakota	28
47	Wyoming	55		50	South Dakota	26
					District of Columbia	134

Source: U.S. Department of Health and Human Services, Centers for Medicare and Medicaid Services
   "State Health Care Expenditures" (http://www.cms.hhs.gov/NationalHealthExpendData/)
*By state of residence. Includes spending for services and products by public and private freestanding home health agencies.
Excludes home health care services provided by hospital-based agencies which are included in hospital expenditures.

Expenditures for Drugs and Other Medical Nondurables in 2004

National Total = $222,412,000,000*

ALPHA ORDER					RANK ORDER			

RANK	STATE	EXPENDITURES	% of USA		RANK	STATE	EXPENDITURES	% of USA
18	Alabama	$4,241,000,000	1.9%		1	California	$20,799,000,000	9.4%
49	Alaska	418,000,000	0.2%		2	New York	17,722,000,000	8.0%
24	Arizona	3,378,000,000	1.5%		3	Florida	15,545,000,000	7.0%
32	Arkansas	1,938,000,000	0.9%		4	Texas	13,870,000,000	6.2%
1	California	20,799,000,000	9.4%		5	Pennsylvania	11,086,000,000	5.0%
28	Colorado	2,346,000,000	1.1%		6	Ohio	9,205,000,000	4.1%
26	Connecticut	3,246,000,000	1.5%		7	Illinois	9,098,000,000	4.1%
44	Delaware	769,000,000	0.3%		8	New Jersey	8,317,000,000	3.7%
3	Florida	15,545,000,000	7.0%		9	Michigan	7,790,000,000	3.5%
11	Georgia	6,493,000,000	2.9%		10	North Carolina	7,445,000,000	3.3%
42	Hawaii	925,000,000	0.4%		11	Georgia	6,493,000,000	2.9%
43	Idaho	834,000,000	0.4%		12	Tennessee	5,785,000,000	2.6%
7	Illinois	9,098,000,000	4.1%		13	Virginia	5,651,000,000	2.5%
15	Indiana	4,951,000,000	2.2%		14	Massachusetts	5,462,000,000	2.5%
31	Iowa	2,021,000,000	0.9%		15	Indiana	4,951,000,000	2.2%
33	Kansas	1,897,000,000	0.9%		16	Missouri	4,664,000,000	2.1%
19	Kentucky	3,917,000,000	1.8%		17	Maryland	4,595,000,000	2.1%
23	Louisiana	3,586,000,000	1.6%		18	Alabama	4,241,000,000	1.9%
40	Maine	1,052,000,000	0.5%		19	Kentucky	3,917,000,000	1.8%
17	Maryland	4,595,000,000	2.1%		20	Wisconsin	3,831,000,000	1.7%
14	Massachusetts	5,462,000,000	2.5%		21	Washington	3,792,000,000	1.7%
9	Michigan	7,790,000,000	3.5%		22	Minnesota	3,639,000,000	1.6%
22	Minnesota	3,639,000,000	1.6%		23	Louisiana	3,586,000,000	1.6%
29	Mississippi	2,208,000,000	1.0%		24	Arizona	3,378,000,000	1.5%
16	Missouri	4,664,000,000	2.1%		25	South Carolina	3,369,000,000	1.5%
46	Montana	499,000,000	0.2%		26	Connecticut	3,246,000,000	1.5%
37	Nebraska	1,288,000,000	0.6%		27	Oklahoma	2,472,000,000	1.1%
34	Nevada	1,786,000,000	0.8%		28	Colorado	2,346,000,000	1.1%
41	New Hampshire	962,000,000	0.4%		29	Mississippi	2,208,000,000	1.0%
8	New Jersey	8,317,000,000	3.7%		30	Oregon	2,042,000,000	0.9%
38	New Mexico	1,127,000,000	0.5%		31	Iowa	2,021,000,000	0.9%
2	New York	17,722,000,000	8.0%		32	Arkansas	1,938,000,000	0.9%
10	North Carolina	7,445,000,000	3.3%		33	Kansas	1,897,000,000	0.9%
45	North Dakota	537,000,000	0.2%		34	Nevada	1,786,000,000	0.8%
6	Ohio	9,205,000,000	4.1%		35	West Virginia	1,627,000,000	0.7%
27	Oklahoma	2,472,000,000	1.1%		36	Utah	1,592,000,000	0.7%
30	Oregon	2,042,000,000	0.9%		37	Nebraska	1,288,000,000	0.6%
5	Pennsylvania	11,086,000,000	5.0%		38	New Mexico	1,127,000,000	0.5%
39	Rhode Island	1,066,000,000	0.5%		39	Rhode Island	1,066,000,000	0.5%
25	South Carolina	3,369,000,000	1.5%		40	Maine	1,052,000,000	0.5%
48	South Dakota	440,000,000	0.2%		41	New Hampshire	962,000,000	0.4%
12	Tennessee	5,785,000,000	2.6%		42	Hawaii	925,000,000	0.4%
4	Texas	13,870,000,000	6.2%		43	Idaho	834,000,000	0.4%
36	Utah	1,592,000,000	0.7%		44	Delaware	769,000,000	0.3%
47	Vermont	444,000,000	0.2%		45	North Dakota	537,000,000	0.2%
13	Virginia	5,651,000,000	2.5%		46	Montana	499,000,000	0.2%
21	Washington	3,792,000,000	1.7%		47	Vermont	444,000,000	0.2%
35	West Virginia	1,627,000,000	0.7%		48	South Dakota	440,000,000	0.2%
20	Wisconsin	3,831,000,000	1.7%		49	Alaska	418,000,000	0.2%
50	Wyoming	302,000,000	0.1%		50	Wyoming	302,000,000	0.1%
						District of Columbia	345,000,000	0.2%

Source: U.S. Department of Health and Human Services, Centers for Medicare and Medicaid Services
 "State Health Care Expenditures" (http://www.cms.hhs.gov/NationalHealthExpendData/)
*Purchases in retail outlets. By state of residence. Includes prescription drugs, over-the-counter drugs, and sundries.

Percent of Total Personal Health Care Expenditures Spent on Drugs and Other Medical Nondurables in 2004
National Percent = 14.3%*

ALPHA ORDER

RANK	STATE	PERCENT
1	Alabama	18.3
50	Alaska	9.9
26	Arizona	14.3
24	Arkansas	14.5
39	California	12.5
47	Colorado	10.8
23	Connecticut	14.6
22	Delaware	14.7
8	Florida	16.3
10	Georgia	15.8
19	Hawaii	14.9
31	Idaho	13.5
31	Illinois	13.5
18	Indiana	15.0
37	Iowa	12.7
36	Kansas	12.9
3	Kentucky	17.3
10	Louisiana	15.8
42	Maine	12.2
21	Maryland	14.8
37	Massachusetts	12.7
14	Michigan	15.3
40	Minnesota	12.3
15	Mississippi	15.1
19	Missouri	14.9
49	Montana	10.6
35	Nebraska	13.2
4	Nevada	16.8
30	New Hampshire	13.6
7	New Jersey	16.5
34	New Mexico	13.3
28	New York	14.1
4	North Carolina	16.8
24	North Dakota	14.5
29	Ohio	14.0
26	Oklahoma	14.3
45	Oregon	11.7
15	Pennsylvania	15.1
9	Rhode Island	16.0
12	South Carolina	15.7
48	South Dakota	10.7
2	Tennessee	18.0
33	Texas	13.4
6	Utah	16.6
44	Vermont	11.8
12	Virginia	15.7
43	Washington	12.0
15	West Virginia	15.1
40	Wisconsin	12.3
46	Wyoming	11.3

RANK ORDER

RANK	STATE	PERCENT
1	Alabama	18.3
2	Tennessee	18.0
3	Kentucky	17.3
4	Nevada	16.8
4	North Carolina	16.8
6	Utah	16.6
7	New Jersey	16.5
8	Florida	16.3
9	Rhode Island	16.0
10	Georgia	15.8
10	Louisiana	15.8
12	South Carolina	15.7
12	Virginia	15.7
14	Michigan	15.3
15	Mississippi	15.1
15	Pennsylvania	15.1
15	West Virginia	15.1
18	Indiana	15.0
19	Hawaii	14.9
19	Missouri	14.9
21	Maryland	14.8
22	Delaware	14.7
23	Connecticut	14.6
24	Arkansas	14.5
24	North Dakota	14.5
26	Arizona	14.3
26	Oklahoma	14.3
28	New York	14.1
29	Ohio	14.0
30	New Hampshire	13.6
31	Idaho	13.5
31	Illinois	13.5
33	Texas	13.4
34	New Mexico	13.3
35	Nebraska	13.2
36	Kansas	12.9
37	Iowa	12.7
37	Massachusetts	12.7
39	California	12.5
40	Minnesota	12.3
40	Wisconsin	12.3
42	Maine	12.2
43	Washington	12.0
44	Vermont	11.8
45	Oregon	11.7
46	Wyoming	11.3
47	Colorado	10.8
48	South Dakota	10.7
49	Montana	10.6
50	Alaska	9.9

District of Columbia 7.2

Source: CQ Press using data from U.S. Department of Health and Human Services, Centers for Medicare and Medicaid Services
"State Health Care Expenditures" (http://www.cms.hhs.gov/NationalHealthExpendData/)
*Purchases in retail outlets. By state of residence. Includes prescription drugs, over-the-counter drugs, and sundries.

Per Capita Expenditures for Drugs and Other Medical Nondurables in 2004

National Per Capita = $757*

ALPHA ORDER

RANK ORDER

RANK	STATE	PER CAPITA
5	Alabama	$939
39	Alaska	636
45	Arizona	588
33	Arkansas	705
46	California	580
50	Colorado	510
6	Connecticut	929
7	Delaware	928
11	Florida	895
29	Georgia	727
28	Hawaii	734
42	Idaho	598
30	Illinois	716
21	Indiana	796
37	Iowa	684
36	Kansas	693
4	Kentucky	946
20	Louisiana	798
19	Maine	800
15	Maryland	827
13	Massachusetts	849
22	Michigan	772
32	Minnesota	714
24	Mississippi	763
16	Missouri	811
49	Montana	539
27	Nebraska	737
23	Nevada	766
26	New Hampshire	741
3	New Jersey	959
44	New Mexico	593
8	New York	919
12	North Carolina	873
14	North Dakota	845
17	Ohio	803
34	Oklahoma	702
48	Oregon	569
10	Pennsylvania	896
1	Rhode Island	988
17	South Carolina	803
47	South Dakota	572
2	Tennessee	983
40	Texas	616
38	Utah	658
31	Vermont	715
25	Virginia	756
41	Washington	611
9	West Virginia	898
35	Wisconsin	697
43	Wyoming	597

RANK	STATE	PER CAPITA
1	Rhode Island	$988
2	Tennessee	983
3	New Jersey	959
4	Kentucky	946
5	Alabama	939
6	Connecticut	929
7	Delaware	928
8	New York	919
9	West Virginia	898
10	Pennsylvania	896
11	Florida	895
12	North Carolina	873
13	Massachusetts	849
14	North Dakota	845
15	Maryland	827
16	Missouri	811
17	Ohio	803
17	South Carolina	803
19	Maine	800
20	Louisiana	798
21	Indiana	796
22	Michigan	772
23	Nevada	766
24	Mississippi	763
25	Virginia	756
26	New Hampshire	741
27	Nebraska	737
28	Hawaii	734
29	Georgia	727
30	Illinois	716
31	Vermont	715
32	Minnesota	714
33	Arkansas	705
34	Oklahoma	702
35	Wisconsin	697
36	Kansas	693
37	Iowa	684
38	Utah	658
39	Alaska	636
40	Texas	616
41	Washington	611
42	Idaho	598
43	Wyoming	597
44	New Mexico	593
45	Arizona	588
46	California	580
47	South Dakota	572
48	Oregon	569
49	Montana	539
50	Colorado	510

District of Columbia 594

Source: U.S. Department of Health and Human Services, Centers for Medicare and Medicaid Services
 "State Health Care Expenditures" (http://www.cms.hhs.gov/NationalHealthExpendData/)
*Purchases in retail outlets. By state of residence. Includes prescription drugs, over-the-counter drugs, and sundries.

Expenditures for Durable Medical Products in 2004

National Total = $23,128,000,000*

ALPHA ORDER

ALPHA ORDER

RANK	STATE	EXPENDITURES	% of USA
24	Alabama	$316,000,000	1.4%
46	Alaska	61,000,000	0.3%
21	Arizona	422,000,000	1.8%
36	Arkansas	164,000,000	0.7%
1	California	2,552,000,000	11.0%
18	Colorado	440,000,000	1.9%
23	Connecticut	317,000,000	1.4%
44	Delaware	78,000,000	0.3%
4	Florida	1,574,000,000	6.8%
11	Georgia	619,000,000	2.7%
39	Hawaii	118,000,000	0.5%
41	Idaho	101,000,000	0.4%
6	Illinois	987,000,000	4.3%
16	Indiana	470,000,000	2.0%
29	Iowa	261,000,000	1.1%
32	Kansas	215,000,000	0.9%
25	Kentucky	281,000,000	1.2%
28	Louisiana	272,000,000	1.2%
42	Maine	92,000,000	0.4%
13	Maryland	503,000,000	2.2%
14	Massachusetts	501,000,000	2.2%
9	Michigan	779,000,000	3.4%
17	Minnesota	456,000,000	2.0%
34	Mississippi	172,000,000	0.7%
20	Missouri	424,000,000	1.8%
43	Montana	85,000,000	0.4%
29	Nebraska	261,000,000	1.1%
33	Nevada	211,000,000	0.9%
40	New Hampshire	116,000,000	0.5%
7	New Jersey	964,000,000	4.2%
37	New Mexico	141,000,000	0.6%
2	New York	1,685,000,000	7.3%
12	North Carolina	524,000,000	2.3%
48	North Dakota	55,000,000	0.2%
8	Ohio	880,000,000	3.8%
31	Oklahoma	239,000,000	1.0%
26	Oregon	279,000,000	1.2%
5	Pennsylvania	1,026,000,000	4.4%
45	Rhode Island	62,000,000	0.3%
27	South Carolina	275,000,000	1.2%
47	South Dakota	60,000,000	0.3%
19	Tennessee	431,000,000	1.9%
3	Texas	1,678,000,000	7.3%
35	Utah	171,000,000	0.7%
50	Vermont	44,000,000	0.2%
10	Virginia	630,000,000	2.7%
15	Washington	485,000,000	2.1%
38	West Virginia	129,000,000	0.6%
22	Wisconsin	419,000,000	1.8%
49	Wyoming	47,000,000	0.2%

RANK ORDER

RANK	STATE	EXPENDITURES	% of USA
1	California	$2,552,000,000	11.0%
2	New York	1,685,000,000	7.3%
3	Texas	1,678,000,000	7.3%
4	Florida	1,574,000,000	6.8%
5	Pennsylvania	1,026,000,000	4.4%
6	Illinois	987,000,000	4.3%
7	New Jersey	964,000,000	4.2%
8	Ohio	880,000,000	3.8%
9	Michigan	779,000,000	3.4%
10	Virginia	630,000,000	2.7%
11	Georgia	619,000,000	2.7%
12	North Carolina	524,000,000	2.3%
13	Maryland	503,000,000	2.2%
14	Massachusetts	501,000,000	2.2%
15	Washington	485,000,000	2.1%
16	Indiana	470,000,000	2.0%
17	Minnesota	456,000,000	2.0%
18	Colorado	440,000,000	1.9%
19	Tennessee	431,000,000	1.9%
20	Missouri	424,000,000	1.8%
21	Arizona	422,000,000	1.8%
22	Wisconsin	419,000,000	1.8%
23	Connecticut	317,000,000	1.4%
24	Alabama	316,000,000	1.4%
25	Kentucky	281,000,000	1.2%
26	Oregon	279,000,000	1.2%
27	South Carolina	275,000,000	1.2%
28	Louisiana	272,000,000	1.2%
29	Iowa	261,000,000	1.1%
29	Nebraska	261,000,000	1.1%
31	Oklahoma	239,000,000	1.0%
32	Kansas	215,000,000	0.9%
33	Nevada	211,000,000	0.9%
34	Mississippi	172,000,000	0.7%
35	Utah	171,000,000	0.7%
36	Arkansas	164,000,000	0.7%
37	New Mexico	141,000,000	0.6%
38	West Virginia	129,000,000	0.6%
39	Hawaii	118,000,000	0.5%
40	New Hampshire	116,000,000	0.5%
41	Idaho	101,000,000	0.4%
42	Maine	92,000,000	0.4%
43	Montana	85,000,000	0.4%
44	Delaware	78,000,000	0.3%
45	Rhode Island	62,000,000	0.3%
46	Alaska	61,000,000	0.3%
47	South Dakota	60,000,000	0.3%
48	North Dakota	55,000,000	0.2%
49	Wyoming	47,000,000	0.2%
50	Vermont	44,000,000	0.2%
	District of Columbia	59,000,000	0.3%

Source: U.S. Department of Health and Human Services, Centers for Medicare and Medicaid Services
"State Health Care Expenditures" (http://www.cms.hhs.gov/NationalHealthExpendData/)
*By state of residence. Includes eyeglasses, hearing aids, surgical appliances and supplies, bulk and cylinder oxygen, and medical equipment rentals.

Percent of Total Personal Health Care Expenditures
Spent on Durable Medical Products in 2004
National Percent = 1.5%*

ALPHA ORDER

RANK	STATE	PERCENT
29	Alabama	1.4
29	Alaska	1.4
6	Arizona	1.8
41	Arkansas	1.2
19	California	1.5
2	Colorado	2.0
29	Connecticut	1.4
19	Delaware	1.5
10	Florida	1.7
19	Georgia	1.5
4	Hawaii	1.9
13	Idaho	1.6
19	Illinois	1.5
29	Indiana	1.4
13	Iowa	1.6
19	Kansas	1.5
41	Kentucky	1.2
41	Louisiana	1.2
49	Maine	1.1
13	Maryland	1.6
41	Massachusetts	1.2
19	Michigan	1.5
19	Minnesota	1.5
41	Mississippi	1.2
29	Missouri	1.4
6	Montana	1.8
1	Nebraska	2.7
2	Nevada	2.0
13	New Hampshire	1.6
4	New Jersey	1.9
10	New Mexico	1.7
36	New York	1.3
41	North Carolina	1.2
19	North Dakota	1.5
36	Ohio	1.3
29	Oklahoma	1.4
13	Oregon	1.6
29	Pennsylvania	1.4
50	Rhode Island	0.9
36	South Carolina	1.3
19	South Dakota	1.5
36	Tennessee	1.3
13	Texas	1.6
6	Utah	1.8
41	Vermont	1.2
10	Virginia	1.7
19	Washington	1.5
41	West Virginia	1.2
36	Wisconsin	1.3
6	Wyoming	1.8

RANK ORDER

RANK	STATE	PERCENT
1	Nebraska	2.7
2	Colorado	2.0
2	Nevada	2.0
4	Hawaii	1.9
4	New Jersey	1.9
6	Arizona	1.8
6	Montana	1.8
6	Utah	1.8
6	Wyoming	1.8
10	Florida	1.7
10	New Mexico	1.7
10	Virginia	1.7
13	Idaho	1.6
13	Iowa	1.6
13	Maryland	1.6
13	New Hampshire	1.6
13	Oregon	1.6
13	Texas	1.6
19	California	1.5
19	Delaware	1.5
19	Georgia	1.5
19	Illinois	1.5
19	Kansas	1.5
19	Michigan	1.5
19	Minnesota	1.5
19	North Dakota	1.5
19	South Dakota	1.5
19	Washington	1.5
29	Alabama	1.4
29	Alaska	1.4
29	Connecticut	1.4
29	Indiana	1.4
29	Missouri	1.4
29	Oklahoma	1.4
29	Pennsylvania	1.4
36	New York	1.3
36	Ohio	1.3
36	South Carolina	1.3
36	Tennessee	1.3
36	Wisconsin	1.3
41	Arkansas	1.2
41	Kentucky	1.2
41	Louisiana	1.2
41	Massachusetts	1.2
41	Mississippi	1.2
41	North Carolina	1.2
41	Vermont	1.2
41	West Virginia	1.2
49	Maine	1.1
50	Rhode Island	0.9

District of Columbia — 1.2

Source: CQ Press using data from U.S. Department of Health and Human Services, Centers for Medicare and Medicaid Services
    "State Health Care Expenditures" (http://www.cms.hhs.gov/NationalHealthExpendData/)
*By state of residence. Includes eyeglasses, hearing aids, surgical appliances and supplies, bulk and cylinder oxygen, and medical equipment rentals.

Per Capita Expenditures for Durable Medical Products in 2004

National Per Capita = $79*

ALPHA ORDER				RANK ORDER		

RANK	STATE	PER CAPITA		RANK	STATE	PER CAPITA
40	Alabama	$70		1	Nebraska	$149
6	Alaska	93		2	New Jersey	111
30	Arizona	74		3	Colorado	96
47	Arkansas	60		4	Delaware	95
37	California	71		5	Hawaii	94
3	Colorado	96		6	Alaska	93
9	Connecticut	91		7	Montana	92
4	Delaware	95		7	Wyoming	92
9	Florida	91		9	Connecticut	91
42	Georgia	69		9	Florida	91
5	Hawaii	94		9	Maryland	91
35	Idaho	72		12	Nevada	90
20	Illinois	78		12	New Hampshire	90
28	Indiana	76		14	Minnesota	89
15	Iowa	88		15	Iowa	88
20	Kansas	78		16	New York	87
43	Kentucky	68		17	North Dakota	86
47	Louisiana	60		18	Virginia	84
40	Maine	70		19	Pennsylvania	83
9	Maryland	91		20	Illinois	78
20	Massachusetts	78		20	Kansas	78
25	Michigan	77		20	Massachusetts	78
14	Minnesota	89		20	Oregon	78
47	Mississippi	60		20	Washington	78
30	Missouri	74		25	Michigan	77
7	Montana	92		25	Ohio	77
1	Nebraska	149		25	South Dakota	77
12	Nevada	90		28	Indiana	76
12	New Hampshire	90		28	Wisconsin	76
2	New Jersey	111		30	Arizona	74
30	New Mexico	74		30	Missouri	74
16	New York	87		30	New Mexico	74
46	North Carolina	61		30	Texas	74
17	North Dakota	86		34	Tennessee	73
25	Ohio	77		35	Idaho	72
43	Oklahoma	68		35	Vermont	72
20	Oregon	78		37	California	71
19	Pennsylvania	83		37	Utah	71
50	Rhode Island	57		37	West Virginia	71
45	South Carolina	66		40	Alabama	70
25	South Dakota	77		40	Maine	70
34	Tennessee	73		42	Georgia	69
30	Texas	74		43	Kentucky	68
37	Utah	71		43	Oklahoma	68
35	Vermont	72		45	South Carolina	66
18	Virginia	84		46	North Carolina	61
20	Washington	78		47	Arkansas	60
37	West Virginia	71		47	Louisiana	60
28	Wisconsin	76		47	Mississippi	60
7	Wyoming	92		50	Rhode Island	57
					District of Columbia	102

Source: U.S. Department of Health and Human Services, Centers for Medicare and Medicaid Services
   "State Health Care Expenditures" (http://www.cms.hhs.gov/NationalHealthExpendData/)
*By state of residence. Includes eyeglasses, hearing aids, surgical appliances and supplies, bulk and cylinder oxygen, and medical equipment rentals.

Projected National Health Care Expenditures in 2010

Total Health Care Expenditures = $2,624,400,000,000*

The 2004 health care expenditures broken down to the state level and shown on pages 305 to 332 were released in February of 2007 and are the most recent state health expenditure data available from the Centers for Medicare and Medicaid Services (CMS).

Given the high level of interest in health care finance data, we have assembled a table showing the most recent national level health care expenditure projections.

	PROJECTED EXPENDITURES IN 2010	PROJECTED PERCENT CHANGE: 2009 TO 2010
Total Health Care Expenditures	$2,624,400,000,000	4.6
Per Capita Total Health Care Expenditures	$8,548	
Personal Health Care Expenditures	$2,191,300,000,000	4.4
Per Capita Personal Health Care Expenditures	$7,138	
Hospital Care Expenditures	$829,700,000,000	3.4
Per Capita Hospital Care Expenditures	$2,703	
Physician Services Expenditures	$551,600,000,000	2.3
Per Capita Physician Services Expenditures	$1,797	
Dental Services Expenditures	$106,300,000,000	4.3
Per Capita Dental Services Expenditures	$346	
Other Professional Services	$71,500,000,000	4.0
Per Capita Other Professional Services	$233	
Home Health Care Expenditures	$74,600,000,000	7.1
Per Capita Home Health Care Expenditures	$243	
Prescription Drugs	$255,900,000,000	4.5
Per Capita Prescription Drugs	$834	
Nursing Home Care	$151,200,000,000	5.1
Per Capita Nursing Home Care	$492	
Other Personal Care Expenditures	$83,500,000,000	9.8
Per Capita Other Personal Care Expenditures	$272	

Source: U.S. Department of Health and Human Services, Centers for Medicare and Medicaid Services
   "National Health Care Expenditures Projections: 2003-2018"
   (http://www.cms.hhs.gov/NationalHealthExpendData/downloads/proj2008.pdf)
*Per Capita figures calculated by CQ Press using 2009 Census population estimates. For definitions see the corresponding 2004 state tables in this chapter.

V. Incidence of Disease

Estimated New Cancer Cases in 2009

National Estimated Total = 1,479,350 New Cases*

ALPHA ORDER

RANK	STATE	CASES	% of USA
21	Alabama	24,090	1.6%
49	Alaska	2,530	0.2%
18	Arizona	27,600	1.9%
31	Arkansas	14,800	1.0%
1	California	152,170	10.3%
27	Colorado	20,340	1.4%
26	Connecticut	20,650	1.4%
45	Delaware	4,690	0.3%
2	Florida	102,210	6.9%
11	Georgia	39,080	2.6%
42	Hawaii	6,400	0.4%
41	Idaho	6,800	0.5%
7	Illinois	60,960	4.1%
16	Indiana	31,320	2.1%
30	Iowa	16,740	1.1%
33	Kansas	13,080	0.9%
22	Kentucky	24,060	1.6%
24	Louisiana	22,170	1.5%
36	Maine	9,000	0.6%
20	Maryland	26,650	1.8%
12	Massachusetts	36,080	2.4%
8	Michigan	53,550	3.6%
23	Minnesota	23,670	1.6%
32	Mississippi	14,150	1.0%
17	Missouri	30,090	2.0%
44	Montana	5,340	0.4%
39	Nebraska	8,810	0.6%
34	Nevada	12,020	0.8%
40	New Hampshire	7,630	0.5%
9	New Jersey	47,920	3.2%
38	New Mexico	8,830	0.6%
3	New York	101,550	6.9%
10	North Carolina	42,270	2.9%
48	North Dakota	3,200	0.2%
6	Ohio	62,420	4.2%
29	Oklahoma	18,110	1.2%
28	Oregon	19,210	1.3%
5	Pennsylvania	74,170	5.0%
43	Rhode Island	6,250	0.4%
25	South Carolina	22,100	1.5%
46	South Dakota	4,120	0.3%
14	Tennessee	32,570	2.2%
4	Texas	98,200	6.6%
37	Utah	8,880	0.6%
47	Vermont	3,550	0.2%
13	Virginia	34,150	2.3%
15	Washington	32,290	2.2%
35	West Virginia	10,230	0.7%
19	Wisconsin	27,560	1.9%
50	Wyoming	2,500	0.2%

RANK ORDER

RANK	STATE	CASES	% of USA
1	California	152,170	10.3%
2	Florida	102,210	6.9%
3	New York	101,550	6.9%
4	Texas	98,200	6.6%
5	Pennsylvania	74,170	5.0%
6	Ohio	62,420	4.2%
7	Illinois	60,960	4.1%
8	Michigan	53,550	3.6%
9	New Jersey	47,920	3.2%
10	North Carolina	42,270	2.9%
11	Georgia	39,080	2.6%
12	Massachusetts	36,080	2.4%
13	Virginia	34,150	2.3%
14	Tennessee	32,570	2.2%
15	Washington	32,290	2.2%
16	Indiana	31,320	2.1%
17	Missouri	30,090	2.0%
18	Arizona	27,600	1.9%
19	Wisconsin	27,560	1.9%
20	Maryland	26,650	1.8%
21	Alabama	24,090	1.6%
22	Kentucky	24,060	1.6%
23	Minnesota	23,670	1.6%
24	Louisiana	22,170	1.5%
25	South Carolina	22,100	1.5%
26	Connecticut	20,650	1.4%
27	Colorado	20,340	1.4%
28	Oregon	19,210	1.3%
29	Oklahoma	18,110	1.2%
30	Iowa	16,740	1.1%
31	Arkansas	14,800	1.0%
32	Mississippi	14,150	1.0%
33	Kansas	13,080	0.9%
34	Nevada	12,020	0.8%
35	West Virginia	10,230	0.7%
36	Maine	9,000	0.6%
37	Utah	8,880	0.6%
38	New Mexico	8,830	0.6%
39	Nebraska	8,810	0.6%
40	New Hampshire	7,630	0.5%
41	Idaho	6,800	0.5%
42	Hawaii	6,400	0.4%
43	Rhode Island	6,250	0.4%
44	Montana	5,340	0.4%
45	Delaware	4,690	0.3%
46	South Dakota	4,120	0.3%
47	Vermont	3,550	0.2%
48	North Dakota	3,200	0.2%
49	Alaska	2,530	0.2%
50	Wyoming	2,500	0.2%
	District of Columbia	2,600	0.2%

Source: American Cancer Society
"Cancer Facts & Figures 2009" (Copyright 2009, American Cancer Society, http://www.cancer.org/docroot/stt/stt_0.asp)
*These estimates are offered as a rough guide and should not be regarded as definitive. They are calculated according to the distribution of estimated 2008 cancer deaths by state. Totals do not include basal and squamous cell skin cancers or in situ carcinomas except urinary bladder.

Estimated Rate of New Cancer Cases in 2009

National Estimated Rate = 481.9 New Cases per 100,000 Population*

ALPHA ORDER			RANK ORDER		
RANK	STATE	RATE	RANK	STATE	RATE
20	Alabama	511.6	1	Maine	682.7
49	Alaska	362.2	2	Rhode Island	593.4
44	Arizona	418.4	3	Pennsylvania	588.4
19	Arkansas	512.2	4	Connecticut	586.9
45	California	411.7	5	New Hampshire	576.0
46	Colorado	404.8	6	Vermont	571.0
4	Connecticut	586.9	7	West Virginia	562.2
16	Delaware	529.9	8	Kentucky	557.7
10	Florida	551.4	9	Iowa	556.5
47	Georgia	397.6	10	Florida	551.4
25	Hawaii	494.1	11	New Jersey	550.3
41	Idaho	439.9	12	Montana	547.7
34	Illinois	472.2	13	Massachusetts	547.2
29	Indiana	487.6	14	Ohio	540.8
9	Iowa	556.5	15	Michigan	537.1
36	Kansas	464.0	16	Delaware	529.9
8	Kentucky	557.7	17	New York	519.7
26	Louisiana	493.5	18	Tennessee	517.3
1	Maine	682.7	19	Arkansas	512.2
35	Maryland	467.6	20	Alabama	511.6
13	Massachusetts	547.2	21	South Dakota	507.1
15	Michigan	537.1	22	Missouri	502.5
40	Minnesota	449.5	23	Oregon	502.1
33	Mississippi	479.3	24	North Dakota	494.7
22	Missouri	502.5	25	Hawaii	494.1
12	Montana	547.7	26	Louisiana	493.5
28	Nebraska	490.4	27	Oklahoma	491.2
38	Nevada	454.8	28	Nebraska	490.4
5	New Hampshire	576.0	29	Indiana	487.6
11	New Jersey	550.3	30	Wisconsin	487.4
42	New Mexico	439.4	31	South Carolina	484.5
17	New York	519.7	31	Washington	484.5
39	North Carolina	450.6	33	Mississippi	479.3
24	North Dakota	494.7	34	Illinois	472.2
14	Ohio	540.8	35	Maryland	467.6
27	Oklahoma	491.2	36	Kansas	464.0
23	Oregon	502.1	37	Wyoming	459.3
3	Pennsylvania	588.4	38	Nevada	454.8
2	Rhode Island	593.4	39	North Carolina	450.6
31	South Carolina	484.5	40	Minnesota	449.5
21	South Dakota	507.1	41	Idaho	439.9
18	Tennessee	517.3	42	New Mexico	439.4
48	Texas	396.3	43	Virginia	433.2
50	Utah	318.9	44	Arizona	418.4
6	Vermont	571.0	45	California	411.7
43	Virginia	433.2	46	Colorado	404.8
31	Washington	484.5	47	Georgia	397.6
7	West Virginia	562.2	48	Texas	396.3
30	Wisconsin	487.4	49	Alaska	362.2
37	Wyoming	459.3	50	Utah	318.9
				District of Columbia	433.6

Source: CQ Press using data from American Cancer Society
"Cancer Facts & Figures 2009" (Copyright 2009, American Cancer Society, http://www.cancer.org/docroot/stt/stt_0.asp)
*These estimates are offered as a rough guide and should not be regarded as definitive. They are calculated according to the distribution of estimated 2009 cancer deaths by state. Totals do not include basal and squamous cell skin cancers or in situ carcinomas except urinary bladder. Rates calculated using 2009 Census resident population estimates.

Age-Adjusted Cancer Incidence Rates for Males in 2005

National Rate = 562.3 New Cases per 100,000 Male Population*

ALPHA ORDER

RANK	STATE	RATE
24	Alabama	555.6
36	Alaska	533.2
45	Arizona	461.7
22	Arkansas	558.2
37	California	518.2
40	Colorado	512.7
11	Connecticut	589.5
8	Delaware	601.7
28	Florida	549.3
16	Georgia	571.3
44	Hawaii	484.9
33	Idaho	543.5
13	Illinois	580.1
26	Indiana	552.3
21	Iowa	560.9
NA	Kansas**	NA
4	Kentucky	612.5
1	Louisiana	624.9
2	Maine	621.6
NA	Maryland**	NA
7	Massachusetts	604.0
6	Michigan	608.0
18	Minnesota	568.8
24	Mississippi	555.6
30	Missouri	545.3
20	Montana	561.2
23	Nebraska	557.0
34	Nevada	539.9
12	New Hampshire	586.7
4	New Jersey	612.5
43	New Mexico	490.7
15	New York	575.7
NA	North Carolina**	NA
31	North Dakota	543.8
31	Ohio	543.8
27	Oklahoma	551.3
35	Oregon	533.4
9	Pennsylvania	593.9
3	Rhode Island	616.7
10	South Carolina	589.6
19	South Dakota	568.5
41	Tennessee	496.9
29	Texas	546.5
42	Utah	493.1
NA	Vermont**	NA
38	Virginia	515.6
17	Washington	571.2
14	West Virginia	576.0
NA	Wisconsin**	NA
39	Wyoming	515.5

RANK ORDER

RANK	STATE	RATE
1	Louisiana	624.9
2	Maine	621.6
3	Rhode Island	616.7
4	Kentucky	612.5
4	New Jersey	612.5
6	Michigan	608.0
7	Massachusetts	604.0
8	Delaware	601.7
9	Pennsylvania	593.9
10	South Carolina	589.6
11	Connecticut	589.5
12	New Hampshire	586.7
13	Illinois	580.1
14	West Virginia	576.0
15	New York	575.7
16	Georgia	571.3
17	Washington	571.2
18	Minnesota	568.8
19	South Dakota	568.5
20	Montana	561.2
21	Iowa	560.9
22	Arkansas	558.2
23	Nebraska	557.0
24	Alabama	555.6
24	Mississippi	555.6
26	Indiana	552.3
27	Oklahoma	551.3
28	Florida	549.3
29	Texas	546.5
30	Missouri	545.3
31	North Dakota	543.8
31	Ohio	543.8
33	Idaho	543.5
34	Nevada	539.9
35	Oregon	533.4
36	Alaska	533.2
37	California	518.2
38	Virginia	515.6
39	Wyoming	515.5
40	Colorado	512.7
41	Tennessee	496.9
42	Utah	493.1
43	New Mexico	490.7
44	Hawaii	484.9
45	Arizona	461.7
NA	Kansas**	NA
NA	Maryland**	NA
NA	North Carolina**	NA
NA	Vermont**	NA
NA	Wisconsin**	NA
	District of Columbia**	NA

Source: American Cancer Society
"Cancer Facts & Figures 2009" (Copyright 2009, American Cancer Society, http://www.cancer.org/docroot/stt/stt_0.asp)
*For 2001 to 2005. Age-adjusted to the 2000 U.S. standard population.
**Not available.

Age-Adjusted Cancer Incidence Rates for Females in 2005

National Rate = 417.3 New Cases per 100,000 Female Population*

ALPHA ORDER

RANK	STATE	RATE
39	Alabama	377.6
24	Alaska	410.6
44	Arizona	363.0
38	Arkansas	381.5
32	California	396.4
29	Colorado	401.7
3	Connecticut	454.3
11	Delaware	438.6
25	Florida	410.1
33	Georgia	395.2
37	Hawaii	385.9
30	Idaho	399.0
16	Illinois	426.8
20	Indiana	414.9
15	Iowa	428.3
NA	Kansas**	NA
7	Kentucky	447.1
26	Louisiana	409.5
1	Maine	460.6
NA	Maryland**	NA
2	Massachusetts	455.9
10	Michigan	440.2
17	Minnesota	418.6
43	Mississippi	365.5
21	Missouri	414.6
23	Montana	412.3
18	Nebraska	417.9
19	Nevada	415.8
4	New Hampshire	451.9
5	New Jersey	451.5
42	New Mexico	367.7
13	New York	432.7
NA	North Carolina**	NA
31	North Dakota	396.7
22	Ohio	413.6
27	Oklahoma	409.2
14	Oregon	430.0
9	Pennsylvania	444.0
8	Rhode Island	446.9
33	South Carolina	395.2
28	South Dakota	406.0
40	Tennessee	377.4
36	Texas	390.9
45	Utah	348.2
NA	Vermont**	NA
41	Virginia	376.4
6	Washington	447.7
12	West Virginia	433.6
NA	Wisconsin**	NA
35	Wyoming	394.8

RANK ORDER

RANK	STATE	RATE
1	Maine	460.6
2	Massachusetts	455.9
3	Connecticut	454.3
4	New Hampshire	451.9
5	New Jersey	451.5
6	Washington	447.7
7	Kentucky	447.1
8	Rhode Island	446.9
9	Pennsylvania	444.0
10	Michigan	440.2
11	Delaware	438.6
12	West Virginia	433.6
13	New York	432.7
14	Oregon	430.0
15	Iowa	428.3
16	Illinois	426.8
17	Minnesota	418.6
18	Nebraska	417.9
19	Nevada	415.8
20	Indiana	414.9
21	Missouri	414.6
22	Ohio	413.6
23	Montana	412.3
24	Alaska	410.6
25	Florida	410.1
26	Louisiana	409.5
27	Oklahoma	409.2
28	South Dakota	406.0
29	Colorado	401.7
30	Idaho	399.0
31	North Dakota	396.7
32	California	396.4
33	Georgia	395.2
33	South Carolina	395.2
35	Wyoming	394.8
36	Texas	390.9
37	Hawaii	385.9
38	Arkansas	381.5
39	Alabama	377.6
40	Tennessee	377.4
41	Virginia	376.4
42	New Mexico	367.7
43	Mississippi	365.5
44	Arizona	363.0
45	Utah	348.2
NA	Kansas**	NA
NA	Maryland**	NA
NA	North Carolina**	NA
NA	Vermont**	NA
NA	Wisconsin**	NA

District of Columbia**   NA

Source: American Cancer Society
   "Cancer Facts & Figures 2009" (Copyright 2009, American Cancer Society, http://www.cancer.org/docroot/stt/stt_0.asp)
*For 2001 to 2005. Age-adjusted to the 2000 U.S. standard population.
**Not available.

Estimated New Cases of Bladder Cancer in 2009

National Estimated Total = 70,980 New Cases*

ALPHA ORDER

RANK	STATE	CASES	% of USA
25	Alabama	960	1.4%
50	Alaska	120	0.2%
15	Arizona	1,460	2.1%
33	Arkansas	610	0.9%
1	California	6,870	9.7%
26	Colorado	940	1.3%
21	Connecticut	1,120	1.6%
45	Delaware	220	0.3%
2	Florida	5,490	7.7%
18	Georgia	1,400	2.0%
45	Hawaii	220	0.3%
42	Idaho	340	0.5%
6	Illinois	3,100	4.4%
13	Indiana	1,550	2.2%
29	Iowa	870	1.2%
32	Kansas	620	0.9%
23	Kentucky	1,070	1.5%
27	Louisiana	910	1.3%
36	Maine	500	0.7%
22	Maryland	1,110	1.6%
10	Massachusetts	2,010	2.8%
8	Michigan	2,810	4.0%
20	Minnesota	1,200	1.7%
34	Mississippi	540	0.8%
16	Missouri	1,450	2.0%
43	Montana	270	0.4%
37	Nebraska	450	0.6%
31	Nevada	630	0.9%
38	New Hampshire	420	0.6%
9	New Jersey	2,640	3.7%
41	New Mexico	350	0.5%
3	New York	5,360	7.6%
11	North Carolina	1,790	2.5%
48	North Dakota	180	0.3%
7	Ohio	2,990	4.2%
30	Oklahoma	770	1.1%
24	Oregon	1,020	1.4%
4	Pennsylvania	4,160	5.9%
39	Rhode Island	370	0.5%
28	South Carolina	880	1.2%
44	South Dakota	230	0.3%
19	Tennessee	1,380	1.9%
5	Texas	3,720	5.2%
40	Utah	360	0.5%
47	Vermont	190	0.3%
17	Virginia	1,430	2.0%
12	Washington	1,660	2.3%
35	West Virginia	510	0.7%
14	Wisconsin	1,530	2.2%
49	Wyoming	130	0.2%

RANK ORDER

RANK	STATE	CASES	% of USA
1	California	6,870	9.7%
2	Florida	5,490	7.7%
3	New York	5,360	7.6%
4	Pennsylvania	4,160	5.9%
5	Texas	3,720	5.2%
6	Illinois	3,100	4.4%
7	Ohio	2,990	4.2%
8	Michigan	2,810	4.0%
9	New Jersey	2,640	3.7%
10	Massachusetts	2,010	2.8%
11	North Carolina	1,790	2.5%
12	Washington	1,660	2.3%
13	Indiana	1,550	2.2%
14	Wisconsin	1,530	2.2%
15	Arizona	1,460	2.1%
16	Missouri	1,450	2.0%
17	Virginia	1,430	2.0%
18	Georgia	1,400	2.0%
19	Tennessee	1,380	1.9%
20	Minnesota	1,200	1.7%
21	Connecticut	1,120	1.6%
22	Maryland	1,110	1.6%
23	Kentucky	1,070	1.5%
24	Oregon	1,020	1.4%
25	Alabama	960	1.4%
26	Colorado	940	1.3%
27	Louisiana	910	1.3%
28	South Carolina	880	1.2%
29	Iowa	870	1.2%
30	Oklahoma	770	1.1%
31	Nevada	630	0.9%
32	Kansas	620	0.9%
33	Arkansas	610	0.9%
34	Mississippi	540	0.8%
35	West Virginia	510	0.7%
36	Maine	500	0.7%
37	Nebraska	450	0.6%
38	New Hampshire	420	0.6%
39	Rhode Island	370	0.5%
40	Utah	360	0.5%
41	New Mexico	350	0.5%
42	Idaho	340	0.5%
43	Montana	270	0.4%
44	South Dakota	230	0.3%
45	Delaware	220	0.3%
45	Hawaii	220	0.3%
47	Vermont	190	0.3%
48	North Dakota	180	0.3%
49	Wyoming	130	0.2%
50	Alaska	120	0.2%
	District of Columbia	90	0.1%

Source: American Cancer Society
"Cancer Facts & Figures 2009" (Copyright 2009, American Cancer Society, http://www.cancer.org/docroot/stt/stt_0.asp)
*These estimates are offered as a rough guide and should be interpreted with caution. They are calculated according to the distribution of estimated 2009 cancer deaths by state.

Estimated Rate of New Bladder Cancer Cases in 2009

National Estimated Rate = 23.1 New Cases per 100,000 Population*

ALPHA ORDER

RANK	STATE	RATE
36	Alabama	20.4
46	Alaska	17.2
30	Arizona	22.1
34	Arkansas	21.1
42	California	18.6
41	Colorado	18.7
4	Connecticut	31.8
21	Delaware	24.9
9	Florida	29.6
49	Georgia	14.2
47	Hawaii	17.0
31	Idaho	22.0
26	Illinois	24.0
25	Indiana	24.1
10	Iowa	28.9
31	Kansas	22.0
23	Kentucky	24.8
37	Louisiana	20.3
1	Maine	37.9
38	Maryland	19.5
7	Massachusetts	30.5
12	Michigan	28.2
29	Minnesota	22.8
43	Mississippi	18.3
24	Missouri	24.2
15	Montana	27.7
20	Nebraska	25.0
28	Nevada	23.8
5	New Hampshire	31.7
8	New Jersey	30.3
45	New Mexico	17.4
16	New York	27.4
40	North Carolina	19.1
14	North Dakota	27.8
19	Ohio	25.9
35	Oklahoma	20.9
18	Oregon	26.7
3	Pennsylvania	33.0
2	Rhode Island	35.1
39	South Carolina	19.3
11	South Dakota	28.3
33	Tennessee	21.9
48	Texas	15.0
50	Utah	12.9
6	Vermont	30.6
44	Virginia	18.1
21	Washington	24.9
13	West Virginia	28.0
17	Wisconsin	27.1
27	Wyoming	23.9

RANK ORDER

RANK	STATE	RATE
1	Maine	37.9
2	Rhode Island	35.1
3	Pennsylvania	33.0
4	Connecticut	31.8
5	New Hampshire	31.7
6	Vermont	30.6
7	Massachusetts	30.5
8	New Jersey	30.3
9	Florida	29.6
10	Iowa	28.9
11	South Dakota	28.3
12	Michigan	28.2
13	West Virginia	28.0
14	North Dakota	27.8
15	Montana	27.7
16	New York	27.4
17	Wisconsin	27.1
18	Oregon	26.7
19	Ohio	25.9
20	Nebraska	25.0
21	Delaware	24.9
21	Washington	24.9
23	Kentucky	24.8
24	Missouri	24.2
25	Indiana	24.1
26	Illinois	24.0
27	Wyoming	23.9
28	Nevada	23.8
29	Minnesota	22.8
30	Arizona	22.1
31	Idaho	22.0
31	Kansas	22.0
33	Tennessee	21.9
34	Arkansas	21.1
35	Oklahoma	20.9
36	Alabama	20.4
37	Louisiana	20.3
38	Maryland	19.5
39	South Carolina	19.3
40	North Carolina	19.1
41	Colorado	18.7
42	California	18.6
43	Mississippi	18.3
44	Virginia	18.1
45	New Mexico	17.4
46	Alaska	17.2
47	Hawaii	17.0
48	Texas	15.0
49	Georgia	14.2
50	Utah	12.9
	District of Columbia	15.0

Source: CQ Press using data from American Cancer Society
"Cancer Facts & Figures 2009" (Copyright 2009, American Cancer Society, http://www.cancer.org/docroot/stt/stt_0.asp)
*These estimates are offered as a rough guide and should be interpreted with caution. They are calculated according to the distribution of estimated 2009 cancer deaths by state. Rates calculated using 2009 Census resident population estimates.

Estimated New Female Breast Cancer Cases in 2009

National Estimated Total = 192,370 New Cases*

ALPHA ORDER

RANK	STATE	CASES	% of USA
22	Alabama	2,970	1.5%
49	Alaska	370	0.2%
20	Arizona	3,470	1.8%
31	Arkansas	1,820	0.9%
1	California	21,740	11.3%
23	Colorado	2,840	1.5%
26	Connecticut	2,790	1.5%
45	Delaware	600	0.3%
4	Florida	12,650	6.6%
11	Georgia	5,370	2.8%
41	Hawaii	870	0.5%
42	Idaho	810	0.4%
6	Illinois	7,610	4.0%
17	Indiana	3,710	1.9%
30	Iowa	2,080	1.1%
33	Kansas	1,790	0.9%
23	Kentucky	2,840	1.5%
27	Louisiana	2,700	1.4%
38	Maine	1,080	0.6%
18	Maryland	3,660	1.9%
13	Massachusetts	4,800	2.5%
8	Michigan	6,480	3.4%
21	Minnesota	3,280	1.7%
31	Mississippi	1,820	0.9%
16	Missouri	3,880	2.0%
44	Montana	640	0.3%
35	Nebraska	1,200	0.6%
34	Nevada	1,350	0.7%
40	New Hampshire	1,010	0.5%
9	New Jersey	6,440	3.3%
37	New Mexico	1,090	0.6%
2	New York	13,530	7.0%
10	North Carolina	5,470	2.8%
48	North Dakota	410	0.2%
7	Ohio	7,340	3.8%
29	Oklahoma	2,340	1.2%
28	Oregon	2,680	1.4%
5	Pennsylvania	9,380	4.9%
42	Rhode Island	810	0.4%
25	South Carolina	2,820	1.5%
46	South Dakota	530	0.3%
15	Tennessee	3,970	2.1%
3	Texas	13,090	6.8%
38	Utah	1,080	0.6%
47	Vermont	480	0.2%
12	Virginia	4,850	2.5%
14	Washington	4,520	2.3%
36	West Virginia	1,180	0.6%
19	Wisconsin	3,480	1.8%
50	Wyoming	300	0.2%

RANK ORDER

RANK	STATE	CASES	% of USA
1	California	21,740	11.3%
2	New York	13,530	7.0%
3	Texas	13,090	6.8%
4	Florida	12,650	6.6%
5	Pennsylvania	9,380	4.9%
6	Illinois	7,610	4.0%
7	Ohio	7,340	3.8%
8	Michigan	6,480	3.4%
9	New Jersey	6,440	3.3%
10	North Carolina	5,470	2.8%
11	Georgia	5,370	2.8%
12	Virginia	4,850	2.5%
13	Massachusetts	4,800	2.5%
14	Washington	4,520	2.3%
15	Tennessee	3,970	2.1%
16	Missouri	3,880	2.0%
17	Indiana	3,710	1.9%
18	Maryland	3,660	1.9%
19	Wisconsin	3,480	1.8%
20	Arizona	3,470	1.8%
21	Minnesota	3,280	1.7%
22	Alabama	2,970	1.5%
23	Colorado	2,840	1.5%
23	Kentucky	2,840	1.5%
25	South Carolina	2,820	1.5%
26	Connecticut	2,790	1.5%
27	Louisiana	2,700	1.4%
28	Oregon	2,680	1.4%
29	Oklahoma	2,340	1.2%
30	Iowa	2,080	1.1%
31	Arkansas	1,820	0.9%
31	Mississippi	1,820	0.9%
33	Kansas	1,790	0.9%
34	Nevada	1,350	0.7%
35	Nebraska	1,200	0.6%
36	West Virginia	1,180	0.6%
37	New Mexico	1,090	0.6%
38	Maine	1,080	0.6%
38	Utah	1,080	0.6%
40	New Hampshire	1,010	0.5%
41	Hawaii	870	0.5%
42	Idaho	810	0.4%
42	Rhode Island	810	0.4%
44	Montana	640	0.3%
45	Delaware	600	0.3%
46	South Dakota	530	0.3%
47	Vermont	480	0.2%
48	North Dakota	410	0.2%
49	Alaska	370	0.2%
50	Wyoming	300	0.2%
	District of Columbia	340	0.2%

Source: American Cancer Society
"Cancer Facts & Figures 2009" (Copyright 2009, American Cancer Society, http://www.cancer.org/docroot/stt/stt_0.asp)
*These estimates are offered as a rough guide and should be interpreted with caution. They are calculated according to the distribution of estimated 2009 cancer deaths by state.

Age-Adjusted Incidence Rate of Female Breast Cancer Cases in 2005

National Rate = 123.6 New Cases per 100,000 Female Population*

ALPHA ORDER

RANK	STATE	RATE
40	Alabama	114.2
9	Alaska	127.9
44	Arizona	109.8
41	Arkansas	114.0
20	California	124.7
16	Colorado	125.9
2	Connecticut	137.4
13	Delaware	126.4
35	Florida	116.7
28	Georgia	120.6
15	Hawaii	126.0
32	Idaho	118.2
22	Illinois	124.1
34	Indiana	117.7
19	Iowa	125.4
NA	Kansas**	NA
29	Kentucky	120.5
27	Louisiana	120.9
6	Maine	130.6
NA	Maryland**	NA
4	Massachusetts	133.8
12	Michigan	127.0
8	Minnesota	129.3
45	Mississippi	105.8
23	Missouri	123.0
24	Montana	122.6
10	Nebraska	127.8
37	Nevada	116.0
5	New Hampshire	132.3
7	New Jersey	129.8
43	New Mexico	111.7
21	New York	124.6
NA	North Carolina**	NA
25	North Dakota	122.5
26	Ohio	121.9
13	Oklahoma	126.4
3	Oregon	134.7
17	Pennsylvania	125.7
11	Rhode Island	127.5
31	South Carolina	119.2
18	South Dakota	125.5
38	Tennessee	115.3
36	Texas	116.3
42	Utah	112.9
NA	Vermont**	NA
30	Virginia	119.5
1	Washington	138.9
38	West Virginia	115.3
NA	Wisconsin**	NA
33	Wyoming	117.9

RANK ORDER

RANK	STATE	RATE
1	Washington	138.9
2	Connecticut	137.4
3	Oregon	134.7
4	Massachusetts	133.8
5	New Hampshire	132.3
6	Maine	130.6
7	New Jersey	129.8
8	Minnesota	129.3
9	Alaska	127.9
10	Nebraska	127.8
11	Rhode Island	127.5
12	Michigan	127.0
13	Delaware	126.4
13	Oklahoma	126.4
15	Hawaii	126.0
16	Colorado	125.9
17	Pennsylvania	125.7
18	South Dakota	125.5
19	Iowa	125.4
20	California	124.7
21	New York	124.6
22	Illinois	124.1
23	Missouri	123.0
24	Montana	122.6
25	North Dakota	122.5
26	Ohio	121.9
27	Louisiana	120.9
28	Georgia	120.6
29	Kentucky	120.5
30	Virginia	119.5
31	South Carolina	119.2
32	Idaho	118.2
33	Wyoming	117.9
34	Indiana	117.7
35	Florida	116.7
36	Texas	116.3
37	Nevada	116.0
38	Tennessee	115.3
38	West Virginia	115.3
40	Alabama	114.2
41	Arkansas	114.0
42	Utah	112.9
43	New Mexico	111.7
44	Arizona	109.8
45	Mississippi	105.8
NA	Kansas**	NA
NA	Maryland**	NA
NA	North Carolina**	NA
NA	Vermont**	NA
NA	Wisconsin**	NA
	District of Columbia**	NA

Source: American Cancer Society

"Cancer Facts & Figures 2009" (Copyright 2009, American Cancer Society, http://www.cancer.org/docroot/stt/stt_0.asp)

*For 2001 to 2005. Age-adjusted to the 2000 U.S. standard population.

**Not available.

Percent of Women 40 and Older Who Have Had a Mammogram in the Past Two Years: 2008
National Median = 76.0% of Women*

<table>
<thead>
<tr><th colspan="3">ALPHA ORDER</th><th colspan="3">RANK ORDER</th></tr>
<tr><th>RANK</th><th>STATE</th><th>PERCENT</th><th>RANK</th><th>STATE</th><th>PERCENT</th></tr>
</thead>
<tbody>
<tr><td>34</td><td>Alabama</td><td>74.1</td><td>1</td><td>Massachusetts</td><td>84.9</td></tr>
<tr><td>49</td><td>Alaska</td><td>67.6</td><td>2</td><td>Connecticut</td><td>84.1</td></tr>
<tr><td>17</td><td>Arizona</td><td>77.4</td><td>3</td><td>Maine</td><td>83.3</td></tr>
<tr><td>42</td><td>Arkansas</td><td>70.9</td><td>4</td><td>New Hampshire</td><td>83.0</td></tr>
<tr><td>12</td><td>California</td><td>78.9</td><td>5</td><td>Delaware</td><td>82.3</td></tr>
<tr><td>38</td><td>Colorado</td><td>72.7</td><td>6</td><td>Rhode Island</td><td>81.8</td></tr>
<tr><td>2</td><td>Connecticut</td><td>84.1</td><td>7</td><td>Vermont</td><td>80.0</td></tr>
<tr><td>5</td><td>Delaware</td><td>82.3</td><td>8</td><td>New York</td><td>79.9</td></tr>
<tr><td>9</td><td>Florida</td><td>79.3</td><td>9</td><td>Florida</td><td>79.3</td></tr>
<tr><td>12</td><td>Georgia</td><td>78.9</td><td>10</td><td>Michigan</td><td>79.2</td></tr>
<tr><td>14</td><td>Hawaii</td><td>78.7</td><td>11</td><td>Minnesota</td><td>79.1</td></tr>
<tr><td>46</td><td>Idaho</td><td>68.1</td><td>12</td><td>California</td><td>78.9</td></tr>
<tr><td>27</td><td>Illinois</td><td>75.8</td><td>12</td><td>Georgia</td><td>78.9</td></tr>
<tr><td>35</td><td>Indiana</td><td>73.9</td><td>14</td><td>Hawaii</td><td>78.7</td></tr>
<tr><td>20</td><td>Iowa</td><td>76.5</td><td>15</td><td>North Carolina</td><td>78.5</td></tr>
<tr><td>31</td><td>Kansas</td><td>74.9</td><td>16</td><td>Virginia</td><td>78.2</td></tr>
<tr><td>30</td><td>Kentucky</td><td>75.0</td><td>17</td><td>Arizona</td><td>77.4</td></tr>
<tr><td>25</td><td>Louisiana</td><td>76.0</td><td>18</td><td>Maryland</td><td>77.0</td></tr>
<tr><td>3</td><td>Maine</td><td>83.3</td><td>19</td><td>North Dakota</td><td>76.9</td></tr>
<tr><td>18</td><td>Maryland</td><td>77.0</td><td>20</td><td>Iowa</td><td>76.5</td></tr>
<tr><td>1</td><td>Massachusetts</td><td>84.9</td><td>21</td><td>Pennsylvania</td><td>76.4</td></tr>
<tr><td>10</td><td>Michigan</td><td>79.2</td><td>22</td><td>Washington</td><td>76.3</td></tr>
<tr><td>11</td><td>Minnesota</td><td>79.1</td><td>22</td><td>Wisconsin</td><td>76.3</td></tr>
<tr><td>44</td><td>Mississippi</td><td>69.0</td><td>24</td><td>Oregon</td><td>76.2</td></tr>
<tr><td>37</td><td>Missouri</td><td>73.5</td><td>25</td><td>Louisiana</td><td>76.0</td></tr>
<tr><td>41</td><td>Montana</td><td>71.8</td><td>25</td><td>New Jersey</td><td>76.0</td></tr>
<tr><td>38</td><td>Nebraska</td><td>72.7</td><td>27</td><td>Illinois</td><td>75.8</td></tr>
<tr><td>47</td><td>Nevada</td><td>68.0</td><td>27</td><td>Ohio</td><td>75.8</td></tr>
<tr><td>4</td><td>New Hampshire</td><td>83.0</td><td>29</td><td>South Dakota</td><td>75.4</td></tr>
<tr><td>25</td><td>New Jersey</td><td>76.0</td><td>30</td><td>Kentucky</td><td>75.0</td></tr>
<tr><td>43</td><td>New Mexico</td><td>70.8</td><td>31</td><td>Kansas</td><td>74.9</td></tr>
<tr><td>8</td><td>New York</td><td>79.9</td><td>31</td><td>South Carolina</td><td>74.9</td></tr>
<tr><td>15</td><td>North Carolina</td><td>78.5</td><td>33</td><td>Tennessee</td><td>74.3</td></tr>
<tr><td>19</td><td>North Dakota</td><td>76.9</td><td>34</td><td>Alabama</td><td>74.1</td></tr>
<tr><td>27</td><td>Ohio</td><td>75.8</td><td>35</td><td>Indiana</td><td>73.9</td></tr>
<tr><td>45</td><td>Oklahoma</td><td>68.9</td><td>36</td><td>West Virginia</td><td>73.7</td></tr>
<tr><td>24</td><td>Oregon</td><td>76.2</td><td>37</td><td>Missouri</td><td>73.5</td></tr>
<tr><td>21</td><td>Pennsylvania</td><td>76.4</td><td>38</td><td>Colorado</td><td>72.7</td></tr>
<tr><td>6</td><td>Rhode Island</td><td>81.8</td><td>38</td><td>Nebraska</td><td>72.7</td></tr>
<tr><td>31</td><td>South Carolina</td><td>74.9</td><td>40</td><td>Texas</td><td>72.6</td></tr>
<tr><td>29</td><td>South Dakota</td><td>75.4</td><td>41</td><td>Montana</td><td>71.8</td></tr>
<tr><td>33</td><td>Tennessee</td><td>74.3</td><td>42</td><td>Arkansas</td><td>70.9</td></tr>
<tr><td>40</td><td>Texas</td><td>72.6</td><td>43</td><td>New Mexico</td><td>70.8</td></tr>
<tr><td>48</td><td>Utah</td><td>67.8</td><td>44</td><td>Mississippi</td><td>69.0</td></tr>
<tr><td>7</td><td>Vermont</td><td>80.0</td><td>45</td><td>Oklahoma</td><td>68.9</td></tr>
<tr><td>16</td><td>Virginia</td><td>78.2</td><td>46</td><td>Idaho</td><td>68.1</td></tr>
<tr><td>22</td><td>Washington</td><td>76.3</td><td>47</td><td>Nevada</td><td>68.0</td></tr>
<tr><td>36</td><td>West Virginia</td><td>73.7</td><td>48</td><td>Utah</td><td>67.8</td></tr>
<tr><td>22</td><td>Wisconsin</td><td>76.3</td><td>49</td><td>Alaska</td><td>67.6</td></tr>
<tr><td>50</td><td>Wyoming</td><td>67.2</td><td>50</td><td>Wyoming</td><td>67.2</td></tr>
<tr><td></td><td></td><td></td><td></td><td>District of Columbia</td><td>80.8</td></tr>
</tbody>
</table>

Source: U.S. Department of Health and Human Services, Centers for Disease Control and Prevention
"2008 Behavioral Risk Factor Surveillance Summary Prevalence Data" (http://apps.nccd.cdc.gov/brfss/)
*Percent of women 40 years and older.

Estimated New Colon and Rectum Cancer Cases in 2009

National Estimated Total = 146,970 New Cases*

ALPHA ORDER

RANK	STATE	CASES	% of USA
23	Alabama	2,480	1.7%
49	Alaska	250	0.2%
19	Arizona	2,680	1.8%
31	Arkansas	1,540	1.0%
1	California	14,680	10.0%
27	Colorado	1,860	1.3%
26	Connecticut	1,950	1.3%
45	Delaware	440	0.3%
2	Florida	10,420	7.1%
11	Georgia	3,750	2.6%
41	Hawaii	710	0.5%
42	Idaho	630	0.4%
6	Illinois	6,430	4.4%
15	Indiana	3,260	2.2%
29	Iowa	1,800	1.2%
33	Kansas	1,290	0.9%
20	Kentucky	2,620	1.8%
24	Louisiana	2,330	1.6%
37	Maine	870	0.6%
20	Maryland	2,620	1.8%
13	Massachusetts	3,380	2.3%
8	Michigan	5,020	3.4%
22	Minnesota	2,520	1.7%
32	Mississippi	1,480	1.0%
16	Missouri	3,100	2.1%
44	Montana	520	0.4%
36	Nebraska	950	0.6%
34	Nevada	1,240	0.8%
40	New Hampshire	730	0.5%
9	New Jersey	4,590	3.1%
38	New Mexico	810	0.6%
3	New York	9,970	6.8%
10	North Carolina	4,230	2.9%
47	North Dakota	350	0.2%
7	Ohio	6,060	4.1%
27	Oklahoma	1,860	1.3%
30	Oregon	1,780	1.2%
5	Pennsylvania	7,590	5.2%
43	Rhode Island	590	0.4%
25	South Carolina	2,150	1.5%
45	South Dakota	440	0.3%
12	Tennessee	3,490	2.4%
4	Texas	9,800	6.7%
39	Utah	770	0.5%
48	Vermont	330	0.2%
13	Virginia	3,380	2.3%
17	Washington	2,890	2.0%
35	West Virginia	1,070	0.7%
18	Wisconsin	2,770	1.9%
50	Wyoming	240	0.2%

RANK ORDER

RANK	STATE	CASES	% of USA
1	California	14,680	10.0%
2	Florida	10,420	7.1%
3	New York	9,970	6.8%
4	Texas	9,800	6.7%
5	Pennsylvania	7,590	5.2%
6	Illinois	6,430	4.4%
7	Ohio	6,060	4.1%
8	Michigan	5,020	3.4%
9	New Jersey	4,590	3.1%
10	North Carolina	4,230	2.9%
11	Georgia	3,750	2.6%
12	Tennessee	3,490	2.4%
13	Massachusetts	3,380	2.3%
13	Virginia	3,380	2.3%
15	Indiana	3,260	2.2%
16	Missouri	3,100	2.1%
17	Washington	2,890	2.0%
18	Wisconsin	2,770	1.9%
19	Arizona	2,680	1.8%
20	Kentucky	2,620	1.8%
20	Maryland	2,620	1.8%
22	Minnesota	2,520	1.7%
23	Alabama	2,480	1.7%
24	Louisiana	2,330	1.6%
25	South Carolina	2,150	1.5%
26	Connecticut	1,950	1.3%
27	Colorado	1,860	1.3%
27	Oklahoma	1,860	1.3%
29	Iowa	1,800	1.2%
30	Oregon	1,780	1.2%
31	Arkansas	1,540	1.0%
32	Mississippi	1,480	1.0%
33	Kansas	1,290	0.9%
34	Nevada	1,240	0.8%
35	West Virginia	1,070	0.7%
36	Nebraska	950	0.6%
37	Maine	870	0.6%
38	New Mexico	810	0.6%
39	Utah	770	0.5%
40	New Hampshire	730	0.5%
41	Hawaii	710	0.5%
42	Idaho	630	0.4%
43	Rhode Island	590	0.4%
44	Montana	520	0.4%
45	Delaware	440	0.3%
45	South Dakota	440	0.3%
47	North Dakota	350	0.2%
48	Vermont	330	0.2%
49	Alaska	250	0.2%
50	Wyoming	240	0.2%
	District of Columbia	260	0.2%

Source: American Cancer Society
   "Cancer Facts & Figures 2009" (Copyright 2009, American Cancer Society, http://www.cancer.org/docroot/stt/stt_0.asp)
*These estimates are offered as a rough guide and should be interpreted with caution. They are calculated according to the distribution of estimated 2009 cancer deaths by state.

Estimated Rate of New Colon and Rectum Cancer Cases in 2009

National Estimated Rate = 47.9 New Cases per 100,000 Population*

ALPHA ORDER

RANK	STATE	RATE
18	Alabama	52.7
49	Alaska	35.8
43	Arizona	40.6
14	Arkansas	53.3
45	California	39.7
48	Colorado	37.0
8	Connecticut	55.4
30	Delaware	49.7
6	Florida	56.2
47	Georgia	38.2
11	Hawaii	54.8
42	Idaho	40.8
29	Illinois	49.8
25	Indiana	50.8
4	Iowa	59.8
37	Kansas	45.8
2	Kentucky	60.7
21	Louisiana	51.9
1	Maine	66.0
36	Maryland	46.0
23	Massachusetts	51.3
26	Michigan	50.4
32	Minnesota	47.9
28	Mississippi	50.1
22	Missouri	51.8
14	Montana	53.3
17	Nebraska	52.9
34	Nevada	46.9
10	New Hampshire	55.1
18	New Jersey	52.7
44	New Mexico	40.3
24	New York	51.0
38	North Carolina	45.1
13	North Dakota	54.1
20	Ohio	52.5
26	Oklahoma	50.4
35	Oregon	46.5
3	Pennsylvania	60.2
7	Rhode Island	56.0
33	South Carolina	47.1
12	South Dakota	54.2
8	Tennessee	55.4
46	Texas	39.5
50	Utah	27.7
16	Vermont	53.1
41	Virginia	42.9
40	Washington	43.4
5	West Virginia	58.8
31	Wisconsin	49.0
39	Wyoming	44.1

RANK ORDER

RANK	STATE	RATE
1	Maine	66.0
2	Kentucky	60.7
3	Pennsylvania	60.2
4	Iowa	59.8
5	West Virginia	58.8
6	Florida	56.2
7	Rhode Island	56.0
8	Connecticut	55.4
8	Tennessee	55.4
10	New Hampshire	55.1
11	Hawaii	54.8
12	South Dakota	54.2
13	North Dakota	54.1
14	Arkansas	53.3
14	Montana	53.3
16	Vermont	53.1
17	Nebraska	52.9
18	Alabama	52.7
18	New Jersey	52.7
20	Ohio	52.5
21	Louisiana	51.9
22	Missouri	51.8
23	Massachusetts	51.3
24	New York	51.0
25	Indiana	50.8
26	Michigan	50.4
26	Oklahoma	50.4
28	Mississippi	50.1
29	Illinois	49.8
30	Delaware	49.7
31	Wisconsin	49.0
32	Minnesota	47.9
33	South Carolina	47.1
34	Nevada	46.9
35	Oregon	46.5
36	Maryland	46.0
37	Kansas	45.8
38	North Carolina	45.1
39	Wyoming	44.1
40	Washington	43.4
41	Virginia	42.9
42	Idaho	40.8
43	Arizona	40.6
44	New Mexico	40.3
45	California	39.7
46	Texas	39.5
47	Georgia	38.2
48	Colorado	37.0
49	Alaska	35.8
50	Utah	27.7
	District of Columbia	43.4

Source: CQ Press using data from American Cancer Society
   "Cancer Facts & Figures 2009" (Copyright 2009, American Cancer Society, http://www.cancer.org/docroot/stt/stt_0.asp)
*These estimates are offered as a rough guide and should be interpreted with caution. They are calculated according to the
distribution of estimated 2009 cancer deaths by state. Rates calculated using 2009 Census resident population estimates.

Percent of Adults Who Have Ever Had a Sigmoidoscopy or Colonoscopy Exam: 2008
National Median = 62.2% of Adults*

ALPHA ORDER

RANK	STATE	PERCENT
30	Alabama	60.7
38	Alaska	58.0
20	Arizona	63.8
47	Arkansas	55.3
32	California	59.8
26	Colorado	61.9
9	Connecticut	69.5
1	Delaware	74.3
19	Florida	64.2
25	Georgia	62.2
31	Hawaii	60.1
46	Idaho	55.6
35	Illinois	59.1
34	Indiana	59.3
20	Iowa	63.8
27	Kansas	61.7
22	Kentucky	63.7
50	Louisiana	52.6
2	Maine	72.6
5	Maryland	71.3
4	Massachusetts	71.4
11	Michigan	68.6
6	Minnesota	71.0
41	Mississippi	56.4
28	Missouri	61.4
40	Montana	56.5
37	Nebraska	58.6
45	Nevada	55.7
3	New Hampshire	71.7
36	New Jersey	58.7
44	New Mexico	55.9
17	New York	65.5
15	North Carolina	66.6
39	North Dakota	57.9
29	Ohio	60.8
48	Oklahoma	55.2
14	Oregon	66.8
23	Pennsylvania	62.5
10	Rhode Island	69.4
17	South Carolina	65.5
24	South Dakota	62.4
33	Tennessee	59.5
42	Texas	56.2
12	Utah	67.2
8	Vermont	69.6
7	Virginia	69.9
16	Washington	66.2
49	West Virginia	54.7
12	Wisconsin	67.2
43	Wyoming	56.0

RANK ORDER

RANK	STATE	PERCENT
1	Delaware	74.3
2	Maine	72.6
3	New Hampshire	71.7
4	Massachusetts	71.4
5	Maryland	71.3
6	Minnesota	71.0
7	Virginia	69.9
8	Vermont	69.6
9	Connecticut	69.5
10	Rhode Island	69.4
11	Michigan	68.6
12	Utah	67.2
12	Wisconsin	67.2
14	Oregon	66.8
15	North Carolina	66.6
16	Washington	66.2
17	New York	65.5
17	South Carolina	65.5
19	Florida	64.2
20	Arizona	63.8
20	Iowa	63.8
22	Kentucky	63.7
23	Pennsylvania	62.5
24	South Dakota	62.4
25	Georgia	62.2
26	Colorado	61.9
27	Kansas	61.7
28	Missouri	61.4
29	Ohio	60.8
30	Alabama	60.7
31	Hawaii	60.1
32	California	59.8
33	Tennessee	59.5
34	Indiana	59.3
35	Illinois	59.1
36	New Jersey	58.7
37	Nebraska	58.6
38	Alaska	58.0
39	North Dakota	57.9
40	Montana	56.5
41	Mississippi	56.4
42	Texas	56.2
43	Wyoming	56.0
44	New Mexico	55.9
45	Nevada	55.7
46	Idaho	55.6
47	Arkansas	55.3
48	Oklahoma	55.2
49	West Virginia	54.7
50	Louisiana	52.6

District of Columbia — 68.6

Source: U.S. Department of Health and Human Services, Centers for Disease Control and Prevention
"2008 Behavioral Risk Factor Surveillance Summary Prevalence Data" (http://apps.nccd.cdc.gov/brfss/)
*Persons 50 and older.

Estimated New Leukemia Cases in 2009

National Estimated Total = 44,790 New Cases*

ALPHA ORDER

RANK	STATE	CASES	% of USA
25	Alabama	590	1.3%
49	Alaska	70	0.2%
20	Arizona	810	1.8%
31	Arkansas	420	0.9%
1	California	4,570	10.2%
21	Colorado	720	1.6%
29	Connecticut	540	1.2%
46	Delaware	120	0.3%
3	Florida	3,180	7.1%
11	Georgia	1,080	2.4%
44	Hawaii	160	0.4%
40	Idaho	250	0.6%
7	Illinois	1,940	4.3%
16	Indiana	930	2.1%
25	Iowa	590	1.3%
32	Kansas	380	0.8%
22	Kentucky	690	1.5%
23	Louisiana	660	1.5%
39	Maine	270	0.6%
24	Maryland	640	1.4%
12	Massachusetts	1,000	2.2%
8	Michigan	1,690	3.8%
17	Minnesota	890	2.0%
34	Mississippi	360	0.8%
18	Missouri	880	2.0%
43	Montana	170	0.4%
37	Nebraska	290	0.6%
32	Nevada	380	0.8%
41	New Hampshire	210	0.5%
9	New Jersey	1,380	3.1%
36	New Mexico	310	0.7%
4	New York	3,140	7.0%
10	North Carolina	1,150	2.6%
47	North Dakota	110	0.2%
6	Ohio	1,950	4.4%
28	Oklahoma	580	1.3%
30	Oregon	490	1.1%
5	Pennsylvania	2,200	4.9%
42	Rhode Island	180	0.4%
25	South Carolina	590	1.3%
45	South Dakota	140	0.3%
12	Tennessee	1,000	2.2%
2	Texas	3,470	7.7%
35	Utah	330	0.7%
48	Vermont	100	0.2%
19	Virginia	840	1.9%
14	Washington	990	2.2%
37	West Virginia	290	0.6%
15	Wisconsin	980	2.2%
49	Wyoming	70	0.2%

RANK ORDER

RANK	STATE	CASES	% of USA
1	California	4,570	10.2%
2	Texas	3,470	7.7%
3	Florida	3,180	7.1%
4	New York	3,140	7.0%
5	Pennsylvania	2,200	4.9%
6	Ohio	1,950	4.4%
7	Illinois	1,940	4.3%
8	Michigan	1,690	3.8%
9	New Jersey	1,380	3.1%
10	North Carolina	1,150	2.6%
11	Georgia	1,080	2.4%
12	Massachusetts	1,000	2.2%
12	Tennessee	1,000	2.2%
14	Washington	990	2.2%
15	Wisconsin	980	2.2%
16	Indiana	930	2.1%
17	Minnesota	890	2.0%
18	Missouri	880	2.0%
19	Virginia	840	1.9%
20	Arizona	810	1.8%
21	Colorado	720	1.6%
22	Kentucky	690	1.5%
23	Louisiana	660	1.5%
24	Maryland	640	1.4%
25	Alabama	590	1.3%
25	Iowa	590	1.3%
25	South Carolina	590	1.3%
28	Oklahoma	580	1.3%
29	Connecticut	540	1.2%
30	Oregon	490	1.1%
31	Arkansas	420	0.9%
32	Kansas	380	0.8%
32	Nevada	380	0.8%
34	Mississippi	360	0.8%
35	Utah	330	0.7%
36	New Mexico	310	0.7%
37	Nebraska	290	0.6%
37	West Virginia	290	0.6%
39	Maine	270	0.6%
40	Idaho	250	0.6%
41	New Hampshire	210	0.5%
42	Rhode Island	180	0.4%
43	Montana	170	0.4%
44	Hawaii	160	0.4%
45	South Dakota	140	0.3%
46	Delaware	120	0.3%
47	North Dakota	110	0.2%
48	Vermont	100	0.2%
49	Alaska	70	0.2%
49	Wyoming	70	0.2%
	District of Columbia	50	0.1%

Source: American Cancer Society
    "Cancer Facts & Figures 2009" (Copyright 2009, American Cancer Society, http://www.cancer.org/docroot/stt/stt_0.asp)
*These estimates are offered as a rough guide and should be interpreted with caution. They are calculated according to the distribution of estimated 2009 cancer deaths by state.

Estimated Rate of New Leukemia Cases in 2009

National Estimated Rate = 14.6 New Cases per 100,000 Population*

ALPHA ORDER

RANK	STATE	RATE
40	Alabama	12.5
50	Alaska	10.0
43	Arizona	12.3
30	Arkansas	14.5
41	California	12.4
33	Colorado	14.3
24	Connecticut	15.3
35	Delaware	13.6
6	Florida	17.2
48	Georgia	11.0
41	Hawaii	12.4
13	Idaho	16.2
26	Illinois	15.0
30	Indiana	14.5
2	Iowa	19.6
36	Kansas	13.5
17	Kentucky	16.0
28	Louisiana	14.7
1	Maine	20.5
47	Maryland	11.2
25	Massachusetts	15.2
9	Michigan	17.0
11	Minnesota	16.9
45	Mississippi	12.2
28	Missouri	14.7
4	Montana	17.4
14	Nebraska	16.1
32	Nevada	14.4
18	New Hampshire	15.9
21	New Jersey	15.8
23	New Mexico	15.4
14	New York	16.1
43	North Carolina	12.3
9	North Dakota	17.0
11	Ohio	16.9
22	Oklahoma	15.7
39	Oregon	12.8
3	Pennsylvania	17.5
8	Rhode Island	17.1
37	South Carolina	12.9
6	South Dakota	17.2
18	Tennessee	15.9
34	Texas	14.0
46	Utah	11.9
14	Vermont	16.1
49	Virginia	10.7
27	Washington	14.9
18	West Virginia	15.9
5	Wisconsin	17.3
37	Wyoming	12.9

RANK ORDER

RANK	STATE	RATE
1	Maine	20.5
2	Iowa	19.6
3	Pennsylvania	17.5
4	Montana	17.4
5	Wisconsin	17.3
6	Florida	17.2
6	South Dakota	17.2
8	Rhode Island	17.1
9	Michigan	17.0
9	North Dakota	17.0
11	Minnesota	16.9
11	Ohio	16.9
13	Idaho	16.2
14	Nebraska	16.1
14	New York	16.1
14	Vermont	16.1
17	Kentucky	16.0
18	New Hampshire	15.9
18	Tennessee	15.9
18	West Virginia	15.9
21	New Jersey	15.8
22	Oklahoma	15.7
23	New Mexico	15.4
24	Connecticut	15.3
25	Massachusetts	15.2
26	Illinois	15.0
27	Washington	14.9
28	Louisiana	14.7
28	Missouri	14.7
30	Arkansas	14.5
30	Indiana	14.5
32	Nevada	14.4
33	Colorado	14.3
34	Texas	14.0
35	Delaware	13.6
36	Kansas	13.5
37	South Carolina	12.9
37	Wyoming	12.9
39	Oregon	12.8
40	Alabama	12.5
41	California	12.4
41	Hawaii	12.4
43	Arizona	12.3
43	North Carolina	12.3
45	Mississippi	12.2
46	Utah	11.9
47	Maryland	11.2
48	Georgia	11.0
49	Virginia	10.7
50	Alaska	10.0

District of Columbia   8.3

Source: CQ Press using data from American Cancer Society
"Cancer Facts & Figures 2009" (Copyright 2009, American Cancer Society, http://www.cancer.org/docroot/stt/stt_0.asp)
*These estimates are offered as a rough guide and should be interpreted with caution. They are calculated according to the distribution of estimated 2009 cancer deaths by state. Rates calculated using 2009 Census resident population estimates.

Estimated New Lung Cancer Cases in 2009

National Estimated Total = 219,440 New Cases*

ALPHA ORDER

RANK	STATE	CASES	% of USA
20	Alabama	4,040	1.8%
49	Alaska	350	0.2%
21	Arizona	3,960	1.8%
30	Arkansas	2,580	1.2%
1	California	17,910	8.2%
32	Colorado	2,240	1.0%
27	Connecticut	2,720	1.2%
42	Delaware	800	0.4%
2	Florida	17,790	8.1%
11	Georgia	6,150	2.8%
43	Hawaii	740	0.3%
41	Idaho	820	0.4%
7	Illinois	9,180	4.2%
14	Indiana	5,360	2.4%
28	Iowa	2,620	1.2%
33	Kansas	2,110	1.0%
17	Kentucky	4,650	2.1%
24	Louisiana	3,650	1.7%
36	Maine	1,390	0.6%
19	Maryland	4,060	1.9%
16	Massachusetts	5,120	2.3%
8	Michigan	8,190	3.7%
25	Minnesota	3,310	1.5%
31	Mississippi	2,340	1.1%
12	Missouri	5,600	2.6%
44	Montana	730	0.3%
37	Nebraska	1,230	0.6%
35	Nevada	1,910	0.9%
38	New Hampshire	1,100	0.5%
10	New Jersey	6,250	2.8%
39	New Mexico	970	0.4%
4	New York	13,550	6.2%
9	North Carolina	6,670	3.0%
48	North Dakota	420	0.2%
5	Ohio	10,690	4.9%
26	Oklahoma	3,220	1.5%
29	Oregon	2,610	1.2%
6	Pennsylvania	10,480	4.8%
40	Rhode Island	900	0.4%
23	South Carolina	3,680	1.7%
46	South Dakota	590	0.3%
13	Tennessee	5,370	2.4%
3	Texas	14,150	6.4%
45	Utah	620	0.3%
47	Vermont	500	0.2%
15	Virginia	5,330	2.4%
18	Washington	4,130	1.9%
34	West Virginia	2,030	0.9%
21	Wisconsin	3,960	1.8%
50	Wyoming	320	0.1%

RANK ORDER

RANK	STATE	CASES	% of USA
1	California	17,910	8.2%
2	Florida	17,790	8.1%
3	Texas	14,150	6.4%
4	New York	13,550	6.2%
5	Ohio	10,690	4.9%
6	Pennsylvania	10,480	4.8%
7	Illinois	9,180	4.2%
8	Michigan	8,190	3.7%
9	North Carolina	6,670	3.0%
10	New Jersey	6,250	2.8%
11	Georgia	6,150	2.8%
12	Missouri	5,600	2.6%
13	Tennessee	5,370	2.4%
14	Indiana	5,360	2.4%
15	Virginia	5,330	2.4%
16	Massachusetts	5,120	2.3%
17	Kentucky	4,650	2.1%
18	Washington	4,130	1.9%
19	Maryland	4,060	1.9%
20	Alabama	4,040	1.8%
21	Arizona	3,960	1.8%
21	Wisconsin	3,960	1.8%
23	South Carolina	3,680	1.7%
24	Louisiana	3,650	1.7%
25	Minnesota	3,310	1.5%
26	Oklahoma	3,220	1.5%
27	Connecticut	2,720	1.2%
28	Iowa	2,620	1.2%
29	Oregon	2,610	1.2%
30	Arkansas	2,580	1.2%
31	Mississippi	2,340	1.1%
32	Colorado	2,240	1.0%
33	Kansas	2,110	1.0%
34	West Virginia	2,030	0.9%
35	Nevada	1,910	0.9%
36	Maine	1,390	0.6%
37	Nebraska	1,230	0.6%
38	New Hampshire	1,100	0.5%
39	New Mexico	970	0.4%
40	Rhode Island	900	0.4%
41	Idaho	820	0.4%
42	Delaware	800	0.4%
43	Hawaii	740	0.3%
44	Montana	730	0.3%
45	Utah	620	0.3%
46	South Dakota	590	0.3%
47	Vermont	500	0.2%
48	North Dakota	420	0.2%
49	Alaska	350	0.2%
50	Wyoming	320	0.1%
	District of Columbia	370	0.2%

Source: American Cancer Society
   "Cancer Facts & Figures 2009" (Copyright 2009, American Cancer Society, http://www.cancer.org/docroot/stt/stt_0.asp)
*These estimates are offered as a rough guide and should be interpreted with caution. They are calculated according to the distribution of estimated 2009 cancer deaths by state.

Estimated Rate of New Lung Cancer Cases in 2009

National Estimated Rate = 71.5 New Cases per 100,000 Population*

<table>
<tr><td colspan="3">ALPHA ORDER</td><td colspan="3">RANK ORDER</td></tr>
<tr><th>RANK</th><th>STATE</th><th>RATE</th><th>RANK</th><th>STATE</th><th>RATE</th></tr>
<tr><td>11</td><td>Alabama</td><td>85.8</td><td>1</td><td>West Virginia</td><td>111.6</td></tr>
<tr><td>46</td><td>Alaska</td><td>50.1</td><td>2</td><td>Kentucky</td><td>107.8</td></tr>
<tr><td>41</td><td>Arizona</td><td>60.0</td><td>3</td><td>Maine</td><td>105.4</td></tr>
<tr><td>8</td><td>Arkansas</td><td>89.3</td><td>4</td><td>Florida</td><td>96.0</td></tr>
<tr><td>47</td><td>California</td><td>48.5</td><td>5</td><td>Missouri</td><td>93.5</td></tr>
<tr><td>49</td><td>Colorado</td><td>44.6</td><td>6</td><td>Ohio</td><td>92.6</td></tr>
<tr><td>23</td><td>Connecticut</td><td>77.3</td><td>7</td><td>Delaware</td><td>90.4</td></tr>
<tr><td>7</td><td>Delaware</td><td>90.4</td><td>8</td><td>Arkansas</td><td>89.3</td></tr>
<tr><td>4</td><td>Florida</td><td>96.0</td><td>9</td><td>Oklahoma</td><td>87.3</td></tr>
<tr><td>39</td><td>Georgia</td><td>62.6</td><td>10</td><td>Iowa</td><td>87.1</td></tr>
<tr><td>43</td><td>Hawaii</td><td>57.1</td><td>11</td><td>Alabama</td><td>85.8</td></tr>
<tr><td>45</td><td>Idaho</td><td>53.0</td><td>12</td><td>Rhode Island</td><td>85.5</td></tr>
<tr><td>30</td><td>Illinois</td><td>71.1</td><td>13</td><td>Tennessee</td><td>85.3</td></tr>
<tr><td>14</td><td>Indiana</td><td>83.4</td><td>14</td><td>Indiana</td><td>83.4</td></tr>
<tr><td>10</td><td>Iowa</td><td>87.1</td><td>15</td><td>Pennsylvania</td><td>83.1</td></tr>
<tr><td>24</td><td>Kansas</td><td>74.9</td><td>16</td><td>New Hampshire</td><td>83.0</td></tr>
<tr><td>2</td><td>Kentucky</td><td>107.8</td><td>17</td><td>Michigan</td><td>82.1</td></tr>
<tr><td>18</td><td>Louisiana</td><td>81.3</td><td>18</td><td>Louisiana</td><td>81.3</td></tr>
<tr><td>3</td><td>Maine</td><td>105.4</td><td>19</td><td>South Carolina</td><td>80.7</td></tr>
<tr><td>29</td><td>Maryland</td><td>71.2</td><td>20</td><td>Vermont</td><td>80.4</td></tr>
<tr><td>22</td><td>Massachusetts</td><td>77.7</td><td>21</td><td>Mississippi</td><td>79.3</td></tr>
<tr><td>17</td><td>Michigan</td><td>82.1</td><td>22</td><td>Massachusetts</td><td>77.7</td></tr>
<tr><td>38</td><td>Minnesota</td><td>62.9</td><td>23</td><td>Connecticut</td><td>77.3</td></tr>
<tr><td>21</td><td>Mississippi</td><td>79.3</td><td>24</td><td>Kansas</td><td>74.9</td></tr>
<tr><td>5</td><td>Missouri</td><td>93.5</td><td>24</td><td>Montana</td><td>74.9</td></tr>
<tr><td>24</td><td>Montana</td><td>74.9</td><td>26</td><td>South Dakota</td><td>72.6</td></tr>
<tr><td>34</td><td>Nebraska</td><td>68.5</td><td>27</td><td>Nevada</td><td>72.3</td></tr>
<tr><td>27</td><td>Nevada</td><td>72.3</td><td>28</td><td>New Jersey</td><td>71.8</td></tr>
<tr><td>16</td><td>New Hampshire</td><td>83.0</td><td>29</td><td>Maryland</td><td>71.2</td></tr>
<tr><td>28</td><td>New Jersey</td><td>71.8</td><td>30</td><td>Illinois</td><td>71.1</td></tr>
<tr><td>48</td><td>New Mexico</td><td>48.3</td><td>30</td><td>North Carolina</td><td>71.1</td></tr>
<tr><td>33</td><td>New York</td><td>69.3</td><td>32</td><td>Wisconsin</td><td>70.0</td></tr>
<tr><td>30</td><td>North Carolina</td><td>71.1</td><td>33</td><td>New York</td><td>69.3</td></tr>
<tr><td>37</td><td>North Dakota</td><td>64.9</td><td>34</td><td>Nebraska</td><td>68.5</td></tr>
<tr><td>6</td><td>Ohio</td><td>92.6</td><td>35</td><td>Oregon</td><td>68.2</td></tr>
<tr><td>9</td><td>Oklahoma</td><td>87.3</td><td>36</td><td>Virginia</td><td>67.6</td></tr>
<tr><td>35</td><td>Oregon</td><td>68.2</td><td>37</td><td>North Dakota</td><td>64.9</td></tr>
<tr><td>15</td><td>Pennsylvania</td><td>83.1</td><td>38</td><td>Minnesota</td><td>62.9</td></tr>
<tr><td>12</td><td>Rhode Island</td><td>85.5</td><td>39</td><td>Georgia</td><td>62.6</td></tr>
<tr><td>19</td><td>South Carolina</td><td>80.7</td><td>40</td><td>Washington</td><td>62.0</td></tr>
<tr><td>26</td><td>South Dakota</td><td>72.6</td><td>41</td><td>Arizona</td><td>60.0</td></tr>
<tr><td>13</td><td>Tennessee</td><td>85.3</td><td>42</td><td>Wyoming</td><td>58.8</td></tr>
<tr><td>43</td><td>Texas</td><td>57.1</td><td>43</td><td>Hawaii</td><td>57.1</td></tr>
<tr><td>50</td><td>Utah</td><td>22.3</td><td>43</td><td>Texas</td><td>57.1</td></tr>
<tr><td>20</td><td>Vermont</td><td>80.4</td><td>45</td><td>Idaho</td><td>53.0</td></tr>
<tr><td>36</td><td>Virginia</td><td>67.6</td><td>46</td><td>Alaska</td><td>50.1</td></tr>
<tr><td>40</td><td>Washington</td><td>62.0</td><td>47</td><td>California</td><td>48.5</td></tr>
<tr><td>1</td><td>West Virginia</td><td>111.6</td><td>48</td><td>New Mexico</td><td>48.3</td></tr>
<tr><td>32</td><td>Wisconsin</td><td>70.0</td><td>49</td><td>Colorado</td><td>44.6</td></tr>
<tr><td>42</td><td>Wyoming</td><td>58.8</td><td>50</td><td>Utah</td><td>22.3</td></tr>
<tr><td></td><td></td><td></td><td></td><td>District of Columbia</td><td>61.7</td></tr>
</table>

Source: CQ Press using data from American Cancer Society

"Cancer Facts & Figures 2009" (Copyright 2009, American Cancer Society, http://www.cancer.org/docroot/stt/stt_0.asp)

*These estimates are offered as a rough guide and should be interpreted with caution. They are calculated according to the distribution of estimated 2009 cancer deaths by state. Rates calculated using 2009 Census resident population estimates.

Estimated New Non-Hodgkin's Lymphoma Cases in 2009

National Estimated Total = 65,980 New Cases*

ALPHA ORDER

RANK	STATE	CASES	% of USA
24	Alabama	950	1.4%
49	Alaska	110	0.2%
18	Arizona	1,250	1.9%
31	Arkansas	680	1.0%
1	California	7,140	10.8%
25	Colorado	920	1.4%
25	Connecticut	920	1.4%
45	Delaware	190	0.3%
2	Florida	4,640	7.0%
12	Georgia	1,560	2.4%
42	Hawaii	260	0.4%
40	Idaho	330	0.5%
6	Illinois	2,900	4.4%
15	Indiana	1,420	2.2%
30	Iowa	750	1.1%
32	Kansas	600	0.9%
22	Kentucky	980	1.5%
23	Louisiana	960	1.5%
38	Maine	360	0.5%
21	Maryland	1,120	1.7%
11	Massachusetts	1,610	2.4%
8	Michigan	2,470	3.7%
20	Minnesota	1,130	1.7%
33	Mississippi	540	0.8%
18	Missouri	1,250	1.9%
44	Montana	240	0.4%
37	Nebraska	400	0.6%
34	Nevada	480	0.7%
41	New Hampshire	310	0.5%
9	New Jersey	2,160	3.3%
38	New Mexico	360	0.5%
3	New York	4,540	6.9%
10	North Carolina	1,730	2.6%
47	North Dakota	140	0.2%
7	Ohio	2,800	4.2%
29	Oklahoma	820	1.2%
27	Oregon	910	1.4%
5	Pennsylvania	3,330	5.0%
42	Rhode Island	260	0.4%
28	South Carolina	870	1.3%
46	South Dakota	180	0.3%
16	Tennessee	1,370	2.1%
4	Texas	4,530	6.9%
35	Utah	440	0.7%
47	Vermont	140	0.2%
14	Virginia	1,450	2.2%
13	Washington	1,540	2.3%
36	West Virginia	420	0.6%
17	Wisconsin	1,310	2.0%
49	Wyoming	110	0.2%

RANK ORDER

RANK	STATE	CASES	% of USA
1	California	7,140	10.8%
2	Florida	4,640	7.0%
3	New York	4,540	6.9%
4	Texas	4,530	6.9%
5	Pennsylvania	3,330	5.0%
6	Illinois	2,900	4.4%
7	Ohio	2,800	4.2%
8	Michigan	2,470	3.7%
9	New Jersey	2,160	3.3%
10	North Carolina	1,730	2.6%
11	Massachusetts	1,610	2.4%
12	Georgia	1,560	2.4%
13	Washington	1,540	2.3%
14	Virginia	1,450	2.2%
15	Indiana	1,420	2.2%
16	Tennessee	1,370	2.1%
17	Wisconsin	1,310	2.0%
18	Arizona	1,250	1.9%
18	Missouri	1,250	1.9%
20	Minnesota	1,130	1.7%
21	Maryland	1,120	1.7%
22	Kentucky	980	1.5%
23	Louisiana	960	1.5%
24	Alabama	950	1.4%
25	Colorado	920	1.4%
25	Connecticut	920	1.4%
27	Oregon	910	1.4%
28	South Carolina	870	1.3%
29	Oklahoma	820	1.2%
30	Iowa	750	1.1%
31	Arkansas	680	1.0%
32	Kansas	600	0.9%
33	Mississippi	540	0.8%
34	Nevada	480	0.7%
35	Utah	440	0.7%
36	West Virginia	420	0.6%
37	Nebraska	400	0.6%
38	Maine	360	0.5%
38	New Mexico	360	0.5%
40	Idaho	330	0.5%
41	New Hampshire	310	0.5%
42	Hawaii	260	0.4%
42	Rhode Island	260	0.4%
44	Montana	240	0.4%
45	Delaware	190	0.3%
46	South Dakota	180	0.3%
47	North Dakota	140	0.2%
47	Vermont	140	0.2%
49	Alaska	110	0.2%
49	Wyoming	110	0.2%
	District of Columbia	90	0.1%

Source: American Cancer Society
"Cancer Facts & Figures 2009" (Copyright 2009, American Cancer Society, http://www.cancer.org/docroot/stt/stt_0.asp)
*These estimates are offered as a rough guide and should be interpreted with caution. They are calculated according to the distribution of estimated 2009 cancer deaths by state.

Estimated Rate of New Non-Hodgkin's Lymphoma Cases in 2009

National Estimated Rate = 21.5 New Cases per 100,000 Population*

<table>
<tr><td colspan="3">ALPHA ORDER</td><td colspan="3">RANK ORDER</td></tr>
<tr><th>RANK</th><th>STATE</th><th>RATE</th><th>RANK</th><th>STATE</th><th>RATE</th></tr>
<tr><td>34</td><td>Alabama</td><td>20.2</td><td>1</td><td>Maine</td><td>27.3</td></tr>
<tr><td>50</td><td>Alaska</td><td>15.7</td><td>2</td><td>Pennsylvania</td><td>26.4</td></tr>
<tr><td>40</td><td>Arizona</td><td>19.0</td><td>3</td><td>Connecticut</td><td>26.1</td></tr>
<tr><td>13</td><td>Arkansas</td><td>23.5</td><td>4</td><td>Florida</td><td>25.0</td></tr>
<tr><td>38</td><td>California</td><td>19.3</td><td>5</td><td>Iowa</td><td>24.9</td></tr>
<tr><td>43</td><td>Colorado</td><td>18.3</td><td>6</td><td>Michigan</td><td>24.8</td></tr>
<tr><td>3</td><td>Connecticut</td><td>26.1</td><td>6</td><td>New Jersey</td><td>24.8</td></tr>
<tr><td>28</td><td>Delaware</td><td>21.5</td><td>8</td><td>Rhode Island</td><td>24.7</td></tr>
<tr><td>4</td><td>Florida</td><td>25.0</td><td>9</td><td>Montana</td><td>24.6</td></tr>
<tr><td>48</td><td>Georgia</td><td>15.9</td><td>10</td><td>Massachusetts</td><td>24.4</td></tr>
<tr><td>36</td><td>Hawaii</td><td>20.1</td><td>11</td><td>Ohio</td><td>24.3</td></tr>
<tr><td>31</td><td>Idaho</td><td>21.3</td><td>12</td><td>Oregon</td><td>23.8</td></tr>
<tr><td>20</td><td>Illinois</td><td>22.5</td><td>13</td><td>Arkansas</td><td>23.5</td></tr>
<tr><td>25</td><td>Indiana</td><td>22.1</td><td>14</td><td>New Hampshire</td><td>23.4</td></tr>
<tr><td>5</td><td>Iowa</td><td>24.9</td><td>15</td><td>New York</td><td>23.2</td></tr>
<tr><td>31</td><td>Kansas</td><td>21.3</td><td>15</td><td>Wisconsin</td><td>23.2</td></tr>
<tr><td>19</td><td>Kentucky</td><td>22.7</td><td>17</td><td>Washington</td><td>23.1</td></tr>
<tr><td>30</td><td>Louisiana</td><td>21.4</td><td>17</td><td>West Virginia</td><td>23.1</td></tr>
<tr><td>1</td><td>Maine</td><td>27.3</td><td>19</td><td>Kentucky</td><td>22.7</td></tr>
<tr><td>37</td><td>Maryland</td><td>19.7</td><td>20</td><td>Illinois</td><td>22.5</td></tr>
<tr><td>10</td><td>Massachusetts</td><td>24.4</td><td>20</td><td>Vermont</td><td>22.5</td></tr>
<tr><td>6</td><td>Michigan</td><td>24.8</td><td>22</td><td>Nebraska</td><td>22.3</td></tr>
<tr><td>28</td><td>Minnesota</td><td>21.5</td><td>23</td><td>Oklahoma</td><td>22.2</td></tr>
<tr><td>43</td><td>Mississippi</td><td>18.3</td><td>23</td><td>South Dakota</td><td>22.2</td></tr>
<tr><td>33</td><td>Missouri</td><td>20.9</td><td>25</td><td>Indiana</td><td>22.1</td></tr>
<tr><td>9</td><td>Montana</td><td>24.6</td><td>26</td><td>Tennessee</td><td>21.8</td></tr>
<tr><td>22</td><td>Nebraska</td><td>22.3</td><td>27</td><td>North Dakota</td><td>21.6</td></tr>
<tr><td>46</td><td>Nevada</td><td>18.2</td><td>28</td><td>Delaware</td><td>21.5</td></tr>
<tr><td>14</td><td>New Hampshire</td><td>23.4</td><td>28</td><td>Minnesota</td><td>21.5</td></tr>
<tr><td>6</td><td>New Jersey</td><td>24.8</td><td>30</td><td>Louisiana</td><td>21.4</td></tr>
<tr><td>47</td><td>New Mexico</td><td>17.9</td><td>31</td><td>Idaho</td><td>21.3</td></tr>
<tr><td>15</td><td>New York</td><td>23.2</td><td>31</td><td>Kansas</td><td>21.3</td></tr>
<tr><td>41</td><td>North Carolina</td><td>18.4</td><td>33</td><td>Missouri</td><td>20.9</td></tr>
<tr><td>27</td><td>North Dakota</td><td>21.6</td><td>34</td><td>Alabama</td><td>20.2</td></tr>
<tr><td>11</td><td>Ohio</td><td>24.3</td><td>34</td><td>Wyoming</td><td>20.2</td></tr>
<tr><td>23</td><td>Oklahoma</td><td>22.2</td><td>36</td><td>Hawaii</td><td>20.1</td></tr>
<tr><td>12</td><td>Oregon</td><td>23.8</td><td>37</td><td>Maryland</td><td>19.7</td></tr>
<tr><td>2</td><td>Pennsylvania</td><td>26.4</td><td>38</td><td>California</td><td>19.3</td></tr>
<tr><td>8</td><td>Rhode Island</td><td>24.7</td><td>39</td><td>South Carolina</td><td>19.1</td></tr>
<tr><td>39</td><td>South Carolina</td><td>19.1</td><td>40</td><td>Arizona</td><td>19.0</td></tr>
<tr><td>23</td><td>South Dakota</td><td>22.2</td><td>41</td><td>North Carolina</td><td>18.4</td></tr>
<tr><td>26</td><td>Tennessee</td><td>21.8</td><td>41</td><td>Virginia</td><td>18.4</td></tr>
<tr><td>43</td><td>Texas</td><td>18.3</td><td>43</td><td>Colorado</td><td>18.3</td></tr>
<tr><td>49</td><td>Utah</td><td>15.8</td><td>43</td><td>Mississippi</td><td>18.3</td></tr>
<tr><td>20</td><td>Vermont</td><td>22.5</td><td>43</td><td>Texas</td><td>18.3</td></tr>
<tr><td>41</td><td>Virginia</td><td>18.4</td><td>46</td><td>Nevada</td><td>18.2</td></tr>
<tr><td>17</td><td>Washington</td><td>23.1</td><td>47</td><td>New Mexico</td><td>17.9</td></tr>
<tr><td>17</td><td>West Virginia</td><td>23.1</td><td>48</td><td>Georgia</td><td>15.9</td></tr>
<tr><td>15</td><td>Wisconsin</td><td>23.2</td><td>49</td><td>Utah</td><td>15.8</td></tr>
<tr><td>34</td><td>Wyoming</td><td>20.2</td><td>50</td><td>Alaska</td><td>15.7</td></tr>
<tr><td></td><td></td><td></td><td></td><td>District of Columbia</td><td>15.0</td></tr>
</table>

Source: CQ Press using data from American Cancer Society
"Cancer Facts & Figures 2009" (Copyright 2009, American Cancer Society, http://www.cancer.org/docroot/stt/stt_0.asp)
*These estimates are offered as a rough guide and should be interpreted with caution. They are calculated according to the distribution of estimated 2009 cancer deaths by state. Rates calculated using 2009 Census resident population estimates.

Estimated New Prostate Cancer Cases in 2009

National Estimated Total = 192,280 New Cases*

ALPHA ORDER					RANK ORDER			
RANK	STATE	CASES	% of USA		RANK	STATE	CASES	% of USA
25	Alabama	2,800	1.5%		1	California	20,790	10.8%
50	Alaska	360	0.2%		2	Texas	13,130	6.8%
19	Arizona	3,530	1.8%		3	New York	12,520	6.5%
31	Arkansas	2,140	1.1%		4	Florida	12,380	6.4%
1	California	20,790	10.8%		5	Pennsylvania	8,130	4.2%
22	Colorado	3,070	1.6%		6	Illinois	7,590	3.9%
28	Connecticut	2,400	1.2%		7	Michigan	7,010	3.6%
47	Delaware	550	0.3%		8	Ohio	6,510	3.4%
4	Florida	12,380	6.4%		9	North Carolina	6,130	3.2%
11	Georgia	5,210	2.7%		10	New Jersey	6,060	3.2%
42	Hawaii	860	0.4%		11	Georgia	5,210	2.7%
39	Idaho	1,170	0.6%		12	Minnesota	4,910	2.6%
6	Illinois	7,590	3.9%		13	Virginia	4,830	2.5%
20	Indiana	3,250	1.7%		14	Tennessee	4,790	2.5%
29	Iowa	2,330	1.2%		15	Washington	4,680	2.4%
33	Kansas	1,970	1.0%		16	Massachusetts	4,200	2.2%
23	Kentucky	2,910	1.5%		17	Missouri	3,620	1.9%
21	Louisiana	3,160	1.6%		18	Maryland	3,580	1.9%
40	Maine	1,130	0.6%		19	Arizona	3,530	1.8%
18	Maryland	3,580	1.9%		20	Indiana	3,250	1.7%
16	Massachusetts	4,200	2.2%		21	Louisiana	3,160	1.6%
7	Michigan	7,010	3.6%		22	Colorado	3,070	1.6%
12	Minnesota	4,910	2.6%		23	Kentucky	2,910	1.5%
32	Mississippi	1,990	1.0%		23	South Carolina	2,910	1.5%
17	Missouri	3,620	1.9%		25	Alabama	2,800	1.5%
43	Montana	810	0.4%		26	Wisconsin	2,770	1.4%
36	Nebraska	1,410	0.7%		27	Oregon	2,510	1.3%
34	Nevada	1,660	0.9%		28	Connecticut	2,400	1.2%
41	New Hampshire	910	0.5%		29	Iowa	2,330	1.2%
10	New Jersey	6,060	3.2%		30	Oklahoma	2,190	1.1%
37	New Mexico	1,400	0.7%		31	Arkansas	2,140	1.1%
3	New York	12,520	6.5%		32	Mississippi	1,990	1.0%
9	North Carolina	6,130	3.2%		33	Kansas	1,970	1.0%
46	North Dakota	560	0.3%		34	Nevada	1,660	0.9%
8	Ohio	6,510	3.4%		35	Utah	1,570	0.8%
30	Oklahoma	2,190	1.1%		36	Nebraska	1,410	0.7%
27	Oregon	2,510	1.3%		37	New Mexico	1,400	0.7%
5	Pennsylvania	8,130	4.2%		38	West Virginia	1,210	0.6%
45	Rhode Island	650	0.3%		39	Idaho	1,170	0.6%
23	South Carolina	2,910	1.5%		40	Maine	1,130	0.6%
44	South Dakota	740	0.4%		41	New Hampshire	910	0.5%
14	Tennessee	4,790	2.5%		42	Hawaii	860	0.4%
2	Texas	13,130	6.8%		43	Montana	810	0.4%
35	Utah	1,570	0.8%		44	South Dakota	740	0.4%
48	Vermont	540	0.3%		45	Rhode Island	650	0.3%
13	Virginia	4,830	2.5%		46	North Dakota	560	0.3%
15	Washington	4,680	2.4%		47	Delaware	550	0.3%
38	West Virginia	1,210	0.6%		48	Vermont	540	0.3%
26	Wisconsin	2,770	1.4%		49	Wyoming	390	0.2%
49	Wyoming	390	0.2%		50	Alaska	360	0.2%
						District of Columbia	380	0.2%

Source: American Cancer Society
    "Cancer Facts & Figures 2009" (Copyright 2009, American Cancer Society, http://www.cancer.org/docroot/stt/stt_0.asp)
*These estimates are offered as a rough guide and should be interpreted with caution. They are calculated according to the distribution of estimated 2009 cancer deaths by state.

Age-Adjusted Incidence Rate of Prostate Cancer Cases in 2005

National Rate = 158.2 New Cases per 100,000 Male Population*

ALPHA ORDER

RANK	STATE	RATE
31	Alabama	150.7
30	Alaska	151.3
45	Arizona	116.6
25	Arkansas	158.1
28	California	152.6
24	Colorado	159.4
16	Connecticut	166.6
8	Delaware	175.5
39	Florida	143.1
18	Georgia	163.6
43	Hawaii	129.3
13	Idaho	168.8
23	Illinois	159.5
41	Indiana	136.9
34	Iowa	147.3
NA	Kansas**	NA
38	Kentucky	144.4
7	Louisiana	180.2
15	Maine	166.8
NA	Maryland**	NA
12	Massachusetts	170.2
1	Michigan	186.4
2	Minnesota	185.9
20	Mississippi	161.9
42	Missouri	131.5
6	Montana	182.4
26	Nebraska	157.3
33	Nevada	148.7
19	New Hampshire	162.7
4	New Jersey	183.9
32	New Mexico	149.3
17	New York	165.9
NA	North Carolina**	NA
11	North Dakota	170.8
37	Ohio	145.6
35	Oklahoma	147.0
29	Oregon	151.4
22	Pennsylvania	161.4
21	Rhode Island	161.6
9	South Carolina	172.3
5	South Dakota	183.0
44	Tennessee	120.3
36	Texas	146.6
3	Utah	185.0
NA	Vermont**	NA
27	Virginia	154.1
14	Washington	167.7
40	West Virginia	139.4
NA	Wisconsin**	NA
10	Wyoming	171.2

RANK ORDER

RANK	STATE	RATE
1	Michigan	186.4
2	Minnesota	185.9
3	Utah	185.0
4	New Jersey	183.9
5	South Dakota	183.0
6	Montana	182.4
7	Louisiana	180.2
8	Delaware	175.5
9	South Carolina	172.3
10	Wyoming	171.2
11	North Dakota	170.8
12	Massachusetts	170.2
13	Idaho	168.8
14	Washington	167.7
15	Maine	166.8
16	Connecticut	166.6
17	New York	165.9
18	Georgia	163.6
19	New Hampshire	162.7
20	Mississippi	161.9
21	Rhode Island	161.6
22	Pennsylvania	161.4
23	Illinois	159.5
24	Colorado	159.4
25	Arkansas	158.1
26	Nebraska	157.3
27	Virginia	154.1
28	California	152.6
29	Oregon	151.4
30	Alaska	151.3
31	Alabama	150.7
32	New Mexico	149.3
33	Nevada	148.7
34	Iowa	147.3
35	Oklahoma	147.0
36	Texas	146.6
37	Ohio	145.6
38	Kentucky	144.4
39	Florida	143.1
40	West Virginia	139.4
41	Indiana	136.9
42	Missouri	131.5
43	Hawaii	129.3
44	Tennessee	120.3
45	Arizona	116.6
NA	Kansas**	NA
NA	Maryland**	NA
NA	North Carolina**	NA
NA	Vermont**	NA
NA	Wisconsin**	NA
	District of Columbia**	NA

Source: American Cancer Society
"Cancer Facts & Figures 2009" (Copyright 2009, American Cancer Society, http://www.cancer.org/docroot/stt/stt_0.asp)
*For 2001 to 2005. Age-adjusted to the 2000 U.S. standard population.
**Not available.

Percent of Males Receiving PSA Test for Prostate Cancer: 2008

National Median = 54.8% of Men*

ALPHA ORDER

RANK	STATE	PERCENT
3	Alabama	61.5
47	Alaska	48.4
7	Arizona	59.3
16	Arkansas	57.4
46	California	48.8
29	Colorado	54.5
15	Connecticut	57.8
18	Delaware	57.1
2	Florida	64.1
4	Georgia	61.0
50	Hawaii	44.9
35	Idaho	52.9
38	Illinois	52.6
22	Indiana	55.3
38	Iowa	52.6
19	Kansas	57.0
36	Kentucky	52.8
44	Louisiana	49.5
17	Maine	57.2
11	Maryland	58.6
12	Massachusetts	58.5
8	Michigan	59.2
45	Minnesota	49.4
29	Mississippi	54.5
26	Missouri	54.6
21	Montana	55.6
32	Nebraska	53.8
24	Nevada	54.8
23	New Hampshire	55.2
31	New Jersey	54.3
43	New Mexico	50.6
12	New York	58.5
6	North Carolina	60.2
26	North Dakota	54.6
26	Ohio	54.6
34	Oklahoma	53.3
33	Oregon	53.5
24	Pennsylvania	54.8
5	Rhode Island	60.4
10	South Carolina	58.8
14	South Dakota	58.2
48	Tennessee	48.1
36	Texas	52.8
49	Utah	47.7
42	Vermont	51.5
9	Virginia	58.9
38	Washington	52.6
20	West Virginia	56.7
41	Wisconsin	51.7
1	Wyoming	64.6

RANK ORDER

RANK	STATE	PERCENT
1	Wyoming	64.6
2	Florida	64.1
3	Alabama	61.5
4	Georgia	61.0
5	Rhode Island	60.4
6	North Carolina	60.2
7	Arizona	59.3
8	Michigan	59.2
9	Virginia	58.9
10	South Carolina	58.8
11	Maryland	58.6
12	Massachusetts	58.5
12	New York	58.5
14	South Dakota	58.2
15	Connecticut	57.8
16	Arkansas	57.4
17	Maine	57.2
18	Delaware	57.1
19	Kansas	57.0
20	West Virginia	56.7
21	Montana	55.6
22	Indiana	55.3
23	New Hampshire	55.2
24	Nevada	54.8
24	Pennsylvania	54.8
26	Missouri	54.6
26	North Dakota	54.6
26	Ohio	54.6
29	Colorado	54.5
29	Mississippi	54.5
31	New Jersey	54.3
32	Nebraska	53.8
33	Oregon	53.5
34	Oklahoma	53.3
35	Idaho	52.9
36	Kentucky	52.8
36	Texas	52.8
38	Illinois	52.6
38	Iowa	52.6
38	Washington	52.6
41	Wisconsin	51.7
42	Vermont	51.5
43	New Mexico	50.6
44	Louisiana	49.5
45	Minnesota	49.4
46	California	48.8
47	Alaska	48.4
48	Tennessee	48.1
49	Utah	47.7
50	Hawaii	44.9

	District of Columbia	61.7

Source: U.S. Department of Health and Human Services, Centers for Disease Control and Prevention
   "2008 Behavioral Risk Factor Surveillance Summary Prevalence Data" (http://apps.nccd.cdc.gov/brfss/)
*Men 40 and older receiving prostate-specific antigen (PSA) test within the past two years.

Estimated New Skin Melanoma Cases in 2009

National Estimated Total = 68,720 New Cases*

ALPHA ORDER

RANK	STATE	CASES	% of USA
26	Alabama	930	1.4%
50	Alaska	80	0.1%
15	Arizona	1,460	2.1%
33	Arkansas	500	0.7%
1	California	9,080	13.2%
18	Colorado	1,260	1.8%
18	Connecticut	1,260	1.8%
44	Delaware	220	0.3%
2	Florida	4,920	7.2%
10	Georgia	2,040	3.0%
43	Hawaii	320	0.5%
40	Idaho	380	0.6%
12	Illinois	2,010	2.9%
23	Indiana	1,170	1.7%
27	Iowa	910	1.3%
31	Kansas	610	0.9%
18	Kentucky	1,260	1.8%
30	Louisiana	630	0.9%
34	Maine	480	0.7%
17	Maryland	1,310	1.9%
11	Massachusetts	2,030	3.0%
7	Michigan	2,240	3.3%
28	Minnesota	890	1.3%
40	Mississippi	380	0.6%
18	Missouri	1,260	1.8%
44	Montana	220	0.3%
39	Nebraska	420	0.6%
34	Nevada	480	0.7%
36	New Hampshire	460	0.7%
6	New Jersey	2,530	3.7%
36	New Mexico	460	0.7%
4	New York	3,710	5.4%
8	North Carolina	2,190	3.2%
49	North Dakota	110	0.2%
9	Ohio	2,080	3.0%
29	Oklahoma	690	1.0%
22	Oregon	1,220	1.8%
5	Pennsylvania	3,440	5.0%
42	Rhode Island	340	0.5%
24	South Carolina	1,090	1.6%
47	South Dakota	180	0.3%
16	Tennessee	1,410	2.1%
3	Texas	3,820	5.6%
32	Utah	600	0.9%
46	Vermont	200	0.3%
14	Virginia	1,790	2.6%
13	Washington	1,970	2.9%
38	West Virginia	450	0.7%
25	Wisconsin	1,040	1.5%
48	Wyoming	130	0.2%

RANK ORDER

RANK	STATE	CASES	% of USA
1	California	9,080	13.2%
2	Florida	4,920	7.2%
3	Texas	3,820	5.6%
4	New York	3,710	5.4%
5	Pennsylvania	3,440	5.0%
6	New Jersey	2,530	3.7%
7	Michigan	2,240	3.3%
8	North Carolina	2,190	3.2%
9	Ohio	2,080	3.0%
10	Georgia	2,040	3.0%
11	Massachusetts	2,030	3.0%
12	Illinois	2,010	2.9%
13	Washington	1,970	2.9%
14	Virginia	1,790	2.6%
15	Arizona	1,460	2.1%
16	Tennessee	1,410	2.1%
17	Maryland	1,310	1.9%
18	Colorado	1,260	1.8%
18	Connecticut	1,260	1.8%
18	Kentucky	1,260	1.8%
18	Missouri	1,260	1.8%
22	Oregon	1,220	1.8%
23	Indiana	1,170	1.7%
24	South Carolina	1,090	1.6%
25	Wisconsin	1,040	1.5%
26	Alabama	930	1.4%
27	Iowa	910	1.3%
28	Minnesota	890	1.3%
29	Oklahoma	690	1.0%
30	Louisiana	630	0.9%
31	Kansas	610	0.9%
32	Utah	600	0.9%
33	Arkansas	500	0.7%
34	Maine	480	0.7%
34	Nevada	480	0.7%
36	New Hampshire	460	0.7%
36	New Mexico	460	0.7%
38	West Virginia	450	0.7%
39	Nebraska	420	0.6%
40	Idaho	380	0.6%
40	Mississippi	380	0.6%
42	Rhode Island	340	0.5%
43	Hawaii	320	0.5%
44	Delaware	220	0.3%
44	Montana	220	0.3%
46	Vermont	200	0.3%
47	South Dakota	180	0.3%
48	Wyoming	130	0.2%
49	North Dakota	110	0.2%
50	Alaska	80	0.1%
	District of Columbia	70	0.1%

Source: American Cancer Society

"Cancer Facts & Figures 2009" (Copyright 2009, American Cancer Society, http://www.cancer.org/docroot/stt/stt_0.asp)
*These estimates are offered as a rough guide and should be interpreted with caution. They are calculated according to the distribution of estimated 2009 cancer deaths by state.

Estimated Rate of New Skin Melanoma Cases in 2009

National Estimated Rate = 22.3 New Cases per 100,000 Population*

ALPHA ORDER

RANK	STATE	RATE
36	Alabama	19.8
50	Alaska	11.5
31	Arizona	22.1
43	Arkansas	17.3
18	California	24.6
14	Colorado	25.1
2	Connecticut	35.8
15	Delaware	24.9
13	Florida	26.5
35	Georgia	20.8
16	Hawaii	24.7
18	Idaho	24.6
46	Illinois	15.6
40	Indiana	18.2
8	Iowa	30.3
32	Kansas	21.6
10	Kentucky	29.2
48	Louisiana	14.0
1	Maine	36.4
24	Maryland	23.0
7	Massachusetts	30.8
28	Michigan	22.5
45	Minnesota	16.9
49	Mississippi	12.9
34	Missouri	21.0
27	Montana	22.6
22	Nebraska	23.4
40	Nevada	18.2
3	New Hampshire	34.7
11	New Jersey	29.1
25	New Mexico	22.9
37	New York	19.0
23	North Carolina	23.3
44	North Dakota	17.0
42	Ohio	18.0
38	Oklahoma	18.7
6	Oregon	31.9
12	Pennsylvania	27.3
4	Rhode Island	32.3
20	South Carolina	23.9
30	South Dakota	22.2
29	Tennessee	22.4
47	Texas	15.4
33	Utah	21.5
5	Vermont	32.2
26	Virginia	22.7
9	Washington	29.6
16	West Virginia	24.7
39	Wisconsin	18.4
20	Wyoming	23.9

RANK ORDER

RANK	STATE	RATE
1	Maine	36.4
2	Connecticut	35.8
3	New Hampshire	34.7
4	Rhode Island	32.3
5	Vermont	32.2
6	Oregon	31.9
7	Massachusetts	30.8
8	Iowa	30.3
9	Washington	29.6
10	Kentucky	29.2
11	New Jersey	29.1
12	Pennsylvania	27.3
13	Florida	26.5
14	Colorado	25.1
15	Delaware	24.9
16	Hawaii	24.7
16	West Virginia	24.7
18	California	24.6
18	Idaho	24.6
20	South Carolina	23.9
20	Wyoming	23.9
22	Nebraska	23.4
23	North Carolina	23.3
24	Maryland	23.0
25	New Mexico	22.9
26	Virginia	22.7
27	Montana	22.6
28	Michigan	22.5
29	Tennessee	22.4
30	South Dakota	22.2
31	Arizona	22.1
32	Kansas	21.6
33	Utah	21.5
34	Missouri	21.0
35	Georgia	20.8
36	Alabama	19.8
37	New York	19.0
38	Oklahoma	18.7
39	Wisconsin	18.4
40	Indiana	18.2
40	Nevada	18.2
42	Ohio	18.0
43	Arkansas	17.3
44	North Dakota	17.0
45	Minnesota	16.9
46	Illinois	15.6
47	Texas	15.4
48	Louisiana	14.0
49	Mississippi	12.9
50	Alaska	11.5
	District of Columbia	11.7

Source: CQ Press using data from American Cancer Society
"Cancer Facts & Figures 2009" (Copyright 2009, American Cancer Society, http://www.cancer.org/docroot/stt/stt_0.asp)
*These estimates are offered as a rough guide and should be interpreted with caution. They are calculated according to the distribution of estimated 2009 cancer deaths by state. Rates calculated using 2009 Census resident population estimates.

Estimated New Cervical Cancer Cases in 2009

National Estimated Total = 11,270 New Cases*

ALPHA ORDER

RANK	STATE	CASES	% of USA
18	Alabama	190	1.7%
NA	Alaska**	NA	NA
16	Arizona	210	1.9%
28	Arkansas	130	1.2%
1	California	1,350	12.0%
25	Colorado	150	1.3%
30	Connecticut	110	1.0%
NA	Delaware**	NA	NA
4	Florida	800	7.1%
9	Georgia	340	3.0%
39	Hawaii	50	0.4%
NA	Idaho**	NA	NA
6	Illinois	480	4.3%
14	Indiana	220	2.0%
33	Iowa	90	0.8%
33	Kansas	90	0.8%
22	Kentucky	180	1.6%
18	Louisiana	190	1.7%
39	Maine	50	0.4%
18	Maryland	190	1.7%
17	Massachusetts	200	1.8%
11	Michigan	320	2.8%
26	Minnesota	140	1.2%
28	Mississippi	130	1.2%
14	Missouri	220	2.0%
NA	Montana**	NA	NA
37	Nebraska	60	0.5%
30	Nevada	110	1.0%
NA	New Hampshire**	NA	NA
7	New Jersey	410	3.6%
35	New Mexico	80	0.7%
3	New York	870	7.7%
9	North Carolina	340	3.0%
NA	North Dakota**	NA	NA
8	Ohio	390	3.5%
26	Oklahoma	140	1.2%
30	Oregon	110	1.0%
5	Pennsylvania	500	4.4%
NA	Rhode Island**	NA	NA
23	South Carolina	170	1.5%
NA	South Dakota**	NA	NA
12	Tennessee	240	2.1%
2	Texas	980	8.7%
37	Utah	60	0.5%
NA	Vermont**	NA	NA
12	Virginia	240	2.1%
18	Washington	190	1.7%
36	West Virginia	70	0.6%
24	Wisconsin	160	1.4%
NA	Wyoming**	NA	NA

RANK ORDER

RANK	STATE	CASES	% of USA
1	California	1,350	12.0%
2	Texas	980	8.7%
3	New York	870	7.7%
4	Florida	800	7.1%
5	Pennsylvania	500	4.4%
6	Illinois	480	4.3%
7	New Jersey	410	3.6%
8	Ohio	390	3.5%
9	Georgia	340	3.0%
9	North Carolina	340	3.0%
11	Michigan	320	2.8%
12	Tennessee	240	2.1%
12	Virginia	240	2.1%
14	Indiana	220	2.0%
14	Missouri	220	2.0%
16	Arizona	210	1.9%
17	Massachusetts	200	1.8%
18	Alabama	190	1.7%
18	Louisiana	190	1.7%
18	Maryland	190	1.7%
18	Washington	190	1.7%
22	Kentucky	180	1.6%
23	South Carolina	170	1.5%
24	Wisconsin	160	1.4%
25	Colorado	150	1.3%
26	Minnesota	140	1.2%
26	Oklahoma	140	1.2%
28	Arkansas	130	1.2%
28	Mississippi	130	1.2%
30	Connecticut	110	1.0%
30	Nevada	110	1.0%
30	Oregon	110	1.0%
33	Iowa	90	0.8%
33	Kansas	90	0.8%
35	New Mexico	80	0.7%
36	West Virginia	70	0.6%
37	Nebraska	60	0.5%
37	Utah	60	0.5%
39	Hawaii	50	0.4%
39	Maine	50	0.4%
NA	Alaska**	NA	NA
NA	Delaware**	NA	NA
NA	Idaho**	NA	NA
NA	Montana**	NA	NA
NA	New Hampshire**	NA	NA
NA	North Dakota**	NA	NA
NA	Rhode Island**	NA	NA
NA	South Dakota**	NA	NA
NA	Vermont**	NA	NA
NA	Wyoming**	NA	NA
	District of Columbia**	NA	NA

Source: American Cancer Society
"Cancer Facts & Figures 2009" (Copyright 2009, American Cancer Society, http://www.cancer.org/docroot/stt/stt_0.asp)
*These estimates are offered as a rough guide and should be interpreted with caution. They are calculated according to the distribution of estimated 2009 cancer deaths by state.
**Not available.

Estimated Rate of New Cervical Cancer Cases in 2009

National Estimated Rate = 7.3 New Cases per 100,000 Female Population*

ALPHA ORDER

RANK	STATE	RATE
11	Alabama	7.9
NA	Alaska**	NA
27	Arizona	6.5
2	Arkansas	8.9
19	California	7.3
31	Colorado	6.1
31	Connecticut	6.1
NA	Delaware**	NA
4	Florida	8.6
23	Georgia	6.9
12	Hawaii	7.8
NA	Idaho**	NA
19	Illinois	7.3
24	Indiana	6.8
35	Iowa	5.9
29	Kansas	6.4
8	Kentucky	8.3
7	Louisiana	8.4
17	Maine	7.4
27	Maryland	6.5
34	Massachusetts	6.0
30	Michigan	6.3
39	Minnesota	5.3
4	Mississippi	8.6
19	Missouri	7.3
NA	Montana**	NA
25	Nebraska	6.7
4	Nevada	8.6
NA	New Hampshire**	NA
1	New Jersey	9.3
9	New Mexico	8.0
3	New York	8.7
22	North Carolina	7.2
NA	North Dakota**	NA
26	Ohio	6.6
14	Oklahoma	7.6
36	Oregon	5.8
12	Pennsylvania	7.8
NA	Rhode Island**	NA
17	South Carolina	7.4
NA	South Dakota**	NA
16	Tennessee	7.5
9	Texas	8.0
40	Utah	4.4
NA	Vermont**	NA
31	Virginia	6.1
36	Washington	5.8
14	West Virginia	7.6
38	Wisconsin	5.7
NA	Wyoming**	NA

RANK ORDER

RANK	STATE	RATE
1	New Jersey	9.3
2	Arkansas	8.9
3	New York	8.7
4	Florida	8.6
4	Mississippi	8.6
4	Nevada	8.6
7	Louisiana	8.4
8	Kentucky	8.3
9	New Mexico	8.0
9	Texas	8.0
11	Alabama	7.9
12	Hawaii	7.8
12	Pennsylvania	7.8
14	Oklahoma	7.6
14	West Virginia	7.6
16	Tennessee	7.5
17	Maine	7.4
17	South Carolina	7.4
19	California	7.3
19	Illinois	7.3
19	Missouri	7.3
22	North Carolina	7.2
23	Georgia	6.9
24	Indiana	6.8
25	Nebraska	6.7
26	Ohio	6.6
27	Arizona	6.5
27	Maryland	6.5
29	Kansas	6.4
30	Michigan	6.3
31	Colorado	6.1
31	Connecticut	6.1
31	Virginia	6.1
34	Massachusetts	6.0
35	Iowa	5.9
36	Oregon	5.8
36	Washington	5.8
38	Wisconsin	5.7
39	Minnesota	5.3
40	Utah	4.4
NA	Alaska**	NA
NA	Delaware**	NA
NA	Idaho**	NA
NA	Montana**	NA
NA	New Hampshire**	NA
NA	North Dakota**	NA
NA	Rhode Island**	NA
NA	South Dakota**	NA
NA	Vermont**	NA
NA	Wyoming**	NA
	District of Columbia**	NA

Source: CQ Press using data from American Cancer Society
   "Cancer Facts & Figures 2009" (Copyright 2009, American Cancer Society, http://www.cancer.org/docroot/stt/stt_0.asp)
*These estimates are offered as a rough guide and should be interpreted with caution. They are calculated according to the distribution of estimated 2009 cancer deaths by state. Rates calculated using 2008 Census female population estimates.
**Not available.

Percent of Women 18 Years Old and Older
Who Had a Pap Smear within the Past Three Years: 2008
National Median = 82.9% of Women 18 Years and Older*

RANK	STATE	PERCENT
39	Alabama	81.3
20	Alaska	83.6
32	Arizona	82.3
40	Arkansas	80.8
12	California	84.1
13	Colorado	84.0
16	Connecticut	83.9
10	Delaware	84.5
21	Florida	83.3
1	Georgia	87.6
26	Hawaii	82.8
48	Idaho	76.8
18	Illinois	83.8
45	Indiana	78.7
13	Iowa	84.0
13	Kansas	84.0
34	Kentucky	81.7
49	Louisiana	76.7
4	Maine	86.3
11	Maryland	84.2
1	Massachusetts	87.6
43	Michigan	80.1
8	Minnesota	86.0
30	Mississippi	82.6
25	Missouri	82.9
36	Montana	81.5
18	Nebraska	83.8
47	Nevada	78.2
5	New Hampshire	86.1
44	New Jersey	79.9
42	New Mexico	80.7
21	New York	83.3
3	North Carolina	86.9
26	North Dakota	82.8
28	Ohio	82.7
38	Oklahoma	81.4
34	Oregon	81.7
33	Pennsylvania	82.0
5	Rhode Island	86.1
5	South Carolina	86.1
31	South Dakota	82.5
16	Tennessee	83.9
36	Texas	81.5
50	Utah	74.2
9	Vermont	85.9
23	Virginia	83.2
28	Washington	82.7
40	West Virginia	80.8
24	Wisconsin	83.1
46	Wyoming	78.4

RANK	STATE	PERCENT
1	Georgia	87.6
1	Massachusetts	87.6
3	North Carolina	86.9
4	Maine	86.3
5	New Hampshire	86.1
5	Rhode Island	86.1
5	South Carolina	86.1
8	Minnesota	86.0
9	Vermont	85.9
10	Delaware	84.5
11	Maryland	84.2
12	California	84.1
13	Colorado	84.0
13	Iowa	84.0
13	Kansas	84.0
16	Connecticut	83.9
16	Tennessee	83.9
18	Illinois	83.8
18	Nebraska	83.8
20	Alaska	83.6
21	Florida	83.3
21	New York	83.3
23	Virginia	83.2
24	Wisconsin	83.1
25	Missouri	82.9
26	Hawaii	82.8
26	North Dakota	82.8
28	Ohio	82.7
28	Washington	82.7
30	Mississippi	82.6
31	South Dakota	82.5
32	Arizona	82.3
33	Pennsylvania	82.0
34	Kentucky	81.7
34	Oregon	81.7
36	Montana	81.5
36	Texas	81.5
38	Oklahoma	81.4
39	Alabama	81.3
40	Arkansas	80.8
40	West Virginia	80.8
42	New Mexico	80.7
43	Michigan	80.1
44	New Jersey	79.9
45	Indiana	78.7
46	Wyoming	78.4
47	Nevada	78.2
48	Idaho	76.8
49	Louisiana	76.7
50	Utah	74.2

	District of Columbia	88.9

Source: U.S. Department of Health and Human Services, Centers for Disease Control and Prevention
"2008 Behavioral Risk Factor Surveillance Summary Prevalence Data" (http://apps.nccd.cdc.gov/brfss/)
*A Pap test is a test for cancer, especially of the female genital tract such as cancer of the cervix. Named after George Papanicolaou (1883-1962), American anatomist.

Estimated New Uterine Cancer Cases in 2009

National Estimated Total = 42,160 New Cases*

ALPHA ORDER

RANK	STATE	CASES	% of USA
27	Alabama	510	1.2%
49	Alaska	70	0.2%
21	Arizona	660	1.6%
33	Arkansas	310	0.7%
1	California	4,230	10.0%
25	Colorado	530	1.3%
21	Connecticut	660	1.6%
44	Delaware	140	0.3%
3	Florida	2,590	6.1%
16	Georgia	930	2.2%
41	Hawaii	200	0.5%
43	Idaho	170	0.4%
6	Illinois	1,960	4.6%
14	Indiana	970	2.3%
28	Iowa	500	1.2%
30	Kansas	400	0.9%
23	Kentucky	590	1.4%
29	Louisiana	430	1.0%
34	Maine	270	0.6%
18	Maryland	840	2.0%
10	Massachusetts	1,140	2.7%
8	Michigan	1,700	4.0%
19	Minnesota	810	1.9%
34	Mississippi	270	0.6%
17	Missouri	870	2.1%
44	Montana	140	0.3%
34	Nebraska	270	0.6%
34	Nevada	270	0.6%
39	New Hampshire	240	0.6%
9	New Jersey	1,620	3.8%
40	New Mexico	210	0.5%
2	New York	3,510	8.3%
11	North Carolina	1,030	2.4%
48	North Dakota	90	0.2%
7	Ohio	1,930	4.6%
30	Oklahoma	400	0.9%
24	Oregon	570	1.4%
4	Pennsylvania	2,550	6.0%
42	Rhode Island	190	0.5%
26	South Carolina	520	1.2%
46	South Dakota	120	0.3%
20	Tennessee	720	1.7%
5	Texas	2,220	5.3%
38	Utah	250	0.6%
46	Vermont	120	0.3%
12	Virginia	1,020	2.4%
15	Washington	960	2.3%
32	West Virginia	330	0.8%
13	Wisconsin	1,000	2.4%
49	Wyoming	70	0.2%

RANK ORDER

RANK	STATE	CASES	% of USA
1	California	4,230	10.0%
2	New York	3,510	8.3%
3	Florida	2,590	6.1%
4	Pennsylvania	2,550	6.0%
5	Texas	2,220	5.3%
6	Illinois	1,960	4.6%
7	Ohio	1,930	4.6%
8	Michigan	1,700	4.0%
9	New Jersey	1,620	3.8%
10	Massachusetts	1,140	2.7%
11	North Carolina	1,030	2.4%
12	Virginia	1,020	2.4%
13	Wisconsin	1,000	2.4%
14	Indiana	970	2.3%
15	Washington	960	2.3%
16	Georgia	930	2.2%
17	Missouri	870	2.1%
18	Maryland	840	2.0%
19	Minnesota	810	1.9%
20	Tennessee	720	1.7%
21	Arizona	660	1.6%
21	Connecticut	660	1.6%
23	Kentucky	590	1.4%
24	Oregon	570	1.4%
25	Colorado	530	1.3%
26	South Carolina	520	1.2%
27	Alabama	510	1.2%
28	Iowa	500	1.2%
29	Louisiana	430	1.0%
30	Kansas	400	0.9%
30	Oklahoma	400	0.9%
32	West Virginia	330	0.8%
33	Arkansas	310	0.7%
34	Maine	270	0.6%
34	Mississippi	270	0.6%
34	Nebraska	270	0.6%
34	Nevada	270	0.6%
38	Utah	250	0.6%
39	New Hampshire	240	0.6%
40	New Mexico	210	0.5%
41	Hawaii	200	0.5%
42	Rhode Island	190	0.5%
43	Idaho	170	0.4%
44	Delaware	140	0.3%
44	Montana	140	0.3%
46	South Dakota	120	0.3%
46	Vermont	120	0.3%
48	North Dakota	90	0.2%
49	Alaska	70	0.2%
49	Wyoming	70	0.2%
	District of Columbia	80	0.2%

Source: American Cancer Society
  "Cancer Facts & Figures 2009" (Copyright 2009, American Cancer Society, http://www.cancer.org/docroot/stt/stt_0.asp)
*These estimates are offered as a rough guide and should be interpreted with caution. They are calculated according to the distribution of estimated 2009 cancer deaths by state.

Estimated Rate of New Uterine Cancer Cases in 2009

National Estimated Rate = 27.4 New Cases per 100,000 Female Population*

ALPHA ORDER

RANK	STATE	RATE
42	Alabama	21.2
40	Alaska	21.3
45	Arizona	20.3
40	Arkansas	21.3
33	California	23.0
39	Colorado	21.6
4	Connecticut	36.8
16	Delaware	31.1
29	Florida	27.8
46	Georgia	18.9
15	Hawaii	31.3
36	Idaho	22.5
18	Illinois	30.0
18	Indiana	30.0
13	Iowa	32.9
27	Kansas	28.4
30	Kentucky	27.1
46	Louisiana	18.9
1	Maine	40.1
25	Maryland	28.9
11	Massachusetts	34.1
12	Michigan	33.5
17	Minnesota	30.9
50	Mississippi	17.8
26	Missouri	28.8
24	Montana	29.0
18	Nebraska	30.0
42	Nevada	21.2
6	New Hampshire	36.0
5	New Jersey	36.6
44	New Mexico	20.9
9	New York	35.0
37	North Carolina	21.9
28	North Dakota	28.2
14	Ohio	32.8
38	Oklahoma	21.7
21	Oregon	29.9
2	Pennsylvania	39.9
9	Rhode Island	35.0
34	South Carolina	22.6
22	South Dakota	29.8
34	Tennessee	22.6
49	Texas	18.2
48	Utah	18.4
3	Vermont	38.0
32	Virginia	25.8
23	Washington	29.3
7	West Virginia	35.6
8	Wisconsin	35.3
31	Wyoming	26.7

RANK ORDER

RANK	STATE	RATE
1	Maine	40.1
2	Pennsylvania	39.9
3	Vermont	38.0
4	Connecticut	36.8
5	New Jersey	36.6
6	New Hampshire	36.0
7	West Virginia	35.6
8	Wisconsin	35.3
9	New York	35.0
9	Rhode Island	35.0
11	Massachusetts	34.1
12	Michigan	33.5
13	Iowa	32.9
14	Ohio	32.8
15	Hawaii	31.3
16	Delaware	31.1
17	Minnesota	30.9
18	Illinois	30.0
18	Indiana	30.0
18	Nebraska	30.0
21	Oregon	29.9
22	South Dakota	29.8
23	Washington	29.3
24	Montana	29.0
25	Maryland	28.9
26	Missouri	28.8
27	Kansas	28.4
28	North Dakota	28.2
29	Florida	27.8
30	Kentucky	27.1
31	Wyoming	26.7
32	Virginia	25.8
33	California	23.0
34	South Carolina	22.6
34	Tennessee	22.6
36	Idaho	22.5
37	North Carolina	21.9
38	Oklahoma	21.7
39	Colorado	21.6
40	Alaska	21.3
40	Arkansas	21.3
42	Alabama	21.2
42	Nevada	21.2
44	New Mexico	20.9
45	Arizona	20.3
46	Georgia	18.9
46	Louisiana	18.9
48	Utah	18.4
49	Texas	18.2
50	Mississippi	17.8

| | District of Columbia | 25.6 |

Source: CQ Press using data from American Cancer Society
"Cancer Facts & Figures 2009" (Copyright 2009, American Cancer Society, http://www.cancer.org/docroot/stt/stt_0.asp)
*These estimates are offered as a rough guide and should be interpreted with caution. They are calculated according to the distribution of estimated 2009 cancer deaths by state. Rates calculated using 2008 Census female population estimates.

AIDS Cases Reported in 2007

National Total = 37,281 New AIDS Cases*

ALPHA ORDER

RANK	STATE	CASES	% of USA
22	Alabama	391	1.0%
44	Alaska	32	0.1%
18	Arizona	585	1.6%
32	Arkansas	196	0.5%
1	California	4,952	13.3%
23	Colorado	355	1.0%
20	Connecticut	528	1.4%
33	Delaware	171	0.5%
3	Florida	3,961	10.6%
5	Georgia	1,877	5.0%
37	Hawaii	78	0.2%
46	Idaho	23	0.1%
8	Illinois	1,348	3.6%
26	Indiana	329	0.9%
38	Iowa	76	0.2%
34	Kansas	132	0.4%
27	Kentucky	292	0.8%
11	Louisiana	879	2.4%
43	Maine	46	0.1%
7	Maryland	1,394	3.7%
17	Massachusetts	612	1.6%
16	Michigan	628	1.7%
31	Minnesota	197	0.5%
24	Mississippi	352	0.9%
19	Missouri	542	1.5%
45	Montana	25	0.1%
36	Nebraska	80	0.2%
25	Nevada	335	0.9%
42	New Hampshire	51	0.1%
9	New Jersey	1,164	3.1%
35	New Mexico	113	0.3%
2	New York	4,810	12.9%
10	North Carolina	1,024	2.7%
49	North Dakota	8	0.0%
13	Ohio	703	1.9%
28	Oklahoma	264	0.7%
29	Oregon	239	0.6%
6	Pennsylvania	1,750	4.7%
41	Rhode Island	66	0.2%
12	South Carolina	742	2.0%
47	South Dakota	15	0.0%
14	Tennessee	658	1.8%
4	Texas	2,964	8.0%
40	Utah	68	0.2%
50	Vermont	6	0.0%
15	Virginia	634	1.7%
21	Washington	427	1.1%
38	West Virginia	76	0.2%
30	Wisconsin	199	0.5%
48	Wyoming	13	0.0%

RANK ORDER

RANK	STATE	CASES	% of USA
1	California	4,952	13.3%
2	New York	4,810	12.9%
3	Florida	3,961	10.6%
4	Texas	2,964	8.0%
5	Georgia	1,877	5.0%
6	Pennsylvania	1,750	4.7%
7	Maryland	1,394	3.7%
8	Illinois	1,348	3.6%
9	New Jersey	1,164	3.1%
10	North Carolina	1,024	2.7%
11	Louisiana	879	2.4%
12	South Carolina	742	2.0%
13	Ohio	703	1.9%
14	Tennessee	658	1.8%
15	Virginia	634	1.7%
16	Michigan	628	1.7%
17	Massachusetts	612	1.6%
18	Arizona	585	1.6%
19	Missouri	542	1.5%
20	Connecticut	528	1.4%
21	Washington	427	1.1%
22	Alabama	391	1.0%
23	Colorado	355	1.0%
24	Mississippi	352	0.9%
25	Nevada	335	0.9%
26	Indiana	329	0.9%
27	Kentucky	292	0.8%
28	Oklahoma	264	0.7%
29	Oregon	239	0.6%
30	Wisconsin	199	0.5%
31	Minnesota	197	0.5%
32	Arkansas	196	0.5%
33	Delaware	171	0.5%
34	Kansas	132	0.4%
35	New Mexico	113	0.3%
36	Nebraska	80	0.2%
37	Hawaii	78	0.2%
38	Iowa	76	0.2%
38	West Virginia	76	0.2%
40	Utah	68	0.2%
41	Rhode Island	66	0.2%
42	New Hampshire	51	0.1%
43	Maine	46	0.1%
44	Alaska	32	0.1%
45	Montana	25	0.1%
46	Idaho	23	0.1%
47	South Dakota	15	0.0%
48	Wyoming	13	0.0%
49	North Dakota	8	0.0%
50	Vermont	6	0.0%
	District of Columbia	871	2.3%

Source: U.S. Department of Health and Human Services, Centers for Disease Control and Prevention
   "HIV/AIDS Surveillance Report, 2007" (Vol. 19, http://www.cdc.gov/hiv/topics/surveillance/resources/reports/index.htm)
*AIDS is Acquired Immunodeficiency Syndrome. It is a specific group of diseases or conditions which are indicative of severe immunosuppression related to infection with the Human Immunodeficiency Virus (HIV). National total does not include 847 new cases in Puerto Rico and 34 in the Virgin Islands.

AIDS Rate in 2007

National Rate = 12.4 New AIDS Cases Reported per 100,000 Population*

ALPHA ORDER

RANK	STATE	RATE
21	Alabama	8.4
36	Alaska	4.7
19	Arizona	9.2
25	Arkansas	6.9
10	California	13.5
23	Colorado	7.3
8	Connecticut	15.1
5	Delaware	19.8
3	Florida	21.7
6	Georgia	19.7
31	Hawaii	6.1
48	Idaho	1.5
17	Illinois	10.5
34	Indiana	5.2
45	Iowa	2.5
35	Kansas	4.8
25	Kentucky	6.9
4	Louisiana	20.5
42	Maine	3.5
2	Maryland	24.8
18	Massachusetts	9.5
29	Michigan	6.2
40	Minnesota	3.8
14	Mississippi	12.1
19	Missouri	9.2
43	Montana	2.6
37	Nebraska	4.5
12	Nevada	13.1
39	New Hampshire	3.9
11	New Jersey	13.4
33	New Mexico	5.7
1	New York	24.9
15	North Carolina	11.3
49	North Dakota	1.3
31	Ohio	6.1
23	Oklahoma	7.3
28	Oregon	6.4
9	Pennsylvania	14.1
29	Rhode Island	6.2
7	South Carolina	16.8
47	South Dakota	1.9
16	Tennessee	10.7
13	Texas	12.4
43	Utah	2.6
50	Vermont	1.0
22	Virginia	8.2
27	Washington	6.6
38	West Virginia	4.2
41	Wisconsin	3.6
45	Wyoming	2.5

RANK ORDER

RANK	STATE	RATE
1	New York	24.9
2	Maryland	24.8
3	Florida	21.7
4	Louisiana	20.5
5	Delaware	19.8
6	Georgia	19.7
7	South Carolina	16.8
8	Connecticut	15.1
9	Pennsylvania	14.1
10	California	13.5
11	New Jersey	13.4
12	Nevada	13.1
13	Texas	12.4
14	Mississippi	12.1
15	North Carolina	11.3
16	Tennessee	10.7
17	Illinois	10.5
18	Massachusetts	9.5
19	Arizona	9.2
19	Missouri	9.2
21	Alabama	8.4
22	Virginia	8.2
23	Colorado	7.3
23	Oklahoma	7.3
25	Arkansas	6.9
25	Kentucky	6.9
27	Washington	6.6
28	Oregon	6.4
29	Michigan	6.2
29	Rhode Island	6.2
31	Hawaii	6.1
31	Ohio	6.1
33	New Mexico	5.7
34	Indiana	5.2
35	Kansas	4.8
36	Alaska	4.7
37	Nebraska	4.5
38	West Virginia	4.2
39	New Hampshire	3.9
40	Minnesota	3.8
41	Wisconsin	3.6
42	Maine	3.5
43	Montana	2.6
43	Utah	2.6
45	Iowa	2.5
45	Wyoming	2.5
47	South Dakota	1.9
48	Idaho	1.5
49	North Dakota	1.3
50	Vermont	1.0

District of Columbia	148.1

Source: U.S. Department of Health and Human Services, Centers for Disease Control and Prevention
"HIV/AIDS Surveillance Report, 2007" (Vol. 19, http://www.cdc.gov/hiv/topics/surveillance/resources/reports/index.htm)
*AIDS is Acquired Immunodeficiency Syndrome. It is a specific group of diseases or conditions which are indicative of severe immunosuppression related to infection with the Human Immunodeficiency Virus (HIV). National rate does not include cases or population in U.S. territories.

AIDS Cases Reported through December 2007

National Total = 998,255 Reported AIDS Cases*

ALPHA ORDER

RANK	STATE	CASES	% of USA
23	Alabama	9,091	0.9%
44	Alaska	689	0.1%
21	Arizona	10,975	1.1%
32	Arkansas	4,119	0.4%
2	California	148,949	14.9%
22	Colorado	9,129	0.9%
16	Connecticut	15,399	1.5%
33	Delaware	3,741	0.4%
3	Florida	109,524	11.0%
8	Georgia	33,847	3.4%
34	Hawaii	3,019	0.3%
45	Idaho	628	0.1%
7	Illinois	35,066	3.5%
24	Indiana	8,628	0.9%
39	Iowa	1,815	0.2%
35	Kansas	2,933	0.3%
30	Kentucky	4,904	0.5%
11	Louisiana	18,612	1.9%
42	Maine	1,163	0.1%
9	Maryland	31,931	3.2%
10	Massachusetts	20,037	2.0%
15	Michigan	15,672	1.6%
29	Minnesota	5,044	0.5%
25	Mississippi	7,032	0.7%
20	Missouri	11,646	1.2%
47	Montana	404	0.0%
41	Nebraska	1,572	0.2%
27	Nevada	6,124	0.6%
43	New Hampshire	1,134	0.1%
5	New Jersey	50,694	5.1%
36	New Mexico	2,721	0.3%
1	New York	181,461	18.2%
13	North Carolina	17,127	1.7%
50	North Dakota	153	0.0%
14	Ohio	15,838	1.6%
28	Oklahoma	5,105	0.5%
26	Oregon	6,248	0.6%
6	Pennsylvania	35,489	3.6%
37	Rhode Island	2,676	0.3%
17	South Carolina	14,163	1.4%
48	South Dakota	275	0.0%
18	Tennessee	13,173	1.3%
4	Texas	72,828	7.3%
38	Utah	2,383	0.2%
46	Vermont	474	0.0%
12	Virginia	17,608	1.8%
19	Washington	12,237	1.2%
40	West Virginia	1,586	0.2%
31	Wisconsin	4,749	0.5%
49	Wyoming	244	0.0%

RANK ORDER

RANK	STATE	CASES	% of USA
1	New York	181,461	18.2%
2	California	148,949	14.9%
3	Florida	109,524	11.0%
4	Texas	72,828	7.3%
5	New Jersey	50,694	5.1%
6	Pennsylvania	35,489	3.6%
7	Illinois	35,066	3.5%
8	Georgia	33,847	3.4%
9	Maryland	31,931	3.2%
10	Massachusetts	20,037	2.0%
11	Louisiana	18,612	1.9%
12	Virginia	17,608	1.8%
13	North Carolina	17,127	1.7%
14	Ohio	15,838	1.6%
15	Michigan	15,672	1.6%
16	Connecticut	15,399	1.5%
17	South Carolina	14,163	1.4%
18	Tennessee	13,173	1.3%
19	Washington	12,237	1.2%
20	Missouri	11,646	1.2%
21	Arizona	10,975	1.1%
22	Colorado	9,129	0.9%
23	Alabama	9,091	0.9%
24	Indiana	8,628	0.9%
25	Mississippi	7,032	0.7%
26	Oregon	6,248	0.6%
27	Nevada	6,124	0.6%
28	Oklahoma	5,105	0.5%
29	Minnesota	5,044	0.5%
30	Kentucky	4,904	0.5%
31	Wisconsin	4,749	0.5%
32	Arkansas	4,119	0.4%
33	Delaware	3,741	0.4%
34	Hawaii	3,019	0.3%
35	Kansas	2,933	0.3%
36	New Mexico	2,721	0.3%
37	Rhode Island	2,676	0.3%
38	Utah	2,383	0.2%
39	Iowa	1,815	0.2%
40	West Virginia	1,586	0.2%
41	Nebraska	1,572	0.2%
42	Maine	1,163	0.1%
43	New Hampshire	1,134	0.1%
44	Alaska	689	0.1%
45	Idaho	628	0.1%
46	Vermont	474	0.0%
47	Montana	404	0.0%
48	South Dakota	275	0.0%
49	Wyoming	244	0.0%
50	North Dakota	153	0.0%
	District of Columbia	18,196	1.8%

Source: U.S. Department of Health and Human Services, Centers for Disease Control and Prevention
  "HIV/AIDS Surveillance Report, 2007" (Vol. 19, http://www.cdc.gov/hiv/topics/surveillance/resources/reports/index.htm)
*Cumulative through December 2007. AIDS is Acquired Immunodeficiency Syndrome. It is a specific group of diseases or
conditions which are indicative of severe immunosuppression related to infection with the Human Immunodeficiency Virus (HIV).
National total does not include 30,736 cases in Puerto Rico, 681 cases in the Virgin Islands and 76 cases in other U.S. territories.

AIDS Cases in Children 12 Years and Younger through December 2007

National Total = 9,156 Juvenile AIDS Cases*

ALPHA ORDER

RANK	STATE	CASES	% of USA
18	Alabama	76	0.8%
43	Alaska	7	0.1%
23	Arizona	46	0.5%
24	Arkansas	36	0.4%
4	California	675	7.4%
28	Colorado	31	0.3%
11	Connecticut	183	2.0%
32	Delaware	26	0.3%
2	Florida	1,544	16.9%
9	Georgia	240	2.6%
36	Hawaii	17	0.2%
48	Idaho	2	0.0%
8	Illinois	283	3.1%
21	Indiana	56	0.6%
38	Iowa	13	0.1%
37	Kansas	14	0.2%
25	Kentucky	35	0.4%
14	Louisiana	132	1.4%
43	Maine	7	0.1%
7	Maryland	320	3.5%
10	Massachusetts	218	2.4%
16	Michigan	114	1.2%
30	Minnesota	28	0.3%
21	Mississippi	56	0.6%
19	Missouri	61	0.7%
47	Montana	3	0.0%
39	Nebraska	11	0.1%
29	Nevada	29	0.3%
41	New Hampshire	10	0.1%
3	New Jersey	787	8.6%
42	New Mexico	9	0.1%
1	New York	2,345	25.6%
15	North Carolina	120	1.3%
48	North Dakota	2	0.0%
13	Ohio	140	1.5%
32	Oklahoma	26	0.3%
35	Oregon	19	0.2%
6	Pennsylvania	369	4.0%
30	Rhode Island	28	0.3%
17	South Carolina	108	1.2%
46	South Dakota	5	0.1%
20	Tennessee	59	0.6%
5	Texas	394	4.3%
34	Utah	20	0.2%
45	Vermont	6	0.1%
12	Virginia	177	1.9%
25	Washington	35	0.4%
39	West Virginia	11	0.1%
27	Wisconsin	33	0.4%
48	Wyoming	2	0.0%

RANK ORDER

RANK	STATE	CASES	% of USA
1	New York	2,345	25.6%
2	Florida	1,544	16.9%
3	New Jersey	787	8.6%
4	California	675	7.4%
5	Texas	394	4.3%
6	Pennsylvania	369	4.0%
7	Maryland	320	3.5%
8	Illinois	283	3.1%
9	Georgia	240	2.6%
10	Massachusetts	218	2.4%
11	Connecticut	183	2.0%
12	Virginia	177	1.9%
13	Ohio	140	1.5%
14	Louisiana	132	1.4%
15	North Carolina	120	1.3%
16	Michigan	114	1.2%
17	South Carolina	108	1.2%
18	Alabama	76	0.8%
19	Missouri	61	0.7%
20	Tennessee	59	0.6%
21	Indiana	56	0.6%
21	Mississippi	56	0.6%
23	Arizona	46	0.5%
24	Arkansas	36	0.4%
25	Kentucky	35	0.4%
25	Washington	35	0.4%
27	Wisconsin	33	0.4%
28	Colorado	31	0.3%
29	Nevada	29	0.3%
30	Minnesota	28	0.3%
30	Rhode Island	28	0.3%
32	Delaware	26	0.3%
32	Oklahoma	26	0.3%
34	Utah	20	0.2%
35	Oregon	19	0.2%
36	Hawaii	17	0.2%
37	Kansas	14	0.2%
38	Iowa	13	0.1%
39	Nebraska	11	0.1%
39	West Virginia	11	0.1%
41	New Hampshire	10	0.1%
42	New Mexico	9	0.1%
43	Alaska	7	0.1%
43	Maine	7	0.1%
45	Vermont	6	0.1%
46	South Dakota	5	0.1%
47	Montana	3	0.0%
48	Idaho	2	0.0%
48	North Dakota	2	0.0%
48	Wyoming	2	0.0%
	District of Columbia	188	2.1%

Source: U.S. Department of Health and Human Services, Centers for Disease Control and Prevention
 "HIV/AIDS Surveillance Report, 2007" (Vol. 19, http://www.cdc.gov/hiv/topics/surveillance/resources/reports/index.htm)
*Cumulative through December 2007. AIDS is Acquired Immunodeficiency Syndrome. It is a specific group of diseases or conditions which are indicative of severe immunosuppression related to infection with the Human Immunodeficiency Virus (HIV).
National total does not include 403 cases in Puerto Rico, 18 cases in the Virgin Islands, and one case in Guam.

Chickenpox (Varicella) Cases Reported in 2009

National Total = 16,944 Cases*

ALPHA ORDER

RANK	STATE	CASES	% of USA
8	Alabama	516	3.0%
23	Alaska	54	0.3%
32	Arizona	0	0.0%
18	Arkansas	115	0.7%
32	California	0	0.0%
9	Colorado	515	3.0%
32	Connecticut	0	0.0%
28	Delaware	12	0.1%
6	Florida	1,129	6.7%
NA	Georgia**	NA	NA
25	Hawaii	35	0.2%
NA	Idaho**	NA	NA
5	Illinois	1,528	9.0%
13	Indiana	392	2.3%
NA	Iowa**	NA	NA
15	Kansas	183	1.1%
NA	Kentucky**	NA	NA
22	Louisiana	76	0.4%
19	Maine	105	0.6%
NA	Maryland**	NA	NA
31	Massachusetts	2	0.0%
3	Michigan	1,857	11.0%
32	Minnesota	0	0.0%
29	Mississippi	5	0.0%
7	Missouri	580	3.4%
19	Montana	105	0.6%
NA	Nebraska**	NA	NA
NA	Nevada**	NA	NA
14	New Hampshire	195	1.2%
NA	New Jersey**	NA	NA
17	New Mexico	134	0.8%
NA	New York**	NA	NA
NA	North Carolina**	NA	NA
21	North Dakota	83	0.5%
2	Ohio	1,916	11.3%
NA	Oklahoma**	NA	NA
NA	Oregon**	NA	NA
4	Pennsylvania	1,537	9.1%
30	Rhode Island	4	0.0%
16	South Carolina	154	0.9%
27	South Dakota	17	0.1%
NA	Tennessee**	NA	NA
1	Texas	4,121	24.3%
12	Utah	485	2.9%
24	Vermont	43	0.3%
26	Virginia	28	0.2%
NA	Washington**	NA	NA
11	West Virginia	493	2.9%
10	Wisconsin	512	3.0%
32	Wyoming	0	0.0%

RANK ORDER

RANK	STATE	CASES	% of USA
1	Texas	4,121	24.3%
2	Ohio	1,916	11.3%
3	Michigan	1,857	11.0%
4	Pennsylvania	1,537	9.1%
5	Illinois	1,528	9.0%
6	Florida	1,129	6.7%
7	Missouri	580	3.4%
8	Alabama	516	3.0%
9	Colorado	515	3.0%
10	Wisconsin	512	3.0%
11	West Virginia	493	2.9%
12	Utah	485	2.9%
13	Indiana	392	2.3%
14	New Hampshire	195	1.2%
15	Kansas	183	1.1%
16	South Carolina	154	0.9%
17	New Mexico	134	0.8%
18	Arkansas	115	0.7%
19	Maine	105	0.6%
19	Montana	105	0.6%
21	North Dakota	83	0.5%
22	Louisiana	76	0.4%
23	Alaska	54	0.3%
24	Vermont	43	0.3%
25	Hawaii	35	0.2%
26	Virginia	28	0.2%
27	South Dakota	17	0.1%
28	Delaware	12	0.1%
29	Mississippi	5	0.0%
30	Rhode Island	4	0.0%
31	Massachusetts	2	0.0%
32	Arizona	0	0.0%
32	California	0	0.0%
32	Connecticut	0	0.0%
32	Minnesota	0	0.0%
32	Wyoming	0	0.0%
NA	Georgia**	NA	NA
NA	Idaho**	NA	NA
NA	Iowa**	NA	NA
NA	Kentucky**	NA	NA
NA	Maryland**	NA	NA
NA	Nebraska**	NA	NA
NA	Nevada**	NA	NA
NA	New Jersey**	NA	NA
NA	New York**	NA	NA
NA	North Carolina**	NA	NA
NA	Oklahoma**	NA	NA
NA	Oregon**	NA	NA
NA	Tennessee**	NA	NA
NA	Washington**	NA	NA
	District of Columbia	13	0.1%

Source: U.S. Department of Health and Human Services, National Center for Health Statistics
  "Morbidity and Mortality Weekly Report" (January 10, 2010, Vol. 58, Nos. 51 & 52, http://www.cdc.gov/mmwr/)
*Provisional data. An illness with acute onset of generalized maculo-papulovesicular rash without other apparent cause.
**Not notifiable.

Chickenpox (Varicella) Rate in 2009

National Rate = 5.5 Cases per 100,000 Population*

ALPHA ORDER				RANK ORDER		
RANK	STATE	RATE		RANK	STATE	RATE
10	Alabama	11.0		1	West Virginia	27.1
16	Alaska	7.7		2	Michigan	18.6
31	Arizona	0.0		3	Utah	17.4
22	Arkansas	4.0		4	Ohio	16.6
31	California	0.0		4	Texas	16.6
12	Colorado	10.2		6	New Hampshire	14.7
31	Connecticut	0.0		7	North Dakota	12.8
27	Delaware	1.4		8	Pennsylvania	12.2
20	Florida	6.1		9	Illinois	11.8
NA	Georgia**	NA		10	Alabama	11.0
24	Hawaii	2.7		11	Montana	10.8
NA	Idaho**	NA		12	Colorado	10.2
9	Illinois	11.8		13	Missouri	9.7
20	Indiana	6.1		14	Wisconsin	9.1
NA	Iowa**	NA		15	Maine	8.0
19	Kansas	6.5		16	Alaska	7.7
NA	Kentucky**	NA		17	Vermont	6.9
26	Louisiana	1.7		18	New Mexico	6.7
15	Maine	8.0		19	Kansas	6.5
NA	Maryland**	NA		20	Florida	6.1
31	Massachusetts	0.0		20	Indiana	6.1
2	Michigan	18.6		22	Arkansas	4.0
31	Minnesota	0.0		23	South Carolina	3.4
30	Mississippi	0.2		24	Hawaii	2.7
13	Missouri	9.7		25	South Dakota	2.1
11	Montana	10.8		26	Louisiana	1.7
NA	Nebraska**	NA		27	Delaware	1.4
NA	Nevada**	NA		28	Rhode Island	0.4
6	New Hampshire	14.7		28	Virginia	0.4
NA	New Jersey**	NA		30	Mississippi	0.2
18	New Mexico	6.7		31	Arizona	0.0
NA	New York**	NA		31	California	0.0
NA	North Carolina**	NA		31	Connecticut	0.0
7	North Dakota	12.8		31	Massachusetts	0.0
4	Ohio	16.6		31	Minnesota	0.0
NA	Oklahoma**	NA		31	Wyoming	0.0
NA	Oregon**	NA		NA	Georgia**	NA
8	Pennsylvania	12.2		NA	Idaho**	NA
28	Rhode Island	0.4		NA	Iowa**	NA
23	South Carolina	3.4		NA	Kentucky**	NA
25	South Dakota	2.1		NA	Maryland**	NA
NA	Tennessee**	NA		NA	Nebraska**	NA
4	Texas	16.6		NA	Nevada**	NA
3	Utah	17.4		NA	New Jersey**	NA
17	Vermont	6.9		NA	New York**	NA
28	Virginia	0.4		NA	North Carolina**	NA
NA	Washington**	NA		NA	Oklahoma**	NA
1	West Virginia	27.1		NA	Oregon**	NA
14	Wisconsin	9.1		NA	Tennessee**	NA
31	Wyoming	0.0		NA	Washington**	NA
					District of Columbia	2.2

Source: CQ Press using data from U.S. Department of Health and Human Services, National Center for Health Statistics
   "Morbidity and Mortality Weekly Report" (January 10, 2010, Vol. 58, Nos. 51 & 52, http://www.cdc.gov/mmwr/)
*Provisional data. An illness with acute onset of generalized maculo-papulovesicular rash without other apparent cause.
**Not notifiable.

E. Coli Cases Reported in 2009

National Total = 4,323 Cases*

ALPHA ORDER

RANK	STATE	CASES	% of USA
30	Alabama	45	1.0%
49	Alaska	0	0.0%
25	Arizona	71	1.6%
31	Arkansas	43	1.0%
2	California	269	6.2%
8	Colorado	166	3.8%
28	Connecticut	65	1.5%
45	Delaware	13	0.3%
7	Florida	177	4.1%
25	Georgia	71	1.6%
46	Hawaii	9	0.2%
19	Idaho	91	2.1%
12	Illinois	138	3.2%
24	Indiana	79	1.8%
10	Iowa	153	3.5%
38	Kansas	32	0.7%
27	Kentucky	70	1.6%
49	Louisiana	0	0.0%
42	Maine	19	0.4%
18	Maryland	93	2.2%
17	Massachusetts	100	2.3%
9	Michigan	158	3.7%
3	Minnesota	222	5.1%
48	Mississippi	6	0.1%
11	Missouri	144	3.3%
34	Montana	35	0.8%
21	Nebraska	87	2.0%
43	Nevada	16	0.4%
33	New Hampshire	36	0.8%
37	New Jersey	33	0.8%
36	New Mexico	34	0.8%
4	New York	203	4.7%
21	North Carolina	87	2.0%
47	North Dakota	8	0.2%
13	Ohio	133	3.1%
34	Oklahoma	35	0.8%
23	Oregon	80	1.9%
16	Pennsylvania	106	2.5%
32	Rhode Island	38	0.9%
40	South Carolina	30	0.7%
29	South Dakota	60	1.4%
19	Tennessee	91	2.1%
6	Texas	186	4.3%
15	Utah	110	2.5%
41	Vermont	24	0.6%
13	Virginia	133	3.1%
5	Washington	200	4.6%
39	West Virginia	31	0.7%
1	Wisconsin	277	6.4%
44	Wyoming	15	0.3%

RANK ORDER

RANK	STATE	CASES	% of USA
1	Wisconsin	277	6.4%
2	California	269	6.2%
3	Minnesota	222	5.1%
4	New York	203	4.7%
5	Washington	200	4.6%
6	Texas	186	4.3%
7	Florida	177	4.1%
8	Colorado	166	3.8%
9	Michigan	158	3.7%
10	Iowa	153	3.5%
11	Missouri	144	3.3%
12	Illinois	138	3.2%
13	Ohio	133	3.1%
13	Virginia	133	3.1%
15	Utah	110	2.5%
16	Pennsylvania	106	2.5%
17	Massachusetts	100	2.3%
18	Maryland	93	2.2%
19	Idaho	91	2.1%
19	Tennessee	91	2.1%
21	Nebraska	87	2.0%
21	North Carolina	87	2.0%
23	Oregon	80	1.9%
24	Indiana	79	1.8%
25	Arizona	71	1.6%
25	Georgia	71	1.6%
27	Kentucky	70	1.6%
28	Connecticut	65	1.5%
29	South Dakota	60	1.4%
30	Alabama	45	1.0%
31	Arkansas	43	1.0%
32	Rhode Island	38	0.9%
33	New Hampshire	36	0.8%
34	Montana	35	0.8%
34	Oklahoma	35	0.8%
36	New Mexico	34	0.8%
37	New Jersey	33	0.8%
38	Kansas	32	0.7%
39	West Virginia	31	0.7%
40	South Carolina	30	0.7%
41	Vermont	24	0.6%
42	Maine	19	0.4%
43	Nevada	16	0.4%
44	Wyoming	15	0.3%
45	Delaware	13	0.3%
46	Hawaii	9	0.2%
47	North Dakota	8	0.2%
48	Mississippi	6	0.1%
49	Alaska	0	0.0%
49	Louisiana	0	0.0%
	District of Columbia	1	0.0%

Source: U.S. Department of Health and Human Services, National Center for Health Statistics
"Morbidity and Mortality Weekly Report" (January 10, 2010, Vol. 58, Nos. 51 & 52, http://www.cdc.gov/mmwr/)
*Escherichia Coli is a common bacterium that normally inhabits the intestinal tracts of humans and animals but can cause infection in other parts of the body, especially the urinary tract. One strain, sometimes transmitted in hamburger meat, can cause serious infection resulting in sickness and death.

E. Coli Rate in 2009

National Rate = 1.4 Cases per 100,000 Population*

ALPHA ORDER				RANK ORDER		
RANK	**STATE**	**RATE**		**RANK**	**STATE**	**RATE**
35	Alabama	1.0		1	South Dakota	7.4
49	Alaska	0.0		2	Idaho	5.9
32	Arizona	1.1		3	Iowa	5.1
24	Arkansas	1.5		4	Wisconsin	4.9
42	California	0.7		5	Nebraska	4.8
11	Colorado	3.3		6	Minnesota	4.2
17	Connecticut	1.8		7	Utah	4.0
24	Delaware	1.5		8	Vermont	3.9
35	Florida	1.0		9	Montana	3.6
42	Georgia	0.7		9	Rhode Island	3.6
42	Hawaii	0.7		11	Colorado	3.3
2	Idaho	5.9		12	Washington	3.0
32	Illinois	1.1		13	Wyoming	2.8
29	Indiana	1.2		14	New Hampshire	2.7
3	Iowa	5.1		15	Missouri	2.4
32	Kansas	1.1		16	Oregon	2.1
21	Kentucky	1.6		17	Connecticut	1.8
49	Louisiana	0.0		18	New Mexico	1.7
27	Maine	1.4		18	Virginia	1.7
21	Maryland	1.6		18	West Virginia	1.7
24	Massachusetts	1.5		21	Kentucky	1.6
21	Michigan	1.6		21	Maryland	1.6
6	Minnesota	4.2		21	Michigan	1.6
48	Mississippi	0.2		24	Arkansas	1.5
15	Missouri	2.4		24	Delaware	1.5
9	Montana	3.6		24	Massachusetts	1.5
5	Nebraska	4.8		27	Maine	1.4
46	Nevada	0.6		27	Tennessee	1.4
14	New Hampshire	2.7		29	Indiana	1.2
47	New Jersey	0.4		29	North Dakota	1.2
18	New Mexico	1.7		29	Ohio	1.2
35	New York	1.0		32	Arizona	1.1
38	North Carolina	0.9		32	Illinois	1.1
29	North Dakota	1.2		32	Kansas	1.1
29	Ohio	1.2		35	Alabama	1.0
38	Oklahoma	0.9		35	Florida	1.0
16	Oregon	2.1		35	New York	1.0
40	Pennsylvania	0.8		38	North Carolina	0.9
9	Rhode Island	3.6		38	Oklahoma	0.9
42	South Carolina	0.7		40	Pennsylvania	0.8
1	South Dakota	7.4		40	Texas	0.8
27	Tennessee	1.4		42	California	0.7
40	Texas	0.8		42	Georgia	0.7
7	Utah	4.0		42	Hawaii	0.7
8	Vermont	3.9		42	South Carolina	0.7
18	Virginia	1.7		46	Nevada	0.6
12	Washington	3.0		47	New Jersey	0.4
18	West Virginia	1.7		48	Mississippi	0.2
4	Wisconsin	4.9		49	Alaska	0.0
13	Wyoming	2.8		49	Louisiana	0.0
					District of Columbia	0.2

Source: CQ Press using data from U.S. Department of Health and Human Services, National Center for Health Statistics "Morbidity and Mortality Weekly Report" (January 10, 2010, Vol. 58, Nos. 51 & 52, http://www.cdc.gov/mmwr/)
*Escherichia Coli is a common bacterium that normally inhabits the intestinal tracts of humans and animals but can cause infection in other parts of the body, especially the urinary tract. One strain, sometimes transmitted in hamburger meat, can cause serious infection resulting in sickness and death.

Hepatitis A and B Cases Reported in 2009

National Total = 4,869 Cases*

ALPHA ORDER

RANK	STATE	CASES	% of USA
20	Alabama	94	1.9%
44	Alaska	7	0.1%
14	Arizona	116	2.4%
28	Arkansas	57	1.2%
1	California	505	10.4%
23	Colorado	74	1.5%
35	Connecticut	32	0.7%
NA	Delaware**	NA	NA
2	Florida	485	10.0%
6	Georgia	188	3.9%
41	Hawaii	11	0.2%
37	Idaho	15	0.3%
6	Illinois	188	3.9%
25	Indiana	71	1.5%
26	Iowa	66	1.4%
40	Kansas	12	0.2%
19	Kentucky	98	2.0%
34	Louisiana	36	0.7%
36	Maine	16	0.3%
15	Maryland	114	2.3%
24	Massachusetts	72	1.5%
8	Michigan	182	3.7%
30	Minnesota	47	1.0%
31	Mississippi	44	0.9%
17	Missouri	109	2.2%
45	Montana	6	0.1%
32	Nebraska	42	0.9%
33	Nevada	39	0.8%
42	New Hampshire	10	0.2%
12	New Jersey	127	2.6%
38	New Mexico	13	0.3%
4	New York	364	7.5%
5	North Carolina	190	3.9%
49	North Dakota	1	0.0%
13	Ohio	122	2.5%
16	Oklahoma	113	2.3%
27	Oregon	60	1.2%
9	Pennsylvania	175	3.6%
43	Rhode Island	8	0.2%
18	South Carolina	108	2.2%
47	South Dakota	5	0.1%
10	Tennessee	140	2.9%
3	Texas	454	9.3%
38	Utah	13	0.3%
48	Vermont	2	0.0%
11	Virginia	132	2.7%
21	Washington	82	1.7%
22	West Virginia	76	1.6%
29	Wisconsin	49	1.0%
45	Wyoming	6	0.1%

RANK ORDER

RANK	STATE	CASES	% of USA
1	California	505	10.4%
2	Florida	485	10.0%
3	Texas	454	9.3%
4	New York	364	7.5%
5	North Carolina	190	3.9%
6	Georgia	188	3.9%
6	Illinois	188	3.9%
8	Michigan	182	3.7%
9	Pennsylvania	175	3.6%
10	Tennessee	140	2.9%
11	Virginia	132	2.7%
12	New Jersey	127	2.6%
13	Ohio	122	2.5%
14	Arizona	116	2.4%
15	Maryland	114	2.3%
16	Oklahoma	113	2.3%
17	Missouri	109	2.2%
18	South Carolina	108	2.2%
19	Kentucky	98	2.0%
20	Alabama	94	1.9%
21	Washington	82	1.7%
22	West Virginia	76	1.6%
23	Colorado	74	1.5%
24	Massachusetts	72	1.5%
25	Indiana	71	1.5%
26	Iowa	66	1.4%
27	Oregon	60	1.2%
28	Arkansas	57	1.2%
29	Wisconsin	49	1.0%
30	Minnesota	47	1.0%
31	Mississippi	44	0.9%
32	Nebraska	42	0.9%
33	Nevada	39	0.8%
34	Louisiana	36	0.7%
35	Connecticut	32	0.7%
36	Maine	16	0.3%
37	Idaho	15	0.3%
38	New Mexico	13	0.3%
38	Utah	13	0.3%
40	Kansas	12	0.2%
41	Hawaii	11	0.2%
42	New Hampshire	10	0.2%
43	Rhode Island	8	0.2%
44	Alaska	7	0.1%
45	Montana	6	0.1%
45	Wyoming	6	0.1%
47	South Dakota	5	0.1%
48	Vermont	2	0.0%
49	North Dakota	1	0.0%
NA	Delaware**	NA	NA
	District of Columbia**	NA	NA

Source: U.S. Department of Health and Human Services, National Center for Health Statistics
   "Morbidity and Mortality Weekly Report" (January 10, 2010, Vol. 58, Nos. 51 & 52, http://www.cdc.gov/mmwr/)
*Provisional data. An inflammation of the liver.
**Not available.

Hepatitis A and B Rate in 2009

National Rate = 1.6 Cases per 100,000 Population*

<table>
<tr><td colspan="3">ALPHA ORDER</td><td colspan="3">RANK ORDER</td></tr>
<tr><td>RANK</td><td>STATE</td><td>RATE</td><td>RANK</td><td>STATE</td><td>RATE</td></tr>
<tr><td>9</td><td>Alabama</td><td>2.0</td><td>1</td><td>West Virginia</td><td>4.2</td></tr>
<tr><td>34</td><td>Alaska</td><td>1.0</td><td>2</td><td>Oklahoma</td><td>3.1</td></tr>
<tr><td>15</td><td>Arizona</td><td>1.8</td><td>3</td><td>Florida</td><td>2.6</td></tr>
<tr><td>9</td><td>Arkansas</td><td>2.0</td><td>4</td><td>South Carolina</td><td>2.4</td></tr>
<tr><td>26</td><td>California</td><td>1.4</td><td>5</td><td>Kentucky</td><td>2.3</td></tr>
<tr><td>21</td><td>Colorado</td><td>1.5</td><td>5</td><td>Nebraska</td><td>2.3</td></tr>
<tr><td>36</td><td>Connecticut</td><td>0.9</td><td>7</td><td>Iowa</td><td>2.2</td></tr>
<tr><td>NA</td><td>Delaware**</td><td>NA</td><td>7</td><td>Tennessee</td><td>2.2</td></tr>
<tr><td>3</td><td>Florida</td><td>2.6</td><td>9</td><td>Alabama</td><td>2.0</td></tr>
<tr><td>13</td><td>Georgia</td><td>1.9</td><td>9</td><td>Arkansas</td><td>2.0</td></tr>
<tr><td>39</td><td>Hawaii</td><td>0.8</td><td>9</td><td>Maryland</td><td>2.0</td></tr>
<tr><td>34</td><td>Idaho</td><td>1.0</td><td>9</td><td>North Carolina</td><td>2.0</td></tr>
<tr><td>21</td><td>Illinois</td><td>1.5</td><td>13</td><td>Georgia</td><td>1.9</td></tr>
<tr><td>30</td><td>Indiana</td><td>1.1</td><td>13</td><td>New York</td><td>1.9</td></tr>
<tr><td>7</td><td>Iowa</td><td>2.2</td><td>15</td><td>Arizona</td><td>1.8</td></tr>
<tr><td>47</td><td>Kansas</td><td>0.4</td><td>15</td><td>Michigan</td><td>1.8</td></tr>
<tr><td>5</td><td>Kentucky</td><td>2.3</td><td>15</td><td>Missouri</td><td>1.8</td></tr>
<tr><td>39</td><td>Louisiana</td><td>0.8</td><td>15</td><td>Texas</td><td>1.8</td></tr>
<tr><td>28</td><td>Maine</td><td>1.2</td><td>19</td><td>Virginia</td><td>1.7</td></tr>
<tr><td>9</td><td>Maryland</td><td>2.0</td><td>20</td><td>Oregon</td><td>1.6</td></tr>
<tr><td>30</td><td>Massachusetts</td><td>1.1</td><td>21</td><td>Colorado</td><td>1.5</td></tr>
<tr><td>15</td><td>Michigan</td><td>1.8</td><td>21</td><td>Illinois</td><td>1.5</td></tr>
<tr><td>36</td><td>Minnesota</td><td>0.9</td><td>21</td><td>Mississippi</td><td>1.5</td></tr>
<tr><td>21</td><td>Mississippi</td><td>1.5</td><td>21</td><td>Nevada</td><td>1.5</td></tr>
<tr><td>15</td><td>Missouri</td><td>1.8</td><td>21</td><td>New Jersey</td><td>1.5</td></tr>
<tr><td>43</td><td>Montana</td><td>0.6</td><td>26</td><td>California</td><td>1.4</td></tr>
<tr><td>5</td><td>Nebraska</td><td>2.3</td><td>26</td><td>Pennsylvania</td><td>1.4</td></tr>
<tr><td>21</td><td>Nevada</td><td>1.5</td><td>28</td><td>Maine</td><td>1.2</td></tr>
<tr><td>39</td><td>New Hampshire</td><td>0.8</td><td>28</td><td>Washington</td><td>1.2</td></tr>
<tr><td>21</td><td>New Jersey</td><td>1.5</td><td>30</td><td>Indiana</td><td>1.1</td></tr>
<tr><td>43</td><td>New Mexico</td><td>0.6</td><td>30</td><td>Massachusetts</td><td>1.1</td></tr>
<tr><td>13</td><td>New York</td><td>1.9</td><td>30</td><td>Ohio</td><td>1.1</td></tr>
<tr><td>9</td><td>North Carolina</td><td>2.0</td><td>30</td><td>Wyoming</td><td>1.1</td></tr>
<tr><td>49</td><td>North Dakota</td><td>0.2</td><td>34</td><td>Alaska</td><td>1.0</td></tr>
<tr><td>30</td><td>Ohio</td><td>1.1</td><td>34</td><td>Idaho</td><td>1.0</td></tr>
<tr><td>2</td><td>Oklahoma</td><td>3.1</td><td>36</td><td>Connecticut</td><td>0.9</td></tr>
<tr><td>20</td><td>Oregon</td><td>1.6</td><td>36</td><td>Minnesota</td><td>0.9</td></tr>
<tr><td>26</td><td>Pennsylvania</td><td>1.4</td><td>36</td><td>Wisconsin</td><td>0.9</td></tr>
<tr><td>39</td><td>Rhode Island</td><td>0.8</td><td>39</td><td>Hawaii</td><td>0.8</td></tr>
<tr><td>4</td><td>South Carolina</td><td>2.4</td><td>39</td><td>Louisiana</td><td>0.8</td></tr>
<tr><td>43</td><td>South Dakota</td><td>0.6</td><td>39</td><td>New Hampshire</td><td>0.8</td></tr>
<tr><td>7</td><td>Tennessee</td><td>2.2</td><td>39</td><td>Rhode Island</td><td>0.8</td></tr>
<tr><td>15</td><td>Texas</td><td>1.8</td><td>43</td><td>Montana</td><td>0.6</td></tr>
<tr><td>46</td><td>Utah</td><td>0.5</td><td>43</td><td>New Mexico</td><td>0.6</td></tr>
<tr><td>48</td><td>Vermont</td><td>0.3</td><td>43</td><td>South Dakota</td><td>0.6</td></tr>
<tr><td>19</td><td>Virginia</td><td>1.7</td><td>46</td><td>Utah</td><td>0.5</td></tr>
<tr><td>28</td><td>Washington</td><td>1.2</td><td>47</td><td>Kansas</td><td>0.4</td></tr>
<tr><td>1</td><td>West Virginia</td><td>4.2</td><td>48</td><td>Vermont</td><td>0.3</td></tr>
<tr><td>36</td><td>Wisconsin</td><td>0.9</td><td>49</td><td>North Dakota</td><td>0.2</td></tr>
<tr><td>30</td><td>Wyoming</td><td>1.1</td><td>NA</td><td>Delaware**</td><td>NA</td></tr>
<tr><td></td><td></td><td></td><td></td><td>District of Columbia**</td><td>NA</td></tr>
</table>

Source: CQ Press using data from U.S. Department of Health and Human Services, National Center for Health Statistics
"Morbidity and Mortality Weekly Report" (January 10, 2010, Vol. 58, Nos. 51 & 52, http://www.cdc.gov/mmwr/)
*Provisional data. An inflammation of the liver.
**Not available.

Legionellosis Cases Reported in 2009

National Total = 3,145 Cases*

ALPHA ORDER

RANK	STATE	CASES	% of USA
27	Alabama	17	0.5%
48	Alaska	1	0.0%
16	Arizona	53	1.7%
37	Arkansas	8	0.3%
5	California	163	5.2%
21	Colorado	31	1.0%
15	Connecticut	55	1.7%
26	Delaware	18	0.6%
4	Florida	202	6.4%
17	Georgia	51	1.6%
48	Hawaii	1	0.0%
37	Idaho	8	0.3%
9	Illinois	105	3.3%
19	Indiana	47	1.5%
24	Iowa	21	0.7%
46	Kansas	3	0.1%
17	Kentucky	51	1.6%
43	Louisiana	4	0.1%
34	Maine	10	0.3%
7	Maryland	151	4.8%
11	Massachusetts	80	2.5%
8	Michigan	147	4.7%
31	Minnesota	12	0.4%
43	Mississippi	4	0.1%
14	Missouri	56	1.8%
37	Montana	8	0.3%
29	Nebraska	13	0.4%
33	Nevada	11	0.3%
31	New Hampshire	12	0.4%
6	New Jersey	155	4.9%
37	New Mexico	8	0.3%
1	New York	562	17.9%
20	North Carolina	40	1.3%
47	North Dakota	2	0.1%
3	Ohio	283	9.0%
42	Oklahoma	6	0.2%
28	Oregon	16	0.5%
2	Pennsylvania	383	12.2%
25	Rhode Island	19	0.6%
29	South Carolina	13	0.4%
48	South Dakota	1	0.0%
12	Tennessee	63	2.0%
10	Texas	102	3.2%
23	Utah	24	0.8%
41	Vermont	7	0.2%
13	Virginia	61	1.9%
22	Washington	25	0.8%
36	West Virginia	9	0.3%
34	Wisconsin	10	0.3%
43	Wyoming	4	0.1%

RANK ORDER

RANK	STATE	CASES	% of USA
1	New York	562	17.9%
2	Pennsylvania	383	12.2%
3	Ohio	283	9.0%
4	Florida	202	6.4%
5	California	163	5.2%
6	New Jersey	155	4.9%
7	Maryland	151	4.8%
8	Michigan	147	4.7%
9	Illinois	105	3.3%
10	Texas	102	3.2%
11	Massachusetts	80	2.5%
12	Tennessee	63	2.0%
13	Virginia	61	1.9%
14	Missouri	56	1.8%
15	Connecticut	55	1.7%
16	Arizona	53	1.7%
17	Georgia	51	1.6%
17	Kentucky	51	1.6%
19	Indiana	47	1.5%
20	North Carolina	40	1.3%
21	Colorado	31	1.0%
22	Washington	25	0.8%
23	Utah	24	0.8%
24	Iowa	21	0.7%
25	Rhode Island	19	0.6%
26	Delaware	18	0.6%
27	Alabama	17	0.5%
28	Oregon	16	0.5%
29	Nebraska	13	0.4%
29	South Carolina	13	0.4%
31	Minnesota	12	0.4%
31	New Hampshire	12	0.4%
33	Nevada	11	0.3%
34	Maine	10	0.3%
34	Wisconsin	10	0.3%
36	West Virginia	9	0.3%
37	Arkansas	8	0.3%
37	Idaho	8	0.3%
37	Montana	8	0.3%
37	New Mexico	8	0.3%
41	Vermont	7	0.2%
42	Oklahoma	6	0.2%
43	Louisiana	4	0.1%
43	Mississippi	4	0.1%
43	Wyoming	4	0.1%
46	Kansas	3	0.1%
47	North Dakota	2	0.1%
48	Alaska	1	0.0%
48	Hawaii	1	0.0%
48	South Dakota	1	0.0%
	District of Columbia	9	0.3%

Source: U.S. Department of Health and Human Services, National Center for Health Statistics
"Morbidity and Mortality Weekly Report" (January 10, 2010, Vol. 58, Nos. 51 & 52, http://www.cdc.gov/mmwr/)
*Provisional data. A pneumonia-like disease (Legionnaire's Disease).

Legionellosis Rate in 2009

National Rate = 1.0 Cases per 100,000 Population*

<table>
<tr><td colspan="3">ALPHA ORDER</td><td colspan="3">RANK ORDER</td></tr>
<tr><th>RANK</th><th>STATE</th><th>RATE</th><th>RANK</th><th>STATE</th><th>RATE</th></tr>
<tr><td>31</td><td>Alabama</td><td>0.4</td><td>1</td><td>Pennsylvania</td><td>3.0</td></tr>
<tr><td>45</td><td>Alaska</td><td>0.1</td><td>2</td><td>New York</td><td>2.9</td></tr>
<tr><td>18</td><td>Arizona</td><td>0.8</td><td>3</td><td>Maryland</td><td>2.6</td></tr>
<tr><td>39</td><td>Arkansas</td><td>0.3</td><td>4</td><td>Ohio</td><td>2.5</td></tr>
<tr><td>31</td><td>California</td><td>0.4</td><td>5</td><td>Delaware</td><td>2.0</td></tr>
<tr><td>27</td><td>Colorado</td><td>0.6</td><td>6</td><td>New Jersey</td><td>1.8</td></tr>
<tr><td>8</td><td>Connecticut</td><td>1.6</td><td>6</td><td>Rhode Island</td><td>1.8</td></tr>
<tr><td>5</td><td>Delaware</td><td>2.0</td><td>8</td><td>Connecticut</td><td>1.6</td></tr>
<tr><td>12</td><td>Florida</td><td>1.1</td><td>9</td><td>Michigan</td><td>1.5</td></tr>
<tr><td>28</td><td>Georgia</td><td>0.5</td><td>10</td><td>Kentucky</td><td>1.2</td></tr>
<tr><td>45</td><td>Hawaii</td><td>0.1</td><td>10</td><td>Massachusetts</td><td>1.2</td></tr>
<tr><td>28</td><td>Idaho</td><td>0.5</td><td>12</td><td>Florida</td><td>1.1</td></tr>
<tr><td>18</td><td>Illinois</td><td>0.8</td><td>12</td><td>Vermont</td><td>1.1</td></tr>
<tr><td>23</td><td>Indiana</td><td>0.7</td><td>14</td><td>Tennessee</td><td>1.0</td></tr>
<tr><td>23</td><td>Iowa</td><td>0.7</td><td>15</td><td>Missouri</td><td>0.9</td></tr>
<tr><td>45</td><td>Kansas</td><td>0.1</td><td>15</td><td>New Hampshire</td><td>0.9</td></tr>
<tr><td>10</td><td>Kentucky</td><td>1.2</td><td>15</td><td>Utah</td><td>0.9</td></tr>
<tr><td>45</td><td>Louisiana</td><td>0.1</td><td>18</td><td>Arizona</td><td>0.8</td></tr>
<tr><td>18</td><td>Maine</td><td>0.8</td><td>18</td><td>Illinois</td><td>0.8</td></tr>
<tr><td>3</td><td>Maryland</td><td>2.6</td><td>18</td><td>Maine</td><td>0.8</td></tr>
<tr><td>10</td><td>Massachusetts</td><td>1.2</td><td>18</td><td>Montana</td><td>0.8</td></tr>
<tr><td>9</td><td>Michigan</td><td>1.5</td><td>18</td><td>Virginia</td><td>0.8</td></tr>
<tr><td>42</td><td>Minnesota</td><td>0.2</td><td>23</td><td>Indiana</td><td>0.7</td></tr>
<tr><td>45</td><td>Mississippi</td><td>0.1</td><td>23</td><td>Iowa</td><td>0.7</td></tr>
<tr><td>15</td><td>Missouri</td><td>0.9</td><td>23</td><td>Nebraska</td><td>0.7</td></tr>
<tr><td>18</td><td>Montana</td><td>0.8</td><td>23</td><td>Wyoming</td><td>0.7</td></tr>
<tr><td>23</td><td>Nebraska</td><td>0.7</td><td>27</td><td>Colorado</td><td>0.6</td></tr>
<tr><td>31</td><td>Nevada</td><td>0.4</td><td>28</td><td>Georgia</td><td>0.5</td></tr>
<tr><td>15</td><td>New Hampshire</td><td>0.9</td><td>28</td><td>Idaho</td><td>0.5</td></tr>
<tr><td>6</td><td>New Jersey</td><td>1.8</td><td>28</td><td>West Virginia</td><td>0.5</td></tr>
<tr><td>31</td><td>New Mexico</td><td>0.4</td><td>31</td><td>Alabama</td><td>0.4</td></tr>
<tr><td>2</td><td>New York</td><td>2.9</td><td>31</td><td>California</td><td>0.4</td></tr>
<tr><td>31</td><td>North Carolina</td><td>0.4</td><td>31</td><td>Nevada</td><td>0.4</td></tr>
<tr><td>39</td><td>North Dakota</td><td>0.3</td><td>31</td><td>New Mexico</td><td>0.4</td></tr>
<tr><td>4</td><td>Ohio</td><td>2.5</td><td>31</td><td>North Carolina</td><td>0.4</td></tr>
<tr><td>42</td><td>Oklahoma</td><td>0.2</td><td>31</td><td>Oregon</td><td>0.4</td></tr>
<tr><td>31</td><td>Oregon</td><td>0.4</td><td>31</td><td>Texas</td><td>0.4</td></tr>
<tr><td>1</td><td>Pennsylvania</td><td>3.0</td><td>31</td><td>Washington</td><td>0.4</td></tr>
<tr><td>6</td><td>Rhode Island</td><td>1.8</td><td>39</td><td>Arkansas</td><td>0.3</td></tr>
<tr><td>39</td><td>South Carolina</td><td>0.3</td><td>39</td><td>North Dakota</td><td>0.3</td></tr>
<tr><td>45</td><td>South Dakota</td><td>0.1</td><td>39</td><td>South Carolina</td><td>0.3</td></tr>
<tr><td>14</td><td>Tennessee</td><td>1.0</td><td>42</td><td>Minnesota</td><td>0.2</td></tr>
<tr><td>31</td><td>Texas</td><td>0.4</td><td>42</td><td>Oklahoma</td><td>0.2</td></tr>
<tr><td>15</td><td>Utah</td><td>0.9</td><td>42</td><td>Wisconsin</td><td>0.2</td></tr>
<tr><td>12</td><td>Vermont</td><td>1.1</td><td>45</td><td>Alaska</td><td>0.1</td></tr>
<tr><td>18</td><td>Virginia</td><td>0.8</td><td>45</td><td>Hawaii</td><td>0.1</td></tr>
<tr><td>31</td><td>Washington</td><td>0.4</td><td>45</td><td>Kansas</td><td>0.1</td></tr>
<tr><td>28</td><td>West Virginia</td><td>0.5</td><td>45</td><td>Louisiana</td><td>0.1</td></tr>
<tr><td>42</td><td>Wisconsin</td><td>0.2</td><td>45</td><td>Mississippi</td><td>0.1</td></tr>
<tr><td>23</td><td>Wyoming</td><td>0.7</td><td>45</td><td>South Dakota</td><td>0.1</td></tr>
</table>

District of Columbia   1.5

Source: CQ Press using data from U.S. Department of Health and Human Services, National Center for Health Statistics
"Morbidity and Mortality Weekly Report" (January 10, 2010, Vol. 58, Nos. 51 & 52, http://www.cdc.gov/mmwr/)
*Provisional data. A pneumonia-like disease (Legionnaire's Disease).

Lyme Disease Cases in 2009

National Total = 29,780 Cases*

ALPHA ORDER

RANK	STATE	CASES	% of USA
36	Alabama	3	0.0%
36	Alaska	3	0.0%
33	Arizona	6	0.0%
44	Arkansas	0	0.0%
15	California	154	0.5%
41	Colorado	1	0.0%
44	Connecticut	0	0.0%
8	Delaware	952	3.2%
16	Florida	127	0.4%
23	Georgia	53	0.2%
NA	Hawaii**	NA	NA
29	Idaho	15	0.1%
17	Illinois	126	0.4%
21	Indiana	62	0.2%
19	Iowa	96	0.3%
31	Kansas	14	0.0%
41	Kentucky	1	0.0%
44	Louisiana	0	0.0%
9	Maine	894	3.0%
6	Maryland	1,775	6.0%
4	Massachusetts	3,662	12.3%
18	Michigan	99	0.3%
14	Minnesota	169	0.6%
44	Mississippi	0	0.0%
36	Missouri	3	0.0%
36	Montana	3	0.0%
28	Nebraska	20	0.1%
34	Nevada	5	0.0%
7	New Hampshire	1,156	3.9%
3	New Jersey	4,163	14.0%
34	New Mexico	5	0.0%
2	New York	4,441	14.9%
20	North Carolina	63	0.2%
44	North Dakota	0	0.0%
22	Ohio	56	0.2%
44	Oklahoma	0	0.0%
26	Oregon	35	0.1%
1	Pennsylvania	8,087	27.2%
12	Rhode Island	212	0.7%
25	South Carolina	39	0.1%
41	South Dakota	1	0.0%
27	Tennessee	32	0.1%
24	Texas	48	0.2%
32	Utah	7	0.0%
11	Vermont	390	1.3%
10	Virginia	579	1.9%
29	Washington	15	0.1%
13	West Virginia	170	0.6%
5	Wisconsin	2,016	6.8%
40	Wyoming	2	0.0%

RANK ORDER

RANK	STATE	CASES	% of USA
1	Pennsylvania	8,087	27.2%
2	New York	4,441	14.9%
3	New Jersey	4,163	14.0%
4	Massachusetts	3,662	12.3%
5	Wisconsin	2,016	6.8%
6	Maryland	1,775	6.0%
7	New Hampshire	1,156	3.9%
8	Delaware	952	3.2%
9	Maine	894	3.0%
10	Virginia	579	1.9%
11	Vermont	390	1.3%
12	Rhode Island	212	0.7%
13	West Virginia	170	0.6%
14	Minnesota	169	0.6%
15	California	154	0.5%
16	Florida	127	0.4%
17	Illinois	126	0.4%
18	Michigan	99	0.3%
19	Iowa	96	0.3%
20	North Carolina	63	0.2%
21	Indiana	62	0.2%
22	Ohio	56	0.2%
23	Georgia	53	0.2%
24	Texas	48	0.2%
25	South Carolina	39	0.1%
26	Oregon	35	0.1%
27	Tennessee	32	0.1%
28	Nebraska	20	0.1%
29	Idaho	15	0.1%
29	Washington	15	0.1%
31	Kansas	14	0.0%
32	Utah	7	0.0%
33	Arizona	6	0.0%
34	Nevada	5	0.0%
34	New Mexico	5	0.0%
36	Alabama	3	0.0%
36	Alaska	3	0.0%
36	Missouri	3	0.0%
36	Montana	3	0.0%
40	Wyoming	2	0.0%
41	Colorado	1	0.0%
41	Kentucky	1	0.0%
41	South Dakota	1	0.0%
44	Arkansas	0	0.0%
44	Connecticut	0	0.0%
44	Louisiana	0	0.0%
44	Mississippi	0	0.0%
44	North Dakota	0	0.0%
44	Oklahoma	0	0.0%
NA	Hawaii**	NA	NA
	District of Columbia	20	0.1%

Source: U.S. Department of Health and Human Services, National Center for Health Statistics
   "Morbidity and Mortality Weekly Report" (January 10, 2010, Vol. 58, Nos. 51 & 52, http://www.cdc.gov/mmwr/)
*Provisional data. Caused by ticks-lesions, followed by arthritis of large joints, myalgia, malaise, and neurologic and cardiac manifestations. Named after Old Lyme, CT, where the disease was first reported.
**Not notifiable.

Lyme Disease Rate in 2009

National Rate = 9.7 Cases per 100,000 Population*

ALPHA ORDER			RANK ORDER		
RANK	STATE	RATE	RANK	STATE	RATE
38	Alabama	0.1	1	Delaware	107.6
29	Alaska	0.4	2	New Hampshire	87.3
38	Arizona	0.1	3	Maine	67.8
42	Arkansas	0.0	4	Pennsylvania	64.2
29	California	0.4	5	Vermont	62.7
42	Colorado	0.0	6	Massachusetts	55.5
42	Connecticut	0.0	7	New Jersey	47.8
1	Delaware	107.6	8	Wisconsin	35.7
23	Florida	0.7	9	Maryland	31.1
25	Georgia	0.5	10	New York	22.7
NA	Hawaii**	NA	11	Rhode Island	20.1
17	Idaho	1.0	12	West Virginia	9.3
17	Illinois	1.0	13	Virginia	7.3
17	Indiana	1.0	14	Iowa	3.2
14	Iowa	3.2	14	Minnesota	3.2
25	Kansas	0.5	16	Nebraska	1.1
42	Kentucky	0.0	17	Idaho	1.0
42	Louisiana	0.0	17	Illinois	1.0
3	Maine	67.8	17	Indiana	1.0
9	Maryland	31.1	17	Michigan	1.0
6	Massachusetts	55.5	21	Oregon	0.9
17	Michigan	1.0	21	South Carolina	0.9
14	Minnesota	3.2	23	Florida	0.7
42	Mississippi	0.0	23	North Carolina	0.7
38	Missouri	0.1	25	Georgia	0.5
32	Montana	0.3	25	Kansas	0.5
16	Nebraska	1.1	25	Ohio	0.5
34	Nevada	0.2	25	Tennessee	0.5
2	New Hampshire	87.3	29	Alaska	0.4
7	New Jersey	47.8	29	California	0.4
34	New Mexico	0.2	29	Wyoming	0.4
10	New York	22.7	32	Montana	0.3
23	North Carolina	0.7	32	Utah	0.3
42	North Dakota	0.0	34	Nevada	0.2
25	Ohio	0.5	34	New Mexico	0.2
42	Oklahoma	0.0	34	Texas	0.2
21	Oregon	0.9	34	Washington	0.2
4	Pennsylvania	64.2	38	Alabama	0.1
11	Rhode Island	20.1	38	Arizona	0.1
21	South Carolina	0.9	38	Missouri	0.1
38	South Dakota	0.1	38	South Dakota	0.1
25	Tennessee	0.5	42	Arkansas	0.0
34	Texas	0.2	42	Colorado	0.0
32	Utah	0.3	42	Connecticut	0.0
5	Vermont	62.7	42	Kentucky	0.0
13	Virginia	7.3	42	Louisiana	0.0
34	Washington	0.2	42	Mississippi	0.0
12	West Virginia	9.3	42	North Dakota	0.0
8	Wisconsin	35.7	42	Oklahoma	0.0
29	Wyoming	0.4	NA	Hawaii**	NA

District of Columbia 3.3

Source: CQ Press using data from U.S. Department of Health and Human Services, National Center for Health Statistics
"Morbidity and Mortality Weekly Report" (January 10, 2010, Vol. 58, Nos. 51 & 52, http://www.cdc.gov/mmwr/)
*Provisional data. Caused by ticks-lesions, followed by arthritis of large joints, myalgia, malaise, and neurologic and cardiac manifestations. Named after Old Lyme, CT, where the disease was first reported.
**Not notifiable.

Malaria Cases Reported in 2009

National Total = 1,169 Cases*

ALPHA ORDER

RANK	STATE	CASES	% of USA
21	Alabama	9	0.8%
39	Alaska	2	0.2%
21	Arizona	9	0.8%
32	Arkansas	4	0.3%
2	California	117	10.0%
24	Colorado	8	0.7%
27	Connecticut	6	0.5%
29	Delaware	5	0.4%
3	Florida	93	8.0%
5	Georgia	69	5.9%
42	Hawaii	1	0.1%
35	Idaho	3	0.3%
7	Illinois	54	4.6%
16	Indiana	17	1.5%
20	Iowa	10	0.9%
32	Kansas	4	0.3%
17	Kentucky	13	1.1%
35	Louisiana	3	0.3%
39	Maine	2	0.2%
4	Maryland	80	6.8%
11	Massachusetts	35	3.0%
13	Michigan	27	2.3%
12	Minnesota	32	2.7%
42	Mississippi	1	0.1%
18	Missouri	12	1.0%
29	Montana	5	0.4%
24	Nebraska	8	0.7%
48	Nevada	0	0.0%
35	New Hampshire	3	0.3%
42	New Jersey	1	0.1%
48	New Mexico	0	0.0%
1	New York	245	21.0%
14	North Carolina	21	1.8%
42	North Dakota	1	0.1%
10	Ohio	37	3.2%
42	Oklahoma	1	0.1%
19	Oregon	11	0.9%
7	Pennsylvania	54	4.6%
29	Rhode Island	5	0.4%
27	South Carolina	6	0.5%
42	South Dakota	1	0.1%
21	Tennessee	9	0.8%
9	Texas	44	3.8%
32	Utah	4	0.3%
35	Vermont	3	0.3%
6	Virginia	56	4.8%
14	Washington	21	1.8%
39	West Virginia	2	0.2%
26	Wisconsin	7	0.6%
48	Wyoming	0	0.0%

RANK ORDER

RANK	STATE	CASES	% of USA
1	New York	245	21.0%
2	California	117	10.0%
3	Florida	93	8.0%
4	Maryland	80	6.8%
5	Georgia	69	5.9%
6	Virginia	56	4.8%
7	Illinois	54	4.6%
7	Pennsylvania	54	4.6%
9	Texas	44	3.8%
10	Ohio	37	3.2%
11	Massachusetts	35	3.0%
12	Minnesota	32	2.7%
13	Michigan	27	2.3%
14	North Carolina	21	1.8%
14	Washington	21	1.8%
16	Indiana	17	1.5%
17	Kentucky	13	1.1%
18	Missouri	12	1.0%
19	Oregon	11	0.9%
20	Iowa	10	0.9%
21	Alabama	9	0.8%
21	Arizona	9	0.8%
21	Tennessee	9	0.8%
24	Colorado	8	0.7%
24	Nebraska	8	0.7%
26	Wisconsin	7	0.6%
27	Connecticut	6	0.5%
27	South Carolina	6	0.5%
29	Delaware	5	0.4%
29	Montana	5	0.4%
29	Rhode Island	5	0.4%
32	Arkansas	4	0.3%
32	Kansas	4	0.3%
32	Utah	4	0.3%
35	Idaho	3	0.3%
35	Louisiana	3	0.3%
35	New Hampshire	3	0.3%
35	Vermont	3	0.3%
39	Alaska	2	0.2%
39	Maine	2	0.2%
39	West Virginia	2	0.2%
42	Hawaii	1	0.1%
42	Mississippi	1	0.1%
42	New Jersey	1	0.1%
42	North Dakota	1	0.1%
42	Oklahoma	1	0.1%
42	South Dakota	1	0.1%
48	Nevada	0	0.0%
48	New Mexico	0	0.0%
48	Wyoming	0	0.0%
	District of Columbia	8	0.7%

Source: U.S. Department of Health and Human Services, National Center for Health Statistics
   "Morbidity and Mortality Weekly Report" (January 10, 2010, Vol. 58, Nos. 51 & 52, http://www.cdc.gov/mmwr/)
*Provisional data. Infectious disease usually transmitted by bites of infected mosquitoes. Symptoms include high fever, shaking chills, sweating, and anemia.

Malaria Rate in 2009

National Rate = 0.4 Cases per 100,000 Population*

ALPHA ORDER			RANK ORDER		
RANK	STATE	RATE	RANK	STATE	RATE
24	Alabama	0.2	1	Maryland	1.4
15	Alaska	0.3	2	New York	1.3
34	Arizona	0.1	3	Georgia	0.7
34	Arkansas	0.1	3	Virginia	0.7
15	California	0.3	5	Delaware	0.6
24	Colorado	0.2	5	Minnesota	0.6
24	Connecticut	0.2	7	Florida	0.5
5	Delaware	0.6	7	Massachusetts	0.5
7	Florida	0.5	7	Montana	0.5
3	Georgia	0.7	7	Rhode Island	0.5
34	Hawaii	0.1	7	Vermont	0.5
24	Idaho	0.2	12	Illinois	0.4
12	Illinois	0.4	12	Nebraska	0.4
15	Indiana	0.3	12	Pennsylvania	0.4
15	Iowa	0.3	15	Alaska	0.3
34	Kansas	0.1	15	California	0.3
15	Kentucky	0.3	15	Indiana	0.3
34	Louisiana	0.1	15	Iowa	0.3
24	Maine	0.2	15	Kentucky	0.3
1	Maryland	1.4	15	Michigan	0.3
7	Massachusetts	0.5	15	Ohio	0.3
15	Michigan	0.3	15	Oregon	0.3
5	Minnesota	0.6	15	Washington	0.3
45	Mississippi	0.0	24	Alabama	0.2
24	Missouri	0.2	24	Colorado	0.2
7	Montana	0.5	24	Connecticut	0.2
12	Nebraska	0.4	24	Idaho	0.2
45	Nevada	0.0	24	Maine	0.2
24	New Hampshire	0.2	24	Missouri	0.2
45	New Jersey	0.0	24	New Hampshire	0.2
45	New Mexico	0.0	24	North Carolina	0.2
2	New York	1.3	24	North Dakota	0.2
24	North Carolina	0.2	24	Texas	0.2
24	North Dakota	0.2	34	Arizona	0.1
15	Ohio	0.3	34	Arkansas	0.1
45	Oklahoma	0.0	34	Hawaii	0.1
15	Oregon	0.3	34	Kansas	0.1
12	Pennsylvania	0.4	34	Louisiana	0.1
7	Rhode Island	0.5	34	South Carolina	0.1
34	South Carolina	0.1	34	South Dakota	0.1
34	South Dakota	0.1	34	Tennessee	0.1
34	Tennessee	0.1	34	Utah	0.1
24	Texas	0.2	34	West Virginia	0.1
34	Utah	0.1	34	Wisconsin	0.1
7	Vermont	0.5	45	Mississippi	0.0
3	Virginia	0.7	45	Nevada	0.0
15	Washington	0.3	45	New Jersey	0.0
34	West Virginia	0.1	45	New Mexico	0.0
34	Wisconsin	0.1	45	Oklahoma	0.0
45	Wyoming	0.0	45	Wyoming	0.0

District of Columbia   1.3

Source: CQ Press using data from U.S. Department of Health and Human Services, National Center for Health Statistics
"Morbidity and Mortality Weekly Report" (January 10, 2010, Vol. 58, Nos. 51 & 52, http://www.cdc.gov/mmwr/)
*Provisional data. Infectious disease usually transmitted by bites of infected mosquitoes. Symptoms include high fever, shaking chills, sweating, and anemia.

Meningococcal Infections Reported in 2009

National Total = 887 Cases*

ALPHA ORDER

RANK ORDER

RANK	STATE	CASES	% of USA		RANK	STATE	CASES	% of USA
23	Alabama	11	1.2%		1	California	118	13.3%
35	Alaska	6	0.7%		2	Florida	51	5.7%
17	Arizona	15	1.7%		3	Pennsylvania	45	5.1%
29	Arkansas	9	1.0%		3	Texas	45	5.1%
1	California	118	13.3%		5	New York	43	4.8%
13	Colorado	24	2.7%		5	Ohio	43	4.8%
36	Connecticut	5	0.6%		5	Oregon	43	4.8%
38	Delaware	4	0.5%		8	Illinois	40	4.5%
2	Florida	51	5.7%		9	Indiana	34	3.8%
11	Georgia	29	3.3%		10	North Carolina	31	3.5%
38	Hawaii	4	0.5%		11	Georgia	29	3.3%
32	Idaho	7	0.8%		12	Missouri	28	3.2%
8	Illinois	40	4.5%		13	Colorado	24	2.7%
9	Indiana	34	3.8%		14	Washington	23	2.6%
22	Iowa	14	1.6%		15	Michigan	20	2.3%
30	Kansas	8	0.9%		16	Massachusetts	17	1.9%
32	Kentucky	7	0.8%		17	Arizona	15	1.7%
23	Louisiana	11	1.2%		17	Minnesota	15	1.7%
38	Maine	4	0.5%		17	Oklahoma	15	1.7%
23	Maryland	11	1.2%		17	Tennessee	15	1.7%
16	Massachusetts	17	1.9%		17	Virginia	15	1.7%
15	Michigan	20	2.3%		22	Iowa	14	1.6%
17	Minnesota	15	1.7%		23	Alabama	11	1.2%
43	Mississippi	3	0.3%		23	Louisiana	11	1.2%
12	Missouri	28	3.2%		23	Maryland	11	1.2%
38	Montana	4	0.5%		23	South Carolina	11	1.2%
27	Nebraska	10	1.1%		27	Nebraska	10	1.1%
43	Nevada	3	0.3%		27	Wisconsin	10	1.1%
43	New Hampshire	3	0.3%		29	Arkansas	9	1.0%
30	New Jersey	8	0.9%		30	Kansas	8	0.9%
43	New Mexico	3	0.3%		30	New Jersey	8	0.9%
5	New York	43	4.8%		32	Idaho	7	0.8%
10	North Carolina	31	3.5%		32	Kentucky	7	0.8%
49	North Dakota	1	0.1%		32	West Virginia	7	0.8%
5	Ohio	43	4.8%		35	Alaska	6	0.7%
17	Oklahoma	15	1.7%		36	Connecticut	5	0.6%
5	Oregon	43	4.8%		36	Wyoming	5	0.6%
3	Pennsylvania	45	5.1%		38	Delaware	4	0.5%
38	Rhode Island	4	0.5%		38	Hawaii	4	0.5%
23	South Carolina	11	1.2%		38	Maine	4	0.5%
47	South Dakota	2	0.2%		38	Montana	4	0.5%
17	Tennessee	15	1.7%		38	Rhode Island	4	0.5%
3	Texas	45	5.1%		43	Mississippi	3	0.3%
47	Utah	2	0.2%		43	Nevada	3	0.3%
49	Vermont	1	0.1%		43	New Hampshire	3	0.3%
17	Virginia	15	1.7%		43	New Mexico	3	0.3%
14	Washington	23	2.6%		47	South Dakota	2	0.2%
32	West Virginia	7	0.8%		47	Utah	2	0.2%
27	Wisconsin	10	1.1%		49	North Dakota	1	0.1%
36	Wyoming	5	0.6%		49	Vermont	1	0.1%
					District of Columbia	0	0.0%

Source: U.S. Department of Health and Human Services, National Center for Health Statistics
"Morbidity and Mortality Weekly Report" (January 10, 2010, Vol. 58, Nos. 51 & 52, http://www.cdc.gov/mmwr/)
*Provisional data. A bacterium (Neisseria meningitidis) that causes cerebrospinal meningitis.

Meningococcal Infection Rate in 2009

National Rate = 0.3 Cases per 100,000 Population*

ALPHA ORDER

RANK ORDER

RANK	STATE	RATE
29	Alabama	0.2
2	Alaska	0.9
29	Arizona	0.2
17	Arkansas	0.3
17	California	0.3
5	Colorado	0.5
45	Connecticut	0.1
5	Delaware	0.5
17	Florida	0.3
17	Georgia	0.3
17	Hawaii	0.3
5	Idaho	0.5
17	Illinois	0.3
5	Indiana	0.5
5	Iowa	0.5
17	Kansas	0.3
29	Kentucky	0.2
29	Louisiana	0.2
17	Maine	0.3
29	Maryland	0.2
17	Massachusetts	0.3
29	Michigan	0.2
17	Minnesota	0.3
45	Mississippi	0.1
5	Missouri	0.5
11	Montana	0.4
4	Nebraska	0.6
45	Nevada	0.1
29	New Hampshire	0.2
45	New Jersey	0.1
45	New Mexico	0.1
29	New York	0.2
17	North Carolina	0.3
29	North Dakota	0.2
11	Ohio	0.4
11	Oklahoma	0.4
1	Oregon	1.1
11	Pennsylvania	0.4
11	Rhode Island	0.4
29	South Carolina	0.2
29	South Dakota	0.2
29	Tennessee	0.2
29	Texas	0.2
45	Utah	0.1
29	Vermont	0.2
29	Virginia	0.2
17	Washington	0.3
11	West Virginia	0.4
29	Wisconsin	0.2
2	Wyoming	0.9

RANK	STATE	RATE
1	Oregon	1.1
2	Alaska	0.9
2	Wyoming	0.9
4	Nebraska	0.6
5	Colorado	0.5
5	Delaware	0.5
5	Idaho	0.5
5	Indiana	0.5
5	Iowa	0.5
5	Missouri	0.5
11	Montana	0.4
11	Ohio	0.4
11	Oklahoma	0.4
11	Pennsylvania	0.4
11	Rhode Island	0.4
11	West Virginia	0.4
17	Arkansas	0.3
17	California	0.3
17	Florida	0.3
17	Georgia	0.3
17	Hawaii	0.3
17	Illinois	0.3
17	Kansas	0.3
17	Maine	0.3
17	Massachusetts	0.3
17	Minnesota	0.3
17	North Carolina	0.3
17	Washington	0.3
29	Alabama	0.2
29	Arizona	0.2
29	Kentucky	0.2
29	Louisiana	0.2
29	Maryland	0.2
29	Michigan	0.2
29	New Hampshire	0.2
29	New York	0.2
29	North Dakota	0.2
29	South Carolina	0.2
29	South Dakota	0.2
29	Tennessee	0.2
29	Texas	0.2
29	Vermont	0.2
29	Virginia	0.2
29	Wisconsin	0.2
45	Connecticut	0.1
45	Mississippi	0.1
45	Nevada	0.1
45	New Jersey	0.1
45	New Mexico	0.1
45	Utah	0.1

District of Columbia	0.0

Source: CQ Press using data from U.S. Department of Health and Human Services, National Center for Health Statistics
"Morbidity and Mortality Weekly Report" (January 10, 2010, Vol. 58, Nos. 51 & 52, http://www.cdc.gov/mmwr/)
*Provisional data. A bacterium (Neisseria meningitidis) that causes cerebrospinal meningitis.

Rabies (Animal) Cases Reported in 2009

National Total = 3,581 Cases*

ALPHA ORDER

RANK	STATE	CASES	% of USA
38	Alabama	0	0.0%
32	Alaska	12	0.3%
NA	Arizona**	NA	NA
21	Arkansas	36	1.0%
5	California	205	5.7%
38	Colorado	0	0.0%
7	Connecticut	150	4.2%
38	Delaware	0	0.0%
6	Florida	156	4.4%
3	Georgia	440	12.3%
38	Hawaii	0	0.0%
38	Idaho	0	0.0%
10	Illinois	87	2.4%
30	Indiana	23	0.6%
28	Iowa	24	0.7%
16	Kansas	60	1.7%
20	Kentucky	46	1.3%
38	Louisiana	0	0.0%
17	Maine	55	1.5%
4	Maryland	379	10.6%
38	Massachusetts	0	0.0%
12	Michigan	66	1.8%
15	Minnesota	61	1.7%
35	Mississippi	4	0.1%
13	Missouri	65	1.8%
27	Montana	25	0.7%
11	Nebraska	77	2.2%
36	Nevada	1	0.0%
23	New Hampshire	33	0.9%
38	New Jersey	0	0.0%
28	New Mexico	24	0.7%
2	New York	458	12.8%
NA	North Carolina**	NA	NA
33	North Dakota	11	0.3%
19	Ohio	47	1.3%
23	Oklahoma	33	0.9%
31	Oregon	15	0.4%
9	Pennsylvania	118	3.3%
18	Rhode Island	51	1.4%
38	South Carolina	0	0.0%
25	South Dakota	27	0.8%
22	Tennessee	34	0.9%
36	Texas	1	0.0%
33	Utah	11	0.3%
14	Vermont	64	1.8%
1	Virginia	536	15.0%
38	Washington	0	0.0%
8	West Virginia	119	3.3%
NA	Wisconsin**	NA	NA
25	Wyoming	27	0.8%

RANK ORDER

RANK	STATE	CASES	% of USA
1	Virginia	536	15.0%
2	New York	458	12.8%
3	Georgia	440	12.3%
4	Maryland	379	10.6%
5	California	205	5.7%
6	Florida	156	4.4%
7	Connecticut	150	4.2%
8	West Virginia	119	3.3%
9	Pennsylvania	118	3.3%
10	Illinois	87	2.4%
11	Nebraska	77	2.2%
12	Michigan	66	1.8%
13	Missouri	65	1.8%
14	Vermont	64	1.8%
15	Minnesota	61	1.7%
16	Kansas	60	1.7%
17	Maine	55	1.5%
18	Rhode Island	51	1.4%
19	Ohio	47	1.3%
20	Kentucky	46	1.3%
21	Arkansas	36	1.0%
22	Tennessee	34	0.9%
23	New Hampshire	33	0.9%
23	Oklahoma	33	0.9%
25	South Dakota	27	0.8%
25	Wyoming	27	0.8%
27	Montana	25	0.7%
28	Iowa	24	0.7%
28	New Mexico	24	0.7%
30	Indiana	23	0.6%
31	Oregon	15	0.4%
32	Alaska	12	0.3%
33	North Dakota	11	0.3%
33	Utah	11	0.3%
35	Mississippi	4	0.1%
36	Nevada	1	0.0%
36	Texas	1	0.0%
38	Alabama	0	0.0%
38	Colorado	0	0.0%
38	Delaware	0	0.0%
38	Hawaii	0	0.0%
38	Idaho	0	0.0%
38	Louisiana	0	0.0%
38	Massachusetts	0	0.0%
38	New Jersey	0	0.0%
38	South Carolina	0	0.0%
38	Washington	0	0.0%
NA	Arizona**	NA	NA
NA	North Carolina**	NA	NA
NA	Wisconsin**	NA	NA
	District of Columbia	0	0.0%

Source: U.S. Department of Health and Human Services, National Center for Health Statistics
"Morbidity and Mortality Weekly Report" (January 10, 2010, Vol. 58, Nos. 51 & 52, http://www.cdc.gov/mmwr/)
*Provisional data. An acute, infectious, often fatal viral disease of most warm-blooded animals, especially wolves, cats, and dogs, that attacks the central nervous system and is transmitted by the bite of infected animals.
**Not notifiable.

Rabies (Animal) Rate in 2009

National Rate = 1.2 Cases per 100,000 Human Population*

ALPHA ORDER

RANK	STATE	RATE
36	Alabama	0.0
16	Alaska	1.7
NA	Arizona**	NA
18	Arkansas	1.2
29	California	0.6
36	Colorado	0.0
8	Connecticut	4.3
36	Delaware	0.0
25	Florida	0.8
7	Georgia	4.5
36	Hawaii	0.0
36	Idaho	0.0
27	Illinois	0.7
31	Indiana	0.4
25	Iowa	0.8
15	Kansas	2.1
21	Kentucky	1.1
36	Louisiana	0.0
10	Maine	4.2
3	Maryland	6.6
36	Massachusetts	0.0
27	Michigan	0.7
18	Minnesota	1.2
35	Mississippi	0.1
21	Missouri	1.1
12	Montana	2.6
8	Nebraska	4.3
36	Nevada	0.0
13	New Hampshire	2.5
36	New Jersey	0.0
18	New Mexico	1.2
14	New York	2.3
NA	North Carolina**	NA
16	North Dakota	1.7
31	Ohio	0.4
23	Oklahoma	0.9
31	Oregon	0.4
23	Pennsylvania	0.9
6	Rhode Island	4.8
36	South Carolina	0.0
11	South Dakota	3.3
30	Tennessee	0.5
36	Texas	0.0
31	Utah	0.4
1	Vermont	10.3
2	Virginia	6.8
36	Washington	0.0
4	West Virginia	6.5
NA	Wisconsin**	NA
5	Wyoming	5.0

RANK ORDER

RANK	STATE	RATE
1	Vermont	10.3
2	Virginia	6.8
3	Maryland	6.6
4	West Virginia	6.5
5	Wyoming	5.0
6	Rhode Island	4.8
7	Georgia	4.5
8	Connecticut	4.3
8	Nebraska	4.3
10	Maine	4.2
11	South Dakota	3.3
12	Montana	2.6
13	New Hampshire	2.5
14	New York	2.3
15	Kansas	2.1
16	Alaska	1.7
16	North Dakota	1.7
18	Arkansas	1.2
18	Minnesota	1.2
18	New Mexico	1.2
21	Kentucky	1.1
21	Missouri	1.1
23	Oklahoma	0.9
23	Pennsylvania	0.9
25	Florida	0.8
25	Iowa	0.8
27	Illinois	0.7
27	Michigan	0.7
29	California	0.6
30	Tennessee	0.5
31	Indiana	0.4
31	Ohio	0.4
31	Oregon	0.4
31	Utah	0.4
35	Mississippi	0.1
36	Alabama	0.0
36	Colorado	0.0
36	Delaware	0.0
36	Hawaii	0.0
36	Idaho	0.0
36	Louisiana	0.0
36	Massachusetts	0.0
36	Nevada	0.0
36	New Jersey	0.0
36	South Carolina	0.0
36	Texas	0.0
36	Washington	0.0
NA	Arizona**	NA
NA	North Carolina**	NA
NA	Wisconsin**	NA

District of Columbia   0.0

Source: CQ Press using data from U.S. Department of Health and Human Services, National Center for Health Statistics
"Morbidity and Mortality Weekly Report" (January 10, 2010, Vol. 58, Nos. 51 & 52, http://www.cdc.gov/mmwr/)
*Provisional data. An acute, infectious, often fatal viral disease of most warm-blooded animals, especially wolves, cats, and dogs, that attacks the central nervous system and is transmitted by the bite of infected animals.
**Not notifiable.

Rocky Mountain Spotted Fever Cases Reported in 2009

National Total = 1,393 Cases*

ALPHA ORDER

RANK	STATE	CASES	% of USA
5	Alabama	65	4.7%
NA	Alaska**	NA	NA
20	Arizona	8	0.6%
4	Arkansas	71	5.1%
33	California	1	0.1%
33	Colorado	1	0.1%
40	Connecticut	0	0.0%
15	Delaware	18	1.3%
18	Florida	12	0.9%
9	Georgia	48	3.4%
NA	Hawaii**	NA	NA
33	Idaho	1	0.1%
8	Illinois	50	3.6%
17	Indiana	13	0.9%
26	Iowa	4	0.3%
30	Kansas	2	0.1%
33	Kentucky	1	0.1%
30	Louisiana	2	0.1%
23	Maine	5	0.4%
11	Maryland	37	2.7%
23	Massachusetts	5	0.4%
23	Michigan	5	0.4%
26	Minnesota	4	0.3%
22	Mississippi	7	0.5%
1	Missouri	319	22.9%
20	Montana	8	0.6%
18	Nebraska	12	0.9%
40	Nevada	0	0.0%
40	New Hampshire	0	0.0%
40	New Jersey	0	0.0%
33	New Mexico	1	0.1%
10	New York	44	3.2%
2	North Carolina	264	19.0%
40	North Dakota	0	0.0%
15	Ohio	18	1.3%
6	Oklahoma	53	3.8%
40	Oregon	0	0.0%
13	Pennsylvania	23	1.7%
40	Rhode Island	0	0.0%
14	South Carolina	19	1.4%
40	South Dakota	0	0.0%
3	Tennessee	184	13.2%
12	Texas	24	1.7%
33	Utah	1	0.1%
33	Vermont	1	0.1%
6	Virginia	53	3.8%
40	Washington	0	0.0%
26	West Virginia	4	0.3%
30	Wisconsin	2	0.1%
29	Wyoming	3	0.2%

RANK ORDER

RANK	STATE	CASES	% of USA
1	Missouri	319	22.9%
2	North Carolina	264	19.0%
3	Tennessee	184	13.2%
4	Arkansas	71	5.1%
5	Alabama	65	4.7%
6	Oklahoma	53	3.8%
6	Virginia	53	3.8%
8	Illinois	50	3.6%
9	Georgia	48	3.4%
10	New York	44	3.2%
11	Maryland	37	2.7%
12	Texas	24	1.7%
13	Pennsylvania	23	1.7%
14	South Carolina	19	1.4%
15	Delaware	18	1.3%
15	Ohio	18	1.3%
17	Indiana	13	0.9%
18	Florida	12	0.9%
18	Nebraska	12	0.9%
20	Arizona	8	0.6%
20	Montana	8	0.6%
22	Mississippi	7	0.5%
23	Maine	5	0.4%
23	Massachusetts	5	0.4%
23	Michigan	5	0.4%
26	Iowa	4	0.3%
26	Minnesota	4	0.3%
26	West Virginia	4	0.3%
29	Wyoming	3	0.2%
30	Kansas	2	0.1%
30	Louisiana	2	0.1%
30	Wisconsin	2	0.1%
33	California	1	0.1%
33	Colorado	1	0.1%
33	Idaho	1	0.1%
33	Kentucky	1	0.1%
33	New Mexico	1	0.1%
33	Utah	1	0.1%
33	Vermont	1	0.1%
40	Connecticut	0	0.0%
40	Nevada	0	0.0%
40	New Hampshire	0	0.0%
40	New Jersey	0	0.0%
40	North Dakota	0	0.0%
40	Oregon	0	0.0%
40	Rhode Island	0	0.0%
40	South Dakota	0	0.0%
40	Washington	0	0.0%
NA	Alaska**	NA	NA
NA	Hawaii**	NA	NA
	District of Columbia	0	0.0%

Source: U.S. Department of Health and Human Services, National Center for Health Statistics
"Morbidity and Mortality Weekly Report" (January 10, 2010, Vol. 58, Nos. 51 & 52, http://www.cdc.gov/mmwr/)
*Provisional data. An illness caused by Rickettsia rickettsii, a bacterial pathogen transmitted to humans through contact with ticks. Characterized by acute onset of fever, and may be accompanied by headache, malaise, myalgia, nausea/vomiting, or neurologic signs. A rash is often present on the palms sond soles.
**Not notifiable.

Rocky Mountain Spotted Fever Rate in 2009

National Rate = 0.5 Cases per 100,000 Population*

ALPHA ORDER

RANK	STATE	RATE
6	Alabama	1.4
NA	Alaska**	NA
24	Arizona	0.1
4	Arkansas	2.5
33	California	0.0
33	Colorado	0.0
33	Connecticut	0.0
5	Delaware	2.0
24	Florida	0.1
13	Georgia	0.5
NA	Hawaii**	NA
24	Idaho	0.1
14	Illinois	0.4
17	Indiana	0.2
24	Iowa	0.1
24	Kansas	0.1
33	Kentucky	0.0
33	Louisiana	0.0
14	Maine	0.4
11	Maryland	0.6
24	Massachusetts	0.1
24	Michigan	0.1
24	Minnesota	0.1
17	Mississippi	0.2
1	Missouri	5.3
8	Montana	0.8
9	Nebraska	0.7
33	Nevada	0.0
33	New Hampshire	0.0
33	New Jersey	0.0
33	New Mexico	0.0
17	New York	0.2
3	North Carolina	2.8
33	North Dakota	0.0
17	Ohio	0.2
6	Oklahoma	1.4
33	Oregon	0.0
17	Pennsylvania	0.2
33	Rhode Island	0.0
14	South Carolina	0.4
33	South Dakota	0.0
2	Tennessee	2.9
24	Texas	0.1
33	Utah	0.0
17	Vermont	0.2
9	Virginia	0.7
33	Washington	0.0
17	West Virginia	0.2
33	Wisconsin	0.0
11	Wyoming	0.6

RANK ORDER

RANK	STATE	RATE
1	Missouri	5.3
2	Tennessee	2.9
3	North Carolina	2.8
4	Arkansas	2.5
5	Delaware	2.0
6	Alabama	1.4
6	Oklahoma	1.4
8	Montana	0.8
9	Nebraska	0.7
9	Virginia	0.7
11	Maryland	0.6
11	Wyoming	0.6
13	Georgia	0.5
14	Illinois	0.4
14	Maine	0.4
14	South Carolina	0.4
17	Indiana	0.2
17	Mississippi	0.2
17	New York	0.2
17	Ohio	0.2
17	Pennsylvania	0.2
17	Vermont	0.2
17	West Virginia	0.2
24	Arizona	0.1
24	Florida	0.1
24	Idaho	0.1
24	Iowa	0.1
24	Kansas	0.1
24	Massachusetts	0.1
24	Michigan	0.1
24	Minnesota	0.1
24	Texas	0.1
33	California	0.0
33	Colorado	0.0
33	Connecticut	0.0
33	Kentucky	0.0
33	Louisiana	0.0
33	Nevada	0.0
33	New Hampshire	0.0
33	New Jersey	0.0
33	New Mexico	0.0
33	North Dakota	0.0
33	Oregon	0.0
33	Rhode Island	0.0
33	South Dakota	0.0
33	Utah	0.0
33	Washington	0.0
33	Wisconsin	0.0
NA	Alaska**	NA
NA	Hawaii**	NA

District of Columbia 0.0

Source: CQ Press using data from U.S. Department of Health and Human Services, National Center for Health Statistics
"Morbidity and Mortality Weekly Report" (January 10, 2010, Vol. 58, Nos. 51 & 52, http://www.cdc.gov/mmwr/)
*Provisional data. An illness caused by Rickettsia rickettsii, a bacterial pathogen transmitted to humans through contact with ticks. Characterized by acute onset of fever, and may be accompanied by headache, malaise, myalgia, nausea/vomiting, or neurologic signs. A rash is often present on the palms and soles.
**Not notifiable.

Salmonellosis Cases Reported in 2009

National Total = 44,468 Cases*

ALPHA ORDER

RANK	STATE	CASES	% of USA
16	Alabama	850	1.9%
49	Alaska	70	0.2%
12	Arizona	1,051	2.4%
25	Arkansas	607	1.4%
2	California	4,757	10.7%
23	Colorado	621	1.4%
30	Connecticut	406	0.9%
43	Delaware	137	0.3%
1	Florida	6,749	15.2%
5	Georgia	2,365	5.3%
35	Hawaii	297	0.7%
41	Idaho	172	0.4%
8	Illinois	1,294	2.9%
32	Indiana	349	0.8%
31	Iowa	398	0.9%
37	Kansas	269	0.6%
28	Kentucky	451	1.0%
26	Louisiana	599	1.3%
45	Maine	119	0.3%
18	Maryland	784	1.8%
9	Massachusetts	1,159	2.6%
14	Michigan	911	2.0%
27	Minnesota	572	1.3%
15	Mississippi	853	1.9%
21	Missouri	667	1.5%
46	Montana	99	0.2%
33	Nebraska	337	0.8%
40	Nevada	173	0.4%
38	New Hampshire	243	0.5%
17	New Jersey	802	1.8%
34	New Mexico	325	0.7%
4	New York	2,492	5.6%
11	North Carolina	1,053	2.4%
48	North Dakota	73	0.2%
7	Ohio	1,407	3.2%
24	Oklahoma	615	1.4%
29	Oregon	416	0.9%
6	Pennsylvania	1,707	3.8%
44	Rhode Island	122	0.3%
10	South Carolina	1,153	2.6%
42	South Dakota	156	0.4%
19	Tennessee	783	1.8%
3	Texas	2,930	6.6%
36	Utah	283	0.6%
50	Vermont	61	0.1%
13	Virginia	1,004	2.3%
20	Washington	760	1.7%
39	West Virginia	217	0.5%
22	Wisconsin	636	1.4%
47	Wyoming	88	0.2%

RANK ORDER

RANK	STATE	CASES	% of USA
1	Florida	6,749	15.2%
2	California	4,757	10.7%
3	Texas	2,930	6.6%
4	New York	2,492	5.6%
5	Georgia	2,365	5.3%
6	Pennsylvania	1,707	3.8%
7	Ohio	1,407	3.2%
8	Illinois	1,294	2.9%
9	Massachusetts	1,159	2.6%
10	South Carolina	1,153	2.6%
11	North Carolina	1,053	2.4%
12	Arizona	1,051	2.4%
13	Virginia	1,004	2.3%
14	Michigan	911	2.0%
15	Mississippi	853	1.9%
16	Alabama	850	1.9%
17	New Jersey	802	1.8%
18	Maryland	784	1.8%
19	Tennessee	783	1.8%
20	Washington	760	1.7%
21	Missouri	667	1.5%
22	Wisconsin	636	1.4%
23	Colorado	621	1.4%
24	Oklahoma	615	1.4%
25	Arkansas	607	1.4%
26	Louisiana	599	1.3%
27	Minnesota	572	1.3%
28	Kentucky	451	1.0%
29	Oregon	416	0.9%
30	Connecticut	406	0.9%
31	Iowa	398	0.9%
32	Indiana	349	0.8%
33	Nebraska	337	0.8%
34	New Mexico	325	0.7%
35	Hawaii	297	0.7%
36	Utah	283	0.6%
37	Kansas	269	0.6%
38	New Hampshire	243	0.5%
39	West Virginia	217	0.5%
40	Nevada	173	0.4%
41	Idaho	172	0.4%
42	South Dakota	156	0.4%
43	Delaware	137	0.3%
44	Rhode Island	122	0.3%
45	Maine	119	0.3%
46	Montana	99	0.2%
47	Wyoming	88	0.2%
48	North Dakota	73	0.2%
49	Alaska	70	0.2%
50	Vermont	61	0.1%
	District of Columbia	26	0.1%

Source: U.S. Department of Health and Human Services, National Center for Health Statistics
    "Morbidity and Mortality Weekly Report" (January 10, 2010, Vol. 58, Nos. 51 & 52, http://www.cdc.gov/mmwr/)
*Provisional data. Any disease caused by a salmonella infection, which may be manifested as food poisoning with acute gastroenteritis, vomiting, and diarrhea.

Salmonellosis Rate in 2009

National Rate = 14.5 Cases per 100,000 Population*

ALPHA ORDER

RANK	STATE	RATE
10	Alabama	18.1
42	Alaska	10.0
15	Arizona	15.9
6	Arkansas	21.0
21	California	12.9
24	Colorado	12.4
30	Connecticut	11.5
16	Delaware	15.5
1	Florida	36.4
4	Georgia	24.1
5	Hawaii	22.9
35	Idaho	11.1
42	Illinois	10.0
50	Indiana	5.4
20	Iowa	13.2
45	Kansas	9.5
39	Kentucky	10.5
19	Louisiana	13.3
48	Maine	9.0
17	Maryland	13.8
11	Massachusetts	17.6
47	Michigan	9.1
37	Minnesota	10.9
2	Mississippi	28.9
35	Missouri	11.1
40	Montana	10.2
8	Nebraska	18.8
49	Nevada	6.5
9	New Hampshire	18.3
46	New Jersey	9.2
13	New Mexico	16.2
22	New York	12.8
33	North Carolina	11.2
32	North Dakota	11.3
26	Ohio	12.2
12	Oklahoma	16.7
37	Oregon	10.9
18	Pennsylvania	13.5
29	Rhode Island	11.6
3	South Carolina	25.3
7	South Dakota	19.2
24	Tennessee	12.4
28	Texas	11.8
40	Utah	10.2
44	Vermont	9.8
23	Virginia	12.7
31	Washington	11.4
27	West Virginia	11.9
33	Wisconsin	11.2
13	Wyoming	16.2

RANK ORDER

RANK	STATE	RATE
1	Florida	36.4
2	Mississippi	28.9
3	South Carolina	25.3
4	Georgia	24.1
5	Hawaii	22.9
6	Arkansas	21.0
7	South Dakota	19.2
8	Nebraska	18.8
9	New Hampshire	18.3
10	Alabama	18.1
11	Massachusetts	17.6
12	Oklahoma	16.7
13	New Mexico	16.2
13	Wyoming	16.2
15	Arizona	15.9
16	Delaware	15.5
17	Maryland	13.8
18	Pennsylvania	13.5
19	Louisiana	13.3
20	Iowa	13.2
21	California	12.9
22	New York	12.8
23	Virginia	12.7
24	Colorado	12.4
24	Tennessee	12.4
26	Ohio	12.2
27	West Virginia	11.9
28	Texas	11.8
29	Rhode Island	11.6
30	Connecticut	11.5
31	Washington	11.4
32	North Dakota	11.3
33	North Carolina	11.2
33	Wisconsin	11.2
35	Idaho	11.1
35	Missouri	11.1
37	Minnesota	10.9
37	Oregon	10.9
39	Kentucky	10.5
40	Montana	10.2
40	Utah	10.2
42	Alaska	10.0
42	Illinois	10.0
44	Vermont	9.8
45	Kansas	9.5
46	New Jersey	9.2
47	Michigan	9.1
48	Maine	9.0
49	Nevada	6.5
50	Indiana	5.4

District of Columbia	4.3

Source: CQ Press using data from U.S. Department of Health and Human Services, National Center for Health Statistics
"Morbidity and Mortality Weekly Report" (January 10, 2010, Vol. 58, Nos. 51 & 52, http://www.cdc.gov/mmwr/)
*Provisional data. Any disease caused by a salmonella infection, which may be manifested as food poisoning with acute gastroenteritis, vomiting, and diarrhea.

Shigellosis Cases Reported in 2009

National Total = 14,581 Cases*

RANK	STATE	CASES	% of USA
25	Alabama	142	1.0%
49	Alaska	2	0.0%
6	Arizona	808	5.5%
16	Arkansas	310	2.1%
5	California	1,014	7.0%
28	Colorado	104	0.7%
35	Connecticut	40	0.3%
23	Delaware	151	1.0%
11	Florida	462	3.2%
8	Georgia	650	4.5%
37	Hawaii	38	0.3%
44	Idaho	9	0.1%
9	Illinois	538	3.7%
32	Indiana	58	0.4%
33	Iowa	54	0.4%
22	Kansas	159	1.1%
19	Kentucky	221	1.5%
27	Louisiana	108	0.7%
45	Maine	5	0.0%
14	Maryland	361	2.5%
18	Massachusetts	243	1.7%
20	Michigan	212	1.5%
30	Minnesota	81	0.6%
34	Mississippi	47	0.3%
4	Missouri	1,037	7.1%
42	Montana	13	0.1%
38	Nebraska	33	0.2%
31	Nevada	68	0.5%
41	New Hampshire	19	0.1%
10	New Jersey	516	3.5%
29	New Mexico	93	0.6%
7	New York	658	4.5%
15	North Carolina	317	2.2%
45	North Dakota	5	0.0%
3	Ohio	1,096	7.5%
17	Oklahoma	308	2.1%
35	Oregon	40	0.3%
2	Pennsylvania	1,468	10.1%
39	Rhode Island	23	0.2%
26	South Carolina	121	0.8%
48	South Dakota	4	0.0%
13	Tennessee	365	2.5%
1	Texas	1,773	12.2%
40	Utah	20	0.1%
45	Vermont	5	0.0%
21	Virginia	188	1.3%
24	Washington	149	1.0%
43	West Virginia	10	0.1%
12	Wisconsin	425	2.9%
49	Wyoming	2	0.0%

RANK	STATE	CASES	% of USA
1	Texas	1,773	12.2%
2	Pennsylvania	1,468	10.1%
3	Ohio	1,096	7.5%
4	Missouri	1,037	7.1%
5	California	1,014	7.0%
6	Arizona	808	5.5%
7	New York	658	4.5%
8	Georgia	650	4.5%
9	Illinois	538	3.7%
10	New Jersey	516	3.5%
11	Florida	462	3.2%
12	Wisconsin	425	2.9%
13	Tennessee	365	2.5%
14	Maryland	361	2.5%
15	North Carolina	317	2.2%
16	Arkansas	310	2.1%
17	Oklahoma	308	2.1%
18	Massachusetts	243	1.7%
19	Kentucky	221	1.5%
20	Michigan	212	1.5%
21	Virginia	188	1.3%
22	Kansas	159	1.1%
23	Delaware	151	1.0%
24	Washington	149	1.0%
25	Alabama	142	1.0%
26	South Carolina	121	0.8%
27	Louisiana	108	0.7%
28	Colorado	104	0.7%
29	New Mexico	93	0.6%
30	Minnesota	81	0.6%
31	Nevada	68	0.5%
32	Indiana	58	0.4%
33	Iowa	54	0.4%
34	Mississippi	47	0.3%
35	Connecticut	40	0.3%
35	Oregon	40	0.3%
37	Hawaii	38	0.3%
38	Nebraska	33	0.2%
39	Rhode Island	23	0.2%
40	Utah	20	0.1%
41	New Hampshire	19	0.1%
42	Montana	13	0.1%
43	West Virginia	10	0.1%
44	Idaho	9	0.1%
45	Maine	5	0.0%
45	North Dakota	5	0.0%
45	Vermont	5	0.0%
48	South Dakota	4	0.0%
49	Alaska	2	0.0%
49	Wyoming	2	0.0%
	District of Columbia	8	0.1%

Source: U.S. Department of Health and Human Services, National Center for Health Statistics
"Morbidity and Mortality Weekly Report" (January 10, 2010, Vol. 58, Nos. 51 & 52, http://www.cdc.gov/mmwr/)
*Provisional data. Dysentery caused by any of various species of shigellae, occurring most frequently in areas where poor sanitation and malnutrition are prevalent, and commonly affecting children and infants.

Shigellosis Rate in 2009

National Rate = 4.7 Cases per 100,000 Population*

RANK	STATE	RATE
21	Alabama	3.0
50	Alaska	0.3
3	Arizona	12.3
5	Arkansas	10.7
23	California	2.7
31	Colorado	2.1
39	Connecticut	1.1
2	Delaware	17.1
26	Florida	2.5
10	Georgia	6.6
22	Hawaii	2.9
45	Idaho	0.6
17	Illinois	4.2
41	Indiana	0.9
33	Iowa	1.8
14	Kansas	5.6
15	Kentucky	5.1
27	Louisiana	2.4
48	Maine	0.4
11	Maryland	6.3
18	Massachusetts	3.7
31	Michigan	2.1
36	Minnesota	1.5
35	Mississippi	1.6
1	Missouri	17.3
38	Montana	1.3
33	Nebraska	1.8
25	Nevada	2.6
37	New Hampshire	1.4
12	New Jersey	5.9
16	New Mexico	4.6
19	New York	3.4
19	North Carolina	3.4
42	North Dakota	0.8
6	Ohio	9.5
7	Oklahoma	8.4
40	Oregon	1.0
4	Pennsylvania	11.6
29	Rhode Island	2.2
23	South Carolina	2.7
46	South Dakota	0.5
13	Tennessee	5.8
9	Texas	7.2
44	Utah	0.7
42	Vermont	0.8
27	Virginia	2.4
29	Washington	2.2
46	West Virginia	0.5
8	Wisconsin	7.5
48	Wyoming	0.4

RANK	STATE	RATE
1	Missouri	17.3
2	Delaware	17.1
3	Arizona	12.3
4	Pennsylvania	11.6
5	Arkansas	10.7
6	Ohio	9.5
7	Oklahoma	8.4
8	Wisconsin	7.5
9	Texas	7.2
10	Georgia	6.6
11	Maryland	6.3
12	New Jersey	5.9
13	Tennessee	5.8
14	Kansas	5.6
15	Kentucky	5.1
16	New Mexico	4.6
17	Illinois	4.2
18	Massachusetts	3.7
19	New York	3.4
19	North Carolina	3.4
21	Alabama	3.0
22	Hawaii	2.9
23	California	2.7
23	South Carolina	2.7
25	Nevada	2.6
26	Florida	2.5
27	Louisiana	2.4
27	Virginia	2.4
29	Rhode Island	2.2
29	Washington	2.2
31	Colorado	2.1
31	Michigan	2.1
33	Iowa	1.8
33	Nebraska	1.8
35	Mississippi	1.6
36	Minnesota	1.5
37	New Hampshire	1.4
38	Montana	1.3
39	Connecticut	1.1
40	Oregon	1.0
41	Indiana	0.9
42	North Dakota	0.8
42	Vermont	0.8
44	Utah	0.7
45	Idaho	0.6
46	South Dakota	0.5
46	West Virginia	0.5
48	Maine	0.4
48	Wyoming	0.4
50	Alaska	0.3

	District of Columbia	1.3

Source: CQ Press using data from U.S. Department of Health and Human Services, National Center for Health Statistics
"Morbidity and Mortality Weekly Report" (January 10, 2010, Vol. 58, Nos. 51 & 52, http://www.cdc.gov/mmwr/)
*Provisional data. Dysentery caused by any of various species of shigellae, occurring most frequently in areas where poor sanitation and malnutrition are prevalent, and commonly affecting children and infants.

West Nile Virus Disease Cases Reported in 2009

National Total = 690 Cases*

RANK	STATE	CASES	% of USA
37	Alabama	0	0.0%
37	Alaska	0	0.0%
10	Arizona	20	2.9%
18	Arkansas	6	0.9%
2	California	105	15.2%
3	Colorado	101	14.6%
37	Connecticut	0	0.0%
37	Delaware	0	0.0%
27	Florida	3	0.4%
24	Georgia	4	0.6%
37	Hawaii	0	0.0%
6	Idaho	38	5.5%
21	Illinois	5	0.7%
24	Indiana	4	0.6%
21	Iowa	5	0.7%
11	Kansas	12	1.7%
27	Kentucky	3	0.4%
8	Louisiana	21	3.0%
37	Maine	0	0.0%
31	Maryland	2	0.3%
37	Massachusetts	0	0.0%
34	Michigan	1	0.1%
24	Minnesota	4	0.6%
4	Mississippi	52	7.5%
21	Missouri	5	0.7%
18	Montana	6	0.9%
5	Nebraska	51	7.4%
11	Nevada	12	1.7%
37	New Hampshire	0	0.0%
31	New Jersey	2	0.3%
16	New Mexico	8	1.2%
18	New York	6	0.9%
37	North Carolina	0	0.0%
34	North Dakota	1	0.1%
31	Ohio	2	0.3%
15	Oklahoma	10	1.4%
14	Oregon	11	1.6%
37	Pennsylvania	0	0.0%
37	Rhode Island	0	0.0%
27	South Carolina	3	0.4%
8	South Dakota	21	3.0%
16	Tennessee	8	1.2%
1	Texas	106	15.4%
37	Utah	0	0.0%
37	Vermont	0	0.0%
27	Virginia	3	0.4%
7	Washington	36	5.2%
37	West Virginia	0	0.0%
34	Wisconsin	1	0.1%
11	Wyoming	12	1.7%

RANK	STATE	CASES	% of USA
1	Texas	106	15.4%
2	California	105	15.2%
3	Colorado	101	14.6%
4	Mississippi	52	7.5%
5	Nebraska	51	7.4%
6	Idaho	38	5.5%
7	Washington	36	5.2%
8	Louisiana	21	3.0%
8	South Dakota	21	3.0%
10	Arizona	20	2.9%
11	Kansas	12	1.7%
11	Nevada	12	1.7%
11	Wyoming	12	1.7%
14	Oregon	11	1.6%
15	Oklahoma	10	1.4%
16	New Mexico	8	1.2%
16	Tennessee	8	1.2%
18	Arkansas	6	0.9%
18	Montana	6	0.9%
18	New York	6	0.9%
21	Illinois	5	0.7%
21	Iowa	5	0.7%
21	Missouri	5	0.7%
24	Georgia	4	0.6%
24	Indiana	4	0.6%
24	Minnesota	4	0.6%
27	Florida	3	0.4%
27	Kentucky	3	0.4%
27	South Carolina	3	0.4%
27	Virginia	3	0.4%
31	Maryland	2	0.3%
31	New Jersey	2	0.3%
31	Ohio	2	0.3%
34	Michigan	1	0.1%
34	North Dakota	1	0.1%
34	Wisconsin	1	0.1%
37	Alabama	0	0.0%
37	Alaska	0	0.0%
37	Connecticut	0	0.0%
37	Delaware	0	0.0%
37	Hawaii	0	0.0%
37	Maine	0	0.0%
37	Massachusetts	0	0.0%
37	New Hampshire	0	0.0%
37	North Carolina	0	0.0%
37	Pennsylvania	0	0.0%
37	Rhode Island	0	0.0%
37	Utah	0	0.0%
37	Vermont	0	0.0%
37	West Virginia	0	0.0%
	District of Columbia	0	0.0%

Source: U.S. Department of Health and Human Services, National Center for Health Statistics
"Morbidity and Mortality Weekly Report" (January 10, 2010, Vol. 58, Nos. 51 & 52, http://www.cdc.gov/mmwr/)
*Provisional data. A flavivirus typically carried by mosquitoes.

West Nile Disease Rate in 2009

National Rate = 0.2 Cases per 100,000 Population*

ALPHA ORDER

RANK	STATE	RATE
27	Alabama	0.0
27	Alaska	0.0
14	Arizona	0.3
18	Arkansas	0.2
14	California	0.3
5	Colorado	2.0
27	Connecticut	0.0
27	Delaware	0.0
27	Florida	0.0
27	Georgia	0.0
27	Hawaii	0.0
3	Idaho	2.5
27	Illinois	0.0
21	Indiana	0.1
18	Iowa	0.2
11	Kansas	0.4
21	Kentucky	0.1
8	Louisiana	0.5
27	Maine	0.0
27	Maryland	0.0
27	Massachusetts	0.0
27	Michigan	0.0
21	Minnesota	0.1
6	Mississippi	1.8
21	Missouri	0.1
7	Montana	0.6
1	Nebraska	2.8
8	Nevada	0.5
27	New Hampshire	0.0
27	New Jersey	0.0
11	New Mexico	0.4
27	New York	0.0
27	North Carolina	0.0
18	North Dakota	0.2
27	Ohio	0.0
14	Oklahoma	0.3
14	Oregon	0.3
27	Pennsylvania	0.0
27	Rhode Island	0.0
21	South Carolina	0.1
2	South Dakota	2.6
21	Tennessee	0.1
11	Texas	0.4
27	Utah	0.0
27	Vermont	0.0
27	Virginia	0.0
8	Washington	0.5
27	West Virginia	0.0
27	Wisconsin	0.0
4	Wyoming	2.2

RANK ORDER

RANK	STATE	RATE
1	Nebraska	2.8
2	South Dakota	2.6
3	Idaho	2.5
4	Wyoming	2.2
5	Colorado	2.0
6	Mississippi	1.8
7	Montana	0.6
8	Louisiana	0.5
8	Nevada	0.5
8	Washington	0.5
11	Kansas	0.4
11	New Mexico	0.4
11	Texas	0.4
14	Arizona	0.3
14	California	0.3
14	Oklahoma	0.3
14	Oregon	0.3
18	Arkansas	0.2
18	Iowa	0.2
18	North Dakota	0.2
21	Indiana	0.1
21	Kentucky	0.1
21	Minnesota	0.1
21	Missouri	0.1
21	South Carolina	0.1
21	Tennessee	0.1
27	Alabama	0.0
27	Alaska	0.0
27	Connecticut	0.0
27	Delaware	0.0
27	Florida	0.0
27	Georgia	0.0
27	Hawaii	0.0
27	Illinois	0.0
27	Maine	0.0
27	Maryland	0.0
27	Massachusetts	0.0
27	Michigan	0.0
27	New Hampshire	0.0
27	New Jersey	0.0
27	New York	0.0
27	North Carolina	0.0
27	Ohio	0.0
27	Pennsylvania	0.0
27	Rhode Island	0.0
27	Utah	0.0
27	Vermont	0.0
27	Virginia	0.0
27	West Virginia	0.0
27	Wisconsin	0.0

District of Columbia   0.0

Source: CQ Press using data from U.S. Department of Health and Human Services, National Center for Health Statistics
"Morbidity and Mortality Weekly Report" (January 10, 2010, Vol. 58, Nos. 51 & 52, http://www.cdc.gov/mmwr/)
*Provisional data. A flavivirus typically carried by mosquitoes.

Whooping Cough (Pertussis) Cases Reported in 2009

National Total = 13,506 Cases*

ALPHA ORDER

RANK	STATE	CASES	% of USA
12	Alabama	285	2.1%
40	Alaska	49	0.4%
18	Arizona	224	1.7%
13	Arkansas	278	2.1%
8	California	473	3.5%
17	Colorado	233	1.7%
41	Connecticut	48	0.4%
48	Delaware	13	0.1%
7	Florida	500	3.7%
22	Georgia	194	1.4%
45	Hawaii	29	0.2%
32	Idaho	99	0.7%
6	Illinois	570	4.2%
11	Indiana	338	2.5%
23	Iowa	192	1.4%
28	Kansas	146	1.1%
20	Kentucky	219	1.6%
33	Louisiana	90	0.7%
34	Maine	78	0.6%
30	Maryland	134	1.0%
9	Massachusetts	348	2.6%
4	Michigan	854	6.3%
26	Minnesota	165	1.2%
37	Mississippi	66	0.5%
3	Missouri	975	7.2%
39	Montana	57	0.4%
29	Nebraska	141	1.0%
50	Nevada	9	0.1%
36	New Hampshire	76	0.6%
27	New Jersey	158	1.2%
37	New Mexico	66	0.5%
10	New York	344	2.5%
19	North Carolina	223	1.7%
45	North Dakota	29	0.2%
2	Ohio	1,096	8.1%
35	Oklahoma	77	0.6%
16	Oregon	246	1.8%
5	Pennsylvania	599	4.4%
43	Rhode Island	31	0.2%
15	South Carolina	252	1.9%
44	South Dakota	30	0.2%
24	Tennessee	190	1.4%
1	Texas	2,437	18.0%
25	Utah	181	1.3%
49	Vermont	11	0.1%
21	Virginia	198	1.5%
14	Washington	265	2.0%
42	West Virginia	34	0.3%
31	Wisconsin	132	1.0%
47	Wyoming	21	0.2%

RANK ORDER

RANK	STATE	CASES	% of USA
1	Texas	2,437	18.0%
2	Ohio	1,096	8.1%
3	Missouri	975	7.2%
4	Michigan	854	6.3%
5	Pennsylvania	599	4.4%
6	Illinois	570	4.2%
7	Florida	500	3.7%
8	California	473	3.5%
9	Massachusetts	348	2.6%
10	New York	344	2.5%
11	Indiana	338	2.5%
12	Alabama	285	2.1%
13	Arkansas	278	2.1%
14	Washington	265	2.0%
15	South Carolina	252	1.9%
16	Oregon	246	1.8%
17	Colorado	233	1.7%
18	Arizona	224	1.7%
19	North Carolina	223	1.7%
20	Kentucky	219	1.6%
21	Virginia	198	1.5%
22	Georgia	194	1.4%
23	Iowa	192	1.4%
24	Tennessee	190	1.4%
25	Utah	181	1.3%
26	Minnesota	165	1.2%
27	New Jersey	158	1.2%
28	Kansas	146	1.1%
29	Nebraska	141	1.0%
30	Maryland	134	1.0%
31	Wisconsin	132	1.0%
32	Idaho	99	0.7%
33	Louisiana	90	0.7%
34	Maine	78	0.6%
35	Oklahoma	77	0.6%
36	New Hampshire	76	0.6%
37	Mississippi	66	0.5%
37	New Mexico	66	0.5%
39	Montana	57	0.4%
40	Alaska	49	0.4%
41	Connecticut	48	0.4%
42	West Virginia	34	0.3%
43	Rhode Island	31	0.2%
44	South Dakota	30	0.2%
45	Hawaii	29	0.2%
45	North Dakota	29	0.2%
47	Wyoming	21	0.2%
48	Delaware	13	0.1%
49	Vermont	11	0.1%
50	Nevada	9	0.1%
	District of Columbia	3	0.0%

Source: U.S. Department of Health and Human Services, National Center for Health Statistics
   "Morbidity and Mortality Weekly Report" (January 10, 2010, Vol. 58, Nos. 51 & 52, http://www.cdc.gov/mmwr/)
*Provisional data. Acute, highly contagious infection of respiratory tract.

Whooping Cough (Pertussis) Rate in 2009

National Rate = 4.4 Cases per 100,000 Population*

ALPHA ORDER

RANK	STATE	RATE
12	Alabama	6.1
7	Alaska	7.0
28	Arizona	3.4
3	Arkansas	9.6
49	California	1.3
22	Colorado	4.6
48	Connecticut	1.4
47	Delaware	1.5
33	Florida	2.7
41	Georgia	2.0
38	Hawaii	2.2
9	Idaho	6.4
24	Illinois	4.4
17	Indiana	5.3
9	Iowa	6.4
19	Kansas	5.2
20	Kentucky	5.1
41	Louisiana	2.0
13	Maine	5.9
35	Maryland	2.4
17	Massachusetts	5.3
5	Michigan	8.6
30	Minnesota	3.1
38	Mississippi	2.2
1	Missouri	16.3
14	Montana	5.8
6	Nebraska	7.8
50	Nevada	0.3
15	New Hampshire	5.7
44	New Jersey	1.8
29	New Mexico	3.3
44	New York	1.8
35	North Carolina	2.4
23	North Dakota	4.5
4	Ohio	9.5
40	Oklahoma	2.1
9	Oregon	6.4
21	Pennsylvania	4.8
32	Rhode Island	2.9
16	South Carolina	5.5
27	South Dakota	3.7
31	Tennessee	3.0
2	Texas	9.8
8	Utah	6.5
44	Vermont	1.8
34	Virginia	2.5
25	Washington	4.0
43	West Virginia	1.9
37	Wisconsin	2.3
26	Wyoming	3.9

RANK ORDER

RANK	STATE	RATE
1	Missouri	16.3
2	Texas	9.8
3	Arkansas	9.6
4	Ohio	9.5
5	Michigan	8.6
6	Nebraska	7.8
7	Alaska	7.0
8	Utah	6.5
9	Idaho	6.4
9	Iowa	6.4
9	Oregon	6.4
12	Alabama	6.1
13	Maine	5.9
14	Montana	5.8
15	New Hampshire	5.7
16	South Carolina	5.5
17	Indiana	5.3
17	Massachusetts	5.3
19	Kansas	5.2
20	Kentucky	5.1
21	Pennsylvania	4.8
22	Colorado	4.6
23	North Dakota	4.5
24	Illinois	4.4
25	Washington	4.0
26	Wyoming	3.9
27	South Dakota	3.7
28	Arizona	3.4
29	New Mexico	3.3
30	Minnesota	3.1
31	Tennessee	3.0
32	Rhode Island	2.9
33	Florida	2.7
34	Virginia	2.5
35	Maryland	2.4
35	North Carolina	2.4
37	Wisconsin	2.3
38	Hawaii	2.2
38	Mississippi	2.2
40	Oklahoma	2.1
41	Georgia	2.0
41	Louisiana	2.0
43	West Virginia	1.9
44	New Jersey	1.8
44	New York	1.8
44	Vermont	1.8
47	Delaware	1.5
48	Connecticut	1.4
49	California	1.3
50	Nevada	0.3

District of Columbia	0.5

Source: CQ Press using data from U.S. Department of Health and Human Services, National Center for Health Statistics
"Morbidity and Mortality Weekly Report" (January 10, 2010, Vol. 58, Nos. 51 & 52, http://www.cdc.gov/mmwr/)
*Provisional data. Acute, highly contagious infection of respiratory tract.

Percent of Children Aged 19 to 35 Months Fully Immunized in 2008

National Percent = 76.1%*

ALPHA ORDER			RANK ORDER		
RANK	STATE	PERCENT	RANK	STATE	PERCENT
25	Alabama	75.1	1	Massachusetts	82.3
44	Alaska	69.2	2	Louisiana	81.9
21	Arizona	76.4	3	Ohio	81.8
23	Arkansas	75.5	4	Tennessee	81.2
10	California	78.7	5	New Hampshire	81.0
9	Colorado	79.4	6	Maryland	80.2
42	Connecticut	69.8	7	Florida	79.9
37	Delaware	71.8	8	Wisconsin	79.6
7	Florida	79.9	9	Colorado	79.4
36	Georgia	71.9	10	California	78.7
15	Hawaii	77.4	11	South Carolina	78.4
49	Idaho	60.4	12	Texas	77.8
26	Illinois	74.8	13	Pennsylvania	77.7
23	Indiana	75.5	14	Rhode Island	77.5
27	Iowa	74.7	15	Hawaii	77.4
18	Kansas	76.7	15	South Dakota	77.4
30	Kentucky	74.1	17	New Mexico	77.0
2	Louisiana	81.9	18	Kansas	76.7
31	Maine	73.6	19	Utah	76.6
6	Maryland	80.2	20	West Virginia	76.5
1	Massachusetts	82.3	21	Arizona	76.4
29	Michigan	74.5	22	Mississippi	75.8
28	Minnesota	74.6	23	Arkansas	75.5
22	Mississippi	75.8	23	Indiana	75.5
34	Missouri	72.9	25	Alabama	75.1
50	Montana	59.2	26	Illinois	74.8
39	Nebraska	71.5	27	Iowa	74.7
46	Nevada	67.8	28	Minnesota	74.6
5	New Hampshire	81.0	29	Michigan	74.5
45	New Jersey	68.5	30	Kentucky	74.1
17	New Mexico	77.0	31	Maine	73.6
33	New York	73.3	32	Washington	73.5
41	North Carolina	70.8	33	New York	73.3
42	North Dakota	69.8	34	Missouri	72.9
3	Ohio	81.8	34	Virginia	72.9
38	Oklahoma	71.7	36	Georgia	71.9
40	Oregon	71.0	37	Delaware	71.8
13	Pennsylvania	77.7	38	Oklahoma	71.7
14	Rhode Island	77.5	39	Nebraska	71.5
11	South Carolina	78.4	40	Oregon	71.0
15	South Dakota	77.4	41	North Carolina	70.8
4	Tennessee	81.2	42	Connecticut	69.8
12	Texas	77.8	42	North Dakota	69.8
19	Utah	76.6	44	Alaska	69.2
48	Vermont	64.5	45	New Jersey	68.5
34	Virginia	72.9	46	Nevada	67.8
32	Washington	73.5	47	Wyoming	64.6
20	West Virginia	76.5	48	Vermont	64.5
8	Wisconsin	79.6	49	Idaho	60.4
47	Wyoming	64.6	50	Montana	59.2

| | | | | District of Columbia | 77.6 |

Source: U.S. Department of Health and Human Services, Centers for Disease Control and Prevention
   "State Vaccination Coverage Levels" (MMWR, Vol. 58, No. 33, August 28, 2009, http://www.cdc.gov/mmwr/)
*Fully immunized (4:3:1:3:3:1 series) children received four doses of DTP/DT/DTaP (Diphtheria, Tetanus, Pertussis [Whooping Cough], Acellular Pertussis), three doses of OPV (Oral Poliovirus Vaccine), one dose of MCV (Measles-Containing Vaccine), three doses of Hib (Haemophilus influenzae type b), three doses of Hepatitis B vaccine, and one dose of Varicella (chickenpox) vaccine. This differs from previous "fully" immunized tables.

Percent of Adults Aged 65 Years and Older Who Received Flu Shots in 2008

National Median = 71.1%*

ALPHA ORDER

RANK	STATE	PERCENT
39	Alabama	68.7
41	Alaska	68.5
22	Arizona	71.4
30	Arkansas	70.5
33	California	70.0
2	Colorado	77.9
8	Connecticut	74.6
37	Delaware	69.6
48	Florida	63.5
47	Georgia	65.2
3	Hawaii	77.1
42	Idaho	68.4
49	Illinois	63.2
40	Indiana	68.6
4	Iowa	76.5
19	Kansas	72.0
11	Kentucky	73.6
43	Louisiana	68.0
8	Maine	74.6
35	Maryland	69.8
19	Massachusetts	72.0
33	Michigan	70.0
5	Minnesota	76.4
45	Mississippi	67.5
24	Missouri	71.3
38	Montana	69.3
7	Nebraska	75.7
50	Nevada	57.1
1	New Hampshire	78.1
46	New Jersey	65.9
36	New Mexico	69.7
27	New York	70.9
17	North Carolina	73.0
14	North Dakota	73.2
31	Ohio	70.3
14	Oklahoma	73.2
32	Oregon	70.1
21	Pennsylvania	71.7
10	Rhode Island	74.0
43	South Carolina	68.0
6	South Dakota	76.3
28	Tennessee	70.8
25	Texas	71.1
13	Utah	73.3
12	Vermont	73.4
16	Virginia	73.1
22	Washington	71.4
25	West Virginia	71.1
17	Wisconsin	73.0
29	Wyoming	70.7

RANK ORDER

RANK	STATE	PERCENT
1	New Hampshire	78.1
2	Colorado	77.9
3	Hawaii	77.1
4	Iowa	76.5
5	Minnesota	76.4
6	South Dakota	76.3
7	Nebraska	75.7
8	Connecticut	74.6
8	Maine	74.6
10	Rhode Island	74.0
11	Kentucky	73.6
12	Vermont	73.4
13	Utah	73.3
14	North Dakota	73.2
14	Oklahoma	73.2
16	Virginia	73.1
17	North Carolina	73.0
17	Wisconsin	73.0
19	Kansas	72.0
19	Massachusetts	72.0
21	Pennsylvania	71.7
22	Arizona	71.4
22	Washington	71.4
24	Missouri	71.3
25	Texas	71.1
25	West Virginia	71.1
27	New York	70.9
28	Tennessee	70.8
29	Wyoming	70.7
30	Arkansas	70.5
31	Ohio	70.3
32	Oregon	70.1
33	California	70.0
33	Michigan	70.0
35	Maryland	69.8
36	New Mexico	69.7
37	Delaware	69.6
38	Montana	69.3
39	Alabama	68.7
40	Indiana	68.6
41	Alaska	68.5
42	Idaho	68.4
43	Louisiana	68.0
43	South Carolina	68.0
45	Mississippi	67.5
46	New Jersey	65.9
47	Georgia	65.2
48	Florida	63.5
49	Illinois	63.2
50	Nevada	57.1

District of Columbia	61.3

Source: U.S. Department of Health and Human Services, Centers for Disease Control and Prevention
"2008 Behavioral Risk Factor Surveillance Summary Prevalence Data" (http://apps.nccd.cdc.gov/brfss/)
*Percent of adults 65 years old and older who reported receiving influenza vaccine during the preceding 12 months.

Percent of Adults Aged 65 Years and Older
Who Have Had a Pneumonia Vaccine: 2008
National Median = 66.9%*

RANK	STATE	PERCENT
28	Alabama	66.8
35	Alaska	66.0
7	Arizona	70.9
44	Arkansas	64.2
46	California	62.7
2	Colorado	72.5
28	Connecticut	66.8
4	Delaware	71.9
48	Florida	61.5
40	Georgia	65.2
37	Hawaii	65.6
41	Idaho	65.1
50	Illinois	57.4
20	Indiana	68.5
14	Iowa	70.0
25	Kansas	67.3
42	Kentucky	65.0
36	Louisiana	65.8
3	Maine	72.3
30	Maryland	66.7
26	Massachusetts	66.9
32	Michigan	66.3
10	Minnesota	70.5
31	Mississippi	66.5
23	Missouri	67.7
16	Montana	69.4
9	Nebraska	70.6
47	Nevada	62.6
1	New Hampshire	73.0
49	New Jersey	60.5
34	New Mexico	66.1
39	New York	65.3
19	North Carolina	68.7
21	North Dakota	68.4
26	Ohio	66.9
5	Oklahoma	71.4
6	Oregon	71.1
8	Pennsylvania	70.7
10	Rhode Island	70.5
33	South Carolina	66.2
38	South Dakota	65.4
43	Tennessee	64.3
45	Texas	63.9
17	Utah	69.2
13	Vermont	70.2
23	Virginia	67.7
15	Washington	69.8
22	West Virginia	68.2
12	Wisconsin	70.3
18	Wyoming	68.9

RANK	STATE	PERCENT
1	New Hampshire	73.0
2	Colorado	72.5
3	Maine	72.3
4	Delaware	71.9
5	Oklahoma	71.4
6	Oregon	71.1
7	Arizona	70.9
8	Pennsylvania	70.7
9	Nebraska	70.6
10	Minnesota	70.5
10	Rhode Island	70.5
12	Wisconsin	70.3
13	Vermont	70.2
14	Iowa	70.0
15	Washington	69.8
16	Montana	69.4
17	Utah	69.2
18	Wyoming	68.9
19	North Carolina	68.7
20	Indiana	68.5
21	North Dakota	68.4
22	West Virginia	68.2
23	Missouri	67.7
23	Virginia	67.7
25	Kansas	67.3
26	Massachusetts	66.9
26	Ohio	66.9
28	Alabama	66.8
28	Connecticut	66.8
30	Maryland	66.7
31	Mississippi	66.5
32	Michigan	66.3
33	South Carolina	66.2
34	New Mexico	66.1
35	Alaska	66.0
36	Louisiana	65.8
37	Hawaii	65.6
38	South Dakota	65.4
39	New York	65.3
40	Georgia	65.2
41	Idaho	65.1
42	Kentucky	65.0
43	Tennessee	64.3
44	Arkansas	64.2
45	Texas	63.9
46	California	62.7
47	Nevada	62.6
48	Florida	61.5
49	New Jersey	60.5
50	Illinois	57.4
	District of Columbia	55.1

Source: U.S. Department of Health and Human Services, Centers for Disease Control and Prevention
  "2008 Behavioral Risk Factor Surveillance Summary Prevalence Data" (http://apps.nccd.cdc.gov/brfss/)
*Percent of adults 65 years old and older who reported ever receiving a pneumonia vaccine.

Sexually Transmitted Diseases in 2008

National Total = 1,560,790 Cases*

<table>
<tr><td colspan="4">ALPHA ORDER</td><td colspan="4">RANK ORDER</td></tr>
<tr><th>RANK</th><th>STATE</th><th>CASES</th><th>% of USA</th><th>RANK</th><th>STATE</th><th>CASES</th><th>% of USA</th></tr>
<tr><td>14</td><td>Alabama</td><td>34,949</td><td>2.2%</td><td>1</td><td>California</td><td>176,791</td><td>11.3%</td></tr>
<tr><td>39</td><td>Alaska</td><td>5,440</td><td>0.3%</td><td>2</td><td>Texas</td><td>134,482</td><td>8.6%</td></tr>
<tr><td>20</td><td>Arizona</td><td>28,535</td><td>1.8%</td><td>3</td><td>New York</td><td>106,686</td><td>6.8%</td></tr>
<tr><td>27</td><td>Arkansas</td><td>18,856</td><td>1.2%</td><td>4</td><td>Florida</td><td>95,387</td><td>6.1%</td></tr>
<tr><td>1</td><td>California</td><td>176,791</td><td>11.3%</td><td>5</td><td>Illinois</td><td>80,397</td><td>5.2%</td></tr>
<tr><td>24</td><td>Colorado</td><td>23,067</td><td>1.5%</td><td>6</td><td>Ohio</td><td>64,272</td><td>4.1%</td></tr>
<tr><td>30</td><td>Connecticut</td><td>15,354</td><td>1.0%</td><td>7</td><td>Michigan</td><td>62,197</td><td>4.0%</td></tr>
<tr><td>40</td><td>Delaware</td><td>4,929</td><td>0.3%</td><td>8</td><td>Georgia</td><td>59,815</td><td>3.8%</td></tr>
<tr><td>4</td><td>Florida</td><td>95,387</td><td>6.1%</td><td>9</td><td>North Carolina</td><td>53,779</td><td>3.4%</td></tr>
<tr><td>8</td><td>Georgia</td><td>59,815</td><td>3.8%</td><td>10</td><td>Pennsylvania</td><td>53,576</td><td>3.4%</td></tr>
<tr><td>37</td><td>Hawaii</td><td>6,621</td><td>0.4%</td><td>11</td><td>Virginia</td><td>41,821</td><td>2.7%</td></tr>
<tr><td>41</td><td>Idaho</td><td>4,388</td><td>0.3%</td><td>12</td><td>Tennessee</td><td>37,231</td><td>2.4%</td></tr>
<tr><td>5</td><td>Illinois</td><td>80,397</td><td>5.2%</td><td>13</td><td>South Carolina</td><td>35,864</td><td>2.3%</td></tr>
<tr><td>18</td><td>Indiana</td><td>31,063</td><td>2.0%</td><td>14</td><td>Alabama</td><td>34,949</td><td>2.2%</td></tr>
<tr><td>34</td><td>Iowa</td><td>11,088</td><td>0.7%</td><td>15</td><td>Missouri</td><td>33,055</td><td>2.1%</td></tr>
<tr><td>33</td><td>Kansas</td><td>11,512</td><td>0.7%</td><td>16</td><td>Louisiana</td><td>32,821</td><td>2.1%</td></tr>
<tr><td>29</td><td>Kentucky</td><td>16,804</td><td>1.1%</td><td>17</td><td>Maryland</td><td>31,713</td><td>2.0%</td></tr>
<tr><td>16</td><td>Louisiana</td><td>32,821</td><td>2.1%</td><td>18</td><td>Indiana</td><td>31,063</td><td>2.0%</td></tr>
<tr><td>46</td><td>Maine</td><td>2,714</td><td>0.2%</td><td>19</td><td>Mississippi</td><td>28,931</td><td>1.9%</td></tr>
<tr><td>17</td><td>Maryland</td><td>31,713</td><td>2.0%</td><td>20</td><td>Arizona</td><td>28,535</td><td>1.8%</td></tr>
<tr><td>26</td><td>Massachusetts</td><td>19,852</td><td>1.3%</td><td>21</td><td>New Jersey</td><td>27,929</td><td>1.8%</td></tr>
<tr><td>7</td><td>Michigan</td><td>62,197</td><td>4.0%</td><td>22</td><td>Wisconsin</td><td>27,148</td><td>1.7%</td></tr>
<tr><td>28</td><td>Minnesota</td><td>17,504</td><td>1.1%</td><td>23</td><td>Washington</td><td>24,711</td><td>1.6%</td></tr>
<tr><td>19</td><td>Mississippi</td><td>28,931</td><td>1.9%</td><td>24</td><td>Colorado</td><td>23,067</td><td>1.5%</td></tr>
<tr><td>15</td><td>Missouri</td><td>33,055</td><td>2.1%</td><td>25</td><td>Oklahoma</td><td>20,074</td><td>1.3%</td></tr>
<tr><td>45</td><td>Montana</td><td>3,230</td><td>0.2%</td><td>26</td><td>Massachusetts</td><td>19,852</td><td>1.3%</td></tr>
<tr><td>36</td><td>Nebraska</td><td>7,048</td><td>0.5%</td><td>27</td><td>Arkansas</td><td>18,856</td><td>1.2%</td></tr>
<tr><td>32</td><td>Nevada</td><td>11,919</td><td>0.8%</td><td>28</td><td>Minnesota</td><td>17,504</td><td>1.1%</td></tr>
<tr><td>47</td><td>New Hampshire</td><td>2,229</td><td>0.1%</td><td>29</td><td>Kentucky</td><td>16,804</td><td>1.1%</td></tr>
<tr><td>21</td><td>New Jersey</td><td>27,929</td><td>1.8%</td><td>30</td><td>Connecticut</td><td>15,354</td><td>1.0%</td></tr>
<tr><td>35</td><td>New Mexico</td><td>10,709</td><td>0.7%</td><td>31</td><td>Oregon</td><td>11,995</td><td>0.8%</td></tr>
<tr><td>3</td><td>New York</td><td>106,686</td><td>6.8%</td><td>32</td><td>Nevada</td><td>11,919</td><td>0.8%</td></tr>
<tr><td>9</td><td>North Carolina</td><td>53,779</td><td>3.4%</td><td>33</td><td>Kansas</td><td>11,512</td><td>0.7%</td></tr>
<tr><td>48</td><td>North Dakota</td><td>2,064</td><td>0.1%</td><td>34</td><td>Iowa</td><td>11,088</td><td>0.7%</td></tr>
<tr><td>6</td><td>Ohio</td><td>64,272</td><td>4.1%</td><td>35</td><td>New Mexico</td><td>10,709</td><td>0.7%</td></tr>
<tr><td>25</td><td>Oklahoma</td><td>20,074</td><td>1.3%</td><td>36</td><td>Nebraska</td><td>7,048</td><td>0.5%</td></tr>
<tr><td>31</td><td>Oregon</td><td>11,995</td><td>0.8%</td><td>37</td><td>Hawaii</td><td>6,621</td><td>0.4%</td></tr>
<tr><td>10</td><td>Pennsylvania</td><td>53,576</td><td>3.4%</td><td>38</td><td>Utah</td><td>6,523</td><td>0.4%</td></tr>
<tr><td>43</td><td>Rhode Island</td><td>3,642</td><td>0.2%</td><td>39</td><td>Alaska</td><td>5,440</td><td>0.3%</td></tr>
<tr><td>13</td><td>South Carolina</td><td>35,864</td><td>2.3%</td><td>40</td><td>Delaware</td><td>4,929</td><td>0.3%</td></tr>
<tr><td>44</td><td>South Dakota</td><td>3,332</td><td>0.2%</td><td>41</td><td>Idaho</td><td>4,388</td><td>0.3%</td></tr>
<tr><td>12</td><td>Tennessee</td><td>37,231</td><td>2.4%</td><td>42</td><td>West Virginia</td><td>4,075</td><td>0.3%</td></tr>
<tr><td>2</td><td>Texas</td><td>134,482</td><td>8.6%</td><td>43</td><td>Rhode Island</td><td>3,642</td><td>0.2%</td></tr>
<tr><td>38</td><td>Utah</td><td>6,523</td><td>0.4%</td><td>44</td><td>South Dakota</td><td>3,332</td><td>0.2%</td></tr>
<tr><td>50</td><td>Vermont</td><td>1,238</td><td>0.1%</td><td>45</td><td>Montana</td><td>3,230</td><td>0.2%</td></tr>
<tr><td>11</td><td>Virginia</td><td>41,821</td><td>2.7%</td><td>46</td><td>Maine</td><td>2,714</td><td>0.2%</td></tr>
<tr><td>23</td><td>Washington</td><td>24,711</td><td>1.6%</td><td>47</td><td>New Hampshire</td><td>2,229</td><td>0.1%</td></tr>
<tr><td>42</td><td>West Virginia</td><td>4,075</td><td>0.3%</td><td>48</td><td>North Dakota</td><td>2,064</td><td>0.1%</td></tr>
<tr><td>22</td><td>Wisconsin</td><td>27,148</td><td>1.7%</td><td>49</td><td>Wyoming</td><td>1,704</td><td>0.1%</td></tr>
<tr><td>49</td><td>Wyoming</td><td>1,704</td><td>0.1%</td><td>50</td><td>Vermont</td><td>1,238</td><td>0.1%</td></tr>
<tr><td></td><td></td><td></td><td></td><td colspan="2">District of Columbia</td><td>9,726</td><td>0.6%</td></tr>
</table>

Source: CQ Press using data from U.S. Dept. of Health and Human Services, National Center for Health Statistics
"Sexually Transmitted Disease Surveillance 2008" (http://www.cdc.gov/STD/stats08/toc.htm)
*Includes chancroid, chlamydia, gonorrhea, and primary and secondary syphilis.

Sexually Transmitted Disease Rate in 2008

National Rate = 517.4 Cases per 100,000 Population*

ALPHA ORDER

RANK	STATE	RATE
5	Alabama	755.2
3	Alaska	795.9
28	Arizona	450.2
6	Arkansas	665.2
25	California	483.6
26	Colorado	474.4
29	Connecticut	438.4
12	Delaware	570.0
21	Florida	522.6
7	Georgia	626.7
22	Hawaii	515.9
45	Idaho	292.7
8	Illinois	625.6
23	Indiana	489.5
36	Iowa	371.0
32	Kansas	414.7
34	Kentucky	396.2
4	Louisiana	764.5
48	Maine	206.1
13	Maryland	564.4
44	Massachusetts	307.8
9	Michigan	617.5
39	Minnesota	336.7
1	Mississippi	991.2
15	Missouri	562.3
38	Montana	337.1
33	Nebraska	397.1
27	Nevada	464.6
50	New Hampshire	169.4
42	New Jersey	321.5
19	New Mexico	543.6
18	New York	552.9
11	North Carolina	593.5
41	North Dakota	322.7
16	Ohio	560.5
17	Oklahoma	554.9
43	Oregon	320.1
30	Pennsylvania	430.9
37	Rhode Island	344.3
2	South Carolina	813.6
31	South Dakota	418.5
10	Tennessee	604.7
14	Texas	562.6
46	Utah	246.5
49	Vermont	199.3
20	Virginia	542.2
35	Washington	382.0
47	West Virginia	224.9
24	Wisconsin	484.7
40	Wyoming	325.9

RANK ORDER

RANK	STATE	RATE
1	Mississippi	991.2
2	South Carolina	813.6
3	Alaska	795.9
4	Louisiana	764.5
5	Alabama	755.2
6	Arkansas	665.2
7	Georgia	626.7
8	Illinois	625.6
9	Michigan	617.5
10	Tennessee	604.7
11	North Carolina	593.5
12	Delaware	570.0
13	Maryland	564.4
14	Texas	562.6
15	Missouri	562.3
16	Ohio	560.5
17	Oklahoma	554.9
18	New York	552.9
19	New Mexico	543.6
20	Virginia	542.2
21	Florida	522.6
22	Hawaii	515.9
23	Indiana	489.5
24	Wisconsin	484.7
25	California	483.6
26	Colorado	474.4
27	Nevada	464.6
28	Arizona	450.2
29	Connecticut	438.4
30	Pennsylvania	430.9
31	South Dakota	418.5
32	Kansas	414.7
33	Nebraska	397.1
34	Kentucky	396.2
35	Washington	382.0
36	Iowa	371.0
37	Rhode Island	344.3
38	Montana	337.1
39	Minnesota	336.7
40	Wyoming	325.9
41	North Dakota	322.7
42	New Jersey	321.5
43	Oregon	320.1
44	Massachusetts	307.8
45	Idaho	292.7
46	Utah	246.5
47	West Virginia	224.9
48	Maine	206.1
49	Vermont	199.3
50	New Hampshire	169.4

	District of Columbia	1,653.3

Source: CQ Press using data from U.S. Dept. of Health and Human Services, National Center for Health Statistics
   "Sexually Transmitted Disease Surveillance 2008" (http://www.cdc.gov/STD/stats08/toc.htm)
*Includes chancroid, chlamydia, gonorrhea, and primary and secondary syphilis.

Chlamydia Cases Reported in 2008

National Total = 1,210,523 Cases*

ALPHA ORDER

RANK	STATE	CASES	% of USA
16	Alabama	24,760	2.0%
39	Alaska	4,861	0.4%
15	Arizona	24,769	2.0%
28	Arkansas	14,136	1.2%
1	California	148,798	12.3%
24	Colorado	19,180	1.6%
29	Connecticut	12,519	1.0%
41	Delaware	3,868	0.3%
4	Florida	71,017	5.9%
8	Georgia	42,629	3.5%
37	Hawaii	5,982	0.5%
40	Idaho	4,194	0.3%
5	Illinois	59,169	4.9%
20	Indiana	22,154	1.8%
33	Iowa	9,372	0.8%
35	Kansas	9,208	0.8%
30	Kentucky	12,163	1.0%
18	Louisiana	22,659	1.9%
46	Maine	2,608	0.2%
17	Maryland	24,669	2.0%
25	Massachusetts	17,503	1.4%
7	Michigan	44,923	3.7%
27	Minnesota	14,351	1.2%
22	Mississippi	21,253	1.8%
14	Missouri	24,817	2.1%
44	Montana	3,101	0.3%
38	Nebraska	5,573	0.5%
32	Nevada	9,670	0.8%
47	New Hampshire	2,109	0.2%
19	New Jersey	22,405	1.9%
34	New Mexico	9,262	0.8%
3	New York	88,359	7.3%
10	North Carolina	37,516	3.1%
48	North Dakota	1,921	0.2%
6	Ohio	47,117	3.9%
26	Oklahoma	14,803	1.2%
31	Oregon	10,744	0.9%
9	Pennsylvania	42,233	3.5%
42	Rhode Island	3,317	0.3%
13	South Carolina	26,323	2.2%
45	South Dakota	2,956	0.2%
12	Tennessee	28,038	2.3%
2	Texas	100,870	8.3%
36	Utah	6,021	0.5%
50	Vermont	1,190	0.1%
11	Virginia	31,218	2.6%
21	Washington	21,402	1.8%
43	West Virginia	3,316	0.3%
23	Wisconsin	20,996	1.7%
49	Wyoming	1,577	0.1%

RANK ORDER

RANK	STATE	CASES	% of USA
1	California	148,798	12.3%
2	Texas	100,870	8.3%
3	New York	88,359	7.3%
4	Florida	71,017	5.9%
5	Illinois	59,169	4.9%
6	Ohio	47,117	3.9%
7	Michigan	44,923	3.7%
8	Georgia	42,629	3.5%
9	Pennsylvania	42,233	3.5%
10	North Carolina	37,516	3.1%
11	Virginia	31,218	2.6%
12	Tennessee	28,038	2.3%
13	South Carolina	26,323	2.2%
14	Missouri	24,817	2.1%
15	Arizona	24,769	2.0%
16	Alabama	24,760	2.0%
17	Maryland	24,669	2.0%
18	Louisiana	22,659	1.9%
19	New Jersey	22,405	1.9%
20	Indiana	22,154	1.8%
21	Washington	21,402	1.8%
22	Mississippi	21,253	1.8%
23	Wisconsin	20,996	1.7%
24	Colorado	19,180	1.6%
25	Massachusetts	17,503	1.4%
26	Oklahoma	14,803	1.2%
27	Minnesota	14,351	1.2%
28	Arkansas	14,136	1.2%
29	Connecticut	12,519	1.0%
30	Kentucky	12,163	1.0%
31	Oregon	10,744	0.9%
32	Nevada	9,670	0.8%
33	Iowa	9,372	0.8%
34	New Mexico	9,262	0.8%
35	Kansas	9,208	0.8%
36	Utah	6,021	0.5%
37	Hawaii	5,982	0.5%
38	Nebraska	5,573	0.5%
39	Alaska	4,861	0.4%
40	Idaho	4,194	0.3%
41	Delaware	3,868	0.3%
42	Rhode Island	3,317	0.3%
43	West Virginia	3,316	0.3%
44	Montana	3,101	0.3%
45	South Dakota	2,956	0.2%
46	Maine	2,608	0.2%
47	New Hampshire	2,109	0.2%
48	North Dakota	1,921	0.2%
49	Wyoming	1,577	0.1%
50	Vermont	1,190	0.1%
	District of Columbia	6,924	0.6%

Source: U.S. Department of Health and Human Services, National Center for Health Statistics
"Sexually Transmitted Disease Surveillance 2008" (http://www.cdc.gov/STD/stats08/toc.htm)
*Any of several common, often asymptomatic, sexually transmitted diseases caused by the microorganism Chlamydia trachomatis, including nonspecific urethritis in men.

Chlamydia Rate in 2008

National Rate = 401.3 Cases per 100,000 Population*

ALPHA ORDER

RANK	STATE	RATE
4	Alabama	535.0
2	Alaska	711.2
24	Arizona	390.8
6	Arkansas	498.7
21	California	407.1
23	Colorado	394.5
29	Connecticut	357.4
12	Delaware	447.3
25	Florida	389.1
13	Georgia	446.6
8	Hawaii	466.1
42	Idaho	279.7
9	Illinois	460.4
30	Indiana	349.1
36	Iowa	313.6
32	Kansas	331.7
40	Kentucky	286.8
5	Louisiana	527.8
47	Maine	198.0
15	Maryland	439.1
44	Massachusetts	271.4
14	Michigan	446.0
43	Minnesota	276.1
1	Mississippi	728.1
16	Missouri	422.2
34	Montana	323.7
35	Nebraska	314.0
26	Nevada	376.9
50	New Hampshire	160.3
45	New Jersey	257.9
7	New Mexico	470.2
10	New York	457.9
18	North Carolina	414.0
39	North Dakota	300.3
19	Ohio	410.9
20	Oklahoma	409.2
41	Oregon	286.7
31	Pennsylvania	339.7
36	Rhode Island	313.6
3	South Carolina	597.2
28	South Dakota	371.3
11	Tennessee	455.4
17	Texas	422.0
46	Utah	227.6
48	Vermont	191.5
22	Virginia	404.8
33	Washington	330.9
49	West Virginia	183.0
27	Wisconsin	374.8
38	Wyoming	301.6

RANK ORDER

RANK	STATE	RATE
1	Mississippi	728.1
2	Alaska	711.2
3	South Carolina	597.2
4	Alabama	535.0
5	Louisiana	527.8
6	Arkansas	498.7
7	New Mexico	470.2
8	Hawaii	466.1
9	Illinois	460.4
10	New York	457.9
11	Tennessee	455.4
12	Delaware	447.3
13	Georgia	446.6
14	Michigan	446.0
15	Maryland	439.1
16	Missouri	422.2
17	Texas	422.0
18	North Carolina	414.0
19	Ohio	410.9
20	Oklahoma	409.2
21	California	407.1
22	Virginia	404.8
23	Colorado	394.5
24	Arizona	390.8
25	Florida	389.1
26	Nevada	376.9
27	Wisconsin	374.8
28	South Dakota	371.3
29	Connecticut	357.4
30	Indiana	349.1
31	Pennsylvania	339.7
32	Kansas	331.7
33	Washington	330.9
34	Montana	323.7
35	Nebraska	314.0
36	Iowa	313.6
36	Rhode Island	313.6
38	Wyoming	301.6
39	North Dakota	300.3
40	Kentucky	286.8
41	Oregon	286.7
42	Idaho	279.7
43	Minnesota	276.1
44	Massachusetts	271.4
45	New Jersey	257.9
46	Utah	227.6
47	Maine	198.0
48	Vermont	191.5
49	West Virginia	183.0
50	New Hampshire	160.3

	District of Columbia	1,177.0

Source: U.S. Department of Health and Human Services, National Center for Health Statistics
"Sexually Transmitted Disease Surveillance 2008" (http://www.cdc.gov/STD/stats08/toc.htm)
*Any of several common, often asymptomatic, sexually transmitted diseases caused by the microorganism Chlamydia trachomatis, including nonspecific urethritis in men.

Gonorrhea Cases Reported in 2008

National Total = 336,742 Cases*

ALPHA ORDER

RANK	STATE	CASES	% of USA
12	Alabama	9,740	2.9%
40	Alaska	578	0.2%
26	Arizona	3,449	1.0%
24	Arkansas	4,514	1.3%
2	California	25,787	7.7%
25	Colorado	3,757	1.1%
29	Connecticut	2,801	0.8%
37	Delaware	1,045	0.3%
3	Florida	23,326	6.9%
8	Georgia	16,272	4.8%
39	Hawaii	610	0.2%
44	Idaho	187	0.1%
4	Illinois	20,674	6.1%
16	Indiana	8,769	2.6%
33	Iowa	1,700	0.5%
30	Kansas	2,274	0.7%
23	Kentucky	4,548	1.4%
13	Louisiana	9,455	2.8%
49	Maine	96	0.0%
19	Maryland	6,666	2.0%
32	Massachusetts	2,129	0.6%
6	Michigan	17,064	5.1%
28	Minnesota	3,037	0.9%
18	Mississippi	7,494	2.2%
17	Missouri	8,014	2.4%
47	Montana	122	0.0%
34	Nebraska	1,460	0.4%
31	Nevada	2,172	0.6%
48	New Hampshire	100	0.0%
21	New Jersey	5,298	1.6%
35	New Mexico	1,403	0.4%
5	New York	17,108	5.1%
9	North Carolina	15,972	4.7%
45	North Dakota	143	0.0%
7	Ohio	16,803	5.0%
22	Oklahoma	5,185	1.5%
36	Oregon	1,225	0.4%
10	Pennsylvania	11,071	3.3%
43	Rhode Island	307	0.1%
14	South Carolina	9,442	2.8%
42	South Dakota	375	0.1%
15	Tennessee	8,780	2.6%
1	Texas	32,199	9.6%
41	Utah	477	0.1%
50	Vermont	37	0.0%
11	Virginia	10,337	3.1%
27	Washington	3,127	0.9%
38	West Virginia	746	0.2%
20	Wisconsin	6,087	1.8%
46	Wyoming	124	0.0%

RANK ORDER

RANK	STATE	CASES	% of USA
1	Texas	32,199	9.6%
2	California	25,787	7.7%
3	Florida	23,326	6.9%
4	Illinois	20,674	6.1%
5	New York	17,108	5.1%
6	Michigan	17,064	5.1%
7	Ohio	16,803	5.0%
8	Georgia	16,272	4.8%
9	North Carolina	15,972	4.7%
10	Pennsylvania	11,071	3.3%
11	Virginia	10,337	3.1%
12	Alabama	9,740	2.9%
13	Louisiana	9,455	2.8%
14	South Carolina	9,442	2.8%
15	Tennessee	8,780	2.6%
16	Indiana	8,769	2.6%
17	Missouri	8,014	2.4%
18	Mississippi	7,494	2.2%
19	Maryland	6,666	2.0%
20	Wisconsin	6,087	1.8%
21	New Jersey	5,298	1.6%
22	Oklahoma	5,185	1.5%
23	Kentucky	4,548	1.4%
24	Arkansas	4,514	1.3%
25	Colorado	3,757	1.1%
26	Arizona	3,449	1.0%
27	Washington	3,127	0.9%
28	Minnesota	3,037	0.9%
29	Connecticut	2,801	0.8%
30	Kansas	2,274	0.7%
31	Nevada	2,172	0.6%
32	Massachusetts	2,129	0.6%
33	Iowa	1,700	0.5%
34	Nebraska	1,460	0.4%
35	New Mexico	1,403	0.4%
36	Oregon	1,225	0.4%
37	Delaware	1,045	0.3%
38	West Virginia	746	0.2%
39	Hawaii	610	0.2%
40	Alaska	578	0.2%
41	Utah	477	0.1%
42	South Dakota	375	0.1%
43	Rhode Island	307	0.1%
44	Idaho	187	0.1%
45	North Dakota	143	0.0%
46	Wyoming	124	0.0%
47	Montana	122	0.0%
48	New Hampshire	100	0.0%
49	Maine	96	0.0%
50	Vermont	37	0.0%
	District of Columbia	2,656	0.8%

Source: U.S. Department of Health and Human Services, National Center for Health Statistics
"Sexually Transmitted Disease Surveillance 2008" (http://www.cdc.gov/STD/stats08/toc.htm)
*Gonorrhea is a sexually transmitted disease caused by gonococcal bacteria that affects the mucous membrane chiefly of the genital and urinary tracts and is characterized by an acute purulent discharge and painful or difficult urination, though women often have no symptoms.

Gonorrhea Rate in 2008

National Rate = 111.6 Cases per 100,000 Population*

ALPHA ORDER				RANK ORDER		
RANK	STATE	RATE		RANK	STATE	RATE
4	Alabama	210.5		1	Mississippi	256.8
25	Alaska	84.6		2	Louisiana	220.2
35	Arizona	54.4		3	South Carolina	214.2
9	Arkansas	159.2		4	Alabama	210.5
31	California	70.5		5	North Carolina	176.3
29	Colorado	77.3		6	Georgia	170.5
28	Connecticut	80.0		7	Michigan	169.4
18	Delaware	120.8		8	Illinois	160.9
17	Florida	127.8		9	Arkansas	159.2
6	Georgia	170.5		10	Ohio	146.5
37	Hawaii	47.5		11	Oklahoma	143.3
47	Idaho	12.5		12	Tennessee	142.6
8	Illinois	160.9		13	Indiana	138.2
13	Indiana	138.2		14	Missouri	136.3
34	Iowa	56.9		15	Texas	134.7
27	Kansas	81.9		16	Virginia	134.0
21	Kentucky	107.2		17	Florida	127.8
2	Louisiana	220.2		18	Delaware	120.8
49	Maine	7.3		19	Maryland	118.6
19	Maryland	118.6		20	Wisconsin	108.7
40	Massachusetts	33.0		21	Kentucky	107.2
7	Michigan	169.4		22	Pennsylvania	89.0
33	Minnesota	58.4		23	New York	88.7
1	Mississippi	256.8		24	Nevada	84.7
14	Missouri	136.3		25	Alaska	84.6
46	Montana	12.7		26	Nebraska	82.3
26	Nebraska	82.3		27	Kansas	81.9
24	Nevada	84.7		28	Connecticut	80.0
48	New Hampshire	7.6		29	Colorado	77.3
32	New Jersey	61.0		30	New Mexico	71.2
30	New Mexico	71.2		31	California	70.5
23	New York	88.7		32	New Jersey	61.0
5	North Carolina	176.3		33	Minnesota	58.4
44	North Dakota	22.4		34	Iowa	56.9
10	Ohio	146.5		35	Arizona	54.4
11	Oklahoma	143.3		36	Washington	48.3
41	Oregon	32.7		37	Hawaii	47.5
22	Pennsylvania	89.0		38	South Dakota	47.1
42	Rhode Island	29.0		39	West Virginia	41.2
3	South Carolina	214.2		40	Massachusetts	33.0
38	South Dakota	47.1		41	Oregon	32.7
12	Tennessee	142.6		42	Rhode Island	29.0
15	Texas	134.7		43	Wyoming	23.7
45	Utah	18.0		44	North Dakota	22.4
50	Vermont	6.0		45	Utah	18.0
16	Virginia	134.0		46	Montana	12.7
36	Washington	48.3		47	Idaho	12.5
39	West Virginia	41.2		48	New Hampshire	7.6
20	Wisconsin	108.7		49	Maine	7.3
43	Wyoming	23.7		50	Vermont	6.0

District of Columbia   451.5

Source: U.S. Department of Health and Human Services, National Center for Health Statistics
"Sexually Transmitted Disease Surveillance 2008" (http://www.cdc.gov/STD/stats08/toc.htm)
*Gonorrhea is a sexually transmitted disease caused by gonococcal bacteria that affects the mucous membrane chiefly of the genital and urinary tracts and is characterized by an acute purulent discharge and painful or difficult urination, though women often have no symptoms.

Syphilis Cases Reported in 2008

National Total = 13,500 Cases*

ALPHA ORDER					RANK ORDER			
RANK	STATE	CASES	% of USA		RANK	STATE	CASES	% of USA
8	Alabama	449	3.3%		1	California	2,204	16.3%
48	Alaska	1	0.0%		2	Texas	1,405	10.4%
12	Arizona	317	2.3%		3	New York	1,217	9.0%
20	Arkansas	206	1.5%		4	Florida	1,044	7.7%
1	California	2,204	16.3%		5	Georgia	914	6.8%
24	Colorado	128	0.9%		6	Louisiana	707	5.2%
32	Connecticut	34	0.3%		7	Illinois	554	4.1%
39	Delaware	16	0.1%		8	Alabama	449	3.3%
4	Florida	1,044	7.7%		9	Tennessee	413	3.1%
5	Georgia	914	6.8%		10	Maryland	378	2.8%
34	Hawaii	29	0.2%		11	Ohio	351	2.6%
45	Idaho	7	0.1%		12	Arizona	317	2.3%
7	Illinois	554	4.1%		13	North Carolina	287	2.1%
23	Indiana	140	1.0%		14	Pennsylvania	272	2.0%
39	Iowa	16	0.1%		15	Virginia	266	2.0%
33	Kansas	30	0.2%		16	New Jersey	226	1.7%
27	Kentucky	93	0.7%		17	Missouri	224	1.7%
6	Louisiana	707	5.2%		18	Massachusetts	216	1.6%
44	Maine	10	0.1%		19	Michigan	210	1.6%
10	Maryland	378	2.8%		20	Arkansas	206	1.5%
18	Massachusetts	216	1.6%		21	Mississippi	184	1.4%
19	Michigan	210	1.6%		22	Washington	181	1.3%
25	Minnesota	116	0.9%		23	Indiana	140	1.0%
21	Mississippi	184	1.4%		24	Colorado	128	0.9%
17	Missouri	224	1.7%		25	Minnesota	116	0.9%
45	Montana	7	0.1%		26	South Carolina	98	0.7%
41	Nebraska	15	0.1%		27	Kentucky	93	0.7%
29	Nevada	77	0.6%		28	Oklahoma	86	0.6%
37	New Hampshire	20	0.1%		29	Nevada	77	0.6%
16	New Jersey	226	1.7%		30	Wisconsin	65	0.5%
31	New Mexico	44	0.3%		31	New Mexico	44	0.3%
3	New York	1,217	9.0%		32	Connecticut	34	0.3%
13	North Carolina	287	2.1%		33	Kansas	30	0.2%
50	North Dakota	0	0.0%		34	Hawaii	29	0.2%
11	Ohio	351	2.6%		35	Oregon	26	0.2%
28	Oklahoma	86	0.6%		36	Utah	25	0.2%
35	Oregon	26	0.2%		37	New Hampshire	20	0.1%
14	Pennsylvania	272	2.0%		38	Rhode Island	18	0.1%
38	Rhode Island	18	0.1%		39	Delaware	16	0.1%
26	South Carolina	98	0.7%		39	Iowa	16	0.1%
48	South Dakota	1	0.0%		41	Nebraska	15	0.1%
9	Tennessee	413	3.1%		42	West Virginia	13	0.1%
2	Texas	1,405	10.4%		43	Vermont	11	0.1%
36	Utah	25	0.2%		44	Maine	10	0.1%
43	Vermont	11	0.1%		45	Idaho	7	0.1%
15	Virginia	266	2.0%		45	Montana	7	0.1%
22	Washington	181	1.3%		47	Wyoming	3	0.0%
42	West Virginia	13	0.1%		48	Alaska	1	0.0%
30	Wisconsin	65	0.5%		48	South Dakota	1	0.0%
47	Wyoming	3	0.0%		50	North Dakota	0	0.0%
						District of Columbia	146	1.1%

Source: U.S. Department of Health and Human Services, National Center for Health Statistics
"Sexually Transmitted Disease Surveillance 2008" (http://www.cdc.gov/STD/stats08/toc.htm)
*Includes only primary and secondary cases. Does not include 32,777 cases in other stages. A chronic infectious disease
caused by a spirochete (Treponema pallidum), either transmitted by direct contact, usually in sexual intercourse, or passed from
mother to child in utero, and progressing through three stages characterized respectively by local formation of chancres, ulcerous
skin eruptions, and systemic infection leading to general paresis.

Syphilis Rate in 2008

National Rate = 4.5 Cases per 100,000 Population*

ALPHA ORDER

RANK	STATE	RATE
2	Alabama	9.7
48	Alaska	0.1
12	Arizona	5.0
4	Arkansas	7.3
9	California	6.0
21	Colorado	2.6
38	Connecticut	1.0
32	Delaware	1.9
11	Florida	5.7
3	Georgia	9.6
24	Hawaii	2.3
46	Idaho	0.5
13	Illinois	4.3
25	Indiana	2.2
46	Iowa	0.5
37	Kansas	1.1
25	Kentucky	2.2
1	Louisiana	16.5
40	Maine	0.8
5	Maryland	6.7
16	Massachusetts	3.3
31	Michigan	2.1
25	Minnesota	2.2
7	Mississippi	6.3
14	Missouri	3.8
42	Montana	0.7
40	Nebraska	0.8
19	Nevada	3.0
35	New Hampshire	1.5
21	New Jersey	2.6
25	New Mexico	2.2
7	New York	6.3
17	North Carolina	3.2
50	North Dakota	0.0
18	Ohio	3.1
23	Oklahoma	2.4
42	Oregon	0.7
25	Pennsylvania	2.2
34	Rhode Island	1.7
25	South Carolina	2.2
48	South Dakota	0.1
5	Tennessee	6.7
10	Texas	5.9
39	Utah	0.9
33	Vermont	1.8
15	Virginia	3.4
20	Washington	2.8
42	West Virginia	0.7
36	Wisconsin	1.2
45	Wyoming	0.6

RANK ORDER

RANK	STATE	RATE
1	Louisiana	16.5
2	Alabama	9.7
3	Georgia	9.6
4	Arkansas	7.3
5	Maryland	6.7
5	Tennessee	6.7
7	Mississippi	6.3
7	New York	6.3
9	California	6.0
10	Texas	5.9
11	Florida	5.7
12	Arizona	5.0
13	Illinois	4.3
14	Missouri	3.8
15	Virginia	3.4
16	Massachusetts	3.3
17	North Carolina	3.2
18	Ohio	3.1
19	Nevada	3.0
20	Washington	2.8
21	Colorado	2.6
21	New Jersey	2.6
23	Oklahoma	2.4
24	Hawaii	2.3
25	Indiana	2.2
25	Kentucky	2.2
25	Minnesota	2.2
25	New Mexico	2.2
25	Pennsylvania	2.2
25	South Carolina	2.2
31	Michigan	2.1
32	Delaware	1.9
33	Vermont	1.8
34	Rhode Island	1.7
35	New Hampshire	1.5
36	Wisconsin	1.2
37	Kansas	1.1
38	Connecticut	1.0
39	Utah	0.9
40	Maine	0.8
40	Nebraska	0.8
42	Montana	0.7
42	Oregon	0.7
42	West Virginia	0.7
45	Wyoming	0.6
46	Idaho	0.5
46	Iowa	0.5
48	Alaska	0.1
48	South Dakota	0.1
50	North Dakota	0.0

District of Columbia   24.8

Source: U.S. Department of Health and Human Services, National Center for Health Statistics
   "Sexually Transmitted Disease Surveillance 2008" (http://www.cdc.gov/STD/stats08/toc.htm)
*Includes only primary and secondary cases. Does not include 32,777 cases in other stages. A chronic infectious disease caused by a spirochete (Treponema pallidum), either transmitted by direct contact, usually in sexual intercourse, or passed from mother to child in utero, and progressing through three stages characterized respectively by local formation of chancres, ulcerous skin eruptions, and systemic infection leading to general paresis.

Percent of Adults Who Have Asthma: 2008

National Median = 8.8% of Adults*

ALPHA ORDER

RANK	STATE	PERCENT
42	Alabama	7.8
8	Alaska	9.6
6	Arizona	9.8
36	Arkansas	8.3
33	California	8.4
38	Colorado	8.1
25	Connecticut	8.8
8	Delaware	9.6
50	Florida	6.6
31	Georgia	8.5
8	Hawaii	9.6
23	Idaho	8.9
40	Illinois	7.9
20	Indiana	9.2
44	Iowa	7.7
27	Kansas	8.7
7	Kentucky	9.7
39	Louisiana	8.0
3	Maine	10.3
15	Maryland	9.4
8	Massachusetts	9.6
4	Michigan	9.9
42	Minnesota	7.8
49	Mississippi	7.0
33	Missouri	8.4
8	Montana	9.6
48	Nebraska	7.1
28	Nevada	8.6
2	New Hampshire	10.4
28	New Jersey	8.6
31	New Mexico	8.5
25	New York	8.8
45	North Carolina	7.6
40	North Dakota	7.9
8	Ohio	9.6
23	Oklahoma	8.9
28	Oregon	8.6
17	Pennsylvania	9.3
1	Rhode Island	10.6
36	South Carolina	8.3
47	South Dakota	7.2
22	Tennessee	9.0
46	Texas	7.3
33	Utah	8.4
4	Vermont	9.9
17	Virginia	9.3
17	Washington	9.3
8	West Virginia	9.6
15	Wisconsin	9.4
20	Wyoming	9.2

RANK ORDER

RANK	STATE	PERCENT
1	Rhode Island	10.6
2	New Hampshire	10.4
3	Maine	10.3
4	Michigan	9.9
4	Vermont	9.9
6	Arizona	9.8
7	Kentucky	9.7
8	Alaska	9.6
8	Delaware	9.6
8	Hawaii	9.6
8	Massachusetts	9.6
8	Montana	9.6
8	Ohio	9.6
8	West Virginia	9.6
15	Maryland	9.4
15	Wisconsin	9.4
17	Pennsylvania	9.3
17	Virginia	9.3
17	Washington	9.3
20	Indiana	9.2
20	Wyoming	9.2
22	Tennessee	9.0
23	Idaho	8.9
23	Oklahoma	8.9
25	Connecticut	8.8
25	New York	8.8
27	Kansas	8.7
28	Nevada	8.6
28	New Jersey	8.6
28	Oregon	8.6
31	Georgia	8.5
31	New Mexico	8.5
33	California	8.4
33	Missouri	8.4
33	Utah	8.4
36	Arkansas	8.3
36	South Carolina	8.3
38	Colorado	8.1
39	Louisiana	8.0
40	Illinois	7.9
40	North Dakota	7.9
42	Alabama	7.8
42	Minnesota	7.8
44	Iowa	7.7
45	North Carolina	7.6
46	Texas	7.3
47	South Dakota	7.2
48	Nebraska	7.1
49	Mississippi	7.0
50	Florida	6.6

District of Columbia	9.6

Source: U.S. Department of Health and Human Services, Centers for Disease Control and Prevention
   "2008 Behavioral Risk Factor Surveillance Summary Prevalence Data" (http://apps.nccd.cdc.gov/brfss/)
*Percent of adults who answered yes to the questions "Have you ever been told by a doctor, nurse, or other health professional that you had asthma?" and "Do you still have asthma?"

Percent of Adults Who Have Been Told They Have Arthritis: 2007

National Median = 27.5%*

ALPHA ORDER				RANK ORDER		
RANK	**STATE**	**PERCENT**		**RANK**	**STATE**	**PERCENT**
2	Alabama	34.7		1	West Virginia	35.5
43	Alaska	24.9		2	Alabama	34.7
41	Arizona	25.3		3	Tennessee	34.0
11	Arkansas	30.7		4	Maine	32.2
50	California	20.8		4	Ohio	32.2
46	Colorado	23.9		6	Pennsylvania	32.1
39	Connecticut	25.5		7	Missouri	31.9
10	Delaware	31.0		8	Kentucky	31.6
44	Florida	24.3		9	Michigan	31.4
26	Georgia	27.5		10	Delaware	31.0
45	Hawaii	24.1		11	Arkansas	30.7
38	Idaho	25.8		12	Mississippi	30.5
32	Illinois	26.9		13	Indiana	30.4
13	Indiana	30.4		14	Oklahoma	30.3
31	Iowa	27.1		15	South Carolina	29.5
26	Kansas	27.5		16	Rhode Island	29.3
8	Kentucky	31.6		17	North Carolina	29.1
40	Louisiana	25.4		18	Montana	29.0
4	Maine	32.2		19	New Hampshire	28.7
24	Maryland	27.8		20	Vermont	28.4
26	Massachusetts	27.5		21	New York	28.1
9	Michigan	31.4		22	Nebraska	28.0
48	Minnesota	22.9		23	Wyoming	27.9
12	Mississippi	30.5		24	Maryland	27.8
7	Missouri	31.9		24	Wisconsin	27.8
18	Montana	29.0		26	Georgia	27.5
22	Nebraska	28.0		26	Kansas	27.5
42	Nevada	25.2		26	Massachusetts	27.5
19	New Hampshire	28.7		29	Washington	27.4
36	New Jersey	26.7		30	New Mexico	27.2
30	New Mexico	27.2		31	Iowa	27.1
21	New York	28.1		32	Illinois	26.9
17	North Carolina	29.1		32	North Dakota	26.9
32	North Dakota	26.9		34	South Dakota	26.8
4	Ohio	32.2		34	Virginia	26.8
14	Oklahoma	30.3		36	New Jersey	26.7
37	Oregon	26.4		37	Oregon	26.4
6	Pennsylvania	32.1		38	Idaho	25.8
16	Rhode Island	29.3		39	Connecticut	25.5
15	South Carolina	29.5		40	Louisiana	25.4
34	South Dakota	26.8		41	Arizona	25.3
3	Tennessee	34.0		42	Nevada	25.2
47	Texas	23.7		43	Alaska	24.9
49	Utah	21.8		44	Florida	24.3
20	Vermont	28.4		45	Hawaii	24.1
34	Virginia	26.8		46	Colorado	23.9
29	Washington	27.4		47	Texas	23.7
1	West Virginia	35.5		48	Minnesota	22.9
24	Wisconsin	27.8		49	Utah	21.8
23	Wyoming	27.9		50	California	20.8
					District of Columbia	23.6

Source: U.S. Department of Health and Human Services, Centers for Disease Control and Prevention
   "2007 Behavioral Risk Factor Surveillance Summary Prevalence Data" (http://apps.nccd.cdc.gov/brfss/)
*Of population 18 years old and older.

Percent of Adults Who Have Been Told They Have Diabetes: 2008

National Median = 8.3% of Adults*

ALPHA ORDER

RANK	STATE	PERCENT
3	Alabama	11.2
44	Alaska	6.7
31	Arizona	7.8
13	Arkansas	9.5
21	California	8.5
49	Colorado	6.0
43	Connecticut	6.8
24	Delaware	8.3
13	Florida	9.5
8	Georgia	9.9
27	Hawaii	8.2
39	Idaho	7.0
24	Illinois	8.3
12	Indiana	9.6
39	Iowa	7.0
28	Kansas	8.1
8	Kentucky	9.9
4	Louisiana	10.7
24	Maine	8.3
19	Maryland	8.7
36	Massachusetts	7.2
16	Michigan	9.1
50	Minnesota	5.9
2	Mississippi	11.3
16	Missouri	9.1
46	Montana	6.5
31	Nebraska	7.8
20	Nevada	8.6
36	New Hampshire	7.2
22	New Jersey	8.4
29	New Mexico	7.9
22	New York	8.4
15	North Carolina	9.3
33	North Dakota	7.6
8	Ohio	9.9
6	Oklahoma	10.1
41	Oregon	6.9
18	Pennsylvania	8.8
34	Rhode Island	7.4
6	South Carolina	10.1
45	South Dakota	6.6
5	Tennessee	10.4
11	Texas	9.7
48	Utah	6.1
47	Vermont	6.4
29	Virginia	7.9
41	Washington	6.9
1	West Virginia	11.9
36	Wisconsin	7.2
34	Wyoming	7.4

RANK ORDER

RANK	STATE	PERCENT
1	West Virginia	11.9
2	Mississippi	11.3
3	Alabama	11.2
4	Louisiana	10.7
5	Tennessee	10.4
6	Oklahoma	10.1
6	South Carolina	10.1
8	Georgia	9.9
8	Kentucky	9.9
8	Ohio	9.9
11	Texas	9.7
12	Indiana	9.6
13	Arkansas	9.5
13	Florida	9.5
15	North Carolina	9.3
16	Michigan	9.1
16	Missouri	9.1
18	Pennsylvania	8.8
19	Maryland	8.7
20	Nevada	8.6
21	California	8.5
22	New Jersey	8.4
22	New York	8.4
24	Delaware	8.3
24	Illinois	8.3
24	Maine	8.3
27	Hawaii	8.2
28	Kansas	8.1
29	New Mexico	7.9
29	Virginia	7.9
31	Arizona	7.8
31	Nebraska	7.8
33	North Dakota	7.6
34	Rhode Island	7.4
34	Wyoming	7.4
36	Massachusetts	7.2
36	New Hampshire	7.2
36	Wisconsin	7.2
39	Idaho	7.0
39	Iowa	7.0
41	Oregon	6.9
41	Washington	6.9
43	Connecticut	6.8
44	Alaska	6.7
45	South Dakota	6.6
46	Montana	6.5
47	Vermont	6.4
48	Utah	6.1
49	Colorado	6.0
50	Minnesota	5.9

	District of Columbia	8.0

Source: U.S. Department of Health and Human Services, Centers for Disease Control and Prevention
   "2008 Behavioral Risk Factor Surveillance Summary Prevalence Data" (http://apps.nccd.cdc.gov/brfss/)
*Of population 18 years old and older. Does not include pregnancy-related diabetes.

Percent of Adults Reporting Serious Psychological Distress: 2007

National Percent = 11.1% of Population*

ALPHA ORDER				RANK ORDER		
RANK	STATE	PERCENT		RANK	STATE	PERCENT
24	Alabama	11.5		1	West Virginia	14.4
28	Alaska	11.3		2	Oklahoma	14.0
18	Arizona	12.0		3	Tennessee	13.7
5	Arkansas	13.0		4	Kentucky	13.6
47	California	9.8		5	Arkansas	13.0
30	Colorado	11.2		5	Missouri	13.0
45	Connecticut	10.1		7	Indiana	12.8
39	Delaware	10.5		7	Rhode Island	12.8
44	Florida	10.2		9	Louisiana	12.7
16	Georgia	12.1		9	New Mexico	12.7
50	Hawaii	8.2		11	Utah	12.6
24	Idaho	11.5		11	Wyoming	12.6
43	Illinois	10.3		13	Maine	12.5
7	Indiana	12.8		14	North Dakota	12.3
27	Iowa	11.4		15	South Carolina	12.2
22	Kansas	11.9		16	Georgia	12.1
4	Kentucky	13.6		16	Nebraska	12.1
9	Louisiana	12.7		18	Arizona	12.0
13	Maine	12.5		18	Michigan	12.0
48	Maryland	9.7		18	Mississippi	12.0
41	Massachusetts	10.4		18	Nevada	12.0
18	Michigan	12.0		22	Kansas	11.9
35	Minnesota	10.9		23	Vermont	11.8
18	Mississippi	12.0		24	Alabama	11.5
5	Missouri	13.0		24	Idaho	11.5
28	Montana	11.3		24	Ohio	11.5
16	Nebraska	12.1		27	Iowa	11.4
18	Nevada	12.0		28	Alaska	11.3
30	New Hampshire	11.2		28	Montana	11.3
48	New Jersey	9.7		30	Colorado	11.2
9	New Mexico	12.7		30	New Hampshire	11.2
33	New York	11.0		32	Wisconsin	11.1
35	North Carolina	10.9		33	New York	11.0
14	North Dakota	12.3		33	Oregon	11.0
24	Ohio	11.5		35	Minnesota	10.9
2	Oklahoma	14.0		35	North Carolina	10.9
33	Oregon	11.0		35	Virginia	10.9
39	Pennsylvania	10.5		38	Texas	10.7
7	Rhode Island	12.8		39	Delaware	10.5
15	South Carolina	12.2		39	Pennsylvania	10.5
45	South Dakota	10.1		41	Massachusetts	10.4
3	Tennessee	13.7		41	Washington	10.4
38	Texas	10.7		43	Illinois	10.3
11	Utah	12.6		44	Florida	10.2
23	Vermont	11.8		45	Connecticut	10.1
35	Virginia	10.9		45	South Dakota	10.1
41	Washington	10.4		47	California	9.8
1	West Virginia	14.4		48	Maryland	9.7
32	Wisconsin	11.1		48	New Jersey	9.7
11	Wyoming	12.6		50	Hawaii	8.2

	District of Columbia	11.5

Source: U.S. Department of Health and Human Services, Substance Abuse and Mental Health Services Administration
"2006-2007 National Surveys on Drug Use and Health" (June 2009, http://www.oas.samhsa.gov/2k7state/toc.cfm)
*Population 18 years and older. Serious psychological distress was previously referred to as serious mental illness. It is defined as having a diagnosable mental, behavioral, or emotional disorder that resulted in functional impairment that substantially interfered with or limited one or more major life activities.

VI. Providers

Health Care Practitioners and Technicians in 2008

National Total = 6,947,090 Practitioners and Technicians*

ALPHA ORDER

RANK ORDER

RANK	STATE	EMPLOYEES	% of USA
22	Alabama	110,320	1.6%
49	Alaska	13,700	0.2%
21	Arizona	118,120	1.7%
33	Arkansas	67,850	1.0%
1	California	641,270	9.2%
25	Colorado	105,140	1.5%
27	Connecticut	89,730	1.3%
45	Delaware	23,590	0.3%
4	Florida	408,110	5.9%
12	Georgia	190,270	2.7%
43	Hawaii	24,590	0.4%
41	Idaho	30,340	0.4%
7	Illinois	304,130	4.4%
16	Indiana	160,980	2.3%
30	Iowa	73,920	1.1%
31	Kansas	69,280	1.0%
24	Kentucky	105,750	1.5%
23	Louisiana	109,400	1.6%
39	Maine	35,310	0.5%
19	Maryland	138,690	2.0%
10	Massachusetts	204,820	2.9%
8	Michigan	237,840	3.4%
17	Minnesota	150,430	2.2%
32	Mississippi	68,810	1.0%
15	Missouri	166,390	2.4%
46	Montana	22,550	0.3%
34	Nebraska	50,350	0.7%
37	Nevada	43,170	0.6%
40	New Hampshire	33,390	0.5%
11	New Jersey	195,020	2.8%
38	New Mexico	39,590	0.6%
3	New York	456,150	6.6%
9	North Carolina	214,050	3.1%
47	North Dakota	19,330	0.3%
6	Ohio	307,730	4.4%
28	Oklahoma	85,150	1.2%
29	Oregon	77,960	1.1%
5	Pennsylvania	343,990	5.0%
42	Rhode Island	29,710	0.4%
26	South Carolina	98,790	1.4%
44	South Dakota	24,160	0.3%
14	Tennessee	168,050	2.4%
2	Texas	487,100	7.0%
35	Utah	48,880	0.7%
48	Vermont	16,390	0.2%
13	Virginia	168,940	2.4%
20	Washington	135,260	1.9%
36	West Virginia	48,030	0.7%
18	Wisconsin	144,790	2.1%
50	Wyoming	11,650	0.2%

RANK	STATE	EMPLOYEES	% of USA
1	California	641,270	9.2%
2	Texas	487,100	7.0%
3	New York	456,150	6.6%
4	Florida	408,110	5.9%
5	Pennsylvania	343,990	5.0%
6	Ohio	307,730	4.4%
7	Illinois	304,130	4.4%
8	Michigan	237,840	3.4%
9	North Carolina	214,050	3.1%
10	Massachusetts	204,820	2.9%
11	New Jersey	195,020	2.8%
12	Georgia	190,270	2.7%
13	Virginia	168,940	2.4%
14	Tennessee	168,050	2.4%
15	Missouri	166,390	2.4%
16	Indiana	160,980	2.3%
17	Minnesota	150,430	2.2%
18	Wisconsin	144,790	2.1%
19	Maryland	138,690	2.0%
20	Washington	135,260	1.9%
21	Arizona	118,120	1.7%
22	Alabama	110,320	1.6%
23	Louisiana	109,400	1.6%
24	Kentucky	105,750	1.5%
25	Colorado	105,140	1.5%
26	South Carolina	98,790	1.4%
27	Connecticut	89,730	1.3%
28	Oklahoma	85,150	1.2%
29	Oregon	77,960	1.1%
30	Iowa	73,920	1.1%
31	Kansas	69,280	1.0%
32	Mississippi	68,810	1.0%
33	Arkansas	67,850	1.0%
34	Nebraska	50,350	0.7%
35	Utah	48,880	0.7%
36	West Virginia	48,030	0.7%
37	Nevada	43,170	0.6%
38	New Mexico	39,590	0.6%
39	Maine	35,310	0.5%
40	New Hampshire	33,390	0.5%
41	Idaho	30,340	0.4%
42	Rhode Island	29,710	0.4%
43	Hawaii	24,590	0.4%
44	South Dakota	24,160	0.3%
45	Delaware	23,590	0.3%
46	Montana	22,550	0.3%
47	North Dakota	19,330	0.3%
48	Vermont	16,390	0.2%
49	Alaska	13,700	0.2%
50	Wyoming	11,650	0.2%
	District of Columbia	25,860	0.4%

Source: U.S. Department of Labor, Bureau of Labor Statistics
    "Occupational Employment and Wages, 2008" (http://www.bls.gov/oes/)
*Does not include self-employed. Includes various doctors, dentists, nurses, therapists, optometrists, paramedics, and technicians. Does not include assistants and aides listed under health care support occupations. Veterinarians and veterinarian technicians have been subtracted from the totals.

Rate of Health Care Practitioners and Technicians in 2008

National Rate = 2,282 Practitioners and Technicians per 100,000 Population*

ALPHA ORDER

RANK	STATE	RATE
27	Alabama	2,359
43	Alaska	1,991
47	Arizona	1,817
26	Arkansas	2,366
49	California	1,753
38	Colorado	2,130
16	Connecticut	2,562
10	Delaware	2,692
34	Florida	2,215
45	Georgia	1,962
46	Hawaii	1,910
44	Idaho	1,986
25	Illinois	2,368
18	Indiana	2,520
20	Iowa	2,469
19	Kansas	2,477
21	Kentucky	2,466
22	Louisiana	2,458
11	Maine	2,676
23	Maryland	2,451
1	Massachusetts	3,130
24	Michigan	2,378
4	Minnesota	2,876
29	Mississippi	2,340
7	Missouri	2,793
31	Montana	2,329
5	Nebraska	2,826
50	Nevada	1,650
17	New Hampshire	2,526
33	New Jersey	2,251
42	New Mexico	1,993
28	New York	2,343
32	North Carolina	2,315
2	North Dakota	3,014
12	Ohio	2,669
30	Oklahoma	2,337
39	Oregon	2,061
8	Pennsylvania	2,737
6	Rhode Island	2,820
35	South Carolina	2,194
3	South Dakota	3,003
9	Tennessee	2,693
41	Texas	2,004
48	Utah	1,792
14	Vermont	2,639
37	Virginia	2,167
40	Washington	2,060
13	West Virginia	2,646
15	Wisconsin	2,573
36	Wyoming	2,186

RANK ORDER

RANK	STATE	RATE
1	Massachusetts	3,130
2	North Dakota	3,014
3	South Dakota	3,003
4	Minnesota	2,876
5	Nebraska	2,826
6	Rhode Island	2,820
7	Missouri	2,793
8	Pennsylvania	2,737
9	Tennessee	2,693
10	Delaware	2,692
11	Maine	2,676
12	Ohio	2,669
13	West Virginia	2,646
14	Vermont	2,639
15	Wisconsin	2,573
16	Connecticut	2,562
17	New Hampshire	2,526
18	Indiana	2,520
19	Kansas	2,477
20	Iowa	2,469
21	Kentucky	2,466
22	Louisiana	2,458
23	Maryland	2,451
24	Michigan	2,378
25	Illinois	2,368
26	Arkansas	2,366
27	Alabama	2,359
28	New York	2,343
29	Mississippi	2,340
30	Oklahoma	2,337
31	Montana	2,329
32	North Carolina	2,315
33	New Jersey	2,251
34	Florida	2,215
35	South Carolina	2,194
36	Wyoming	2,186
37	Virginia	2,167
38	Colorado	2,130
39	Oregon	2,061
40	Washington	2,060
41	Texas	2,004
42	New Mexico	1,993
43	Alaska	1,991
44	Idaho	1,986
45	Georgia	1,962
46	Hawaii	1,910
47	Arizona	1,817
48	Utah	1,792
49	California	1,753
50	Nevada	1,650

	District of Columbia	4,383

Source: CQ Press using data from U.S. Department of Labor, Bureau of Labor Statistics
"Occupational Employment and Wages, 2008" (http://www.bls.gov/oes/)
*Does not include self-employed. Includes various doctors, dentists, nurses, therapists, optometrists, paramedics, and technicians. Does not include assistants and aides listed under health care support occupations. Veterinarians and veterinarian technicians have been subtracted from the totals.

Average Annual Wages of Health Care Practitioners and Technicians in 2008

National Average = $67,890*

<table>
<tr><td colspan="3"><u>ALPHA ORDER</u></td><td colspan="3"><u>RANK ORDER</u></td></tr>
<tr><td>RANK</td><td>STATE</td><td>WAGES</td><td>RANK</td><td>STATE</td><td>WAGES</td></tr>
<tr><td>45</td><td>Alabama</td><td>$57,410</td><td>1</td><td>Hawaii</td><td>$80,410</td></tr>
<tr><td>7</td><td>Alaska</td><td>76,600</td><td>2</td><td>California</td><td>80,090</td></tr>
<tr><td>20</td><td>Arizona</td><td>67,610</td><td>3</td><td>New Jersey</td><td>78,450</td></tr>
<tr><td>43</td><td>Arkansas</td><td>57,780</td><td>4</td><td>Maryland</td><td>78,400</td></tr>
<tr><td>2</td><td>California</td><td>80,090</td><td>5</td><td>Massachusetts</td><td>77,300</td></tr>
<tr><td>17</td><td>Colorado</td><td>68,600</td><td>6</td><td>Oregon</td><td>76,760</td></tr>
<tr><td>10</td><td>Connecticut</td><td>74,700</td><td>7</td><td>Alaska</td><td>76,600</td></tr>
<tr><td>12</td><td>Delaware</td><td>73,900</td><td>8</td><td>Nevada</td><td>76,050</td></tr>
<tr><td>27</td><td>Florida</td><td>64,760</td><td>9</td><td>New York</td><td>75,400</td></tr>
<tr><td>25</td><td>Georgia</td><td>64,960</td><td>10</td><td>Connecticut</td><td>74,700</td></tr>
<tr><td>1</td><td>Hawaii</td><td>80,410</td><td>11</td><td>Washington</td><td>74,350</td></tr>
<tr><td>35</td><td>Idaho</td><td>60,920</td><td>12</td><td>Delaware</td><td>73,900</td></tr>
<tr><td>24</td><td>Illinois</td><td>65,950</td><td>13</td><td>Minnesota</td><td>72,850</td></tr>
<tr><td>31</td><td>Indiana</td><td>62,530</td><td>14</td><td>Rhode Island</td><td>71,830</td></tr>
<tr><td>49</td><td>Iowa</td><td>56,930</td><td>15</td><td>New Hampshire</td><td>69,310</td></tr>
<tr><td>36</td><td>Kansas</td><td>60,740</td><td>16</td><td>Wisconsin</td><td>68,880</td></tr>
<tr><td>38</td><td>Kentucky</td><td>60,010</td><td>17</td><td>Colorado</td><td>68,600</td></tr>
<tr><td>41</td><td>Louisiana</td><td>58,380</td><td>18</td><td>Michigan</td><td>67,920</td></tr>
<tr><td>19</td><td>Maine</td><td>67,850</td><td>19</td><td>Maine</td><td>67,850</td></tr>
<tr><td>4</td><td>Maryland</td><td>78,400</td><td>20</td><td>Arizona</td><td>67,610</td></tr>
<tr><td>5</td><td>Massachusetts</td><td>77,300</td><td>21</td><td>Virginia</td><td>66,810</td></tr>
<tr><td>18</td><td>Michigan</td><td>67,920</td><td>22</td><td>Vermont</td><td>66,420</td></tr>
<tr><td>13</td><td>Minnesota</td><td>72,850</td><td>23</td><td>New Mexico</td><td>66,190</td></tr>
<tr><td>44</td><td>Mississippi</td><td>57,690</td><td>24</td><td>Illinois</td><td>65,950</td></tr>
<tr><td>40</td><td>Missouri</td><td>58,650</td><td>25</td><td>Georgia</td><td>64,960</td></tr>
<tr><td>39</td><td>Montana</td><td>58,970</td><td>26</td><td>Ohio</td><td>64,900</td></tr>
<tr><td>42</td><td>Nebraska</td><td>58,340</td><td>27</td><td>Florida</td><td>64,760</td></tr>
<tr><td>8</td><td>Nevada</td><td>76,050</td><td>28</td><td>North Carolina</td><td>64,390</td></tr>
<tr><td>15</td><td>New Hampshire</td><td>69,310</td><td>29</td><td>Texas</td><td>64,080</td></tr>
<tr><td>3</td><td>New Jersey</td><td>78,450</td><td>30</td><td>Pennsylvania</td><td>63,200</td></tr>
<tr><td>23</td><td>New Mexico</td><td>66,190</td><td>31</td><td>Indiana</td><td>62,530</td></tr>
<tr><td>9</td><td>New York</td><td>75,400</td><td>32</td><td>Utah</td><td>62,510</td></tr>
<tr><td>28</td><td>North Carolina</td><td>64,390</td><td>33</td><td>Wyoming</td><td>62,350</td></tr>
<tr><td>48</td><td>North Dakota</td><td>57,200</td><td>34</td><td>South Carolina</td><td>61,340</td></tr>
<tr><td>26</td><td>Ohio</td><td>64,900</td><td>35</td><td>Idaho</td><td>60,920</td></tr>
<tr><td>50</td><td>Oklahoma</td><td>56,680</td><td>36</td><td>Kansas</td><td>60,740</td></tr>
<tr><td>6</td><td>Oregon</td><td>76,760</td><td>37</td><td>Tennessee</td><td>60,110</td></tr>
<tr><td>30</td><td>Pennsylvania</td><td>63,200</td><td>38</td><td>Kentucky</td><td>60,010</td></tr>
<tr><td>14</td><td>Rhode Island</td><td>71,830</td><td>39</td><td>Montana</td><td>58,970</td></tr>
<tr><td>34</td><td>South Carolina</td><td>61,340</td><td>40</td><td>Missouri</td><td>58,650</td></tr>
<tr><td>47</td><td>South Dakota</td><td>57,270</td><td>41</td><td>Louisiana</td><td>58,380</td></tr>
<tr><td>37</td><td>Tennessee</td><td>60,110</td><td>42</td><td>Nebraska</td><td>58,340</td></tr>
<tr><td>29</td><td>Texas</td><td>64,080</td><td>43</td><td>Arkansas</td><td>57,780</td></tr>
<tr><td>32</td><td>Utah</td><td>62,510</td><td>44</td><td>Mississippi</td><td>57,690</td></tr>
<tr><td>22</td><td>Vermont</td><td>66,420</td><td>45</td><td>Alabama</td><td>57,410</td></tr>
<tr><td>21</td><td>Virginia</td><td>66,810</td><td>45</td><td>West Virginia</td><td>57,410</td></tr>
<tr><td>11</td><td>Washington</td><td>74,350</td><td>47</td><td>South Dakota</td><td>57,270</td></tr>
<tr><td>45</td><td>West Virginia</td><td>57,410</td><td>48</td><td>North Dakota</td><td>57,200</td></tr>
<tr><td>16</td><td>Wisconsin</td><td>68,880</td><td>49</td><td>Iowa</td><td>56,930</td></tr>
<tr><td>33</td><td>Wyoming</td><td>62,350</td><td>50</td><td>Oklahoma</td><td>56,680</td></tr>
<tr><td></td><td></td><td></td><td colspan="2">District of Columbia</td><td>73,570</td></tr>
</table>

Source: U.S. Department of Labor, Bureau of Labor Statistics
  "Occupational Employment and Wages, 2008" (http://www.bls.gov/oes/)
*Does not include self-employed. Includes various doctors, dentists, nurses, therapists, optometrists, paramedics, and technicians. Does not include assistants and aides listed under health care support occupations.

Physicians in 2008

National Total = 940,171 Physicians*

ALPHA ORDER					RANK ORDER			
RANK	STATE	PHYSICIANS	% of USA		RANK	STATE	PHYSICIANS	% of USA
27	Alabama	11,371	1.2%		1	California	114,490	12.2%
49	Alaska	1,730	0.2%		2	New York	85,142	9.1%
19	Arizona	16,133	1.7%		3	Texas	57,939	6.2%
31	Arkansas	6,631	0.7%		4	Florida	56,027	6.0%
1	California	114,490	12.2%		5	Pennsylvania	43,726	4.7%
23	Colorado	14,870	1.6%		6	Illinois	40,255	4.3%
22	Connecticut	14,931	1.6%		7	Ohio	34,743	3.7%
46	Delaware	2,477	0.3%		8	Massachusetts	33,815	3.6%
4	Florida	56,027	6.0%		9	New Jersey	30,700	3.3%
14	Georgia	23,714	2.5%		10	Michigan	28,567	3.0%
39	Hawaii	4,723	0.5%		11	North Carolina	26,744	2.8%
43	Idaho	3,063	0.3%		12	Maryland	26,602	2.8%
6	Illinois	40,255	4.3%		13	Virginia	24,634	2.6%
21	Indiana	15,642	1.7%		14	Georgia	23,714	2.5%
32	Iowa	6,564	0.7%		15	Washington	20,842	2.2%
29	Kansas	7,325	0.8%		16	Tennessee	18,416	2.0%
28	Kentucky	11,099	1.2%		17	Minnesota	17,462	1.9%
24	Louisiana	13,009	1.4%		18	Wisconsin	16,718	1.8%
42	Maine	4,304	0.5%		19	Arizona	16,133	1.7%
12	Maryland	26,602	2.8%		20	Missouri	16,110	1.7%
8	Massachusetts	33,815	3.6%		21	Indiana	15,642	1.7%
10	Michigan	28,567	3.0%		22	Connecticut	14,931	1.6%
17	Minnesota	17,462	1.9%		23	Colorado	14,870	1.6%
34	Mississippi	6,023	0.6%		24	Louisiana	13,009	1.4%
20	Missouri	16,110	1.7%		25	Oregon	12,466	1.3%
45	Montana	2,604	0.3%		26	South Carolina	11,747	1.2%
37	Nebraska	5,042	0.5%		27	Alabama	11,371	1.2%
35	Nevada	5,697	0.6%		28	Kentucky	11,099	1.2%
41	New Hampshire	4,377	0.5%		29	Kansas	7,325	0.8%
9	New Jersey	30,700	3.3%		30	Oklahoma	7,317	0.8%
36	New Mexico	5,612	0.6%		31	Arkansas	6,631	0.7%
2	New York	85,142	9.1%		32	Iowa	6,564	0.7%
11	North Carolina	26,744	2.8%		33	Utah	6,467	0.7%
48	North Dakota	1,787	0.2%		34	Mississippi	6,023	0.6%
7	Ohio	34,743	3.7%		35	Nevada	5,697	0.6%
30	Oklahoma	7,317	0.8%		36	New Mexico	5,612	0.6%
25	Oregon	12,466	1.3%		37	Nebraska	5,042	0.5%
5	Pennsylvania	43,726	4.7%		38	West Virginia	4,798	0.5%
40	Rhode Island	4,452	0.5%		39	Hawaii	4,723	0.5%
26	South Carolina	11,747	1.2%		40	Rhode Island	4,452	0.5%
47	South Dakota	2,046	0.2%		41	New Hampshire	4,377	0.5%
16	Tennessee	18,416	2.0%		42	Maine	4,304	0.5%
3	Texas	57,939	6.2%		43	Idaho	3,063	0.3%
33	Utah	6,467	0.7%		44	Vermont	2,762	0.3%
44	Vermont	2,762	0.3%		45	Montana	2,604	0.3%
13	Virginia	24,634	2.6%		46	Delaware	2,477	0.3%
15	Washington	20,842	2.2%		47	South Dakota	2,046	0.2%
38	West Virginia	4,798	0.5%		48	North Dakota	1,787	0.2%
18	Wisconsin	16,718	1.8%		49	Alaska	1,730	0.2%
50	Wyoming	1,212	0.1%		50	Wyoming	1,212	0.1%
					District of Columbia		5,244	0.6%

Source: American Medical Association (Chicago, Illinois)
   "Physician Characteristics and Distribution in the U.S." (2010 Edition)
*As of December 31, 2008. Total does not include 14,053 physicians in the U.S. territories and possessions, at APOs and FPOs, or whose addresses are unknown.

Rate of Physicians in 2008

National Rate = 309 Physicians per 100,000 Population*

<table>
<tr><td colspan="3">ALPHA ORDER</td><td colspan="3">RANK ORDER</td></tr>
<tr><th>RANK</th><th>STATE</th><th>RATE</th><th>RANK</th><th>STATE</th><th>RATE</th></tr>
<tr><td>41</td><td>Alabama</td><td>243</td><td>1</td><td>Massachusetts</td><td>517</td></tr>
<tr><td>37</td><td>Alaska</td><td>251</td><td>2</td><td>Maryland</td><td>470</td></tr>
<tr><td>38</td><td>Arizona</td><td>248</td><td>3</td><td>Vermont</td><td>445</td></tr>
<tr><td>44</td><td>Arkansas</td><td>231</td><td>4</td><td>New York</td><td>437</td></tr>
<tr><td>16</td><td>California</td><td>313</td><td>5</td><td>Connecticut</td><td>426</td></tr>
<tr><td>19</td><td>Colorado</td><td>301</td><td>6</td><td>Rhode Island</td><td>423</td></tr>
<tr><td>5</td><td>Connecticut</td><td>426</td><td>7</td><td>Hawaii</td><td>367</td></tr>
<tr><td>26</td><td>Delaware</td><td>283</td><td>8</td><td>New Jersey</td><td>354</td></tr>
<tr><td>18</td><td>Florida</td><td>304</td><td>9</td><td>Pennsylvania</td><td>348</td></tr>
<tr><td>39</td><td>Georgia</td><td>245</td><td>10</td><td>Minnesota</td><td>334</td></tr>
<tr><td>7</td><td>Hawaii</td><td>367</td><td>11</td><td>New Hampshire</td><td>331</td></tr>
<tr><td>49</td><td>Idaho</td><td>201</td><td>12</td><td>Oregon</td><td>330</td></tr>
<tr><td>16</td><td>Illinois</td><td>313</td><td>13</td><td>Maine</td><td>326</td></tr>
<tr><td>39</td><td>Indiana</td><td>245</td><td>14</td><td>Washington</td><td>317</td></tr>
<tr><td>46</td><td>Iowa</td><td>219</td><td>15</td><td>Virginia</td><td>316</td></tr>
<tr><td>33</td><td>Kansas</td><td>262</td><td>16</td><td>California</td><td>313</td></tr>
<tr><td>35</td><td>Kentucky</td><td>259</td><td>16</td><td>Illinois</td><td>313</td></tr>
<tr><td>23</td><td>Louisiana</td><td>292</td><td>18</td><td>Florida</td><td>304</td></tr>
<tr><td>13</td><td>Maine</td><td>326</td><td>19</td><td>Colorado</td><td>301</td></tr>
<tr><td>2</td><td>Maryland</td><td>470</td><td>19</td><td>Ohio</td><td>301</td></tr>
<tr><td>1</td><td>Massachusetts</td><td>517</td><td>21</td><td>Wisconsin</td><td>297</td></tr>
<tr><td>25</td><td>Michigan</td><td>286</td><td>22</td><td>Tennessee</td><td>295</td></tr>
<tr><td>10</td><td>Minnesota</td><td>334</td><td>23</td><td>Louisiana</td><td>292</td></tr>
<tr><td>48</td><td>Mississippi</td><td>205</td><td>24</td><td>North Carolina</td><td>289</td></tr>
<tr><td>30</td><td>Missouri</td><td>270</td><td>25</td><td>Michigan</td><td>286</td></tr>
<tr><td>31</td><td>Montana</td><td>269</td><td>26</td><td>Delaware</td><td>283</td></tr>
<tr><td>26</td><td>Nebraska</td><td>283</td><td>26</td><td>Nebraska</td><td>283</td></tr>
<tr><td>47</td><td>Nevada</td><td>218</td><td>28</td><td>New Mexico</td><td>282</td></tr>
<tr><td>11</td><td>New Hampshire</td><td>331</td><td>29</td><td>North Dakota</td><td>279</td></tr>
<tr><td>8</td><td>New Jersey</td><td>354</td><td>30</td><td>Missouri</td><td>270</td></tr>
<tr><td>28</td><td>New Mexico</td><td>282</td><td>31</td><td>Montana</td><td>269</td></tr>
<tr><td>4</td><td>New York</td><td>437</td><td>32</td><td>West Virginia</td><td>264</td></tr>
<tr><td>24</td><td>North Carolina</td><td>289</td><td>33</td><td>Kansas</td><td>262</td></tr>
<tr><td>29</td><td>North Dakota</td><td>279</td><td>34</td><td>South Carolina</td><td>261</td></tr>
<tr><td>19</td><td>Ohio</td><td>301</td><td>35</td><td>Kentucky</td><td>259</td></tr>
<tr><td>49</td><td>Oklahoma</td><td>201</td><td>36</td><td>South Dakota</td><td>254</td></tr>
<tr><td>12</td><td>Oregon</td><td>330</td><td>37</td><td>Alaska</td><td>251</td></tr>
<tr><td>9</td><td>Pennsylvania</td><td>348</td><td>38</td><td>Arizona</td><td>248</td></tr>
<tr><td>6</td><td>Rhode Island</td><td>423</td><td>39</td><td>Georgia</td><td>245</td></tr>
<tr><td>34</td><td>South Carolina</td><td>261</td><td>39</td><td>Indiana</td><td>245</td></tr>
<tr><td>36</td><td>South Dakota</td><td>254</td><td>41</td><td>Alabama</td><td>243</td></tr>
<tr><td>22</td><td>Tennessee</td><td>295</td><td>42</td><td>Texas</td><td>238</td></tr>
<tr><td>42</td><td>Texas</td><td>238</td><td>43</td><td>Utah</td><td>237</td></tr>
<tr><td>43</td><td>Utah</td><td>237</td><td>44</td><td>Arkansas</td><td>231</td></tr>
<tr><td>3</td><td>Vermont</td><td>445</td><td>45</td><td>Wyoming</td><td>227</td></tr>
<tr><td>15</td><td>Virginia</td><td>316</td><td>46</td><td>Iowa</td><td>219</td></tr>
<tr><td>14</td><td>Washington</td><td>317</td><td>47</td><td>Nevada</td><td>218</td></tr>
<tr><td>32</td><td>West Virginia</td><td>264</td><td>48</td><td>Mississippi</td><td>205</td></tr>
<tr><td>21</td><td>Wisconsin</td><td>297</td><td>49</td><td>Idaho</td><td>201</td></tr>
<tr><td>45</td><td>Wyoming</td><td>227</td><td>49</td><td>Oklahoma</td><td>201</td></tr>
<tr><td></td><td></td><td></td><td></td><td>District of Columbia</td><td>889</td></tr>
</table>

Source: CQ Press using data from American Medical Association (Chicago, Illinois)
   "Physician Characteristics and Distribution in the U.S." (2010 Edition)
*As of December 31, 2008. National rate does not include physicians in the U.S. territories and possessions, at APOs and FPOs, or whose addresses are unknown.

Percent of Physicians Who Are Female: 2008

National Percent = 28.9% of Physicians*

ALPHA ORDER

RANK ORDER

RANK	STATE	PERCENT	RANK	STATE	PERCENT
39	Alabama	23.2	1	Massachusetts	35.4
9	Alaska	31.6	2	Maryland	33.5
30	Arizona	26.0	3	New York	33.1
45	Arkansas	22.6	4	Illinois	33.0
17	California	29.4	4	Rhode Island	33.0
13	Colorado	30.0	6	New Jersey	32.2
10	Connecticut	30.7	7	New Mexico	32.0
11	Delaware	30.4	8	Vermont	31.8
44	Florida	22.7	9	Alaska	31.6
25	Georgia	28.0	10	Connecticut	30.7
21	Hawaii	28.4	11	Delaware	30.4
50	Idaho	18.7	11	Virginia	30.4
4	Illinois	33.0	13	Colorado	30.0
31	Indiana	25.9	14	Michigan	29.6
36	Iowa	23.9	15	Minnesota	29.5
29	Kansas	26.4	15	Pennsylvania	29.5
32	Kentucky	25.5	17	California	29.4
33	Louisiana	25.4	18	Oregon	29.3
28	Maine	27.3	19	Washington	29.1
2	Maryland	33.5	20	Ohio	28.8
1	Massachusetts	35.4	21	Hawaii	28.4
14	Michigan	29.6	22	Missouri	28.2
15	Minnesota	29.5	22	North Carolina	28.2
49	Mississippi	20.8	24	Texas	28.1
22	Missouri	28.2	25	Georgia	28.0
46	Montana	22.3	26	New Hampshire	27.9
33	Nebraska	25.4	27	Wisconsin	27.4
38	Nevada	23.4	28	Maine	27.3
26	New Hampshire	27.9	29	Kansas	26.4
6	New Jersey	32.2	30	Arizona	26.0
7	New Mexico	32.0	31	Indiana	25.9
3	New York	33.1	32	Kentucky	25.5
22	North Carolina	28.2	33	Louisiana	25.4
43	North Dakota	22.8	33	Nebraska	25.4
20	Ohio	28.8	35	Tennessee	24.3
39	Oklahoma	23.2	36	Iowa	23.9
18	Oregon	29.3	36	South Carolina	23.9
15	Pennsylvania	29.5	38	Nevada	23.4
4	Rhode Island	33.0	39	Alabama	23.2
36	South Carolina	23.9	39	Oklahoma	23.2
42	South Dakota	22.9	39	West Virginia	23.2
35	Tennessee	24.3	42	South Dakota	22.9
24	Texas	28.1	43	North Dakota	22.8
48	Utah	21.1	44	Florida	22.7
8	Vermont	31.8	45	Arkansas	22.6
11	Virginia	30.4	46	Montana	22.3
19	Washington	29.1	47	Wyoming	21.7
39	West Virginia	23.2	48	Utah	21.1
27	Wisconsin	27.4	49	Mississippi	20.8
47	Wyoming	21.7	50	Idaho	18.7

District of Columbia   38.4

Source: CQ Press using data from American Medical Association (Chicago, Illinois)
"Physician Characteristics and Distribution in the U.S." (2010 Edition)
*As of December 31, 2008. National percent does not include physicians in the U.S. territories and possessions, at APOs and FPOs, or whose addresses are unknown.

Percent of Physicians Under 35 Years Old in 2008

National Percent = 15.1% of Physicians*

ALPHA ORDER

RANK	STATE	PERCENT
16	Alabama	15.1
47	Alaska	6.7
38	Arizona	11.1
27	Arkansas	13.9
33	California	12.5
37	Colorado	11.4
11	Connecticut	16.3
20	Delaware	14.7
44	Florida	9.4
30	Georgia	13.0
38	Hawaii	11.1
48	Idaho	6.2
5	Illinois	19.2
29	Indiana	13.4
20	Iowa	14.7
22	Kansas	14.6
19	Kentucky	14.8
10	Louisiana	16.8
46	Maine	7.8
17	Maryland	15.0
4	Massachusetts	19.4
6	Michigan	18.8
13	Minnesota	16.2
34	Mississippi	12.0
2	Missouri	19.6
50	Montana	4.4
8	Nebraska	18.4
45	Nevada	8.3
41	New Hampshire	11.0
31	New Jersey	12.9
35	New Mexico	11.8
2	New York	19.6
14	North Carolina	15.6
36	North Dakota	11.5
8	Ohio	18.4
32	Oklahoma	12.8
42	Oregon	10.6
7	Pennsylvania	18.5
1	Rhode Island	19.8
15	South Carolina	15.3
43	South Dakota	9.6
22	Tennessee	14.6
11	Texas	16.3
24	Utah	14.4
28	Vermont	13.7
26	Virginia	14.0
38	Washington	11.1
17	West Virginia	15.0
25	Wisconsin	14.1
49	Wyoming	5.7

RANK ORDER

RANK	STATE	PERCENT
1	Rhode Island	19.8
2	Missouri	19.6
2	New York	19.6
4	Massachusetts	19.4
5	Illinois	19.2
6	Michigan	18.8
7	Pennsylvania	18.5
8	Nebraska	18.4
8	Ohio	18.4
10	Louisiana	16.8
11	Connecticut	16.3
11	Texas	16.3
13	Minnesota	16.2
14	North Carolina	15.6
15	South Carolina	15.3
16	Alabama	15.1
17	Maryland	15.0
17	West Virginia	15.0
19	Kentucky	14.8
20	Delaware	14.7
20	Iowa	14.7
22	Kansas	14.6
22	Tennessee	14.6
24	Utah	14.4
25	Wisconsin	14.1
26	Virginia	14.0
27	Arkansas	13.9
28	Vermont	13.7
29	Indiana	13.4
30	Georgia	13.0
31	New Jersey	12.9
32	Oklahoma	12.8
33	California	12.5
34	Mississippi	12.0
35	New Mexico	11.8
36	North Dakota	11.5
37	Colorado	11.4
38	Arizona	11.1
38	Hawaii	11.1
38	Washington	11.1
41	New Hampshire	11.0
42	Oregon	10.6
43	South Dakota	9.6
44	Florida	9.4
45	Nevada	8.3
46	Maine	7.8
47	Alaska	6.7
48	Idaho	6.2
49	Wyoming	5.7
50	Montana	4.4

District of Columbia	26.7

Source: CQ Press using data from American Medical Association (Chicago, Illinois)
   "Physician Characteristics and Distribution in the U.S." (2010 Edition)
*As of December 31, 2008. National percent does not include physicians in the U.S. territories and possessions, at APOs and FPOs, or whose addresses are unknown.

Percent of Physicians 65 Years Old and Older in 2008

National Percent = 20.3% of Physicians*

ALPHA ORDER

RANK	STATE	PERCENT
44	Alabama	17.3
50	Alaska	16.3
7	Arizona	22.5
29	Arkansas	19.3
4	California	24.1
25	Colorado	19.9
22	Connecticut	20.5
19	Delaware	20.8
1	Florida	27.2
37	Georgia	17.8
8	Hawaii	22.4
9	Idaho	22.1
35	Illinois	18.0
39	Indiana	17.6
31	Iowa	18.8
17	Kansas	20.9
41	Kentucky	17.5
33	Louisiana	18.4
3	Maine	24.3
21	Maryland	20.7
38	Massachusetts	17.7
28	Michigan	19.4
49	Minnesota	16.9
23	Mississippi	20.2
48	Missouri	17.1
2	Montana	25.0
44	Nebraska	17.3
9	Nevada	22.1
15	New Hampshire	21.1
19	New Jersey	20.8
13	New Mexico	21.2
17	New York	20.9
44	North Carolina	17.3
39	North Dakota	17.6
32	Ohio	18.5
16	Oklahoma	21.0
12	Oregon	21.5
27	Pennsylvania	19.7
24	Rhode Island	20.1
30	South Carolina	19.2
33	South Dakota	18.4
43	Tennessee	17.4
44	Texas	17.3
41	Utah	17.5
6	Vermont	22.7
25	Virginia	19.9
13	Washington	21.2
11	West Virginia	22.0
36	Wisconsin	17.9
5	Wyoming	23.8

RANK ORDER

RANK	STATE	PERCENT
1	Florida	27.2
2	Montana	25.0
3	Maine	24.3
4	California	24.1
5	Wyoming	23.8
6	Vermont	22.7
7	Arizona	22.5
8	Hawaii	22.4
9	Idaho	22.1
9	Nevada	22.1
11	West Virginia	22.0
12	Oregon	21.5
13	New Mexico	21.2
13	Washington	21.2
15	New Hampshire	21.1
16	Oklahoma	21.0
17	Kansas	20.9
17	New York	20.9
19	Delaware	20.8
19	New Jersey	20.8
21	Maryland	20.7
22	Connecticut	20.5
23	Mississippi	20.2
24	Rhode Island	20.1
25	Colorado	19.9
25	Virginia	19.9
27	Pennsylvania	19.7
28	Michigan	19.4
29	Arkansas	19.3
30	South Carolina	19.2
31	Iowa	18.8
32	Ohio	18.5
33	Louisiana	18.4
33	South Dakota	18.4
35	Illinois	18.0
36	Wisconsin	17.9
37	Georgia	17.8
38	Massachusetts	17.7
39	Indiana	17.6
39	North Dakota	17.6
41	Kentucky	17.5
41	Utah	17.5
43	Tennessee	17.4
44	Alabama	17.3
44	Nebraska	17.3
44	North Carolina	17.3
44	Texas	17.3
48	Missouri	17.1
49	Minnesota	16.9
50	Alaska	16.3

District of Columbia	20.6

Source: CQ Press using data from American Medical Association (Chicago, Illinois)
"Physician Characteristics and Distribution in the U.S." (2010 Edition)
*As of December 31, 2008. National percent does not include physicians in the U.S. territories and possessions, at APOs and FPOs, or whose addresses are unknown.

Physicians in Patient Care in 2008

National Total = 730,435 Physicians*

ALPHA ORDER

RANK	STATE	PHYSICIANS	% of USA
27	Alabama	9,310	1.3%
49	Alaska	1,445	0.2%
21	Arizona	12,280	1.7%
31	Arkansas	5,350	0.7%
1	California	86,980	11.9%
22	Colorado	11,520	1.6%
23	Connecticut	11,498	1.6%
46	Delaware	1,967	0.3%
4	Florida	41,686	5.7%
14	Georgia	18,892	2.6%
39	Hawaii	3,682	0.5%
43	Idaho	2,425	0.3%
6	Illinois	31,824	4.4%
20	Indiana	12,744	1.7%
33	Iowa	5,051	0.7%
30	Kansas	5,749	0.8%
28	Kentucky	9,014	1.2%
24	Louisiana	10,598	1.5%
42	Maine	3,266	0.4%
12	Maryland	19,498	2.7%
8	Massachusetts	25,407	3.5%
10	Michigan	22,349	3.1%
17	Minnesota	13,784	1.9%
34	Mississippi	4,839	0.7%
19	Missouri	12,914	1.8%
45	Montana	2,016	0.3%
37	Nebraska	4,014	0.5%
35	Nevada	4,501	0.6%
41	New Hampshire	3,372	0.5%
9	New Jersey	24,140	3.3%
36	New Mexico	4,246	0.6%
2	New York	65,512	9.0%
11	North Carolina	21,064	2.9%
48	North Dakota	1,470	0.2%
7	Ohio	27,204	3.7%
29	Oklahoma	5,797	0.8%
26	Oregon	9,439	1.3%
5	Pennsylvania	33,171	4.5%
40	Rhode Island	3,485	0.5%
25	South Carolina	9,447	1.3%
47	South Dakota	1,676	0.2%
16	Tennessee	14,927	2.0%
3	Texas	46,768	6.4%
32	Utah	5,067	0.7%
44	Vermont	2,021	0.3%
13	Virginia	19,237	2.6%
15	Washington	15,842	2.2%
38	West Virginia	3,795	0.5%
18	Wisconsin	13,348	1.8%
50	Wyoming	947	0.1%

RANK ORDER

RANK	STATE	PHYSICIANS	% of USA
1	California	86,980	11.9%
2	New York	65,512	9.0%
3	Texas	46,768	6.4%
4	Florida	41,686	5.7%
5	Pennsylvania	33,171	4.5%
6	Illinois	31,824	4.4%
7	Ohio	27,204	3.7%
8	Massachusetts	25,407	3.5%
9	New Jersey	24,140	3.3%
10	Michigan	22,349	3.1%
11	North Carolina	21,064	2.9%
12	Maryland	19,498	2.7%
13	Virginia	19,237	2.6%
14	Georgia	18,892	2.6%
15	Washington	15,842	2.2%
16	Tennessee	14,927	2.0%
17	Minnesota	13,784	1.9%
18	Wisconsin	13,348	1.8%
19	Missouri	12,914	1.8%
20	Indiana	12,744	1.7%
21	Arizona	12,280	1.7%
22	Colorado	11,520	1.6%
23	Connecticut	11,498	1.6%
24	Louisiana	10,598	1.5%
25	South Carolina	9,447	1.3%
26	Oregon	9,439	1.3%
27	Alabama	9,310	1.3%
28	Kentucky	9,014	1.2%
29	Oklahoma	5,797	0.8%
30	Kansas	5,749	0.8%
31	Arkansas	5,350	0.7%
32	Utah	5,067	0.7%
33	Iowa	5,051	0.7%
34	Mississippi	4,839	0.7%
35	Nevada	4,501	0.6%
36	New Mexico	4,246	0.6%
37	Nebraska	4,014	0.5%
38	West Virginia	3,795	0.5%
39	Hawaii	3,682	0.5%
40	Rhode Island	3,485	0.5%
41	New Hampshire	3,372	0.5%
42	Maine	3,266	0.4%
43	Idaho	2,425	0.3%
44	Vermont	2,021	0.3%
45	Montana	2,016	0.3%
46	Delaware	1,967	0.3%
47	South Dakota	1,676	0.2%
48	North Dakota	1,470	0.2%
49	Alaska	1,445	0.2%
50	Wyoming	947	0.1%
	District of Columbia	3,857	0.5%

Source: American Medical Association (Chicago, Illinois)
"Physician Characteristics and Distribution in the U.S." (2010 Edition)
*As of December 31, 2008. Total does not include 10,432 physicians in U.S. territories and possessions.

Rate of Physicians in Patient Care in 2008

National Rate = 240 Physicians per 100,000 Population*

ALPHA ORDER

RANK	STATE	RATE
38	Alabama	199
31	Alaska	210
42	Arizona	189
43	Arkansas	187
18	California	238
22	Colorado	233
5	Connecticut	328
27	Delaware	224
25	Florida	226
40	Georgia	195
7	Hawaii	286
49	Idaho	159
13	Illinois	248
38	Indiana	199
47	Iowa	169
37	Kansas	206
31	Kentucky	210
18	Louisiana	238
14	Maine	247
2	Maryland	345
1	Massachusetts	388
28	Michigan	223
9	Minnesota	264
48	Mississippi	165
29	Missouri	217
35	Montana	208
26	Nebraska	225
46	Nevada	172
11	New Hampshire	255
8	New Jersey	279
30	New Mexico	214
3	New York	337
24	North Carolina	228
23	North Dakota	229
21	Ohio	236
49	Oklahoma	159
12	Oregon	250
9	Pennsylvania	264
4	Rhode Island	331
31	South Carolina	210
35	South Dakota	208
17	Tennessee	239
41	Texas	192
44	Utah	186
6	Vermont	325
14	Virginia	247
16	Washington	241
34	West Virginia	209
20	Wisconsin	237
45	Wyoming	178

RANK ORDER

RANK	STATE	RATE
1	Massachusetts	388
2	Maryland	345
3	New York	337
4	Rhode Island	331
5	Connecticut	328
6	Vermont	325
7	Hawaii	286
8	New Jersey	279
9	Minnesota	264
9	Pennsylvania	264
11	New Hampshire	255
12	Oregon	250
13	Illinois	248
14	Maine	247
14	Virginia	247
16	Washington	241
17	Tennessee	239
18	California	238
18	Louisiana	238
20	Wisconsin	237
21	Ohio	236
22	Colorado	233
23	North Dakota	229
24	North Carolina	228
25	Florida	226
26	Nebraska	225
27	Delaware	224
28	Michigan	223
29	Missouri	217
30	New Mexico	214
31	Alaska	210
31	Kentucky	210
31	South Carolina	210
34	West Virginia	209
35	Montana	208
35	South Dakota	208
37	Kansas	206
38	Alabama	199
38	Indiana	199
40	Georgia	195
41	Texas	192
42	Arizona	189
43	Arkansas	187
44	Utah	186
45	Wyoming	178
46	Nevada	172
47	Iowa	169
48	Mississippi	165
49	Idaho	159
49	Oklahoma	159

	District of Columbia	654

Source: CQ Press using data from American Medical Association (Chicago, Illinois)
    "Physician Characteristics and Distribution in the U.S." (2010 Edition)
*As of December 31, 2008. National rate does not include physicians in the U.S. territories and possessions.

Physicians in Primary Care in 2008

National Total = 299,832 Physicians*

<table>
<tr><th colspan="4">ALPHA ORDER</th><th colspan="4">RANK ORDER</th></tr>
<tr><th>RANK</th><th>STATE</th><th>PHYSICIANS</th><th>% of USA</th><th>RANK</th><th>STATE</th><th>PHYSICIANS</th><th>% of USA</th></tr>
<tr><td>27</td><td>Alabama</td><td>3,941</td><td>1.3%</td><td>1</td><td>California</td><td>36,531</td><td>12.2%</td></tr>
<tr><td>48</td><td>Alaska</td><td>706</td><td>0.2%</td><td>2</td><td>New York</td><td>26,333</td><td>8.8%</td></tr>
<tr><td>21</td><td>Arizona</td><td>4,925</td><td>1.6%</td><td>3</td><td>Texas</td><td>18,750</td><td>6.3%</td></tr>
<tr><td>31</td><td>Arkansas</td><td>2,357</td><td>0.8%</td><td>4</td><td>Florida</td><td>16,117</td><td>5.4%</td></tr>
<tr><td>1</td><td>California</td><td>36,531</td><td>12.2%</td><td>5</td><td>Illinois</td><td>13,779</td><td>4.6%</td></tr>
<tr><td>22</td><td>Colorado</td><td>4,731</td><td>1.6%</td><td>6</td><td>Pennsylvania</td><td>12,584</td><td>4.2%</td></tr>
<tr><td>23</td><td>Connecticut</td><td>4,576</td><td>1.5%</td><td>7</td><td>Ohio</td><td>11,014</td><td>3.7%</td></tr>
<tr><td>47</td><td>Delaware</td><td>749</td><td>0.2%</td><td>8</td><td>New Jersey</td><td>9,967</td><td>3.3%</td></tr>
<tr><td>4</td><td>Florida</td><td>16,117</td><td>5.4%</td><td>9</td><td>Massachusetts</td><td>9,510</td><td>3.2%</td></tr>
<tr><td>13</td><td>Georgia</td><td>8,054</td><td>2.7%</td><td>10</td><td>Michigan</td><td>9,430</td><td>3.1%</td></tr>
<tr><td>38</td><td>Hawaii</td><td>1,634</td><td>0.5%</td><td>11</td><td>North Carolina</td><td>8,710</td><td>2.9%</td></tr>
<tr><td>43</td><td>Idaho</td><td>1,020</td><td>0.3%</td><td>12</td><td>Virginia</td><td>8,146</td><td>2.7%</td></tr>
<tr><td>5</td><td>Illinois</td><td>13,779</td><td>4.6%</td><td>13</td><td>Georgia</td><td>8,054</td><td>2.7%</td></tr>
<tr><td>19</td><td>Indiana</td><td>5,323</td><td>1.8%</td><td>14</td><td>Maryland</td><td>7,818</td><td>2.6%</td></tr>
<tr><td>32</td><td>Iowa</td><td>2,141</td><td>0.7%</td><td>15</td><td>Washington</td><td>6,837</td><td>2.3%</td></tr>
<tr><td>30</td><td>Kansas</td><td>2,417</td><td>0.8%</td><td>16</td><td>Tennessee</td><td>6,115</td><td>2.0%</td></tr>
<tr><td>28</td><td>Kentucky</td><td>3,660</td><td>1.2%</td><td>17</td><td>Minnesota</td><td>5,937</td><td>2.0%</td></tr>
<tr><td>24</td><td>Louisiana</td><td>4,227</td><td>1.4%</td><td>18</td><td>Wisconsin</td><td>5,694</td><td>1.9%</td></tr>
<tr><td>40</td><td>Maine</td><td>1,448</td><td>0.5%</td><td>19</td><td>Indiana</td><td>5,323</td><td>1.8%</td></tr>
<tr><td>14</td><td>Maryland</td><td>7,818</td><td>2.6%</td><td>20</td><td>Missouri</td><td>4,967</td><td>1.7%</td></tr>
<tr><td>9</td><td>Massachusetts</td><td>9,510</td><td>3.2%</td><td>21</td><td>Arizona</td><td>4,925</td><td>1.6%</td></tr>
<tr><td>10</td><td>Michigan</td><td>9,430</td><td>3.1%</td><td>22</td><td>Colorado</td><td>4,731</td><td>1.6%</td></tr>
<tr><td>17</td><td>Minnesota</td><td>5,937</td><td>2.0%</td><td>23</td><td>Connecticut</td><td>4,576</td><td>1.5%</td></tr>
<tr><td>33</td><td>Mississippi</td><td>2,021</td><td>0.7%</td><td>24</td><td>Louisiana</td><td>4,227</td><td>1.4%</td></tr>
<tr><td>20</td><td>Missouri</td><td>4,967</td><td>1.7%</td><td>25</td><td>Oregon</td><td>4,098</td><td>1.4%</td></tr>
<tr><td>45</td><td>Montana</td><td>858</td><td>0.3%</td><td>26</td><td>South Carolina</td><td>3,966</td><td>1.3%</td></tr>
<tr><td>37</td><td>Nebraska</td><td>1,789</td><td>0.6%</td><td>27</td><td>Alabama</td><td>3,941</td><td>1.3%</td></tr>
<tr><td>36</td><td>Nevada</td><td>1,898</td><td>0.6%</td><td>28</td><td>Kentucky</td><td>3,660</td><td>1.2%</td></tr>
<tr><td>41</td><td>New Hampshire</td><td>1,445</td><td>0.5%</td><td>29</td><td>Oklahoma</td><td>2,452</td><td>0.8%</td></tr>
<tr><td>8</td><td>New Jersey</td><td>9,967</td><td>3.3%</td><td>30</td><td>Kansas</td><td>2,417</td><td>0.8%</td></tr>
<tr><td>35</td><td>New Mexico</td><td>1,924</td><td>0.6%</td><td>31</td><td>Arkansas</td><td>2,357</td><td>0.8%</td></tr>
<tr><td>2</td><td>New York</td><td>26,333</td><td>8.8%</td><td>32</td><td>Iowa</td><td>2,141</td><td>0.7%</td></tr>
<tr><td>11</td><td>North Carolina</td><td>8,710</td><td>2.9%</td><td>33</td><td>Mississippi</td><td>2,021</td><td>0.7%</td></tr>
<tr><td>49</td><td>North Dakota</td><td>685</td><td>0.2%</td><td>34</td><td>Utah</td><td>1,982</td><td>0.7%</td></tr>
<tr><td>7</td><td>Ohio</td><td>11,014</td><td>3.7%</td><td>35</td><td>New Mexico</td><td>1,924</td><td>0.6%</td></tr>
<tr><td>29</td><td>Oklahoma</td><td>2,452</td><td>0.8%</td><td>36</td><td>Nevada</td><td>1,898</td><td>0.6%</td></tr>
<tr><td>25</td><td>Oregon</td><td>4,098</td><td>1.4%</td><td>37</td><td>Nebraska</td><td>1,789</td><td>0.6%</td></tr>
<tr><td>6</td><td>Pennsylvania</td><td>12,584</td><td>4.2%</td><td>38</td><td>Hawaii</td><td>1,634</td><td>0.5%</td></tr>
<tr><td>42</td><td>Rhode Island</td><td>1,409</td><td>0.5%</td><td>39</td><td>West Virginia</td><td>1,591</td><td>0.5%</td></tr>
<tr><td>26</td><td>South Carolina</td><td>3,966</td><td>1.3%</td><td>40</td><td>Maine</td><td>1,448</td><td>0.5%</td></tr>
<tr><td>46</td><td>South Dakota</td><td>765</td><td>0.3%</td><td>41</td><td>New Hampshire</td><td>1,445</td><td>0.5%</td></tr>
<tr><td>16</td><td>Tennessee</td><td>6,115</td><td>2.0%</td><td>42</td><td>Rhode Island</td><td>1,409</td><td>0.5%</td></tr>
<tr><td>3</td><td>Texas</td><td>18,750</td><td>6.3%</td><td>43</td><td>Idaho</td><td>1,020</td><td>0.3%</td></tr>
<tr><td>34</td><td>Utah</td><td>1,982</td><td>0.7%</td><td>44</td><td>Vermont</td><td>915</td><td>0.3%</td></tr>
<tr><td>44</td><td>Vermont</td><td>915</td><td>0.3%</td><td>45</td><td>Montana</td><td>858</td><td>0.3%</td></tr>
<tr><td>12</td><td>Virginia</td><td>8,146</td><td>2.7%</td><td>46</td><td>South Dakota</td><td>765</td><td>0.3%</td></tr>
<tr><td>15</td><td>Washington</td><td>6,837</td><td>2.3%</td><td>47</td><td>Delaware</td><td>749</td><td>0.2%</td></tr>
<tr><td>39</td><td>West Virginia</td><td>1,591</td><td>0.5%</td><td>48</td><td>Alaska</td><td>706</td><td>0.2%</td></tr>
<tr><td>18</td><td>Wisconsin</td><td>5,694</td><td>1.9%</td><td>49</td><td>North Dakota</td><td>685</td><td>0.2%</td></tr>
<tr><td>50</td><td>Wyoming</td><td>456</td><td>0.2%</td><td>50</td><td>Wyoming</td><td>456</td><td>0.2%</td></tr>
<tr><td></td><td></td><td></td><td></td><td></td><td>District of Columbia</td><td>1,430</td><td>0.5%</td></tr>
</table>

Source: American Medical Association (Chicago, Illinois)
   "Physician Characteristics and Distribution in the U.S." (2010 Edition)
*As of December 31, 2008. National total does not include 5,432 physicians in U.S. territories and possessions. Primary Care Specialties include Family Practice, General Practice, Internal Medicine, Obstetrics/Gynecology, and Pediatrics excluding subspecialties within each category.

Rate of Physicians in Primary Care in 2008

National Rate = 99 Physicians per 100,000 Population*

ALPHA ORDER

RANK	STATE	RATE
38	Alabama	84
17	Alaska	103
44	Arizona	76
42	Arkansas	82
19	California	100
24	Colorado	96
6	Connecticut	131
36	Delaware	85
33	Florida	87
39	Georgia	83
7	Hawaii	127
49	Idaho	67
13	Illinois	107
39	Indiana	83
47	Iowa	72
34	Kansas	86
36	Kentucky	85
26	Louisiana	95
10	Maine	110
3	Maryland	138
2	Massachusetts	145
28	Michigan	94
9	Minnesota	114
48	Mississippi	69
39	Missouri	83
30	Montana	89
19	Nebraska	100
45	Nevada	73
11	New Hampshire	109
8	New Jersey	115
23	New Mexico	97
4	New York	135
28	North Carolina	94
13	North Dakota	107
24	Ohio	96
49	Oklahoma	67
12	Oregon	108
19	Pennsylvania	100
5	Rhode Island	134
31	South Carolina	88
26	South Dakota	95
22	Tennessee	98
43	Texas	77
45	Utah	73
1	Vermont	147
15	Virginia	104
15	Washington	104
31	West Virginia	88
18	Wisconsin	101
34	Wyoming	86

RANK ORDER

RANK	STATE	RATE
1	Vermont	147
2	Massachusetts	145
3	Maryland	138
4	New York	135
5	Rhode Island	134
6	Connecticut	131
7	Hawaii	127
8	New Jersey	115
9	Minnesota	114
10	Maine	110
11	New Hampshire	109
12	Oregon	108
13	Illinois	107
13	North Dakota	107
15	Virginia	104
15	Washington	104
17	Alaska	103
18	Wisconsin	101
19	California	100
19	Nebraska	100
19	Pennsylvania	100
22	Tennessee	98
23	New Mexico	97
24	Colorado	96
24	Ohio	96
26	Louisiana	95
26	South Dakota	95
28	Michigan	94
28	North Carolina	94
30	Montana	89
31	South Carolina	88
31	West Virginia	88
33	Florida	87
34	Kansas	86
34	Wyoming	86
36	Delaware	85
36	Kentucky	85
38	Alabama	84
39	Georgia	83
39	Indiana	83
39	Missouri	83
42	Arkansas	82
43	Texas	77
44	Arizona	76
45	Nevada	73
45	Utah	73
47	Iowa	72
48	Mississippi	69
49	Idaho	67
49	Oklahoma	67

District of Columbia   242

Source: CQ Press using data from American Medical Association (Chicago, Illinois)
    "Physician Characteristics and Distribution in the U.S." (2010 Edition)
*As of December 31, 2008. National rate does not include physicians in U.S. territories and possessions. Primary Care Specialties include Family Practice, General Practice, Internal Medicine, Obstetrics/Gynecology, and Pediatrics excluding subspecialties within each category.

Percent of Physicians in Primary Care in 2008

National Percent = 31.9% of Physicians*

ALPHA ORDER

RANK	STATE	PERCENT
7	Alabama	34.7
1	Alaska	40.8
45	Arizona	30.5
5	Arkansas	35.5
37	California	31.9
38	Colorado	31.8
43	Connecticut	30.6
46	Delaware	30.2
48	Florida	28.8
12	Georgia	34.0
8	Hawaii	34.6
19	Idaho	33.3
10	Illinois	34.2
12	Indiana	34.0
32	Iowa	32.6
25	Kansas	33.0
25	Kentucky	33.0
34	Louisiana	32.5
16	Maine	33.6
47	Maryland	29.4
50	Massachusetts	28.1
25	Michigan	33.0
12	Minnesota	34.0
16	Mississippi	33.6
42	Missouri	30.8
29	Montana	32.9
5	Nebraska	35.5
19	Nevada	33.3
25	New Hampshire	33.0
34	New Jersey	32.5
9	New Mexico	34.3
41	New York	30.9
32	North Carolina	32.6
2	North Dakota	38.3
39	Ohio	31.7
18	Oklahoma	33.5
29	Oregon	32.9
48	Pennsylvania	28.8
40	Rhode Island	31.6
15	South Carolina	33.8
4	South Dakota	37.4
21	Tennessee	33.2
36	Texas	32.4
43	Utah	30.6
23	Vermont	33.1
23	Virginia	33.1
31	Washington	32.8
21	West Virginia	33.2
11	Wisconsin	34.1
3	Wyoming	37.6

RANK ORDER

RANK	STATE	PERCENT
1	Alaska	40.8
2	North Dakota	38.3
3	Wyoming	37.6
4	South Dakota	37.4
5	Arkansas	35.5
5	Nebraska	35.5
7	Alabama	34.7
8	Hawaii	34.6
9	New Mexico	34.3
10	Illinois	34.2
11	Wisconsin	34.1
12	Georgia	34.0
12	Indiana	34.0
12	Minnesota	34.0
15	South Carolina	33.8
16	Maine	33.6
16	Mississippi	33.6
18	Oklahoma	33.5
19	Idaho	33.3
19	Nevada	33.3
21	Tennessee	33.2
21	West Virginia	33.2
23	Vermont	33.1
23	Virginia	33.1
25	Kansas	33.0
25	Kentucky	33.0
25	Michigan	33.0
25	New Hampshire	33.0
29	Montana	32.9
29	Oregon	32.9
31	Washington	32.8
32	Iowa	32.6
32	North Carolina	32.6
34	Louisiana	32.5
34	New Jersey	32.5
36	Texas	32.4
37	California	31.9
38	Colorado	31.8
39	Ohio	31.7
40	Rhode Island	31.6
41	New York	30.9
42	Missouri	30.8
43	Connecticut	30.6
43	Utah	30.6
45	Arizona	30.5
46	Delaware	30.2
47	Maryland	29.4
48	Florida	28.8
48	Pennsylvania	28.8
50	Massachusetts	28.1

District of Columbia 27.3

Source: CQ Press using data from American Medical Association (Chicago, Illinois)
"Physician Characteristics and Distribution in the U.S." (2010 Edition)
*As of December 31, 2008. National percent does not include physicians in U.S. territories and possessions. Primary Care Specialties include Family Practice, General Practice, Internal Medicine, Obstetrics/Gynecology, and Pediatrics excluding subspecialties within each category.

Percent of Population Lacking Access to Primary Care in 2010

National Percent = 11.5% of Population*

ALPHA ORDER				RANK ORDER		
RANK	**STATE**	**PERCENT**		**RANK**	**STATE**	**PERCENT**
9	Alabama	18.4		1	Louisiana	33.3
16	Alaska	14.0		2	New Mexico	31.5
12	Arizona	16.4		3	Mississippi	31.3
31	Arkansas	9.9		4	South Dakota	26.5
29	California	10.0		5	Montana	23.7
22	Colorado	11.7		6	North Dakota	22.3
33	Connecticut	9.0		7	Missouri	21.2
17	Delaware	13.6		8	Wyoming	19.0
13	Florida	14.9		9	Alabama	18.4
15	Georgia	14.3		10	Illinois	17.5
48	Hawaii	2.8		11	Idaho	16.7
11	Idaho	16.7		12	Arizona	16.4
10	Illinois	17.5		13	Florida	14.9
37	Indiana	7.1		14	Oklahoma	14.5
25	Iowa	10.8		15	Georgia	14.3
20	Kansas	12.5		16	Alaska	14.0
23	Kentucky	11.4		17	Delaware	13.6
1	Louisiana	33.3		18	South Carolina	13.0
42	Maine	5.8		19	Nevada	12.6
43	Maryland	5.7		20	Kansas	12.5
38	Massachusetts	6.9		21	Texas	12.4
25	Michigan	10.8		22	Colorado	11.7
45	Minnesota	5.4		23	Kentucky	11.4
3	Mississippi	31.3		24	New York	11.3
7	Missouri	21.2		25	Iowa	10.8
5	Montana	23.7		25	Michigan	10.8
46	Nebraska	4.7		27	Wisconsin	10.6
19	Nevada	12.6		28	Tennessee	10.4
47	New Hampshire	4.1		29	California	10.0
50	New Jersey	1.7		29	Utah	10.0
2	New Mexico	31.5		31	Arkansas	9.9
24	New York	11.3		32	Washington	9.4
43	North Carolina	5.7		33	Connecticut	9.0
6	North Dakota	22.3		34	West Virginia	8.8
40	Ohio	6.0		35	Virginia	8.2
14	Oklahoma	14.5		36	Oregon	7.8
36	Oregon	7.8		37	Indiana	7.1
41	Pennsylvania	5.9		38	Massachusetts	6.9
39	Rhode Island	6.3		39	Rhode Island	6.3
18	South Carolina	13.0		40	Ohio	6.0
4	South Dakota	26.5		41	Pennsylvania	5.9
28	Tennessee	10.4		42	Maine	5.8
21	Texas	12.4		43	Maryland	5.7
29	Utah	10.0		43	North Carolina	5.7
49	Vermont	2.7		45	Minnesota	5.4
35	Virginia	8.2		46	Nebraska	4.7
32	Washington	9.4		47	New Hampshire	4.1
34	West Virginia	8.8		48	Hawaii	2.8
27	Wisconsin	10.6		49	Vermont	2.7
8	Wyoming	19.0		50	New Jersey	1.7

District of Columbia   25.2

Source: CQ Press using data from U.S. Department of Health and Human Services, Division of Shortage Designation
"Selected Statistics on Health Professional Shortage Areas" (as of January 15, 2010)
(http://datawarehouse.hrsa.gov/HPSADownload.aspx)
*Percent of population considered under-served by primary medical practitioners (Family and General Practice doctors, Internists, Ob/Gyns, and Pediatricians). An under-served population does not have primary medical care within reasonable economic and geographic bounds.

Physicians in General/Family Practice in 2008

National Total = 92,536 Physicians*

ALPHA ORDER

RANK	STATE	PHYSICIANS	% of USA
26	Alabama	1,362	1.5%
45	Alaska	407	0.4%
20	Arizona	1,561	1.7%
28	Arkansas	1,265	1.4%
1	California	10,941	11.8%
17	Colorado	1,880	2.0%
38	Connecticut	598	0.6%
49	Delaware	247	0.3%
3	Florida	5,033	5.4%
15	Georgia	2,379	2.6%
43	Hawaii	418	0.5%
40	Idaho	576	0.6%
4	Illinois	3,937	4.3%
14	Indiana	2,420	2.6%
30	Iowa	1,159	1.3%
29	Kansas	1,167	1.3%
25	Kentucky	1,371	1.5%
23	Louisiana	1,373	1.5%
37	Maine	625	0.7%
23	Maryland	1,373	1.5%
27	Massachusetts	1,361	1.5%
10	Michigan	2,881	3.1%
11	Minnesota	2,860	3.1%
33	Mississippi	806	0.9%
22	Missouri	1,402	1.5%
42	Montana	454	0.5%
32	Nebraska	889	1.0%
39	Nevada	585	0.6%
41	New Hampshire	499	0.5%
19	New Jersey	1,619	1.7%
34	New Mexico	788	0.9%
5	New York	3,895	4.2%
9	North Carolina	2,998	3.2%
46	North Dakota	383	0.4%
7	Ohio	3,444	3.7%
31	Oklahoma	1,089	1.2%
21	Oregon	1,469	1.6%
6	Pennsylvania	3,795	4.1%
50	Rhode Island	218	0.2%
18	South Carolina	1,637	1.8%
44	South Dakota	411	0.4%
16	Tennessee	1,974	2.1%
2	Texas	6,493	7.0%
35	Utah	766	0.8%
47	Vermont	333	0.4%
12	Virginia	2,765	3.0%
8	Washington	3,034	3.3%
36	West Virginia	662	0.7%
13	Wisconsin	2,477	2.7%
48	Wyoming	262	0.3%

RANK ORDER

RANK	STATE	PHYSICIANS	% of USA
1	California	10,941	11.8%
2	Texas	6,493	7.0%
3	Florida	5,033	5.4%
4	Illinois	3,937	4.3%
5	New York	3,895	4.2%
6	Pennsylvania	3,795	4.1%
7	Ohio	3,444	3.7%
8	Washington	3,034	3.3%
9	North Carolina	2,998	3.2%
10	Michigan	2,881	3.1%
11	Minnesota	2,860	3.1%
12	Virginia	2,765	3.0%
13	Wisconsin	2,477	2.7%
14	Indiana	2,420	2.6%
15	Georgia	2,379	2.6%
16	Tennessee	1,974	2.1%
17	Colorado	1,880	2.0%
18	South Carolina	1,637	1.8%
19	New Jersey	1,619	1.7%
20	Arizona	1,561	1.7%
21	Oregon	1,469	1.6%
22	Missouri	1,402	1.5%
23	Louisiana	1,373	1.5%
23	Maryland	1,373	1.5%
25	Kentucky	1,371	1.5%
26	Alabama	1,362	1.5%
27	Massachusetts	1,361	1.5%
28	Arkansas	1,265	1.4%
29	Kansas	1,167	1.3%
30	Iowa	1,159	1.3%
31	Oklahoma	1,089	1.2%
32	Nebraska	889	1.0%
33	Mississippi	806	0.9%
34	New Mexico	788	0.9%
35	Utah	766	0.8%
36	West Virginia	662	0.7%
37	Maine	625	0.7%
38	Connecticut	598	0.6%
39	Nevada	585	0.6%
40	Idaho	576	0.6%
41	New Hampshire	499	0.5%
42	Montana	454	0.5%
43	Hawaii	418	0.5%
44	South Dakota	411	0.4%
45	Alaska	407	0.4%
46	North Dakota	383	0.4%
47	Vermont	333	0.4%
48	Wyoming	262	0.3%
49	Delaware	247	0.3%
50	Rhode Island	218	0.2%
	District of Columbia	195	0.2%

Source: American Medical Association (Chicago, Illinois)
"Physician Characteristics and Distribution in the U.S." (2010 Edition)
*As of December 31, 2008. Total does not include 2,420 physicians in U.S. territories and possessions.

Rate of Physicians in General/Family Practice in 2008

National Rate = 30 Physicians per 100,000 Population*

ALPHA ORDER

RANK	STATE	RATE
34	Alabama	29
2	Alaska	59
42	Arizona	24
11	Arkansas	44
30	California	30
17	Colorado	38
50	Connecticut	17
36	Delaware	28
38	Florida	27
41	Georgia	25
24	Hawaii	32
17	Idaho	38
28	Illinois	31
17	Indiana	38
15	Iowa	39
13	Kansas	42
24	Kentucky	32
28	Louisiana	31
8	Maine	47
42	Maryland	24
46	Massachusetts	21
34	Michigan	29
3	Minnesota	55
38	Mississippi	27
42	Missouri	24
8	Montana	47
6	Nebraska	50
45	Nevada	22
17	New Hampshire	38
49	New Jersey	19
14	New Mexico	40
48	New York	20
24	North Carolina	32
1	North Dakota	60
30	Ohio	30
30	Oklahoma	30
15	Oregon	39
30	Pennsylvania	30
46	Rhode Island	21
21	South Carolina	36
5	South Dakota	51
24	Tennessee	32
38	Texas	27
36	Utah	28
4	Vermont	54
23	Virginia	35
10	Washington	46
21	West Virginia	36
11	Wisconsin	44
7	Wyoming	49

RANK ORDER

RANK	STATE	RATE
1	North Dakota	60
2	Alaska	59
3	Minnesota	55
4	Vermont	54
5	South Dakota	51
6	Nebraska	50
7	Wyoming	49
8	Maine	47
8	Montana	47
10	Washington	46
11	Arkansas	44
11	Wisconsin	44
13	Kansas	42
14	New Mexico	40
15	Iowa	39
15	Oregon	39
17	Colorado	38
17	Idaho	38
17	Indiana	38
17	New Hampshire	38
21	South Carolina	36
21	West Virginia	36
23	Virginia	35
24	Hawaii	32
24	Kentucky	32
24	North Carolina	32
24	Tennessee	32
28	Illinois	31
28	Louisiana	31
30	California	30
30	Ohio	30
30	Oklahoma	30
30	Pennsylvania	30
34	Alabama	29
34	Michigan	29
36	Delaware	28
36	Utah	28
38	Florida	27
38	Mississippi	27
38	Texas	27
41	Georgia	25
42	Arizona	24
42	Maryland	24
42	Missouri	24
45	Nevada	22
46	Massachusetts	21
46	Rhode Island	21
48	New York	20
49	New Jersey	19
50	Connecticut	17

District of Columbia   33

Source: CQ Press using data from American Medical Association (Chicago, Illinois)
"Physician Characteristics and Distribution in the U.S." (2010 Edition)
*As of December 31, 2008. National rate does not include physicians in the U.S. territories and possessions.

Average Annual Wages of Family and General Practitioners in 2008

National Average = $161,490*

ALPHA ORDER

RANK	STATE	WAGES
45	Alabama	$142,670
48	Alaska	138,380
38	Arizona	153,540
2	Arkansas	188,880
46	California	142,620
33	Colorado	158,050
28	Connecticut	160,830
16	Delaware	168,570
44	Florida	145,070
8	Georgia	177,700
31	Hawaii	159,010
18	Idaho	168,140
43	Illinois	147,840
32	Indiana	158,950
10	Iowa	175,500
5	Kansas	180,690
23	Kentucky	163,760
12	Louisiana	173,040
41	Maine	151,500
35	Maryland	157,060
4	Massachusetts	185,200
15	Michigan	169,760
20	Minnesota	165,290
11	Mississippi	174,870
42	Missouri	150,980
49	Montana	135,220
26	Nebraska	162,320
25	Nevada	162,850
29	New Hampshire	160,540
34	New Jersey	158,010
36	New Mexico	156,200
47	New York	142,510
7	North Carolina	178,960
21	North Dakota	164,690
30	Ohio	160,140
17	Oklahoma	168,440
24	Oregon	163,750
19	Pennsylvania	167,050
3	Rhode Island	185,840
14	South Carolina	170,410
37	South Dakota	153,680
40	Tennessee	153,080
27	Texas	161,600
13	Utah	172,880
50	Vermont	128,910
22	Virginia	164,100
39	Washington	153,450
6	West Virginia	179,380
1	Wisconsin	192,180
9	Wyoming	175,630

RANK ORDER

RANK	STATE	WAGES
1	Wisconsin	$192,180
2	Arkansas	188,880
3	Rhode Island	185,840
4	Massachusetts	185,200
5	Kansas	180,690
6	West Virginia	179,380
7	North Carolina	178,960
8	Georgia	177,700
9	Wyoming	175,630
10	Iowa	175,500
11	Mississippi	174,870
12	Louisiana	173,040
13	Utah	172,880
14	South Carolina	170,410
15	Michigan	169,760
16	Delaware	168,570
17	Oklahoma	168,440
18	Idaho	168,140
19	Pennsylvania	167,050
20	Minnesota	165,290
21	North Dakota	164,690
22	Virginia	164,100
23	Kentucky	163,760
24	Oregon	163,750
25	Nevada	162,850
26	Nebraska	162,320
27	Texas	161,600
28	Connecticut	160,830
29	New Hampshire	160,540
30	Ohio	160,140
31	Hawaii	159,010
32	Indiana	158,950
33	Colorado	158,050
34	New Jersey	158,010
35	Maryland	157,060
36	New Mexico	156,200
37	South Dakota	153,680
38	Arizona	153,540
39	Washington	153,450
40	Tennessee	153,080
41	Maine	151,500
42	Missouri	150,980
43	Illinois	147,840
44	Florida	145,070
45	Alabama	142,670
46	California	142,620
47	New York	142,510
48	Alaska	138,380
49	Montana	135,220
50	Vermont	128,910

District of Columbia 166,740

Source: U.S. Department of Labor, Bureau of Labor Statistics
   "Occupational Employment and Wages, 2008" (http://www.bls.gov/oes/)
*Does not include self-employed.

Percent of Physicians Who Are Specialists in 2008

National Percent = 72.4% of Physicians*

ALPHA ORDER

RANK	STATE	PERCENT
13	Alabama	73.3
46	Alaska	63.9
25	Arizona	70.4
43	Arkansas	65.1
23	California	71.0
29	Colorado	69.4
1	Connecticut	78.9
13	Delaware	73.3
33	Florida	68.7
9	Georgia	74.2
11	Hawaii	73.6
48	Idaho	62.6
13	Illinois	73.3
27	Indiana	69.9
47	Iowa	63.8
40	Kansas	66.2
18	Kentucky	72.3
8	Louisiana	74.3
42	Maine	65.9
6	Maryland	77.3
4	Massachusetts	77.8
17	Michigan	72.4
36	Minnesota	67.0
26	Mississippi	70.0
7	Missouri	75.9
48	Montana	62.6
40	Nebraska	66.2
21	Nevada	71.3
30	New Hampshire	69.3
2	New Jersey	78.2
39	New Mexico	66.5
5	New York	77.5
20	North Carolina	72.2
45	North Dakota	64.1
18	Ohio	72.3
35	Oklahoma	68.0
34	Oregon	68.1
16	Pennsylvania	72.5
3	Rhode Island	77.9
27	South Carolina	69.9
44	South Dakota	64.5
9	Tennessee	74.2
12	Texas	73.4
22	Utah	71.2
37	Vermont	66.7
23	Virginia	71.0
37	Washington	66.7
31	West Virginia	69.2
32	Wisconsin	69.0
50	Wyoming	59.2

RANK ORDER

RANK	STATE	PERCENT
1	Connecticut	78.9
2	New Jersey	78.2
3	Rhode Island	77.9
4	Massachusetts	77.8
5	New York	77.5
6	Maryland	77.3
7	Missouri	75.9
8	Louisiana	74.3
9	Georgia	74.2
9	Tennessee	74.2
11	Hawaii	73.6
12	Texas	73.4
13	Alabama	73.3
13	Delaware	73.3
13	Illinois	73.3
16	Pennsylvania	72.5
17	Michigan	72.4
18	Kentucky	72.3
18	Ohio	72.3
20	North Carolina	72.2
21	Nevada	71.3
22	Utah	71.2
23	California	71.0
23	Virginia	71.0
25	Arizona	70.4
26	Mississippi	70.0
27	Indiana	69.9
27	South Carolina	69.9
29	Colorado	69.4
30	New Hampshire	69.3
31	West Virginia	69.2
32	Wisconsin	69.0
33	Florida	68.7
34	Oregon	68.1
35	Oklahoma	68.0
36	Minnesota	67.0
37	Vermont	66.7
37	Washington	66.7
39	New Mexico	66.5
40	Kansas	66.2
40	Nebraska	66.2
42	Maine	65.9
43	Arkansas	65.1
44	South Dakota	64.5
45	North Dakota	64.1
46	Alaska	63.9
47	Iowa	63.8
48	Idaho	62.6
48	Montana	62.6
50	Wyoming	59.2

District of Columbia 79.5

Source: CQ Press using data from American Medical Association (Chicago, Illinois)
"Physician Characteristics and Distribution in the U.S." (2010 Edition)
*As of December 31, 2008. National percent does not include physicians in the U.S. territories and possessions. Includes physicians in medical, surgical, and other specialties.

Physicians in Medical Specialties in 2008

National Total = 295,094 Physicians*

ALPHA ORDER					RANK ORDER			

RANK	STATE	PHYSICIANS	% of USA		RANK	STATE	PHYSICIANS	% of USA
25	Alabama	3,549	1.2%		1	California	34,704	11.8%
49	Alaska	353	0.1%		2	New York	31,120	10.5%
20	Arizona	4,759	1.6%		3	Texas	17,619	6.0%
33	Arkansas	1,711	0.6%		4	Florida	16,860	5.7%
1	California	34,704	11.8%		5	Pennsylvania	13,732	4.7%
24	Colorado	4,047	1.4%		6	Illinois	13,460	4.6%
17	Connecticut	5,523	1.9%		7	Massachusetts	12,458	4.2%
43	Delaware	775	0.3%		8	New Jersey	11,711	4.0%
4	Florida	16,860	5.7%		9	Ohio	10,965	3.7%
13	Georgia	7,511	2.5%		10	Maryland	9,457	3.2%
38	Hawaii	1,471	0.5%		11	Michigan	8,998	3.0%
45	Idaho	618	0.2%		12	North Carolina	8,236	2.8%
6	Illinois	13,460	4.6%		13	Georgia	7,511	2.5%
22	Indiana	4,387	1.5%		14	Virginia	7,256	2.5%
36	Iowa	1,555	0.5%		15	Tennessee	5,984	2.0%
30	Kansas	1,843	0.6%		16	Washington	5,542	1.9%
27	Kentucky	3,307	1.1%		17	Connecticut	5,523	1.9%
23	Louisiana	4,054	1.4%		18	Missouri	5,443	1.8%
42	Maine	1,128	0.4%		19	Minnesota	4,945	1.7%
10	Maryland	9,457	3.2%		20	Arizona	4,759	1.6%
7	Massachusetts	12,458	4.2%		21	Wisconsin	4,676	1.6%
11	Michigan	8,998	3.0%		22	Indiana	4,387	1.5%
19	Minnesota	4,945	1.7%		23	Louisiana	4,054	1.4%
35	Mississippi	1,673	0.6%		24	Colorado	4,047	1.4%
18	Missouri	5,443	1.8%		25	Alabama	3,549	1.2%
46	Montana	557	0.2%		26	Oregon	3,446	1.2%
40	Nebraska	1,295	0.4%		27	Kentucky	3,307	1.1%
32	Nevada	1,728	0.6%		28	South Carolina	3,246	1.1%
41	New Hampshire	1,273	0.4%		29	Oklahoma	1,978	0.7%
8	New Jersey	11,711	4.0%		30	Kansas	1,843	0.6%
37	New Mexico	1,543	0.5%		31	Utah	1,750	0.6%
2	New York	31,120	10.5%		32	Nevada	1,728	0.6%
12	North Carolina	8,236	2.8%		33	Arkansas	1,711	0.6%
48	North Dakota	442	0.1%		34	Rhode Island	1,685	0.6%
9	Ohio	10,965	3.7%		35	Mississippi	1,673	0.6%
29	Oklahoma	1,978	0.7%		36	Iowa	1,555	0.5%
26	Oregon	3,446	1.2%		37	New Mexico	1,543	0.5%
5	Pennsylvania	13,732	4.7%		38	Hawaii	1,471	0.5%
34	Rhode Island	1,685	0.6%		39	West Virginia	1,343	0.5%
28	South Carolina	3,246	1.1%		40	Nebraska	1,295	0.4%
47	South Dakota	507	0.2%		41	New Hampshire	1,273	0.4%
15	Tennessee	5,984	2.0%		42	Maine	1,128	0.4%
3	Texas	17,619	6.0%		43	Delaware	775	0.3%
31	Utah	1,750	0.6%		44	Vermont	755	0.3%
44	Vermont	755	0.3%		45	Idaho	618	0.2%
14	Virginia	7,256	2.5%		46	Montana	557	0.2%
16	Washington	5,542	1.9%		47	South Dakota	507	0.2%
39	West Virginia	1,343	0.5%		48	North Dakota	442	0.1%
21	Wisconsin	4,676	1.6%		49	Alaska	353	0.1%
50	Wyoming	214	0.1%		50	Wyoming	214	0.1%
					District of Columbia		1,902	0.6%

Source: American Medical Association (Chicago, Illinois)
   "Physician Characteristics and Distribution in the U.S." (2010 Edition)
*As of December 31, 2008. Total does not include 3,550 physicians in U.S. territories and possessions. Medical Specialties are Allergy/Immunology, Cardiovascular Diseases, Dermatology, Gastroenterology, Internal Medicine, Pediatrics, Pediatric Cardiology, and Pulmonary Diseases.

Rate of Nonfederal Physicians in Medical Specialties in 2008

National Rate = 97 Physicians per 100,000 Population*

ALPHA ORDER

RANK	STATE	RATE
31	Alabama	76
48	Alaska	51
33	Arizona	73
43	Arkansas	60
13	California	95
27	Colorado	82
5	Connecticut	158
23	Delaware	88
17	Florida	92
29	Georgia	77
8	Hawaii	114
49	Idaho	40
10	Illinois	105
37	Indiana	69
47	Iowa	52
39	Kansas	66
29	Kentucky	77
18	Louisiana	91
24	Maine	85
2	Maryland	167
1	Massachusetts	190
21	Michigan	90
13	Minnesota	95
45	Mississippi	57
18	Missouri	91
44	Montana	58
33	Nebraska	73
39	Nevada	66
11	New Hampshire	96
6	New Jersey	135
28	New Mexico	78
3	New York	160
22	North Carolina	89
37	North Dakota	69
13	Ohio	95
46	Oklahoma	54
18	Oregon	91
9	Pennsylvania	109
3	Rhode Island	160
35	South Carolina	72
42	South Dakota	63
11	Tennessee	96
35	Texas	72
41	Utah	64
7	Vermont	122
16	Virginia	93
25	Washington	84
32	West Virginia	74
26	Wisconsin	83
49	Wyoming	40

RANK ORDER

RANK	STATE	RATE
1	Massachusetts	190
2	Maryland	167
3	New York	160
3	Rhode Island	160
5	Connecticut	158
6	New Jersey	135
7	Vermont	122
8	Hawaii	114
9	Pennsylvania	109
10	Illinois	105
11	New Hampshire	96
11	Tennessee	96
13	California	95
13	Minnesota	95
13	Ohio	95
16	Virginia	93
17	Florida	92
18	Louisiana	91
18	Missouri	91
18	Oregon	91
21	Michigan	90
22	North Carolina	89
23	Delaware	88
24	Maine	85
25	Washington	84
26	Wisconsin	83
27	Colorado	82
28	New Mexico	78
29	Georgia	77
29	Kentucky	77
31	Alabama	76
32	West Virginia	74
33	Arizona	73
33	Nebraska	73
35	South Carolina	72
35	Texas	72
37	Indiana	69
37	North Dakota	69
39	Kansas	66
39	Nevada	66
41	Utah	64
42	South Dakota	63
43	Arkansas	60
44	Montana	58
45	Mississippi	57
46	Oklahoma	54
47	Iowa	52
48	Alaska	51
49	Idaho	40
49	Wyoming	40

District of Columbia	322

Source: CQ Press using data from American Medical Association (Chicago, Illinois)
"Physician Characteristics and Distribution in the U.S." (2010 Edition)

*As of December 31, 2008. National rate does not include physicians in U.S. territories and possessions. Medical Specialties are Allergy/Immunology, Cardiovascular Diseases, Dermatology, Gastroenterology, Internal Medicine, Pediatrics, Pediatric Cardiology, and Pulmonary Diseases.

Physicians in Internal Medicine in 2008

National Total = 158,355 Physicians*

ALPHA ORDER

RANK	STATE	PHYSICIANS	% of USA
26	Alabama	1,899	1.2%
49	Alaska	167	0.1%
21	Arizona	2,502	1.6%
37	Arkansas	765	0.5%
1	California	18,519	11.7%
23	Colorado	2,094	1.3%
15	Connecticut	3,233	2.0%
44	Delaware	360	0.2%
4	Florida	8,647	5.5%
13	Georgia	3,920	2.5%
35	Hawaii	821	0.5%
45	Idaho	310	0.2%
5	Illinois	7,700	4.9%
22	Indiana	2,206	1.4%
38	Iowa	759	0.5%
32	Kansas	918	0.6%
27	Kentucky	1,635	1.0%
25	Louisiana	1,989	1.3%
42	Maine	634	0.4%
10	Maryland	5,347	3.4%
7	Massachusetts	7,253	4.6%
11	Michigan	5,064	3.2%
19	Minnesota	2,600	1.6%
33	Mississippi	867	0.5%
18	Missouri	2,825	1.8%
46	Montana	298	0.2%
41	Nebraska	668	0.4%
30	Nevada	1,001	0.6%
39	New Hampshire	713	0.5%
8	New Jersey	6,290	4.0%
34	New Mexico	840	0.5%
2	New York	17,832	11.3%
12	North Carolina	4,244	2.7%
48	North Dakota	268	0.2%
9	Ohio	5,751	3.6%
29	Oklahoma	1,036	0.7%
24	Oregon	2,038	1.3%
6	Pennsylvania	7,492	4.7%
31	Rhode Island	949	0.6%
28	South Carolina	1,596	1.0%
47	South Dakota	293	0.2%
16	Tennessee	3,071	1.9%
3	Texas	8,650	5.5%
36	Utah	767	0.5%
43	Vermont	429	0.3%
14	Virginia	3,770	2.4%
17	Washington	2,989	1.9%
40	West Virginia	701	0.4%
20	Wisconsin	2,503	1.6%
50	Wyoming	120	0.1%

RANK ORDER

RANK	STATE	PHYSICIANS	% of USA
1	California	18,519	11.7%
2	New York	17,832	11.3%
3	Texas	8,650	5.5%
4	Florida	8,647	5.5%
5	Illinois	7,700	4.9%
6	Pennsylvania	7,492	4.7%
7	Massachusetts	7,253	4.6%
8	New Jersey	6,290	4.0%
9	Ohio	5,751	3.6%
10	Maryland	5,347	3.4%
11	Michigan	5,064	3.2%
12	North Carolina	4,244	2.7%
13	Georgia	3,920	2.5%
14	Virginia	3,770	2.4%
15	Connecticut	3,233	2.0%
16	Tennessee	3,071	1.9%
17	Washington	2,989	1.9%
18	Missouri	2,825	1.8%
19	Minnesota	2,600	1.6%
20	Wisconsin	2,503	1.6%
21	Arizona	2,502	1.6%
22	Indiana	2,206	1.4%
23	Colorado	2,094	1.3%
24	Oregon	2,038	1.3%
25	Louisiana	1,989	1.3%
26	Alabama	1,899	1.2%
27	Kentucky	1,635	1.0%
28	South Carolina	1,596	1.0%
29	Oklahoma	1,036	0.7%
30	Nevada	1,001	0.6%
31	Rhode Island	949	0.6%
32	Kansas	918	0.6%
33	Mississippi	867	0.5%
34	New Mexico	840	0.5%
35	Hawaii	821	0.5%
36	Utah	767	0.5%
37	Arkansas	765	0.5%
38	Iowa	759	0.5%
39	New Hampshire	713	0.5%
40	West Virginia	701	0.4%
41	Nebraska	668	0.4%
42	Maine	634	0.4%
43	Vermont	429	0.3%
44	Delaware	360	0.2%
45	Idaho	310	0.2%
46	Montana	298	0.2%
47	South Dakota	293	0.2%
48	North Dakota	268	0.2%
49	Alaska	167	0.1%
50	Wyoming	120	0.1%
	District of Columbia	1,012	0.6%

Source: American Medical Association (Chicago, Illinois)
"Physician Characteristics and Distribution in the U.S." (2010 Edition)
*As of December 31, 2008. Total does not include 1,749 physicians in U.S. territories and possessions. Internal Medicine includes Diabetes, Endocrinology, Geriatrics, Hematology, Infectious Diseases, Nephrology, Nutrition, Medical Oncology, and Rheumatology.

Rate of Physicians in Internal Medicine in 2008

National Rate = 52 Physicians per 100,000 Population*

ALPHA ORDER

RANK	STATE	RATE
29	Alabama	41
48	Alaska	24
33	Arizona	38
46	Arkansas	27
13	California	51
26	Colorado	42
3	Connecticut	92
29	Delaware	41
20	Florida	47
31	Georgia	40
8	Hawaii	64
50	Idaho	20
9	Illinois	60
39	Indiana	35
47	Iowa	25
41	Kansas	33
33	Kentucky	38
24	Louisiana	45
18	Maine	48
2	Maryland	94
1	Massachusetts	111
13	Michigan	51
15	Minnesota	50
43	Mississippi	29
20	Missouri	47
42	Montana	31
36	Nebraska	37
33	Nevada	38
11	New Hampshire	54
6	New Jersey	73
26	New Mexico	42
3	New York	92
22	North Carolina	46
26	North Dakota	42
15	Ohio	50
44	Oklahoma	28
11	Oregon	54
9	Pennsylvania	60
5	Rhode Island	90
39	South Carolina	35
37	South Dakota	36
17	Tennessee	49
37	Texas	36
44	Utah	28
7	Vermont	69
18	Virginia	48
22	Washington	46
32	West Virginia	39
25	Wisconsin	44
49	Wyoming	23

RANK ORDER

RANK	STATE	RATE
1	Massachusetts	111
2	Maryland	94
3	Connecticut	92
3	New York	92
5	Rhode Island	90
6	New Jersey	73
7	Vermont	69
8	Hawaii	64
9	Illinois	60
9	Pennsylvania	60
11	New Hampshire	54
11	Oregon	54
13	California	51
13	Michigan	51
15	Minnesota	50
15	Ohio	50
17	Tennessee	49
18	Maine	48
18	Virginia	48
20	Florida	47
20	Missouri	47
22	North Carolina	46
22	Washington	46
24	Louisiana	45
25	Wisconsin	44
26	Colorado	42
26	New Mexico	42
26	North Dakota	42
29	Alabama	41
29	Delaware	41
31	Georgia	40
32	West Virginia	39
33	Arizona	38
33	Kentucky	38
33	Nevada	38
36	Nebraska	37
37	South Dakota	36
37	Texas	36
39	Indiana	35
39	South Carolina	35
41	Kansas	33
42	Montana	31
43	Mississippi	29
44	Oklahoma	28
44	Utah	28
46	Arkansas	27
47	Iowa	25
48	Alaska	24
49	Wyoming	23
50	Idaho	20

	District of Columbia	172

Source: CQ Press using data from American Medical Association (Chicago, Illinois)
   "Physician Characteristics and Distribution in the U.S." (2010 Edition)

*As of December 31, 2008. National rate does not include physicians in U.S. territories and possessions. Internal Medicine includes Diabetes, Endocrinology, Geriatrics, Hematology, Infectious Diseases, Nephrology, Nutrition, Medical Oncology, and Rheumatology.

Physicians in Pediatrics in 2008

National Total = 73,920 Physicians*

ALPHA ORDER

RANK	STATE	PHYSICIANS	% of USA
27	Alabama	864	1.2%
46	Alaska	122	0.2%
20	Arizona	1,170	1.6%
30	Arkansas	527	0.7%
1	California	9,003	12.2%
24	Colorado	1,067	1.4%
22	Connecticut	1,150	1.6%
43	Delaware	257	0.3%
4	Florida	3,927	5.3%
13	Georgia	2,024	2.7%
33	Hawaii	418	0.6%
45	Idaho	140	0.2%
5	Illinois	3,167	4.3%
19	Indiana	1,172	1.6%
38	Iowa	382	0.5%
31	Kansas	488	0.7%
25	Kentucky	915	1.2%
23	Louisiana	1,089	1.5%
42	Maine	263	0.4%
10	Maryland	2,269	3.1%
9	Massachusetts	2,771	3.7%
11	Michigan	2,207	3.0%
18	Minnesota	1,192	1.6%
34	Mississippi	415	0.6%
16	Missouri	1,405	1.9%
47	Montana	121	0.2%
40	Nebraska	341	0.5%
37	Nevada	386	0.5%
41	New Hampshire	305	0.4%
8	New Jersey	2,984	4.0%
36	New Mexico	395	0.5%
2	New York	7,309	9.9%
12	North Carolina	2,159	2.9%
49	North Dakota	90	0.1%
6	Ohio	3,015	4.1%
32	Oklahoma	474	0.6%
28	Oregon	745	1.0%
7	Pennsylvania	3,009	4.1%
35	Rhode Island	412	0.6%
26	South Carolina	879	1.2%
48	South Dakota	101	0.1%
15	Tennessee	1,608	2.2%
3	Texas	5,001	6.8%
29	Utah	565	0.8%
44	Vermont	184	0.2%
14	Virginia	1,967	2.7%
17	Washington	1,386	1.9%
39	West Virginia	345	0.5%
21	Wisconsin	1,160	1.6%
50	Wyoming	53	0.1%

RANK ORDER

RANK	STATE	PHYSICIANS	% of USA
1	California	9,003	12.2%
2	New York	7,309	9.9%
3	Texas	5,001	6.8%
4	Florida	3,927	5.3%
5	Illinois	3,167	4.3%
6	Ohio	3,015	4.1%
7	Pennsylvania	3,009	4.1%
8	New Jersey	2,984	4.0%
9	Massachusetts	2,771	3.7%
10	Maryland	2,269	3.1%
11	Michigan	2,207	3.0%
12	North Carolina	2,159	2.9%
13	Georgia	2,024	2.7%
14	Virginia	1,967	2.7%
15	Tennessee	1,608	2.2%
16	Missouri	1,405	1.9%
17	Washington	1,386	1.9%
18	Minnesota	1,192	1.6%
19	Indiana	1,172	1.6%
20	Arizona	1,170	1.6%
21	Wisconsin	1,160	1.6%
22	Connecticut	1,150	1.6%
23	Louisiana	1,089	1.5%
24	Colorado	1,067	1.4%
25	Kentucky	915	1.2%
26	South Carolina	879	1.2%
27	Alabama	864	1.2%
28	Oregon	745	1.0%
29	Utah	565	0.8%
30	Arkansas	527	0.7%
31	Kansas	488	0.7%
32	Oklahoma	474	0.6%
33	Hawaii	418	0.6%
34	Mississippi	415	0.6%
35	Rhode Island	412	0.6%
36	New Mexico	395	0.5%
37	Nevada	386	0.5%
38	Iowa	382	0.5%
39	West Virginia	345	0.5%
40	Nebraska	341	0.5%
41	New Hampshire	305	0.4%
42	Maine	263	0.4%
43	Delaware	257	0.3%
44	Vermont	184	0.2%
45	Idaho	140	0.2%
46	Alaska	122	0.2%
47	Montana	121	0.2%
48	South Dakota	101	0.1%
49	North Dakota	90	0.1%
50	Wyoming	53	0.1%
	District of Columbia	522	0.7%

Source: American Medical Association (Chicago, Illinois)
   "Physician Characteristics and Distribution in the U.S." (2010 Edition)

*As of December 31, 2008. Total does not include 1,209 physicians in U.S. territories and possessions. Pediatrics includes Adolescent Medicine, Neonatal-Perinatal, Pediatric Allergy, Pediatric Endocrinology, Pediatric Pulmonology, Pediatric Hematology-Oncology, and Pediatric Nephrology.

Rate of Physicians in Pediatrics in 2008

National Rate = 100 Physicians per 100,000 Population 17 Years and Younger*

ALPHA ORDER

RANK	STATE	RATE
33	Alabama	77
40	Alaska	68
39	Arizona	69
35	Arkansas	75
19	California	96
27	Colorado	88
8	Connecticut	142
9	Delaware	125
17	Florida	98
31	Georgia	79
5	Hawaii	147
50	Idaho	34
15	Illinois	100
36	Indiana	74
45	Iowa	54
38	Kansas	70
24	Kentucky	91
17	Louisiana	98
19	Maine	96
3	Maryland	169
1	Massachusetts	194
23	Michigan	92
22	Minnesota	95
45	Mississippi	54
16	Missouri	99
44	Montana	55
34	Nebraska	76
43	Nevada	58
14	New Hampshire	104
6	New Jersey	146
31	New Mexico	79
4	New York	166
19	North Carolina	96
42	North Dakota	63
10	Ohio	110
47	Oklahoma	52
29	Oregon	86
11	Pennsylvania	109
2	Rhode Island	180
30	South Carolina	82
48	South Dakota	51
11	Tennessee	109
36	Texas	74
41	Utah	66
7	Vermont	143
13	Virginia	108
25	Washington	90
26	West Virginia	89
27	Wisconsin	88
49	Wyoming	41

RANK ORDER

RANK	STATE	RATE
1	Massachusetts	194
2	Rhode Island	180
3	Maryland	169
4	New York	166
5	Hawaii	147
6	New Jersey	146
7	Vermont	143
8	Connecticut	142
9	Delaware	125
10	Ohio	110
11	Pennsylvania	109
11	Tennessee	109
13	Virginia	108
14	New Hampshire	104
15	Illinois	100
16	Missouri	99
17	Florida	98
17	Louisiana	98
19	California	96
19	Maine	96
19	North Carolina	96
22	Minnesota	95
23	Michigan	92
24	Kentucky	91
25	Washington	90
26	West Virginia	89
27	Colorado	88
27	Wisconsin	88
29	Oregon	86
30	South Carolina	82
31	Georgia	79
31	New Mexico	79
33	Alabama	77
34	Nebraska	76
35	Arkansas	75
36	Indiana	74
36	Texas	74
38	Kansas	70
39	Arizona	69
40	Alaska	68
41	Utah	66
42	North Dakota	63
43	Nevada	58
44	Montana	55
45	Iowa	54
45	Mississippi	54
47	Oklahoma	52
48	South Dakota	51
49	Wyoming	41
50	Idaho	34

District of Columbia 466

Source: CQ Press using data from American Medical Association (Chicago, Illinois)
"Physician Characteristics and Distribution in the U.S." (2010 Edition)
*As of December 31, 2008. National rate does not include physicians in U.S. territories and possessions. Pediatrics includes Adolescent Medicine, Neonatal-Perinatal, Pediatric Allergy, Pediatric Endocrinology, Pediatric Pulmonology, Pediatric Hematology-Oncology, and Pediatric Nephrology.

Physicians in Surgical Specialties in 2008

National Total = 161,168 Physicians*

ALPHA ORDER

RANK	STATE	PHYSICIANS	% of USA
25	Alabama	2,300	1.4%
48	Alaska	331	0.2%
22	Arizona	2,658	1.6%
34	Arkansas	1,156	0.7%
1	California	18,793	11.7%
23	Colorado	2,541	1.6%
24	Connecticut	2,518	1.6%
45	Delaware	428	0.3%
4	Florida	9,431	5.9%
12	Georgia	4,472	2.8%
39	Hawaii	814	0.5%
43	Idaho	594	0.4%
6	Illinois	6,555	4.1%
21	Indiana	2,716	1.7%
33	Iowa	1,160	0.7%
30	Kansas	1,291	0.8%
27	Kentucky	2,094	1.3%
20	Louisiana	2,727	1.7%
42	Maine	687	0.4%
14	Maryland	4,272	2.7%
11	Massachusetts	4,794	3.0%
9	Michigan	4,923	3.1%
19	Minnesota	2,769	1.7%
31	Mississippi	1,232	0.8%
17	Missouri	2,928	1.8%
44	Montana	491	0.3%
36	Nebraska	927	0.6%
35	Nevada	960	0.6%
40	New Hampshire	775	0.5%
8	New Jersey	5,226	3.2%
38	New Mexico	832	0.5%
2	New York	13,781	8.6%
10	North Carolina	4,854	3.0%
49	North Dakota	304	0.2%
7	Ohio	6,143	3.8%
29	Oklahoma	1,351	0.8%
28	Oregon	2,092	1.3%
5	Pennsylvania	7,276	4.5%
41	Rhode Island	739	0.5%
26	South Carolina	2,249	1.4%
47	South Dakota	388	0.2%
15	Tennessee	3,593	2.2%
3	Texas	10,970	6.8%
32	Utah	1,195	0.7%
46	Vermont	427	0.3%
13	Virginia	4,330	2.7%
16	Washington	3,231	2.0%
37	West Virginia	907	0.6%
18	Wisconsin	2,812	1.7%
50	Wyoming	237	0.1%

RANK ORDER

RANK	STATE	PHYSICIANS	% of USA
1	California	18,793	11.7%
2	New York	13,781	8.6%
3	Texas	10,970	6.8%
4	Florida	9,431	5.9%
5	Pennsylvania	7,276	4.5%
6	Illinois	6,555	4.1%
7	Ohio	6,143	3.8%
8	New Jersey	5,226	3.2%
9	Michigan	4,923	3.1%
10	North Carolina	4,854	3.0%
11	Massachusetts	4,794	3.0%
12	Georgia	4,472	2.8%
13	Virginia	4,330	2.7%
14	Maryland	4,272	2.7%
15	Tennessee	3,593	2.2%
16	Washington	3,231	2.0%
17	Missouri	2,928	1.8%
18	Wisconsin	2,812	1.7%
19	Minnesota	2,769	1.7%
20	Louisiana	2,727	1.7%
21	Indiana	2,716	1.7%
22	Arizona	2,658	1.6%
23	Colorado	2,541	1.6%
24	Connecticut	2,518	1.6%
25	Alabama	2,300	1.4%
26	South Carolina	2,249	1.4%
27	Kentucky	2,094	1.3%
28	Oregon	2,092	1.3%
29	Oklahoma	1,351	0.8%
30	Kansas	1,291	0.8%
31	Mississippi	1,232	0.8%
32	Utah	1,195	0.7%
33	Iowa	1,160	0.7%
34	Arkansas	1,156	0.7%
35	Nevada	960	0.6%
36	Nebraska	927	0.6%
37	West Virginia	907	0.6%
38	New Mexico	832	0.5%
39	Hawaii	814	0.5%
40	New Hampshire	775	0.5%
41	Rhode Island	739	0.5%
42	Maine	687	0.4%
43	Idaho	594	0.4%
44	Montana	491	0.3%
45	Delaware	428	0.3%
46	Vermont	427	0.3%
47	South Dakota	388	0.2%
48	Alaska	331	0.2%
49	North Dakota	304	0.2%
50	Wyoming	237	0.1%
	District of Columbia	894	0.6%

Source: American Medical Association (Chicago, Illinois)
"Physician Characteristics and Distribution in the U.S." (2010 Edition)
*As of December 31, 2008. Total does not include 1,767 physicians in U.S. territories and possessions. Surgical Specialties include Colon and Rectal, General, Neurological, Obstetrics and Gynecology, Ophthalmology, Orthopedic, Otolaryngology, Plastic, Thoracic, and Urological Surgeries.

Rate of Physicians in Surgical Specialties in 2008

National Rate = 53 Physicians per 100,000 Population*

ALPHA ORDER

RANK	STATE	RATE
28	Alabama	49
34	Alaska	48
45	Arizona	41
46	Arkansas	40
20	California	51
20	Colorado	51
3	Connecticut	72
28	Delaware	49
20	Florida	51
37	Georgia	46
7	Hawaii	63
47	Idaho	39
20	Illinois	51
42	Indiana	43
47	Iowa	39
37	Kansas	46
28	Kentucky	49
8	Louisiana	61
17	Maine	52
1	Maryland	75
2	Massachusetts	73
28	Michigan	49
15	Minnesota	53
43	Mississippi	42
28	Missouri	49
20	Montana	51
17	Nebraska	52
49	Nevada	37
10	New Hampshire	59
9	New Jersey	60
43	New Mexico	42
4	New York	71
17	North Carolina	52
36	North Dakota	47
15	Ohio	53
49	Oklahoma	37
14	Oregon	55
11	Pennsylvania	58
5	Rhode Island	70
25	South Carolina	50
34	South Dakota	48
11	Tennessee	58
39	Texas	45
40	Utah	44
6	Vermont	69
13	Virginia	56
28	Washington	49
25	West Virginia	50
25	Wisconsin	50
40	Wyoming	44

RANK ORDER

RANK	STATE	RATE
1	Maryland	75
2	Massachusetts	73
3	Connecticut	72
4	New York	71
5	Rhode Island	70
6	Vermont	69
7	Hawaii	63
8	Louisiana	61
9	New Jersey	60
10	New Hampshire	59
11	Pennsylvania	58
11	Tennessee	58
13	Virginia	56
14	Oregon	55
15	Minnesota	53
15	Ohio	53
17	Maine	52
17	Nebraska	52
17	North Carolina	52
20	California	51
20	Colorado	51
20	Florida	51
20	Illinois	51
20	Montana	51
25	South Carolina	50
25	West Virginia	50
25	Wisconsin	50
28	Alabama	49
28	Delaware	49
28	Kentucky	49
28	Michigan	49
28	Missouri	49
28	Washington	49
34	Alaska	48
34	South Dakota	48
36	North Dakota	47
37	Georgia	46
37	Kansas	46
39	Texas	45
40	Utah	44
40	Wyoming	44
42	Indiana	43
43	Mississippi	42
43	New Mexico	42
45	Arizona	41
46	Arkansas	40
47	Idaho	39
47	Iowa	39
49	Nevada	37
49	Oklahoma	37

District of Columbia 152

Source: CQ Press using data from American Medical Association (Chicago, Illinois)
"Physician Characteristics and Distribution in the U.S." (2010 Edition)
*As of December 31, 2008. National rate does not include physicians in U.S. territories and possessions. Surgical Specialties include Colon and Rectal, General, Neurological, Obstetrics and Gynecology, Ophthalmology, Orthopedic, Otolaryngology, Plastic, Thoracic, and Urological Surgeries.

Average Annual Wages of Surgeons in 2008

National Average = $206,770*

ALPHA ORDER

RANK	STATE	WAGES
13	Alabama	$212,750
NA	Alaska**	NA
29	Arizona	190,110
NA	Arkansas**	NA
23	California	202,940
10	Colorado	215,160
9	Connecticut	215,370
25	Delaware	201,870
31	Florida	185,810
NA	Georgia**	NA
35	Hawaii	177,110
20	Idaho	208,270
32	Illinois	184,730
NA	Indiana**	NA
24	Iowa	202,020
3	Kansas	217,490
15	Kentucky	211,540
NA	Louisiana**	NA
NA	Maine**	NA
NA	Maryland**	NA
12	Massachusetts	213,850
NA	Michigan**	NA
NA	Minnesota**	NA
7	Mississippi	216,380
NA	Missouri**	NA
NA	Montana**	NA
34	Nebraska	177,990
11	Nevada	214,690
NA	New Hampshire**	NA
NA	New Jersey**	NA
5	New Mexico	217,380
33	New York	178,960
NA	North Carolina**	NA
16	North Dakota	211,360
21	Ohio	206,570
19	Oklahoma	208,760
6	Oregon	216,820
27	Pennsylvania	194,990
8	Rhode Island	216,010
4	South Carolina	217,450
17	South Dakota	210,770
22	Tennessee	203,650
28	Texas	194,670
2	Utah	218,200
30	Vermont	190,050
26	Virginia	198,620
14	Washington	212,350
18	West Virginia	209,530
1	Wisconsin	218,610
NA	Wyoming**	NA

RANK ORDER

RANK	STATE	WAGES
1	Wisconsin	$218,610
2	Utah	218,200
3	Kansas	217,490
4	South Carolina	217,450
5	New Mexico	217,380
6	Oregon	216,820
7	Mississippi	216,380
8	Rhode Island	216,010
9	Connecticut	215,370
10	Colorado	215,160
11	Nevada	214,690
12	Massachusetts	213,850
13	Alabama	212,750
14	Washington	212,350
15	Kentucky	211,540
16	North Dakota	211,360
17	South Dakota	210,770
18	West Virginia	209,530
19	Oklahoma	208,760
20	Idaho	208,270
21	Ohio	206,570
22	Tennessee	203,650
23	California	202,940
24	Iowa	202,020
25	Delaware	201,870
26	Virginia	198,620
27	Pennsylvania	194,990
28	Texas	194,670
29	Arizona	190,110
30	Vermont	190,050
31	Florida	185,810
32	Illinois	184,730
33	New York	178,960
34	Nebraska	177,990
35	Hawaii	177,110
NA	Alaska**	NA
NA	Arkansas**	NA
NA	Georgia**	NA
NA	Indiana**	NA
NA	Louisiana**	NA
NA	Maine**	NA
NA	Maryland**	NA
NA	Michigan**	NA
NA	Minnesota**	NA
NA	Missouri**	NA
NA	Montana**	NA
NA	New Hampshire**	NA
NA	New Jersey**	NA
NA	North Carolina**	NA
NA	Wyoming**	NA

District of Columbia — 169,440

Source: U.S. Department of Labor, Bureau of Labor Statistics
    "Occupational Employment and Wages, 2008" (http://www.bls.gov/oes/)
*Does not include self-employed.
**Not available.

Physicians in General Surgery in 2008

National Total = 37,354 Physicians*

<table>
<tr><td colspan="4">ALPHA ORDER</td><td colspan="4">RANK ORDER</td></tr>
<tr><td>RANK</td><td>STATE</td><td>PHYSICIANS</td><td>% of USA</td><td>RANK</td><td>STATE</td><td>PHYSICIANS</td><td>% of USA</td></tr>
<tr><td>27</td><td>Alabama</td><td>533</td><td>1.4%</td><td>1</td><td>California</td><td>4,029</td><td>10.8%</td></tr>
<tr><td>49</td><td>Alaska</td><td>75</td><td>0.2%</td><td>2</td><td>New York</td><td>3,287</td><td>8.8%</td></tr>
<tr><td>20</td><td>Arizona</td><td>621</td><td>1.7%</td><td>3</td><td>Texas</td><td>2,368</td><td>6.3%</td></tr>
<tr><td>32</td><td>Arkansas</td><td>275</td><td>0.7%</td><td>4</td><td>Florida</td><td>1,928</td><td>5.2%</td></tr>
<tr><td>1</td><td>California</td><td>4,029</td><td>10.8%</td><td>5</td><td>Pennsylvania</td><td>1,891</td><td>5.1%</td></tr>
<tr><td>23</td><td>Colorado</td><td>557</td><td>1.5%</td><td>6</td><td>Ohio</td><td>1,553</td><td>4.2%</td></tr>
<tr><td>24</td><td>Connecticut</td><td>551</td><td>1.5%</td><td>7</td><td>Illinois</td><td>1,512</td><td>4.0%</td></tr>
<tr><td>45</td><td>Delaware</td><td>103</td><td>0.3%</td><td>8</td><td>Michigan</td><td>1,252</td><td>3.4%</td></tr>
<tr><td>4</td><td>Florida</td><td>1,928</td><td>5.2%</td><td>9</td><td>Massachusetts</td><td>1,245</td><td>3.3%</td></tr>
<tr><td>12</td><td>Georgia</td><td>1,036</td><td>2.8%</td><td>10</td><td>New Jersey</td><td>1,195</td><td>3.2%</td></tr>
<tr><td>42</td><td>Hawaii</td><td>171</td><td>0.5%</td><td>11</td><td>North Carolina</td><td>1,124</td><td>3.0%</td></tr>
<tr><td>43</td><td>Idaho</td><td>136</td><td>0.4%</td><td>12</td><td>Georgia</td><td>1,036</td><td>2.8%</td></tr>
<tr><td>7</td><td>Illinois</td><td>1,512</td><td>4.0%</td><td>13</td><td>Maryland</td><td>970</td><td>2.6%</td></tr>
<tr><td>22</td><td>Indiana</td><td>591</td><td>1.6%</td><td>14</td><td>Virginia</td><td>960</td><td>2.6%</td></tr>
<tr><td>30</td><td>Iowa</td><td>300</td><td>0.8%</td><td>15</td><td>Tennessee</td><td>914</td><td>2.4%</td></tr>
<tr><td>31</td><td>Kansas</td><td>298</td><td>0.8%</td><td>16</td><td>Washington</td><td>751</td><td>2.0%</td></tr>
<tr><td>25</td><td>Kentucky</td><td>542</td><td>1.5%</td><td>17</td><td>Missouri</td><td>660</td><td>1.8%</td></tr>
<tr><td>21</td><td>Louisiana</td><td>598</td><td>1.6%</td><td>18</td><td>Minnesota</td><td>659</td><td>1.8%</td></tr>
<tr><td>40</td><td>Maine</td><td>181</td><td>0.5%</td><td>19</td><td>Wisconsin</td><td>642</td><td>1.7%</td></tr>
<tr><td>13</td><td>Maryland</td><td>970</td><td>2.6%</td><td>20</td><td>Arizona</td><td>621</td><td>1.7%</td></tr>
<tr><td>9</td><td>Massachusetts</td><td>1,245</td><td>3.3%</td><td>21</td><td>Louisiana</td><td>598</td><td>1.6%</td></tr>
<tr><td>8</td><td>Michigan</td><td>1,252</td><td>3.4%</td><td>22</td><td>Indiana</td><td>591</td><td>1.6%</td></tr>
<tr><td>18</td><td>Minnesota</td><td>659</td><td>1.8%</td><td>23</td><td>Colorado</td><td>557</td><td>1.5%</td></tr>
<tr><td>33</td><td>Mississippi</td><td>265</td><td>0.7%</td><td>24</td><td>Connecticut</td><td>551</td><td>1.5%</td></tr>
<tr><td>17</td><td>Missouri</td><td>660</td><td>1.8%</td><td>25</td><td>Kentucky</td><td>542</td><td>1.5%</td></tr>
<tr><td>46</td><td>Montana</td><td>102</td><td>0.3%</td><td>26</td><td>South Carolina</td><td>538</td><td>1.4%</td></tr>
<tr><td>35</td><td>Nebraska</td><td>246</td><td>0.7%</td><td>27</td><td>Alabama</td><td>533</td><td>1.4%</td></tr>
<tr><td>37</td><td>Nevada</td><td>211</td><td>0.6%</td><td>28</td><td>Oregon</td><td>502</td><td>1.3%</td></tr>
<tr><td>39</td><td>New Hampshire</td><td>191</td><td>0.5%</td><td>29</td><td>Oklahoma</td><td>302</td><td>0.8%</td></tr>
<tr><td>10</td><td>New Jersey</td><td>1,195</td><td>3.2%</td><td>30</td><td>Iowa</td><td>300</td><td>0.8%</td></tr>
<tr><td>38</td><td>New Mexico</td><td>203</td><td>0.5%</td><td>31</td><td>Kansas</td><td>298</td><td>0.8%</td></tr>
<tr><td>2</td><td>New York</td><td>3,287</td><td>8.8%</td><td>32</td><td>Arkansas</td><td>275</td><td>0.7%</td></tr>
<tr><td>11</td><td>North Carolina</td><td>1,124</td><td>3.0%</td><td>33</td><td>Mississippi</td><td>265</td><td>0.7%</td></tr>
<tr><td>48</td><td>North Dakota</td><td>95</td><td>0.3%</td><td>34</td><td>West Virginia</td><td>247</td><td>0.7%</td></tr>
<tr><td>6</td><td>Ohio</td><td>1,553</td><td>4.2%</td><td>35</td><td>Nebraska</td><td>246</td><td>0.7%</td></tr>
<tr><td>29</td><td>Oklahoma</td><td>302</td><td>0.8%</td><td>36</td><td>Utah</td><td>230</td><td>0.6%</td></tr>
<tr><td>28</td><td>Oregon</td><td>502</td><td>1.3%</td><td>37</td><td>Nevada</td><td>211</td><td>0.6%</td></tr>
<tr><td>5</td><td>Pennsylvania</td><td>1,891</td><td>5.1%</td><td>38</td><td>New Mexico</td><td>203</td><td>0.5%</td></tr>
<tr><td>41</td><td>Rhode Island</td><td>180</td><td>0.5%</td><td>39</td><td>New Hampshire</td><td>191</td><td>0.5%</td></tr>
<tr><td>26</td><td>South Carolina</td><td>538</td><td>1.4%</td><td>40</td><td>Maine</td><td>181</td><td>0.5%</td></tr>
<tr><td>46</td><td>South Dakota</td><td>102</td><td>0.3%</td><td>41</td><td>Rhode Island</td><td>180</td><td>0.5%</td></tr>
<tr><td>15</td><td>Tennessee</td><td>914</td><td>2.4%</td><td>42</td><td>Hawaii</td><td>171</td><td>0.5%</td></tr>
<tr><td>3</td><td>Texas</td><td>2,368</td><td>6.3%</td><td>43</td><td>Idaho</td><td>136</td><td>0.4%</td></tr>
<tr><td>36</td><td>Utah</td><td>230</td><td>0.6%</td><td>44</td><td>Vermont</td><td>119</td><td>0.3%</td></tr>
<tr><td>44</td><td>Vermont</td><td>119</td><td>0.3%</td><td>45</td><td>Delaware</td><td>103</td><td>0.3%</td></tr>
<tr><td>14</td><td>Virginia</td><td>960</td><td>2.6%</td><td>46</td><td>Montana</td><td>102</td><td>0.3%</td></tr>
<tr><td>16</td><td>Washington</td><td>751</td><td>2.0%</td><td>46</td><td>South Dakota</td><td>102</td><td>0.3%</td></tr>
<tr><td>34</td><td>West Virginia</td><td>247</td><td>0.7%</td><td>48</td><td>North Dakota</td><td>95</td><td>0.3%</td></tr>
<tr><td>19</td><td>Wisconsin</td><td>642</td><td>1.7%</td><td>49</td><td>Alaska</td><td>75</td><td>0.2%</td></tr>
<tr><td>50</td><td>Wyoming</td><td>58</td><td>0.2%</td><td>50</td><td>Wyoming</td><td>58</td><td>0.2%</td></tr>
<tr><td></td><td></td><td></td><td></td><td colspan="2">District of Columbia</td><td>255</td><td>0.7%</td></tr>
</table>

Source: American Medical Association (Chicago, Illinois)
   "Physician Characteristics and Distribution in the U.S." (2010 Edition)
*As of December 31, 2008. Total does not include 443 physicians in U.S. territories and possessions. General Surgery includes
Abdominal, Cardiovascular, Hand, Head and Neck, Pediatric, Traumatic, and Vascular Surgeries.

Rate of Physicians in General Surgery in 2008

National Rate = 12 Physicians per 100,000 Population*

<table>
<tr><td colspan="3">ALPHA ORDER</td><td colspan="3">RANK ORDER</td></tr>
<tr><th>RANK</th><th>STATE</th><th>RATE</th><th>RANK</th><th>STATE</th><th>RATE</th></tr>
<tr><td>28</td><td>Alabama</td><td>11</td><td>1</td><td>Massachusetts</td><td>19</td></tr>
<tr><td>28</td><td>Alaska</td><td>11</td><td>1</td><td>Vermont</td><td>19</td></tr>
<tr><td>39</td><td>Arizona</td><td>10</td><td>3</td><td>Maryland</td><td>17</td></tr>
<tr><td>39</td><td>Arkansas</td><td>10</td><td>3</td><td>New York</td><td>17</td></tr>
<tr><td>28</td><td>California</td><td>11</td><td>3</td><td>Rhode Island</td><td>17</td></tr>
<tr><td>28</td><td>Colorado</td><td>11</td><td>6</td><td>Connecticut</td><td>16</td></tr>
<tr><td>6</td><td>Connecticut</td><td>16</td><td>7</td><td>North Dakota</td><td>15</td></tr>
<tr><td>23</td><td>Delaware</td><td>12</td><td>7</td><td>Pennsylvania</td><td>15</td></tr>
<tr><td>39</td><td>Florida</td><td>10</td><td>7</td><td>Tennessee</td><td>15</td></tr>
<tr><td>28</td><td>Georgia</td><td>11</td><td>10</td><td>Maine</td><td>14</td></tr>
<tr><td>15</td><td>Hawaii</td><td>13</td><td>10</td><td>Nebraska</td><td>14</td></tr>
<tr><td>45</td><td>Idaho</td><td>9</td><td>10</td><td>New Hampshire</td><td>14</td></tr>
<tr><td>23</td><td>Illinois</td><td>12</td><td>10</td><td>New Jersey</td><td>14</td></tr>
<tr><td>45</td><td>Indiana</td><td>9</td><td>10</td><td>West Virginia</td><td>14</td></tr>
<tr><td>39</td><td>Iowa</td><td>10</td><td>15</td><td>Hawaii</td><td>13</td></tr>
<tr><td>28</td><td>Kansas</td><td>11</td><td>15</td><td>Kentucky</td><td>13</td></tr>
<tr><td>15</td><td>Kentucky</td><td>13</td><td>15</td><td>Louisiana</td><td>13</td></tr>
<tr><td>15</td><td>Louisiana</td><td>13</td><td>15</td><td>Michigan</td><td>13</td></tr>
<tr><td>10</td><td>Maine</td><td>14</td><td>15</td><td>Minnesota</td><td>13</td></tr>
<tr><td>3</td><td>Maryland</td><td>17</td><td>15</td><td>Ohio</td><td>13</td></tr>
<tr><td>1</td><td>Massachusetts</td><td>19</td><td>15</td><td>Oregon</td><td>13</td></tr>
<tr><td>15</td><td>Michigan</td><td>13</td><td>15</td><td>South Dakota</td><td>13</td></tr>
<tr><td>15</td><td>Minnesota</td><td>13</td><td>23</td><td>Delaware</td><td>12</td></tr>
<tr><td>45</td><td>Mississippi</td><td>9</td><td>23</td><td>Illinois</td><td>12</td></tr>
<tr><td>28</td><td>Missouri</td><td>11</td><td>23</td><td>North Carolina</td><td>12</td></tr>
<tr><td>28</td><td>Montana</td><td>11</td><td>23</td><td>South Carolina</td><td>12</td></tr>
<tr><td>10</td><td>Nebraska</td><td>14</td><td>23</td><td>Virginia</td><td>12</td></tr>
<tr><td>48</td><td>Nevada</td><td>8</td><td>28</td><td>Alabama</td><td>11</td></tr>
<tr><td>10</td><td>New Hampshire</td><td>14</td><td>28</td><td>Alaska</td><td>11</td></tr>
<tr><td>10</td><td>New Jersey</td><td>14</td><td>28</td><td>California</td><td>11</td></tr>
<tr><td>39</td><td>New Mexico</td><td>10</td><td>28</td><td>Colorado</td><td>11</td></tr>
<tr><td>3</td><td>New York</td><td>17</td><td>28</td><td>Georgia</td><td>11</td></tr>
<tr><td>23</td><td>North Carolina</td><td>12</td><td>28</td><td>Kansas</td><td>11</td></tr>
<tr><td>7</td><td>North Dakota</td><td>15</td><td>28</td><td>Missouri</td><td>11</td></tr>
<tr><td>15</td><td>Ohio</td><td>13</td><td>28</td><td>Montana</td><td>11</td></tr>
<tr><td>48</td><td>Oklahoma</td><td>8</td><td>28</td><td>Washington</td><td>11</td></tr>
<tr><td>15</td><td>Oregon</td><td>13</td><td>28</td><td>Wisconsin</td><td>11</td></tr>
<tr><td>7</td><td>Pennsylvania</td><td>15</td><td>28</td><td>Wyoming</td><td>11</td></tr>
<tr><td>3</td><td>Rhode Island</td><td>17</td><td>39</td><td>Arizona</td><td>10</td></tr>
<tr><td>23</td><td>South Carolina</td><td>12</td><td>39</td><td>Arkansas</td><td>10</td></tr>
<tr><td>15</td><td>South Dakota</td><td>13</td><td>39</td><td>Florida</td><td>10</td></tr>
<tr><td>7</td><td>Tennessee</td><td>15</td><td>39</td><td>Iowa</td><td>10</td></tr>
<tr><td>39</td><td>Texas</td><td>10</td><td>39</td><td>New Mexico</td><td>10</td></tr>
<tr><td>48</td><td>Utah</td><td>8</td><td>39</td><td>Texas</td><td>10</td></tr>
<tr><td>1</td><td>Vermont</td><td>19</td><td>45</td><td>Idaho</td><td>9</td></tr>
<tr><td>23</td><td>Virginia</td><td>12</td><td>45</td><td>Indiana</td><td>9</td></tr>
<tr><td>28</td><td>Washington</td><td>11</td><td>45</td><td>Mississippi</td><td>9</td></tr>
<tr><td>10</td><td>West Virginia</td><td>14</td><td>48</td><td>Nevada</td><td>8</td></tr>
<tr><td>28</td><td>Wisconsin</td><td>11</td><td>48</td><td>Oklahoma</td><td>8</td></tr>
<tr><td>28</td><td>Wyoming</td><td>11</td><td>48</td><td>Utah</td><td>8</td></tr>
</table>

District of Columbia   43

Source: CQ Press using data from American Medical Association (Chicago, Illinois)
"Physician Characteristics and Distribution in the U.S." (2010 Edition)
*As of December 31, 2008. National rate does not include physicians in U.S. territories and possessions. General Surgery includes Abdominal, Cardiovascular, Hand, Head and Neck, Pediatric, Traumatic, and Vascular Surgeries.

Physicians in Obstetrics and Gynecology in 2008

National Total = 41,992 Physicians*

ALPHA ORDER

RANK	STATE	PHYSICIANS	% of USA
26	Alabama	576	1.4%
47	Alaska	79	0.2%
17	Arizona	721	1.7%
34	Arkansas	270	0.6%
1	California	5,009	11.9%
22	Colorado	684	1.6%
19	Connecticut	718	1.7%
46	Delaware	105	0.3%
4	Florida	2,293	5.5%
10	Georgia	1,352	3.2%
35	Hawaii	255	0.6%
43	Idaho	137	0.3%
5	Illinois	1,831	4.4%
20	Indiana	707	1.7%
37	Iowa	214	0.5%
31	Kansas	294	0.7%
27	Kentucky	533	1.3%
21	Louisiana	703	1.7%
42	Maine	163	0.4%
13	Maryland	1,163	2.8%
14	Massachusetts	1,132	2.7%
9	Michigan	1,372	3.3%
23	Minnesota	645	1.5%
30	Mississippi	321	0.8%
18	Missouri	719	1.7%
45	Montana	109	0.3%
39	Nebraska	204	0.5%
33	Nevada	282	0.7%
41	New Hampshire	199	0.5%
7	New Jersey	1,507	3.6%
36	New Mexico	232	0.6%
2	New York	3,685	8.8%
11	North Carolina	1,325	3.2%
50	North Dakota	52	0.1%
8	Ohio	1,498	3.6%
29	Oklahoma	328	0.8%
27	Oregon	533	1.3%
6	Pennsylvania	1,694	4.0%
39	Rhode Island	204	0.5%
25	South Carolina	586	1.4%
48	South Dakota	75	0.2%
15	Tennessee	912	2.2%
3	Texas	3,032	7.2%
32	Utah	287	0.7%
44	Vermont	114	0.3%
12	Virginia	1,250	3.0%
16	Washington	772	1.8%
38	West Virginia	205	0.5%
23	Wisconsin	645	1.5%
49	Wyoming	59	0.1%

RANK ORDER

RANK	STATE	PHYSICIANS	% of USA
1	California	5,009	11.9%
2	New York	3,685	8.8%
3	Texas	3,032	7.2%
4	Florida	2,293	5.5%
5	Illinois	1,831	4.4%
6	Pennsylvania	1,694	4.0%
7	New Jersey	1,507	3.6%
8	Ohio	1,498	3.6%
9	Michigan	1,372	3.3%
10	Georgia	1,352	3.2%
11	North Carolina	1,325	3.2%
12	Virginia	1,250	3.0%
13	Maryland	1,163	2.8%
14	Massachusetts	1,132	2.7%
15	Tennessee	912	2.2%
16	Washington	772	1.8%
17	Arizona	721	1.7%
18	Missouri	719	1.7%
19	Connecticut	718	1.7%
20	Indiana	707	1.7%
21	Louisiana	703	1.7%
22	Colorado	684	1.6%
23	Minnesota	645	1.5%
23	Wisconsin	645	1.5%
25	South Carolina	586	1.4%
26	Alabama	576	1.4%
27	Kentucky	533	1.3%
27	Oregon	533	1.3%
29	Oklahoma	328	0.8%
30	Mississippi	321	0.8%
31	Kansas	294	0.7%
32	Utah	287	0.7%
33	Nevada	282	0.7%
34	Arkansas	270	0.6%
35	Hawaii	255	0.6%
36	New Mexico	232	0.6%
37	Iowa	214	0.5%
38	West Virginia	205	0.5%
39	Nebraska	204	0.5%
39	Rhode Island	204	0.5%
41	New Hampshire	199	0.5%
42	Maine	163	0.4%
43	Idaho	137	0.3%
44	Vermont	114	0.3%
45	Montana	109	0.3%
46	Delaware	105	0.3%
47	Alaska	79	0.2%
48	South Dakota	75	0.2%
49	Wyoming	59	0.1%
50	North Dakota	52	0.1%
	District of Columbia	207	0.5%

Source: American Medical Association (Chicago, Illinois)
   "Physician Characteristics and Distribution in the U.S." (2010 Edition)
*As of December 31, 2008. Total does not include 643 physicians in U.S. territories and possessions. Obstetrics and Gynecology includes Gynecology and Oncology, Maternal and Fetal Medicine, and Reproductive Endocrinology.

Rate of Physicians in Obstetrics and Gynecology in 2008

National Rate = 27 Physicians per 100,000 Female Population*

ALPHA ORDER

RANK	STATE	RATE
26	Alabama	24
26	Alaska	24
37	Arizona	22
45	Arkansas	19
17	California	27
13	Colorado	28
1	Connecticut	40
32	Delaware	23
21	Florida	25
17	Georgia	27
1	Hawaii	40
47	Idaho	18
13	Illinois	28
37	Indiana	22
50	Iowa	14
42	Kansas	21
26	Kentucky	24
10	Louisiana	31
26	Maine	24
1	Maryland	40
7	Massachusetts	34
17	Michigan	27
21	Minnesota	25
42	Mississippi	21
26	Missouri	24
32	Montana	23
32	Nebraska	23
37	Nevada	22
11	New Hampshire	30
7	New Jersey	34
32	New Mexico	23
5	New York	37
13	North Carolina	28
49	North Dakota	16
21	Ohio	25
47	Oklahoma	18
13	Oregon	28
17	Pennsylvania	27
4	Rhode Island	38
21	South Carolina	25
45	South Dakota	19
12	Tennessee	29
21	Texas	25
42	Utah	21
6	Vermont	36
9	Virginia	32
26	Washington	24
37	West Virginia	22
32	Wisconsin	23
37	Wyoming	22

RANK ORDER

RANK	STATE	RATE
1	Connecticut	40
1	Hawaii	40
1	Maryland	40
4	Rhode Island	38
5	New York	37
6	Vermont	36
7	Massachusetts	34
7	New Jersey	34
9	Virginia	32
10	Louisiana	31
11	New Hampshire	30
12	Tennessee	29
13	Colorado	28
13	Illinois	28
13	North Carolina	28
13	Oregon	28
17	California	27
17	Georgia	27
17	Michigan	27
17	Pennsylvania	27
21	Florida	25
21	Minnesota	25
21	Ohio	25
21	South Carolina	25
21	Texas	25
26	Alabama	24
26	Alaska	24
26	Kentucky	24
26	Maine	24
26	Missouri	24
26	Washington	24
32	Delaware	23
32	Montana	23
32	Nebraska	23
32	New Mexico	23
32	Wisconsin	23
37	Arizona	22
37	Indiana	22
37	Nevada	22
37	West Virginia	22
37	Wyoming	22
42	Kansas	21
42	Mississippi	21
42	Utah	21
45	Arkansas	19
45	South Dakota	19
47	Idaho	18
47	Oklahoma	18
49	North Dakota	16
50	Iowa	14
	District of Columbia	66

Source: CQ Press using data from American Medical Association (Chicago, Illinois)
"Physician Characteristics and Distribution in the U.S." (2010 Edition)
*As of December 31, 2008. National rate does not include physicians in U.S. territories and possessions. Obstetrics and Gynecology includes Gynecology and Oncology, Maternal and Fetal Medicine, and Reproductive Endocrinology.

Physicians in Ophthalmology in 2008

National Total = 18,037 Physicians*

ALPHA ORDER

RANK	STATE	PHYSICIANS	% of USA
27	Alabama	224	1.2%
48	Alaska	32	0.2%
24	Arizona	267	1.5%
32	Arkansas	133	0.7%
1	California	2,232	12.4%
23	Colorado	277	1.5%
20	Connecticut	300	1.7%
44	Delaware	49	0.3%
3	Florida	1,178	6.5%
14	Georgia	416	2.3%
35	Hawaii	103	0.6%
43	Idaho	57	0.3%
6	Illinois	732	4.1%
22	Indiana	278	1.5%
29	Iowa	157	0.9%
30	Kansas	143	0.8%
28	Kentucky	189	1.0%
19	Louisiana	301	1.7%
40	Maine	72	0.4%
11	Maryland	532	2.9%
10	Massachusetts	537	3.0%
9	Michigan	560	3.1%
21	Minnesota	299	1.7%
32	Mississippi	133	0.7%
18	Missouri	325	1.8%
44	Montana	49	0.3%
37	Nebraska	99	0.5%
37	Nevada	99	0.5%
42	New Hampshire	67	0.4%
8	New Jersey	604	3.3%
39	New Mexico	74	0.4%
2	New York	1,750	9.7%
12	North Carolina	497	2.8%
49	North Dakota	31	0.2%
7	Ohio	639	3.5%
31	Oklahoma	142	0.8%
26	Oregon	231	1.3%
5	Pennsylvania	846	4.7%
41	Rhode Island	70	0.4%
25	South Carolina	254	1.4%
46	South Dakota	40	0.2%
16	Tennessee	342	1.9%
4	Texas	1,149	6.4%
34	Utah	132	0.7%
47	Vermont	36	0.2%
13	Virginia	455	2.5%
15	Washington	349	1.9%
36	West Virginia	101	0.6%
17	Wisconsin	326	1.8%
50	Wyoming	17	0.1%

RANK ORDER

RANK	STATE	PHYSICIANS	% of USA
1	California	2,232	12.4%
2	New York	1,750	9.7%
3	Florida	1,178	6.5%
4	Texas	1,149	6.4%
5	Pennsylvania	846	4.7%
6	Illinois	732	4.1%
7	Ohio	639	3.5%
8	New Jersey	604	3.3%
9	Michigan	560	3.1%
10	Massachusetts	537	3.0%
11	Maryland	532	2.9%
12	North Carolina	497	2.8%
13	Virginia	455	2.5%
14	Georgia	416	2.3%
15	Washington	349	1.9%
16	Tennessee	342	1.9%
17	Wisconsin	326	1.8%
18	Missouri	325	1.8%
19	Louisiana	301	1.7%
20	Connecticut	300	1.7%
21	Minnesota	299	1.7%
22	Indiana	278	1.5%
23	Colorado	277	1.5%
24	Arizona	267	1.5%
25	South Carolina	254	1.4%
26	Oregon	231	1.3%
27	Alabama	224	1.2%
28	Kentucky	189	1.0%
29	Iowa	157	0.9%
30	Kansas	143	0.8%
31	Oklahoma	142	0.8%
32	Arkansas	133	0.7%
32	Mississippi	133	0.7%
34	Utah	132	0.7%
35	Hawaii	103	0.6%
36	West Virginia	101	0.6%
37	Nebraska	99	0.5%
37	Nevada	99	0.5%
39	New Mexico	74	0.4%
40	Maine	72	0.4%
41	Rhode Island	70	0.4%
42	New Hampshire	67	0.4%
43	Idaho	57	0.3%
44	Delaware	49	0.3%
44	Montana	49	0.3%
46	South Dakota	40	0.2%
47	Vermont	36	0.2%
48	Alaska	32	0.2%
49	North Dakota	31	0.2%
50	Wyoming	17	0.1%
	District of Columbia	112	0.6%

Source: American Medical Association (Chicago, Illinois)
   "Physician Characteristics and Distribution in the U.S." (2010 Edition)
*As of December 31, 2008. Total does not include 180 physicians in U.S. territories and possessions. Ophthalmology is the branch of medicine dealing with the anatomy, functions, and diseases of the eye.

Rate of Physicians in Ophthalmology in 2008

National Rate = 6 Physicians per 100,000 Population*

<table>
<tr><td colspan="3">ALPHA ORDER</td><td colspan="3">RANK ORDER</td></tr>
<tr><td>RANK</td><td>STATE</td><td>RATE</td><td>RANK</td><td>STATE</td><td>RATE</td></tr>
<tr><td>25</td><td>Alabama</td><td>5</td><td>1</td><td>Connecticut</td><td>9</td></tr>
<tr><td>25</td><td>Alaska</td><td>5</td><td>1</td><td>Maryland</td><td>9</td></tr>
<tr><td>42</td><td>Arizona</td><td>4</td><td>1</td><td>New York</td><td>9</td></tr>
<tr><td>25</td><td>Arkansas</td><td>5</td><td>4</td><td>Hawaii</td><td>8</td></tr>
<tr><td>10</td><td>California</td><td>6</td><td>4</td><td>Massachusetts</td><td>8</td></tr>
<tr><td>10</td><td>Colorado</td><td>6</td><td>6</td><td>Louisiana</td><td>7</td></tr>
<tr><td>1</td><td>Connecticut</td><td>9</td><td>6</td><td>New Jersey</td><td>7</td></tr>
<tr><td>10</td><td>Delaware</td><td>6</td><td>6</td><td>Pennsylvania</td><td>7</td></tr>
<tr><td>10</td><td>Florida</td><td>6</td><td>6</td><td>Rhode Island</td><td>7</td></tr>
<tr><td>42</td><td>Georgia</td><td>4</td><td>10</td><td>California</td><td>6</td></tr>
<tr><td>4</td><td>Hawaii</td><td>8</td><td>10</td><td>Colorado</td><td>6</td></tr>
<tr><td>42</td><td>Idaho</td><td>4</td><td>10</td><td>Delaware</td><td>6</td></tr>
<tr><td>10</td><td>Illinois</td><td>6</td><td>10</td><td>Florida</td><td>6</td></tr>
<tr><td>42</td><td>Indiana</td><td>4</td><td>10</td><td>Illinois</td><td>6</td></tr>
<tr><td>25</td><td>Iowa</td><td>5</td><td>10</td><td>Michigan</td><td>6</td></tr>
<tr><td>25</td><td>Kansas</td><td>5</td><td>10</td><td>Minnesota</td><td>6</td></tr>
<tr><td>42</td><td>Kentucky</td><td>4</td><td>10</td><td>Nebraska</td><td>6</td></tr>
<tr><td>6</td><td>Louisiana</td><td>7</td><td>10</td><td>Ohio</td><td>6</td></tr>
<tr><td>25</td><td>Maine</td><td>5</td><td>10</td><td>Oregon</td><td>6</td></tr>
<tr><td>1</td><td>Maryland</td><td>9</td><td>10</td><td>South Carolina</td><td>6</td></tr>
<tr><td>4</td><td>Massachusetts</td><td>8</td><td>10</td><td>Vermont</td><td>6</td></tr>
<tr><td>10</td><td>Michigan</td><td>6</td><td>10</td><td>Virginia</td><td>6</td></tr>
<tr><td>10</td><td>Minnesota</td><td>6</td><td>10</td><td>West Virginia</td><td>6</td></tr>
<tr><td>25</td><td>Mississippi</td><td>5</td><td>10</td><td>Wisconsin</td><td>6</td></tr>
<tr><td>25</td><td>Missouri</td><td>5</td><td>25</td><td>Alabama</td><td>5</td></tr>
<tr><td>25</td><td>Montana</td><td>5</td><td>25</td><td>Alaska</td><td>5</td></tr>
<tr><td>10</td><td>Nebraska</td><td>6</td><td>25</td><td>Arkansas</td><td>5</td></tr>
<tr><td>42</td><td>Nevada</td><td>4</td><td>25</td><td>Iowa</td><td>5</td></tr>
<tr><td>25</td><td>New Hampshire</td><td>5</td><td>25</td><td>Kansas</td><td>5</td></tr>
<tr><td>6</td><td>New Jersey</td><td>7</td><td>25</td><td>Maine</td><td>5</td></tr>
<tr><td>42</td><td>New Mexico</td><td>4</td><td>25</td><td>Mississippi</td><td>5</td></tr>
<tr><td>1</td><td>New York</td><td>9</td><td>25</td><td>Missouri</td><td>5</td></tr>
<tr><td>25</td><td>North Carolina</td><td>5</td><td>25</td><td>Montana</td><td>5</td></tr>
<tr><td>25</td><td>North Dakota</td><td>5</td><td>25</td><td>New Hampshire</td><td>5</td></tr>
<tr><td>10</td><td>Ohio</td><td>6</td><td>25</td><td>North Carolina</td><td>5</td></tr>
<tr><td>42</td><td>Oklahoma</td><td>4</td><td>25</td><td>North Dakota</td><td>5</td></tr>
<tr><td>10</td><td>Oregon</td><td>6</td><td>25</td><td>South Dakota</td><td>5</td></tr>
<tr><td>6</td><td>Pennsylvania</td><td>7</td><td>25</td><td>Tennessee</td><td>5</td></tr>
<tr><td>6</td><td>Rhode Island</td><td>7</td><td>25</td><td>Texas</td><td>5</td></tr>
<tr><td>10</td><td>South Carolina</td><td>6</td><td>25</td><td>Utah</td><td>5</td></tr>
<tr><td>25</td><td>South Dakota</td><td>5</td><td>25</td><td>Washington</td><td>5</td></tr>
<tr><td>25</td><td>Tennessee</td><td>5</td><td>42</td><td>Arizona</td><td>4</td></tr>
<tr><td>25</td><td>Texas</td><td>5</td><td>42</td><td>Georgia</td><td>4</td></tr>
<tr><td>25</td><td>Utah</td><td>5</td><td>42</td><td>Idaho</td><td>4</td></tr>
<tr><td>10</td><td>Vermont</td><td>6</td><td>42</td><td>Indiana</td><td>4</td></tr>
<tr><td>10</td><td>Virginia</td><td>6</td><td>42</td><td>Kentucky</td><td>4</td></tr>
<tr><td>25</td><td>Washington</td><td>5</td><td>42</td><td>Nevada</td><td>4</td></tr>
<tr><td>10</td><td>West Virginia</td><td>6</td><td>42</td><td>New Mexico</td><td>4</td></tr>
<tr><td>10</td><td>Wisconsin</td><td>6</td><td>42</td><td>Oklahoma</td><td>4</td></tr>
<tr><td>50</td><td>Wyoming</td><td>3</td><td>50</td><td>Wyoming</td><td>3</td></tr>
</table>

District of Columbia   19

Source: CQ Press using data from American Medical Association (Chicago, Illinois)
"Physician Characteristics and Distribution in the U.S." (2010 Edition)
*As of December 31, 2008. National rate does not include physicians in U.S. territories and possessions. Ophthalmology is the branch of medicine dealing with the anatomy, functions, and diseases of the eye.

Physicians in Orthopedic Surgery in 2008

National Total = 24,651 Physicians*

ALPHA ORDER				RANK ORDER			
RANK	STATE	PHYSICIANS	% of USA	RANK	STATE	PHYSICIANS	% of USA
24	Alabama	380	1.5%	1	California	2,911	11.8%
46	Alaska	70	0.3%	2	New York	1,854	7.5%
23	Arizona	394	1.6%	3	Texas	1,634	6.6%
34	Arkansas	176	0.7%	4	Florida	1,366	5.5%
1	California	2,911	11.8%	5	Pennsylvania	1,088	4.4%
21	Colorado	449	1.8%	6	Illinois	961	3.9%
25	Connecticut	373	1.5%	7	Ohio	932	3.8%
48	Delaware	64	0.3%	8	Massachusetts	773	3.1%
4	Florida	1,366	5.5%	9	North Carolina	759	3.1%
12	Georgia	635	2.6%	10	New Jersey	731	3.0%
41	Hawaii	123	0.5%	11	Virginia	654	2.7%
39	Idaho	128	0.5%	12	Georgia	635	2.6%
6	Illinois	961	3.9%	13	Michigan	629	2.6%
20	Indiana	463	1.9%	14	Maryland	599	2.4%
32	Iowa	200	0.8%	15	Washington	577	2.3%
30	Kansas	228	0.9%	16	Tennessee	557	2.3%
28	Kentucky	319	1.3%	17	Minnesota	510	2.1%
22	Louisiana	403	1.6%	18	Wisconsin	502	2.0%
40	Maine	125	0.5%	19	Missouri	473	1.9%
14	Maryland	599	2.4%	20	Indiana	463	1.9%
8	Massachusetts	773	3.1%	21	Colorado	449	1.8%
13	Michigan	629	2.6%	22	Louisiana	403	1.6%
17	Minnesota	510	2.1%	23	Arizona	394	1.6%
33	Mississippi	180	0.7%	24	Alabama	380	1.5%
19	Missouri	473	1.9%	25	Connecticut	373	1.5%
44	Montana	113	0.5%	26	South Carolina	354	1.4%
35	Nebraska	164	0.7%	27	Oregon	326	1.3%
38	Nevada	139	0.6%	28	Kentucky	319	1.3%
36	New Hampshire	148	0.6%	29	Oklahoma	234	0.9%
10	New Jersey	731	3.0%	30	Kansas	228	0.9%
37	New Mexico	141	0.6%	31	Utah	219	0.9%
2	New York	1,854	7.5%	32	Iowa	200	0.8%
9	North Carolina	759	3.1%	33	Mississippi	180	0.7%
50	North Dakota	51	0.2%	34	Arkansas	176	0.7%
7	Ohio	932	3.8%	35	Nebraska	164	0.7%
29	Oklahoma	234	0.9%	36	New Hampshire	148	0.6%
27	Oregon	326	1.3%	37	New Mexico	141	0.6%
5	Pennsylvania	1,088	4.4%	38	Nevada	139	0.6%
43	Rhode Island	119	0.5%	39	Idaho	128	0.5%
26	South Carolina	354	1.4%	40	Maine	125	0.5%
47	South Dakota	67	0.3%	41	Hawaii	123	0.5%
16	Tennessee	557	2.3%	42	West Virginia	121	0.5%
3	Texas	1,634	6.6%	43	Rhode Island	119	0.5%
31	Utah	219	0.9%	44	Montana	113	0.5%
45	Vermont	78	0.3%	45	Vermont	78	0.3%
11	Virginia	654	2.7%	46	Alaska	70	0.3%
15	Washington	577	2.3%	47	South Dakota	67	0.3%
42	West Virginia	121	0.5%	48	Delaware	64	0.3%
18	Wisconsin	502	2.0%	49	Wyoming	57	0.2%
49	Wyoming	57	0.2%	50	North Dakota	51	0.2%
					District of Columbia	100	0.4%

Source: American Medical Association (Chicago, Illinois)
"Physician Characteristics and Distribution in the U.S." (2010 Edition)
*As of December 31, 2008. Total does not include 171 physicians in U.S. territories and possessions. Orthopedics is the branch of medicine dealing with the skeletal system.

Rate of Physicians in Orthopedic Surgery in 2008

National Rate = 8 Physicians per 100,000 Population*

ALPHA ORDER

RANK	STATE	RATE
22	Alabama	8
9	Alaska	10
45	Arizona	6
45	Arkansas	6
22	California	8
13	Colorado	9
4	Connecticut	11
35	Delaware	7
35	Florida	7
35	Georgia	7
9	Hawaii	10
22	Idaho	8
35	Illinois	7
35	Indiana	7
35	Iowa	7
22	Kansas	8
35	Kentucky	7
13	Louisiana	9
13	Maine	9
4	Maryland	11
2	Massachusetts	12
45	Michigan	6
9	Minnesota	10
45	Mississippi	6
22	Missouri	8
2	Montana	12
13	Nebraska	9
50	Nevada	5
4	New Hampshire	11
22	New Jersey	8
35	New Mexico	7
9	New York	10
22	North Carolina	8
22	North Dakota	8
22	Ohio	8
45	Oklahoma	6
13	Oregon	9
13	Pennsylvania	9
4	Rhode Island	11
22	South Carolina	8
22	South Dakota	8
13	Tennessee	9
35	Texas	7
22	Utah	8
1	Vermont	13
22	Virginia	8
13	Washington	9
35	West Virginia	7
13	Wisconsin	9
4	Wyoming	11

RANK ORDER

RANK	STATE	RATE
1	Vermont	13
2	Massachusetts	12
2	Montana	12
4	Connecticut	11
4	Maryland	11
4	New Hampshire	11
4	Rhode Island	11
4	Wyoming	11
9	Alaska	10
9	Hawaii	10
9	Minnesota	10
9	New York	10
13	Colorado	9
13	Louisiana	9
13	Maine	9
13	Nebraska	9
13	Oregon	9
13	Pennsylvania	9
13	Tennessee	9
13	Washington	9
13	Wisconsin	9
22	Alabama	8
22	California	8
22	Idaho	8
22	Kansas	8
22	Missouri	8
22	New Jersey	8
22	North Carolina	8
22	North Dakota	8
22	Ohio	8
22	South Carolina	8
22	South Dakota	8
22	Utah	8
22	Virginia	8
35	Delaware	7
35	Florida	7
35	Georgia	7
35	Illinois	7
35	Indiana	7
35	Iowa	7
35	Kentucky	7
35	New Mexico	7
35	Texas	7
35	West Virginia	7
45	Arizona	6
45	Arkansas	6
45	Michigan	6
45	Mississippi	6
45	Oklahoma	6
50	Nevada	5

District of Columbia	17

Source: CQ Press using data from American Medical Association (Chicago, Illinois)
"Physician Characteristics and Distribution in the U.S." (2010 Edition)

*As of December 31, 2008. National rate does not include physicians in U.S. territories and possessions. Orthopedics is the branch of medicine dealing with the skeletal system.

Physicians in Plastic Surgery in 2008

National Total = 7,180 Physicians*

ALPHA ORDER

RANK	STATE	PHYSICIANS	% of USA
27	Alabama	81	1.1%
49	Alaska	6	0.1%
15	Arizona	140	1.9%
34	Arkansas	32	0.4%
1	California	1,106	15.4%
19	Colorado	105	1.5%
23	Connecticut	95	1.3%
42	Delaware	22	0.3%
3	Florida	605	8.4%
10	Georgia	197	2.7%
40	Hawaii	29	0.4%
43	Idaho	19	0.3%
6	Illinois	261	3.6%
20	Indiana	103	1.4%
34	Iowa	32	0.4%
30	Kansas	63	0.9%
24	Kentucky	93	1.3%
26	Louisiana	86	1.2%
44	Maine	17	0.2%
12	Maryland	187	2.6%
10	Massachusetts	197	2.7%
9	Michigan	206	2.9%
22	Minnesota	96	1.3%
32	Mississippi	47	0.7%
17	Missouri	139	1.9%
45	Montana	15	0.2%
36	Nebraska	31	0.4%
31	Nevada	49	0.7%
41	New Hampshire	27	0.4%
7	New Jersey	224	3.1%
36	New Mexico	31	0.4%
2	New York	621	8.6%
13	North Carolina	186	2.6%
48	North Dakota	9	0.1%
8	Ohio	222	3.1%
33	Oklahoma	46	0.6%
29	Oregon	70	1.0%
5	Pennsylvania	267	3.7%
36	Rhode Island	31	0.4%
25	South Carolina	88	1.2%
46	South Dakota	11	0.2%
15	Tennessee	140	1.9%
4	Texas	579	8.1%
28	Utah	78	1.1%
47	Vermont	10	0.1%
14	Virginia	180	2.5%
18	Washington	130	1.8%
39	West Virginia	30	0.4%
21	Wisconsin	99	1.4%
50	Wyoming	4	0.1%

RANK ORDER

RANK	STATE	PHYSICIANS	% of USA
1	California	1,106	15.4%
2	New York	621	8.6%
3	Florida	605	8.4%
4	Texas	579	8.1%
5	Pennsylvania	267	3.7%
6	Illinois	261	3.6%
7	New Jersey	224	3.1%
8	Ohio	222	3.1%
9	Michigan	206	2.9%
10	Georgia	197	2.7%
10	Massachusetts	197	2.7%
12	Maryland	187	2.6%
13	North Carolina	186	2.6%
14	Virginia	180	2.5%
15	Arizona	140	1.9%
15	Tennessee	140	1.9%
17	Missouri	139	1.9%
18	Washington	130	1.8%
19	Colorado	105	1.5%
20	Indiana	103	1.4%
21	Wisconsin	99	1.4%
22	Minnesota	96	1.3%
23	Connecticut	95	1.3%
24	Kentucky	93	1.3%
25	South Carolina	88	1.2%
26	Louisiana	86	1.2%
27	Alabama	81	1.1%
28	Utah	78	1.1%
29	Oregon	70	1.0%
30	Kansas	63	0.9%
31	Nevada	49	0.7%
32	Mississippi	47	0.7%
33	Oklahoma	46	0.6%
34	Arkansas	32	0.4%
34	Iowa	32	0.4%
36	Nebraska	31	0.4%
36	New Mexico	31	0.4%
36	Rhode Island	31	0.4%
39	West Virginia	30	0.4%
40	Hawaii	29	0.4%
41	New Hampshire	27	0.4%
42	Delaware	22	0.3%
43	Idaho	19	0.3%
44	Maine	17	0.2%
45	Montana	15	0.2%
46	South Dakota	11	0.2%
47	Vermont	10	0.1%
48	North Dakota	9	0.1%
49	Alaska	6	0.1%
50	Wyoming	4	0.1%
	District of Columbia	38	0.5%

Source: American Medical Association (Chicago, Illinois)
   "Physician Characteristics and Distribution in the U.S." (2010 Edition)
*As of December 31, 2008. Total does not include 36 physicians in U.S. territories and possessions.

Rate of Physicians in Plastic Surgery in 2008

National Rate = 2 Physicians per 100,000 Population*

<table>
<tr><td colspan="3">ALPHA ORDER</td><td colspan="3">RANK ORDER</td></tr>
<tr><th>RANK</th><th>STATE</th><th>RATE</th><th>RANK</th><th>STATE</th><th>RATE</th></tr>
<tr><td>11</td><td>Alabama</td><td>2</td><td>1</td><td>California</td><td>3</td></tr>
<tr><td>42</td><td>Alaska</td><td>1</td><td>1</td><td>Connecticut</td><td>3</td></tr>
<tr><td>11</td><td>Arizona</td><td>2</td><td>1</td><td>Delaware</td><td>3</td></tr>
<tr><td>42</td><td>Arkansas</td><td>1</td><td>1</td><td>Florida</td><td>3</td></tr>
<tr><td>1</td><td>California</td><td>3</td><td>1</td><td>Maryland</td><td>3</td></tr>
<tr><td>11</td><td>Colorado</td><td>2</td><td>1</td><td>Massachusetts</td><td>3</td></tr>
<tr><td>1</td><td>Connecticut</td><td>3</td><td>1</td><td>New Jersey</td><td>3</td></tr>
<tr><td>1</td><td>Delaware</td><td>3</td><td>1</td><td>New York</td><td>3</td></tr>
<tr><td>1</td><td>Florida</td><td>3</td><td>1</td><td>Rhode Island</td><td>3</td></tr>
<tr><td>11</td><td>Georgia</td><td>2</td><td>1</td><td>Utah</td><td>3</td></tr>
<tr><td>11</td><td>Hawaii</td><td>2</td><td>11</td><td>Alabama</td><td>2</td></tr>
<tr><td>42</td><td>Idaho</td><td>1</td><td>11</td><td>Arizona</td><td>2</td></tr>
<tr><td>11</td><td>Illinois</td><td>2</td><td>11</td><td>Colorado</td><td>2</td></tr>
<tr><td>11</td><td>Indiana</td><td>2</td><td>11</td><td>Georgia</td><td>2</td></tr>
<tr><td>42</td><td>Iowa</td><td>1</td><td>11</td><td>Hawaii</td><td>2</td></tr>
<tr><td>11</td><td>Kansas</td><td>2</td><td>11</td><td>Illinois</td><td>2</td></tr>
<tr><td>11</td><td>Kentucky</td><td>2</td><td>11</td><td>Indiana</td><td>2</td></tr>
<tr><td>11</td><td>Louisiana</td><td>2</td><td>11</td><td>Kansas</td><td>2</td></tr>
<tr><td>42</td><td>Maine</td><td>1</td><td>11</td><td>Kentucky</td><td>2</td></tr>
<tr><td>1</td><td>Maryland</td><td>3</td><td>11</td><td>Louisiana</td><td>2</td></tr>
<tr><td>1</td><td>Massachusetts</td><td>3</td><td>11</td><td>Michigan</td><td>2</td></tr>
<tr><td>11</td><td>Michigan</td><td>2</td><td>11</td><td>Minnesota</td><td>2</td></tr>
<tr><td>11</td><td>Minnesota</td><td>2</td><td>11</td><td>Mississippi</td><td>2</td></tr>
<tr><td>11</td><td>Mississippi</td><td>2</td><td>11</td><td>Missouri</td><td>2</td></tr>
<tr><td>11</td><td>Missouri</td><td>2</td><td>11</td><td>Montana</td><td>2</td></tr>
<tr><td>11</td><td>Montana</td><td>2</td><td>11</td><td>Nebraska</td><td>2</td></tr>
<tr><td>11</td><td>Nebraska</td><td>2</td><td>11</td><td>Nevada</td><td>2</td></tr>
<tr><td>11</td><td>Nevada</td><td>2</td><td>11</td><td>New Hampshire</td><td>2</td></tr>
<tr><td>11</td><td>New Hampshire</td><td>2</td><td>11</td><td>New Mexico</td><td>2</td></tr>
<tr><td>1</td><td>New Jersey</td><td>3</td><td>11</td><td>North Carolina</td><td>2</td></tr>
<tr><td>11</td><td>New Mexico</td><td>2</td><td>11</td><td>Ohio</td><td>2</td></tr>
<tr><td>1</td><td>New York</td><td>3</td><td>11</td><td>Oregon</td><td>2</td></tr>
<tr><td>11</td><td>North Carolina</td><td>2</td><td>11</td><td>Pennsylvania</td><td>2</td></tr>
<tr><td>42</td><td>North Dakota</td><td>1</td><td>11</td><td>South Carolina</td><td>2</td></tr>
<tr><td>11</td><td>Ohio</td><td>2</td><td>11</td><td>Tennessee</td><td>2</td></tr>
<tr><td>42</td><td>Oklahoma</td><td>1</td><td>11</td><td>Texas</td><td>2</td></tr>
<tr><td>11</td><td>Oregon</td><td>2</td><td>11</td><td>Vermont</td><td>2</td></tr>
<tr><td>11</td><td>Pennsylvania</td><td>2</td><td>11</td><td>Virginia</td><td>2</td></tr>
<tr><td>1</td><td>Rhode Island</td><td>3</td><td>11</td><td>Washington</td><td>2</td></tr>
<tr><td>11</td><td>South Carolina</td><td>2</td><td>11</td><td>West Virginia</td><td>2</td></tr>
<tr><td>42</td><td>South Dakota</td><td>1</td><td>11</td><td>Wisconsin</td><td>2</td></tr>
<tr><td>11</td><td>Tennessee</td><td>2</td><td>42</td><td>Alaska</td><td>1</td></tr>
<tr><td>11</td><td>Texas</td><td>2</td><td>42</td><td>Arkansas</td><td>1</td></tr>
<tr><td>1</td><td>Utah</td><td>3</td><td>42</td><td>Idaho</td><td>1</td></tr>
<tr><td>11</td><td>Vermont</td><td>2</td><td>42</td><td>Iowa</td><td>1</td></tr>
<tr><td>11</td><td>Virginia</td><td>2</td><td>42</td><td>Maine</td><td>1</td></tr>
<tr><td>11</td><td>Washington</td><td>2</td><td>42</td><td>North Dakota</td><td>1</td></tr>
<tr><td>11</td><td>West Virginia</td><td>2</td><td>42</td><td>Oklahoma</td><td>1</td></tr>
<tr><td>11</td><td>Wisconsin</td><td>2</td><td>42</td><td>South Dakota</td><td>1</td></tr>
<tr><td>42</td><td>Wyoming</td><td>1</td><td>42</td><td>Wyoming</td><td>1</td></tr>
<tr><td></td><td></td><td></td><td></td><td>District of Columbia</td><td>6</td></tr>
</table>

Source: CQ Press using data from American Medical Association (Chicago, Illinois)
"Physician Characteristics and Distribution in the U.S." (2010 Edition)
*As of December 31, 2008. National rate does not include physicians in U.S. territories and possessions.

Physicians in Other Specialties in 2008

National Total = 224,473 Physicians*

ALPHA ORDER

RANK	STATE	PHYSICIANS	% of USA
28	Alabama	2,487	1.1%
48	Alaska	422	0.2%
19	Arizona	3,938	1.8%
33	Arkansas	1,452	0.6%
1	California	27,781	12.4%
23	Colorado	3,737	1.7%
22	Connecticut	3,739	1.7%
45	Delaware	613	0.3%
4	Florida	12,199	5.4%
14	Georgia	5,607	2.5%
37	Hawaii	1,193	0.5%
43	Idaho	705	0.3%
6	Illinois	9,497	4.2%
21	Indiana	3,826	1.7%
32	Iowa	1,475	0.7%
29	Kansas	1,718	0.8%
27	Kentucky	2,622	1.2%
25	Louisiana	2,887	1.3%
41	Maine	1,023	0.5%
10	Maryland	6,830	3.0%
7	Massachusetts	9,065	4.0%
11	Michigan	6,763	3.0%
18	Minnesota	3,978	1.8%
36	Mississippi	1,313	0.6%
20	Missouri	3,858	1.7%
46	Montana	581	0.3%
38	Nebraska	1,116	0.5%
34	Nevada	1,375	0.6%
42	New Hampshire	984	0.4%
9	New Jersey	7,072	3.2%
35	New Mexico	1,358	0.6%
2	New York	21,043	9.4%
12	North Carolina	6,219	2.8%
49	North Dakota	399	0.2%
8	Ohio	8,020	3.6%
31	Oklahoma	1,646	0.7%
24	Oregon	2,948	1.3%
5	Pennsylvania	10,685	4.8%
40	Rhode Island	1,046	0.5%
26	South Carolina	2,712	1.2%
47	South Dakota	424	0.2%
16	Tennessee	4,085	1.8%
3	Texas	13,928	6.2%
30	Utah	1,660	0.7%
44	Vermont	660	0.3%
13	Virginia	5,905	2.6%
15	Washington	5,119	2.3%
39	West Virginia	1,070	0.5%
17	Wisconsin	4,051	1.8%
50	Wyoming	266	0.1%

RANK ORDER

RANK	STATE	PHYSICIANS	% of USA
1	California	27,781	12.4%
2	New York	21,043	9.4%
3	Texas	13,928	6.2%
4	Florida	12,199	5.4%
5	Pennsylvania	10,685	4.8%
6	Illinois	9,497	4.2%
7	Massachusetts	9,065	4.0%
8	Ohio	8,020	3.6%
9	New Jersey	7,072	3.2%
10	Maryland	6,830	3.0%
11	Michigan	6,763	3.0%
12	North Carolina	6,219	2.8%
13	Virginia	5,905	2.6%
14	Georgia	5,607	2.5%
15	Washington	5,119	2.3%
16	Tennessee	4,085	1.8%
17	Wisconsin	4,051	1.8%
18	Minnesota	3,978	1.8%
19	Arizona	3,938	1.8%
20	Missouri	3,858	1.7%
21	Indiana	3,826	1.7%
22	Connecticut	3,739	1.7%
23	Colorado	3,737	1.7%
24	Oregon	2,948	1.3%
25	Louisiana	2,887	1.3%
26	South Carolina	2,712	1.2%
27	Kentucky	2,622	1.2%
28	Alabama	2,487	1.1%
29	Kansas	1,718	0.8%
30	Utah	1,660	0.7%
31	Oklahoma	1,646	0.7%
32	Iowa	1,475	0.7%
33	Arkansas	1,452	0.6%
34	Nevada	1,375	0.6%
35	New Mexico	1,358	0.6%
36	Mississippi	1,313	0.6%
37	Hawaii	1,193	0.5%
38	Nebraska	1,116	0.5%
39	West Virginia	1,070	0.5%
40	Rhode Island	1,046	0.5%
41	Maine	1,023	0.5%
42	New Hampshire	984	0.4%
43	Idaho	705	0.3%
44	Vermont	660	0.3%
45	Delaware	613	0.3%
46	Montana	581	0.3%
47	South Dakota	424	0.2%
48	Alaska	422	0.2%
49	North Dakota	399	0.2%
50	Wyoming	266	0.1%
	District of Columbia	1,373	0.6%

Source: American Medical Association (Chicago, Illinois)
  "Physician Characteristics and Distribution in the U.S." (2010 Edition)
*As of December 31, 2008. Total does not include 3,204 physicians in U.S. territories and possessions. Other Specialties include Aerospace Medicine, Anatomic/Clinical Pathology, Anesthesiology, Child Psychiatry, Diagnostic Radiology, Emergency Medicine, Forensic Pathology, Nuclear Medicine, Occupational Medicine, Neurology, Psychiatry, Public Health, Radiation Oncology, Radiology, and other specialties.

Rate of Physicians in Other Specialties in 2008

National Rate = 74 Physicians per 100,000 Population*

ALPHA ORDER			RANK ORDER		
RANK	STATE	RATE	RANK	STATE	RATE
42	Alabama	53	1	Massachusetts	139
31	Alaska	61	2	Maryland	121
31	Arizona	61	3	New York	108
45	Arkansas	51	4	Connecticut	107
13	California	76	5	Vermont	106
13	Colorado	76	6	Rhode Island	99
4	Connecticut	107	7	Hawaii	93
20	Delaware	70	8	Pennsylvania	85
25	Florida	66	9	New Jersey	82
40	Georgia	58	10	Maine	78
7	Hawaii	93	10	Oregon	78
48	Idaho	46	10	Washington	78
17	Illinois	74	13	California	76
36	Indiana	60	13	Colorado	76
47	Iowa	49	13	Minnesota	76
31	Kansas	61	13	Virginia	76
31	Kentucky	61	17	Illinois	74
26	Louisiana	65	17	New Hampshire	74
10	Maine	78	19	Wisconsin	72
2	Maryland	121	20	Delaware	70
1	Massachusetts	139	20	Ohio	70
22	Michigan	68	22	Michigan	68
13	Minnesota	76	22	New Mexico	68
49	Mississippi	45	24	North Carolina	67
26	Missouri	65	25	Florida	66
36	Montana	60	26	Louisiana	65
29	Nebraska	63	26	Missouri	65
42	Nevada	53	26	Tennessee	65
17	New Hampshire	74	29	Nebraska	63
9	New Jersey	82	30	North Dakota	62
22	New Mexico	68	31	Alaska	61
3	New York	108	31	Arizona	61
24	North Carolina	67	31	Kansas	61
30	North Dakota	62	31	Kentucky	61
20	Ohio	70	31	Utah	61
49	Oklahoma	45	36	Indiana	60
10	Oregon	78	36	Montana	60
8	Pennsylvania	85	36	South Carolina	60
6	Rhode Island	99	39	West Virginia	59
36	South Carolina	60	40	Georgia	58
42	South Dakota	53	41	Texas	57
26	Tennessee	65	42	Alabama	53
41	Texas	57	42	Nevada	53
31	Utah	61	42	South Dakota	53
5	Vermont	106	45	Arkansas	51
13	Virginia	76	46	Wyoming	50
10	Washington	78	47	Iowa	49
39	West Virginia	59	48	Idaho	46
19	Wisconsin	72	49	Mississippi	45
46	Wyoming	50	49	Oklahoma	45
				District of Columbia	233

Source: CQ Press using data from American Medical Association (Chicago, Illinois)
"Physician Characteristics and Distribution in the U.S." (2010 Edition)
*As of December 31, 2008. National rate does not include physicians in U.S. territories and possessions. Other Specialties include Aerospace Medicine, Anatomic/Clinical Pathology, Anesthesiology, Child Psychiatry, Diagnostic Radiology, Emergency Medicine, Forensic Pathology, Nuclear Medicine, Occupational Medicine, Neurology, Psychiatry, Public Health, Radiation Oncology, Radiology, and other specialties.

Physicians in Anesthesiology in 2008

National Total = 42,005 Physicians*

ALPHA ORDER

RANK	STATE	PHYSICIANS	% of USA
27	Alabama	493	1.2%
47	Alaska	85	0.2%
17	Arizona	922	2.2%
34	Arkansas	298	0.7%
1	California	5,303	12.6%
20	Colorado	752	1.8%
24	Connecticut	591	1.4%
46	Delaware	96	0.2%
4	Florida	2,638	6.3%
14	Georgia	1,005	2.4%
40	Hawaii	158	0.4%
44	Idaho	110	0.3%
5	Illinois	1,880	4.5%
16	Indiana	979	2.3%
33	Iowa	308	0.7%
32	Kansas	330	0.8%
25	Kentucky	533	1.3%
26	Louisiana	522	1.2%
39	Maine	173	0.4%
10	Maryland	1,066	2.5%
9	Massachusetts	1,367	3.3%
13	Michigan	1,006	2.4%
23	Minnesota	592	1.4%
35	Mississippi	260	0.6%
21	Missouri	711	1.7%
42	Montana	135	0.3%
36	Nebraska	238	0.6%
30	Nevada	369	0.9%
38	New Hampshire	191	0.5%
7	New Jersey	1,534	3.7%
37	New Mexico	210	0.5%
2	New York	3,475	8.3%
12	North Carolina	1,012	2.4%
49	North Dakota	60	0.1%
8	Ohio	1,515	3.6%
31	Oklahoma	365	0.9%
22	Oregon	595	1.4%
6	Pennsylvania	1,760	4.2%
43	Rhode Island	120	0.3%
28	South Carolina	484	1.2%
48	South Dakota	74	0.2%
19	Tennessee	773	1.8%
3	Texas	3,221	7.7%
29	Utah	380	0.9%
44	Vermont	110	0.3%
15	Virginia	987	2.3%
11	Washington	1,013	2.4%
41	West Virginia	150	0.4%
18	Wisconsin	844	2.0%
50	Wyoming	53	0.1%

RANK ORDER

RANK	STATE	PHYSICIANS	% of USA
1	California	5,303	12.6%
2	New York	3,475	8.3%
3	Texas	3,221	7.7%
4	Florida	2,638	6.3%
5	Illinois	1,880	4.5%
6	Pennsylvania	1,760	4.2%
7	New Jersey	1,534	3.7%
8	Ohio	1,515	3.6%
9	Massachusetts	1,367	3.3%
10	Maryland	1,066	2.5%
11	Washington	1,013	2.4%
12	North Carolina	1,012	2.4%
13	Michigan	1,006	2.4%
14	Georgia	1,005	2.4%
15	Virginia	987	2.3%
16	Indiana	979	2.3%
17	Arizona	922	2.2%
18	Wisconsin	844	2.0%
19	Tennessee	773	1.8%
20	Colorado	752	1.8%
21	Missouri	711	1.7%
22	Oregon	595	1.4%
23	Minnesota	592	1.4%
24	Connecticut	591	1.4%
25	Kentucky	533	1.3%
26	Louisiana	522	1.2%
27	Alabama	493	1.2%
28	South Carolina	484	1.2%
29	Utah	380	0.9%
30	Nevada	369	0.9%
31	Oklahoma	365	0.9%
32	Kansas	330	0.8%
33	Iowa	308	0.7%
34	Arkansas	298	0.7%
35	Mississippi	260	0.6%
36	Nebraska	238	0.6%
37	New Mexico	210	0.5%
38	New Hampshire	191	0.5%
39	Maine	173	0.4%
40	Hawaii	158	0.4%
41	West Virginia	150	0.4%
42	Montana	135	0.3%
43	Rhode Island	120	0.3%
44	Idaho	110	0.3%
44	Vermont	110	0.3%
46	Delaware	96	0.2%
47	Alaska	85	0.2%
48	South Dakota	74	0.2%
49	North Dakota	60	0.1%
50	Wyoming	53	0.1%
	District of Columbia	159	0.4%

Source: American Medical Association (Chicago, Illinois)
"Physician Characteristics and Distribution in the U.S." (2010 Edition)
*As of December 31, 2008. Total does not include 225 physicians in U.S. territories and possessions.

Rate of Physicians in Anesthesiology in 2008

National Rate = 14 Physicians per 100,000 Population*

ALPHA ORDER

RANK	STATE	RATE
33	Alabama	11
26	Alaska	12
13	Arizona	14
40	Arkansas	10
13	California	14
8	Colorado	15
6	Connecticut	17
33	Delaware	11
13	Florida	14
40	Georgia	10
26	Hawaii	12
50	Idaho	7
8	Illinois	15
8	Indiana	15
40	Iowa	10
26	Kansas	12
26	Kentucky	12
26	Louisiana	12
21	Maine	13
2	Maryland	19
1	Massachusetts	21
40	Michigan	10
33	Minnesota	11
46	Mississippi	9
26	Missouri	12
13	Montana	14
21	Nebraska	13
13	Nevada	14
13	New Hampshire	14
3	New Jersey	18
33	New Mexico	11
3	New York	18
33	North Carolina	11
46	North Dakota	9
21	Ohio	13
40	Oklahoma	10
7	Oregon	16
13	Pennsylvania	14
33	Rhode Island	11
33	South Carolina	11
46	South Dakota	9
26	Tennessee	12
21	Texas	13
13	Utah	14
3	Vermont	18
21	Virginia	13
8	Washington	15
49	West Virginia	8
8	Wisconsin	15
40	Wyoming	10

RANK ORDER

RANK	STATE	RATE
1	Massachusetts	21
2	Maryland	19
3	New Jersey	18
3	New York	18
3	Vermont	18
6	Connecticut	17
7	Oregon	16
8	Colorado	15
8	Illinois	15
8	Indiana	15
8	Washington	15
8	Wisconsin	15
13	Arizona	14
13	California	14
13	Florida	14
13	Montana	14
13	Nevada	14
13	New Hampshire	14
13	Pennsylvania	14
13	Utah	14
21	Maine	13
21	Nebraska	13
21	Ohio	13
21	Texas	13
21	Virginia	13
26	Alaska	12
26	Hawaii	12
26	Kansas	12
26	Kentucky	12
26	Louisiana	12
26	Missouri	12
26	Tennessee	12
33	Alabama	11
33	Delaware	11
33	Minnesota	11
33	New Mexico	11
33	North Carolina	11
33	Rhode Island	11
33	South Carolina	11
40	Arkansas	10
40	Georgia	10
40	Iowa	10
40	Michigan	10
40	Oklahoma	10
40	Wyoming	10
46	Mississippi	9
46	North Dakota	9
46	South Dakota	9
49	West Virginia	8
50	Idaho	7

District of Columbia — 27

Source: CQ Press using data from American Medical Association (Chicago, Illinois)
  "Physician Characteristics and Distribution in the U.S." (2010 Edition)
*As of December 31, 2008. National rate does not include physicians in U.S. territories and possessions.

Physicians in Psychiatry in 2008

National Total = 40,402 Physicians*

ALPHA ORDER					RANK ORDER			
RANK	STATE		PHYSICIANS	% of USA	RANK	STATE	PHYSICIANS	% of USA
28	Alabama		352	0.9%	1	California	5,604	13.9%
47	Alaska		79	0.2%	2	New York	5,430	13.4%
22	Arizona		564	1.4%	3	Massachusetts	2,120	5.2%
33	Arkansas		238	0.6%	4	Pennsylvania	1,954	4.8%
1	California		5,604	13.9%	5	Texas	1,883	4.7%
17	Colorado		609	1.5%	6	Florida	1,745	4.3%
15	Connecticut		920	2.3%	7	Illinois	1,537	3.8%
44	Delaware		96	0.2%	8	New Jersey	1,398	3.5%
6	Florida		1,745	4.3%	9	Maryland	1,367	3.4%
14	Georgia		937	2.3%	10	Ohio	1,159	2.9%
32	Hawaii		260	0.6%	11	North Carolina	1,112	2.8%
45	Idaho		80	0.2%	12	Virginia	1,072	2.7%
7	Illinois		1,537	3.8%	13	Michigan	1,064	2.6%
26	Indiana		463	1.1%	14	Georgia	937	2.3%
36	Iowa		208	0.5%	15	Connecticut	920	2.3%
30	Kansas		300	0.7%	16	Washington	791	2.0%
27	Kentucky		381	0.9%	17	Colorado	609	1.5%
25	Louisiana		466	1.2%	18	Tennessee	599	1.5%
35	Maine		229	0.6%	19	Missouri	593	1.5%
9	Maryland		1,367	3.4%	20	Wisconsin	591	1.5%
3	Massachusetts		2,120	5.2%	21	Minnesota	581	1.4%
13	Michigan		1,064	2.6%	22	Arizona	564	1.4%
21	Minnesota		581	1.4%	23	South Carolina	474	1.2%
37	Mississippi		201	0.5%	24	Oregon	467	1.2%
19	Missouri		593	1.5%	25	Louisiana	466	1.2%
45	Montana		80	0.2%	26	Indiana	463	1.1%
42	Nebraska		172	0.4%	27	Kentucky	381	0.9%
39	Nevada		190	0.5%	28	Alabama	352	0.9%
40	New Hampshire		186	0.5%	29	Oklahoma	301	0.7%
8	New Jersey		1,398	3.5%	30	Kansas	300	0.7%
31	New Mexico		276	0.7%	31	New Mexico	276	0.7%
2	New York		5,430	13.4%	32	Hawaii	260	0.6%
11	North Carolina		1,112	2.8%	33	Arkansas	238	0.6%
48	North Dakota		78	0.2%	34	Rhode Island	232	0.6%
10	Ohio		1,159	2.9%	35	Maine	229	0.6%
29	Oklahoma		301	0.7%	36	Iowa	208	0.5%
24	Oregon		467	1.2%	37	Mississippi	201	0.5%
4	Pennsylvania		1,954	4.8%	38	Utah	197	0.5%
34	Rhode Island		232	0.6%	39	Nevada	190	0.5%
23	South Carolina		474	1.2%	40	New Hampshire	186	0.5%
49	South Dakota		59	0.1%	41	West Virginia	174	0.4%
18	Tennessee		599	1.5%	42	Nebraska	172	0.4%
5	Texas		1,883	4.7%	43	Vermont	158	0.4%
38	Utah		197	0.5%	44	Delaware	96	0.2%
43	Vermont		158	0.4%	45	Idaho	80	0.2%
12	Virginia		1,072	2.7%	45	Montana	80	0.2%
16	Washington		791	2.0%	47	Alaska	79	0.2%
41	West Virginia		174	0.4%	48	North Dakota	78	0.2%
20	Wisconsin		591	1.5%	49	South Dakota	59	0.1%
50	Wyoming		49	0.1%	50	Wyoming	49	0.1%
						District of Columbia	326	0.8%

Source: American Medical Association (Chicago, Illinois)
   "Physician Characteristics and Distribution in the U.S." (2010 Edition)
*As of December 31, 2008. Total does not include 502 physicians in U.S. territories and possessions. Psychiatry includes psychoanalysis.

Rate of Physicians in Psychiatry in 2008

National Rate = 13 Physicians per 100,000 Population*

ALPHA ORDER			RANK ORDER		
RANK	STATE	RATE	RANK	STATE	RATE
39	Alabama	8	1	Massachusetts	32
21	Alaska	11	2	New York	28
35	Arizona	9	3	Connecticut	26
39	Arkansas	8	4	Vermont	25
11	California	15	5	Maryland	24
15	Colorado	12	6	Rhode Island	22
3	Connecticut	26	7	Hawaii	20
21	Delaware	11	8	Maine	17
35	Florida	9	9	New Jersey	16
28	Georgia	10	9	Pennsylvania	16
7	Hawaii	20	11	California	15
50	Idaho	5	12	New Hampshire	14
15	Illinois	12	12	New Mexico	14
44	Indiana	7	12	Virginia	14
44	Iowa	7	15	Colorado	12
21	Kansas	11	15	Illinois	12
35	Kentucky	9	15	North Carolina	12
28	Louisiana	10	15	North Dakota	12
8	Maine	17	15	Oregon	12
5	Maryland	24	15	Washington	12
1	Massachusetts	32	21	Alaska	11
21	Michigan	11	21	Delaware	11
21	Minnesota	11	21	Kansas	11
44	Mississippi	7	21	Michigan	11
28	Missouri	10	21	Minnesota	11
39	Montana	8	21	South Carolina	11
28	Nebraska	10	21	Wisconsin	11
44	Nevada	7	28	Georgia	10
12	New Hampshire	14	28	Louisiana	10
9	New Jersey	16	28	Missouri	10
12	New Mexico	14	28	Nebraska	10
2	New York	28	28	Ohio	10
15	North Carolina	12	28	Tennessee	10
15	North Dakota	12	28	West Virginia	10
28	Ohio	10	35	Arizona	9
39	Oklahoma	8	35	Florida	9
15	Oregon	12	35	Kentucky	9
9	Pennsylvania	16	35	Wyoming	9
6	Rhode Island	22	39	Alabama	8
21	South Carolina	11	39	Arkansas	8
44	South Dakota	7	39	Montana	8
28	Tennessee	10	39	Oklahoma	8
39	Texas	8	39	Texas	8
44	Utah	7	44	Indiana	7
4	Vermont	25	44	Iowa	7
12	Virginia	14	44	Mississippi	7
15	Washington	12	44	Nevada	7
28	West Virginia	10	44	South Dakota	7
21	Wisconsin	11	44	Utah	7
35	Wyoming	9	50	Idaho	5
				District of Columbia	55

Source: CQ Press using data from American Medical Association (Chicago, Illinois)
"Physician Characteristics and Distribution in the U.S." (2010 Edition)
*As of December 31, 2008. National rate does not include physicians in U.S. territories and possessions. Psychiatry includes psychoanalysis.

Percent of Population Lacking Access to Mental Health Care in 2010

National Percent = 18.4% of Population*

<table>
<tr><td colspan="3">ALPHA ORDER</td><td colspan="3">RANK ORDER</td></tr>
<tr><th>RANK</th><th>STATE</th><th>PERCENT</th><th>RANK</th><th>STATE</th><th>PERCENT</th></tr>
<tr><td>7</td><td>Alabama</td><td>41.7</td><td>1</td><td>Wyoming</td><td>69.2</td></tr>
<tr><td>31</td><td>Alaska</td><td>15.2</td><td>2</td><td>Louisiana</td><td>62.3</td></tr>
<tr><td>28</td><td>Arizona</td><td>17.1</td><td>3</td><td>Idaho</td><td>61.5</td></tr>
<tr><td>5</td><td>Arkansas</td><td>45.9</td><td>4</td><td>South Dakota</td><td>48.8</td></tr>
<tr><td>38</td><td>California</td><td>9.1</td><td>5</td><td>Arkansas</td><td>45.9</td></tr>
<tr><td>36</td><td>Colorado</td><td>10.2</td><td>6</td><td>Iowa</td><td>42.4</td></tr>
<tr><td>48</td><td>Connecticut</td><td>1.9</td><td>7</td><td>Alabama</td><td>41.7</td></tr>
<tr><td>50</td><td>Delaware</td><td>0.0</td><td>7</td><td>New Mexico</td><td>41.7</td></tr>
<tr><td>39</td><td>Florida</td><td>8.8</td><td>9</td><td>Montana</td><td>41.2</td></tr>
<tr><td>20</td><td>Georgia</td><td>28.8</td><td>10</td><td>Nebraska</td><td>40.9</td></tr>
<tr><td>45</td><td>Hawaii</td><td>5.9</td><td>11</td><td>Mississippi</td><td>40.8</td></tr>
<tr><td>3</td><td>Idaho</td><td>61.5</td><td>12</td><td>Missouri</td><td>36.0</td></tr>
<tr><td>26</td><td>Illinois</td><td>22.2</td><td>13</td><td>Kansas</td><td>35.7</td></tr>
<tr><td>32</td><td>Indiana</td><td>14.9</td><td>14</td><td>Oklahoma</td><td>34.6</td></tr>
<tr><td>6</td><td>Iowa</td><td>42.4</td><td>15</td><td>North Dakota</td><td>33.5</td></tr>
<tr><td>13</td><td>Kansas</td><td>35.7</td><td>16</td><td>Tennessee</td><td>31.9</td></tr>
<tr><td>21</td><td>Kentucky</td><td>26.6</td><td>17</td><td>Utah</td><td>30.9</td></tr>
<tr><td>2</td><td>Louisiana</td><td>62.3</td><td>18</td><td>Wisconsin</td><td>29.8</td></tr>
<tr><td>36</td><td>Maine</td><td>10.2</td><td>19</td><td>South Carolina</td><td>29.4</td></tr>
<tr><td>43</td><td>Maryland</td><td>7.4</td><td>20</td><td>Georgia</td><td>28.8</td></tr>
<tr><td>47</td><td>Massachusetts</td><td>3.0</td><td>21</td><td>Kentucky</td><td>26.6</td></tr>
<tr><td>34</td><td>Michigan</td><td>11.3</td><td>22</td><td>Minnesota</td><td>26.5</td></tr>
<tr><td>22</td><td>Minnesota</td><td>26.5</td><td>23</td><td>West Virginia</td><td>25.7</td></tr>
<tr><td>11</td><td>Mississippi</td><td>40.8</td><td>24</td><td>Texas</td><td>25.2</td></tr>
<tr><td>12</td><td>Missouri</td><td>36.0</td><td>25</td><td>Washington</td><td>25.0</td></tr>
<tr><td>9</td><td>Montana</td><td>41.2</td><td>26</td><td>Illinois</td><td>22.2</td></tr>
<tr><td>10</td><td>Nebraska</td><td>40.9</td><td>27</td><td>Oregon</td><td>22.1</td></tr>
<tr><td>40</td><td>Nevada</td><td>7.9</td><td>28</td><td>Arizona</td><td>17.1</td></tr>
<tr><td>46</td><td>New Hampshire</td><td>4.3</td><td>29</td><td>Rhode Island</td><td>15.6</td></tr>
<tr><td>49</td><td>New Jersey</td><td>1.3</td><td>29</td><td>Virginia</td><td>15.6</td></tr>
<tr><td>7</td><td>New Mexico</td><td>41.7</td><td>31</td><td>Alaska</td><td>15.2</td></tr>
<tr><td>41</td><td>New York</td><td>7.7</td><td>32</td><td>Indiana</td><td>14.9</td></tr>
<tr><td>42</td><td>North Carolina</td><td>7.5</td><td>32</td><td>Ohio</td><td>14.9</td></tr>
<tr><td>15</td><td>North Dakota</td><td>33.5</td><td>34</td><td>Michigan</td><td>11.3</td></tr>
<tr><td>32</td><td>Ohio</td><td>14.9</td><td>35</td><td>Pennsylvania</td><td>10.7</td></tr>
<tr><td>14</td><td>Oklahoma</td><td>34.6</td><td>36</td><td>Colorado</td><td>10.2</td></tr>
<tr><td>27</td><td>Oregon</td><td>22.1</td><td>36</td><td>Maine</td><td>10.2</td></tr>
<tr><td>35</td><td>Pennsylvania</td><td>10.7</td><td>38</td><td>California</td><td>9.1</td></tr>
<tr><td>29</td><td>Rhode Island</td><td>15.6</td><td>39</td><td>Florida</td><td>8.8</td></tr>
<tr><td>19</td><td>South Carolina</td><td>29.4</td><td>40</td><td>Nevada</td><td>7.9</td></tr>
<tr><td>4</td><td>South Dakota</td><td>48.8</td><td>41</td><td>New York</td><td>7.7</td></tr>
<tr><td>16</td><td>Tennessee</td><td>31.9</td><td>42</td><td>North Carolina</td><td>7.5</td></tr>
<tr><td>24</td><td>Texas</td><td>25.2</td><td>43</td><td>Maryland</td><td>7.4</td></tr>
<tr><td>17</td><td>Utah</td><td>30.9</td><td>43</td><td>Vermont</td><td>7.4</td></tr>
<tr><td>43</td><td>Vermont</td><td>7.4</td><td>45</td><td>Hawaii</td><td>5.9</td></tr>
<tr><td>29</td><td>Virginia</td><td>15.6</td><td>46</td><td>New Hampshire</td><td>4.3</td></tr>
<tr><td>25</td><td>Washington</td><td>25.0</td><td>47</td><td>Massachusetts</td><td>3.0</td></tr>
<tr><td>23</td><td>West Virginia</td><td>25.7</td><td>48</td><td>Connecticut</td><td>1.9</td></tr>
<tr><td>18</td><td>Wisconsin</td><td>29.8</td><td>49</td><td>New Jersey</td><td>1.3</td></tr>
<tr><td>1</td><td>Wyoming</td><td>69.2</td><td>50</td><td>Delaware</td><td>0.0</td></tr>
<tr><td></td><td></td><td></td><td></td><td>District of Columbia</td><td>13.1</td></tr>
</table>

Source: CQ Press using data from U.S. Department of Health and Human Services, Division of Shortage Designation
  "Selected Statistics on Health Professional Shortage Areas" (as of January 15, 2010)
    (http://datawarehouse.hrsa.gov/HPSADownload.aspx)
*Percent of population considered under-served by mental health practitioners. An under-served population does not have
primary medical care within reasonable economic and geographic bounds.

International Medical School Graduates in 2008

National Total = 237,963 Nonfederal Physicians*

<table>
<tr><td colspan="4">ALPHA ORDER</td><td colspan="4">RANK ORDER</td></tr>
<tr><td>RANK</td><td>STATE</td><td>PHYSICIANS</td><td>% of USA</td><td>RANK</td><td>STATE</td><td>PHYSICIANS</td><td>% of USA</td></tr>
<tr><td>25</td><td>Alabama</td><td>1,823</td><td>0.8%</td><td>1</td><td>New York</td><td>35,219</td><td>14.8%</td></tr>
<tr><td>49</td><td>Alaska</td><td>118</td><td>0.0%</td><td>2</td><td>California</td><td>26,613</td><td>11.2%</td></tr>
<tr><td>15</td><td>Arizona</td><td>3,638</td><td>1.5%</td><td>3</td><td>Florida</td><td>20,672</td><td>8.7%</td></tr>
<tr><td>35</td><td>Arkansas</td><td>1,059</td><td>0.4%</td><td>4</td><td>Texas</td><td>14,075</td><td>5.9%</td></tr>
<tr><td>2</td><td>California</td><td>26,613</td><td>11.2%</td><td>5</td><td>New Jersey</td><td>13,795</td><td>5.8%</td></tr>
<tr><td>34</td><td>Colorado</td><td>1,107</td><td>0.5%</td><td>6</td><td>Illinois</td><td>13,592</td><td>5.7%</td></tr>
<tr><td>14</td><td>Connecticut</td><td>4,361</td><td>1.8%</td><td>7</td><td>Pennsylvania</td><td>11,279</td><td>4.7%</td></tr>
<tr><td>38</td><td>Delaware</td><td>761</td><td>0.3%</td><td>8</td><td>Ohio</td><td>9,973</td><td>4.2%</td></tr>
<tr><td>3</td><td>Florida</td><td>20,672</td><td>8.7%</td><td>9</td><td>Michigan</td><td>9,791</td><td>4.1%</td></tr>
<tr><td>13</td><td>Georgia</td><td>4,717</td><td>2.0%</td><td>10</td><td>Massachusetts</td><td>7,393</td><td>3.1%</td></tr>
<tr><td>39</td><td>Hawaii</td><td>720</td><td>0.3%</td><td>11</td><td>Maryland</td><td>7,215</td><td>3.0%</td></tr>
<tr><td>49</td><td>Idaho</td><td>118</td><td>0.0%</td><td>12</td><td>Virginia</td><td>5,255</td><td>2.2%</td></tr>
<tr><td>6</td><td>Illinois</td><td>13,592</td><td>5.7%</td><td>13</td><td>Georgia</td><td>4,717</td><td>2.0%</td></tr>
<tr><td>18</td><td>Indiana</td><td>3,268</td><td>1.4%</td><td>14</td><td>Connecticut</td><td>4,361</td><td>1.8%</td></tr>
<tr><td>31</td><td>Iowa</td><td>1,305</td><td>0.5%</td><td>15</td><td>Arizona</td><td>3,638</td><td>1.5%</td></tr>
<tr><td>30</td><td>Kansas</td><td>1,365</td><td>0.6%</td><td>16</td><td>Missouri</td><td>3,574</td><td>1.5%</td></tr>
<tr><td>24</td><td>Kentucky</td><td>2,293</td><td>1.0%</td><td>17</td><td>North Carolina</td><td>3,549</td><td>1.5%</td></tr>
<tr><td>23</td><td>Louisiana</td><td>2,559</td><td>1.1%</td><td>18</td><td>Indiana</td><td>3,268</td><td>1.4%</td></tr>
<tr><td>42</td><td>Maine</td><td>622</td><td>0.3%</td><td>19</td><td>Wisconsin</td><td>3,095</td><td>1.3%</td></tr>
<tr><td>11</td><td>Maryland</td><td>7,215</td><td>3.0%</td><td>20</td><td>Tennessee</td><td>3,088</td><td>1.3%</td></tr>
<tr><td>10</td><td>Massachusetts</td><td>7,393</td><td>3.1%</td><td>21</td><td>Washington</td><td>2,631</td><td>1.1%</td></tr>
<tr><td>9</td><td>Michigan</td><td>9,791</td><td>4.1%</td><td>22</td><td>Minnesota</td><td>2,583</td><td>1.1%</td></tr>
<tr><td>22</td><td>Minnesota</td><td>2,583</td><td>1.1%</td><td>23</td><td>Louisiana</td><td>2,559</td><td>1.1%</td></tr>
<tr><td>37</td><td>Mississippi</td><td>799</td><td>0.3%</td><td>24</td><td>Kentucky</td><td>2,293</td><td>1.0%</td></tr>
<tr><td>16</td><td>Missouri</td><td>3,574</td><td>1.5%</td><td>25</td><td>Alabama</td><td>1,823</td><td>0.8%</td></tr>
<tr><td>48</td><td>Montana</td><td>123</td><td>0.1%</td><td>26</td><td>Nevada</td><td>1,743</td><td>0.7%</td></tr>
<tr><td>40</td><td>Nebraska</td><td>709</td><td>0.3%</td><td>27</td><td>West Virginia</td><td>1,697</td><td>0.7%</td></tr>
<tr><td>26</td><td>Nevada</td><td>1,743</td><td>0.7%</td><td>28</td><td>South Carolina</td><td>1,559</td><td>0.7%</td></tr>
<tr><td>41</td><td>New Hampshire</td><td>652</td><td>0.3%</td><td>29</td><td>Oklahoma</td><td>1,439</td><td>0.6%</td></tr>
<tr><td>5</td><td>New Jersey</td><td>13,795</td><td>5.8%</td><td>30</td><td>Kansas</td><td>1,365</td><td>0.6%</td></tr>
<tr><td>36</td><td>New Mexico</td><td>963</td><td>0.4%</td><td>31</td><td>Iowa</td><td>1,305</td><td>0.5%</td></tr>
<tr><td>1</td><td>New York</td><td>35,219</td><td>14.8%</td><td>32</td><td>Rhode Island</td><td>1,176</td><td>0.5%</td></tr>
<tr><td>17</td><td>North Carolina</td><td>3,549</td><td>1.5%</td><td>33</td><td>Oregon</td><td>1,130</td><td>0.5%</td></tr>
<tr><td>44</td><td>North Dakota</td><td>473</td><td>0.2%</td><td>34</td><td>Colorado</td><td>1,107</td><td>0.5%</td></tr>
<tr><td>8</td><td>Ohio</td><td>9,973</td><td>4.2%</td><td>35</td><td>Arkansas</td><td>1,059</td><td>0.4%</td></tr>
<tr><td>29</td><td>Oklahoma</td><td>1,439</td><td>0.6%</td><td>36</td><td>New Mexico</td><td>963</td><td>0.4%</td></tr>
<tr><td>33</td><td>Oregon</td><td>1,130</td><td>0.5%</td><td>37</td><td>Mississippi</td><td>799</td><td>0.3%</td></tr>
<tr><td>7</td><td>Pennsylvania</td><td>11,279</td><td>4.7%</td><td>38</td><td>Delaware</td><td>761</td><td>0.3%</td></tr>
<tr><td>32</td><td>Rhode Island</td><td>1,176</td><td>0.5%</td><td>39</td><td>Hawaii</td><td>720</td><td>0.3%</td></tr>
<tr><td>28</td><td>South Carolina</td><td>1,559</td><td>0.7%</td><td>40</td><td>Nebraska</td><td>709</td><td>0.3%</td></tr>
<tr><td>45</td><td>South Dakota</td><td>285</td><td>0.1%</td><td>41</td><td>New Hampshire</td><td>652</td><td>0.3%</td></tr>
<tr><td>20</td><td>Tennessee</td><td>3,088</td><td>1.3%</td><td>42</td><td>Maine</td><td>622</td><td>0.3%</td></tr>
<tr><td>4</td><td>Texas</td><td>14,075</td><td>5.9%</td><td>43</td><td>Utah</td><td>564</td><td>0.2%</td></tr>
<tr><td>43</td><td>Utah</td><td>564</td><td>0.2%</td><td>44</td><td>North Dakota</td><td>473</td><td>0.2%</td></tr>
<tr><td>46</td><td>Vermont</td><td>244</td><td>0.1%</td><td>45</td><td>South Dakota</td><td>285</td><td>0.1%</td></tr>
<tr><td>12</td><td>Virginia</td><td>5,255</td><td>2.2%</td><td>46</td><td>Vermont</td><td>244</td><td>0.1%</td></tr>
<tr><td>21</td><td>Washington</td><td>2,631</td><td>1.1%</td><td>47</td><td>Wyoming</td><td>134</td><td>0.1%</td></tr>
<tr><td>27</td><td>West Virginia</td><td>1,697</td><td>0.7%</td><td>48</td><td>Montana</td><td>123</td><td>0.1%</td></tr>
<tr><td>19</td><td>Wisconsin</td><td>3,095</td><td>1.3%</td><td>49</td><td>Alaska</td><td>118</td><td>0.0%</td></tr>
<tr><td>47</td><td>Wyoming</td><td>134</td><td>0.1%</td><td>49</td><td>Idaho</td><td>118</td><td>0.0%</td></tr>
<tr><td></td><td></td><td></td><td></td><td colspan="2">District of Columbia</td><td>1,047</td><td>0.4%</td></tr>
</table>

Source: American Medical Association (Chicago, Illinois)
"Physician Characteristics and Distribution in the U.S." (2010 Edition)
*As of December 31, 2008. Total does not include 7,042 physicians in U.S. territories and possessions.

International Medical School Graduates as a Percent of Physicians in 2008

National Percent = 25.3% of Physicians*

ALPHA ORDER

RANK	STATE	PERCENT
31	Alabama	16.0
48	Alaska	6.8
17	Arizona	22.6
31	Arkansas	16.0
16	California	23.2
47	Colorado	7.4
9	Connecticut	29.2
7	Delaware	30.7
3	Florida	36.9
23	Georgia	19.9
33	Hawaii	15.2
50	Idaho	3.9
6	Illinois	33.8
21	Indiana	20.9
23	Iowa	19.9
27	Kansas	18.6
22	Kentucky	20.7
25	Louisiana	19.7
36	Maine	14.5
11	Maryland	27.1
19	Massachusetts	21.9
5	Michigan	34.3
35	Minnesota	14.8
39	Mississippi	13.3
18	Missouri	22.2
49	Montana	4.7
37	Nebraska	14.1
8	Nevada	30.6
34	New Hampshire	14.9
1	New Jersey	44.9
29	New Mexico	17.2
2	New York	41.4
39	North Carolina	13.3
12	North Dakota	26.5
10	Ohio	28.7
25	Oklahoma	19.7
44	Oregon	9.1
14	Pennsylvania	25.8
13	Rhode Island	26.4
39	South Carolina	13.3
38	South Dakota	13.9
30	Tennessee	16.8
15	Texas	24.3
46	Utah	8.7
45	Vermont	8.8
20	Virginia	21.3
42	Washington	12.6
4	West Virginia	35.4
28	Wisconsin	18.5
43	Wyoming	11.1

RANK ORDER

RANK	STATE	PERCENT
1	New Jersey	44.9
2	New York	41.4
3	Florida	36.9
4	West Virginia	35.4
5	Michigan	34.3
6	Illinois	33.8
7	Delaware	30.7
8	Nevada	30.6
9	Connecticut	29.2
10	Ohio	28.7
11	Maryland	27.1
12	North Dakota	26.5
13	Rhode Island	26.4
14	Pennsylvania	25.8
15	Texas	24.3
16	California	23.2
17	Arizona	22.6
18	Missouri	22.2
19	Massachusetts	21.9
20	Virginia	21.3
21	Indiana	20.9
22	Kentucky	20.7
23	Georgia	19.9
23	Iowa	19.9
25	Louisiana	19.7
25	Oklahoma	19.7
27	Kansas	18.6
28	Wisconsin	18.5
29	New Mexico	17.2
30	Tennessee	16.8
31	Alabama	16.0
31	Arkansas	16.0
33	Hawaii	15.2
34	New Hampshire	14.9
35	Minnesota	14.8
36	Maine	14.5
37	Nebraska	14.1
38	South Dakota	13.9
39	Mississippi	13.3
39	North Carolina	13.3
39	South Carolina	13.3
42	Washington	12.6
43	Wyoming	11.1
44	Oregon	9.1
45	Vermont	8.8
46	Utah	8.7
47	Colorado	7.4
48	Alaska	6.8
49	Montana	4.7
50	Idaho	3.9

| | District of Columbia | 20.0 |

Source: CQ Press using data from American Medical Association (Chicago, Illinois)
    "Physician Characteristics and Distribution in the U.S." (2010 Edition)
*As of December 31, 2008. National percent does not include physicians in the U.S. territories and possessions.

Osteopathic Physicians in 2009

National Total = 59,936 Osteopathic Physicians*

ALPHA ORDER

RANK	STATE	OSTEOPATHS	% of USA
33	Alabama	395	0.7%
44	Alaska	156	0.3%
11	Arizona	1,639	2.7%
37	Arkansas	264	0.4%
3	California	4,282	7.1%
14	Colorado	992	1.7%
31	Connecticut	472	0.8%
38	Delaware	255	0.4%
6	Florida	3,986	6.7%
19	Georgia	815	1.4%
42	Hawaii	213	0.4%
36	Idaho	265	0.4%
9	Illinois	2,516	4.2%
17	Indiana	848	1.4%
13	Iowa	1,144	1.9%
23	Kansas	684	1.1%
30	Kentucky	507	0.8%
45	Louisiana	148	0.2%
25	Maine	644	1.1%
21	Maryland	761	1.3%
24	Massachusetts	678	1.1%
2	Michigan	5,156	8.6%
29	Minnesota	510	0.9%
34	Mississippi	329	0.5%
10	Missouri	1,892	3.2%
45	Montana	148	0.2%
43	Nebraska	185	0.3%
28	Nevada	530	0.9%
39	New Hampshire	248	0.4%
8	New Jersey	3,092	5.2%
40	New Mexico	222	0.4%
4	New York	4,087	6.8%
18	North Carolina	822	1.4%
49	North Dakota	62	0.1%
5	Ohio	4,002	6.7%
12	Oklahoma	1,617	2.7%
26	Oregon	597	1.0%
1	Pennsylvania	5,962	9.9%
41	Rhode Island	217	0.4%
32	South Carolina	440	0.7%
47	South Dakota	109	0.2%
27	Tennessee	594	1.0%
7	Texas	3,558	5.9%
34	Utah	329	0.5%
50	Vermont	61	0.1%
15	Virginia	980	1.6%
16	Washington	859	1.4%
22	West Virginia	728	1.2%
20	Wisconsin	786	1.3%
48	Wyoming	82	0.1%

RANK ORDER

RANK	STATE	OSTEOPATHS	% of USA
1	Pennsylvania	5,962	9.9%
2	Michigan	5,156	8.6%
3	California	4,282	7.1%
4	New York	4,087	6.8%
5	Ohio	4,002	6.7%
6	Florida	3,986	6.7%
7	Texas	3,558	5.9%
8	New Jersey	3,092	5.2%
9	Illinois	2,516	4.2%
10	Missouri	1,892	3.2%
11	Arizona	1,639	2.7%
12	Oklahoma	1,617	2.7%
13	Iowa	1,144	1.9%
14	Colorado	992	1.7%
15	Virginia	980	1.6%
16	Washington	859	1.4%
17	Indiana	848	1.4%
18	North Carolina	822	1.4%
19	Georgia	815	1.4%
20	Wisconsin	786	1.3%
21	Maryland	761	1.3%
22	West Virginia	728	1.2%
23	Kansas	684	1.1%
24	Massachusetts	678	1.1%
25	Maine	644	1.1%
26	Oregon	597	1.0%
27	Tennessee	594	1.0%
28	Nevada	530	0.9%
29	Minnesota	510	0.9%
30	Kentucky	507	0.8%
31	Connecticut	472	0.8%
32	South Carolina	440	0.7%
33	Alabama	395	0.7%
34	Mississippi	329	0.5%
34	Utah	329	0.5%
36	Idaho	265	0.4%
37	Arkansas	264	0.4%
38	Delaware	255	0.4%
39	New Hampshire	248	0.4%
40	New Mexico	222	0.4%
41	Rhode Island	217	0.4%
42	Hawaii	213	0.4%
43	Nebraska	185	0.3%
44	Alaska	156	0.3%
45	Louisiana	148	0.2%
45	Montana	148	0.2%
47	South Dakota	109	0.2%
48	Wyoming	82	0.1%
49	North Dakota	62	0.1%
50	Vermont	61	0.1%
	District of Columbia	68	0.1%

Source: American Osteopathic Association
"Osteopathic Medical Profession Report" (https://www.do-online.org/index.cfm?PageID=aoa_ompreport_us)
*Active osteopaths under age 65 as of May 31, 2009. National total does not include 248 osteopaths not shown by state. Osteopaths practice a system of medicine based on the theory that disturbances in the musculoskeletal system affect other body parts, causing many disorders that can be corrected by various manipulative techniques in conjunction with conventional medical, surgical, pharmacological, and other therapeutic procedures.

Rate of Osteopathic Physicians in 2009

National Rate = 20 Osteopaths per 100,000 Population*

ALPHA ORDER

RANK	STATE	RATE
48	Alabama	8
13	Alaska	22
11	Arizona	25
45	Arkansas	9
33	California	12
17	Colorado	20
28	Connecticut	13
10	Delaware	29
13	Florida	22
48	Georgia	8
22	Hawaii	16
21	Idaho	17
19	Illinois	19
28	Indiana	13
6	Iowa	38
12	Kansas	24
33	Kentucky	12
50	Louisiana	3
2	Maine	49
28	Maryland	13
39	Massachusetts	10
1	Michigan	52
39	Minnesota	10
37	Mississippi	11
9	Missouri	32
24	Montana	15
39	Nebraska	10
17	Nevada	20
19	New Hampshire	19
7	New Jersey	36
37	New Mexico	11
15	New York	21
45	North Carolina	9
39	North Dakota	10
8	Ohio	35
4	Oklahoma	44
22	Oregon	16
3	Pennsylvania	47
15	Rhode Island	21
39	South Carolina	10
28	South Dakota	13
45	Tennessee	9
26	Texas	14
33	Utah	12
39	Vermont	10
33	Virginia	12
28	Washington	13
5	West Virginia	40
26	Wisconsin	14
24	Wyoming	15

RANK ORDER

RANK	STATE	RATE
1	Michigan	52
2	Maine	49
3	Pennsylvania	47
4	Oklahoma	44
5	West Virginia	40
6	Iowa	38
7	New Jersey	36
8	Ohio	35
9	Missouri	32
10	Delaware	29
11	Arizona	25
12	Kansas	24
13	Alaska	22
13	Florida	22
15	New York	21
15	Rhode Island	21
17	Colorado	20
17	Nevada	20
19	Illinois	19
19	New Hampshire	19
21	Idaho	17
22	Hawaii	16
22	Oregon	16
24	Montana	15
24	Wyoming	15
26	Texas	14
26	Wisconsin	14
28	Connecticut	13
28	Indiana	13
28	Maryland	13
28	South Dakota	13
28	Washington	13
33	California	12
33	Kentucky	12
33	Utah	12
33	Virginia	12
37	Mississippi	11
37	New Mexico	11
39	Massachusetts	10
39	Minnesota	10
39	Nebraska	10
39	North Dakota	10
39	South Carolina	10
39	Vermont	10
45	Arkansas	9
45	North Carolina	9
45	Tennessee	9
48	Alabama	8
48	Georgia	8
50	Louisiana	3

District of Columbia	11

Source: CQ Press using data from American Osteopathic Association
    "Osteopathic Medical Profession Report" (https://www.do-online.org/index.cfm?PageID=aoa_ompreport_us)
*Active osteopaths under age 65 as of May 31, 2009. National rate does not include osteopaths not shown by state.
Osteopaths practice a system of medicine based on the theory that disturbances in the musculoskeletal system affect other
body parts, causing many disorders that can be corrected by various manipulative techniques in conjunction with conventional
medical, surgical, pharmacological, and other therapeutic procedures.

Podiatrists in 2008

National Total = 9,670 Podiatrists*

ALPHA ORDER				RANK ORDER			
RANK	STATE	PODIATRISTS	% of USA	RANK	STATE	PODIATRISTS	% of USA
21	Alabama	110	1.1%	1	New York	1,090	11.3%
NA	Alaska**	NA	NA	2	California	760	7.9%
9	Arizona	390	4.0%	3	Pennsylvania	700	7.2%
34	Arkansas	40	0.4%	4	Florida	610	6.3%
2	California	760	7.9%	5	Ohio	560	5.8%
30	Colorado	70	0.7%	6	New Jersey	540	5.6%
21	Connecticut	110	1.1%	7	Texas	520	5.4%
26	Delaware	80	0.8%	8	Illinois	410	4.2%
4	Florida	610	6.3%	9	Arizona	390	4.0%
13	Georgia	180	1.9%	10	Michigan	360	3.7%
NA	Hawaii**	NA	NA	11	Maryland	340	3.5%
NA	Idaho**	NA	NA	12	Virginia	280	2.9%
8	Illinois	410	4.2%	13	Georgia	180	1.9%
17	Indiana	140	1.4%	13	Massachusetts	180	1.9%
23	Iowa	100	1.0%	13	Tennessee	180	1.9%
30	Kansas	70	0.7%	16	Washington	150	1.6%
26	Kentucky	80	0.8%	17	Indiana	140	1.4%
33	Louisiana	60	0.6%	17	North Carolina	140	1.4%
37	Maine	30	0.3%	19	Minnesota	130	1.3%
11	Maryland	340	3.5%	20	Missouri	120	1.2%
13	Massachusetts	180	1.9%	21	Alabama	110	1.1%
10	Michigan	360	3.7%	21	Connecticut	110	1.1%
19	Minnesota	130	1.3%	23	Iowa	100	1.0%
34	Mississippi	40	0.4%	23	Oklahoma	100	1.0%
20	Missouri	120	1.2%	25	Wisconsin	90	0.9%
NA	Montana**	NA	NA	26	Delaware	80	0.8%
NA	Nebraska**	NA	NA	26	Kentucky	80	0.8%
26	Nevada	80	0.8%	26	Nevada	80	0.8%
NA	New Hampshire**	NA	NA	26	New Mexico	80	0.8%
6	New Jersey	540	5.6%	30	Colorado	70	0.7%
26	New Mexico	80	0.8%	30	Kansas	70	0.7%
1	New York	1,090	11.3%	30	South Carolina	70	0.7%
17	North Carolina	140	1.4%	33	Louisiana	60	0.6%
NA	North Dakota**	NA	NA	34	Arkansas	40	0.4%
5	Ohio	560	5.8%	34	Mississippi	40	0.4%
23	Oklahoma	100	1.0%	34	Rhode Island	40	0.4%
NA	Oregon**	NA	NA	37	Maine	30	0.3%
3	Pennsylvania	700	7.2%	NA	Alaska**	NA	NA
34	Rhode Island	40	0.4%	NA	Hawaii**	NA	NA
30	South Carolina	70	0.7%	NA	Idaho**	NA	NA
NA	South Dakota**	NA	NA	NA	Montana**	NA	NA
13	Tennessee	180	1.9%	NA	Nebraska**	NA	NA
7	Texas	520	5.4%	NA	New Hampshire**	NA	NA
NA	Utah**	NA	NA	NA	North Dakota**	NA	NA
NA	Vermont**	NA	NA	NA	Oregon**	NA	NA
12	Virginia	280	2.9%	NA	South Dakota**	NA	NA
16	Washington	150	1.6%	NA	Utah**	NA	NA
NA	West Virginia**	NA	NA	NA	Vermont**	NA	NA
25	Wisconsin	90	0.9%	NA	West Virginia**	NA	NA
NA	Wyoming**	NA	NA	NA	Wyoming**	NA	NA
					District of Columbia**	NA	NA

Source: U.S. Department of Labor, Bureau of Labor Statistics
"Occupational Employment and Wages, 2008" (http://www.bls.gov/oes/)
*Does not include self-employed.
**Not available.

Rate of Podiatrists in 2008

National Rate = 3 Podiatrists per 100,000 Population*

<table>
<tr><td colspan="3">ALPHA ORDER</td><td colspan="3">RANK ORDER</td></tr>
<tr><td>RANK</td><td>STATE</td><td>RATE</td><td>RANK</td><td>STATE</td><td>RATE</td></tr>
<tr><td>21</td><td>Alabama</td><td>2</td><td>1</td><td>Delaware</td><td>9</td></tr>
<tr><td>NA</td><td>Alaska**</td><td>NA</td><td>2</td><td>Arizona</td><td>6</td></tr>
<tr><td>2</td><td>Arizona</td><td>6</td><td>2</td><td>Maryland</td><td>6</td></tr>
<tr><td>34</td><td>Arkansas</td><td>1</td><td>2</td><td>New Jersey</td><td>6</td></tr>
<tr><td>21</td><td>California</td><td>2</td><td>2</td><td>New York</td><td>6</td></tr>
<tr><td>34</td><td>Colorado</td><td>1</td><td>2</td><td>Pennsylvania</td><td>6</td></tr>
<tr><td>12</td><td>Connecticut</td><td>3</td><td>7</td><td>Ohio</td><td>5</td></tr>
<tr><td>1</td><td>Delaware</td><td>9</td><td>8</td><td>Michigan</td><td>4</td></tr>
<tr><td>12</td><td>Florida</td><td>3</td><td>8</td><td>New Mexico</td><td>4</td></tr>
<tr><td>21</td><td>Georgia</td><td>2</td><td>8</td><td>Rhode Island</td><td>4</td></tr>
<tr><td>NA</td><td>Hawaii**</td><td>NA</td><td>8</td><td>Virginia</td><td>4</td></tr>
<tr><td>NA</td><td>Idaho**</td><td>NA</td><td>12</td><td>Connecticut</td><td>3</td></tr>
<tr><td>12</td><td>Illinois</td><td>3</td><td>12</td><td>Florida</td><td>3</td></tr>
<tr><td>21</td><td>Indiana</td><td>2</td><td>12</td><td>Illinois</td><td>3</td></tr>
<tr><td>12</td><td>Iowa</td><td>3</td><td>12</td><td>Iowa</td><td>3</td></tr>
<tr><td>12</td><td>Kansas</td><td>3</td><td>12</td><td>Kansas</td><td>3</td></tr>
<tr><td>21</td><td>Kentucky</td><td>2</td><td>12</td><td>Massachusetts</td><td>3</td></tr>
<tr><td>34</td><td>Louisiana</td><td>1</td><td>12</td><td>Nevada</td><td>3</td></tr>
<tr><td>21</td><td>Maine</td><td>2</td><td>12</td><td>Oklahoma</td><td>3</td></tr>
<tr><td>2</td><td>Maryland</td><td>6</td><td>12</td><td>Tennessee</td><td>3</td></tr>
<tr><td>12</td><td>Massachusetts</td><td>3</td><td>21</td><td>Alabama</td><td>2</td></tr>
<tr><td>8</td><td>Michigan</td><td>4</td><td>21</td><td>California</td><td>2</td></tr>
<tr><td>21</td><td>Minnesota</td><td>2</td><td>21</td><td>Georgia</td><td>2</td></tr>
<tr><td>34</td><td>Mississippi</td><td>1</td><td>21</td><td>Indiana</td><td>2</td></tr>
<tr><td>21</td><td>Missouri</td><td>2</td><td>21</td><td>Kentucky</td><td>2</td></tr>
<tr><td>NA</td><td>Montana**</td><td>NA</td><td>21</td><td>Maine</td><td>2</td></tr>
<tr><td>NA</td><td>Nebraska**</td><td>NA</td><td>21</td><td>Minnesota</td><td>2</td></tr>
<tr><td>12</td><td>Nevada</td><td>3</td><td>21</td><td>Missouri</td><td>2</td></tr>
<tr><td>NA</td><td>New Hampshire**</td><td>NA</td><td>21</td><td>North Carolina</td><td>2</td></tr>
<tr><td>2</td><td>New Jersey</td><td>6</td><td>21</td><td>South Carolina</td><td>2</td></tr>
<tr><td>8</td><td>New Mexico</td><td>4</td><td>21</td><td>Texas</td><td>2</td></tr>
<tr><td>2</td><td>New York</td><td>6</td><td>21</td><td>Washington</td><td>2</td></tr>
<tr><td>21</td><td>North Carolina</td><td>2</td><td>21</td><td>Wisconsin</td><td>2</td></tr>
<tr><td>NA</td><td>North Dakota**</td><td>NA</td><td>34</td><td>Arkansas</td><td>1</td></tr>
<tr><td>7</td><td>Ohio</td><td>5</td><td>34</td><td>Colorado</td><td>1</td></tr>
<tr><td>12</td><td>Oklahoma</td><td>3</td><td>34</td><td>Louisiana</td><td>1</td></tr>
<tr><td>NA</td><td>Oregon**</td><td>NA</td><td>34</td><td>Mississippi</td><td>1</td></tr>
<tr><td>2</td><td>Pennsylvania</td><td>6</td><td>NA</td><td>Alaska**</td><td>NA</td></tr>
<tr><td>8</td><td>Rhode Island</td><td>4</td><td>NA</td><td>Hawaii**</td><td>NA</td></tr>
<tr><td>21</td><td>South Carolina</td><td>2</td><td>NA</td><td>Idaho**</td><td>NA</td></tr>
<tr><td>NA</td><td>South Dakota**</td><td>NA</td><td>NA</td><td>Montana**</td><td>NA</td></tr>
<tr><td>12</td><td>Tennessee</td><td>3</td><td>NA</td><td>Nebraska**</td><td>NA</td></tr>
<tr><td>21</td><td>Texas</td><td>2</td><td>NA</td><td>New Hampshire**</td><td>NA</td></tr>
<tr><td>NA</td><td>Utah**</td><td>NA</td><td>NA</td><td>North Dakota**</td><td>NA</td></tr>
<tr><td>NA</td><td>Vermont**</td><td>NA</td><td>NA</td><td>Oregon**</td><td>NA</td></tr>
<tr><td>8</td><td>Virginia</td><td>4</td><td>NA</td><td>South Dakota**</td><td>NA</td></tr>
<tr><td>21</td><td>Washington</td><td>2</td><td>NA</td><td>Utah**</td><td>NA</td></tr>
<tr><td>NA</td><td>West Virginia**</td><td>NA</td><td>NA</td><td>Vermont**</td><td>NA</td></tr>
<tr><td>21</td><td>Wisconsin</td><td>2</td><td>NA</td><td>West Virginia**</td><td>NA</td></tr>
<tr><td>NA</td><td>Wyoming**</td><td>NA</td><td>NA</td><td>Wyoming**</td><td>NA</td></tr>
<tr><td></td><td></td><td></td><td></td><td>District of Columbia**</td><td>NA</td></tr>
</table>

Source: CQ Press using data from U.S. Department of Labor, Bureau of Labor Statistics
    "Occupational Employment and Wages, 2008" (http://www.bls.gov/oes/)
*Does not include self-employed.
**Not available.

Average Annual Wages of Podiatrists in 2008

National Average = $125,760*

ALPHA ORDER

RANK	STATE	WAGES
20	Alabama	$124,270
NA	Alaska**	NA
38	Arizona	95,180
4	Arkansas	171,820
25	California	121,450
12	Colorado	142,500
18	Connecticut	128,460
34	Delaware	108,230
23	Florida	122,270
9	Georgia	150,930
41	Hawaii	57,800
1	Idaho	184,040
37	Illinois	101,440
22	Indiana	122,490
29	Iowa	118,270
5	Kansas	160,390
8	Kentucky	152,900
7	Louisiana	156,880
28	Maine	119,970
13	Maryland	142,010
30	Massachusetts	115,400
2	Michigan	173,440
6	Minnesota	158,740
36	Mississippi	105,260
14	Missouri	140,270
11	Montana	142,640
24	Nebraska	121,870
15	Nevada	138,590
17	New Hampshire	128,950
32	New Jersey	114,360
33	New Mexico	113,890
19	New York	126,710
10	North Carolina	145,300
NA	North Dakota**	NA
27	Ohio	120,060
NA	Oklahoma**	NA
NA	Oregon**	NA
39	Pennsylvania	94,960
35	Rhode Island	107,920
31	South Carolina	114,540
NA	South Dakota**	NA
21	Tennessee	123,820
NA	Texas**	NA
40	Utah	92,160
NA	Vermont**	NA
26	Virginia	120,380
16	Washington	132,760
NA	West Virginia**	NA
3	Wisconsin	172,920
NA	Wyoming**	NA

RANK ORDER

RANK	STATE	WAGES
1	Idaho	$184,040
2	Michigan	173,440
3	Wisconsin	172,920
4	Arkansas	171,820
5	Kansas	160,390
6	Minnesota	158,740
7	Louisiana	156,880
8	Kentucky	152,900
9	Georgia	150,930
10	North Carolina	145,300
11	Montana	142,640
12	Colorado	142,500
13	Maryland	142,010
14	Missouri	140,270
15	Nevada	138,590
16	Washington	132,760
17	New Hampshire	128,950
18	Connecticut	128,460
19	New York	126,710
20	Alabama	124,270
21	Tennessee	123,820
22	Indiana	122,490
23	Florida	122,270
24	Nebraska	121,870
25	California	121,450
26	Virginia	120,380
27	Ohio	120,060
28	Maine	119,970
29	Iowa	118,270
30	Massachusetts	115,400
31	South Carolina	114,540
32	New Jersey	114,360
33	New Mexico	113,890
34	Delaware	108,230
35	Rhode Island	107,920
36	Mississippi	105,260
37	Illinois	101,440
38	Arizona	95,180
39	Pennsylvania	94,960
40	Utah	92,160
41	Hawaii	57,800
NA	Alaska**	NA
NA	North Dakota**	NA
NA	Oklahoma**	NA
NA	Oregon**	NA
NA	South Dakota**	NA
NA	Texas**	NA
NA	Vermont**	NA
NA	West Virginia**	NA
NA	Wyoming**	NA
	District of Columbia**	NA

Source: U.S. Department of Labor, Bureau of Labor Statistics
   "Occupational Employment and Wages, 2008" (http://www.bls.gov/oes/)
*Does not include self-employed.
**Not available.

Doctors of Chiropractic in 2008

National Total = 87,724 Chiropractors*

<table>
<tr><td colspan="4">ALPHA ORDER</td><td colspan="4">RANK ORDER</td></tr>
<tr><th>RANK</th><th>STATE</th><th>CHIROPRACTORS</th><th>% of USA</th><th>RANK</th><th>STATE</th><th>CHIROPRACTORS</th><th>% of USA</th></tr>
<tr><td>28</td><td>Alabama</td><td>815</td><td>0.9%</td><td>1</td><td>California</td><td>13,851</td><td>15.8%</td></tr>
<tr><td>48</td><td>Alaska</td><td>240</td><td>0.3%</td><td>2</td><td>New York</td><td>5,830</td><td>6.6%</td></tr>
<tr><td>12</td><td>Arizona</td><td>2,463</td><td>2.8%</td><td>3</td><td>Florida</td><td>4,824</td><td>5.5%</td></tr>
<tr><td>33</td><td>Arkansas</td><td>556</td><td>0.6%</td><td>4</td><td>Texas</td><td>4,602</td><td>5.2%</td></tr>
<tr><td>1</td><td>California</td><td>13,851</td><td>15.8%</td><td>5</td><td>Pennsylvania</td><td>3,914</td><td>4.5%</td></tr>
<tr><td>11</td><td>Colorado</td><td>2,480</td><td>2.8%</td><td>6</td><td>Illinois</td><td>3,848</td><td>4.4%</td></tr>
<tr><td>25</td><td>Connecticut</td><td>1,017</td><td>1.2%</td><td>7</td><td>New Jersey</td><td>3,372</td><td>3.8%</td></tr>
<tr><td>44</td><td>Delaware</td><td>332</td><td>0.4%</td><td>8</td><td>Georgia</td><td>3,075</td><td>3.5%</td></tr>
<tr><td>3</td><td>Florida</td><td>4,824</td><td>5.5%</td><td>9</td><td>Michigan</td><td>2,938</td><td>3.3%</td></tr>
<tr><td>8</td><td>Georgia</td><td>3,075</td><td>3.5%</td><td>10</td><td>Minnesota</td><td>2,563</td><td>2.9%</td></tr>
<tr><td>38</td><td>Hawaii</td><td>487</td><td>0.6%</td><td>11</td><td>Colorado</td><td>2,480</td><td>2.8%</td></tr>
<tr><td>35</td><td>Idaho</td><td>534</td><td>0.6%</td><td>12</td><td>Arizona</td><td>2,463</td><td>2.8%</td></tr>
<tr><td>6</td><td>Illinois</td><td>3,848</td><td>4.4%</td><td>13</td><td>Washington</td><td>2,288</td><td>2.6%</td></tr>
<tr><td>24</td><td>Indiana</td><td>1,068</td><td>1.2%</td><td>14</td><td>Ohio</td><td>2,235</td><td>2.5%</td></tr>
<tr><td>19</td><td>Iowa</td><td>1,520</td><td>1.7%</td><td>15</td><td>Missouri</td><td>2,187</td><td>2.5%</td></tr>
<tr><td>30</td><td>Kansas</td><td>775</td><td>0.9%</td><td>16</td><td>Wisconsin</td><td>2,181</td><td>2.5%</td></tr>
<tr><td>26</td><td>Kentucky</td><td>866</td><td>1.0%</td><td>17</td><td>Massachusetts</td><td>2,039</td><td>2.3%</td></tr>
<tr><td>34</td><td>Louisiana</td><td>552</td><td>0.6%</td><td>18</td><td>North Carolina</td><td>1,946</td><td>2.2%</td></tr>
<tr><td>40</td><td>Maine</td><td>370</td><td>0.4%</td><td>19</td><td>Iowa</td><td>1,520</td><td>1.7%</td></tr>
<tr><td>29</td><td>Maryland</td><td>785</td><td>0.9%</td><td>20</td><td>South Carolina</td><td>1,441</td><td>1.6%</td></tr>
<tr><td>17</td><td>Massachusetts</td><td>2,039</td><td>2.3%</td><td>21</td><td>Oregon</td><td>1,378</td><td>1.6%</td></tr>
<tr><td>9</td><td>Michigan</td><td>2,938</td><td>3.3%</td><td>22</td><td>Virginia</td><td>1,155</td><td>1.3%</td></tr>
<tr><td>10</td><td>Minnesota</td><td>2,563</td><td>2.9%</td><td>23</td><td>Tennessee</td><td>1,125</td><td>1.3%</td></tr>
<tr><td>43</td><td>Mississippi</td><td>334</td><td>0.4%</td><td>24</td><td>Indiana</td><td>1,068</td><td>1.2%</td></tr>
<tr><td>15</td><td>Missouri</td><td>2,187</td><td>2.5%</td><td>25</td><td>Connecticut</td><td>1,017</td><td>1.2%</td></tr>
<tr><td>41</td><td>Montana</td><td>366</td><td>0.4%</td><td>26</td><td>Kentucky</td><td>866</td><td>1.0%</td></tr>
<tr><td>37</td><td>Nebraska</td><td>506</td><td>0.6%</td><td>27</td><td>Utah</td><td>827</td><td>0.9%</td></tr>
<tr><td>32</td><td>Nevada</td><td>600</td><td>0.7%</td><td>28</td><td>Alabama</td><td>815</td><td>0.9%</td></tr>
<tr><td>39</td><td>New Hampshire</td><td>450</td><td>0.5%</td><td>29</td><td>Maryland</td><td>785</td><td>0.9%</td></tr>
<tr><td>7</td><td>New Jersey</td><td>3,372</td><td>3.8%</td><td>30</td><td>Kansas</td><td>775</td><td>0.9%</td></tr>
<tr><td>36</td><td>New Mexico</td><td>508</td><td>0.6%</td><td>31</td><td>Oklahoma</td><td>773</td><td>0.9%</td></tr>
<tr><td>2</td><td>New York</td><td>5,830</td><td>6.6%</td><td>32</td><td>Nevada</td><td>600</td><td>0.7%</td></tr>
<tr><td>18</td><td>North Carolina</td><td>1,946</td><td>2.2%</td><td>33</td><td>Arkansas</td><td>556</td><td>0.6%</td></tr>
<tr><td>46</td><td>North Dakota</td><td>286</td><td>0.3%</td><td>34</td><td>Louisiana</td><td>552</td><td>0.6%</td></tr>
<tr><td>14</td><td>Ohio</td><td>2,235</td><td>2.5%</td><td>35</td><td>Idaho</td><td>534</td><td>0.6%</td></tr>
<tr><td>31</td><td>Oklahoma</td><td>773</td><td>0.9%</td><td>36</td><td>New Mexico</td><td>508</td><td>0.6%</td></tr>
<tr><td>21</td><td>Oregon</td><td>1,378</td><td>1.6%</td><td>37</td><td>Nebraska</td><td>506</td><td>0.6%</td></tr>
<tr><td>5</td><td>Pennsylvania</td><td>3,914</td><td>4.5%</td><td>38</td><td>Hawaii</td><td>487</td><td>0.6%</td></tr>
<tr><td>47</td><td>Rhode Island</td><td>263</td><td>0.3%</td><td>39</td><td>New Hampshire</td><td>450</td><td>0.5%</td></tr>
<tr><td>20</td><td>South Carolina</td><td>1,441</td><td>1.6%</td><td>40</td><td>Maine</td><td>370</td><td>0.4%</td></tr>
<tr><td>42</td><td>South Dakota</td><td>338</td><td>0.4%</td><td>41</td><td>Montana</td><td>366</td><td>0.4%</td></tr>
<tr><td>23</td><td>Tennessee</td><td>1,125</td><td>1.3%</td><td>42</td><td>South Dakota</td><td>338</td><td>0.4%</td></tr>
<tr><td>4</td><td>Texas</td><td>4,602</td><td>5.2%</td><td>43</td><td>Mississippi</td><td>334</td><td>0.4%</td></tr>
<tr><td>27</td><td>Utah</td><td>827</td><td>0.9%</td><td>44</td><td>Delaware</td><td>332</td><td>0.4%</td></tr>
<tr><td>49</td><td>Vermont</td><td>224</td><td>0.3%</td><td>45</td><td>West Virginia</td><td>327</td><td>0.4%</td></tr>
<tr><td>22</td><td>Virginia</td><td>1,155</td><td>1.3%</td><td>46</td><td>North Dakota</td><td>286</td><td>0.3%</td></tr>
<tr><td>13</td><td>Washington</td><td>2,288</td><td>2.6%</td><td>47</td><td>Rhode Island</td><td>263</td><td>0.3%</td></tr>
<tr><td>45</td><td>West Virginia</td><td>327</td><td>0.4%</td><td>48</td><td>Alaska</td><td>240</td><td>0.3%</td></tr>
<tr><td>16</td><td>Wisconsin</td><td>2,181</td><td>2.5%</td><td>49</td><td>Vermont</td><td>224</td><td>0.3%</td></tr>
<tr><td>50</td><td>Wyoming</td><td>200</td><td>0.2%</td><td>50</td><td>Wyoming</td><td>200</td><td>0.2%</td></tr>
<tr><td></td><td></td><td></td><td></td><td colspan="2">District of Columbia</td><td>70</td><td>0.1%</td></tr>
</table>

Source: Federation of Chiropractic Licensing Boards
  "Official Directory" (http://directory.fclb.org/)
*As of December 2008. Licensed active doctors. There is some duplication as some doctors are licensed in more than one state.

Rate of Doctors of Chiropractic in 2008

National Rate = 29 Chiropractors per 100,000 Population*

ALPHA ORDER

RANK	STATE	RATE
45	Alabama	17
17	Alaska	35
8	Arizona	38
40	Arkansas	19
8	California	38
2	Colorado	50
28	Connecticut	29
8	Delaware	38
33	Florida	26
21	Georgia	32
8	Hawaii	38
17	Idaho	35
25	Illinois	30
45	Indiana	17
1	Iowa	51
30	Kansas	28
39	Kentucky	20
49	Louisiana	12
30	Maine	28
48	Maryland	14
23	Massachusetts	31
28	Michigan	29
3	Minnesota	49
50	Mississippi	11
14	Missouri	37
8	Montana	38
30	Nebraska	28
36	Nevada	23
20	New Hampshire	34
6	New Jersey	39
33	New Mexico	26
25	New York	30
37	North Carolina	21
4	North Dakota	45
40	Ohio	19
37	Oklahoma	21
15	Oregon	36
23	Pennsylvania	31
35	Rhode Island	25
21	South Carolina	32
5	South Dakota	42
43	Tennessee	18
40	Texas	19
25	Utah	30
15	Vermont	36
47	Virginia	15
17	Washington	35
43	West Virginia	18
6	Wisconsin	39
8	Wyoming	38

RANK ORDER

RANK	STATE	RATE
1	Iowa	51
2	Colorado	50
3	Minnesota	49
4	North Dakota	45
5	South Dakota	42
6	New Jersey	39
6	Wisconsin	39
8	Arizona	38
8	California	38
8	Delaware	38
8	Hawaii	38
8	Montana	38
8	Wyoming	38
14	Missouri	37
15	Oregon	36
15	Vermont	36
17	Alaska	35
17	Idaho	35
17	Washington	35
20	New Hampshire	34
21	Georgia	32
21	South Carolina	32
23	Massachusetts	31
23	Pennsylvania	31
25	Illinois	30
25	New York	30
25	Utah	30
28	Connecticut	29
28	Michigan	29
30	Kansas	28
30	Maine	28
30	Nebraska	28
33	Florida	26
33	New Mexico	26
35	Rhode Island	25
36	Nevada	23
37	North Carolina	21
37	Oklahoma	21
39	Kentucky	20
40	Arkansas	19
40	Ohio	19
40	Texas	19
43	Tennessee	18
43	West Virginia	18
45	Alabama	17
45	Indiana	17
47	Virginia	15
48	Maryland	14
49	Louisiana	12
50	Mississippi	11

District of Columbia	12

Source: CQ Press using data from Federation of Chiropractic Licensing Boards
"Official Directory" (http://directory.fclb.org/)
*As of December 2008. Licensed active doctors. There is some duplication as some doctors are licensed in more than one state.

Average Annual Wages of Chiropractors in 2008

National Average = $81,340*

ALPHA ORDER

RANK	STATE	WAGES
1	Alabama	$126,950
12	Alaska	94,410
47	Arizona	56,560
15	Arkansas	91,930
36	California	72,160
NA	Colorado**	NA
19	Connecticut	89,860
16	Delaware	91,440
28	Florida	79,410
43	Georgia	62,360
46	Hawaii	57,360
42	Idaho	65,470
13	Illinois	93,520
21	Indiana	89,400
29	Iowa	79,270
30	Kansas	78,430
4	Kentucky	108,430
38	Louisiana	70,670
37	Maine	72,010
9	Maryland	99,230
20	Massachusetts	89,720
35	Michigan	73,250
18	Minnesota	90,840
44	Mississippi	61,220
40	Missouri	68,030
49	Montana	38,420
22	Nebraska	88,000
2	Nevada	114,360
23	New Hampshire	85,610
27	New Jersey	79,610
41	New Mexico	66,770
25	New York	84,800
8	North Carolina	101,500
34	North Dakota	73,270
5	Ohio	107,150
33	Oklahoma	73,410
48	Oregon	48,850
32	Pennsylvania	74,790
17	Rhode Island	91,090
39	South Carolina	69,220
10	South Dakota	97,240
3	Tennessee	113,710
31	Texas	75,290
45	Utah	59,890
11	Vermont	95,380
26	Virginia	79,870
7	Washington	104,780
14	West Virginia	92,180
6	Wisconsin	107,060
24	Wyoming	85,580

RANK ORDER

RANK	STATE	WAGES
1	Alabama	$126,950
2	Nevada	114,360
3	Tennessee	113,710
4	Kentucky	108,430
5	Ohio	107,150
6	Wisconsin	107,060
7	Washington	104,780
8	North Carolina	101,500
9	Maryland	99,230
10	South Dakota	97,240
11	Vermont	95,380
12	Alaska	94,410
13	Illinois	93,520
14	West Virginia	92,180
15	Arkansas	91,930
16	Delaware	91,440
17	Rhode Island	91,090
18	Minnesota	90,840
19	Connecticut	89,860
20	Massachusetts	89,720
21	Indiana	89,400
22	Nebraska	88,000
23	New Hampshire	85,610
24	Wyoming	85,580
25	New York	84,800
26	Virginia	79,870
27	New Jersey	79,610
28	Florida	79,410
29	Iowa	79,270
30	Kansas	78,430
31	Texas	75,290
32	Pennsylvania	74,790
33	Oklahoma	73,410
34	North Dakota	73,270
35	Michigan	73,250
36	California	72,160
37	Maine	72,010
38	Louisiana	70,670
39	South Carolina	69,220
40	Missouri	68,030
41	New Mexico	66,770
42	Idaho	65,470
43	Georgia	62,360
44	Mississippi	61,220
45	Utah	59,890
46	Hawaii	57,360
47	Arizona	56,560
48	Oregon	48,850
49	Montana	38,420
NA	Colorado**	NA
	District of Columbia**	NA

Source: U.S. Department of Labor, Bureau of Labor Statistics
   "Occupational Employment and Wages, 2008" (http://www.bls.gov/oes/)
*Does not include self-employed.
**Not available.

Physician Assistants in Clinical Practice in 2008

National Total = 73,506 Physician Assistants*

ALPHA ORDER

RANK	STATE	PAs	% of USA
38	Alabama	485	0.7%
41	Alaska	376	0.5%
15	Arizona	1,668	2.3%
49	Arkansas	155	0.2%
2	California	7,115	9.7%
13	Colorado	1,792	2.4%
19	Connecticut	1,375	1.9%
46	Delaware	215	0.3%
5	Florida	4,324	5.9%
8	Georgia	2,369	3.2%
48	Hawaii	158	0.2%
37	Idaho	511	0.7%
12	Illinois	1,950	2.7%
32	Indiana	621	0.8%
26	Iowa	765	1.0%
25	Kansas	796	1.1%
23	Kentucky	866	1.2%
34	Louisiana	545	0.7%
33	Maine	555	0.8%
9	Maryland	1,978	2.7%
14	Massachusetts	1,725	2.3%
7	Michigan	3,015	4.1%
20	Minnesota	1,251	1.7%
50	Mississippi	86	0.1%
31	Missouri	635	0.9%
42	Montana	353	0.5%
28	Nebraska	731	1.0%
35	Nevada	517	0.7%
39	New Hampshire	420	0.6%
18	New Jersey	1,434	2.0%
36	New Mexico	516	0.7%
1	New York	7,916	10.8%
6	North Carolina	3,586	4.9%
43	North Dakota	243	0.3%
11	Ohio	1,960	2.7%
21	Oklahoma	1,072	1.5%
24	Oregon	853	1.2%
4	Pennsylvania	4,357	5.9%
44	Rhode Island	226	0.3%
27	South Carolina	743	1.0%
40	South Dakota	409	0.6%
22	Tennessee	954	1.3%
3	Texas	4,696	6.4%
30	Utah	693	0.9%
45	Vermont	219	0.3%
16	Virginia	1,611	2.2%
10	Washington	1,967	2.7%
29	West Virginia	719	1.0%
17	Wisconsin	1,557	2.1%
47	Wyoming	192	0.3%

RANK ORDER

RANK	STATE	PAs	% of USA
1	New York	7,916	10.8%
2	California	7,115	9.7%
3	Texas	4,696	6.4%
4	Pennsylvania	4,357	5.9%
5	Florida	4,324	5.9%
6	North Carolina	3,586	4.9%
7	Michigan	3,015	4.1%
8	Georgia	2,369	3.2%
9	Maryland	1,978	2.7%
10	Washington	1,967	2.7%
11	Ohio	1,960	2.7%
12	Illinois	1,950	2.7%
13	Colorado	1,792	2.4%
14	Massachusetts	1,725	2.3%
15	Arizona	1,668	2.3%
16	Virginia	1,611	2.2%
17	Wisconsin	1,557	2.1%
18	New Jersey	1,434	2.0%
19	Connecticut	1,375	1.9%
20	Minnesota	1,251	1.7%
21	Oklahoma	1,072	1.5%
22	Tennessee	954	1.3%
23	Kentucky	866	1.2%
24	Oregon	853	1.2%
25	Kansas	796	1.1%
26	Iowa	765	1.0%
27	South Carolina	743	1.0%
28	Nebraska	731	1.0%
29	West Virginia	719	1.0%
30	Utah	693	0.9%
31	Missouri	635	0.9%
32	Indiana	621	0.8%
33	Maine	555	0.8%
34	Louisiana	545	0.7%
35	Nevada	517	0.7%
36	New Mexico	516	0.7%
37	Idaho	511	0.7%
38	Alabama	485	0.7%
39	New Hampshire	420	0.6%
40	South Dakota	409	0.6%
41	Alaska	376	0.5%
42	Montana	353	0.5%
43	North Dakota	243	0.3%
44	Rhode Island	226	0.3%
45	Vermont	219	0.3%
46	Delaware	215	0.3%
47	Wyoming	192	0.3%
48	Hawaii	158	0.2%
49	Arkansas	155	0.2%
50	Mississippi	86	0.1%

District of Columbia	231	0.3%

Source: The American Academy of Physician Assistants
    "Projected Number of People in Clinical Practice as PAs as of December 31, 2008" (http://www.aapa.org/research/)
*Projected. National total does not include 387 physician assistants who work outside the United States or whose location is unknown.

Rate of Physician Assistants in Clinical Practice in 2008

National Rate = 24 PAs per 100,000 Population*

ALPHA ORDER			RANK ORDER		
RANK	STATE	RATE	RANK	STATE	RATE
47	Alabama	10	1	Alaska	55
1	Alaska	55	2	South Dakota	51
24	Arizona	26	3	Maine	42
49	Arkansas	5	4	Nebraska	41
37	California	19	4	New York	41
10	Colorado	36	6	West Virginia	40
7	Connecticut	39	7	Connecticut	39
26	Delaware	25	7	North Carolina	39
29	Florida	24	9	North Dakota	38
29	Georgia	24	10	Colorado	36
44	Hawaii	12	10	Montana	36
16	Idaho	34	10	Wyoming	36
42	Illinois	15	13	Maryland	35
47	Indiana	10	13	Pennsylvania	35
26	Iowa	25	13	Vermont	35
21	Kansas	28	16	Idaho	34
35	Kentucky	20	17	New Hampshire	32
44	Louisiana	12	18	Michigan	30
3	Maine	42	18	Washington	30
13	Maryland	35	20	Oklahoma	29
23	Massachusetts	27	21	Kansas	28
18	Michigan	30	21	Wisconsin	28
29	Minnesota	24	23	Massachusetts	27
50	Mississippi	3	24	Arizona	26
46	Missouri	11	24	New Mexico	26
10	Montana	36	26	Delaware	25
4	Nebraska	41	26	Iowa	25
35	Nevada	20	26	Utah	25
17	New Hampshire	32	29	Florida	24
39	New Jersey	17	29	Georgia	24
24	New Mexico	26	29	Minnesota	24
4	New York	41	32	Oregon	23
7	North Carolina	39	33	Rhode Island	22
9	North Dakota	38	34	Virginia	21
39	Ohio	17	35	Kentucky	20
20	Oklahoma	29	35	Nevada	20
32	Oregon	23	37	California	19
13	Pennsylvania	35	37	Texas	19
33	Rhode Island	22	39	New Jersey	17
39	South Carolina	17	39	Ohio	17
2	South Dakota	51	39	South Carolina	17
42	Tennessee	15	42	Illinois	15
37	Texas	19	42	Tennessee	15
26	Utah	25	44	Hawaii	12
13	Vermont	35	44	Louisiana	12
34	Virginia	21	46	Missouri	11
18	Washington	30	47	Alabama	10
6	West Virginia	40	47	Indiana	10
21	Wisconsin	28	49	Arkansas	5
10	Wyoming	36	50	Mississippi	3
				District of Columbia	39

Source: CQ Press using data from The American Academy of Physician Assistants
   "Projected Number of People in Clinical Practice as PAs as of December 31, 2008" (http://www.aapa.org/research/)
*Projected. Rates calculated using 2008 Census population figures.

Average Annual Wages of Physician Assistants in 2008

National Average = $81,610*

ALPHA ORDER

RANK	STATE	WAGES
29	Alabama	$79,830
1	Alaska	97,750
34	Arizona	76,490
45	Arkansas	68,990
8	California	87,410
31	Colorado	78,710
3	Connecticut	94,360
18	Delaware	83,380
19	Florida	82,160
13	Georgia	85,000
33	Hawaii	77,190
42	Idaho	71,590
37	Illinois	75,630
41	Indiana	73,410
32	Iowa	78,160
27	Kansas	80,470
26	Kentucky	80,510
44	Louisiana	69,630
15	Maine	84,740
10	Maryland	85,880
12	Massachusetts	85,540
14	Michigan	84,840
16	Minnesota	84,600
50	Mississippi	48,190
47	Missouri	65,590
43	Montana	70,860
25	Nebraska	80,880
2	Nevada	95,160
22	New Hampshire	81,780
5	New Jersey	88,540
49	New Mexico	63,000
11	New York	85,810
21	North Carolina	81,810
39	North Dakota	74,900
24	Ohio	81,190
36	Oklahoma	76,210
7	Oregon	87,720
46	Pennsylvania	68,210
20	Rhode Island	82,050
40	South Carolina	73,460
28	South Dakota	80,430
35	Tennessee	76,250
17	Texas	84,360
8	Utah	87,410
6	Vermont	88,130
48	Virginia	63,940
4	Washington	91,800
38	West Virginia	75,320
23	Wisconsin	81,670
30	Wyoming	79,240

RANK ORDER

RANK	STATE	WAGES
1	Alaska	$97,750
2	Nevada	95,160
3	Connecticut	94,360
4	Washington	91,800
5	New Jersey	88,540
6	Vermont	88,130
7	Oregon	87,720
8	California	87,410
8	Utah	87,410
10	Maryland	85,880
11	New York	85,810
12	Massachusetts	85,540
13	Georgia	85,000
14	Michigan	84,840
15	Maine	84,740
16	Minnesota	84,600
17	Texas	84,360
18	Delaware	83,380
19	Florida	82,160
20	Rhode Island	82,050
21	North Carolina	81,810
22	New Hampshire	81,780
23	Wisconsin	81,670
24	Ohio	81,190
25	Nebraska	80,880
26	Kentucky	80,510
27	Kansas	80,470
28	South Dakota	80,430
29	Alabama	79,830
30	Wyoming	79,240
31	Colorado	78,710
32	Iowa	78,160
33	Hawaii	77,190
34	Arizona	76,490
35	Tennessee	76,250
36	Oklahoma	76,210
37	Illinois	75,630
38	West Virginia	75,320
39	North Dakota	74,900
40	South Carolina	73,460
41	Indiana	73,410
42	Idaho	71,590
43	Montana	70,860
44	Louisiana	69,630
45	Arkansas	68,990
46	Pennsylvania	68,210
47	Missouri	65,590
48	Virginia	63,940
49	New Mexico	63,000
50	Mississippi	48,190
	District of Columbia	86,890

Source: U.S. Department of Labor, Bureau of Labor Statistics
"Occupational Employment and Wages, 2008" (http://www.bls.gov/oes/)
*Does not include self-employed.

Registered Nurses in 2008

National Total = 2,542,760 Registered Nurses*

ALPHA ORDER

RANK	STATE	NURSES	% of USA
21	Alabama	41,560	1.6%
49	Alaska	5,350	0.2%
25	Arizona	37,780	1.5%
33	Arkansas	23,000	0.9%
1	California	240,470	9.5%
24	Colorado	39,440	1.6%
27	Connecticut	35,370	1.4%
44	Delaware	9,060	0.4%
4	Florida	146,040	5.7%
12	Georgia	64,920	2.6%
45	Hawaii	8,760	0.3%
42	Idaho	10,850	0.4%
7	Illinois	108,820	4.3%
16	Indiana	56,500	2.2%
28	Iowa	30,170	1.2%
32	Kansas	25,020	1.0%
22	Kentucky	41,080	1.6%
23	Louisiana	39,610	1.6%
38	Maine	14,050	0.6%
20	Maryland	50,780	2.0%
10	Massachusetts	79,670	3.1%
8	Michigan	86,580	3.4%
17	Minnesota	55,730	2.2%
30	Mississippi	27,350	1.1%
14	Missouri	60,100	2.4%
46	Montana	7,480	0.3%
34	Nebraska	18,930	0.7%
37	Nevada	15,950	0.6%
39	New Hampshire	13,110	0.5%
11	New Jersey	75,590	3.0%
40	New Mexico	11,900	0.5%
2	New York	168,850	6.6%
9	North Carolina	84,230	3.3%
47	North Dakota	6,340	0.2%
6	Ohio	114,930	4.5%
31	Oklahoma	26,760	1.1%
29	Oregon	29,980	1.2%
5	Pennsylvania	129,060	5.1%
41	Rhode Island	11,360	0.4%
26	South Carolina	36,880	1.5%
43	South Dakota	10,010	0.4%
13	Tennessee	61,570	2.4%
3	Texas	164,400	6.5%
35	Utah	17,230	0.7%
48	Vermont	5,900	0.2%
15	Virginia	60,040	2.4%
18	Washington	52,020	2.0%
36	West Virginia	16,910	0.7%
19	Wisconsin	51,700	2.0%
50	Wyoming	4,300	0.2%

RANK ORDER

RANK	STATE	NURSES	% of USA
1	California	240,470	9.5%
2	New York	168,850	6.6%
3	Texas	164,400	6.5%
4	Florida	146,040	5.7%
5	Pennsylvania	129,060	5.1%
6	Ohio	114,930	4.5%
7	Illinois	108,820	4.3%
8	Michigan	86,580	3.4%
9	North Carolina	84,230	3.3%
10	Massachusetts	79,670	3.1%
11	New Jersey	75,590	3.0%
12	Georgia	64,920	2.6%
13	Tennessee	61,570	2.4%
14	Missouri	60,100	2.4%
15	Virginia	60,040	2.4%
16	Indiana	56,500	2.2%
17	Minnesota	55,730	2.2%
18	Washington	52,020	2.0%
19	Wisconsin	51,700	2.0%
20	Maryland	50,780	2.0%
21	Alabama	41,560	1.6%
22	Kentucky	41,080	1.6%
23	Louisiana	39,610	1.6%
24	Colorado	39,440	1.6%
25	Arizona	37,780	1.5%
26	South Carolina	36,880	1.5%
27	Connecticut	35,370	1.4%
28	Iowa	30,170	1.2%
29	Oregon	29,980	1.2%
30	Mississippi	27,350	1.1%
31	Oklahoma	26,760	1.1%
32	Kansas	25,020	1.0%
33	Arkansas	23,000	0.9%
34	Nebraska	18,930	0.7%
35	Utah	17,230	0.7%
36	West Virginia	16,910	0.7%
37	Nevada	15,950	0.6%
38	Maine	14,050	0.6%
39	New Hampshire	13,110	0.5%
40	New Mexico	11,900	0.5%
41	Rhode Island	11,360	0.4%
42	Idaho	10,850	0.4%
43	South Dakota	10,010	0.4%
44	Delaware	9,060	0.4%
45	Hawaii	8,760	0.3%
46	Montana	7,480	0.3%
47	North Dakota	6,340	0.2%
48	Vermont	5,900	0.2%
49	Alaska	5,350	0.2%
50	Wyoming	4,300	0.2%
	District of Columbia	9,240	0.4%

Source: U.S. Department of Labor, Bureau of Labor Statistics
   "Occupational Employment and Wages, 2008" (http://www.bls.gov/oes/)
*Does not include self-employed.

Rate of Registered Nurses in 2008

National Rate = 835 Nurses per 100,000 Population*

RANK	STATE	RATE
25	Alabama	889
38	Alaska	777
50	Arizona	581
33	Arkansas	802
46	California	657
34	Colorado	799
9	Connecticut	1,010
7	Delaware	1,034
35	Florida	793
45	Georgia	669
43	Hawaii	680
42	Idaho	710
30	Illinois	847
26	Indiana	884
11	Iowa	1,008
23	Kansas	894
16	Kentucky	958
24	Louisiana	890
4	Maine	1,065
22	Maryland	897
2	Massachusetts	1,218
29	Michigan	866
4	Minnesota	1,065
19	Mississippi	930
10	Missouri	1,009
39	Montana	773
6	Nebraska	1,062
48	Nevada	610
13	New Hampshire	992
27	New Jersey	873
49	New Mexico	599
28	New York	867
21	North Carolina	911
14	North Dakota	988
12	Ohio	997
41	Oklahoma	734
36	Oregon	792
8	Pennsylvania	1,027
3	Rhode Island	1,078
31	South Carolina	819
1	South Dakota	1,244
15	Tennessee	987
44	Texas	676
47	Utah	632
17	Vermont	950
40	Virginia	770
36	Washington	792
18	West Virginia	932
20	Wisconsin	919
32	Wyoming	807

RANK	STATE	RATE
1	South Dakota	1,244
2	Massachusetts	1,218
3	Rhode Island	1,078
4	Maine	1,065
4	Minnesota	1,065
6	Nebraska	1,062
7	Delaware	1,034
8	Pennsylvania	1,027
9	Connecticut	1,010
10	Missouri	1,009
11	Iowa	1,008
12	Ohio	997
13	New Hampshire	992
14	North Dakota	988
15	Tennessee	987
16	Kentucky	958
17	Vermont	950
18	West Virginia	932
19	Mississippi	930
20	Wisconsin	919
21	North Carolina	911
22	Maryland	897
23	Kansas	894
24	Louisiana	890
25	Alabama	889
26	Indiana	884
27	New Jersey	873
28	New York	867
29	Michigan	866
30	Illinois	847
31	South Carolina	819
32	Wyoming	807
33	Arkansas	802
34	Colorado	799
35	Florida	793
36	Oregon	792
36	Washington	792
38	Alaska	777
39	Montana	773
40	Virginia	770
41	Oklahoma	734
42	Idaho	710
43	Hawaii	680
44	Texas	676
45	Georgia	669
46	California	657
47	Utah	632
48	Nevada	610
49	New Mexico	599
50	Arizona	581
	District of Columbia	1,566

Source: CQ Press using data from U.S. Department of Labor, Bureau of Labor Statistics
"Occupational Employment and Wages, 2008" (http://www.bls.gov/oes/)
*Does not include self-employed.

Average Annual Wages of Registered Nurses in 2008

National Average = $65,130*

ALPHA ORDER

RANK	STATE	WAGES
38	Alabama	$56,670
7	Alaska	72,820
15	Arizona	64,740
41	Arkansas	55,280
1	California	83,040
16	Colorado	64,280
12	Connecticut	70,350
13	Delaware	68,900
24	Florida	61,290
27	Georgia	59,960
3	Hawaii	77,950
34	Idaho	57,770
17	Illinois	64,020
36	Indiana	57,160
50	Iowa	50,700
45	Kansas	54,500
37	Kentucky	56,780
29	Louisiana	59,320
28	Maine	59,520
4	Maryland	74,370
2	Massachusetts	79,390
18	Michigan	63,100
11	Minnesota	70,560
40	Mississippi	56,160
38	Missouri	56,670
43	Montana	55,060
46	Nebraska	53,490
10	Nevada	70,700
26	New Hampshire	60,210
6	New Jersey	72,870
20	New Mexico	61,830
5	New York	73,160
33	North Carolina	57,790
42	North Dakota	55,260
31	Ohio	58,750
49	Oklahoma	51,880
8	Oregon	71,210
23	Pennsylvania	61,390
14	Rhode Island	67,810
35	South Carolina	57,610
47	South Dakota	52,600
30	Tennessee	59,000
21	Texas	61,780
32	Utah	58,050
25	Vermont	60,610
21	Virginia	61,780
9	Washington	71,140
48	West Virginia	52,340
19	Wisconsin	62,140
44	Wyoming	54,880

RANK ORDER

RANK	STATE	WAGES
1	California	$83,040
2	Massachusetts	79,390
3	Hawaii	77,950
4	Maryland	74,370
5	New York	73,160
6	New Jersey	72,870
7	Alaska	72,820
8	Oregon	71,210
9	Washington	71,140
10	Nevada	70,700
11	Minnesota	70,560
12	Connecticut	70,350
13	Delaware	68,900
14	Rhode Island	67,810
15	Arizona	64,740
16	Colorado	64,280
17	Illinois	64,020
18	Michigan	63,100
19	Wisconsin	62,140
20	New Mexico	61,830
21	Texas	61,780
21	Virginia	61,780
23	Pennsylvania	61,390
24	Florida	61,290
25	Vermont	60,610
26	New Hampshire	60,210
27	Georgia	59,960
28	Maine	59,520
29	Louisiana	59,320
30	Tennessee	59,000
31	Ohio	58,750
32	Utah	58,050
33	North Carolina	57,790
34	Idaho	57,770
35	South Carolina	57,610
36	Indiana	57,160
37	Kentucky	56,780
38	Alabama	56,670
38	Missouri	56,670
40	Mississippi	56,160
41	Arkansas	55,280
42	North Dakota	55,260
43	Montana	55,060
44	Wyoming	54,880
45	Kansas	54,500
46	Nebraska	53,490
47	South Dakota	52,600
48	West Virginia	52,340
49	Oklahoma	51,880
50	Iowa	50,700

	District of Columbia	73,040

Source: U.S. Department of Labor, Bureau of Labor Statistics
"Occupational Employment and Wages, 2008" (http://www.bls.gov/oes/)
*Does not include self-employed.

Licensed Practical and Licensed Vocational Nurses in 2008

National Total = 733,500 LPN/LVNs*

ALPHA ORDER

RANK	STATE	NURSES	% of USA
19	Alabama	15,720	2.2%
50	Alaska	480	0.1%
24	Arizona	10,490	1.4%
21	Arkansas	11,760	1.6%
2	California	62,350	8.5%
32	Colorado	7,060	1.0%
29	Connecticut	7,940	1.1%
43	Delaware	2,140	0.3%
3	Florida	46,750	6.4%
7	Georgia	24,980	3.4%
46	Hawaii	1,650	0.2%
37	Idaho	2,940	0.4%
9	Illinois	23,980	3.3%
10	Indiana	19,760	2.7%
31	Iowa	7,290	1.0%
30	Kansas	7,480	1.0%
25	Kentucky	10,300	1.4%
13	Louisiana	19,140	2.6%
45	Maine	1,710	0.2%
23	Maryland	10,710	1.5%
17	Massachusetts	16,850	2.3%
14	Michigan	19,000	2.6%
11	Minnesota	19,590	2.7%
26	Mississippi	10,080	1.4%
15	Missouri	18,010	2.5%
38	Montana	2,780	0.4%
34	Nebraska	5,430	0.7%
41	Nevada	2,470	0.3%
40	New Hampshire	2,500	0.3%
18	New Jersey	15,840	2.2%
35	New Mexico	4,830	0.7%
4	New York	46,160	6.3%
16	North Carolina	17,260	2.4%
36	North Dakota	3,250	0.4%
5	Ohio	40,180	5.5%
20	Oklahoma	13,600	1.9%
39	Oregon	2,510	0.3%
6	Pennsylvania	37,140	5.1%
47	Rhode Island	1,610	0.2%
28	South Carolina	9,800	1.3%
44	South Dakota	1,950	0.3%
8	Tennessee	24,390	3.3%
1	Texas	67,150	9.2%
42	Utah	2,250	0.3%
48	Vermont	1,500	0.2%
12	Virginia	19,560	2.7%
27	Washington	9,880	1.4%
33	West Virginia	6,510	0.9%
22	Wisconsin	11,040	1.5%
49	Wyoming	690	0.1%

RANK ORDER

RANK	STATE	NURSES	% of USA
1	Texas	67,150	9.2%
2	California	62,350	8.5%
3	Florida	46,750	6.4%
4	New York	46,160	6.3%
5	Ohio	40,180	5.5%
6	Pennsylvania	37,140	5.1%
7	Georgia	24,980	3.4%
8	Tennessee	24,390	3.3%
9	Illinois	23,980	3.3%
10	Indiana	19,760	2.7%
11	Minnesota	19,590	2.7%
12	Virginia	19,560	2.7%
13	Louisiana	19,140	2.6%
14	Michigan	19,000	2.6%
15	Missouri	18,010	2.5%
16	North Carolina	17,260	2.4%
17	Massachusetts	16,850	2.3%
18	New Jersey	15,840	2.2%
19	Alabama	15,720	2.2%
20	Oklahoma	13,600	1.9%
21	Arkansas	11,760	1.6%
22	Wisconsin	11,040	1.5%
23	Maryland	10,710	1.5%
24	Arizona	10,490	1.4%
25	Kentucky	10,300	1.4%
26	Mississippi	10,080	1.4%
27	Washington	9,880	1.4%
28	South Carolina	9,800	1.3%
29	Connecticut	7,940	1.1%
30	Kansas	7,480	1.0%
31	Iowa	7,290	1.0%
32	Colorado	7,060	1.0%
33	West Virginia	6,510	0.9%
34	Nebraska	5,430	0.7%
35	New Mexico	4,830	0.7%
36	North Dakota	3,250	0.4%
37	Idaho	2,940	0.4%
38	Montana	2,780	0.4%
39	Oregon	2,510	0.3%
40	New Hampshire	2,500	0.3%
41	Nevada	2,470	0.3%
42	Utah	2,250	0.3%
43	Delaware	2,140	0.3%
44	South Dakota	1,950	0.3%
45	Maine	1,710	0.2%
46	Hawaii	1,650	0.2%
47	Rhode Island	1,610	0.2%
48	Vermont	1,500	0.2%
49	Wyoming	690	0.1%
50	Alaska	480	0.1%
	District of Columbia	2,040	0.3%

Source: U.S. Department of Labor, Bureau of Labor Statistics
    "Occupational Employment and Wages, 2008" (http://www.bls.gov/oes/)
*Does not include self-employed.

Rate of Licensed Practical and Licensed Vocational Nurses in 2008

National Rate = 240 LPN/LVNs per 100,000 Population*

ALPHA ORDER

RANK	STATE	RATE
10	Alabama	336
49	Alaska	70
40	Arizona	161
3	Arkansas	410
39	California	170
43	Colorado	143
29	Connecticut	227
22	Delaware	244
20	Florida	254
18	Georgia	258
46	Hawaii	128
32	Idaho	192
36	Illinois	187
11	Indiana	309
23	Iowa	243
17	Kansas	267
27	Kentucky	240
2	Louisiana	430
44	Maine	130
34	Maryland	189
18	Massachusetts	258
33	Michigan	190
5	Minnesota	375
9	Mississippi	343
13	Missouri	302
15	Montana	287
12	Nebraska	305
47	Nevada	94
34	New Hampshire	189
38	New Jersey	183
23	New Mexico	243
28	New York	237
36	North Carolina	187
1	North Dakota	507
8	Ohio	349
6	Oklahoma	373
50	Oregon	66
14	Pennsylvania	296
41	Rhode Island	153
30	South Carolina	218
25	South Dakota	242
4	Tennessee	391
16	Texas	276
48	Utah	82
25	Vermont	242
21	Virginia	251
42	Washington	150
7	West Virginia	359
31	Wisconsin	196
45	Wyoming	129

RANK ORDER

RANK	STATE	RATE
1	North Dakota	507
2	Louisiana	430
3	Arkansas	410
4	Tennessee	391
5	Minnesota	375
6	Oklahoma	373
7	West Virginia	359
8	Ohio	349
9	Mississippi	343
10	Alabama	336
11	Indiana	309
12	Nebraska	305
13	Missouri	302
14	Pennsylvania	296
15	Montana	287
16	Texas	276
17	Kansas	267
18	Georgia	258
18	Massachusetts	258
20	Florida	254
21	Virginia	251
22	Delaware	244
23	Iowa	243
23	New Mexico	243
25	South Dakota	242
25	Vermont	242
27	Kentucky	240
28	New York	237
29	Connecticut	227
30	South Carolina	218
31	Wisconsin	196
32	Idaho	192
33	Michigan	190
34	Maryland	189
34	New Hampshire	189
36	Illinois	187
36	North Carolina	187
38	New Jersey	183
39	California	170
40	Arizona	161
41	Rhode Island	153
42	Washington	150
43	Colorado	143
44	Maine	130
45	Wyoming	129
46	Hawaii	128
47	Nevada	94
48	Utah	82
49	Alaska	70
50	Oregon	66

	District of Columbia	346

Source: CQ Press using data from U.S. Department of Labor, Bureau of Labor Statistics
"Occupational Employment and Wages, 2008" (http://www.bls.gov/oes/)
*Does not include self-employed.

Average Annual Wages of Licensed Practical and Licensed Vocational Nurses in 2008
National Average = $40,110*

ALPHA ORDER

RANK	STATE	WAGES
47	Alabama	$32,760
8	Alaska	47,860
15	Arizona	42,980
46	Arkansas	33,300
4	California	48,400
19	Colorado	40,870
1	Connecticut	51,780
10	Delaware	46,420
25	Florida	39,600
36	Georgia	35,800
14	Hawaii	43,220
32	Idaho	37,690
17	Illinois	41,370
30	Indiana	37,820
40	Iowa	35,430
37	Kansas	35,780
35	Kentucky	35,850
38	Louisiana	35,770
23	Maine	39,720
6	Maryland	48,030
2	Massachusetts	49,690
16	Michigan	41,900
28	Minnesota	38,860
44	Mississippi	34,090
43	Missouri	34,180
45	Montana	33,900
41	Nebraska	35,280
9	Nevada	46,610
11	New Hampshire	43,690
3	New Jersey	49,570
7	New Mexico	47,880
18	New York	41,120
26	North Carolina	39,240
42	North Dakota	34,270
24	Ohio	39,700
49	Oklahoma	32,500
13	Oregon	43,420
22	Pennsylvania	39,920
5	Rhode Island	48,330
34	South Carolina	36,720
48	South Dakota	32,570
39	Tennessee	35,440
27	Texas	39,080
31	Utah	37,790
21	Vermont	40,320
33	Virginia	37,330
12	Washington	43,520
50	West Virginia	31,620
20	Wisconsin	40,670
29	Wyoming	38,590

RANK ORDER

RANK	STATE	WAGES
1	Connecticut	$51,780
2	Massachusetts	49,690
3	New Jersey	49,570
4	California	48,400
5	Rhode Island	48,330
6	Maryland	48,030
7	New Mexico	47,880
8	Alaska	47,860
9	Nevada	46,610
10	Delaware	46,420
11	New Hampshire	43,690
12	Washington	43,520
13	Oregon	43,420
14	Hawaii	43,220
15	Arizona	42,980
16	Michigan	41,900
17	Illinois	41,370
18	New York	41,120
19	Colorado	40,870
20	Wisconsin	40,670
21	Vermont	40,320
22	Pennsylvania	39,920
23	Maine	39,720
24	Ohio	39,700
25	Florida	39,600
26	North Carolina	39,240
27	Texas	39,080
28	Minnesota	38,860
29	Wyoming	38,590
30	Indiana	37,820
31	Utah	37,790
32	Idaho	37,690
33	Virginia	37,330
34	South Carolina	36,720
35	Kentucky	35,850
36	Georgia	35,800
37	Kansas	35,780
38	Louisiana	35,770
39	Tennessee	35,440
40	Iowa	35,430
41	Nebraska	35,280
42	North Dakota	34,270
43	Missouri	34,180
44	Mississippi	34,090
45	Montana	33,900
46	Arkansas	33,300
47	Alabama	32,760
48	South Dakota	32,570
49	Oklahoma	32,500
50	West Virginia	31,620
	District of Columbia	49,830

Source: U.S. Department of Labor, Bureau of Labor Statistics
"Occupational Employment and Wages, 2008" (http://www.bls.gov/oes/)
*Does not include self-employed.

Physical Therapists in 2008

National Total = 167,300 Physical Therapists*

ALPHA ORDER

RANK	STATE	THERAPISTS	% of USA
27	Alabama	1,790	1.1%
49	Alaska	350	0.2%
23	Arizona	2,610	1.6%
32	Arkansas	1,530	0.9%
1	California	13,680	8.2%
21	Colorado	3,240	1.9%
20	Connecticut	3,270	2.0%
47	Delaware	510	0.3%
3	Florida	10,640	6.4%
18	Georgia	3,690	2.2%
37	Hawaii	1,000	0.6%
42	Idaho	840	0.5%
7	Illinois	6,940	4.1%
12	Indiana	4,110	2.5%
31	Iowa	1,620	1.0%
30	Kansas	1,660	1.0%
27	Kentucky	1,790	1.1%
26	Louisiana	2,150	1.3%
39	Maine	970	0.6%
14	Maryland	4,010	2.4%
9	Massachusetts	6,270	3.7%
8	Michigan	6,390	3.8%
22	Minnesota	2,940	1.8%
33	Mississippi	1,430	0.9%
15	Missouri	4,000	2.4%
44	Montana	680	0.4%
34	Nebraska	1,150	0.7%
38	Nevada	990	0.6%
36	New Hampshire	1,100	0.7%
10	New Jersey	5,760	3.4%
40	New Mexico	880	0.5%
2	New York	12,780	7.6%
11	North Carolina	4,210	2.5%
48	North Dakota	410	0.2%
6	Ohio	6,970	4.2%
29	Oklahoma	1,770	1.1%
25	Oregon	2,160	1.3%
5	Pennsylvania	8,780	5.2%
43	Rhode Island	750	0.4%
24	South Carolina	2,190	1.3%
46	South Dakota	560	0.3%
19	Tennessee	3,490	2.1%
4	Texas	10,250	6.1%
35	Utah	1,110	0.7%
45	Vermont	620	0.4%
17	Virginia	3,740	2.2%
16	Washington	3,950	2.4%
41	West Virginia	850	0.5%
13	Wisconsin	4,100	2.5%
50	Wyoming	330	0.2%

RANK ORDER

RANK	STATE	THERAPISTS	% of USA
1	California	13,680	8.2%
2	New York	12,780	7.6%
3	Florida	10,640	6.4%
4	Texas	10,250	6.1%
5	Pennsylvania	8,780	5.2%
6	Ohio	6,970	4.2%
7	Illinois	6,940	4.1%
8	Michigan	6,390	3.8%
9	Massachusetts	6,270	3.7%
10	New Jersey	5,760	3.4%
11	North Carolina	4,210	2.5%
12	Indiana	4,110	2.5%
13	Wisconsin	4,100	2.5%
14	Maryland	4,010	2.4%
15	Missouri	4,000	2.4%
16	Washington	3,950	2.4%
17	Virginia	3,740	2.2%
18	Georgia	3,690	2.2%
19	Tennessee	3,490	2.1%
20	Connecticut	3,270	2.0%
21	Colorado	3,240	1.9%
22	Minnesota	2,940	1.8%
23	Arizona	2,610	1.6%
24	South Carolina	2,190	1.3%
25	Oregon	2,160	1.3%
26	Louisiana	2,150	1.3%
27	Alabama	1,790	1.1%
27	Kentucky	1,790	1.1%
29	Oklahoma	1,770	1.1%
30	Kansas	1,660	1.0%
31	Iowa	1,620	1.0%
32	Arkansas	1,530	0.9%
33	Mississippi	1,430	0.9%
34	Nebraska	1,150	0.7%
35	Utah	1,110	0.7%
36	New Hampshire	1,100	0.7%
37	Hawaii	1,000	0.6%
38	Nevada	990	0.6%
39	Maine	970	0.6%
40	New Mexico	880	0.5%
41	West Virginia	850	0.5%
42	Idaho	840	0.5%
43	Rhode Island	750	0.4%
44	Montana	680	0.4%
45	Vermont	620	0.4%
46	South Dakota	560	0.3%
47	Delaware	510	0.3%
48	North Dakota	410	0.2%
49	Alaska	350	0.2%
50	Wyoming	330	0.2%
	District of Columbia	300	0.2%

Source: U.S. Department of Labor, Bureau of Labor Statistics
"Occupational Employment and Wages, 2008" (http://www.bls.gov/oes/)
*Does not include self-employed.

Rate of Physical Therapists in 2008

National Rate = 55 Physical Therapists per 100,000 Population*

RANK	STATE	RATE
47	Alabama	38
34	Alaska	51
46	Arizona	40
33	Arkansas	53
50	California	37
14	Colorado	66
3	Connecticut	93
25	Delaware	58
25	Florida	58
47	Georgia	38
5	Hawaii	78
30	Idaho	55
31	Illinois	54
18	Indiana	64
31	Iowa	54
24	Kansas	59
43	Kentucky	42
38	Louisiana	48
6	Maine	74
8	Maryland	71
2	Massachusetts	96
18	Michigan	64
28	Minnesota	56
35	Mississippi	49
13	Missouri	67
10	Montana	70
17	Nebraska	65
47	Nevada	38
4	New Hampshire	83
14	New Jersey	66
42	New Mexico	44
14	New York	66
41	North Carolina	46
18	North Dakota	64
22	Ohio	60
35	Oklahoma	49
27	Oregon	57
10	Pennsylvania	70
8	Rhode Island	71
35	South Carolina	49
10	South Dakota	70
28	Tennessee	56
43	Texas	42
45	Utah	41
1	Vermont	100
38	Virginia	48
22	Washington	60
40	West Virginia	47
7	Wisconsin	73
21	Wyoming	62

RANK	STATE	RATE
1	Vermont	100
2	Massachusetts	96
3	Connecticut	93
4	New Hampshire	83
5	Hawaii	78
6	Maine	74
7	Wisconsin	73
8	Maryland	71
8	Rhode Island	71
10	Montana	70
10	Pennsylvania	70
10	South Dakota	70
13	Missouri	67
14	Colorado	66
14	New Jersey	66
14	New York	66
17	Nebraska	65
18	Indiana	64
18	Michigan	64
18	North Dakota	64
21	Wyoming	62
22	Ohio	60
22	Washington	60
24	Kansas	59
25	Delaware	58
25	Florida	58
27	Oregon	57
28	Minnesota	56
28	Tennessee	56
30	Idaho	55
31	Illinois	54
31	Iowa	54
33	Arkansas	53
34	Alaska	51
35	Mississippi	49
35	Oklahoma	49
35	South Carolina	49
38	Louisiana	48
38	Virginia	48
40	West Virginia	47
41	North Carolina	46
42	New Mexico	44
43	Kentucky	42
43	Texas	42
45	Utah	41
46	Arizona	40
47	Alabama	38
47	Georgia	38
47	Nevada	38
50	California	37
	District of Columbia	51

Source: CQ Press using data from U.S. Department of Labor, Bureau of Labor Statistics
"Occupational Employment and Wages, 2008" (http://www.bls.gov/oes/)
*Does not include self-employed.

Average Annual Wages of Physical Therapists in 2008

National Average = $74,410*

<table>
<tr><td colspan="3">ALPHA ORDER</td><td colspan="3">RANK ORDER</td></tr>
<tr><th>RANK</th><th>STATE</th><th>WAGES</th><th>RANK</th><th>STATE</th><th>WAGES</th></tr>
<tr><td>15</td><td>Alabama</td><td>$75,630</td><td>1</td><td>Nevada</td><td>$87,160</td></tr>
<tr><td>10</td><td>Alaska</td><td>78,450</td><td>2</td><td>California</td><td>83,180</td></tr>
<tr><td>27</td><td>Arizona</td><td>71,730</td><td>3</td><td>New Jersey</td><td>82,800</td></tr>
<tr><td>32</td><td>Arkansas</td><td>69,690</td><td>4</td><td>Rhode Island</td><td>81,980</td></tr>
<tr><td>2</td><td>California</td><td>83,180</td><td>5</td><td>Illinois</td><td>80,310</td></tr>
<tr><td>41</td><td>Colorado</td><td>66,860</td><td>6</td><td>Maryland</td><td>79,620</td></tr>
<tr><td>7</td><td>Connecticut</td><td>79,540</td><td>7</td><td>Connecticut</td><td>79,540</td></tr>
<tr><td>11</td><td>Delaware</td><td>77,990</td><td>8</td><td>West Virginia</td><td>78,850</td></tr>
<tr><td>13</td><td>Florida</td><td>76,190</td><td>9</td><td>Texas</td><td>78,550</td></tr>
<tr><td>17</td><td>Georgia</td><td>74,920</td><td>10</td><td>Alaska</td><td>78,450</td></tr>
<tr><td>50</td><td>Hawaii</td><td>54,490</td><td>11</td><td>Delaware</td><td>77,990</td></tr>
<tr><td>31</td><td>Idaho</td><td>69,880</td><td>12</td><td>Louisiana</td><td>77,840</td></tr>
<tr><td>5</td><td>Illinois</td><td>80,310</td><td>13</td><td>Florida</td><td>76,190</td></tr>
<tr><td>30</td><td>Indiana</td><td>70,120</td><td>14</td><td>Tennessee</td><td>75,910</td></tr>
<tr><td>35</td><td>Iowa</td><td>68,270</td><td>15</td><td>Alabama</td><td>75,630</td></tr>
<tr><td>36</td><td>Kansas</td><td>68,210</td><td>16</td><td>Michigan</td><td>75,150</td></tr>
<tr><td>24</td><td>Kentucky</td><td>72,440</td><td>17</td><td>Georgia</td><td>74,920</td></tr>
<tr><td>12</td><td>Louisiana</td><td>77,840</td><td>18</td><td>Ohio</td><td>74,710</td></tr>
<tr><td>43</td><td>Maine</td><td>64,780</td><td>19</td><td>Virginia</td><td>74,170</td></tr>
<tr><td>6</td><td>Maryland</td><td>79,620</td><td>20</td><td>North Carolina</td><td>73,580</td></tr>
<tr><td>28</td><td>Massachusetts</td><td>71,160</td><td>21</td><td>New York</td><td>72,900</td></tr>
<tr><td>16</td><td>Michigan</td><td>75,150</td><td>22</td><td>Pennsylvania</td><td>72,820</td></tr>
<tr><td>37</td><td>Minnesota</td><td>68,160</td><td>23</td><td>Washington</td><td>72,550</td></tr>
<tr><td>25</td><td>Mississippi</td><td>72,390</td><td>24</td><td>Kentucky</td><td>72,440</td></tr>
<tr><td>48</td><td>Missouri</td><td>62,220</td><td>25</td><td>Mississippi</td><td>72,390</td></tr>
<tr><td>49</td><td>Montana</td><td>55,380</td><td>26</td><td>South Carolina</td><td>72,240</td></tr>
<tr><td>39</td><td>Nebraska</td><td>67,030</td><td>27</td><td>Arizona</td><td>71,730</td></tr>
<tr><td>1</td><td>Nevada</td><td>87,160</td><td>28</td><td>Massachusetts</td><td>71,160</td></tr>
<tr><td>38</td><td>New Hampshire</td><td>67,100</td><td>29</td><td>Wisconsin</td><td>70,530</td></tr>
<tr><td>3</td><td>New Jersey</td><td>82,800</td><td>30</td><td>Indiana</td><td>70,120</td></tr>
<tr><td>44</td><td>New Mexico</td><td>64,520</td><td>31</td><td>Idaho</td><td>69,880</td></tr>
<tr><td>21</td><td>New York</td><td>72,900</td><td>32</td><td>Arkansas</td><td>69,690</td></tr>
<tr><td>20</td><td>North Carolina</td><td>73,580</td><td>33</td><td>Oregon</td><td>69,520</td></tr>
<tr><td>45</td><td>North Dakota</td><td>63,740</td><td>34</td><td>Oklahoma</td><td>69,250</td></tr>
<tr><td>18</td><td>Ohio</td><td>74,710</td><td>35</td><td>Iowa</td><td>68,270</td></tr>
<tr><td>34</td><td>Oklahoma</td><td>69,250</td><td>36</td><td>Kansas</td><td>68,210</td></tr>
<tr><td>33</td><td>Oregon</td><td>69,520</td><td>37</td><td>Minnesota</td><td>68,160</td></tr>
<tr><td>22</td><td>Pennsylvania</td><td>72,820</td><td>38</td><td>New Hampshire</td><td>67,100</td></tr>
<tr><td>4</td><td>Rhode Island</td><td>81,980</td><td>39</td><td>Nebraska</td><td>67,030</td></tr>
<tr><td>26</td><td>South Carolina</td><td>72,240</td><td>40</td><td>Wyoming</td><td>66,970</td></tr>
<tr><td>46</td><td>South Dakota</td><td>63,570</td><td>41</td><td>Colorado</td><td>66,860</td></tr>
<tr><td>14</td><td>Tennessee</td><td>75,910</td><td>42</td><td>Utah</td><td>66,410</td></tr>
<tr><td>9</td><td>Texas</td><td>78,550</td><td>43</td><td>Maine</td><td>64,780</td></tr>
<tr><td>42</td><td>Utah</td><td>66,410</td><td>44</td><td>New Mexico</td><td>64,520</td></tr>
<tr><td>47</td><td>Vermont</td><td>63,110</td><td>45</td><td>North Dakota</td><td>63,740</td></tr>
<tr><td>19</td><td>Virginia</td><td>74,170</td><td>46</td><td>South Dakota</td><td>63,570</td></tr>
<tr><td>23</td><td>Washington</td><td>72,550</td><td>47</td><td>Vermont</td><td>63,110</td></tr>
<tr><td>8</td><td>West Virginia</td><td>78,850</td><td>48</td><td>Missouri</td><td>62,220</td></tr>
<tr><td>29</td><td>Wisconsin</td><td>70,530</td><td>49</td><td>Montana</td><td>55,380</td></tr>
<tr><td>40</td><td>Wyoming</td><td>66,970</td><td>50</td><td>Hawaii</td><td>54,490</td></tr>
<tr><td></td><td></td><td></td><td></td><td>District of Columbia</td><td>67,710</td></tr>
</table>

Source: U.S. Department of Labor, Bureau of Labor Statistics
   "Occupational Employment and Wages, 2008" (http://www.bls.gov/oes/)
*Does not include self-employed.

Dentists in 2007

National Total = 181,725 Dentists*

RANK	STATE	DENTISTS	% of USA
27	Alabama	2,032	1.1%
45	Alaska	519	0.3%
16	Arizona	3,225	1.8%
35	Arkansas	1,162	0.6%
1	California	27,654	15.2%
19	Colorado	3,181	1.8%
23	Connecticut	2,710	1.5%
46	Delaware	403	0.2%
4	Florida	9,640	5.3%
13	Georgia	4,295	2.4%
37	Hawaii	1,043	0.6%
39	Idaho	863	0.5%
5	Illinois	8,268	4.5%
21	Indiana	3,035	1.7%
31	Iowa	1,610	0.9%
32	Kansas	1,437	0.8%
25	Kentucky	2,356	1.3%
26	Louisiana	2,118	1.2%
42	Maine	662	0.4%
14	Maryland	4,212	2.3%
10	Massachusetts	5,314	2.9%
8	Michigan	6,126	3.4%
17	Minnesota	3,196	1.8%
34	Mississippi	1,190	0.7%
22	Missouri	2,813	1.5%
44	Montana	549	0.3%
36	Nebraska	1,111	0.6%
33	Nevada	1,285	0.7%
41	New Hampshire	830	0.5%
7	New Jersey	7,042	3.9%
38	New Mexico	907	0.5%
2	New York	15,184	8.4%
15	North Carolina	4,108	2.3%
49	North Dakota	326	0.2%
9	Ohio	6,063	3.3%
29	Oklahoma	1,804	1.0%
24	Oregon	2,551	1.4%
6	Pennsylvania	7,747	4.3%
43	Rhode Island	569	0.3%
28	South Carolina	2,026	1.1%
47	South Dakota	397	0.2%
20	Tennessee	3,076	1.7%
3	Texas	10,981	6.0%
30	Utah	1,713	0.9%
48	Vermont	361	0.2%
11	Virginia	4,563	2.5%
12	Washington	4,528	2.5%
40	West Virginia	847	0.5%
18	Wisconsin	3,186	1.8%
50	Wyoming	269	0.1%

RANK	STATE	DENTISTS	% of USA
1	California	27,654	15.2%
2	New York	15,184	8.4%
3	Texas	10,981	6.0%
4	Florida	9,640	5.3%
5	Illinois	8,268	4.5%
6	Pennsylvania	7,747	4.3%
7	New Jersey	7,042	3.9%
8	Michigan	6,126	3.4%
9	Ohio	6,063	3.3%
10	Massachusetts	5,314	2.9%
11	Virginia	4,563	2.5%
12	Washington	4,528	2.5%
13	Georgia	4,295	2.4%
14	Maryland	4,212	2.3%
15	North Carolina	4,108	2.3%
16	Arizona	3,225	1.8%
17	Minnesota	3,196	1.8%
18	Wisconsin	3,186	1.8%
19	Colorado	3,181	1.8%
20	Tennessee	3,076	1.7%
21	Indiana	3,035	1.7%
22	Missouri	2,813	1.5%
23	Connecticut	2,710	1.5%
24	Oregon	2,551	1.4%
25	Kentucky	2,356	1.3%
26	Louisiana	2,118	1.2%
27	Alabama	2,032	1.1%
28	South Carolina	2,026	1.1%
29	Oklahoma	1,804	1.0%
30	Utah	1,713	0.9%
31	Iowa	1,610	0.9%
32	Kansas	1,437	0.8%
33	Nevada	1,285	0.7%
34	Mississippi	1,190	0.7%
35	Arkansas	1,162	0.6%
36	Nebraska	1,111	0.6%
37	Hawaii	1,043	0.6%
38	New Mexico	907	0.5%
39	Idaho	863	0.5%
40	West Virginia	847	0.5%
41	New Hampshire	830	0.5%
42	Maine	662	0.4%
43	Rhode Island	569	0.3%
44	Montana	549	0.3%
45	Alaska	519	0.3%
46	Delaware	403	0.2%
47	South Dakota	397	0.2%
48	Vermont	361	0.2%
49	North Dakota	326	0.2%
50	Wyoming	269	0.1%
	District of Columbia	614	0.3%

Source: American Dental Association
    "Distribution of Dentists, by Region and State, 2007"
*Professionally active dentists. Total includes 24 dentists for whom state is not known.

Rate of Dentists in 2007

National Rate = 60 Dentists per 100,000 Population*

RANK	STATE	RATE
48	Alabama	44
6	Alaska	76
30	Arizona	51
49	Arkansas	41
6	California	76
11	Colorado	66
4	Connecticut	78
41	Delaware	47
27	Florida	53
46	Georgia	45
1	Hawaii	82
20	Idaho	58
12	Illinois	65
38	Indiana	48
25	Iowa	54
29	Kansas	52
24	Kentucky	55
38	Louisiana	48
33	Maine	50
8	Maryland	75
1	Massachusetts	82
18	Michigan	61
16	Minnesota	62
49	Mississippi	41
38	Missouri	48
22	Montana	57
14	Nebraska	63
33	Nevada	50
14	New Hampshire	63
1	New Jersey	82
43	New Mexico	46
4	New York	78
46	North Carolina	45
30	North Dakota	51
27	Ohio	53
33	Oklahoma	50
10	Oregon	68
16	Pennsylvania	62
25	Rhode Island	54
43	South Carolina	46
33	South Dakota	50
33	Tennessee	50
43	Texas	46
13	Utah	64
20	Vermont	58
19	Virginia	59
9	Washington	70
41	West Virginia	47
22	Wisconsin	57
30	Wyoming	51

RANK	STATE	RATE
1	Hawaii	82
1	Massachusetts	82
1	New Jersey	82
4	Connecticut	78
4	New York	78
6	Alaska	76
6	California	76
8	Maryland	75
9	Washington	70
10	Oregon	68
11	Colorado	66
12	Illinois	65
13	Utah	64
14	Nebraska	63
14	New Hampshire	63
16	Minnesota	62
16	Pennsylvania	62
18	Michigan	61
19	Virginia	59
20	Idaho	58
20	Vermont	58
22	Montana	57
22	Wisconsin	57
24	Kentucky	55
25	Iowa	54
25	Rhode Island	54
27	Florida	53
27	Ohio	53
29	Kansas	52
30	Arizona	51
30	North Dakota	51
30	Wyoming	51
33	Maine	50
33	Nevada	50
33	Oklahoma	50
33	South Dakota	50
33	Tennessee	50
38	Indiana	48
38	Louisiana	48
38	Missouri	48
41	Delaware	47
41	West Virginia	47
43	New Mexico	46
43	South Carolina	46
43	Texas	46
46	Georgia	45
46	North Carolina	45
48	Alabama	44
49	Arkansas	41
49	Mississippi	41

	District of Columbia	105

Source: CQ Press using data from American Dental Association
   "Distribution of Dentists, by Region and State, 2007"
*Professionally active dentists. Total includes 24 dentists for whom state is not known.

Average Annual Wages of Dentists in 2008

National Average = $154,270*

RANK	STATE	WAGES
28	Alabama	$156,370
1	Alaska	203,000
37	Arizona	150,530
13	Arkansas	166,500
44	California	140,990
27	Colorado	157,340
22	Connecticut	161,420
2	Delaware	187,600
36	Florida	150,940
8	Georgia	171,280
43	Hawaii	144,280
30	Idaho	154,090
38	Illinois	149,840
26	Indiana	158,080
32	Iowa	152,830
23	Kansas	161,410
29	Kentucky	156,010
46	Louisiana	138,550
5	Maine	180,690
41	Maryland	145,060
33	Massachusetts	152,260
18	Michigan	162,930
14	Minnesota	166,480
40	Mississippi	147,480
12	Missouri	166,830
45	Montana	139,380
10	Nebraska	169,230
21	Nevada	161,830
15	New Hampshire	166,330
39	New Jersey	149,760
35	New Mexico	151,860
34	New York	151,880
3	North Carolina	182,500
4	North Dakota	181,380
16	Ohio	165,400
48	Oklahoma	130,710
19	Oregon	162,720
47	Pennsylvania	131,410
11	Rhode Island	167,710
20	South Carolina	162,250
17	South Dakota	164,900
24	Tennessee	161,150
31	Texas	153,560
50	Utah	116,000
7	Vermont	177,070
9	Virginia	170,040
6	Washington	178,700
42	West Virginia	144,900
25	Wisconsin	158,340
49	Wyoming	128,120

RANK	STATE	WAGES
1	Alaska	$203,000
2	Delaware	187,600
3	North Carolina	182,500
4	North Dakota	181,380
5	Maine	180,690
6	Washington	178,700
7	Vermont	177,070
8	Georgia	171,280
9	Virginia	170,040
10	Nebraska	169,230
11	Rhode Island	167,710
12	Missouri	166,830
13	Arkansas	166,500
14	Minnesota	166,480
15	New Hampshire	166,330
16	Ohio	165,400
17	South Dakota	164,900
18	Michigan	162,930
19	Oregon	162,720
20	South Carolina	162,250
21	Nevada	161,830
22	Connecticut	161,420
23	Kansas	161,410
24	Tennessee	161,150
25	Wisconsin	158,340
26	Indiana	158,080
27	Colorado	157,340
28	Alabama	156,370
29	Kentucky	156,010
30	Idaho	154,090
31	Texas	153,560
32	Iowa	152,830
33	Massachusetts	152,260
34	New York	151,880
35	New Mexico	151,860
36	Florida	150,940
37	Arizona	150,530
38	Illinois	149,840
39	New Jersey	149,760
40	Mississippi	147,480
41	Maryland	145,060
42	West Virginia	144,900
43	Hawaii	144,280
44	California	140,990
45	Montana	139,380
46	Louisiana	138,550
47	Pennsylvania	131,410
48	Oklahoma	130,710
49	Wyoming	128,120
50	Utah	116,000
	District of Columbia	155,400

Source: U.S. Department of Labor, Bureau of Labor Statistics
  "Occupational Employment and Wages, 2008" (http://www.bls.gov/oes/)
*Does not include self-employed.

Percent of Population Lacking Access to Dental Care in 2010

National Percent = 10.1% of Population*

ALPHA ORDER			RANK ORDER		
RANK	STATE	PERCENT	RANK	STATE	PERCENT
3	Alabama	26.4	1	Louisiana	32.8
23	Alaska	10.5	2	Mississippi	32.0
25	Arizona	9.9	3	Alabama	26.4
40	Arkansas	5.7	4	New Mexico	23.7
45	California	3.8	5	South Carolina	20.4
39	Colorado	5.9	6	Montana	19.8
32	Connecticut	7.9	7	Tennessee	19.5
12	Delaware	16.2	8	Missouri	17.6
13	Florida	15.8	9	Idaho	17.1
27	Georgia	9.4	10	Maine	16.9
17	Hawaii	13.0	11	Kansas	16.5
9	Idaho	17.1	12	Delaware	16.2
16	Illinois	13.4	13	Florida	15.8
46	Indiana	3.0	14	Nevada	15.1
23	Iowa	10.5	15	Oregon	14.0
11	Kansas	16.5	16	Illinois	13.4
43	Kentucky	4.9	17	Hawaii	13.0
1	Louisiana	32.8	18	South Dakota	11.9
10	Maine	16.9	19	Michigan	11.5
37	Maryland	6.5	20	Texas	10.8
29	Massachusetts	8.5	21	Rhode Island	10.7
19	Michigan	11.5	22	North Carolina	10.6
43	Minnesota	4.9	23	Alaska	10.5
2	Mississippi	32.0	23	Iowa	10.5
8	Missouri	17.6	25	Arizona	9.9
6	Montana	19.8	25	Pennsylvania	9.9
49	Nebraska	1.6	27	Georgia	9.4
14	Nevada	15.1	28	Virginia	8.6
48	New Hampshire	2.1	29	Massachusetts	8.5
50	New Jersey	0.9	30	Washington	8.4
4	New Mexico	23.7	31	Wisconsin	8.0
38	New York	6.0	32	Connecticut	7.9
22	North Carolina	10.6	33	North Dakota	7.5
33	North Dakota	7.5	34	West Virginia	7.3
35	Ohio	7.2	35	Ohio	7.2
42	Oklahoma	5.3	36	Wyoming	7.1
15	Oregon	14.0	37	Maryland	6.5
25	Pennsylvania	9.9	38	New York	6.0
21	Rhode Island	10.7	39	Colorado	5.9
5	South Carolina	20.4	40	Arkansas	5.7
18	South Dakota	11.9	41	Utah	5.6
7	Tennessee	19.5	42	Oklahoma	5.3
20	Texas	10.8	43	Kentucky	4.9
41	Utah	5.6	43	Minnesota	4.9
47	Vermont	2.5	45	California	3.8
28	Virginia	8.6	46	Indiana	3.0
30	Washington	8.4	47	Vermont	2.5
34	West Virginia	7.3	48	New Hampshire	2.1
31	Wisconsin	8.0	49	Nebraska	1.6
36	Wyoming	7.1	50	New Jersey	0.9
				District of Columbia	3.7

Source: CQ Press using data from U.S. Department of Health and Human Services, Division of Shortage Designation
   "Selected Statistics on Health Professional Shortage Areas" (as of January 15, 2010)
   (http://datawarehouse.hrsa.gov/HPSADownload.aspx)
*Percent of population considered under-served by dental practitioners. An under-served population does not have primary medical care within reasonable economic and geographic bounds.

Pharmacists in 2008

National Total = 266,410 Pharmacists*

ALPHA ORDER

ALPHA ORDER

RANK	STATE	PHARMACISTS	% of USA	RANK	STATE	PHARMACISTS	% of USA
23	Alabama	4,330	1.6%	1	California	24,830	9.3%
50	Alaska	390	0.1%	2	Texas	19,820	7.4%
20	Arizona	4,790	1.8%	3	Florida	16,720	6.3%
30	Arkansas	2,770	1.0%	4	New York	16,020	6.0%
1	California	24,830	9.3%	5	Ohio	11,610	4.4%
25	Colorado	4,230	1.6%	6	Pennsylvania	11,590	4.4%
31	Connecticut	2,750	1.0%	7	Illinois	10,250	3.8%
47	Delaware	780	0.3%	8	Michigan	8,480	3.2%
3	Florida	16,720	6.3%	8	New Jersey	8,480	3.2%
10	Georgia	8,210	3.1%	10	Georgia	8,210	3.1%
45	Hawaii	1,050	0.4%	11	North Carolina	7,900	3.0%
40	Idaho	1,480	0.6%	12	Virginia	7,210	2.7%
7	Illinois	10,250	3.8%	13	Massachusetts	6,710	2.5%
14	Indiana	6,660	2.5%	14	Indiana	6,660	2.5%
29	Iowa	3,090	1.2%	15	Tennessee	6,640	2.5%
32	Kansas	2,730	1.0%	16	Missouri	5,810	2.2%
24	Kentucky	4,270	1.6%	17	Minnesota	5,620	2.1%
26	Louisiana	4,140	1.6%	17	Washington	5,620	2.1%
41	Maine	1,220	0.5%	19	Wisconsin	4,920	1.8%
21	Maryland	4,780	1.8%	20	Arizona	4,790	1.8%
13	Massachusetts	6,710	2.5%	21	Maryland	4,780	1.8%
8	Michigan	8,480	3.2%	22	South Carolina	4,450	1.7%
17	Minnesota	5,620	2.1%	23	Alabama	4,330	1.6%
33	Mississippi	2,300	0.9%	24	Kentucky	4,270	1.6%
16	Missouri	5,810	2.2%	25	Colorado	4,230	1.6%
43	Montana	1,090	0.4%	26	Louisiana	4,140	1.6%
35	Nebraska	2,050	0.8%	27	Oregon	3,310	1.2%
34	Nevada	2,260	0.8%	28	Oklahoma	3,190	1.2%
39	New Hampshire	1,490	0.6%	29	Iowa	3,090	1.2%
8	New Jersey	8,480	3.2%	30	Arkansas	2,770	1.0%
38	New Mexico	1,740	0.7%	31	Connecticut	2,750	1.0%
4	New York	16,020	6.0%	32	Kansas	2,730	1.0%
11	North Carolina	7,900	3.0%	33	Mississippi	2,300	0.9%
46	North Dakota	880	0.3%	34	Nevada	2,260	0.8%
5	Ohio	11,610	4.4%	35	Nebraska	2,050	0.8%
28	Oklahoma	3,190	1.2%	36	Utah	2,010	0.8%
27	Oregon	3,310	1.2%	37	West Virginia	1,910	0.7%
6	Pennsylvania	11,590	4.4%	38	New Mexico	1,740	0.7%
42	Rhode Island	1,130	0.4%	39	New Hampshire	1,490	0.6%
22	South Carolina	4,450	1.7%	40	Idaho	1,480	0.6%
44	South Dakota	1,070	0.4%	41	Maine	1,220	0.5%
15	Tennessee	6,640	2.5%	42	Rhode Island	1,130	0.4%
2	Texas	19,820	7.4%	43	Montana	1,090	0.4%
36	Utah	2,010	0.8%	44	South Dakota	1,070	0.4%
48	Vermont	490	0.2%	45	Hawaii	1,050	0.4%
12	Virginia	7,210	2.7%	46	North Dakota	880	0.3%
17	Washington	5,620	2.1%	47	Delaware	780	0.3%
37	West Virginia	1,910	0.7%	48	Vermont	490	0.2%
19	Wisconsin	4,920	1.8%	49	Wyoming	460	0.2%
49	Wyoming	460	0.2%	50	Alaska	390	0.1%
					District of Columbia	670	0.3%

RANK ORDER

Source: U.S. Department of Labor, Bureau of Labor Statistics
   "Occupational Employment and Wages, 2008" (http://www.bls.gov/oes/)
*Does not include self-employed.

Rate of Pharmacists in 2008

National Rate = 88 Pharmacists per 100,000 Population*

RANK	STATE	RATE
21	Alabama	93
50	Alaska	57
47	Arizona	74
19	Arkansas	97
49	California	68
32	Colorado	86
44	Connecticut	79
27	Delaware	89
26	Florida	91
36	Georgia	85
40	Hawaii	82
19	Idaho	97
43	Illinois	80
10	Indiana	104
11	Iowa	103
16	Kansas	98
14	Kentucky	100
21	Louisiana	93
23	Maine	92
39	Maryland	84
11	Massachusetts	103
36	Michigan	85
6	Minnesota	107
46	Mississippi	78
16	Missouri	98
4	Montana	113
3	Nebraska	115
32	Nevada	86
4	New Hampshire	113
16	New Jersey	98
28	New Mexico	88
40	New York	82
36	North Carolina	85
1	North Dakota	137
13	Ohio	101
28	Oklahoma	88
30	Oregon	87
23	Pennsylvania	92
6	Rhode Island	107
15	South Carolina	99
2	South Dakota	133
8	Tennessee	106
40	Texas	82
47	Utah	74
44	Vermont	79
23	Virginia	92
32	Washington	86
9	West Virginia	105
30	Wisconsin	87
32	Wyoming	86

RANK	STATE	RATE
1	North Dakota	137
2	South Dakota	133
3	Nebraska	115
4	Montana	113
4	New Hampshire	113
6	Minnesota	107
6	Rhode Island	107
8	Tennessee	106
9	West Virginia	105
10	Indiana	104
11	Iowa	103
11	Massachusetts	103
13	Ohio	101
14	Kentucky	100
15	South Carolina	99
16	Kansas	98
16	Missouri	98
16	New Jersey	98
19	Arkansas	97
19	Idaho	97
21	Alabama	93
21	Louisiana	93
23	Maine	92
23	Pennsylvania	92
23	Virginia	92
26	Florida	91
27	Delaware	89
28	New Mexico	88
28	Oklahoma	88
30	Oregon	87
30	Wisconsin	87
32	Colorado	86
32	Nevada	86
32	Washington	86
32	Wyoming	86
36	Georgia	85
36	Michigan	85
36	North Carolina	85
39	Maryland	84
40	Hawaii	82
40	New York	82
40	Texas	82
43	Illinois	80
44	Connecticut	79
44	Vermont	79
46	Mississippi	78
47	Arizona	74
47	Utah	74
49	California	68
50	Alaska	57
	District of Columbia	114

Source: CQ Press using data from U.S. Department of Labor, Bureau of Labor Statistics
   "Occupational Employment and Wages, 2008" (http://www.bls.gov/oes/)
*Does not include self-employed.

Average Annual Wages of Pharmacists in 2008

National Average = $104,260*

ALPHA ORDER

RANK	STATE	WAGES
11	Alabama	$108,160
4	Alaska	110,610
20	Arizona	103,800
42	Arkansas	96,120
1	California	116,960
13	Colorado	106,660
12	Connecticut	107,810
36	Delaware	100,290
21	Florida	103,580
32	Georgia	100,940
27	Hawaii	102,600
24	Idaho	103,220
29	Illinois	102,300
37	Indiana	100,200
47	Iowa	91,280
34	Kansas	100,750
14	Kentucky	106,560
39	Louisiana	97,990
2	Maine	112,450
33	Maryland	100,900
41	Massachusetts	96,230
31	Michigan	101,330
5	Minnesota	109,760
22	Mississippi	103,510
15	Missouri	106,240
48	Montana	91,080
49	Nebraska	90,160
23	Nevada	103,370
3	New Hampshire	111,050
28	New Jersey	102,340
30	New Mexico	101,620
18	New York	103,910
8	North Carolina	108,990
50	North Dakota	86,930
38	Ohio	99,470
43	Oklahoma	95,590
17	Oregon	105,070
44	Pennsylvania	93,280
45	Rhode Island	92,790
25	South Carolina	103,000
46	South Dakota	91,560
6	Tennessee	109,370
9	Texas	108,630
35	Utah	100,530
16	Vermont	105,310
10	Virginia	108,250
25	Washington	103,000
19	West Virginia	103,840
7	Wisconsin	109,350
40	Wyoming	97,890

RANK ORDER

RANK	STATE	WAGES
1	California	$116,960
2	Maine	112,450
3	New Hampshire	111,050
4	Alaska	110,610
5	Minnesota	109,760
6	Tennessee	109,370
7	Wisconsin	109,350
8	North Carolina	108,990
9	Texas	108,630
10	Virginia	108,250
11	Alabama	108,160
12	Connecticut	107,810
13	Colorado	106,660
14	Kentucky	106,560
15	Missouri	106,240
16	Vermont	105,310
17	Oregon	105,070
18	New York	103,910
19	West Virginia	103,840
20	Arizona	103,800
21	Florida	103,580
22	Mississippi	103,510
23	Nevada	103,370
24	Idaho	103,220
25	South Carolina	103,000
25	Washington	103,000
27	Hawaii	102,600
28	New Jersey	102,340
29	Illinois	102,300
30	New Mexico	101,620
31	Michigan	101,330
32	Georgia	100,940
33	Maryland	100,900
34	Kansas	100,750
35	Utah	100,530
36	Delaware	100,290
37	Indiana	100,200
38	Ohio	99,470
39	Louisiana	97,990
40	Wyoming	97,890
41	Massachusetts	96,230
42	Arkansas	96,120
43	Oklahoma	95,590
44	Pennsylvania	93,280
45	Rhode Island	92,790
46	South Dakota	91,560
47	Iowa	91,280
48	Montana	91,080
49	Nebraska	90,160
50	North Dakota	86,930
	District of Columbia	97,790

Source: U.S. Department of Labor, Bureau of Labor Statistics
   "Occupational Employment and Wages, 2008" (http://www.bls.gov/oes/)
*Does not include self-employed.

Optometrists in 2008

National Total = 25,970 Optometrists*

RANK	STATE	OPTOMETRISTS	% of USA
30	Alabama	270	1.0%
49	Alaska	60	0.2%
9	Arizona	730	2.8%
28	Arkansas	290	1.1%
1	California	2,580	9.9%
15	Colorado	650	2.5%
38	Connecticut	170	0.7%
49	Delaware	60	0.2%
6	Florida	1,090	4.2%
16	Georgia	600	2.3%
28	Hawaii	290	1.1%
37	Idaho	190	0.7%
4	Illinois	1,670	6.4%
11	Indiana	670	2.6%
26	Iowa	310	1.2%
22	Kansas	420	1.6%
26	Kentucky	310	1.2%
33	Louisiana	240	0.9%
41	Maine	120	0.5%
23	Maryland	410	1.6%
13	Massachusetts	660	2.5%
7	Michigan	1,040	4.0%
19	Minnesota	490	1.9%
30	Mississippi	270	1.0%
10	Missouri	700	2.7%
43	Montana	100	0.4%
36	Nebraska	220	0.8%
34	Nevada	230	0.9%
40	New Hampshire	140	0.5%
17	New Jersey	540	2.1%
39	New Mexico	160	0.6%
3	New York	1,680	6.5%
11	North Carolina	670	2.6%
43	North Dakota	100	0.4%
8	Ohio	1,010	3.9%
20	Oklahoma	480	1.8%
18	Oregon	510	2.0%
5	Pennsylvania	1,240	4.8%
43	Rhode Island	100	0.4%
25	South Carolina	350	1.3%
42	South Dakota	110	0.4%
30	Tennessee	270	1.0%
2	Texas	1,790	6.9%
34	Utah	230	0.9%
48	Vermont	70	0.3%
13	Virginia	660	2.5%
24	Washington	370	1.4%
43	West Virginia	100	0.4%
21	Wisconsin	430	1.7%
47	Wyoming	90	0.3%

RANK	STATE	OPTOMETRISTS	% of USA
1	California	2,580	9.9%
2	Texas	1,790	6.9%
3	New York	1,680	6.5%
4	Illinois	1,670	6.4%
5	Pennsylvania	1,240	4.8%
6	Florida	1,090	4.2%
7	Michigan	1,040	4.0%
8	Ohio	1,010	3.9%
9	Arizona	730	2.8%
10	Missouri	700	2.7%
11	Indiana	670	2.6%
11	North Carolina	670	2.6%
13	Massachusetts	660	2.5%
13	Virginia	660	2.5%
15	Colorado	650	2.5%
16	Georgia	600	2.3%
17	New Jersey	540	2.1%
18	Oregon	510	2.0%
19	Minnesota	490	1.9%
20	Oklahoma	480	1.8%
21	Wisconsin	430	1.7%
22	Kansas	420	1.6%
23	Maryland	410	1.6%
24	Washington	370	1.4%
25	South Carolina	350	1.3%
26	Iowa	310	1.2%
26	Kentucky	310	1.2%
28	Arkansas	290	1.1%
28	Hawaii	290	1.1%
30	Alabama	270	1.0%
30	Mississippi	270	1.0%
30	Tennessee	270	1.0%
33	Louisiana	240	0.9%
34	Nevada	230	0.9%
34	Utah	230	0.9%
36	Nebraska	220	0.8%
37	Idaho	190	0.7%
38	Connecticut	170	0.7%
39	New Mexico	160	0.6%
40	New Hampshire	140	0.5%
41	Maine	120	0.5%
42	South Dakota	110	0.4%
43	Montana	100	0.4%
43	North Dakota	100	0.4%
43	Rhode Island	100	0.4%
43	West Virginia	100	0.4%
47	Wyoming	90	0.3%
48	Vermont	70	0.3%
49	Alaska	60	0.2%
49	Delaware	60	0.2%
	District of Columbia	80	0.3%

Source: U.S. Department of Labor, Bureau of Labor Statistics
  "Occupational Employment and Wages, 2008" (http://www.bls.gov/oes/)
*Does not include self-employed.

Rate of Optometrists in 2008

National Rate = 9 Optometrists per 100,000 Population*

ALPHA ORDER

RANK	STATE	RATE
42	Alabama	6
23	Alaska	9
13	Arizona	11
16	Arkansas	10
36	California	7
6	Colorado	13
48	Connecticut	5
36	Delaware	7
42	Florida	6
42	Georgia	6
1	Hawaii	23
10	Idaho	12
6	Illinois	13
16	Indiana	10
16	Iowa	10
4	Kansas	15
36	Kentucky	7
48	Louisiana	5
23	Maine	9
36	Maryland	7
16	Massachusetts	10
16	Michigan	10
23	Minnesota	9
23	Mississippi	9
10	Missouri	12
16	Montana	10
10	Nebraska	12
23	Nevada	9
13	New Hampshire	11
42	New Jersey	6
31	New Mexico	8
23	New York	9
36	North Carolina	7
3	North Dakota	16
23	Ohio	9
6	Oklahoma	13
6	Oregon	13
16	Pennsylvania	10
23	Rhode Island	9
31	South Carolina	8
5	South Dakota	14
50	Tennessee	4
36	Texas	7
31	Utah	8
13	Vermont	11
31	Virginia	8
42	Washington	6
42	West Virginia	6
31	Wisconsin	8
2	Wyoming	17

RANK ORDER

RANK	STATE	RATE
1	Hawaii	23
2	Wyoming	17
3	North Dakota	16
4	Kansas	15
5	South Dakota	14
6	Colorado	13
6	Illinois	13
6	Oklahoma	13
6	Oregon	13
10	Idaho	12
10	Missouri	12
10	Nebraska	12
13	Arizona	11
13	New Hampshire	11
13	Vermont	11
16	Arkansas	10
16	Indiana	10
16	Iowa	10
16	Massachusetts	10
16	Michigan	10
16	Montana	10
16	Pennsylvania	10
23	Alaska	9
23	Maine	9
23	Minnesota	9
23	Mississippi	9
23	Nevada	9
23	New York	9
23	Ohio	9
23	Rhode Island	9
31	New Mexico	8
31	South Carolina	8
31	Utah	8
31	Virginia	8
31	Wisconsin	8
36	California	7
36	Delaware	7
36	Kentucky	7
36	Maryland	7
36	North Carolina	7
36	Texas	7
42	Alabama	6
42	Florida	6
42	Georgia	6
42	New Jersey	6
42	Washington	6
42	West Virginia	6
48	Connecticut	5
48	Louisiana	5
50	Tennessee	4

	District of Columbia	14

Source: CQ Press using data from U.S. Department of Labor, Bureau of Labor Statistics
"Occupational Employment and Wages, 2008" (http://www.bls.gov/oes/)
*Does not include self-employed.

Average Annual Wages of Optometrists in 2008

National Average = $105,200*

ALPHA ORDER

RANK	STATE	WAGES
38	Alabama	$93,920
16	Alaska	114,450
15	Arizona	116,940
29	Arkansas	102,910
28	California	103,120
47	Colorado	73,800
26	Connecticut	103,930
25	Delaware	104,300
24	Florida	106,740
19	Georgia	111,580
41	Hawaii	92,260
48	Idaho	62,650
32	Illinois	100,130
22	Indiana	107,710
36	Iowa	94,690
12	Kansas	118,370
5	Kentucky	122,620
3	Louisiana	143,980
30	Maine	100,870
31	Maryland	100,350
20	Massachusetts	108,910
18	Michigan	111,660
9	Minnesota	120,420
46	Mississippi	85,580
42	Missouri	92,120
NA	Montana**	NA
37	Nebraska	94,580
13	Nevada	117,860
21	New Hampshire	107,870
34	New Jersey	97,040
40	New Mexico	93,550
23	New York	107,160
8	North Carolina	120,430
10	North Dakota	119,160
7	Ohio	121,240
45	Oklahoma	86,290
NA	Oregon**	NA
39	Pennsylvania	93,730
4	Rhode Island	126,130
43	South Carolina	89,860
27	South Dakota	103,790
6	Tennessee	121,670
14	Texas	117,630
17	Utah	112,830
1	Vermont	146,820
33	Virginia	100,080
2	Washington	144,060
11	West Virginia	118,540
35	Wisconsin	96,170
44	Wyoming	87,860

RANK ORDER

RANK	STATE	WAGES
1	Vermont	$146,820
2	Washington	144,060
3	Louisiana	143,980
4	Rhode Island	126,130
5	Kentucky	122,620
6	Tennessee	121,670
7	Ohio	121,240
8	North Carolina	120,430
9	Minnesota	120,420
10	North Dakota	119,160
11	West Virginia	118,540
12	Kansas	118,370
13	Nevada	117,860
14	Texas	117,630
15	Arizona	116,940
16	Alaska	114,450
17	Utah	112,830
18	Michigan	111,660
19	Georgia	111,580
20	Massachusetts	108,910
21	New Hampshire	107,870
22	Indiana	107,710
23	New York	107,160
24	Florida	106,740
25	Delaware	104,300
26	Connecticut	103,930
27	South Dakota	103,790
28	California	103,120
29	Arkansas	102,910
30	Maine	100,870
31	Maryland	100,350
32	Illinois	100,130
33	Virginia	100,080
34	New Jersey	97,040
35	Wisconsin	96,170
36	Iowa	94,690
37	Nebraska	94,580
38	Alabama	93,920
39	Pennsylvania	93,730
40	New Mexico	93,550
41	Hawaii	92,260
42	Missouri	92,120
43	South Carolina	89,860
44	Wyoming	87,860
45	Oklahoma	86,290
46	Mississippi	85,580
47	Colorado	73,800
48	Idaho	62,650
NA	Montana**	NA
NA	Oregon**	NA
	District of Columbia	95,580

Source: U.S. Department of Labor, Bureau of Labor Statistics
   "Occupational Employment and Wages, 2008" (http://www.bls.gov/oes/)
*Does not include self-employed.

Emergency Medical Technicians and Paramedics in 2008

National Total = 207,610 Technicians and Paramedics*

ALPHA ORDER

RANK	STATE	PARAMEDICS	% of USA
22	Alabama	3,230	1.6%
NA	Alaska**	NA	NA
21	Arizona	3,540	1.7%
33	Arkansas	1,790	0.9%
3	California	13,220	6.4%
23	Colorado	3,210	1.5%
27	Connecticut	2,760	1.3%
42	Delaware	730	0.4%
6	Florida	9,010	4.3%
9	Georgia	7,590	3.7%
49	Hawaii	270	0.1%
43	Idaho	680	0.3%
5	Illinois	10,440	5.0%
16	Indiana	5,110	2.5%
30	Iowa	2,130	1.0%
28	Kansas	2,330	1.1%
17	Kentucky	4,630	2.2%
26	Louisiana	3,020	1.5%
36	Maine	1,260	0.6%
24	Maryland	3,180	1.5%
14	Massachusetts	6,150	3.0%
12	Michigan	6,410	3.1%
18	Minnesota	4,110	2.0%
35	Mississippi	1,700	0.8%
11	Missouri	7,250	3.5%
41	Montana	740	0.4%
47	Nebraska	560	0.3%
38	Nevada	1,130	0.5%
37	New Hampshire	1,150	0.6%
10	New Jersey	7,410	3.6%
39	New Mexico	1,040	0.5%
1	New York	13,380	6.4%
8	North Carolina	8,490	4.1%
44	North Dakota	610	0.3%
7	Ohio	8,530	4.1%
29	Oklahoma	2,240	1.1%
32	Oregon	2,010	1.0%
3	Pennsylvania	13,220	6.4%
48	Rhode Island	500	0.2%
19	South Carolina	4,030	1.9%
40	South Dakota	770	0.4%
13	Tennessee	6,200	3.0%
2	Texas	13,230	6.4%
33	Utah	1,790	0.9%
45	Vermont	580	0.3%
20	Virginia	3,620	1.7%
25	Washington	3,050	1.5%
31	West Virginia	2,090	1.0%
15	Wisconsin	5,520	2.7%
45	Wyoming	580	0.3%

RANK ORDER

RANK	STATE	PARAMEDICS	% of USA
1	New York	13,380	6.4%
2	Texas	13,230	6.4%
3	California	13,220	6.4%
3	Pennsylvania	13,220	6.4%
5	Illinois	10,440	5.0%
6	Florida	9,010	4.3%
7	Ohio	8,530	4.1%
8	North Carolina	8,490	4.1%
9	Georgia	7,590	3.7%
10	New Jersey	7,410	3.6%
11	Missouri	7,250	3.5%
12	Michigan	6,410	3.1%
13	Tennessee	6,200	3.0%
14	Massachusetts	6,150	3.0%
15	Wisconsin	5,520	2.7%
16	Indiana	5,110	2.5%
17	Kentucky	4,630	2.2%
18	Minnesota	4,110	2.0%
19	South Carolina	4,030	1.9%
20	Virginia	3,620	1.7%
21	Arizona	3,540	1.7%
22	Alabama	3,230	1.6%
23	Colorado	3,210	1.5%
24	Maryland	3,180	1.5%
25	Washington	3,050	1.5%
26	Louisiana	3,020	1.5%
27	Connecticut	2,760	1.3%
28	Kansas	2,330	1.1%
29	Oklahoma	2,240	1.1%
30	Iowa	2,130	1.0%
31	West Virginia	2,090	1.0%
32	Oregon	2,010	1.0%
33	Arkansas	1,790	0.9%
33	Utah	1,790	0.9%
35	Mississippi	1,700	0.8%
36	Maine	1,260	0.6%
37	New Hampshire	1,150	0.6%
38	Nevada	1,130	0.5%
39	New Mexico	1,040	0.5%
40	South Dakota	770	0.4%
41	Montana	740	0.4%
42	Delaware	730	0.4%
43	Idaho	680	0.3%
44	North Dakota	610	0.3%
45	Vermont	580	0.3%
45	Wyoming	580	0.3%
47	Nebraska	560	0.3%
48	Rhode Island	500	0.2%
49	Hawaii	270	0.1%
NA	Alaska**	NA	NA
	District of Columbia	1,140	0.5%

Source: U.S. Department of Labor, Bureau of Labor Statistics
"Occupational Employment and Wages, 2008" (http://www.bls.gov/oes/)
*Does not include self-employed.
**Not available.

Rate of Emergency Medical Technicians and Paramedics in 2008

National Rate = 68 Technicians and Paramedics per 100,000 Population*

ALPHA ORDER

RANK	STATE	RATE
27	Alabama	69
NA	Alaska**	NA
37	Arizona	54
33	Arkansas	62
47	California	36
31	Colorado	65
21	Connecticut	79
17	Delaware	83
41	Florida	49
23	Georgia	78
49	Hawaii	21
45	Idaho	45
19	Illinois	81
20	Indiana	80
26	Iowa	71
17	Kansas	83
4	Kentucky	108
29	Louisiana	68
9	Maine	95
36	Maryland	56
11	Massachusetts	94
32	Michigan	64
21	Minnesota	79
35	Mississippi	58
1	Missouri	122
24	Montana	76
48	Nebraska	31
46	Nevada	43
15	New Hampshire	87
16	New Jersey	86
40	New Mexico	52
27	New York	69
13	North Carolina	92
9	North Dakota	95
25	Ohio	74
34	Oklahoma	61
39	Oregon	53
5	Pennsylvania	105
42	Rhode Island	47
14	South Carolina	89
8	South Dakota	96
6	Tennessee	99
37	Texas	54
30	Utah	66
12	Vermont	93
43	Virginia	46
43	Washington	46
2	West Virginia	115
7	Wisconsin	98
3	Wyoming	109

RANK ORDER

RANK	STATE	RATE
1	Missouri	122
2	West Virginia	115
3	Wyoming	109
4	Kentucky	108
5	Pennsylvania	105
6	Tennessee	99
7	Wisconsin	98
8	South Dakota	96
9	Maine	95
9	North Dakota	95
11	Massachusetts	94
12	Vermont	93
13	North Carolina	92
14	South Carolina	89
15	New Hampshire	87
16	New Jersey	86
17	Delaware	83
17	Kansas	83
19	Illinois	81
20	Indiana	80
21	Connecticut	79
21	Minnesota	79
23	Georgia	78
24	Montana	76
25	Ohio	74
26	Iowa	71
27	Alabama	69
27	New York	69
29	Louisiana	68
30	Utah	66
31	Colorado	65
32	Michigan	64
33	Arkansas	62
34	Oklahoma	61
35	Mississippi	58
36	Maryland	56
37	Arizona	54
37	Texas	54
39	Oregon	53
40	New Mexico	52
41	Florida	49
42	Rhode Island	47
43	Virginia	46
43	Washington	46
45	Idaho	45
46	Nevada	43
47	California	36
48	Nebraska	31
49	Hawaii	21
NA	Alaska**	NA

	District of Columbia	193

Source: CQ Press using data from U.S. Department of Labor, Bureau of Labor Statistics
   "Occupational Employment and Wages, 2008" (http://www.bls.gov/oes/)
*Does not include self-employed.
**Not available.

Average Annual Wages of
Emergency Medical Technicians and Paramedics in 2008
National Average = $31,980*

ALPHA ORDER

RANK	STATE	WAGES
38	Alabama	$27,870
2	Alaska	46,490
35	Arizona	28,950
46	Arkansas	26,470
23	California	31,110
13	Colorado	35,470
8	Connecticut	37,560
6	Delaware	38,220
20	Florida	32,190
24	Georgia	30,960
1	Hawaii	48,780
15	Idaho	34,300
10	Illinois	36,760
33	Indiana	29,340
40	Iowa	27,720
42	Kansas	26,960
40	Kentucky	27,720
22	Louisiana	31,220
37	Maine	28,370
4	Maryland	41,630
9	Massachusetts	37,340
26	Michigan	30,720
27	Minnesota	30,560
47	Mississippi	26,310
18	Missouri	33,390
49	Montana	25,900
43	Nebraska	26,950
11	Nevada	35,950
14	New Hampshire	34,930
17	New Jersey	33,590
31	New Mexico	29,650
7	New York	37,900
29	North Carolina	30,450
44	North Dakota	26,650
38	Ohio	27,870
45	Oklahoma	26,560
3	Oregon	44,380
32	Pennsylvania	29,490
12	Rhode Island	35,740
30	South Carolina	30,340
48	South Dakota	25,940
21	Tennessee	31,860
34	Texas	29,000
28	Utah	30,510
24	Vermont	30,960
19	Virginia	33,180
5	Washington	39,020
50	West Virginia	23,510
36	Wisconsin	28,710
16	Wyoming	33,640

RANK ORDER

RANK	STATE	WAGES
1	Hawaii	$48,780
2	Alaska	46,490
3	Oregon	44,380
4	Maryland	41,630
5	Washington	39,020
6	Delaware	38,220
7	New York	37,900
8	Connecticut	37,560
9	Massachusetts	37,340
10	Illinois	36,760
11	Nevada	35,950
12	Rhode Island	35,740
13	Colorado	35,470
14	New Hampshire	34,930
15	Idaho	34,300
16	Wyoming	33,640
17	New Jersey	33,590
18	Missouri	33,390
19	Virginia	33,180
20	Florida	32,190
21	Tennessee	31,860
22	Louisiana	31,220
23	California	31,110
24	Georgia	30,960
24	Vermont	30,960
26	Michigan	30,720
27	Minnesota	30,560
28	Utah	30,510
29	North Carolina	30,450
30	South Carolina	30,340
31	New Mexico	29,650
32	Pennsylvania	29,490
33	Indiana	29,340
34	Texas	29,000
35	Arizona	28,950
36	Wisconsin	28,710
37	Maine	28,370
38	Alabama	27,870
38	Ohio	27,870
40	Iowa	27,720
40	Kentucky	27,720
42	Kansas	26,960
43	Nebraska	26,950
44	North Dakota	26,650
45	Oklahoma	26,560
46	Arkansas	26,470
47	Mississippi	26,310
48	South Dakota	25,940
49	Montana	25,900
50	West Virginia	23,510
	District of Columbia	45,110

Source: U.S. Department of Labor, Bureau of Labor Statistics
  "Occupational Employment and Wages, 2008" (http://www.bls.gov/oes/)
*Does not include self-employed.

Employment in Health Care Support Industries in 2008

National Total = 3,779,280 Aides and Assistants*

ALPHA ORDER

RANK	STATE	EMPLOYEES	% of USA
24	Alabama	51,930	1.4%
50	Alaska	6,610	0.2%
20	Arizona	67,400	1.8%
33	Arkansas	32,170	0.9%
1	California	350,910	9.3%
27	Colorado	46,850	1.2%
23	Connecticut	54,110	1.4%
46	Delaware	10,810	0.3%
4	Florida	212,990	5.6%
14	Georgia	82,650	2.2%
43	Hawaii	14,460	0.4%
41	Idaho	16,760	0.4%
8	Illinois	145,030	3.8%
17	Indiana	75,250	2.0%
28	Iowa	46,680	1.2%
31	Kansas	40,870	1.1%
26	Kentucky	48,900	1.3%
22	Louisiana	55,640	1.5%
38	Maine	22,320	0.6%
21	Maryland	66,780	1.8%
11	Massachusetts	100,040	2.6%
9	Michigan	132,590	3.5%
12	Minnesota	91,080	2.4%
32	Mississippi	33,570	0.9%
16	Missouri	78,340	2.1%
44	Montana	12,780	0.3%
35	Nebraska	26,310	0.7%
39	Nevada	22,100	0.6%
42	New Hampshire	16,670	0.4%
10	New Jersey	116,810	3.1%
36	New Mexico	24,770	0.7%
2	New York	313,210	8.3%
7	North Carolina	146,300	3.9%
45	North Dakota	12,260	0.3%
6	Ohio	189,860	5.0%
29	Oklahoma	44,680	1.2%
30	Oregon	43,340	1.1%
5	Pennsylvania	195,080	5.2%
40	Rhode Island	19,420	0.5%
25	South Carolina	49,180	1.3%
47	South Dakota	10,380	0.3%
19	Tennessee	72,120	1.9%
3	Texas	262,440	6.9%
34	Utah	28,860	0.8%
48	Vermont	7,030	0.2%
15	Virginia	81,520	2.2%
18	Washington	72,820	1.9%
37	West Virginia	23,480	0.6%
13	Wisconsin	89,230	2.4%
49	Wyoming	6,670	0.2%

RANK ORDER

RANK	STATE	EMPLOYEES	% of USA
1	California	350,910	9.3%
2	New York	313,210	8.3%
3	Texas	262,440	6.9%
4	Florida	212,990	5.6%
5	Pennsylvania	195,080	5.2%
6	Ohio	189,860	5.0%
7	North Carolina	146,300	3.9%
8	Illinois	145,030	3.8%
9	Michigan	132,590	3.5%
10	New Jersey	116,810	3.1%
11	Massachusetts	100,040	2.6%
12	Minnesota	91,080	2.4%
13	Wisconsin	89,230	2.4%
14	Georgia	82,650	2.2%
15	Virginia	81,520	2.2%
16	Missouri	78,340	2.1%
17	Indiana	75,250	2.0%
18	Washington	72,820	1.9%
19	Tennessee	72,120	1.9%
20	Arizona	67,400	1.8%
21	Maryland	66,780	1.8%
22	Louisiana	55,640	1.5%
23	Connecticut	54,110	1.4%
24	Alabama	51,930	1.4%
25	South Carolina	49,180	1.3%
26	Kentucky	48,900	1.3%
27	Colorado	46,850	1.2%
28	Iowa	46,680	1.2%
29	Oklahoma	44,680	1.2%
30	Oregon	43,340	1.1%
31	Kansas	40,870	1.1%
32	Mississippi	33,570	0.9%
33	Arkansas	32,170	0.9%
34	Utah	28,860	0.8%
35	Nebraska	26,310	0.7%
36	New Mexico	24,770	0.7%
37	West Virginia	23,480	0.6%
38	Maine	22,320	0.6%
39	Nevada	22,100	0.6%
40	Rhode Island	19,420	0.5%
41	Idaho	16,760	0.4%
42	New Hampshire	16,670	0.4%
43	Hawaii	14,460	0.4%
44	Montana	12,780	0.3%
45	North Dakota	12,260	0.3%
46	Delaware	10,810	0.3%
47	South Dakota	10,380	0.3%
48	Vermont	7,030	0.2%
49	Wyoming	6,670	0.2%
50	Alaska	6,610	0.2%
	District of Columbia	7,200	0.2%

Source: U.S. Department of Labor, Bureau of Labor Statistics
  "Occupational Employment and Wages, 2008" (http://www.bls.gov/oes/)
*Does not include self-employed. Includes various health care assistants and aides not included in the category of health care practitioners and technicians. Among the included occupations are home health aides, nursing aides, psychiatric aides, dental assistants, and pharmacy aides.

Rate of Employees in Health Care Support Industries in 2008

National Rate = 1,242 Aides and Assistants per 100,000 Population*

ALPHA ORDER				RANK ORDER		
RANK	STATE	RATE		RANK	STATE	RATE
38	Alabama	1,110		1	North Dakota	1,911
46	Alaska	961		2	Rhode Island	1,843
45	Arizona	1,037		3	Minnesota	1,741
37	Arkansas	1,122		4	Maine	1,691
47	California	959		5	Ohio	1,647
48	Colorado	949		6	New York	1,609
11	Connecticut	1,545		7	Wisconsin	1,586
25	Delaware	1,234		8	North Carolina	1,582
29	Florida	1,156		9	Iowa	1,559
49	Georgia	852		10	Pennsylvania	1,552
36	Hawaii	1,123		11	Connecticut	1,545
40	Idaho	1,097		12	Massachusetts	1,529
35	Illinois	1,129		13	Nebraska	1,476
28	Indiana	1,178		14	Kansas	1,461
9	Iowa	1,559		15	New Jersey	1,348
14	Kansas	1,461		16	Michigan	1,326
33	Kentucky	1,140		17	Montana	1,320
23	Louisiana	1,250		18	Missouri	1,315
4	Maine	1,691		19	West Virginia	1,294
27	Maryland	1,180		20	South Dakota	1,290
12	Massachusetts	1,529		21	New Hampshire	1,261
16	Michigan	1,326		22	Wyoming	1,251
3	Minnesota	1,741		23	Louisiana	1,250
32	Mississippi	1,142		24	New Mexico	1,247
18	Missouri	1,315		25	Delaware	1,234
17	Montana	1,320		26	Oklahoma	1,226
13	Nebraska	1,476		27	Maryland	1,180
50	Nevada	845		28	Indiana	1,178
21	New Hampshire	1,261		29	Florida	1,156
15	New Jersey	1,348		29	Tennessee	1,156
24	New Mexico	1,247		31	Oregon	1,146
6	New York	1,609		32	Mississippi	1,142
8	North Carolina	1,582		33	Kentucky	1,140
1	North Dakota	1,911		34	Vermont	1,132
5	Ohio	1,647		35	Illinois	1,129
26	Oklahoma	1,226		36	Hawaii	1,123
31	Oregon	1,146		37	Arkansas	1,122
10	Pennsylvania	1,552		38	Alabama	1,110
2	Rhode Island	1,843		39	Washington	1,109
41	South Carolina	1,092		40	Idaho	1,097
20	South Dakota	1,290		41	South Carolina	1,092
29	Tennessee	1,156		42	Texas	1,080
42	Texas	1,080		43	Utah	1,058
43	Utah	1,058		44	Virginia	1,046
34	Vermont	1,132		45	Arizona	1,037
44	Virginia	1,046		46	Alaska	961
39	Washington	1,109		47	California	959
19	West Virginia	1,294		48	Colorado	949
7	Wisconsin	1,586		49	Georgia	852
22	Wyoming	1,251		50	Nevada	845
					District of Columbia	1,220

Source: CQ Press using data from U.S. Department of Labor, Bureau of Labor Statistics
"Occupational Employment and Wages, 2008" (http://www.bls.gov/oes/)
*Does not include self-employed. Includes various health care assistants and aides not included in the category of health care practitioners and technicians. Among the included occupations are home health aides, nursing aides, psychiatric aides, dental assistants, and pharmacy aides.

Average Annual Wages of Employees in Health Care Support Industries in 2008

National Average = $26,340*

ALPHA ORDER

RANK	STATE	WAGES
46	Alabama	$22,080
1	Alaska	35,150
20	Arizona	26,430
47	Arkansas	21,730
6	California	29,710
10	Colorado	29,160
2	Connecticut	31,530
8	Delaware	29,400
22	Florida	25,760
33	Georgia	24,440
4	Hawaii	30,380
31	Idaho	24,720
17	Illinois	27,290
24	Indiana	25,690
29	Iowa	24,940
37	Kansas	24,060
32	Kentucky	24,680
50	Louisiana	21,010
27	Maine	25,340
9	Maryland	29,350
3	Massachusetts	31,060
20	Michigan	26,430
16	Minnesota	27,760
49	Mississippi	21,020
40	Missouri	23,870
41	Montana	23,720
30	Nebraska	24,780
7	Nevada	29,520
11	New Hampshire	29,140
14	New Jersey	28,490
36	New Mexico	24,100
15	New York	27,940
43	North Carolina	23,530
39	North Dakota	23,950
28	Ohio	24,990
45	Oklahoma	22,790
13	Oregon	28,590
23	Pennsylvania	25,720
12	Rhode Island	29,010
42	South Carolina	23,590
38	South Dakota	23,990
34	Tennessee	24,390
44	Texas	23,420
35	Utah	24,180
18	Vermont	27,200
24	Virginia	25,690
5	Washington	29,990
48	West Virginia	21,110
19	Wisconsin	26,600
26	Wyoming	25,510

RANK ORDER

RANK	STATE	WAGES
1	Alaska	$35,150
2	Connecticut	31,530
3	Massachusetts	31,060
4	Hawaii	30,380
5	Washington	29,990
6	California	29,710
7	Nevada	29,520
8	Delaware	29,400
9	Maryland	29,350
10	Colorado	29,160
11	New Hampshire	29,140
12	Rhode Island	29,010
13	Oregon	28,590
14	New Jersey	28,490
15	New York	27,940
16	Minnesota	27,760
17	Illinois	27,290
18	Vermont	27,200
19	Wisconsin	26,600
20	Arizona	26,430
20	Michigan	26,430
22	Florida	25,760
23	Pennsylvania	25,720
24	Indiana	25,690
24	Virginia	25,690
26	Wyoming	25,510
27	Maine	25,340
28	Ohio	24,990
29	Iowa	24,940
30	Nebraska	24,780
31	Idaho	24,720
32	Kentucky	24,680
33	Georgia	24,440
34	Tennessee	24,390
35	Utah	24,180
36	New Mexico	24,100
37	Kansas	24,060
38	South Dakota	23,990
39	North Dakota	23,950
40	Missouri	23,870
41	Montana	23,720
42	South Carolina	23,590
43	North Carolina	23,530
44	Texas	23,420
45	Oklahoma	22,790
46	Alabama	22,080
47	Arkansas	21,730
48	West Virginia	21,110
49	Mississippi	21,020
50	Louisiana	21,010
	District of Columbia	31,990

Source: U.S. Department of Labor, Bureau of Labor Statistics
 "Occupational Employment and Wages, 2008" (http://www.bls.gov/oes/)
*Does not include self-employed. Includes various health care assistants and aides not included in the category of health care practitioners and technicians. Among the included occupations are home health aides, nursing aides, psychiatric aides, dental assistants, and pharmacy aides.

VII. Physical Fitness

Users of Exercise Equipment in 2007

National Total = 52,827,000 Users

ALPHA ORDER

RANK	STATE	USERS	% of USA
25	Alabama	666,000	1.3%
NA	Alaska*	NA	NA
13	Arizona	1,381,000	2.6%
34	Arkansas	336,000	0.6%
1	California	6,077,000	11.5%
18	Colorado	1,177,000	2.2%
28	Connecticut	553,000	1.0%
46	Delaware	110,000	0.2%
4	Florida	2,877,000	5.5%
14	Georgia	1,357,000	2.6%
NA	Hawaii*	NA	NA
43	Idaho	144,000	0.3%
6	Illinois	2,377,000	4.5%
15	Indiana	1,296,000	2.5%
33	Iowa	361,000	0.7%
23	Kansas	728,000	1.4%
20	Kentucky	1,074,000	2.0%
26	Louisiana	621,000	1.2%
40	Maine	214,000	0.4%
17	Maryland	1,245,000	2.4%
12	Massachusetts	1,533,000	2.9%
8	Michigan	1,822,000	3.5%
19	Minnesota	1,164,000	2.2%
39	Mississippi	219,000	0.4%
22	Missouri	938,000	1.8%
41	Montana	175,000	0.3%
36	Nebraska	284,000	0.5%
27	Nevada	588,000	1.1%
38	New Hampshire	235,000	0.4%
9	New Jersey	1,688,000	3.2%
37	New Mexico	244,000	0.5%
3	New York	3,455,000	6.5%
10	North Carolina	1,668,000	3.2%
44	North Dakota	142,000	0.3%
7	Ohio	2,096,000	4.0%
32	Oklahoma	401,000	0.8%
35	Oregon	331,000	0.6%
5	Pennsylvania	2,576,000	4.9%
48	Rhode Island	93,000	0.2%
24	South Carolina	699,000	1.3%
41	South Dakota	175,000	0.3%
29	Tennessee	552,000	1.0%
2	Texas	4,131,000	7.8%
31	Utah	433,000	0.8%
47	Vermont	108,000	0.2%
11	Virginia	1,583,000	3.0%
16	Washington	1,254,000	2.4%
30	West Virginia	446,000	0.8%
21	Wisconsin	1,017,000	1.9%
45	Wyoming	140,000	0.3%

RANK ORDER

RANK	STATE	USERS	% of USA
1	California	6,077,000	11.5%
2	Texas	4,131,000	7.8%
3	New York	3,455,000	6.5%
4	Florida	2,877,000	5.5%
5	Pennsylvania	2,576,000	4.9%
6	Illinois	2,377,000	4.5%
7	Ohio	2,096,000	4.0%
8	Michigan	1,822,000	3.5%
9	New Jersey	1,688,000	3.2%
10	North Carolina	1,668,000	3.2%
11	Virginia	1,583,000	3.0%
12	Massachusetts	1,533,000	2.9%
13	Arizona	1,381,000	2.6%
14	Georgia	1,357,000	2.6%
15	Indiana	1,296,000	2.5%
16	Washington	1,254,000	2.4%
17	Maryland	1,245,000	2.4%
18	Colorado	1,177,000	2.2%
19	Minnesota	1,164,000	2.2%
20	Kentucky	1,074,000	2.0%
21	Wisconsin	1,017,000	1.9%
22	Missouri	938,000	1.8%
23	Kansas	728,000	1.4%
24	South Carolina	699,000	1.3%
25	Alabama	666,000	1.3%
26	Louisiana	621,000	1.2%
27	Nevada	588,000	1.1%
28	Connecticut	553,000	1.0%
29	Tennessee	552,000	1.0%
30	West Virginia	446,000	0.8%
31	Utah	433,000	0.8%
32	Oklahoma	401,000	0.8%
33	Iowa	361,000	0.7%
34	Arkansas	336,000	0.6%
35	Oregon	331,000	0.6%
36	Nebraska	284,000	0.5%
37	New Mexico	244,000	0.5%
38	New Hampshire	235,000	0.4%
39	Mississippi	219,000	0.4%
40	Maine	214,000	0.4%
41	Montana	175,000	0.3%
41	South Dakota	175,000	0.3%
43	Idaho	144,000	0.3%
44	North Dakota	142,000	0.3%
45	Wyoming	140,000	0.3%
46	Delaware	110,000	0.2%
47	Vermont	108,000	0.2%
48	Rhode Island	93,000	0.2%
NA	Alaska*	NA	NA
NA	Hawaii*	NA	NA
	District of Columbia*	NA	NA

Source: The National Sporting Goods Association
   "NSGA Sports Participation Survey, January-December 2007" (Copyright 2008, reprinted with permission)
*Not available.

Participants in Golf in 2007

National Total = 22,729,000 Golfers

RANK	STATE	GOLFERS	% of USA
26	Alabama	245,000	1.1%
NA	Alaska*	NA	NA
18	Arizona	401,000	1.8%
35	Arkansas	139,000	0.6%
1	California	2,340,000	10.3%
21	Colorado	318,000	1.4%
33	Connecticut	160,000	0.7%
47	Delaware	12,000	0.1%
4	Florida	1,545,000	6.8%
12	Georgia	572,000	2.5%
NA	Hawaii*	NA	NA
24	Idaho	267,000	1.2%
5	Illinois	1,464,000	6.4%
17	Indiana	431,000	1.9%
38	Iowa	90,000	0.4%
27	Kansas	235,000	1.0%
22	Kentucky	295,000	1.3%
29	Louisiana	195,000	0.9%
46	Maine	50,000	0.2%
19	Maryland	392,000	1.7%
13	Massachusetts	570,000	2.5%
3	Michigan	1,557,000	6.9%
14	Minnesota	518,000	2.3%
40	Mississippi	76,000	0.3%
15	Missouri	479,000	2.1%
45	Montana	52,000	0.2%
41	Nebraska	75,000	0.3%
34	Nevada	154,000	0.7%
42	New Hampshire	63,000	0.3%
10	New Jersey	808,000	3.6%
25	New Mexico	246,000	1.1%
2	New York	1,685,000	7.4%
11	North Carolina	599,000	2.6%
NA	North Dakota*	NA	NA
7	Ohio	1,159,000	5.1%
37	Oklahoma	117,000	0.5%
28	Oregon	204,000	0.9%
8	Pennsylvania	1,056,000	4.6%
36	Rhode Island	134,000	0.6%
23	South Carolina	271,000	1.2%
39	South Dakota	81,000	0.4%
32	Tennessee	186,000	0.8%
6	Texas	1,296,000	5.7%
31	Utah	191,000	0.8%
44	Vermont	58,000	0.3%
20	Virginia	348,000	1.5%
16	Washington	435,000	1.9%
30	West Virginia	193,000	0.8%
9	Wisconsin	900,000	4.0%
42	Wyoming	63,000	0.3%

RANK	STATE	GOLFERS	% of USA
1	California	2,340,000	10.3%
2	New York	1,685,000	7.4%
3	Michigan	1,557,000	6.9%
4	Florida	1,545,000	6.8%
5	Illinois	1,464,000	6.4%
6	Texas	1,296,000	5.7%
7	Ohio	1,159,000	5.1%
8	Pennsylvania	1,056,000	4.6%
9	Wisconsin	900,000	4.0%
10	New Jersey	808,000	3.6%
11	North Carolina	599,000	2.6%
12	Georgia	572,000	2.5%
13	Massachusetts	570,000	2.5%
14	Minnesota	518,000	2.3%
15	Missouri	479,000	2.1%
16	Washington	435,000	1.9%
17	Indiana	431,000	1.9%
18	Arizona	401,000	1.8%
19	Maryland	392,000	1.7%
20	Virginia	348,000	1.5%
21	Colorado	318,000	1.4%
22	Kentucky	295,000	1.3%
23	South Carolina	271,000	1.2%
24	Idaho	267,000	1.2%
25	New Mexico	246,000	1.1%
26	Alabama	245,000	1.1%
27	Kansas	235,000	1.0%
28	Oregon	204,000	0.9%
29	Louisiana	195,000	0.9%
30	West Virginia	193,000	0.8%
31	Utah	191,000	0.8%
32	Tennessee	186,000	0.8%
33	Connecticut	160,000	0.7%
34	Nevada	154,000	0.7%
35	Arkansas	139,000	0.6%
36	Rhode Island	134,000	0.6%
37	Oklahoma	117,000	0.5%
38	Iowa	90,000	0.4%
39	South Dakota	81,000	0.4%
40	Mississippi	76,000	0.3%
41	Nebraska	75,000	0.3%
42	New Hampshire	63,000	0.3%
42	Wyoming	63,000	0.3%
44	Vermont	58,000	0.3%
45	Montana	52,000	0.2%
46	Maine	50,000	0.2%
47	Delaware	12,000	0.1%
NA	Alaska*	NA	NA
NA	Hawaii*	NA	NA
NA	North Dakota*	NA	NA
	District of Columbia*	NA	NA

Source: The National Sporting Goods Association
"NSGA Sports Participation Survey, January-December 2007" (Copyright 2008, reprinted with permission)
*Not available.

Participants in Running/Jogging in 2007

National Total = 30,372,000 Runners/Joggers

ALPHA ORDER					RANK ORDER			
RANK	STATE	RUNNERS	% of USA		RANK	STATE	RUNNERS	% of USA
19	Alabama	494,000	1.6%		1	California	4,563,000	15.0%
NA	Alaska*	NA	NA		2	Texas	2,142,000	7.1%
13	Arizona	694,000	2.3%		3	New York	1,930,000	6.4%
35	Arkansas	200,000	0.7%		4	Georgia	1,633,000	5.4%
1	California	4,563,000	15.0%		5	Florida	1,520,000	5.0%
16	Colorado	578,000	1.9%		6	Illinois	1,347,000	4.4%
31	Connecticut	275,000	0.9%		7	Pennsylvania	1,287,000	4.2%
40	Delaware	101,000	0.3%		8	Michigan	1,193,000	3.9%
5	Florida	1,520,000	5.0%		9	Ohio	1,099,000	3.6%
4	Georgia	1,633,000	5.4%		10	Virginia	914,000	3.0%
NA	Hawaii*	NA	NA		11	New Jersey	911,000	3.0%
36	Idaho	187,000	0.6%		12	North Carolina	757,000	2.5%
6	Illinois	1,347,000	4.4%		13	Arizona	694,000	2.3%
14	Indiana	679,000	2.2%		14	Indiana	679,000	2.2%
28	Iowa	369,000	1.2%		15	Maryland	656,000	2.2%
32	Kansas	242,000	0.8%		16	Colorado	578,000	1.9%
27	Kentucky	372,000	1.2%		17	Washington	565,000	1.9%
29	Louisiana	363,000	1.2%		18	Oregon	527,000	1.7%
42	Maine	95,000	0.3%		19	Alabama	494,000	1.6%
15	Maryland	656,000	2.2%		20	Utah	487,000	1.6%
25	Massachusetts	432,000	1.4%		21	Wisconsin	470,000	1.5%
8	Michigan	1,193,000	3.9%		22	Tennessee	464,000	1.5%
23	Minnesota	453,000	1.5%		23	Minnesota	453,000	1.5%
38	Mississippi	116,000	0.4%		24	Missouri	440,000	1.4%
24	Missouri	440,000	1.4%		25	Massachusetts	432,000	1.4%
37	Montana	156,000	0.5%		26	South Carolina	380,000	1.3%
43	Nebraska	88,000	0.3%		27	Kentucky	372,000	1.2%
33	Nevada	223,000	0.7%		28	Iowa	369,000	1.2%
45	New Hampshire	71,000	0.2%		29	Louisiana	363,000	1.2%
11	New Jersey	911,000	3.0%		30	West Virginia	287,000	0.9%
34	New Mexico	207,000	0.7%		31	Connecticut	275,000	0.9%
3	New York	1,930,000	6.4%		32	Kansas	242,000	0.8%
12	North Carolina	757,000	2.5%		33	Nevada	223,000	0.7%
39	North Dakota	110,000	0.4%		34	New Mexico	207,000	0.7%
9	Ohio	1,099,000	3.6%		35	Arkansas	200,000	0.7%
46	Oklahoma	59,000	0.2%		36	Idaho	187,000	0.6%
18	Oregon	527,000	1.7%		37	Montana	156,000	0.5%
7	Pennsylvania	1,287,000	4.2%		38	Mississippi	116,000	0.4%
47	Rhode Island	30,000	0.1%		39	North Dakota	110,000	0.4%
26	South Carolina	380,000	1.3%		40	Delaware	101,000	0.3%
44	South Dakota	80,000	0.3%		40	Wyoming	101,000	0.3%
22	Tennessee	464,000	1.5%		42	Maine	95,000	0.3%
2	Texas	2,142,000	7.1%		43	Nebraska	88,000	0.3%
20	Utah	487,000	1.6%		44	South Dakota	80,000	0.3%
48	Vermont	24,000	0.1%		45	New Hampshire	71,000	0.2%
10	Virginia	914,000	3.0%		46	Oklahoma	59,000	0.2%
17	Washington	565,000	1.9%		47	Rhode Island	30,000	0.1%
30	West Virginia	287,000	0.9%		48	Vermont	24,000	0.1%
21	Wisconsin	470,000	1.5%		NA	Alaska*	NA	NA
40	Wyoming	101,000	0.3%		NA	Hawaii*	NA	NA
						District of Columbia*	NA	NA

Source: The National Sporting Goods Association
   "NSGA Sports Participation Survey, January-December 2007" (Copyright 2008, reprinted with permission)
*Not available.

Participants in Swimming in 2007

National Total = 52,346,000 Swimmers

ALPHA ORDER

RANK	STATE	SWIMMERS	% of USA
25	Alabama	746,000	1.4%
NA	Alaska*	NA	NA
16	Arizona	1,142,000	2.2%
40	Arkansas	256,000	0.5%
1	California	5,651,000	10.8%
23	Colorado	772,000	1.5%
35	Connecticut	341,000	0.7%
44	Delaware	124,000	0.2%
4	Florida	2,889,000	5.5%
13	Georgia	1,510,000	2.9%
NA	Hawaii*	NA	NA
34	Idaho	434,000	0.8%
6	Illinois	2,538,000	4.8%
21	Indiana	866,000	1.7%
26	Iowa	703,000	1.3%
32	Kansas	520,000	1.0%
20	Kentucky	867,000	1.7%
29	Louisiana	608,000	1.2%
37	Maine	285,000	0.5%
14	Maryland	1,505,000	2.9%
15	Massachusetts	1,323,000	2.5%
7	Michigan	2,142,000	4.1%
19	Minnesota	975,000	1.9%
38	Mississippi	284,000	0.5%
17	Missouri	1,061,000	2.0%
42	Montana	158,000	0.3%
48	Nebraska	62,000	0.1%
31	Nevada	534,000	1.0%
36	New Hampshire	304,000	0.6%
10	New Jersey	1,673,000	3.2%
41	New Mexico	160,000	0.3%
2	New York	4,016,000	7.7%
9	North Carolina	1,684,000	3.2%
43	North Dakota	129,000	0.2%
8	Ohio	1,897,000	3.6%
22	Oklahoma	822,000	1.6%
24	Oregon	762,000	1.5%
3	Pennsylvania	2,918,000	5.6%
47	Rhode Island	95,000	0.2%
28	South Carolina	620,000	1.2%
45	South Dakota	99,000	0.2%
27	Tennessee	647,000	1.2%
5	Texas	2,657,000	5.1%
30	Utah	592,000	1.1%
45	Vermont	99,000	0.2%
12	Virginia	1,526,000	2.9%
11	Washington	1,563,000	3.0%
33	West Virginia	505,000	1.0%
18	Wisconsin	978,000	1.9%
39	Wyoming	261,000	0.5%

RANK ORDER

RANK	STATE	SWIMMERS	% of USA
1	California	5,651,000	10.8%
2	New York	4,016,000	7.7%
3	Pennsylvania	2,918,000	5.6%
4	Florida	2,889,000	5.5%
5	Texas	2,657,000	5.1%
6	Illinois	2,538,000	4.8%
7	Michigan	2,142,000	4.1%
8	Ohio	1,897,000	3.6%
9	North Carolina	1,684,000	3.2%
10	New Jersey	1,673,000	3.2%
11	Washington	1,563,000	3.0%
12	Virginia	1,526,000	2.9%
13	Georgia	1,510,000	2.9%
14	Maryland	1,505,000	2.9%
15	Massachusetts	1,323,000	2.5%
16	Arizona	1,142,000	2.2%
17	Missouri	1,061,000	2.0%
18	Wisconsin	978,000	1.9%
19	Minnesota	975,000	1.9%
20	Kentucky	867,000	1.7%
21	Indiana	866,000	1.7%
22	Oklahoma	822,000	1.6%
23	Colorado	772,000	1.5%
24	Oregon	762,000	1.5%
25	Alabama	746,000	1.4%
26	Iowa	703,000	1.3%
27	Tennessee	647,000	1.2%
28	South Carolina	620,000	1.2%
29	Louisiana	608,000	1.2%
30	Utah	592,000	1.1%
31	Nevada	534,000	1.0%
32	Kansas	520,000	1.0%
33	West Virginia	505,000	1.0%
34	Idaho	434,000	0.8%
35	Connecticut	341,000	0.7%
36	New Hampshire	304,000	0.6%
37	Maine	285,000	0.5%
38	Mississippi	284,000	0.5%
39	Wyoming	261,000	0.5%
40	Arkansas	256,000	0.5%
41	New Mexico	160,000	0.3%
42	Montana	158,000	0.3%
43	North Dakota	129,000	0.2%
44	Delaware	124,000	0.2%
45	South Dakota	99,000	0.2%
45	Vermont	99,000	0.2%
47	Rhode Island	95,000	0.2%
48	Nebraska	62,000	0.1%
NA	Alaska*	NA	NA
NA	Hawaii*	NA	NA
	District of Columbia*	NA	NA

Source: The National Sporting Goods Association
"NSGA Sports Participation Survey, January-December 2007" (Copyright 2008, reprinted with permission)
*Not available.

Participants in Tennis in 2007

National Total = 12,290,000 Tennis Players

ALPHA ORDER

RANK	STATE	PLAYERS	% of USA
24	Alabama	132,000	1.1%
NA	Alaska*	NA	NA
20	Arizona	171,000	1.4%
31	Arkansas	67,000	0.5%
1	California	2,527,000	20.6%
14	Colorado	300,000	2.4%
19	Connecticut	176,000	1.4%
34	Delaware	44,000	0.4%
6	Florida	575,000	4.7%
3	Georgia	831,000	6.8%
NA	Hawaii*	NA	NA
43	Idaho	9,000	0.1%
7	Illinois	544,000	4.4%
15	Indiana	261,000	2.1%
23	Iowa	134,000	1.1%
22	Kansas	135,000	1.1%
27	Kentucky	104,000	0.8%
35	Louisiana	39,000	0.3%
37	Maine	32,000	0.3%
33	Maryland	52,000	0.4%
17	Massachusetts	199,000	1.6%
10	Michigan	428,000	3.5%
25	Minnesota	128,000	1.0%
30	Mississippi	70,000	0.6%
16	Missouri	218,000	1.8%
NA	Montana*	NA	NA
42	Nebraska	11,000	0.1%
40	Nevada	16,000	0.1%
NA	New Hampshire*	NA	NA
9	New Jersey	485,000	3.9%
36	New Mexico	38,000	0.3%
5	New York	579,000	4.7%
8	North Carolina	521,000	4.2%
28	North Dakota	87,000	0.7%
4	Ohio	673,000	5.5%
NA	Oklahoma*	NA	NA
29	Oregon	79,000	0.6%
11	Pennsylvania	354,000	2.9%
38	Rhode Island	31,000	0.3%
18	South Carolina	181,000	1.5%
NA	South Dakota*	NA	NA
39	Tennessee	26,000	0.2%
2	Texas	1,003,000	8.2%
32	Utah	65,000	0.5%
NA	Vermont*	NA	NA
13	Virginia	328,000	2.7%
26	Washington	121,000	1.0%
12	West Virginia	337,000	2.7%
21	Wisconsin	167,000	1.4%
41	Wyoming	13,000	0.1%

RANK ORDER

RANK	STATE	PLAYERS	% of USA
1	California	2,527,000	20.6%
2	Texas	1,003,000	8.2%
3	Georgia	831,000	6.8%
4	Ohio	673,000	5.5%
5	New York	579,000	4.7%
6	Florida	575,000	4.7%
7	Illinois	544,000	4.4%
8	North Carolina	521,000	4.2%
9	New Jersey	485,000	3.9%
10	Michigan	428,000	3.5%
11	Pennsylvania	354,000	2.9%
12	West Virginia	337,000	2.7%
13	Virginia	328,000	2.7%
14	Colorado	300,000	2.4%
15	Indiana	261,000	2.1%
16	Missouri	218,000	1.8%
17	Massachusetts	199,000	1.6%
18	South Carolina	181,000	1.5%
19	Connecticut	176,000	1.4%
20	Arizona	171,000	1.4%
21	Wisconsin	167,000	1.4%
22	Kansas	135,000	1.1%
23	Iowa	134,000	1.1%
24	Alabama	132,000	1.1%
25	Minnesota	128,000	1.0%
26	Washington	121,000	1.0%
27	Kentucky	104,000	0.8%
28	North Dakota	87,000	0.7%
29	Oregon	79,000	0.6%
30	Mississippi	70,000	0.6%
31	Arkansas	67,000	0.5%
32	Utah	65,000	0.5%
33	Maryland	52,000	0.4%
34	Delaware	44,000	0.4%
35	Louisiana	39,000	0.3%
36	New Mexico	38,000	0.3%
37	Maine	32,000	0.3%
38	Rhode Island	31,000	0.3%
39	Tennessee	26,000	0.2%
40	Nevada	16,000	0.1%
41	Wyoming	13,000	0.1%
42	Nebraska	11,000	0.1%
43	Idaho	9,000	0.1%
NA	Alaska*	NA	NA
NA	Hawaii*	NA	NA
NA	Montana*	NA	NA
NA	New Hampshire*	NA	NA
NA	Oklahoma*	NA	NA
NA	South Dakota*	NA	NA
NA	Vermont*	NA	NA
	District of Columbia*	NA	NA

Source: The National Sporting Goods Association
   "NSGA Sports Participation Survey, January-December 2007" (Copyright 2008, reprinted with permission)
*Not available.

Alcohol Consumption in 2007

National Total = 564,410,000 Gallons*

ALPHA ORDER

RANK	STATE	GALLONS	% of USA
26	Alabama	7,602,000	1.3%
47	Alaska	1,540,000	0.3%
16	Arizona	12,366,000	2.2%
35	Arkansas	4,204,000	0.7%
1	California	68,375,000	12.1%
18	Colorado	10,789,000	1.9%
28	Connecticut	6,747,000	1.2%
43	Delaware	2,275,000	0.4%
3	Florida	41,098,000	7.3%
10	Georgia	15,576,000	2.8%
39	Hawaii	2,769,000	0.5%
38	Idaho	3,051,000	0.5%
5	Illinois	24,506,000	4.3%
19	Indiana	10,750,000	1.9%
31	Iowa	5,464,000	1.0%
34	Kansas	4,379,000	0.8%
29	Kentucky	6,414,000	1.1%
23	Louisiana	9,365,000	1.7%
40	Maine	2,764,000	0.5%
21	Maryland	10,167,000	1.8%
14	Massachusetts	13,357,000	2.4%
8	Michigan	17,962,000	3.2%
20	Minnesota	10,354,000	1.8%
32	Mississippi	5,275,000	0.9%
17	Missouri	11,528,000	2.0%
45	Montana	2,214,000	0.4%
37	Nebraska	3,325,000	0.6%
27	Nevada	7,362,000	1.3%
33	New Hampshire	4,603,000	0.8%
9	New Jersey	16,532,000	2.9%
36	New Mexico	3,836,000	0.7%
4	New York	33,159,000	5.9%
11	North Carolina	14,656,000	2.6%
48	North Dakota	1,526,000	0.3%
7	Ohio	19,019,000	3.4%
30	Oklahoma	5,614,000	1.0%
25	Oregon	7,983,000	1.4%
6	Pennsylvania	22,350,000	4.0%
44	Rhode Island	2,251,000	0.4%
24	South Carolina	8,782,000	1.6%
46	South Dakota	1,669,000	0.3%
22	Tennessee	9,494,000	1.7%
2	Texas	41,921,000	7.4%
41	Utah	2,696,000	0.5%
49	Vermont	1,403,000	0.2%
13	Virginia	13,386,000	2.4%
15	Washington	12,403,000	2.2%
42	West Virginia	2,675,000	0.5%
12	Wisconsin	13,689,000	2.4%
50	Wyoming	1,205,000	0.2%

RANK ORDER

RANK	STATE	GALLONS	% of USA
1	California	68,375,000	12.1%
2	Texas	41,921,000	7.4%
3	Florida	41,098,000	7.3%
4	New York	33,159,000	5.9%
5	Illinois	24,506,000	4.3%
6	Pennsylvania	22,350,000	4.0%
7	Ohio	19,019,000	3.4%
8	Michigan	17,962,000	3.2%
9	New Jersey	16,532,000	2.9%
10	Georgia	15,576,000	2.8%
11	North Carolina	14,656,000	2.6%
12	Wisconsin	13,689,000	2.4%
13	Virginia	13,386,000	2.4%
14	Massachusetts	13,357,000	2.4%
15	Washington	12,403,000	2.2%
16	Arizona	12,366,000	2.2%
17	Missouri	11,528,000	2.0%
18	Colorado	10,789,000	1.9%
19	Indiana	10,750,000	1.9%
20	Minnesota	10,354,000	1.8%
21	Maryland	10,167,000	1.8%
22	Tennessee	9,494,000	1.7%
23	Louisiana	9,365,000	1.7%
24	South Carolina	8,782,000	1.6%
25	Oregon	7,983,000	1.4%
26	Alabama	7,602,000	1.3%
27	Nevada	7,362,000	1.3%
28	Connecticut	6,747,000	1.2%
29	Kentucky	6,414,000	1.1%
30	Oklahoma	5,614,000	1.0%
31	Iowa	5,464,000	1.0%
32	Mississippi	5,275,000	0.9%
33	New Hampshire	4,603,000	0.8%
34	Kansas	4,379,000	0.8%
35	Arkansas	4,204,000	0.7%
36	New Mexico	3,836,000	0.7%
37	Nebraska	3,325,000	0.6%
38	Idaho	3,051,000	0.5%
39	Hawaii	2,769,000	0.5%
40	Maine	2,764,000	0.5%
41	Utah	2,696,000	0.5%
42	West Virginia	2,675,000	0.5%
43	Delaware	2,275,000	0.4%
44	Rhode Island	2,251,000	0.4%
45	Montana	2,214,000	0.4%
46	South Dakota	1,669,000	0.3%
47	Alaska	1,540,000	0.3%
48	North Dakota	1,526,000	0.3%
49	Vermont	1,403,000	0.2%
50	Wyoming	1,205,000	0.2%
	District of Columbia	1,981,000	0.4%

Source: U.S. Department of Health and Human Services, National Institute on Alcohol Abuse and Alcoholism
"Volume Beverage and Ethanol Consumption for States" (http://www.niaaa.nih.gov/Resources/)
*This is apparent consumption of actual alcohol, not entire volume of an alcoholic beverage (for example, wine is roughly 11% absolute alcohol content). Apparent consumption is based on several sources which together approximate sales but do not actually measure consumption. Accordingly, figures for some states may be skewed by purchases by nonresidents.

Adult Per Capita Alcohol Consumption in 2007

National Per Capita = 2.6 Gallons Consumed per Adult 21 Years and Older*

ALPHA ORDER

RANK	STATE	PER CAPITA
40	Alabama	2.3
5	Alaska	3.3
18	Arizona	2.8
46	Arkansas	2.1
24	California	2.7
9	Colorado	3.1
24	Connecticut	2.7
3	Delaware	3.7
10	Florida	3.0
37	Georgia	2.4
15	Hawaii	2.9
10	Idaho	3.0
24	Illinois	2.7
37	Indiana	2.4
30	Iowa	2.6
44	Kansas	2.2
46	Kentucky	2.1
10	Louisiana	3.0
18	Maine	2.8
34	Maryland	2.5
18	Massachusetts	2.8
34	Michigan	2.5
18	Minnesota	2.8
30	Mississippi	2.6
24	Missouri	2.7
7	Montana	3.2
24	Nebraska	2.7
2	Nevada	4.1
1	New Hampshire	4.8
30	New Jersey	2.6
18	New Mexico	2.8
40	New York	2.3
40	North Carolina	2.3
5	North Dakota	3.3
40	Ohio	2.3
44	Oklahoma	2.2
15	Oregon	2.9
34	Pennsylvania	2.5
15	Rhode Island	2.9
18	South Carolina	2.8
10	South Dakota	3.0
46	Tennessee	2.1
30	Texas	2.6
50	Utah	1.6
10	Vermont	3.0
37	Virginia	2.4
24	Washington	2.7
49	West Virginia	2.0
4	Wisconsin	3.4
7	Wyoming	3.2

RANK ORDER

RANK	STATE	PER CAPITA
1	New Hampshire	4.8
2	Nevada	4.1
3	Delaware	3.7
4	Wisconsin	3.4
5	Alaska	3.3
5	North Dakota	3.3
7	Montana	3.2
7	Wyoming	3.2
9	Colorado	3.1
10	Florida	3.0
10	Idaho	3.0
10	Louisiana	3.0
10	South Dakota	3.0
10	Vermont	3.0
15	Hawaii	2.9
15	Oregon	2.9
15	Rhode Island	2.9
18	Arizona	2.8
18	Maine	2.8
18	Massachusetts	2.8
18	Minnesota	2.8
18	New Mexico	2.8
18	South Carolina	2.8
24	California	2.7
24	Connecticut	2.7
24	Illinois	2.7
24	Missouri	2.7
24	Nebraska	2.7
24	Washington	2.7
30	Iowa	2.6
30	Mississippi	2.6
30	New Jersey	2.6
30	Texas	2.6
34	Maryland	2.5
34	Michigan	2.5
34	Pennsylvania	2.5
37	Georgia	2.4
37	Indiana	2.4
37	Virginia	2.4
40	Alabama	2.3
40	New York	2.3
40	North Carolina	2.3
40	Ohio	2.3
44	Kansas	2.2
44	Oklahoma	2.2
46	Arkansas	2.1
46	Kentucky	2.1
46	Tennessee	2.1
49	West Virginia	2.0
50	Utah	1.6

| | District of Columbia | 4.5 |

Source: CQ Press using data from U.S. Dept of Health and Human Services, National Institute on Alcohol Abuse and Alcoholism
"Volume Beverage and Ethanol Consumption for States" (http://www.niaaa.nih.gov/Resources/)
*This is apparent consumption of actual alcohol, not entire volume of an alcoholic beverage (for example, wine is roughly 11% absolute alcohol content). Apparent consumption is based on several sources which together approximate sales but do not actually measure consumption. Accordingly, figures for some states may be skewed by purchases by nonresidents.

Apparent Beer Consumption in 2007

National Total = 6,550,633,000 Gallons of Beer Consumed*

ALPHA ORDER

RANK	STATE	GALLONS	% of USA
24	Alabama	103,905,000	1.6%
49	Alaska	15,930,000	0.2%
13	Arizona	152,116,000	2.3%
34	Arkansas	54,473,000	0.8%
1	California	694,575,000	10.6%
22	Colorado	112,196,000	1.7%
32	Connecticut	59,186,000	0.9%
45	Delaware	21,735,000	0.3%
3	Florida	436,764,000	6.7%
9	Georgia	195,525,000	3.0%
40	Hawaii	31,358,000	0.5%
42	Idaho	30,810,000	0.5%
6	Illinois	282,149,000	4.3%
17	Indiana	129,115,000	2.0%
30	Iowa	75,735,000	1.2%
33	Kansas	58,017,000	0.9%
27	Kentucky	80,559,000	1.2%
19	Louisiana	122,963,000	1.9%
41	Maine	31,275,000	0.5%
25	Maryland	103,401,000	1.6%
20	Massachusetts	121,219,000	1.9%
8	Michigan	202,770,000	3.1%
23	Minnesota	108,608,000	1.7%
31	Mississippi	75,600,000	1.2%
15	Missouri	141,305,000	2.2%
43	Montana	27,900,000	0.4%
36	Nebraska	46,013,000	0.7%
28	Nevada	77,411,000	1.2%
37	New Hampshire	42,075,000	0.6%
14	New Jersey	145,932,000	2.2%
35	New Mexico	49,608,000	0.8%
4	New York	328,061,000	5.0%
10	North Carolina	189,055,000	2.9%
47	North Dakota	18,427,000	0.3%
7	Ohio	277,088,000	4.2%
29	Oklahoma	76,208,000	1.2%
26	Oregon	88,380,000	1.3%
5	Pennsylvania	306,675,000	4.7%
44	Rhode Island	22,005,000	0.3%
21	South Carolina	114,300,000	1.7%
46	South Dakota	21,668,000	0.3%
18	Tennessee	126,428,000	1.9%
2	Texas	585,365,000	8.9%
39	Utah	33,615,000	0.5%
48	Vermont	15,975,000	0.2%
11	Virginia	158,732,000	2.4%
16	Washington	130,388,000	2.0%
38	West Virginia	41,648,000	0.6%
12	Wisconsin	157,185,000	2.4%
50	Wyoming	14,147,000	0.2%

RANK ORDER

RANK	STATE	GALLONS	% of USA
1	California	694,575,000	10.6%
2	Texas	585,365,000	8.9%
3	Florida	436,764,000	6.7%
4	New York	328,061,000	5.0%
5	Pennsylvania	306,675,000	4.7%
6	Illinois	282,149,000	4.3%
7	Ohio	277,088,000	4.2%
8	Michigan	202,770,000	3.1%
9	Georgia	195,525,000	3.0%
10	North Carolina	189,055,000	2.9%
11	Virginia	158,732,000	2.4%
12	Wisconsin	157,185,000	2.4%
13	Arizona	152,116,000	2.3%
14	New Jersey	145,932,000	2.2%
15	Missouri	141,305,000	2.2%
16	Washington	130,388,000	2.0%
17	Indiana	129,115,000	2.0%
18	Tennessee	126,428,000	1.9%
19	Louisiana	122,963,000	1.9%
20	Massachusetts	121,219,000	1.9%
21	South Carolina	114,300,000	1.7%
22	Colorado	112,196,000	1.7%
23	Minnesota	108,608,000	1.7%
24	Alabama	103,905,000	1.6%
25	Maryland	103,401,000	1.6%
26	Oregon	88,380,000	1.3%
27	Kentucky	80,559,000	1.2%
28	Nevada	77,411,000	1.2%
29	Oklahoma	76,208,000	1.2%
30	Iowa	75,735,000	1.2%
31	Mississippi	75,600,000	1.2%
32	Connecticut	59,186,000	0.9%
33	Kansas	58,017,000	0.9%
34	Arkansas	54,473,000	0.8%
35	New Mexico	49,608,000	0.8%
36	Nebraska	46,013,000	0.7%
37	New Hampshire	42,075,000	0.6%
38	West Virginia	41,648,000	0.6%
39	Utah	33,615,000	0.5%
40	Hawaii	31,358,000	0.5%
41	Maine	31,275,000	0.5%
42	Idaho	30,810,000	0.5%
43	Montana	27,900,000	0.4%
44	Rhode Island	22,005,000	0.3%
45	Delaware	21,735,000	0.3%
46	South Dakota	21,668,000	0.3%
47	North Dakota	18,427,000	0.3%
48	Vermont	15,975,000	0.2%
49	Alaska	15,930,000	0.2%
50	Wyoming	14,147,000	0.2%
	District of Columbia	15,053,000	0.2%

Source: U.S. Department of Health and Human Services, National Institute on Alcohol Abuse and Alcoholism
    "Volume Beverage and Ethanol Consumption for States" (http://www.niaaa.nih.gov/Resources/)
*This is apparent consumption and is based on several sources which together approximate sales but do not actually measure consumption. Reported state volumes reflect only in-state purchases. Accordingly, figures for some states may be skewed by purchases by nonresidents.

Adult Per Capita Beer Consumption in 2007

National Per Capita = 30.5 Gallons Consumed per Adult 21 Years and Older*

ALPHA ORDER

RANK ORDER

RANK	STATE	PER CAPITA	RANK	STATE	PER CAPITA
27	Alabama	31.4	1	New Hampshire	43.8
18	Alaska	33.9	2	Nevada	42.6
17	Arizona	34.3	3	North Dakota	40.1
43	Arkansas	27.0	4	Louisiana	40.0
42	California	27.4	4	Montana	40.0
23	Colorado	32.3	6	Wisconsin	38.9
47	Connecticut	23.4	7	South Dakota	38.5
15	Delaware	35.1	8	Wyoming	37.7
23	Florida	32.3	9	Mississippi	37.4
33	Georgia	29.5	10	Nebraska	36.9
22	Hawaii	33.3	11	South Carolina	36.2
30	Idaho	30.0	12	Texas	36.1
28	Illinois	31.1	13	New Mexico	36.0
36	Indiana	28.8	14	Iowa	35.5
14	Iowa	35.5	15	Delaware	35.1
32	Kansas	29.7	16	Vermont	34.7
44	Kentucky	26.2	17	Arizona	34.3
4	Louisiana	40.0	18	Alaska	33.9
26	Maine	31.7	19	Pennsylvania	33.7
45	Maryland	25.7	20	Ohio	33.6
46	Massachusetts	25.6	21	Missouri	33.5
40	Michigan	28.2	22	Hawaii	33.3
34	Minnesota	29.3	23	Colorado	32.3
9	Mississippi	37.4	23	Florida	32.3
21	Missouri	33.5	23	Oregon	32.3
4	Montana	40.0	26	Maine	31.7
10	Nebraska	36.9	27	Alabama	31.4
2	Nevada	42.6	28	Illinois	31.1
1	New Hampshire	43.8	29	West Virginia	30.8
48	New Jersey	23.3	30	Idaho	30.0
13	New Mexico	36.0	31	Oklahoma	29.8
49	New York	23.2	32	Kansas	29.7
34	North Carolina	29.3	33	Georgia	29.5
3	North Dakota	40.1	34	Minnesota	29.3
20	Ohio	33.6	34	North Carolina	29.3
31	Oklahoma	29.8	36	Indiana	28.8
23	Oregon	32.3	37	Rhode Island	28.7
19	Pennsylvania	33.7	38	Virginia	28.6
37	Rhode Island	28.7	39	Tennessee	28.4
11	South Carolina	36.2	40	Michigan	28.2
7	South Dakota	38.5	41	Washington	27.9
39	Tennessee	28.4	42	California	27.4
12	Texas	36.1	43	Arkansas	27.0
50	Utah	19.6	44	Kentucky	26.2
16	Vermont	34.7	45	Maryland	25.7
38	Virginia	28.6	46	Massachusetts	25.6
41	Washington	27.9	47	Connecticut	23.4
29	West Virginia	30.8	48	New Jersey	23.3
6	Wisconsin	38.9	49	New York	23.2
8	Wyoming	37.7	50	Utah	19.6

District of Columbia 33.9

Source: CQ Press using data from U.S. Dept of Health and Human Services, National Institute on Alcohol Abuse and Alcoholism
"Volume Beverage and Ethanol Consumption for States" (http://www.niaaa.nih.gov/Resources/)
*This is apparent consumption and is based on several sources which together approximate sales but do not actually measure consumption. Reported state volumes reflect only in-state purchases. Accordingly, figures for some states may be skewed by purchases by nonresidents.

Wine Consumption in 2007

National Total = 711,788,000 Gallons of Wine Consumed*

ALPHA ORDER

RANK	STATE	GALLONS	% of USA
29	Alabama	6,381,000	0.9%
46	Alaska	1,874,000	0.3%
16	Arizona	13,032,000	1.8%
39	Arkansas	3,008,000	0.4%
1	California	125,250,000	17.6%
15	Colorado	14,120,000	2.0%
17	Connecticut	12,827,000	1.8%
37	Delaware	3,250,000	0.5%
3	Florida	57,313,000	8.1%
14	Georgia	14,995,000	2.1%
32	Hawaii	4,008,000	0.6%
28	Idaho	6,735,000	0.9%
5	Illinois	32,742,000	4.6%
24	Indiana	9,699,000	1.4%
38	Iowa	3,220,000	0.5%
40	Kansas	2,560,000	0.4%
31	Kentucky	4,679,000	0.7%
26	Louisiana	7,531,000	1.1%
36	Maine	3,668,000	0.5%
18	Maryland	12,738,000	1.8%
7	Massachusetts	25,546,000	3.6%
11	Michigan	19,018,000	2.7%
22	Minnesota	10,520,000	1.5%
44	Mississippi	2,171,000	0.3%
21	Missouri	11,017,000	1.5%
45	Montana	2,165,000	0.3%
43	Nebraska	2,272,000	0.3%
23	Nevada	10,061,000	1.4%
30	New Hampshire	6,252,000	0.9%
6	New Jersey	30,240,000	4.2%
34	New Mexico	3,784,000	0.5%
2	New York	57,880,000	8.1%
13	North Carolina	15,636,000	2.2%
49	North Dakota	959,000	0.1%
12	Ohio	18,121,000	2.5%
33	Oklahoma	3,936,000	0.6%
19	Oregon	11,794,000	1.7%
10	Pennsylvania	19,176,000	2.7%
35	Rhode Island	3,669,000	0.5%
27	South Carolina	6,825,000	1.0%
48	South Dakota	1,092,000	0.2%
25	Tennessee	7,784,000	1.1%
4	Texas	39,223,000	5.5%
41	Utah	2,490,000	0.3%
42	Vermont	2,462,000	0.3%
9	Virginia	20,053,000	2.8%
8	Washington	20,435,000	2.9%
47	West Virginia	1,215,000	0.2%
20	Wisconsin	11,758,000	1.7%
50	Wyoming	766,000	0.1%

RANK ORDER

RANK	STATE	GALLONS	% of USA
1	California	125,250,000	17.6%
2	New York	57,880,000	8.1%
3	Florida	57,313,000	8.1%
4	Texas	39,223,000	5.5%
5	Illinois	32,742,000	4.6%
6	New Jersey	30,240,000	4.2%
7	Massachusetts	25,546,000	3.6%
8	Washington	20,435,000	2.9%
9	Virginia	20,053,000	2.8%
10	Pennsylvania	19,176,000	2.7%
11	Michigan	19,018,000	2.7%
12	Ohio	18,121,000	2.5%
13	North Carolina	15,636,000	2.2%
14	Georgia	14,995,000	2.1%
15	Colorado	14,120,000	2.0%
16	Arizona	13,032,000	1.8%
17	Connecticut	12,827,000	1.8%
18	Maryland	12,738,000	1.8%
19	Oregon	11,794,000	1.7%
20	Wisconsin	11,758,000	1.7%
21	Missouri	11,017,000	1.5%
22	Minnesota	10,520,000	1.5%
23	Nevada	10,061,000	1.4%
24	Indiana	9,699,000	1.4%
25	Tennessee	7,784,000	1.1%
26	Louisiana	7,531,000	1.1%
27	South Carolina	6,825,000	1.0%
28	Idaho	6,735,000	0.9%
29	Alabama	6,381,000	0.9%
30	New Hampshire	6,252,000	0.9%
31	Kentucky	4,679,000	0.7%
32	Hawaii	4,008,000	0.6%
33	Oklahoma	3,936,000	0.6%
34	New Mexico	3,784,000	0.5%
35	Rhode Island	3,669,000	0.5%
36	Maine	3,668,000	0.5%
37	Delaware	3,250,000	0.5%
38	Iowa	3,220,000	0.5%
39	Arkansas	3,008,000	0.4%
40	Kansas	2,560,000	0.4%
41	Utah	2,490,000	0.3%
42	Vermont	2,462,000	0.3%
43	Nebraska	2,272,000	0.3%
44	Mississippi	2,171,000	0.3%
45	Montana	2,165,000	0.3%
46	Alaska	1,874,000	0.3%
47	West Virginia	1,215,000	0.2%
48	South Dakota	1,092,000	0.2%
49	North Dakota	959,000	0.1%
50	Wyoming	766,000	0.1%
	District of Columbia	3,836,000	0.5%

Source: U.S. Department of Health and Human Services, National Institute on Alcohol Abuse and Alcoholism
"Volume Beverage and Ethanol Consumption for States" (http://www.niaaa.nih.gov/Resources/)
*This is apparent consumption and is based on several sources which together approximate sales but do not actually measure consumption. Reported state volumes reflect only in-state purchases. Accordingly, figures for some states may be skewed by purchases by nonresidents.

Adult Per Capita Wine Consumption in 2007

National Per Capita = 3.3 Gallons Consumed per Adult 21 Years and Older*

ALPHA ORDER

RANK	STATE	PER CAPITA
39	Alabama	1.9
17	Alaska	4.0
23	Arizona	2.9
43	Arkansas	1.5
8	California	4.9
15	Colorado	4.1
7	Connecticut	5.1
6	Delaware	5.2
14	Florida	4.2
32	Georgia	2.3
12	Hawaii	4.3
1	Idaho	6.6
19	Illinois	3.6
33	Indiana	2.2
43	Iowa	1.5
48	Kansas	1.3
43	Kentucky	1.5
29	Louisiana	2.5
18	Maine	3.7
21	Maryland	3.2
4	Massachusetts	5.4
27	Michigan	2.6
25	Minnesota	2.8
49	Mississippi	1.1
27	Missouri	2.6
22	Montana	3.1
41	Nebraska	1.8
3	Nevada	5.5
2	New Hampshire	6.5
9	New Jersey	4.8
26	New Mexico	2.7
15	New York	4.1
30	North Carolina	2.4
36	North Dakota	2.1
33	Ohio	2.2
43	Oklahoma	1.5
12	Oregon	4.3
36	Pennsylvania	2.1
9	Rhode Island	4.8
33	South Carolina	2.2
39	South Dakota	1.9
42	Tennessee	1.7
30	Texas	2.4
47	Utah	1.4
5	Vermont	5.3
19	Virginia	3.6
11	Washington	4.4
50	West Virginia	0.9
23	Wisconsin	2.9
38	Wyoming	2.0

RANK ORDER

RANK	STATE	PER CAPITA
1	Idaho	6.6
2	New Hampshire	6.5
3	Nevada	5.5
4	Massachusetts	5.4
5	Vermont	5.3
6	Delaware	5.2
7	Connecticut	5.1
8	California	4.9
9	New Jersey	4.8
9	Rhode Island	4.8
11	Washington	4.4
12	Hawaii	4.3
12	Oregon	4.3
14	Florida	4.2
15	Colorado	4.1
15	New York	4.1
17	Alaska	4.0
18	Maine	3.7
19	Illinois	3.6
19	Virginia	3.6
21	Maryland	3.2
22	Montana	3.1
23	Arizona	2.9
23	Wisconsin	2.9
25	Minnesota	2.8
26	New Mexico	2.7
27	Michigan	2.6
27	Missouri	2.6
29	Louisiana	2.5
30	North Carolina	2.4
30	Texas	2.4
32	Georgia	2.3
33	Indiana	2.2
33	Ohio	2.2
33	South Carolina	2.2
36	North Dakota	2.1
36	Pennsylvania	2.1
38	Wyoming	2.0
39	Alabama	1.9
39	South Dakota	1.9
41	Nebraska	1.8
42	Tennessee	1.7
43	Arkansas	1.5
43	Iowa	1.5
43	Kentucky	1.5
43	Oklahoma	1.5
47	Utah	1.4
48	Kansas	1.3
49	Mississippi	1.1
50	West Virginia	0.9

District of Columbia 8.6

Source: CQ Press using data from U.S. Dept of Health and Human Services, National Institute on Alcohol Abuse and Alcoholism "Volume Beverage and Ethanol Consumption for States" (http://www.niaaa.nih.gov/Resources/)

*This is apparent consumption and is based on several sources which together approximate sales but do not actually measure consumption. Reported state volumes reflect only in-state purchases. Accordingly, figures for some states may be skewed by purchases by nonresidents.

Distilled Spirits Consumption in 2007

National Total = 432,629,000 Gallons of Distilled Spirits Consumed*

ALPHA ORDER					RANK ORDER			
RANK	STATE	GALLONS	% of USA		RANK	STATE	GALLONS	% of USA
29	Alabama	5,117,000	1.2%		1	California	51,001,000	11.8%
46	Alaska	1,415,000	0.3%		2	Florida	34,186,000	7.9%
18	Arizona	9,341,000	2.2%		3	New York	26,594,000	6.1%
35	Arkansas	3,320,000	0.8%		4	Texas	25,595,000	5.9%
1	California	51,001,000	11.8%		5	Illinois	18,455,000	4.3%
15	Colorado	9,535,000	2.2%		6	Michigan	15,532,000	3.6%
27	Connecticut	5,909,000	1.4%		7	Pennsylvania	14,784,000	3.4%
39	Delaware	2,135,000	0.5%		8	New Jersey	14,754,000	3.4%
2	Florida	34,186,000	7.9%		9	Wisconsin	12,405,000	2.9%
10	Georgia	11,784,000	2.7%		10	Georgia	11,784,000	2.7%
41	Hawaii	2,046,000	0.5%		11	Massachusetts	11,210,000	2.6%
42	Idaho	1,935,000	0.4%		12	Ohio	10,249,000	2.4%
5	Illinois	18,455,000	4.3%		13	North Carolina	10,052,000	2.3%
20	Indiana	8,975,000	2.1%		14	Minnesota	9,999,000	2.3%
32	Iowa	3,992,000	0.9%		15	Colorado	9,535,000	2.2%
34	Kansas	3,500,000	0.8%		16	Washington	9,488,000	2.2%
28	Kentucky	5,318,000	1.2%		17	Maryland	9,418,000	2.2%
22	Louisiana	6,959,000	1.6%		18	Arizona	9,341,000	2.2%
38	Maine	2,149,000	0.5%		19	Missouri	9,118,000	2.1%
17	Maryland	9,418,000	2.2%		20	Indiana	8,975,000	2.1%
11	Massachusetts	11,210,000	2.6%		21	Virginia	8,897,000	2.1%
6	Michigan	15,532,000	3.6%		22	Louisiana	6,959,000	1.6%
14	Minnesota	9,999,000	2.3%		23	Tennessee	6,814,000	1.6%
33	Mississippi	3,876,000	0.9%		24	South Carolina	6,711,000	1.6%
19	Missouri	9,118,000	2.1%		25	Nevada	6,280,000	1.5%
44	Montana	1,652,000	0.4%		26	Oregon	6,045,000	1.4%
37	Nebraska	2,339,000	0.5%		27	Connecticut	5,909,000	1.4%
25	Nevada	6,280,000	1.5%		28	Kentucky	5,318,000	1.2%
30	New Hampshire	4,631,000	1.1%		29	Alabama	5,117,000	1.2%
8	New Jersey	14,754,000	3.4%		30	New Hampshire	4,631,000	1.1%
36	New Mexico	2,714,000	0.6%		31	Oklahoma	4,080,000	0.9%
3	New York	26,594,000	6.1%		32	Iowa	3,992,000	0.9%
13	North Carolina	10,052,000	2.3%		33	Mississippi	3,876,000	0.9%
47	North Dakota	1,394,000	0.3%		34	Kansas	3,500,000	0.8%
12	Ohio	10,249,000	2.4%		35	Arkansas	3,320,000	0.8%
31	Oklahoma	4,080,000	0.9%		36	New Mexico	2,714,000	0.6%
26	Oregon	6,045,000	1.4%		37	Nebraska	2,339,000	0.5%
7	Pennsylvania	14,784,000	3.4%		38	Maine	2,149,000	0.5%
43	Rhode Island	1,916,000	0.4%		39	Delaware	2,135,000	0.5%
24	South Carolina	6,711,000	1.6%		40	Utah	2,097,000	0.5%
48	South Dakota	1,346,000	0.3%		41	Hawaii	2,046,000	0.5%
23	Tennessee	6,814,000	1.6%		42	Idaho	1,935,000	0.4%
4	Texas	25,595,000	5.9%		43	Rhode Island	1,916,000	0.4%
40	Utah	2,097,000	0.5%		44	Montana	1,652,000	0.4%
50	Vermont	891,000	0.2%		45	West Virginia	1,566,000	0.4%
21	Virginia	8,897,000	2.1%		46	Alaska	1,415,000	0.3%
16	Washington	9,488,000	2.2%		47	North Dakota	1,394,000	0.3%
45	West Virginia	1,566,000	0.4%		48	South Dakota	1,346,000	0.3%
9	Wisconsin	12,405,000	2.9%		49	Wyoming	1,142,000	0.3%
49	Wyoming	1,142,000	0.3%		50	Vermont	891,000	0.2%
						District of Columbia	1,967,000	0.5%

Source: U.S. Department of Health and Human Services, National Institute on Alcohol Abuse and Alcoholism
"Volume Beverage and Ethanol Consumption for States" (http://www.niaaa.nih.gov/Resources/)
*This is apparent consumption and is based on several sources which together approximate sales but do not actually measure consumption. Reported state volumes reflect only in-state purchases. Accordingly, figures for some states may be skewed by purchases by nonresidents.

Adult Per Capita Distilled Spirits Consumption in 2007

National Per Capita = 2.0 Gallons Consumed per Adult 21 Years and Older*

ALPHA ORDER				RANK ORDER		
RANK	STATE	PER CAPITA		RANK	STATE	PER CAPITA
46	Alabama	1.5		1	New Hampshire	4.8
5	Alaska	3.0		2	Nevada	3.5
24	Arizona	2.1		3	Delaware	3.4
40	Arkansas	1.6		4	Wisconsin	3.1
26	California	2.0		5	Alaska	3.0
8	Colorado	2.7		5	North Dakota	3.0
16	Connecticut	2.3		5	Wyoming	3.0
3	Delaware	3.4		8	Colorado	2.7
10	Florida	2.5		8	Minnesota	2.7
37	Georgia	1.8		10	Florida	2.5
19	Hawaii	2.2		10	Rhode Island	2.5
31	Idaho	1.9		12	Massachusetts	2.4
26	Illinois	2.0		12	Montana	2.4
26	Indiana	2.0		12	New Jersey	2.4
31	Iowa	1.9		12	South Dakota	2.4
37	Kansas	1.8		16	Connecticut	2.3
39	Kentucky	1.7		16	Louisiana	2.3
16	Louisiana	2.3		16	Maryland	2.3
19	Maine	2.2		19	Hawaii	2.2
16	Maryland	2.3		19	Maine	2.2
12	Massachusetts	2.4		19	Michigan	2.2
19	Michigan	2.2		19	Missouri	2.2
8	Minnesota	2.7		19	Oregon	2.2
31	Mississippi	1.9		24	Arizona	2.1
19	Missouri	2.2		24	South Carolina	2.1
12	Montana	2.4		26	California	2.0
31	Nebraska	1.9		26	Illinois	2.0
2	Nevada	3.5		26	Indiana	2.0
1	New Hampshire	4.8		26	New Mexico	2.0
12	New Jersey	2.4		26	Washington	2.0
26	New Mexico	2.0		31	Idaho	1.9
31	New York	1.9		31	Iowa	1.9
40	North Carolina	1.6		31	Mississippi	1.9
5	North Dakota	3.0		31	Nebraska	1.9
48	Ohio	1.2		31	New York	1.9
40	Oklahoma	1.6		31	Vermont	1.9
19	Oregon	2.2		37	Georgia	1.8
40	Pennsylvania	1.6		37	Kansas	1.8
10	Rhode Island	2.5		39	Kentucky	1.7
24	South Carolina	2.1		40	Arkansas	1.6
12	South Dakota	2.4		40	North Carolina	1.6
46	Tennessee	1.5		40	Oklahoma	1.6
40	Texas	1.6		40	Pennsylvania	1.6
48	Utah	1.2		40	Texas	1.6
31	Vermont	1.9		40	Virginia	1.6
40	Virginia	1.6		46	Alabama	1.5
26	Washington	2.0		46	Tennessee	1.5
48	West Virginia	1.2		48	Ohio	1.2
4	Wisconsin	3.1		48	Utah	1.2
5	Wyoming	3.0		48	West Virginia	1.2
					District of Columbia	4.4

Source: CQ Press using data from U.S. Dept of Health and Human Services, National Institute on Alcohol Abuse and Alcoholism
"Volume Beverage and Ethanol Consumption for States" (http://www.niaaa.nih.gov/Resources/)
*This is apparent consumption and is based on several sources which together approximate sales but do not actually measure consumption. Reported state volumes reflect only in-state purchases. Accordingly, figures for some states may be skewed by purchases by nonresidents.

Percent of Adults Who Do Not Drink Alcohol: 2008

National Median = 45.5% of Adults*

ALPHA ORDER

RANK	STATE	PERCENT
5	Alabama	61.8
22	Alaska	46.8
28	Arizona	45.3
7	Arkansas	58.6
21	California	47.6
43	Colorado	38.5
49	Connecticut	34.3
34	Delaware	42.8
19	Florida	48.7
12	Georgia	53.2
16	Hawaii	50.8
13	Idaho	53.1
36	Illinois	42.2
18	Indiana	48.8
38	Iowa	42.0
17	Kansas	50.2
6	Kentucky	61.4
11	Louisiana	53.5
42	Maine	41.1
30	Maryland	43.8
46	Massachusetts	36.4
33	Michigan	43.0
45	Minnesota	36.7
4	Mississippi	62.3
20	Missouri	48.0
39	Montana	41.7
35	Nebraska	42.6
32	Nevada	43.1
47	New Hampshire	35.7
26	New Jersey	45.5
14	New Mexico	52.9
29	New York	44.4
10	North Carolina	55.7
36	North Dakota	42.2
24	Ohio	46.4
8	Oklahoma	58.5
31	Oregon	43.7
27	Pennsylvania	45.4
44	Rhode Island	37.3
9	South Carolina	56.8
39	South Dakota	41.7
3	Tennessee	66.4
15	Texas	51.5
1	Utah	74.6
48	Vermont	35.1
23	Virginia	46.6
41	Washington	41.4
2	West Virginia	69.0
50	Wisconsin	33.4
25	Wyoming	45.9

RANK ORDER

RANK	STATE	PERCENT
1	Utah	74.6
2	West Virginia	69.0
3	Tennessee	66.4
4	Mississippi	62.3
5	Alabama	61.8
6	Kentucky	61.4
7	Arkansas	58.6
8	Oklahoma	58.5
9	South Carolina	56.8
10	North Carolina	55.7
11	Louisiana	53.5
12	Georgia	53.2
13	Idaho	53.1
14	New Mexico	52.9
15	Texas	51.5
16	Hawaii	50.8
17	Kansas	50.2
18	Indiana	48.8
19	Florida	48.7
20	Missouri	48.0
21	California	47.6
22	Alaska	46.8
23	Virginia	46.6
24	Ohio	46.4
25	Wyoming	45.9
26	New Jersey	45.5
27	Pennsylvania	45.4
28	Arizona	45.3
29	New York	44.4
30	Maryland	43.8
31	Oregon	43.7
32	Nevada	43.1
33	Michigan	43.0
34	Delaware	42.8
35	Nebraska	42.6
36	Illinois	42.2
36	North Dakota	42.2
38	Iowa	42.0
39	Montana	41.7
39	South Dakota	41.7
41	Washington	41.4
42	Maine	41.1
43	Colorado	38.5
44	Rhode Island	37.3
45	Minnesota	36.7
46	Massachusetts	36.4
47	New Hampshire	35.7
48	Vermont	35.1
49	Connecticut	34.3
50	Wisconsin	33.4

	District of Columbia	38.7

Source: U.S. Department of Health and Human Services, Centers for Disease Control and Prevention
"2008 Behavioral Risk Factor Surveillance Summary Prevalence Data" (http://apps.nccd.cdc.gov/brfss/)
*Persons 18 and older reporting not having at least one drink of alcohol in the past 30 days.

Percent of Adults Who Are Binge Drinkers: 2008

National Median = 15.6% of Adults*

RANK	STATE	PERCENT		RANK	STATE	PERCENT
44	Alabama	12.0		1	Wisconsin	22.8
21	Alaska	15.9		2	North Dakota	21.6
24	Arizona	15.6		3	Iowa	20.2
41	Arkansas	12.6		4	Minnesota	19.8
24	California	15.6		5	Illinois	19.4
20	Colorado	16.0		6	Nebraska	19.1
17	Connecticut	16.6		7	Nevada	18.8
8	Delaware	17.9		8	Delaware	17.9
38	Florida	13.0		9	South Dakota	17.8
31	Georgia	14.0		10	Massachusetts	17.7
13	Hawaii	17.6		10	Michigan	17.7
37	Idaho	13.1		10	Montana	17.7
5	Illinois	19.4		13	Hawaii	17.6
19	Indiana	16.1		14	Rhode Island	17.5
3	Iowa	20.2		15	Vermont	17.4
33	Kansas	13.8		16	Pennsylvania	16.7
46	Kentucky	11.3		17	Connecticut	16.6
36	Louisiana	13.5		18	New Hampshire	16.5
22	Maine	15.8		19	Indiana	16.1
33	Maryland	13.8		20	Colorado	16.0
10	Massachusetts	17.7		21	Alaska	15.9
10	Michigan	17.7		22	Maine	15.8
4	Minnesota	19.8		22	Ohio	15.8
47	Mississippi	10.8		24	Arizona	15.6
27	Missouri	15.3		24	California	15.6
10	Montana	17.7		26	Wyoming	15.4
6	Nebraska	19.1		27	Missouri	15.3
7	Nevada	18.8		28	Washington	15.1
18	New Hampshire	16.5		29	New York	14.7
31	New Jersey	14.0		29	Texas	14.7
45	New Mexico	11.4		31	Georgia	14.0
29	New York	14.7		31	New Jersey	14.0
39	North Carolina	12.9		33	Kansas	13.8
2	North Dakota	21.6		33	Maryland	13.8
22	Ohio	15.8		35	Virginia	13.7
43	Oklahoma	12.2		36	Louisiana	13.5
40	Oregon	12.8		37	Idaho	13.1
16	Pennsylvania	16.7		38	Florida	13.0
14	Rhode Island	17.5		39	North Carolina	12.9
42	South Carolina	12.3		40	Oregon	12.8
9	South Dakota	17.8		41	Arkansas	12.6
48	Tennessee	10.5		42	South Carolina	12.3
29	Texas	14.7		43	Oklahoma	12.2
50	Utah	8.2		44	Alabama	12.0
15	Vermont	17.4		45	New Mexico	11.4
35	Virginia	13.7		46	Kentucky	11.3
28	Washington	15.1		47	Mississippi	10.8
49	West Virginia	8.8		48	Tennessee	10.5
1	Wisconsin	22.8		49	West Virginia	8.8
26	Wyoming	15.4		50	Utah	8.2

ALPHA ORDER

RANK ORDER

District of Columbia   17.9

Source: U.S. Department of Health and Human Services, Centers for Disease Control and Prevention
    "2008 Behavioral Risk Factor Surveillance Summary Prevalence Data" (http://apps.nccd.cdc.gov/brfss/)
*Persons 18 and older reporting consumption of five or more alcoholic drinks on one or more occasions during the previous month.

Percent of Adults Who Smoke: 2008

National Median = 18.4% of Adults*

ALPHA ORDER				RANK ORDER		
RANK	STATE	PERCENT		RANK	STATE	PERCENT
10	Alabama	22.1		1	West Virginia	26.5
11	Alaska	21.5		2	Indiana	26.0
43	Arizona	15.9		3	Kentucky	25.2
8	Arkansas	22.3		4	Missouri	25.0
49	California	14.0		5	Oklahoma	24.7
31	Colorado	17.6		6	Tennessee	23.1
43	Connecticut	15.9		7	Mississippi	22.7
30	Delaware	17.8		8	Arkansas	22.3
33	Florida	17.5		9	Nevada	22.2
20	Georgia	19.5		10	Alabama	22.1
46	Hawaii	15.4		11	Alaska	21.5
37	Idaho	16.9		12	Illinois	21.3
12	Illinois	21.3		12	Pennsylvania	21.3
2	Indiana	26.0		14	North Carolina	20.9
23	Iowa	18.8		15	Louisiana	20.5
29	Kansas	17.9		15	Michigan	20.5
3	Kentucky	25.2		17	Ohio	20.1
15	Louisiana	20.5		18	South Carolina	20.0
27	Maine	18.2		19	Wisconsin	19.9
47	Maryland	14.9		20	Georgia	19.5
42	Massachusetts	16.1		21	New Mexico	19.4
15	Michigan	20.5		21	Wyoming	19.4
31	Minnesota	17.6		23	Iowa	18.8
7	Mississippi	22.7		24	Montana	18.5
4	Missouri	25.0		24	Texas	18.5
24	Montana	18.5		26	Nebraska	18.4
26	Nebraska	18.4		27	Maine	18.2
9	Nevada	22.2		28	North Dakota	18.1
36	New Hampshire	17.1		29	Kansas	17.9
48	New Jersey	14.8		30	Delaware	17.8
21	New Mexico	19.4		31	Colorado	17.6
38	New York	16.8		31	Minnesota	17.6
14	North Carolina	20.9		33	Florida	17.5
28	North Dakota	18.1		33	South Dakota	17.5
17	Ohio	20.1		35	Rhode Island	17.4
5	Oklahoma	24.7		36	New Hampshire	17.1
41	Oregon	16.3		37	Idaho	16.9
12	Pennsylvania	21.3		38	New York	16.8
35	Rhode Island	17.4		38	Vermont	16.8
18	South Carolina	20.0		40	Virginia	16.4
33	South Dakota	17.5		41	Oregon	16.3
6	Tennessee	23.1		42	Massachusetts	16.1
24	Texas	18.5		43	Arizona	15.9
50	Utah	9.3		43	Connecticut	15.9
38	Vermont	16.8		45	Washington	15.7
40	Virginia	16.4		46	Hawaii	15.4
45	Washington	15.7		47	Maryland	14.9
1	West Virginia	26.5		48	New Jersey	14.8
19	Wisconsin	19.9		49	California	14.0
21	Wyoming	19.4		50	Utah	9.3

District of Columbia   16.2

Source: U.S. Department of Health and Human Services, Centers for Disease Control and Prevention
"2008 Behavioral Risk Factor Surveillance Summary Prevalence Data" (http://apps.nccd.cdc.gov/brfss/)
*Persons 18 and older who have smoked more than 100 cigarettes during their lifetime and who currently smoke every day or some days.

Percent of Men Who Smoke: 2008

National Median = 20.3% of Men*

ALPHA ORDER				RANK ORDER		
RANK	STATE	PERCENT		RANK	STATE	PERCENT
9	Alabama	25.2		1	Indiana	28.3
12	Alaska	23.7		2	Missouri	27.3
39	Arizona	18.1		3	Tennessee	26.6
10	Arkansas	24.3		4	Oklahoma	26.5
42	California	17.8		5	Kentucky	26.3
31	Colorado	19.7		6	West Virginia	26.0
45	Connecticut	17.3		7	Illinois	25.4
27	Delaware	20.3		7	Mississippi	25.4
34	Florida	18.8		9	Alabama	25.2
19	Georgia	21.8		10	Arkansas	24.3
38	Hawaii	18.2		10	Nevada	24.3
37	Idaho	18.3		12	Alaska	23.7
7	Illinois	25.4		12	North Carolina	23.7
1	Indiana	28.3		14	Louisiana	23.5
25	Iowa	20.9		15	Pennsylvania	23.4
30	Kansas	19.8		16	Michigan	22.6
5	Kentucky	26.3		17	Texas	22.3
14	Louisiana	23.5		18	New Mexico	22.0
20	Maine	21.6		19	Georgia	21.8
49	Maryland	16.1		20	Maine	21.6
48	Massachusetts	16.9		20	Wisconsin	21.6
16	Michigan	22.6		22	South Carolina	21.5
32	Minnesota	19.3		23	Ohio	21.4
7	Mississippi	25.4		23	Oregon	21.4
2	Missouri	27.3		25	Iowa	20.9
35	Montana	18.7		26	North Dakota	20.4
28	Nebraska	20.1		27	Delaware	20.3
10	Nevada	24.3		28	Nebraska	20.1
39	New Hampshire	18.1		29	Wyoming	19.9
44	New Jersey	17.4		30	Kansas	19.8
18	New Mexico	22.0		31	Colorado	19.7
42	New York	17.8		32	Minnesota	19.3
12	North Carolina	23.7		33	South Dakota	18.9
26	North Dakota	20.4		34	Florida	18.8
23	Ohio	21.4		35	Montana	18.7
4	Oklahoma	26.5		36	Vermont	18.4
23	Oregon	21.4		37	Idaho	18.3
15	Pennsylvania	23.4		38	Hawaii	18.2
41	Rhode Island	18.0		39	Arizona	18.1
22	South Carolina	21.5		39	New Hampshire	18.1
33	South Dakota	18.9		41	Rhode Island	18.0
3	Tennessee	26.6		42	California	17.8
17	Texas	22.3		42	New York	17.8
50	Utah	10.6		44	New Jersey	17.4
36	Vermont	18.4		45	Connecticut	17.3
46	Virginia	17.1		46	Virginia	17.1
47	Washington	17.0		47	Washington	17.0
6	West Virginia	26.0		48	Massachusetts	16.9
20	Wisconsin	21.6		49	Maryland	16.1
29	Wyoming	19.9		50	Utah	10.6
					District of Columbia	19.2

Source: U.S. Department of Health and Human Services, Centers for Disease Control and Prevention
  "2008 Behavioral Risk Factor Surveillance Summary Prevalence Data" (http://apps.nccd.cdc.gov/brfss/)
*Males 18 and older who have smoked more than 100 cigarettes during their lifetime and who currently smoke every day or some days.

Percent of Women Who Smoke: 2008

National Median = 16.7% of Women*

ALPHA ORDER

RANK	STATE	PERCENT
11	Alabama	19.3
12	Alaska	19.2
45	Arizona	13.8
6	Arkansas	20.4
49	California	10.3
36	Colorado	15.5
43	Connecticut	14.7
37	Delaware	15.4
28	Florida	16.4
23	Georgia	17.4
47	Hawaii	12.7
37	Idaho	15.4
22	Illinois	17.5
3	Indiana	23.9
26	Iowa	16.7
30	Kansas	16.1
2	Kentucky	24.2
21	Louisiana	17.7
41	Maine	15.0
45	Maryland	13.8
37	Massachusetts	15.4
17	Michigan	18.4
32	Minnesota	15.8
7	Mississippi	20.3
5	Missouri	22.8
17	Montana	18.4
26	Nebraska	16.7
8	Nevada	20.0
31	New Hampshire	16.0
48	New Jersey	12.3
24	New Mexico	16.8
32	New York	15.8
19	North Carolina	18.3
32	North Dakota	15.8
13	Ohio	19.0
4	Oklahoma	23.1
13	Oregon	19.0
10	Pennsylvania	19.4
24	Rhode Island	16.8
16	South Carolina	18.6
29	South Dakota	16.2
9	Tennessee	19.9
42	Texas	14.8
50	Utah	8.0
40	Vermont	15.3
32	Virginia	15.8
44	Washington	14.4
1	West Virginia	27.0
20	Wisconsin	18.2
15	Wyoming	18.8

RANK ORDER

RANK	STATE	PERCENT
1	West Virginia	27.0
2	Kentucky	24.2
3	Indiana	23.9
4	Oklahoma	23.1
5	Missouri	22.8
6	Arkansas	20.4
7	Mississippi	20.3
8	Nevada	20.0
9	Tennessee	19.9
10	Pennsylvania	19.4
11	Alabama	19.3
12	Alaska	19.2
13	Ohio	19.0
13	Oregon	19.0
15	Wyoming	18.8
16	South Carolina	18.6
17	Michigan	18.4
17	Montana	18.4
19	North Carolina	18.3
20	Wisconsin	18.2
21	Louisiana	17.7
22	Illinois	17.5
23	Georgia	17.4
24	New Mexico	16.8
24	Rhode Island	16.8
26	Iowa	16.7
26	Nebraska	16.7
28	Florida	16.4
29	South Dakota	16.2
30	Kansas	16.1
31	New Hampshire	16.0
32	Minnesota	15.8
32	New York	15.8
32	North Dakota	15.8
32	Virginia	15.8
36	Colorado	15.5
37	Delaware	15.4
37	Idaho	15.4
37	Massachusetts	15.4
40	Vermont	15.3
41	Maine	15.0
42	Texas	14.8
43	Connecticut	14.7
44	Washington	14.4
45	Arizona	13.8
45	Maryland	13.8
47	Hawaii	12.7
48	New Jersey	12.3
49	California	10.3
50	Utah	8.0

	District of Columbia	13.7

Source: U.S. Department of Health and Human Services, Centers for Disease Control and Prevention
  "2008 Behavioral Risk Factor Surveillance Summary Prevalence Data" (http://apps.nccd.cdc.gov/brfss/)
*Females 18 and older who have smoked more than 100 cigarettes during their lifetime and who currently smoke every day or some days.

Percent of Adults Who Are Former Smokers: 2008

National Median = 25.2% of Adults*

ALPHA ORDER				RANK ORDER		
RANK	STATE	PERCENT		RANK	STATE	PERCENT
44	Alabama	21.9		1	Vermont	32.2
6	Alaska	28.4		2	Maine	31.7
9	Arizona	27.4		3	New Hampshire	31.1
14	Arkansas	26.3		4	Connecticut	30.1
40	California	23.3		5	Delaware	28.5
30	Colorado	24.9		6	Alaska	28.4
4	Connecticut	30.1		7	Massachusetts	28.1
5	Delaware	28.5		7	Rhode Island	28.1
15	Florida	26.1		9	Arizona	27.4
48	Georgia	21.4		10	Minnesota	27.1
18	Hawaii	25.4		11	Montana	26.8
44	Idaho	21.9		12	Washington	26.7
39	Illinois	23.4		12	Wisconsin	26.7
42	Indiana	23.0		14	Arkansas	26.3
33	Iowa	24.7		15	Florida	26.1
41	Kansas	23.2		15	South Dakota	26.1
24	Kentucky	25.3		17	Michigan	25.5
49	Louisiana	19.9		18	Hawaii	25.4
2	Maine	31.7		18	New York	25.4
37	Maryland	24.2		18	North Dakota	25.4
7	Massachusetts	28.1		18	Ohio	25.4
17	Michigan	25.5		18	West Virginia	25.4
10	Minnesota	27.1		18	Wyoming	25.4
43	Mississippi	22.2		24	Kentucky	25.3
28	Missouri	25.0		24	Pennsylvania	25.3
11	Montana	26.8		26	South Carolina	25.2
28	Nebraska	25.0		27	Nevada	25.1
27	Nevada	25.1		28	Missouri	25.0
3	New Hampshire	31.1		28	Nebraska	25.0
36	New Jersey	24.3		30	Colorado	24.9
30	New Mexico	24.9		30	New Mexico	24.9
18	New York	25.4		32	North Carolina	24.8
32	North Carolina	24.8		33	Iowa	24.7
18	North Dakota	25.4		33	Oklahoma	24.7
18	Ohio	25.4		33	Oregon	24.7
33	Oklahoma	24.7		36	New Jersey	24.3
33	Oregon	24.7		37	Maryland	24.2
24	Pennsylvania	25.3		38	Virginia	24.0
7	Rhode Island	28.1		39	Illinois	23.4
26	South Carolina	25.2		40	California	23.3
15	South Dakota	26.1		41	Kansas	23.2
46	Tennessee	21.8		42	Indiana	23.0
47	Texas	21.5		43	Mississippi	22.2
50	Utah	16.1		44	Alabama	21.9
1	Vermont	32.2		44	Idaho	21.9
38	Virginia	24.0		46	Tennessee	21.8
12	Washington	26.7		47	Texas	21.5
18	West Virginia	25.4		48	Georgia	21.4
12	Wisconsin	26.7		49	Louisiana	19.9
18	Wyoming	25.4		50	Utah	16.1
					District of Columbia	22.5

Source: U.S. Department of Health and Human Services, Centers for Disease Control and Prevention
   "2008 Behavioral Risk Factor Surveillance Summary Prevalence Data" (http://apps.nccd.cdc.gov/brfss/)
*Persons 18 and older who have smoked more than 100 cigarettes during their lifetime and who currently do not smoke.

Percent of Adults Who Have Never Smoked: 2008

National Median = 55.4% of Adults*

ALPHA ORDER

RANK ORDER

RANK	STATE	PERCENT		RANK	STATE	PERCENT
22	Alabama	56.0		1	Utah	74.5
48	Alaska	50.0		2	California	62.7
16	Arizona	56.7		3	Idaho	61.2
42	Arkansas	51.4		4	Maryland	60.9
2	California	62.7		4	New Jersey	60.9
15	Colorado	57.5		6	Texas	60.0
36	Connecticut	54.0		7	Louisiana	59.7
37	Delaware	53.7		8	Virginia	59.5
20	Florida	56.4		9	Hawaii	59.2
10	Georgia	59.1		10	Georgia	59.1
9	Hawaii	59.2		11	Kansas	59.0
3	Idaho	61.2		11	Oregon	59.0
26	Illinois	55.3		13	New York	57.8
44	Indiana	51.0		14	Washington	57.6
17	Iowa	56.6		15	Colorado	57.5
11	Kansas	59.0		16	Arizona	56.7
49	Kentucky	49.5		17	Iowa	56.6
7	Louisiana	59.7		17	Nebraska	56.6
46	Maine	50.1		19	North Dakota	56.5
4	Maryland	60.9		20	Florida	56.4
23	Massachusetts	55.8		20	South Dakota	56.4
35	Michigan	54.1		22	Alabama	56.0
25	Minnesota	55.4		23	Massachusetts	55.8
28	Mississippi	55.1		24	New Mexico	55.7
46	Missouri	50.1		25	Minnesota	55.4
30	Montana	54.7		26	Illinois	55.3
17	Nebraska	56.6		27	Wyoming	55.2
40	Nevada	52.7		28	Mississippi	55.1
41	New Hampshire	51.9		29	Tennessee	55.0
4	New Jersey	60.9		30	Montana	54.7
24	New Mexico	55.7		30	South Carolina	54.7
13	New York	57.8		32	Rhode Island	54.5
34	North Carolina	54.3		33	Ohio	54.4
19	North Dakota	56.5		34	North Carolina	54.3
33	Ohio	54.4		35	Michigan	54.1
45	Oklahoma	50.6		36	Connecticut	54.0
11	Oregon	59.0		37	Delaware	53.7
39	Pennsylvania	53.3		38	Wisconsin	53.5
32	Rhode Island	54.5		39	Pennsylvania	53.3
30	South Carolina	54.7		40	Nevada	52.7
20	South Dakota	56.4		41	New Hampshire	51.9
29	Tennessee	55.0		42	Arkansas	51.4
6	Texas	60.0		43	Vermont	51.1
1	Utah	74.5		44	Indiana	51.0
43	Vermont	51.1		45	Oklahoma	50.6
8	Virginia	59.5		46	Maine	50.1
14	Washington	57.6		46	Missouri	50.1
50	West Virginia	48.1		48	Alaska	50.0
38	Wisconsin	53.5		49	Kentucky	49.5
27	Wyoming	55.2		50	West Virginia	48.1

District of Columbia — 61.2

Source: U.S. Department of Health and Human Services, Centers for Disease Control and Prevention
"2008 Behavioral Risk Factor Surveillance Summary Prevalence Data" (http://apps.nccd.cdc.gov/brfss/)
*Persons 18 and older who have not smoked more than 100 cigarettes during their lifetime.

Percent of Population Who Are Illicit Drug Users: 2007

National Percent = 8.1% of Population*

ALPHA ORDER				RANK ORDER		
RANK	STATE	PERCENT		RANK	STATE	PERCENT
40	Alabama	7.0		1	Rhode Island	12.5
4	Alaska	10.7		2	Vermont	11.5
12	Arizona	9.1		3	Colorado	11.0
19	Arkansas	8.6		4	Alaska	10.7
12	California	9.1		5	Montana	10.3
3	Colorado	11.0		6	Oregon	10.2
29	Connecticut	7.9		6	Washington	10.2
19	Delaware	8.6		8	Massachusetts	9.8
31	Florida	7.7		8	New Hampshire	9.8
32	Georgia	7.5		10	Maine	9.6
32	Hawaii	7.5		10	New Mexico	9.6
34	Idaho	7.4		12	Arizona	9.1
37	Illinois	7.3		12	California	9.1
22	Indiana	8.4		12	Michigan	9.1
50	Iowa	5.2		12	New York	9.1
34	Kansas	7.4		16	Nevada	9.0
27	Kentucky	8.1		17	Tennessee	8.8
24	Louisiana	8.2		18	Wyoming	8.7
10	Maine	9.6		19	Arkansas	8.6
40	Maryland	7.0		19	Delaware	8.6
8	Massachusetts	9.8		21	Oklahoma	8.5
12	Michigan	9.1		22	Indiana	8.4
23	Minnesota	8.3		23	Minnesota	8.3
39	Mississippi	7.1		24	Louisiana	8.2
28	Missouri	8.0		24	Virginia	8.2
5	Montana	10.3		24	Wisconsin	8.2
43	Nebraska	6.7		27	Kentucky	8.1
16	Nevada	9.0		28	Missouri	8.0
8	New Hampshire	9.8		29	Connecticut	7.9
47	New Jersey	6.5		29	Ohio	7.9
10	New Mexico	9.6		31	Florida	7.7
12	New York	9.1		32	Georgia	7.5
38	North Carolina	7.2		32	Hawaii	7.5
49	North Dakota	6.2		34	Idaho	7.4
29	Ohio	7.9		34	Kansas	7.4
21	Oklahoma	8.5		34	West Virginia	7.4
6	Oregon	10.2		37	Illinois	7.3
40	Pennsylvania	7.0		38	North Carolina	7.2
1	Rhode Island	12.5		39	Mississippi	7.1
46	South Carolina	6.6		40	Alabama	7.0
43	South Dakota	6.7		40	Maryland	7.0
17	Tennessee	8.8		40	Pennsylvania	7.0
43	Texas	6.7		43	Nebraska	6.7
48	Utah	6.4		43	South Dakota	6.7
2	Vermont	11.5		43	Texas	6.7
24	Virginia	8.2		46	South Carolina	6.6
6	Washington	10.2		47	New Jersey	6.5
34	West Virginia	7.4		48	Utah	6.4
24	Wisconsin	8.2		49	North Dakota	6.2
18	Wyoming	8.7		50	Iowa	5.2
					District of Columbia	12.1

Source: U.S. Department of Health and Human Services, Substance Abuse and Mental Health Services Administration
"2006-2007 National Surveys on Drug Use and Health" (June 2009, http://www.oas.samhsa.gov/2k7state/toc.cfm)
*Population 12 years and older who used any illicit drug at least once within month of survey.

Percent of Adults Overweight: 2008

National Median = 36.5% of Adults*

RANK	STATE	PERCENT
37	Alabama	35.7
3	Alaska	38.4
37	Arizona	35.7
29	Arkansas	36.2
13	California	37.1
29	Colorado	36.2
4	Connecticut	38.3
32	Delaware	36.0
45	Florida	35.0
16	Georgia	36.9
47	Hawaii	34.2
14	Idaho	37.0
27	Illinois	36.4
24	Indiana	36.6
7	Iowa	37.6
7	Kansas	37.6
26	Kentucky	36.5
46	Louisiana	34.8
32	Maine	36.0
22	Maryland	36.7
24	Massachusetts	36.6
40	Michigan	35.2
7	Minnesota	37.6
49	Mississippi	34.1
27	Missouri	36.4
11	Montana	37.4
16	Nebraska	36.9
14	Nevada	37.0
5	New Hampshire	38.2
2	New Jersey	38.5
47	New Mexico	34.2
40	New York	35.2
29	North Carolina	36.2
1	North Dakota	39.6
49	Ohio	34.1
39	Oklahoma	35.6
22	Oregon	36.7
32	Pennsylvania	36.0
6	Rhode Island	37.9
40	South Carolina	35.2
20	South Dakota	36.8
20	Tennessee	36.8
12	Texas	37.3
44	Utah	35.1
40	Vermont	35.2
35	Virginia	35.8
35	Washington	35.8
16	West Virginia	36.9
10	Wisconsin	37.5
16	Wyoming	36.9

RANK	STATE	PERCENT
1	North Dakota	39.6
2	New Jersey	38.5
3	Alaska	38.4
4	Connecticut	38.3
5	New Hampshire	38.2
6	Rhode Island	37.9
7	Iowa	37.6
7	Kansas	37.6
7	Minnesota	37.6
10	Wisconsin	37.5
11	Montana	37.4
12	Texas	37.3
13	California	37.1
14	Idaho	37.0
14	Nevada	37.0
16	Georgia	36.9
16	Nebraska	36.9
16	West Virginia	36.9
16	Wyoming	36.9
20	South Dakota	36.8
20	Tennessee	36.8
22	Maryland	36.7
22	Oregon	36.7
24	Indiana	36.6
24	Massachusetts	36.6
26	Kentucky	36.5
27	Illinois	36.4
27	Missouri	36.4
29	Arkansas	36.2
29	Colorado	36.2
29	North Carolina	36.2
32	Delaware	36.0
32	Maine	36.0
32	Pennsylvania	36.0
35	Virginia	35.8
35	Washington	35.8
37	Alabama	35.7
37	Arizona	35.7
39	Oklahoma	35.6
40	Michigan	35.2
40	New York	35.2
40	South Carolina	35.2
40	Vermont	35.2
44	Utah	35.1
45	Florida	35.0
46	Louisiana	34.8
47	Hawaii	34.2
47	New Mexico	34.2
49	Mississippi	34.1
49	Ohio	34.1

	District of Columbia	32.8

Source: U.S. Department of Health and Human Services, Centers for Disease Control and Prevention
   "2008 Behavioral Risk Factor Surveillance Summary Prevalence Data" (http://apps.nccd.cdc.gov/brfss/)
*Persons 18 and older. Does not include obese adults. Overweight is defined as a Body Mass Index (BMI) of 25.0 to 29.9
regardless of sex. BMI is a ratio of height to weight. As an example, a person 5' 8" and weighing 171 pounds has a BMI of 26.
See http://www.cdc.gov/healthyweight/assessing/bmi/index.html.

Percent of Adults Obese: 2008

National Median = 26.7% of Adults*

ALPHA ORDER

RANK	STATE	PERCENT
2	Alabama	32.2
22	Alaska	27.1
32	Arizona	25.6
8	Arkansas	29.5
41	California	24.3
50	Colorado	19.1
49	Connecticut	21.4
18	Delaware	27.8
34	Florida	25.2
18	Georgia	27.8
45	Hawaii	23.1
34	Idaho	25.2
24	Illinois	26.9
23	Indiana	27.0
25	Iowa	26.7
16	Kansas	28.1
7	Kentucky	30.3
13	Louisiana	29.0
29	Maine	25.9
25	Maryland	26.7
48	Massachusetts	21.5
8	Michigan	29.5
34	Minnesota	25.2
1	Mississippi	33.4
12	Missouri	29.1
41	Montana	24.3
21	Nebraska	27.2
32	Nevada	25.6
40	New Hampshire	24.9
43	New Jersey	23.6
31	New Mexico	25.7
38	New York	25.1
8	North Carolina	29.5
18	North Dakota	27.8
11	Ohio	29.3
5	Oklahoma	31.0
39	Oregon	25.0
15	Pennsylvania	28.4
47	Rhode Island	22.1
6	South Carolina	30.7
16	South Dakota	28.1
4	Tennessee	31.2
14	Texas	28.9
45	Utah	23.1
44	Vermont	23.3
30	Virginia	25.8
28	Washington	26.0
3	West Virginia	31.9
27	Wisconsin	26.1
34	Wyoming	25.2

RANK ORDER

RANK	STATE	PERCENT
1	Mississippi	33.4
2	Alabama	32.2
3	West Virginia	31.9
4	Tennessee	31.2
5	Oklahoma	31.0
6	South Carolina	30.7
7	Kentucky	30.3
8	Arkansas	29.5
8	Michigan	29.5
8	North Carolina	29.5
11	Ohio	29.3
12	Missouri	29.1
13	Louisiana	29.0
14	Texas	28.9
15	Pennsylvania	28.4
16	Kansas	28.1
16	South Dakota	28.1
18	Delaware	27.8
18	Georgia	27.8
18	North Dakota	27.8
21	Nebraska	27.2
22	Alaska	27.1
23	Indiana	27.0
24	Illinois	26.9
25	Iowa	26.7
25	Maryland	26.7
27	Wisconsin	26.1
28	Washington	26.0
29	Maine	25.9
30	Virginia	25.8
31	New Mexico	25.7
32	Arizona	25.6
32	Nevada	25.6
34	Florida	25.2
34	Idaho	25.2
34	Minnesota	25.2
34	Wyoming	25.2
38	New York	25.1
39	Oregon	25.0
40	New Hampshire	24.9
41	California	24.3
41	Montana	24.3
43	New Jersey	23.6
44	Vermont	23.3
45	Hawaii	23.1
45	Utah	23.1
47	Rhode Island	22.1
48	Massachusetts	21.5
49	Connecticut	21.4
50	Colorado	19.1
	District of Columbia	22.3

Source: U.S. Department of Health and Human Services, Centers for Disease Control and Prevention
"2008 Behavioral Risk Factor Surveillance Summary Prevalence Data" (http://apps.nccd.cdc.gov/brfss/)
*Persons 18 and older.   Obese is defined as a Body Mass Index (BMI) of 30.0 or more regardless of sex. BMI is a ratio of height to weight. As an example, a person 5' 8" and weighing 197 pounds has a BMI of 30. See
http://www.cdc.gov/healthyweight/assessing/bmi/index.html.

Percent of Adults Overweight or Obese: 2008

National Median = 63.2% of Adults*

ALPHA ORDER

RANK	STATE	PERCENT
3	Alabama	67.9
13	Alaska	65.5
40	Arizona	61.3
10	Arkansas	65.7
39	California	61.4
50	Colorado	55.3
45	Connecticut	59.7
21	Delaware	63.8
42	Florida	60.2
16	Georgia	64.7
49	Hawaii	57.3
31	Idaho	62.2
27	Illinois	63.3
23	Indiana	63.6
19	Iowa	64.3
10	Kansas	65.7
6	Kentucky	66.8
21	Louisiana	63.8
34	Maine	61.9
25	Maryland	63.4
48	Massachusetts	58.1
16	Michigan	64.7
29	Minnesota	62.8
4	Mississippi	67.5
13	Missouri	65.5
36	Montana	61.7
20	Nebraska	64.1
30	Nevada	62.6
28	New Hampshire	63.1
32	New Jersey	62.1
44	New Mexico	59.9
41	New York	60.3
10	North Carolina	65.7
5	North Dakota	67.4
25	Ohio	63.4
7	Oklahoma	66.6
36	Oregon	61.7
18	Pennsylvania	64.4
43	Rhode Island	60.0
9	South Carolina	65.9
15	South Dakota	64.9
2	Tennessee	68.0
8	Texas	66.2
47	Utah	58.2
46	Vermont	58.5
38	Virginia	61.6
35	Washington	61.8
1	West Virginia	68.8
23	Wisconsin	63.6
32	Wyoming	62.1

RANK ORDER

RANK	STATE	PERCENT
1	West Virginia	68.8
2	Tennessee	68.0
3	Alabama	67.9
4	Mississippi	67.5
5	North Dakota	67.4
6	Kentucky	66.8
7	Oklahoma	66.6
8	Texas	66.2
9	South Carolina	65.9
10	Arkansas	65.7
10	Kansas	65.7
10	North Carolina	65.7
13	Alaska	65.5
13	Missouri	65.5
15	South Dakota	64.9
16	Georgia	64.7
16	Michigan	64.7
18	Pennsylvania	64.4
19	Iowa	64.3
20	Nebraska	64.1
21	Delaware	63.8
21	Louisiana	63.8
23	Indiana	63.6
23	Wisconsin	63.6
25	Maryland	63.4
25	Ohio	63.4
27	Illinois	63.3
28	New Hampshire	63.1
29	Minnesota	62.8
30	Nevada	62.6
31	Idaho	62.2
32	New Jersey	62.1
32	Wyoming	62.1
34	Maine	61.9
35	Washington	61.8
36	Montana	61.7
36	Oregon	61.7
38	Virginia	61.6
39	California	61.4
40	Arizona	61.3
41	New York	60.3
42	Florida	60.2
43	Rhode Island	60.0
44	New Mexico	59.9
45	Connecticut	59.7
46	Vermont	58.5
47	Utah	58.2
48	Massachusetts	58.1
49	Hawaii	57.3
50	Colorado	55.3

District of Columbia   55.1

Source: CQ Press using data from U.S. Department of Health and Human Services, Centers for Disease Control and Prevention
"2008 Behavioral Risk Factor Surveillance Summary Prevalence Data" (http://apps.nccd.cdc.gov/brfss/)
*Persons 18 and older. Overweight is defined as a Body Mass Index (BMI) of 25.0 to 29.9 regardless of sex. Obese is a BMI of 30.0 or greater. BMI is a ratio of height to weight. As an example, a person 5' 8" and weighing 165 pounds has a BMI of 25. The same height at 197 pounds has a BMI of 30. See http://www.cdc.gov/healthyweight/assessing/bmi/index.html.

Percent of Adults Who Do Not Exercise: 2008

National Median = 24.6% of Adults*

RANK	STATE	PERCENT
7	Alabama	29.5
29	Alaska	24.1
35	Arizona	23.2
6	Arkansas	29.7
34	California	23.3
49	Colorado	18.9
39	Connecticut	22.4
29	Delaware	24.1
19	Florida	25.9
36	Georgia	23.1
45	Hawaii	19.6
43	Idaho	21.1
10	Illinois	28.0
11	Indiana	27.7
24	Iowa	25.0
22	Kansas	25.5
4	Kentucky	30.5
5	Louisiana	29.8
38	Maine	22.8
31	Maryland	24.0
40	Massachusetts	22.1
23	Michigan	25.1
50	Minnesota	18.1
1	Mississippi	32.5
12	Missouri	27.6
36	Montana	23.1
25	Nebraska	24.6
12	Nevada	27.6
42	New Hampshire	21.5
15	New Jersey	26.9
32	New Mexico	23.9
17	New York	26.4
25	North Carolina	24.6
21	North Dakota	25.6
18	Ohio	26.0
2	Oklahoma	31.5
48	Oregon	19.0
20	Pennsylvania	25.7
28	Rhode Island	24.2
14	South Carolina	27.2
15	South Dakota	26.9
8	Tennessee	28.9
9	Texas	28.5
44	Utah	19.8
46	Vermont	19.4
33	Virginia	23.6
47	Washington	19.3
3	West Virginia	31.1
41	Wisconsin	22.0
27	Wyoming	24.4

RANK	STATE	PERCENT
1	Mississippi	32.5
2	Oklahoma	31.5
3	West Virginia	31.1
4	Kentucky	30.5
5	Louisiana	29.8
6	Arkansas	29.7
7	Alabama	29.5
8	Tennessee	28.9
9	Texas	28.5
10	Illinois	28.0
11	Indiana	27.7
12	Missouri	27.6
12	Nevada	27.6
14	South Carolina	27.2
15	New Jersey	26.9
15	South Dakota	26.9
17	New York	26.4
18	Ohio	26.0
19	Florida	25.9
20	Pennsylvania	25.7
21	North Dakota	25.6
22	Kansas	25.5
23	Michigan	25.1
24	Iowa	25.0
25	Nebraska	24.6
25	North Carolina	24.6
27	Wyoming	24.4
28	Rhode Island	24.2
29	Alaska	24.1
29	Delaware	24.1
31	Maryland	24.0
32	New Mexico	23.9
33	Virginia	23.6
34	California	23.3
35	Arizona	23.2
36	Georgia	23.1
36	Montana	23.1
38	Maine	22.8
39	Connecticut	22.4
40	Massachusetts	22.1
41	Wisconsin	22.0
42	New Hampshire	21.5
43	Idaho	21.1
44	Utah	19.8
45	Hawaii	19.6
46	Vermont	19.4
47	Washington	19.3
48	Oregon	19.0
49	Colorado	18.9
50	Minnesota	18.1
	District of Columbia	21.2

Source: U.S. Department of Health and Human Services, Centers for Disease Control and Prevention
"2008 Behavioral Risk Factor Surveillance Summary Prevalence Data" (http://apps.nccd.cdc.gov/brfss/)
*Persons 18 and older who, in the previous month, did not participate in any physical activities.

Percent of Adults Who Exercise Vigorously: 2007

National Median = 28.3% of Adults*

ALPHA ORDER

RANK	STATE	PERCENT
45	Alabama	21.7
1	Alaska	39.5
19	Arizona	29.5
42	Arkansas	24.3
11	California	31.3
5	Colorado	33.0
16	Connecticut	30.2
32	Delaware	26.7
34	Florida	26.0
26	Georgia	28.1
15	Hawaii	30.4
3	Idaho	33.4
24	Illinois	28.3
33	Indiana	26.5
40	Iowa	25.0
35	Kansas	25.8
45	Kentucky	21.7
47	Louisiana	20.5
9	Maine	31.9
28	Maryland	27.7
18	Massachusetts	29.7
19	Michigan	29.5
44	Minnesota	22.8
48	Mississippi	19.7
36	Missouri	25.5
6	Montana	32.8
14	Nebraska	30.6
24	Nevada	28.3
12	New Hampshire	31.2
31	New Jersey	27.3
21	New Mexico	29.2
30	New York	27.5
43	North Carolina	23.4
22	North Dakota	28.9
27	Ohio	28.0
41	Oklahoma	24.9
10	Oregon	31.5
23	Pennsylvania	28.6
28	Rhode Island	27.7
38	South Carolina	25.4
38	South Dakota	25.4
50	Tennessee	18.5
36	Texas	25.5
2	Utah	35.8
4	Vermont	33.2
17	Virginia	30.0
13	Washington	30.8
49	West Virginia	19.2
8	Wisconsin	32.1
7	Wyoming	32.7

RANK ORDER

RANK	STATE	PERCENT
1	Alaska	39.5
2	Utah	35.8
3	Idaho	33.4
4	Vermont	33.2
5	Colorado	33.0
6	Montana	32.8
7	Wyoming	32.7
8	Wisconsin	32.1
9	Maine	31.9
10	Oregon	31.5
11	California	31.3
12	New Hampshire	31.2
13	Washington	30.8
14	Nebraska	30.6
15	Hawaii	30.4
16	Connecticut	30.2
17	Virginia	30.0
18	Massachusetts	29.7
19	Arizona	29.5
19	Michigan	29.5
21	New Mexico	29.2
22	North Dakota	28.9
23	Pennsylvania	28.6
24	Illinois	28.3
24	Nevada	28.3
26	Georgia	28.1
27	Ohio	28.0
28	Maryland	27.7
28	Rhode Island	27.7
30	New York	27.5
31	New Jersey	27.3
32	Delaware	26.7
33	Indiana	26.5
34	Florida	26.0
35	Kansas	25.8
36	Missouri	25.5
36	Texas	25.5
38	South Carolina	25.4
38	South Dakota	25.4
40	Iowa	25.0
41	Oklahoma	24.9
42	Arkansas	24.3
43	North Carolina	23.4
44	Minnesota	22.8
45	Alabama	21.7
45	Kentucky	21.7
47	Louisiana	20.5
48	Mississippi	19.7
49	West Virginia	19.2
50	Tennessee	18.5

	District of Columbia	30.9

Source: U.S. Department of Health and Human Services, Centers for Disease Control and Prevention
"2007 Behavioral Risk Factor Surveillance Summary Prevalence Data" (http://apps.nccd.cdc.gov/brfss/)
*Persons 18 and older. Vigorous exercise is activity that caused large increases in breathing or heart rate at least 20 minutes three or more times per week (such as running, aerobics, or heavy yard work).

Percent of Adults Who Are Disabled: 2008

National Median = 20.6%*

ALPHA ORDER				RANK ORDER		

RANK	STATE	PERCENT		RANK	STATE	PERCENT
4	Alabama	25.1		1	West Virginia	29.5
16	Alaska	21.9		2	Oklahoma	26.1
18	Arizona	21.6		3	Kentucky	25.5
5	Arkansas	25.0		4	Alabama	25.1
40	California	18.8		5	Arkansas	25.0
37	Colorado	19.0		5	Missouri	25.0
40	Connecticut	18.8		7	Mississippi	24.2
28	Delaware	20.3		8	Oregon	23.9
35	Florida	19.2		8	Washington	23.9
42	Georgia	18.5		10	Montana	22.9
50	Hawaii	16.8		11	Tennessee	22.8
12	Idaho	22.6		12	Idaho	22.6
44	Illinois	18.2		12	Michigan	22.6
30	Indiana	20.0		14	Maine	22.2
48	Iowa	17.0		14	New Mexico	22.2
25	Kansas	20.8		16	Alaska	21.9
3	Kentucky	25.5		17	South Carolina	21.7
24	Louisiana	20.9		18	Arizona	21.6
14	Maine	22.2		19	Ohio	21.5
27	Maryland	20.5		20	New Hampshire	21.4
46	Massachusetts	17.5		21	North Carolina	21.3
12	Michigan	22.6		21	Vermont	21.3
31	Minnesota	19.9		23	Pennsylvania	21.1
7	Mississippi	24.2		24	Louisiana	20.9
5	Missouri	25.0		25	Kansas	20.8
10	Montana	22.9		26	Wyoming	20.6
43	Nebraska	18.3		27	Maryland	20.5
28	Nevada	20.3		28	Delaware	20.3
20	New Hampshire	21.4		28	Nevada	20.3
47	New Jersey	17.1		30	Indiana	20.0
14	New Mexico	22.2		31	Minnesota	19.9
33	New York	19.4		32	Utah	19.5
21	North Carolina	21.3		33	New York	19.4
48	North Dakota	17.0		34	Virginia	19.3
19	Ohio	21.5		35	Florida	19.2
2	Oklahoma	26.1		35	Texas	19.2
8	Oregon	23.9		37	Colorado	19.0
23	Pennsylvania	21.1		37	South Dakota	19.0
39	Rhode Island	18.9		39	Rhode Island	18.9
17	South Carolina	21.7		40	California	18.8
37	South Dakota	19.0		40	Connecticut	18.8
11	Tennessee	22.8		42	Georgia	18.5
35	Texas	19.2		43	Nebraska	18.3
32	Utah	19.5		44	Illinois	18.2
21	Vermont	21.3		44	Wisconsin	18.2
34	Virginia	19.3		46	Massachusetts	17.5
8	Washington	23.9		47	New Jersey	17.1
1	West Virginia	29.5		48	Iowa	17.0
44	Wisconsin	18.2		48	North Dakota	17.0
26	Wyoming	20.6		50	Hawaii	16.8

District of Columbia	17.4

Source: U.S. Department of Health and Human Services, Centers for Disease Control and Prevention
  "2008 Behavioral Risk Factor Surveillance Summary Prevalence Data" (http://apps.nccd.cdc.gov/brfss/)
*Persons 18 and older. Adults who are limited in any activities because of physical, mental, or emotional problems.

Percent of Adults with High Blood Pressure: 2007

National Median = 27.8% of Adults*

ALPHA ORDER				RANK ORDER		
RANK	**STATE**	**PERCENT**		**RANK**	**STATE**	**PERCENT**
4	Alabama	33.1		1	Tennessee	33.8
45	Alaska	24.9		2	Mississippi	33.7
46	Arizona	24.8		3	West Virginia	33.3
7	Arkansas	31.3		4	Alabama	33.1
42	California	25.2		5	Louisiana	32.1
49	Colorado	21.2		6	Oklahoma	31.5
36	Connecticut	26.2		7	Arkansas	31.3
12	Delaware	29.3		8	Georgia	30.4
20	Florida	28.2		8	South Carolina	30.4
8	Georgia	30.4		10	Kentucky	30.0
14	Hawaii	28.8		11	Missouri	29.4
38	Idaho	25.9		12	Delaware	29.3
23	Illinois	28.0		13	Maryland	29.1
24	Indiana	27.9		14	Hawaii	28.8
29	Iowa	26.8		14	North Carolina	28.8
29	Kansas	26.8		16	Maine	28.7
10	Kentucky	30.0		17	Michigan	28.6
5	Louisiana	32.1		18	Ohio	28.4
16	Maine	28.7		18	Rhode Island	28.4
13	Maryland	29.1		20	Florida	28.2
33	Massachusetts	26.4		20	New Jersey	28.2
17	Michigan	28.6		22	Pennsylvania	28.1
48	Minnesota	21.4		23	Illinois	28.0
2	Mississippi	33.7		24	Indiana	27.9
11	Missouri	29.4		25	Texas	27.8
42	Montana	25.2		26	New York	27.2
31	Nebraska	26.5		27	Virginia	27.1
28	Nevada	27.0		28	Nevada	27.0
34	New Hampshire	26.3		29	Iowa	26.8
20	New Jersey	28.2		29	Kansas	26.8
39	New Mexico	25.6		31	Nebraska	26.5
26	New York	27.2		31	Oregon	26.5
14	North Carolina	28.8		33	Massachusetts	26.4
37	North Dakota	26.0		34	New Hampshire	26.3
18	Ohio	28.4		34	Wisconsin	26.3
6	Oklahoma	31.5		36	Connecticut	26.2
31	Oregon	26.5		37	North Dakota	26.0
22	Pennsylvania	28.1		38	Idaho	25.9
18	Rhode Island	28.4		39	New Mexico	25.6
8	South Carolina	30.4		40	South Dakota	25.5
40	South Dakota	25.5		41	Washington	25.4
1	Tennessee	33.8		42	California	25.2
25	Texas	27.8		42	Montana	25.2
50	Utah	19.7		44	Wyoming	25.1
46	Vermont	24.8		45	Alaska	24.9
27	Virginia	27.1		46	Arizona	24.8
41	Washington	25.4		46	Vermont	24.8
3	West Virginia	33.3		48	Minnesota	21.4
34	Wisconsin	26.3		49	Colorado	21.2
44	Wyoming	25.1		50	Utah	19.7
					District of Columbia	28.6

Source: U.S. Department of Health and Human Services, Centers for Disease Control and Prevention
  "2007 Behavioral Risk Factor Surveillance Summary Prevalence Data" (http://apps.nccd.cdc.gov/brfss/)
*Persons 18 and older who have been told by a doctor, nurse, or other health professional that they have high blood pressure.

Percent of Adults with High Cholesterol: 2007

National Median = 37.6% of Adults*

ALPHA ORDER			RANK ORDER		
RANK	STATE	PERCENT	RANK	STATE	PERCENT
10	Alabama	39.4	1	West Virginia	42.4
25	Alaska	37.6	2	Oklahoma	41.0
18	Arizona	38.3	3	Maine	40.2
4	Arkansas	40.1	4	Arkansas	40.1
41	California	34.9	5	Michigan	39.9
48	Colorado	33.5	6	Pennsylvania	39.7
18	Connecticut	38.3	7	North Carolina	39.6
18	Delaware	38.3	7	Ohio	39.6
30	Florida	37.1	9	Missouri	39.5
28	Georgia	37.4	10	Alabama	39.4
37	Hawaii	36.3	11	South Carolina	39.2
25	Idaho	37.6	12	New Hampshire	38.7
37	Illinois	36.3	13	New Jersey	38.6
14	Indiana	38.5	14	Indiana	38.5
23	Iowa	37.8	14	Kentucky	38.5
35	Kansas	36.6	14	Mississippi	38.5
14	Kentucky	38.5	14	Texas	38.5
47	Louisiana	33.7	18	Arizona	38.3
3	Maine	40.2	18	Connecticut	38.3
33	Maryland	36.9	18	Delaware	38.3
39	Massachusetts	35.6	21	Wyoming	38.1
5	Michigan	39.9	22	Rhode Island	38.0
50	Minnesota	32.4	23	Iowa	37.8
14	Mississippi	38.5	24	New York	37.7
9	Missouri	39.5	25	Alaska	37.6
43	Montana	34.6	25	Idaho	37.6
35	Nebraska	36.6	25	Oregon	37.6
30	Nevada	37.1	28	Georgia	37.4
12	New Hampshire	38.7	28	Virginia	37.4
13	New Jersey	38.6	30	Florida	37.1
44	New Mexico	34.5	30	Nevada	37.1
24	New York	37.7	30	North Dakota	37.1
7	North Carolina	39.6	33	Maryland	36.9
30	North Dakota	37.1	34	Washington	36.7
7	Ohio	39.6	35	Kansas	36.6
2	Oklahoma	41.0	35	Nebraska	36.6
25	Oregon	37.6	37	Hawaii	36.3
6	Pennsylvania	39.7	37	Illinois	36.3
22	Rhode Island	38.0	39	Massachusetts	35.6
11	South Carolina	39.2	40	Vermont	35.1
46	South Dakota	34.0	41	California	34.9
45	Tennessee	34.2	41	Wisconsin	34.9
14	Texas	38.5	43	Montana	34.6
49	Utah	32.6	44	New Mexico	34.5
40	Vermont	35.1	45	Tennessee	34.2
28	Virginia	37.4	46	South Dakota	34.0
34	Washington	36.7	47	Louisiana	33.7
1	West Virginia	42.4	48	Colorado	33.5
41	Wisconsin	34.9	49	Utah	32.6
21	Wyoming	38.1	50	Minnesota	32.4
				District of Columbia	34.1

Source: U.S. Department of Health and Human Services, Centers for Disease Control and Prevention
"2007 Behavioral Risk Factor Surveillance Summary Prevalence Data" (http://apps.nccd.cdc.gov/brfss/)
*Persons 18 and older who have had their cholesterol checked and have been told that they have high blood cholesterol.

Percent of Adults Who Have Visited a Dentist or Dental Clinic: 2008

National Median = 71.3%*

ALPHA ORDER				RANK ORDER		
RANK	STATE	PERCENT		RANK	STATE	PERCENT
42	Alabama	65.0		1	Connecticut	80.3
39	Alaska	66.3		2	Massachusetts	79.3
34	Arizona	68.3		3	Rhode Island	79.0
45	Arkansas	63.5		4	Delaware	76.9
27	California	70.3		5	New Hampshire	76.8
32	Colorado	68.5		6	Michigan	76.0
1	Connecticut	80.3		7	New Jersey	75.9
4	Delaware	76.9		8	Vermont	75.5
30	Florida	69.1		9	Hawaii	75.4
22	Georgia	71.8		10	Minnesota	75.3
9	Hawaii	75.4		11	Virginia	75.2
29	Idaho	69.5		12	New York	74.2
31	Illinois	68.9		13	North Dakota	74.1
34	Indiana	68.3		14	Iowa	73.4
14	Iowa	73.4		15	Washington	73.3
21	Kansas	71.9		15	Wisconsin	73.3
43	Kentucky	64.4		17	Utah	72.7
28	Louisiana	69.8		18	Maryland	72.6
23	Maine	71.5		18	South Dakota	72.6
18	Maryland	72.6		20	Ohio	72.2
2	Massachusetts	79.3		21	Kansas	71.9
6	Michigan	76.0		22	Georgia	71.8
10	Minnesota	75.3		23	Maine	71.5
49	Mississippi	59.5		24	Oregon	71.4
46	Missouri	62.7		25	Nebraska	71.3
40	Montana	66.0		26	Pennsylvania	71.1
25	Nebraska	71.3		27	California	70.3
44	Nevada	63.7		28	Louisiana	69.8
5	New Hampshire	76.8		29	Idaho	69.5
7	New Jersey	75.9		30	Florida	69.1
40	New Mexico	66.0		31	Illinois	68.9
12	New York	74.2		32	Colorado	68.5
32	North Carolina	68.5		32	North Carolina	68.5
13	North Dakota	74.1		34	Arizona	68.3
20	Ohio	72.2		34	Indiana	68.3
50	Oklahoma	57.9		36	Wyoming	68.0
24	Oregon	71.4		37	South Carolina	67.7
26	Pennsylvania	71.1		38	Tennessee	66.8
3	Rhode Island	79.0		39	Alaska	66.3
37	South Carolina	67.7		40	Montana	66.0
18	South Dakota	72.6		40	New Mexico	66.0
38	Tennessee	66.8		42	Alabama	65.0
47	Texas	62.6		43	Kentucky	64.4
17	Utah	72.7		44	Nevada	63.7
8	Vermont	75.5		45	Arkansas	63.5
11	Virginia	75.2		46	Missouri	62.7
15	Washington	73.3		47	Texas	62.6
48	West Virginia	60.7		48	West Virginia	60.7
15	Wisconsin	73.3		49	Mississippi	59.5
36	Wyoming	68.0		50	Oklahoma	57.9
					District of Columbia	72.6

Source: U.S. Department of Health and Human Services, Centers for Disease Control and Prevention
"2008 Behavioral Risk Factor Surveillance Summary Prevalence Data" (http://apps.nccd.cdc.gov/brfss/)
*Persons 18 and older who have visited a dentist within the past year for any reason.

Percent of Adults 65 Years Old and Older
Who Have Lost All Their Natural Teeth: 2008
National Median = 18.5%*

ALPHA ORDER

RANK	STATE	PERCENT
6	Alabama	26.0
17	Alaska	20.7
45	Arizona	13.5
9	Arkansas	23.1
49	California	10.1
40	Colorado	15.0
46	Connecticut	13.2
36	Delaware	16.7
36	Florida	16.7
9	Georgia	23.1
50	Hawaii	9.6
32	Idaho	17.3
21	Illinois	19.1
13	Indiana	21.7
25	Iowa	18.5
18	Kansas	20.5
7	Kentucky	23.7
8	Louisiana	23.2
12	Maine	21.9
48	Maryland	12.4
27	Massachusetts	18.3
39	Michigan	15.6
47	Minnesota	13.0
3	Mississippi	27.3
5	Missouri	26.2
23	Montana	18.7
33	Nebraska	17.2
29	Nevada	17.7
25	New Hampshire	18.5
33	New Jersey	17.2
28	New Mexico	18.1
35	New York	17.0
15	North Carolina	21.3
19	North Dakota	20.1
16	Ohio	20.8
4	Oklahoma	26.8
38	Oregon	16.0
14	Pennsylvania	21.5
29	Rhode Island	17.7
11	South Carolina	22.7
24	South Dakota	18.6
2	Tennessee	31.5
31	Texas	17.5
43	Utah	13.9
20	Vermont	19.8
41	Virginia	14.6
44	Washington	13.8
1	West Virginia	37.8
42	Wisconsin	14.5
21	Wyoming	19.1

RANK ORDER

RANK	STATE	PERCENT
1	West Virginia	37.8
2	Tennessee	31.5
3	Mississippi	27.3
4	Oklahoma	26.8
5	Missouri	26.2
6	Alabama	26.0
7	Kentucky	23.7
8	Louisiana	23.2
9	Arkansas	23.1
9	Georgia	23.1
11	South Carolina	22.7
12	Maine	21.9
13	Indiana	21.7
14	Pennsylvania	21.5
15	North Carolina	21.3
16	Ohio	20.8
17	Alaska	20.7
18	Kansas	20.5
19	North Dakota	20.1
20	Vermont	19.8
21	Illinois	19.1
21	Wyoming	19.1
23	Montana	18.7
24	South Dakota	18.6
25	Iowa	18.5
25	New Hampshire	18.5
27	Massachusetts	18.3
28	New Mexico	18.1
29	Nevada	17.7
29	Rhode Island	17.7
31	Texas	17.5
32	Idaho	17.3
33	Nebraska	17.2
33	New Jersey	17.2
35	New York	17.0
36	Delaware	16.7
36	Florida	16.7
38	Oregon	16.0
39	Michigan	15.6
40	Colorado	15.0
41	Virginia	14.6
42	Wisconsin	14.5
43	Utah	13.9
44	Washington	13.8
45	Arizona	13.5
46	Connecticut	13.2
47	Minnesota	13.0
48	Maryland	12.4
49	California	10.1
50	Hawaii	9.6

	District of Columbia	15.9

Source: U.S. Department of Health and Human Services, Centers for Disease Control and Prevention
    "2008 Behavioral Risk Factor Surveillance Summary Prevalence Data" (http://apps.nccd.cdc.gov/brfss/)
*Those who have had all their natural teeth extracted.

Percent of Adults Who Average Five or More Servings of Fruits and Vegetables Each Day: 2007
National Median = 24.4%*

ALPHA ORDER

RANK	STATE	PERCENT
39	Alabama	20.6
26	Alaska	24.2
7	Arizona	28.3
34	Arkansas	21.8
2	California	28.9
17	Colorado	25.8
5	Connecticut	28.5
36	Delaware	21.4
15	Florida	26.2
22	Georgia	25.0
3	Hawaii	28.7
31	Idaho	22.3
23	Illinois	24.6
28	Indiana	22.8
41	Iowa	19.9
45	Kansas	18.8
48	Kentucky	18.4
43	Louisiana	19.6
4	Maine	28.6
12	Maryland	26.6
8	Massachusetts	27.5
37	Michigan	21.3
44	Minnesota	19.4
49	Mississippi	18.1
40	Missouri	20.2
20	Montana	25.3
27	Nebraska	24.1
32	Nevada	21.9
5	New Hampshire	28.5
8	New Jersey	27.5
30	New Mexico	22.4
10	New York	27.4
35	North Carolina	21.6
32	North Dakota	21.9
38	Ohio	20.8
50	Oklahoma	16.3
11	Oregon	27.0
19	Pennsylvania	25.4
18	Rhode Island	25.6
46	South Carolina	18.7
47	South Dakota	18.6
13	Tennessee	26.4
21	Texas	25.2
28	Utah	22.8
1	Vermont	30.0
14	Virginia	26.3
16	Washington	26.0
42	West Virginia	19.7
24	Wisconsin	24.4
24	Wyoming	24.4

RANK ORDER

RANK	STATE	PERCENT
1	Vermont	30.0
2	California	28.9
3	Hawaii	28.7
4	Maine	28.6
5	Connecticut	28.5
5	New Hampshire	28.5
7	Arizona	28.3
8	Massachusetts	27.5
8	New Jersey	27.5
10	New York	27.4
11	Oregon	27.0
12	Maryland	26.6
13	Tennessee	26.4
14	Virginia	26.3
15	Florida	26.2
16	Washington	26.0
17	Colorado	25.8
18	Rhode Island	25.6
19	Pennsylvania	25.4
20	Montana	25.3
21	Texas	25.2
22	Georgia	25.0
23	Illinois	24.6
24	Wisconsin	24.4
24	Wyoming	24.4
26	Alaska	24.2
27	Nebraska	24.1
28	Indiana	22.8
28	Utah	22.8
30	New Mexico	22.4
31	Idaho	22.3
32	Nevada	21.9
32	North Dakota	21.9
34	Arkansas	21.8
35	North Carolina	21.6
36	Delaware	21.4
37	Michigan	21.3
38	Ohio	20.8
39	Alabama	20.6
40	Missouri	20.2
41	Iowa	19.9
42	West Virginia	19.7
43	Louisiana	19.6
44	Minnesota	19.4
45	Kansas	18.8
46	South Carolina	18.7
47	South Dakota	18.6
48	Kentucky	18.4
49	Mississippi	18.1
50	Oklahoma	16.3

	District of Columbia	32.5

Source: U.S. Department of Health and Human Services, Centers for Disease Control and Prevention
"2007 Behavioral Risk Factor Surveillance Summary Prevalence Data" (http://apps.nccd.cdc.gov/brfss/)
*Persons 18 and older.

Percent of Adults Rating Their Health as Fair or Poor in 2008

National Median = 14.4% of Adults*

<table>
<tr><td colspan="3">ALPHA ORDER</td><td colspan="3">RANK ORDER</td></tr>
<tr><th>RANK</th><th>STATE</th><th>PERCENT</th><th>RANK</th><th>STATE</th><th>PERCENT</th></tr>
<tr><td>2</td><td>Alabama</td><td>21.2</td><td>1</td><td>West Virginia</td><td>24.1</td></tr>
<tr><td>27</td><td>Alaska</td><td>14.2</td><td>2</td><td>Alabama</td><td>21.2</td></tr>
<tr><td>19</td><td>Arizona</td><td>16.0</td><td>2</td><td>Mississippi</td><td>21.2</td></tr>
<tr><td>6</td><td>Arkansas</td><td>19.3</td><td>4</td><td>Tennessee</td><td>20.5</td></tr>
<tr><td>10</td><td>California</td><td>18.6</td><td>5</td><td>Kentucky</td><td>20.3</td></tr>
<tr><td>34</td><td>Colorado</td><td>13.3</td><td>6</td><td>Arkansas</td><td>19.3</td></tr>
<tr><td>49</td><td>Connecticut</td><td>11.1</td><td>7</td><td>Texas</td><td>19.1</td></tr>
<tr><td>36</td><td>Delaware</td><td>13.1</td><td>8</td><td>Nevada</td><td>18.7</td></tr>
<tr><td>20</td><td>Florida</td><td>15.6</td><td>8</td><td>Oklahoma</td><td>18.7</td></tr>
<tr><td>16</td><td>Georgia</td><td>16.4</td><td>10</td><td>California</td><td>18.6</td></tr>
<tr><td>25</td><td>Hawaii</td><td>14.8</td><td>11</td><td>Louisiana</td><td>18.3</td></tr>
<tr><td>28</td><td>Idaho</td><td>14.0</td><td>12</td><td>New Mexico</td><td>18.2</td></tr>
<tr><td>24</td><td>Illinois</td><td>15.3</td><td>13</td><td>North Carolina</td><td>17.5</td></tr>
<tr><td>15</td><td>Indiana</td><td>16.7</td><td>14</td><td>Missouri</td><td>16.8</td></tr>
<tr><td>40</td><td>Iowa</td><td>12.5</td><td>15</td><td>Indiana</td><td>16.7</td></tr>
<tr><td>30</td><td>Kansas</td><td>13.5</td><td>16</td><td>Georgia</td><td>16.4</td></tr>
<tr><td>5</td><td>Kentucky</td><td>20.3</td><td>17</td><td>Pennsylvania</td><td>16.3</td></tr>
<tr><td>11</td><td>Louisiana</td><td>18.3</td><td>18</td><td>South Carolina</td><td>16.2</td></tr>
<tr><td>36</td><td>Maine</td><td>13.1</td><td>19</td><td>Arizona</td><td>16.0</td></tr>
<tr><td>40</td><td>Maryland</td><td>12.5</td><td>20</td><td>Florida</td><td>15.6</td></tr>
<tr><td>42</td><td>Massachusetts</td><td>12.3</td><td>20</td><td>New Jersey</td><td>15.6</td></tr>
<tr><td>26</td><td>Michigan</td><td>14.4</td><td>20</td><td>Ohio</td><td>15.6</td></tr>
<tr><td>47</td><td>Minnesota</td><td>11.4</td><td>23</td><td>New York</td><td>15.5</td></tr>
<tr><td>2</td><td>Mississippi</td><td>21.2</td><td>24</td><td>Illinois</td><td>15.3</td></tr>
<tr><td>14</td><td>Missouri</td><td>16.8</td><td>25</td><td>Hawaii</td><td>14.8</td></tr>
<tr><td>28</td><td>Montana</td><td>14.0</td><td>26</td><td>Michigan</td><td>14.4</td></tr>
<tr><td>45</td><td>Nebraska</td><td>11.9</td><td>27</td><td>Alaska</td><td>14.2</td></tr>
<tr><td>8</td><td>Nevada</td><td>18.7</td><td>28</td><td>Idaho</td><td>14.0</td></tr>
<tr><td>47</td><td>New Hampshire</td><td>11.4</td><td>28</td><td>Montana</td><td>14.0</td></tr>
<tr><td>20</td><td>New Jersey</td><td>15.6</td><td>30</td><td>Kansas</td><td>13.5</td></tr>
<tr><td>12</td><td>New Mexico</td><td>18.2</td><td>30</td><td>Rhode Island</td><td>13.5</td></tr>
<tr><td>23</td><td>New York</td><td>15.5</td><td>32</td><td>North Dakota</td><td>13.4</td></tr>
<tr><td>13</td><td>North Carolina</td><td>17.5</td><td>32</td><td>Washington</td><td>13.4</td></tr>
<tr><td>32</td><td>North Dakota</td><td>13.4</td><td>34</td><td>Colorado</td><td>13.3</td></tr>
<tr><td>20</td><td>Ohio</td><td>15.6</td><td>35</td><td>Oregon</td><td>13.2</td></tr>
<tr><td>8</td><td>Oklahoma</td><td>18.7</td><td>36</td><td>Delaware</td><td>13.1</td></tr>
<tr><td>35</td><td>Oregon</td><td>13.2</td><td>36</td><td>Maine</td><td>13.1</td></tr>
<tr><td>17</td><td>Pennsylvania</td><td>16.3</td><td>36</td><td>Wyoming</td><td>13.1</td></tr>
<tr><td>30</td><td>Rhode Island</td><td>13.5</td><td>39</td><td>Virginia</td><td>12.7</td></tr>
<tr><td>18</td><td>South Carolina</td><td>16.2</td><td>40</td><td>Iowa</td><td>12.5</td></tr>
<tr><td>44</td><td>South Dakota</td><td>12.1</td><td>40</td><td>Maryland</td><td>12.5</td></tr>
<tr><td>4</td><td>Tennessee</td><td>20.5</td><td>42</td><td>Massachusetts</td><td>12.3</td></tr>
<tr><td>7</td><td>Texas</td><td>19.1</td><td>42</td><td>Wisconsin</td><td>12.3</td></tr>
<tr><td>50</td><td>Utah</td><td>10.6</td><td>44</td><td>South Dakota</td><td>12.1</td></tr>
<tr><td>46</td><td>Vermont</td><td>11.5</td><td>45</td><td>Nebraska</td><td>11.9</td></tr>
<tr><td>39</td><td>Virginia</td><td>12.7</td><td>46</td><td>Vermont</td><td>11.5</td></tr>
<tr><td>32</td><td>Washington</td><td>13.4</td><td>47</td><td>Minnesota</td><td>11.4</td></tr>
<tr><td>1</td><td>West Virginia</td><td>24.1</td><td>47</td><td>New Hampshire</td><td>11.4</td></tr>
<tr><td>42</td><td>Wisconsin</td><td>12.3</td><td>49</td><td>Connecticut</td><td>11.1</td></tr>
<tr><td>36</td><td>Wyoming</td><td>13.1</td><td>50</td><td>Utah</td><td>10.6</td></tr>
</table>

District of Columbia   13.9

Source: CQ Press using data from U.S. Department of Health and Human Services, Centers for Disease Control and Prevention
"2008 Behavioral Risk Factor Surveillance Summary Prevalence Data" (http://apps.nccd.cdc.gov/brfss/)
*Persons 18 and older.

Safety Belt Usage Rate in 2008

National Rate = 83.0% Use Safety Belts

ALPHA ORDER			RANK ORDER		
RANK	STATE	PERCENT	RANK	STATE	PERCENT
22	Alabama	86.1	1	Michigan	97.2
25	Alaska	84.9	2	Hawaii	97.0
35	Arizona	79.9	3	Washington	96.5
47	Arkansas	70.4	4	Oregon	96.3
5	California	95.7	5	California	95.7
30	Colorado	81.7	6	Maryland	93.3
19	Connecticut	88.0	7	Iowa	92.9
9	Delaware	91.3	8	New Jersey	91.8
30	Florida	81.7	9	Delaware	91.3
16	Georgia	89.6	10	Indiana	91.2
2	Hawaii	97.0	10	Texas	91.2
39	Idaho	76.9	12	New Mexico	91.1
14	Illinois	90.5	13	Nevada	90.9
10	Indiana	91.2	14	Illinois	90.5
7	Iowa	92.9	15	North Carolina	89.8
38	Kansas	77.4	16	Georgia	89.6
43	Kentucky	73.3	17	West Virginia	89.5
41	Louisiana	75.5	18	New York	89.1
27	Maine	83.0	19	Connecticut	88.0
6	Maryland	93.3	20	Vermont	87.3
50	Massachusetts	66.8	21	Minnesota	86.7
1	Michigan	97.2	22	Alabama	86.1
21	Minnesota	86.7	23	Utah	86.0
46	Mississippi	71.3	24	Pennsylvania	85.1
40	Missouri	75.8	25	Alaska	84.9
36	Montana	79.3	26	Oklahoma	84.3
29	Nebraska	82.6	27	Maine	83.0
13	Nevada	90.9	28	Ohio	82.7
48	New Hampshire	69.2	29	Nebraska	82.6
8	New Jersey	91.8	30	Colorado	81.7
12	New Mexico	91.1	30	Florida	81.7
18	New York	89.1	32	North Dakota	81.6
15	North Carolina	89.8	33	Tennessee	81.5
32	North Dakota	81.6	34	Virginia	80.6
28	Ohio	82.7	35	Arizona	79.9
26	Oklahoma	84.3	36	Montana	79.3
4	Oregon	96.3	37	South Carolina	79.0
24	Pennsylvania	85.1	38	Kansas	77.4
44	Rhode Island	72.0	39	Idaho	76.9
37	South Carolina	79.0	40	Missouri	75.8
45	South Dakota	71.8	41	Louisiana	75.5
33	Tennessee	81.5	42	Wisconsin	74.2
10	Texas	91.2	43	Kentucky	73.3
23	Utah	86.0	44	Rhode Island	72.0
20	Vermont	87.3	45	South Dakota	71.8
34	Virginia	80.6	46	Mississippi	71.3
3	Washington	96.5	47	Arkansas	70.4
17	West Virginia	89.5	48	New Hampshire	69.2
42	Wisconsin	74.2	49	Wyoming	68.6
49	Wyoming	68.6	50	Massachusetts	66.8
				District of Columbia	90.0

Source: U.S. Department of Transportation, National Highway Traffic Safety Administration
  "Occupant Protection" (http://www-nrd.nhtsa.dot.gov/Pubs/811160.PDF)

VIII. Appendix

Population in 2009

National Total = 307,006,550*

ALPHA ORDER

RANK	STATE	POPULATION	% of USA
23	Alabama	4,708,708	1.5%
47	Alaska	698,473	0.2%
14	Arizona	6,595,778	2.1%
32	Arkansas	2,889,450	0.9%
1	California	36,961,664	12.0%
22	Colorado	5,024,748	1.6%
29	Connecticut	3,518,288	1.1%
45	Delaware	885,122	0.3%
4	Florida	18,537,969	6.0%
9	Georgia	9,829,211	3.2%
42	Hawaii	1,295,178	0.4%
39	Idaho	1,545,801	0.5%
5	Illinois	12,910,409	4.2%
16	Indiana	6,423,113	2.1%
30	Iowa	3,007,856	1.0%
33	Kansas	2,818,747	0.9%
26	Kentucky	4,314,113	1.4%
25	Louisiana	4,492,076	1.5%
41	Maine	1,318,301	0.4%
19	Maryland	5,699,478	1.9%
15	Massachusetts	6,593,587	2.1%
8	Michigan	9,969,727	3.2%
21	Minnesota	5,266,214	1.7%
31	Mississippi	2,951,996	1.0%
18	Missouri	5,987,580	2.0%
44	Montana	974,989	0.3%
38	Nebraska	1,796,619	0.6%
35	Nevada	2,643,085	0.9%
40	New Hampshire	1,324,575	0.4%
11	New Jersey	8,707,739	2.8%
36	New Mexico	2,009,671	0.7%
3	New York	19,541,453	6.4%
10	North Carolina	9,380,884	3.1%
48	North Dakota	646,844	0.2%
7	Ohio	11,542,645	3.8%
28	Oklahoma	3,687,050	1.2%
27	Oregon	3,825,657	1.2%
6	Pennsylvania	12,604,767	4.1%
43	Rhode Island	1,053,209	0.3%
24	South Carolina	4,561,242	1.5%
46	South Dakota	812,383	0.3%
17	Tennessee	6,296,254	2.1%
2	Texas	24,782,302	8.1%
34	Utah	2,784,572	0.9%
49	Vermont	621,760	0.2%
12	Virginia	7,882,590	2.6%
13	Washington	6,664,195	2.2%
37	West Virginia	1,819,777	0.6%
20	Wisconsin	5,654,774	1.8%
50	Wyoming	544,270	0.2%

RANK ORDER

RANK	STATE	POPULATION	% of USA
1	California	36,961,664	12.0%
2	Texas	24,782,302	8.1%
3	New York	19,541,453	6.4%
4	Florida	18,537,969	6.0%
5	Illinois	12,910,409	4.2%
6	Pennsylvania	12,604,767	4.1%
7	Ohio	11,542,645	3.8%
8	Michigan	9,969,727	3.2%
9	Georgia	9,829,211	3.2%
10	North Carolina	9,380,884	3.1%
11	New Jersey	8,707,739	2.8%
12	Virginia	7,882,590	2.6%
13	Washington	6,664,195	2.2%
14	Arizona	6,595,778	2.1%
15	Massachusetts	6,593,587	2.1%
16	Indiana	6,423,113	2.1%
17	Tennessee	6,296,254	2.1%
18	Missouri	5,987,580	2.0%
19	Maryland	5,699,478	1.9%
20	Wisconsin	5,654,774	1.8%
21	Minnesota	5,266,214	1.7%
22	Colorado	5,024,748	1.6%
23	Alabama	4,708,708	1.5%
24	South Carolina	4,561,242	1.5%
25	Louisiana	4,492,076	1.5%
26	Kentucky	4,314,113	1.4%
27	Oregon	3,825,657	1.2%
28	Oklahoma	3,687,050	1.2%
29	Connecticut	3,518,288	1.1%
30	Iowa	3,007,856	1.0%
31	Mississippi	2,951,996	1.0%
32	Arkansas	2,889,450	0.9%
33	Kansas	2,818,747	0.9%
34	Utah	2,784,572	0.9%
35	Nevada	2,643,085	0.9%
36	New Mexico	2,009,671	0.7%
37	West Virginia	1,819,777	0.6%
38	Nebraska	1,796,619	0.6%
39	Idaho	1,545,801	0.5%
40	New Hampshire	1,324,575	0.4%
41	Maine	1,318,301	0.4%
42	Hawaii	1,295,178	0.4%
43	Rhode Island	1,053,209	0.3%
44	Montana	974,989	0.3%
45	Delaware	885,122	0.3%
46	South Dakota	812,383	0.3%
47	Alaska	698,473	0.2%
48	North Dakota	646,844	0.2%
49	Vermont	621,760	0.2%
50	Wyoming	544,270	0.2%
	District of Columbia	599,657	0.2%

Source: U.S. Bureau of the Census
"Population Estimates" (December 23, 2009, http://www.census.gov/popest/estimates.php)
*Resident population.

Population in 2008

National Total = 304,374,846*

ALPHA ORDER

RANK	STATE	POPULATION	% of USA
23	Alabama	4,677,464	1.5%
47	Alaska	688,125	0.2%
15	Arizona	6,499,377	2.1%
32	Arkansas	2,867,764	0.9%
1	California	36,580,371	12.0%
22	Colorado	4,935,213	1.6%
29	Connecticut	3,502,932	1.2%
45	Delaware	876,211	0.3%
4	Florida	18,423,878	6.1%
9	Georgia	9,697,838	3.2%
42	Hawaii	1,287,481	0.4%
39	Idaho	1,527,506	0.5%
5	Illinois	12,842,954	4.2%
16	Indiana	6,388,309	2.1%
30	Iowa	2,993,987	1.0%
33	Kansas	2,797,375	0.9%
26	Kentucky	4,287,931	1.4%
25	Louisiana	4,451,513	1.5%
41	Maine	1,319,691	0.4%
19	Maryland	5,658,655	1.9%
14	Massachusetts	6,543,595	2.1%
8	Michigan	10,002,486	3.3%
21	Minnesota	5,230,567	1.7%
31	Mississippi	2,940,212	1.0%
18	Missouri	5,956,335	2.0%
44	Montana	968,035	0.3%
38	Nebraska	1,781,949	0.6%
35	Nevada	2,615,772	0.9%
40	New Hampshire	1,321,872	0.4%
11	New Jersey	8,663,398	2.8%
36	New Mexico	1,986,763	0.7%
3	New York	19,467,789	6.4%
10	North Carolina	9,247,134	3.0%
48	North Dakota	641,421	0.2%
7	Ohio	11,528,072	3.8%
28	Oklahoma	3,644,025	1.2%
27	Oregon	3,782,991	1.2%
6	Pennsylvania	12,566,368	4.1%
43	Rhode Island	1,053,502	0.3%
24	South Carolina	4,503,280	1.5%
46	South Dakota	804,532	0.3%
17	Tennessee	6,240,456	2.1%
2	Texas	24,304,290	8.0%
34	Utah	2,727,343	0.9%
49	Vermont	621,049	0.2%
12	Virginia	7,795,424	2.6%
13	Washington	6,566,073	2.2%
37	West Virginia	1,814,873	0.6%
20	Wisconsin	5,627,610	1.8%
50	Wyoming	532,981	0.2%

RANK ORDER

RANK	STATE	POPULATION	% of USA
1	California	36,580,371	12.0%
2	Texas	24,304,290	8.0%
3	New York	19,467,789	6.4%
4	Florida	18,423,878	6.1%
5	Illinois	12,842,954	4.2%
6	Pennsylvania	12,566,368	4.1%
7	Ohio	11,528,072	3.8%
8	Michigan	10,002,486	3.3%
9	Georgia	9,697,838	3.2%
10	North Carolina	9,247,134	3.0%
11	New Jersey	8,663,398	2.8%
12	Virginia	7,795,424	2.6%
13	Washington	6,566,073	2.2%
14	Massachusetts	6,543,595	2.1%
15	Arizona	6,499,377	2.1%
16	Indiana	6,388,309	2.1%
17	Tennessee	6,240,456	2.1%
18	Missouri	5,956,335	2.0%
19	Maryland	5,658,655	1.9%
20	Wisconsin	5,627,610	1.8%
21	Minnesota	5,230,567	1.7%
22	Colorado	4,935,213	1.6%
23	Alabama	4,677,464	1.5%
24	South Carolina	4,503,280	1.5%
25	Louisiana	4,451,513	1.5%
26	Kentucky	4,287,931	1.4%
27	Oregon	3,782,991	1.2%
28	Oklahoma	3,644,025	1.2%
29	Connecticut	3,502,932	1.2%
30	Iowa	2,993,987	1.0%
31	Mississippi	2,940,212	1.0%
32	Arkansas	2,867,764	0.9%
33	Kansas	2,797,375	0.9%
34	Utah	2,727,343	0.9%
35	Nevada	2,615,772	0.9%
36	New Mexico	1,986,763	0.7%
37	West Virginia	1,814,873	0.6%
38	Nebraska	1,781,949	0.6%
39	Idaho	1,527,506	0.5%
40	New Hampshire	1,321,872	0.4%
41	Maine	1,319,691	0.4%
42	Hawaii	1,287,481	0.4%
43	Rhode Island	1,053,502	0.3%
44	Montana	968,035	0.3%
45	Delaware	876,211	0.3%
46	South Dakota	804,532	0.3%
47	Alaska	688,125	0.2%
48	North Dakota	641,421	0.2%
49	Vermont	621,049	0.2%
50	Wyoming	532,981	0.2%
	District of Columbia	590,074	0.2%

Source: U.S. Bureau of the Census
  "Population Estimates" (December 23, 2009, http://www.census.gov/popest/estimates.php)
*Resident population. Revised estimates.

Male Population in 2008

National Total = 149,924,604 Males

<table>
<tr><td colspan="4">ALPHA ORDER</td><td colspan="4">RANK ORDER</td></tr>
<tr><td>RANK</td><td>STATE</td><td>MALES</td><td>% of USA</td><td>RANK</td><td>STATE</td><td>MALES</td><td>% of USA</td></tr>
<tr><td>23</td><td>Alabama</td><td>2,258,087</td><td>1.5%</td><td>1</td><td>California</td><td>18,388,022</td><td>12.3%</td></tr>
<tr><td>47</td><td>Alaska</td><td>357,607</td><td>0.2%</td><td>2</td><td>Texas</td><td>12,143,558</td><td>8.1%</td></tr>
<tr><td>14</td><td>Arizona</td><td>3,256,691</td><td>2.2%</td><td>3</td><td>New York</td><td>9,462,063</td><td>6.3%</td></tr>
<tr><td>32</td><td>Arkansas</td><td>1,398,635</td><td>0.9%</td><td>4</td><td>Florida</td><td>9,005,282</td><td>6.0%</td></tr>
<tr><td>1</td><td>California</td><td>18,388,022</td><td>12.3%</td><td>5</td><td>Illinois</td><td>6,359,906</td><td>4.2%</td></tr>
<tr><td>22</td><td>Colorado</td><td>2,491,041</td><td>1.7%</td><td>6</td><td>Pennsylvania</td><td>6,060,170</td><td>4.0%</td></tr>
<tr><td>29</td><td>Connecticut</td><td>1,707,410</td><td>1.1%</td><td>7</td><td>Ohio</td><td>5,603,768</td><td>3.7%</td></tr>
<tr><td>45</td><td>Delaware</td><td>423,336</td><td>0.3%</td><td>8</td><td>Michigan</td><td>4,923,929</td><td>3.3%</td></tr>
<tr><td>4</td><td>Florida</td><td>9,005,282</td><td>6.0%</td><td>9</td><td>Georgia</td><td>4,764,975</td><td>3.2%</td></tr>
<tr><td>9</td><td>Georgia</td><td>4,764,975</td><td>3.2%</td><td>10</td><td>North Carolina</td><td>4,516,987</td><td>3.0%</td></tr>
<tr><td>40</td><td>Hawaii</td><td>649,519</td><td>0.4%</td><td>11</td><td>New Jersey</td><td>4,251,782</td><td>2.8%</td></tr>
<tr><td>39</td><td>Idaho</td><td>766,580</td><td>0.5%</td><td>12</td><td>Virginia</td><td>3,817,042</td><td>2.5%</td></tr>
<tr><td>5</td><td>Illinois</td><td>6,359,906</td><td>4.2%</td><td>13</td><td>Washington</td><td>3,269,925</td><td>2.2%</td></tr>
<tr><td>16</td><td>Indiana</td><td>3,142,510</td><td>2.1%</td><td>14</td><td>Arizona</td><td>3,256,691</td><td>2.2%</td></tr>
<tr><td>30</td><td>Iowa</td><td>1,482,872</td><td>1.0%</td><td>15</td><td>Massachusetts</td><td>3,153,176</td><td>2.1%</td></tr>
<tr><td>33</td><td>Kansas</td><td>1,391,821</td><td>0.9%</td><td>16</td><td>Indiana</td><td>3,142,510</td><td>2.1%</td></tr>
<tr><td>26</td><td>Kentucky</td><td>2,088,142</td><td>1.4%</td><td>17</td><td>Tennessee</td><td>3,029,115</td><td>2.0%</td></tr>
<tr><td>25</td><td>Louisiana</td><td>2,140,798</td><td>1.4%</td><td>18</td><td>Missouri</td><td>2,887,907</td><td>1.9%</td></tr>
<tr><td>42</td><td>Maine</td><td>642,369</td><td>0.4%</td><td>19</td><td>Wisconsin</td><td>2,797,649</td><td>1.9%</td></tr>
<tr><td>20</td><td>Maryland</td><td>2,727,323</td><td>1.8%</td><td>20</td><td>Maryland</td><td>2,727,323</td><td>1.8%</td></tr>
<tr><td>15</td><td>Massachusetts</td><td>3,153,176</td><td>2.1%</td><td>21</td><td>Minnesota</td><td>2,599,899</td><td>1.7%</td></tr>
<tr><td>8</td><td>Michigan</td><td>4,923,929</td><td>3.3%</td><td>22</td><td>Colorado</td><td>2,491,041</td><td>1.7%</td></tr>
<tr><td>21</td><td>Minnesota</td><td>2,599,899</td><td>1.7%</td><td>23</td><td>Alabama</td><td>2,258,087</td><td>1.5%</td></tr>
<tr><td>31</td><td>Mississippi</td><td>1,423,841</td><td>0.9%</td><td>24</td><td>South Carolina</td><td>2,181,278</td><td>1.5%</td></tr>
<tr><td>18</td><td>Missouri</td><td>2,887,907</td><td>1.9%</td><td>25</td><td>Louisiana</td><td>2,140,798</td><td>1.4%</td></tr>
<tr><td>44</td><td>Montana</td><td>484,485</td><td>0.3%</td><td>26</td><td>Kentucky</td><td>2,088,142</td><td>1.4%</td></tr>
<tr><td>38</td><td>Nebraska</td><td>884,280</td><td>0.6%</td><td>27</td><td>Oregon</td><td>1,882,731</td><td>1.3%</td></tr>
<tr><td>35</td><td>Nevada</td><td>1,324,590</td><td>0.9%</td><td>28</td><td>Oklahoma</td><td>1,798,841</td><td>1.2%</td></tr>
<tr><td>41</td><td>New Hampshire</td><td>649,087</td><td>0.4%</td><td>29</td><td>Connecticut</td><td>1,707,410</td><td>1.1%</td></tr>
<tr><td>11</td><td>New Jersey</td><td>4,251,782</td><td>2.8%</td><td>30</td><td>Iowa</td><td>1,482,872</td><td>1.0%</td></tr>
<tr><td>36</td><td>New Mexico</td><td>978,326</td><td>0.7%</td><td>31</td><td>Mississippi</td><td>1,423,841</td><td>0.9%</td></tr>
<tr><td>3</td><td>New York</td><td>9,462,063</td><td>6.3%</td><td>32</td><td>Arkansas</td><td>1,398,635</td><td>0.9%</td></tr>
<tr><td>10</td><td>North Carolina</td><td>4,516,987</td><td>3.0%</td><td>33</td><td>Kansas</td><td>1,391,821</td><td>0.9%</td></tr>
<tr><td>48</td><td>North Dakota</td><td>321,933</td><td>0.2%</td><td>34</td><td>Utah</td><td>1,381,261</td><td>0.9%</td></tr>
<tr><td>7</td><td>Ohio</td><td>5,603,768</td><td>3.7%</td><td>35</td><td>Nevada</td><td>1,324,590</td><td>0.9%</td></tr>
<tr><td>28</td><td>Oklahoma</td><td>1,798,841</td><td>1.2%</td><td>36</td><td>New Mexico</td><td>978,326</td><td>0.7%</td></tr>
<tr><td>27</td><td>Oregon</td><td>1,882,731</td><td>1.3%</td><td>37</td><td>West Virginia</td><td>888,696</td><td>0.6%</td></tr>
<tr><td>6</td><td>Pennsylvania</td><td>6,060,170</td><td>4.0%</td><td>38</td><td>Nebraska</td><td>884,280</td><td>0.6%</td></tr>
<tr><td>43</td><td>Rhode Island</td><td>508,705</td><td>0.3%</td><td>39</td><td>Idaho</td><td>766,580</td><td>0.5%</td></tr>
<tr><td>24</td><td>South Carolina</td><td>2,181,278</td><td>1.5%</td><td>40</td><td>Hawaii</td><td>649,519</td><td>0.4%</td></tr>
<tr><td>46</td><td>South Dakota</td><td>400,861</td><td>0.3%</td><td>41</td><td>New Hampshire</td><td>649,087</td><td>0.4%</td></tr>
<tr><td>17</td><td>Tennessee</td><td>3,029,115</td><td>2.0%</td><td>42</td><td>Maine</td><td>642,369</td><td>0.4%</td></tr>
<tr><td>2</td><td>Texas</td><td>12,143,558</td><td>8.1%</td><td>43</td><td>Rhode Island</td><td>508,705</td><td>0.3%</td></tr>
<tr><td>34</td><td>Utah</td><td>1,381,261</td><td>0.9%</td><td>44</td><td>Montana</td><td>484,485</td><td>0.3%</td></tr>
<tr><td>49</td><td>Vermont</td><td>305,723</td><td>0.2%</td><td>45</td><td>Delaware</td><td>423,336</td><td>0.3%</td></tr>
<tr><td>12</td><td>Virginia</td><td>3,817,042</td><td>2.5%</td><td>46</td><td>South Dakota</td><td>400,861</td><td>0.3%</td></tr>
<tr><td>13</td><td>Washington</td><td>3,269,925</td><td>2.2%</td><td>47</td><td>Alaska</td><td>357,607</td><td>0.2%</td></tr>
<tr><td>37</td><td>West Virginia</td><td>888,696</td><td>0.6%</td><td>48</td><td>North Dakota</td><td>321,933</td><td>0.2%</td></tr>
<tr><td>19</td><td>Wisconsin</td><td>2,797,649</td><td>1.9%</td><td>49</td><td>Vermont</td><td>305,723</td><td>0.2%</td></tr>
<tr><td>50</td><td>Wyoming</td><td>270,190</td><td>0.2%</td><td>50</td><td>Wyoming</td><td>270,190</td><td>0.2%</td></tr>
<tr><td></td><td></td><td></td><td></td><td colspan="2">District of Columbia</td><td>279,880</td><td>0.2%</td></tr>
</table>

Source: CQ Press using data from U.S. Bureau of the Census
   "SC-EST2008-AGESEX_RES - State Characteristic Estimates" (http://www.census.gov/popest/datasets.html)

Female Population in 2008

National Total = 154,135,120 Females

ALPHA ORDER

RANK	STATE	FEMALES	% of USA
23	Alabama	2,403,813	1.6%
47	Alaska	328,686	0.2%
15	Arizona	3,243,489	2.1%
32	Arkansas	1,456,755	0.9%
1	California	18,368,644	11.9%
22	Colorado	2,448,415	1.6%
29	Connecticut	1,793,842	1.2%
45	Delaware	449,756	0.3%
4	Florida	9,323,058	6.0%
9	Georgia	4,920,769	3.2%
42	Hawaii	638,679	0.4%
39	Idaho	757,236	0.5%
5	Illinois	6,541,657	4.2%
16	Indiana	3,234,282	2.1%
30	Iowa	1,519,683	1.0%
33	Kansas	1,410,313	0.9%
26	Kentucky	2,181,103	1.4%
25	Louisiana	2,269,998	1.5%
40	Maine	674,087	0.4%
19	Maryland	2,906,274	1.9%
13	Massachusetts	3,344,791	2.2%
8	Michigan	5,079,493	3.3%
21	Minnesota	2,620,494	1.7%
31	Mississippi	1,514,777	1.0%
18	Missouri	3,023,698	2.0%
44	Montana	482,955	0.3%
38	Nebraska	899,152	0.6%
35	Nevada	1,275,577	0.8%
41	New Hampshire	666,722	0.4%
11	New Jersey	4,430,879	2.9%
36	New Mexico	1,006,030	0.7%
3	New York	10,028,234	6.5%
10	North Carolina	4,705,427	3.1%
48	North Dakota	319,548	0.2%
7	Ohio	5,882,142	3.8%
28	Oklahoma	1,843,520	1.2%
27	Oregon	1,907,329	1.2%
6	Pennsylvania	6,388,109	4.1%
43	Rhode Island	542,083	0.4%
24	South Carolina	2,298,522	1.5%
46	South Dakota	403,333	0.3%
17	Tennessee	3,185,773	2.1%
2	Texas	12,183,416	7.9%
34	Utah	1,355,163	0.9%
49	Vermont	315,547	0.2%
12	Virginia	3,952,047	2.6%
14	Washington	3,279,299	2.1%
37	West Virginia	925,772	0.6%
20	Wisconsin	2,830,318	1.8%
50	Wyoming	262,478	0.2%

RANK ORDER

RANK	STATE	FEMALES	% of USA
1	California	18,368,644	11.9%
2	Texas	12,183,416	7.9%
3	New York	10,028,234	6.5%
4	Florida	9,323,058	6.0%
5	Illinois	6,541,657	4.2%
6	Pennsylvania	6,388,109	4.1%
7	Ohio	5,882,142	3.8%
8	Michigan	5,079,493	3.3%
9	Georgia	4,920,769	3.2%
10	North Carolina	4,705,427	3.1%
11	New Jersey	4,430,879	2.9%
12	Virginia	3,952,047	2.6%
13	Massachusetts	3,344,791	2.2%
14	Washington	3,279,299	2.1%
15	Arizona	3,243,489	2.1%
16	Indiana	3,234,282	2.1%
17	Tennessee	3,185,773	2.1%
18	Missouri	3,023,698	2.0%
19	Maryland	2,906,274	1.9%
20	Wisconsin	2,830,318	1.8%
21	Minnesota	2,620,494	1.7%
22	Colorado	2,448,415	1.6%
23	Alabama	2,403,813	1.6%
24	South Carolina	2,298,522	1.5%
25	Louisiana	2,269,998	1.5%
26	Kentucky	2,181,103	1.4%
27	Oregon	1,907,329	1.2%
28	Oklahoma	1,843,520	1.2%
29	Connecticut	1,793,842	1.2%
30	Iowa	1,519,683	1.0%
31	Mississippi	1,514,777	1.0%
32	Arkansas	1,456,755	0.9%
33	Kansas	1,410,313	0.9%
34	Utah	1,355,163	0.9%
35	Nevada	1,275,577	0.8%
36	New Mexico	1,006,030	0.7%
37	West Virginia	925,772	0.6%
38	Nebraska	899,152	0.6%
39	Idaho	757,236	0.5%
40	Maine	674,087	0.4%
41	New Hampshire	666,722	0.4%
42	Hawaii	638,679	0.4%
43	Rhode Island	542,083	0.4%
44	Montana	482,955	0.3%
45	Delaware	449,756	0.3%
46	South Dakota	403,333	0.3%
47	Alaska	328,686	0.2%
48	North Dakota	319,548	0.2%
49	Vermont	315,547	0.2%
50	Wyoming	262,478	0.2%
	District of Columbia	311,953	0.2%

Source: CQ Press using data from U.S. Bureau of the Census
"SC-EST2008-AGESEX_RES - State Characteristic Estimates" (http://www.census.gov/popest/datasets.html)

Sources

American Academy of Physicians Assistants
950 North Washington Street
Alexandria, VA 22314-1552
703-836-2272
www.aapa.org

American Cancer Society, Inc.
1599 Clifton Road, NE.
Atlanta, GA 30329-4251
800-227-2345
www.cancer.org

American Dental Association
211 E. Chicago Ave.
Chicago, IL 60611-2678
312-440-2500
www.ada.org

American Hospital Association
One North Franklin
Chicago, IL 60606-3421
312-422-3000
www.aha.org

American Medical Association
515 North State Street
Chicago, IL 60610
800-621-8335
www.ama-assn.org

American Osteopathic Association
142 East Ontario Street
Chicago, IL 60611
800-621-1773
www.osteopathic.org

Bureau of Labor Statistics
2 Massachusetts Ave., NE
Washington, DC 20212-0001
202-691-5200
www.bls.gov

Bureau of the Census
4600 Silver Hill Road
Washington, DC 20233-0001
800-923-8282
www.census.gov

Centers for Disease Control and Prevention
1600 Clifton Road
Atlanta, GA 30333
800-232-4636
www.cdc.gov

Centers for Medicare and Medicaid Services
7500 Security Boulevard
Baltimore, MD 21244-1850
877-267-2323
www.cms.hhs.gov

Federation of Chiropractic Licensing Boards
5401 W 10th Street, Ste 101
Greeley, CO 80634
970-356-3500
www.fclb.org

HealthLeaders/InterStudy
One Vantage Way, B-300
Nashville TN 37228
615-385-4131
http://home.healthleaders-interstudy.com

Health Resources and Services Administration
Division of Practitioner Data Banks
5600 Fishers Lane
Rockville MD 20857
800-767-6732
www.hrsa.gov

Medical Expenditure Panel Survey
Agency for Healthcare Research and Quality
540 Gaither Road
Rockville MD 20850
301-427-1364
www.meps.ahrq.gov

National Association of State Budget Officers
444 N Capitol St., NW, Ste 642
Washington DC 20001-1551
202-624-5382
www.nasbo.org

National Center for Health Statistics
U.S. Department of Health and Human Services
3311 Toledo Road
Hyattsville, MD   20782
800-232-4636
www.cdc.gov/nchs/

National Highway Traffic Safety Admin.
1200 New Jersey Ave., SE
West Building
Washington, DC 20590
888-327-4236
www.nhtsa.dot.gov

National Institute on Alcohol Abuse and Alcoholism
National Institutes of Health
5635 Fishers Lane, MSC 9304
Bethesda, MD 20892-9304
301-443-3860
www.niaaa.nih.gov/

National Sporting Goods Association
1601 Feehanville Drive, Ste 300
Mt. Prospect, IL   60056
800-815-5422
www.nsga.org

Substance Abuse and Mental Health Services Admin.
U.S. Department of Health and Human Services
P.O. Box 2345
Rockville MD 20847
877-726-4727
www.samhsa.gov

Index